Rick Steves®

CROATIA
& SLOVENIA

Rick Steves & Cameron Hewitt

P9-CRM-704

CONTENTS

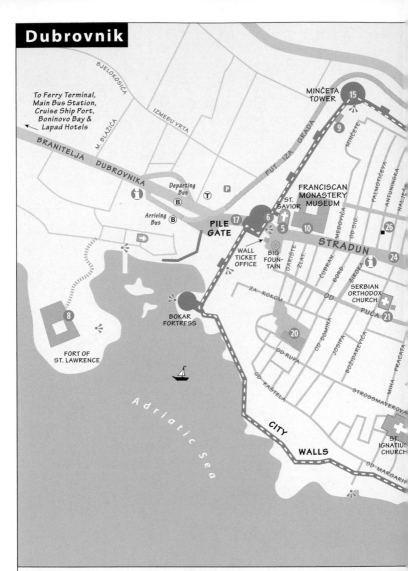

Dubrovnik

To Ferry Terminal,
Main Bus Station,
Cruise Ship Port,
Boninovo Bay &
Lapad Hotels

BJELOKOSIĆA

IZMEĐU VRTA

M. BLAŽIĆA

BRANITELJA DUBROVNIKA

PUT IZA GRADA

MINČETA
TOWER

15

9

MINČETE

Departing
Bus

P

T

B

Arriving
Bus

B

PILE
GATE

17

6

5

ST.
SAVIOR

FRANCISCAN
MONASTERY
MUSEUM

10

26

PALMOTIĆEVA

ANTUNINSKA

NALJEŠKO

OD SIG.

MEDOVIĆA

STRADUN

24

WALL
TICKET
OFFICE

BIG
FOUN-
TAIN

GARIŠTE

ZLAT.

ČUBRAN.

ĐORĐ.

ŠIROKA

OD

SERBIAN
ORTHODOX
CHURCH

21

PUĆA

ZA ROKOM

OD DOMINA

OD

BOKAR
FORTRESS

8

FORT OF
ST. LAWRENCE

20

OD JOSIPA

OD RUPA

BOŽIDAREVIĆA

MIHA PRACATA

STROSSMAYEROVA

OD KAŠTELA

A d r i a t i c   S e a

CITY

WALLS

ST.
IGNATIUS
CHURCH

OD MARGARIT

SIGHTS

1. Bell Tower
2. Buža Gate
3. Cable Car
4. Cathedral
5. Church of St. Savior
6. City Wall Entrances (3)
7. Dominican Monastery Museum & Church
8. Fort of St. Lawrence
9. Foundry Museum
10. Franciscan Monastery Museum & Church
11. Jesuit St. Ignatius' Church
12. Lazareti (Old Quarantine Building)
13. Luža Square & Orlando's Column
14. Maritime Museum & Aquarium
15. Minčeta Tower
16. Old Port
17. Pile Gate
18. Ploče Gate
19. Rector's Palace
20. Rupe Granary & Ethnographic Museum
21. Serbian Orthodox Church & Icon Museum
22. Sponza Palace & Memorial Room of Dubrovnik Defenders
23. St. Blaise's Church
24. Stradun (a.k.a. Placa)
25. Synagogue Museum
26. War Photo Limited

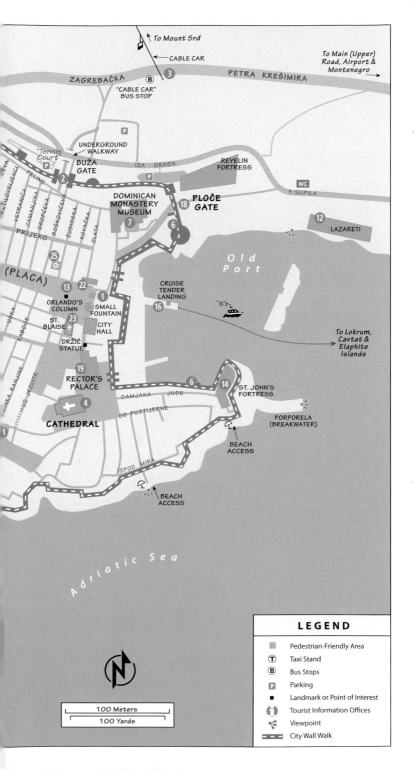

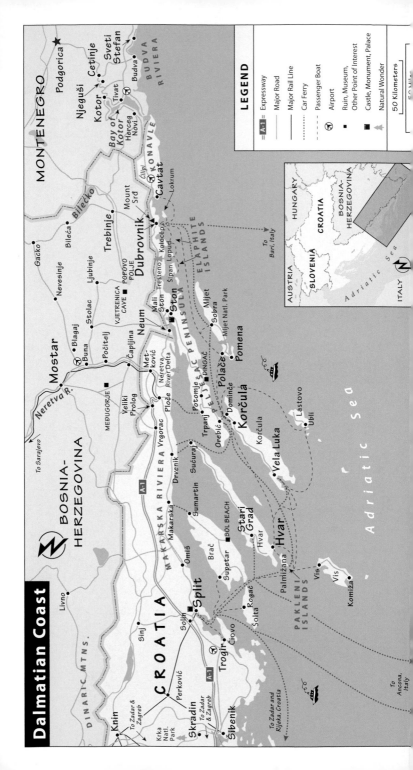

Rick Steves

CROATIA
& SLOVENIA

Top Destinations in Croatia & Slovenia

INTRODUCTION

Set sail on the shimmering Adriatic, for a remote island whose name you can't pronounce but whose wonders you'll never forget. Corkscrew your way up impossibly twisty mountain roads to panoramic vistas of cut-glass peaks. Lie on a beach in the hot summer sun, listening to the lapping waves as a Venetian-style bell tower clangs out the hour. Ponder the fading scars of the Yugoslav Wars, and admire how skillfully the locals have revitalized their once-troubled region. Dine on a seafood feast and sip a glass of local wine as you watch the sunset dip into the watery horizon...feeling smug for discovering this place before all your friends did. Unfamiliar as they might seem, Croatia and Slovenia have what you've been looking for: some of Europe's most spectacular natural wonders, a fascinating recent history, and a spirit of adventure—much of it still off the beaten path.

Here in the land where the Adriatic meets the Alps, there are countless ways to have fun. Begin your adventure by flipping through this book, which covers Croatia's and Slovenia's best big-city, small-town, and back-to-nature destinations. You'll get all the specifics and opinions necessary to wring the maximum value out of your limited time and money. If you're planning a trip of a month or less, this book is all you need.

Croatia and Slovenia were once part of the union called Yugoslavia. But today, that feels like ancient history, as each country is proudly independent. Carefree Croatia, with its long and enticing coastline, beckons vacationers with dramatically scenic terrain, romantic old towns, sunshine-bathed pebbly beaches, and an irrepressible seafaring spirit. Perky Slovenia surprises travelers with its tidy quaintness, breathtaking mountainscapes, colorful towns, and impossibly friendly natives. And for good measure, I've also included detours into two other parts of the former Yugoslavia, each

INTRODUCTION

Map Legend

⚡	Viewpoint	✈	Airport	) (	Tunnel
↑	Entrance	Ⓣ	Taxi Stand	———	Pedestrian Zone
✚	Tourist Info	Ⓣ	Tram Stop	------	Railway
WC	Restroom	Ⓑ	Bus Stop	··········	Ferry/Boat Route
🏰	Castle	Ⓟ	Parking	├──┼──┤	Tram
⛪	Church	)(	Mtn. Pass	▥▥▥▥	Stairs
🕌	Mosque	▣	Park	······	Walk/Tour Route
◎	Fountain	▪	Statue/Point of Interest	------	Trail
🍷	Winery				

Use this legend to help you navigate the maps in this book.

one offering a striking contrast to Croatia or Slovenia: the craggy coast of Montenegro, and a pair of diverse and fascinating Bosnian cities: bite-sized Mostar and bustling Sarajevo.

Experiencing Europe's culture, people, and natural wonders economically and hassle-free has been my goal for much of my life traveling, tour guiding, and writing. With this book, I pass on to you all the lessons I've learned, painstakingly updated—in person—for this edition.

Rick Steves Croatia & Slovenia covers the predictable biggies and adds a healthy dose of "Back Door" intimacy. Along with strolling the walls around Dubrovnik's peerless Old Town, you'll poke your way into a hidden little tavern clinging like a barnacle over the sea. I've been selective, including only the top destinations and sights. For example, Croatia has over a thousand islands. But why not focus on the very best? That's Korčula, Hvar, and Mljet.

The best is, of course, only my opinion. But after spending my adult life researching Europe, I've developed a sixth sense for what travelers enjoy. Just thinking about the places featured in this book makes me want to sing *klapa* music.

ABOUT THIS BOOK

Rick Steves Croatia & Slovenia is a personal tour guide in your pocket. Better yet, it's actually two tour guides in your pocket: The co-author of this book is Cameron Hewitt. Cameron writes and edits guidebooks for my travel company, Rick Steves' Europe. Inspired by his Slavic roots and by the enduring charm of the Slovenian and Croatian people, Cameron has spent the past 15 years closely tracking the exciting changes in this part of the world. Together, Cameron and I keep this book up-to-date and accurate (though for simplicity we've shed our respective egos to become "I" in this book).

This book is organized by destinations. Each is a minivacation

Key to This Book

Updates

This book is updated regularly—but things change. For the latest, visit www.ricksteves.com/update.

Abbreviations and Times

I use the following symbols and abbreviations in this book:

Sights are rated:

▲▲▲	**Don't miss**
▲▲	**Try hard to see**
▲	**Worthwhile if you can make it**
No rating	**Worth knowing about**

Tourist information offices are abbreviated as **TI,** and bathrooms are **WCs.** To categorize accommodations, I use a **Sleep Code** (described on page 762).

Like Europe, this book uses the **24-hour clock.** It's the same through 12:00 noon, then keeps going: 13:00, 14:00, and so on. For anything over 12, subtract 12 and add p.m. (14:00 is 2:00 p.m.).

When giving **opening times,** I include both peak season and off-season hours if they differ. So, if a museum is listed as "May-Oct daily 9:00-16:00," it should be open from 9 a.m. until 4 p.m. from the first day of May until the last day of October (but expect exceptions).

For **transit** or **tour departures,** I first list the frequency, then the duration. So, a train connection listed as "2/hour, 1.5 hours" departs twice each hour and the journey lasts an hour and a half.

on its own, filled with exciting sights, strollable neighborhoods, affordable places to stay, and memorable places to eat.

In the following chapters, you'll find these sections:

Planning Your Time suggests a schedule for how to best use your limited time.

Orientation has specifics on public transportation, helpful hints, local tour options, easy-to-read maps, and tourist information.

Sights describes the top attractions and includes their cost and hours.

Self-Guided Walks take you through interesting neighborhoods, pointing out sights and fun stops.

Sleeping describes my favorite accommodations, from good-value private rooms to cushy splurges.

Eating serves up a buffet of options, from inexpensive eateries to fancy restaurants.

Connections outlines your options for traveling to destina-

INTRODUCTION

tions by train, bus, and boat. In car-friendly areas, I've also included route tips for drivers.

Country Introductions for Croatia, Slovenia, and Bosnia give you an overview of each country's culture, customs, money, history, current events, cuisine, language, and other useful practicalities.

The **Understanding Yugoslavia** chapter sorts out the various countries and conflicts, giving you a good picture of how Yugoslavia was formed, and why it broke apart.

Practicalities is a traveler's tool kit, with my best tips about money, sightseeing, sleeping, eating, staying connected, and transportation (trains, buses, boats, car rentals, driving, and flights).

The **appendix** has the nuts-and-bolts: useful phone numbers and websites, a holiday and festival list, recommended books and films, a climate chart, a handy packing checklist, and Croatian and Slovenian survival phrases.

Browse through this book, choose your favorite destinations, and link them up. Then have a great trip! Traveling like a temporary local, you'll get the absolute most out of every mile, minute, and dollar. And, as you visit places I know and love, I'm happy that you'll be meeting some of my favorite Croatians, Slovenes, Bosnians, and Montenegrins.

Planning

This section will help you get started planning your trip—with advice on trip costs, when to go, and what you should know before you take off.

TRAVEL SMART

Your trip to this region is like a complex play—it's easier to follow and really appreciate on a second viewing. While no one does the same trip twice to gain that advantage, reading this book in its entirety before your trip accomplishes much the same thing.

Design an itinerary that enables you to visit sights at the best possible times. Note festivals, holidays, specifics on sights, and days when sights are closed or most crowded (all covered in this book). For example, avoid coastal resort towns off-season (when they're deserted) and during the busy months of July and August (when they're miserably crammed). To connect the dots smoothly, read the tips in this book's appendix on taking trains, buses, boats, or renting a car and driving. Designing a smart trip is a fun, doable, and worthwhile challenge.

Make your itinerary a mix of intense and relaxed stretches. To maximize rootedness, minimize one-night stands. It's worth taking a long drive or bus ride after dinner to be settled into a town for two nights. Accommodations are more likely to give a good price to someone staying more than one night. Every trip—and every traveler—needs slack time (laundry, picnics, people-watching, and so on). Pace yourself. Assume you will return.

Reread this book as you travel, and visit local tourist information offices (abbreviated as TI in this book). Upon arrival in a new town, lay the groundwork for a smooth departure; confirm the train, bus, boat, or road you'll take when you leave.

Even with the best-planned itinerary, you'll need to be flexible. Update your plans as you travel. Get online or call ahead to double-check tourist information, learn the latest on sights (special events, tour schedules, and so on), book tickets and tours, make reservations, reconfirm accommodations, and research transportation connections.

Enjoy the friendliness of the local people. Connect with the culture. Set up your own quest for the best bell tower, mountain vista, or scenic seafront perch. Slow down and be open to unexpected experiences. Ask questions—most locals are eager to point you toward their idea of the right direction. Keep a notepad in your pocket for noting directions, organizing your thoughts, and confirming prices. Wear your money belt, learn the local currencies, and figure out how to estimate prices in dollars. Those who expect to travel smart, do.

TRIP COSTS

Despite their heritage as formerly communist countries, Croatia and Slovenia are no longer Europe's bargain basement. In fact, the cost of traveling here rivals neighboring Austria and Italy. Still, if you're careful to avoid inflated tourist-trap prices (by following my tips on where to stay and where to eat), a trip to this region can be a good value. If you detour into Bosnia-Herzegovina, you'll find prices substantially lower (though Montenegro is, if anything, pricier than Croatia and Slovenia).

Five components make up your trip costs: airfare, surface transportation, room and board, sightseeing and entertainment, and shopping and miscellany.

Airfare: A basic round-trip flight from the US to Ljubljana or Dubrovnik can cost $1,000-2,000, depending on where you fly from and when (cheaper in winter). Consider saving time and money in Europe by flying into one city and out of another; for instance, flying into Ljubljana and out of Dubrovnik often saves the extra cost (not to mention wasted time) of a 12-hour overland return trip to Ljubljana.

Surface Transportation: For the two-week whirlwind trip described in this chapter, allow $150 per person for public transportation (train, bus, and boat tickets). Train travelers will probably save money by simply buying tickets along the way, rather than

Croatia & Slovenia at a Glance

Croatia

▲▲**Zagreb** Croatia's underrated capital city, with interesting museums (the best feature Naive Art and Broken Relationships), lush parks, and a lively urban bustle.

▲▲▲**Plitvice Lakes National Park** Arguably Europe's most breathtaking natural wonder: a forested canyon filled with crystal-clear lakes, stunning waterfalls, and easy-to-hike boardwalks and trails.

▲▲**Istria** Croatia's most Italian-feeling corner, with the super-romantic, Venetian-flavored coastal town of Rovinj; top Roman ruins in the city of Pula; and a rolling interior of vineyards and picturesque hill towns (including Motovun). Nearby are the genteel Habsburg resort of Opatija and the port city of Rijeka.

▲▲**Split** Unofficial capital city and transit hub of the Dalmatian Coast, with a bustling urban vibe, people-filled seaside promenade, and lived-in warren of twisting lanes sprouting out of a massive Roman palace, plus the nearby town of Trogir and the waterfalls of Krka National Park.

▲▲**Hvar** Ritzy island and Old Town known for its jet-set appeal, high prices, rugged interior, seductively relaxing beaches, and easy escapes to nearby islets.

▲▲**Korčula** Low-key island and walled peninsular Old Town with a fjord-like backdrop, a lush islandscape, a fish-skeleton street plan, and quirky, offbeat museums.

▲▲▲**Dubrovnik** The "Pearl of the Adriatic": a giant walled Old Town with a scenic wall walk, tons of crowds, great beaches, modest but engaging museums, a stunning mountaintop viewpoint, an epic past and difficult but inspiring recent history, and a well-earned reputation as Croatia's single best destination.

Near Dubrovnik Boat excursions from Dubrovnik's Old Port, the art-packed resort village of Cavtat, the nearby Trsteno Arboretum, the walled town of Ston, the vineyard-draped Pelješac Peninsula, and the giant national park at Mljet Island.

Bosnia-Herzegovina

▲▲▲**Mostar** An easy taste of Bosnia-Herzegovina, with a striking setting, vivid Muslim culture, old Turkish architecture, evocative war damage, and an inspiring, rebuilt Old Bridge; plus nearby

Muslim sights (scenic gorge and dervish house at Blagaj, hill town of Počitelj, workaday burg of Stolac) and the famous Catholic pilgrimage site of Međugorje.

▲▲▲**Sarajevo** Formerly war-torn, now rejuvenated Bosnian capital, with a fascinating layered history and a spectacular mountain-valley setting.

Montenegro
▲▲**The Bay of Kotor** Steep bay with fjord-like inlets, visit-worthy towns and sights, and the remarkably fortified Old Town of Kotor.

The Montenegrin Interior Rugged mountain road leading up the cliffs into the Montenegrin heartland, ending at the historic capital of Cetinje.

The Budva Riviera Glitzy emerging beach resort zone with a mix of cheap and luxury resort hotels.

Slovenia
▲▲**Ljubljana** Slovenia's vibrant yet relaxing capital, with a fun-to-browse riverside market, scintillating architecture, and inviting riverside promenade.

▲▲▲**Lake Bled** Photogenic lake resort huddled in the foothills of the Julian Alps, with a church-topped island, cliff-hanging castle, lakefront walkway, tasty desserts, and appealing side-trips.

▲▲**The Julian Alps** Cut-glass peaks easily conquered by a twisty and scenic mountain road over the Vršič Pass, ending in the tranquil Soča River Valley, with the fine WWI museum in Kobarid.

▲**Logarska Dolina and the Northern Valleys** Remote mountain valleys with grand vistas and traditional farming lifestyles.

Ptuj and Maribor In Ptuj, a charming-if-sleepy historic town topped by a castle; and Maribor, Slovenia's "second city."

▲**The Karst** Windblown limestone plateau with world-class caves (Škocjan and Postojna), the Lipizzaner Stallion stud farm at Lipica, and the dramatically situated Predjama Castle.

▲**Piran** Slovenia's adorable, charming Adriatic resort town—a Back Door gem.

purchasing a rail pass (see "Transportation," page 779). If you'll be renting a car, allow at least $230 per week, not including tolls, gas, and insurance. Car rentals are cheapest if arranged from the US, but exorbitant fees for dropping off in a different country can make it prohibitively expensive if you're going to both Croatia and Slovenia (for strategies to avoid this headache, see "Renting a Car," page 784). Don't hesitate to consider flying, as budget airlines are often cheaper than taking the train (check www.skyscanner.com for intra-European flights). For more on public transportation and car rental, see "Transportation" in Practicalities.

Room and Board: You can thrive in Croatia and Slovenia on $100 a day per person for room and board (much less in Bosnia-Herzegovina). This allows $15 for lunch, $25 for dinner, and $60 for lodging (based on two people splitting the cost of a $120 double room that includes breakfast). Students and tightwads can eat and sleep for as little as $50 a day ($30 per hostel bed, $20 for groceries and snacks).

Sightseeing and Entertainment: Sightseeing is cheap here. Figure about $3-6 per major sight (museums), and $10-25 for splurge experiences (e.g., watching the *Moreška* sword dance in Korčula, or seeing Slovenia's Lipizzaner stallions). You can hire your own private guide for three or four hours for about $100-150—a good value when divided among two or more people. An overall average of $20 a day works for most people. Don't skimp here. After all, this category is the driving force behind your trip—you came to sightsee, enjoy, and experience Croatia and Slovenia. Fortunately for you, the region's best attractions—the sea, mountains, and sunshine—are free.

Shopping and Miscellany: Figure $2-3 per postcard, coffee, beer, and ice-cream cone. Shopping can vary in cost from nearly nothing to a small fortune. Good budget travelers find that this category has little to do with assembling a trip full of lifelong memories.

SIGHTSEEING PRIORITIES

Depending on the length of your trip, and taking geographic proximity into account, here are my recommended priorities:

3 days:	Dubrovnik
5 days, add:	Mostar, Split
7 days, add:	Korčula or Hvar (for a relaxing island experience); Montenegro's Bay of Kotor (for dramatic scenery); or Sarajevo (for a more in-depth look at Bosnia)
8 days, add:	Plitvice Lakes
10 days, add:	Lake Bled and the Julian Alps
12 days, add:	Ljubljana, more time for Dalmatian islands

Top 10 Small Coastal Towns

1. Rovinj (Croatia)   6. Opatija (Croatia)
2. Korčula (Croatia)   7. Cavtat (Croatia)
3. Hvar (Croatia)   8. Perast (Montenegro)
4. Piran (Slovenia)   9. Trogir (Croatia)
5. Kotor (Montenegro)   10. Poreč (Croatia)

14 days, add: Istria
16 days, add: Whatever you skipped on day 7 (Korčula/Hvar, Montenegro, or Sarajevo)
18 days, add: The Karst, Zagreb
21 days, add: More mountains (Logarska Dolina) or coastal villages (Piran, Mljet)
More time, add: Ptuj, Opatija, and even more islands and coastal villages

The map and the two-week itinerary above include all of the stops in the first 14 days.

As you plan your trip, don't underestimate the long distances. (For example, Lake Bled and Dubrovnik are a full day's drive apart.) If you have a week or less, focus on either the south (Dalmatian Coast—Dubrovnik, Split, and the islands—plus Mostar and Montenegro) or the north (Slovenia, Istria, and Zagreb). The worth-a-detour Plitvice Lakes are stranded in no-man's land between these two areas, but reachable from either one (easiest by car, possible by bus). Sarajevo also requires a detour (2.5 hours beyond Mostar)—but those who make the trek won't regret it. (Frequent, affordable flights between Sarajevo and Zagreb make it more convenient than it seems.)

Where Should I Go?

The perfect Croatian vacation is like a carefully refined recipe—a dash of this, a pinch of that, a slow simmer...and before long, you've got a delicious feast. Here's my tried-and-true recipe for how to prioritize your time:

Begin with the biggies. Dubrovnik is a must, period. If you like big cities, Split is entertaining. Plitvice Lakes National Park, while difficult to reach, rarely disappoints. The bustling capital city, Zagreb—while far from Croatia's famed beaches—is vastly underrated, and much appreciated by urbanites.

Fold in one or two seafront villages. Adriatic coastal towns are all variations on the same theme: A warm stone Old Town with a Venetian bell tower, a tidy boat-speckled harbor, ample seafood restaurants, a few hulking communist-era resort hotels on the edge of town, and *soba* and *apartman* signs by every other doorbell. Of

Croatia and Slovenia: Best Two-Week Trip by Car

Day	Plan	Sleep in
1	Arrive at Ljubljana's airport and take a taxi to Lake Bled	Lake Bled
2	Relax at Lake Bled	Lake Bled
3	Pick up car, drive through Julian Alps, end in Ljubljana	Ljubljana
4	Ljubljana	Ljubljana
5	Drive through the Karst and Piran to Rovinj*	Rovinj
6	Tour Istria	Rovinj
7	Drive to Plitvice Lakes via Istria's hill towns	Plitvice
8	Hike the lakes, then drive to Split and drop car	Split
9	Split	Split
10	To Hvar or Korčula	Hvar/Korčula
11	Relax on Hvar or Korčula	Hvar/Korčula
12	To Dubrovnik	Dubrovnik
13	Dubrovnik	Dubrovnik
14	Rent a car or hire a driver to daytrip to Mostar or to Montenegro's Bay of Kotor	Dubrovnik

* To save the substantial extra cost of picking up your car in one country and then dropping it off in another (see page 786), come up with a strategy for turning in your rental car in Slovenia and then taking public transportation to Croatia, where you can pick up a different rental car for your time there. For example, you could take the bus from Ljubljana or Portorož (near Piran) to Rovinj, then pick up a rental car in nearby Pula or Poreč; or take the train from Ljubljana to Zagreb or Rijeka, then pick up your rental car in one of those cities.

course, each town has its own personality and claims to fame (for a quick run-down, see the "Croatia & Slovenia at a Glance" sidebar). Beach bums, sightseers, yachters, historians, partiers—everyone you'll talk to has their own favorite town. Don't trust this advice blindly, and don't sweat the decision too much. If a beach vacation is your goal, you can hardly go wrong.

Sprinkle liberally with Slovenia. You won't regret splicing Slovenia into your itinerary. Its spectacular mountain scenery,

By Public Transportation

This itinerary can be done entirely by public transportation, with a few modifications. Skip (or hire a driver for) the Julian Alps, and take the bus from Lake Bled to Ljubljana. Skip Istria; instead, take the train from Ljubljana to Zagreb, see that city, then take a bus to Plitvice. The bus connects Plitvice to Split, and from there, you'll continue down the Dalmatian Coast by boat or bus.

Even if you're using public transportation, seriously consider periodically renting a car for the day; this is most useful to reach the Julian Alps, Istria, Mostar, and Montenegro's Bay of Kotor.

colorful capital (Ljubljana), Germanic efficiency, and extremely friendly natives are a pleasant contrast to Croatia. In hindsight, most travelers cite Slovenia as the biggest pleasant surprise of their itinerary—and wish they'd budgeted more time there.

Add some spice. This is my secret ingredient. After you've been to one or two of the coastal resorts, you could head for another one...or you could use that time for something completely different. Some of these options are easy and convenient—the Roman ruins

Rick Steves Audio Europe

My **Rick Steves Audio Europe app** makes it easy to download audio content to enhance your trip. This includes my audio tours of many of Europe's top destinations, as well as a far-reaching library of insightful travel interviews from my public radio show with experts from around the globe—including many of the places in this book. The app and all of its content are entirely free. You can download Rick Steves Audio Europe via Apple's App Store, Google Play, or the Amazon Appstore. For more information, see www. ricksteves.com/audioeurope.

of Pula, the hilltop hamlets of the Istrian interior, the imported-Austrian-resort feel of Opatija. But my favorites involve crossing borders and broadening horizons: the cities of Mostar and Sarajevo, in Bosnia-Herzegovina; and Montenegro's spectacular Bay of Kotor. A year from now, you'll barely remember the difference between all those little seaside towns you toured. But you'll never forget the mosques of Mostar.

WHEN TO GO

Tourist traffic in this part of Europe (especially the coastal towns) is extremely seasonal. The peak season hits suddenly and floods the towns like a tidal wave, only to recede a couple months later—leaving empty streets and dazed locals. In general, the tourist season runs roughly from mid-May through early October, cresting in early August. (If you're staying in bigger cities or landlocked towns, the seasonal influence is much less pronounced.) You may find the climate chart in the appendix helpful.

Peak Season: July and especially August are top-of-top season—boats, buses, and budget accommodations are packed to the gills. Visiting Croatia in July or August is like spending spring break in Florida—fun, but miserably crowded and hot. Hotels charge top dollar, and you'll miss out on the "undiscovered" quality that pervades most of the region the rest of the year.

Shoulder Season: Early May through June, and September through early October are shoulder seasons. Within these time spans, late June and early September are nearly as crowded as peak season (particularly on weekends at seaside towns), but the rush subsides substantially in May and October; by the second week of October, restaurants are already starting to close down for the winter. Shoulder season is my favorite time to visit—I enjoy the smaller crowds, milder weather, and less-frenzied locals.

Off-Season: Mid-October through early May is dead as a doornail. Many small coastal towns close down entirely, with only one hotel and one restaurant remaining open during the lean winter months; many residents move to the interior to hibernate. Anything that's open keeps very limited hours (weekday mornings only). The weather can be cool and dreary, and night will draw the shades on your sightseeing before dinnertime. If traveling in the winter, skip the coast (or limit yourself to bigger towns like Split and Dubrovnik), and focus on the cities and the interior.

Seasonal Changes: Because of this region's extreme seasonality, opening times and prices are especially flexible. It's not unusual for a hotel to charge six different rates for the same room, depending on the time of year. (A hotel receptionist once showed me an entire book with literally hundreds of potential rates they could charge, based on room size, type, views, season, and length of stay.) With every visit, I dutifully hike around these towns trying to pin down hours for tourist offices, travel agencies, and museums. And every time, they change. It's always smart to call ahead to double-check opening times.

KNOW BEFORE YOU GO
Check this list of things to arrange while you're still at home.

You need a **passport**—but no visa or shots—to travel in Croatia, Slovenia, Bosnia-Herzegovina, and Montenegro. You may be denied entry into certain European countries if your passport is due to expire within three months of your ticketed date of return. Get it renewed if you'll be cutting it close. It can take up to six weeks to get or renew a passport (for more on passports, see www.travel.state.gov). Pack a photocopy of your passport in your luggage in case the original is lost or stolen.

Book rooms well in advance if you'll be traveling during peak season (July and August) or any major holidays or festivals (see page 798). Many of my favorite accommodations are quite small, with only a few rooms, so they fill up early.

Call your **debit- and credit-card companies** to let them know the countries you'll be visiting, to ask about fees, request your PIN code (it will be mailed to you), and more. See page 754 for details.

Do your homework if you want to buy **travel insurance.** Compare the cost of the insurance to the cost of your potential loss. Also, check whether your existing insurance (health, homeowners, or renters) covers you and your possessions overseas. For more tips, see www.ricksteves.com/insurance.

If you're planning on **renting a car** in Croatia or Slovenia,

INTRODUCTION

How Was Your Trip?

Were your travels fun, smooth, and meaningful? If you'd like to share your tips, concerns, and discoveries, please fill out the survey at www.ricksteves.com/feedback. To check out readers' hotel and restaurant reviews—or leave one yourself—visit my travel forum at www.ricksteves.com/travel-forum. I value your feedback. Thanks in advance.

---

bring your driver's license and an International Driving Permit (see page 784). Driving on Slovenia's expressways requires a €15 toll sticker (*vinjeta*, most Slovenian rental cars come with one, otherwise available at shops in Slovenia; see page 791); failure to display one could cost you a €150 fine.

If you plan to hire a **local guide,** reserve ahead by email. Popular guides can get booked up.

If you're bringing a **mobile device,** consider signing up for an international plan for cheaper calls, texts, and data (see page 772). Download any apps you might want to use on the road, such as translators, maps, transit schedules, and **Rick Steves Audio Europe** (see page 12).

Check the **Rick Steves guidebook updates** page for any recent changes to this book (www.ricksteves.com/update).

Croatia is known for its glimmering **beaches.** However, most are pebbly or rocky rather than sandy—and spiny sea urchins are not uncommon. In addition to your swimsuit, pack (or buy in Europe) a pair of water shoes for wading, as well as a beach towel (many of my recommended accommodations don't provide these). Good sunscreen, a sun hat, and bug spray can also be handy. And if you'll be hiking on Croatia's many scenic coastal trails, which can be rugged, pack sturdy shoes.

Traveling as a Temporary Local

We travel all the way to Croatia and Slovenia to enjoy differences—to become temporary locals. You'll experience frustrations. Certain truths that we find "God-given" or "self-evident," such as cold beer, ice in drinks, bottomless cups of coffee, "the customer is king," and bigger being better, are suddenly not so true.

One of the benefits of travel is the eye-opening realization that there are logical, civil, and even better alternatives. A willingness to go local ensures that you'll enjoy a full dose of Croatian and Slovenian hospitality.

Most American travelers find Slovenes to be extremely gregarious and Croatians relatively brusque. While tourism is big in Croatia, the finer points of service and hospitality sometimes get lost. Before losing your patience (as I sometimes do), try to remember that these people lived under a communist regime 25 years ago, followed by a devastating war, and today are coping with an unprecedented tourist crush. They're scrambling to keep up.

Europeans generally like Americans. But if there is a negative aspect to their image of us, it's that we are loud, wasteful, ethnocentric, too informal (which can seem disrespectful), and a bit naive.

While Europeans look bemusedly at some of our Yankee excesses—and worriedly at others—they nearly always afford us individual travelers all the warmth we deserve.

Judging from all the happy feedback I receive from travelers who have used this book, it's safe to assume you'll enjoy a great, affordable vacation—with the finesse of an independent, experienced traveler.

Thanks, and *sretan put*—happy travels!

Rick Steves

Back Door Travel Philosophy

From *Rick Steves Europe Through the Back Door*

Travel is intensified living—maximum thrills per minute and one of the last great sources of legal adventure. Travel is freedom. It's recess, and we need it.

Experiencing the real Europe requires catching it by surprise, going casual..."through the Back Door."

Affording travel is a matter of priorities. (Make do with the old car.) You can eat and sleep—simply, safely, and enjoyably—anywhere in Europe for $100 a day plus transportation costs. In many ways, spending more money only builds a thicker wall between you and what you traveled so far to see. Europe is a cultural carnival, and time after time, you'll find that its best acts are free and the best seats are the cheap ones.

A tight budget forces you to travel close to the ground, meeting and communicating with the people. Never sacrifice sleep, nutrition, safety, or cleanliness to save money. Simply enjoy the local-style alternatives to expensive hotels and restaurants.

Connecting with people carbonates your experience. Extroverts have more fun. If your trip is low on magic moments, kick yourself and make things happen. If you don't enjoy a place, maybe you don't know enough about it. Seek the truth. Recognize tourist traps. Give a culture the benefit of your open mind. See things as different, but not better or worse. Any culture has plenty to share. When an opportunity presents itself, make it a habit to say "yes."

Of course, travel, like the world, is a series of hills and valleys. Be fanatically positive and militantly optimistic. If something's not to your liking, change your liking.

Travel can make you a happier American, as well as a citizen of the world. Our Earth is home to seven billion equally precious people. It's humbling to travel and find that other people don't have the "American Dream"—they have their own dreams. Europeans like us, but with all due respect, they wouldn't trade passports.

Thoughtful travel engages us with the world. It reminds us what is truly important. By broadening perspectives, travel teaches new ways to measure quality of life.

Globetrotting destroys ethnocentricity, helping us understand and appreciate other cultures. Rather than fear the diversity on this planet, celebrate it. Among your most prized souvenirs will be the strands of different cultures you choose to knit into your own character. The world is a cultural yarn shop, and Back Door travelers are weaving the ultimate tapestry. Join in!

CROATIA
Hrvatska

CROATIA

Sunny beaches, succulent seafood, and a taste of *la dolce vita*...in Eastern Europe?

With thousands of miles of seafront and more than a thousand islands, Croatia's coastline is Eastern Europe's Riviera. Holiday-makers love its pebbly beaches, predictably balmy summer weather, and dramatic mountains. Croatia is also historic. From ruined Roman arenas and Byzantine mosaics to Venetian bell towers, Habsburg villas, and even communist concrete, past rulers have left their mark.

Croatia feels more Mediterranean than "Eastern European." Historically, Croatia has more in common with Venice and Rome than Vienna or Budapest; especially on the coast, it's sometimes difficult to distinguish this lively place from Italy. If you've become accustomed to the Germanic efficiency of Slovenia, Croatia's relaxed and unpredictable style can come as a shock.

Aside from its fun-in-the-sun status, Croatia is notorious as one of the sites, just two decades ago, of the most violent European war in generations. Locals call it "The Homeland War" or, more casually, "The Last War" (though it's ambiguous whether they mean "final" or "most recent"). Thankfully, the bloodshed is in the past. While a trip to Croatia offers thoughtful travelers the opportunity to understand a complicated chapter of recent history, most visitors focus instead on its substantial natural wonders: mountains, waterfalls, sun, sand, and sea.

Croatia's 3,600 miles of coastline—its main draw for tourists—is loosely divided into three regions. Most people flock to the Dalmatian Coast, in the south—where dramatic limestone cliffs rise from the watery deep and islands are scattered just offshore (the most appealing are Hvar and Korčula). Here you'll find Croatia's top tourist town, Dubrovnik, and the big city of Split, with its impressive Roman ruins. Way up in the northern corner of the country is the flatter, wedge-shaped peninsula called Istria, which has

arguably even more romantic towns—including my favorite, the Venetian-flavored Rovinj—along with the city of Pula (more great Roman ruins) and a rolling interior blanketed with vineyards and topped with hill towns (Motovun is the best). Wedged between Dalmatia and Istria is the Kvarner Gulf, a windy, arid no-man's-land that has few worthwhile attractions, but ample rugged scenery and a few fine islands offshore.

Enjoy the coast, but don't ignore the interior. The bustling capital of Zagreb is urban, engaging, and full of great museums and foodie restaurants. And Croatia's single best natural wonder (in this country that's so full of them) are the stunning waterfalls at Plitvice Lakes National Park.

It's possible to blow a lot of money here. Croatian hotels, especially on the coast, are a rotten value, and the many touristy restaurants are happy to overcharge you. But if you know where to look, you can find some wonderful budget alternatives—foremost among them *sobe* (rooms in private homes). *Sobe* are a comfortable compromise: fresh, hotelesque doubles with a private bathroom, air-conditioning, and TV, for a fraction of the cost of an anonymous hotel room (for details, see page 764).

Europeans are reverent sun-worshippers, and on clear days, virtually every square inch of coastal Croatia is occupied by a sunbather on a beach towel. Nude

beaches are a big deal, especially for vacationing Germans and Austrians. If you want to work on an all-around tan, seek out a beach marked *FKK* (from the German *Freikörper Kultur,* or "free body culture"). First-timers get comfortable in a hurry, finding they're not the only pink novices on the rocks. But don't get too excited—these beaches are most beloved by people you'd rather see with their clothes on.

Perhaps because sunshine and fishing are so important to the economy, Croatians are particularly affected by weather. They complain that the once-predictable climate has become erratic, with surprise rainy spells or heat waves in the once perfectly consistent, balmy summer months. Locals—and, often, tourists—find that their mood can literally be affected by which way the wind is blowing (for more, see page 164). The Croatian weather report includes a *biometeorološka prognoza* that indicates how the day's weather will affect your mood. Weather maps come with smiley or frowny faces, and forecasts predict, "People will be tired in the afternoon and not feel like working." Hmm...good excuse.

Every Croatian coastal town has two parts: The time-warp old town, and the obnoxious resort sprawl. Main drags are clogged

with gift shops selling shell sculptures and tasteless T-shirts. While many European visitors enjoy this tacky-trinket tourism, Americans are generally more interested in Old World charm. Fortunately, it's relatively easy to ignore the touristy scene and instead poke your way into twisty old medieval lanes, draped with drying laundry and populated by gossiping neighbors, humble fishermen's taverns, and soccer-playing kids.

Croatian popular music, the mariachi music of Europe, is the ever-present soundtrack of a Dalmatian vacation. Oliver Dragojević—singing soulful Mediterranean ballads with his gravelly, passionate voice—is the Croatian Tom Jones. Known simply as "Oliver," this beloved crooner gets airplay across Europe

CROATIA

and has spawned many imitators (such as the almost-as-popular Gibonni).

More traditional is the hauntingly beautiful *klapa* music—men's voices harmonizing a cappella, like a barbershop quartet

with a soothing Adriatic flavor. Typically the leader begins the song, and the rest of the group (usually 3 to 12 singers) follows behind him with a slight delay. You'll see mariachi-style *klapa* groups performing in touristy areas; a CD of one of these performances is a fun souvenir.

Croatia may be Europe's second most ardently Catholic country (after Poland). Under communism, religion was downplayed and many people gave up the habit of attending Mass regularly. But as the wars raged in the early 1990s, many Croatians rediscovered religion. You may be surprised by how many people you see worshipping in Croatia's churches today.

In the Yugoslav era, Croatia was flooded with tourists—both European and American—who fell in love with its achingly beautiful beaches and coves. In its heyday, Croatia hosted about 10 million visitors a year, who provided the country with about a third of its income. But then, for several years after the war, Croatia floundered: In the late 1990s, the streets of Dubrovnik were empty, lined with souvenir shops tended by desperate-looking vendors. More recently, locals are breathing a sigh of relief as the number of visitors has far exceeded prewar highs. With astonishing speed, Croatia is becoming one of Europe's top vacation destinations.

Even so, the standards for service (at restaurants, hotels, and so on) may be lower than you might expect. Service can be relaxed... *too* relaxed by American standards, thanks to the local philosophy of *malo po malo*, "little by little"—the easygoing, no-worries, *mañana* Dalmatian lifestyle. While you'll meet plenty of wonderfully big-hearted Croatians, some of my readers characterize Croatian waiters or hotel receptionists as "gruff" or even "rude." Be prepared for what I call the "Croatian Shrug"—a simple gesture meaning, "Don't know, don't care." If you run into this attitude, put the shoe on the other foot: How would you like it if a tidal wave of sweaty, ill-behaved, clueless tourists took over your town for the nicest months of each year? (No, I'm not talking about you...but just look around you.)

Today's Croatia is crawling with a Babel of international guests speaking German, French, Italian, every accent of English...and a smattering of Croatian. And yet, despite the tourists, this place

Croatia Almanac

Official Name: Republika Hrvatska, or just Hrvatska for short.

Snapshot History: After losing their independence to Hungary in 1102, the Croats watched as most of their coastline became Venetian and their interior was conquered by Ottomans. Croatia was "rescued" by the Habsburgs, but after World War I it became part of Yugoslavia—a decision many Croats regretted until they finally gained independence in 1991 through a bitter war with their Serb neighbors.

Population: Of the country's 4.5 million people, 90 percent are ethnic Croats (Catholic) and 4.5 percent are Serbs (Orthodox). (The Serb population was more than double that before the ethnic cleansing of the 1991-1995 war.) The population also includes ethnic Bosniaks, Hungarians, and Slovenes. "Croatians" are citizens of Croatia; "Croats" are a distinct ethnic group made up of Catholic South Slavs. So Orthodox Serbs living in Croatia are Croatians (specifically "Croatian Serbs")...but they aren't Croats.

Latitude and Longitude: 45°N and 15°E (similar latitude to Venice, Italy or Portland, Oregon).

Area: 22,000 square miles, similar to West Virginia.

Geography: This boomerang-shaped country has two terrains: Stretching north to south is the long, rugged Mediterranean coastline (3,600 miles of beach, including more than 1,100 offshore islands), which is warm and dry. Rising up from the sea are the rocky Dinaric Mountains. To the northeast, beginning at about Zagreb, Croatia's flat, inland "panhandle" (called Slavonia) is an extension of the Great Hungarian Plain, with hot summers and cold winters.

Biggest Cities: The capital, Zagreb (in the northern interior), has 790,000 people; Split (along the Dalmatian Coast) has 178,000; and Rijeka (on the northern coast) has 129,000.

Economy: Much of the country's wealth (about $90 billion GDP, or $20,000 GDP per capita) comes from tourism, banking, and trade with Italy. Unemployment is a stiff 20 percent.

Currency: 1 kuna (kn, or HRK) = about 14 cents, and 7 kunas = about $1. One kuna is broken down into 100 lipas. *Kuna* is Croatian for "marten" (a foxlike animal), recalling a time when fur pelts were used as currency. A *lipa* is a linden tree.

remains distinctly and stubbornly Croatian. You'd have to search pretty hard to find a McDonald's.

HELPFUL HINTS

Telephones: Mobile phone numbers begin with 09. Numbers beginning with 060 are pricey toll lines. For more details on how to dial to, from, and within Croatia, see page 776.

Government: The single-house assembly (Sabor) of 153 legislators is elected by popular vote. The country's prime minister (the head of the majority party in parliament, the center-left SDP party) is currently Zoran Milanović; the directly elected (but more figurehead) president is Kolinda Grabar-Kitarović (Croatia's first female president—and fourth overall), from the right-leaning HDZ party.

Flag: The flag has three horizontal bands (red on top, white, and blue) with a traditional red-and-white checkerboard shield in the center.

The Average Croatian: The average Croatian will live to age 76 and have 1.4 children. The average Croatian absolutely adores the soccer team Dinamo Zagreb and absolutely despises Hajduk Split...or vice versa.

Notable Croatians: A pair of big-league historical figures were born in Croatia: Roman Emperor **Diocletian** (A.D. 245-313) and—supposedly—explorer **Marco Polo** (1254?-1324). More recently, many Americans whose names end in "-ich" have Croatian roots, including actor **John Malkovich** and Ohio politicians **Dennis Kucinich** and **John Kasich**, not to mention baseball legend **Roger** Marich...I mean, **Maris**. More Croatian athletes abound: tennis star **Goran Ivanišević** is internationally known; NBA fans might recognize **Toni Kukoč** or **Gordan Giricek**; and at the 2002 and 2006 Winter Olympic Games, the women's downhill skiing events were dominated by **Janica Kostelić** (her brother **Ivica Kostelić** medaled in 2006, 2010, and 2014). Actor **Goran Višnjić** (from TV's *ER*) was born and raised in Croatia, and served in the army as a paratrooper. You've likely never heard of the beloved Croatian sculptor **Ivan Meštrović**, but you'll see his expressive works all over the country (see page 194). Inventor **Nikola Tesla** (1856-1943)—who, as a rival of Thomas Edison's, invented alternating current (AC)—was a Croatian-born Serb. And a band of well-dressed 17th-century Croatian soldiers stationed in France gave the Western world a new fashion accessory—the cravat, or necktie (for the full story, see page 188).

Addresses: Addresses listed with a street name and followed by "b.b." have no street number. In most small towns, locals ignore not only street numbers but also street names—navigate with a map or by asking for directions.

Slick Pavement: Old towns, with their well-polished pavement stones and many slick stairs, can be quite treacherous, especially after a rainstorm. (On a recent trip, one of your co-authors nearly broke his arm slipping down a flight of stairs.) Tread with care.

Siesta: Croatians eat their big meal at lunch, then take a traditional Mediterranean siesta. This means that many stores, museums, and churches are closed in the mid-afternoon.

Landmine Warning: Certain parts of the Croatian interior were once full of landmines. Most of these mines have been removed, and fields that may still be dangerous are usually clearly marked. As a precaution, if you're in a former war zone, stay on roads and paths, and don't go wandering through overgrown fields and deserted villages.

CROATIA

CROATIAN HISTORY

For nearly a millennium, bits and pieces of what we today call "Croatia" were batted back and forth between foreign powers: Hungarians, Venetians, Ottomans, Habsburgs, and Yugoslavs. Only in 1991 did Croatia (violently) regain its independence.

Early History

Croatia's first inhabitants were the mysterious Illyrians. While they left behind a few scant artifacts, little is known about this group (except that they were likely the ancestors of today's Albanians).

During antiquity, the Greeks and Romans both sailed ships up and down the strategic Dalmatian Coast. They founded many towns that still exist today, introduced winemaking and other agriculture, and littered the Adriatic seabed with shipwrecks. Romans built larger settlements on the Dalmatian Coast as early as 229 B.C., and in the fourth century A.D., Emperor Diocletian—who was born in what's now Croatia, and rose through the military ranks to become the most powerful man on earth—built his retirement palace in the coastal town of Split.

As Rome fell in the fifth century, Slavs (the ancestors of today's Croatians) and other barbarians flooded Europe. They moved into deserted Roman settlements (including Diocletian's Palace) and made them their own. The northern part of Croatia's coast fell briefly under the Byzantines, who slathered churches with shimmering mosaics (the best are in the Euphrasian Basilica in Poreč, Istria).

Beginning in the seventh century, Slavic Croats began to control most of the land that is today's Croatia. In A.D. 925, the Dalmatian Duke Tomislav united the disparate Croat tribes into a single kingdom. By consolidating and extending Croat-held territory and centralizing power, Tomislav created what many consider to be the first "Croatia."

Loss of Independence

By the early 12th century, the Croatian kings had died out, and neighboring powers (Hungary, Venice, and Byzantium) threatened the Croats. For the sake of self-preservation, Croatia entered an alliance with the Hungarians in 1102—and for the next 900 years, the Croats were ruled by foreign states. The Hungarians gradually took more and more power from the Croats, exerting control over the majority of inland Croatia. Meanwhile, the Venetian Republic conquered most of the coast and peppered the Croatian Adriatic with bell towers and the winged lion of St. Mark.

The Ottomans (from today's Turkey) conquered most of inland Croatia by the 15th century and challenged the Venetians—unsuccessfully—for control of the coastline. Most of the stout walls, fortresses, and other fortifications you'll see all along the Croatian coast date from this time, built by the Venetians to defend against Ottoman attack.

Through it all, the tiny Republic of Dubrovnik flourished—paying off whomever necessary to maintain its independence and becoming one of Europe's most important shipbuilding and maritime powers. Although it was surrounded on all sides by the Ottoman threat, Dubrovnik persisted as a plucky rival to powerful Venice.

In the 17th century, the Habsburgs forced the Ottomans out of inland Croatia. Then, after Venice and Dubrovnik fell to Napoleon in the early 19th century, the coast also went to the Habsburgs—beginning a long tradition of Austrians basking on Croatian beaches.

The Yugoslav Era, World War II, and the Ustaše

When the Austro-Hungarian Empire broke up at the end of World War I, the Croats banded together with the Serbs, Slovenes, and Bosnians in the union that would become Yugoslavia. But virtually as soon as the Kingdom of Yugoslavia was formed, many Croats began to fear that the Serbs would steer Yugoslavia to their own purposes.

The parliamentarian Stjepan Radić spoke out passionately for Croat rights within the kingdom—until he was assassinated by a Serb on the morning of June 20, 1928, during a parliamentary session. This outbreak of violence alarmed Yugoslavia's Serb king, Alexander Karađorđević, who abolished the parliament and declared himself absolute ruler of the kingdom—squelching the Croats' fervently desired autonomy.

It was in this political climate, during the 1930s, that the Ustaše ("Uprisers")—a nationalistic, fascist movement bent on creating an ethnically pure "Greater Croatia"—gained popularity among a small but dangerous fringe of Croats. On September 9, 1934, Ustaše operatives assassinated King Alexander.

On April 6, 1941, Hitler's Luftwaffe began aerial bombardment of Belgrade; less than two weeks later, Nazi Germany controlled Yugoslavia. Hitler divvied up the territory among his Italian, Hungarian, and Bulgarian allies. He created the misnamed "Independent State of Croatia"—encompassing much of today's Croatia and Bosnia-Herzegovina, and parts of Serbia—to be led by Ante Pavelić and the Croatian Ustaše Party. The Ustaše operated one of the most brutal Nazi puppet states during World War II. Ustaše concentration camps—including the notorious Jasenovac extermination camp—were used to murder tens of thousands of Jews and Roma (Gypsies), as well as hundreds of thousands of Serbs.

The Croatian Catholic leader Cardinal Alojzije Stepinac was one Croat who made the mistake of backing the Ustaše. By most accounts, Stepinac was a mild-mannered, extremely devout man who didn't agree with the extremism of the Ustaše...but also did little to fight it. Following the war, Stepinac was arrested, tried, and imprisoned, dying under house arrest in 1960. In the years since, Stepinac has become a martyr for Catholics and Croat nationalists.

At the end of World War II, the Ustaše and the Nazis were forced out by Yugoslavia's homegrown Partisan Army, led by a charismatic war hero named Josip Broz, who went by his nickname, "Tito." Tito became "president for life," and Croatia once again became part of a united Yugoslavia. The union would hold together for more than 40 years, until it broke apart amid squabbles between Serbian President Slobodan Milošević and Croatian President Franjo Tuđman.

For more details on Yugoslavia and its breakup, see the Understanding Yugoslavia chapter.

Independence Regained

Croatia's declaration of independence from Yugoslavia in 1991 was met with fear and anger on the part of its more than half-million Serb residents. Even before independence, the first volleys of a bloody war had been fired. The conflict had two phases: First, in 1991, Croatian Serbs declared independence from the new nation of Croatia, forming their own state and forcing out or murdering any Croats in "their" territory (with thinly disguised military support from Slobodan Milošević). Then a tense cease-fire fell over the region until 1995, when the second phase of the war ignited: Croatia pushed back through the Serb-dominated territory, reclaiming it for Croatia and forcing out or murdering Serbs living there.

Imagine becoming an independent nation after nine centuries

of foreign domination. Croatians seized their hard-earned freedom with a nationalist fervor that bordered on fascism. It was a heady and absurd time, which today's Croatians recall with disbelief, sadness...and maybe a tinge of nostalgia.

In the Croatia of the early 1990s, even the most bizarre notions seemed possible. Croatia's first post-Yugoslav president, the extreme nationalist Franjo Tuđman (see sidebar), proposed bold directives for the new nation—such as privatizing all of the nation's resources and handing them over to 200 super-elite oligarchs. While this never quite happened, privatization relied heavily on nepotism, and Tuđman's highly placed allies enjoyed a windfall.

The government began calling the language "Croatian" rather than "Serbo-Croatian" and created new words from specifically Croat roots. Some outside-the-box thinkers even briefly considered replacing the Roman alphabet with the ninth-century Glagolitic script to invoke Croat culture and further differentiate Croatian from Serbia's Cyrillic alphabet. (Fortunately for tourists, this plan didn't take off.)

After Tuđman's death in 1999, Croatia began the new millennium with a more truly democratic leader, Stipe Mesić. The popular Mesić, who was once aligned with Tuđman, had split off and formed his own political party when Tuđman's politics grew too extreme. Tuđman spent years tampering with the constitution to give himself more and more power, but when Mesić took over, he reversed those changes and handed more authority back to the parliament.

After a successful decade as president, the term-limited Stipe Mesić stepped down in 2010. Ivo Josipović, running on a strong anti-corruption platform, won by a landslide.

Croatia Today

In 2013, Croatia joined the European Union—a benchmark of the progress the nation has made since Tuđman. But the road to EU membership has been a rocky one, and several thorny issues face contemporary Croatians.

The legacy of the Yugoslav Wars has yet to fully resolve itself in Croatia. The then-popular president, Franjo Tuđman, is now viewed with regret and suspicion by a significant segment of Croatian society (see sidebar). Others feel shame about reports that have emerged about Croatian soldiers' ethnic-cleansing activities during the war. Several Croatian officers were indicted for war crimes by the International Criminal Tribunal for the Former Yugoslavia (ICTY) in The Hague, Netherlands. The highest-profile of these—Lieutenant General Ante Gotovina—was discovered hiding in Spain in 2005, arrested, extradited, tried, convicted...and then acquitted on appeal in 2012. Yet to this day, many Croatians

Franjo Tuđman (1922-1999)

Independent Croatia's first president was the controversial Franjo Tuđman (FRAHN-yoh TOOJ-mahn). Tuđman began his career fighting for Tito on the left, but later made a dramatic ideological swing to the far right. His anticommunist, highly nationalistic HDZ party was the driving force for Croatian statehood, making him the young nation's first poster boy. But even as he fought for independence from Yugoslavia, his own ruling style grew more and more authoritarian. Today, years after his death, Tuđman remains a divisive figure.

Before entering politics, Tuđman was a military officer. He fought for Tito's Partisans in World War II, and was the youngest general in the Yugoslav People's Army. But later in life, Tuđman—now a professional historian—became a Croatian nationalist who revered the Ustaše, Croatia's Nazi-affiliated government during World War II. Because the Ustaše governed the first "independent" Croatian state since the 12th century, Tuđman considered them Croatian "freedom fighters." But that same state had murdered hundreds of thousands of Serbs in its concentration camps. (In a history book he authored, Tuđman controversially deflated this estimate to between 30,000 and 60,000—a figure no legitimate historian accepts.)

In the 1980s—following Tito's death, and as Yugoslavia began to unravel—Tuđman gained support for his nationalistic, anticommunist political party, the Croatian Democratic Union (*Hrvatska Demokratska Zajednica*, HDZ). In 1990, Croatia's first free elections of the post-Tito era, voters decisively supported Tuđman and the HDZ—effectively voting out the communists. In 1992, Tuđman was formally elected president.

As Tuđman took power, he wasted no time in reintroducing many Ustaše symbols, including their currency (the kuna, still used today). These provocative actions raised eyebrows worldwide, and raised alarms in Croatia's Serb communities.

Tuđman espoused many of the same single-minded attitudes about ethnic divisions as the ruthless Serbian leader Slobodan

feel that the soldiers branded as "war criminals" by The Hague are instead heroes of their war of independence.

Croatia's relations with its neighbors—many of whom were involved in the Yugoslav Wars—are also sometimes problematic. While Croatia and Slovenia shared the same goal (separating from Yugoslavia), many Croatians resent Slovenia's lack of military support for Croatian independence. Decades later, tensions still persist. Slovenia briefly blocked Croatia's EU membership bid in an effort to resolve a longstanding border dispute (described on page 746). Ironically, even many Croatians who were vehemently opposed to EU membership were outraged that Slovenia tried to pre-

Milošević. Croat forces—which may or may not have been acting under Tuđman's orders—carried out wide-scale ethnic cleansing, targeting Serb and Muslim minorities. Tuđman and Milošević had secret, Hitler-and-Stalin-esque negotiations even as they were ripping into each other rhetorically. According to some reports, at one meeting they divvied up a map of Bosnia-Herzegovina on a cocktail napkin. Their so-called "Karađorđevo Agreement" completely left out the Bosniaks, who constituted the largest ethnic group within the nation whose fate was being decided.

To ensure that he stayed in power, Tuđman played fast and loose with his new nation's laws. He was notorious for changing the constitution as it suited him. By the late 1990s, when his popularity was slipping, Tuđman extended Croatian citizenship to anyone in the world who had Croatian heritage—a ploy aimed at gathering votes from Croats living in Bosnia-Herzegovina, who were sure to line up with him on the far right.

Tuđman kept a tight grip on the media, making it illegal to report anything that would disturb the public—even if true. When Croatians turned on their TV sets and saw the flag flapping in the breeze to the strains of the national anthem, they knew something was up...and switched to CNN to get the real story. In this oppressive environment, many bright, young Croatians fled the country, causing a "brain drain" that hampered the postwar recovery.

Tuđman died of cancer at the end of 1999. While history will probably judge him harshly, the opinion in today's Croatia is qualified. Most agree that Tuđman was an important and even admirable figure in the struggle for Croatian statehood, but he ultimately went too far and got too greedy. The most elaborate tomb in Zagreb's national cemetery (Mirogoj) honors this "Croatian founding father." And yet, prosecutors at the International Criminal Tribunal in The Hague have said that if Tuđman were alive, he would be standing trial for war crimes.

vent it. On recent trips to this region, when I show people the cover of this book, people in both countries express displeasure about being grouped together.

Another vexing issue in today's Croatia is government corruption—perhaps best embodied by the country's previous prime minister, Ivo Sanader, who abruptly resigned in 2009, and soon after was arrested, convicted, and sent to prison.

Croatians—and especially expats living here—report that the country is excessively bureaucratic, and can be a tough place to do business. Laws tend to be implemented, then quickly overturned. In the last few years, a ban on shops being open on Sundays, a smoking ban, and a zero blood-alcohol limit for drivers have all come and gone.

In 2012, two-thirds of Croatians voted in favor of EU membership. But when it went into effect on July 1, 2013, some were caught off guard by the stringent new lifestyle that came with it. As if eager to prove they were upstanding citizens, Croatian government officials ratcheted up enforcement of often-ignored laws and regulations. Undercover tax inspectors were deployed throughout the country, ensuring that businesses small and large were properly issuing receipts and reporting their earnings. A strange paranoia swept over small-business owners during the summer of 2013, as rumors spread like wildfire about shops and restaurants being shut down for days at a time because of just a few kunas' discrepancy in their books. Given the nation's recent corruption woes, some pragmatists argue that these heightened regulations—while troublesome for a few legitimate businesspeople—may be a necessary evil.

The reality of EU membership rocked Croatia again in the fall of 2015, when a wave of immigrants from war-torn Syria (as well as many other Middle Eastern and Balkan nations) began to flood into Europe. When neighboring Hungary closed its borders to refugees, many began to spill into northern Croatia. While refugees camped out at the borders, Croatian government agencies and NGOs alike scrambled to deal with simultaneous humanitarian and diplomatic crises.

Despite such geopolitical challenges, Croatia continues to emerge as a red-hot destination for holiday-makers, and with some of the growing pains of new nationhood behind it, seems poised for an ever-brighter future.

CROATIAN FOOD

Most Croatians eat to live, rather than the other way around. This is not quite the "foodie" destination that the tourist board likes to promote. While there are delicious exceptions, the cuisine tends to fall into a predictable rut of pizza, pasta, and no-frills seafood (especially along the coast). Expect good, solid, fill-the-tank meals; if you care about food, try to seek out something more imaginative—especially in the cities. (My restaurant listings attempt to highlight the best of both functional and memorable eateries.)

Two staples in Croatia, as in most Mediterranean lands, are wine and olive oil. You'll see vineyards and olive groves blanketing the Croatian countryside and islandscapes. Croatians joke that grapes are like a new bride—they demand a lot of attention, while olives are like a mother—low-maintenance. Another major part of the local diet is the air-dried ham called *pršut* (a.k.a. prosciutto—see sidebar on page 530).

While you'll find places called *restaurant*, you'll more often see the name *konoba*—which means an unpretentious tradition-al restaurant, like an inn. To request a menu, say, *"Meni, molim"* (MEH-nee, MOH-leem; "Menu, please"). To get the attention of your waiter, say *"Konobar"* (KOH-noh-bahr; "Waiter"). When he's ready to take your order, he'll say, *"Izvolite."* When he brings your food, he'll likely say, *"Dobar tek!"* ("Enjoy your meal!"). When you're ready for the bill, ask for the *račun* (RAH-choon).

CROATIA

Main Dishes

On the coast, seafood is a specialty, and the Italian influence is ob-vious. According to Dalmatians, "Eating meat is food; eating fish is pleasure." They also say that a fish should swim three times: first in the sea, then in olive oil, and finally in wine—when you eat it. If you see something described as "Dalmatian-style," it usually means with lots of olive oil, parsley, and garlic.

You can get all kinds of seafood: fish, scampi, mussels, squid, octopus, you name it. Keep in mind that prices for fish dishes are listed either by the kilogram (1,000 grams) or by the 100-gram unit (figure about a half-kilo, or 500 grams—that's about one pound—for a large portion). While this is a land of fisherfolk, frozen fish is not unheard of—if you want something fresh from the market, ask. When ordering, be prepared for surprises. For example, *škampi* (shrimp) often come still in their shells (sometimes with crayfish-like claws), which can be messy and time-consuming to eat. Before you order shrimp, ask if it's shelled. The menu item called "small fried fish" is generally a plate of deep-fried minnows. If you're not clear on exactly what something is, feel free to ask for clarification (though some waiters are more forthcoming than others).

Sometimes it's a pleasant surprise—many menu items that don't sound appetizing can be delicious. Jump at the chance to sample a

good, fresh anchovy—which, when done right, has a pleasant flavor and a melt-in-your-mouth texture that's a world away from the salty, withered little fish you might find topping a pizza back home. Those not accustomed to eating octopus might want to try octopus salad: a flavorful mix of

CROATIA

Croatian Wine

For gourmands, one of the most pleasant surprises about a trip to Croatia is the quality of the wines. While much of the industry was state-run and focused on mass production during communist times, today vintner families are returning to their roots—literally—and making Croatian wines something to be proud of. Thanks partly to the interest and investment of American vintners, Croatian wines are gaining respect worldwide. Because very few Croatian wines are exported, a visit here is a good chance to sample some new tastes.

The northern part of the country primarily produces whites (*bijelo vino*, bee-YEH-loh VEE-noh), usually dry (*suho*, SOO-hoh) but sometimes semi-dry (*polusuho*, POHL-soo-hoh) or sweet (*slatko*, SLAHT-koh). The sunny mountains just north of Zagreb are covered with vineyards producing whites. From Slavonia (Croatia's inland panhandle), you'll find *graševina*—crisp, dry, and acidic (like a dry Riesling). Well-respected brands include Krauthaker and Enjingi (whose prizewinning Venje wine is a blend of five white grape varieties). The Istrian Peninsula corks up some good whites, including *malvazija*, a very popular, light, mid-range wine (Muscat is also popular). The best reds from this region are made from the *teran* grape, though you'll find some cabernet sauvignon and merlot as well. Top  producers here include Degrassi (try their Terre Bianche white and red blends), Kabola, Kozlović, and Matošević (all of these can be visited for a tasting—see page 156).

As you move south, along the Dalmatian Coast, the wines turn red—which Croatians call "black wine" (*crno vino*, TSUR-noh VEE-noh). The dominant grape here is *plavac mali* ("little blue")—a distant relative of Californian zinfandel. Many of the best coastal reds are produced on the long Pelješac Peninsula, across from Korčula (the most well-respected regions are Dingač and Postup; see page 357). But each island also produces its own good wines. Korčula (especially near the villages of Čara and Smokvica) makes excellent white wine from *pošip* grapes (which are high alcohol and low acidity—locals like to cut this with carbonated water), as well as *grk* ("Greek" grapes that grow only around Lumbarda—try it at the Bire winery, page 264) and *korčulanka*. Hvar's wines tend to be fruitier and less tannic; they specialize in *pošip*, as well as *bogdanuša* ("from the gods")—which has low alcohol and high acidity. On Hvar, good places to try wines include the Tomić winery, in the village of

Jelsa (see page 238), and at Vina Pinjata in Vrboska (see page 236).

Other wines to look for include the heavenly, sweet dessert wine called *prošek* (similar to port wine or Italian *vin santo*). While rosés aren't a big business here, some producers make them to keep up with winemaking trends; you may see them called Opolo (*pol* means "half").

When looking at wine labels, watch for these three official classifications: *stolno* ("table," the lowest grade), *kvalitento* ("quality"—actually mid-range), and *vrhunsko* (top-quality). In general, if only the grape is listed (e.g., *mali plavac*), the quality isn't as good as when the region is prominently noted (e.g., Dingač or Postup). You may also see the words *vinogorje* (vineyard), *položaj* (location), and *barrique* (barrel-aged).

The big name in Croatian wines is Miljenko Grgić. Born in Croatia in 1923, Grgić emigrated from communist Yugoslavia to the US and—as "Mike Grgich"—worked at the Chateau Montelena Winery in Napa Valley. In the famous "Judgment of Paris" in 1976, Grgić's 1973 chardonnay beat out several well-respected French wines in a blind taste test. Considered a turning point in the winemaking world, this event brought new respect to American winemakers and put Napa on the mapa.

Having revolutionized American winemaking, Grgić turned his sights on his Croatian homeland. He imported California know-how to the slopes of the Pelješac Peninsula, where he set about making some of Croatia's first truly well-respected wines. Grgić grows his red *plavac mali* on the Pelješac Peninsula (at Dingač and nearby, at Trstanik), and his white *pošip* wine on Korčula Island.

The prices for Grgić's wines match his reputation; for producers that are comparable but a bit more affordable, look for these red-wine alternatives: Madirazza (they make a great Postup), Frano Miloš (try the full-bodied Stagnum), and Matuško and Skaramuća (good Dingač). Philipp, by a famously meticulous Swiss-Croatian vintner, produces a good Postup, as well as a fine summer white that blends *rukatac* and chardonnay.

While Croatian wines are impressive, don't overlook their neighbors' vintages as well. Slovenia corks up some excellent bottles (especially in the western and eastern reaches of the country—see page 532), and Montenegro has some of the best wines in the entire region (see page 398).

octopus, tomatoes, onions, capers, and spices. In the interior, trout is popular.

Croatia also has plenty of meat options. A delicious Dalmatian specialty is *pašticada*—braised beef in a slightly sweet wine-and-herb sauce, usually served with gnocchi. Dalmatia is also known for its mutton. Since the lambs graze on salty seaside herbs, the meat—often served on a spit—has a distinctive flavor. Throughout Croatia, look for the spicy, flavorful stewed pork-and-vegetables dish called *mućkalica*. The most widely available meat dish is the "mixed grill"—a combination of various Balkan grilled meats, best accompanied by the eggplant-and-red-pepper condiment *ajvar* (see the "Balkan Flavors" sidebar on page 421).

The best meat dish in Croatia is veal or lamb prepared under a *peka*—a metal baking lid that's covered with red-hot coals, to allow

the meat to gradually cook to tender perfection. (*Ispod peka* means "under the bell.") Available only in traditional restaurants, this dish typically must be ordered in advance and for multiple people. You'll also find a break from seafood in the north (Zagreb) and east (Slavonia), where the food has more of a Hungarian flavor—heavy on meat served with cabbage, noodles, or potatoes.

Budget-conscious tourists reserve meat and fish for splurge dinners and mostly dine on cheaper and faster pastas and pizzas. You'll see familiar dishes, such as spaghetti Bolognese (with meat sauce) and spaghetti carbonara (with a sauce of egg, parmesan, and bacon), gnocchi (*njoki*, potato dumplings), and lasagna. Risotto (*rižoto*, a rice dish) is popular here; most common is "black risotto," mixed with squid ink and various kinds of seafood.

Side Dishes

There are many good local varieties of cheese made with sheep's or goat's milk. Pag, an island in the Kvarner Gulf, produces a famous, very salty, fairly dry sheep's-milk cheese *(paški sir)*, which is said to be flavored by the herbs the sheep eat.

A common side dish is boiled potatoes and mangold *(bltiva)*; sometimes identified as "Dalmatian chard," this green is similar to Swiss chard. When ordering salad, choose between mixed (julienned cabbage, carrots, and turnips, often with some tomatoes or beets, and occasionally with a bit of lettuce) or green (mostly lettuce). Throughout Croatia, salad is typically served with the main dish unless you request that it be brought beforehand.

Dessert and Beverages

For dessert, look no further than the mountains of delicious, homemade ice cream *(sladoled)* that line every street in coastal Croatia. While most *sladoled* isn't quite gourmet (don't expect the *artigianale* brilliance of Italian *gelaterias*), I've worked hard to sample and recommend the best ice-cream parlors in each town. (Poor me.) Dalmatia's typical dessert is a flan-like, crème caramel custard, called *rozata*. *Prošek* is a sweet dessert wine.

Water is *voda,* and mineral water is *mineralna voda.* Jamnica is the main Croatian brand of bottled water, but you'll also see Bistra and Studenac. Many restaurants—especially fancier ones—might not want to bring you a glass of tap water, but you can try asking for *voda iz slavine.* For coffee *(kava),* the easiest choice is *bijela kava* (BEE-yeh-lah KAH-vah)—"white coffee," or espresso with lots of milk (similar to a *caffè latte*). To get it black, ask for *crna kava* (TSUR-nah KAH-vah).

The most popular Croatian beers *(pivo)* are Ožujsko and Karlovačko, but you'll also see the Slovenian brand Laško (which is also brewed here in Croatia). Fans of dark beer *(crno pivo)* enjoy Tomislav. Most places also serve nonalcoholic beers *(bezalkoholno pivo);* most common are Ožujsko Cool and Stella Artois NA.

Even more beloved in Croatia is wine *(vino;* see "Croatian Wine" sidebar, page 32). Along the coast, locals find it refreshing to drink wine mixed with mineral water (called, as in English, *špricer*). When toasting with some new Croatian friends, raise your glass with a hearty *"Živjeli!"* (ZHEE-vyeh-lee).

CROATIAN LANGUAGE

Croatian was once known as "Serbo-Croatian," the official language of Yugoslavia. Most Yugoslav republics—including Croatia, Serbia, and Bosnia-Herzegovina—spoke this same language. And while each of these countries has tried to distance its language from that of its neighbors since the war, the languages spoken in all of these places are still very similar. The biggest difference is in the writing: Croatians and Bosniaks use our Roman alphabet, while Serbs use Cyrillic letters.

In recent years, Croatia has attempted to artificially make its vocabulary different from Serbian. In Yugoslav times, you'd catch a plane at the *aerodrom.* Today, you'll catch that same flight at the *zračna luka*—a new coinage that combines the old Croatian words for "air" and "port." These new words, once created, are actively injected into the lexicon. Croatians watching their favorite TV show will suddenly hear a character use a word they've never heard before...and think, "Oh, we have another new word." In this way, Croatian really is becoming quite different from Serbian (in much the same way Norwegian evolved apart from Swedish a century ago).

Remember, *c* is pronounced "ts" (as in "bats"). The letter *j* is pronounced as "y." The letters *č* and *ć* are slightly different, but they both sound more or less like "ch"; *š* sounds like "sh," and *ž* sounds like "zh" (as in "leisure"). One Croatian letter that you won't see in other languages is *đ*, which sounds like the "dj" sound in "jeans." In fact, this letter is often replaced with "dj" in English.

When attempting to pronounce an unfamiliar word, remember that the accent is usually on the first syllable (and never on the last). Confusingly, Croatian pronunciation—even of the same word—can vary in different parts of the country. This is because modern Croatian has three distinct dialects, called Kajkavian, Shtokavian, and Chakavian—based on how you say "what?" (*kaj?*, *što?*, and *ča?*, respectively). That's a lot of variety for a language with only five million speakers.

Attentive travelers will frequently hear two Croatian phrases that are used as enthusiastic affirmatives, like "sure" or "OK": *može* (MOH-zheh; can do) and *ajde* (EYE-deh; let's go).

For a smoother trip, take some time to learn a few key Croatian phrases (see the Croatian survival phrases on the next page).

Croatian Survival Phrases

In the phonetics, ī sounds like the long i in "light," and bolded
syllables are stressed.

English	Croatian	Pronunciation
Hello. (formal)	Dobar dan.	**doh**-bahr dahn
Hi. / Bye. (informal)	Bok.	bohk
Do you speak English?	Govorite li engleski?	**goh**-voh-ree-teh lee **ehn**-glehs-kee
Yes. / No.	Da. / Ne.	dah / neh
I (don't) understand.	(Ne) razumijem.	(neh) rah-**zoo**-mee-yehm
Please. / You're welcome.	Molim.	**moh**-leem
Thank you (very much).	Hvala (ljepa).	**hvah**-lah (**lyeh**-pah)
Excuse me. / I'm sorry.	Oprostite.	oh-**proh**-stee-teh
problem	problem	proh-**blehm**
No problem.	Nema problema.	**neh**-mah proh-**bleh**-mah
Good.	Dobro.	**doh**-broh
Goodbye.	Do viđenija.	doh veed-**jay**-neeah
one / two	jedan / dva	**yeh**-dahn / dvah
three / four	tri / četiri	tree / **cheh**-teh-ree
five / six	pet / šest	peht / shehst
seven / eight	sedam / osam	**seh**-dahm / **oh**-sahm
nine / ten	devet / deset	**deh**-veht / **deh**-seht
hundred / thousand	sto / tisuća	stoh / **tee**-soo-chah
How much?	Koliko?	**koh**-lee-koh
local currency	kuna	**koo**-nah
Write it?	Napišite?	nah-**peesh**-ee-teh
Is it free?	Da li je besplatno?	dah lee yeh **beh**-splaht-noh
Is it included?	Da li je uključeno?	dah lee yeh **ook**-lyoo-cheh-noh
Where can I find / buy...?	Gdje mogu pronaći / kupiti...?	guh-**dyeh** moh-goo **proh**-nah-chee / **koo**-pee-tee
I'd like / We'd like...	Želio bih / Željeli bismo...	**zheh**-lee-oh bee / **zheh**-lyeh-lee **bees**-moh
...a room.	...sobu.	**soh**-boo
...a ticket to ___.	...kartu do ___.	**kar**-too doh ___
Is it possible?	Da li je moguće?	dah lee yeh **moh**-goo-cheh
Where is...?	Gdje je...?	guh-**dyeh** yeh
...the train station	...kolodvor	**koh**-loh-dvor
...the bus station	...autobusni kolodvor	ow-toh-boos-nee **koh**-loh-dvor
...the tourist information office	...turističko informativni centar	**too**-ree-steech-koh **een**-for-mah-teev-nee **tsehn**-tahr
...the toilet	...vece (WC)	**veht**-seh
men / women	muški / ženski	**moosh**-kee / **zhehn**-skee
left / right / straight	lijevo / desno / ravno	**lee**-yeh-voh / **dehs**-noh / **rahv**-noh
At what time...?	U koliko sati...?	oo **koh**-lee-koh **sah**-tee
...does this open / close	...otvara / zatvara	**oht**-vah-rah / **zaht**-vah-rah
(Just) a moment.	(Samo) trenutak.	(**sah**-moh) treh-**noo**-tahk
now / soon / later	sada / uskoro / kasnije	**sah**-dah / **oos**-koh-roh / **kahs**-nee-yeh
today / tomorrow	danas / sutra	**dah**-nahs / **soo**-trah

In a Croatian Restaurant

English	Croatian	Pronunciation
I'd like to reserve…	Rezervirao bih…	reh-zehr-**veer**-ow bee
We'd like to reserve…	Rezervirali bismo…	reh-zehr-**vee**-rah-lee bees-moh
…a table for one / two.	…stol za jednog / dva.	stohl zah yehd-nog / dvah
Is this table free?	Da li je ovaj stol slobodan?	dah lee yeh oh-vī stohl sloh-boh-dahn
Can I help you?	Izvolite?	eez-voh-lee-teh
The menu (in English), please.	Jelovnik (na engleskom), molim.	yeh-**lohv**-neek (nah ehn-glehs-kohm) moh-leem
service (not) included	posluga (nije) uključena	poh-sloo-gah (**nee**-yeh) ook-lyoo-cheh-nah
cover charge	couvert	**koo**-vehr
"to go"	za ponjeti	zah **pohn**-yeh-tee
with / without	sa / bez	sah / behz
and / or	i / ili	ee / **ee**-lee
fixed-price meal (of the day)	(dnevni) meni	(duh-**nehv**-nee) meh-nee
specialty of the house	specijalitet kuće	speht-see-yah-**lee**-teht **koo**-cheh
half portion	pola porcije	**poh**-lah **port**-see-yeh
daily special	jelo dana	**yeh**-loh **dah**-nah
fixed-price meal for tourists	turistički meni	**too**-ree-steech-kee **meh**-nee
appetizers	predjela	**prehd**-yeh-lah
bread	kruh	kroo
cheese	sir	seer
sandwich	sendvič	**send**-veech
soup	juha	**yoo**-hah
salad	salata	sah-**lah**-tah
meat / poultry	meso / perad	**may**-soh / **peh**-rahd
fish / seafood	riba / morska hrana	**ree**-bah **mor**-skah **hrah**-nah
fruit	voće	**voh**-cheh
vegetables	povrće	**poh**-vur-cheh
dessert	desert	deh-**sayrt**
(tap) water	voda (od slavine)	**voh**-dah (ohd **slah**-vee-neh)
mineral water	mineralna voda	**mee**-neh-rahl-nah **voh**-dah
milk	mlijeko	mlee-**yeh**-koh
(orange) juice	sok (od naranče)	sohk (ohd **nah**-rahn-cheh)
coffee	kava	**kah**-vah
tea	čaj	chī
wine	vino	**vee**-noh
red / white	crno / bijelo	**tsehr**-noh / bee-**yeh**-loh
sweet / dry / semi-dry	slatko / suho / polusuho	**slaht**-koh / **soo**-hoh / **poh**-loo-soo-hoh
glass / bottle	čaša / boca	**chah**-shah / **boht**-sah
beer	pivo	**pee**-voh
Cheers!	Živjeli!	**zhee**-vyeh-lee
More. / Another.	Još. / Još jedno.	yohsh / yohsh **yehd**-noh
The same.	Isto.	**ees**-toh
Bill, please.	Račun, molim.	rah-**choon** **moh**-leem
tip	napojnica	**nah**-poy-neet-sah
Delicious!	Izvrsno!	**eez**-vur-snoh

ZAGREB

Surprise: The landlocked Croatian capital is, quite possibly, the country's most underrated destination. In this land of time-passed coastal villages, Zagreb (ZAH-grehb) offers a welcome jolt of big-city sophistication. You can't get a complete picture of modern Croatia without a visit here—away from the touristy resorts, in the lively and livable city that is home to one out of every six Croatians (pop. 790,000). Think of it as a palate cleanser before or after your time on the coast.

In Zagreb, you'll find historic neighborhoods, a thriving café culture, an impressive variety of good restaurants, my favorite urban people-watching in Croatia, a nearly Prague-like Old World streetscape, and virtually no tourists. The city is also the country's best destination for museum-going, with wonderful collections highlighting distinctively Croatian artists (the Naive Art movement and sculptor Ivan Meštrović), a quirky exhibit telling the tales of fractured relationships, and a smattering of other fine options (modern art, city history, arts and crafts, and much more). Get your fill here before heading to smaller cities and towns, where worthwhile museums are in short supply.

Zagreb began as two walled medieval towns, Gradec and Kaptol, separated by a river. As Croatia fell under the control of various foreign powers—Budapest, Vienna, Berlin, and Belgrade—the two hill towns that would become Zagreb gradually took on more religious and civic importance. Kaptol became a bishopric in 1094, and it's still home to Croatia's most important church. In the 16th century, the Ban (Croatia's governor) and the Sabor (parliament) called Gradec home. The two towns officially merged in 1850, and soon after, the railroad connecting Budapest with the Adriatic port city of Rijeka was built through the city. Zagreb prospered. After centuries of being the de facto religious, cultural, and political center of Croatia, Zagreb officially became a European capital when the country declared its independence in 1991. Today, while tourism is on the rise, Zagreb may be the only destination in this book that still feels undiscovered. The city richly rewards those who choose to visit.

PLANNING YOUR TIME

Many visitors just pass through Zagreb, but the city is worth a look. Throw your bag in a locker at the station and zip into the center for a quick visit—or, better yet, spend a night or two. If you enjoy urban bustle and good museums, you won't regret spending a full day (or more) here.

If you're very tight on time, make a beeline for Jelačić Square to visit the TI and get oriented. Take the funicular up to Gradec, visit the excellent Croatian Museum of Naive Art and/or the Museum of Broken Relationships, and stroll St. Mark's Square. Then wander down through the Stone Gate to the lively Tkalčićeva scene (good for a drink or meal), through the market (winds down at 14:00), and on to Kaptol and the cathedral. Depending on how much you linger, this loop can take anywhere from three hours to a full day.

With additional time, visit more of Zagreb's museums (the Meštrović Atelier and City Museum, both in the compact Gradec zone, are both worthwhile), wander the series of parks called the "Green Horseshoe" (with even more museums), pay a visit to the beautiful Mirogoj Cemetery (one of Europe's finest final resting places), or head to the enjoyable nearby town of Samobor.

If you're heading to Plitvice Lakes National Park (described in the next chapter), be warned that the last bus leaves Zagreb in the late afternoon (usually around 16:00); confirm your bus departure carefully to ensure that you don't get stranded in Zagreb.

Orientation to Zagreb

Zagreb, just 30 minutes from the Slovenian border, stretches from the foothills of Medvednica ("Bear Mountain") to the Sava River. In the middle of the sprawl, you'll find the modern **Lower Town** (Donji Grad)—centered on **Jelačić Square** (YEH-lah-cheech)—and the two parts of the historic **Upper Town** (Gornji Grad): **Gradec** (GRAH-dehts) and **Kaptol** (KAHP-tohl). To the south is a

U-shaped belt of parks, squares, and museums that make up the **"Green Horseshoe."** The east side of the U is a series of three parks, with the train station at the bottom (south) and Jelačić Square at the top (north).

Zagrebians have devised a brilliant scheme for confusing tourists: Street names can be given several different ways. For example, the street that is signed as ulica Kralja Držislava ("King Držislav Street") is often called simply Držislavova ("Držislav's") by locals. So if you're looking for a street, don't search for an exact match—be willing to settle for something that has a lot of the same letters.

TOURIST INFORMATION

Zagreb has Croatia's best-organized TI, right on Jelačić Square (June-Sept Mon-Fri 8:30-21:00, Sat-Sun 9:00-18:00; Oct-May Mon-Fri 8:30-20:00, Sat 9:00-18:00, Sun 10:00-16:00; Trg bana Jelačića 11, tel. 01/481-4051, www.zagreb-touristinfo.hr). More TIs are in the train station, bus station, and airport (all open Mon-Fri 9:00-21:00, Sat-Sun 10:00-17:00). There's also a branch in the Burglars' Tower at the top of the funicular in Gradec (daily 9:00-21:00 in summer, shorter hours off-season). Pick up the monthly events guide and the great *Step by Step* brochure (with a couple of good self-guided walking tours). I'd skip the Zagreb Card (free transportation and discounts at most Zagreb museums, 60 kn/24 hours, 90 kn/72 hours, sold at kiosk inside main TI).

ARRIVAL IN ZAGREB

By Train: Zagreb's main train station (Glavni Kolodvor) is a few long blocks south of Jelačić Square, at the base of the Green Horseshoe. The straightforward arrivals hall has a train information desk, ticket windows, luggage lockers (lining the hallway to the left as you exit the platform), ATMs, pay WCs, a Konzum grocery store, and newsstands. To reach the city center, go straight out the front door. You'll run into a taxi stand and then the tracks for **tram** #6 (direction: Črnomerec zips you to Jelačić Square; direction: Sopot takes you to the bus station—the third stop, just after you turn right and go under the big overpass). You can also take tram #13 to Jelačić Square (direction: Žitnjak). For either tram, buy a 10-kn ticket from the kiosk, and validate it when you board the tram—use the yellow box nearest the driver. If you **walk** straight ahead through the long, lush park, you'll wind up at the bottom of Jelačić Square in 10 minutes.

By Bus: The user-friendly but inconveniently located bus station (Autobusni Kolodvor) is a few long blocks southeast of the main train station. The station has all the essentials—ATMs, post office, mini grocery store, left-luggage counter...everything from a smut store to a chapel. Upstairs, you'll find ticket windows and ac-

ZAGREB

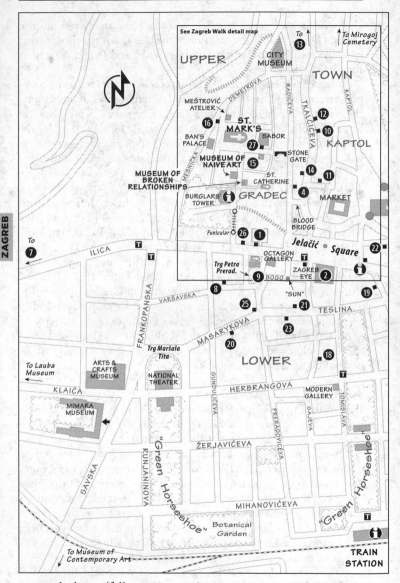

cess to the buses (follow signs to *izlaz na perone;* wave ticket in front of turnstile to open gate). Tram #6 (direction: Črnomerec) takes you to the main train station, then on to Jelačić Square. Walking from the bus station to Jelačić Square takes about 25 minutes.

By Plane: Zagreb's small airport is 10 miles south of the center (airport code: ZAG, tel. 01/626-5222, www.zagreb-airport.hr). If you have time to kill, head up the stairs (near the main security checkpoint) to the rooftop café view-terrace, where you can enjoy

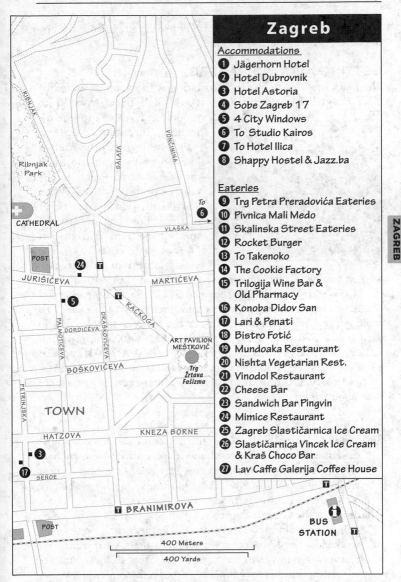

ZAGREB

Zagreb

Accommodations
1. Jägerhorn Hotel
2. Hotel Dubrovnik
3. Hotel Astoria
4. Sobe Zagreb 17
5. 4 City Windows
6. To Studio Kairos
7. To Hotel Ilica
8. Shappy Hostel & Jazz.ba

Eateries
9. Trg Petra Preradovića Eateries
10. Pivnica Mali Medo
11. Skalinska Street Eateries
12. Rocket Burger
13. To Takenoko
14. The Cookie Factory
15. Trilogija Wine Bar & Old Pharmacy
16. Konoba Didov San
17. Lari & Penati
18. Bistro Fotić
19. Mundoaka Restaurant
20. Nishta Vegetarian Rest.
21. Vinodol Restaurant
22. Cheese Bar
23. Sandwich Bar Pingvin
24. Mimice Restaurant
25. Zagreb Slastičarnica Ice Cream
26. Slastičarnica Vincek Ice Cream & Kraš Choco Bar
27. Lav Caffe Galerija Coffee House

a drink while watching planes take off and land, with the Zagreb skyline on the distant horizon. A shuttle bus connects the airport to the bus station (2/hour, 30 minutes, 30 kn); from there, you can walk outside and hop on a tram into town (see "By Bus," earlier). It can be worth the convenience to pay for a taxi right to your hotel (30 minutes; the fair metered rate is around 180-200 kn, but some crooked cabbies might try to charge more—to avoid this, ask for an estimate before you get in). It's cheaper to take a taxi from the city to the airport—figure 100-150 kn.

GETTING AROUND ZAGREB

The main mode of public transportation is the **tram,** operated by ZET (Zagreb Electrical Transport). A single ticket costs 10 kn

(good for 1.5 hours in one direction, including transfers). You can buy tickets from a kiosk near the tram stop (ask for *ZET karta*—zeht KAR-tah), or from the driver. When you board, punch your ticket in the yellow box nearest the front of the tram. A day ticket *(dnevna karta)* costs 30 kn. The most useful tram for tourists is #6, connecting Jelačić Square with the train and bus stations.

Taxis start at 10-15 kn, then run 5-7 kn per kilometer (exact rate depends on company, 3 kn extra for each piece of baggage). To avoid getting overcharged, call one of the main companies: Radio Taxi (tel. 1717 or 01/660-0671 or 060-800-800), Cammeo (tel. 1212 or 060-7100), or Ekotaxi (tel. 1414 or 060-7777). If you hail a cab on the street, beware of corrupt cabbies; ask for an estimate up front. A typical ride within the city center shouldn't run more than about 30 kn.

HELPFUL HINTS

Sight Hours: Virtually all of Zagreb's museums are closed on Sunday afternoon and all day Monday; most also close early Saturday afternoon. Some museums stay open late one night a week in summer (usually Thu). On Sunday morning, the city is thriving—but by afternoon, it's extremely quiet.

Changing of the Guard: Zagreb's "Changing of the Guard" ceremony (a recent innovation) enlivens the city center on summer weekends. The 17th-century-costumed guards wear jaunty red scarves (an homage to the tale of how Croat soldiers "invented" the necktie) as they proceed through the center of town—passing landmarks such as St. Mark's Square, Tkalčićeva street, Jelačić Square, and the statue of Mary in front of the cathedral (mid-April-Sept only, Sat-Sun, begins at 12:00 on St. Mark's Square, ask for complete schedule at TI). While little more than a photo op, this ceremony is one of the many ways Zagreb is working hard to please visitors.

Tours in Zagreb

Local Guides

While I've covered the basics in my self-guided walk, Zagreb gets even more interesting with a good tour guide. I recommend two knowledgeable guides who know their city well and enjoy sharing its charms with visitors: **Darija Gotić** (550 kn/2-3-hour tour, mobile 098-186-7719, darija@assistere.biz) or **Dijana Bebek Miletić** (630 kn/3-hour tour, mobile 091-303-3979, dijana.bebek.miletic@ live.com).

Night Walks

Various after-hours walking tours are a popular way to get some post-dinner infotainment. The **Zagreb Ghost Tour** focuses on spooky stories (75 kn, nightly at 21:00, 2 hours, mobile 097-673-8738, www.secret-zagreb.com), while the **Secrets of Grič Tour** ("Grič" is the nickname for Gradec) brings that historic quarter to life with a costumed guide imparting local legends (150 kn, May-mid-Sept Sat only at 21:00, one hour, mobile 091-461-5677, www. tajnegrica.hr). Both of these require reservations.

Segway Tour

Already popular in many other cities, Segway tours have come to Zagreb, offering a low-impact, narrated zip around town on a stand-up motorized scooter (see options on their website, tel. 01/301-0390, mobile 095-903-4227, www.segway.hr, zagreb@ segway.hr).

Bike Tours

Blue Bike runs a variety of different bike-tour routes through the city, starting on Jelačić Square (175 kn, daily at 10:00 and 17:00— or at 14:00 off-season, reservations required, mobile 098-188-3344, www.zagrebbybike.com). They also rent bikes (100 kn/day).

Zagreb Walk

The following self-guided orientation walk, rated ▲▲, begins and ends at Jelačić Square, linking almost everything that's worth seeing in this city, including the two hilltop towns that merged in 1850 to become Zagreb: Gradec and Kaptol. If you don't enter any of the sights, the entire route takes about 1.5 hours. But if you take your time, you can use it as a framework for a full day of sightseeing. If you want to explore the market—which is near the end of this walk—keep in mind that it becomes quiet after about 14:00. To avoid feeling rushed, you may want to tour the market first (just a block away from our starting point), then embark on this walk.

▲▲Jelačić Square (Trg bana Jelačića)

The "Times Square" of Zagreb bustles with life. Watching the crowds pile in and out of trams and seeing the city buzz with ac-

tivity, you'll feel the energy of an on-the-rise capital of a vibrant nation. This is also a popular place for any kind of special event in town—from concerts and sporting events, to folk festivals, protests, and rallies. The city's busy pedestrian scene, sense of style, and utter lack of tourists make it arguably Croatia's best people-watching destination.

It's hard to believe that this frenetic Donji Grad ("lower town") once held the townspeople's farm fields. Our walk takes you from here up to two towns—Gradec and Kaptol—that merged in 1850 to become the city of Zagreb. At that time, it was a small settlement of about 16,000 people. But under the auspices of the Austro-Hungarian Empire, the newly united Zagreb began to industrialize and grow like mad. These former fields sprouted aristocratic villas as well as low-rent housing for factory workers.

Today, the square features a prominent equestrian statue of national hero **Josip Jelačić** (YOH-seep YEH-lah-cheech, 1801-

1859), a 19th-century governor who extended citizens' rights and did much to unite the Croats within the Habsburg Empire. In Jelačić's time, the Hungarians were exerting extensive control over Croatia, even trying to make Hungarian the official language. Meanwhile, Budapesters revolted against Habsburg rule in 1848. Jelačić, ever mindful of the need to protect Croatian cultural autonomy, knew that he'd have a better shot at getting his way from Austria than from Hungary. Jelačić chose the lesser of two evils and fought alongside the

Habsburgs to put down the Hungarian uprising. A century later, in the Yugoslav era, Jelačić was considered a dangerously nationalistic symbol, and this statue was dismantled and stored away. But when Croatia broke away in 1991, Croatian patriotism was in the air, and Jelačić returned. Though Jelačić originally faced his Hungarian foes to the north, today he's staring down the Serbs to the south.

Get oriented. As you face Jelačić's statue, down a long block to your left is a funicular that takes you up to one of Zagreb's original villages, Gradec. To the right, look for the TI. If you exit the

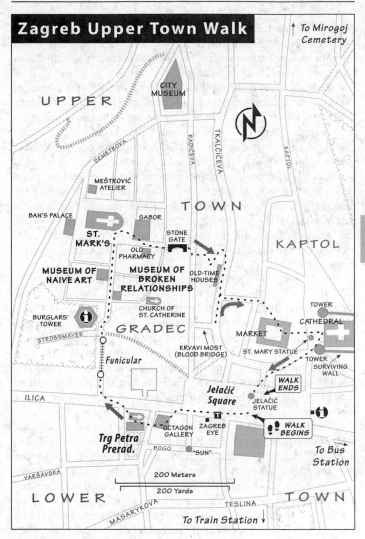

square ahead and to the right, you'll reach the city's other original village, Kaptol, and the cathedral (you can't miss its huge, pointy, Neo-Gothic spires—visible from virtually everywhere in Zagreb). And if you just need a break, several fine cafés ring the square. For the best view in town, you can pay 20 kn to ascend to the **"Zagreb 360°"** viewing platform at the top of the tallest glass skyscraper at the bottom of the square (ride elevator to 16th floor, daily 10:00-24:00, café, www.zagrebeye.hr).

Taking the small street behind Jelačić and then going a little to the left would lead you to the market (best in the morning—depending on the time, consider visiting the market now, using the tips on page 61, before continuing on the walk) and the enticing café-and-restaurant street, Tkalčićeva (lively any time of day or night; we'll circle back here later on the walk).

To see a unique bit of public art on this small street, pause at the modern building with an arcade of blocky pillars. Look closely at the first pillar (closest to Jelačić Square) and find the small silver plaque with a little ball labeled *Venus* (about eight feet up, facing the building). This is one piece of the 10-part work called **"Zagreb's Solar System."** Its center lies a short walk away, two blocks in front of Jelačić (on Bogovićeva street): a large spherical sculpture called *The Grounded Sun*. Scattered around the city are each of the nine planets, completely to scale—from the size of a marble to the size of a basketball—and each one at the appropriate distance from the "sun." The artist did the project in secret, so Zagrebians had to seek out each of the nine planets on their own, in a kind of citywide scavenger hunt.

But for now, head up to the hill called Gradec.

Walk from Jelačić Square to Gradec

Go a long block down busy Ilica street (to the left as you face Jelačić), then enter the big **"Octagon" shopping gallery** on the left (at #5, enter under *Privedna Banka Zagreb* sign). This was the ultimate in iron-and-glass shopping elegance a century ago, and still features a few of the city's top shops (including Croata, the tie store that loves to explain how Croatians invented the necktie; for the whole story, see page 188).

Walk all the way through the gallery, exiting into the inviting café-lined square called **Trg Petra Preradovića.** It hosts a flower market all day, and inviting al fresco cafés throughout the day and into the night. Survey your options for a coffee break, then turn right and head back out to Ilica street, where you'll turn left and continue the way you were headed.

After another block, cross the tram tracks and turn right up Tomića, where you'll see a small **funicular** (ZET Uspinjača) crawling up the hill. Dating from the late 19th century, this funicular is looked upon fondly by Zagrebians—both as a bit of nostalgia and as a way to avoid some steps. You can walk up if you want, but the ride is more fun and takes only 55 seconds. Locals claim this is the "shortest funicular in the world" (4 kn, validate ticket in yellow box before you board, leaves every 10 minutes or with demand, daily 6:30-22:00).

Gradec

From the top of the funicular, you'll enjoy a fine panorama over Zagreb. The tall tower on the left as you exit is one of Gradec's original watchtowers, the **Burglars' Tower** (Kula Lotršćak). After the Tatars ransacked Central Europe in the early 13th century, King Béla IV decreed that towns be fortified—so Gradec built a wall and guard towers (just like Kraków and Budapest did).

Look for the little cannon in the top-floor window. Every day at noon, this cannon fires a shot to commemorate a 15th-century victory over the besieging Ottomans.

The **Strossmayer Promenade** runs along the top of the hill, overlooking the city. The fenced section next to the funicular station is dubbed Strossmartre (a pun on "Montmartre"), which, in good summer weather, hosts a fun little outdoor café, and often features works by local artists and live music. This fine promenade is just the start; along the outside of Gradec is a forested green belt that—while just a few minutes' walk away—feels miles from the city. It's a favorite place for locals to go for an urban hike, walk their dogs, or get away from the asphalt heat of summer.

Head up the street to the right of the tower, entering Gradec (often called "Grič" for short). Although this is one of the oldest parts of Zagreb, it lacks the cutesy cobbled charm you might expect. That's because little remains of medieval Gradec. When the Ottomans overran Europe, they never managed to take Zagreb, but the threat was enough to scare the nobility into the countryside. When the Ottomans left, the nobles came back, and they replaced the medieval buildings here with Baroque mansions.

At the first square, to the right, you'll see the Jesuit **Church of St. Catherine.** It's not much to look at from the outside, but the interior is intricately decorated—bubbly pink-and-white Baroque, dripping with stucco (only open to visitors during Mass). The same applies to several mansions on Gradec. This austere-outside, ornate-inside style is known as "Zagreb Baroque."

As you continue up the street, notice the old-timey **street signs,** holdovers from the Austro-Hungarian era: in both Croatian (Gospodzka ulicza) and German (Herren Gasse).

From here, you're a few steps from Zagreb's two most interesting museums: On the right is the **Museum of Broken Relationships,** and at the end of the block, on the left, is the **Croatian Museum of Naive Art** (both listed later, under "Sights in Zagreb"). Now's the time to visit these, before continuing on our walk.

In the next block, on the left, is the yellow **"city parliament"** building (basically the Town Hall, and a popular place for weddings on summer Saturdays). To the left of the door, look for the plaque honoring **Nikola Tesla** (1856-1943), the prominent scientist who championed alternating current (AC) as a better electrical system than Thomas Edison's direct current (DC). Although Tesla was an ethnic Serb (his father was an Orthodox priest), he was born in a remote village in central Croatia, so both Serbs and Croats claim him. (Today, Tesla is a rare figure who is revered both in Zagreb and in Belgrade.) This plaque proudly trumpets that on May 24, 1892, Tesla came to this building and suggested that Zagreb become the first city in the world to build an AC power station. But the plaque fails to mention that the city parliament rejected this suggestion...so Tesla went to the US, where he successfully pitched the same idea to Buffalo, New York.

While Zagreb eventually did adopt AC, this part of town still clings to a much, much older form of lighting. Flanking the doors of the city parliament are two of the 217 old-fashioned **gaslights** that illuminate Gradec. These are lit and extinguished each day by two city employees. Notice that each lamp is numbered.

At the end of the block, you'll come to **St. Mark's Square** (Markov trg), centered on the **Church of St. Mark.** The origi-

nal church here was from the 13th century, but only a few fragments remain. The present church's colorful tile roof, from 1880, depicts two coats of arms. On the left, the red-and-white checkerboard symbolizes north-central Croatia, the three lions' heads stand for the Dalmatian Coast, and the marten (*kuna*, like the money) running between the two rivers (Sava and Drava) represents Slavonia—Croatia's northern, inland panhandle. On the right is the seal of Zagreb, featuring a walled city.

In the years since these tiles were laid, the **city seal** has changed in two ways (as you can see by comparing it to the city flag that flies from the city parliament building). First, while the castle doors are closed on the roof, today's seal shows wide-open doors—to demonstrate that Zagreb is strong, but still welcoming to visitors. Second, the city color has been changed from red to blue. If you pay attention around town, you'll notice the liberal use of Zagreb's distinctive hue of blue—for example, on city buses and trams. And devoted fans of the immensely popular local soccer team, Dinamo Zagreb, are called the "Bad Blue Boys."

While it would be nice to see the inside of St. Mark's Church, the priest doesn't appreciate tourists, so it's closed except during services. (If you manage to slip in, you'll see frescoes with Bible scenes, and sculptures by the talented 20th-century sculptor Ivan Meštrović: the crucifix over the main altar, a *pietà* on the left, and on the right, Madonna and Child sitting cross-legged, in a typical Meštrović pose. If you can't get in, you can still enjoy some Meštrović works at his nearby museum, described later.)

As you face the church, the long building on the right is the **Sabor,** or parliament. From the 12th century, Croatian noblemen would gather here to make important decisions regarding their territories. This gradually evolved into today's modern parliament. While this square used to be a congested parking lot, Zagreb's mayor declared it a traffic-free zone; now members of parliament either have to be bussed in from off-site parking lots (watch for the cute little blue bus that comes and goes periodically), or have their drivers sit tight nearby (look for unmarked black cars patiently waiting on the street in front of the city parliament).

Across the square from the Sabor (to your left as you face the church) is **Ban's Palace** (Banski Dvori), today the offices for the prime minister. This was one of the few buildings in central Zagreb damaged in the war following Croatia's independence. In October of 1991, Yugoslav People's Army pilots targeted this building in an airstrike. (Notice the different-colored tiles where the roof had to be patched.) They landed a direct hit on the room where Croatian President Franjo Tuđman and his right-hand man, Stipe Mesić (who would later succeed him as president), were scheduled to be meeting. But coincidentally, the meeting had been moved to another location at the last minute—so Croatia's first two presidents survived. (It's eerie to think what might have become of this fledgling nation if its leadership had been wiped out at this early stage.)

Before moving on, consider visiting two more excellent museums, which sit just a short walk away (both described in detail later, under "Sights in Zagreb"). The talented 20th-century sculptor **Ivan Meštrović's former home and studio** is now a museum of his works. It's about a block away: Go down the street behind the church on the left-hand side, and you'll see the museum on the right. And the extensive, well-presented **Zagreb City Museum** explains the story of this town from prehistoric times to the modern day. To reach it, walk along the front of the Sabor and continue straight ahead two blocks, watching for the museum on your right.

Walk from Gradec to Kaptol

For an interesting stroll from St. Mark's Square to the cathedral, head down the street (Kamenita ulica) to the right of the parliament building. Near the end of the street, on the right, you'll see the oldest **pharmacy** in town—recently restored and gleaming (c. 1355, marked *gradska ljekarna*). Across the street is **Lav Caffe Galerija,** a fun, relaxing coffee house and art gallery; this is just one of many inviting coffee-break opportunities you'll see between here and the end of this walk.

Just beyond, you'll reach Gradec's only surviving town gate, the **Stone Gate** (Kamenita Vrata). Inside is an evocative chapel. The focal point is a painting of Mary that miraculously survived a major fire in the house up above in 1731. When this medieval gate was reconstructed in the Baroque style, they decided to turn it into a makeshift chapel. The candles (purchased in the little shop and lit in the big metal bin) represent Zagrebians' prayers. Notice the soot-blackened ceiling over the forest

fire of blazing candles in the bin. The stone plaques on the wall give thanks *(hvala)* for prayers that were answered. You may notice people making the sign of the cross as they walk through here, and often a crowd of worshippers gathers, gazing intently at the painting. Mary was made the official patron saint of Zagreb in 1990.

As you leave the Stone Gate and come to **Radićeva,** turn right and begin walking downhill. Looking down to the bottom of Radićeva, you'll see where this street is becoming a popular shopping zone, with local boutiques popping up all the time—a fun area to browse later.

But for now, head just a few steps down Radićeva, then watch for the orange building at **#30** on your left. Go through the big, arched entryway and bear right down the wooden steps. At the bottom of these stairs, you'll come to a little row of evocative **old-time houses.** In times past, this was one of the most popular areas in town...as home of the red light district. While prostitution is illegal now, it was once allowed and carefully regulated, with routine medical examinations for the working girls. Legally, only a woman (over age 30) could own and operate a brothel. Locals note, with some irony, that the balconies on the opposite side of these houses of ill repute—which we'll see in a moment—face the stern spires of the cathedral.

Turn left, walking along the row of old houses (and noticing the remains of the old Gradec town wall on your left), then turn right down the stairs. You've just dropped down into the middle of Zagreb's most appealing street, **Tkalčićeva** (tuh-KAHL-chee-chay-vah). Do a slow spin to savor this in-love-with-life drag. This traffic-free street combines some of the most atmospheric old homes of Zagreb with some of its most enticing eateries and people-watching. (For starters, you're literally surrounded by tables for the recommended Pivnica Mali Medo brewpub.)

If you need a break from sightseeing, Tkalčićeva is just the ticket: Nurse a coffee, beer, or meal anywhere along this street (I've listed several recommendations under "Eating in Zagreb," later).

If you stood here 200 years ago, you'd be washed away by a rushing river that separated Gradec (behind you) and Kaptol (in front of you). In the Middle Ages, the two towns were at odds and sometimes fought. ("Downriver" from here is a cross street that's still called Krvavi Most—"Blood Bridge.") But in 1850, after the towns had long since set aside their differences, they merged to become Zagreb. The polluted, stinky river had become a nuisance, so they diverted its flow and covered over the valley to create Tkalčićeva.

Turn right and enjoy a stroll down Tkalčićeva (toward the onion-domed church tower of Holy Mary Church). You'll pass (on the right) the balconies of the brothels we saw earlier, then a fine park on the right with a genteel lady prepared for rain. Just beyond the park, next to the door for the recommended Cookie Factory, is the *Mars* plaque for the solar system sculpture. Directly across the street, walk up the hill toward the cathedral towers (on Skalinska, passing outdoor restaurant tables).

Kaptol

As you walk uphill, you're entering Kaptol, the second of medieval Zagreb's twin towns.

At the top of the street, turn right and go down the stairs to find Zagreb's lively-in-the-morning **market** *(dolac)*. If you're here at prime time, browse the market's double-decker delights (noticing that the meat and cheese halls are below your feet—use the stairs or elevator in the blocky white building to get there). For pointers on what to see at the market, see "Sights in Zagreb."

When you're done at the market, go through the gap between the buildings toward the **cathedral** spires. Crossing the square, you can enter Croatia's most important house of worship (described later, under "Sights in Zagreb"). From here, you can head downhill one block to Jelačić Square—where our walk began.

Sights in Zagreb

MUSEUMS IN THE CENTER

Zagreb has more than its share of museums, and many of them are excellent—making up for the lack of great Croatian museums outside the capital. It would take you days to see all the city's museums; I've selected the most worthwhile (still enough to fill a couple of days—choose the ones that interest you the most).

Origins of Naive Art

Starting in the late 19th century, the art world began to broaden its definition of great art, seeking out worthy art originating outside the esteemed academies and salons of the day. The goal: to demonstrate that art was not simply a trained skill, but an inborn talent. Intellectuals began to embrace an "anti-intellectual" approach to art. Interest grew in the indigenous art of Africa, Mesoamerica, and Polynesia (Picasso

went through an African mask phase, and Gauguin went to live in Tahiti); composer Béla Bartok collected traditional folk melodies from the Hungarian countryside; the Art Brut movement preserved artwork by people deemed "insane" by mainstream society; the autodidactic (self-taught) painter Grandma Moses became well known in the US and Europe; and art by children gained acclaim.

Here in Croatia in the 1930s, the focus was on art by untrained peasants. At that time, as in much of rural Europe, 85 percent of Croatians lived virtually medieval lifestyles—with no electricity or other modern conveniences—and a majority were illiterate and uneducated. These artists captured this humble reality, creating figurative works in an increasingly abstract age. By the 1950s and 1960s, Croatian naive art had emerged at the forefront of a Europe-wide phenomenon.

▲▲▲Croatian Museum of Naive Art (Hrvatski Muzej Naivne Umjetnosti)

This remarkable spot, founded in 1952 as the "Peasant Art Gallery," is one of the most enjoyable little museums in Croatia. It features expressionistic paintings by untrained peasant artists. On one easy floor, the museum displays 80 paintings made mostly by Croatians from the 1930s to the 1980s. This museum presents an easily digestible sampling of the top names from the Naive Art movement. Viewing these evocative works, it's important to remember that this isn't considered "folk art" or "amateur art," but top-quality works by great artists who were, by fluke or fate, never formally trained.

Cost and Hours: 20 kn; July-Sept Mon-Sat 10:00-18:00, Sun 10:00-13:00; Oct-June Tue-Fri 10:00-18:00, Sat-Sun 10:00-13:00, closed Mon; pick up the English explanations as you enter, ulica Sv. Ćirila i Metoda 3, tel. 01/485-1911, www.hmnu.org.

Visiting the Museum: Buy your ticket and follow the one-way route through the six numbered rooms, which you'll circle counterclockwise.

Room 1: Immediately to the right as you enter is the first of many paintings by **Ivan Generalić** (1914-1992), the founder and

star of Croatian naive art (his self-portrait, with a blue background, dominates the room). Generalić was discovered in the 1930s by a Paris-trained Croatian artist. The first few paintings show his evolution as an artist (and the evolution of Croatian naive art in general): While his early works come with a social or political agenda (such as *Requisition,* where two policemen repo a cow from an impoverished couple), he eventually mellows his focus to show simple, typical village scenes that gradually become more and more fantastical *(Harvesters),* and eventually strips away people entirely to focus on the land (on the opposite wall, see 1938's *Cows in the Forest* and 1959's *Flood*). In 1953, Generalić—still relatively unknown outside his homeland—did a show in Paris, sold everything, and came home rich. This put Croatian naive art on the international map and kick-started a new vigor in the movement.

Woodcutters, from 1959, shows the next phase, as Generalić's works became even more rich with fantasy—the peacock, the men clinging to tree tops, and the

trademark "coral trees." Instead of showing, Generalić is evoking; naive art strove to capture the spirit and emotion of peasant life. Paintings such as this one inspired Generalić's followers (called the "Hlebine School," for the village where Generalić lived). In the adjacent painting, *Solar Eclipse* (1961), villagers cower and roosters crow as the sun is mysteriously gobbled up by a black disc. People respond in different

ways: some by staging impromptu religious processionals, others by clutching their belongings close and fleeing.

Flanking the door to the next room are works by the next generation of naive art—two big-name followers who were inspired (if not trained) by Generalić: on the left, the gruesome *Evangelists on Calvary* crucifix, by **Ivan Večenaj,** who focused on religious scenes; and on the right, *Winter Landscape with Woman,* by **Mijo Kovačić,** who specialized in peasant landscapes.

Room 2: The next room features more works by Večenaj and Kovačić. Studying Kovačić's many landscapes, notice how he took a style of painting pioneered by Generalić and brought it to the next level. Winter scenes were most common, because the peasant artists were busy working the fields the rest of the year. (Early on, such artists were sometimes called "Sunday painters," because they had to work their "real" jobs from Monday to Saturday.) Kovačić also enjoyed winter scenes for the evocative black-and-white contrast they allowed. Like Dalí, Magritte, and other surrealists, Kovačić juxtaposed super-realism (look at each individual hair on the swine in his painting *Swineherd,* pictured below) with fantastical, almost otherworldly settings. Also in this room are some landscapes and portraits by **Dragan Gaži,** a friend and neighbor of Generalić's. His *The Wind in Winter* (1973) is an intoxicating landscape.

You may notice that these supposedly "untrained" artists seem to borrow from other painters—most notably, the countryside peasant scenes often feel ripped from a Pieter Bruegel canvas. While these artists were not formally schooled, there's no doubt that they were aware of, and often inspired by, their artistic forebears.

Also notice that naive artists in Croatia frequently painted on glass. It was cheaper and more readily available in rural areas than art canvases, and—because it required no special technique—was an easier medium for the untrained naive artists to work on.

Room 3: On the right, find the portraits of Roma (Gypsy) people by **Martin Mehkek.** For the one depicting his cross-eyed neighbor Steve, Mehkek mostly painted with his fingers, using brushes only for fine details (such as the Hitler-style moustache). On the other side of the room is *Guiana '78*—by **Josip Generalić,** the founder's less-talented son—showing the gruesome aftermath of the Jim Jones mass suicide, with a pair of monkeys surveying the smiling corpses. (While vivid, this painting doesn't reflect the Croatian peasant experience, and the curator admits it's not the best representative of naive art.) Filling out the room are more of those distinctively spiny, bonsai-like trees that pervade naive works, these by **Ivan Lacković Croata.** Notice that Croata's fine works focus on different seasons.

But this room's highlight is Večenaj's *Moses and the Red Sea*

(1973), an expressionistic retelling of the familiar biblical story. Moses, glowing against an inky black sky and with feet muddy from having just crossed the seabed, watches the sea—literally red with Egyptian blood—washing away his pursuers. The footprints emerging from the sea (at the bottom) suggest that the Israelites' exodus has been a successful one. On the left, see the pyramids (Egypt), and on the right, the cozy village (the Promised Land). Flying around Moses are 10 birds (representing the Commandments); he's equipped with some of his typical symbols, including the horn around his neck, the ram, and the snake (which, as

the story goes, he had conjured from a staff to convince the pharaoh to allow the Israelites to leave Egypt).

Room 4: This room shows off two big names from the latter part of the movement. On the left are lyrical landscapes by Ivan Rabuzin, arguably the movement's second most important artist, after Ivan Generalić. Like a visual haiku, Rabuzin's dreamlike world of hills, trees, and clouds is reminiscent of Marc Chagall. Rabuzin's works are especially popular among the museum's many Japanese visitors. On the right are Emerik Fejes's

colorful scenes of famous monuments from around Europe—Paris, Venice, Vienna, and Milan. Feješ never traveled to any of these places—his paintings are based on romantic black-and-white postcards of the era, which Feješ "colorized" in his unique style.

Room 5: On the left, see **Matija Skurjeni**'s almost crayon-like *Animal World* (1961). While it looks like the roll call for Noah's ark, it's loaded with symbolism. The dinosaur is Skurjeni's self-portrait, the other large animals are his friends and artistic colleagues, the butterflies fluttering around represent spirituality (a new spin on the white dove of the Holy Spirit)...and the devil in the base of the tree, with wings and a crown, is one of Skurjeni's harshest critics—who also happened to be the curator of this museum at the time. Also here is **Drago Jurak**'s *Luxury Boat* (1974), which looks like a Bollywood *Titanic*. On the right are works by naive artists from other countries (Russia, Japan, France, and Poland).

Room 6: Here you'll see pencil sketches used by naive artists to create their works (including one for Generalić's *Solar Eclipse*). After the sketch was complete, the artist would put it against a pane of glass to paint the scene—small details first, gradually filling in more and more of the background. Then the glass painting would literally be flipped over to be viewed. All of the works on glass you've seen in this collection were actually painted backward.

▲▲Museum of Broken Relationships

Opened in 2010 by a couple who had recently broken up, this extremely clever museum lives up to all the attention it's received in the international press. The museum's mission is simple: collect true stories of failed couples from around the world, tell their story in their own words, and display the tale alongside an actual item that embodies the relationship. The items and stories provide insights into a shared human experience—we can all relate to the anger, sadness, and relief expressed in these poignant, at times hilarious, displays. In addition to the predictable "he cheated on me so I broke his favorite fill-in-the-blank" items, the ever-changing collection delves into other types of fractured connections: an unrequited childhood crush, the slow fade of lovers who  gradually grew apart, disappointment in a politician who failed to live up to lofty expectations, the premature end of a love cut short by death, and so on. You'll see discarded wedding albums, sex toys with stories about unreasonable requests for kinky acts, films that attempt to capture the essence of a relationship, children's playthings representing the innocence of young love (and, perhaps, the universality of stuffed animals), and plenty of items broken with vengeful wrath. The museum is small—just a few rooms—but rewards those who take the time to read each story. The collection has been such a hit, they've taken it on the road, garnering fans in cities worldwide. If you enjoy the collection, the 280-kn "diary"— with all the stories and photos—is a good souvenir.

Cost and Hours: 25 kn, daily June-Sept 9:00-22:30, Oct-May 9:00-21:00, café, Sv. Ćirila i Metoda 2, tel. 01/485-1021, https://brokenships.com.

▲Ivan Meštrović Atelier

Ivan Meštrović—Croatia's most famous artist—lived here from 1922 until 1942 (before he fled to the US after World War II). The house, carefully decorated by Meštrović himself, has been converted into a delightful gallery of the artist's works, displayed in two parts: residence and studio. Split's Meštrović Gallery (described on page 192) is the definitive museum of this 20th-century Croatian sculptor, but if you're not going there, Zagreb's gallery is a convenient place to gain an appreciation for this prolific, thoughtful artist. For more on Meštrović, see page 194.

Cost and Hours: 30 kn, Tue-Fri 10:00-18:00, Sat-Sun 10:00-14:00, closed Mon, 20-kn English catalog, behind St. Mark's Square at Mletačka 8, tel. 01/485-1123, www.mestrovic.hr.

Visiting the Museum: When you buy your ticket, be sure to pick up the large floor plan—it's the only way to identify the

pieces on display here (they're marked only by number; I've noted the numbers for important works in this description). Then enter the high-ceilinged dining room of Meštrović's **home.** He designed the crucifix on the wall (#83, Christ being supported by an angel), the wood-carved chandeliers, and the furniture, right down to the carvings on the backs of the chairs. Overlooking the table is a sculpture of his mother (#59), wearing the traditional headdress of her Dalmatian village homeland, legs crossed, hands clasped in intent prayer—a favorite pose of Meštrović's. At the other end of the table is a self-portrait bust of Meštrović, head cocked quizzically (#76). In the alcove at the bottom of the stairs, see the *Madonna and Baby,* tenderly kissing (#38).

Head **upstairs** to see sketches and plaster casts Meštrović did in preparation for some of his larger works. The rooms on this floor are filled with busts and small, characteristically elongated statues, all of them expressive. In the far room, appreciate his fine ceiling frescoes; in the adjoining room, find Meštrović's powerful sculpture depicting his mentor and friend, Auguste Rodin, furiously at work (#26).

Continue up to the **top floor,** where you'll find several evocative pieces: Meštrović's wife breastfeeding their son (#54); a portrait of Michelangelo, Meštrović's artistic ancestor, holding a chisel and hammer, and portrayed with his trademark high forehead and smashed nose (#56); and a copy of the powerful *pietà* from St. Mark's Church (#89). The next room holds a cowering *Job* (#88), the head of an archangel (#97), a tender portrait of a mother teaching her child to pray (#55), and a small model of one of Meštrović's

biggest and best-known works, *Bishop Gregory of Nin* (#61, in Split, described on page 186). In the small, final room is a woman with a beehive 'do praying (#33).

Back downstairs, you'll cross through the **garden** to reach the studio. Outside are several more fine pieces, including another one of the museum's top works: *The History of the Croats* (#90), with a woman sitting cross-legged (remember this pose?) with a book resting on her lap. The top of the book has a unique Croatian spiral design, and along the front of it are the letters of Croatia's Glagolitic alphabet. Back against the wall, *John the Evangelist* studiously takes notes, looking up for divine inspiration (#71). And the small *Prince Marko on Šarac* (#16)—while clearly a Croatian theme—evokes two of Meštrović's most famous works, the giant Native Americans on horseback that stand in Chicago's Grant Park. Those towering sculptures were created in this very studio, and later transported (in pieces) to the United States. Originally, those sculptures were commissioned to be a cowboy and an Indian...but Meštrović said, "How about *two* Native Americans...?"

Go into Meštrović's **studio.** Next to the door to the inner courtyard is a skinny, Modigliani-esque sculpture of Meštrović's first wife, Ruža (#70). In the middle of the room are two sculptures modeled after his second wife, Olga: the unfinished, walnut-carved *Mother and Child* (#100), and the exquisite, white-marble *Woman Beside the Sea* (#58, one of the collection's highlights). Nearby is a sculpture of the *Evangelist Luke* (#72)—the twin of John out in the garden. Upstairs around the gallery are smaller pieces, including a study for the spiny-fingered hand of Split's *Bishop Gregory of Nin* (#62).

On your way out, take a moment to linger in the **courtyard**—with the large *Woman in Agony* (#67) in the center, and less-agonized women all around.

▲Zagreb City Museum (Muzej Grada Zagreba)

This collection, with a modern, well-presented exhibit that sprawls over two floors of an old convent, traces the history of the city through town models, paintings, furniture, clothing, and lots of fascinating artifacts.

Cost and Hours: 30 kn, Tue-Fri 10:00-18:00, Sat 11:00-19:00, Sun 10:00-14:00, closed Mon, 20-kn audioguide nicely supplements the posted descriptions, at north end of Gradec at Opatička 20, tel. 01/485-1361, www.mgz.hr.

Visiting the Museum: After buying your ticket, head through the door and turn left, then work your way up through the ages. Each display has a fine English description. On the largely skippable ground floor, you'll loop through the prehistoric and Roman periods, and the medieval growth of the twin towns of Gradec and Kaptol. You'll see city symbols and flags, a town model from 1795, statues from the main portal of the cathedral (17th-century Baroque) and other religious art, and a small collection of cleverly decorated 18th-century weathervanes.

Upstairs, the exhibit lingers on Zagreb's boom time in the 19th century, when it was an increasingly spruced-up and genteel outpost of the Austro-Hungarian Empire. The exhibits consider various facets of society during that era. You'll see more religious art, furniture, aristocratic portraits, another town model (from the 1860s), a life-size portrait of national hero Josip Jelačić (and his actual uniform), and colorfully painted shooting targets. One room has a giant city map on the floor, punctuated with models of key buildings. You'll also find models of old storefronts, theater costumes, and exhibits on public utilities and social life.

The coverage of the tumultuous 20th century is perhaps most engaging, evincing an understandably bad attitude about the Serb-dominated first Yugoslav period. Propaganda posters cheer on the communist period, while all of this historical heaviness is balanced by a lighthearted exhibit about Zagreb's popular cartoon industry. The finale is a room dedicated to the creation of independent Croatia, including an exhibit on damage sustained during the war and a film with clips from various landmarks in Croatian independence: a violent riot at a heated 1990 soccer match between Dinamo Zagreb and Belgrade's Crvena Zvezda ("Red Star") team; the election and arrival in parliament of the pro-independence Franjo Tuđman; and the return of the statue of Jelačić to his namesake square.

OTHER SIGHTS IN THE CENTER
▲▲Market (Dolac)

In 1930, Zagreb tore down much of Kaptol's rickety old medieval Old Town to build this as-central-as-possible market. Today, it's jammed with producers from the surrounding countryside—and all over Croatia—selling all manner of fruits, vegetables, meats, cheeses, fish, and other foodstuffs. A stroll through the market offers insight into the colorful local culture, and the chance to pick up a few picnic items. To reach the market easily from Jelačić Square, walk one block up the street to the left of the Jelačić statue, and climb up the stairs (open Mon-Sat 7:00-14:00, Sun 7:00-13:00).

Visiting the Market: The market has two sections—indoor (with meat and cheese) and outdoor (produce, just above). Begin by exploring the outdoor section, then head inside. At the top of the stairs coming up from Jelačić Square, notice the statue of the *kumica*—a villager wearing a traditional dress (with a head scarf) and balancing a basket of produce on her head.

Filling the square is the **produce market,** with vendors from all around selling what's fresh. What you'll see changes with the season (for instance, in late summer, you'll see plums and grapes; in fall, look for nuts and mushrooms), but a few things are mainstays. The honey *(med)* is a reminder that the mountain behind Zagreb is called Medvednica. In Croatian, a bear is poetically called a *medved*—literally "honey-seer." So *Medvednica* means "place of the honey-seer." The big red umbrellas with white, yellow, and green stripes evoke the parasols that are part of the traditional costume for the region around Zagreb. The stalls behind the boxy white building (which is the entrance to the lower, indoor market) sell various components of that same costume (such as embroidered scarves); while tourists can buy them, most customers are locals. Nearby, the few "souvenir" stands (at the top part of the market, near the cathedral) show off colorful, traditional wooden toys, still made the way they have been for centuries (men do the carving, women do the painting); the wooden birds on sticks—which flap their wings when you roll them along the floor—are a favorite.

As you face the top of the market, to the left you'll see the fragrant **fish market** *(ribarnica)*. While Zagreb is far from the sea, the freshest catch is trucked in daily.

To get to the indoor market *(tržnica)*, enter the boxy white building and descend using the stairs or elevator. You'll pop out in the **meat market.** Stroll the stalls, noticing—in addition to the typical array of sausages, salamis, and *pršut* (cured ham)—the local affection for horsemeat (from a young horse—*ždrebetina,* or an adult—*konjetina*). Also watch for piles of a local delicacy called *čvarci*. Vaguely similar to pork rinds, these were created as a way to use up otherwise unused bits and pieces of pork; they'd press all of the fat out of them, creating a crispy snack. While this used to be simple peasant food, these days meat production is streamlined to process pork leftovers in other ways—and so *čvarci* are considered a rare and expensive delicacy (*prešani čvarci* are even more pressed—and more expensive).

From the meat market, look for the **dairy** section (marked *mlijenči proizvodi,* on the left from where you entered). Most cheese here is cow cheese *(kravlji),* typically very fresh and soft, and sometimes with flavorings (such as paprika or chives) mixed in. Goat cheese *(kozji)* is more rare. In this area, you'll also see some local starches. The extremely skinny noodles called *rezanci* are used in soups; the big, flat squares that look like tortillas *(mlinci)* are served with poultry—they soak up drippings to become soft and delicious.

▲▲Cathedral (Katedrala)

The most important church in a very devoutly Catholic country, Zagreb's cathedral is worth a visit. The full name is the Cathedral of the Assumption of the Blessed Virgin Mary and the Saintly Kings Stephen and Ladislav (whew!)—but most locals just call it "the cathedral." Inside, you'll see monuments to many late, great Croatians, and get a taste of the faith that pervades in this country.

Cost and Hours: Free, Mon-Sat 10:00-17:00, Sun 13:00-17:00.

Visiting the Cathedral: Before entering, stand in the **square** in front of the cathedral (near the gilded Madonna on a pillar—sculpted by the same artist who did the Jelačić statue on the main square) to ponder the history of this site. In 1094, when a diocese was established at Kaptol, this church quickly became a major center of high-ranking church officials. In the mid-13th century, the original cathedral was destroyed by invading Tatars, who used it as a stable. It was rebuilt and surrounded by a stout medieval wall—practically turning it into a castle to defend against potential Ottoman invasion. You can still see the pointy tops of the round guard towers on either side of the church; until a century ago, this wall ran along the road behind you, completely enclosing the building. (The St. Mary pillar stands upon the round footprint of another one of the towers.) The church was severely damaged again, this time by an earthquake, in 1880. The current version is Neo-Gothic (completed in 1902), incorporating a few original Gothic elements. Much of the wall was torn down to allow the town to grow.

Walking closer to the main door, look to the left to see the **two spires** displayed just inside the wall. The one on the left, eroded down to a pathetic nub, demonstrates what happens when you use abundant—but porous—limestone to build a church in a climate with cold, freezing winters. (They can get away with using limestone on the coast, but in chilly Zagreb, it's just not the right material.) Some part of the church will certainly be covered by scaffolding during your visit—as it has been for decades, as restorers have gradually been replacing worn elements with new ones...this time, using a more durable stone.

Just before entering the church, appreciate the modern tympanum (carved semicircular section over the door). Then step inside and wander down the nave, taking in the opulence of the church. When it was completed, Zagreb was a small city of about 70,000 people; the construction of a church this finely decorated hints at the wealth of the city during its boom time. (In later times, that money dried up; the big chandeliers hanging in the nave were reportedly imported from Las Vegas—the best source for affordable glitz—in the 1970s.)

First, head to the **main altar** and look closely at the silver relief: a whimsical scene of the Holy Family doing chores around the house (Mary sewing, Joseph and Jesus building a fence...and angels helping out).

From the altar, turn left, then head to the front of the church. In the front-left corner (on the wall, between the confessionals), find **Ivan Meštrović's monument to Alojzije Stepinac.** We'll learn more about Stepinac in a moment, but for now pay attention to this beautifully carved piece of sculpture. Meštrović, the talented Croatian sculptor, worked in the early 20th century before fleeing communist Yugoslavia. Notice that this work was carved in "Detroit, Mich, USA," where Meštrović lived out his days in a self-imposed exile. Meštrović was a close friend of Stepinac, and carved this monument from half a world away.

Facing the nearby altar, on the right look for the bronze monument to **Josip Jelačić,** the statesman whose statue adorns Zagreb's main square. Remember that Jelačić gained fame fighting against the Hungarians during the Habsburg era; the monument explains that his efforts allowed Zagreb to become an archbishopric, increasing its independence. But the large altar next to him celebrates three early Hungarian sainted kings, who (back when Croatia was part of Hungary, centuries before Jelačić) founded this church. You can imagine a Croat viewing this and thinking, "Those wonderful Hungarians, to whom we owe this church—thank God we defeated them."

Walk up the steps to the area behind the main altar. Here you'll find a glass case containing a waxy, eerily lifelike sculpture of **Alojzije Stepinac.** (His actual remains are below.) Stepinac was the Archbishop of Zagreb during World War II, when he short-sightedly supported the Ustaše (Nazi puppet government in Croatia)—thinking, like many Croatians, that this was the ticket to greater independence from Serbia. When Tito came to power, he put Stepinac on trial and sent him to jail for five years, before he was banished to live out his life in the remote, poor village where he had been born. But Stepinac never lost his faith, and many Croatian Catholics consider him something of a martyr—and arguably the most inspirational figure of their faith. He's also respected in the US, where some Catholic schools bear his name. But many Serbs today consider Stepinac a villain who cooperated with the brutal Ustaše.

Before leaving, pull up a pew and ponder the role of faith in contemporary Croatian life. By definition, Croats are Catholics. And, although religion was not encouraged in communist Yugoslavia, it was also not prohibited (as it was in most Warsaw Pact countries). Politicians, military officers, and civil servants (such as teachers) couldn't publicly profess their faith, but many were privately devout. And with the breakup of Yugoslavia and the ensuing wars, Catholicism has seen a huge boost. In this part of the world, where ethnicity is tied to faith, nationalism (which is also on the rise) hews closely to religion—too closely, many impartial observers fear. The increasing influence of the Catholic Church on Croatian politics will be a hot potato here for years to come.

As you leave the cathedral, look high on the wall to the left of the door. This strange script is the **Glagolitic alphabet** *(glagoljca)*,

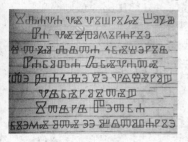

invented by Byzantine missionaries Cyril and Methodius in the ninth century to translate the Bible into Slavic languages. Though these missionaries worked mostly in Moravia (today's eastern Czech Republic), their alphabet caught on only here, in Croatia. (Glagolitic was later adapted in Bulgaria to become the Cyrillic alphabet—still used in Serbia, Russia, and other parts east.) In 1991, when Croatia became its own country and nationalism surged, some Croats flirted with the idea of making this the official alphabet.

ELSEWHERE IN ZAGREB
▲Mirogoj Cemetery (Groblje Mirogoj)
Of Europe's many evocative cemeteries, Mirogoj (MEE-roh-goy) is one of the finest, studded with great architecture and beautifully designed tombs. This peaceful spot, a short bus ride from the city center, memorializes many of the greats who built the Croatian nation. Anyone can enjoy a quiet walk here, but to provide context to your stroll, stop by the TI first for their free, thorough booklet of maps and descriptions identifying the most significant graves.

The cemetery was designed by Herman Bollé, an Austrian architect who lived and worked for most of his career in Zagreb, leaving his mark all over the city before becoming a permanent resident in this cemetery. From the stately, domed main mausoleum, a long arcade (with VIP tombs) stretches along the road in both directions, punctuated by smaller domes. Entering through the main gate, circle behind the mausoleum to find the biggest tomb here: Franjo Tuđman, the leader who spearheaded the creation of independent Croatia but left behind a questionable legacy (for more on Tuđman, see page 28). Continuing straight past Tuđman's grave, you'll reach the Central Cross, which usually has a field of flowers around it, and beyond that, a monument to the dead of World War I. In every direction, as far as the eye can see, are the final resting places of great Croatians.

Cost and Hours: Free, daily April-Sept 6:00-20:00, Oct-March 7:30-18:00.

Getting There: Catch bus #106 from in front of the cathedral (3/hour) and ride six stops, or about 10 minutes, to the stop called simply "Mirogoj" (the one *after* the stop called "Mirogoj Arkada"). The return bus leaves from across the street.

Sights in and near the Green Horseshoe

With extra time, stroll around the Green Horseshoe (the U-shaped belt of parks and museums near the city center). The museums on

and near this park aren't as interesting as those on Gradec, but may be worth a peek on a rainy day. Like most museums in Zagreb, these close early on Sundays and all day Monday. The Modern Gallery, described later, is also in this area.

The **Mimara Museum** (Muzej Mimara) fills a grand, empty-feeling building with the eclectic art collection of a wealthy Dalmatian, ranging from ancient artifacts to paintings by European masters. While the names in the second-floor painting gallery are major—Rubens, Rembrandt, Velázquez, Renoir, Manet—the paintings themselves are minor. The first floor displays sculpture and applied arts, while the ground floor has vases, carpets, and objects from the Far East (Rooseveltov trg 5, www.mimara.hr).

The **Arts and Crafts Museum** (Muzej za Umjetnost i Obrt) features furniture, ceramics, and fashion, all well-displayed chronologically (Trg Maršala Tita 10, www.muo.hr).

The **Botanical Garden** (Botanički Vrt), run by the University of Zagreb, offers a back-to-nature change of pace from the urban bustle (free, closed Nov-March, at southwest corner of the Green 'Shoe, Marulicev trg 9A).

Art Museums

In addition to the art gallery at the Mimara Museum (described above), art lovers may want to visit the following museums. Three different collections cover works from the 20th century through today: The **Modern Gallery** features art from the early 20th century (a few blocks south of Jelačić Square at Andrije Hebranga 1, www.moderna-galerija.hr); the **Museum of Contemporary Art** focuses on mid-century art (south of the river and not as convenient to visit, avenija Dubrovnik 17, www.msu.hr); and the innovative **Lauba,** with more cutting-edge works from the past few years (Baruna Filipovića 23A, www.lauba.hr). For details on any of these, check their websites or ask at the TI.

Sleeping in Zagreb

Zagreb is a convention and business town, so rates at business-oriented hotels are highest on weekdays mid-February through mid-July, then again from September through October. At other times of year, and weekends year-round, you'll generally enjoy lower rates. I've listed the average rates—they may be slightly higher or lower with demand. If I've listed two sets of rates separated by slashes, the first is for high season and the second is for low season.

$$$ Jägerhorn Hotel is the top choice in Zagreb for affordable elegance in an excellent location (one long block from Jelačić Square, along the busy Ilica boulevard but tucked back on a quieter courtyard). Its 18 rooms are small but well-appointed, and provide a fine downtown refuge (Sb-€119/€90, Db-€129/€100, air-con, free parking a few blocks away, Ilica 14, tel. 01/483-3877, www. hotel-jagerhorn.hr, info@hotel-jagerhorn.hr).

$$$ Hotel Dubrovnik is a business-class hotel with 245 rooms. While lacking personality, it's comfortable and ideally located at the bottom of Jelačić Square (small Sb-€95, bigger Sb-€110, Db-€135, bigger and nicer "deluxe" Db-€175, suite-€200-220, extra bed-€20, rooms overlooking the square don't cost extra but can come with some noise, often cheaper on weekends, prices can flex up or down with demand, air-con, nonsmoking floors, elevator, Gajeva 1, tel. 01/486-3555, www.hotel-dubrovnik.hr, reservations@hotel-dubrovnik.hr).

$$$ Hotel Astoria, a Best Western, offers 100 smallish but plush rooms and a high-class lobby. It feels professional and polished, but still friendly. It's on a humdrum street that's handy to the train station (about a 10-minute walk from Jelačić Square)—ideal if you want to sleep near the station (Sb-€89/€79, Db-€103/€93, rates flex up or down with demand—lower rates more likely on weekends, various discounts offered—including military, fancier suites also available, air-con, elevator, nonsmoking rooms, some free parking—first come, first served, Petrinjska 71, tel. 01/480-8900, www.hotelastoria.hr, sales@hotelastoria.hr).

$$ Sobe Zagreb 17 rents seven cute and colorful rooms in a wonderfully located old building, just steps from Gradec, the Tkalčićeva restaurant street, and Jelačić Square (Db-€60-100 de-

ZAGREB

Sleep Code

Abbreviations   **(7 kn=about $1, €1=about $1.10, country code: 385)**
S=Single, **D**=Double/Twin, **T**=Triple, **Q**=Quad, **b**=bathroom
Price Rankings
 $$$ Higher Priced—Most rooms €100 or more
  $$ Moderately Priced—Most rooms €60-100
   $ Lower Priced—Most rooms €60 or less
Unless otherwise noted, credit cards are accepted, Wi-Fi is generally free, and breakfast is included, but the modest tourist tax (about 7 kn/person per night) is not. While rates are listed in euros, you'll pay in kunas. English is spoken at each place listed here. Prices change; verify current rates online or by email. For the best prices, always book directly with the hotel.

pending on size and demand, Qb apartment-€80-120, no breakfast, cash only, reception open 8:00-20:00, air-con, laundry service, airport transfers, Radićeva 22, mobile 091-170-0000, www. sobezagreb17.com, info@sobezagreb17.com, Irena).

$$ 4 City Windows is well-located just a few minutes' walk from Jelačić Square. The four rooms are bursting with creativity, each designed by owner Tanja, who also provides a warm welcome along with her husband, Ivo (small Sb-€58, Sb-€66, small Db-€76, Db-€90, Tb-€100, lower off-season, Palmotićeva 13, tel. 01/889-7999, mobile 091-383-8110, www.4citywindows.com, tanja@4citywindows.com).

$$ InZagreb, run by Ivana and Ksandro Kovačić, rents 10 one- and two-bedroom apartments scattered around the city. The units are nicely equipped and come with several welcoming touches, including kitchens with basic supplies and fresh fruit. Visit their website, find the apartment that appeals to you (noting the location of each one—some are close to the main square, while others are quite far out), and make a reservation. Clearly communicate your arrival time, and they'll pick you up at the train or bus station (no extra charge) or at the airport (150 kn extra) and take you to your home-away-from-home in Zagreb (Db-€65-95 depending on apartment and location, no one-night stays, no breakfast, air-con, laundry machine, mobile 091-652-3201, www.inzagreb.com, info@inzagreb.com). Ivana, a licensed guide, also offers a variety of custom tours around town.

$$ Studio Kairos has affordable prices, classy comfort, a warm welcome, and four creatively decorated rooms—all with different themes. It's a bit less conveniently located than my other listings, on a pleasant shopping street about a 15-minute walk from Jelačić Square (Sb-€58-69, Db-€75-87, price depends on room size, cash only, shared kitchen, air-con, self-service pay laundry, Vlaška 92, tel. 01/464-0680, mobile 091-464-0690, www.studio-kairos.com, danijela@studio-kairos.com, Danijela).

$ Hotel Ilica is a 15-minute walk or short tram ride from Jelačić Square. The hotel's idiosyncratic sense of style—with chandeliers and Roman busts that Liberace would find gaudy—helps compensate for its dull urban neighborhood. It's set back on its own courtyard with a garden behind it, making it an oasis of quiet in the heart of the city. With 25 rooms and four apartments, this quirky place is a fine value if you don't mind commuting to your sightseeing by tram (Sb-€25, Db-€45, larger twin Db-€49, big apartment-€65, 10 percent discount for Rick Steves readers who book directly, air-con, off-street courtyard parking-39 kn/day, Ilica 102, two tram stops from Jelačić Square near Britanski trg stop, tel. 01/377-7522, www.hotel-ilica.hr, info@hotel-ilica.hr).

$ Shappy Hostel—slick, shabby-chic, and modern—is the most appealing of Zagreb's many new design hostels. Surrounding a courtyard in a very central, urban-feeling area, it has 41 beds in 13 rooms, including 9 private, sleek, stylish, hotelesque doubles that are well worth considering, even for nonhostelers (bunk in dorm room-€17-25 depending on size and season, Db-€70/€50, no breakfast, air-con, free parking, lockers, Varšavska 8, tel. 01/483-0483, mobile 091-405-0511, www.hostel-shappy.com, info@hostel-shappy.com).

Eating in Zagreb

As a cosmopolitan European capital, Zagreb enjoys a refreshingly varied restaurant scene. It's also a good value; while most of the touristy towns in this book have inflated-for-tourists prices, most diners here are natives, and competition to lure value-conscious local foodies keeps things affordable. Traditional Zagreb-area cuisine is hearty peasant grub—sausage, sauerkraut, potatoes, *sarma* (cabbage rolls)—that seems more "Eastern European" than the seafood, pizza, and pastas of the coast. But consider skipping traditional Croatian food altogether here in Zagreb—the city provides some desperately needed variety (which is rare everywhere else in the country). Look beyond restaurants, too: Several enticing sandwich shops, chichi bakeries, burger joints, and gourmet coffee bars are scattered around the center, catering to businesspeople on their lunch breaks. Many of Zagreb's best eateries are closed on Sundays.

PEOPLE-WATCHING AND COFFEE-SIPPING

One of my favorite Zagreb pastimes is lingering over a drink or meal along its thriving people zones, watching an endless parade of fashionable locals saunter past, and wondering why they don't create such an inviting space in my hometown. The best place is on **Tkalčićeva street,** Zagreb's main café street and urban promenade rolled into one (starts a block behind Jelačić Square, next to the market; I've listed my favorite Tkalčićeva eateries next). Honorable mention goes to **Trg Petra Preradovića,** an inviting square just a short walk from Jelačić Square (up Ilica street) that bustles with appealing outdoor cafés and bars.

It's generally fine to buy a pastry at one of Zagreb's many boutique bakeries and dessert shops, then eat it with coffee ordered at an outdoor café—provided that café doesn't serve food of its own.

ON OR NEAR TKALČIĆEVA STREET

Tkalčićeva has the highest concentration of inviting restaurants in town. Strolling its entire length (about a 10-minute walk),

you'll pass plenty of drinks-only cafés, but also pizzerias, Turkish eateries, *ćevapi* (grilled meat) joints, cake and dessert shops, *fritule* (doughnut) windows, and the restaurants listed below. Keep an eye out for the drinks-only **Melin** bar, set just above the bustle of the street; it's the hipster's choice, with mismatched secondhand furniture and a mellower vibe.

Pivnica Mali Medo ("Little Bear") is a rollicking brewpub serving five different beers from the Medvedgrad brewery ("Bear Town"—named for a fortress near Zagreb). The heavy, stick-to-your-ribs pub grub feels closer to Prague than to Dubrovnik. The outdoor seating right on Tkalčićeva's most colorful stretch will seduce you into staying for another beer. The pubby interior is convivial, but less enticing (30-60-kn meals, daily 10:00-24:00, food served until 22:00, Tkalčićeva 36, tel. 01/492-9613).

Skalinska Street: This tight, steep lane connects Tkalčićeva to the market and cathedral. Tucked between the sprawling pizzerias are two gems: **La Štruk** is a great place to try several varieties of the local ravioli, called *štrukli*. While most eateries along here have seating out on the street, this one has its own little garden tucked inside the courtyard (25-35-kn meals, closed Sun, at #5). **Umami** is an order-at-the-counter Asian grill with indoor and sidewalk seating (35-40-kn meals, daily, at #3).

Burgers: **Rocket Burger,** an unpretentious American-style diner, dishes up decent 30-40-kn burgers at outdoor tables with prime Tkalčićeva views (daily 9:00-23:00, Tkalčićeva 44).

Asian: **Takenoko,** in the glitzy modern shopping mall at the very top end of Tkalčićeva, is a good chance for high-quality pan-Asian (mostly Japanese) cuisine with a pinch of Mediterranean fusion. The classy atmosphere and stiff service make it feel like a splurge. Choose between their sushi menu (105-175-kn combos) and their Asian fusion menu (105-140-kn dishes). Reservations are advised (Mon-Sat 12:00-24:00, Sun 12:00-18:00, in Centar Kaptol at Nova Ves 17, tel. 01/486-0530, www.takenoko.hr). Lots of other sophisticated bars and cafés are nearby.

At the Market (**Dolac**): Zagreb's busy market offers plenty of options. Assemble a fresh picnic direct from the producers; for pointers on local ingredients to look for, see page 61. Or, for something already prepared, duck into one of the many cheap restaurants and cafés on the streets around the market. The middle level of the market, facing Jelačić Square, is home to a line of places with cheap food and indoor or outdoor seating.

Dessert: **The Cookie Factory** has a wide array of delicious American-style cookies, brownies, smoothies, and other goodies. Pull up a table for a brownie à la mode, or get a cookie sandwich to go. They have outdoor tables along a delightful stretch of Tkalčićeva (10-20-kn treats, Sun-Thu 9:00-22:00, Fri-Sat 9:00-23:00, Tkalčićeva 21, mobile 099-494-9400).

IN THE UPPER TOWN (GRADEC)

Trilogija, just above the Stone Gate, is a casual wine bar serving up delicious, well-presented, and affordable international dishes made with local ingredients. There's no printed menu because they cook what they find at the market—your server can explain the chalkboard menu. As this place is deservedly popular, reservations are smart (40-70-kn small dishes, 90-130-kn large dishes, Mon-Sat 11:00-24:00, Sun 11:00-16:00—except closed Sun Nov-April, Kamenita 5, tel. 01/485-1394, www.trilogija.com).

Konoba Didov San ("Grandfather's Dream") offers traditional food from the Dalmatian hinterland (specifically the Neretva River Delta, near Metković). You'll find the normal Dalmatian specialties, plus eel, frog, and snail. Choose between the homey, traditional interior and the outdoor tables. Reservations are smart on weekends (25-60-kn starters, 65-130-kn main courses, daily 10:00-24:00, a few steps up from the Ivan Meštrović Atelier at Mletačka 11, tel. 01/485-1154).

IN THE LOWER TOWN, NEAR JELAČIĆ SQUARE

Lari & Penati is a gem hiding a couple of blocks from the train station, about a 10-minute walk from Jelačić Square. Modern and foodie, yet unpretentious and laid-back, they dish up eclectic and affordable 50-60-kn meals (Mon-Sat 12:00-22:30, closed Sun, Petrinjska 42A, tel. 01/465-5776).

Bistro Fotić is another good foodie choice, with country-classy decor under butterflies and a few outdoor tables on a dull street. The menu (with a focus on Mediterranean fare) changes daily, based on what's fresh at the market. They share the space with a local photography club, whose members display their works on the walls (Mon-Sat 8:00-23:00, closed Sun, Ljudevita Gaja 25, tel. 01/481-0476, www.bistrofotic.com).

Mundoaka is a youthful, lively spot dishing up international street food in a local-feeling pedestrian zone a block from Jelačić Square. Squeeze into the tight, trendy interior, or enjoy the outdoor tables. While the service can be a little overwhelmed, the comfort food hits the spot (80-95-kn meals, Mon-Sat 9:00-22:30, closed Sun, Petrinjska 2, tel. 01/788-8777).

Nishta, the highly recommended vegetarian restaurant in Dubrovnik (see page 334), also has a branch in Zagreb, with an eclectic menu of international meatless cuisine and an extensive salad bar (20-30-kn starters, 50-70-kn main dishes, Tue-Sun 11:00-22:00, closed Mon, Masarykova 11, tel. 01/889-7444).

Vinodol is a sprawling, white-tablecloth-classy dinner spot, with a peaceful covered terrace and a smartly appointed dining room under an impressive vaulted ceiling. The good, reasonably priced cuisine includes lamb or veal prepared *peka*-style, under a baking lid covered with hot coals (*peka* portion costs 90 kn, served only at certain times—generally at 13:00 and 19:00; 50-90-kn main courses, open daily 10:00-24:00, Teslina 10, tel. 01/481-1427).

Cheese Bar offers an easy opportunity to sample Croatian wines (45 bottles available by the glass, most 20-30 kn) accompanied by a plate of local cheeses with olives (60 kn). While the cheese isn't quite the gourmet experience you'd hope for (most taste about the same, with different spices), the stay-a-while ambience is pleasant—both in the sleek, contemporary interior, or outside, on a cobbled square just off Jelačić Square (daily 8:00-24:00, Cesarčeva 4, mobile 091-888-8628).

Fast and Cheap: **Sandwich Bar Pingvin,** busy with locals dropping by for takeaway, is a favorite for quick, cheap, tasty sandwiches with chicken, turkey, steak, or fish. They'll wrap it all in a piece of grilled bread and top it with your choice of veggies and sauces to go—or, to eat here, sit at one of the few tiny tables or stools (17-26 kn, Mon-Sat 10:00-late, Sun 18:00-late, about a block below Jelačić Square at Teslina 7). For *ćevapčići*—the classic Balkan grilled-meat dish (described on page 421)—drop by the Sarajevan-owned **Jazz.ba,** hiding in a very central, nondescript neighborhood (18-36-kn meals, daily 10:00-23:00, Varšavska 8, mobile 091-955-5001).

Fried and Fishy: **Mimice** is a local institution and an old-habits-die-hard favorite of the older generation. Although it's quite tired and dreary, I like it as a cheap and memorable time-warp serving up simple fish dishes (16-31 kn, order starches and sauces separately). Choose what you want from the limited menu (if confused, survey the room for a plate that looks good and ask what it is), pay, and take your receipt to the next counter to claim your food. Order the smelt to get a plate of tiny deep-fried fish (Mon-Fri 7:00-21:00, Sat 8:00-19:00, closed Sun, Jurišićeva 21). As Zagreb is a Catholic town, you'll have to wait in line if you're here on a Friday.

Dessert: Several inviting places in the center offer good *sladoled* (Italian gelato-style ice cream). Three central locations are **Zagreb Slastičarnica,** which usually features some creative and unusual flavors (hiding behind the statue of Tesla just past the bottom of the Trg Petra Preradovića café square at Masarykova 4); **Slastičarnica Vincek,** whose specialty is the chocolate-and-walnuts Vincek flavor (closed Sun, two blocks west of Jelačić Square on the busy tram-lined Ilica street at #18); and, across the street, **Kraš Choco Bar**, the flagship store of the Croatian candy empire, with ice-cream flavors that match its candies (closed Sun, Ilica 15).

Zagreb Connections

From Zagreb by Train to: Rijeka (3/day direct, 4-5 hours), **Pula** (3/day, 6 hours, transfer in Rijeka), **Split** (3/day, 6.5 hours, plus 1 direct night train, 9 hours), **Sarajevo** (1/day, 9 hours), **Mostar** (1/day, 11.5 hours, bus is faster), **Ptuj** (3/day, 3.5-4.5 hours, usually requires 2 transfers), **Ljubljana** (4/day direct, 2.5 hours), **Vienna** (2/day with change in Budapest or Sevnica, 8-10 hours, more with multiple changes), **Budapest** (2/day direct, 6-7 hours), **Lake Bled** (via Lesce-Bled, 4/day, 3-3.5 hours), **Munich** (2/day direct, including a night train, 9 hours). Train info: Tel. 060-333-444.

By Bus to: Samobor (about 2-3/hour, 30-50 minutes), **Plitvice Lakes National Park** (about hourly until around 16:00, 2.5 hours; the best choice is the express bus operated by Prijevoz Knežević—see page 79), **Rijeka** (hourly, 2-3.5 hours), **Rovinj** (6-9/day, 3-6 hours), **Pula** (almost hourly, 4 hours), **Split** (at least hourly, 5-8 hours), **Mostar** (7/day, 9 hours, includes a night bus), **Sarajevo** (5/day, 8 hours, includes night bus), **Dubrovnik** (10/day including some overnight options, 10 hours), **Korčula** (1/day, 9-13.5 hours depending on route), **Kotor** (1/night, 14.5 hours).

Bus schedules can be sporadic (for example, several departures clustered around the same time, then nothing for hours)—confirm your plans carefully (inquire locally, or use the good online schedules at www.akz.hr). The TI is very helpful with providing bus information. Popular buses, such as the afternoon express to Split, can fill up quickly in peak season. Book ahead on the website www.akz.hr—you can even select a seat. If you don't have a ticket, get to the station early (two hours in advance on summer days). For train information, call 060-313-333 (from abroad, dial +385-1-611-2789).

Near Zagreb

SAMOBOR

ZAGREB

This charming little town, tucked in the hills between Zagreb and the Slovenian border, is where city dwellers head to unwind,

get away from the clattering trams, and gorge themselves on sausages and cream cakes. While popular with Croatian and German tourists, Samobor is virtually undiscovered by Americans. Cuddled by hiker-friendly hills, bisected by a gurgling and promenade-lined stream, favored by artists and poets, and proud of its tidy square, Samobor is made to order for a break from the big city. Samobor works as a small-town home base near Zagreb, but it's perhaps best suited for a low-impact lunch or dinner stop en route between Zagreb and points west or north.

Samobor (with 15,000 people, plus 20,000 more in the surrounding area) has a pleasantly compact tourist zone. Virtually anything you'd want to see or do is within sight of its centerpiece, King Tomislav Square (Trg Kralja Tomislava). A stream called Gradna cuts through the middle of town. The **TI,** dead center on the main square, hands out town maps and is eager to offer hiking advice (daily, Trg Kralja Tomislava 5, tel. 01/336-0044, www.tz-samobor.hr).

Getting There: You can reach Samobor by **bus** from Zagreb's main bus station (2-3/hour, 25 kn). The trip takes 30-50 minutes, depending on traffic and the route (if possible, avoid slower buses that stop in smaller villages, such as Novaki and Rakitije). Samobor's bus station is three-quarters of a mile from the main square; take a taxi or walk, following *Centar* signs for about 15 minutes. By **car,** Samobor is just off the main Zagreb-Ljubljana expressway. Exit following signs for *Samobor,* then follow the bull's-eyes to the *Centar.* Head for the yellow steeple, then carry on past the steeple and the main square; just after the square, watch for the covered bridge on your left, which leads to a handy pay parking lot.

Visiting Samobor: Samobor is more about ambience than about sightseeing. Stroll the main square, sit at a café, gaze at the surrounding hills, and contemplate a hike.

For extra credit, drop into the sleepy **Samobor Museum,** an old mansion with miscellaneous bric-a-brac from the town's history (closed Mon, across the covered bridge from the main square at Livadićeva 7, tel. 01/336-1014, www.samoborskimuzej. hr). Samobor also boasts the exquisite **Marton Museum,** with a particularly notable porcelain collection—but most of its items are usually out on loan, and its Samobor home is rarely open except by prior arrangement (Jurjevska 7, tel. 01/332-6426, www. muzej-marton.hr).

Those interested in **hiking** find Samobor a pleasant base for venturing into the hills that begin just west of town. One popular option is to drive up to the Šoićeva Kuća mountain lodge, then hike to a nearby peak (either Oštrc or Japetić). Another popular option is to walk from Samobor to Okić and back. You can get specifics and buy hiking maps at the TI.

Sleeping in Samobor: If you'd prefer a cheaper, small-town home base, Samobor is a decent alternative to Zagreb. Consider **$ Hotel Livadić** (21 elegant rooms and a garden courtyard located over a classy café right on the main square, Trg Kralja Tomislava 1, tel. 01/336-5850, www.hotel-livadic.hr, bubbly Maja).

Eating in Samobor: Samobor is highly regarded among Zagrebians for its filling, rustic cuisine. First, an apéritif: Samobor's own Bermet is a sweet red wine made with fruits and grasses from the Samobor hills. As it's an acquired taste, start with just a sip. The local sausage, *češnjovke* (sometimes translated on menus as "garlic sausage"), is traditionally  eaten with the town's own mustard, *Samoborska Muštarda* (Dijonesque but without much kick, also sold around town in little ceramic pots). Round out your meal with a piece of *kremšnita* cream cake (curiously similar to Lake Bled's specialty).

Gabreku, every local's top recommendation for good Samobor cooking, serves the classics described above, a delicious mushroom soup, veal brains and liver, and plenty of other (mostly meat-centric) options (at far end of town, 15-minute walk from main square—head upriver on path after covered bridge then cross second bridge; free parking, Starogradska 46, tel. 01/336-0722, www. gabrek.hr).

Pri Staroj Vuri ("By the Old Clock"), with a similar menu of regional dishes, as well as homemade *štrukli* (cheese ravioli), has a traditional interior with a wall of namesake old clocks and a fine outdoor terrace in a tranquil garden (5-minute walk from square—from small fountain at intersection near end of church, head uphill for a couple of blocks, veering right at the fork; Giznik 2, tel. 01/336-0548).

Samoborska Klet ("Samobor Cellar") is the most convenient option, tucked in a courtyard on the main square, with a meaty menu, a modern dining room, and a more rustic tavern in the back, but no seating on the square itself (Trg Kralja Tomislava 7, tel. 01/332-6536).

ZAGREB

PLITVICE LAKES NATIONAL PARK

Nacionalni Park Plitvička Jezera

Plitvice (PLEET-veet-seh) is one of Europe's most spectacular natural wonders. Imagine Niagara Falls diced and sprinkled over a heavily forested Grand Canyon. There's nothing like this lush valley of 16 terraced lakes, separated by natural travertine dams and laced together by waterfalls, boat rides, and miles of pleasant plank walks. Countless cascades and water that's both strangely clear and full of vibrant colors make this park a misty natural wonderland. Over time, the water has simultaneously carved out, and, with the help of mineral deposits, built up this fluid landscape. Decades ago, after eight or nine visits, I thought I really knew Europe. Then I discovered Plitvice and realized you can never exhaust Europe's surprises.

Plitvice became Croatia's first national park in 1949, and was a popular destination during the Yugoslav period. On Easter Sunday in 1991, the first shots of Croatia's war with Yugoslavia were fired right here—in fact, the war's first casualty was a park policeman, Josip Jović. The Serbs held Plitvice until 1995, and most of the Croatians you'll meet here were evacuated and lived near the coast as refugees. During those five years, the park saw virtually no tourists, and was allowed to grow wild—allowing the ecosystem to recover from the impact of so many visitors. Today, the park is again a hugely popular tourist destination, with more than a million visitors each year (still, relatively few are from the US).

While Plitvice never fails to blow visitors away, a trip here brings you through one of the poorest, remotest areas of inland Croatia. This part of the country is still war-torn: You'll see bombed-out churches and homes in many villages, most of which likely belonged to local Serbs who fled after the war. The national park represents the only real industry for miles around, which can make locals insular and a bit greedy. Public transportation is workable, but requires some effort—this region is easiest by car.

PLANNING YOUR TIME

You can see all the best scenery at Plitvice in a three- to four-hour, mostly level hike. If your time or energy is short, you can still see

a lot in just 90 minutes. While you can give yourself more time here, it's not necessary. Other trails pale in comparison to this convenient main route.

Since it takes some time to get here (about two hours by car or bus from Zagreb), the most sensible plan is to spend the night in the area—either at one of the park's hotels, or at a guesthouse nearby. If you're coming from the north (e.g., Ljubljana), you can take the train to Zagreb in the morning, spend a few hours seeing the Croatian capital, then take the bus (generally no buses after about 16:00) or pick up a rental car and head to Plitvice in the late afternoon. To avoid crowds, hit the trails early (see tips below); by early afternoon, you'll be ready to move on (south to the coast, or north to Zagreb). Two nights and a full day at Plitvice is overkill for all but the most avid hikers.

Crowd-Beating Tips: Plitvice is swamped with international tour groups, many of which aren't shy about elbowing into position for the best photos. Work at finding ways to dodge the groups and find quiet time with a waterfall. While it's impossible to avoid crowds entirely, you'll get at least some of the park to yourself if you hike early or late. The park's trails are most crowded between 10:00 and 15:00. I try to hit the trails by 8:30—or in the peak month of August, as early as 7:30—and begin with the Lower Lakes; that way, the crowds are moving in just as I'm finishing up. If you arrive in the afternoon, starting the hike after 15:00 also works well (though off-season, be careful to check when buses and boats stop running). The Upper Lakes are often less crowded later in the day, especially in the afternoon.

GETTING TO PLITVICE

Plitvice Lakes National Park, a few miles from the Bosnian border, is located on the old highway between Zagreb and Split. Driving is the easiest option, but the park is also reachable by bus.

If taking a bus to Plitvice, confirm schedules locally or online, and also confirm that your bus will actually stop at Plitvice. The park's official bus stop is along the main road, about a 5- to 10-minute walk from the park's hotels.

From Zagreb

By **car,** Plitvice is two hours south of Zagreb on the old highway #1 (a.k.a. D-1). Leaving Zagreb, take the A-1 expressway south for about an hour, exiting at Karlovac (marked for *1* and *Plitvice*). From here, follow yellow signs to Split to get through Karlovac. Once you pop out the other side, you'll track brown signs to Plitvice along D-1. This takes you directly south about another hour to the park (for a description of what you'll pass on the way, see "En Route," below). If you're staying at the official park hotels, you can park for free at the hotel lot; to park at the lots at Entrance 1 or Entrance 2, you'll have to pay. For information about driving onward from Plitvice, see "Route Tips for Drivers" at the end of this chapter.

Buses leave from Zagreb's main bus station in the direction of Plitvice (trip takes 2-2.5 hours). Various bus companies handle the route; the best option is an **express bus** operated by a Plitvice-based company, Prijevoz Knežević (3/day in July-Aug, 1-2/day in shoulder season, first bus likely departing around 8:00, bus does not run late Oct-April; also see page 92). You can check schedules and book tickets for this bus at www.getbybus.com (look for buses operated by "PKN"). If they won't sell you a ticket for the Prijevoz Knežević express at the main ticket window, ask for "Croatia Zovko Bus." If the express doesn't suit your schedule, you can just go to any ticket window and ask for the next departure. Nonexpress buses run from Zagreb about hourly until around 16:00; avoid the sporadic late-night buses, which don't get you to the park until after midnight (for schedules, see www.autobusni-kolodvor.com or www.akz.hr; look for "Plitvička Jezera").

En Route: By car or bus, you'll see some thought-provoking terrain between Zagreb and Plitvice. Exiting the expressway at Karlovac, then heading south on D-1, you'll pass through the village of **Turanj**—part of the war zone from two decades ago. Notice the military museum (on the right as you drive through), with tanks, heavy-artillery cannons, and other war machines that actually saw action. The destroyed, derelict houses belonged to Serbs who have not come back to reclaim and repair them. Farther along, about 25 miles before Plitvice, you'll pass through the striking village of **Slunj,** perched picturesquely on travertine formations (like

Plitvice's) and surrounded by sparkling streams and waterfalls. The most traditional part of the town, perched just above the water, is called **Rastoke,** which has a memorable restaurant (see page 91). If you're driving, this is worth a photo stop. This town, too, looks very different from how it did before the war—when it was 30 percent Serb. As in countless other villages in the Croatian interior, the Orthodox church has been destroyed.

From Split

Drivers head north on the A-1 expressway, exiting at Gornja Ploča; from here, follow road D-1 about an hour north (passing Udbina and Korenica) to the park.

Various **buses** run from Split to Plitvice (5-7/day in summer, 4/day in winter, 4-6 hours). The best option is the express bus operated by Plitvice-based Prijevoz Knežević (3/day in July-Aug, 1/day in shoulder season, does not run late Sept-late June, 4.5 hours, check schedule and buy tickets at www.getbybus.com—look for buses operated by "PKN").

Orientation to Plitvice

Plitvice's 16 lakes are divided into the Upper Lakes (Gornja Jezera) and the Lower Lakes (Donja Jezera). The park officially has two entrances *(ulaz),* each with ticket windows and snack and gift shops (see the sidebar and the map). There is no town at Plitvice. The nearest village, Mukinje, is a residential community mostly for park workers; Rakovica, about a 10-minute drive north, has a grocery store.

Cost: The price to enter the park varies by season: 180 kn July-Aug, 110 kn April-June and Sept-Oct, and 55 kn Nov-March. This price covers park entry, boats, and shuttle buses. Park hotel guests pay the entry fee only once for their entire stay; if you're staying off-site and want to enter the park on several days, you'll have to buy a two-day ticket (280 kn/180 kn/90 kn).

Hours: The park is open every day, but the hours vary by season. In summer, it's generally open 7:00-20:00; in spring and fall, 8:00-18:00; and in winter, 8:00-16:00. The last boats and shuttle buses depart earlier (generally 30-60 minutes before the park closes—if hiking late in the day, ask about this before you head out). The quick boat ride between P-1 (below the hotels) and P-2 (at the Upper Lakes) runs later.

Maps and Information: A handy map of the trails is on the back of your ticket, and big maps are posted all over the park. Unless you're planning a more ambitious hike than the usual circuit I describe, I'd skip the big map and the various English-language guidebooks (both sold at entrances, hotels, and shops throughout

Park Signs and Symbols

While spectacular, Plitvice has a long history of poor management by government bureaucrats and could be more user-friendly. The trails can be confusingly marked. These symbols—which you'll see throughout the park—are much easier to grasp with the help of a map.

There are two official **entrances** to the park:

Entrance 1 is a steep 10-minute hike above the Lower Lakes.

Entrance 2, about a mile and a half south, sits just below the park's three official hotels (Jezero, Plitvice, and Bellevue). It's about a 10-minute walk downhill to the dock, where you can take a quick boat ride to the Upper Lakes or a longer boat ride to the Lower Lakes.

Boat icons point you to one of the park's three boat docks:

P-1 is the dock that's a steep hike below Entrance 2.

P-2 is just across the water from the P-1 dock, at the bottom of the Upper Lakes.

P-3 is all the way across the biggest lake, at the top of the Lower Lakes.

Train icons direct you to one of the three stops for the shuttle buses (not actual trains) that move visitors around the park:

ST-1 is a 10-minute walk below Entrance 1 (Lower Lakes).

ST-2 is below Entrance 2 (a short boat ride from the Upper Lakes).

ST-3 is at the very top of the Upper Lakes.

Letters denote various recommended hiking routes. These are largely nonsensical; while I mention these letters occasionally to help you find your way, don't get too hung up on them.

the park). The park has a good website: www.np-plitvicka-jezera.hr.

Services: While you'll find WCs at both entrances, once you're on the trails, they're rare: The only convenient one is near the P-3 boat dock (the Kozjak Lake boat dock for the Lower Lakes). There is no WC at the P-2 boat dock—the only WC at the Upper Lakes is at the ST-3 bus stop, at the very top of these lakes.

GETTING AROUND PLITVICE

Plitvice is designed for hikers. But the park has a few other ways (included in entry cost) to help you connect the best parts. Use this chapter's map and the "Park Signs and Symbols" sidebar to get oriented to your options.

By Shuttle Bus: These rubber-tired trains are useful mostly for guests at the official park hotels, or for returning to your car at the end of the hike—saving you a 40-minute walk along a boring highway. Buses start running early and continue until late after-

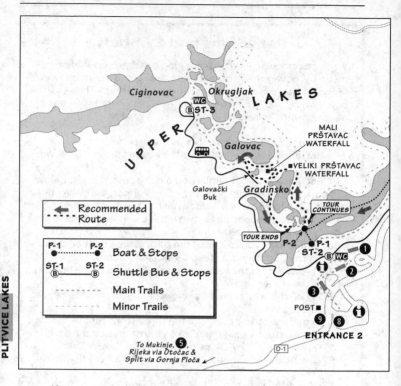

Recommended Route ········

P-1 ●········● P-2 Boat & Stops

ST-1 ⒷーーーⒷ ST-2 Shuttle Bus & Stops

--------- Main Trails

-·-·-·-·- Minor Trails

noon (frequency depends on demand—generally 3-4/hour; buses run from March until the first snow—often Dec).

By Boat: Low-impact electric boats ply the waters of the biggest lake, Kozjak, with three stops: a steep hike below Entrance 2

and the park hotels (stop P-1), at the bottom of the Upper Lakes (P-2), and at the far end of Kozjak, at the top of the Lower Lakes (P-3). From Hotel Jezero to the Upper Lakes, it's a quick five-minute ride; the boat goes back and forth continuously. The trip from the Upper Lakes to the Lower Lakes takes closer

to 20 minutes, and the boat goes about twice per hour—often at the top and bottom of every hour. (You may have to wait for a seat on this boat.)

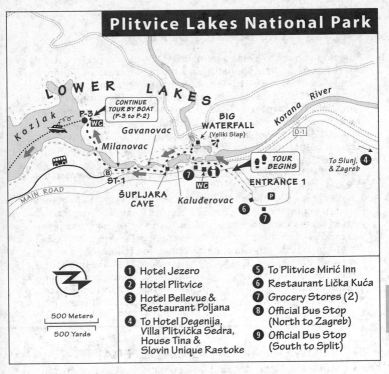

Plitvice Lakes National Park

L O W E R   L A K E S

Kozjak

CONTINUE TOUR BY BOAT (P-3 to P-2)

P-3 WC

Gavanovac

Milanovac

BIG WATERFALL (Veliki Slap)

Korana River

D-1

B

ST-1

7

WC

TOUR BEGINS

To Slunj, & Zagreb 4

MAIN ROAD

ŠUPLJARA CAVE

Kaluđerovac

ENTRANCE 1

P

6

7

500 Meters

500 Yards

1 Hotel Jezero
2 Hotel Plitvice
3 Hotel Bellevue & Restaurant Poljana
4 To Hotel Degenija, Villa Plitvička Sedra, House Tina & Slovin Unique Rastoke

5 To Plitvice Mirić Inn
6 Restaurant Lička Kuća
7 Grocery Stores (2)
8 Official Bus Stop (North to Zagreb)
9 Official Bus Stop (South to Split)

PLITVICE LAKES

Plitvice Lakes Hike

Plitvice's ▲▲▲ system of trails and boardwalks makes it easy for visitors to immerse themselves in nature. In some places, the path leads literally right up the middle of a waterfall. The official park map and signage recommend a variety of hikes, but there's no need to adhere strictly to these suggestions if you want to create your own route.

Planning Your Time: You can see everything—Upper Lakes and Lower Lakes—in a few hours. You can do these areas in either order. I prefer doing the Lower Lakes first, which offers slightly better head-on views of the best scenery and saves the most picturesque stretch for last. (That's the route I've described next.) Figure about an hour for the Lower Lakes, about an hour for the Upper Lakes, and a half-hour to connect them by boat—though it can take longer than this when the park is crowded, which it often is.

The Science of Plitvice

A geologist once explained to me that Plitvice is a perfect storm of unique geological, climatic, and biological features found in very few places on earth. Plitvice's magic ingredient is calcium carbonate ($CaCO_3$), a mineral deposit from the limestone. It's the same thing that makes "hard water" hard—and leaves calcium deposits on your cold-water faucet. But these deposits build up only at the faucet, not inside the pipes. That's because when hard water is motionless (as it usually is in the pipes), it holds on to the calcium. But at the point where the water is subjected to pressure and movement—as it pours out of the faucet—it releases the calcium.

Plitvice works the same way. As water flows over the park's limestone formations, it dissolves the rock, and the water becomes supersaturated with calcium carbonate. Then, when the water spills over the edges of the lakes, it releases carbon dioxide gas, depositing the calcium carbonate on the lake bed and at the edges of the lakes. Eventually, these deposits build up to form a rock called travertine. As the travertine thickens, barriers—and eventually dams and new waterfalls—are formed. In some places, the stone hangs down like foliage, because moss and grass pro-

PART 1: LOWER LAKES (DONJA JEZERA)

From Entrance 1, you'll descend a steep path with lots of switchbacks, as well as thrilling postcard views over the canyon of the Lower Lakes. As you reach the lakes and begin to follow the boardwalks (use the route marked *B*), you'll have great up-close views of the travertine formations that make up Plitvice's many waterfalls. Count the trout. If you're tempted to throw in a line, don't. Fishing is strictly forbidden.

After you cross the path over the first lake, an optional 10-minute detour (to the right) takes you down to the **Big Waterfall** (Veliki Slap). It's the biggest of Plitvice's waterfalls, where the Plitvica River plunges 250 feet over a cliff into the valley below. Depending on recent rainfall, the force of the Big Waterfall varies from a light mist to a thundering deluge.

If you're a hardy hiker, consider climbing the steep steps from the Big Waterfall up to a **viewpoint** at the top of the canyon (marked *Sightseeing Point/Vidikovac*; it's a strenuous 10-minute hike to the top). Take the stairs up, bearing to the right at the top (near the shelter) to find a nice viewpoint overlooking the Big

vide a framework that guides the growth of the stone. Because of this ongoing process, Plitvice's landscape is perpetually changing.

And why is the water so clear? For one thing, it comes directly from high-mountain runoff. And because the water calcifies everything it touches, it prevents the creation of mud—so the bottoms of the lakes are entirely stone. A different mineral in the water, magnesium carbonate, both gives the water its special color (which changes with the direction of the sunshine) and makes it highly basic, preventing the growth of algae and other plant life that could cloud the water.

The park contains nearly 1,300 species of plants. Wildlife found in the park include deer, wolves, wildcats, lynx, wild boar, voles, otters, snakes, 350 species of butterflies, 42 types of dragonflies, 21 species of bats, and more than 160 species of birds (including eagles, herons, owls, grouse, and storks). The lakes (and local menus) are full of trout, and you'll also see smaller, red-finned fish called *klen* ("chub" in English). Perhaps most importantly, Plitvice is home to about 40 or 50 brown bears—a species now extremely endangered in Europe. You'll see this park mascot plastered everywhere.

PLITVICE LAKES

Waterfall. From here, you can carry on along the road that actually goes up over the top of the Big Waterfall, offering more views over the park. (Go as far as you like, then return the way you came.) The giant mill perched at the top of the Big Waterfall was used to grind grains; this very poor part of Croatia was traditionally inhabited by farmers.

When you're done at the Big Waterfall, backtrack up to the main trail and continue on the boardwalks. You'll skirt the rim of Kaluđerovac Lake; then, after you pass another bank of waterfalls, a smaller trail branches off (on the left) toward **Šupljara** ("Bottomless") **Cave.** You can actually climb through this slippery cave all the way up to the trail overlooking the Lower Lakes (though it's not recommended). This unassuming cavern is a big draw. In the 1960s, several German and Italian "Spaghetti Westerns" were filmed at Plitvice and in other parts of Croatia (which, to European eyes, has terrain similar to the American West). The most famous, *Der Schatz im Silbersee (The Treasure in Silver Lake)*, was filmed here at Plitvice, and the treasure was hidden in this cave. The movie—complete with *Deutsch*-speaking "Native Americans"—is still a favorite in Germany, and popular theme tours bring German tourists to movie locations here in Croatia. (If you drive the roads near Plitvice, keep an eye out for strange, Native American-sounding names such as Winnetou—fictional characters from these beloved stories of the Old West, by the German writer Karl May.)

After Šupljara Cave, you'll stick to the east side of Gavanovac Lake, pass some picturesque terraces, then walk along the shore of Milanovac Lake, before crossing over one more time to the west, where you'll cut through a comparatively dull forest. You'll head up the paved road, branching off to the left (following the boat icon) to emerge at a pit-stop-perfect clearing with WCs, picnic tables, a souvenir shop, and a self-service restaurant.

From here you can catch the shuttle boat across **Lake Kozjak** (Jezero Kozjak) to the bottom of the Upper Lakes (usually every 30 minutes, 20-minute ride). The ride across Kozjak, the park's biggest lake, offers a great chance for a breather.

PART 2: UPPER LAKES (GORNJA JEZERA)

Focus on the lower half of the Upper Lakes, where nearly all the exotic beauty is (between P-2 and Lake Galovac). You'll soon experience some of the most striking waterfalls in the whole park.

Climbing up steeply on stepped boardwalks from the boat dock (following signs for *C*), you'll pass deep pools with fallen trees stretching along the bottom, illustrating just how magnificently clear the water here is. Soon you'll curl along the waterline of Gradinsko Lake. At the end of the lake, you'll come to the park's finest cascades, which tumble dramatically from Galovac into Gradinsko. You'll hear the waterfalls, then you'll see them, and finally you'll feel them, as the spray pelts your face while you stroll the boardwalks. First you'll pass by thundering **Veliki ("Big") Prštavac,** then hook up a tight-and-steep uphill bend—literally walking in the middle of a waterfall—to the nearly as spectacular **Mali ("Small") Prštavac.** Then you'll stroll along a whole wall of other waterfalls. Continuing up, you'll weave through another grand set of pools and falls, with views down on the pond of **Galovački Buk.** Walk along here, enjoying more ponds and cascades. Eventually you'll emerge at a fork in the path. Here, you have two options:

1. Make your hike a loop by turning left (following signs for the boat icon, *P-2*, and *E, H*, and *K*). This is the easiest and most enjoyable choice for most hikers. First, you'll walk down a stepped boardwalk with gurgling water underfoot. Then you'll circle back around the far (south) side of Gradinsko Lake and through a forest. Finally you'll pass a small picnic shelter, then walk down past one last set of falls to the P-2 boat dock, where you can take the boat back over to the hotels (P-1 stop). From here, hike up to Entrance 2; if you left your car back at Entrance 1, you can hop on the shuttle bus to get there.

2. Turn right (following the icon for the shuttle bus and *C*) to continue hiking up to the top of the Upper Lakes. I'd choose this option only if you have energy and time to burn. This route leads

you along the top of the best waterfalls (heard, but not seen), then loops you the long way around Galovac Lake and eventually to the ST-3 bus stop. From here on up, the scenery is less stunning, and the waterfalls are fewer and farther between. At the top, you'll finish at shuttle bus stop ST-3 (with food stalls and a WC), where the bus zips you back to the entrances and hotels.

Nice work!

Sleeping in and near Plitvice

AT THE PARK

The most convenient place to sleep is at one of Plitvice's official park lodges, which are all run by the same office (reservation tel. 053/751-015, www.np-plitvicka-jezera.hr). It's best to book on their website (emails may go unanswered in busy times). These are all located a few minutes' walk apart, along the main highway and just above the park's Entrance 2. Note that none of these hotels has air-conditioning (which is rarely needed in this climate), and all of them include breakfast.

$$$ Hotel Jezero is big and modern, with all the comfort—and charm—of a Holiday Inn. It's well-situated right at the park entrance and offers 200 rooms that feel newish, but generally have at least one thing that's broken. Rooms facing the park have big glass doors and balconies (Db-€120/€110/€85; elevator, reception tel. 053/751-400).

$$ Hotel Plitvice, a better value than Jezero, offers 57 rooms and mod, wide-open public spaces on two floors with no elevator. For rooms, choose from economy (fine, older-feeling; Db-€97/€87/€70), standard (just a teeny bit bigger; Db-€107/€97/€74), or superior (bigger still, with a sitting area; Db-€117/€107/€84, reception tel. 053/751-100).

$$ Hotel Bellevue, dated and faded, feels like a Tito-era leftover, with a musty orange-and-dark-brown color scheme in its 77 rooms. While not up to the standards of the other park hotels, it's cheap (Db-€75/€70/€54, no elevator, closed Nov-March, reception tel. 053/751-700).

OUTSIDE THE PARK

Drivers should consider sleeping at one of the many options near the park. Prices here are also high, but these choices have a bit more personality.

North of Plitvice

Dozens of midsize hotels and small *sobe* line the highway for about 10 miles north of the national park. Options are so abundant here that spontaneous travelers can show up without reservations and

PLITVICE LAKES

Sleep Code

Abbreviations   (7 kn=about $1, €1=about $1.10, country code: 385)
S=Single, **D**=Double/Twin, **T**=Triple, **Q**=Quad, **b**=bathroom
Price Rankings
  $$$ Higher Priced—Most rooms €100 or more
   $$ Moderately Priced—Most rooms €60-100
    $ Lower Priced—Most rooms €60 or less

If I've listed three sets of rates, separated by slashes, the first is for peak season (July-Aug), the second is for shoulder season (May-June and Sept-Oct), and the third is for off-season (Nov-April). The dates for seasonal rates vary by hotel. These rates do not include the modest tourist tax (about 7 kn/person per day). Unless otherwise noted, credit cards are accepted, free Wi-Fi is generally available, and breakfast is included. While rates are listed in euros, you'll pay in kunas. Everyone listed here speaks English (or has a relative or neighbor who can help translate). Prices change; verify current rates online or by email. For the best prices, always book directly with the hotel.

---

take their pick. I've listed some favorites below. To reach Plitvička Sedra and Tina, turn left off the main road toward *Bihać*, after entering the town of Rakovica. The Degenija is right along the main road, a bit closer to Plitvice.

$$$ Hotel Degenija is pricey, but offers all the big hotel comforts in a homier package than the park lodges. Its 20 modern, stylish rooms are in a building behind the bustling roadside restaurant (economy Db-€90/€84/€78, comfort Db-€110/€92/€85, superior Db-€120/€100/€90, bigger suites also available, air-con, elevator, bikes available, Selište Drežničko 57a, tel. 047/782-143, www.hotel-degenija.com, rezervacije.degenija@email.t-com.hr). The busy restaurant is justifiably popular with tour groups (45-60-kn pastas and pizzas, 75-100-kn main courses, daily 7:00-23:00).

$$ Villa Plitvička Sedra may be the best value around. It's a homey yet modern-feeling stone-and-wood complex that sits in a pleasant parklike setting, with tennis courts and a billiards pavilion, just off the main road. The 23 rooms have all the comforts you'll need for an overnight near the park (standard Db-€75/€45, larger superior Db with balcony-€120/€75, air-con, Irinovac 149, tel. 047/784-401, www.restoran-sedra.hr, info@restoran-sedra.hr). The restaurant is also inviting (40-90-kn meals, open long hours daily).

$$ House Tina is a neon-yellow farmhouse surrounded by fields (and a dozen other B&Bs) just off the main road. They have 11 rooms, including two nicely woody bungalows that sleep four each (Db-€80/€70/€55, bungalow-€90/€80/€70, studio apartment-€110/€100/€90, some with air-con, Grabovac 175, Rakovica, tel. 04/778-4197, mobile 098-963-4048, www.housetina.com, ljubica.vukovic@ka.t-com.hr).

In Rastoke: **$ Slovin Unique Rastoke**—described later, under "Eating in and near Plitvice"—also rents two rooms above the restaurant (Db-€40-50/€30-40/€30-35, price depends on size), along with a cozy, primitive bungalow with modern features, such as air-conditioning, TV, and Wi-Fi (Db-€65/€50/€45).

A Few Minutes South of Plitvice

$$$ Plitvice Mirić Inn offers the friendliest welcome in the region. The Mirić family (daughter Lili speaks great English, mom cooks fine meals) offers 13 smallish, modern-chalet rooms, lots of good travel advice, and a not-to-be-missed, home-cooked dinner for €20—guests only (standard Db-€100/€85/€68, Db with balcony-€120/€103/€84, air-con, Jezerce 18/1, watch for it along the main road on the left as you head south from the park, mobile 098-930-6508, www.plitvice-croatia.com, info@plitvice-croatia.com). While better for drivers, this can work by bus: It's 300 yards from the nearest bus stop (Mukinje village) and about a mile and a half from Entrance 2.

In Mukinje Village: Just south of the park is the village of Mukinje, which feels like a holdover from communist times: It's basically a planned workers' town, where crumbling concrete apartment blocks mingle with newer chalet-style homes renting rooms to travelers. Unfortunately, attitudes here seem trapped in communist times, too; most of the *sobe* I've inspected here are run by locals who are grouchy and indifferent, and the prices are too high. While you could drive into town and check a few options, you'll find a warmer welcome at some of the places listed above.

Eating in and near Plitvice

Local cuisine is hearty countryside grub, offering a nice, landlocked change of pace from the seafood-heavy and Italian-flavored menus of most of Croatia's tourist towns. You'll see mushroom soups, soft spreadable cheeses, and grilled trout, with the fish pulled fresh from the lakes. Restaurants here are functional—don't expect high cuisine.

AT THE NATIONAL PARK

The park runs a variety of uninspired restaurants, with institutional food and ambience. If you're staying at the hotels, you have the option of paying for half-board with your room (lunch or dinner, 90 kn each). The half-board option is worth doing if you're here for dinner, but don't lock yourself in for lunch—you'll want more flexibility as you explore Plitvice (excellent picnic spots and decent food stands abound inside the park). All of these eateries are open long hours daily.

Near Entrance 1, the rustic **Restaurant Lička Kuća** has more character than the other park eateries. It's across the highway from the entrance and gift shop (40-100-kn starters, 100-160-kn main dishes).

Near Entrance 2, most people opting for half-board dine at the restaurants inside **Hotel Jezero** and **Hotel Plitvice,** but you can also use the voucher at other park eateries (you'll pay the difference if the bill is more). **Restaurant Poljana,** behind Hotel Bellevue, has the same park-lodge atmosphere in both of its sections: cheap, self-service cafeteria (30-45-kn meals) and sit-down "national restaurant" with open wood-fired grill (65-110-kn meals); both parts have dreary communist decor.

For **picnic** fixings, there's a tiny grocery store at Entrance 1 and another one with a larger selection across road D-1 (use the pedestrian overpass). If you're driving in from the north, consider getting your provisions at the better-stocked grocery store in the village of Rakovica on your way through. Once inside the park, at the P-3 boat dock, you can buy grilled meat and drinks. Friendly old ladies sell homemade goodies (such as strudel and hunks of cheese) throughout the park, including at Entrance 1.

OUTSIDE THE PARK

Many truck stop-type restaurants line the highway for miles in both directions from Plitvice. These cater primarily to tour buses... and their drivers, who dine like kings in exchange for bringing in so much business. Most of these places are unexciting, but two good options are at the recommended **Hotel Degenija** and **Villa Plitvička Sedra** (for details, see listings earlier). Many countryside accommodations also have a half-board option; ask about this when you book.

Eating in Bosnia: Adventurous drivers may want to make a short drive across the border for a bite in the town of Bihać (BEE-hahch). This small Bosnian city is about a 30-minute drive from the national park (be sure to bring your passport and "green card"/proof of car insurance). If this is your only chance to dip into Bosnia, and you have an evening to kill, it can be a fun option. For more on Bosnian food, see page 420.

A MEMORABLE MEAL SURROUNDED BY WATERFALLS 30 MINUTES NORTH OF PLITVICE

On the main highway between Zagreb and Plitvice, about 30 minutes from the national park, you'll pass above, then through, the striking town of Slunj (pronounced "sloon"), which is surrounded by its own little "mini-Plitvice" ecosystem of waterfalls. This can be an enjoyable pit stop, whether or not you eat here. The lower part of the town—buried deep amid all those cascades—is the village of Rastoke (meaning roughly "beautiful water"), which has its share of touristy restaurants. The most elaborate is the complex of **Slovin Unique Rastoke,** where you can explore a series of canals, waterfalls, canyons, and viewpoints. The grounds also have an old mill, a small "ethno collection" (traditional local furniture, tools, and so on), and a trail down to the Korona River canyon. While you can pay 25 kn to explore (they'll give you a map), it's free for those who dine at their restaurant, **Pod Rastočkim Krovom** ("Under Rastoke's Roof"). They specialize in trout—you can see their ponds out back—and also have a wide range of other local dishes, including some prepared with grains ground by traditional mills (20-35-kn soups and pastas, 60-80-kn main courses, open long hours daily, Rastoke 25B, mobile 099-215-0907, www.slunj-rastoke.com). While a bit hokey and tour group-oriented, Rastoke gives you a chance to see some bonus waterfalls.

Getting There: Approaching the town of Slunj from the north, you'll see Rastoke filling the valley below. After crossing the first bridge, turn right at the *Rastoke* sign, then park next to—and walk over—the dilapidated old concrete bridge; finally, turn right and walk down the hill to Slovin Unique Rastoke.

Plitvice Connections

To reach the park, see "Getting to Plitvice" on page 79. Moving on from Plitvice is trickier.

BY BUS

Bus Schedules and Options: Buses pass by the park in each direction—northbound (to **Zagreb,** 2-2.5 hours) and southbound (to coastal destinations such as **Split,** 4-6 hours). The park lodge reception desk should have a printout of the specific bus schedule, or you can check at www.autobusni-kolodvor.com (look for "Plitvička Jezera").

In summer, the best choice is the **Prijevoz Knežević express bus,** designed to zip Plitvice hikers directly to major destinations. (The regular buses take longer, make several stops en route, and can fill up before even reaching the park.) The express bus connects the park to Zagreb in the north (2 hours) and to Split in the south (4.5 hours; connections to Zadar and Skradin at Krka National Park are also possible). Each bus runs 3 times per day in summer (July-Aug), and 1-2 times per day in shoulder season (no buses in off-season). You can check schedules and buy tickets at www.getbybus.com (look for buses operated by "PKN"). Or you can buy tickets for express buses at the little sales kiosks next to the bus stops at both Plitvice entrances (daily 8:00-17:00, mobile 098-650-757); for other buses, buy your ticket on board.

Catching the Bus: There is no bus station at the park—just a low-profile *Plitvice Centar* bus stop shelter near Entrance 2. To reach it from the park, go out to the main road from either Hotel Jezero or Hotel Plitvice, then turn right; the bus stops are just after the pedestrian overpass. The one on the hotel side of the road is for buses headed for the coast (southbound); the stop on the opposite side is for Zagreb (northbound). Confirm the bus schedule with the park or hotel staff, then head out to the bus stop and wave down the bus. (It's easy to confuse public buses with private tour buses, so don't panic if a bus doesn't stop for you—look for a bus with your final destination marked in the windshield.)

Here's the catch: If the bus is full, they won't stop at Plitvice to pick you up. This is most common on days when the buses are jammed with people headed to or from the coast. For example, on Fridays—when everyone is going from Zagreb to Split—you're unlikely to have any luck catching a southbound bus at Plitvice after 12:00, as they tend to be full. Similarly, on Sunday afternoons, northbound buses are often full. In general, don't plan on taking the last bus of the day. One advantage of the Prijevoz Knežević express buses is that they originate at Plitvice, so they don't arrive full.

While there's a chance you'll miss a bus and have to wait for the next one, bus travel from Plitvice usually works fine...if you're patient.

ROUTE TIPS FOR DRIVERS

Plitvice is an hour away from the handy A-1 expressway that connects northern Croatia to the Dalmatian Coast. You have three ways to get from Plitvice to the expressway, depending on which direction you're heading.

Going North: If you're heading north (to Zagreb or Slovenia), get on the expressway at **Karlovac:** From Plitvice, drive about one hour north on D-1 to the town of Karlovac, where you can access A-1 northbound. Alternatively, you can take A-1 southbound to A-6, which leads west to Rijeka, Opatija, and

Istria (though this route is more boring and only slightly faster than the route via Otočac, described below).

Going South: If you're heading south (to Split and the rest of Dalmatia), catch the expressway at **Gornja Ploča.** Drive south from Plitvice on D-1—through Korenica, Pećane, and Udbina—then follow signs for the A-1 expressway (and *Lovinac*) via Kurjak to the Gornja Ploča on-ramp. Once on A-1, you'll twist south through the giant Sveti Rok tunnel to Dalmatia.

Going to Central Croatia: If you're going to central destinations on the coast—such as Istria, Rijeka, or Opatija—get on the expressway at **Otočac.** From Plitvice, go south on D-1, then turn west on road #52 to the town of Otočac (about an hour through the mountains from Plitvice to Otočac). After Otočac, you can get on A-1 (north to Zagreb, south to the Dalmatian Coast) or continue west and twist down the mountain road to the seaside town of Senj, on the main coastal road of the Kvarner Gulf. From Senj, it's about an hour north along the coast to Rijeka, then on to Opatija or Istria.

During the Yugoslav Wars, the front line between the Croats and Serbs ran just east of **Otočac** (OH-toh-chawts), and a few bullet holes still mar the town's facades. (Watch for minefield warning signs just east of Otočac. While it's perfectly safe to drive here, don't get out of your car and wander through the fields.) Today Otočac is putting itself back together, and it's a fine place to drop in to a café for a coffee, or pick up some produce at the outdoor market. The Catholic church in the center of town, destroyed in the war but now rebuilt, displays its damaged church bells in a memorial out back. Notice that the crucifix nearby is made of old artillery shells. Also in the churchyard are big white blocks, each one honoring a Croatian hero; notice that a character from Glagolitic script (the ancient Croatian alphabet) is carved in the top of each one.

Just up the main street, you'll come to a fine, manicured park, dominated by a huge monument honoring the lives lost in the fight to create a free Croatian nation. It reads: "In order to make real the vision of a Croatian homeland, they laid upon the altar their dreams, their hopes, and their lives." Noticing the giant block splintering into four pieces, it's easy to imagine how this might illustrate the splitting up of the Yugoslav state...and might make you wonder how local Serbs feel about this provocative monument.

At the far end of the park is the Orthodox church. Otočac used to be about one-third Serb, but the Serbs were forced out during the war, and this church fell into disrepair. But, as Otočac and Croatia show signs of healing, about two dozen Serbs have returned to town and reopened their church (for more on the Serbian Orthodox Church, see page 316).

ISTRIA

*Rovinj • Pula • The Brijuni Islands • Poreč • Hill Towns
• Opatija and Rijeka*

Idyllic Istria (EE-stree-ah; "Istra" in Croatian), at Croatia's northwest corner, reveals itself to you gradually and seductively. Pungent truffles, Roman ruins, striking hill towns, quaint coastal villages, carefully cultivated food and wine, and breezy Italian culture all compete for your attention. The wedge-shaped Istrian Peninsula, while not as famous as its southern rival (the much-hyped Dalmatian Coast), is giving Dalmatia a run for its money.

The Istrian coast, with gentle green slopes instead of the sheer limestone cliffs found along the rest of the Croatian shoreline, is more serene than sensational. It's lined with pretty, interchangeably tacky resort towns, such as the tourist mecca Poreč (worthwhile only for its mosaic-packed Byzantine basilica). But one seafront village reaches the ranks of greatness: romantically creaky Rovinj, my favorite little town on the Adriatic. Down at the tip of Istria is big, industrial Pula, offering a bustling urban contrast to the rest of the time-passed coastline, plus some impressive Roman ruins (including an amphitheater so remarkably intact, you'll marvel that you haven't heard of it before). Just offshore are the Brijuni Islands—once the stomping grounds of Marshal Tito, whose ghost still haunts a national park peppered with unexpected attractions.

But Croatia is more than the sea, and diverse Istria offers some of the country's most appealing reasons to head inland. In the Istrian interior, between humble concrete towns crying out for a paint job, you'll find vintners painstakingly reviving a delicate winemaking tradition, farmers pressing that last drop of oil out of their olives, trained dogs sniffing out truffles in primeval forests, and a smattering of fortified medieval hill towns with sweeping

ISTRIA

views over the surrounding terrain—including the justifiably popular village of Motovun.

PLANNING YOUR TIME

Istria offers an exciting variety of attractions compared to the relatively uniform, if beautiful, string of island towns farther south. While some travelers wouldn't trade a sunny island day for anything, I prefer to sacrifice a little time on the Dalmatian Coast for the diversity that comes with a day or two exploring Istria's hill towns and other unique sights.

Istria's main logistical advantage is that it's easy to reach and to

Istria at a Glance

▲▲▲**Rovinj** Extremely romantic, Venetian-style coastal town with an atmospheric Old Town and salty harbor. See page 99.

▲▲**Pula** Big, industrial port city with one of the world's best-preserved Roman amphitheaters. See page 125.

▲▲**Motovun** Touristy but enjoyable hill town with a fun rampart walk offering sweeping views over inland Istria. See page 144.

▲**Opatija** Former Austrian beach resort (just outside Istria) with sparkling beaches and a touch of classy Viennese-style architecture. See page 160.

▲**Završje** Picturesque, mostly deserted hill town overlooking Motovun and its valley. See page 154.

▲**Brijuni Islands** Tito's former summer residence, now a national park with a Tito museum, mini safari, and other offbeat sights. See page 137.

▲**Grožnjan** Sleepy artists' colony hill town in the interior. See page 153.

Buje Big hill town mingling charm with urban flair. See page 152.

Hum Minuscule, touristy town deep in the interior. See page 159.

Poreč Big coastal resort squeezed full of European holiday makers, plus a church with remarkably intact Byzantine mosaics. See page 141.

Oprtalj Hill town that's striking from afar but all business up close. See page 155.

Livade Modest valley village with some top-notch truffle eateries. See page 158.

Brtonigla Hill town worth visiting only for its great restaurants. See page 151.

Rijeka Hulking transit-hub metropolis sitting on a pretty bay just outside Istria. See page 165.

explore by car. Just a quick hop from Venice or Slovenia, compact little Istria is made-to-order for a quick, efficient road trip.

With a car and two weeks to spend in Croatia and Slovenia, Istria deserves two days, divided between its two big attractions: the coastal town of Rovinj and the hill towns of the interior. Ideally, make your home base for two nights in Rovinj or in Motovun, and day-trip to the region's other attractions. To wring the most out of limited Istrian time, the city of Pula and its Roman amphitheater are well worth a few hours. If you have a car, it's easy to go for a joyride through the Istrian countryside, visiting a few hill towns and wineries en route. The town of Poreč and the fun but time-consuming Brijuni Islands merit a detour only if you've got at least three days.

GETTING AROUND ISTRIA

Istria is a cinch for **drivers,** who find distances short and roads and attractions well-marked. Summer traffic, however, can be miserable (especially on weekends), and parking can be tricky—and expensive—in some towns. Istria is neatly connected by a speedy highway nicknamed the *ipsilon* (the Croatian word for the letter Y, which is what the highway is shaped like). One branch of the "Y" (A-9) runs roughly parallel to the coast from Slovenia to Pula, about six miles inland; the other branch (A-8) cuts diagonally northeast to the Učka Tunnel (leading to Rijeka). You'll periodically come to toll booths, where you'll pay a modest fee for using the *ipsilon*. Following road signs here is easy (navigate by town names), but if you'll be driving a lot, pick up a good map to more easily navigate the back roads. As you drive, keep an eye out for characteristic stone igloos called *kažun* (a symbol of Istria). Formerly used as very humble residences, now the few surviving structures—sometimes built right into a dry-stone wall—are mostly used as shelter for farmers caught in the rain.

If you're relying on **public transportation,** Istria can be frustrating: The towns that are easiest to reach (Poreč and Pula) are less appealing than Istria's highlights (Rovinj and Motovun). Linking up the coastal towns by bus is doable if you're patient and check schedules carefully, but the hill towns probably aren't worth the hassle. Even if you're doing the rest of your trip by public transportation, consider renting a car for a day or two in Istria.

Driving from Istria to Rijeka (and the Rest of Croatia): Istria meets the rest of Croatia at the big port city of Rijeka (described at the end of this chapter). There are two ways to get to Rijeka: The faster alternative is to take the *ipsilon* road via Pazin to the Učka Tunnel (28-kn toll), which emerges just above Rijeka and Opatija (for Rijeka, you'll follow the road more or less straight on; for Opatija, you'll twist down to the right, backtracking slightly to the seashore below you). Or you can take the slower but more scenic **coastal road** from Pula via Labin. After going inland for about 25 miles, this road jogs to the east coast of Istria, which it hugs all the way into Opatija, then Rijeka.

From Rijeka, you can easily hook into Croatia's expressway network (for example, take A-6 east to A-1, which zips you north to Zagreb or south to the Dalmatian Coast). For more driving tips, see the end of this chapter.

By Boat to Venice, Piran, or Trieste: Various companies connect Venice daily in summer with Rovinj, Poreč, and Pula (about three hours). While designed for day-trippers from Istria to Venice, these services can be used for one-way travel. As the companies and specific routes change from year to year, check each of these websites to see what might work for your itinerary: **Venezia Lines** (www.venezialines.com), **Adriatic Lines** (www.adriatic-lines.com), and **Commodore Cruises** (www.commodore-cruises.hr). **Trieste Lines** (www.triestelines.it) connects Rovinj and Poreč to Piran (Slovenia), then Trieste (Italy).

Rovinj

Rising dramatically from the Adriatic as though being pulled up to heaven by its grand bell tower, Rovinj (roh-VEEN; in Italian: Rovigno/roh-VEEN-yoh) is a welcoming Old World oasis. Among the villages of Croatia's coast, there's something particularly romantic about Rovinj—the most Italian town in Croatia's most Italian region. Rovinj's streets are delightfully twisty, its ancient houses are characteristically crumbling, and its harbor—lively with real-life fishermen—is as salty as they come. Like a little Venice on a hill, Rovinj is the atmospheric setting of your Croatian seaside dreams.

Rovinj was prosperous and well-fortified in the Middle Ages. It boomed in the 16th and 17th centuries, when it was flooded with

refugees fleeing both the Ottoman invasions and the plague. Because the town was part of the Republic of Venice for five centuries (13th to 18th century), its architecture, culture, and even language are strongly Venetian. The local folk groups sing in a dialect actually considered more Venetian than what the Venetians themselves speak these days. (You can even see Venice from Rovinj's church bell tower on a very clear day.)

ISTRIA

Istrian Food and Wine

Foodies consider Istria the best part of Croatia. Though much of the rest of the country is arid and barren, Istria is notice-ably greener—its fertile soil bursts with a cornucopia of delicious ingredients. Like the Istrian people, Istrian cuisine is a mix of various cultural influences, including Italian-style elements, farmer fare, game, and seafood. Truffles are used liberally, and are a big hit with the many tourists who come here for their pungent flavor (see sidebar on page 150).

Istrian menus come with an enticing list of pastas. You'll see familiar dishes such as gnocchi and risotto, but Istria also adds some unique noodles to the mix. *Fuži* are little pasta squares that are rolled up to create hollow noodles, roughly shaped like penne; *pljukanci* are short, thick, nearly transpar-ent twists (similar to Italian *trofie*).

Pršut is the air-cured ham that is Istria's answer to pro-sciutto (see sidebar on page 530). You'll often find game on the menu, as well as *boškarin*—the meat of an indigenous Istrian longhorn cattle. *Ombolo* is pork loin—a locally beloved dish.

Istria is also a major wine-growing region. And—now that they've made progress repairing the damage done by com-munist-era winemaking cooperatives—Istrian wines are begin-ning to get some international attention. Relatively few Istrian wines are exported (though the number is growing), so this region gives wine lovers a good opportunity to discover some new bouquets.

About 80 percent of Istrian wines are white, many made with the grape called *malvazija* (mahl-VAH-zee-yah; better known to English-speakers as malvasia)—producing a de-licious, light white wine that can be either sweet *(slatko)* or dry *(suho)*. *Malvazija* wines are produced throughout Europe, but Istria's *malvazija* is indigenous. *Malvazija* comes in several forms: "fresh" (table wine, aged in stainless steel) or aged in barrels (often in French oak or in local Istrian acacia; look for *barrique* on the label). White blends (usually including some *malvazija*) are also common.

Red wines are made from the *teran* grape, which produc-es a "big" wine that you can chew on. Because *teran* is full-bodied, it's often blended with merlot or other grapes, result-ing in some softer, lovely flavors and a finer wine. *Teran* pairs well with *pršut*.

For more on Istrian wines—including several winer-ies where drivers can stop off for a taste—see page 156. If you're carless, consider the two wine bars in Rovinj, described on page 115.

After Napoleon seized the region, then was defeated, Rovinj became part of the Austro-Hungarian Empire. The Venetians had neglected Istria, but the Austrians invested in it, bringing the railroad, gas lights, and a huge Ronhill tobacco factory. (This factory—recently replaced by an enormous, state-of-the-art facility you'll pass on the highway farther inland—is one of the town's most elegant structures, and is slated for extensive renovation in the coming years.) The Habsburgs tapped Pula and Trieste to be the empire's major ports—cursing those cities with pollution and sprawl, while allowing Rovinj to linger in its trapped-in-the-past quaintness.

Before long, Austrians discovered Istria as a handy escape for a beach holiday. Tourism came to Rovinj in the late 1890s, when a powerful Austrian baron bought one of the remote, barren islands offshore and brought it back to life with gardens and a grand villa. Soon another baron bought another island...and a tourist boom was under way. In more recent times, Rovinj has become a top destination for nudists. The resort of Valalta, just to the north, is a popular spot for those seeking "southern exposure"...as a very revealing brochure at the TI illustrates (www.valalta.hr). Whether you want to find PNBs (pudgy nude bodies) or avoid them, remember that *FKK*

is international shorthand for nudism.

Rovinj is the most atmospheric of all of Croatia's small coastal towns. Maybe that's because it's always been a real town, where poor people lived. You'll find no fancy old palaces here—just narrow streets lined with skinny houses that have sheltered humble families for generations. While it's becoming known on the tourist circuit, Rovinj retains the soul of a fishermen's village; notice that the harbor is still filled not with glitzy yachts, but with a busy fishing fleet.

ISTRIA

PLANNING YOUR TIME

Rovinj is hardly packed with diversions. You can get the gist of the town in a one-hour wander. The rest of your time is for enjoying the ambience, savoring a slow meal, or pedaling a rental bike to a nearby beach. When you're ready to overcome your inertia, there's no shortage of day trips (the best are outlined in this chapter). Be aware that much of Rovinj (like other small Croatian coastal towns) closes down from mid-October through Easter.

Orientation to Rovinj

Rovinj's Old Town is divided in two parts: a particularly charismatic chunk on the oval-shaped peninsula, and the rest on the
mainland (with similarly time-worn buildings, but without the
commercial cuteness that comes with lots of tourist money). Where
the mainland meets the peninsula is a broad, bustling public space
called Tito Square (Trg Maršala Tita). The Old Town peninsula—
traffic-free except for the occasional moped—is topped by the massive bell tower of the Church of St. Euphemia. At the very tip of
the peninsula is a small park.

TOURIST INFORMATION

Rovinj's TI, facing the harbor, has a town map and an info book-
let (May-Oct daily 8:00-20:00; Nov-April Mon-Fri 8:00-16:00,
Sat 8:00-13:00, closed Sun; along the embankment at Obala Pina
Budičina 12, tel. 052/811-566, www.tzgrovinj.hr).

ARRIVAL IN ROVINJ

By Car: Only local cars are allowed to enter the Old Town area
(though if you're overnighting in this area, they may let you drive in
just long enough to drop off your bags—ask your host for details). To
get as close as possible—whether you're staying in the Old Town or
just visiting for the day—use the big waterfront Valdibora parking
lots just north of the Old Town, which come with the classic Rovinj
view (5-7 kn/hour, 120 kn/24 hours; much cheaper off-season). As
you drive in from the highway through the outskirts of Rovinj,
the road forks, sending most hotel traffic to the left (turn off here
if you're staying outside the Old Town); but if you want to reach
the Old Town, go right instead, then follow *Centar* signs, which
eventually lead you directly to the two Valdibora lots: "Valdibora 1"
(a.k.a. "Big Valdibora," farther from the Old Town), then "Valdibora 2" (a.k.a. "Little Valdibora," closer to the Old Town). During
busy times, the slightly closer Valdibora 2 is reserved for residents;
in this case, signs will divert you into Valdibora 1.

If both Valdibora lots are full, you'll be pushed to another pay
lot farther out, along the bay northwest of the Old Town (a scenic
15-minute walk from town, 6 kn/hour, free 23:00-6:00, cheaper
off-season). Yet another option is to use the free lot above Hotel
Park at the corner of ulica Stjepana Radića and ulica Franje Iskre, a
20-minute walk from the Old Town (see map on page 104). Even if
the Valdibora lots are available, budget-oriented drivers may prefer
these somewhat cheaper outer lots—the cost adds up fast if you're
parking over several nights. Accommodations outside the Old
Town generally have on-site (or nearby streetside) parking, often

free; a few places in the Old Town have parking available outside of town.

By Bus: The bus station is on the south side of the Old Town, close to the harbor. Leave the station to the left, then walk on busy Carera street directly into the center of town.

By Boat: The few boats connecting Rovinj to Venice, Piran, Trieste, and other Istrian towns dock at the long pier protruding from the Old Town peninsula. Just walk up the pier, and you're in the heart of town.

HELPFUL HINTS

Laundry: The full-service **Galax** launderette hides up the street beyond the bus station. You can usually pick up your laundry after 24 hours, though same-day service might be possible if you drop it off early enough in the morning (90 kn/load wash and dry; Easter-Sept daily 6:00-20:00, until later in summer; Oct-Easter Mon-Fri 7:00-19:00, Sat 9:00-15:00, closed Sun; up Benussia street past the bus station, on the left after the post office, tel. 052/816-130).

Local Guide: Vukica Palčić knows her town intimately and loves to share it with visitors (€50 for a 1.5-hour tour, mobile 098-794-003, vukica.palcic@gmail.com).

Best Views: The town is full of breathtaking views. Photography buffs will be busy in the magic hours of early morning and evening, and even by moonlight. The postcard view of Rovinj is from the parking lot embankment at the north end of the Old Town (at the start of the "Rovinj Ramble," next). For a different perspective on the Old Town, head for the far side of the harbor on the opposite (south) end of town. The church bell tower provides an almost aerial view of the town and a grand vista of the outlying islands.

Rovinj Ramble

This self-guided walk, rated ▲▲▲, introduces you to Rovinj in about an hour. Begin at the parking lot just north of the Old Town ("Little Valdibora").

Old Town View

Many places offer fine views of Rovinj's Old Town, but this is the most striking. Boats bob in the harbor, and behind them Venetian-looking homes seem to rise from

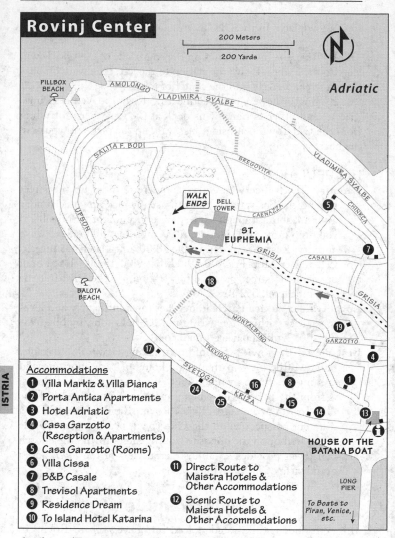

ISTRIA

the deep. (For an aerial perspective, notice the big billboard overhead and to the left.)

The Old Town is topped by the church, whose bell tower is capped by a weathervane in the shape of Rovinj's patron saint, Euphemia. Local fishermen look to this saintly weathervane for direction: When Euphemia is looking out to sea, it means the stiff, fresh Bora wind is blowing, bringing dry air from the interior...a sailor's delight. But if she's facing the land, the humid Jugo wind will soon bring bad weather from the sea. After a day or so, even a tourist learns to look to St. Euphemia for the weather forecast. (For more on Croatian winds and weather, see the sidebar on page 164.)

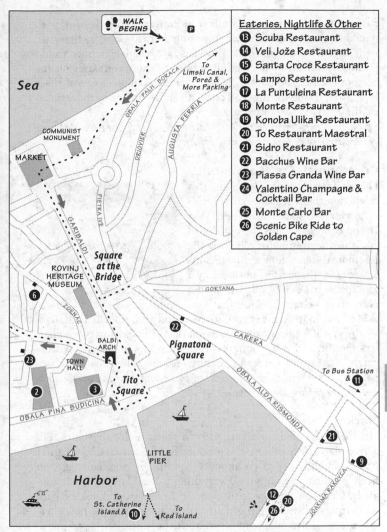

WALK BEGINS

P

Sea

To Limski Canal, Poreč & More Parking

OBALA PALIH BORACA

AUGUSTA FERRIA

DRIOVIER

COMMUNIST MONUMENT

MARKET

PIETRA IVE

GARIBALDI

ZDENAC

ROVINJ HERITAGE MUSEUM

6

Square at the Bridge

GORTANA

22

BALBI ARCH

Pignatona Square

CARERA

23

TOWN HALL

Tito Square

To Bus Station & 11

OBALA ALDA RISMONDA

2

3

OBALA PINA BUDICINA

LITTLE PIER

21

9

Harbor

To St. Catherine Island & 10

To Red Island

12

20

26

JOAKIMA RAKOVCA

Eateries, Nightlife & Other

13 Scuba Restaurant
14 Veli Jože Restaurant
15 Santa Croce Restaurant
16 Lampo Restaurant
17 La Puntuleina Restaurant
18 Monte Restaurant
19 Konoba Ulika Restaurant
20 To Restaurant Maestral
21 Sidro Restaurant
22 Bacchus Wine Bar
23 Piassa Granda Wine Bar
24 Valentino Champagne & Cocktail Bar
25 Monte Carlo Bar
26 Scenic Bike Ride to Golden Cape

ISTRIA

As you soak in this scene, ponder how the town's history created its current shape. In the Middle Ages, Rovinj was an island, rather than a peninsula, and it was surrounded by a double wall—a protective inner wall and an outer seawall. Because it was defended so well against pirates and other marauders (and carefully quarantined from the plague), it was extremely desirable real estate. And yet, it was easy to reach from the mainland, allowing it to thrive as a trading town. With more than 10,000 residents at its peak, Rovinj became immensely crowded, which explains today's pleasantly claustrophobic Old Town.

Over the centuries—as demand for living space trumped security concerns—the town walls were converted into houses, with windows grafted on to their imposing frame. Gaps in the wall, with steps that seem to end at the water, are where fishermen would pull in to unload their catch directly into the warehouses on the bottom level of the houses. (Later you can explore some of these lanes from inside the town.) Today, if you live in one of these houses, the Adriatic is your backyard.

• Now head into town. In the little park near the sea, just beyond the end of the parking lot, look for the big, blocky...

Communist-Era Monument

Dating from the time of Tito, this celebrates the Partisan Army's victory over the Nazis in World War II and commemorates the victims of fascism. The minimalist reliefs on the ceremonial tomb show a slow prisoners' parade, the victims prodded by a gun in the back from a figure with a Nazi-style helmet. Notice that one side of the monument is in Croatian, and the other is in Italian. With typical Yugoslav grace and subtlety, this jarring block shatters the otherwise harmonious time-warp vibe of Rovinj. Fortunately, it's the only modern structure near the Old Town.

• Now walk a few more steps toward town and past the playground, stopping to explore the covered...

Market

The front part of the market, near the water, is for souvenirs. But natives delve deeper in, to the produce stands. Separating the gifty stuff from the nitty-gritty produce is a line of merchants aggressively pushing free samples. Everything is local and mostly homemade. Consider this snack-time tactic: Loiter around, joking with the farmers while sampling their various tasty walnuts, figs, cherries, grapes, olive oils, honey, *rakija* (the powerful schnapps popular throughout the Balkans), and more. If the sample is good, buy some more for a picnic. In the center of the market, a delightful and practical fountain from 1908 reminds locals of the infrastructure brought in by their Habsburg rulers a century ago. The hall labeled *Ribarnica/Pescheria* at the back of the market is where you'll find fresh, practically wriggling fish. This is where locals gather ingredients for their favorite dish, *brodet*—a stew of various kinds of seafood mixed with olive oil and wine...all of Istria's best bits rolled into one dish. It's slowly simmered and generally served with polenta (unfortunately, it's rare in restaurants).

• Continue up the broad street, named for **Giuseppe Garibaldi**—*one*

of the major players in late 19th-century Italian unification. Imagine: Even though you're in Croatia, Italian patriots are celebrated in this very Italian-feeling town (see the "Italo-Croatia" sidebar). After one long block, on your left, you'll come to the wide cross street called...

Square at the Bridge (Trg na Mostu)

This marks the site of the medieval bridge that once connected the fortified island of Rovinj to the mainland (as illustrated in the small painting above the door of the Kavana al Ponto—"Bridge Café"— on your left). Back then, the island was populated mostly by Italians, while the mainland was the territory of Slavic farmers. But as Rovinj's strategic importance waned, and its trading status rose, the need for easy access became more important than the canal's protective purpose—so in 1763, it was filled in. The two populations integrated, creating the bicultural mix that survives today.

Notice the breeze? Via Garibaldi is nicknamed Val di Bora ("Valley of the Bora Wind") for the constant cooling wind that blows here. On the right side of Trg na Mostu is the Rovinj Heritage Museum (described later, under "Sights in Rovinj"). Next door, the town's cultural center posts lovingly hand-lettered signs in Croatian and Italian announcing upcoming musical events (generally free, designed for locals, and worth noting and enjoying).

Nearby (just past Kavana al Ponto, on the left), the Viecia Batana Café—named for Rovinj's unique, flat-bottomed little fishing boats—has a retro interior with a circa-1960 fishermen's mural that evokes an earlier age. The café is popular for its desserts (the chocolate cake is tasty).

• *Now proceed down Garibaldi to the little fountain in the middle of the square, facing the harbor.*

Tito Square (Trg Maršala Tita)

This wide-open square at the entrance to the Old Town is the crossroads of Rovinj. The **fountain,** with a little boy holding a water-spouting fish, celebrates the government-funded water system that finally brought running water to the Old Town in 1959. Walk around the fountain, with your eyes on the relief, to see a successful socialist society at the inauguration of this new water system.

Despite the happy occasion, the figures are pretty stiff—conformity trumped most other virtues in Tito's world.

Now walk out along the concrete pier, called the **Mali Molo ("Little Pier").** From here, you're surrounded by Rovinj's crowded harbor, with fishing vessels and

ISTRIA

Italo-Croatia

Apart from its tangible attractions, one of Istria's hallmarks is its biculturalism: It's an engaging hybrid of Croatia and Italy. Like most of the Croatian Coast, Istria has variously been controlled by Illyrians, Romans, Byzantines, Slavs, Venetians, and Austrians. After the Habsburgs lost World War I, most of today's Croatia joined Yugoslavia—but Istria became part of Italy. During this time, the Croatian vernacular was suppressed, while the Italian language and culture flourished. But this extra chapter of Italian rule was short-lived. After World War II, Istria joined Yugoslavia, and Croatian culture and language returned. What followed was a so-called Italian exodus, during which many Istrian Italians chose to relocate to Italy—leaving behind hill towns, valley villages, and farm estates that are abandoned even to this day.

The Istrians who stayed behind were saddled with an identity crisis. Many people here found it difficult to abandon their ties to Italy, and continued to speak the language and embrace the culture. Today, depending on whom you ask, Istria is the most Italian part of Croatia...or the most Croatian part of Italy. Istria pops up on Italian weather reports. A few years ago, Italy's then-Prime Minister Silvio Berlusconi declared that he still considered Istria part of Italy—and he wanted it back. When I wrote an article about Istria for a newspaper, some Italian readers complained that I made it sound "too Croatian," while some Croatians claimed my depiction was "too Italian."

People who actually live here typically don't worry about the distinction. Locals insist that they're not Croatians and not Italians—they're Istrians. They don't mind straddling two cultures. Both languages are official (and often taught side-by-side in schools), street signs are bilingual, and most Istrians dabble in each tongue—often seeming to foreign ears as though they're mixing the two at once.

As a result of their tangled history, Istrians have learned how to be mellow and take things as they come. They're gregarious, open-minded, and sometimes seem to thrive on chaos. A twentysomething local told me, "My ancestors lived in Venice. My great-grandfather lived in Austria. My grandfather lived in Italy. My father lived in Yugoslavia. I live in Croatia. My son will live in the European Union. And we've all lived in the same town."

excursion boats that shuttle tourists out to the offshore islands. If the weather's good, a **boat trip** can be a fun way to get out on the water for a different angle on Rovinj (see "Activities in Rovinj," later, for details).

Scan the **harbor.** On the left is the MMC, the local meeting and concert hall (described later, under "Nightlife in Rovinj"). Along the waterfront to the right of the MMC is the multicolored Hotel Park, a monstrosity from the communist era, now tastefully renovated inside. A recommended bike path starts just past this hotel, leading into a nature preserve and the best nearby beaches (which you can see in the distance; for more on bike rentals, see "Activities in Rovinj," later).

Now head back to the base of the pier. A short walk to the left are the TI, the House of the Batana Boat museum, and a de-

lightful "restaurant row" with several tempting places for a drink or a meal. Many fishermen pull their boats into this harbor and carry their catch across the street to a waiting restaurateur.

Next, walk straight past the fountain and face the Old Town entrance gate, called the **Balbi Arch.** On top, the winged lion of St. Mark is a reminder that this was Venetian territory for centuries.

• *Head through the gate into the Old Town. Inside and on the left is the red...*

Town Hall

On the old Town Hall, notice another Venetian lion, as well as other historic crests embedded in the wall. Along with flags for Rovinj, Croatia, and the EU, the Town Hall sports an Italian flag, and faces a square named for Giacomo Matteotti, a much-revered Italian patriot.

Continue a few more steps into town. You'll find another little square, which once functioned as a cistern (collecting rainwater, which was pulled from a subterranean reservoir through the well you see today). The building on your left is the Italian Union—yet another reminder of how Istria has an important bond with Italy.

• *Now begin walking up the street to the left. Passing the recommended Piassa Granda wine bar on your left (consider pausing here for a glass of refreshing white wine), veer right up...*

Grisia Street

The main "street" (actually a tight lane) leading through the middle of the island is choked with tourists during the midday rush and lined with art galleries and souvenir kitsch. This inspiring town has

attracted many artists, some of whom display their works along this colorful stretch. Notice the rusty little nails speckling the walls—each year in August, an art festival invites locals to hang their best art on this street. With paintings lining the lane, the entire community comes out to enjoy each other's creations.

As you walk, keep your camera ready, as you can find delightful scenes down every side lane. Remember that, as crowded as it is today, little Rovinj was even more packed in the Middle Ages. Keep an eye out for arches that span narrow lanes (such as on the right, at Arsenale street)—the only way a walled city could grow was up. Many of these additions created hidden little courtyards, nooks, and crannies that make it easy to get away from the crowds and claim a corner of the town for yourself. The distinctive chimneys poking up above the rooftops are another sign of Rovinj's overcrowding. These chimneys, added long after the buildings were first constructed, made it possible to heat previously underutilized rooms...and squeeze in even more people.

• *Continue up to the top of Grisia. Capping the town is the can't-miss-it...*

ISTRIA

▲Church of St. Euphemia (Sv. Eufemija)

Rovinj's landmark Baroque church dates from 1754. It's watched over by an enormous 190-foot-tall campanile, a replica of the famous bell tower on St. Mark's Square in Venice. The tower is topped by a copper weathervane with the weather-predicting St. Euphemia, the church's namesake.

Cost and Hours: Free, generally open May-Sept daily 10:00-18:00, Easter-April and Oct-Nov open only for Mass and with demand, generally closed Dec-Easter.

Visiting the Church: Enter the church through its right transept. The vast, somewhat gloomy interior boasts some fine altars of Carrara marble (a favorite medium of Michelangelo's). Services here are celebrated using a combination of Croatian and Italian, suiting the town's mixed population.

Walk to the right of the main altar to find the church's highlight: the chapel containing the **relics of St. Euphemia.** Before stepping into the chapel, notice the altar featuring Euphemia—depicted, as she usually is, with her wheel (a reminder of her torture) and a palm frond (symbolic of her martyrdom), and holding the fortified town of Rovinj, of which she is the protector.

Head into the little chapel. In the center is a gigantic tomb, and on the walls above are large paintings that illustrate two significant events from the life of this important local figure. St. Euphemia was the virtuous daughter of a prosperous early fourth-century family in Chalcedon (near today's Istanbul). Euphemia used her family's considerable wealth to help the poor. Unfortunately, her pious philanthropy happened to coincide with anti-Christian purges by the Roman Emperor Diocletian. When she was 15 years old, Euphemia was arrested for refusing to worship the local pagan idol. She was brutally tortured, her bones broken on a wheel. Finally she was thrown to the lions as a public spectacle. But, the story goes, the lions miraculously refused to attack her. You can see this moment depicted in one of the paintings above—as a bored-looking lion tenderly nibbles at her right bicep.

Flash forward to the year 800, when a gigantic marble sarcophagus containing St. Euphemia's relics somehow found its way into the Adriatic and floated all the way up to Istria, where Rovinj fishermen discovered it bobbing in the sea. They tugged it back to town, where a crowd gathered. The townspeople realized what it was and wanted to take it up to the hilltop church. But nobody could move it...until a young boy with two young calves showed up. He said he'd had a dream of St. Euphemia—and, sure enough, he succeeded in dragging her relics to where they still lie. In the painting above, see the burly fishermen looking astonished as the boy succeeds in moving the giant sarcophagus. Note the depiction of Rovinj fortified by a double crenellated wall—looking more like a castle than like the creaky fishing village of today. At the top of the hill is an earlier version of today's church.

Now turn your attention to Euphemia's famous sarcophagus. The front panel (with the painting of Euphemia) is opened with much fanfare every September 16, St. Euphemia's feast day, to display the small, withered, waxen face of Rovinj's favorite saint.

• *If you have time and energy, consider climbing the...*

Bell Tower

Scaling the church bell tower's creaky wooden stairway requires an enduring faith in the reliability of wood. It rewards those who brave its 192 stairs with a commanding view of the town and surrounding islands. The climb doubles your altitude, and from this perch you

can also look down—taking advantage of the quirky little round hole in the floor to photograph the memorable staircase you just climbed.

Cost and Hours: 15 kn, same hours as church, enter from inside church—to the left of the main altar.

• *Leave the church and head out to the plaza in front of the bell tower. Your walk is over. A peaceful café on a park terrace (once a cemetery) is just ahead of and below you. Just to the right, a winding, cobbled lane leads past the café entrance and down toward the water, then forks. A left turn here zigzags you past a WWII pillbox and leads along the "restaurant row," where you can survey your options for a drink or a meal (see "Eating in Rovinj," later). A right turn curls you down along the quieter northern side of the Old Town peninsula. Either way, Rovinj is yours to enjoy.*

Sights in Rovinj

▲House of the Batana Boat (Kuća o Batani)

Rovinj has a long, noble shipbuilding tradition, and this tiny but interesting museum gives you the story of the town's distinctive *batana* boats. The flat-bottomed vessels are favored by local fishermen for their ability to reach rocky areas close to shore that are rich with certain shellfish. The museum explains how the boats are built, with the help of an entertaining time-lapse video showing a boat built from scratch in five minutes. You'll also meet some of the salty old sailors who use these vessels (find the placemat with wine stains, and put the glass in different red circles to hear various seamen talk in the Rovinj dialect). Another movie shows the boats at work. Upstairs is a wall of photos of *batana* boats still in active use, a tiny library (peruse photos of the town from a century ago), and a video screen displaying *bitinada* music—local music with harmonizing voices that imitate instruments. Sit down and listen to several (there's a button for skipping ahead). The museum has no posted English information, so pick up the comprehensive English flier as you enter.

Cost and Hours: 10 kn; June-Sept daily 10:00-14:00 & 19:00-23:00; Oct-Dec and March-May Tue-Sun 10:00-13:00 & generally 16:00-18:00, closed Mon; closed Jan-Feb; Obala Pina Budicina 2, tel. 052/812-593, mobile 091-154-6598, www.batana.org, Ornela.

Activities: The museum, which serves as a sort of cultural heritage center for the town, also presents a variety of engaging *batana*-related activities. For details, see "Nightlife in Rovinj," later.

Rovinj Heritage Museum (Zavičajni Muzej Grada Rovinja)

This ho-hum museum combines art old (obscure classic painters) and new (obscure contemporary painters from Rovinj) in an old mansion. Rounding out the collection are some model ships, a small archaeological exhibit, and temporary exhibits.

Cost and Hours: 15 kn; daily 10:00-18:00; shorter hours off-season and closed Sun-Mon; Trg Maršala Tita 11, tel. 052/816-720, www.muzej-rovinj.com.

Aquarium (Akvarij)

This century-old collection of local sea life is one of Europe's oldest aquariums. Unfortunately, it's also tiny (with three sparse rooms holding a few tanks of what you'd see if you snorkeled here), disappointing, and overpriced.

Cost and Hours: 30 kn, daily June-Aug 9:00-21:00, Sept 9:00-20:00, Oct-May 10:00-16:00 or longer depending on demand, across the street from the end of the waterfront parking lot at Obala G. Paliage 5, tel. 052/804-712.

Activities in Rovinj

Boat Trips

For a different view of Rovinj, consider a boat trip. The scenery is pleasant rather than thrilling, but the craggy and tree-lined coastline and offshore islets are a lovely backdrop for an hour or two at sea. You'll see captains hawking boat excursions at little shacks all along Rovinj's harbor. The most common option is a loop around the "Golden Cape" (Zlatni Rt) and through Rovinj's own little **archipelago;** this is most popular at sunset (75 kn/1 hour, 100 kn/1.5 hours). For a longer cruise, consider the four-hour, 150-200-kn sail north along the coast and into the underwhelming **Limski Canal** (a.k.a. "Limski Fjord"), where you'll have one to two hours of free time. Dolphin sightings are not unusual, and some outfits throw in a "fish picnic" en route for extra. Stroll the harbor and comparison-shop.

You can also take a boat to one of the larger offshore islands. This lets you get away from the crowds and explore some relatively untrampled beaches. These boats—run by the big hotel chain with branches on those islands—depart about hourly from the end of the concrete pier (known as the Mali Molo, or "Little Pier") in the Old Town. The two choices are **St. Catherine** (Sv. Katarina—the lush, green island with a recommended hotel, just across the harbor, about a 5-minute trip, 25 kn) and **Red Island** (Crveni Otok—

farther out, about a 15-minute trip, boats may be marked "Hotel Istra," 40 kn).

▲Swimming and Sunbathing

Rovinj doesn't have any sandy beaches—just rocky ones. (The nearest thing to a sandy beach is the small, finely pebbled beach on Red

Island/Crveni Otok.) The most central spot to swim or sunbathe is at **Balota Beach,** on the rocks along the embankment on the south side of the Old Town peninsula, just past La Puntuleina restaurant (no showers, but scenic and central). On nice days, Balota can get crowded; if you continue around Rovinj's peninsula to the tip, just before the old WWII pillbox, you'll find the more secluded **"Pillbox Beach,"** where steps lead steeply down to a cluster of more secluded rocks. For bigger beaches, go to the wooded **Golden Cape** (Zlatni Rt) south of the harbor (past the big, waterfront Hotel Park). This cape is lined with walking paths and beaches, and shaded by a wide variety of trees and plants. For a scenic sunbathing spot, choose a perch facing Rovinj on the north side of the Golden Cape. Another beach, called **Kuvi,** is beyond the Golden Cape. To get away from it all, take a boat to an island on Rovinj's little archipelago (see previous listing).

▲Bike Ride

The TI's free, handy biking map suggests a variety of short and long bike rides. The easiest and most scenic is a quick loop around the Golden Cape (Zlatni Rt, described above).

You can do this circuit and return to the Old Town in about an hour (without stops). Start by biking south around the harbor and past the waterfront Hotel Park, where you leave the cars and enter the wooded Golden Cape. Peaceful miniature beaches abound. The lane climbs to a quarry (much of Venice was paved with Istrian stone), where you're likely to see beginning rock climbers inching their way up and down. Cycling downhill from the quarry and circling the peninsula, you hit the Lovor Grill (open daily in summer 10:00-16:00 for drinks and light meals)—a cute little restaurant housed in the former stables of the Austrian countess who planted what today is called "Wood Park." From there, you can continue farther along the coast or return to town (backtrack two minutes and take the right fork through the woods back to the waterfront path).

For a more ambitious, inland pedal, pick up the TI's free *Basìlica* bike map, which narrates a 12-mile loop that connects several old churches.

Bike Rental: Bikes are rented at subsidized prices from the city parking lot kiosk (5 kn/hour, open 24 hours daily except no rentals in winter, fast and easy process; choose a bike with enough air in its tires or have them pumped up, as the path is rocky and gravelly). Various travel agencies around town rent bikes for much more (around 20 kn/hour); look for signs—especially near the bus station—or ask around.

Nightlife in Rovinj

ROVINJ AFTER DARK

Rovinj is a delight after dark. Views that are great by day become magical in the moonlight and floodlight. The streets of the Old

Town are particularly inviting when empty and starlit.

Concerts

Lots of low-key, small-time music events take place right in town (ask at the TI, check the events calendar at www.tzgrovinj.hr, and look for handwritten signs in Croatian and Italian on Garibaldi Street

near the Square at the Bridge). Groups perform at various venues around town: right along the harborfront (you'll see the bandstand set up); in the town's churches (especially St. Euphemia and the Franciscan church); in the old cinema/theater by the market; at the pier in front of the House of the Batana Boat (described earlier, under "Sights in Rovinj"); and at the Multi-Media Center (a.k.a. the "MMC," which locals call "Cinema Belgrade"—its former name), in a cute little hall above a bank across the harbor from the Old Town.

Wine Bars

Rovinj has two good places to sample Istrian and Croatian wines (25-35-kn glasses), along with light, basic food—such as *pršut*, truffles, and olive oil. Remember, two popular local wines worth trying are *malvazija* (a crisp white) and *teran* (a heavy red). At **Bacchus Wine Bar,** owner Paolo serves about 80 percent Istrian wines, with the rest from elsewhere in Croatia and international vintners (daily 7:00-24:00, Carera 5, tel. 052/812-154). **Piassa Granda,** on a charming little square right in the heart of the Old Town, has

ISTRIA

good outdoor seating and a cozy, well-stocked interior with more than 100 types of wine (40-70-kn Istrian small plates, more food than Bacchus, daily 12:00-16:00 & 18:00-24:00, Veli trg 1, mobile 098-824-322, Helena).

Lounging

Valentino Champagne and Cocktail Bar is a romantic, justifiably pretentious place for an expensive late-night waterfront drink. Fish, attracted by its underwater lights, swim by from all over the bay...to the enjoyment of those nursing a cocktail on the rocks (literally—you'll be given a small seat cushion to plunk down in your own seaside niche). Or you can choose to sit on one of the terraces. Classy candelabras twinkle in the twilight, as couples cozy up to each other and

the view. While the drinks are extremely pricey, this place is unforgettably cool (65-80-kn cocktails, 65-kn nonalcoholic drinks, daily April-May 12:00-24:00, June-Sept 18:00-24:00, closed Oct-March, Via Santa Croce 28, tel. 052/830-683, Patricia).

If Valentino is too pricey, too chichi, or too crowded for your tastes, a couple of alternatives are nearby. The **Monte Carlo** bar, along the same drag but a bit closer to the harbor, is fun-loving and serves much cheaper drinks (25-35 kn), but it lacks the atmospheric "on the rocks" setting of Valentino (daily 8:00-late, closed Oct-Easter, mobile 091-579-1813). Or consider **La Puntuleina,** beyond Valentino, with a similarly rocky ambience but lower prices (25-45-kn drinks) and a bit less panache (listed later, under "Eating in Rovinj"). I'd scout all three and pick the ambience you prefer.

Batana Boat Activities

In summer, the House of the Batana Boat (described earlier, under "Sights in Rovinj") often hosts special events. On some summer evenings, you can take a boat trip on a *batana* from the pier near the museum. The trip, which is accompanied by traditional music, circles around the end of the Old Town peninsula and docks on the far side, where a traditional wine cellar has a fresh fish dinner ready, with local wine and more live music (June-mid-Sept, generally Tue and Thu at 20:30, boat trip-60 kn, dinner-160 kn extra, visit or call the museum the day before to reserve). Also on some summer evenings, you can enjoy an outdoor food market with traditional Rovinj foods and live *bitinada* music. The centerpiece is a *batana* boat being refurbished before your eyes (in front of museum, light food, mid-June-early Sept generally Tue and Sat

Sleep Code

Abbreviations **(7 kn=about $1, €1=about $1.10, country code: 385)**
S=Single, **D**=Double/Twin, **T**=Triple, **Q**=Quad, **b**=bathroom
Price Rankings
 $$$ **Higher Priced**—Most rooms €110 or more
  $$ **Moderately Priced**—Most rooms €70-110
   $ **Lower Priced**—Most rooms €70 or less

If I've listed three sets of rates, separated by slashes, the first is for peak season (typically mid-July through late Aug), the second is for shoulder season (roughly June-mid-July and late Aug-Sept), and the third is for off-season (Oct-May). If I've listed only two rates, the first is for peak season and the second for shoulder/off-season. The dates for seasonal rates vary by hotel.

The modest tourist tax (about 7 kn/person, per night) is not included in these rates. Hotels generally accept credit cards and include breakfast in their rates, while most *sobe* accept only cash and don't offer breakfast. While rates are listed in euros, you'll pay in kunas. Unless I note otherwise, English is spoken and Wi-Fi is generally free. Prices change; verify current rates online or by email. For the best prices, always book directly with the hotel.

20:00-23:00). Even if you're here off-season, ask at the museum if anything special is planned.

Sleeping in Rovinj

As throughout Croatia, most Rovinj accommodations (both hotels and *sobe*) prefer multinight stays—especially in peak season (July-Aug). While a few places levy surcharges for shorter stays, many are fine with even one-night stays (I've noted this in each listing). Don't show up here without a room in August, when Rovinj is packed. Finding these places will challenge even the ablest of route finders. Don't be proud, ask—locals are happy to help point you in the right direction.

IN THE OLD TOWN

All of these accommodations (with one exception) are on the Old Town peninsula, rather than the mainland section of the Old Town. Residence Dream is just around the atmospheric harbor, an easy five-minute walk away. Rovinj has no real hostel, but *sobe* are a good budget option.

$$$ Villa Markiz, run by Andrej with the help of eager-to-please Ivana, has four extremely mod, stylish apartments in an old shell in a quiet corner of the Old Town. You'll climb a steep and narrow staircase to reach the apartments, each of which has a small terrace (Db-€130/€80-100/€60). Only the gorgeous top-floor, two-story penthouse apartment has sea views (€250/€150-180/€140; no breakfast, air-con, Pod Lukovima 1, Ivana mobile 099-652-7660, Andrej mobile 098-934-0321, www.markizrovinj. com, dani7cro@msn.com). Their next-door **Villa Bianca** has three one-bedroom apartments (Db-€150/€90-120/€70).

$$$ Porta Antica rents 16 comfortable, nicely decorated apartments in five different buildings around the Old Town (all except La Carera are on the peninsula)—but conveniently, all are managed from a single reception. Review your options on their website and be specific in your request (Db-€110-200/€90-170/€80-120, price depends on size and views, extra person-€25, no extra charge for 1-night stays, no breakfast, air-con, nonsmoking, reception and main building next door to TI on Obala Pina Budičina, mobile 099-680-1101, www.portaantica.com, portaantica@yahoo. it, Claudia).

$$$ Hotel Adriatic features 18 suites overlooking the main square, where the Old Town peninsula meets the mainland. The only Old Town branch of the big chain of Maistra hotels (described on page 121), this was recently renovated to four-star status. That, combined with the couldn't-be-more-central location, makes this a plush splurge (Db-€450 in peak season—but can be much less, air-con, Trg Maršala Tita, tel. 052/803-510, www.maistra.hr, adriatic@maistra.hr).

$$$ Casa Garzotto is an appealing option, with four apartments, four rooms, and one large family apartment in three different Old Town buildings. These classy and classic lodgings have modern facilities but old-fashioned charm, with antique furniture and historic family portraits on the walls. Thoughtfully run by a friendly staff, it's a winner (rooms—Sb-€80/€80/€70, Db-€120/€105/€90; apartments—Db-€180/€160/€140; 2-bedroom family apartment—Db-€260/€230/€120, extra person-€35; includes breakfast, off-site parking, loaner bikes, and other thoughtful extras; 30 percent extra for 1-night stays, air-con, lots of stairs, reception and most apartments are at Garzotto 8, others are a short walk away, tel. 052/811-884, mobile 099-800-7338, www.casa-garzotto.com, casagarzotto@gmail.com).

$$ Villa Cissa, run by Zagreb transplant Veljko Despot, has three apartments with contemporary decor above an art gallery in the Old Town. Kind Veljko is a fascinating guy who had an illustrious career as a rock-and-roll journalist (he was the only Eastern Bloc reporter to interview the Beatles) and record-company executive. Veljko lives off-site, so be sure to clearly communicate your arrival time (smaller apartment-€108/€98/€88 plus €30 one-time cleaning fee—best for a couple; bigger apartment-€218/€208/€198 plus €50 one-time cleaning fee—good for up to 6 people; extra person-20 percent more, cash only, air-con, Zdenac 14, tel. 052/813-080, www.villacissa.com, info@villacissa.com).

$$ B&B Casale has three simple but affordable and nicely appointed rooms atmospherically located in a tight lane in the heart of the Old Town. As there's no air-conditioning, thin windows, and lots of outdoor cafés nearby, it can be noisy at night (Db-€80/€55/€46, breakfast-€9, cash only, Casale 2, tel. 052/814-828, mobile 091-601-6784, info.casale2@gmail.com, Adriano).

$$ Trevisol Apartments has four modern units on a sleepy Old Town street, plus a few others around town. Check your options on their website, reserve your apartment, and arrange a time to meet (Db-€110/€85/€65; bigger seaview Db-€150/€120/€80; extra charge for 1-night stays: 50 percent in peak season, 30 percent off-season; no breakfast, air-con, Trevisol 40, main office at Sv. Križa 33, mobile 098-177-7404, www.lvi.hr, Adriano).

$$ Residence Dream, tucked in a tight warren of lanes in the touristy restaurant ghetto just around the harbor from the Old Town peninsula, has three modern, pleasantly furnished rooms above a busy restaurant. While you're not right in the heart of the Old Town, it's close enough, and it's worth considering if other midrange places are full (Db-€100/€85/€70, extra bed-€15, breakfast-€8, air-con, good windows but may have some restaurant noise, Rakovca 18, tel. 052/830-613, mobile 091-579-9239, www. dream.hr, dream@dream.hr).

ON THE MAINLAND, SOUTHEAST OF THE OLD TOWN

To escape the high prices of Rovinj's Old Town, consider the resort neighborhood just south of the harbor. These are a 10- to 20-minute walk from the Old Town (in most cases, at least partly uphill), but most of that walk is along the very scenic harborfront—hardly an unpleasant commute. While the big Maistra hotels are an option, I prefer cheaper alternatives in the same area. Given the cost and inconvenience of parking if you're sleeping in the Old Town (see "Arrival in Rovinj," earlier, for details), accommodations in this area are handy for drivers. The big hotels are signposted as you approach town (follow signs for *hoteli,* then your specific hotel). Once you're on the road to Hotels Eden and Park, the smaller ones are easy to reach: Villa Baron Gautsch is right on the road to Hotel Park; Hotel Vila Lili and Vila Kristina are a little farther on the main road toward Eden (to the left just after turnoff for Hotel Park, look for signs).

Guesthouses and Small Hotels

These are a bit closer to the Old Town than the Maistra hotels, and offer much lower rates and more personality. The first three are hotelesque and sit up on the hill behind the big resort hotels, while the last two choices lack personality but are a great budget option relatively close to the Old Town (an easy and scenic 10-minute walk).

$$ Villa Baron Gautsch, named for a shipwreck, is a German-owned pension with 16 bright, crisp, comfortable rooms and an inviting, shared view terrace (Db-€90/€80/€65, €10 more for balcony, they also have two Sb for half the Db price, no extra charge for 1-night stays, closed late Oct-Easter, cash only, air-con, no elevator, free but limited street parking, Ronjgova 7, tel. 052/840-538, www.baron-gautsch.com, baron.gautsch@gmx.net, Sanja).

$$ Hotel Vila Lili is a family-run hotel with 20 nicely decorated but slightly faded rooms on a quiet lane. The rooms are pricey, but the extra cost buys you more hotel amenities than the cheaper guesthouses listed here (Sb-€65/€55, Db-€110/€100, pricier suites also available, no extra charge for 1-night stays, includes a good breakfast, elevator, air-con, parking-35 kn/day, Mohorovičića 16, tel. 052/840-940, www.hotel-vilalili.hr, vila-lili@pu.t-com.hr, Petričević family).

$$ Vila Kristina, run by Kristina Kiš and her family, has 10 rooms and five apartments along a busy road. All but one of the units has a balcony. I'd skip the overpriced apartments (Db-€105/€90, apartment Db-€140/€120, no extra charge for 1-night stays, includes breakfast, air-con, no elevator, Luje Adamovića 16, tel. 052/815-537, www.kis-rovinj.com, kristinakis@mail.inet.hr).

$ Elda Markulin, whose son runs the Baccus Wine Bar, rents three rooms and four apartments in a new, modern house a short walk up from the main harborfront road (Db-€50/€45/€40, apartment-€75/€60/€50, cash only, air-con, free parking, Mate Balote 12, tel. 052/811-018, mobile 095-900-8654, markulin@hi.t-com.hr). To reach it from the Old Town, walk along the waterfront; after you pass the recommended Maestral restaurant on your right, turn left just before the park onto the uphill Mate Balote and follow the road as it curves.

$ Apartmani Tomo, next door to Elda (see directions above), is run with Albanian pride by Tomo Lleshdedaj, who rents seven rooms and nine studio apartments. While the lodgings are basic and communication can be a bit challenging, it's a handy location for a budget last resort (Db-€50/€40/€35, Db with kitchen-€70/€60/€50, smaller studio Db-€75/€65/€55, bigger studio Db-€85/€75/€65, extra person-€10, cash only, air-con, free parking, Mate Balote 10, tel. 052/813-457, mobile 091-578-1518, mtomoll@net.hr).

Maistra Hotels

The local hotel conglomerate, Maistra, has several overpriced hotels in the lush parklands just south of the Old Town and one on a nearby island. Most of my readers will prefer to spend less money for more character at one of my other listings. However, the Maistra hotels are worth considering if you can get a deal. These hotels have extremely slippery pricing, based on the type of room, the season, and how far ahead you book. (I've listed the starting rate for a 1- or 2-night stay in July-Aug. Complete rates are explained on the website, www.maistra.hr.) All hotels have air-conditioning, elevators, and include breakfast in their rates; most have free parking and close during the winter.

$$$ Island Hotel Katarina is the castaway's choice, with 110 rooms occupying the hotel's own little island just offshore from the Old Town—complete with a park, beaches, and swimming pool. It's connected by an hourly boat (free for guests) to the Old Town pier; some find this inconvenient, but most who opt to sleep here consider it romantic (Db-€160).

$$$ Hotel Park has 202 modest rooms in a colorized communist-era hull, and a huge seaside swimming pool with sweeping views to the Old Town. This is the handiest for walking into town—it's a 10-minute stroll, entirely along the stunning harborfront promenade (Db-€180, about €50 more for sea view).

$$$ Hotel Monte Mulini is the fanciest of the bunch, with five stars, 99 rooms and 14 suites (all with seaview balconies), a beautiful atrium with a huge glass wall overlooking the cove, an infinity pool, and over-the-top prices (Db-€550).

$$$ Hotel Lone (LOH-neh), with 248 rooms, is the most striking in the collection—the soaring atrium of this "design hotel" feels like a modern art museum (Db-€325).

$$$ Hotel Eden offers four stars and 325 upscale, imaginatively updated rooms with oodles of contemporary style behind a brooding communist facade (Db-€210).

The chain has other branches, but I wouldn't consider them.

Eating in Rovinj

It's expensive to dine in Rovinj, but the food is generally good, with a few truffle dishes on most menus (see "Istrian Food and Wine" sidebar on page 100). Interchangeable restaurants cluster where Rovinj's Old Town peninsula meets the mainland, and all around the harbor. Be warned that most eateries—like much of Rovinj—close for the winter (roughly mid-Oct to Easter). If you're day-tripping into the Istrian interior, consider dining at one of the excellent restaurants in or near Moto- vun (see page 149), then returning to Rovinj after dark.

ALONG ROVINJ'S "RESTAURANT ROW"

The easiest dining option is to stroll the Old Town embankment overlooking the harbor. Window shop the pricey but scenic eater- ies along here, each of which has its own personality: Some have sea views, others are set back on charming squares, and still others have atmospheric interiors. I've listed these in the order you'll reach them (all open long hours daily).

Scuba, at the start of the row, is closest to the harbor—so, they claim, they get first pick of the daily catch from arriving fish- ing boats. They serve both seafood and tasty Italian dishes in a plain contemporary interior or at outdoor tables with harbor views (75-kn pastas, 60-150-kn main courses, daily 11:00-24:00, Obala Pina Budičina 6, mobile 098-219-446).

Veli Jože has a smattering of outdoor tables (no real views) and a rollicking, folksy interior decorated to the hilt. They offer a wide variety of pastas and tasty, traditional Istrian cuisine (50-80- kn pastas, 55-kn basic grill dishes, 110-160-kn main courses, daily 11:00-24:00, Sv. Križa 1, tel. 052/816-337).

Santa Croce, with tables scenically scattered along a terraced incline that looks like a stage set, is well-respected for its seafood and pastas. Classy and sedate, and with attentive service, it attracts a slightly older clientele (45-60-kn pastas, 70-150-kn main cours- es, no sea views, daily 18:00-23:00, Sv. Križa 11, tel. 052/842-240).

Lampo is simpler, with a basic menu of salads, pizzas, and pastas. The only reason to come here is for the fine waterfront seat- ing at a reasonable price (45-65-kn pastas, 60-120-kn main cours- es, daily 11:00-24:00, Sv. Križa 22, tel. 052/811-186).

La Puntuleina, at the end of the row, is the most scenic op- tion. This upscale restaurant/wine bar features Istrian, Italian, and Mediterranean cuisine served in the contemporary dining room or outside—either on one of the many terraces, or at tables scattered along the rocks overlooking a swimming hole. The menu is short, and Miriam and Giovanni occasionally add seasonal specials, though the cuisine can suffer during busy times. As the outdoor seating is deservedly popular, reserve ahead (10-kn cover charge, 80-110-kn pastas, 130-190-kn main courses, daily 12:00-23:00, closed Nov-Easter, on the Old Town embankment past the harbor at Sv. Križa 38, tel. 052/813-186). You can also order just a drink to sip while sitting down on the rocks.

Just before La Puntuleina, don't miss the inviting **Valentino Champagne and Cocktail Bar**—with no food but similar "drinks on the rocks" ambience (described earlier, under "Nightlife in

Rovinj"). If you're on a tight budget, dine cheaply elsewhere, then come here for an after-dinner finale.

INTERNATIONAL FARE ON THE OLD TOWN PENINSULA

Offering upscale, international (rather than strictly Croatian) food and presentation, these options are expensive but creative.

Monte Restaurant is your upscale, white-tablecloth splurge—made-to-order for a fine dinner out. With tables strewn around a covered terrace just under the town bell tower, this atmospheric place features inventive cuisine that melds Istrian products with international techniques. Come here only if you value a fine dining experience, polished service, and the chance to learn about local food and wines without regard for price (plan to spend 350-700 kn per person for dinner, daily 12:00-14:30 & 18:30-23:00, reserve ahead in peak season, Montalbano 75, tel. 052/830-203, www. monte.hr, Đekić family).

Konoba Ulika, a classy hole-in-the-wall run by Inja Tucman, has a mellow, cozy, art-strewn interior. Inja enjoys surprising diners with unexpected flavor combinations. The food is a bit overpriced and can be hit-or-miss, but the experience feels like an innovative break from traditional Croatian fare. As portions are small (Inja encourages diners to order two courses), the price can add up (15-kn cover, 75-95-kn starters and pastas, 170-200-kn main courses, fine wine list, daily 13:00-15:00 & 18:30-23:00—except closed for lunch in Aug, closed mid-Oct-April, cash only, Porečka 6, tel. 052/651-985, mobile 098-929-7541).

AFFORDABLE ALTERNATIVES ON THE MAINLAND

These options are a bit less expensive than most of those described above. I've listed them in the order you'll reach them as you walk around Rovinj's harbor.

Maestral combines affordable, straightforward pizzas and seafood with Rovinj's best view. If you want an outdoor table overlooking bobbing boats and the Old Town's skyline—without breaking the bank—this is the place. It fills a big building sur-rounded by workaday shipyards about a 10-minute walk from the Old Town, around the harbor toward Hotel Park (45-kn sandwich-es, 45-65-kn pizzas and pastas, 60-100-kn fish and meat courses, daily 9:00-24:00, closed Oct-March, Obala N. Nazora b.b., look for *Bavaria* beer sign, tel. 052/830-565).

Sidro, around the harbor with views back on the Old Town, has a typical menu of pasta, pizza, and fish. But it's particularly well-respected for its Balkan meat dishes such as *ćevapčići* (see the "Balkan Flavors" sidebar on page 421) and a spicy pork-and-onion stew called *mućkalica*. With unusually polite service and a long tradition (run by three generations of the Paoletti family since 1966), it's a popular local hangout (50-75-kn pastas, 60-90-kn grilled meat dishes, 110-140-kn steaks and fish, daily 11:00-23:00, closed Nov-Feb, harborfront at Rismondo 14, tel. 052/813-471).

BREAKFAST
Most rental apartments come with a kitchenette handy for breakfasts (stock up at a neighborhood grocery). Cafés and bars along the waterfront serve little more than an expensive croissant with coffee. The best budget breakfast (and a fun experience) is a picnic. Within a block of the market, you have all the necessary stops: the Brionka bakery (fresh-baked cheese or apple strudel); mini grocery stores (juice, milk, drinkable yogurt, and so on); market stalls (cherries, strawberries, walnuts, and more, as well as an elegant fountain for washing); an Albanian-run bread kiosk, Pekarna Laste, between the market and the water...plus benches with birds chirping, children playing, and fine Old Town views along the water.

Rovinj Connections

BY BUS
Rovinj's bus station is open daily 6:30-9:15 & 9:45-16:30 & 17:00-21:30. As always, confirm the following times before planning your trip. Bus schedules are dramatically reduced on Saturdays and especially on Sundays, as well as (in some cases) off-season. Bus information: Tel. 060-333-111 or 052/811-453, www.autobusni-kolodvor.com.

From Rovinj by Bus to: Pula (about hourly, 45 minutes), Poreč (3-6/day, 1 hour), Rijeka (10/day, 2-3.5 hours), Zagreb (6-9/day, 3-6 hours), Venice (2/day Mon-Sat departing very early in the morning—likely at 5:40, arriving Venice at 10:00, none Sun).

To Slovenia: In summer, daily buses connect Rovinj to Slovenia (3-4/day late June-Aug, 1/day Sept, none Oct-late June, 2-3 hours to Piran, 4-5.5 hours to Ljubljana); as this connection is changeable, confirm schedules at www.ap-ljubljana.si. Twice weekly off-season (generally Mon and Fri), an early morning bus begins in Pula, then heads to Poreč, Portorož (with an easy transfer to Piran), and Ljubljana. You can also reach Piran (and other Slovenian destinations) with transfers in Umag and Portorož.

To the Dalmatian Coast: A bus departs Rovinj every evening at 19:00 for the Dalmatian Coast, arriving in Split at 6:00 and Dubrovnik at 11:00. (If this direct bus isn't running, you can take an earlier bus to Pula, from where this night bus leaves at 20:00; also note that Pula has two daytime connections to Split.) Or, for a splurge, European Coastal Airlines offers **seaplanes** from Pula to Dalmatian destinations (www.ec-air.eu; for details, see page 214).

ROUTE TIPS FOR DRIVERS

Just north of Rovinj, on the coastal road to Poreč, you'll drive briefly along a seven-mile-long inlet dubbed the **Limski Canal** (Limski Kanal—sometimes called "Limski Fjord"...but only to infuriate Norwegians). Named for the border (*Lim*-it) between Rovinj and Poreč, this jagged slash in the landscape was created when an underground karstic river collapsed. Keen-eyed arborists will notice that the canal's southern bank has deciduous trees, and the northern bank, evergreens. Many Venetian quarries once pulled stone from the walls of this canal to build houses and embankments. Supposedly the famed pirate Captain Morgan was so enchanted by this canal that he retired here, founding the nearby namesake town of Mrgani. Local tour companies sell boat excursions into the fjord, which is used to raise much of the shellfish that's slurped down at local restaurants. While the canal isn't worth going out of your way to see, you may skirt it anyway. Along the road above the canal, you'll pass kiosks selling grappa (firewater, a.k.a. *rakija*), honey, and other homemade concoctions. The recommended Matošević winery is a two-minute drive away (see page 156).

Pula

ISTRIA

Pula (POO-lah, Pola in Italian)—Istria's biggest city—is an industrial port town with traffic, smog, and sprawl...but it has the soul of a Roman poet. Between the shipyards, you'll discover some of the top Roman ruins in Croatia, including a stately amphitheater: a fully intact mini-Colosseum that marks the entry to a seedy Old Town with ancient temples, arches, and columns.

Strategically situated at the southern tip of the Istrian Peninsula, Pula has long been a center of industry, trade, and military

might. In 177 B.C., the city became an important outpost of the Roman Empire. It was destroyed during the wars following Julius Caesar's death, then rebuilt by Emperor Augustus. Many of Pula's most important Roman features—including its amphitheater—date from this time (early first century A.D.). But as Rome fell, so did Pula's fortunes. The town changed hands repeatedly, caught in the crossfire of wars between greater powers—Byzantines, Venetians, and Habsburgs. After being dev-astated by Venice's enemy, Genoa, in the 14th century, Pula gath-ered dust as a ghost town...still of strategic military importance, but otherwise abandoned.

In the mid-19th century, Italian unification forced the Aus-trian Habsburgs—whose navy had been based in Venice—to look for a new home for their fleet. In 1856, they chose Pula, and over the next 60 years, the town's population grew thirtyfold. (Despite the many Roman and Venetian artifacts littering the Old Town, most of modern Pula is essentially Austrian.) By the dawn of the 20th century, Pula's harbor bristled with Austro-Hungarian war-ships, and it had become the crucial link in a formidable line of imperial defenses that stretched from here to Montenegro. As one of the most important port cities of the Austro-Hungarian Empire, Pula attracted naval officers, royalty...and a young Irishman named James Joyce who was on the verge of revolutionizing the literary world.

Today's Pula, while no longer quite so important, remains a vi-brant port town and the de facto capital of Istria. It offers an enjoy-ably urban antidote to the rest of this stuck-in-the-past peninsula.

PLANNING YOUR TIME

Pula's sights, while top-notch, are quickly exhausted. Two or three hours should do it: Visit the amphitheater, stroll the circular Old Town, and maybe see a museum or two. As it's less than an hour from Rovinj, there's no reason to spend the night.

ISTRIA

Orientation to Pula

Although the city itself is big, the tourist's Pula is compact: the amphitheater and, beside it, the ring-shaped Old Town circling the base of an old hilltop fortress. The Old Town's main square, the Forum, dates back to Roman times.

TOURIST INFORMATION

Pula's TI sits on the Old Town's main square, the Forum. It offers information on the town and all of Istria (May-Oct Mon-Sat 8:00-18:00, until 21:00 June-Sept, Sun 10:00-18:00; Nov-April Mon-Sat 9:00-16:00, Sun 10:00-16:00, Forum 3, tel. 052/219-197, www.pulainfo.hr).

ARRIVAL IN PULA

By Car: Pula is about a 45-minute drive south of Rovinj. Ap-proaching town, follow *Centar* signs, then watch for the amphithe-ater. Parking is plentiful on the streets around the amphitheater; if it's parked up, head for the large pay lot just below the amphithe-

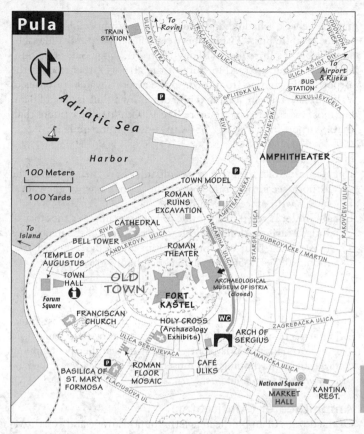

ater, toward the waterfront. This lot, and any street spaces marked in blue, cost the same (5 kn/hour, free on Sun; if parking on street, pay at meter or buy parking voucher at newsstand to display in window).

By Bus: As you exit the bus station, walk toward the yellow mansion, then turn left onto the major street (ulica 43 Istarske Divizije); at the roundabout, bear left again, and you'll be headed for the amphitheater (about a 10-minute walk total).

By Train: The train station is a 15-minute walk from the amphitheater, near the waterfront (in the opposite direction from the Old Town). Walk with the coast on your right until you see the amphitheater.

By Plane: Pula's small airport, which is served by various low-cost airlines, is about 3.5 miles northeast of the center. A handy and affordable **shuttle bus** is coordinated to depart 20 minutes after many budget flights arrive—check for details with your airline (30 kn to downtown Pula, 150 kn to Rovinj, run by two different companies—check schedule and prebook at www.brioni.hr or www.fils.hr). **Public bus #23** goes between the airport and Pula's bus station, but it's infrequent (10/day Mon-Fri, 4/day Sat, none Sun) and stops along the road in front of the airport rather than at the airport itself (coming from town to the airport, watch for buses to Valtura). The fair rate for a **taxi** into downtown Pula is about 80 kn, but most manage to charge more like 100 kn (don't pay more than that). Airport info: Tel. 052/530-105, www.airport-pula.hr.

HELPFUL HINTS

Car Rental: All of the big rental companies have their offices at the airport (see airport info above); the TI has a list of a few local outfits with offices downtown.

Local Guide: If you'd like a guide to help you uncover the story of Pula, **Mariam Abdelghani** leads great tours of the major sites (€80 for a 2-hour city tour, €160 for an all-day tour of Istria, mobile 098-419-560, mariam.abdelghani@gmail.com).

Pula Walk

This self-guided walk is divided between Pula's two most interesting attractions: the Roman amphitheater and the circular Old Town. Two hours total is plenty. More time can be spent sipping coffee al fresco or dipping into museums.

• *Begin at Pula's main landmark, its...*

Amphitheater (Amfiteatar)

Of the dozens of amphitheaters left around Europe and North Africa by Roman engineers, Pula's is the sixth-largest (435 feet long and 345 feet wide) and one of the best-preserved anywhere. This is the top place in Croatia to resurrect the age of the gladiators.

Cost and Hours: 40 kn, daily May-Sept 8:00-21:00—often later in July-Aug and for special events, April 8:00-20:00, Oct 9:00-19:00, Nov-March 9:00-17:00. The 40-kn audioguide, available at the kiosk inside, narrates 20 stops with 30 minutes of flat, basic data on the structure.

Gladiator Shows: About once each week in the summer, costumed gladiators reenact the glory days of the amphitheater in a show called *Spectacvla Antiqva* (70 kn, 1/week late June-mid-Sept, details at www.pulainfo.hr).

Visiting the Amphitheater: Go inside and explore the interior, climbing up the seats as you like. An "amphi-theater" is literally a "double theater"—imagine two theaters, without the back wall behind the stage, stuck together to maximize seating. Pula's amphitheater was built over several decades (first century A.D.) under the reign of three of Rome's top-tier emperors: Augustus, Claudius, and Vespasian. It was completed around A.D. 80, about the same time as the Colosseum in Rome. It remained in active use until the beginning of the fifth century, when gladiator battles were outlawed. The location is unusual but sensible: It was built just outside town (too big for tiny Pula, with just 5,000 people) and near the sea (so its giant limestone blocks could be transported here more easily from the quarry six miles away).

Notice that the amphitheater is built into the gentle incline of a hill. This economical plan, unusual for Roman amphitheaters, saved on the amount of stone needed, and provided a natural foundation for some of the seats (notice how the upper seats incorporate the slope). It may seem like the architects were cutting corners, but they actually had to raise the ground level at the lower end of the amphitheater to give it a level foundation. The four rectangular towers anchoring the amphitheater's facade are also unique (two of them are mostly gone). These once held wooden staircases for loading and unloading the amphitheater more quickly—like the massive corkscrew ramps in  many modern stadiums. At the top of each tower was a water reservoir, used for powering fountains that sprayed refreshing scents over the crowd to mask the stench of blood.

And there was plenty of blood. Imagine this scene in the days of the gladiators. More than 25,000 cheering fans from all social classes filled the seats. The Romans made these spectacles cheap or even free—distracting commoners with a steady diet of mindless entertainment prevented discontent and rebellion. (Hmm... *The Voice,* anyone?) Canvas awnings rigged around the top of the amphitheater shaded many seats. The fans surrounded the "slaying field," which was covered with sand to absorb blood spilled by man and beast, making it easier to clean up after the fight. This sand *(harena)* gave the amphitheater its nickname...arena.

The amphitheater's "entertainers" were gladiators (named for the *gladius,* a short sword that was tucked into a fighter's boot). Some gladiators were criminals, but most were prisoners of war from lands conquered by Rome, who dressed and used weapons according to their country of origin. A colorful parade kicked off the spectacle, followed by simulated fights with fake weapons. Then the real battles began. Often the fights represented stories from mythology or Greek or Roman history. Most ended in death for the loser. Sometimes gladiators fought exotic animals—gathered at great expense from far corners of the empire—which would enter the arena from the two far ends (through the biggest arches). There were female gladiators, as well, but they always fought other women.

While the life of a gladiator seems difficult, consider that it wasn't such a bad gig—compared to, say, being a soldier. Gladiators were often better paid than soldiers, enjoyed terrific celebrity (both in life and in death), and only had to fight a few times each year.

Ignore the modern seating, and imagine when the arena (sandy oval area in the center) was ringed with two levels of stone seating and a top level of wooden bleachers. Notice that the outline of the arena is marked by a small moat (now covered with wooden slats)—just wide enough to keep the animals off the laps of those with the best seats, but close enough so that blood still sprayed their togas.

After the fall of Rome, builders looking for ready-cut stone picked apart structures like this one—scraping it as clean as a neat slice of cantaloupe. Sometimes the scavengers were seeking the iron hooks that were used to connect the stone; in those oh-so "Dark Ages," the method for smelting iron from ore was lost. Most of this amphitheater's interior structures—such as steps and seats—are now in the foundations and walls of Pula's

buildings...not to mention palaces in Venice, across the Adriatic. In fact, in the late 16th century, the Venetians planned to take this entire amphitheater apart, stone by stone, and reassemble it on the island of Lido on the Venetian lagoon. A heroic Venetian senator—still revered in Pula—convinced them to leave it where it is.

Despite these and other threats, the amphitheater's exterior has been left gloriously intact. The 1999 film *Titus* (with Anthony Hopkins and Jessica Lange) was filmed here, and today the amphitheater is still used to stage spectacles—from Placido Domingo to Elton John—with seating for about 5,000 fans. Recently, the loudest concerts were banned, because the vibrations were damaging the old structure.

Before leaving, don't miss the museum exhibit (in the "subterranean hall"—follow *exhibition* signs down the chute marked #17). This takes you to the lower level of the amphitheater, where gladiators and animals were kept between fights. When the fight began,

ISTRIA

Amphorae

In museums, hotels, and restaurants all along the Croatian coast, you'll see amphorae. An amphora is a jug that was used  to transport goods when the ancient Greeks ruled the seas, through about the second century B.C. Later, the Romans also used their own amphorae. These tall and skinny ceramic jugs—many of them lost in ancient shipwrecks—litter the Adriatic coastline.

Amphorae were used to carry oil, wine, and fish on long sea journeys. They're tapered at the bottom because they were stuck into sand (or placed on a stand) to keep them upright in transit. They also have a narrow neck at the top, often with two large handles. In fact, the name comes from the Greek *amphi pherein*, "to carry from both sides." The taller, skinnier amphorae were generally used for wine, while the fat, short ones were for olive oil. Because amphorae differ according to their purpose and nationality, archaeologists find them to be a particularly useful clue for dating shipwrecks and determining the country of origin of lost ships. This is made easier by later Roman amphorae, which are actually stamped with the place they came from and what they held.

ISTRIA

gladiators would charge up a chute and burst into the arena, like football players being introduced at the Super Bowl. As you go down the passage, you'll walk on a grate over an even lower tunnel. Pula is honeycombed with tunnels like these, originally used for sewers and as a last-ditch place of refuge in case of attack. Inside, check out the extensive collection of amphorae (see sidebar), find your location on the replica of a fourth-century A.D. Roman map (oriented with east on top), and ogle the gigantic grape press and two olive-oil mills.

On your way out, check the corridor across from the ticket booth to see if there are any temporary exhibits.

• *From the amphitheater, it's a few minutes' walk to Pula's Old Town, where more Roman sights await. Exit the amphitheater, cross the street, turn left, and walk one long block along the small wall up the busy road (Amfiteatarska ulica). When you reach the park on your right, look for the car-sized...*

Town Model

Use this handy model of Pula to get oriented. Next to the amphitheater, the little water cannon spouting into the air marks the pale-blue house nearby, the site of a freshwater spring (which makes this location even more strategic). The big star-shaped fortress on the hill is Fort Kaštel, designed by a French architect during the Venetian era (1630). Read the street plan of the Roman town into this model: At the center (on the hill) was the *castrum*, or military base. At the base of the hill (the far side from the amphitheater) was the forum, or town square. During Pula's Roman glory days, the hillsides around the *castrum* were blanketed with the villas of rich merchants. The Old Town, which clusters around the base of the fortress-topped hill, still features many fragments of the Roman period, as well as Pula's later occupiers. We'll take a counterclockwise stroll around the fortified old hill through this ancient zone.

The huge anchor across the street from the model celebrates Pula's number-one employer—its shipyards.

• *Continue along the street. At the fork, bear right (on Kandlerova ulica—level, not uphill). Notice the* **Roman ruins** *on your right. Just about any time someone wants to put up a new building, they find ruins like these. Work screeches to a halt while the valuable remains are excavated. In this case, they've discovered three Roman houses, two churches, and 2,117 amphorae—the largest stash found anywhere in the world. (The harbor is just behind, which suggests this might have been a storehouse for off-loaded amphorae.) I guess the new parking garage has to wait.*

After about three more blocks strolling through gritty, slice-of-life Pula, on your right-hand side, you'll see Pula's...

Cathedral (Katedrala)

This church combines elements of the two big Italian influences on Pula: Roman and Venetian. Dating from the fifth century A.D., the

Romanesque core of the church (notice the skinny, slitlike windows) marks the site of an early-Christian seafront settlement in Pula. The Venetian Baroque facade and bell tower are much more recent (early 18th century). Typical of the Venetian style, notice how far away the austere bell tower is from the body of the church. The bell tower's foundation is made of stones that were scavenged from the amphitheater. The church's sparsely decorated interior features a classic Roman-style basilica floor plan, with a single grand hall—the side naves were added in the 15th century, after a fire.

Cost and Hours: Free, generally open daily 10:00-18:00 in summer, less off-season.

• *Keep walking through the main pedestrian zone, passing tacky souve-*

nir shops and Albanian-run fast-food and ice-cream joints. After a few more blocks, you emerge into the...

Forum

Every Roman town had a forum, or main square. Twenty centuries later, Pula's Forum not only serves the same function but has kept the old Roman name.

Two important buildings front the north end of the square, where you enter. The smaller building (on the left, with the col-

umns) is the first-century A.D. Roman **Temple of Augustus** (Augustov Hram). Built during the reign of, and dedicated to, Augustus Caesar, this temple took a direct hit from an Allied bomb in World War II. After the war, the Allied occupiers rebuilt it as a sort of mea culpa—notice the patchwork repair job. It's the only one remaining of three such temples that once lined this side of the square. Inside the temple is a single room with fragments of ancient sculptures (10 kn, May-Sept Mon-Sat 9:00-21:00, Sun 9:00-15:00, often closed Oct-April, sparse English labels). The surviving torso from a statue of Augustus, which likely stood on or near this spot, dates from the time of Christ. Other evocative chips and bits of Roman Pula include the feet of a powerful commander with a pathetic little vanquished barbarian obediently at his knee (perhaps one of the Histri—the indigenous Istrians that the Romans conquered in 177 B.C.).

Head back out to the square. As Rome fell, its long-subjugated subjects in Pula had little respect for the former empire's symbols, and many temples didn't survive. Others were put to new use: Part of an adjacent temple (likely dedicated to Diana) was incorporated into the bigger building on the right, Pula's medieval **Town Hall** (Gradska Palača). If you circle around behind this building, you can still see Roman fragments embedded in the back. The Town Hall encapsulates many centuries of Pula architecture: Romanesque core, Gothic reliefs, Renaissance porch, Baroque windows... and a few Roman bits and pieces. Notice the interesting combination of flags above the door: Pula, Croatia, Istria (with its mascot goat), Italy (for the large ethnic minority here), and the European Union (which Croatia joined in 2013).

• *Consider dropping by the TI on this square before continuing our stroll down the main drag, Sergijevaca. You'll pass by a small park on your right. For an optional detour to Byzantine times, angle through the park and find a parking lot. Near the end of the lot, on the left-hand side, is a fenced-off grassy field. At the far end of the field is the small...*

Basilica of St. Mary Formosa
(Kapela Marije Formoze)

We've seen plenty of Roman and Venetian bric-a-brac, but this chapel survives from the time of another Istrian occupier: Byzantium. For about 170 years after Rome fell (the sixth and seventh centuries A.D.), this region came under the control of the Byzantine Empire and was ruled from Ravenna (now in Italy, across the Adriatic, south of Venice). Much of this field was once occupied by a vast, richly decorated basilica. This lonely chapel is all that's left, but it still gives a feel for the architecture of that era—including the Greek-cross floor plan (with four equal arms) and heavy brick vaulting.

• *From here, follow brown* Rimski Mozaik *signs through a dusty parking lot and into a small yard. Walk to the metal grille, and look down to see the...*

Roman Floor Mosaic (Rimski Mozaik)

This hidden mosaic is a great example of the Roman treasures that lie below the old center of Pula. Uncovered by locals who were cleaning up from WWII bombs, this third-century floor was carefully excavated and cleaned up for display right where it was laid nearly two millennia ago. (Notice that the Roman floor level was about six feet below today's.) The centerpiece of the mosaic depicts the punishment of Dirce. According to the ancient Greek legend, King Lykos of Thebes was bewitched by Dirce and abandoned his pregnant queen. The queen gave birth to twin boys (depicted in this mosaic), who grew up to kill their deadbeat dad and tie Dirce to the horns of a bull, to be bashed against a mountain. This same story is famously depicted in the twisty *Toro Farnese* sculpture partly carved by Michelangelo (on display in Naples' Archaeological Museum).

• *Find your way through the adjacent passage to return to the main drag* (Sergijevaca). *Turn right and continue through Pula's most colorful (and most touristy) neighborhood. After a block, the stepped lane on the left leads up to the deconsecrated Church of the Holy Cross, which is now a state-of-the-art museum space housing temporary exhibits from the Archaeological Museum (explained on page 136).*

Continuing along Sergijevaca, in a few short blocks you'll arrive at the...

Arch of Sergius
(Slavoluk Sergijevaca)

This triumphal arch, from the first century B.C., was Michelangelo's favorite Roman artifact in Pula. Marking the edge of the original Roman town, it was built to honor Lucius Sergius Lepidus. He fought on the side of Augustus in the civil wars that swept the empire after Julius Caesar's assassination. The proto-feminist inscription proudly explains, "Silvia of the Sergius family paid for this with her own money." Statues of Silvia's husband, Lucius, plus her son and her brother-in-law, once stood on the three blocks at the top of the arch. (Squint to see the *Sergivs* name on each block.) On the underside of the arch is a relief of an eagle (the symbol of Rome) clutching an evil snake in its talons.

• *Before going under the arch, look to your left to see a famous Irishman appreciating the view from the terrace of...*

Café Uliks

In October 1904, a young writer named James Joyce moved from Dublin to Pula with his girlfriend, Nora Barnacle. By day, he taught English to Austro-Hungarian naval of-  ficers at the Berlitz language school (in the yellow building nearby). By night, he imagined strolling through his home-town as he penned short stories that would eventually become the collection *Dubliners*. But James and Nora quickly grew bored with little Pula and moved to Trieste in March 1905. Even so, Pula remains proud of its literary connections.

• *Now pass through the arch, into a square next to some remains of the town wall. Continue straight ahead for two bustling blocks, along Flanatička street, to...*

National Square (Narodni Trg) and Market Hall

Pula's market hall was an iron-and-glass marvel when inaugurated in the 19th century. This structure is yet another reminder of the

 way the Austro-Hungarian Empire modernized Pula with grace and gentility. You'll find meats, cheeses, and smelly fish on the ground floor (Mon-Sat 7:00-13:30, Sun 7:00-12:00), and an inviting food circus upstairs (Mon-Fri 7:00-15:00, Sat 7:00-14:00, sleepy on Sun). All around is a busy and colorful farmers market that bustles until about 13:00, when things quiet down.

• *Our tour is finished. If you're ready for lunch, consider one of the cheap options inside or near the market hall, or walk one block to Kantina (see "Eating in Pula," later).*

  When you're done here, backtrack to the town wall. As you face the Arch of Sergius, take a right and walk uphill under the leafy canopy *next to the wall. Keep an eye out (mostly on your left, along the wall) for more Roman remains. Among these are the **Twin Gates** (Porta Gemina), marking the entrance to a garden that's home to the **Archaeological Museum of Istria** (one long block after the cafés, described next). You'll also see entrances to the Austro-Hungarian-era **tunnels** that burrow under the hill; called Zerostrasse, this space often hosts special exhibits. With more time, you can also consider a trip to the hilltop fortress, **Fort Kaštel**. Otherwise, we've completed our circular tour—the amphitheater is just around the corner.*

Sights in Pula

Archaeological Museum of Istria (Arheološki Muzej Istre) in the Church of the Holy Cross (Sv. Srca)

Pula's century-old archaeological museum (at Carrarina 3) is closed for renovation for several years. When open, it shows off some of what you've seen in the streets, plus lots more: stone monuments, classical statues, ancient pottery, you name it. While it's closed, temporary exhibits drawing from the collection's highlights are displayed a few blocks away, inside the Church of the Holy Cross. Beautifully restored and repurposed as a modern exhibition space, and with good English descriptions, the church is arguably a more satisfying home for the collection. Historians will want to check out the latest exhibits (www.ami-pula.hr).

Roman Theater (Rimsko Kazalište)

The remains of an ancient theater are free to visit, on the hill behind the (currently closed) Archaeological Museum. Part of the stage is still intact, along with the semicircle of stone seats (some of which are still engraved with the names of the wealthy theatergoers who once sat in them). To find it, go up the hill around the right side of the museum. This was the smaller of the two theaters in Roman Pula; the second was south of the center (and is no longer intact).

Fort Kaštel

For a bird's-eye view over the town, head up to its centerpiece fortress. This deserted-feeling place, hosting the Historical Museum of Istria, is worth visiting only for the chance to wander the ramparts and enjoy the views over the town and amphitheater (various trails lead up from the streets below).

Eating in Pula

The best lunch options are in and near the town's **market hall** (which is also where my self-guided walk ends). The top floor of the market is a food circus with a number of cheap and tempting eateries with both indoor and terrace seating. Back outside, around the right side of the market hall, you'll find a pair of fiercely competitive bakeries serving fresh batches of cheap and delicious *burek*, the savory phyllo-dough pastry: One no-name bakery is built into the market hall itself, and Pekarna Corona faces it from across the market square.

Kantina Restaurant, a block away, serves good lunches (including veggie options) and hearty, creative 35-kn salads, in an elegant vaulted cellar and on a lazy shady terrace. The service can be slow—if you're in a rush, eat at the market hall instead (60-85-kn pastas, 90-150-kn meat dishes, daily 12:00-23:00, closed Sun off-season, at the end of the pedestrian zone at Flanatička 16, tel. 052/214-054).

Pula Connections

By Bus from Pula to: Rovinj (about hourly, 45 minutes), **Poreč** (9/day, 1.5 hours), **Opatija** (12 day, 2 hours), **Rijeka** (nearly hourly, 2-2.5 hours), **Zagreb** (almost hourly, 4 hours), **Split** (1/day, 10 hours), **Venice** (1/day departing at about 6:00, arrives Venice 11:00). To reach destinations in **Slovenia** (including Piran and Ljubljana), most connections require a change in Umag. Year-round, two days a week you can take a very early bus from Pula to Portorož (with a connection to Piran) and then on to Ljubljana (departs Pula at 5:30). Slovenia connections are run by Fils Pula (confirm schedules at www.fils.hr). In the summer, be aware that bus connections are more frequent on weekdays (fewer departures Sat-Sun). Bus info: Toll tel. 060-304-090.

By Train to: Zagreb (3/day, 6 hours, transfer in Rijeka), **Ljubljana** (1/day in late June-late Sept only, 5 hours, transfer in Hrpelje-Kozina).

ISTRIA

The Brijuni Islands

The Brijuni Islands (bree-YOO-nee, Brioni in Italian)—an archipelago of 14 islands just offshore from the southern tip of the Istrian Peninsula—were a favorite haunt of Marshal Tito, the leader of communist Yugoslavia. The main island, called Great Brijuni (Veli Brijun), was where Tito liked to show off the natural wonders of his beloved Yugoslavia to visiting dignitaries and world leaders. Today the island is a national park that combines serene natural beauty with quirky Yugoslav sights, offering a strange but enjoyable time capsule of the Tito years.

Tito wasn't the first to fall in love with Brijuni; visitors see the remains of many previous occupants (Romans, Byzantines, Ve-

Brijuni: Center of the Nonaligned World

Many visitors to the former Yugoslavia mistakenly assume this country was part of the Soviet Bloc. It most decidedly wasn't. While the rest of "Eastern Europe" was liberated by the Soviets at the end of World War II, Yugoslavia's own, homegrown Partisan Army forced the Nazis out themselves. This allowed the country—and its new leader, the war hero Marshal Tito—a certain degree of self-determination following the war. Though the new Yugoslavia was socialist, it was not Soviet-style socialism. After formally breaking ties with Moscow in 1948, Tito steered his country toward a "third way" between the strict and stifling communism of the East and the capitalist free-for-all of the West. (For more on Tito's system, see the Understanding Yugoslavia chapter.)

Many other countries also didn't quite fit into the easy East-versus-West dichotomy embraced by the US, USSR, and Europe. On July 19, 1956, the Brijuni Declaration—signed by Tito, Jawaharlal Nehru of India, and Abdel Nasser of Egypt—created the Non-Aligned Movement (NAM). Members recognized each other's sovereignty and respected each leader's right to handle domestic issues however he or she saw fit.

As Tito's international prominence grew, so did the list of visitors to his Brijuni Islands hideaway. In addition to Nehru and Nasser, Tito hosted Haile Selassie (Ethiopia), Yasser Arafat (Palestine Liberation Organization), Fidel Castro (Cuba), Indira Gandhi (India), Muammar al-Gaddafi (Libya), Queen Elizabeth II (Great Britain), Willy Brandt (West Germany), Leonid Brezhnev (USSR)...not to mention Elizabeth Taylor (US) and Sophia Loren (Italy).

In principle, the NAM was envisioned as a competitor of NATO and the Warsaw Pact. But as the world's politics have changed, many NAM members are now closely allied with other, more powerful nations. And when Yugoslavia broke up, most of the countries that emerged preferred to join NATO and the EU.

So whatever happened to the rest of the NAM? It's still going strong, with 120 member states encompassing virtually all of Africa, the Middle East, Southeast Asia, and Latin America. While the EU and the US wrestle for bragging rights as the world's superpower, the NAM represents more than half of the world's population.

netians, Austrians—even dinosaurs). Between the World Wars, a health resort here hosted many notables, from Douglas Fairbanks and John D. Rockefeller to Richard Strauss and Hirohito. But when Tito took power, he made Brijuni his summer residence from 1949 until 1979—hosting a steady stream of VIP visitors from the East, the West, and the nonaligned world (see sidebar). Just three years after Tito's death, in October 1983, Brijuni opened to the public as a national park.

Getting There: You can get to Great Brijuni Island only on one of the national park's boats. These depart from the town of Fažana, five miles north of Pula and 20 miles south of Rovinj. From Rovinj, drive southeast to Bale, where you'll get on the *ipsilon* highway and continue south. In Vodnjan, watch for the easy-to-miss turnoff (on the right) marked for Fažana and Brijuni. Once in Fažana, follow brown *Brijuni* signs and park along the water (confirm with park ticket office that your parking spot is OK).

Cost and Information: The price varies depending on the time of year: July-Aug-210 kn, June and Sept-200 kn, April-May and Oct-170 kn, Nov-March-125 kn; includes park entry, round-trip by boat to the island, and a guide (see "English Tour," below). Tel. 052/525-882, www.brijuni.hr.

Hours: From April through October, the first boat departure from Fažana is at 6:45 and the last trip is at 21:45 (last return from Brijuni at 23:00). The number of departures varies with the time of year: May-Sept about hourly, 12/day; March-April and Oct 8/day; Nov-Feb 4/day.

English Tour: You're required to go to the island with a four-hour guided tour, much of which is spent on a little tourist train. The only English-language tour usually departs Fažana daily at 11:30. It's essential to call ahead to confirm the schedule and reserve a space on the tour (call or email at least a day before, or three days ahead in peak season, tel. 052/525-883, izleti@np-brijuni.hr).

If you can't make it on the English tour, you're welcome to join any tour you like (Croatian, German, Italian, etc.). While it's easy to slip away from your group and explore the island on your own, park officials discourage it. Staying with the tour for most of the trip is wise in any event, as there's lots of ground to cover in a limited amount of time. It's possible to rent bikes at the hotel where the boat puts in. You're technically required to take the same boat back with the rest of your tour, but this isn't closely monitored.

Visiting the Island: Great Brijuni Island can be visited only with a tour (described above). After a 15-minute crossing from the mainland town of Fažana, visitors arrive at the island's main harbor, which is a hub of activity and the site of its two hotels. Outside this area, the island is largely undeveloped. There are virtually no cars—most people get around by bike, golf cart, or the little tourist train you'll board to begin your tour. As you spin around the island, you'll enjoy views over its endlessly twisty coast, with cove after tranquil cove. Your guide will impart both dry facts and eye-rolling legends while you putter past several intriguing sights, periodically giving you a chance to get off the train and explore a few of them up close.

The tour's highlight is the **"Tito on Brijuni"** exhibit. Dating from 1984—four years after his death, but before the end of Yugoslavia—this exhibit celebrates the cult of personality surrounding the head of this now-deceased nation. The museum (with English descriptions) features countless photos of Tito in every Brijuni context imaginable—strolling, sunbathing, skeet shooting, schmoozing with world leaders and movie stars, inspecting military officers, playing with camels given to him by Muammar al-Gaddafi, and so on. (For more on Tito, and why this former dictator remains so beloved in his former lands, see the sidebar on page 734.)

Another high point of the island tour is the **safari,** featuring a diverse menagerie of animals (or their descendants) brought here for Tito as gifts by visiting heads of state. Because many of the nonaligned nations are in Africa, Asia, or other non-European regions, many of these beasts are exotic. Aside from the Istrian ox and Istria's trademark goat, you'll see llamas, Somali sheep, Shetland ponies, chamois, and more. There once were elephants, camels, cheetahs, ostriches, monkeys, bears, and bobcats as well, but most of these have gone to the great nonaligned safari in the sky, and their bodies are now preserved at the "Tito on Brijuni" exhibit.

Other attractions you may see on Brijuni: an ancient, gnarled olive tree supposedly dating from the fourth century A.D.; the remains of a mostly first-century A.D. Roman *villa rustica* (country estate); the ruined street plan of a Byzantine fort; a 15th-century Gothic church with an exhibit on frescoes and Glagolitic (early Croatian) script; a Venetian summer house that hosts an archaeology museum; an Austro-Hungarian naval fort (Brijuni was strategically important back when Pula was Austria's main naval base); and footprints left by a dinosaur who vacationed here 120 million years before Tito.

Birders can look for some of the 250 avian species that live on the island in the summer. Gardeners may spot some exotic, nonnative plant species (more gifts, to go along with all those animals), such as Australian eucalyptus. And Republicans can drool over the golf course, a reminder that Brijuni is attempting to cultivate a ritzy image. Your tour's lengthy stop at the bar/gift shop is yet another indication that, while some remember Tito fondly, good ol' capitalism is here to stay.

Poreč

Poreč (poh-RETCH, Parenzo in Italian), the tourist capital of the Istrian coast, is the kind of resort that brags about how many hotel beds it has, rather than how many museums or churches pack the cobbled streets of its Old Town. (Think of it as the Croatian Acapulco.) The town is too big to be charming, but too small to be exciting. The only reason to come is to see its landmark basilica, slathered with exquisite mosaics. But if you're in a hurry or churched out, I'd skip it.

Getting There: Surrounding Poreč's peninsular Old Town are miles of hotels-and-concrete sprawl. Drivers follow *Centar* and blue *P* signs to the big pay parking lot, then head up to the big boulevard called Zagrebačka (with the grass median). This leads past the **TI** (Zagrebačka 9, tel. 052/451-293, www.to-porec.com) to the spacious square named Trg Slobode. From here, Decumanus street marches straight through the middle of the Old Town. To find the basilica, look for the archway with gold mosaics down Sv. Eleuterija street.

▲Euphrasian Basilica (Eufrazijeva Bazilika)

This sixth-century church is a gold mine for fans of Byzantine mosaics.

Cost and Hours: 30 kn, basilica open long hours daily, no shorts; museum and tower open April-Sept daily 10:00-17:00, likely closed Oct-March.

Visiting the Basilica: The interior is dominated by gorgeous, glittering mosaics in the apse surrounding the main altar. The top row depicts Jesus surrounded by the 12 apostles, the medallions around the arch celebrate 12 female martyrs, and front and center are Mary and Jesus surrounded

by angels and martyrs—including Bishop Euphrasius, holding his namesake basilica in his arms (second from left). These date from the 170-year period after the fall of Rome (roughly 530-700 A.D.), when Istria was part of the Byzantine Empire and was ruled from Ravenna (near Venice, across the Adriatic). The more recent (13th-century) canopy over the altar was inspired by the one in St. Mark's Basilica in Venice. Don't miss another set of mosaics in the floor just inside the door.

For more mosaics, drop into the attached **museum,** with several mosaic fragments scattered around two floors. Or climb the **bell tower** to get a bird's-eye view of Poreč. Both are included in the basilica ticket.

ISTRIA

Hill Towns of the Istrian Interior

Most tourists in Croatia focus on the coast. For a dash of variety, head inland. Some of the best bits of the Croatian interior lie just a short drive from Rovinj. Dotted with sleepy, picturesque hill towns, speckled with wineries and olive-oil farms, embedded with precious truffles, and grooved by meandering rural roads, the Istrian interior is worth a detour. Tucked below, between, and on top of the many hills are characteristic stone-walled villages, designed to stay cool in summer and warm in winter. Visitors find themselves

seduced by the *malvazija* wine, truffles, picturesque tableaus, and laid-back ambience of the Istrian hill towns.

Poking around and exploring on your own is a good option here. For a quick visit, focus on the best hill town: Motovun, a popular little burg with sweeping views. With more time, consider venturing deeper into the smaller villages that sit above the Mirna River Valley—the scenic, deserted, lost-in-a-time-warp village of Završje; the rugged, relatively untrampled artists' colony of Grožnjan; or the bigger towns of Buje and Oprtalj. Farther east—on the way to Rijeka—is the extremely remote and miniscule, yet touristy, hamlet of Hum.

One of the interior's main draws is its cuisine—especially the truffles that are found right here, as fresh as you can get. While Rovinj has some fine restaurants, it's worth planning your day around having lunch or dinner in the interior. Motovun has several excellent options—Mondo Konoba is tops—or you can head for the countryside: For the ultimate rustic rest stop (but with few truffles), dine at Konoba Astarea in Brtonigla; for truffle dishes surrounded by the forests in which they're foraged, you can go upscale at Zigante in Livade, or venture into the nearby countryside to enjoy the more rustic truffle dishes at Konoba Dolina in Gradinje. All of these are described later in more detail.

During the glory days of the Austro-Hungarian Empire, a twisty railway called La Parenzana (Porečanka in Croatian) connected

Trieste to Poreč by way of many of northwest Istria's hill towns. While the train itself is long gone, part of its route has been converted to a "rails-to-trails" path (you'll see signs for this around the area, and a small museum in Livade). The many bridges and tunnels engineered to make the train line possible have become nostalgic icons of an earlier time. While Croatia hasn't yet developed a serious bicycle-tourism culture, La Parenzana is an impressive first effort. Ask locally for the free, EU-funded map of La Parenzana's route, which spans three countries (Italy, Slovenia, and Croatia).

Istrian hill towns can be pretty rough and rugged. Many are abandoned, only recently having been rediscovered by artists. Remember that after Istria shifted from Italy to Yugoslavia following World War II, the "Italian exodus" saw many local peasants leave their homes behind and move into Italy proper—one reason many of these towns are still in such disrepair. Stumbling over cobbles between desolate buildings in a village that once must have been humming with life, you may find yourself thinking about the sadness that comes with forced population shifts.

As you explore, you'll see frequent signs for wineries, olive-oil producers, and truffle shops. There's an itinerary for every interest, and the Istrian tourist board publishes a stack of well-produced brochures on every topic you can imagine (available at local TIs). One recent trend in Istria is the emergence of *agroturizams*. Like Italian *agriturismos* or Slovenian tourist farms, these are working farms that try to involve tourists in a meaningful way—sometimes just for a meal or overnight stay, but occasionally actually participating in the daily workings of the farm. For more information, pick up the free brochure (available locally), or visit www.istra.hr.

GETTING AROUND THE ISTRIAN INTERIOR

By Public Transportation: While it's possible to see some parts of inland Istria by public transportation, the rewards are not worth the headaches. The large hill town of Pazin is the region's transit hub, with buses to Rovinj, Pula, Poreč, and Motovun—but not the smaller villages.

By Car: The region is ideal by car. For a quick visit to only the best hill town (Motovun), just zip on the *ipsilon* highway (A-9) to the *Nova Vas* exit, and take the mercifully flat road 44 along the Mirna River Valley straight to Motovun. But for a full day of hill town-hopping in the Istrian interior, follow my suggested route in the "More Hill Towns" section, later.

Motovun

Dramatically situated a thousand feet above vineyards and a truffle-filled forest, Motovun (moh-toh-VOON, Montona in Italian, pop. 531) is the best-known and most-touristed of the Istrian hill towns. And for good reason: Its hilltop Old Town is particularly evocative, with a colorful old church and a rampart walk with the best spine-tingling vistas in the Istrian interior. It's hard to believe that race-car driver Mario Andretti was born in such a tranquil little traffic-free hamlet. Today Motovun's quiet lanes are shared by locals, tourists, and artists—who began settling here a generation ago, when it was nearly deserted.

Orientation to Motovun

Motovun is steep. Most everything of interest to tourists is huddled around its tippy-top. The main, upper entrance gate into town deposits you at the main square, with the church on your left and Hotel Kaštel on the right. From there, you're just about two blocks in every direction from a sheer drop-off. This hilltop zone is
circled by an old rampart that today offers Motovun's most scenic stroll.

Motovun's **TI** comes and goes (tel. 052/681-726, www.tz-motovun.hr). Fortunately, the reception desk at Hotel Kaštel kindly dispenses tourist information and town maps.

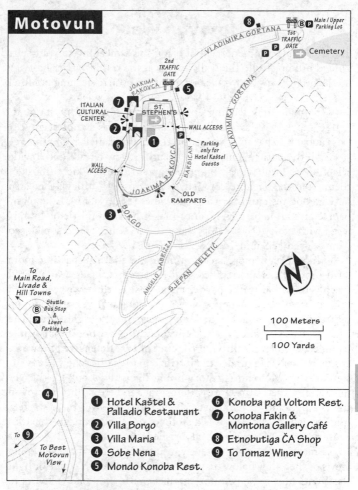

Motovun

Map Legend:
1. Hotel Kaštel & Palladio Restaurant
2. Villa Borgo
3. Villa Maria
4. Sobe Nena
5. Mondo Konoba Rest.
6. Konoba pod Voltom Rest.
7. Konoba Fakin & Montona Gallery Café
8. Etnobutiga ČA Shop
9. To Tomaz Winery

ISTRIA

ARRIVAL IN MOTOVUN

Motovun's striking hilltop setting comes with a catch: Visitors usually have to hike up part of the way. A steep, twisty road connects the base of the hill with the Old Town up top. Drive as far up this road as possible until you're directed to park in the lot partway up (by the traffic gate and near the lower church, a steep 10-minute uphill walk to the main square, 22 kn/day). On busy days, you'll be forced to park in the lower lot (along the main road), then ride the shuttle bus up. If you're staying at Hotel Kaštel, follow the procedure explained under "Sleeping in Motovun," later. If staying elsewhere, ask your *soba* host for advice.

Motovun Walk

The following commentary will bring some meaning to your self-guided hilltop stroll. The walk begins at the traffic barrier halfway up the hill (the highest you can drive unless you're sleeping at Hotel Kaštel).

The main drag leading up into town is lined with wine-and-truffle shops. My favorite is the Lanča family's **Etnobutiga ČA** (just above the parking lot on the right, at Gradiziol 33). This restored 17th-century house has a beautiful view terrace and a wide selection of local wines, brandies, and truffle products (most of them from the Zigante company, just across the valley); they also have a good restaurant with grand views (Pod Napun). Like many people around here, Livio Lanča makes his own mistletoe brandy laced with honey (Easter-Oct daily 10:00-22:00, off-season closed Mon, closed Feb-mid-March, tel. 052/681-767).

Hike several more steep minutes up the hill, passing more local-products shops, truffles, and jewelry boutiques. Soon you'll reach yet another traffic barrier at the base of the town's wall (and the recommended Mondo Konoba restaurant). Continuing up past the barrier, you'll earn grand views on the right—the little town across the valley floor is Livade, the heart of all that truffle commerce—then go through the first of two **defensive gateways.** Inside this passage (under the fortified gate), notice the various insignias from Motovun's history lining the walls: Look for the Venetian lion, the Latin family tombstone, and the seal of Motovun (with a pyramid of five towers being watched over by an angel). The area above the gate was a storehouse for weapons in the 15th century, when Motovun first flourished.

Emerging from the gateway, you're greeted by more sweeping views of the valley below on your right-hand side. (A coffee or light meal with this view is unforgettable; the town's lone ATM is to your left.) Just up and to the left, you'll find another defensive gateway, which is the main entrance into the heart of the **Old Town.** (Inside this gateway, notice the recommended Konoba pod Voltom restaurant.)

To your left as you come through the main gate is the yellow town church, **St. Stephen's.** The crenellated tower is a reminder of a time when this hilltop town needed to be defended. While unassuming from the outside, this austere house of worship has an impressive pedigree: It's based on designs by the famous Venetian architect Andrea Palladio (1508-1580), who greatly influenced the Neoclassical architecture of Washington, DC. The interior is a little gloomy but refreshingly lived-in—used more by locals than by tourists. On the left, notice a painting of the heart of Jesus, its eyes following you around the church (free, generally open daily 10:00-18:00 and during frequent services).

As you stand on the square in front of the church, imagine Motovun during its annual **film festival,** when it's filled with 20,000 movie lovers from throughout the region and around the world—often including a minor celebrity or two. This square fills to capacity, and films are projected on a giant screen at the far end (generally late July or early Aug, www.motovunfilmfestival.com).

Facing the church is the **Italian Cultural Center,** which plays an important role in this very Italian corner of Croatia. While the building is not open to the public, if your timing is right you'll enjoy beautiful music spilling out from its windows and filling the square. The local *klapa* music troupe—with men's voices harmonizing a cappella—practices here twice weekly (usually Mon and Fri evenings, at 21:00 in summer and 20:00 in winter). If you hear them, grab a bench and enjoy the show.

At the other end of the square is a leafy little piazza dominated by the big, pink **Hotel Kaštel**—the main industry in town. This is also where bigwigs in town for the local film festival call home—ask the staff about recent sightings of B-, C-, and D-list celebrities. (For example, if you're staying here, you may be showering in the same bathroom once graced by Jason Biggs, star of *American Pie.* Lucky you.)

Between the church and Hotel Kaštel, follow the lane to the **ramparts.** Take the five-minute stroll around the Old Town on these fortifications. While most of Croatia is overrun by stray cats, Motovun seems populated by dog lovers. If you see or hear dogs in people's backyards, it's a safe bet that they are trained to hunt for truffles in the surrounding forest.

As you breathe in the stunning panorama, notice that well-defended Motovun has been fortified three times—two layers of wall up top, and a third down below.

Sleeping in Motovun

Except for the big hotel, all of the places here keep the same rates all year long. Most Motovun accommodations lack air-conditioning; thick old walls and a nice breeze generally keep things cool.

$$$ Hotel Kaštel, dominating Motovun's hilltop (and its tourist industry), is can-do, ideally located, and the only real hotel in this little burg. Most of the 33 colorful rooms have views. True to its name, the building used to be a castle, so the floor plan can be confusing (Sb-€66/€62/€58, standard Db-€112/€106/€96, Db suite or "superior" Db with air-con-€140/€130/€116, "exclusive" Db with air-con and balcony-€170/€154/€130; 10 percent discount with this book if you reserve direct, elevator, air-con in some rooms, laundry service, bike rental, Trg Andrea Antico 7, tel. 052/681-607, www.hotel-kastel-motovun.hr, info@hotel-kastel-motovun.hr). Guests have free access to part of the spa facilities, with a beautiful indoor pool and a spa offering a wide range of massages (starting at 150 kn/30 min, 10 percent discount with this book). Guests with cars should tell the attendant at the traffic barrier that you have a reservation here; if there's room on top, he'll let you drive up. Otherwise he'll tell you where to park and call the hotel, which will send down a free car to shuttle you up (runs until about 18:00); either way, call ahead to the hotel to figure out your options.

$$ Villa Borgo, beautifully located next to the loggia just below Motovun's uppermost gate, has 10 simple but stylish rooms. There are several types of rooms, all of which are discounted 10 percent for Rick Steves readers who book direct: with grand views (Db-€84/€68), with no views (Db-€73/€62), top-floor rooms that share a bathroom (D-€46), and a big apartment (Db-€87/€67, extra bed-€16). All rooms share a spectacular view terrace (lower prices are for Nov-May, includes breakfast, no air-con but built-in ventilators, April-Oct staffed until 20:00, off-season call first, Borgo 4, mobile 098-434-797, tel. 052/681-708, www.villaborgo.com, info@villaborgo.com).

$ Villa Maria is a good value, offering two fine rooms with view terraces, plus a third nonview room, in the Sviličić family home on a quiet back lane a steep five-minute walk below the main part of town (Db-€50, breakfast-€5, cash only, air-con, facing the defensive gate turn right and go down and around to Borgo 32, tel. 052/681-559, lorenasvilicic@gmail.com, minimal English).

$ Sobe Nena, run by Nevija and Ricardo, is a good budget option in a tidy house at the very bottom of Motovun's hill. The two rooms are old-fashioned and basic, sharing a bathroom, but there's a fine garden to relax in. Ricardo speaks only a little English (Nevija speaks none), but they can call their daughter Doris to translate. If you lack a car, you'll have to get to town on the shuttle bus from the lower parking lot (if it's running)—or you're in for a loooong hike up (S-€30, D-€60, cash only, no Wi-Fi, across from the gas station at Kanal 32, tel. 052/681-719, mobile 099-609-0883, sobe.nena@gmail.com).

Eating in Motovun

This small hill town has just a few real restaurants, and all of them are quite good; the first two listings are particularly notable. Every menu is topped by pricey (but tasty) truffle dishes—but keep in mind that these are a better investment when truffles are in season and the flavors are pungent (see sidebar); otherwise, you'll get older, blander truffles. Remember, there are also several excellent restaurants in the countryside near Motovun—if you're serious about food, before choosing, be sure to peruse your options in the "More Hill Towns" section, later.

Mondo Konoba, run by a Croatian-Italian hybrid family and located just below the lower town gate (on the left, at the base of the wall), serves up Sicilian-Istrian fusion cuisine that ranks with any restaurant in the region. Most diners skip the unpretentious, pastel-blue dining room in favor of the inviting little outdoor terrace, with more tables across the street at the base of the town wall. The Mondo family's pack of five truffle-hunting dogs occasionally pays a visit (35-50-kn salads, 60-100-kn pastas, 75-125-kn main courses, June-Sept daily 12:00-15:30 & 18:00-22:00, closed Tue Oct-May and all of Jan, Barbakan 1, tel. 052/681-791).

Konoba pod Voltom is actually inside the town's upper, main gate (on the right, with the *Taberna* sign above the door). Motovun's most traditional eatery serves excellent, well-presented Istrian food in a cozy dining room. In good weather (June-Sept only), it's hard to beat their view loggia, just below and outside the gate (45-60-kn pastas, 60-110-kn main courses, 80-260-kn truffle splurges, daily 12:00-22:00, closed Jan, tel. 052/681-923).

Other Scenic Eateries: Two other, simpler places also have seating along the wall, with these same mammoth views. **Konoba Fakin,** run by the winemaking family of the same name, offers a menu of Istrian dishes (35-65-kn salads, 55-90-kn pastas, 65-145-kn main courses, daily 10:00-24:00, tel. 052/681-598). The **Montona Gallery** café, with tables along the rampart between the two gates, serves drinks, ice cream, snacks, and 40- to 60-kn pizzas, pastas, and burgers (daily 9:00-24:00, tel. 052/681-754).

On the Main Square: Hotel Kaštel's **Palladio Restaurant** has ambitiously executed food and delightful seating right on the leafy main square—but I'd skip the dull interior (65-100-kn pastas, 90-175-kn main courses, 10 percent discount with this book, daily 7:00-22:00; also listed under "Sleeping in Motovun," earlier).

Truffle Mania

A mysterious fungus with a pungent, unmistakable flavor is all the rage in Istria. Called *tartufi* in both Croatian and Italian, these precious tubers have been gathered here since Roman times and were favored by the region's Venetian and Austrian rulers. More recently, local peasants ate them as a substitute for meat (often mixed with polenta) during the lean days after World War II.

In 1999, local entrepreneur Giancarlo Zigante discovered a nearly three-pound white truffle. In addition to making Zigante a very wealthy man (see page 158), this giant truffle legitimized Istria on the world truffle scene. Today, Istria rivals France's Provence and Italy's Piedmont in truffle production. Most of Istria's truffles are concentrated in the Motovun Forest, the damp, oak-tree-filled terrain surrounding Motovun, Livade, and Buzet.

A truffle is a tuber that grows entirely underground, usually at a depth of eight inches, near the roots of oak trees. Since no part of the plant grows aboveground, they're difficult to find... and, therefore, extremely expensive. Traditionally, Istrian truffle-gatherers use specially trained dogs to find truffles. This is best

More Hill Towns

While Motovun is the top hill town, a charm bracelet of appealing villages sits close by. Dropping by several as you drive can make for a perfect day. Some are better for exploring (Grožnjan, Završje), others better for a meal (Brtonigla, Livade), and others worth a quick stop if you're passing through (Buje, Oprtalj, Hum). I've listed these roughly in the order you'll reach them, coming from the highway and working your way toward Motovun. While you'll traverse some slow and windy roads, this entire trip is quick—you could do the full circle (including Hum) without stops in less than three hours. This route is just a rough framework. Venture off it. Run down leads from locals. Follow intriguing signs to wine tastings, restaurants, and *agroturizams*. Sniff out some truffles in the Motovun Forest. You will see some other tourists, but this area isn't overrun...yet. There may just be some overlooked gems in the Istrian interior waiting for you to discover.

• *From Rovinj, take the fast* ipsilon *highway (A-9) north. You have two exit options for this area. If you want to enjoy a meal in Brtonigla, take the* Nova Vas *exit, drive into Nova Vas, then follow signs for five minutes into Brtonigla. But if you want to head straight to the other towns, take the exit for* Buje *and skip down to that section.*

done at night, when the dog has to rely more on its sense of smell.

There are two general types of truffles: white (more valuable and with a deeper and more pungent flavor—*Tuber magnatum*, known as the "Queen of the Truffles") and black. Each type of truffle has a season when its scent is released, making it easier to find (May-Nov for black, mid-Sept-Jan for white). Once dug up, they look like a tough, dirty pinecone.

Thanks to their powerful and distinctive kick, truffles are often used sparingly for flavor—grated like parmesan cheese, or infused in truffle oil that's sprinkled over a dish. But you'll also find them in cheese, salami, olive oil, tapenade, pâté, and even ice cream. Truffle is commonly served with pasta—sometimes in a rich cream sauce, and other times more simply, just with olive oil. Truffle soufflé and truffle frittata (scrambled eggs) are also popular. Some people find that the pungent, musty aftertaste follows them around all day...and all night, when its supposed aphrodisiac qualities kick in.

If you're a truffle nut, you'll be in heaven here; if not, you may still appreciate the chance to sample a taste. While you do that, ponder how one giant tuber changed the economy of an entire region.

BRTONIGLA

Brtonigla (bur-toh-NEEG-lah, Verteneglio in Italian, literally "black soil") is a tiny wine village surrounded by vineyards. It's a bit closer to the sea than the other hill towns in this chapter, and sits above gentle slopes rather than on a dramatic hilltop. But this empty-feeling place is home to a luxurious hotel/restaurant and a well-regarded local eatery. Still, if you're not eating or sleeping here, give it a pass. Once in town, you'll find just a handful of haphazard streets.

Sleeping and Eating in Brtonigla: $$$ San Rocco Hotel and Restaurant is a family-run hotel suitable for a serious splurge. Not long ago, this was the abandoned shell of a traditional Istrian house. Now it's a cushy and elegant hotel with traditional beams-and-stone decor and all the modern amenities. With 14 rooms, an outdoor pool, a big indoor hot tub and sauna, and distant views of the Adriatic, it's a welcoming retreat. "Tradition" rooms come with views or Jacuzzi tubs (Db-€209/€199/€179), but the simpler and smaller "classic" (Db-€189/€179/€139) and midsized "comfort" (Db-€199/€189/€159) rooms are plenty comfortable (Sb costs 35 percent less than Db, no extra charge for 1- or 2-night stays, aircon, elevator, loaner bikes, Srednja ulica 2, tel. 052/725-000, www.san-rocco.hr, info@san-rocco.hr, Rita and the Fernetich family).

Its well-regarded, upmarket **restaurant**—open to guests and non-guests alike—features Istrian cuisine served with a modern twist, in a dressy dining room or outside, with poolside elegance (450-500-kn fixed-price meals—or more with truffles, à la carte dishes for 110-120 kn, daily 13:00-24:00).

Konoba Astarea, down the street and around the corner (on the main road toward Buje), is a local favorite for traditional, take-

your-time Istrian cuisine with a focus on fish and lamb. While this isn't gourmet cooking (truffles are an afterthought), it's rustic food done very, very well. Anton and Alma Kernjus cultivate a convivial atmosphere that feels like a well-worn neighborhood hangout. Anton ignores the long menu; he'd rather pull up a chair to explain your options. Choose between the warmly cluttered, borderline-kitschy dining room huddled around the blazing open fire, where Alma does a lot of the cooking; the cool and welcoming terrace with faraway sea views; or the relaxing back garden. It's smart to reserve ahead (figure 200-300 kn per person for a full-blown multicourse meal, or order à la carte: 45-80-kn pastas, 60-180-kn main courses, daily 11:00-23:00, closed Nov, tel. 052/774-384, www.konoba-astarea-brtonigla.com).

• *From Brtonigla, simply follow signs into...*

BUJE

Close to the Slovenian border, Buje (BOO-yeh, Buie in Italian) is big and striking from afar, but functional up close. Still, it's worth a visit if you're passing through and curious to take a stroll through a hill town that feels more alive and workaday than the norm. Just above the parking lot are the small TI and the town museum (facing each other across the street), and higher up is another parking-lot plaza in front of Buje's pastel-yellow Church of Our Mother of Mercy (marked in Latin, *Mater Misericordiae*). From the nearby terrace, you have (distant) views of the sea. From this square, you can hike on cobbles through everyday neighborhoods. Up and to the left you'll find the squat remains of a mid-15th-century octagonal defensive tower, the small Sv. Martin church with its evocative graveyard, and a viewpoint overlooking the countryside. Up and to the right from the main square is the main Sv. Servol Church, whose

big bell tower—visible from miles around—dominates the hilltop. With a rough, unfinished facade, the church shares a fine little piazza with the local elementary school.

    Sleeping and Eating near Buje: In Volpia, a nondescript village five minutes outside of Buje (toward Slovenia), you'll find a charming stone country house offering reasonably priced rooms and good food. **$$ La Parenzana,** named for the long-extinct and lamented Istrian rail line, rents 16 woody, simple-but-comfortable, Germanic-feeling rooms (Sb-€39, Db-€78, includes breakfast, no air-con, rental bikes, Volpia 3, tel. 052/777-460, www.parenzana.com.hr, info@parenzana.com.hr, Jozo) and also runs a restaurant serving up truffle specialties and other dishes cooked over an open fire (60-110-kn pastas, 60-190-kn main courses, daily 12:00-23:00). The former route of the Parenzana rail line—now a handy hiking and biking trail—runs just behind the property, and Guido runs a sweet little minimuseum about that nostalgic train trip. To get here from Buje, leave town following signs for *Trieste* and *Koper*, then turn off toward *Plovanija, Portorož,* and the Slovenian border; after a couple of minutes, watch for *Casa Parenzana* signs to the right.

    • *If you're interested in a wine-tasting detour to two of Istria's swankiest wineries (**Kabola** and **Kozlović**, both described on page 156), now's your chance: Drive by the entrance to Buje on the main road past the Grožnjan turnoff, then watch for signs on the right to* Momjan/Momiano. *Take this road through the village of Kremenje; soon after, you'll pass Kabola on the right. Kozlović is across the valley around the far side of Momjan.*

    To skip the wines and continue on our route, leaving Buje, look for signs that take you along a twisty, narrow road (via Triban) right to Grožnjan.

▲GROŽNJAN

Grožnjan (grohzh-NYAHN, Grisignana in Italian) is your trapped-in-a-time-warp Istrian hill town. Its setting, artfully balanced on the tip of a vine-and-olive-tree-covered promontory, is pleasing, if not thrilling. The time-passed character of its sleepy, rough-cobbled lanes invites you to get lost and leave your itinerary on your dashboard. Not long ago, Grožnjan was virtually forgotten. But now several artists have taken up residence here, keeping it Old World but with a spiffed-up, bohemian ambience. If gallery-browsing is your idea of fun, you'll like this place.

    Grožnjan has no "sights," but it's a delightful place to go for a stroll. All roads lead to the convenient and free parking lot, a few steps from the traffic-free village. Distant sea views from the main terrace at the entrance to town (with a modern café) remind you that you're not far from the Adriatic. A few English panels are posted around town, identifying what passes for "important" buildings in this sleepy burg. The town church's bell tower is its only landmark. Inside the church, the big wall painting over the altar shows angels intervening in the Pula amphitheater to save Christians who were thrown to the lions and tigers.

To get the lay of the land, take a 10-minute town wander: Facing the church's front door, go left and loop clockwise through town (you'll pass the town's lone ATM on your right as you start down the street). Walking along the main street, ulica Umberta Gorjana, you'll pass the Enoteka Zigante truffle shop (one of many outposts of the truffle magnate described on page 158), then the **TI** (which doesn't have a lot to do; closed Mon, Gorjan 3, tel. 052/776-131, www.tz-groznjan.hr). Then you'll reach the shaded square with Café Pintur and the Bastia restaurant, then the Italian Cultural Center. Don't worry about addresses or finding a particular place; you'll find yourself walking in circles, and quickly see what there is to see. Let your pulse slow and enjoy being a castaway on this isolated, tranquil hilltop.

Sleeping and Eating in Grožnjan: **$ Café Pintur,** on a cozy Grožnjan square just downhill from the church, rents four tiny and basic but comfy top-floor rooms. The Černeka family doesn't speak much English, but the rooms are cheap and work in a pinch (Sb-€28, Db-€50, includes breakfast Sept-May, or €5 extra June-Aug; cash only, lots of stairs with no elevator, air-con, Mate Gorjana 9, mobile 098-586-188, tel. 052/776-397, ivan.cerneka@pu.t-com.hr).

Café Pintur's restaurant, open long hours daily in summer, serves basic pasta and grilled meats (40-50-kn pastas, 40-95-kn main courses, 80-kn truffle omelet).

Bastia, across the square and sharing a leafy terrace with Pintur, is a bit more comfortable, with a menu focusing on truffles and a lovely courtyard (55-110-kn pastas, 75-160-kn main courses, daily 8:00-23:00, 1 Svibnja 1, tel. 052/776-370).

• *From Grožnjan, follow signs for* Oprtalj. *Along the way, you'll see* Završje *signs directing you to the right.*

▲ZAVRŠJE

If you'd like to visit a nearly deserted hill town, Završje (ZAH-vur-shyeh) is your place. Called "Piemonte d'Istria" in *Italiano,* this mini-Motovun seems to have more truffle-hunting dogs than people. One of the smallest, most compact, and most picturesquely set hill towns in the area, Završje was once just a double-walled fortress clinging to the top of its bulbous hill. Over time it sprawled just a bit outside its original walls, but it was deserted after the post-

WWII Italian exodus and remains almost uninhabited today; only a few locals live here, and virtually all of the buildings are abandoned skeletons. There's very little to see or do here—no museums, no restaurants, and a sporadically open church with a leaning tower and a colorfully painted Baroque altar. But the EU has taken notice of this precious little burg, and has invested in restoring its pretty pink schoolhouse (at the base of the hill, near the parking lot) and posting informative English descriptions scattered around town. Walk up through the village on the main cobbled lane, peering into ruined stone houses and pondering their potential. If I were an entrepreneurial Istrian restaurateur, I'd set up a fancy truffle restaurant here posthaste. A stroll through here today will have a big payoff a decade from now, after little Završje has been rediscovered and repopulated with artists, hotels, and restaurants—as it surely will. You'll be able to say, "Yeah, I was there back when it was a ghost town."

• *If you want to head directly to Motovun, you can simply proceed on the road past Završje and twist down into the valley. Or, for a more scenic approach, backtrack the way you came for a couple of minutes, turning right to follow signs to* Oprtalj.

ISTRIA

OPRTALJ

Oprtalj (oh-per-TAL; Porotole in Italian) has a particularly scenic approach, along a twisting driveway lined with pointy cypress trees.

But once in the town itself, there's not much to see. Oprtalj lines up along a plateau with a busy road ripping through its middle. Like Motovun, it has a pink loggia across from its main gate, containing an old stone-carved winged lion of St. Mark and other stony fragments from the town's history. If you poke up through the gate and wander the town, you'll find a fairly nondescript, largely deserted burg. Near the gate is the town's *konoba*, with seating under a tree out on the view terrace across the street. The fancy yellow building at the Motovun end of town is the elementary school, named for local hero Milan Šorgo, a Partisan who was killed during the fighting to retake his native Istria from the Nazis.

• *The road through Oprtalj leads directly down into Livade, then across the valley highway to Motovun.*

Istrian Wine Tastings

Istrian wines are beginning to get some attention on the world stage. A few high-class restaurants in New York and London are adding vintages ending in -ić to their wine lists, and German, Austrian, and Italian tourists are starting to discover Istria's wine roads (even if the French remain aloof to them).

A few local wineries have opened classy tasting rooms that invite passing motorists in for a sample. As this is an emerging scene, wine lovers should do their homework before arriving. But if you simply want to splice a few sips into your itinerary, the options below are worth considering. At most places you can drop by for a few free tastes, though they'd like you to buy a bottle or two for your picnic. They understand that it's tough for Americans to carry wine home, so producers that are exporters hope you'll look for their wines back home. It's good form to call ahead and let them know you're coming (hotels can help)—particularly if you want to pay for a more serious visit, with a guided tour of the cellar, and local cheeses and other bites paired with each wine. I've organized the wine-tasting options below by area within Istria.

Near Momjan, just north of the Hill Town Loop: An easy 10-minute detour from my recommended hill-town driving loop is the village of Momjan, which is surrounded by some of the

most striking vineyards I've seen here. While humble Momjan itself doesn't have much to see, it's flanked by two well-regarded wineries with state-of-the-art tasting facilities. Traditional **Kabola,** near the village of Kremenje (just toward Buje from Momjan), owns the most striking setting, with a cypress-lined driveway leading to a cluster of picture-perfect stone buildings overlooking gorgeous vineyard tableaus that feel like Provence. Kabola produces a wide variety of whites, including several made from malvazija, pisak (pinot grigio), and muscat. They also have a full palette of reds—100 percent teran and teran blends with cabernet sauvignon and merlot. (They also make a 100 percent cabernet sauvignon that's very nice.) Try the rosé that blends teran and muscat (free tastings, drop-ins welcome, 60-100-kn bottles, summer daily 10:00-18:00, off-season Mon-Sat 10:00-16:00, closed Sun, Kanedolo 90, tel. 052/779-208, www.kabola.hr). **Kozlović** has a sophisticated, super-modern tasting facility, dramatically perched on a hill overlooking the valley behind Momjan.

Arguably Istria's most well-regarded winery, most of their wines are whites (about 85 percent, including lots of *malvazija* and some muscat). They also make exquisite reds (*teran* and blends that knocked my socks off). The staff is more formal, and you must call ahead to make an appointment—tastings are all prearranged to match with light foods (75 kn for a one-hour tasting of three wines, more elaborate options available—see details on their website; Mon-Sat 10:00-19:00, closed Sun, Vale 78, tel. 052/779-177, mobile 099-277-9177, www.kozlovic.hr).

Near Motovun: The hillsides below Motovun are draped in enticing vineyards and fine views back to Motovun. While none of these is as slick, professional, or well-regarded as the ones near Momjan listed above, some of them do welcome travelers for a sample. As these are hardworking facilities, they offer a more intimate and personal experience. From Motovun, head south (turning left as you come down from the hill) along the humble street at the very bottom of town, then watch for the turn-off on the right just past the gas station. Wineries are well-signposted from here, all within a few minutes' drive. My favorite is **Tomaz**, where Klaudio, Pilato, and Danijela Tomaz produce *malvazija*, *teran*, muscat, and a rosé made with *teran* grapes. They offer samples in a cozy setting (best to call ahead, free tasting, 60-130-kn bottles, Kanal 36, tel. 052/681-717, mobile 098-335-769, www.vina-tomaz.hr).

Between Rovinj and Poreč: Just a minute's drive off the Limski Canal (described on page 125), in the village of Krunčići, Ivica **Matošević** turns out well-respected wines and offers tastings in a humble space without pretense (it's a working facility rather than a snazzy showroom). Its proximity to Rovinj makes it an easy choice if you want a winery visit without scouring the back lanes. Matošević corks up mostly whites, with several varieties of *malvazija* (which they call Alba—Italian for "dawn"), as well as a red blend of *teran* and merlot called Grimalda (after the place where the grapes are grown). They offer free tastings (and sell 60-115-kn bottles), or you can pay for a cellar tour and a more elaborate tasting paired with local snacks (150 kn for a group of up to 5 people); in either case, call ahead (June-mid-Sept Mon-Fri 9:00-19:00, Sat-Sun 10:00-18:00; mid-Sept-May Mon-Sat 9:00-16:00, closed Sun; Krunčići 2, tel. 052/448-558, mobile 098-367-339, www.matosevic.com). From Rovinj, head up to the Limski Canal (following signs for *Poreč*, but without getting on the highway). After driving along the rim of the canal, then heading inland, watch for the turn-off on the right for *Krunčići* and *Matošević*.

ISTRIA

LIVADE

The flat little crossroads village of Livade, sitting in the valley facing the back of Motovun's hill, is home to the first and last name in Istrian truffles. In 1999, Giancarlo Zigante unearthed the biggest white truffle the world had ever seen—2.9 pounds, as verified by *The Guinness Book of World Records.* (In 2007, the record was broken by a 3.3-pound Tuscan truffle.) Zigante's hunk of fungus—now revered as though it was a religious relic—kicked off a truffle craze that continues in Istria today (see sidebar on page 150). Today Zigante has a virtual monopoly on Istria's truffle industry, producing a wide range of truffle goodies. If you're a connoisseur, or just curious, make a pilgrimage to this truffle mecca. The valley is enlivened by Livade's White Truffle Days, which take place on weekends from late September through early November; white tents are filled with local producers showing off their truffles, wines, olive oils, and more. While here, you can also drop into Livade's little museum about La Parenzana, the railway that once linked these hill towns.

Eating in Livade: Zigante's large facility here is divided into two parts: The **Zigante Tartufi shop** offers shelves upon shelves of both fresh and packaged truffle products (plus local wines, olive oils, brandies, and more). There's also a little tasting table where you can sample the earthy goods, and a brain-sized replica of that famously massive chunk of white truffle (daily 9:00-21:00, off-season 10:00-20:00, Livade 7, tel. 052/664-030, www.zigantetartufi.com). The adjacent **Restaurant Zigante,** one of Istria's fanciest, dishes up all manner of truffle specialties. The decor—inside, or out on the terrace—is white-tablecloth classy, the service is deliberate but friendly, and the truffles, as if on a cooking game show, are prepared in a dizzying variety of ways. If you want the full dose of this local delicacy from a place that knows its truffles, this is a worthwhile splurge (190-300-kn main courses, 400-600-kn fixed-price meals—even more during white truffle season, daily 12:00-23:00, until 22:00 in winter, Livade 7, tel. 052/664-302).

Eating near Livade, in Gradinje: A five-minute drive east of Livade, in the hamlet of Gradinje, is a rustic, unpretentious eatery serving up the most affordable truffle dishes around. **Konoba Dolina** ("Valley Inn") has a nondescript interior and a pleasant terrace out front. Because it's just beyond the tourist trail, the prices are reasonable and the ambience feels authentic (45-95-kn meals, truffle splurges up to 120 kn, Wed-Mon 12:00-21:00, closed Tue, tel. 052/664-091). First make your way to Gradinje (go into Livade and turn right at the main roundabout, then drive through the countryside for a few minutes). Once in Gradinje, go all the way through town, then look for signs on the left.

• **Motovun** *hovers on the hill just across the valley from Livade (described earlier in this chapter).*

Once you've seen this area, if you have more time and interest, you can carry on another 40 minutes to reach Hum (follow the main valley road east to Buzet, then to Roč, then look for the turn-off on the right to Hum, along the Glagolitic Lane). Most people won't find the Hum detour worth the miles, but it works great if you're headed east anyway (such as to Opatija or Rijeka).

HUM

According to its marketing plan, Hum (pronounced "hoom," Colmo in Italian) is the "smallest town in the world." Despite its

 tiny population of 16 people, Hum has a Town Hall, church, school, post office, and all the other trappings of a "town." Smart gimmick. Unfortunately, Hum is also, per capita, the most touristy town in the world—crammed with visitors who come to stroll through its streets, drop some kunas in its souvenir shops, or dine at its lone

restaurant, **Humska Konoba,** with fine outdoor terrace seating (tel. 052/660-005). But despite its quirks and its one-trick commercialism, Hum is engaging. At the far corner of Istria—just up the road from Mount Učka, which forms the natural boundary with the neighboring Kvarner Gulf—Hum feels incredibly remote, rugged, and (if you don't run into any tour buses) forgotten by modern times.

Getting There: From Motovun, follow the Mirna Valley road east. After you go through Buzet, you'll pass under the village of Roč; watch for the turnoff to Hum on the right. From here, you'll follow the Glagolitic Lane (described next) through the wilderness to Hum.

Nearby: The road between Hum and the Mirna Valley—called the **Glagolitic Lane** (Aleja Glagoljaša)—commemorates a ninth-century alphabet once used for written Croatian. Driving here, watch for giant Glagolitic characters and a sort of "Rosetta Stone" on top of a hill comparing the Glagolitic, Cyrillic, and Roman alphabets. While Glagolitic was abandoned centuries ago in most of Croatia, the area around Hum used it well into modern times. And since the rise of Croatian nationalism during the Yugoslav Wars, the Glagolitic alphabet has been in vogue—schoolchildren even have Glagolitic poetry contests and spelling bees.

• *From Hum, you're very close to the northeast branch of the* ipsilon *highway (A-8). You can take this either west to Rovinj (via Pazin), or east to the Učka Tunnel, Opatija, and Rijeka.*

ISTRIA

Near Istria

The towering Mount Učka separates Istria from the rest of Croatia. And just on the other side of that mountain are a pair of former Habsburg towns that offer a dose of variety (and a convenient pit stop on the way to other Croatian towns). Shot through with the faded elegance of an upper-crust history, **Opatija** is a welcome change of pace from the salty towns along the rest of the Croatian coast. Its elegant Viennese-style cafés delight coffee-sippers, its parks tickle gardeners, and its beaches lure sunbathers. Nearby, the big industrial port city of **Rijeka** is an important transit hub; if you wind up changing buses or boats here, consider a quick stroll through its run-down but gentrifying urban core.

Opatija

Opatija (oh-PAH-tee-yah) is not your typical Croatian beach town. In the late 19th-century golden age of the Austro-Hungarian Empire, this unassuming village was transformed into the Eastern Riviera—one of the swankiest resorts on the Mediterranean. While the French, British, and German aristocracy sunbathed on France's Côte d'Azur, the wealthy elite from the eastern half of Europe—the Habsburg Empire, Scandinavia, and Russia—partied in Opatija. Baroque, Neoclassical, and Art Nouveau villas popped up along its coastline as it became *the* sunny aristocratic playground.

Though the Habsburgs are long gone, Opatija retains the trappings of its genteel past. Most of Croatia evokes the time-passed Mediterranean, but Opatija whispers "belle époque." It may be the classiest resort town in Croatia, with more taste and less fixation on postcards and seashells. Most people don't come to Croatia for this chic scene. But if rustic seaside villages are wearing on you, cosmopolitan Opatija—which hosts equal numbers of tourists and convention-going businesspeople—is a pleasant return to high-class civilization.

The town is also strikingly situated: tucked beneath thickly forested mountains, with a view across the bay of Rijeka's sprawl. Thanks to its sheltered location nestled under towering peaks, Opatija is protected from the Bora wind, enjoying instead a light, refreshing breeze. This gives Opatija a particularly mild and enjoyable climate—the perfect match for its refined ambience.

Orientation to Opatija

Opatija is basically a one-street town: Ulica Maršala Tita, lined on both sides by stately hotels, follows the seafront. The town's focal point is its beach area, called Slatina. You can walk from one end of the tourist zone to the other in about 20 minutes. (For a handy loop, walk along the bustling main street in one direction, then back along the waterfront promenade—or vice versa.)

TOURIST INFORMATION

Opatija's TI, across from the big Hotel Milenij, is a short walk up ulica Maršala Tita from Slatina (mid-July-Aug daily 8:00-21:00, progressively shorter hours off-season until Nov-Easter Mon-Sat 8:00-17:00, closed Sun; from Slatina, just head a block toward Rijeka and look on the left side of road, Maršala Tita 128; tel. 051/271-310, www.opatija-tourism.hr).

ARRIVAL IN OPATIJA

Driving in from either Istria or Rijeka, just follow *Opatija* and bull's-eye signs and switchback down, down, down to the water. There's a parking lot at Slatina (the bus-station zone above the main beach), another one behind Hotel Imperial, and ample street parking; all of it costs the same (12 kn/hour). Tow trucks are at the ready for drivers looking for a free ride at the meters. The TI can change bills to coins for meters.

Sights in Opatija

Begin at Opatija's centerpiece, the waterfront beach-and-park area called **Slatina,** with sweeping sea views, a marbled Croatian "Walk of Fame" (with one or two names you might recognize), and a sea-water swimming pool. From here, Opatija lines up along its main drag, **ulica Maršala Tita,** still fronted by ornate villas that would seem more at home in Vienna than they do in Croatia. Tourists stroll here hand-in-hand, taking in the views, dipping into high-class boutiques, and snapping photos of the fancy facades as they go. Joining them, you, too, may soon find yourself thinking of this place as the "Monte Carlo of Croatia."

A few steps toward the sea, stretching in either direction along the waterfront, is a scenic promenade called the **Lungomare.** This is another wonderful spot for rocky seafront strolling, and it offers striking views across the bay to

Rijeka (which looks much better from afar). Partway along the Lungomare is one of Opatija's trademarks: a **statue** of a woman surrounded by seagulls, called *Greetings to the Sea*. Much as I'd like to relay some romantic legend behind this evocative monument, the truth is that there's no story behind it—like Opatija itself, it's just pretty to look at. Farther along, you'll pass the **Juraj Šporer Art Pavilion,** which generally hosts free art installations.

As for sightseeing...well, Opatija is not that kind of place. But if the spirit moves you, a 10-kn ticket allows entry to the three places described below (all open daily June-Sept 10:00-22:00, Oct-May until 18:00). Drop into the *opatija* (abbey) that gave the town its name, the **Abbey of St. James** (Opatija Sv. Jakov, right along the Lungomare below the TI). On the dome above the altar is a strangely eerie relief showing

St. James standing in a boat, cradling this church in his arm, accompanied by his trademark gourd-on-a-stick, and flanked by palm trees.

Beyond the abbey, the Lungomare cuts through one of Opatija's many manicured parks—the large Angiolina Park—and hits the harbor. Near where you enter the park, look for **Villa Angiolina,** a recently restored mansion with a gorgeous lobby (free to view) and intriguing exhibits upstairs about the history of tourism in Croatia. Just uphill through the same garden is **Swiss House,** with a permanent exhibit about the history of Opatija as a tourist destination. Downhill (toward the water) from both of these, you'll find an outdoor theater that shows movies or concerts nightly in peak season.

Sleeping in Opatija

Opatija is chock-a-block full of swanky resort-slash-business hotels. While prices are high, you get a lot of luxury for your money (unlike hotels in most small coastal villages). The busiest—and most expensive—times are August (tourists) and September through late October (conventions).

$$$ Big and Fancy Chain Hotels: These have the most striking Habsburg facades in town, and both have luxurious rooms with all the amenities: **Hotel Bristol,** part of the Vienna International chain, has 78 rooms. It's gone to great pains to maintain its late 19th-century decor inside and out—mixing modern comfort with period moldings, chandeliers, and a cheery yellow facade (Sb-€132/€110/€95, Db-€163/€130/€113, bigger "deluxe" rooms for

€10 more, last-minute deals possible, gorgeously restored coffee shop in lobby, parking-€12, Maršala Tita 108, tel. 051/706-300, www.hotel-bristol.hr, info@hotel-bristol.hr). **Hotel Agava,** part of the Milenij chain, also has an impressively restored old shell with a handsome lobby and café, but its 76 rooms feel more business-like and contemporary (Sb-€100/€90/€80, Db-€165/€145/€120, sea view-€10 extra, parking garage-€13, Maršala Tita 89, tel. 051/278-200, www.milenijhoteli.hr, info@milenijhoteli.hr).

$$$ *Smaller and Family-Run:* These two small hotels, run by the Brko family, are well-located a few steps from the lively Slatina scene (to the right as you face the water; both have air-con, elevators, and a parking garage for €11). **Hotel Galeb,** with 25 comfortable rooms and three stars, has character but feels overpriced. Guests at the Galeb have access to the pool and beach at the Savoy, described next (Sb-€100/€79/€71, Db-€136/€106/€95, €10 more for "superior" room with sea view and balcony, 10 percent less if you pay cash, pricier suites also available, Maršala Tita 160, tel. 051/271-177, www.hotel-galeb.hr, info@hotel-galeb.hr). **Hotel Savoy,** across the street, comes with four stars, more class, 32 nicely appointed rooms, an enticing swimming pool with a great view, a private beach, and higher prices. Request the type of room you want when you reserve: Most rooms have balconies and sea views for no extra charge, but many of these face a noisy nightclub; for more quiet, you can request a back (nonview) room facing the street (Db-€148/€108, Maršala Tita 129, tel. 051/710-500, www.hotel-savoy.hr, info@hotel-savoy.hr).

Eating in Opatija

For a good, unpretentious sit-down meal, consider one of the following options. Several hotel lobbies also have refined Vienna-style coffee houses with late 19th-century appeal.

Ružmarin, tucked in a residential zone just behind and above a row of big hotels, is a sane oasis with an inviting covered terrace, a modern dining room, and good pizzas, pastas, and other dishes (35-70-kn pizzas, 55-85-kn pastas, 60-160-kn main courses, daily 10:00-24:00, up the road behind Grand Hotel Palace at Veprinački put 2, tel. 051/712-673).

Roko has two popular places side-by-side along the busy main drag. I prefer the cozy stone-and-brick interior at #114, with a small terrace, and a busy wood-fired oven turning out tasty Italian meals. If you find this place calming, it may be because it was the home of Opatija native Leo Henryk Sternbach, who invented Valium (50-90-kn pizzas and pastas, 75-150-kn main courses, daily 11:00-24:00, Maršala Tita 112/114, tel. 051/711-500).

Picnic: To browse for your own picnic, drop by the old-fash-

The Bora
Or, How to Predict Croatian Coastal Weather

When asked what tomorrow's weather will bring, a salty Croatian fisherman looks to the mountains and feels the stiff wind on his face. "Sun," he says. "The Bora brings good weather."

Like any people whose fate is tied to the sea, coastal Croatians can extrapolate a breeze or a front of clouds into a full-blown weather report. While this is a precise art cultivated over a lifetime, even the casual tourist can learn a few tricks from the natives.

Croatian coastal weather is shaped by a mighty wind called the Bora (named for the Greek Boreas, the North Wind; sometimes called "Bura" in Croatian, or "Burja" in Slovene). Much like France's infamous mistral wind, the Bora has an indelible impact on this region's weather, vegetation, architecture, and tourism.

The Dinaric Mountains, which rise sharply up from the sea along the Croatian Coast, act as a barrier for cold, cloudy weather. As the air on the coastal side of the mountains heats up, the air behind the snow-capped peaks stays cool. To equalize the temperature and pressure differential, the cool air begins to move toward the warm air, creating a white fringe of clouds along the ridge of the mountains—a sure sign that the Bora is about to blow. When all that pent-up air finally escapes, the Bora comes screaming down the slopes to the sea.

The Bora's power is at its peak along the Kvarner Gulf—especially where a gap in the mountains provides a natural funnel toward the sea (such as at Senj and at Karlobag). Farther south, such as in Dalmatia, the inland remains warmer and the Bora is milder (but still strong—Bora winds blowing through the "funnel" near Dubrovnik's airport occasionally force incoming flights to divert to Split).

The Bora is not constant—it's strongest at midday and made

ioned indoor market hall (*tržnica*, on the left a 10-minute walk up Maršala Tita from Slatina).

Opatija Connections

Intercity buses leave Opatija from the big Slatina square, just above the beach (next to Grand Hotel Palace); before boarding, buy tickets at the Autotrans office just up the steep road out of town.

From Opatija by Bus to: Rijeka (2/hour, 30 minutes), **Pula** (12-14/day, 2 hours), **Rovinj** (3/day, 3 hours), **Zagreb** (7/day, 3 hours), **Split** (3/day in summer, fewer on weekends and off-season, 8 hours), and **Dubrovnik** (1/night, departs around 22:00, 12 hours). Info: Mobile 060-306-010, www.autobusni-kolodvor.com.

up of intermittent, fierce gusts that can reach 150 miles per hour. Young children have been known to "fly" through the air for short distances because of the Bora. The Kvarner coastal road is closed several times each year to trucks, buses, and other high-profile vehicles, which can be tipped over by the gusts. The Bora can also wreak havoc on car ferries. After a day or two of a stiff winter Bora, everything is coated with a thin layer of salt, like ash after a volcano.

The good news: As the Bora rushes toward the coast, it sweeps bad-weather clouds away with it—leaving in its wake clear, cooler air and sunshine.

In summer, the much milder version of this wind—which usually bathes the coast in a refreshing breeze each evening, when the interior cools faster than the sea—is called a Maestral. Sporadic mini-Bora gusts at night are known as Burin.

The Bora's unpopular cousin is the wind called Jugo (YOO-goh, meaning "south"). The Jugo originates as a moist air mass gathering over the Adriatic, which creates a low-pressure vortex. Finally it blows northward toward Croatia, bringing with it hot, humid, and stormy weather. Because humid conditions foster disease, an ancient superstition considers the Jugo wind evil, and the refreshing Bora wind good. The Bora and the Jugo are the yin and yang of Croatian winds, blowing in opposite directions and with opposite effects.

Of course, the weather here is anything but predictable. Croatia's coast is made up of a series of microclimates. Each island has its own very specific weather conditions, which is why one island may excel at growing olives, the next one lavender, the next red wine grapes, and the next white wine grapes. If you really want to know what sort of weather is on the way, ask a local.

Rijeka

The industrial city of Rijeka (ree-YAY-kah; it translates as "River") became Croatia's biggest port under Austro-Hungarian rule. It's dainty little Opatija's bigger, burlier brother, with a population of 129,000. Like Opatija, much of Rijeka's architecture is reminiscent of the glory days of the Habsburgs. But unlike Opatija, most of Rijeka's buildings haven't been renovated, giving it a seedy, gritty, past-its-prime feel. Since it's a major transportation hub, there's a good chance you'll pass through. Here are the basics.

The bus station, train station, and ferry terminal are within a few blocks of each other in a bustling waterfront business zone. The sector is crossed by two one-way streets (going in opposite directions): Ivana Zajca (or the "Riva," along the waterfront, runs west to east) and Adamićeva (which changes its name a few times as it cuts east to west through town).

A block above these two streets is the **Korzo,** an almost-charming pedestrianized zone packed with shops, restaurants, and the **TI** (Korzo 14, tel. 051/335-882, www.tz-rijeka.hr).

The **train station** is a few blocks west of the Korzo. On arrival, exit the station to the right and walk 10 minutes to the water. You'll first come to the bus station, then the ferry terminal. The Korzo is just above them.

The **bus station** is a big parking lot in the middle of the chaos, near the west end of the Korzo. You'll see the big boats along the waterfront as you exit your bus. To get to the train station, face the water and turn right, following the busy street about 10 minutes.

The **ferry terminal** is at the east end of the waterfront. The Jadrolinija ticket office is in the building with the big *Jadrolinija* sign (at Riva 16, second building east of bus station, ticket office at far right end of building as you face it).

Rijeka's downtown **car-rental** offices—including **Avis** (tel. 051/311-135), **Hertz** (tel. 051/311-098), and **Thrifty** (tel. 051/325-900)—tend to move around, so be sure to call first to ask for the location. Additional car-rental offices are at the airport.

Rijeka Connections

From Rijeka by Train to: Zagreb (3/day direct, 4-5 hours), **Ljubljana** (2/day direct, 3 hours).

From Rijeka by Bus to: Opatija (2/hour, 30 minutes), **Senj** (hourly, 1.5 hours), **Pula** (nearly hourly, 2-2.5 hours), **Rovinj** (10/day, 2-3.5 hours), **Zagreb** (hourly, 2-3.5 hours), **Split** (7-10/day, 7 hours), **Dubrovnik** (4/day, 12.5-13 hours, includes night buses), **Ljubljana** (1/day in summer, none off-season, 2.5 hours). For schedules, see www.autotrans.hr or call 051/213-821.

ROUTE TIPS FOR DRIVERS: DRIVING BETWEEN NORTHERN CROATIA AND DALMATIA

The long stretch of Croatian coast from Istria to Dalmatia—between the cities of Rijeka and Zadar—offers twisty seaside roads, functional port towns and fishing villages, some of the country's most rugged scenery, and no real knockout sights. South of Opatija and Rijeka, the Kvarner coastline is stark and desolate—most traces of settlement have been long since blown away by the battering Bora wind (see sidebar on page 164). Offshore, sheltered from the elements, are several islands—Krk, Cres, Lošinj, Rab, and Pag—each with its own character and appeal. Still, Croatia offers more bang for your buck to the north (Istria) and the south (Dalmatia).

If you're driving between northern Croatia (Zagreb, Plitvice, Istria, or Opatija) and the Dalmatian Coast (Zadar, from where the expressway zips to Split), you have two options: Use the fast inland A-1 expressway, or follow the slow Kvarner Gulf coastal road all the way down.

The **A-1 expressway** option is boring but faster and far more efficient, especially from Zagreb or Plitvice. If you're coming from Zagreb, just take A-1 directly to Split; from Plitvice, drive south through Korenica to access A-1 at Gornja Ploča (see page 92). From Istria or Opatija, you have two options for accessing A-1 that take about the same amount of time: Head east (inland) from Rijeka on A-6 to join A-1; or, more interesting (and better for southern destinations), drive the Kvarner coastal road as far south as Senj, then cut inland and up over the mountains to Otočac, where you can get on A-1.

The two-lane **Kvarner coastal road** (national road #8, a.k.a. E-65) is twisty and slow, but more scenic. Speedy sightseers won't find it worth the time. Compared to the expressway, you'll lose at least an hour if you're coming from Istria or Opatija, and much more if you're starting in Zagreb or Plitvice. Along this road, you'll enjoy good but not spectacular views—similar to what you'll see in Dalmatia, but less developed. To find this road from Rijeka, just follow signs for *Split* and *Zadar* (being careful not to get on the expressway).

It's striking how desolate it feels as you drive along the Kvarner coastal road. The most appealing spot for a break is **Senj** (pronounced "sehn"—the j is mostly silent, but has a slight *y* sound). Senj has a little harbor and a modest square with a jumble of outdoor cafés. The town is watched over by the boxy fortress of a band of pirates called the Uskoks. These were Serb and Croat refugees forced out of their homes in the interior when the Ottomans invaded in the 16th century. After resettling here in Senj, they became pirates and began terrorizing the Adriatic coastline. While they claimed to target only Ottoman ships, they also harassed anyone who traded with the Ottomans—including the Venetians. Finally the Austrians—bowed by political pressure from Venice—put down the Uskoks. Today Senj is the best jolt of civilization along this road, with busloads of tour groups constantly dropping off here for a coffee-and-WC break. This means that the natives of

ISTRIA

Senj—perhaps harkening back to their pirate ancestors—are adept at overcharging and shortchanging visitors. Check your bill carefully against the posted menu prices.

Senj is also the easiest point where the Kvarner coastal road connects to the speedy A-1 expressway that runs parallel to the coast inland. From Senj, a well-traveled road cuts away from the coast and soon begins twisting up the coastal mountain range. After about an hour, you'll arrive at the A-1 expressway, followed by the war-scarred town of **Otočac**. (For more on Otočac, see page 92.)

ISTRIA

SPLIT

Dubrovnik is the darling of the Dalmatian Coast, but Split (pronounced as it's spelled) is Croatia's second city, bustling with 178,000 people. If you've been hopping along the coast, landing in urban Split feels like a return to civilization. While most Dalmatian coastal towns seem made for tourists, Split is real and vibrant—a shipbuilding city with ugly sprawl surrounding an atmospheric Old Town, which teems with Croatians living life to the fullest.

Though today's Split throbs to a modern, youthful beat, its history goes way back—all the way to the Roman Empire. Along with all the trappings of a modern city, Split has some of the best Roman ruins this side of Italy. In the fourth century A.D., the Roman Emperor Diocletian (245-313) wanted to retire in his native Dalmatia, so he built a huge palace here. Eventually, the palace was abandoned. Then locals, fleeing seventh-century Slavic invaders, moved in and made themselves at home, and a medieval town sprouted from the rubble of the old palace. In the 15th century, the Venetians took over the Dalmatian Coast. They developed and fortified Split, slathering the city with a new layer of Gothic-Renaissance architecture.

But even as Split grew, the nucleus remained the ruins of Diocletian's Palace. To this day, 2,000 people live or work inside the former palace walls. A maze of narrow alleys is home to fashionable boutiques

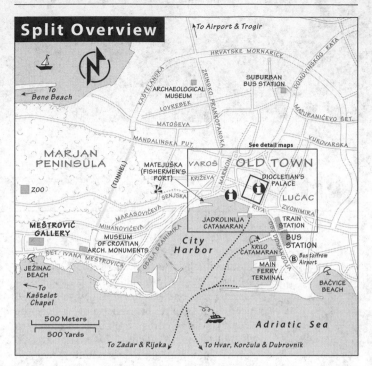

Split Overview

To Airport & Trogir

HRVATSKE MORNARICE

To Bene Beach

KAŠTELANSKA
LOVREBEK
MATOŠEVA
MANDALINSKA PUT

ARCHAEOLOGICAL MUSEUM
ZRINSKO FRANKOPANSKA

SUBURBAN BUS STATION
DOMOVINSKOG RATA
MAŽURANIĆEVO ŠET.
VUKOVARSKA

See detail maps

MARJAN PENINSULA

(TUNNEL)

ZOO

MATEJUŠKA (FISHERMEN'S PORT)
KRIŽEVA
SENJSKA

VAROŠ
MARMON

OLD TOWN

DIOCLETIAN'S PALACE
LUČAC
ZVONIMIRA

RIVA

MARASOVIĆEVA

MEŠTROVIĆ GALLERY

MIHANOVIĆEVA

MUSEUM OF CROATIAN ARCH. MONUMENTS

OPAT BRANIMIRA

City Harbor

JADROLINIJA CATAMARAN

TRAIN STATION

ŠET. IVANA MEŠTROVIĆA

JEŽINAC BEACH

To Kaštelet Chapel

KRILO CATAMARAN
DUJMANOVIĆA

BUS STATION

Bus to/from Airport

MAIN FERRY TERMINAL

BAČVICE BEACH

500 Meters
500 Yards

Adriatic Sea

To Zadar & Rijeka

To Hvar, Korčula & Dubrovnik

and galleries, wonderfully atmospheric cafés, and Roman artifacts around every corner.

Today's Split has a split personality, as it struggles to decide how it fits into Croatia's tourist-mecca image: Is it a no-nonsense, metropolitan transit point; an impressive destination in its own right, with sights to rival Dubrovnik's—or both? While largely lacking Dubrovnik's over-the-top romance, Split settles for being nobody's "second-best." It is its own city—the antidote to all that's quaint and cutesy in Dalmatia.

PLANNING YOUR TIME

Split is southern Croatia's hub for bus, boat, train, and flight connections to other destinations in the country and abroad. This means that many visitors stop in Split only long enough to change boats. But the city deserves at least a full day. Begin by strolling Diocletian's Palace, then take a coffee break along the Riva promenade or have lunch in the Old Town. In the afternoon, browse the shops or visit a couple of Split's museums (the Meštrović Gallery, which is a long walk or short bus or taxi ride from the Old Town, is tops). Promenading along the Riva with the natives is *the* evening activity; nursing a drink at an atmospheric open-air café is a close second.

With a second day (or en route to or from northern destinations), you could spend some time in nearby Trogir—an enjoyable Dalmatian seaside village. And if you're connecting to points north on the expressway, you could stop off for a waterfall dip at Krka National Park. (Both are described at the end of this chapter.)

Orientation to Split

Split sprawls, but almost everything of interest to travelers is close to the City Harbor (Gradska Luka, GRAHD-skah LOO-kah).

At the top of this harbor is the Old Town (Stari Grad, STAH-ree grahd). Stretching out between the Old Town and the sea is the Riva, a waterfront pedestrian promenade lined with cafés and shaded by palm trees. The main ferry terminal (Trajektni Terminal) juts into the harbor from the east side. Along the harborfront embankment between the ferry terminal and the Old Town are the long-distance bus station (Autobusni Kolodvor) and the forlorn little train station (Željeznička Stanica). West of the Old Town, poking into the Adriatic, is the lush and hilly Marjan peninsula.

Split's domino-shaped Old Town is made up of two square sections. The east half was once Diocletian's Palace, and the west half is the medieval town that sprang up next door. The shell of Diocletian's ruined palace provides a checkerboard street plan, with a gate at each end. But the streets built since are anything but straight, making the Old Town a delightfully convoluted maze (double-decker in some places). At the center of the former palace is a square called the Peristyle (Peristil), where you'll find the TI, cathedral, and highest concentration of Roman ruins.

TOURIST INFORMATION

Split has two TI locations: One is in the little chapel on the square called the Peristyle, in the very center of Diocletian's Palace; the other is on the Riva at #9, facing the harbor (same hours for both: May-Sept daily 8:00-21:00—longer if there's a cruise ship in town; April and Oct Mon-Sat 8:00-20:00, Sun 8:00-13:00; Nov-March Mon-Fri 9:00-16:00, Sat 9:00-13:00, closed Sun; Peristyle tel. 021/345-606, Riva tel. 021/360-066, www.visitsplit.com). The TIs hand out good town maps, the *Discover Split* newspaper (with an even more detailed map), *Split in Your Pocket* guidebooks and maps, and piles of brochures.

Sightseeing Pass: If you're staying in town at least three

SPLIT

nights, bring your hotel reservation to the TI to claim your **Splitcard,** which covers free admission to several sights (including the City Museum, Ethnographic Museum, and cathedral) and offers a 50 percent discount at other sights (including the Meštrović Gallery, Archaeological Museum, and Gallery of Fine Arts), plus minor discounts at other attractions, shops, car rental agencies, and restaurants around town. If you're staying fewer than three nights, the card is still worth paying for if you're planning to do much sightseeing (35 kn/72 hours, buy one a few doors down from the Riva TI at Turistički Biro, at #12 on the Riva).

ARRIVAL IN SPLIT

By Boat, Bus, or Train: Split's ferry terminal (Trajektni Terminal), main bus station (Autobusni Kolodvor), and train station (Željeznička Stanica) all share a busy and prac-

tical strip of land called Obala Kneza Domagoja, on the east side of the City Harbor. From any of them, you can see the Old Town and Riva; just **walk** 10 minutes toward the big bell tower. You'll pass travel agencies, baggage-storage offices, people trying to rent rooms, a post office, Internet cafés, shops, and cafés.

Boats arrive at various piers. The **Jadrolinija passenger catamaran** to and from Hvar and Korčula usually docks at the Obala Lazareta embankment, right in front of the Old Town. The *Krilo* **passenger catamaran** to those destinations— and, sometimes, the Jadrolinija catamaran as well—uses pier #11, partway along the harbor. Bigger **car ferries** use various docks along the harbor. The main terminal, at the far end, has ATMs, WCs, a grocery store, and the large Jadrolinija ticket and information office, which is open long hours daily and generally has an English-speaking staff.

By Cruise Ship: In recent years—as packed-to-the-gills Dubrovnik has had to turn away cruise ships—Split has become a popular port of call for Mediterranean cruises. Ships either dock along the main harbor in front of the Old Town or anchor in the harbor and send tenders into the harbor (for directions on the short walk to the Old Town, see above).

By Plane: Split's airport (Zračna Luka Split-Kaštela) is across the big bay, 15 miles northwest of the center, near the town of Trogir (airport code: SPU, tel. 021/203-506, www.split-airport.hr). **Buses** operated by two different companies (Croatia Airlines and Promet) connect the airport to the main bus station along Split's harbor (see arrival instructions earlier). Between them, at least one departs every 30 minutes or so, and they cost about the same (35 kn); just take whichever bus is leaving next. A **taxi** costs a hefty 300 kn between the airport and downtown Split.

By Car: For details on arriving in Split by car, driving between northern Croatia and Split, and driving south to the rest of the Dalmatian Coast, see "Route Tips for Drivers," on page 215. Dropping rental cars at the airport rather than downtown is wise, as navigating Split's one-way street grid is challenging.

HELPFUL HINTS

Festivals: For one week in late August, Split celebrates Diocletian Days, when 50 actors from Rome walk the streets in ancient garb. A boat brings "Diocletian" to the Riva, people wearing togas attend dinner in the palace cellars, and the Diocletian Games are staged along the Riva.

Post Office: A modern little post office is next to the bus station (Mon-Fri 7:00-20:00, Sat 7:00-13:00, closed Sun, on Obala Kneza Domagoja).

Luggage Storage: Seemingly custom-made for a quick stopover between Dalmatian destinations, this transit hub has no shortage of luggage-storage options. The train station has lockers, and the adjacent bus station has a left-luggage desk *(garderoba)*. A small luggage-storage kiosk is along the sidewalk between the stations and the Old Town. Just west of the Old Town, Modrulj Launderette (described next) also has a left-luggage service.

Laundry: Modrulj Launderette, a rare self-service launderette, is conveniently located in the Varoš neighborhood at the west end of the Old Town, near several recommended restaurants—handy if multitasking is your style (self-service-50 kn/load, full-service-75 kn/load, air-con, Internet access, left-luggage service; April-Oct daily 8:00-21:00; Nov-March Mon-Sat 9:00-17:00, closed Sun; Šperun 1—see map on page 174, tel. 021/315-888).

Bike Rental: There are plenty of choices for bike rentals in Split. One good—if moderately strenuous—option for a ride is a loop around the nearby Marjan peninsula, with a stop at a beach.

Who's Hajduk?: You'll see the word *Hajduk* (HIGH-dook), and a distinctive red-and-white checkerboard circle design (or red-and-blue stripes), all over town and throughout northern Dalmatia. Hajduk Split is the fervently supported soccer team, named for a band of highwaymen bandits who rebelled against Ottoman rule in the 17th-19th centuries. Most locals adore Hajduk as much as they loathe their bitter rivals, Dinamo Zagreb.

G'day, *Gospod:* You may notice a surprising concentration of Aus-

SPLIT

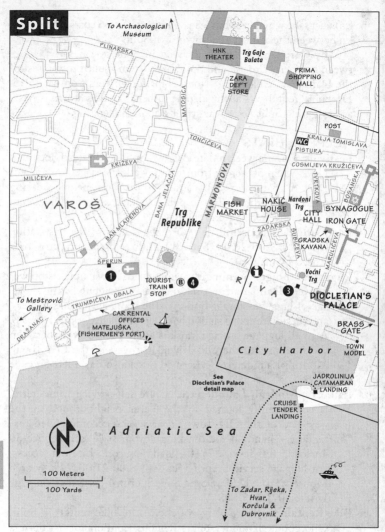

Split

To Archaeological Museum

PLINARSKA

HNK THEATER · Trg Gaje Bulata

PRIMA SHOPPING MALL

ZARA DEP'T STORE

MATOSICA

POST

KRALJA TOMISLAVA

WC PISTURA

COSMIJEVA KRUŽIĆEVA

TONČIĆEVA

IVETKOVA

BOSANSKA

KRIŽEVA

MARMONTOVA

NAKIĆ HOUSE

Nardoni Trg

SYNAGOGUE

MILIČEVA

BANA JELAČIĆA

FISH MARKET

CITY HALL

IRON GATE

VAROŠ

BAN MLADENOVA

Trg Republike

ZADARSKA

SUPILOVA

GRADSKA KAVANA

MARULIĆEVA

ŠPERUN

TOURIST TRAIN STOP

B **4**

R I V A

i

Voćni Trg

3

DIOCLETIAN'S PALACE

To Meštrović Gallery

TRUMBIĆEVA OBALA

CAR RENTAL OFFICES

MATEJUŠKA (FISHERMEN'S PORT)

BRASS GATE

DRAŽANAC

City Harbor

TOWN MODEL

See Diocletian's Palace detail map

JADROLINIJA CATAMARAN LANDING

CRUISE TENDER LANDING

N

Adriatic Sea

100 Meters

100 Yards

To Zadar, Rijeka, Hvar, Korčula & Dubrovnik

SPLIT

tralians in Split. Many of them are actually Australian-born Croats, returning to the cosmopolitan capital city of their parents' Dalmatian homeland.

GETTING AROUND SPLIT

Most of what you'll want to see is within walking distance, but some sights (such as the Meštrović Gallery) are more easily reached by bus or taxi.

By Bus: Local buses, run by Promet, cost 11 kn per ride (or 10 kn if you buy a ticket at a newsstand or Promet kiosk, ask for a *putna karta;* zone I is fine for any ride within Split, but you need

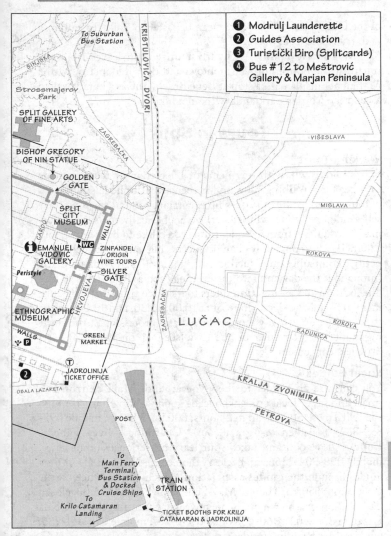

1. Modrulj Launderette
2. Guides Association
3. Turistički Biro (Splitcards)
4. Bus #12 to Meštrović Gallery & Marjan Peninsula

the 21-kn zone IV ticket for the ride to Trogir). For a round-trip within the city, buy a 17-kn transfer ticket, which works like two individual tickets (must buy at kiosk). Validate your ticket in the machine or with the driver as you board the bus. Suburban buses to towns near Split (such as Trogir) generally use the suburban bus station (Prigradski Autobusni Kolodvor), a 10-minute walk due north of the Old Town on Domovinskog rata. Bus information: www.promet-split.hr.

By Taxi: Taxis start at 20 kn, then cost around 8 kn per kilometer. Figure 60 kn for most rides within the city (for example, from the ferry terminal to most hotels)—but if going from one end of the Old Town to the other, it can be faster to walk. To call for a taxi, try Radio Taxi (tel. 021/1777).

By Tourist Train: An hourly tourist train leaves from the square at the bottom of Marmontova and does a loop around the Marjan peninsula with a stop at Bene Beach. This is a handy way to ascend the Marjan parklands without a hike.

Tours in Split

Walking Tours

Split's Old Town, with fragments of Diocletian's Palace, is made to order for a walking tour, and it seems that Split has hundreds of tour guides leading cruise-ship excursions around the town. My self-guided walk (described later) covers basically the same information you'll get from a guide. But if you'd like to hear it live, join a tour. This is a constantly changing scene, but various fiercely competitive companies offer dueling 1.25-hour walks, leaving regularly throughout the day and into the evening (generally around 90 kn). The local **guides association** offers tours three times daily in summer (100 kn, May-Sept Mon-Sat at 10:00, 11:30, and 13:00); while these guides are usually more polished and professional, the starting point—at their office on the Riva (see map on page 174)—is a little less convenient.

Local Guides

You can hire an insider to show you around. **Maja Benzon** is a smart and savvy local guide who leads good walking tours through the Old Town (500 kn/up to 2 hours, 600 kn/3 hours, mobile 098-852-869, maja.benzon@gmail.com). Charming **Nives Fabečić Bojić** is also good and takes your learning seriously (same rates, mobile 098-904-3366, nfabecic@yahoo.com). You can also hire a guide through the **guides association,** which has an office on the Riva (about 550 kn/2 hours, May-Sept Mon-Fri 9:00-15:00, closed Sat-Sun, off-season generally open weekday mornings only, Obala Lazareta 3, tel. 021/360-058 or 021/346-267, mobile 098-361-936, www.guides.hr, info@guides.hr).

EXCURSIONS FROM SPLIT

A staggering variety of pop-up travel agencies sell tickets for bus or boat **excursions** to nearby destinations. There's no shortage of enticing side-trips: the town of Trogir; the Roman ruins of Solin (ancient Salona); whitewater rafting on the Cetina River; the islands of Brač, Hvar, and Šolta (either separately or together; the "Blue Cave" on Vis is another favorite); the pilgrimage site at Međugorje; Dubrovnik; and the waterfalls at Krka National Park or Plitvice Lakes National Park. New companies come and go every year; read online reviews and comparison-shop for a tour that suits your interests.

Various **tour boats** line up along the Riva each morning and evening, hawking trips to nearby islands. Popular itineraries include a combination cruise to Hvar and the "Green Cave" and "Blue Cave" on Vis, all in one day. Aside from the standard side-trips, there are a few more interesting or adventurous alternatives. For example, the **Summer Blues** catamaran does party-oriented "sail 'n swim" cruises with swimming stops, dancing, food, and lots of drinks (www.summer-blues. com). Various companies also offer **kayaking tours** from Split.

If you'd like a **wine-tasting tour**, consider **Zinfandel Origin Wine Tours** (named for the historical link between the local *plavac mali* grape and zinfandel). They offer relaxed, small-group wine excursions into the area around Split that weave some history with sampling wine (includes visits to three wineries, appetizers, and two minor museums; €80/person, 4/week at 16:00 or 17:00, 4-5 hours, office at Papalićeva 2, tel. 02/134-5244, www. zinfandelorigin.com, zinorigin@opcijatours.hr).

Split Walk

▲▲▲DIOCLETIAN'S PALACE (DIOKLECIJANOVA PALAČA)

Split's top activity is visiting the remains of Roman Emperor Diocletian's enormous retirement palace, which sits on the harbor in the heart of the city. This monstrous complex was two impressive structures in one: luxurious villa and fortified Roman town. My self-guided walk takes you through Diocletian's back door; down into the labyrinth of cellars that supported the palace; up to the Peristyle (the center of the palace); into Diocletian's mausoleum—now the town's cathedral, with a crypt, treasury/museum, and climbable tower; over to Jupiter's Temple (later converted into a baptistery); down the main artery of the palace; and finally to what was once the palace's front entrance. The ruins themselves are now integrated with the city's street plan, so exploring them is free—except for the cellars and the cathedral sights/temple, which you'll pay to enter. In peak season, the cellars are open until 21:00, and the cathedral sights generally close at 19:00. If visiting off-season, do this walk as early as possible, because the cathedral sights close at noon. For exact hours, see the individual sight listings.

Fragments of the palace are poorly marked, and there are no good guidebooks or audioguides for understanding the remains. For most visitors, this walk provides enough details; for more in-depth information, you could join a walking tour or hire a guide (see "Tours in Split," earlier).

Background

Diocletian grew up just inland from Split, in the town of Salona (Solin in Croatian), which was then the capital of the Roman province of Dalmatia. He worked his way up

the Roman hierarchy and ruled as emperor for the unusually long tenure of 20 years (A.D. 284-305). Despite all of his achievements, Diocletian is best remembered for two questionable legacies: dividing the huge empire among four emperors (which helped administer it more efficiently, but began a splintering effect that arguably led to the empire's decline); and torturing and executing Christians, including thousands right here on the Dalmatian Coast. Diocletian's successor, Constantine, not only legalized Christianity, but made it the official religion of the empire—effectively making Diocletian's purges some of the last in Roman history.

Diocletian decided to return to his homeland for retirement. Since he was in poor health, the medicinal sulfur spring here was another plus. His massive palace took only 11 years to build—and this fast pace required a big push (more than 2,000 slaves died during construction). Huge sections of his palace still exist, modified by medieval and modern developers alike.

• *Start in front of the palace, at the east end of the Riva. Cross the street toward the harbor and find the big illustration to get a sense of the original palace. Nearby, notice the car-size model of today's Old Town, which is helpful for orientation. Now study the...*

Palace Facade

The "front" of today's Split—facing the harbor—was actually the back door of Diocletian's Palace. There was no embankment in front of the palace back then, so the water came right up to this door—sort of an emergency exit by boat. Looking out to the water, appreciate the palace's strategic location: It's easy to fortify, and to spot enemies approaching either by land or by sea.

Visually trace the outline of the gigantic palace, which was more than 600 feet long on each side. On the corner to the right stands a stumpy, rectangular guard tower (one of the original 16). To the left, the tower is gone and the corner is harder to pick out (look for the beginning of the newer-looking buildings). Mentally erase the ramshackle two-story buildings added 200 years ago, which obscure the grandeur of the palace wall.

Halfway up the facade, notice the row of 42 arched window

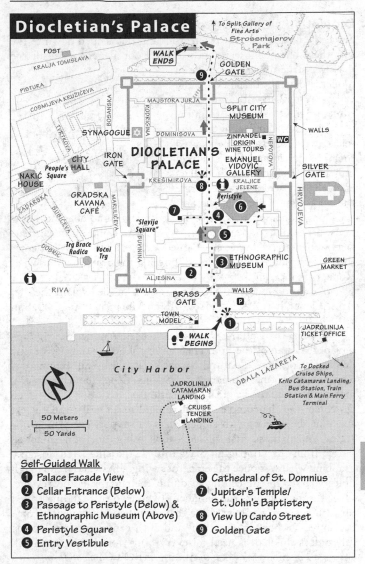

Self-Guided Walk

1. Palace Facade View
2. Cellar Entrance (Below)
3. Passage to Peristyle (Below) & Ethnographic Museum (Above)
4. Peristyle Square
5. Entry Vestibule
6. Cathedral of St. Domnius
7. Jupiter's Temple/ St. John's Baptistery
8. View Up Cardo Street
9. Golden Gate

frames (mostly filled in today). Diocletian and his family lived in the seaside half of the palace. Imagine him strolling back and forth along this fine arcade, enjoying the views of his Adriatic homeland. The inland, nonview half of the palace was home to 700 servants, bodyguards, and soldiers.

• Go through the door in the middle of the palace (known as the "Brass Gate," located under The Substructure of Diocletian's Palace banner). Just inside the door and to the left is the entrance to...

Diocletian's Cellars (Podrumi)

Since the palace was constructed on land that sloped down to the sea, these chambers were built to level out a foundation for the massive structure above (like a modern "daylight basement"). The cellars were filled with water from three different sources: a freshwater spring, a sulfur spring, and the sea. Later, medieval residents used them as a dump. Rediscovered only in the last century, the cellars enabled archaeologists to derive the floor plan of some of the palace's long-gone upper sections. These underground chambers now house art exhibits and a little strip of souvenir stands. One particularly well-preserved stretch—immediately to the left as you enter the long corridor—can be toured, offering the best look in town at Roman engineering.

Cost and Hours: 40 kn, some posters inside explain the site; April-Oct daily 8:30-21:00; Nov-March Mon-Sat 9:00-18:00, Sun 9:00-14:00.

Visiting the Cellars: Near the ticket seller, notice the big **topographical map** of the Split area, clearly showing the city's easily defensible location: a natural harbor sheltered by tall mountains. You'll see the former Roman city of Salona, Diocletian's birthplace, just inland (read the English explanation).

Step into the complex's vast, vaulted **main hall**—the biggest space in the cellars, with stout pillars to support everything upstairs. When those first villagers took refuge in the abandoned palace from the rampaging Slavs in 641, the elite lived upstairs, grabbing what was once the emperor's wing. They carved the rough holes you see in the ceiling to dump their garbage and sewage. Over the generations, the basement (where you're standing) filled up with layers of pungent waste that solidified, ultimately becoming a precious bonanza for 19th- and 20th-century archaeologists. These days this hall is used for everything from flower and book shows, to fashion catwalks, to filming HBO's *Game of Thrones* (it's where Daenerys Targaryen locked up her dragons).

From here, explore the cellars. Which rooms are open can change from year to year, but you can enjoy a scavenger hunt looking for the following items:

In many rooms, look overhead to see the **holes** that once held beams to support floorboards, creating an efficient two-story space.

The headless, pawless black granite **sphinx** is one of 13 that Diocletian brought home from Egypt (only four survive, including a mostly intact one we'll see soon on the Peristyle).

One small room displays a stone **olive-oil press**—a reminder of a local industry that has remained much the same since Roman times.

Look for two **petrified beams**, like the ones that once filled those double-decker holes. Likely in the same room, you'll see an **unexcavated wing**—a compost pile of ancient lifestyles, awaiting the tiny shovels and toothbrushes of future archaeologists.

The **bust of Diocletian** (or is it Sean Connery?) helps you visualize the emperor who left his mark on Split—and on the entire empire.

Near the WCs, look for **original Roman sewer pipes**—square outside and round inside—designed to fit into each other to create long pipes.

When you're finished, your ticket gets you into a whole other labyrinth of chambers—mostly with their ceilings missing, so they're open to the air. To enter this area, walk directly across the main passage and into the **eastern cellars**.

• *When you're finished, head back to the main gallery. Ignore the tacky made-in-Malaysia trinket shops as you head down the passage and up the chunky stairs into the...*

Peristyle (Peristil)

This square was the centerpiece of Diocletian's Palace. As you walk up the stairs, the entry vestibule into the residence is above your

head, Diocletian's mausoleum (today's Cathedral of St. Domnius) is to your right, and the street to Jupiter's Temple (supported by wooden beams) is on your left. The TI is in the small chapel, at the end of the square on the right. Straight ahead, beyond the TI/chapel, is the narrow street that leads to the palace's former main entrance, the Golden Gate.

Go to the middle of the square and take it all in. The red granite pillars—which you'll see all over Diocletian's Palace—are from Egypt, where Diocletian spent many of his preretirement years. Imagine the pillars defining fine arcades—now obscured by medieval houses. The black sphinx is the only one of Diocletian's collection of 13 that's still (mostly) intact.

"Roman soldiers" pose for tips (daily 9:00-17:00), and every day at noon in summer (mid-June-mid-Sept), an actor playing Diocletian appears at the top of the stairs to address the crowd in Latin. The event lasts 10 minutes and is a fun experience.

Without realizing it, you're standing in the middle of one of Split's most inviting bars, Luxor. The red cushions on the steps ringing the square belong to the bar; if you want to sit on one, you have to buy a drink. To really lounge in Roman style, this is well worth paying for—especially in the cool of the evening, when the Peristyle is less crowded and there's often live music. Come back tonight for a pre- or post-dinner drink.

• Climb the stairs (above where you came in) into the domed, open-ceilinged...

Entry Vestibule

Impressed? That's the idea. This was the grand entry to Diocletian's living quarters, meant to wow visitors. Emperors were be-

lieved to be gods. Diocletian called himself "Jovius"—the son of Jupiter, the most powerful of all gods. Four times a year (at the changing of the seasons), Diocletian would stand here and overlook the Peristyle. His subjects would lie on the ground in worship, praising his name and kissing his scarlet robe. Notice the four big niches at floor level, which once held statues of the four tetrarchs who ruled the unwieldy empire after Diocletian retired. The empty hole in the ceiling was once capped by a dome (long since collapsed), and the ceiling itself was covered with frescoes and mosaics.

In this grand space, you'll likely run into an all-male band of *klapa* singers, performing traditional a cappella harmonies. Just stand and enjoy a few glorious tunes—you'll rarely find a better group or acoustics. A 100-kn *klapa* CD is the perfect souvenir.

• Now go back into the Peristyle and turn right, climbing the steps to the...

Cathedral of St. Domnius (Katedrala Sv. Duje)

The original octagonal structure was Diocletian's elaborate mauso-

leum, built in the fourth century. But after the fall of Rome, it was converted into the town's cathedral (the Venetian-style bell tower was added in the 13th to 16th century). Before you go inside, notice the sarcophagi ringing the cathedral. In the late Middle Ages, this was prime postmortem real estate: Being buried closer to a cathedral improved your chances of getting to heaven.

Cost and Hours: Several sights associated with the cathedral require tickets: the cathedral interior, the unimpressive treasury/

museum, the crypt, the tower climb, and—a block away—Jupiter's Temple (described next). Options generally include paying 25 kn for the cathedral, crypt, and baptistery (the three most worthwhile parts); a 45-kn ticket adds the skippable treasury/museum and steep-but-scenic bell tower. (You can also pay 15 kn just for the tower climb—buy ticket at tower door.) All of the sights are open similar hours (summer Mon-Sat 8:00-19:00, Sun 12:30-18:30, cathedral often closed Sat afternoons for weddings; winter daily 7:00-12:00, maybe later on request)—but the cathedral can close unexpectedly anytime for services.

Visiting the Cathedral: To get inside, you usually have to enter from behind: Facing the main door at the bottom of the stairs, circle around the right side—passing the crypt (we'll return here later)—to find the door in the building behind. Buy your ticket here and climb up the stairs.

Once inside, the first flight of stairs leads to the cathedral interior (described below). But first, if you bought the 45-kn ticket and want to see the **treasury/museum**, head up one more flight. The single-room museum contains dusty display cases of vestments, giant psalter books, icon-like paintings, reliquaries, chalices, monstrances, and other church art, with very sparse English descriptions. After visiting, head back down to the cathedral.

Step into the tiny but evocative church **interior.** You'll enter into the apse; head around the side of the altar to reach the main part of the church. This is the oldest—and likely smallest—building used as a cathedral anywhere in Christendom. Imagine the place in pre-Christian times, with Diocletian's tomb in the center. The only surviving pieces of decor from those days are the granite columns and the relief circling the base of the dome (about 50 feet up)—a ring of carvings heralding the greatness of the emperor. The small red-marble pillars around the top of the pulpit (near the main door) were the only thing scavenged from Diocletian's sarcophagus—his actual remains have never been found.

Diocletian brutally persecuted his Christian subjects. Just before he moved to the Dalmatian Coast, he had Bishop Domnius of Salona killed, along with several thousand Christians. When Diocletian died, there were riotous celebrations. In the seventh century, his mausoleum became a cathedral dedicated to the martyred bishop. Posthumous poetic justice: Now Christian saints are entombed in Diocletian's mausoleum...and Diocletian is nowhere to be found.

The **sarcophagus of St. Domnius** (to the right of the altar, with early-Christian carvings) was once the cathedral's high altar. To the left of today's main altar is the impressively detailed, Renaissance-era **altar of St. Anastasius,** who is lying on a millstone that is tied to his neck. On Diocletian's orders, this Christian martyr was drowned in A.D. 302. To the left of St. Anastasius' altar is the **"new" altar of St. Domnius**; his relics lie in the 18th-century Baroque silver reliquary, above a stone relief showing him about to be beheaded.

As you exit through the 13th-century **main doors**, notice the 14 panels on each of the two wings—showing 28 scenes from the life of Christ.

Exiting the church, you'll see the entrance to the **bell tower** on your right. Climbing the 183 steep steps to the top of the 200-foot-tall bell tower rewards you with sweeping views of Split, but it's not for claustrophobes or those scared of heights.

To visit the **crypt** *(kripta)*, also included with your ticket, exit the main door of the cathedral, go down the stairs, and loop left to find its low-profile entrance. This musty, domed cellar (with eerie acoustics) was originally used to level the foundation of Diocletian's mausoleum. Later, Christians turned it into another chapel, dedicated to the Italian Saint Lucia, who was martyred by Diocletian. (The legend you'll likely hear about Diocletian torturing and murdering Christians in this very crypt is probably false.) Lucia stands above a small altar where the faithful have left scraps of paper scrawled with their prayers and their thanks. Ponder the contrast of this dark and gloomy space with Santa Lucia, whose name means "light." Notice the freshwater well in the middle of the room. Because this water was believed to have healing properties, the faithful would wash their eyes with it (Santa Lucia is also the patron saint of eyesight).

• *Return to the middle of the Peristyle square. Remember that Diocletian believed himself to be Jovius (Jupiter, Jr.). As worshippers exited the mausoleum of Jovius, they would look straight ahead to the temple of Jupiter. (Back then, there were none of these medieval buildings cluttering up the view.) Make your way through the narrow alley (directly across from the cathedral entry) to explore the small...*

Jupiter's Temple/St. John's Baptistery

About the time the mausoleum became a cathedral, this temple was converted into a baptistery (same ticket and hours as cathedral, or 10 kn on its own). Inside, the big 12th-century baptismal font—large enough to immerse someone (as was the tradition in those days)—is decorated with the intricate, traditional woven-rope *pleter* design that evokes Croatia's nautical heritage. Observant travelers will see examples of this motif all over the country. On the font, notice the engraving: a bishop (on the left) and the king on his throne (on the right). Liter-

ally under the feet of the bishop is a submissive commoner—neatly summing up the social structure of the Middle Ages. Standing above the font is a statue of St. John the Baptist counting to four, done by the great Croatian sculptor Ivan Meštrović (see page 194). The half-barrel vaulted ceiling, completed later, is considered the best-preserved of its kind anywhere. Every face and each patterned box is different.

• *Back at the Peristyle, stand in front of the TI/chapel with your back to the square. The small street just beyond the chapel (going left to right) connects the east and west gates. If you've had enough Roman history, head right (east) to go through the Silver Gate and find Split's busy, open-air Green Market. Or, head to the left (west), which takes you to the Iron Gate and People's Square (see "Sights in Split," later) and, beyond that, the fresh-and-smelly fish market. But if you want to see one last bit of Roman history, continue straight ahead up the...*

Cardo

A traditional Roman street plan has two roads: Cardo (the north-south axis) and Decumanus (the east-west axis). Split's Cardo street was the most important in Diocletian's Palace, connecting the main entry with the heart of the complex. As you walk, you'll pass several noteworthy sights: in the first building on the right, a bank with modern computer gear all around its exposed Roman ruins (look through window); at the first gate on the left, the courtyard of a Venetian merchant's palace (a reminder that Split was dominated by Venice from the 15th century until Napoleon); farther along on the right, an alley to the **City Museum** (described later, under "Sights in Split"); and, beyond that on the right, **Nadalina,** an artisan chocolatier selling mostly dark chocolate creations with some innovative Dalmatian flavors—such as dried fig and prosecco (Mon-Fri 8:00-20:00, Sat-Sun 9:00-14:00, mobile 091-210-8889).

At the end of the street, just before the Golden Gate, detour a few steps to the left along covered **Majstora Jurja** street—lined with some of the most appealing outdoor cafés in town, lively both

SPLIT

day and night (described later, under "Nightlife in Split"). Near the start of this street, just after its initial jog, stairs climb to the miniscule **St. Martin's Chapel,** burrowed into the city wall. Dating from the fifth century, this is one of the earliest Christian chapels anywhere. St. Martin is the patron saint of soldiers, and the chapel was built for the troops who guarded this gate (free, sporadic hours—just climb the stairs to see if it's open).

• *Backtrack to the main drag and go inside the huge...*

Golden Gate (Zlatna Vrata)

This great gate was the main entry of Diocletian's Palace. Its name wasn't literal—rather, the "gold" suggests the importance of this gateway to Salona, the Roman provincial capital at the time. Standing inside the gate itself, you can appreciate the double-door design that kept the palace safe. Also notice how this ancient building has been repurposed: Above, on the outer wall, you can see the bricked-in windows that contain part of a Dominican convent. And at the top of the inner wall is somebody's garden terrace.

Go outside the gate and look back at the fortification. This mostly uncluttered facade helps you visualize how the palace looked before so many other buildings were grafted on. Four miles straight ahead as you exit this gate was Salona, which was a major city of 60,000 (and Diocletian's hometown) before there was a Split. The big statue by Ivan Meštrović is **Bishop Gregory of Nin,** a 10th-century Croatian priest who tried to convince the Vatican to allow sermons during Mass to be said in Croatian, rather than Latin. People rub his toe for good luck (though only nonmaterial wishes are given serious consideration). Beyond the statue you'll find Split's **Gallery of Fine Arts** (described later, under "Sights in Split").

• *Your tour is finished. Now enjoy the rest of Split.*

Sights in Split

OLD TOWN PUBLIC SPACES

My self-guided walk (described earlier) takes you through the main artery of town, but just a few steps away are some delightful public zones that are worth exploring.

▲▲▲The Riva

The official name for this seaside pedestrian drag is the "Croatian National Revival Embankment" (Obala Hrvatskog Narodnog

Preporoda)—but locals just call it "Riva" (REE-vah, Italian for "harbor"). This is the town's promenade, an integral part of Mediterranean culture. After dinner, Split residents collect their families and friends for a stroll on the Riva. It offers some of the best people-watching in Croatia; make it a point to be here for an hour or two in the evening. The stinky smell that sometimes accompanies the stroll (especially at the west end) isn't from a sewer. It's sulfur—a reminder that the town's medicinal sulfur spas have attracted people here since the days of Diocletian.

At the west end of the Riva, the people-parade of Croatian culture turns right and heads away from the water, up **Marmontova.** Although it lacks the seafront cachet, this drag is equally enjoyable and feels more local. As you walk up Marmontova, on the left is the plain-Jane outer facade of the arcade that defines Trg Republike, a grand and genteel Napoleonic-era square. Duck through the passage across from the fish market to bask in its "poor man's St. Mark's Square" ambience, and maybe to linger over a drink at the recommended Bajamonti café. A bit farther up Marmontova, on the right, look for the whimsical fountain nicknamed "The Teacup," with a hand squirting water across the sidewalk into a funnel. At the top of Marmontova are some department stores, a lively café square, and the Croatian National Theater (Hrvatsko Narodno Kazalište, HNK).

▲People's Square (Narodni Trg)

Locals call this lively square at the center of the Old Town "Pjaca," pronounced the same as the Italian *piazza.* Stand in the center and enjoy the bustle. When Diocletian lived in his palace, a Roman

village popped up here, just outside the wall. By the 14th century, a medieval town had developed, making this the main square of Split.

The square has some quirky decorative flourishes. On the wall just to the right of the lane leading to the

Peristyle, look for the life-size relief of St. Anthony. Notice the creepy "mini-me" clutching the saint's left leg—depicting the sculptor's donor, who didn't want his gift to be forgotten. Above this strange statue, notice the smaller, faded relief of a man and a woman arguing.

Turn around and face the square. On your left is the city's grand old café, **Gradska Kavana,** which has been the Old Town's venerable meeting point for generations. Today it's both a café and a restaurant, with disappointing food but some of the best outdoor ambience in town.

Across the square, the white building jutting into the square was once the **City Hall,** and now houses temporary exhibitions. The loggia is all that remains of the original Gothic building.

At the far end of the square is the out-of-place **Nakić House,** built in the early 20th-century Viennese Secession style—a reminder that Dalmatia was part of the Habsburg Empire, and ruled by Vienna, from Napoleon's downfall through World War I.

The lane on the right side of the Nakić House leads to Split's **fish market** (Ribarnica), where you can see piles of the still-wriggling catch of the day. Why no flies? It's thanks to the sulfur spring in the nearby spa building (with the gray statues, on the corner). Just beyond the fish market is the pedestrian boulevard, Marmontova (described earlier).

Radić Brothers Square (Trg Braće Radića)

This little piazza hides just off the Riva, between the two halves of the Old Town. Overhead is a **Venetian citadel.** After Split became part of the Venetian Republic, there was a serious danger of attack by the Ottomans, so octagonal towers like this were built all along the coast. But this imposing tower had a second purpose: to encourage citizens of Split to forget about any plans of rebellion. At its base is an inviting juice bar, invoking the more popular nickname of the square—Voćni Trg ("Fruit Square"), for the produce that was once sold here.

In the middle of the square is a studious sculpture by Ivan Meštrović of the 16th-century poet **Marko Marulić,** who is considered the father of the Croatian language. Marulić was the first to write literature in the Croatian vernacular, which before then had generally been considered a backward peasants' tongue.

On the downhill (harbor) side of the square is **Croata,** a necktie boutique that loves to explain how Croatian soldiers who fought with the French in the Thirty Years' War (1618-1648) had a distinctive way of tying their scarves. The French found it stylish, adopted it, and called it *à la Croate*—or eventually, *cravate*—thus creating the modern necktie. Croata's selection includes ties with traditional Croatian motifs, such as the checkerboard pattern from the flag or characters from the ninth-century Glagolitic alphabet. Though pricey, these ties make nice souvenirs. Basic ties run about 500 kn, while handmade ones with 24-carat gold accents can run up to 4,000 kn. The shop also sells women's scarves (Mon-Fri

8:00-20:00, Sat 8:00-13:00, closed Sun, Mihovilova Širina 7, tel. 021/346-336). Croata has a bigger, second location on the Peristyle.

Green Market

This lively open-air market bustles at the east end of Diocletian's Palace. Residents shop for produce and clothes here, and there are plenty of tourist souvenirs as well. Browse the wide selection of T-shirts, and ignore the sleazy black-market tobacco salesmen who mutter at you: *"Cigaretta?"*

Matejuška Fishermen's Port

While Split's harborfront Riva is where the beautiful people stroll, the city's fishermen roots still thrive just to the west. The neighborhood called Matejuška—at the little harbor where the Varoš district hits the water (a five-minute walk beyond the end of the Riva, with the water on your left)—

has long been Split's working fishermen's harbor. While the area has received a facelift to match the one along the Riva, it still retains its striped-collar character. The enclosed harbor area is filled with working fishing boats and colorful dinghies that bob in unison. Along the breakwater, notice the fishermen's lockers, where people who earn their living from the Adriatic still keep their supplies. You'll see the most fishing action here in the mornings.

The far side of the breakwater—all glitzy white marble—is another world, with a pebbly beach, attractive plaza, and some of the best views looking back on the Riva. This jetty has recently become a popular open-air, after-hours hangout for young people. Like Split itself, these two worlds—the grizzled fishermen mending their nets, and the teenagers laughing and flirting—coexist more smoothly than anyone might have guessed.

Beyond Matejuška, the harborfront embankment (which runs toward the Marjan peninsula) has also been rejuvenated and is now spiffed up with cafés facing moored sailboats, creating a relaxing, scenic, largely tourist-free zone. (Ignore the eyesore of an abandoned skyscraper, formerly the Hotel Marjan; corruption and intrigue swirl around this prime real estate, which is the biggest political hot potato in town.)

MUSEUMS AND OTHER SIGHTS

Ethnographic Museum (Etnografski Muzej)

This museum shows off the culture, costumes, furniture, tools, jewelry, weapons, and paintings of Dalmatia, all with good English explanations. The modest but vibrant collection, with a confusing treehouse floor plan, is displayed in a gorgeously renovated early-medieval palace (parts of which once formed the private residential halls of Diocletian). You'll find it in the upper level of the Old Town, behind Diocletian's entry vestibule. Check out the artsy "golden fleece" entry door. The ground floor sports the remains of a seventh-century church, and the exhibits usually include a good look at traditional folk dress. Your ticket also includes access to the roof of the vestibule (find the stairs outside at the far end of the museum); while it's not high enough to be thrilling, it provides a nice view over the rooftops of Split, and you can peer into the top of the vestibule.

Cost and Hours: 15 kn; June-Sept Mon-Sat 9:30-19:00, Sun 10:00-13:00; Oct-May Mon-Fri 9:00-16:00, Sat 9:00-13:00, closed Sun; Severova 7, tel. 021/344-164, www.etnografski-muzej-split.hr.

Split City Museum (Muzej Grada Splita)

This museum traces how the city grew over the centuries. While the collection is a bit dull, the good English descriptions can help you better appreciate the layers of history you're seeing in the streets.

Cost and Hours: 20 kn, April-Oct daily 9:00-21:00, Nov-March generally Tue-Sat 9:00-17:00, Sun 10:00-14:00, closed Mon, free audioguide to use on your smartphone; Papalićeva 1, tel. 021/360-171, www.mgst.net.

Visiting the Museum: The ground floor displays Roman fragments (including coins from the days of Diocletian that resemble the kunas in your pocket), temporary exhibits, a model of the Peristyle during Diocletian's time, and the museum's highlight: a semicircular marble table (called a "mensa") used by the Romans. As depicted in Hollywood movies, the Romans ate lying down (multiple people would lounge and feast, while servants dished things up from the straight side). This table has been painstakingly reconstructed from shards and splinters discovered in the cellars.

The next floor focuses on the Middle Ages, with a beautifully restored Gothic ballroom, medieval weapons, and a terrace displaying carved stone monuments. The top floor covers the 16th century to the present.

The 15th-century Papalić Palace, which houses the City Museum, is a sight all its own. At the end of the palace, near Cardo street, look up to see several typical Venetian-style Gothic-Renaissance windows. The stone posts sticking out of the wall next to them were used to hang curtains.

Emanuel Vidović Gallery

This small, somber museum celebrates the work of Split native Emanuel Vidović (1870-1953), who gained fame as a Post-Impres-

SPLIT

sionist painter. Start with the video about the artist on the first floor up, then find the reconstruction of his cluttered studio; notice the creepy dolls' heads. Elsewhere on the first floor—and upstairs—hang many of his works: hazy, Turner-esque landscapes; church interiors; shimmering street and village scenes from Split and around Dalmatia; and paintings of those bizarre dolls. Located just a few steps off the Peristyle, it's an easy opportunity to get to know an unfamiliar but locally respected artist.

Cost and Hours: 20 kn; May-Oct Tue-Fri 9:00-21:00, Sat-Mon 9:00-16:00; Nov-April Tue-Sat 9:00-17:00, Sun 9:00-14:00, closed Mon; Poljana Kraljice Jelene b.b., tel. 021/360-155, www.galerija-vidovic.com.

Split Synagogue

The tiny, modest synagogue of Split is hidden down a small side street, not coincidentally located just outside the walls of Diocletian's Palace. Ring the bell and climb the stairs to step into the unassuming, lived-in religious home of Split's Jewish community, which numbered around 300 before the Holocaust (and about a hundred today). You'll see a replica of a little, clay menorah lamp that was discovered in the ruins of ancient Salona, indicating that the Jewish presence here goes back to Roman times. This is the third-oldest practicing synagogue in Europe (after Prague and Dubrovnik); a rabbi comes from Zagreb a few times each year.

Cost and Hours: Free but donations requested, loaner yarmulkes, Mon-Fri 10:00-14:00, closed Sat-Sun, Židovski Prolaz 1, tel. 021/345-672, www.zost.hr.

Split Gallery of Fine Arts (Galerija Umjetnina Split)

This collection, beautifully displayed in a finely restored old hospital just behind Diocletian's Palace, features mostly Croatian artwork from the 14th to the 21st century. It's basically a hodgepodge with few highlights—best reserved for art lovers. Cross through the courtyard, climb up the stairs, and follow the one-way route through the chronologically displayed collection, which is heavy on the 20th century.

Cost and Hours: 20 kn, Tue-Fri 10:00-18:00, Sat-Sun 10:00-14:00, closed Mon; mod café, go straight out the Golden Gate and a bit to the left—behind the statue of Gregory of Nin—to Kralja Tomislava 15, tel. 021/350-110, www.galum.hr.

Archaeological Museum (Arheološki Muzej)

If you're intrigued by all the "big stuff" from Split's past (buildings and ruins), consider paying a visit to this collection of its "little stuff." A good exhibit of artifacts (mostly everyday domestic items) traces this region's history chronologically, from its Illyrian beginnings through its notable Roman period (items from Split and Salona) to the Middle Ages. About a 10-minute walk north of the Old Town, it's worth the trip for archaeology fans. Don't confuse this with the less-interesting Museum of Croatian Archaeological Monuments, on the way to the Ivan Meštrović Gallery.

Cost and Hours: 20 kn; June-Sept Mon-Sat 9:00-14:00 & 16:00-20:00, closed Sun; Oct-May Mon-Fri 9:00-14:00 & 16:00-20:00, Sat 9:00-14:00, closed Sun; Zrinsko Frankopanska 25, tel. 021/329-340, www.mdc.hr/split-arheoloski/eng/index.html.

IVAN MEŠTROVIĆ SIGHTS, WEST OF THE OLD TOWN

The Meštrović Gallery and nearby Kaštelet Chapel are just outside the Old Town. Both sights are covered by the same ticket and have the same hours.

Cost and Hours: 30 kn, covers both the gallery and the chapel, 10 kn more during special exhibits; May-Sept Tue-Sun 9:00-19:00, closed Mon; Oct-April Tue-Sat 9:00-16:00, Sun 10:00-15:00, closed Mon; gallery tel. 021/340-800, chapel tel. 021/358-185, www.mdc. hr. At the information desk, confirm the departure time for the return bus and ask for the brochure explaining the Kaštelet Chapel, which may not be available once you get there.

Getting There: Both sights are located along Šetalište Ivana Meštrovića. You can take **bus** #12 from the little cul-de-sac at the west end of the Riva (departs hourly, likely at :50 past the hour—schedule posted in the blue shelter; get off at the stop in front of the gallery, just after your bus passes a museum prominently marked *Muzej Hrvatskih Arheoloških Spomenika*). The return bus generally leaves at :10 past the hour. You can also **walk** (about 30 minutes): Follow the harbor west of town toward the big marina, swing right with the road, and follow the park until you see the gallery on your right (at #46). A **taxi** from the west end of the Old Town to the gallery costs about 60 kn (much more from the east end of the Old Town).

To reach the **chapel**, it's a five-minute walk past the gallery down Šetalište Ivana Meštrovića to #39 (on the left, in an olive grove).

Cuisine Art: Café Galerija is just above the ticket office.

▲▲Meštrović Gallery (Galerija Meštrović)

Split's best art museum is dedicated to the sculptor Ivan Meštrović, the most important of all Croatian artists. Many of Meštrović's finest works are housed in this palace, designed by the sculptor himself to serve as his residence, studio, and exhibition space. If you have time, it's worth the trek.

Visiting the Gallery: Each work is labeled, but there's very little description otherwise (and the 80-kn guidebook is overkill for most visitors).

The following tour will help you navigate the highlights. Before you begin, read the sidebar (see page 194) for background on Meštrović's life; while the collection is presented thematically rather than chronologically, knowing the artist's journey helps to make sense of what you'll see.

From the ticket office, climb the stairs toward Meštrović's house, pausing in the **garden** to admire a smattering of sculptures. On the right, see Persephone reaching skyward for freedom—an idea that came to Meštrović while he was imprisoned by the Ustaše in World War II. Beyond her, you'll see Cyclops struggling to hurl a giant shot put—in keeping with Meštrović's theme of the struggles of great men. Tucked behind the trees nearby is an eagle, which was a study for a mountaintop monument honoring one great man in particular, the Montenegrin King Petar II Petrović-Njegoš (see page 402). To the left as you face the building is a statue of a woman playing a lute, and reliefs of women playing a lute and harp flank the door of the villa. Much as he enjoyed depicting the travails of men, Meštrović also often sculpted women serenely engaging in music.

Go up another set of stairs to reach the **Entrance Hall.** The sculptures here evoke some of Michelangelo's nudes and were fittingly carved from that great sculptor's favorite medium: Carrara marble. The head of a woman glancing pensively out a window is Meštrović's second wife, Olga, who was one of his favorite models. Notice the smaller black sculptures by the two staircases: on the left, representing birth, and on the right, representing death—Meštrović strove to capture the full range of human experience in his work.

Go to the left to find a pyramid of maternal love called *Madonna and Children*. While the woman is clearly garbed in the head-scarf of the Virgin Mary, she cradles not one, but two children; these are Olga and Meštrović's first two kids.

Now enter the **Dining Room** at the end of the main floor. This is the most intimate space in the villa—the only room that still feels even a little bit lived-in. It's decorated with more sculptures of Meštrović and his family. Entering, go straight ahead to the windows, then do a clockwise loop around the room. First look for the self-portrait bust of Meštrović and the bust of a woman in a traditional Dalmatian head scarf—this is Meštrović's mother, another one of his favorite models. Notice that the two giant caryatids carved from Dalmatian stone (embedded with fragments of sea-

Ivan Meštrović
(1883-1962)

Ivan Meštrović (EE-vahn MESH-troh-veech), who achieved international fame for his talents as a sculptor, was Croatia's answer to Rodin. You'll see Meštrović's works everywhere, in the streets, squares, and museums of Croatia.

Meštrović grew up in a family of poor, nomadic farm workers just inland from Split. At an early age, his drawings and wooden carvings showed promise, and a wealthy family took him in and made sure he was properly trained. He eventually went off to school in Vienna, where he fell in with the Secession movement and found fame and fortune. He lived in Prague, Paris, and Switzerland, fully engaged in the flourishing European artistic culture at the turn of the 20th century (he counted Rodin among his friends). After World War I, Meštrović moved back to Croatia and established an atelier, or workshop, in Zagreb (now a museum—see page 58).

Later in life—like Diocletian before him—Meštrović returned to Split and built a huge seaside mansion (today's Meštrović Gallery). The years between the World Wars were Meštrović's happiest and most productive. It was during this time that he sculpted his most internationally famous works, a pair of giant Native American warriors on horseback in Chicago's Grant Park. But when World War II broke out, Meštrović—an outspoken supporter of the ideals of a united Yugoslavia—was briefly imprisoned by the anti-Yugoslav Ustaše (Croatia's Nazi puppet government).

After his release, Meštrović fled to Italy, then to the US, where he lectured at prominent universities including Notre Dame and Syracuse. (President Eisenhower personally handed Meštrović his new US passport in 1954.) After the war, the Yugoslav dictator Tito invited Meštrović to return, but the very religious artist refused to cooperate with an atheistic regime. (Meštrović was friends with the Archbishop Alojzije Stepinac, who was imprisoned by Tito.) Meštrović died in South Bend, Indiana.

Viewing Meštrović's works, his abundant talent is evident. He worked in wood, plaster, marble, and bronze, and dabbled in painting. Meštrović's figures typically have long, angular fingers, arms, and legs. Whether whimsical or emotional, Meštrović's expressive, elongated faces—often with prominent noses—powerfully connect with the viewer.

Here are a few themes you'll see recurring in Meštrović's works as you tour his museum:

Religion: Meštrović was a devout Catholic.

Dalmatian Traditions: Meštrović felt a poignant nostalgia for the simple lifestyles and customs of his home region of Drniš, and he used his art to elevate them to be on par with religious and mythological themes. This is most evident in the angular scarves many of his female subjects wear around their heads.

Yugoslav Symbolism: Meštrović was a strong supporter of the first (interwar) incarnation of Yugoslavia. He created sculptures not only in Croatia, but throughout Yugoslavia, many of them honoring heroes of Yugoslav tradition.

The Secession: Living and studying in Vienna in the early 20th century, Meštrović was exposed to the slinky cultural milieu of the likes of Gustav Klimt.

Struggling Men, Serene Women: While Meštrović frequently sculpted both male and female nudes, they often carry starkly different tones: Meštrović's ripped men tend to be toiling against an insurmountable challenge; his smooth and supple women are celebrating life, often through the medium of music (dancing, singing, playing instruments, and so on).

Tumult: Meštrović's life coincided with a time of great turmoil in Europe. He lived through World War I, the creation of the first Yugoslavia, World War II, the postwar/communist Yugoslavia, and the dawn of the Atomic Age in the United States. This 20th-century angst—particularly surrounding his arrest and exile during World War II—comes through in his work.

Meštrović's works can be found throughout Split, Croatia, and the former Yugoslavia. In Split, in addition to the Meštrović Gallery and Kaštelet Chapel, you'll find his statues of Marko Marulić (see page 188), Gregory of Nin (page 186), and John the Baptist (page 184). Zagreb has another fine atelier/museum of Meštrović's works (see page 58), and the seaside village of Cavtat, just outside Dubrovnik, has one of the sculptor's most cohesive and poignant works, the Račić Mausoleum (see page 351). And sitting high above Montenegro is the mountaintop Njegoš monument at Lovćen.

shells) are also clad in this traditional garb. On the wall to the right of the fireplace, you'll see two painted portraits of Meštrović—one as a young man (by his contemporary, Vlaho Bukovac—see page 350), and another shortly before his death. Other busts in the room depict Meštrović's children. A painting of the *Last Supper* hangs in virtually every Dalmatian dining room, and Meštrović's is no exception—he painted this version himself, on wood. He also designed the furniture in this room.

Now climb the stairs. On the **landing,** look for a large bronze relief panel called *My People's Artist.* The old man and the young boy are linked by the *gusle,* a traditional Balkan stringed instrument. Here, Meštrović uses the *gusle* to represent the oral transmission of history (and specifically, the story of the pivotal Battle of Kosovo in 1389—a date etched into the minds of all Yugoslavs, particularly Serbs). Much as Meštrović dresses his women in traditional peasant clothes, he deeply believes in the regeneration of culture and customs over time. Meštrović's detailed drawings in this room—including some inspired by Dante's *Divine Comedy*—are worth a look.

Next, turn right into the **Secession Room.** Two of the finest works in this room—*Little Girl Singing* and *The Katunarić Family*—show the influence of Meštrović's contemporary, Rodin: smoothed rather than angular features, which make the final product less strictly lifelike, but also more expressive and visually pleasing. Other pieces in this room include several small studies for larger statues, some of which were never completed.

Pass through the room of drawings into the **Long Hall,** lined with life-size figures and a view terrace. The *Vestal Virgin,* sitting with her knees apart and feet together, is demonstrating a favorite pose of Meštrović's. And, once again, we see women finding solace and joy in music: dancing (while playfully tossing her hair), playing a lute, and so on. For contrast, look at the facing wall to see sketches of male nudes struggling. Step out onto the terrace to enjoy the Dalmatian views that inspired the artist.

At the end of the hall—past another small landing with drawings—is the **Study Room,** filled with miniature sculptures Meštrović created to prepare for larger-scale works: *Moses, Prometheus* (the figure tied to a rock, to be eaten by birds for eternity), and *Cyclops* (a large version of which we saw outside). Notice the small study of *Job,* then go into the small side room to see the much larger final version.

One of Meštrović's most powerful works, *Job*—howling with an agony verging on insanity—was carved by the artist in exile, as his country was turned upside down by World War II. Like Picasso's *Guernica,* it's a silent scream against the inanity of war. The curator has intentionally placed it in a separate room to emphasize the feeling of alienation. Meštrović sketched his inspiration for this piece (displayed on the wall) while he was imprisoned by the Ustaše.

Head down the stairs and make a U-turn left into the **Sacral Room.** Meštrović was very religious, and here you can see some of his many works depicting biblical figures. The giant, wood-carved *Adam* and *Eve* dominate the room. Also notice the wood-carved relief panels of *Merry Angels* and *Grieving Angels*. (These are similar to the panels you'll see at the Kaštelet Chapel down the road.) Smaller statues around the room include four evangelists (Matthew, John, and two Lukes—but no Mark), Moses, a *pietà*, and both bronze and wooden heads of Christ.

The smaller side room displays another of the gallery's highlights: the quietly poignant **Roman Pietà.** Meštrović follows the

classical pyramid form, with Joseph of Arimathea (top), Mary (left), and Mary Magdalene (right) surrounding the limp body of Christ. But the harmony is broken by the painful angles of the mourning faces. Also notice how Jesus' oversized, ruined body drags down those trying to support his dead weight; if he stood up, he'd be towering over all of them. For Meštrović, Christ's suffering was personal: The women wear those traditional Dalmatian head scarves, the features of Joseph are a self-portrait, and Mary Magdalene is modeled after Meštrović's daughter Marija. This sculpture is plaster; there's a bronze version at the Vatican and a marble one on the campus of the University of Notre Dame in the US.

To Kaštelet Chapel: To reach the last part of the Meštrović experience, head down the stairs to the road, cross the street, turn right, and walk about five minutes. You'll see the low-profile entrance to the chapel on the left, through a doorway marked *39*, in an olive grove.

▲▲Kaštelet Chapel

If you're enjoying Meštrović's works, don't miss the nearby Kaštelet Chapel ("Chapel of the Holy Cross"), which brings a new dimen-

sion to his oeuvre. Meštrović bought this 16th-century fortified palace to display his 28 wood reliefs of Jesus' life.

You can see how Meštrović's style changed over time, as he carved these over a nearly 30-year span, com-

SPLIT

pleting the last 12 when he was in the US. (However, he didn't carve the reliefs in chronological order; the gallery's ticket office has a booklet dating each one.) While the earlier pieces are well-composed and powerful, the later ones seem more hastily done, as Meštrović rushed to complete his opus. He started with the crucifix in 1916. His last two panels, completed in 1953, are on the right as you face the crucifix (the second one, showing the Deposition; and the fourth, showing the Last Supper).

Work clockwise around the room, tracing the life of Christ. Notice that some of the Passion scenes are out of order (a side effect of Meštrović's nonlinear schedule). The beautiful *pietà* back near the entrance still shows some of the original surface of the wood, demonstrating the skill required to create depth and emotion in just a few inches of medium. Dominating the chapel is an extremely powerful wooden crucifix, with Christ's emaciated arms, legs, fingers, and toes bent at unnatural angles—a typically expressionistic flair Meštrović used to exaggerate suffering.

Activities in Split

▲Hiking the Marjan Peninsula

This huge, hilly, and relatively undeveloped spit of parkland feels like a chunk of Dalmatian island wilderness, a stone's throw from the big city. With out-of-the-way beaches and miles of hiking trails, the Marjan (MAR-yahn) peninsula is where residents go to relax; most people here seem to have their favorite hidden paths and beach coves, so ask around for tips.

From the Šperun neighborhood at the west end of the Old Town, you can hike to various lookout points. If you're in shape, figure about an hour to hike to the top viewpoint, then another 45 minutes back down—but some of the best views are from partway up.

Start by climbing the stairs past the recommended Šperun Restaurant, and continue straight up Senjska ulica. Follow the stairs all the way up for 15 steep minutes to reach a spectacular view terrace (with sweeping vistas over Split's Old Town), next to a little café.

If you like, you can keep ascending for more good views (though you can't really see the Old Town beyond here). To continue on, curl around past the restaurant (following signs for *Crkva sv. Nikole* and *Sedlo*) and follow the steep pathway up, passing the fenced-in park on your right. Soon you'll reach the small chapel of St. Nicholas. Just behind it, find the steps up and to the right (look for *Marjanske Skale* signs). At the top of these stairs is Split's very humble zoo. From here, a broad path cuts through the woods, with smaller paths branching off downhill. For the highest viewpoint, follow signs for *Sedlo* up the steps to the terrace. This top-of-the-world perch offers a 360-degree panorama of Split's urban sprawl, receding layers of jagged and majestic mountains, offshore islands, and the bay behind the Marjan peninsula (but little in the way of Old Town views).

It's easiest to go back down the way you came. But for a longer hike, continue down the stairs at the far end of the view terrace, and follow signs for *Crkva sv. Jere.* This path takes you along the length of the peninsula, mostly through trees (read: no views). A series of switchbacks leads back down to the main road running along the perimeter of Marjan; from here, you can turn left to get back to town or right for an even longer walk around the far end of Marjan.

The peninsula also has a pair of good beaches (Ježinac and Bene, described next).

Hitting the Beach

Since it's more of a big city than a resort, Split's beaches are less scenic (and less pristine) than small towns elsewhere along the coast. I'd use my Split time for big-city sights and culture. However, if the weather's great and you want to go for a dip, here are a few ideas.

The most popular, most crowded beach is **Bačvice,** in a pebbly cove just a short walk east of the main ferry terminal. As it's very shallow, it's often unpleasantly jammed with kids. After dark, it becomes a hopping meat-market nightlife zone for older "kids."

Less crowded beaches lie just to the east of Bačvice. Each cove has its own little swimming zone; the fourth cove over, called **Trstenik,** is perhaps the most inviting. A pebbly beach—with free access—flanks the big deck in front of the Radisson Hotel, where you can rent a chair, buy a drink at the bar, and use the showers.

Or head in the other direction to Marjan, the peninsular city park, which is ringed with several sunbathing beaches. Along the southern edge of Marjan, just below the Meštrović Gallery, is a rocky but more local-feeling and less crowded beach called **Ježinac** (Croatian for "sea urchin"...be sure to wear water shoes). **Bene Beach** is along the northern edge of Marjan—so it offers more shade. You can get to Bene Beach by bus #12 (the same one that goes to the Meštrović Gallery), tourist train, bike, or foot (about a 45-minute walk from the Old Town).

Nightlife in Split

The Riva

Every night, the sea of Croatian humanity laps at the walls of Diocletian's Palace along the town's pedestrian promenade. Choose a bench and watch life go by, or enjoy a drink at one of the many outdoor cafés. Live music (funded by the tourist board) enlivens the Riva nightly through the summer (Junemid-Sept).

Old Town Bars

The labyrinthine lanes of the Old Town are packed with mostly interchangeable bars and cafés featuring pleasant tables crammed between ancient stone buildings under a starry Croatian sky. Even if you're not interested in drinking, make a point to wander some of these areas after dark just to people-watch and take in the hubbub in these otherwise hidden pockets. If you're staying in the Old Town, you'll hear bar-goers late into the night. If you can't beat 'em, join 'em. One way is to simply lose yourself in the twisty lanes by following the music and the sound of socializing Croatians to the spot you like best. Or, if you prefer a little direction to your ramblings, explore the following neighborhoods. Note that, while each of the bars listed here has an interior, there's little reason to sit anywhere but under the open sky. Prices and menus are similar at most places (beer, wine, cocktails, coffee drinks); ordering something simply gives you an excuse to sit in a gorgeous outdoor space, nurse a drink, and focus on your travel partner. The action at these places really gets rolling around 22:00 and peaks around 23:00 or 24:00. Bars are supposed to close their outdoor seating areas at 2:00.

On the Peristyle: The obvious choice, particularly for the not-so-young set, is right on the main square of the Old Town, Diocletian's former entry hall. All day long, the Peristyle steps serve as makeshift café tables for the bar called **Luxor,** with red cushions and small tables scattered along the steps. If you sit on a cushion, you're expected to order a drink (but you can sit or stand elsewhere for free). In the evening—as twilight encroaches and floodlights transform the square into one of the most atmospheric public spaces in Europe—live music breaks out (generally starting between 20:00 and 21:00 and continuing until around midnight). The smooth marble tiles of the Peristyle—worn to a slippery sheen by two millennia of visitors—becomes a dance floor, as people salsa, foxtrot, or pop-and-lock their way around the majestic space. Where else can you cut a rug in the grand entry hall of a Roman palace?

Majstora Jurja: This street, which runs along the north edge of Diocletian's Palace (just inside the wall), is lined with a mellow gaggle of youthful hangouts. Some mood music plays, but the soundtrack here is mostly chatting, laughing, and flirting. West of the Golden Gate, the lineup of café/bars includes the nondescript **Kala** and **Mosquito.** Two better options are nearby: Up the side street at Dominisova 9, **Galerija** has the classiest atmosphere, with an upscale-feeling (but not stuffy), gallery-like ambience and a display case of cakes. A bit farther along Majstora Jurja is **Teak,** with a namesake woody interior that feels almost distinguished. East of the Golden Gate is a tamer zone, with the soccer-themed **Mali Flek** and then the **Red Room,** filling a large square with tables.

"Slavija Square": This is my own nickname for the tight, stepped area that's squeezed in front of Hotel Slavija, near Radić Brothers Square (Trg Braće Radića; from the square's statue of Marulić, enter the Old Town and bear right, following the beat). This area is more youthful and rowdy, with throbbing techno music and cocktails that flow freely. Clambering up the steps are several bars, including the mellow **Figa** and the hip **Fluid,** with predictable thumpa-thumpa atmosphere. Near the top of the stairs, the engagingly scruffy **Split Circus** boasts magic-marker walls and several varieties of *rakija*, the ubiquitous Balkan firewater. A few steps beyond, through the enclosed courtyard on the right, **Ghetto** has a mellower, sailors' bordello-theme interior, with heart-shaped chairs, red velvet, and vivid graffiti.

Behind the Loggia: For the youngest, trendiest scene in the Old Town, head for the zone locals call *Iza Lođa* ("Behind the Loggia"). From the grand People's Square, follow the beat behind the former City Hall loggia to discover a well-dressed meat market populated by sleazy young men and tipsy American girls determined to make bad decisions. The main magnet here is the standing-room-only **Gaga,** with a pounding dance beat, indoor and outdoor bar areas, and a laser-light show on the ancient stones above. At the far end of the little square, like a mellow grandparent observing the rowdy younger generation, is **La Linea** (which locals call simply "taverna")—an old sailors' pub decorated with nautical flags.

Other Areas: The large square at the top of Marmontova, just before the **Zara** store, is crammed with tables belonging to a half-dozen identical-feeling cafés. And with the arrival of the recommended Bajamonti café, **Trg Republike** (the grand Napoleonic square just west of the Riva) could also become a happening nightlife option.

Clubbing at Bačvice Beach

This family-friendly beach by day becomes a throbbing party area for young locals late at night. Since all Old Town bars have to close by 2:00 in the morning, night owls hike on over to the Bačvice crescent of clubs. The three-floor club complex is a cacophony of music, with the beat of one club melting into the next—all with breezy terraces overlooking the harbor.

Sleeping in Split

Split has more and more sleeping options every year, as little guest-houses frequently pop up. But even with the abundance of beds, prices can be high in this big city. Split also suffers from perhaps the worst nighttime noise of any destination in this book—bring earplugs, and always ask for a quiet room (if possible). If you're on your own for breakfast, see my suggestions on page 208.

OUTSIDE THE OLD TOWN

These good values are within a five-minute walk of the Old Town. They're nearly as convenient as the Old Town options, but cheaper. Of these places, only Hotel Luxe has a full-time reception desk; for the others, call ahead to arrange your arrival time.

In the Lučac Neighborhood, East of the Old Town

The Lučac neighborhood—which lines up along the busy street called Kralja Zvonimira—feels urban and a bit gritty, but it's handy to the Old Town.

$$$ Hotel Luxe, a modern hotel with a shiny lobby and 30 upscale-mod rooms, is a comfy splurge that combines a convenient location (near the Old Town) with sea views—rare in this city. While it fronts a dreary, busy street, all of its rooms face the quieter back side, and most have views over the harbor (nonview "classic" Db-€165/€115/€85, partial-view Db-€205/€150/€110, bigger "comfort" Db with view and small balcony-€245/€165/€115, "superior" Db with view and big balcony-€315/€195/€135, includes good breakfast, small gym, Jacuzzi, parking, cheaper Nov-Feb, air-con, elevator, Kralja Zvonimira 6, tel. 021/314-444, www.hotelluxesplit.com, reservations@hotelluxesplit.com).

$$ Villa Ana has five spacious, comfortable rooms with hotelesque amenities in a smart, little, freestanding stone house (Sb-€80, Db-€100, Tb-€115, can be cheaper at last minute in shoulder season, roughly €20 less Nov-March, includes breakfast, air-con, reception open 7:00-22:00, a few tight free parking spots out front; 2 long blocks east of Old Town up busy Kralja Zvonimira, follow the driveway-like lane opposite the lonely skyscraper to Vrh Lučac 16; if using GPS, enter the address Kralja Zvonimira 14 to

---

Sleep Code

Abbreviations   (7 kn=about $1, €1=about $1.10, country code: 385)
S=Single, **D**=Double/Twin, **T**=Triple, **Q**=Quad, **b**=bathroom
Price Rankings
  $$$ Higher Priced—Most rooms €125 or more
   $$ Moderately Priced—Most rooms €70-125
    $ Lower Priced—Most rooms €70 or less
If I've listed two sets of rates, I've noted when the second rate applies (generally off-season, Oct-May); if I've listed three sets of rates, the first is for peak season (July-Sept), the second is shoulder season (May-June and Oct), and the third is off-season (Nov-April). The dates for seasonal rates vary by hotel.
   These rates do not include the modest tourist tax (about 7 kn/person, per night). Hotels generally accept credit cards and include breakfast in their rates; most *sobe* accept only cash and don't offer breakfast. While rates are listed in euros, you'll pay in kunas. Free Wi-Fi and/or a guest computer is generally available, and English is spoken. Prices change; verify current rates online or by email. For the best prices, always book directly with the hotel.

---

get close; tel. 021/482-715, www.villaana-split.hr, info@villaana-split.hr, Danijel Bilobrk).

In the Varoš Neighborhood, West of the Old Town

In addition to hosting the following accommodations, the atmospheric Varoš neighborhood—with twisty lanes climbing up toward the forested peak of the Marjan peninsula—is also home to several recommended eateries and the self-service Modrulj Launderette.

$$ Villa Matejuška, run by sweet Andreja, has six apartments with old-fashioned beams and stone walls on a tight lane just up from the fishermen's port (Db-€110-135/€80-105/€60-85, price depends on size, cash only, no extra charge for 1-night stays, no breakfast, air-con, Tomića Stine 3, mobile 098-222-822, www.villamatejuska.hr, villamatejuska97@gmail.com).

$$ Villa Urbi et Orbi has six units a steep five-minute hike up the street—ideal for those wanting to explore the Marjan peninsula (Db-€100-110/€70-80/€50-60, price depends on size, 4-person apartment-€200/€160/€120, same owners and amenities as Villa Matejuška; from Villa Matejuška, continue up Senjska, head straight up the stairs, then turn right on Šenoina to #2; mobile 099-734-2777, www.villaurbietorbi.hr, villaurbietorbi97@gmail.com).

$$ Villa Varoš, run with class by Croatian-American Joanne and her sons Jure and Gregory, has seven rooms and two apartments (with private terraces) on a residential lane just beyond the restau-

SPLIT

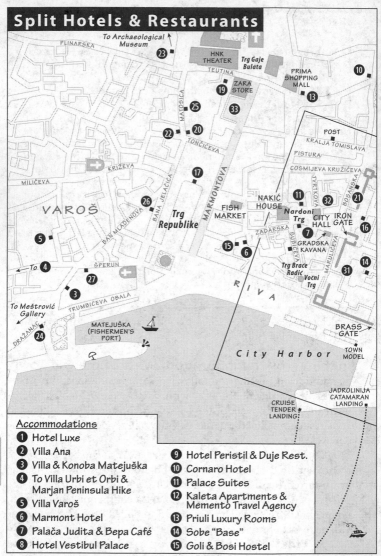

Split Hotels & Restaurants

Accommodations

1. Hotel Luxe
2. Villa Ana
3. Villa & Konoba Matejuška
4. To Villa Urbi et Orbi & Marjan Peninsula Hike
5. Villa Varoš
6. Marmont Hotel
7. Palača Judita & Bepa Café
8. Hotel Vestibul Palace
9. Hotel Peristil & Duje Rest.
10. Cornaro Hotel
11. Palace Suites
12. Kaleta Apartments & Memento Travel Agency
13. Priuli Luxury Rooms
14. Sobe "Base"
15. Goli & Bosi Hostel

rant-lined Šperun street. Thin walls and echoey halls can make for a noisy night (Db-€80/€65, Tb-€90/€70, apartment-€125/€90, big apartment for up to 6-€180, lower prices are for Oct-March, no breakfast, air-con, stairs with no elevator, loaner bikes, Miljenka Smoje 1, tel. 021/483-469, Joanne's mobile 098-469-681, Gregory's mobile 099-215-9538, www.villavaros.hr).

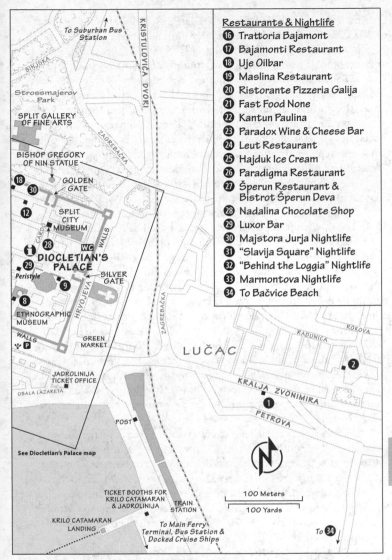

To Suburban Bus Station

KRISTULOVIĆA DVORI

SINJSKA

Strossmajerov Park

SPLIT GALLERY OF FINE ARTS

ZAGREBAČKA

BISHOP GREGORY OF NIN STATUE

18

30

GOLDEN GATE

12

CARDO

SPLIT CITY MUSEUM

28

WALLS

WC

DIOCLETIAN'S PALACE

29

HRVOJEVA

SILVER GATE

Peristyle

9

8

ETHNOGRAPHIC MUSEUM

WALLS

P

GREEN MARKET

ZAGREBAČKA

LUČAC

RADUNIČA

ROKOVA

2

KRALJA ZVONIMIRA

1

PETROVA

JADROLINIJA TICKET OFFICE

OBALA LAZARETA

POST

See Diocletian's Palace map

TICKET BOOTHS FOR KRILO CATAMARAN & JADROLINIJA

TRAIN STATION

KRILO CATAMARAN LANDING

To Main Ferry Terminal, Bus Station & Docked Cruise Ships

N

100 Meters

100 Yards

To 34

Restaurants & Nightlife
16 Trattoria Bajamont
17 Bajamonti Restaurant
18 Uje Oilbar
19 Maslina Restaurant
20 Ristorante Pizzeria Galija
21 Fast Food None
22 Kantun Paulina
23 Paradox Wine & Cheese Bar
24 Leut Restaurant
25 Hajduk Ice Cream
26 Paradigma Restaurant
27 Šperun Restaurant & Bistrot Šperun Deva
28 Nadalina Chocolate Shop
29 Luxor Bar
30 Majstora Jurja Nightlife
31 "Slavija Square" Nightlife
32 "Behind the Loggia" Nightlife
33 Marmontova Nightlife
34 To Bačvice Beach

SPLIT

INSIDE THE OLD TOWN

While the Old Town is convenient and atmospheric, it's also a happening nightlife zone, so you're likely to encounter some noise (especially on weekends).

$$$ Marmont Hotel is a sophisticated oasis offering four-star comfort, with 21 classy rooms in a quiet corner of the Old Town. The slight aroma you may notice is from the fish market, just around the corner (standard Sb-€195/€150/€120, superior Sb-€245/€190/€155, Db-€220/€180/€140, superior Db-€270/€220/€180, pricier "deluxe" rooms also available, air-con, elevator, sun terrace, Zadarska 13, tel. 021/308-060, www.marmonthotel.com, booking@marmonthotel.com).

$$$ Palača Judita is a splurge, designed for people who are willing to pay plenty extra for personal service and serenity in a cozy B&B atmosphere. Its 11 rooms are housed in a 16th-century Renaissance palace on the appealing "People's Square," with solid windows to help block out the after-hours ruckus (Db-€300-380 in June-Sept—but price varies dramatically depending on size, amenities, and when you book; includes breakfast, air-con, free parking and porter service, Narodni Trg 4, tel. 021/420-220, www.juditapalace.com, booking@juditapalace.com).

$$$ Hotel Vestibul Palace is the swankiest spot in Split's Old Town, with modern decor in an old shell. Tucked in a corner just behind the entry vestibule on the upper level of Diocletian's Palace, this plush place offers seven rooms with maximum style and service for maximum prices. Throughout the day, you'll hear the harmonious voices of the *klapa* singers echoing up from the vestibule below; they take their breaks at the hotel's outdoor tables. Sleep here only if you value location, comfort, and service without regard for the price tag (Sb-€355/€255/€140, small "standard" Db-€375/€275/€160, superior Db-€475/€380/€200, pricier suites also available, air-con, no elevator, valet parking, Iza Vestibula 4, tel. 021/329-329, www.vestibulpalace.com, info@vestibulpalace.com). They also have four more rooms in a nearby annex, called Villa Vestibul, and plan even more in a new property just outside the Old Town.

$$$ Hotel Peristil has 12 classy rooms over a restaurant just steps from the couldn't-be-more-central square of the same name. Run by the Caktaš family, it's homey and convenient, if pricey (Sb-€135/€110/€95, Db-€165/€135/€120, extra bed-€35, includes breakfast, air-con, stairs with no elevator, some noise from nearby bars, just behind TI and inside the Silver Gate at Poljana Kraljice Jelene 5, tel. 021/329-070, www.hotelperistil.com, booking@hotelperistil.com).

$$$ Cornaro Hotel is a well-polished, four-star, business-class hotel with 74 spacious rooms, generous public areas, and a view terrace (Db-€150-230, Db suite-€220-360, includes breakfast, parking-€15, Sinjska 6, tel. 021/644-200, www.cornarohotel.com, booking@cornarohotel.com).

$$$ Palace Suites is a 14-room boutique hotel overlooking People's Square with stone walls, mahogany floors, and contemporary furnishings (Db-€140-190, suites-€160-290, includes breakfast, Nardoni Trg 13, tel. 021/339-040, mobile 091-444-4065, www.palacesuites.com, info@palacesuites.com).

$$ Kaleta Apartments, run by the Raić family, consists of five tastefully decorated apartments in two buildings. Two of the comfortable apartments, with stone walls and beamed ceilings, are squeezed between cafés along a lively area at the back of the Old Town (the good windows do a heroic job of keeping noise to a minimum). Their other three units, including a larger one with a couch and eat-in space, share a common lounge in a quieter building a few blocks away, near People's Square (Db-€75-110/€45-80, cash only, air-con, Majstora Jurja 4, mobile 099-509-4299, www.kaletaapartments.com, kaletaapartments@email.t-com.hr).

$$-$$$ Memento Travel Agency manages several apartments, all well-located in the old city. They rent three rooms near People's Square, called Split City Breaks (Db-€60-100/€40-60/€40, no breakfast, air-con, 10 percent less for Rick Steves readers); and two rooms and a snazzy apartment called Villa Marta (Db-€130-180/€90-130/€70-90). Memento Travel Agency can also arrange a room for you elsewhere for similar prices (you pay 20 percent, then the rest to the owner, cash only, check in or get information at Majstora Jurja 4, mobile 091-390-9416, www.split-apartment.com, info@split-apartment.com).

$$ Priuli Luxury Rooms—managed by Memento Travel Agency (see above)—feels like a minihotel, with five elegant, nicely equipped rooms just north of the Old Town (Db-€100-130, larger Db-€110-150/€70-100/€40-60, 10 percent less for Rick Steves readers, Sinjska 1, tel. 091-390-9416, www.priulisplit.com, info@priulisplit.com).

$$ Sobe "Base" has three good rooms in the Old Town. Tina and her dad, Ivo, run a small travel agency where you'll check in. All of the colorful rooms overlook the front steps of the cute little Jupiter's Temple. Although this place is in the midst of some bustling bar action, the double-paned windows provide reasonable peace; earplugs help, too (Db-€80/€70, lower price is for Sept-June, cash only, no extra charge for 1- or 2-night stays, no breakfast, clearly communicate your arrival time if arriving early or late, air-con, Kraj Svetog Ivana 3, tel. 021/317-375, mobile 098-361-387, www.base-rooms.com, mail@base-rooms.com).

$ Goli & Bosi Hostel ("Nude and Barefoot") is a design hostel filling an old shopping mall in a hidden square in Split's Old Town, just off Marmontova. It's big (135 beds in 25 rooms), industrial-strength, and unabashedly stylish. The neon-yellow halls (inspired by the sulfur springs that lured Diocletian here)—scrawled with important dates from Croatian history—give way to white, minimalist rooms. It's expensive (the private rooms are downright overpriced), but it offers lots of fun amenities, including shared view balconies, an "auditorium" for watching movies, a restaurant out front, and lots of parties (bunk in dorm room-€33/€28/€26, small

Sb-€90/€72/€60, small Db-€110/€90/€82, larger "premium" Db-€150/€135, cheaper mid-Oct-mid-April, breakfast-€5, elevator, air-con, tries to be soundproof in sleeping areas, Morpurgova Poljana 2, tel. 021/510-999, www.golibosi.com, info@golibosi.com).

Eating in Split

I've concentrated my listings inside Split's Old Town and within the adjacent Varoš district, just a couple of blocks west, which has several characteristic *konobas* (traditional restaurants). Reservations are wise, especially for dinner.

IN AND NEAR THE OLD TOWN

Trattoria Bajamont, not to be confused with Bajamonti (listed below), is buried on a narrow lane deep in the Old Town. They offer unpretentious, affordable Dalmatian home cooking with an emphasis on fish. The handwritten menu informs you of the day's options—all fresh from the market. In this tight and casual eatery, the busy kitchen and seven tables are all crammed into a single room (with more tables on the alley outside). Because the place can be crowded, you may have to share your table—and be prepared for the service to be a bit quirky (90-120-kn pastas, 90-150-kn fish dishes, cash only, daily 8:00-24:00—but closed Sun outside peak season, Bajamontijeva 3, tel. 021/355-356).

Bajamonti sits regally at the top of Split's beautiful, arcaded square, Trg Republike, just off the west end of the Riva. This place brings a certain grand-café class to Split's otherwise rustic-*konoba*-heavy dining scene. The interior is classy, with checkerboard-tiled, split-level elegance, but the best seating is on the grand square out front, facing the sea. The food is pricey, with an emphasis on fish, but the outside setting is worth the extra kunas (90-120-kn pastas, 120-170-kn main courses, 75-95-kn lunches, daily 7:30-24:00, Trg Republike 1, tel. 021/341-033).

Bepa is a simple place with a great outdoor-only setting on a popular square. It's family-friendly and reasonably priced, serving several types of burgers (40-60 kn) and a variety of omelets and salads (35-80 kn; daily 8:00-24:00, Narodni Trg 1, tel. 021/355-546).

Uje Oilbar is the flagship restaurant of Croatia's popular chain of upscale olive-oil boutiques. Tucked away in a hidden corner of the Old Town, it serves simple plates and boards of Dalmatian *pršut* (prosciutto), cheeses, olives, and, of course, olive oils—50 different types. Dinner here feels more like a big snack than a hearty meal; to assemble a filling meal, you'll run up quite a bill. But the rustic-mod interior, pleasant (if cramped) outdoor seating, and re-freshingly good-quality local flavors can make a light meal here worthwhile (40-70-kn olive-oil tastings, 70-100-kn small plates and taster boards, daily 12:00-24:00, Dominisova 3, mobile 095-200-8008).

Maslina ("Olive"), an unpretentious family-run spot filled with locals, hides behind a shopping mall on the busy Marmontova pedestrian street. They serve a wide range of 50-75-kn pizzas, pastas, and big salads, plus 80-130-kn meat and fish dishes (Tue-Sat 11:00-24:00, Sun-Mon 12:00-24:00, Teutina 1A, tel. 021/314-988, Pezo family). It's virtually impossible to find on your own, so follow these directions carefully: Approaching the top of Marmontova from the harbor, look for the low-profile archway on the left beyond the café tables (just before the big Zara store). Walk along the skinny path between the building and the old wall to reach the restaurant.

Pizzerias: **Ristorante Pizzeria Galija,** at the west end of the Old Town, has a boisterous local following and good wood-fired pizzas, pastas, and salads. They have a woody interior and a terrace (45-85 kn, Mon-Sat 9:00-24:00, Sun 12:00-24:00, air-con, just a block off Marmontova at Tončićeva 12, tel. 021/347-932; the recommended Hajduk ice-cream shop is nearby).

Takeaway: **Fast Food None** ("Grandma's") is a stand-up or takeaway pizza joint handy for a quick bite in the Old Town. In addition to pizzas and bruschettas with various toppings, they serve up a pair of traditional pizza-like specialties (with crust on bottom and top, like a filled pizza): *viška pogača,* with tomatoes, onion, and anchovy; and *soparnik,* with a thin layer of spinach, onion, and olive oil. They can also make you a grilled sandwich—just point to what you want (10-30 kn, Mon-Sat 7:00-23:00, closed Sun, just outside Diocletian's Palace on the skinny street that runs along the wall at Bosanska 4, tel. 021/347-252). **Kantun Paulina** ("Paulina's Corner") is a local favorite for takeaway *ćevapčići*—Balkan grilled meats (18-22 kn, Mon-Sat 8:30-24:00, Sun 10:00-24:00, Matošića 1). For descriptions of your options, see the "Balkan Flavors" sidebar on page 421.

Wine Bar: **Paradox Wine & Cheese Bar,** in an unassuming urban zone behind the National Theater, offers an inviting opportunity to sample some local wines and appetizers. Their well-structured menu lists 120 wines, 50 of which are available by the glass (most about 30 kn). Sit either in the cozy old-meets-modern interior or out on the terrace (also 25-80-kn light bites, including cheese and prosciutto, daily 9:00-24:00, Dubrovačka 18, mobile 099-817-0711).

Breakfast: The budget choice is to simply buy some pastries at a bakery and eat them on a harborfront bench. **Hotel Peristil** serves an all-you-can-eat breakfast—including eggs—to nonguests for 60 kn (daily 7:00-11:00); the adjacent **Duje Restaurant,** just behind the cathedral, has a similar deal. For a cheap alternative, head over to the Matejuška fishermen's port, where **Leut** restaurant serves a 30-45-kn breakfast on their terrace (from 9:30). Several of my recommended restaurants also offer breakfast.

Gelato: Split has several spots for delicious ice cream *(sladoled).* Most ice-cream parlors *(kuća sladoleda)* are open daily 8:00-24:00. Natives recommend **Hajduk,** named for Split's soccer team; ask them to dip your cone in milk chocolate for no extra charge (a block off the main Marmontova pedestrian drag, around the corner from Pizzeria Galija at Matošićeva 4).

IN VAROŠ,
WEST OF THE OLD TOWN

Paradigma is the place to go for fine cuisine. The food here is carefully prepared and served in a blue marine interior, or (better) on the broad upstairs terrace. Chef Ante Udovičić trained under famous French chef Paul Bocuse and seems to have learned his trade well (€40 five-course meal, €60 tasting menu, wine pairings available, Mon-Sat 11:30-24:00, Sun 18:00-24:00, Bana Jelačića ulica 3, tel. 021/645-103, www.restoranparadigma.hr).

Konoba Matejuška offers charm, good food, and fair prices in a cozy, mellow, five-table cellar. This place is tiny and justifiably popular, so reserve at least a day before (60-80-kn starters, 60-150 kn main courses, daily 12:00-23:00, Tomića Stine 3, tel. 021/355-152).

Šperun Restaurant has a cozy, Old World ambience and a passion for good Dalmatian food. Owner Damir Banović (with the help of his animated dad, Zdravko) serves a mix of Croatian and "eclectic Mediterranean," specializing in seafood. A modest "buffet" table of *antipasti* (starters) in the lower dining room shows you what you're getting, so you can select your ideal meal (not self-service—order from the waiter). This place is known for its warm welcome and reasonable prices (40-90-kn pastas, 60-130-kn meat and seafood dishes, daily 9:00-23:00—but likely closed Sun Nov-March, air-con, a few sidewalk tables, reservations wise in summer, Šperun 3, tel. 021/346-999). Their annex across the street, **Bistrot Šperun Deva,** has a simpler and cheaper menu, lots of outdoor seating, and a handy à la carte breakfast for *soba*-dwellers (20-50-kn salads, 60-75-kn main courses, daily 8:00-23:00—except closed 13:00-18:00 Mon-Tue, closed off-season, Šperun 2).

Split Connections

BY BOAT

As the transport hub for the Dalmatian Coast, Split has good boat connections to nearly anywhere you want to go. But things change, so confirm anything listed here before you make your plans. To check Jadrolinija schedules, see www.jadrolinija.hr; for *Krilo* catamaran schedules, see www. krilo.hr. You can also drop by Split's helpful, air-conditioned, and typically uncrowded Jadrolinija main ticket office, in the ferry terminal (open 24/7 in summer, daily 5:30-24:00 off-season, tel. 021/338-333).

Finding Your Boat: The fast passenger **catamarans** dock close to the Old Town: the *Krilo* catamaran uses dock #11 (a.k.a. Gat Sv. Petra), which is across from the train station, halfway between the main ferry terminal and the Old Town; and the Jadrolinija catamaran usually arrives and departs at the handy Obala Lazareta embankment just in front of the Old Town (although it may sometimes use dock #11 instead—ask when you buy your ticket). On the catamarans, boarding typically begins 30 minutes before departure; arrive early in peak season to snare a window seat. Big **car ferries** can arrive or depart from all along the harbor (electronic boards display which dock each boat leaves from). Note that these locations sometimes change according to boat traffic.

Fares: Walk-on passage for both catamarans and ferries is affordable. The passenger fare on a trip from Split to Hvar or Korčula costs only around 55-70 kn, depending on the type of boat and season. (For a car, figure 265-530 kn for a similar trip.)

Buying Tickets: If you want to take a fast passenger catamaran (either *Krilo* or Jadrolinija), buy your tickets in advance. Both companies allow online ticket purchase. Tickets sell out quickly—especially for weekend departures. To avoid disappointment, book at least three or four days ahead in July and August, and at least the day before in shoulder season. Both companies also have ticket offices in Split.

Krilo **tickets** can be bought anytime at www.krilo.hr. You can also look for the *sales* kiosk marked *Kapetan Luka* at the departure dock.

Jadrolinija catamaran tickets for most departures can be purchased online at www.jadrolinija.hr, starting one month before departure. However, you cannot buy online tickets for same-day departures. If any tickets are left, they can be purchased starting

Sailing Between Croatia and Italy

While adding a dash of Italy to your Croatian vacation is a romantic notion, it can be more complicated than it sounds. Most sea crossings are overnight, and the Italian towns best connected to Croatia—Ancona, Pescara, and Bari—are each a lengthy train ride away from Italy's top sights.

Split is the primary hub for boats to Italy, but there are sometimes also connections from Dubrovnik or Zadar. (Note that in Italian, Split is called "Spalato"...which is also the sound you hear if seasickness gets the best of you.) Almost all boats go to Ancona, Italy, which is on the calf of Italy's "boot." Others go to Pescara, about 100 miles south of Ancona (the "cankle"), and to Bari, near the southeastern tip of Italy (the "heel"). Most trips are overnight and last 8-10 hours; faster daytime catamarans run sporadically. Note that these connections are highly subject to change from year to year; do an Internet search to be confident you know all your options.

Slow Night Boats: The lineup of companies that operate night boats to Italy includes **Jadrolinija** (www.jadrolinija.hr), **SNAV** (www.snav.it), and **Blue Line** (www.blueline-ferries.com). Other lines serving these routes come and go each year—for the latest, search online, ask the Split TI, or poke around Split's main

at 6:00 in the morning at one of three ticket points: the kiosk on the parking island right in front of the Old Town; next to the *Krilo* kiosk alongside the harbor; and in the main terminal (which is air-conditioned and may have a shorter line than the other kiosks). Note: A few Jadrolinija departures, designated for island residents (rather than "commercial"), can't be purchased online—only in person.

If catamaran tickets do sell out, you're not entirely out of luck. Each route is also operated by slower **car ferries** with unlimited room for walk-on passengers. The downside is that car ferries drop you off at ports that are not convenient to the main town on each island (Stari Grad on Hvar, Vela Luka on Korčula), requiring an additional bus trip to your final destination. The ticket seller can advise you on alternatives. Car ferries always have room for foot passengers, so you can buy tickets anytime (sold at the same three locations noted above). However, if you're driving onto a car ferry, it's smart to line up early—ask locally for advice on your particular boat.

Weather Disruptions: Catamarans are the quickest way to the islands, but they're also the most susceptible to inclement weather. In very rough or windy weather, cancellations are possible (decisions are made a couple of hours before departure—ask at the ticket booth what time you should come back to check). In poor

terminal building. Figure about €50-60 per person for one-way deck passage (about 10-20 percent more in July-Aug, sometimes even more on weekends). Onboard accommodation costs extra (about €20 per person for a couchette in a 4-berth compartment, €60-75 per person in 2-bed compartment with private shower and WC, up to €100 per person in a seaview double).

Fast Catamaran: So far, only SNAV (listed above) runs a faster daytime catamaran from Split to Ancona, which takes 4.5 hours (July-Aug only).

Trains Within Italy: From **Ancona**, trains zip to Florence (3 hours, change in Bologna), Venice (4 hours, change in Bologna), and Rome (4 hours). From **Pescara**, it's about 4.5 hours to either Rome (direct) or Florence (via Bologna). And from **Bari**, you can hop a train to Naples (4 hours, most transfer in Caserta), Rome (4 hours direct), or Florence (7 hours, most transfer in Bologna). For timetables, check www.trenitalia.com or www.bahn.com.

Northern Italy/Croatia: If you're heading to Istria (in northern Croatia), you may find it's easier to side-trip from there to Venice than it is to head across the Adriatic from Dalmatia. Venice is connected by boat to several seaside towns in northern Croatia and Slovenia. For details, see page 98.

weather, the *Krilo* is more stable (and provides a more comfortable ride) than Jadrolinija's catamaran; if you have an option, go with *Krilo*. If the catamarans aren't running, look into taking the slower car ferries instead (which typically go in any weather).

Getting from Split to Dalmatian Destinations

To Hvar Island: Note that Hvar Island has two commonly used ports. Ideally, make sure your boat goes to simply "Hvar" (that is, Hvar town), rather than "Stari Grad." Two different companies run speedy catamarans from Split to Hvar town in about an hour: The national ferry operator, **Jadrolinija** (June-Sept at least 3/day—often more sailings July-Aug; Oct-May 2/day); and the smaller, private company called *Krilo* (1/day June-Sept, 3-4/week May and Oct, none Nov-April; an additional catamaran, bound for Vis, runs year-round but stops at Hvar only on Tue). *Krilo's* schedules are changeable—confirm details at www.krilo.hr. Alternatively, you can reach Hvar Island on a **local car ferry** from Split (7/day in summer, 3/day in winter, operated by Jadrolinija). These car ferries are frequent but take longer (2 hours) and are less convenient, since they take you to the town of Stari Grad. From Stari Grad, it's a 20-minute drive or public bus ride across the island to Hvar town (public buses generally meet most arriving ferries).

To Korčula Island: As with Hvar, it's important to pay attention to which port on Korčula Island your boat uses: "Korčula" (that is, Korčula town) is far more convenient than "Vela Luka," at the opposite end of the island (a 1-hour bus ride away). To reach Korčula town from Split (about 2.5 hours), the most convenient options are the direct **catamarans:** *Krilo* runs in the early morning (1/day June-Sept, 3-4/week May and Oct, none Nov-April), while Jadrolinija's catamaran goes daily year-round in the late afternoon (they may also have a morning run mid-June-early Sept). If you're desperate, additional boats head to Vela Luka, including a different Jadrolinija catamaran (generally 1/day, 2 hours) or on Jadrolinija's slower **local car ferries** (2/day, 2-3 hours).

To Dubrovnik and Mljet National Park: The Split-Hvar-Korčula *Krilo* catamaran line, described above, also continues to Mljet National Park (3 hours) and Dubrovnik (4 hours; for details, see www.krilo.hr).

BY BUS

Each of the following routes is served by multiple companies. Always ask about the fastest option—which can save hours of bus time. It's smart to arrive about 30 minutes before your bus departs to buy tickets (better yet, during peak season, come to the station to buy them earlier in the day). The generally English-speaking staff at Split's bus station gives out handy little schedules for popular journeys. Bus info: www.ak-split.hr, toll tel. 060-327-777.

By Bus to: Zagreb (at least hourly, 5-8 hours depending on route), **Dubrovnik** (at least hourly, less off-season, 4.5 hours), **Korčula** (1 night bus leaves at 1:00 in the morning and arrives around 7:00), **Trogir** (1-2/hour, 30 minutes), **Zadar** (at least hourly, 3 hours), **Mostar** (7/day, 4 hours), **Međugorje** (4/day, 3 hours), **Sarajevo** (2/day, 7.5-8 hours), **Rijeka** (7-10/day, 7 hours). Zagreb-bound buses sometimes also stop at **Plitvice** (confirm with driver and ask him to stop at the national park entrance; about 7/ day in summer—the best are the direct connections with Prijevoz Knežević, described on page 91; 4/day in winter, 4-6 hours).

BY TRAIN

From Split, trains go to **Zagreb** (3/day, 6.5 hours; 1 direct night train, 9 hours); in Zagreb, you can transfer to **Ljubljana** (4/day, 9 hours total). Train info: tel. 021/338-525 or toll tel. 060-333-444, www.hznet.hr.

BY SEAPLANE

European Coastal Airlines offers a speedy, scenic, and expensive way to connect coastal destinations. They operate 19-passeger propeller seaplanes, serving big cities (Split, Pula, Rijeka, Zadar, Dubrovnik) as well as sleepy island villages (Hvar, Korčula, Vis, Rab, and so on). Readers have reported that the seats are a tight squeeze, and unpredictable weather can delay or reroute scheduled flights. But if you're in a hurry, this is a memorable and efficient way to connect the dots—especially for long journeys, such as Dalmatia to Istria (www.ec-air.eu, tel. 021/444-813).

ROUTE TIPS FOR DRIVERS

Driving in the city center can be challenging. Split is split by its Old Town, which is welded to the harbor by the pedestrian-only Riva promenade. This means drivers needing to get 300 yards from one side of the Old Town to the other must drive about 15 minutes entirely around the center, which can be miserably clogged with traffic. A semicircular ring road and a tunnel under the Marjan peninsula help relieve the situation a bit.

Arriving in Split: Drivers are treated to the ugly side of Split as they approach town (don't worry—it gets better). From the expressway, you'll pass through an industrial zone, then curl through a few tunnels as you twist your way down into Split's striking, bowl-like setting. While you're still quite a distance from downtown, you'll come to a fork where you'll have to make a decision about which side of town you want to drive to (east or west); ask your hotel in advance for directions, and be ready for your turn. (While many hotels are individually signposted at the fork, it's a long list and hard to read quickly as you zip past.)

At the main fork, turning to the right (marked with *Centar* signs) takes you to the **west end** of the Old Town, including the Varoš neighborhood. Or, if you continue straight (marked *Trajekt*—"ferry"), you'll eventually reach other *Centar* signs and the **east end** of the Old Town, with the ferry terminal, the bus and train stations, and the Lučac neighborhood. You'll pop out right at the southeast corner of Diocletian's Palace (by the Green Market). For handy but expensive parking, when the road swings left to the ferry terminal, continue straight, and then turn right into a parking lot just outside the palace walls. I'd park here only to unload and find my hotel, then ask about cheaper long-term parking elsewhere.

Connecting Split with Destinations to the North: Thanks to Croatia's A-1 super-expressway, the road trip from Zagreb to Split takes less than five hours. If you're heading north from Split, simply drive up out of the city's bowl-like setting and follow signs to the A-1 expressway north (toward Zagreb; if you're going to Plitvice, get off at Otočac and drive east from there).

Connecting Split with Destinations to the South: If you're heading to Dubrovnik, other Dalmatian Coast destinations, or Mostar, it's a bit more complicated, as the expressway southbound from Split is only partially completed (to check the latest progress,

SPLIT

see www.hac.hr or www.hak.hr). You have two options: the scenic coastal road or the speedy expressway.

The main **coastal road** twists slowly but scenically along some fantastic scenery, in an area dubbed the "Makarska Riviera." (Along this road is the town of Drvenik, where you can take a ferry to Sućuraj on Hvar Island; from Sućuraj, a long and twisty road traverses the length of the island to Hvar town. If you're going to Hvar Island, taking a car ferry directly from Split to Stari Grad is much faster and less stressful.) Continuing south, you'll wind up in the town of Ploče (described later).

To save some time, most travelers prefer to take the **expressway** part of the way. To do this, as you leave Split, follow blue expressway signs to *Dubrovnik*. You can take A-1 south as far as it goes; it cuts inland from the sea, running behind the tall coastal mountain range, near the Bosnian border, all the way to the city of Ploče. (If you're headed to Mostar, get off the expressway and cross the border just south of Vrgorac, at Veliki Prolog, then follow signs to *Mostar* from there.)

Ploče has a ferry that runs to the town of Trpanj, on the landward side of the Pelješac Peninsula—not far from Orebić, where another boat plods across to Korčula town. If you're headed to Korčula and plan your timing to catch this ferry, it could save you some driving.

Just south of Ploče is the dramatic Neretva River Delta, a scenic and lush zone of farmland (described on page 453). This also marks the end of the A-1 expressway. Here you'll hop on the main Dalmatian coastal road. Halfway along the delta, you'll see the turnoff to Metković, the gateway town on the main, heavily touristed road between Croatia and Mostar.

South of the Neretva River Delta—after twisting up to a high perch overlooking the delta—is a border crossing. Here begins an odd little stretch of coastline that's technically in Bosnia, around the town of Neum (for details on Neum—and the bridge Croatia is building to bypass it—see "A Bridge Too Far?" on page 355). Have your passport ready, but don't panic—the border is generally a quick wave-through. After a few more miles, you'll cross back into Croatia, and shortly come to a crossroads where, if you like, you can turn right and detour a few minutes to the impressively walled little villages of Ston and Mali Ston, at the base of the Pelješac Peninsula (all described on page 354). If you're headed to Korčula, continue beyond Ston to the far end of the Pelješac Peninsula, where the ferry plods from Orebić to Dominče, near Korčula town.

After Ston, you're less than an hour from Dubrovnik. Along the way, you'll have fine views of Mljet and the Elaphite Islands. As you near Dubrovnik, you'll pass through the town of Trsteno, which has a good arboretum (described on page 353). When you cross the giant, modern bridge, you'll know Dubrovnik is just around the bend; for arrival tips, see page 280.

Near Split

Two destinations are easy, worthwhile side-trips from Split: the small town of Trogir, and farther north, the swimmable waterfalls at Krka National Park.

Trogir

Just 12 miles northwest of Split, across a giant bay, is Trogir, a tiny, medieval-architecture-packed town surrounded by water.

This made-for-tourists village is appealing, though it lacks the real-world heart and soul of Split. Trogir is popular with yachters; the proud masts of tall ships line the harbor three deep. Although Trogir is nothing to jump ship for, it's an easy day trip for those looking to get away from urban Split.

GETTING THERE

The easiest option in summer is to take the Bura Line **boat,** which avoids traffic and includes a minicruise on the Adriatic. The boat departs from the embankment in front of the Riva (24 kn one-way, 4/day June-Sept only, 1 hour, stops at Čiovo Island en route, www.buraline.com).

You also have two bus options for reaching Trogir from Split, both roughly the same price (20-25 kn): The faster, easier option is to take a bus from Split's **main bus station,** next to the City Harbor. Any bus going north (for example, to Šibenik, Zadar, or even Rijeka) will usually stop at Trogir (1-2/hour, 30 minutes, simply go to ticket window and ask for next bus to Trogir). Note that in the busiest summer months, long-distance bus drivers may not want to take you (preferring to give your seat instead to someone paying for a longer trip). The other, slower option is **local bus #37;** because this bus makes several stops along the way, it can take longer (3/hour Mon-Fri, 2/hour Sat-Sun; 45-60 minutes, depending on traffic; departs from Split's suburban bus station—Prigradski Autobusni Kolodvor, a 10-minute walk north of Old Town on Domovinskog rata; buy 20-kn ticket for zone IV at ticket window or on bus). Note that bus #37 also stops at the **airport** on its way between Split and Trogir; if you're sleeping in Trogir before catching a flight, this bus is handy (about 10 minutes from Trogir; taxis from Trogir to the airport are exorbitantly priced).

Drivers will find a handy pay parking lot on the left just before Trogir; you can walk into town in five minutes (pass the bus station and cross the bridge).

Orientation to Trogir

Trogir is a small island wedged between the mainland and the much bigger Čiovo Island. Busy bridges connect it to the rest of the world at its east end, and a big soccer field squeezed between imposing watchtowers anchors the west end. In the middle is a tight medieval maze of twisty marble-stone lanes.

Tourist Information: At the main square, named for Pope John Paul II (Trg Ivana Pavla II), you'll find the TI (open long hours daily except closed Sun off-season, tel. 021/885-628).

Arrival in Trogir: Buses drop you off at the mainland market, just across the canal from the island. Cross the bridge into town and wander straight ahead for two blocks (bearing left); you'll run into the main square.

Sights in Trogir

On the main square is the town's centerpiece, the **Cathedral of St. Lawrence** (Katedrala Sv. Lovre). Built from the 13th through the 17th century, the cathedral drips with history. The bell tower alone took 200 years to build, leaving it a textbook lesson in Dalmatian architectural styles: straightforward Gothic at the bottom, Venetian Gothic in the middle, and Renaissance at the top. The cathedral's front entryway—the ornately decorated, recently restored Radovan's Portal—is worth a gander. Inside, it's dark, very old-feeling, and packed with altars. The treasury features some beautiful 15th-century carved-wood cabinets filled with ecclesiastical art and gear.

The town's other sights are the **Town Museum** (Muzej Grada), a few blocks north (toward the mainland) from the main square; and the **Monastery of St. Nikola** (Samostan Sv. Nikole), a few blocks south (toward Čiovo Island).

But Trogir isn't for museum going; it's for aimless strolling. And the best place for that is the wide, beautifully manicured **harborfront promenade** along the southern edge of town (Obala bana Berislavića). Lined with expensive restaurants, and clogged with giddy, ice-cream-licking tourists, this promenade is the highlight of a visit to Trogir. Often the enormous yachts of the rich and famous stern-tie into the good life here, giving wanderers something to gaze at and yak about. At the far end of the promenade, the

Kamerlengo Fortress has a lookout tower with fine views over the town and region.

Sleeping in Trogir

Some travelers prefer sleepy Trogir to bustling Split. But since Trogir is also lively after-hours, and is in the airport's flight path, it's hardly the quietest place in Dalmatia.

$$$ Hotel Pašike is a family-run boutique hotel with lots of character. Situated over a restaurant in the Old Town, its 13 rooms come with over-the-top traditional formality (standard Db-€135/€118/€100, superior Db-€150/€135/€115, less Nov-April, 10 percent cheaper if you pay cash or stay longer than 3 nights, air-con, Splitska 4, tel. 021/885-185, mobile 091-484-8434, www.hotelpasike.com, info@hotelpasike.com, Buble family).

$$ Hotel Concordia, with 11 outmoded-but-tidy, slightly overpriced rooms at the end of the embankment, is run with warmth by the Bulum family (Sb-€65/€60, small Db with view or bigger Db without view-€80/€75, big Db with view-€100/€90, lower prices are for Sept-June, includes breakfast, air-con, Obala bana Berislavića 22, tel. 021/885-400, www.concordia-hotel.net, concordia-hotel@st.t-com.hr).

$ Palaća Stafileo, well-run by gentle Thomas, has six apartments in a 15th-century Venetian palace buried in a quiet part of town (Db-€60-70/€55-65/€50-60, price depends on size of apartment, cash only, no breakfast, air-con, lots of stairs, Subićeva 7a, tel. 021/885-680, mobile 098-131-3171, www.trogironline.com/stafileo, stafileo@vip.hr).

Krka National Park

While Plitvice has Croatia's best waterfalls, they're not the only game in town. An hour north of Split, an easy detour off the ex-

pressway, is the glittering canyon of Krka National Park. This sprawling park—where the Krka (pronounced KUR-kah) River spreads out and splits into many fingers cut deep into the parched limestone, with shimmering blue waters and forested walls—could occupy a nature lover for days. But its claim to fame is simple to reach and enjoy in just a few hours: the multitiered Skradinski Buk waterfall. While not as magical or as expansive as Plitvice's cascades, Skradinski Buk is bigger (a single grand run, rather than sprinkled throughout a canyon) and less crowded. And, crucially, at Skradinski Buk, swimmers are allowed to dive into its lowest pool. If you could barely resist the urge to jump into the ponds at Plitvice, this is your chance. (Because the footing is uneven and the services for swimmers are basically nonexistent, I'd recommend this only for hardy paddlers who enjoy a good, rugged swimmin' hole.)

Cost and Hours: The ticket price changes by season—110 kn (June-Sept), 90 kn (March-May and Oct), or 30 kn (Nov-Feb)—and includes the boat from Skradin to Skradinski Buk and the shuttle bus from Lozovac to Skradinski Buk, but not boats or shuttle buses to other parts of the park. The park is open daily June-Aug 8:00-20:00, May and Sept 8:00-18:00, and Oct-April 9:00-16:00. The last boat from Skradinski Buk back to Skradin departs 30 minutes before closing time. Information: www.npkrka.hr, tel. 022/771-688.

Getting There: By **car,** it's easy—about an hour north of Split, just off the expressway (see exit information for both major park entrances below). By **public transportation,** the easiest option is to take the direct bus from Split to Skradin, where you can buy your park ticket and hop on the boat to Lozovac and the waterfalls (5-6/day in summer, first departure around 8:00, 1.5 hours; you can ride the boat back to return on this same bus, or you can take the bus from Lozovac to Šibenik and return to Split from there). The other option is to first take the bus from Split to the city of Šibenik; from there, buses go to both the Skradin entrance (for the boat trip) and the Lozovac entrance (closer to the waterfalls). Check the specifics for any of these connections locally (at the Split TI or bus station). Alternatively, consider paying for an **excursion** from Split (or other cities in Dalmatia), which includes door-to-door transportation and the park entrance fee; this often doesn't cost much more than doing it on your own, but you'll have to stick to a set itinerary.

Visiting the National Park: The national park sprawls over 42 square miles, with five entrances; assuming your interest is the Skradinski Buk waterfall, you can ignore all but two of them. The most efficient entrance for most travelers is the **Lozovac entrance** ("Šibenik" exit from A-1 expressway, then a 7-mile, 15-minute drive). Here you'll find a large and free parking lot, and you can take a shuttle bus straight down to the waterfalls (leaves every 15 minutes or so, 10-minute ride on a very twisty and steep road). If you have more time and would prefer to approach the falls by boat, you can use the **Skradin entrance** ("Skradin" exit from A-1, then a 3-mile, 5-minute drive). From the glassy new visitors center here, you can hop on an hourly boat for the 20-minute trip to Skradinski Buk (included in your park ticket; boats depart every 2 hours off-season, Oct-April).

Skradinski Buk: Once at Skradinski Buk, you'll find a roughly circular, 1.5-mile boardwalk path that takes you up, down, and around the various cascades, through forests, over gurgling streams, and to a variety of thrilling viewpoints. Near the top of the falls—where the shuttle bus from Lozovac arrives—is a restaurant, an "ethno village" (with a few houses displaying traditional lifestyles), and a large terrace with free WCs and grand views of the falls. Near the bottom of the falls—where the boat from Skradin arrives—is a pay WC popular with swimmers, a large outdoor eating area (mostly table-service restaurants and a few snack stands), and the bridge that cuts across the pool at the bottom of the falls. From this bridge, you'll spot people enjoying the park's most popular activity: swimming near the falls.

Swimmers are allowed only in this one, large pool at the bottom of the final cascade. While swimming is permitted, it's not exactly encouraged; there are no lifeguards, no real beach, no showers, and no official changing rooms (you have several options: wear your swimsuit to the park; pay a small fee to change in the cramped WC 100 yards away from the pool; or awkwardly change into your suit under a towel...or do as many Europeans do, and just skip the towel). When you're ready to get in, make your way across the uneven, root-embedded ground and find a place to gingerly slip in. The water can be chilly, and you'll smell the fishy aroma from the pounding spray, but it's generally clean. As you wade into the pool, watch your footing—the same travertine dams that create those grand waterfalls can be very treacherous to walk on, with dramatically uneven surfaces, occasional sharp edges, and slippery moss. Once you've tiptoed past the initial rocky gauntlet, you can plunge into the deeper section—noticing that the closer you get to the falls, the stronger the current pushes you back.

Other Excursions in the Park: Aside from hiking and swimming, another popular attraction at Krka is its variety of excursions by boat or minibus to farther-flung parts of the park. These excursions are not covered by the entrance ticket. Options include a two-hour cruise to **Visovac Island,** with its picturesque Franciscan monastery; a 3.5-hour cruise to **Visovac Island and Roški Slap** (another, less striking waterfall where you can swim); and a 2.5-hour trip to the **Krka Monastery** and ruins of two fortresses. Other excursions take you to the ancient Roman ruins (amphitheater and military camp) at **Burnum.**

SPLIT

HVAR

Hvar's hip cachet, upscale-ritzy "Croatian Riviera" buzz, and easy proximity to Split have quickly turned this tidy Dalmatian fishing village into one of the most popular destinations in Croatia. The island desperately wants to be thought of as Croatia's answer to Mykonos or St-Tropez...and it's getting there. While the infrastructure lags a bit behind, the rows of yachts tied up five deep in the harbor—and the steady string of wealthy yuppies dressing up for a night on the town—don't seem to notice. Budget travelers may be stymied by Hvar's pervasive "quality is worth paying for" mantra. But while some may find Hvar's relative glitz off-putting, the setting is undeniably gorgeous, and the island provides a cosmopolitan contrast to its lowbrow rival, Korčula.

Hvar's straightforward main town, also called Hvar, melts into the harbor rather than dominating it. And as you get to know it, Hvar reveals itself to be a fun-loving, easygoing place to be on vacation. Its quirky museums, while far from time-consuming, are enjoyable. The formidable fortress hovering above town provides restless beach bums with a good excuse for a hike—and rewards hikers with stunning views.

If you're seeking nightlife, you'll find that happening Hvar becomes a rollicking party town after hours. In jam-packed August, the entire town seems to be hopping to the same thumpa-thumpa beat...much to the aggravation of those looking for a sleepy island getaway. Hvar has become popular for celebrity-spotting—from Beyoncé, Tom Cruise, and Bill Gates to Giorgio Armani, Ellen DeGeneres, and Britain's Prince Harry. Locals claim their laid-back attitude is perfect for high-profile visitors who just want to be left alone.

Despite Hvar's newfound fame, it has plenty of history. Its tongue-twisting name comes from the ancient Greek settlement here: Pharos. Greeks from the island of Paros migrated here in the fourth century B.C., attracted by the fertile farmland. Since then, it's been occupied by Slavs, Venetians, Habsburgs, and—today—tourists, all of whom have left their mark.

But Hvar town is just the beginning. Hvar Island—which insists it's both the sunniest and greenest in Dalmatia—entertains those who stay here long enough to do some exploring. Known for its excellent wines (grapes love the island's perfect combination of wind and sunshine), stony terraces, and smattering of fragrant lavender fields, Hvar Island's gentle climate is appreciated by tourists and farmers alike. Every corner and cove of Hvar has something to offer, but for speedy tourists, the most obvious and easiest side-trip from Hvar town is the Pakleni Islands, a small archipelago just offshore.

PLANNING YOUR TIME

Don't overdose on Dalmatian islands. On a quick visit, overnighting on one island is enough—choose either Hvar or Korčula, and give it at least two nights and a full day. (If you're efficient, you can squeeze in a brief visit to Hvar on the way to Korčula—see strategies next.) On a longer, more relaxed vacation, sleep in both towns.

With a full day on Hvar, do your sightseeing—or hike to the fortress (with little shade)—in the morning, before the weather gets too hot and while the sights are open (many close for an afternoon siesta). Use the rest of the day to relax, swim at the beaches, explore the Old Town, or take a trip out to Palmižana on the Pakleni Islands (this excursion works well in the late afternoon—take a dip while it's still hot, then hike over to Vlaka for your dinner reservation at Dionis).

If time is short, well-connected Hvar is easier to see on the run (for example, a few hours en route between Split and Korčula—just keep in mind that many sights close at 12:00 or 13:00).

Be warned that July and especially August are peak-of-the-peak season. When you ask locals about crowds in August, they just roll their eyes and groan. It can be impossible to find a room, and the "undiscovered" back lanes and "hidden" offshore islands are jam-packed with loud, partying tourists. In August, consider giving Hvar a miss. Conversely, the town is completely dead off-season (roughly from the second or third week of Oct until the third or fourth week of May), when many hotels, restaurants, and even museums shut their doors for winter hibernation. The best times to visit Hvar are late May through the end of June, and September through early October.

Orientation to Hvar

First off, "Hvar" is pronounced like it's spelled, but the H is nearly silent. If you struggle with it, just say "var" (but don't say "huh-var," which just sounds silly to locals).

Hvar town (with about 3,600 residents) clusters around its harbor. The harbor's eastern embankment (to the right, with your back to the water) is where the big boats put in, and is home to the Jadrolinija boat ticket office, most travel agencies and tourist services, and the post office. At the top of the harbor is Hvar's generous main square, St. Stephen's Square (Trg Svetog Stjepana). The Old Town scampers up the hills in either direction from the square. Overlooking the town and harbor is a mighty hilltop fortress. Sprawling in both directions from the Old Town are nondescript residential zones packed with good-value apartment rentals, many with sensational sea views.

TOURIST INFORMATION

Hvar's TI is in the big Arsenal building right on the main square, a few steps from the harbor. Ask about events, and confirm details for your day trips and ferry connections (mid-June-Aug daily 8:00-14:00 & 15:00-21:00; May-mid-June and Sept-Oct Mon-Sat 8:00-14:00 & 16:00-20:00, Sun 8:00-12:00; Nov-April Mon-Sat 8:00-14:00, closed Sun; off-season hours can vary with demand; Trg Svetog Stjepana, tel. 021/741-059 or 021/742-977, www.tzhvar.hr).

ARRIVAL IN HVAR

If you're staying at one of the private rooms or apartments outside the Old Town, clearly communicate your arrival time to your host, and ask for directions. Some hosts may offer to come pick you up, but because only a few vehicles have permission to enter the Old Town area, most will need to meet you at the bus station (a scenic 10-minute stroll from the harbor, through the middle of the main square—see details next).

By Boat: Passenger boats to **Hvar town** arrive on the harbor's eastern embankment. Simply exit and walk to the left—you'll run right into St. Stephen's Square. To continue to the bus station (where taxis wait), walk the length of St. Stephen's Square, jog left around the cathedral, then angle left through the big open square.

Car ferries to Hvar Island (including the big Jadrolinija coastal ferries) arrive just outside the town of **Stari Grad,** across the island from Hvar town. Buses are timed to meet arriving boats and take passengers over the island's picturesque spine to Hvar town (20 minutes, 30 kn; off-season, not every car ferry is met by a bus—confirm before booking your ticket).

By Bus: Hvar's bus station is just beyond the far end of St. Stephen's Square from the harbor. As you get off your bus, you can see the main tower of the cathedral—marking the town center, a two-minute walk away. The island's few **taxis** usually hang out at the bus station.

By Car: Car ferries from Split and most other destinations arrive on Hvar Island at the town of Stari Grad. There are two ways to drive from Stari Grad to Hvar town: the speedy, newer road via Dubovica (and a long tunnel) to the south; or the slower, windy road (through prettier, less-traveled terrain) via Brusje to the north. In Hvar, you can park by the bus station. Be warned that the car ferries can be crowded in summer—waiting two hours or more is not unusual.

A second ferry crossing is at the opposite tip of Hvar Island, connecting the island's settlement of Sućuraj to the mainland town of Drvenik. But the road connecting Sućuraj to Hvar town is long, twisty, and challenging to drive—most visitors prefer arriving and departing at Stari Grad instead. If you do need to drive from Hvar town to Sućuraj, give yourself about 1.5 hours, and add about an hour to get to the boat dock before everyone else making the same trip. There are plans to straighten some stretches of this road, which may make the trip easier and slightly shorter.

HELPFUL HINTS

Boat Tickets: Tickets for the fast catamarans to Split and Korčula Island sell out quickly in peak season—buy them as early as possible; see page 784 for details.

Live Music: The Hvar Summer Festival fills the entire peak season (mid-May–early Oct) with frequent concerts. Ask the TI for a Summer Festival *Program* with the latest schedule. Other festivals include the Lavender Fest, which packs the little village of Velo Grablje with demonstrations and a general celebration of the traditional harvesting of the fragrant herb (last weekend in June).

Addresses: Everyone in Hvar ignores house numbers (you'll constantly see *b.b.*, meaning "without number") and even street names. Making things more complicated, the town recently renamed and renumbered many streets and addresses...so you now have twice as many ways to get lost. (Locals tend to ignore both the old and the new systems.) Navigate with maps

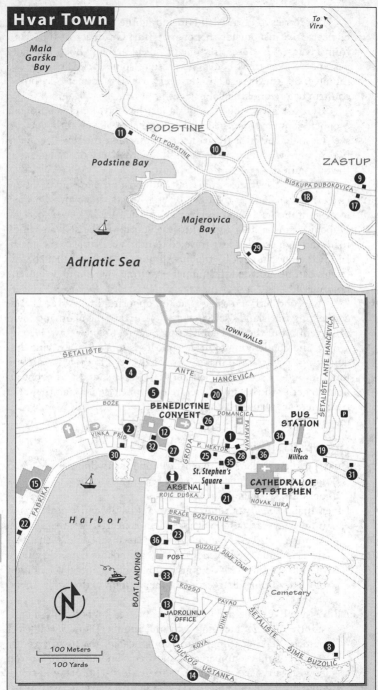

Hvar Town

Mala Garška Bay

PODSTINE

To Vira

11

PUT PODSTINE

10

ZASTUP

9

Podstine Bay

BISKUPA DUBOKOVIĆA

18

17

Majerovica Bay

29

Adriatic Sea

ŠETALIŠTE

TOWN WALLS

ŠETALIŠTE ANTE HANČEVIĆA

4

ANTE HANČEVIĆA

5

BOŽE

BENEDICTINE CONVENT

20

26

3

DOMANČIĆA

BUS STATION

P

2

VINKA PRIB

12

32

GRODA

PAPAFAVA

19

30

27

1

34

Trg. Miličača

P. HEKTOR

25

28

36

15

FABRIKA

ARSENAL

St. Stephen's Square

35

31

ROIĆ DUŠKA

21

CATHEDRAL OF ST. STEPHEN

Harbor

BRAĆE BOŽITKOVIĆ

NOVAK JURA

22

36

23

BUZOLIĆ ŠIME TOME

BOAT LANDING

POST

33

ROSSO

Cemetery

13

JADROLINIJA OFFICE

PAVAO

DINKA

ŠETALIŠTE ŠIME BUZOLIĆ

24

KOVA

8

100 Meters

100 Yards

PUČKOG USTANKA

14

HVAR

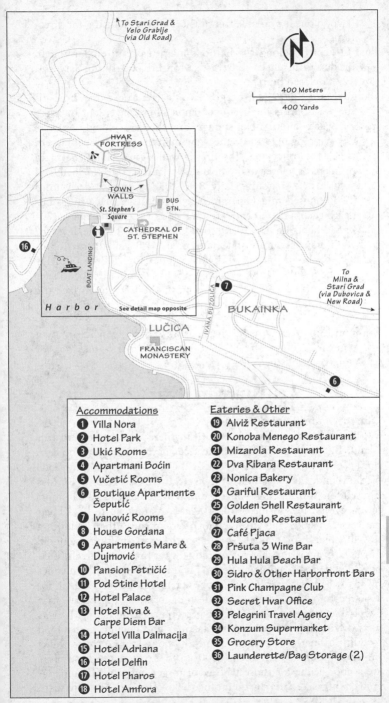

Accommodations
1. Villa Nora
2. Hotel Park
3. Ukić Rooms
4. Apartmani Boćin
5. Vučetić Rooms
6. Boutique Apartments Šeputić
7. Ivanović Rooms
8. House Gordana
9. Apartments Mare & Dujmović
10. Pansion Petričić
11. Pod Stine Hotel
12. Hotel Palace
13. Hotel Riva & Carpe Diem Bar
14. Hotel Villa Dalmacija
15. Hotel Adriana
16. Hotel Delfin
17. Hotel Pharos
18. Hotel Amfora

Eateries & Other
19. Alviž Restaurant
20. Konoba Menego Restaurant
21. Mizarola Restaurant
22. Dva Ribara Restaurant
23. Nonica Bakery
24. Gariful Restaurant
25. Golden Shell Restaurant
26. Macondo Restaurant
27. Café Pjaca
28. Pršuta 3 Wine Bar
29. Hula Hula Beach Bar
30. Sidro & Other Harborfront Bars
31. Pink Champagne Club
32. Secret Hvar Office
33. Pelegrini Travel Agency
34. Konzum Supermarket
35. Grocery Store
36. Launderette/Bag Storage (2)

HVAR

(a good one is available free at the TI) and by asking for directions.

Post Office: It's along the harbor's main (eastern) embankment, inside a little fenced courtyard (Mon-Fri 7:00-19:00, Sat 8:00-12:00, closed Sun).

Laundry and Baggage Storage: Two different no-name, hole-in-the-wall outfits in the town center offer convenient but very expensive laundry, bag storage, and showers—handy if you're day-tripping here and want to swim in the sea. If one is closed, check the other one. The first is well-signed along the main promenade, closer to the boat dock (laundry-110 kn/load, full service in 2-3 hours, daily 8:30-20:00, summer daily until 21:00, closed mid-Oct-mid-May). The other place hides beneath the market at the cathedral end of the main square (70-kn wash, 50-kn dry, 10-kn soap, they'll stick it in the dryer for you if you ask nicely and thank them with a small tip; unpredictable hours, but generally daily June-Aug 7:00-23:00, May and Sept 7:00-21:00, Oct 8:00-13:30 & 16:00-19:00, shorter hours and no laundry off-season, to the left as you face the cathedral at Trg Svetog Stjepana 1—look for big, blue *toilet* sign).

Summer Fun: You name it, Hvar has it. Various agencies in town rent cars, scooters, bikes, motorboats, and more—just look for signs or ask at the TI.

Tours in Hvar

Old Town and Island Tours

While the town of Hvar is beautiful, there's much more to this island. But most tourists without a car never get to see the rest. For an insightful, affordable peek at the refreshingly unglitzy side of the island, take a tour with **Secret Hvar.** Owner Siniša prides himself on introducing you to undiscovered corners that most tourists miss. He or one of his guides—guaranteed to be a Hvar native—can take you on a **"Hvar off-road tour"** that includes a *peka* lunch and some off-the-beaten-path sights, making use of old gravel farming roads that you wouldn't want to drive yourself (€85/person, 8 hours). They also offer a **"Hvar island tour"** that includes Hvar town, Jelsa, Stari Grad, Vroboska, and more (€65/person for a shared tour, or arrange a private tour for a small group—price negotiable, tour lasts up to 5 hours); a **wine-tasting** trip with visits to two wineries, including eight tastings and enough finger food to call it dinner (€75/person for up to 4 hours); or a private **walking tour** around Hvar town (€100/up to 2.5 hours). These tours are a good value for those who want to get out and see some island countryside. Stop by their office below the Park Hotel to learn more or contact Siniša to arrange a meeting time and place (Trg Sv. Stjepana 4A, office tel. 021/717-615, Siniša mobile 095-805-9075, www.secrethvar.com, info@secrethvar.com). Siniša can also arrange hiking, biking, boating, and other trips.

Other Excursions from Hvar

Joining a day-trip excursion is a handy way to reach nearby destinations (generally available June-Oct). The best-selling options for getting off Hvar Island include the nearby Pakleni Islands (described later); Vis Island and its "Blue Cave" and "Green Cave"; Brač Island and the beach at Bol; Korčula; Mljet National Park; Dubrovnik; river-rafting; and more. Multiple companies around town offer these and other excursions, and salespeople along the embankment hawk various boat excursions. I'd simply shop around for an itinerary and price that suits your travel dreams.

Sights and Activities in Hvar

IN AND NEAR THE OLD TOWN

▲▲St. Stephen's Square (Trg Svetog Stjepana)

Hvar's main square, which is supposedly Dalmatia's biggest, is a relaxed and relaxing people zone surrounded by inviting cafés filled with deliriously sunbaked tourists. For a quick tour, begin by the harbor and face the cathedral. Sit on the stone wall with your back to the water.

To your right is the **Arsenal** building (housing the TI)—a reminder of Hvar's nautical importance through history, thanks to its ideal location on the sailing route between Venice and the Mediterranean. During the town's seafaring heyday, ships were repaired and supplied in this huge building that still dominates the town. The Arsenal was recently restored in honor of its 400th anniversary. The beautiful barrel-vaulted space inside is used for special exhibits and private events. You can climb the stairs to the terrace atop the Arsenal for fine views over the square.

Many of Hvar's buildings date from the 16th and 17th centuries, when it was an important outpost of the Venetian Repub-

lic. During the Venetian period, the population was segregated: To the left of the square lived the well-to-do patricians, protected within the city wall (from the fortress, crenellated walls reach down to embrace this neighborhood—not quite visible from here). To the right, outside the wall, dwelled the humble plebeians—who worked hard and paid

HVAR

high taxes, but had no say in government. In the 16th century, these two populations came to blows. The Venetians finally decided enough was enough and sent a moderator to restore peace. As a symbol of the reconciliation, part of the Arsenal building was converted into a **communal theater.** Built in 1612, this was the first municipal theater in Europe. Like the Loggia (described next), it has recently undergone an extensive renovation.

Looking left, the building with the arches and short tower is the **Loggia,** all that remains of a 15th-century palace for the rector (who ruled the island as a representative of Venice). This was the town's court of justice, and important decisions were announced from the stepped pillar in front (with the flagpole). This pillar also served as the town pillory, for publicly humiliating prisoners. During Habsburg control in the early 20th century, most of the palace was torn down to build the town's first resort hotel; today, that building—appropriately called the Palace Hotel—still stands just behind the Loggia.

Walk toward the cathedral, stopping at the first street on the left. You can see the top of a **Venetian palace,** with its distinctive Venetian-style windows. A descendant of the former owner recently bought back this palace and has restored it. The renovation took longer than expected when workers began to uncover layer after layer of Hvar's history: blocks of stone from the Greek island of Paros, Illyrian coins, and Roman mosaics. If you were to head two blocks up this street, you'd run into the yellow **Benedictine Convent** and its loveable lace museum; if you continued beyond the convent, you'd reach the trailhead for the **fortress** up above (all described later). But before leaving the square, visit the cathedral (see below).

Then poke around Hvar's **back streets.** As you wander, especially on the left (north) side of the square, look up to find more characteristic Venetian windows. You'll also spot stone tabs jutting from house facades. The ones with holes were used to hang color-coded curtains: white for a birth, black for a death. Also notice the gleaming white limestone everywhere, which is quarried locally. An often-repeated (but false) legend that the US White House was built of this same stone is temptingly plausible.

Cathedral of St. Stephen (Sv. Stjepan)

Hvar's centerpiece is its Renaissance-era cathedral, with a distinctive three-humped gable (representing the Holy Trinity) and open-work steeple. The interior comes with a few tales from Hvar's storied past; you can see the bronze doors (described next) without buying a ticket.

Cost and Hours: 10 kn, daily 9:00-13:00 & 17:00-19:00 except closed to tourists during services Sun 10:00-11:00 year-round. If you'd like to attend a service, pick up the English outline inside.

Visiting the Cathedral: The **bronze entrance doors,** completed by a popular Croatian sculptor in 1990, combine religious

themes with important elements of life on Hvar. On the left door, top to bottom, you'll see the Creation; Madonna and Baby Jesus surrounded by the circle of stars (representing the European Union—reflecting Croatians' desire to be considered part of Europe); vineyards (both literal and as a symbol of heaven); and a procession of penitence, a fixture of life among religious locals. On the right door, you'll see a dove (representing peace and the Holy Spirit); the crucified Christ; fishermen (an actual part of Hvar life, but also representing the Church's "fishers of men" evangelical philosophy); and a boat, sailing into the future.

Inside, buy your ticket, pick up a free English information sheet, and work your way counterclockwise around the church **interior.** If you're lucky, you'll meet the chatty caretaker, Boris, who moonlights as a fisherman. At the right transept chapel, the tabernacle embedded in the yellow marble "cloth" (under the big crucifix) holds an important piece of Hvar history: a crucifix that supposedly shed tears of blood on the eve of a major 1510 uprising of the plebeians against the patricians. (This spooked the rebels enough to postpone the uprising a few months.)

Behind the main altar are wooden choir stalls rescued from an earlier Gothic church that was destroyed during an Ottoman attack in 1571. Notice the two pulpits: The right one, with St. Paul and his sword, is for reading or singing the Epistles; the left one, with the eagle (representing St. John), is used for reading the Gospels. The left-front chapel features the tomb of St. Prosperus, Hvar's "co-patron saint," who shares the credit with the more famous St. Stephen. People pray to Prosperus for good health. On his feast day, May 10, the lid is opened and you can actually see his preserved body. The figures flanking the tomb represent Faith and Strength.

▲Benedictine Convent (Benediktinski Samostan) and Lace Museum

Hvar's most endearingly quirky sight is this nun-run attraction, inside a convent where 13 Benedictine sisters spend their lives (they never go outside). When they're not praying, the sisters make lace by using fibers from the *agava* (a cactus-like plant with broad, flat, tapered, spiny leaves—see the sample just outside the door). First, they tease the delicate threads out of the plant, then wash, bleach, and dry them. Finally, they weave the threads into intricate lace designs. The painstaking procedure is made even more challenging by Hvar's unpredictable weather: The humid, southerly Jugo wind causes tangles, while the dry northern Bora wind makes the fibers stiff and difficult to work with.

Cost and Hours: 10 kn, skimpy 15-kn multilingual booklet, extremely expensive samples for sale; June-Sept Mon-Sat 10:00-12:00 & 17:00-19:00, closed Sun; generally closed Oct-May, but try ringing the bell to the right of the main door to get in during these same hours—use the door in the yellow building; tel. 021/741-052.

Visiting the Convent: You'll see astonishingly delicate samples of the nuns' work, both new and old—some yellowed specimens date from the late 19th century (the oldest ones are in the back room). The sisters are particularly happy to make lace for bishops and cardinals. And when the *other* Benedict—the XVI—became pope in 2005, they created a lace papal emblem for him as a gift.

Rounding out the museum are ecclesiastical gear, some bishops' vestments (with the Baby Jesus below them wearing an *agava*-lace shirt), ancient kitchenware discovered in this house, a stone sink and baptismal font, an actual well, and some amphora jugs. Out in front of the building is a statue of St. Benedict, the patron saint of Europe, reading his daily routine in a book: *ora et labora* ("pray and work"). You'll notice the museum is also called the Hanibal Lucić Museum, for a prominent Renaissance poet whose daughter-in-law donated this property to the church.

▲Franciscan Monastery (Franjevački Samostan)

Starting in the 15th century, this monastery was a hospice for sailors who contracted illness on treacherous sea journeys. These days it's worth the 10-minute stroll from the Old Town to visit its off-beat museum, Hvar's most famous painting, an ancient tree, and a pair of monks.

Cost and Hours: 25 kn; May-Oct Mon-Sat 9:00-15:00 & 17:00-19:00, closed Sun except in July-Aug; usually closed Nov-April but the TI can call to see if they'll let you in during these hours.

Visiting the Monastery: Out front, notice the statue of a kneeling St. Francis—the twin of the prayerful St. Benedict, who stands in front of the Benedictine Convent. As you enter, notice that the cloister's floor is slanted inward to capture rainwater. Pipes took this pure water out to the waterfront, where ships could use it to replenish their supplies.

Inside, the focal point of the monastery is its impressive painting of *The Last Supper* (c. 1640). The U-shaped table in the painting provides the framework for some bold experimentation with perspective. Facing Jesus, front and center, is Judas, identified by several clues. In his left hand (hard to see) is a bag of coins, and his right hand is dipping bread into wine (after Jesus had predicted that the one who did this would betray him). The yellow of his garment symbolizes betrayal, and the red indicates that the betrayal led to the spilling of blood. Under the table by Judas is a cat, representing lust. On the lower right, we see a beggar (accompanied by a dog, symbolizing fidelity)—likely a self-portrait by the artist, grateful to the monks who nursed him back to health.

Through the door to the right of *The Last Supper*, look for the exhibit of currency from the fourth century B.C. (Greek coins with an image of Zeus) through today (see the rapid evolution of Croatia's currency since the country's independence), as well as a collection of amphora jugs. Also keep an eye out for a **wooden dragon masthead** called Zvir ("The Beast"), which came from a ship that Hvar sent to fight in the famous Battle of Lepanto in 1571. (This may be gone for restoration.)

You'll pass a room filled with paintings by Venetian masters and modern Croatian artists (and see interpretations of Jesus, from medieval to modern times). Next, head into the relaxing garden to find the outside attraction: an enormous **cypress tree** whose gnarled branches are held up by big supports. Scientists believe this ancient tree—probably around 250 years old—was struck by lightning, which caused the branches to spread out and become flatter than usual.

Wrap up your visit with a peek into the colorful and unusual little **chapel** off the cloister, with a separated choir.

Nearby: On the way to or returning from the monastery, peek inside the recommended Gariful Restaurant to see fish swimming around inside the floor. This is a good place for a pricey but scenic meal.

▲Hvar Fortress (Fortica Hvar)

Visiting this mighty castle above the Old Town is a good excuse for a sturdy 45-minute hike to break up your lazy Hvar day.

Cost and Hours: 30 kn, daily June-mid-Sept 8:00-22:00, Easter-May and mid-Sept-Oct 8:30-20:00, Nov-Easter much shorter hours and sometimes closed.

Getting There: From the Old Town, hike up the steep street called Groda to the road passing above town. Once on that road, look for the nearby gate with the picture of a castle for another steep hike up a switchback trail (stay on the main path—side paths that seem like shortcuts are actually dead-ends).

Visiting the Fortress: This huge fortification was built over several generations, beginning in the 13th century. In the 14th century, Spanish engineers did their part to bulk up the fortress (giving it the nickname "Španjola"). In 1571, the townspeople fled here for sanctuary during an attack by the Ottomans (on their way to the famous Battle of Lepanto). Just a few years later, the fortress was devastated when lightning hit a gunpowder store. In the 19th century, the occupying Austrians put their own touches on the castle. Today it's used as a catering facility and tourist attraction.

Inside the fort, there's little in the way of posted descriptions, but the views over town are terrific. You can also climb down into

the prison, sip a drink at the café/bar, and visit the one-room "Marine Archaeological Collection" (hiding inside the blocky central part of the fortress; look for *amphorae* and *muzej* signs). This display features booty found at three different Dalmatian shipwrecks, including a collection of amphora jugs (for more on these jugs, see the sidebar on page 131). According to the exhibit, one out of every 50 voyages in antiquity ended in a shipwreck. (And you thought flying was dangerous.)

The complex on the higher hill nearby was built by Napoleon (which is also its nickname amongst locals). In the 1970s, it was converted into an astronomic and seismographic observatory.

Strolling and Swimming

With typically Dalmatian crystal-clear water, Hvar is a great place to swim. Also typically Dalmatian, virtually all of the swimming areas are rocky or pebbly. As you walk along the coastline in either direction from town, you'll spot concrete pads and ladders trying to seduce you into the cool blue (these are generally open to the public; you may have the option of renting a beach chair).

East of the Old Town: Whether or not you plan to swim, take a waterfront walk east of town (past the Franciscan Monastery). This delightful path leads past swimmers, sunbathers, and boats bobbing just offshore. After about a 20-minute walk, you'll reach the town's main beach, **Pokonji Dol,** which faces a small, barren island of the same name topped with a lonely little lighthouse. After Pokonji Dol, the path becomes more challenging and is not as well-marked, offering little shade. Bring water and wear good shoes if planning to venture this far. If you continue eastward along the coast, you'll find more beaches—first the one nicknamed **"Robinson,"** then the even better one at the charming resort village of **Milna** (2.5 miles from Hvar town). Beyond Robinson, the waterfront path to Milna is challenging and very poorly marked, so if you want to go to the beach there, consider taking a taxi, water taxi (about 50 kn one-way between Hvar and Milna), or the bus (any bus taking the new road to Stari Grad stops at Milna).

West of the Old Town: This path leads past a cactus garden and children's play area, then along a series of bays—one of them dominated by the huge Hotel Amfora (with a row of private cabanas, below the trail). On the next bay over, the popular **Hula Hula** beach bar serves light meals and cocktails on platforms and rocks over the beach, with chill-out music all day and a live DJ starting at 17:00 (see "Nightlife in Hvar," later). The farther you get from town, the more remote-feeling the beaches become, ending at the mellow cocktail bar under **Pod Stine Hotel.** The hotel's private beach is another inviting place for a swim; you'll pay royally to rent a chair, but it's comfortable, scenic, and offers easy access to the water. The rocky floor here is perfect for snorkeling, and a nearby dive shop rents gear.

Many sun worshippers—especially the clothing-optional crowd—prefer to take a water taxi to the beaches of the nearby **Pakleni Islands,** across the bay from Hvar town (described later).

MORE SIGHTS ON HVAR ISLAND

If you have more time, Hvar is an interesting island to explore. The best way to efficiently hit several sights in a single day is to take a trip with Secret Hvar (listed earlier, under "Tours in Hvar"). Otherwise, consider one of these outings.

If you do leave town, you'll quickly reach a dramatically mountainous landscape with a rugged soil that has been carefully worked by centuries of Hvarins. Heaps of stones big and small—like hundreds of giant molehills—pockmark the landscape. These piles of unwanted rocks were created when the land was cleared for farming. You'll also see a few little stone huts (called *trim*), some of them centuries old. These provided farmers with shelter from sun or storms and gave them a cool place to take a nap during a hot day's work.

Stari Grad

Literally "Old Town," this was the island's original settlement, dating back some 2,400 years. Today it's a likeably humble, workaday port town almost entirely lacking Hvar's glamor-girl charm...and crowds. Simple fishing boats rather than luxury yachts bob in its harbor, and its flat, labyrinthine street plan disperses the few tourists who venture here.

From the harbor, head up through town to the tallest **bell tower;** it marks the Church of St. Stephen, which watches over its own quiet little square. Beyond that is the much smaller Church of St. John, the core of which likely dates from the fifth or sixth century. Recently restored, it offers great acoustics and displays a replica of a Roman mosaic that was discovered during excavations just behind the building. (Loop around behind the church to see the scant foundations.)

Closer to the harbor is a large square fronted by a long, stout **fortress,** which was the personal palace of local landowner and poet Petar Hektorović, who dominates much of the story of Stari Grad. Of the many covered canals leaving the harbor and twisting through town, one runs right into this palace.

Running parallel to the harbor is the street called **Srinjo Kola,** which means "Middle Street" in the local dialect. This was once the town's main street for commerce—notice the display windows that abut many of the doorways. These days, many homes here are abandoned.

Finally, back near the harbor, seek out the shop called **Fantazam,** where artist Zoran Tadić assembles various discarded organic materials (bones, hair, feathers, and other animal body parts) into wholly unique and grotesque statues of mythical beasts. Zoran hangs out in his courtyard working "anytime there's good weather," and invites in the curious to peek at his gallery (Ivana Gundulića 6, mobile 098-953-2967, www.fantazam.com).

While many visitors to Hvar see only the main town and the road to Stari Grad (where the island's main car-ferry port is), drivers may enjoy heading east of Stari Grad to some nearby settlements. Driving eastbound on the main road from Stari Grad takes you into a plain with fertile **farm fields.** This unassuming patch of land is one of the only agricultural areas in Europe that's still divided according to its original plots, dating all the way back to the first ancient Greek settlers.

Vrboska

On the opposite side of the farm fields from Stari Grad is the seafront village of Vrboska, nicknamed "Little Venice" (this endearing

HVAR

hyperbole is typical of local pride). While the name is a stretch, this appealing town does have a canal with picturesque bridges, the fortress/church of St. Mary's (built during a time of Turkish naval threat), a good wine-tasting opportunity, and an island with a lone palm tree. Even better, there are no tourists here. This is where locals from the town of Hvar go to escape the crowds.

To sample some of the island's well-reputed wines in a fun, rustic setting, find **Vina Pinjata**, 30 paces above the Church of St. Mary. Call or email ahead to be sure Marija is available, and enjoy the warm reception (tel. 021/774-262, konobapinjata@net.fr).

Hike from Velo Grablje to Milna

For a vigorous but mostly downhill hike in the interior of Hvar Island, you can bus to a partially abandoned town, hike down through a ravine to a nearly empty village, then pop out along the sea at Milna for a bus ride back to Hvar. Allow a half-day for the whole trip, including about two hours for the hike itself. This is best for hardy hikers and those who enjoy getting away from touristy beaches to explore the artifacts of an earlier age of Hvar; most of the route is in a ravine without sea views. As this is a challenging trail with little shade, wear good shoes and load up on water, sunscreen, and anything else you might need before setting out.

To reach the start of the hike, take the one daily bus that uses the scenic old road to Stari Grad (generally departs Hvar town at 12:20 in summer, 12:10 in winter—confirm at TI or bus station), and get off about five miles east of Hvar town at the village of Velo Grablje. From the Velo Grablje stop, hike down the switchback road into the town. For a more scenic arrival, stay on the bus a few hundred yards longer and ask the driver to let you off at Vidikovac (vee-DEE-koh-vats), a viewpoint restaurant with panoramic vistas across the far side of the island; from here, cross the road and walk down the gravel path into town.

Velo Grablje, once famous for its lavender oil production, is now a near-ghost town on a rugged plateau with far-off views of

the sea. Most people migrated to Hvar town in the 1970s and 1980s, though seven natives still reside here.

From Velo Grablje, follow the medieval footpath through the ravine downhill about two miles to the abandoned village of **Malo Grablje.** After the phylloxera epidemic, most people from this village moved down to Milna, on the sea (where tourism provided them with better prospects for earning income).

Hvar Wine and Lavender

The hillsides of Hvar Island are striped with the faint outlines of an elaborate network of terraces, once used to cultivate grapes for wine. But in 1910, a phylloxera pest infestation devastated vineyards and decimated the island's winemaking industry. Many vintners moved to the US, Australia, and Argentina, where they became pioneers in wine production. Today winemaking on Hvar is at only about 5 percent of its historic peak, and the focus is on quality, not quantity. In general, the south side of the island gets more intense sun, which leads to smaller and sweeter grapes—and, in turn, higher-alcohol and better-quality wine.

Several well-respected vintners are putting Hvar on the oenophiles' map. Top producers include the large Plinković operation (which also has vineyards on the mainland) and Andro Tomić. The **Tomić** winery is well set up for visitors curious to taste a few wines, including their fruity rosé, their Beleca red blend, and their exquisite *prošek* dessert wine, called Hektorovich. While it's smart to call ahead to tell them you're coming, drop-ins are typically welcome (65-250-kn bottles, daily 9:00-20:00, on the road into the town of Jelsa, just above the Hvar Hotel, tel. 021/768-160, www.bastijana.hr).

In the 1930s, in an effort to boost the economy, the island began producing lavender. This was mostly exported for industrial use to Germany and the UK (peaking in the 1960s and 1970s, when Hvar Island was responsible for 10 percent of the world's total lavender production). The lavender industry dramatically improved the quality of life on Hvar, but devastating forest fires in 1984, 1997, 2003, and 2007 burned up much of this cash crop. As the island's tourism industry expands, it has become less critical to the economy to replant after each fire, so many lavender farmers have left their fields fallow. These days most lavender is produced for the sake of tradition...and for tourists.

The last holdout left in 1968. But recently the grandson of the first villager who left returned to Malo Grablje and opened a rustic restaurant called Konoba Stori Komin (open 16:00-22:00 only, run by Berti Tudor—the surname of virtually everyone who originated in this village, possible to call ahead to arrange a *peka* dinner, mobile 091-527-6408). Even if the *konoba* is closed, you can explore the streets of Malo Grablje. Poke into the ruined buildings to find a giant, still-functioning olive press. The humble church hosts a Mass twice per year, when people from Milna return to their ancestral village. Next to the church is a huge reservoir and cistern for catching rainwater.

Leaving Malo Grablje, follow the gravel road down into the beach town of **Milna.** The seafront path from Milna back to Hvar (about 2.5 miles) is extremely rugged and can be nearly impossible to follow; unless you're very adventurous, it's best to walk along the main road (not very scenic) or take a public bus back to Hvar (any bus that goes between Stari Grad and Hvar along the new road stops along the road above Milna—departs Stari Grad in summer at 16:05 and 18:40, in winter at 16:00, reaches Milna about 10-15 minutes later, but confirm times at Hvar TI before heading out). You can also take a water taxi between Milna and Hvar for about 50 kn one-way.

Note: It's possible to drive from Milna up to Malo Grablje and Velo Grablje, but the road consists of very rough gravel and rock—not advisable with a rental car.

NEAR HVAR
Pakleni Islands (Pakleni Otoci)

These islands, just offshore from Hvar town, are a popular and easy back-to-nature day-trip destination. The name means the "Devil's

Islands" in Croatian, but in the local dialect, *pakleni* refers to the resin used to seal the hulls of ships (which had to be boiled—hence the hellish connection). These days, the islands harbor some popular nude beaches: The island of Jerolim and the bay of Stipanska (or is it *Strip*anska?) on the island of Marinkovac are particularly good places to spot—or sport—some bare skin. While the beaches used to be predominantly nude, local captains have recently figured out that they get more business if they don't advertise the nudist connection—so the beaches are now more mixed than they once were. For a bit more civilization, set your sights on the biggest island, known as **"Palmižana"** (pahl-mee-ZHAH-nah; sounds like "parmesan-a") for its main settlement (the island's official name is Svetog Klement, but nobody calls it that). The beach at Palmižana is a popular swim destination because it's partly "sandy" (translation: smaller pebbles). The only real town on this island is Palmižana, which is basically a modest marina and a handful of cafés huddled around a beach. From there, you can hike through the woods and scramble your way to some postcard-perfect hidden coves.

Getting There: Excursion boats ferry tourists out to the islands every summer morning from the harbor in front of the Hvar TI—just look for signs to the specific island, beach, or cove that you want. It costs about 60 kn round-trip per person to Palmižana; most boats take people over between 9:00 and 14:00, then go back

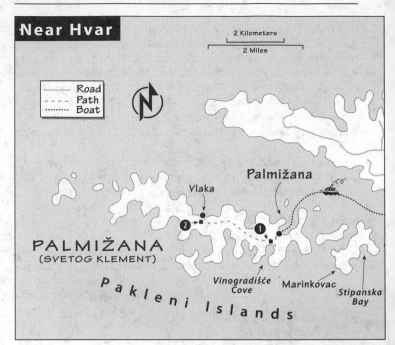

Near Hvar

Road
Path
Boat

2 Kilometers

2 Miles

Vlaka

Palmižana

PALMIŽANA
(SVETOG KLEMENT)

Vinogradišće
Cove

Marinkovac

Stipanska
Bay

P a k l e n i   I s l a n d s

to fetch them around 16:00 or 19:00 (schedule fluctuates wildly with demand—they run more or less constantly in peak season; figure about 20 minutes each way to Palmižana). This works well, provided you want to spend the entire day stranded on a tropical island. Visiting Jerolim or Marinkovac costs 35 kn round-trip.

An efficient sightseer might prefer just a few hours of island time—enough for a quick dip, a hike, and maybe a meal. For this purpose, you can pay double for a faster, private **water taxi** to zip you there in just 15 minutes, and then pick you up whenever you like. I had a good experience with one of these speedy taxis, helmed by English-speaking Luka. I called him 15 minutes before I wanted to head over, and again 15 minutes before I came back—door-to-door service to any island you like (300 kn round-trip for up to 3 people, mobile 098-959-5094, www.water-taxi-hvar.com). Luka's small, inflatable boat is built for speed rather than comfort, so the ride can be rough.

Planning Your Time: If you're relatively fit and have a few hours to spare, try this plan: Ride with Luka to Palmižana, hit the Vinogradišće beach, hike across the island to the settlement of Vlaka, have lunch or dinner at Konoba Dionis, call Luka, and ride with him from Vlaka back to Hvar.

Beach at Vinogradišće Cove: The most popular spot for swimming on the island is the beach at Vinogradišće. To get here from the Palmižana marina, hike up the trail (to the left, past the

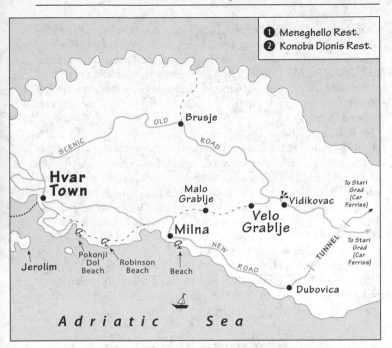

1 Meneghello Rest.
2 Konoba Dionis Rest.

SCENIC

OLD ROAD

Brusje

Hvar Town

Malo Grablje

Vidikovac

To Stari Grad (Car Ferries)

Velo Grablje

Milna

NEW ROAD

TUNNEL

To Stari Grad (Car Ferries)

Jerolim

Pokonji Dol Beach

Robinson Beach

Beach

Dubovica

A d r i a t i c   S e a

little cantina). When the road forks, take the middle fork and follow the restaurant signs (they're all at the beach). While it's not as
"undiscovered" as you might hope, Vinogradišće is a picturesque
spot, with a small patch of semi-sand surrounded by rocks and concrete pads for catching some rays. A smattering of sailboats on the
horizon rounds out the idyllic Croatian scene.

Hike to Vlaka: For a hardy 45-minute (2-mile) hike on a
rough trail with some pleasant views—and a restaurant reward at
the end (Konoba Dionis, described later)—trek across the top of
the island to the little settlement of Vlaka (wear good shoes and
bring water). From Palmižana, first follow signs to *Meneghello*.
After you pass Meneghello Restaurant and some of its bungalows
(described next), go right at the fork in the path (following the faint
red marking on the wall to *Vlaka*). You'll climb up to the crest
of the island, on a very narrow and rocky trail. A few side paths
fork down to various bays, but stay on the main trail along the
top of the island (generally marked with red-painted rocks). You'll
periodically break through the trees for views over secluded coves
and nearby islands. Finally, the path leads down along yet another
pretty cove before sending you back over the top of the island to
Vlaka and Konoba Dionis.

Eating at Palmižana: Several lazy cafés surround the
Vinogradišće beach at Palmižana. A bit higher on the hill is
Meneghello, run by a family of the same name that's been in

HVAR

Palmižana for over a century. They serve mostly seafood on a colorful, funky terrace (open long hours daily April-Oct, reservations smart for dinner, follow signs from the Palmižana marina, tel. 021/717-270). Meneghello Restaurant is the centerpiece of a complex of rentable, color-coded bungalows that bunny-hop through an overgrown botanical garden down to the beach (www. palmizana.hr).

Eating at Vlaka: The culinary highlight of the island is at the other end, in Vlaka. **Konoba Dionis** is a charming stone hut with just six tables on a covered terrace, overlooking vineyards, an olive grove, and the distant sea. The electricity comes from a generator, and the water comes from the sky—so the cuisine is straightforward, traditional Dalmatian dishes, and the focus is on relaxation. Their "aubergine pie" is a tasty eggplant lasagna (figure about 250 kn per person for a meal, mid-May-mid-Oct daily 12:00-23:00, closed off-season, mobile 098-167-1016 or 091-765-6044). Tourists often make the long journey over to Dionis, only to find it's already full—reservations (especially for lunch) are a must. Note that there are boats from Hvar to Vlaka in peak season (but the schedule is sparse; ask at TI).

Shopping in Hvar

Little souvenir kiosks are everywhere on Hvar. The big item here is lavender, produced on the island for the last century or so (see "Hvar Wine and Lavender" sidebar, earlier). In addition to making things smell good, lavender is acclaimed by some locals for its medicinal properties: Massage some lavender oil on your temples to cure a headache, or rub it on your chest for asthma. You'll see it sold in bottles or sachets—a fragrant souvenir that helps keep your luggage smelling fresh, too. Hvar town also has plenty of jewelry shops selling coral and other pieces made from semiprecious stones.

Nightlife in Hvar

This island town is known for its nightlife, so it teems with the young and the restless (i.e., the loud).

Mellow Nightlife
Strolling the harbor, then continuing out of town along the waterfront promenade, is a fine way to pass a warm, starry evening. The best views are from the harbor's east side.

Consider a pre- or post-dinner drink with the best view over the harbor from the fourth-floor bar/terrace at the recommended **Hotel Adriana** (on the waterfront at Obala Fabrika 28, tel. 021/750-200). Slip into your comfortable chair and watch the lights of the village glimmer below.

Pršuta 3 wine bar, right in the heart of town, is a cozy and chill place to hang out, socialize, and sip some of the island's wines with light food (about 25 wines available by the glass, cash only, nightly 18:00-late, mobile 098-969-6193).

Lively Nightlife

Hvar probably has Dalmatia's most happening "après-beach" scene. Expect very high prices for drinks, and prepare to share the night-spots with a very flush international jet-set crowd. On balmy summer evenings, partying is best enjoyed in three stages. (Note that virtually all the places below are closed from about early October through early May.)

Stage 1: Watch the sunset from the groovy **Hula Hula** beach bar, with drinks—and tables—"on the rocks" (literally). Don't expect a relaxed vibe here—in summer, it's absolutely jam-packed (drinks with light food and snacks, open daily from 9:00, "chill-out music" until 17:00, then a live DJ with dance-club ambience, hopping until about 23:00; for directions, see page 235). When I asked if older guests would be comfortable here, they smirked and said, "When they come here, everybody feels young!"

Stage 2: Head for the bars in the center of town, along the harbor (including **Sidro**—known for its cheap drinks and friendly service—as well as **Nautica, Aloha Bar,** and so on). Just above this strip of bars, on the ground floor of Hotel Park, is **Central Park Bar,** with elegant Tuscan living-room ambience.

Stage 3: If you're still going strong, continue to one of the late-night options. While these places brag about their rich and famous guests, many travelers find them overpriced and overrated. But, when in Hvar... **Carpe Diem** is an exclusive-feeling cocktail bar along the harbor, a few doors down from Hotel Riva (Carpe Diem also has their own beach bar on Stipanska Island, www.carpe-diem-hvar.com). **Pink Champagne,** the most chichi of the bunch, is up the lane beyond the bus station and parking lot, near the police station.

Sleeping in Hvar

In keeping with its posh reputation, Hvar has some of the most expensive accommodations in Croatia. As usual, *sobe* and apartments are a more affordable option (see page 764) than hotels, but there are relatively few in the center of town; you'll have to walk 10 to 20 minutes to reach many of them. The ones I've listed are cozy, well-equipped, well-run, and worth the walk. Plan on climbing several steps and/or trudging up steep and dull suburban streets to

Sleep Code

Abbreviations **(7 kn=about $1, €1=about $1.10, country code: 385)**
S=Single, **D**=Double/Twin, **T**=Triple, **Q**=Quad, **b**=bathroom
Price Rankings
  $$$ **Higher Priced**—Most rooms €100 or more
   $$ **Moderately Priced**—Most rooms €55-100
    $ **Lower Priced**—Most rooms €55 or less

If I've listed two sets of rates for an accommodation, the first price is for peak season (mid-July-late Aug) and the second is for shoulder season (May-mid-July and late Aug-Oct); those open in winter are often even cheaper. If I've listed three sets of rates, the third is for off-season (Nov-April). The dates for seasonal rates vary by hotel.

These rates do not include the modest tourist tax (about 7 kn/person, per night). Hotels generally accept credit cards and include breakfast, while most *sobe* accept only cash and don't offer breakfast. While rates are listed in euros, you'll pay in kunas. Unless noted otherwise, free Wi-Fi and/or a guest computer is generally available, and English is spoken.

Prices change; verify current rates online or by email. For the best prices, always book directly with the hotel.

reach most places. The farther and steeper you're willing to walk, the better the price and views (some come with glorious seaview balconies on a pauper's budget). Many of my listings are tucked away in residential areas, so they can be very tricky to find (refer to the map on page 226); get clear directions from your host, ask locals as you go, or—better yet—arrange to be met at the boat. It's challenging to find a room in July and especially August (when all accommodations boost their rates); book as far ahead as possible for these times.

Soba **Tips:** It's standard for *sobe* and apartments to charge 30 percent more for stays shorter than three nights. This is rarely waived in high season, but you can try to negotiate your way out of this at other times. In addition to the places I've listed, you can search for more *soba* options on the TI's website (www.tzhvar.hr; click "Accommodation," then "Private Accommodation").

IN THE OLD TOWN

Note that some of the branches of the Sunčani Hvar chain, described later, are also located in or near the Old Town.

$$$ Villa Nora is a splurge for those willing to pay extra for an ideally located hotel. Its nine handsome rooms—with stone walls and hardwoods—are in the center of Hvar's Old Town, surrounded by cafés and bars. Petar and Natalja are helpful hosts (Db-€250/€150/€100, gigantic family suite-€350/€250/€150, includes

HVAR

breakfast, 10 percent less if you pay cash, air-con, Frane Primija 2, tel. 021/742-498, mobile 092-217-7466, www.villanora.eu, info@villanora.eu).

$$$ Hotel Park sits right in the heart of town, above the harbor and next to Hotel Palace. While quite expensive, its 15 rooms (most of them very spacious suites) offer a small-hotel alternative to the big boys. Its restaurant/breakfast terrace, overlooking the harbor, will slow your pulse. Despite its bottom-floor nightclub and locale near the harborfront disco zone, good windows minimize the noise (standard Db-€250/€200/€150, a variety of pricier suites also available—see website, includes breakfast, air-con, Bankete, tel. 021/718-337, www.hotelparkhvar.com, park.hvar@st.t-com.hr).

$$ Ivana and Paško Ukić offer four small, simple, but cozy apartments (with kitchens), one double room, and a shared rooftop terrace with fine views. The house has one of Hvar's most convenient locations, buried deep in the Old Town and sharing a quiet square with a little church a few steep blocks above the main square (apartment-€90/€80/€70, no breakfast, 30 percent extra for 1-night stays, no extra charge for 2-night stays, air-con, Matija Ivanića 10, tel. 021/741-810, Ivana speaks just enough English to make a reservation but it's better to call daughter Lidija at mobile 097-780-3700, www.hvar-apartments-center.com, ivanaukic@net.hr). From the cathedral, walk three blocks up toward the fortress, then look for the little church (Sv. Duh) to your left.

Higher Up, on the Main Road, in the Gojava Neighborhood

Two places sit near the main road above the Old Town (halfway up to the castle). While these are a bit older than some of the options listed later, their relative proximity to town (10-minute-or-less uphill walk) makes them worth considering.

$$ Apartmani Boćin, run by Eta Rosso Domančić, has two spacious one-bedroom apartments and one rustic studio apartment, all with seaview terraces (Db-€100/€80, €10-20 less for studio, air-con, Marina Carića 6, mobile 091-536-1744, www.hvar-rosso.com, josip.rosso@st.t-com.hr).

$ Jozo and Danica Vučetić offer a great value around the corner and a few steps down toward town. They rent one room (€50/€40, no air-con) and one apartment (€70/€60, air-con, kitchen, and view). They don't speak much English, but their English-speaking daughter-in-law Katija is helpful (Skaline od Gojave 6—just below #10, tel. 021/741-051, katija.vucetic@yahoo.com).

HVAR

EAST OF THE OLD TOWN, IN BUKAINKA

The quiet residential neighborhood called Bukainka sits on a high plateau just east of the harbor, hemmed in by the main road to Stari Grad. To reach this area, figure on a steep 10- to 15-minute uphill walk from the Old Town and waterfront.

$$ Boutique Apartments Šeputić is run by an enterprising Hvarin named Dino, who rents seven modern, colorful apartments, all with kitchens and most with balconies offering exceptional views. This listing is the farthest from the Old Town, but Dino can pick you up on arrival at the bus station (small-view Db-€70/€50/€35, big-view Db-€100/€80/€45, more for larger apartment, rates flexible with demand, air-con, car and scooter rentals; walk straight uphill from the Franciscan Monastery, then twist up through the lanes to reach busy Domovinskog Rata, and head left at the fork to Ive Roića 16; mobile 098-526-099, www.seputic.hr, info@seputic.hr).

$ Charming Ivanka Ivanović rents five pleasantly low-key apartments and two rooms in a big, modern house with view balconies at great rates (Db-€50-60/€40, price depends on size, extra person-€30, no breakfast, cash only, air-con, Ivana Buzolića 9, tel. 021/741-332, mobile 091-517-7038, www.ivanovic-hvar.com, ivanka.ivanovic@st.t-com.hr).

$ House Gordana is a great budget option sitting above the little bay in front of the Franciscan Monastery. Kind Marija Barbarić's five rooms are modest and old-fashioned, but they're well-kept and offer amenities unusual in this price range—including air-conditioning and a shared kitchen. All rooms come with balconies, and some have views (Db-€45-50/€40, extra bed-€20, optional breakfast-€7, Šima Buzolića Tome 49, mobile 098-923-4823, tel. 021/742-182, www.house-gordana-hvar.com.hr, marija.barbaric@st.t-com.hr).

WEST OF THE OLD TOWN
In Zastup

These places are along the street called ulica Biskupa Jurja Dubokovića, the main drag leading west of town, about a 10- to 15-minute walk from the Old Town (directly above and behind Hotel Amfora), though Pansion Petričić is a bit farther out and higher up.

$$ Apartments Mare, warmly run by Marica and Gianni Dujmović, has three small houses that bunny-hop up through a delightful garden behind the main house, which has three more apartments. All come with seaview terraces and the aroma of a well-tended garden. They make their own olive oil, wine, and grappa that you can sample in their atmospheric cellar (Db-€70-80/€40-50, more for larger apartments, cash only, air-con, Biskupa Jurja Dubokovića 34, tel. 021/741-454, mobile 091-552-2014, www.apartments-mare-hvar.com, maricadujmovic@gmail.com).

$$ Ana Dujmović, next door, has one knock-out apartment and seven older but well-appointed apartments with balconies, all overlooking an olive grove and most with sea views (standard Db-€75/€65, big Db-€130/€100, €10 more per extra person, air-con, loaner swim gear, BBQ terrace, Biskupa Jurja Dubokovića 36, tel. 021/742-010, mobile 098-838-434, www.hvar-croatia.com/dujmovic, ana.dujmovic@st.t-com.hr).

$ Pansion Petričić, high up in a residential zone, has four rooms—each with incredible views—that share a full kitchen. The kindly owners, Živko and Marija, enjoy getting to know their guests—and so does their big but friendly dog, Lex. Their rates greatly favor longer stays—these prices are for four nights (Db-€54/€48/€28/€24, 2-person apartment-€64/€56/€36/€30, 4-person apartment-€120/€100/€68/€60, air-con, Biskupa Jurja Dubokovića 25, tel. 021/742-481, www.hvar-petricic.com, z.petricic@inet.hr).

In Podstine, Beyond Zastup

Podstine is a quiet, nondescript residential neighborhood just beyond the big Hotel Amfora west of the Old Town (about a 15- to 20-minute walk).

$$$ Pod Stine Hotel ("Under Stones") feels like the sunny hideout of a reclusive writer. At the edge of town overlooking a tiny arboretum and a beautiful cove, this small resort features smart contemporary decor, 52 upscale-feeling rooms, a cocktail terrace, pool, and a gorgeous, momentum-killing private beach. If you don't mind the 20-minute walk into town, it's a more intimate and enjoyable splurge than the big hotels (nonview Db-€266/€239/€149, seaview Db-€285/€258/€212, bigger seaview Db-€449/€399/€279, pricier suites, cheaper Oct and May, closed Nov-late April, no extra charge for 1- or 2-night stays, air-con, elevator, parking, free use of spa facilities—including gym and swimming pool, good restaurant, Put Podstina 11, tel. 021/740-400, hotel@podstine.com).

SUNČANI HVAR HOTELS

Most of the big hotels in town are operated by the same company, Sunčani Hvar. About half of the chain's hotels have been elaborately renovated with strikingly contemporary decor; the unrenovated hotels offer a taste of the drab old communist days. Prices vary dramatically depending on the season, view, size, how recently the rooms were renovated, and the direction the wind is blowing. I've listed the price per night in peak season (July-Aug) for a two-night stay in a standard double room with no view. You'll pay more for a one-night stay, a sea view, a balcony, a "superior" room, or other special features, but prices can be much lower off-season—check specific rates on their website (www.suncanihvar.com). I'd save some kunas and enjoy more local color by sleeping in one of the *sobe* or apartments listed earlier instead, but if you prefer a well-located home base with big-hotel amenities, here are your options: **$$$ Hotel Palace,** a few steps off the main square, at the end of the harbor (not yet fully renovated but extremely central, some rooms get noise from nearby bars—request a quieter room, 73 rooms, Db-€200); **$$$ Hotel Riva,** along the embankment where the big boats dock (renovated to top-class quality, with artsy, mod decor and nude sketches in the halls, suffers from disco noise from the adjacent Carpe Diem nightclub—try requesting a quieter room, 54 rooms, Db-€320); **$$$ Hotel Villa Dalmacija,** around the corner from Hotel Riva, just east of the Old Town (21 rooms in main hotel and 37 rooms in adjacent "beach lodge," just renovated); **$$$ Hotel Adriana,** across the harbor from Hotel Riva (recently renovated and even more plush than the Riva, full-service spa and 59 rooms, killer views from rooftop bar, Db-€450); **$$ Hotel Delfin,** just beyond the Adriana (55 unrenovated rooms, Db-€75-95); and two others farther along past the Adriana and Delfin, a 5- to 10-minute walk from the Old Town: **$$$ Hotel Pharos** (200 unrenovated rooms, Db-€75-95) and **$$$ Hotel Amfora** (nicely renovated but not quite as fancy as the Riva or Adriana, great resort vibe with wonderful swimming-pool complex that reaches down to the beach, 324 rooms, Db-€250-300). You can book any of the Sunčani Hvar hotels through the same office: tel. 021/750-555, www.suncanihvar.com, reservations@suncanihvar.com.

Eating in Hvar

Like everything else in Hvar, restaurants are pricey. I've broken my listings into two general categories: more affordable places with traditional Croatian menus (which often include pizzas, pastas, basic seafood dishes, and so on), and splurges with a more international/Mediterranean line-up of dishes that seem designed to pad the final bill. No matter where you dine, reservations are smart July through September.

AFFORDABLE, LOCAL ALTERNATIVES

Alviž is a lowbrow restaurant that owns Hvar's most unromantic location—just outside the Old Town near the bus station—but the food and welcoming atmosphere more than compensate. This is where locals mingle with tourists. Say hello to owner Katarina, then dine on affordable pizzas, pastas, and other dishes in a woody interior or on a welcoming terrace out back with a busy open grill. The food is unpretentious but delicious, including one of the best *pašticadas* I've had (50-80-kn pizzas and pasta, 70-140-kn meat and fish dishes, daily 18:00-24:00, closed mid-Oct-April, across parking lot from bus station, Hanibala Lucića 1, tel. 021/742-797).

Konoba Menego, owned by the Kovačević family and run by English-speaking Martin, offers the chance to try typical cuisine from Dalmatia and throughout Croatia. (Owner Dinko stubbornly refuses to serve anything that's not authentically Dalmatian—including Coca-Cola, spaghetti, or beer.) The user-friendly menu lists the town or region of origin for each specialty. Portions are small, so think of it as Croatian tapas: Two people can order three or four dishes to share, or they can split a larger combination plate—the fisherman's plate is excellent. Dine in the cozy, cave-like terrace or in the atmospheric dining room, with air-dried ham *(pršut)* hanging from the rafters; both have rustic bench seating (50-80-kn small plates, 130-140-kn combination plates, 90-130-kn main dishes, Mon-Sat 11:30-14:30 & 18:00-24:00, Sun 18:00-24:00 only, closed mid-Oct-March, on the steep lane called Groda leading up to the fortress, reservations smart, tel. 021/742-036 or 021/717-411, www.menego.hr).

Mizarola is surprisingly affordable given its prime outdoor seating right on Hvar's atmospheric main square. While it seems more or less interchangeable with its neighbors, it has earned a good reputation for its affordable pizzas and pastas. Its tables surround the stone cistern—*mizarola*—in the middle of the square (50-80-kn pizzas and pastas, a few 80-150-kn main courses, daily 10:00-24:00, Trg Sv. Stjepana b.b., mobile 098-799-978).

With a View, West of Town: The best views are had from the harbor's west side. Troll the handful of places past the Hotel Adriana and choose what looks best. You're here for the view, not high cuisine. **Dva Ribara** ("Two Fishermen") has fair prices, reasonable quality, and fine views (70-110-kn pastas, 80-150-kn main courses, Obala Fabrika 31, tel. 021/741-109).

Dessert: Although the ice-cream joints in Hvar are underwhelming, the town has one of the most appealing cake shops in Dalmatia. **Nonica** ("Granny's") serves up a delectable assortment of cakes and cookies—many based on traditional Croatian recipes (just like Granny used to make)—and other international crowd-pleasers. Get your treat to go, or linger over it at the outdoor seating, on a tight lane next to a church just a block off the harbor (10-24-kn treats, Mon-Sat 8:00-22:00, Sun 15:00-22:00, closed Nov-Easter, Kroz Burak 23, mobile 091-739-2390).

Picnics: A big, handy **Konzum** supermarket is near the bus station (Mon-Sat 7:00-21:00, Sun 7:00-13:00), and a smaller grocery store is on the town square, across from the recommended Mizarola. There's no shortage of scenic places to enjoy an al fresco munch: on a stone bench by the arsenal, overlooking the main square, or on the embankment that runs along the harbor.

INTERNATIONAL SPLURGES

Gariful Restaurant ("Carnation") has Hvar's best waterfront location, at the end of the yacht-lined embankment. They have a fine outdoor terrace and a small dining room, and the service is crisp and helpful. You know the fish is fresh, because it's swimming around beneath the floor inside (75-115-kn pastas, 80-240-kn meat or seafood dishes, daily 10:00-23:00, several doors past the Hotel Riva heading east, tel. 021/742-999).

Hvar's "Restaurant Row": The streets just above the main square (to the left as you face the cathedral) are full of restaurants slinging similar Dalmatian and Mediterranean fare in an upscale atmosphere. Outdoor tables make it easy to window shop and find your favorite. Most places here value style over substance. In this zone, one place bucks the trend: **Golden Shell** is owned by a renowned local chef, a Slow Food advocate who also offers cooking courses and enjoys creating inventive dishes mixing local and international flavors (75-110-kn starters, 100-160-kn main courses, 5-hour cooking class for about 750-kn, daily 12:00-15:00 & 19:00-23:00, Petra Hektorovića 8, mobile 098-917-7386, www.zlatna.skoljka.com). Also in this area, **Macondo** offers fun, tight sidewalk seating and a nondescript dining room serving mostly fish dishes (110-kn pastas, 110-150-kn main courses, defiantly cash only, Mon-Sat 12:00-14:00 & 18:30-24:00, Sun 18:30-24:00, closed Nov-March, tel. 021/742-850).

BREAKFAST

If you're sleeping in a *soba*, you're on your own for breakfast. Small **bakeries** are scattered around town. For something more substantial, drop into **Café Pjaca,** with ideal outdoor seating on the main square across from the TI (35-65-kn options, daily 7:00-23:00, cool modern decor). **Hotel Park** costs more, but its enticing terrace—overlooking the square and harbor—may be worth the expense (59-79 kn, daily 7:00-11:00).

Hvar Connections

BY BOAT

For nondrivers, the handiest boat connections from Hvar are on speedy catamarans, which not only are faster but leave from the harbor in the heart of Hvar town. The big car ferries depart from the port of Stari Grad, a 20-minute drive or bus ride from Hvar town. Note that these boat schedules are subject to great variation;

HVAR

confirm departure and ticketing information on each company's website.

Buying Tickets: Remember, it's smart to buy tickets for the catamarans as early as possible—these often sell out, especially in peak season. Both *Krilo* and Jadrolinija tickets can be booked in advance on their websites (*Krilo*: www.krilo.hr; Jadrolinija: www.jadrolinija.hr). Each also has a ticket office in town. *Krilo* tickets are sold at the Pelegrini travel agency facing the harbor at the opposite end of Hotel Riva (long hours daily in peak season but closes for a brief lunch break, in shoulder season daily 7:30-13:00 & 16:00-20:00, Riva 20, tel. 021/742-743, www.pelegrini-hvar.hr). The Jadrolinija ticket office is on the embankment where the catamarans dock; you must buy tickets in person within 24 hours of departure (open long hours daily in summer but closed about 13:00-15:00, tel. 021/741-132).

Fast Catamarans from Hvar Town: The handy *Krilo* catamaran runs in the summer (daily June-Sept, 3-4/week May and Oct, none Nov-April). Each morning, it departs from Hvar town southbound to Korčula (1 hour), Mljet National Park (1.75 hours), and Dubrovnik (3 hours); each evening, it goes north to Split (1 hour; *Krilo* also runs a morning catamaran to Split on Tuesdays). **Jadrolinija catamarans** also connect Hvar town to Split (June-Sept at least 3/day—often more sailings in July-Aug; Oct-May 2/day) and to Korčula (1/day year-round, about 1 hour; additional catamarans use the less convenient port of Vela Luka on Korčula Island, a 1-hour bus ride from Korčula town).

Slower Car Ferries from Stari Grad: If you're in a pinch, you can head to Stari Grad to catch a big Jadrolinija car ferry to Split (7/day in summer, 3/day in winter, 2 hours).

OVERLAND CONNECTIONS

Hvar's **buses** only connect you to other parts of the island. For farther-flung destinations (such as Dubrovnik, Mostar, Sarajevo, or Zagreb), you'll take a boat to Split, then connect by bus from there. In summer, frequent buses cross the island between Hvar town and Stari Grad, and there's always a bus coordinated to meet the big ferries at Stari Grad (in which case you want Stari Grad's "Trajekt" stop rather than its Old Town stop); off-season, not every boat is coordinated with a bus. Most of the Stari Grad buses use the new road and stop at Milna, while one per day uses the old road.

Drivers heading north can drive 20 minutes to Stari Grad and catch the car ferry right to Split. If you're heading south (or to Mostar), you can also drive the very twisty roads (about 1.5 hours) down the length of Hvar Island to the town of Sućuraj, where you can catch the car ferry to Drvenik; from Drvenik, you can drive along the mainland or catch a different ferry to Korčula town (before making the trip, confirm all ferry schedules at the Hvar TI and get advice about how long in advance you need to line up).

BY SEAPLANE

European Coastal Airlines connects Hvar to multiple other points in Croatia. For details, see page 214, or visit www.ec-air.eu.

KORČULA

The island town of Korčula (KOHR-choo-lah) boasts an atmospheric Old Town, a smattering of little museums, and a dramatic, fjord-like mountain backdrop. Humbler than its glitzy big sister Hvar, Korčula—while certainly on the tourist trail—is much sleepier and has an appealing (and occasionally frustrating) backwater charm. At its heart, Korčula is a traditional, blue-collar, salt-of-the-earth shipbuilding and fishing town with a dim patina of tourism. All things considered, Korčula is the most enjoyable Back Door stopover between Split and Dubrovnik.

Like so many other small Croatian coastal towns, Korčula was founded by the ancient Greeks. It became part of the Roman Empire and was eventually a key southern outpost of the Venetian Republic. The town's "mini-Dubrovnik" vibe isn't an accident: Venice would have liked to claim the *real* Dubrovnik, but when that failed, they fortified Korčula instead...as if to create a Dubrovnik of their very own. Four centuries of Venetian rule left Korčula with a quirky Gothic-Renaissance mix and a strong siesta tradition. Korčulans take great pride in the claim that Marco Polo was born here in 1254—the explorer remains the town's poster boy. Korčula is also known for its traditional *Moreška* sword dance.

You'll discover that there are two Korčulas: the tacky seaside resort and the historic Old Town. Savvy visitors ignore the tourist sprawl and focus on Korčula's medieval quarter, which pokes into the sea on a picture-perfect peninsula. Tiny lanes branch off the humble main drag like ribs on a fishbone, a street plan that's designed to catch both the breeze and the shade. All in all, this laid-back island village is an ideal place to take a vacation from your busy vacation.

PLANNING YOUR TIME

For general Dalmatian Island tips, see "Planning Your Time" for Hvar (page 223).

Korčula deserves the better part of a day. Spend the morning wandering the medieval Old Town and exploring the handful of tiny museums (many close for siesta in the early afternoon, especially outside peak season). In the afternoon, kick back at a café or restaurant and bask on the beach. If you're here on a Thursday, be sure to catch the performance of the *Moreška* dance (also Mon July-Aug). With a second day, unwind more, or consider an excursion—either a trip around the island or a side-trip to Mljet Island and its national park (both are sold by various travel agencies around town, including Korkyra Info—see page 257).

If you're trying to choose between Hvar and Korčula, why not do both? For example, if heading south, you can take an early boat from Split to Hvar, have much of the day there, then take the evening boat on to Korčula to set up for a day or two of vacation. If you're in a rush, you could spend one night on Korčula, see the town in the morning, then zip out on the afternoon *Nona Ana* boat to Dubrovnik (runs only July-Aug 4/week)...but I wouldn't rush. Find time to hang out here for two nights.

Off-Season Challenges: While Korčula is reasonably well-connected to the rest of Dalmatia in the summertime, things get more challenging off-season. The express catamarans to Dubrovnik run only in high season (*Krilo* in May-Oct, *Nona Ana* in July-Aug). In winter, boat options dry up, and even the bus connections to Dubrovnik are cut in half (leaving only one early-morning option). You may find that you'll have to spend two nights in Korčula just to have any daylight time here. Before committing to how long you'll stay, double-check transportation options.

Orientation to Korčula

The long, skinny island of Korčula runs alongside the even longer, skinnier Pelješac Peninsula. The main town and best destination on the island—just across a narrow strait from Pelješac—is also called Korčula.

Korčula town is centered on its compact **Old Town** (Stari Grad) peninsula, which is connected to the mainland at a big staircase leading to the Great Land Gate. In the area in front of this staircase, you'll find ATMs, travel agencies, the Jadrolinija ferry office, the Konzum supermarket, a colorful outdoor produce market, and other handy tourist services.

Stretching to the south and east of the Old Town is **"Shell Bay,"** surrounded by a strip of tourist shops and resort hotels. This tacky zone is best avoided.

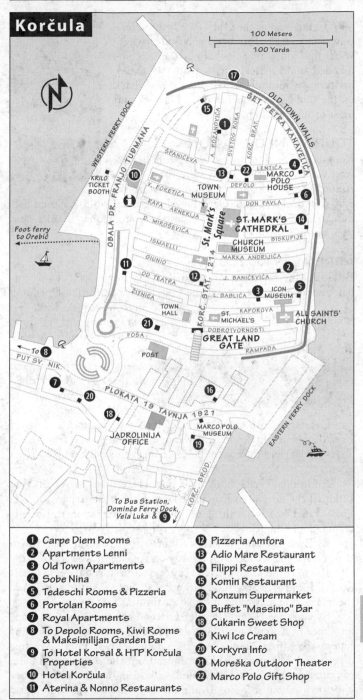

Korčula

100 Meters
100 Yards

1 Carpe Diem Rooms
2 Apartments Lenni
3 Old Town Apartments
4 Sobe Nina
5 Tedeschi Rooms & Pizzeria
6 Portolan Rooms
7 Royal Apartments
8 To Depolo Rooms, Kiwi Rooms & Maksimilijan Garden Bar
9 To Hotel Korsal & HTP Korčula Properties
10 Hotel Korčula
11 Aterina & Nonno Restaurants
12 Pizzeria Amfora
13 Adio Mare Restaurant
14 Filippi Restaurant
15 Komin Restaurant
16 Konzum Supermarket
17 Buffet "Massimo" Bar
18 Cukarin Sweet Shop
19 Kiwi Ice Cream
20 Korkyra Info
21 Moreška Outdoor Theater
22 Marco Polo Gift Shop

KORČULA

To the west of the Old Town is the serene waterfront street **Put Svetog Nikole,** where you'll find a few *sobe* (including some recommended under "Sleeping in Korčula," later), inviting swimming areas, great views back on the Old Town, benches placed just so, and more locals than tourists.

TOURIST INFORMATION

Korčula's TI is next to Hotel Korčula on the west side of the Old Town waterfront (July-Aug daily 8:00-21:00; June and Sept Mon-Sat 8:00-15:00, closed Sun; Oct-May Mon-Fri 8:00-14:00, closed Sat-Sun; tel. 020/715-701, www.visitkorcula.eu; Hana, Stanka, and slyly smiling Smilija).

ARRIVAL IN KORČULA

By Boat: The fast catamarans to **Korčula town** dock at the embankments on either side of the Old Town peninsula (depending

on conditions). From either catamaran landing, it's just a two-minute walk to where the peninsula meets the mainland and all the services described under "Orientation to Korčula," earlier.

Car ferries use the **Dominče** dock two peninsulas east of Korčula, about a five-minute drive (or 30-minute walk) from town. Taxis (70 kn) and infrequent buses connect this dock with Korčula town.

Additional boats from Split and Hvar town arrive at **Vela Luka**, at the far end of Korčula Island. Each boat arriving at Vela Luka is met by a bus waiting to bring arriving travelers to Korčula town (about 1 hour).

By Bus: The bus station is a short stroll from the Old Town. If you leave the station with the bay on your right, you'll reach the Old Town. If you leave with the bay on your left, you'll get to hotels Korsal, Liburna, Park, and Marko Polo. (Note that the location of the bus station may move in the near future.)

By Car: See "Route Tips for Drivers" at the end of this chapter. Once in Korčula town, you can park on top of the big Tommy supermarket (first 2 hours free, then 5 kn/hour, 50 kn/all day, free if you show receipts of 50 kn or more from the shop). From here, you can ride the elevator down and walk straight out the front door into town (about a 5- to 10-minute downhill walk). There's also parking along the marina, but it's pricey and jammed (June-Sept 25 kn/hour, free 24:00-6:00; Oct-May 5 kn/hour, free Mon-Fri 20:00-6:00, Sat 16:00-6:00, and all day Sun).

HELPFUL HINTS

Boat Tickets: On arrival, plan for your departure. Don't dawdle buying your boat tickets to leave Korčula—they can sell out. For details on the three boat companies that serve Korčula (Jadrolinija, *Krilo*, and *Nona Ana*)—and where, when, and how to buy tickets for each one—see "Korčula Connections," later.

Travel Agencies: Korčula has several travel agencies where you can book an excursion, browse shelves of books and souvenirs, and get information about car rental and other activities. **Korkyra Info,** well-run by Vlado, seems to have a knack for creating services that fill travelers' needs. They offer a variety of activities for €12—one hour of car rental, all-day bike rental, kayak rental, city tour, and so on. They also sell a variety of enticing excursions (described on page 263; also ask about their wine-tasting tour) and run a handy shuttle bus to Dubrovnik (office open June-Sept daily 9:00-22:00, until 20:00 in May, usually closed for midafternoon break off-season, main location facing the Old Town at Trg Petra Šegedina 3A, free Wi-Fi and computers, possibly second location just outside the Great Land Gate, tel. 020/711-750, mobile 091-571-4355, www.korkyra.info, info@korkyra.info).

Laundry: **Šugaman** ("Towel") is an innovative and very useful laundry service: Call to arrange a time for them to pick up your laundry, and they return it clean in a few hours. Since they work closely with Korkyra Info, that's likely the easiest place to drop off (small load-100 kn, more for larger loads, mobile 091-529-4631).

Sights in Korčula

Korčula's few sights cluster close to one another in the Old Town. I've listed them roughly in order from the Great Land Gate (the Old Town's main entry) to the tip of the Old Town peninsula. All museums are officially "closed" November through April, but most will usually open by request (ask the TI to call for you...or just try knocking on the door).

▲▲*Moreška* Dance

Lazy Korčula snaps to life when locals perform a medieval folk dance called the *Moreška* (moh-REHSH-kah). The plot helps Korčulans remember their hard-fought past: A bad king takes the good king's bride, the dancing forces of good and evil battle, and there's always a happy ending.

Cost and Hours: 100 kn, June-mid-Oct every Thu at 21:00, July-Aug also Mon at 21:00, in outdoor theater next to the Great Land Gate—to the left as you face the gate, or in a nearby congress center in bad weather; buy tickets from travel agency, at your hotel, or at the door.

▲Great Land Gate (Veliki Revelin)

A noble staircase leads up to the main entrance to the Old Town. Like all of the town's towers, it's adorned with the Venetian winged

lion and the coats of arms of the doge of Venice (left) and the rector of Korčula (right). You may be able to climb the tower (find the stairs around the left side) to visit a small exhibit with costumes and photos from the *Moreška* dance, then head up to the top level to enjoy panoramic town views.

Nearby: On the left inside the gate is the 16th-century **Town Hall and Rector's Palace.** The seal of Korčula (over the center arch) symbolizes the town's importance as the southernmost bastion of the Venetian Republic: St. Mark standing below three defensive towers. The little church on the other side of the square is dedicated to **St. Michael** (Crkva Sv. Mihovila). Throughout Croatia, many towns have churches dedicated to St. Michael just inside the town gates, as he is believed to offer saintly protection from enemies. Notice that a passageway connects the church to the building across the street—home to the Brotherhood of St. Michael, one of Korčula's many religious fraternal organizations. (Another such organization, located farther down this street, hosts the Icon Museum, described later.)

• *Now begin walking up the...*

Street of the Korčulan Statute of 1214 (Ulica Korčulanskog Statuta 1214)

This street is Korčula's backbone, in more ways than one: While most medieval towns slowly evolved with twisty, mazelike lanes, Korčula was carefully planned to resemble a fish skeleton. The streets to the west (left) of this one are straight, to allow the refreshing northwesterly Maestral winds into town. To the east (right), they're curved (notice you can't see the sea) to keep out the bad-vibe southeasterly Jugo winds. As in Croatia's other seafaring towns, the various winds—and weather in general—are highly important to locals. For more on this phenomenon, see the sidebar on page 164.

The street's complicated name honors a 1214 statute—the oldest known written law in Central Europe—with regulations about everyday life and instructions on maintaining the city walls, protecting nature, keeping animals, building a house, and so on. As you head up the street, look up to notice some interesting decorations on the houses' upper floors—artifacts from an earlier time, when residents were proud and wealthy citizens of the Republic of Venice.

• *Speaking of Venice, if you continue up the street, you'll reach St. Mark's Square (Trg Sv. Marka). From here, you're a few steps from the next four sights.*

▲St. Mark's Cathedral (Katedrala Sv. Marka)

Korčula became a bishopric in the 14th century. In the 19th century—36 bishops later—the Habsburgs decided to centralize ecclesiastical power in their empire, and they removed Korčula's bishop. The town still has this beautiful "cathedral"... but no bishop. On the tympanum above the main door (outside), you'll see another Venetian statue of St. Mark (flanked by Adam and Eve). Inside, notice the pointed Gothic arches on the ground floor and the rounded Romanesque arches above. Churches like this were commonly built entirely in the Romanesque style, but later retrofitted with some pointed arches for better support. Above the main altar, you'll find an original Tintoretto painting. At the altar to the far left, find the statue of St. Rok (better known by his Italian name, San Rocco) pointing to a wound in his leg. This French saint is very popular in Croatia; it's believed he helps cure disease. As you leave, notice the weapons on the wall near the door; these were used in pivotal battles near strategically situated Korčula.

Cost and Hours: 10 kn, 25 kn combo-ticket with Church Museum described next; open May-Oct daily 9:00-19:00, closed during church services, generally closed Nov-April but may be open Mon-Fri 9:00-12:00 after Easter. You can pay 20 kn to climb the bell tower.

▲Church Museum (Opatska Riznica)

This small museum has an eclectic and fascinating collection. Go on a scavenger hunt for the following items: a ceremonial necklace from Mother Teresa (who came from Macedonia, not far from here—she gave this necklace to a friend from Korčula), some 12th-century hymnals, a coin collection (including a 2,400-year-old Greek coin minted here in Korčula), some Croatian modern

Marco Polo

Korčula's favorite son is the great 13th-century explorer Marco Polo. Though Polo sailed under the auspices of the Venetian Republic (which included Korčula), locals proudly claim him as their own. Marco Polo was the first Westerner to chronicle his travels to China; he brought back amazing stories and exotic goods (like silk) that Europeans had never seen before. After his trip, Marco Polo fought in an important naval battle against the Genoese near Korčula. He was captured, taken to Genoa, and imprisoned. He told his story to a cellmate, who wrote it down, published it, and made the explorer a world-class and much-in-demand celebrity. To this day, kids in swimming pools around the world try to find him with their eyes closed.

paintings, a bishop's throne, three amphora jugs, and two framed reliquaries with dozens of miniscule relics. Lovers of clay pots and old kitchen stuff should ask at the gift shop to see the kitchen.

Cost and Hours: 25 kn combo-ticket with cathedral, 25-kn guidebook covers both museum and cathedral; May-Oct Mon-Sat 9:00-19:00, sometimes open Sun morning; generally closed Nov-April but may be open Mon-Fri 9:00-12:00 after Easter.

▲Town Museum (Gradski Muzej)

Housed in an old mansion, this museum does a fine job of bringing together Korčula's various claims to fame.

Cost and Hours: 20 kn, good posted English information but free smartphone audiotour available for download on their Wi-Fi network; June-Sept Mon-Fri 10:00-15:00, off-season until 14:00, closed Sat-Sun year-round; tel. 020/711-420. If it's locked, try knocking.

Visiting the Museum: It's arranged like a traditional Dalmatian home: shop on the ground floor, living quarters in the middle floors, kitchen on top. Notice that some of the walls near the entry have holes in them. Archaeologists are continually doing "digs" into these walls to learn how medieval houses here were built. On the ground floor is a lapidarium, featuring fragments of Korčula's stone past (see the first-century Roman amphora jugs).

Upstairs is a display on Korčula's long-standing shipbuilding industry, including models of two modern steel ships built here (the town still builds ship parts today). There's also a furnished living room and, in the attic, a kitchen. This was a smart place for the kitchen—if it caught fire, it was less likely to destroy the whole building. Notice the little WC in the corner. A network of pipes took kitchen and other waste through town and out to sea.

KORČULA

Marco Polo's House (Kuća Marka Pola)

Actually a more recent building on the site of what may or may not have been the property of the adventurer's family, "Marco Polo's House" has a stubby tower you can climb for an uninspiring view... and nothing else. There's little reason to pay admission here. In the future, the town hopes to turn the complex into a world-class museum about the explorer, with exhibits about Polo himself, Korčula in the 13th century, the big 1298 naval battle during which Polo was taken prisoner, and the Silk Road trading route. Progress has been slow on an official museum, but in the meantime, a local entrepreneur has opened an engaging exhibition about the explorer's life—see "Marco Polo Museum," later.

Cost and Hours: 20 kn, daily Easter-June and Sept-Oct 9:00-15:00, July-Aug 9:00-21:00, closed Nov-Easter, just north of cathedral on—where else?—ulica Depolo.

Nearby: Across the street from the house's entrance, you'll find a clever **Marco Polo gift shop** selling various items related to the explorer—herbs, brandies, honey, and so on. Each one comes with a little tag telling a legend about M.P.—for example, how the word "million" was based on his middle name, Emilio (because no existing word was superlative enough for his discoveries). This is one of five such shops, which you'll see all over town (ulica Depolo 1A, mobile 091-189-8048).

▲Icon Museum (Zbirka Ikona)

Korčula is known for its many brotherhoods—centuries-old fraternal organizations that have sprung up around churches. The Brotherhood of All Saints has been meeting every Sunday after Mass since the 14th century, and they run a small but interesting museum of icons. Maja, who lives upstairs, speaks no English but will point out what's worth seeing (ask her to explain the object in the ballot box by the entry). These golden religious images were brought back from Greece in the 17th century by Korčulans who fought the Ottomans on a Venetian warship.

Brotherhoods' meeting halls are often connected to their church by a second-story walkway. Use this one to step in to the Venetian-style **All Saints' Church** (Crkva Svih Svetih). Under the loft in the back of the church, notice the models of boats and tools—donated by Korčula's shipbuilders. Above the loft, notice the KKK-like white cloaks of the brotherhood. Look closely at the painting to the right of the altar. See the guys in the white robes kneeling under Jesus? That's the Brotherhood, who commissioned this painting.

Cost and Hours: 15 kn, hours depend on demand—generally May-Oct Mon-Sat 9:00-13:00 & 17:00-18:00, may be open all day in peak season, closed Sun except in July-Aug, closed Nov-

KORČULA

April—but try ringing the bell, on Kaprova ulica at the Old Town's southeast tip—look for *Ikone* sign.

▲Old Town Walls

For several centuries, strategic Korčula was one of the most important southern outposts of the Venetian Republic. The Republic of Dubrovnik began at the Pelješac Peninsula, just across the channel. Korčula's original town walls date from at least the 13th century, but the fortifications were expanded over several centuries to defend against various foes of Venice—mostly Ottomans, pirates, and Ottoman pirates.

By the late 19th century, Korčula was an unimportant Habsburg beach town, and the walls had no strategic value. The town decided to quarry the top half of its old walls to build new homes (and to improve air circulation inside the city). Though today's walls are half as high as they used to be, the town has restored many of the towers, giving Korčula its fortified feel. Each one has a winged lion—a symbol of Venice—and the seal of the rector of Korčula when the tower was built.

• *Back out near the main gate of town, you'll find Korčula's final—and newest—sight.*

▲Marco Polo Museum

While not quite a serious "museum," this exhibit offers an engaging interpretation of the life story of the (supposedly) Korčula-born explorer. Considering that this attraction is basically a kid-friendly publicity stunt for the local chain of Marco Polo gift shops, it's far better than it could be. You'll be treated to the adventure, suspense, and romance of one of the Western world's most swashbuckling characters.

Cost and Hours: 60 kn, discounted if you purchase something at one of the town's Marco Polo gift shops, daily mid-June-late Sept 9:00-24:00, until 21:00 in shoulder season, closed Nov-April, Plokata 33, mobile 098-970-5334.

Visiting the Museum: You'll borrow a long-winded but evocative audioguide (or, if you're impatient, just read the descriptions) and walk past life-size dioramas of seven scenes from Marco Polo's adventures, including setting sail from Korčula on his 24-year eastern odyssey, crossing the deserts of Asia, coming to the court of Kublai Khan, falling in love with Princess Cocacine, fighting a naval battle—and being captured—off the coast of Korčula, and telling his tales in prison. While pretty low-tech (it feels a bit like a walk-through *Pirates of the Caribbean*, but with figures that don't move), it more than compensates for the otherwise near-total lack of information about this town's favorite son. Although it's a bit pricey, the museum is worthwhile if you're curious to learn more about Marco Polo, or simply as an excuse to get in out of the blazing sun or pouring rain.

ACTIVITIES IN KORČULA

Swimming

The water around Korčula is clean and suitable for swimming. You'll find pebbly beaches strewn with holiday-goers all along Put Svetog Nikole, the street that runs west from the Old Town. (The big, circular plaza where the embankment meets the Old Town is a pebbly kids' beach.) While this shoreline doesn't have much flat land for sunning yourself, you can generally find a relatively comfy rock to recline on. Another good swimming spot is at the tip of the Old Town peninsula. Or better, trek to the beaches near Lumbarda (described later, under "More Sights on Korčula Island").

Excursions

Various companies offer day-long excursions, including trips around the island (either by car or by boat) and side-trips to Dubrovnik or the national park on Mljet Island. Korkyra Info runs their own tours, which are affordably designed with the needs of travelers in mind. Their Mljet day trip, for €47, includes round-trip boat transfers, park admission, and a guide; you can also do a transportation-only option (€20 one-way, €27 round-trip; tour typically runs 3/week in high season, generally Mon/Wed/Fri, departs at 8:30, returns at 18:00). Closer to home, you can take a one-hour boat trip to some of the nearer, smaller islands, with the option to go ashore at a secluded beach to do some swimming and be picked up later (€12, also offered—without swimming option—as a sunset cruise). Their four-hour driving tour (€42) around the island includes a wine tasting, and you have the option of hopping off to enjoy the beach at Lumbarda and returning on a later shuttle bus. For more on their tours, see www.korkyra.info or visit their office.

Several more active tour companies have popped up recently, offering canoe trips, snorkeling, kayaking, and other "adventures"—look for fliers around town.

Other Activities

All over town, you'll see travel agencies where you can rent a car, bike, scooter, boat, sea kayak, or anything else you want for some vacation fun. Local captains take tourists on cruises to nearby bays and islands to get out on the water, swim, and enjoy a local-style "fish picnic." Inquire at any travel agency, or

simply talk to a captain at the harbor (near the eastern ferry dock, at Shell Bay; figure about 200 kn per hour regardless of number of people). If you're a wine lover, consider hiring a driver to take you on a tour of Korčula Island, including stops at some wineries (ask at TI or travel agency).

MORE SIGHTS ON KORČULA ISLAND

Korčula Island may be one of Croatia's most beautiful. It mingles rugged mountains, lush forests, picturesque and tasty vineyards, gorgeous hidden beaches, and an almost Hawaiian ambience. If you have a car, the island is worth a half-day spin. Or you can easily take the bus or a taxi boat to Lumbarda.

▲Lumbarda

For a break from Korčula town, venture about three miles southeast to Lumbarda, a tranquil and tidy, end-of-the-road resort village. Lumbarda makes up for its lack of the stirring, fortified old-town vibe of Korčula town by offering a lazy vacation personality that encourages visitors to linger.

There's not much to see in the town itself; most visitors come to hit the **beach.** While you can swim around Lumbarda's wide harbor, it's worth venturing farther out of town to one of its pleasant and pristine beaches. The two best cling to the little peninsula that juts out east of town: the pebbly **Bilin Žal** (literally "White Stone") to the north, and the sandy **Vela Pržina** ("Old Sand") to the south. Both beaches are about a 20- to 30-minute walk (or a short drive) from town. If you're coming on the bus from Korčula town, stay on the bus through Lumbarda's town-center stop, and carry on one more stop to the end of the line, which is a bit closer to the beaches. With your back to Lumbarda, walk right for sand, left for pebbles (ask locals—or other beachgoers—for specific directions).

Lumbarda is also known for its **wine**—specifically the *grk* white wine, the grapes for which grow only in this village's unique climate. It's named for the Greeks who first introduced it. Several wineries drape the hillsides above Lumbarda; my favorite for a visit and tasting is **Bire** (BEE-reh; drivers will see the turnoff on the right just before entering the town of Lumbarda). The setting is beautiful: a series of stone buildings bunny-hopping down the hill toward town, with an inviting tasting room. You can sample their *grk, plavac,* and rosé wines for 10 kn apiece (Mon-Sat 10:00-12:00 & 18:00-20:00, closed Sun, generally closed Oct-May, mobile 098-344-712, www.bire.hr).

Getting There: From Korčula town, you can get to Lumbarda by water taxi (50 kn) or by bus (hourly Mon-Sat in summer, fewer buses Sun, 15 minutes, 17 kn one-way, 25 kn round-trip).

North Coast

On the road that hugs the island's northern coast, from Korčula town to the village of Račišće, you'll find a series of beautiful tableaux over tranquil coves and tiny offshore islands, with the looming Pelješac Peninsula as a dramatic backdrop.

Korčula Island Spin

If you'd like to see the island (beyond Lumbarda and the coastal zones described above), head west and drive the length of this long (29 miles) and skinny (5 miles) island.

Driving up and out of Korčula (pausing for grand views at the pullout just above the Tommy supermarket), you'll pass through Žrnovo and eventually twist your way up to humble **Pupnat.** This oldest village on the island has a Tito-era Partisan monument and a cluster of old 12th- and 13th-century slate-roof houses. From here, you can continue along the main road, or wind down the steep side road to the tranquil and gorgeous bay of **Pupnatska Luka,** with an inviting pebbly beach fronted by beach bars. Ponder how the ancient Greeks—impressed by the thick forests here—called this island "Black Korkyra."

Farther west are two of Korčula island's main winegrowing towns: **Čara,** an otherwise nondescript concrete town, overlooks a broad basin striped with vineyards. Farther along, **Smokvica** is also all about grapes. In both towns, you'll spot several wineries that invite passersby in for a sample. Korčula produces mostly white wines, using local grapes called *pošip* (which tend to produce dry wines), *korčulanka*, and *rukatac* (smaller grapes that produce sweeter, higher-alcohol wines).

From Smokvica, detour down along the south coastal road, via **Brna** (deep yet sheltered, this stunning cove is a favorite spot for super-wealthy yachters to drop anchor) and then **Prižba.** The scenic road passes the parking pads of cantilevered rental villas that are a popular place for Czechs, Poles, and other Central Europeans to set up for a week or two of fun in the Adriatic sun. A string of tiny islets hovers just offshore, and farther behind is the big island of Lastovo. Facing the open sea, this area is popular for fishing.

Then twist your way back up into the interior (passing old terraces), dropping down into the island's biggest town, **Blato**—filling a low-slung valley and huddled around the base of a small hill. Its atmospheric tree-lined streets take you through a landlocked, workaday town that seems blissfully oblivious to the tourism all around it. Literally "Mud," Blato is named for the flood plain that surrounds it—now efficiently drained and used for abundant agriculture.

The road ends at **Vela Luka,** a working-class town surrounding a picturesque harbor. Enjoy a coffee, wine, or beer as you watch the bobbing fishing vessels, then head back across the island to Korčula town.

Nightlife in Korčula

This town is much sleepier than Hvar, but you'll still find a fair number of late-night discos in the summertime, including one near the eastern base of the Old Town peninsula, and others along the waterfront between the Old Town and the resort hotels (east of town). Just below the Great Land Gate, Caffe Bar Step often has live music outside.

The best setting for drinks is at **Buffet "Massimo,"** a youthful-feeling cocktail bar in a city-wall tower at the very tip of the Old Town peninsula. You can have a drink on one of three levels: the downstairs bar, the main-floor lounge, or the tower-top terrace (terrace is only for cocktail-sippers—no beer or wine; climb the ladder at your own risk). If you're up top, notice the simple dumb-waiter for hauling up drinks (55-65-kn cocktails, 20-kn beer, daily 17:00-1:00 in the morning, closed Nov-April, tel. 020/715-073).

A scenic 10-minute walk from town, **Maksimilijan Garden** perches at the tip of land just below the Franciscan monastery bell tower—perfectly situated for sipping a pricey cocktail in a classy outdoor setting while enjoying the sunset (head out Put Svetog Nikole and find the garden just in front of the church, mobile 091-170-2567).

Sleeping in Korčula

SOBE

My favorite *sobe* in Korčula offer similar comfort to the hotels at far lower prices. Unless otherwise noted, these places accept only cash (no credit cards) and don't provide breakfast. Apartments come equipped with kitchens, and *sobe* often have refrigerators and kettles. For something more substantial, several cafés in town offer a basic breakfast for 30-40 kn; ask your *soba* host for suggestions.

In the Old Town

Sleeping in the Old Town nestles you squarely in the historic heart of Korčula, in immediate proximity to all the sights. The likely trade-offs: steep and tight staircases, small rooms in centuries-old houses, and (with a few exceptions) no sea views.

$$$ **Carpe Diem** sits deep in the center of Korčula's Old Town. Rather than individual rooms, you rent out the entire beautifully restored townhouse, which sleeps up to five on four steep floors: The first floor is a bedroom; the next is another bedroom; the next is an old-fashioned kitchen souped up with all the latest

Sleep Code

Abbreviations   (7 kn=about $1, €1=about $1.10, country code: 385)
S=Single, **D**=Double/Twin, **T**=Triple, **Q**=Quad, **b**=bathroom
Price Rankings
 $$$ **Higher Priced**—Most rooms €100 or more
  $$ **Moderately Priced**—Most rooms €55-100
   $ **Lower Priced**—Most rooms €55 or less

   If I've listed two sets of rates for an accommodation, prices for peak season (generally July and August) precede those for shoulder season (May-June and Sept-Oct). The few places that remain open through the winter charge even less during those months. The dates for seasonal rates vary by hotel.

   These rates do not include the modest tourist tax (about 7 kn/person, per night). Hotels generally accept credit cards and include breakfast in their rates, while most *sobe* accept only cash and don't offer breakfast. While rates are listed in euros, you'll pay in kunas. Unless otherwise noted, free Wi-Fi and/or a guest computer is generally available, and English is spoken.

   Prices change; verify current rates online or by email. For the best prices, always book directly with the hotel.

gadgets; and the top floor is a loft living room with a tiny terrace. It's a worthwhile splurge for those wanting to have their own traditional Korčula home that's thoughtfully appointed with modern conveniences, including a washing machine (same price for up to 5 people-€250 in July-Aug, 15 percent less off-season, 20 percent extra for 1-night stays, air-con, Antuna Rozanovića 8, mobile 091-769-7007, nikola.curac@du.htnet.hr, Nikola and Marija Curać).

$$ Apartments Lenni is run by Lenni and Pero Modrinić, both of whom are outgoing and speak good English. They rent four apartments in a nicely renovated house right in the middle of the Old Town (Db-€99/€79); a fifth apartment next door with two bedrooms and a sea view (€149/€129); and a small, budget double with a private bathroom across the hall (D-€63/€50). Since they

live off-site, confirm your reservation the day before and let them know your arrival time (email them and book directly—not through a booking site—to get these discounted rates; air-con, all apartments have laundry facilities—washing machine and drying lines, near Konoba Marko Polo restaurant at Jakova Baničevića 13, tel. 020/721-444, mobile 091-551-6592, www.ikorcula.net/lenni, perisa.modrinic@du.t-com.hr).

$$ Old Town Apartments, well-run by Branko and Ulrike Ristić (who lived in Germany for many years), has three modern apartments wedged into an old shell in the heart of town (studio-€75/€55, bigger "comfort" studio-€85/€65, one-bedroom apartment-€105/€85, 10 percent discount for Rick Steves readers who book directly, air-con, Don Iva Matijace 14, tel. 020/711-320, mobile 098-180-2553, www.juristic.de/korcula, branko.r@onlinehome.de).

$$ Sobe Nina, run by Nina and her son Mate, offers five rooms and two apartments in a building along the seawall (non-view Db-€60/€45, seaview Db-€65/€55, 2-bedroom seaview family apartment-€140/€115, €20 less for nonview apartment, breakfast-€4, air-con, cheap self-serve washing machine, next to Marco Polo shop at Šetalište Petra Kanavelića 3, tel. 020/711-743, mobile 098-912-7638, matekurtovic@yahoo.com).

$$ Ivo and Katja Tedeschi, who also run a recommended pizzeria, rent three small, simple rooms (two with views) and a big, low-ceilinged, top-floor seaview apartment up lots of steep stairs just inside the seawall (Db-€60/€43, €5 less for nonview room, apartment-€100/€60, breakfast-30 kn, air-con, Don Iva Matijace 26, tel. 020/711-354, mobile 091-566-6924, acc.tedeschi@gmail.com).

$ Anka Portolan rents two older-feeling rooms located near the wall in the Old Town. Communication can be a challenge, but the price is right (Db-€35/€30, bigger apartment-€50/€40, cash only, air-con, Don Pavla Poše 7, tel. 020/711-711, ankaportolan.apartmani@gmail.com).

West of the Old Town

The pleasant residential neighborhood west of the Old Town, along the waterfront drag called Put Svetog Nikole, comes with an easy, level walk into town and gorgeous views of the Old Town peninsula. The main advantages to sleeping here are a bit more space and (in many cases) sea views. I've listed places in the order you'll reach them as you walk along the water—from one minute (the first listing) to 10 minutes (last listing) away from the Old Town.

$$ Royal Apartments are conscientiously run by Zvonko and Marija Jelavić, who winter in Toronto and have built some of the most spacious, hotelesque rooms in town. Zvonko and Marija enjoy socializing with their guests in the small square out front (small apartment-€90/€75, big apartment-€115/€90, closed mid-Oct-mid-April, air-con, easy breakfast at café below, car rental possible, well-marked with green awning just west of Old Town at Trg Petra

Šegedina 4, mobile 098-184-0444, www.korcularoyalapartments. com, royalapt@ica.net).

$ Rezi and Andro Depolo, probably distant relatives of Marco, rent four comfy, good-value rooms on the bay west of the Old Town. Three of the rooms offer beautiful views to the Old Town, and the five-minute stroll into town is pleasant and scenic. Friendly, English-speaking Rezi works to make her guests feel welcome (Db-€45/€40, room with kitchen-€5 more, about €3 cheaper without sea view, 30 percent more for 1-night stays, air-con; walk along waterfront from Old Town with bay on your right to the yellow house at Put Svetog Nikole 28—it's set back from the street but well-signed; tel. 020/711-621, mobile 098-964-3687, rezi.depolo@ gmail.com).

$ Kiwi Rooms, run by gregarious English-speaking Nado Andrijić and his artist wife Marica, has two bright, tight, and nicely decorated rooms with gorgeous seaview balconies facing the monastery steeple. While there's no air-conditioning, they often get a good breeze and there's only a bit of road noise (Db-€55/€45, 25 percent more for 1-night stays, Put Svetog Nikole 42, tel. 020/711-608, mobile 091-543-8265, kiwirooms@yahoo.com).

HOTELS

$$$ Hotel Korsal is an overpriced splurge hotel—and the only one in town not owned by HTP Korčula. Its 18 rooms fill three buildings just above the touristy promenade connecting the Old Town to the resort area, a 10-minute walk from downtown. The "standard seaview" rooms (Db-€180/€160) are tight but tastefully designed; the "comfort" rooms (Db-€230/€210) are big and very sharp—choose between sea view or "comfort garden," which are big and have private decks, but lack views (20 percent more for 1-night stays, includes breakfast, air-con, closed Nov-April, Šetalište Frana Kršinića 80, tel. 020/715-722, mobile 091-533-8302, www.hotel-korsal.com, info@hotel-korsal.com).

HTP Korčula

This company owns Korčula's five big hotels. Holdovers from the communist era, these are in varying stages of renovation. While overpriced, they have high capacity and could work in a pinch. You can reserve rooms at any of them through the main office (tel. 020/726-336, www.korcula-hotels.com, marketing@htp-korcula. hr). **$$$ Hotel Korčula** has by far the best location, right on the waterfront alongside the Old Town. It has a fine seaside terrace restaurant and friendly staff. The rooms are on two floors: The more expensive "first-floor" rooms (actually on the third floor) have big windows and views (Db-€130/€100); the cheaper "second-floor" rooms (actually on the fourth floor) have tiny windows and no views

(Db-€100/€80, reception tel. 020/711-078). Three more HTP hotels cluster a 15-minute walk away, around the far side of Shell Bay; while relatively inconvenient to the Old Town, they share a nice beach: **Hotel Marko Polo** has 94 rooms, air-conditioning, an elevator, and a big pool; **Hotel Liburna,** with a clever split-level design that reflects the skyline of the Old Town, has 109 rooms, most of them accessible by elevator; and **Hotel Park** has 134 cheaper rooms. The fifth hotel, **Hotel Bon Repos**—another 15 minutes by foot from the Old Town—is, in every sense, the last resort.

Eating in Korčula

Korčula lacks the burgeoning culinary scene of Hvar; things are pretty static here, and the place is awash in interchangeable *konobas*—simple restaurants serving pastas and seafood dishes. Note that almost all these places close from mid-October to Easter. Skip the eateries around Shell Bay, east of the Old Town.

"Hipster Square": For years, I searched for something youthful and trendy in Korčula. I finally found it. Tucked in a forgotten little square just inside the town wall, two eateries with personality attract a local following. Both offer good vegetarian options. **Aterina** is deservedly proud of its original recipes, fresh products, and warm welcome (assured by Nataša). Here you can assemble small plates of local Dalmatian bites (mostly seafood-based) or order full courses. Their "a little bit of everything" sampler plate (70 kn/person) makes a fine meal. Ask about the day's specials (30-45-kn small plates, 65-100-kn hot dishes, daily 12:00-24:00, Trg Korčulanskih Klesara i Kipara 2, mobile 091-799-5549 or 099-232-7890). **Nonno** ("Grandpa") is popular for its handmade pastas prepared with delicious sauces (70-120-kn pastas, 90-150-kn main courses, daily 18:00-23:00, ulica od Teatra 12, mobile 091-660-8276).

Pizzeria Amfora, on a side lane off the people-parade up Korčula's main drag in the Old Town, features delicious and well-priced pastas and pizzas—nothing fancy, just good ol' comfort food. Squeeze into the small dining room or enjoy the sidewalk tables (60-90-kn pizzas and pastas, 60-150-kn main courses, daily 10:00-24:00, closed 15:00-18:00 for a few weeks at start and end of season, closed mid-Oct-mid-April, ulica od Teatra 4, tel. 020/711-739).

Adio Mare, with fine seafood and friendly service, greets diners with a stone tavern-like dining room sporting long, shared tables and a thick vine scaling one wall. Or you can sit in the enchanting rooftop garden terrace, where you'll dine romantically above the fray below (12-kn cover, 60-70-kn pastas, 50-130-kn main courses, descriptive menu, Mon-Sat 12:00-23:00, Sun 17:00-23:00, on the main drag just past Marco Polo's House, tel. 020/711-253).

Along the Seawall: Various restaurants line up scenically along the Old Town's seawall, providing al fresco dining with salty views. Their tables, spilling out along the seafront, are ideal for romantic harborside meals. Dine here if it's hot, as there's often a pleasant breeze. Try easygoing **Pizzeria Tedeschi,** which serves up good pizzas closer to the base of the peninsula (the "small" is plenty big, 50-60-kn pizzas and pastas, daily 9:00-24:00, closed mid-Oct-April, tel. 020/711-586). **Filippi** is a white-tablecloth-meets-soft-candlelight splurge. Serving a limited but enticing menu of quality Dalmatian cuisine, the portions are small but delicious (70-kn appetizers, 100-kn pastas, 160-190-kn main courses, assemble your own wine flight from the wine list, daily 12:00-24:00, closed Nov-March, tel. 020/711-690, www.restaurantfilippi.com). On the western side of town, near the tip and perfectly situated for viewing the sunset, **Komin** offers traditional Dalmatian meals cooked on a grill inside (55-65-kn pastas, 70-120-kn main dishes, daily 12:00-24:00, Šetalište Petra Kanavelica 26, mobile 098-847-057).

Picnics: Just outside the main gate, you'll find a lively produce market and a big, modern, air-conditioned **Konzum** supermarket (Mon-Sat 7:00-20:00, Sun 8:00-13:00). A short stroll from there down Put Svetog Nikole takes you to rocky seafront perches with the best Korčula views. Otherwise, there are many inviting picnic spots along the Old Town embankment.

Sweet Shop: For good (if pricey) local sweets, stop by **Cukarin,** which sells tasty traditional cookies such as the delicious flourless (and gluten-free) *amareta* almond cake; the Marko Polo cake (flourless chocolate cake with buttercream); and the walnut-cream-filled *klašun*. They also sell homemade wine, liqueur, honey, and jam (Mon-Sat 8:30-12:00 & 17:00-20:00, closed Sun and Jan-Feb, a block behind the Jadrolinija office on Hrvatske Bratske Zajednice, tel. 020/711-055).

Ice Cream: My favorite *sladoled* in Korčula is at **Kiwi** (just up the lane across from Konzum supermarket, open long hours daily).

Korčula Connections

Korčula is tethered to the rest of the Dalmatian Coast by a few tenuous boat connections. Service becomes even more sparse off-season, and everything has been in flux in recent years, so it's important to research your options carefully online. If you're here during a lull in the sailing schedule, buses (which make the short crossing on the Dominče-Orebić ferry) are your ticket out of town.

BY BOAT

The speedy coastal catamarans and the passenger ferry to Orebić (on the Pelješac Peninsula) depart from the embankment sur-

KORČULA

rounding Korčula's Old Town peninsula (which side depends on weather conditions). Car ferries, including those to Orebić and Drvenik (described later, under "Route Tips for Drivers"), leave from the Dominče dock, about a five-minute drive east of Korčula town. And a few boats leave from the town of Vela Luka (at the opposite tip of the island, a 1-hour bus or taxi ride from Korčula town—described later).

Buying Tickets: Three different companies operate boats to and from Korčula. (For a complete understanding of the up-to-date schedules, check each company's website.) The handy catamarans can sell out quickly, so plan ahead to buy your tickets—ideally a few days in advance in peak season. Between late May and late September, waiting to book your catamaran is a mistake.

The catamarans operated by **Jadrolinija** (www.jadrolinija.hr) and *Krilo* (www.krilo.hr) can be booked online. (Within 24 hours of departure, you must buy Jadrolinija tickets in person—see office location on the map on page 255.) The *Nona Ana* catamaran (www.gv-line.hr) sells its tickets exclusively through the Korkyra Info travel agency (see "Helpful Hints," earlier). These often sell out, and the agency doesn't know the number of tickets they have available until midmorning on the day of departure. Drop by Korkyra Info as early as possible (ideally the day before) and ask to be added to their waiting list. Then show up around 9:00 or 10:00 the morning of departure to see whether tickets are available.

Catamarans from Korčula Town North to Hvar and Split: Jadrolinija and *Krilo* run fast catamarans north, stopping first at Hvar town (1 hour), then at Split (2.5 hours). Jadrolinija typically departs early in the morning (year-round, but departs Sun afternoon off-season), while the *Krilo* goes in the late afternoon (daily June-Sept, 3-4/week May and Oct, none Nov-April). Note: In peak season (mid-June-early Sept), Jadrolinija may run an additional afternoon catamaran to Hvar and Split.

Catamarans from Korčula Town South to Dubrovnik: In high season only, *Krilo* and *Nona Ana* make the 2.5-hour trip to Dubrovnik. The *Krilo* catamaran heads south midmorning (daily June-Sept, 3-4/week May and Oct, none Nov-April). The *Nona Ana* catamaran departs in the afternoon, but only four times per week in July and August. Both of these also stop en route at Mljet National Park.

Passenger Ferry from Korčula Town to Orebić: Državna Brodska boats leave from the Old Town's western embankment (near the TI), connecting Korčula with Orebić on the Pelješac Peninsula in 15 minutes (15 kn, July-Aug: 14/day, June and Sept: 10/day, Oct and March-May: 7/day). This is handy mostly for those meeting a driver on Orebić for a wine-tasting Pelješac drive on the way to Dubrovnik.

Boats from Vela Luka North to Hvar Town and Split: Additional boats connect to points north, but they depart from the port at Vela Luka, an hour away from Korčula town, at the opposite end of the island. A Jadrolinija **fast catamaran** goes daily from Vela Luka to both Hvar town and Split; unfortunately, on most days it departs extremely early, with no bus connection from Korčula to get you there in time—if you're desperate, you could pay about 400 kn for an early-morning taxi or sleep overnight in Vela Luka (Mon-Sat departs at 5:30, Sun at 8:05; 45 minutes to Hvar, 2 hours to Split). A **car ferry** also travels daily from Vela Luka to Split—it's slower, but generally departs at a more convenient time and is coordinated with a bus from Korčula (2/day, 3 hours, no stop at Hvar town). Since getting to Vela Luka from Korčula town is a hassle, carefully confirm these boat schedules at the Korčula TI or Jadrolinija office, and understand all of your options before you get up early to make the trip.

BUS CONNECTIONS

All buses from Korčula town (except those to Vela Luka) first drive to Dominče, where they meet the car ferry to cross over to Orebić, on the Pelješac Peninsula. Once across, it takes just over an hour to drive the length of the Pelješac Peninsula and meet the main coastal road.

From Korčula Town by Bus to: Dubrovnik (peak season: 1/day, 3.5 hours, likely departs at 6:45, possibly an additional departure at 8:50; off-season: 1/day, Mon-Sat generally at 6:45, Sun at 14:45), **Vela Luka** (at far end of island, Mon-Fri 6/day, Sat 5/day, Sun 3/day, 1 hour). An inconveniently timed bus departs Korčula nightly at 19:45, stopping in **Split** (5 hours, arrives after midnight), and then continuing overnight to **Zagreb** (arrives around 7:00 the next morning).

Shuttle Bus to Dubrovnik: Korkyra Info travel agency runs a designed-for-travelers minibus shuttle that costs only about 50 percent more than the public bus, leaves at a more convenient time (8:00 or 10:00), and takes you right to your accommodations in Dubrovnik (150 kn one-way, runs daily May-Sept generally around 9:00, Oct-April by request only, 2 hours, reserve ahead, mobile 091-571-4355, www.korkyra.info, info@korkyra.info).

BY SEAPLANE

European Coastal Airlines flies from Korčula to a variety of Croatian destinations. For details, see page 214, or visit www.ec-air.eu.

ROUTE TIPS FOR DRIVERS

The island of Korčula is connected to the mainland by a small car ferry that runs between Dominče—about a mile east of Korčula town—and Orebić, across the channel on the Pelješac Peninsula (15-minute crossing, departs Dominče at the top of most but not all hours—check carefully in Korčula, departs Orebić at :30 past most hours).

If you're driving via the mainland, you'll first cross on this car ferry to Orebić on the vineyard-strewn Pelješac Peninsula. Consider dropping into a winery as you traverse the long, narrow Pelješac Peninsula (about a 1.5-hour drive to the main coastal road). Where the peninsula meets the mainland, you'll see the cute little "Great Wall of Croatia" town of Ston. For more on the Pelješac Peninsula and Ston—including a self-guided driving tour of the vineyards between here and Dubrovnik—see page 354.

If you're heading south to **Dubrovnik,** the coastal road zips you right there (about an hour from Ston). If you're heading north to **Split,** soon after joining the coastal road you'll actually pass through Bosnia-Herzegovina for a few miles (around the town of Neum; for details, see page 453).

Because of the ferry crossing and the long drive along the Pelješac Peninsula, driving **between Split and Korčula** is time-consuming and tiring. Instead, I prefer to take the longer car ferry the whole way between Split and Vela Luka, at the far end of Korčula Island (described earlier; allow 1 hour for the drive from Korčula town to Vela Luka, costs about 300 kn per car for ferry ride). The scenic and relaxing three-hour boat ride from Vela Luka to Split saves you more than that much driving time.

If you're headed north, note that there's also a car ferry from Dominče north to **Drvenik** on the mainland (about halfway to Split).

DUBROVNIK

Dubrovnik is a living fairy tale that shouldn't be missed. It feels like a small town today, but 500 years ago, Dubrovnik was a major maritime power, with the third-biggest navy in the Mediterranean. Still jutting confidently into the sea and ringed by thick medieval walls, Dubrovnik deserves its nickname: the Pearl of the Adriatic. Within the ramparts, the traffic-free Old Town is a fun jumble of steep alleys, low-impact museums, al fresco cafés, and kid-friendly squares. After all these centuries, the buildings still hint at old-time wealth, and the central promenade (Stradun) remains the place to see and be seen.

The city's charm is the result of its no-nonsense past. Busy merchants, the salt trade, and shipbuilding made Dubrovnik rich. But Dubrovnik's most valued commodity was always its freedom—even today, you'll see the proud motto *Libertas* displayed all over town (see *"Libertas"* sidebar).

Dubrovnik flourished in the 15th and 16th centuries, but an earthquake (and ensuing fire) destroyed nearly everything in 1667. Most of today's buildings in the Old Town are post-quake Baroque, although a few palaces, monasteries, and convents displaying a rich Gothic-Renaissance mix survive from Dubrovnik's earlier Golden Age. Dubrovnik remained a big tourist draw through the Tito years, bringing in much-needed hard currency from Western visitors. Consequently, the city never acquired the hard socialist patina of many other Yugoslav cities.

As Croatia violently separated from Yugoslavia in 1991, Dubrovnik became the only coastal city to be pulled into the fighting (see the sidebar on page 296). Imagine having your youthful memories of good times spent romping in the surrounding hills

DUBROVNIK

Libertas

Libertas—liberty—has always been close to the heart of every Dubrovnik citizen. Dubrovnik was a proudly independent republic for centuries, even as most of Croatia became Venetian and then Hungarian.

In the Middle Ages, the city-state of Dubrovnik (then called Ragusa) bought its independence from whichever power was strongest—Byzantium, Venice, Hungary, the Ottomans, the Vatican—sometimes paying off more than one at a time. Dubrovnik's ships flew whichever flags were necessary to stay free, earning the derisive nickname "Town of Seven Flags." It was sort of a Hong Kong or Singapore of the Middle Ages—a spunky, trading-oriented statelet that maintained its sovereignty while being completely surrounded by an often-hostile mega-state (in Dubrovnik's case, the Ottoman Empire). Dubrovnik persevered partly because of the inherently corrupt nature of the Ottomans; always susceptible to bribery (or "tribute"), the sultans were more than happy to let Dubrovnik thrive...provided they got their cut.

As time went on, Dubrovnik's status grew. Europe's big-league nations were glad to have a second major seafaring power in the Adriatic to balance the Venetian threat; Dubrovnik emerged as an attractive alternative at times when Venetian ports were blockaded by the Ottomans. A free Dubrovnik was more valuable than a pillaged, plundered Dubrovnik.

In 1808, Napoleon conquered the Adriatic and abolished the Republic of Dubrovnik. After Napoleon was defeated, the fate of the continent was decided at the Congress of Vienna. But Dubrovnik's delegate was denied a seat at the table. The more powerful nations, no longer concerned about Venice and fed up after years of being sweet-talked by Dubrovnik, were afraid that the delegate would play old alliances off each other to reestablish an independent Republic of Dubrovnik. Instead, the city became a part of the Habsburg Empire and entered a long period of decline.

Libertas still hasn't died in Dubrovnik. In the surreal days of the early 1990s, when Yugoslavia was reshuffling itself, a movement for the creation of a new Republic of Dubrovnik gained some momentum (led by a judge who, in earlier times, had convicted others for the same ideas). Another movement pushed for Dalmatia to secede as its own nation. But now that the dust has settled, today's locals are content and proud to be part of an independent Republic of Croatia.

replaced by visions of tanks and warships shelling your hometown. The city was devastated, but Dubrovnik was repaired with amazing speed. The only physical reminders of the war are lots of new, bright-orange roof tiles. Locals are often willing to talk openly about the experience with visitors—offering a rare opportunity to grasp the realities of war from an eyewitness perspective.

Though the war killed tourism in the 1990s, today the crowds are most decidedly back—far exceeding prewar levels. In fact, Dubrovnik's biggest downside is its popularity. When several cruise ships are in town, it can be mobbed. And, with more and more locals priced out of the Old Town and moving to the suburbs, the center can feel, at times, like a very pretty but soulless theme park. But those who dig deeper find that the city still has its own personality. And, like Venice, Dubrovnik rewards those who get off the beaten path and savor the town early and late, when cruisers and day-trippers have cleared out. If you haven't discovered your own secluded, laundry-draped back lane...then you haven't looked hard enough.

For many, Dubrovnik makes an ideal home base. Build some slack into your Dubrovnik time for a wide array of worthwhile side-trips (outlined in the Near Dubrovnik, Montenegro, and Mostar chapters).

PLANNING YOUR TIME

While Dubrovnik's museums are nothing special, the real attraction here is the Old Town and its relaxing, breezy ambience. While Dubrovnik could easily be "seen" in a day, a second or third day to unwind (or even more time, for side-trips) makes the long trip here more worthwhile. I enjoy staying at least three or four nights, for maximum side-tripping flexibility.

To hit all the key sights in a single day, start at the Pile Gate, just outside the Old Town. Walk around the city's walls to get your bearings (before it gets too hot and crowded), then work your way down the main drag (following my "Stradun Stroll"). As you explore, drop in at any museums or churches that appeal to you. Ride the cable car to the top of Mount Srđ for the sunset, then descend to the Old Town for dinner. With a second day, spread out these activities, hit the beach, or take a boat excursion from the Old Port (Lokrum Island, just offshore, requires the least brainpower). With even more time, fit in side-trips to a pair of particularly striking international destinations: Bosnia-Herzegovina's Mostar and Montenegro's Bay of Kotor.

DUBROVNIK

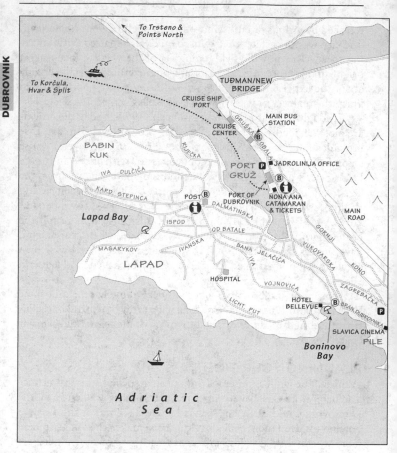

Orientation to Dubrovnik

Nearly all of the sights worth seeing are in Dubrovnik's traffic-free, walled **Old Town** (Stari Grad, STAH-ree grahd) peninsula. The main pedestrian promenade through the middle of town is called the **Stradun** (STRAH-doon); from this artery, the Old Town climbs steeply uphill in both directions to the walls. The Old Town connects to the mainland through three gates: the **Pile Gate,** to the west; the **Ploče Gate,** to the east; and the smaller **Buža Gate,** at the top of the stepped lane called Boškovićeva. The **Old Port** (Gradska Luka), with leisure boats to nearby destinations, is at the east end of town. While greater Dubrovnik has about 50,000 people, the population within the Old Town is around a thousand; most property owners here have converted their homes into tourist apartment rentals.

The **Pile** (PEE-leh) neighborhood, a pincushion of tourist ser-

DUBROVNIK

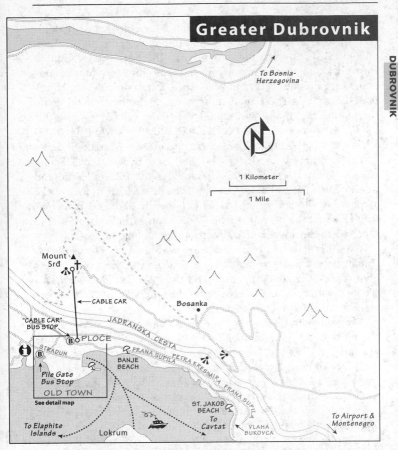

Greater Dubrovnik

To Bosnia-Herzegovina

1 Kilometer

1 Mile

Mount Srđ

CABLE CAR

Bosanka

"CABLE CAR" BUS STOP

JADRANSKA CESTA

PLOČE

STRADUN

FRANA SUPILA

PETRA KREŠIMIRA FRANA SUPILA

Pile Gate Bus Stop

BANJE BEACH

OLD TOWN

See detail map

To Elaphite Islands

Lokrum

ST. JAKOB BEACH

To Cavtat

VLAHA BUKOVCA

To Airport & Montenegro

vices, is just outside the western end of the Old Town (through the Pile Gate). In front of the gate, you'll find the main TI, ATMs, a post office, taxis, buses (fanning out to all the outlying neighborhoods), a bus ticket kiosk, a cheap Konzum grocery store, and a DM pharmacy. This is also the starting point for my "Stradun Stroll".

A mile or two away from the Old Town are beaches peppered with expensive resort hotels. The closest area is **Boninovo Bay** (a 20-minute walk or 5-minute bus trip from the Old Town), but most cluster on the lush **Lapad Peninsula** to the west (a 15-minute bus trip from the Old Town). Across the bay from the Lapad Peninsula is **Port Gruž,** with the main bus station, ferry terminal, and main cruise port. (Additional cruise ships tender to the Old Port.)

TOURIST INFORMATION

Dubrovnik's main TI is just outside the Old Town's **Pile Gate,** at the far end of the big terrace with the modern video-screens sculpture (June-Sept daily 8:00-21:00; May and Oct daily 8:00-20:00; Nov-April Mon-Sat 8:00-19:00, Sun 9:00-15:00; Brsalje 5, tel. 020/312-011, www.tzdubrovnik.hr). There are also locations at **Port Gruž,** across the street from the Jadrolinija ferry dock (same hours except closes earlier in Nov-April, Obala Ivana Pavla II, tel. 020/417-983); in the **Lapad** resort area, at the head of the main drag (June-Sept daily 8:00-20:00; May and Oct Mon-Fri 8:00-20:00, Sat-Sun 9:00-12:00 & 17:00-20:00; April Mon-Sat 9:00-12:00 & 17:00-20:00, closed Sun; closed Nov-March; Šetalište Kralja Zvonimira 7, tel. 020/437-460); on two of the Elaphite Islands, **Lopud** (Obala Iva Kuljevana 12, tel. 020/759-086) and **Šipan** (Luka b.b., tel. 020/758-084); and at the arrivals area of the **airport.** While not an official TI, the handy **Cultural Information Desk** (at the base of the Bell Tower, on Luža Square) is more central and can answer many questions (open long hours daily).

All TIs sell the Dubrovnik Card and hand out copies of two similar booklets: the annual *Dubrovnik Riviera Info* (lots of glossy photos and telephone directory) and the monthly *The Best in Dubrovnik* (with tons of ads, a current schedule of events and performances, and bus and ferry schedules).

Sightseeing Passes: If you'll be doing any sightseeing at all, choose between Dubrovnik's two passes. The 100-kn **"nine museum ticket"** is good for a week and covers several major museums, including the Rector's Palace, Rupe Museum, and Maritime Museum. Since you can't buy individual tickets at these sights, you'll have to get this ticket to see any of them. But assuming you're climbing the City Walls—Dubrovnik's top attraction—you might as well buy the **Dubrovnik Card** instead, which includes the same museums, the walls, and public transit. To squeeze all of your sightseeing into one day, get the 24-hour pass (170 kn, includes unlimited transit); with more time, consider one of the longer tickets (250 kn/3 days includes 10 transit rides, 350 kn/7 days includes 20 transit rides; cards sold at TIs and many sights and hotels; slightly cheaper if you prebook online).

ARRIVAL IN DUBROVNIK

As is the case throughout Croatia, you'll be met at the boat dock or bus station by locals trying to get you to rent a room *(soba)* at their house. If you've already reserved elsewhere, honor your reservation; if not, consider the offer (but be very clear on the location before you accept—many are nowhere near the Old Town).

By Bus

Dubrovnik's main bus station (Autobusni Kolodvor) is just beyond the ferry terminal along the Port Gruž embankment (about 2.5 miles northwest of the Old Town). It's straightforward and user-friendly, with pay toilets, baggage storage, and a helpful bus information window. To reach the Old Town's Pile Gate, walk straight ahead through the bus stalls, then bear right at the main road to the city bus stop, where you can hop on a bus (#1a, #1b, #1c, #3, and #8) to the Pile stop. A taxi from the main bus station to the Old Town and most accommodations runs about 75 kn.

Alternate Bus Stop for Outbound Buses: For buses that are leaving Dubrovnik toward regional destinations to the south (such as the airport or Cavtat), there's another bus stop that's much closer to the Old Town, saving you the long journey out to the main bus station. The **"cable car" bus stop** (a.k.a. "fire station" bus stop) is just uphill from the Buža Gate, overlooking the old wall, right next to the bottom station of the cable car up to Mount Srđ.

By Boat

Passenger **catamarans** and car **ferries** all arrive at Port Gruž, two miles northwest of the Old Town. On the road in front of the ferry terminal, you'll find a bus stop (#1a, #1b, #1c, #3, and #8 go to the Old Town's Pile Gate; wait on the embankment side of the street) and a taxi stand (figure 70 kn to the Old Town and most accommodations). Across the street is the Jadrolinija office (with an ATM out front) and a TI. Note: Due to a redevelopment of the port area, this arrival point may shift to under the big bridge at the end of the port.

Some **cruise ships** anchor just offshore from the Old Port, then send their passengers into the Old Town on tenders. Others put in at Port Gruž, just beyond the bus station. To reach the Old Town, take a bus (described earlier, under "By Bus") or pay 80 kn for a taxi.

By Plane

Dubrovnik's small airport (Zračna Luka) is near a village called Čilipi, 13 miles south of the city. A bus meets arriving flights for most major airlines at the airport, and brings you to the Pile Gate just outside the Old Town, then continues to the main bus station (40 kn, 40 minutes). Legitimate cabbies charge around 250-270 kn for the ride between the airport and the center (though some cabbies charge more than 300 kn; consider arranging your transfer in advance with one of the drivers listed on page 288, or through your *soba* host; airport code: DBV, tel. 020/773-333, www.airport-dubrovnik.hr).

To get *to* the airport, you can take the same bus, which typically leaves from Dubrovnik's main bus station 1.5 hours before each Croatia Airlines or Austrian Airlines flight, or two hours before other airlines' international flights (the schedule is posted the day before—you must ask at the TI). The airport-bound bus stops

Dubrovnik at a Glance

▲▲▲**Stradun Stroll** Charming walk through Dubrovnik's vibrant Old Town, ideal for coffee, ice cream, and people-watching. **Hours:** Always open. See page 289.

▲▲▲**City Walls** Scenic mile-long walk along top of 15th-century fortifications encircling the city. **Hours:** June-mid-Aug daily 8:00-19:30, progressively shorter hours off-season. See page 300.

▲▲▲**Mount Srđ** Napoleonic fortress above Dubrovnik with spectacular views and a modest museum to the recent war. **Hours:** Mountaintop—always open; cable car—daily June-Aug 9:00-24:00, Sept 9:00-22:00, April-May and Oct 9:00-20:00, Feb-March and Nov 9:00-17:00, Dec-Jan 9:00-16:00; museum—same hours as cable car. See page 315.

▲**Franciscan Monastery Museum** Tranquil cloister, medieval pharmacy-turned-museum, and a century-old pharmacy still serving residents today. **Hours:** Daily April-Oct 9:00-18:00, Nov-March 9:00-14:00. See page 305.

▲**Rector's Palace** Sparse antiques collection in the former home of rectors who ruled Dubrovnik in the Middle Ages. **Hours:** Daily May-Oct 9:00-18:00, Nov-April 9:00-16:00. See page 307.

▲**Cathedral** Eighteenth-century Roman Baroque cathedral and treasury filled with unusual relics, such as a swatch of Jesus' swaddling clothes. **Hours:** Church—daily 8:00-17:00, treasury—generally open same hours as church, both have shorter hours off-season. See page 309.

▲**Dominican Monastery Museum** Another relaxing cloister with precious paintings, altarpieces, and manuscripts. **Hours:** Daily April-Oct 9:00-18:00, Nov-March 9:00-17:00. See page 310.

at the main bus station and at the "cable car" bus stop just above the Old Town's Buža Gate (see "By Bus," earlier)—but *not* at Pile Gate.

By Car

Coming from the north, you'll drive over the modern Tuđman Bridge (which most locals, mindful of their former president's tarnished legacy, call simply "the New Bridge"). Immediately after crossing the bridge, you have two options: To get to the main bus station, ferry terminal (with some car-rental drop-off offices nearby), and Lapad Peninsula, take the left turn just after the bridge, wind down to the waterfront, then turn left and follow this road along the Port Gruž embankment.

▲**Synagogue Museum** Europe's second-oldest synagogue and Croatia's only Jewish museum, with 13th-century Torahs and Holocaust-era artifacts. **Hours:** May-mid-Nov daily 9:00-21:00; mid-Nov-April Mon-Fri 10:00-13:00, closed Sat-Sun. See page 312.

▲**War Photo Limited** Thought-provoking photographic look at contemporary warfare. **Hours:** June-Sept daily 10:00-22:00; May and Oct Wed-Mon 10:00-16:00, closed Tue; closed Nov-April. See page 313.

▲**Foundry Museum** Excavated foundry with explanation of medieval metalworking. **Hours:** April-Oct daily 10:00-17:00, closed Nov-March. See page 313.

▲**Serbian Orthodox Church and Icon Museum** Active church serving Dubrovnik's Serbian Orthodox community and museum with traditional religious icons. **Hours:** Church—daily May-Sept 8:00-14:00 & 16:00-21:00 or 22:00, closes earlier in off-season; museum—may be closed for renovation, ask at icon shop near cathedral for status. See page 314.

▲**Rupe Granary and Ethnographic Museum** Good folk museum with tools, jewelry, clothing, and painted eggs above immense underground grain stores. **Hours:** Wed-Mon 9:00-18:00, off-season until 14:00, closed Tue year-round. See page 315.

Maritime Museum Contracts, maps, paintings, and models from Dubrovnik's days as a maritime power and shipbuilding center. **Hours:** Flex with demand, usually March-Oct Tue-Sun 9:00-18:00, Nov-Feb until 16:00, closed Mon year-round. See page 312.

Alternatively, to head to the **Old Town,** continue straight after the bridge. You'll pass above the Port Gruž area, then take the right turn-off marked *Dubrovnik* (with the little bull's-eye). You'll go through a tunnel, then turn left for *Grad/Old City.* This road passes the big Old Town parking garage (described later), then twists around over the top of the Old Town, until you can see the lower station for the cable car. Here you have two choices, which will determine which one-way loop you'll get stuck in: If you want to reach the Pile Gate (at the eastern end of the Old Town), make a sharp right turn just before the cable car (watch for *Grad/Old City* signs), then turn right again (passing the entrance to the small "tennis court" parking lot) to curl around the back of the city wall and pop out at the Pile Gate (with another small parking lot), then back up out of town toward Boninovo Bay and Lapad. Or, if you want to head east of the Old Town, continue straight past the cable-car station for a long, scenic drive above the Viktorija area, then (after looping down again) past luxury hotels and to the Ploče Gate.

Parking: Near the Old Town, parking costs are exorbitant (rates constantly in flux and may exceed what's listed here). Ideally, make Dubrovnik either the first or last stop of your car rental, so you won't have to pay to park here. But if you must, ask your *soba* host for their best advice (many have a line on relatively reasonable options not far away). There are a few small parking lots surrounding the City Walls, charging a hefty 40 kn/hour (or 600 kn/24 hours—you have to buy the daily ticket at a Tisak kiosk, www.sanitat.hr). Useful only for dropping off your luggage before retreating to a more affordable alternative, the handiest are "the tennis court" lot, huddled behind the wall at the Buža Gate, or the small lot just behind the DM pharmacy near the Pile Gate. For longer-term parking, choose between close and expensive or far and cheap: The Old Town parking garage costs 30 kn/hour or 360 kn/day (cheaper Oct-May). If you'll be staying overnight, request a daily ticket *(dnevna karta)* at the ticket office within 15 minutes of when you park—this is essential to avoid exorbitant hourly rates. From this garage, it's about a 10-minute downhill walk to the Old Town—and a much steeper, 20-minute hike back up. Or you can park at the big lot at Port Gruž, just north of the Jadrolinija ferry terminal (10 kn/hour, 100 kn/day); from here, you can take a bus or taxi to the Old Town's Pile Gate (see "By Boat," earlier).

HELPFUL HINTS

Festivals: Dubrovnik is most crowded during its **Summer Festival,** a month and a half of theater and musical performances held annually (July 10-Aug 25, www.dubrovnik-festival.hr). This is quickly followed by the **Late Summer Festival,** designed to continue the festivities into September. For other options, see page 798.

Crowd-Beating Tips: Dubrovnik has been discovered—especially by cruise ships (hundreds of which visit each year, bringing more than one million passengers—on very busy days, there may be five or six ships in at once, sending 15,000-plus passengers ashore). Cruise-ship crowds descend on the Old Town roughly between 8:30 and 14:00 (the streets are most crowded 9:00-13:00). On busy days, try to avoid the big sights—especially walking around the City Walls—during these peak times, and hit the beach or take a siesta midday, when the town is hottest and most crowded. It can also make sense to schedule out-of-town sightseeing for busy cruise days; you can check the day-by-day cruise schedule at www. portdubrovnik.hr.

No Euros: Dubrovnik's merchants (even some of the city's top sights, such as the City Walls and cable car) can be stubborn about accepting only kunas—no euros.

Wine Shop: For the best wine-tasting selection in a cool bar atmosphere, don't miss **D'Vino Wine Bar** (described on page 335). If you want to shop rather than taste, **Vinoteka Miličić** offers a nice variety of local wines in a shoebox space. Jolly Dolores can explain your options, most of which are their own Miličić wines, and she can bubble-wrap bottles—handy to travel with (daily June-Aug 9:00-23:00, April-May and Sept-Oct 9:00-20:00, Nov-March 9:00-15:00, near the Pile Gate end of the Stradun, tel. 020/321-777).

English Bookstore: The **Algoritam** shop, right on the Stradun, has a wide variety of guidebooks, nonfiction books about Croatia and the former Yugoslavia, novels, and magazines—all in English (July-Aug Mon-Sat 9:00-23:00, Sun 10:00-13:00 & 18:00-22:00; June and Sept Mon-Sat 9:00-21:00, Sun 10:00-13:00; shorter hours off-season; Placa 8, tel. 020/322-044).

Laundry: Lavaman is most central. Drop your clothes and let them do the dirty work (100 kn/load, daily 9:00-20:00, allow 2 hours, Dropčeva ulica 2, tel. 020/321-233). The retro, self-service **Sanja and Rosie's Launderette** is just outside the Ploče Gate (cross the bridge and look left; 50-kn wash, 30-40-kn dry, clear English instructions, machines take bills, daily 8:00-22:00, put od Bosanke 2, mobile 091-896-7509). If you're sleeping near the top of town, it may be easier to hike up to the self-service **Laundry Spin** at the Buža Gate, behind the ticket desk for the cable car (wash-50 kn, dry-10 kn/10 minutes, daily 8:00-20:00, Wi-Fi, Iza Grada b.b., tel. 020/456-855).

Car Rental: The big international chains have offices at the airport; a few also have branches near the Port Gruž embankment where the big ships come in. In addition, the many travel agencies closer to the Old Town also have a line on rental cars. Be sure the agency knows if you're crossing a border (such as Bosnia-Herzegovina or Montenegro) to ensure you have the proper paperwork.

Best Views: Walking the **City Walls** late in the day, when the city is bathed in rich light, is a treat. The cable car up to **Mount Srđ** provides bird's-eye panoramas over the entire region, from the highest vantage point without wings. The **Fort of St. Lawrence,** perched above the Pile neighborhood cove, has great views over the Old Town. The **panoramic cruises** that loop around the Old Town are another fine choice. A stroll up the road east of the walls offers nice views back on the Old Town (best light early in the day). Better yet, if you have a car, head south of the city in the morning for gorgeously lit Old Town views over your right shoulder; various turn-offs along this road are ideal photo stops. The best one, known locally simply as **"panorama point,"** is where the road leading up and out of Dubrovnik meets the main road that passes above the town (look for the pull-out on the right, usually crowded with tour buses). Even if you're heading north, in good weather it's worth a quick detour south for this view.

GETTING AROUND DUBROVNIK

If you're staying in or near the Old Town, everything is easily walkable. But those sleeping on Boninovo Bay or the Lapad Peninsula will want to get comfortable using the buses. Once you understand the system, commuting to the Old Town is a breeze.

By Bus: Libertas runs Dubrovnik's public buses. Tickets, which are good for an hour, are cheaper if you buy them in advance from a newsstand or your hotel (12 kn, ask for *autobusna karta*, ow-toh-BOOS-nah KAR-tah) than if you buy them from the bus driver (15 kn). A 24-hour ticket costs 30 kn (only sold at special bus-ticket kiosks, such as the one near the Pile Gate bus stop).

When you enter the bus, validate your ticket in the machine next to the driver (insert it with the orange arrow facing out and pointing down). Because most tourists can't figure out how to validate their tickets, it can take a long time to load the bus (which means drivers are understandably grumpy, and locals aren't shy about cutting in line).

All buses stop near the Old Town, just in front of the Pile Gate (buy tickets at the newsstand). From here, they fan out to various parts of town; the routes you're most likely to use are buses #1a, #1b, #1c, #3, and #8 to Port Gruž (cruise port, ferry terminal), or buses #4 or #6 to the resort cove at Lapad. For more information, visit www.libertasdubrovnik.hr.

By Taxi: Taxis start at 25 kn, then charge 8 kn per kilometer. The handiest taxi stand for the Old Town is just outside the Pile Gate. The biggest operation is Radio Taxi (tel. 0800-0970 or 020/435-650).

Tours in Dubrovnik

Walking Tours

Three companies—**Dubrovnik Walks** (www.dubrovnikwalks.com), **Dubrovnik Walking Tours** (www.dubrovnik-walking-tours.com), and **Dubrovnik Tour** (www.dubrovnik-tour.com)—offer similar one-hour walking tours of the Old Town several times

Game of Thrones in Dubrovnik

Fans of the HBO television series *Game of Thrones* may feel the tingle of déjà vu during their visit to Dubrovnik. For years, much of the series was filmed here. Many locals have been extras, and they've become accustomed to seeing Peter Dinklage strolling down the Stradun in full costume. In 2015, HBO incited a minor riot when they decided *not* to film in Croatia, but they could return—ask around for the latest gossip.

On the show, Dubrovnik and the surrounding coastline and islands provide a setting for two main storylines: the royal family intrigue at King's Landing; and Daenerys Targaryen's conquest of the continent of Essos, from idyllic Qarth to the cities of Slaver's Bay. Of course, in most cases, the real-life Croatian settings are dressed up with special effects—the sea, rocks, and bottoms of the buildings are real, while the fanciful towers and spires (and the dragons) are pure fantasy.

For die-hard *GoT* geeks, here are some specifics (spoilers ahead!): The real-life Fort of St. Lawrence looks over a pleasant cove that becomes Blackwater Bay. Trsteno Arboretum (described in the next chapter) is where Sansa Stark had many heart-to-hearts with Olenna and Margaery Tyrell. The eventful royal wedding of Joffrey and Margaery was filmed in Gradac Park. The epic duel between Oberyn Martell and The Mountain was filmed at the amphitheater below Hotel Belvedere, facing Dubrovnik's Old Port. The island of Lokrum played host to the Qarth garden party, and the tower where Daenerys' dragons were held captive was Minčeta Tower (in the City Walls). And one character was humiliated by being forced to walk naked through town, beginning at the top of the grand staircase below the Jesuit Church (which I now think of as the "Steps of Shame! Shame! Shame!").

Filming has also taken place in Split, where Diocletian's cellars became the dungeon where Daenerys safely locked up her dragons. And the fortified town of Klis, just north of Split, was the location for the slaving town of Mereen.

To please *GoT* pilgrims, various companies offer walking tours of filming locations (see "Tours in Dubrovnik"), while another does a *GoT*-themed cruise (see page 344). A shop on Boškovićeva street (just above Prijeko street) has a replica of the Iron Throne (a great photo op, but only if you buy an overpriced souvenir). And the monastery on Lokrum Island may host a small museum of *Game of Thrones* memorabilia.

In March 2016, Dubrovnik had another brush with Hollywood when scenes from *Star Wars: Episode VIII* were filmed here. For the latest on both of these major franchises—and related attractions in Dubrovnik—ask around town.

daily (90-100 kn). I'd skip these tours—they're pricey and brief, touching lightly on the same information explained in this chapter. All three companies also offer themed tours covering *Game of Thrones* locations, wartime Dubrovnik, and the historic Jewish quarter. For the latest offerings, pick up their fliers (sales kiosks by Pile Gate bus stop) or check their websites. For a *Game of Thrones*-themed boat cruise that also includes a town walk, see page 344.

Local Guides

For an in-depth look at the city, consider hiring your own local guide. **Roberto de Lorenzo** and his mother **Marija Tiberi** are both warm people enthusiastic about telling evocative stories from medieval Dubrovnik, including some off-the-beaten-path stops tailored to your interests (500 kn/2 hours, mobile 091-541-6637, dubrovnikgardens@gmail.com); ask about guided transfers to Bosnia-Herzegovina, Split, or beyond. **Štefica Curić Lenert** is a sharp professional guide who offers a great by-the-book tour and an insider's look at the city (550 kn/1.5 hours, other tour options explained on her website, reserve at least one day ahead, mobile 091-345-0133, www.dubrovnikprivateguide.com, stefe@dubrovnikprivateguide.com). If these guides are busy, they can refer you to another good guide for a similar price.

FROM DUBROVNIK

For information on tour boats and guided big-bus excursions from Dubrovnik to nearby destinations, see the next chapter.

Private Drivers

If you're more comfortable having someone else do the driving to sights near Dubrovnik, hire your own driver. While the drivers listed here are not licensed tour guides, they speak great English and offer commentary as you roll, and can help you craft a good day-long itinerary to Mostar, Montenegro, or anywhere else near Dubrovnik (typically departing around 8:00 and returning in the early evening). They're flexible about tailoring the tour to your interests: Because there are lots of options en route to either Mostar or Montenegro, do your homework so you can tell them what you'd like to see (for example, I'd skip Međugorje to have maximum time in Mostar).

Friendly **Pepo Klaić** is enjoyable to get to know and has a knack for making the experience both informative and meaningful. Ask about his tennis-phenom son (€250/day, €125 for half-day trip to nearer destinations, airport transfer for about €30—cheaper than a taxi, these prices for up to four people—more expensive for bigger group, mobile 098-427-301, www.dubrovnikshoretrip.com, pepoklaic@yahoo.com). **Petar Vlašić** does similar tours for similar prices, and specializes in wine tours to the Pelješac Peninsula, with stops at various wineries along the way (€30 airport trans-fers, €190-200 for 2-person trip to Pelješac wineries, €230 to Mo-star or €250 to Montenegro including local guide, these prices for 1-3 people—more for larger groups, mobile 091-580-8721, www.dubrovnikrivieratours.com, info@dubrovnikrivieratours.com).

If your destination is Mostar, likeable Bosnian driver **Ermin Elezović** will happily come pick you up for less than the Du-brovnik-based drivers (for up to 3 people: €120 for one-way trans-fer from Dubrovnik to Mostar with a few brief sightseeing stops en route, €240 for round-trip to Mostar with same-day return to Dubrovnik; for contact information and details, see page 428).

Recommended local guide **Roberto de Lorenzo,** listed earlier, also offers guided transfers to Mostar, Sarajevo, Split, and beyond, peppered with historical commentary en route.

Stradun Stroll

Running through the heart of Dubrovnik's Old Town is the 300-yard-long Stradun promenade—packed with people and lined with sights. This self-guided walk (rated ▲▲▲) offers an ideal in-troduction to Dubrovnik's charms. It takes about a half-hour, not counting sightseeing stops.

• *Begin at the busy square in front of the west entrance to the Old Town, the Pile Gate.*

Pile Neighborhood

This bustling area is the nerve center of Dubrovnik's tourist indus-try—it's where the real world meets the fantasy of Dubrovnik (for details on services offered here, see "Ori-entation to Dubrovnik," earlier). Behind the odd, modern, mirrors-and-LED-screens monument (which honors the "Dubrovnik Defenders" who protected the city during the 1991-1992 siege) is a long and leafy café terrace. Wander over to the balustrade at the terrace's end and take in the imposing walls of the Pearl of the Adriatic. The huge, fortified pen-insula just outside the City Walls is the **Fort of St. Lawrence** (Tvrđava Lovri-
jenac), Dubrovnik's oldest fortress. Imagine how this fort and the stout walls worked together to fortify the little harbor—and the gate just behind you. You can climb this fortress for great views over the Old Town (30 kn, or covered by same ticket as City Walls on the same day).

DUBROVNIK

• *Back along the busy main drag, cross over the moat (now a shady park) to the round entrance tower in the City Walls. This is the...*

Pile Gate (Gradska Vrata Pile)

Just before you enter the gate, notice the image above the entrance of **St. Blaise** (Sveti Vlaho in Croatian) cradling Dubrovnik in his

arm. You'll see a lot more of Blaise, the protector of Dubrovnik, during your time here—he is to Dubrovnik what the winged lion of St. Mark is to Venice.

Inside the first part of the gate, dead ahead you'll see another image of Blaise. Down the ramp to your left, notice the little hole in the wall. Step through it to enter a tranquil **playground park,** where locals play with their toddlers in serenity (surrounded on all sides by tourists). Back inside the gate, look for the **white map** (next to the tourist map) that shows where each bomb dropped on the Old Town during the siege. Once inside town, you'll see virtually no signs of the war—a testament to the townspeople's impressive resilience in rebuilding so well and so quickly.

• *Passing the rest of the way through the gate, you'll find a lively little square surrounded by landmarks.*

St. Savior Square

The giant, round structure in the middle of the square is **Onofrio's Big Fountain** (Velika Onofrijea Fontana). In the Middle Ages,

Dubrovnik had a complicated aqueduct system that brought water from the mountains seven miles away. The water ended up here, at the town's biggest fountain, before continuing through the city. Three things helped make little, independent Dubrovnik very siege-resistant: this plentiful supply of water, large reserves of salt (a key

source of Dubrovnik's wealth, from the town of Ston—see page 354), and a massive granary (now the Rupe Granary and Ethnographic Museum, described later).

Stand with your back to the fountain and face the small **Church of St. Savior** (Crkva Svetog Spasa). Townspeople built this votive church to thank God after Dubrovnik made it through a 1520 earthquake. When the massive 1667 quake destroyed the city, this church was one of the only buildings left intact—its Renaissance interior stands at odds against the predominantly Baroque styles in other town churches. And during the Yugoslav Wars, the church survived another close call when a shell exploded on the ground right in front of it (you can still see faint pockmarks from the shrapnel).

To the left of the church, a steep stairway leads up to the imposing **Minčeta Tower.** It's possible to enter here to begin Dubrovnik's best activity, walking around the top of the City Walls (described later, under "Sights in Dubrovnik")—but this walk ends near a better, less crowded entry point.

The big building to the right of the Church of St. Savior is the **Franciscan Monastery Museum.** This tourable building has a delightful cloister and one of Europe's oldest continually operating pharmacies (see page 305 for a description; enter through the gap between the small church and the door of the big church). Historically, the monastery's **Franciscan Church** was the house of worship for Dubrovnik's poor people, while the Dominican Church (down at the far end of the Stradun, where our walk ends) was for the wealthy. Services were staggered by 15 minutes to allow servants to drop off their masters there, then rush up the Stradun for their own service here. If you peek inside the church, you'll find a Baroque interior—typical of virtually all of the town's churches, which were rebuilt after the 1667 quake.

Back outside, still with your back to the round fountain, look up and notice the **bell tower** of the Franciscan Church—with its rounded top—which is integrated into the structure of the building. If your travels have taken you beyond Dubrovnik, you'll notice the difference from other Croatian towns, where church steeples follow Venetian convention: Set apart from the church, and with a pointy top. This is just the first of many contrasts we'll see between Dubrovnik and Venice—two powerful maritime republics who were rivals for control of the Adriatic.

Finally, notice the stubby little, shin-high, mustachioed **gargoyle** embedded in the wall, just left of the Franciscan Church's door. You may see a commotion of tourists trying to balance on the small, slippery surface of the gargoyle's head. Tour guides enjoy spinning a variety of tall tales about this creature—if you can balance on one leg for three seconds, your fondest wish comes true— but these are a recent innovation.

• *When you're finished taking in the sights on this square, continue along...*

The Stradun

Dubrovnik's main promenade—officially called the Placa, but better known as the Stradun—is alive with locals and tourists alike.

DUBROVNIK

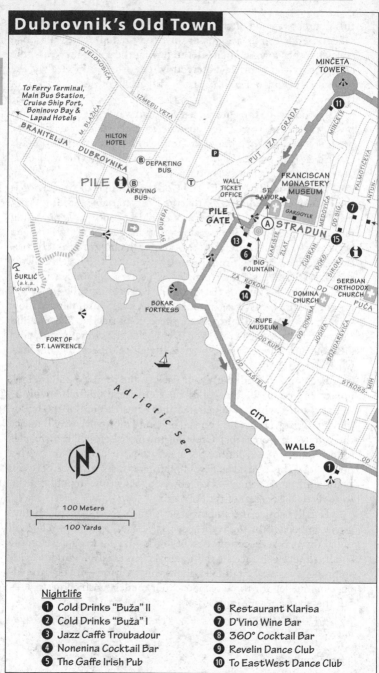

Dubrovnik's Old Town

To Ferry Terminal,
Main Bus Station,
Cruise Ship Port,
Boninovo Bay &
Lapad Hotels

BJELOKOSIĆA

IZMEĐU VRTA

M. BLAŽIĆA

BRANITELJA DUBROVNIKA

HILTON HOTEL

MINČETA TOWER

PUT IZA GRADA

PALMOTIĆEVA

MINČETE

⓫

ANTUN.

FRANCISCAN MONASTERY MUSEUM

OD SIG.

MEDOVIĆA

⓼

DEPARTING BUS

P

T

PILE ⓘ

ARRIVING BUS

SV. ĐURĐA

WALL TICKET OFFICE

ST. SAVIOR

GARGOYLE

PILE GATE

Ⓐ STRADUN

GARIŠTE

ZLAT.

ĐUĐAN

POR.B.

OD SIG.

⓭

⓮

⓯

SIROKA

ⓘ

ŠURLIĆ (a.k.a. Kolorina)

⓺

BIG FOUNTAIN

ZA ROKOM

SERBIAN ORTHODOX CHURCH

BOKAR FORTRESS

⓮

DOMINA CHURCH

OD DOMINA

OD PUČA

FORT OF ST. LAWRENCE

RUPE MUSEUM

OD DOMINA

JOSIPA

OD RUPE

BOŽIDAREVIĆA

STROSS. MIH.

Adriatic Sea

OD KAŠTELA

CITY

WALLS

OD

⓵

N

100 Meters

100 Yards

DUBROVNIK

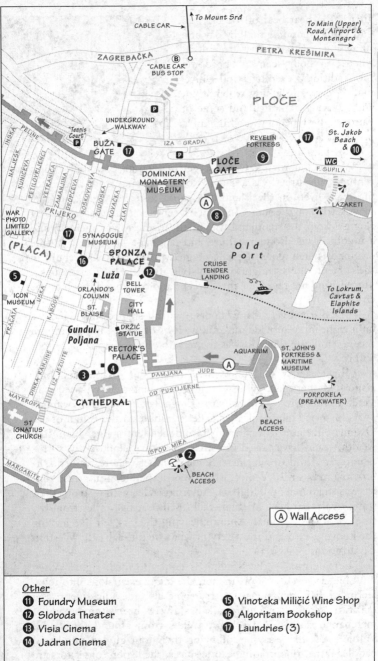

DUBROVNIK

This is the heartbeat of the city: an Old World shopping mall by day and sprawling cocktail party after dark, when everybody seems to be doing the traditional evening stroll—flirting, ice-cream-licking, flaunting, and gawking. A coffee and some of Europe's best people-watching in a prime Stradun café is one of travel's great $5 bargains.

When Dubrovnik was just getting its start in the seventh century, this street was a canal. Romans fleeing from the invading Slavs lived on the island of Ragusa (on your right), and the Slavs settled on the shore. In the 11th century, the canal separating Ragusa from the mainland was filled in, the towns merged, and a unique Slavic-Roman culture and language blossomed. While originally much more higgledy-piggledy, this street was rebuilt in the current, more straightforward style after the 1667 earthquake. The ensuing fire raged for three weeks and consumed much of the city.

The distinctively shaped doors—with P-shaped shop windows built right in, to provide maximum views of goods, but minimum access—indicate that this was the terrain of the merchants...and it still is.

The austerity of Dubrovnik's main drag disappoints some visitors. Rather than lavishing funds on ostentatious palaces, as in Venice, Dubrovnik seems eager to downplay its wealth. For much of its history, Dubrovnik paid a hefty tribute to the sultan of the Ottoman Empire to maintain its independent status. Flaunting wealth would have raised Ottoman eyebrows...and, likely, Ottoman taxes. Think about the stark contrast between restrained Dubrovnik and its rival Venice, which was desperate to impress. Venice was surrounded by Italians, Austrians, Germans—some allies, some rivals, but all Christian. Dubrovnik sat five miles from the frontier of the Ottoman Empire; leaving the city felt like leaving the known world and the safety of what we'd today call "Western Civilization."

Let me guess—the Stradun is quite crowded, right? When multiple cruise ships drop anchor, the many excursions into town feel more like incursions. But try some attitude adjustment: The maritime republic of Dubrovnik has always been a crossroads of merchants, sailors, and other travelers from around the world. While today they may be following their tour guides' numbered paddles rather than trading exotic spices, the legions of visitors are still part of the city's tapestry of history.

If you're here in the summer (June-Sept), you'll periodically hear the rat-a-tat-tat of a drum echoing through the streets from the Stradun. This means it's time to head for this main drag to get a glimpse of the colorfully costumed **"town guards"** parading through (and the cavalcade of tourists running alongside them, trying to snap a clear picture). You'll also see some of these characters standing guard outside the town gates. Begun only recently, this "tradition" is part of the local tourist board's efforts to make their town even more atmospheric.

• *Branching off from this promenade are several museums and other attractions. At the end of the Stradun is the lively Luža Square. Its centerpiece is the 20-foot-tall...*

Orlando's Column (Orlandov Stup)

Dubrovnik erected this column—a northern European symbol—in 1417, soon after it had shifted allegiances from the oppressive Venetians to the Hungarians. Whenever a decision was made by the Republic, the town crier came to Orlando's Column and announced the news. The step he stood on indicated the importance of his message—the higher up, the more important the news. It was also used as the pillory, where people were publicly punished. The thin line on the top step in front of Orlando is exactly as long as the statue's forearm. This mark was Dubrovnik's standard measurement—not for a foot, but for an "elbow."

• *Now stand in front of Orlando's Column and orient yourself with a...*

Luža Square Spin-Tour

Orlando is looking toward the **Sponza Palace** (Sponza-Povijesni Arhiv). This building, from 1522, is the finest surviving example of Dubrovnik's Golden Age in the 15th and 16th centuries. It's a combination of Renaissance (ground-floor arcade) and Venetian Gothic (upstairs windows). Houses up and down the main promenade used to look like this, before the 1667 earthquake and fire. This used to be the customs office *(dogana),* but now it's an exhaustive archive of the city's history, with temporary art exhibits and a war memorial. The poignant **Memorial Room of Dubrovnik Defenders** (inside  and on the left) has photos of dozens of people from Dubrovnik who were killed fighting Yugoslav forces in 1991. A TV screen and images near the ceiling show the devastation of the city. Though the English descriptions are pointedly—if unavoidably—slanted to the Croat perspective, it's compelling to look in the eyes of the brave young men who didn't start this war...but were willing to fin-

DUBROVNIK

The Siege of Dubrovnik

In June 1991, Croatia declared independence from Yugoslavia. Within weeks, the nations were at war (for more on the war, see the Understanding Yugoslavia chapter). Though warfare raged in the Croatian interior, nobody expected that it would reach Dubrovnik.

As refugees from Vukovar (in northeastern Croatia) arrived in Dubrovnik that fall, telling horrific stories of the warfare there, local residents began fearing the worst. Warplanes from the Serb-dominated Yugoslav People's Army buzzed threateningly low over the town, as if to signal an impending attack.

Then, at 6:00 in the morning on October 1, 1991, Dubrovnik residents awoke to explosions on nearby hillsides. The first attacks were focused on Mount Srđ, high above the Old Town. First the giant cross was destroyed, then a communications tower (both have been rebuilt and are visible today). This first wave of attacks cleared the way for Yugoslav land troops—mostly Serbs and Montenegrins—who surrounded the city. The ragtag, newly formed Croatian army quickly dug in at the old Napoleonic-era fortress at the top of Mount Srđ, where just 25 or 30 soldiers fended off a Yugoslav takeover of this highly strategic position.

At first, shelling targeted military positions on the outskirts of town. But soon, Yugoslav forces began bombing residential neighborhoods, then the Pearl of the Adriatic itself: Dubrovnik's Old Town. Defenseless townspeople took shelter in their cellars, and sometimes even huddled together in the city wall's 15th-century forts. It was the first time in Dubrovnik's long history that the walls were actually used to defend against an attack.

The people of Dubrovnik refused to flee their town. Though severely outgunned and outnumbered, Dubrovnik's defenders managed to hold the fort atop Mount Srđ, while Yugoslav forces controlled the nearby mountaintops. All supplies had to be carried up to the fort by foot or by donkey. Dubrovnik wasn't prepared for war, so its citizens had to improvise their defense. Many brave young locals lost their lives when they slung old hunting rifles over their shoulders and, under cover of darkness, climbed the hills above Dubrovnik to meet Yugoslav soldiers face-to-face.

After eight months of bombing, Dubrovnik was liberated by the Croatian army, which attacked Yugoslav positions from the north. By the end of the siege, 100 civilians were dead, as well as more than 200 Dubrovnik citizens who lost their lives actively fighting for their hometown (much revered today as "Dubrovnik Defenders"); in the greater Dubrovnik area, 420 "Defenders" were killed, and another 900 wounded. More than two-thirds of Dubrovnik's buildings had been damaged, and more than 30,000 people had to flee their homes—but the failed siege was finally over.

Why was Dubrovnik—so far from the rest of the fighting—dragged into the conflict? Yugoslavia wanted to catch the city off-guard, gaining a toehold on the southern Dalmatian Coast so they could push north to Split. They also hoped to ignite pro-Serb passions in the nearby Serb-dominated areas of Bosnia-Herzegovina and Montenegro. But perhaps most of all, Yugoslavia wanted to hit Croatia where it hurt—its proudest, most historic, and most beautiful city, the tourist capital of a nation dependent on tourism. It seems their plan backfired. Locals now say, "When Yugoslavia attacked Dubrovnik, they lost the war"—because images of the historic city under siege swayed international public opinion *against* Yugoslavia.

The war initially devastated the tourist industry. Now, to the casual observer, Dubrovnik seems virtually back to normal. Aside from a few pockmarks and bright, new roof tiles, there are scant reminders of what happened here more than two decades ago. But even though the city itself has been repaired, the people of Dubrovnik are forever changed. Imagine living in an idyllic paradise, a place that attracted and awed visitors from around the world...and then watching it gradually blown to bits. It's understandable if Dubrovnik's citizens are a little less in love with life than they once were.

It's clear that in the case of this siege, the Croats of Dubrovnik were the largely innocent victims of a brutal surprise attack. But keep in mind the larger context of the war: The cousins of these Croats, who were defending the glorious monument that is Dubrovnik, bombarded another glorious monument—the Old Bridge of Mostar (see page 433). It's just another reminder that the "good guys" and "bad guys" in these wars are far from clear-cut.

Dubrovnik has several low-key attractions related to its recent war, including the museum in the ruined fortress atop Mount Srđ and the Memorial Room of Dubrovnik Defenders in the Sponza Palace on Luža Square. Another sight, War Photo Limited, expands the scope to war photography from around the world.

ish it (free, long hours daily in peak season). Beyond the memorial room, the impressive **courtyard,** which hosts temporary exhibits, is worth a peek (25 kn, generally free after-hours).

To the right of Sponza Palace is the town's **Bell Tower** (Gradski Zvonik). The original dated from 1444, but it was rebuilt when it started to lean in the 1920s. The big clock may be an octopus, but only one of its hands tells time. Below that, the golden circle shows the phase of the moon. At the bottom, the old-fashioned digital readout tells the hour (in Roman numerals) and the minutes (in five-minute increments). At the top of each hour (and again three minutes later), the time is clanged out on the bell up top by two bronze bell-ringers, Maro and Baro. (If this all seems like a copy of the very similar clock on St. Mark's Square in Venice, locals are quick to point out that this clock predates that one by several decades.)

The clock still has to be wound every two days. Notice the little window between the moon phase and the "digital" readout: The clock-winder opens this window to get some light. The Krasovac family was in charge of winding the clock for generations. During the 1991-1992 siege, their house was destroyed—with the winding keys inside. For days, the clock bell didn't run. But then, miraculously, the keys were discovered lying in the street. The excited Dubrovnik citizens came together in this square and cheered as the clock was wound and the bell chimed, signaling to the soldiers surrounding the city that they hadn't won yet.

To the right of the Bell Tower, you'll see the entrance to the **Sloboda theater,** which hosts cultural events (such as folk-dancing shows) in the summer, and movies year-round. There's also the helpful Cultural Information Desk inside. Next to that, **Onofrio's Little Fountain** (Mala Onofrijea Fontana) is the little brother of the one at the other end of the Stradun. The big building beyond the fountain is the **City Hall** (Vijećnica). The terrace at the near end of City Hall is occupied by the **Gradska Kavana,** or "Town Café." This hangout—historically Dubrovnik's favorite spot for gossiping and people-watching—has seating all the way through the wall to the Old Port.

Behind Orlando is **St. Blaise's Church** (Crkva Sv. Vlaha), dedicated to the patron saint of Dubrovnik. You'll see statues and paintings of St. Blaise all over town, always holding a model of the city in his left hand. According to legend, a millennium ago St. Blaise came to a local priest in a dream and warned him that the up-and-coming Venetians would soon attack the city. The priest alerted the authorities, who

prepared for war. Of course, the prediction came true. St. Blaise has been a Dubrovnik symbol—and locals have resented Venice—ever since.

The church, like most churches in this city, was built following the 1667 earthquake and fire. And, while we've heard plenty on this walk about Dubrovnik's rivalry with Venice, there's no denying that the Venetians were some of Europe's top cultural trendsetters at that time. So Dubrovnik invited a Venetian architect to design the church dedicated to their favorite saint. That's why St. Blaise's looks like it would be right at home reflected in a Venetian canal...right down to its bulbous dome, which seems to have been transplanted here from the top of St. Mark's.

Just down the street from the "Town Café" is the Rector's Palace, and then the cathedral (both described later, under "Sights in Dubrovnik"). Just before the palace, on the left, notice the statue of Dubrovnik poet **Marin Držić** (1508-1567). This beloved bard's most famous work concerns "Uncle Maro," an aristocrat who's as stingy as he is wealthy. His son cleans out his savings account and goes on a bender in Rome...until his father gets wind of it and comes calling. The shiny lap and bright nose of this statue, erected in 2008, might lead you to believe it's good luck to rub his schnozz—and, sure enough, you'll see a steady stream of tourists doing just that. But the truth is that when the statue went up, local kids were drawn to his prominent proboscis, and couldn't resist climbing up on his lap and grabbing it. Tourists saw the shine and assumed they were supposed to do it, too. A legend was born.

• *Your walk is finished. From here, you've got plenty of sightseeing options (all described next, under "Sights in Dubrovnik"). As you face the Bell Tower, you can go up the street to the right to reach the Rector's Palace and cathedral; you can walk straight ahead through the gate to reach the Old Port; or you can head through the gate and jog left to find the Dominican Monastery Museum. Even more sights—including an old synagogue, an Orthodox church, a modern exhibit of war photography, the medieval granary, and the ruins of an old foundry—are in the steep streets between the Stradun and the walls.*

Sights in Dubrovnik

Keep in mind that many of Dubrovnik's museums require you to have either a "nine museum ticket" or a Dubrovnik Card (which also covers the City Walls and public transit); for details on both options, see page 279.

▲▲▲CITY WALLS (GRADSKE ZIDINE)

Dubrovnik's single best attraction is strolling the scenic mile-and-a-quarter around the City Walls. As you meander along this lofty perch—with a sea of orange roofs on one side and the azure sea on the other—you'll get your bearings, peer into secluded gardens, and snap pictures like mad of the ever-changing views. Bring your map, which you can use to pick out landmarks and get the lay of the land. Speed demons can walk the walls in about an hour; strollers and shutterbugs should plan on longer.

Cost: 120 kn to enter walls, also includes the Fort of St. Lawrence outside the Pile Gate (kunas or credit cards only—no euros).

Hours: From April through October, the walls open daily at 8:00; the closing time depends on the season (June-mid-Aug

until 19:30, late Aug until 19:00, May and Sept until 18:30, Oct and April until 18:00). Off-season (Nov-March), the walls are open daily 10:00-15:00. Since the hours are always in flux, confirm them by checking signs posted at the entrance. The "closing time" indicates when the walls shut down, *not* the last entry. Attendants begin circling the walls 30 minutes after the posted closing time to lock the gates, so if you want to make it all the way around, ascend at least 30 minutes before the posted closing if you're speedy, and an hour or more before if you want to linger.

Entrances and Strategies: There are three entry points for the wall (see map on page 328), and wall walkers are required to follow the one-way route counterclockwise. One good strategy is to begin at the far side of the Old Town, using the entrance **near the Ploče Gate** and Dominican Monastery (this is where my self-guided tour of the walls begins). This entrance is the least crowded, and you'll tackle the steepest part (and enjoy some of the best views) first. The most popular—and most crowded—entrance is **just inside the Pile Gate**, next to the Church of St. Savior (for this location, you must buy your tickets at the desk across the square from the stairway entry). If you manage to arrive before the hordes descend, it can make sense to enter here and get this (most congested) section out of the way first. Finally, there's a small entrance **near St. John's Fort** overlooking the Old Port (next to the Maritime Museum).

Crowd Control: Because this is Dubrovnik's top attraction, it's extremely crowded. Your best strategy is to avoid the walls during the times when the cruise ships are in town. If you expect crowds, don't dillydally—enter soon after the 8:00 opening time. The walls are the most crowded from about 9:30 until 11:00. There's generally an afternoon lull (13:00-14:00)—but that's also the hottest time to be atop the walls. Crowds pick up again in the late afternoon (around 17:00), peaking about an hour before closing time (18:30 in high season). During busy times, your best bet is to hit the walls around 8:00, or just before 17:00 (to avoid both the worst heat and the worst crowds).

Tips: Because your ticket is scanned as you enter, you can't leave and re-enter the wall later; you have to do it all in one go. If you have a Dubrovnik Card—even a multiple-day one—you can only use it once to ascend the walls.

Heat Warning: The walls can get deliriously hot—all that white stone and seawater reflect blazing sunshine something fierce, and there's virtually no shade (except at a few wall-top cafés). It's essential to bring sunscreen, a hat, and water. Pace yourself: There are several steep stretches, and you'll be climbing up and down the whole way around. A few shops and cafés along the top of the wall (mostly on the sea side) sell water and other drinks, but it's cheaper to bring what you'll need with you. If you have trouble with the heat, save the walls for a cloudy day. In that hazy light, the red roof tiles seem more vivid, since they're not washed out by glaring sunshine.

Background: There have been walls here almost as long as there's been a Dubrovnik. As with virtually all fortifications on the Croatian Coast, these walls were beefed up in the 15th century, when the Ottoman navy became a threat. Around the perimeter are several substantial forts, with walls rounded so that cannonballs would glance off harmlessly. These stout forts intimidated would-be invaders during the Republic of Dubrovnik's Golden Age, and protected residents during the 1991-1992 siege.

❷ Self-Guided Tour: It's perfectly fine to just wander the walls and snap photos like crazy as you go. And trying to hew too closely to guided commentary kind of misses the point of being high above the Dubrovnik rooftops. But this brief tour should help give you bearings to what you're seeing, as you read Dubrovnik's unique and illustrious history into its street plan.

Part 1—Ploče Gate to Pile Gate: Begin by ascending near the **Ploče Gate** (go through the gate under the Bell Tower, walk along the stoutly walled passageway between the port and the Dominican Monastery, and look for the wall entrance on your right).

Buy your ticket, head up, turn left, and start walking counterclockwise. Climbing stairs, you'll walk with Mount Srđ and the cable car on your right. After passing the roofline of the Dominican Monastery's cloister on the left, you're walking above what was the poorest part of medieval Dubrovnik, the domain of the craftsmen—with narrow, stepped lanes that had shops on the ground floor and humble dwellings up above. Peering down all of the tight lanes, look for the many little stone ledges sticking out next to windows. These were used to hang banners during the city's Golden Age.

As you walk, keep an eye on the different-colored **rooftops** for an illustration of the damage Dubrovnik sustained during the 1991-1992 siege. It's easy to see that nearly two-thirds of Dubrovnik's roofs were replaced after the bombings (notice the new, bright-orange tiles—and how some buildings salvaged the old tiles, but have 20th-century ones underneath). The pristine-seeming Old Town was rebuilt using exactly the same materials and methods with which it was originally constructed.

The path you're on alternates between straight stretches and stairs; as you walk you're rewarded with higher and higher views. Nearing the summit, you pass a juice bar (you can use the WCs if you buy a drink). At the very top, enjoy the best possible view of the Old Town—you can see the rooftops, churches, and the sea. Stuck behind a traffic jam of selfie sticks, ponder the increasing narcissism of our age...then snap a selfie to post to Facebook. For an even better view, huff up the steep stairs to the (empty) **Minčeta Tower.** From either viewpoint, observe the valley-like shape of Dubrovnik. It's easy to imagine how it began as two towns—one where you are now, and the other on the hilly island with the church spires across the way—originally separated by a seawater canal. Notice the relatively regular, grid-like pattern of houses on this side, and the more higgledy-piggledy arrangement on the far side (a visual clue that the far side is older).

The **sports court** at your feet is a reminder that Dubrovnik is a living city. (Anyone can play here, but you need a ball.) Underneath the sports court are the remains of a medieval foundry—the centerpiece of Dubrovnik's least-known museum. To learn how the casting process worked right here in the 16th century, visit the

Foundry Museum later, after you've descended the walls (see page 313).

While officially 2,000 people live within these walls, most locals estimate the real number at about half that; the rest rent out their homes to tourists. And with good reason: Imagine the challenges that come with living in such a steep medieval townscape well into the 21st century. Delivery trucks rumble up and down the Stradun early each morning, and you'll see hardworking young men delivering goods on hand carts throughout the day.

Looking up at the fortress atop **Mount Srđ**—seemingly custom-made for keeping an eye on a large swathe of coastline—the strategic position of Dubrovnik is clear. Independent Dubrovnik was not just this walled city, but an entire region.

Now continue downhill (you've earned it), noticing views on your right of the bustling Pile Gate area and the Fort of St. Lawrence (we'll reach better views of both of these soon). As the wall walk levels off, you'll pass an exit (on the left); if you're bushed and ready to head back to town, you can leave here—but once you leave, you can't reenter on the same ticket, and some of the best views lie ahead. It's much better to carry on straight for part 2.

Part 2—Pile Gate to Old Port: This is the most crowded section, where many people enter—be patient. While you're waiting, pause to enjoy the full frontal view of the **Stradun,** barreling right at you. In the Middle Ages, merchants lined this drag, and before that, this was a canal. At your feet is Onofrio's Big Fountain, which supplied water to a thirsty town. From here, you can see a wide range of church steeples representing the cosmopolitan makeup of a thriving medieval trade town (from left to right): Dominican, Franciscan (near you), the town Bell Tower, St. Blaise's (the round dome—hard to see from here), Serbian

Orthodox (twin domed steeples), Cathedral, and (high on the hill) Jesuit St. Ignatius. Sit and watch the river of humanity, flowing constantly up and down one of Europe's finest main streets. Now do a 180 for a good view of the Pile Gate chaos, with a steady stream of buses lumbering up and down the hill, tethering the Old Town to Port Gruž and the Lapad resort zone.

Carry on through the guard tower and along the wall, climb-

...uphill again. Looking to the wall ahead of you, notice that—after we passed along a straighter, lower stretch—this wall is scampering up a mighty foundation of solid rock. We've left the canal that once separated the two parts of Dubrovnik, and now we're ascending what used to be a separate, very steep, rocky island. This stretch tickles *Game of Thrones* fantasies—many King's Landing scenes were filmed along here.

On the right, across the little cove, is the **Fort of St. Lawrence**, which worked in concert with these stout walls to make Dubrovnik virtually impenetrable. (That fort is also climbable, and covered by the same ticket as the walls.) Climbing higher and looking to your left, into town, you'll see that this area is still damaged—not from the 1991-1992 siege, but from the 1667 earthquake. Notice that, unlike the extremely dense construction on the poorer far side of town, this area has more breathing space and larger gardens. Originally this was also densely populated, but after the quake, rather than rebuild, the wealthy folks who lived here decided to maximize green space. Grates cover the openings to old wells and grain stores that once supplied homes here—essential for surviving a siege.

As the walkway summits and levels out, you pass a drink stand. You'll stroll past local residents' backyards, peering into their inviting gardens and checking the status of their drying laundry. Farther along, at the picturesque little turret, is an artsy souvenir boutique. Looking outside the wall, you'll spot tables and umbrellas clinging to the rocks at the base of the wall. This is the recommended Cold Drinks "Buža" II, the best spot in town for a scenic

drink. (You can't enter from atop the wall—you'll have to wait until later.) On the horizon is the isle of Lokrum and—often—cruise ships at anchor, sending passengers to and fro on tenders. After passing Buža, look down on the left to see another sports court, wedged between the walls—the best they can do in this vertical town.

Rounding the bend, look left to see the facade of the Jesuit St. Ignatius Church. Notice that the homes in this area are much larger. These are aristocratic palaces—VIPs wanted to live as close as possible to the Cathedral and Rector's Palace, which are just below—and this also happens to be the oldest part of town, where "Ragusa" was born on a steep offshore island.

Soon you'll see the "other" Buža (technically Buža I); just above it, notice the little statue of St. Blaise, Dubrovnik's patron, enjoying some shade under the turret.

Continue around the wall, passing two more snack bars (the second is more elaborate, with a better menu, more shade, and pay WCs). Next, pass more quake-ruined houses and eventually pop out at a high plateau, where *The City Walls—Continuation* signs lead down to the next part. From here you could drop down to the exit (though the final stretch of our wall walk is a snap). In the little plant-filled square at the bottom of the next staircase is a sweet cat hospice, with a donation box for feeding some homeless feline residents.

Part 3—Old Port to Ploče Gate: At the start of the next stretch, you'll come to the entrance of the **Maritime Museum**. If you have a museum ticket or Dubrovnik Pass, here's a chance to escape the sun, use a clean WC, and learn about Dubrovnik's 2,500-year seafaring past (see my description on page 312).

Next, walk along the top of the wall overlooking the **Old Port**. Imagine how this heavily fortified little harbor (facing away from Dubrovnik's historic foes, the Venetians) was busy with trade in the Middle Ages. Today it's still the economic lifeline for town—watch the steady stream of cruise-ship tenders injecting dose after dose of tourist cash into town. Circling your way to the middle of the port, the path turns sharply left and heads straight for the Bell Tower—with a good glimpse of the bell ringers, Maro and Baro. Continuing, you'll look down into the inner passage that insulated the wall from the town center. On the sea side, look for the outdoor tables of the unsigned **360°**, a cocktail bar/restaurant catering to high rollers. Gussied-up jet-set diners enjoy coming here for good but extremely expensive designer fare.

Just past 360°, you'll come face to face with the vertical walls of the Dominican Church before finding the stairs back down to where you started this wall walk. Nice work. Now head on down and reward yourself with an ice-cream cone...and some shade.

The "Other" Wall Climb: Your ticket for the City Walls also includes the Fort of St. Lawrence just outside the Old Town (valid same day only; fort described on page 289). If you've already bought a 30-kn ticket there, show it when buying your main wall ticket and you'll pay only the difference.

NEAR THE PILE GATE
▲Franciscan Monastery Museum
(Franjevački Samostan-Muzej)
In the Middle Ages, Dubrovnik's monasteries flourished. And, as a part of their charity work, the monks at this monastery took on the responsibility of serving as pharmacists for the community. Visiting here today, you'll stroll through a delightful cloister and walk through a one-room museum with an old pharmacy.

Cost and Hours: 30 kn, daily April-Oct 9:00-18:00, Nov-March 9:00-14:00, Placa 2, tel. 020/321-410.

Visiting the Museum: Enter through the gap between the small church and the big monastery. Just inside the door (before the ticket-seller), a century-old **pharmacy** still serves residents. Notice the antique jars, advertisements (including one of the first known aspirin ads), and other vintage pharmacist gear. By keeping this open, the monastery maintains one of the world's oldest continually operating pharmacies.

Explore the peaceful, sun-dappled **cloister,** walking clockwise. Examine the capitals at the tops of the 60 Romanesque-Gothic double pillars. Each one is

different. Notice that some parts of the portals inside the courtyard are made with a lighter-colored stone—these had to be repaired after being hit during the 1991-1992 siege. The damaged 19th-century frescoes along the tops of the walls depict the life of St. Francis, who supposedly visited Dubrovnik in the early 13th century. If you look closely, in a few panels you may see two layers of (different) scenes; beneath the 19th-century frescoes, restorers have found even more precious fragments of some early 18th-century paintings; where possible, these are also being resurrected.

In the far corner stands the monastery's original medieval **pharmacy.** The Franciscans opened this pharmacy in 1317, and it's

been in continual operation ever since. On display are jars, pots, and other medieval pharmacists' tools. Notice the display of old pharmacists' books from the 16th, 17th, and 18th centuries—expertise imported from as far away as Venice, Frankfurt, Amsterdam, and Bologna. The sick would come to get their medicine at the little window (on the left side), which limited contact with the pharmacist and reduced the risk of passing on disease. On the right wall, look for the glass case marked *venena*—where poisons were locked away and carefully doled out, with a record of who had what (if only modern gun dealers were so carefully regulated).

Around the room, you'll also find some relics, old manuscripts, and a detailed painting of early 17th-century Dubrovnik.

In the painting, notice that at the top of Mount Srđ—the highly strategic locale where Napoleon built a fortress that was key during the 1991 siege (see page 296)—is a chapel. Though Dubrovnik was always heavily fortified, they avoided putting a fortress on the mountaintop—fearing it might seem overly provocative to the Ottoman Empire that surrounded them, and upon whose favor they depended for their autonomy.

Leaving the museum room, turn left and walk to the end of this corridor. Look up to see a tomb with a privileged position, affixed high on the wall. The **Gučetić-Gozze** family donated vast sums to help rebuild the monastery after the devastating 1667 earthquake. As thanks, the Franciscans helped them get just that much closer to God when they passed on, offering them this final resting place that was elevated...in every sense.

NEAR LUŽA SQUARE

These sights are at the far end of the Stradun (nearest the Old Port). As you stand on Luža Square facing the Bell Tower, the Rector's Palace and cathedral are up the wide street called Pred Dvorom to the right, and the Dominican Monastery Museum is through the gate by the Bell Tower and to the left.

▲Rector's Palace (Knežev Dvor)

In the Middle Ages, the Republic of Dubrovnik was ruled by a rector (similar to a Venetian doge), who was elected by the nobility.

To prevent any one person from becoming too powerful, the rector's term was limited to one month. Most rectors were in their 50s—near the end of the average life span and when they were less likely to shake things up. During his term, a rector lived upstairs in this palace. Because it's been plundered twice (most recently by Napoleon's forces, who stole all the furniture), this empty-feeling museum isn't as interesting as most other European palaces. What little you'll see was donated by local aristocrats to flesh out the pathetically empty complex.

The palace collection (with paid admission and good English explanations) is skippable, but it does offer a glimpse of Dubrovnik in its glory days. The palace's exterior and courtyard are viewable at no charge.

Cost and Hours: Covered by 100-kn "nine museum ticket" or by Dubrovnik Card, daily May-Oct 9:00-18:00, Nov-April 9:00-16:00, posted English information, 10-kn English booklet is helpful, Pred Dvorom 3, tel. 020/322-096.

Visiting the Palace: The **exterior** is decorated in the Gothic-

Renaissance mix (with particularly finely carved capitals) that was so common in Dubrovnik before the 1667 earthquake. Above the entrance is the message *Obliti privatorum publica curate*—loosely translated, "Forget your personal affairs and concern yourself with the affairs of state." This was a bold statement in a feudal era before democracy, when aristocrats were preoccupied exclusively with their self-interests.

Standing at the main door, get a free look at the palace's impressive **courtyard**—a venue for the Summer Festival, hosting music groups ranging from the local symphony to the Vienna Boys' Choir. During Dubrovnik's Golden Age, this courtyard was open to the public. People would wander in and out—gossiping, washing their laundry in the fountain, and bringing food to family members imprisoned in the cells. In the courtyard (and also visible from the door) is the only secular statue created during the centuries-long Republic. Dubrovnik republicans, mindful of the dangers of hero-worship, didn't believe that any one citizen should be singled out. They made only one exception—for Miho Pracat (a.k.a. Michaeli Prazatto), a rich citizen who donated vast sums to charity and willed a fleet of ships to the city. But notice that Pracat's statue is displayed in here, behind closed doors, not out in public.

If you pay to go **inside,** you'll find good English explanations posted in the first section. Start on the ground floor, where you'll

ramble through a few rooms of dull paintings, and then go into the green-stucco courtroom (with explanations of the Republic's unique judiciary system and bios of some of its key politicians). Next, find one of the palace's highlights, the original bronze bell-ringers from the town Bell Tower (Maro and Baro). Like antique robots (from the Renaissance, 1477-1478), these eerily lifelike sculptures could pivot at the waist to ring the bell. Nearby you'll see stonework that used to decorate city buildings. Massive iron chests (including a few with elaborate locking mechanisms) are displayed inside some old prison cells, which supposedly were placed within earshot of the rector's quarters, so he would hear the moans of the prisoners...and stay honest. Leaving the prison, you'll enter the courtyard described earlier, where you can get a better look at the Pracat statue.

On the mezzanine level (stairs near the main entrance, above the prison—notice the "hand" rails), you'll find a decent display of furniture, beautiful 18th-century sedans used to tote around V.I.R.s

(Very Important Ragusans), a wimpy gun exhibit, votive offerings (mostly silver), an 18th-century coin collection (with magnifying glasses to make out the detail), and an interesting painting of "Ragusa" in the early 17th century—back when its stout walls were surrounded by a moat.

Head back down to the courtyard and ascend the grand stairway to the upper floor (with more "hand" rails). Upstairs, you'll explore old apartments that serve as a painting gallery. The only vaguely authentic room is the red room in the corner, decorated more or less as it was in 1500, when it was the rector's office. Mihajlo Hamzić's exquisite *Baptism of Christ* painting, inspired by Italian painter Andrea Mantegna, is an early Renaissance work from the "Dubrovnik School" (see "Dominican Monastery Museum" listing, later). This area also often displays temporary exhibits.

Back in the courtyard, you can go up the smaller stairs to the Domus Christi collection of old pharmacist tools and pots (well-explained in English).

Handy WCs are just off the courtyard next to the shop, through which you'll exit.

▲Cathedral (Katedrala)

Dubrovnik's original 12th-century cathedral was funded largely by the English King Richard the Lionheart. On his way back from

the Third Crusade, Richard was shipwrecked nearby. He promised God that if he survived, he'd build a church on the spot where he landed—which happened to be on Lokrum Island, just offshore. At Dubrovnik's request, Richard agreed to build his token of thanks inside the city instead. It was the finest Romanesque church on the Adriatic...before it was destroyed by the 1667 earthquake. This version is 18th-century Roman Baroque.

Cost and Hours: Church—free, open daily 8:00-17:00; treasury—20 kn, generally open same hours as church; both have shorter hours off-season.

Visiting the Cathedral: Inside, you'll find a painting from the school of Titian *(Assumption of the Virgin)* over the stark contemporary altar. Behind the altar is a quirky treasury *(riznica)* packed with 187 relics.

Examining the treasury collection, notice that there are three locks on the treasury door—the stuff in here was so valuable, three different VIPs (the rector, the bishop, and a local aristocrat) had to agree before it could be opened. On the table near the door are several of St. Blaise's body parts (pieces of his arm, skull, and leg—all encased in gold and silver). In the middle of the wall directly opposite the door, look for the crucifix with a piece of the True Cross. On a dig in Jerusalem, St. Helen (Emperor Constantine's mother) discovered what she believed to be the cross that Jesus was crucified on. It was brought to Constantinople, and the Byzantine czars doled out pieces of it to Balkan kings. Note the folding three-paneled altar painting (underneath the cross). Dubrovnik ambassadors packed this on road trips (such as their annual trip to pay off the Ottomans) so they could worship wherever they traveled.

On the right side of the room, the silver casket supposedly holds the actual swaddling clothes of the Baby Jesus. Dubrovnik bishops secretly passed these clothes down from generation to generation...until a nun got wind of it and told the whole town. Pieces of the cloth were cut off to miraculously heal the sick, especially new mothers recovering from a difficult birth. No matter how often it was cut, the cloth always went back to its original form. Then someone tried to use it on the wife of a Bosnian king. Since she was Muslim, it couldn't help her, and it never worked again. True or not, this legend hints at the prickly relationships between faiths (not to mention the male chauvinism) here in the Balkans.

▲Dominican Monastery Museum (Dominikanski Samostan-Muzej)

You'll find many of Dubrovnik's art treasures—paintings, altarpieces, and manuscripts—gathered around the peaceful Domini-

can Monastery cloister inside the Ploče Gate. As you climb the stairs up to the monastery, notice that the spindles supporting the railing are solid up until about two feet above the ground. This was to provide a modicum of modesty to ladies on their way to church—and to prevent creeps down below from looking up their skirts.

Cost and Hours: 30 kn, daily April-Oct 9:00-18:00, Nov-March 9:00-17:00, no English explanations, art buffs enjoy the 50-kn English book.

Visiting the Museum: Turn left from the entry and work your way clockwise around the cloister. The room in the far corner contains paintings from the **"Dubrovnik School,"** the Republic's circa-1500 answer to the art boom in Florence and Venice. Though the 1667 earthquake destroyed most of these paintings, about a dozen survive, and five of those are in this room. Don't miss the triptych by Nikola Božidarović with St. Blaise holding a detailed model of 16th-century Dubrovnik (left panel)—the most famous depiction of Dubrovnik's favorite saint. You'll also see reliquaries shaped like the hands and feet that they hold.

Continuing around the courtyard, duck into the next room. Here you'll see a painting by **Titian** depicting St. Blaise, Mary Magdalene, and the donor who financed this work.

At the next corner of the courtyard is the entrance to the striking **church** at the heart of this still-active monastery. Step inside and face the altar. The interior is deco-rated with modern stained glass, a fine 13th-century stone pulpit that survived the earthquake (reminding visitors of the intellectual approach to scripture that characterized the Dominicans), and a precious 14th-century Paolo Veneziano crucifix hanging in the arch above the altar. Perhaps the finest piece of art in the church is the *Miracle of St. Dominic*, showing the founder of the order bringing a child back to life (to the left as you face the main altar). Behind the altar, find the Vukovar Cross, embedded with panels painted by different artists from the Croatian school of Naive Art—offering an enticing taste of this unique and fascinating style (for more on Naive Art, see page 54). It was painted in the Realist style (late 19th century) by Vlaho Bukovac.

NEAR THE OLD PORT (STARA LUKA)

The picturesque Old Port, carefully nestled behind St. John's Fort, faces away from what was Dubrovnik's biggest threat, the Vene-tians. At the port, you can haggle with captains selling excursions to nearby towns and islands (described in the next chapter) and watch cruise-ship passengers coming and going on their tenders. The long seaside building across the bay on the left is the Lazareti, once the medieval quarantine house. In those days, all visitors were locked in here for 40 days before entering town. A bench-lined harborside walk leads around the fort to a breakwater, providing a peaceful perch. From the breakwater, rocky beaches curl around the outside of the wall.

Maritime Museum (Pomorski Muzej)

In the 15th century, when Venice's nautical dominance was peaking, Dubrovnik emerged as another maritime power and the Mediterranean's leading shipbuilding center. The Dubrovnik-built "argosy" boat (from "Ragusa," an early name for the city) was the Cadillac of ships, even mentioned by Shakespeare. This worthwhile museum, built into Dubrovnik's walls, fits in tidily with a wall walk. It traces the long history of Dubrovnik's most important industry with contracts, maps, paintings, navigational devices, and models—all well-described in English. The main floor takes you through the 18th century, and the easy-to-miss upstairs covers the 19th and 20th centuries.

Cost and Hours: Covered by 100-kn "nine museum ticket" or by Dubrovnik Card; hours flex on demand—usually March-Oct Tue-Sun 9:00-18:00, Nov-Feb until 16:00, closed Mon year-round; 7-kn English booklet or elaborate 60-kn book, good WCs at entry, upstairs in St. John's Fort, at far/south end of Old Port, tel. 020/323-904.

Aquarium (Akvarij)

Dubrovnik's aquarium, housed in the cavernous St. John's Fort, is an old-school place, with 31 tanks on one floor. A visit here allows you a close look at the local marine life and provides a cool refuge from the midday heat.

Cost and Hours: 60 kn, kids-20 kn, daily July-Aug 9:00-21:00, progressively shorter hours off-season until 9:00-16:00 Nov-March, English descriptions, ground floor of St. John's Fort, enter from Old Port, tel. 020/323-978.

BETWEEN THE STRADUN AND THE MAINLAND

The first two museums are a few steps off the main promenade toward the mainland.

▲Synagogue Museum (Sinagoga-Muzej)

When the Jews were forced out of Spain in 1492, a steady stream of them passed through here en route to today's Turkey. Finding Dubrovnik to be a flourishing and relatively tolerant city, many stayed. Žudioska ulica ("Jewish Street"), just inside the Ploče Gate, became the ghetto in 1546. It was walled at one end and had a gate (which would be locked at night) at the other end. Today, the same street is home to the second-oldest continuously functioning synagogue in Europe (after Prague's), which contains Croatia's only Jewish museum. The top floor houses the synagogue itself. Notice the lattice windows that separated the women from the men (in accordance with Orthodox Jewish tradition). Below that, a small museum with good English descriptions gives meaning to the various Torahs (including a 14th-century one from Spain) and other items—such as the written orders *(naredba)* from Nazi-era Yugoslavia, stating that Jews were to identify their shops as Jewish-owned and wear armbands. (The Ustaše—the Nazi puppet government in Croatia—interned and executed not only Jews and Roma/Gypsies, but also Serbs and other people they considered undesirable; see page 25.) Of Croatia's 24,000 Jews, only 4,000 survived the Holocaust. Today Croatia has about 2,000 Jews, including a dozen Jewish families who call Dubrovnik home.

Cost and Hours: 35 kn; May-mid-Nov daily 9:00-21:00; mid-Nov-April Mon-Fri 10:00-13:00, closed Sat-Sun; 10-kn English booklet (unnecessary), Žudioska ulica 5, tel. 020/321-204.

▲War Photo Limited

If the tragic story of wartime Dubrovnik has you in a pensive mood, drop by this gallery with images of warfare from around the world. The brainchild of Kiwi-turned-Croatian photojournalist Wade Goddard, this thought-provoking museum attempts to show the ugly reality of war through raw, often disturbing photographs taken in the field. Use the loaner guide to understand the well-displayed images on two floors; a small permanent exhibit (on the top floor) captures the Yugoslav Wars through photography and video footage. Each summer, the gallery also houses various temporary exhibits. Note that the focus is not solely on Dubrovnik, but on war anywhere and everywhere.

Cost and Hours: 40 kn; June-Sept daily 10:00-22:00; May and Oct Wed-Mon 10:00-16:00, closed Tue; closed Nov-April; Antuninska 6, tel. 020/322-166, www.warphotoltd.com.

▲Foundry Museum (a.k.a. Gornji Ugao Tower)

This easy-to-miss sight, tucked below the City Walls' tallest tower, offers a fascinating glimpse at a medieval foundry that was established here in 1545. Used for the production of cannonballs and gunpowder (essential elements of an independent ministate), the foundry was intentionally located at the very top of town—still barely within the walls, but a safe distance from most residents. Damaged in the great 1667 quake, it was buried under a garbage dump and then under a playground, until it was finally excavated in 2008.

Inside, enthusiastic Đivo (JEE-voh) sells tickets; if he has time, he'll give you a tour of the foundry's foundations, including its four furnaces, molds for church bells and gigantic cannonballs, and a pile of original casting sand (a volcanic material imported from Italy, essential for the working of any foundry). You'll find out how aqueducts powered the foundry's equipment (harnessing water as it flowed past on its way down to Onofrio's Big Fountain), and see a few of the original items that were cast here, such as buckles, keys, needles, horseshoes, and musket shot.

Cost and Hours: 30 kn, April-Oct daily 10:00-17:00, closed Nov-March.

Getting There: Head up the stairs to the top (northernmost) point of the Old Town (directly below the Minčeta Tower). Walk all the way across the orange sports court, and find the poorly marked door. Đivo may be hanging out at the corner, hoping to snare passing tourists.

BETWEEN THE STRADUN AND THE SEA
▲Serbian Orthodox Church and Icon Museum
(Srpska Pravoslavna Crkva i Muzej Ikona)

Round out your look at Dubrovnik's major faiths (Catholic, Jewish, and Orthodox) with a visit to this house of worship—one of the most convenient places in Croatia to learn about Orthodox Christianity. Remember that people from the former Yugoslavia who follow the Orthodox faith are, by definition, ethnic Serbs. With all the hard feelings about the Yugoslav Wars, this church serves as an important reminder that all Serbs aren't bloodthirsty killers.

Dubrovnik never had a very large Serb population (an Orthodox church wasn't even allowed inside the town walls until the mid-19th century). During the Yugoslav Wars, most Serbs fled, created new lives for themselves elsewhere, and saw little reason to return. But some old-timers remain, and Dubrovnik's dwindling, aging Orthodox population is still served by this **church.** The candles stuck in the sand (to prevent fire outbreaks) represent prayers: The ones at knee level are for the deceased, while the ones higher up are for the living. The gentleman selling candles encourages you to buy and light one, regardless of your faith, so long as you do so with the proper intentions and reverence. To better appreciate this church, read the sidebar.

Cost and Hours: Free but donations accepted, daily May-Sept 8:00-14:00 & 16:00-21:00 or 22:00, closes earlier in off-season, liturgy Sun 10:00-11:00, Od Puča.

Nearby: A few doors down (at Od Puča 8) is the **Icon Museum,** which may be closed for renovation—ask at the icon shop next door to the cathedral entrance. When open, this small collection features 78 different icons (stylized paintings of saints, generally on a golden background—a common feature of Orthodox churches) from the 15th through the 19th centuries, all identified in English. In the library—crammed with old shelves holding some 12,000 books—look for the astonishingly detailed calendar, with portraits of hundreds of saints.

▲Rupe Granary and Ethnographic Museum (Etnografski Muzej Rupe)

This huge, 16th-century building was Dubrovnik's biggest granary, and today houses the best folk museum I've seen in Croatia. *Rupe* means "holes"—and it's worth the price of entry just to peer down into these 15 cavernous underground grain stores, designed to maintain the perfect temperature to preserve the seeds (63 degrees Fahrenheit). When the grain had to be dried, it was moved upstairs—where today you'll find a surprisingly well-presented Ethnographic Museum covering Dubrovnik's many traditions and festivals, and displaying tools, jewelry, clothing, instruments, painted eggs, and other folk artifacts from its colorful history. English explanations are posted in many places (or fork over 7 kn for the booklet at the entry). The museum hides several blocks uphill from the main promenade, toward the sea (climb up Široka—the widest side street from the Stradun—which becomes Od Domina on the way to the museum).

Cost and Hours: Covered by 100-kn "nine museum ticket" or by Dubrovnik Card; open Wed-Mon 9:00-18:00, off-season until 14:00, closed Tue year-round; Od Rupa 3, tel. 020/323-013.

ABOVE DUBROVNIK
▲▲▲Mount Srđ

After adding Dubrovnik to his holdings, Napoleon built a fortress atop the hill behind the Old Town to keep an eye on his new subjects (in 1810). During the city's 20th-century tourism heyday, a cable car was built to effortlessly whisk visitors to the top so they could enjoy the fine views from the fortress and the giant cross nearby. Then, when war broke out in the 1990s, Mount Srđ (pronounced like "surge") became a crucial link in the defense of Dubrovnik—the only high land that locals were able to hold. The fortress was shelled and damaged, and the cross and cable car were destroyed. Minefields and unexploded ordnance left the hilltop a dangerous no-man's land. But more recently, the mountain's fortunes have reversed. The landmines have been removed, and in 2010, the cable car was rebuilt to once again connect Dubrovnik's Old Town to its mountaintop. Visitors head to the top both for the spectacular sweeping views and to ponder the exhibits in a ragtag museum about the war.

Warning: While this area has officially been cleared of land-

DUBROVNIK

The Serbian Orthodox Church

The emphasis of this book is on the Catholic areas of the former Yugoslavia, but don't overlook the rich diversity of faiths in this region. Dubrovnik's Serbian Orthodox church, as well as Orthodox churches in Kotor, Montenegro (see page 394); Sarajevo, Bosnia-Herzegovina (pages 480 and 491); and Ljubljana, Slovenia (page 563); offer invaluable opportunities to learn about a faith that's often unfamiliar to American visitors.

As you explore an Orthodox church, keep in mind that these churches carry on the earliest traditions of the Christian faith. Orthodox and Catholic Christianity came from the same roots, so the oldest surviving early-Christian churches (such as the stave churches of Norway) have many of the same features as today's Orthodox churches.

Notice that there are no pews. Worshippers stand through the service, as a sign of respect (though some older parishioners sit on the seats along the walls). Women stand on the left side, men on the right (equal distance from the altar—to represent that all are equal before God). The Orthodox Church uses essentially the same Bible as Catholics, but it's written in the Cyrillic alphabet, which you'll see displayed around any Orthodox church. Following Old Testament Judeo-Christian tradition, the Bible is kept on the altar behind the iconostasis, the big screen in the middle of the room covered with curtains and icons (golden paintings

mines, nervous locals remind visitors that this was once a war zone. Be sure to stay on clearly defined paths and roads.

Expect Changes: International developers have plans to build a luxury golf resort on the mountain plateau behind Mount Srđ. You may see construction and, while it likely won't affect the cable car, it may eventually take over the fort and museum.

Getting to the Top: The **cable car** is easily the best option for reaching the summit of Mount Srđ (108 kn round-trip, 60 kn one-way, kunas or credit cards only—no euros; at least 2/hour—generally departing at :00 and :30 past each hour, more frequent with demand, 3-minute ride; daily from 9:00, June-Aug until 24:00, Sept until 22:00, April-May and Oct until 20:00, Feb-March and Nov until 17:00, Dec-Jan until 16:00; doesn't run in Bora wind or heavy rain, last ascent 30 minutes before closing, tel. 020/325-393, www.dubrovnikcablecar.com). The lower station is just above the Buža Gate at the top of the Old Town (from the main drag, huff all the way to the top of Boškovićeva, exit through gate, and climb uphill one block, then look right). You may see travel agencies selling tickets elsewhere in town, but there's no advantage to buying them anywhere but here. The line you may see at the cable-car station is

of saints), which separates the material world from the spiritual one. At certain times during the service, the curtains or doors are opened so the congregation can see the Holy Book.

Unlike the decorations in many Catholic churches, Orthodox icons are not intended to be lifelike. Packed with intricate symbolism, and cast against a shimmering golden background, they're meant to remind viewers of the metaphysical nature of Jesus and the saints rather than of their physical form, which is considered irrelevant. You'll almost never see a statue, which is thought to overemphasize the physical world...and, to Orthodox people, feels a little too close to violating the commandment, "Thou shalt not worship graven images." Orthodox services generally involve chanting (a dialogue that goes back and forth between the priest and the congregation), and the church is filled with the evocative aroma of incense.

The incense, chanting, icons, and standing up are all intended to heighten the experience of worship. While many Catholic and Protestant services tend to be more of a theoretical and rote consideration of religious issues (come on—don't tell me you've never dozed through the sermon), Orthodox services are about creating a religious experience. Each of these elements does its part to help the worshipper transcend the physical world and join in communion with the spiritual one.

not to buy tickets, but to actually ride up. For tips on avoiding a long wait, see below.

If you have a **car**, it's possible to drive up—though the road can be crowded. From the high road above the Old Town, watch for the turnoff to *Bosanka*, which leads you to that village, then up to the fortress and cross—follow signs for *Srđ* (it's twisty but not far—figure a 20-minute drive from the Old Town area). If you're coming south from the Old Town, once you reach the main road above, you'll have to turn left and backtrack a bit to reach the *Bosanka* turnoff. For **hikers,** a switchback trail (used to supply the fortress during the siege) connects the Old Town to the mountaintop—but it's very steep and provides minimal shade. (If your knees are solid and it's not too hot, you could ride the cable car up, then hike down.)

Crowd-Beating Tips: The cable car has a limited capacity, and lines can get long when several cruise ships are in town. If you come during peak times, you may have to wait to board a cable car. Cruise passengers tend to come here first thing upon disembarking, so it can be quite crowded around 9:30-10:00, and stay busy through the morning. Things may quiet down in the mid- to late-afternoon. But then there's another rush before sunset—which is, understandably, the most popular time to ascend.

Mountaintop: From the top cable-car station, head up the stairs to the panoramic terrace. The bird's-eye **view** is truly spectacular, looking straight down to the street plan of Dubrovnik's Old Town. From this lofty perch, you can see north to the Dalmatian islands (the Elaphite archipelago, Mljet, Korčula, and beyond); south to Montenegro; and east into Bosnia-Herzegovina. Gazing upon those looming mountains that define the

border with Bosnia-Herzegovina—which, centuries ago, was also the frontier of the huge and powerful Ottoman Empire—you can appreciate how impressive it was that stubborn little Dubrovnik managed to remain independent for so much of its history.

The **cross** was always an important symbol in this very Catholic town. After it was destroyed, a temporary wooden one was

erected to encourage the townspeople who were waiting out the siege below. During a visit in 2003, Pope John Paul II blessed the rubble from the old cross; those fragments are now being used in the foundations of the city's newest churches. Nearby stands a huge red, white, and blue flagpole—the colors of the Croatian flag.

To reach the museum in the old fortress, walk behind the cable-car station along the rocky red soil.

Fort and Museum: The Napoleonic-era Fort Imperial (Trđava Imperijal) houses the **Dubrovnik During the Homeland War (1991-1995) Museum** (30 kn, various books for sale, same hours as cable car). As you enter, temporary exhibits are on the right, and the permanent exhibit is to the left. Photos, documents, and artifacts tell the story (with English descriptions) of the overarching war with Yugoslavia and how the people defended this fortress. The descriptions are too dense and tactical for casual visitors, but you'll see lots of photos and some actual items used in the fighting: primitive, rusty rifles (some dating from World War II) that the Croatians used for their improvised defense, and piles of spent mortar shells and other projectiles that Yugoslav forces hurled at the fortress and the city. Look for the wire-guided Russian rockets. After being launched at their target, the rockets would burrow into a wall, waiting to be detonated once their operators saw the opportunity for maximum destruction. The tattered Croatian flag seems soaked in local patriotism. A video screen shows breathless international news reports from the front line during the bombing. You'll also learn how a squadron of armed supply ships became besieged, Dubrovnik's only tether to the outside world.

While the devastation of Dubrovnik was disturbing, this museum could do a far better job of fostering at least an illusion of impartiality. Instead, descriptions rant one-sidedly against "Serbian and Montenegrin aggression" and the "Serbian imperialist war," and the exhibits self-righteously depict Croats exclusively as victims (which was essentially true here in Dubrovnik, but ignores Croat atrocities elsewhere). All of this serves only to trivialize and distract from the human tragedy of this war.

After seeing the exhibit, climb up a few flights of stairs to the **rooftop** for the view. The giant communications tower overhead flew the Croatian flag during the war, to inspire the besieged residents below. You might see some charred trees around here—these were claimed not by the war, but more recently, by forest fires. (Fear of landmines and other explosives prevented locals from fighting the wildfires as aggressively as they might otherwise, making these fires more dangerous than ever.)

Eating: Boasting undoubtedly the best view in Dubrovnik, **Restaurant/Snack Bar Panorama** has reasonable prices and drop-dead, astonishing views over the rooftops of the Old Town and to the most beautiful parts of three different countries. While there's glassed-in seating inside, in good weather I'd exit the building to find the outdoor terrace—the Old Town floats just under your nose (35-kn drinks, 60-80-kn cocktails, 90-100-kn pastas, 110-170-kn main dishes, open same hours as cable car).

Activities in Dubrovnik

Swimming and Sunbathing

If the weather's good and you've had enough of museums, spend a sunny afternoon at the beach. There are no sandy beaches on the mainland near Dubrovnik, but there are lots of suitable pebbly options, plus several concrete perches.

The easiest and most atmospheric place to take a dip is right off the **Old Town.** From the Old Port and its breakwater, uneven steps clinging to the outside of the wall lead to a series of great sunbathing and swimming coves (and

DUBROVNIK

even a showerhead sticking out of the town wall). Another delightful rocky beach hangs onto the outside of the Old Town's wall (at the bar called Cold Drinks "Buža" I; for more on this bar, and how to find it, see page 323).

A more convenient—and crowded—public beach is **Banje,** just outside the Ploče Gate, east of Old Town. While this is dominated by the EastWest nightclub, by day it's a public beach with an inviting swath of sand and pebbles, ideal for sunbathing and wading, with a spectacular backdrop of Dubrovnik's Old Town. To reach the beach, leave the Old Town through the Ploče Gate, walk about five minutes gradually uphill on the main road, then watch for the two staircases marked *EastWest* and climb down. (While the stair nearer the Old Town passes through the EastWest café/bar, it is public access.) The café/bar itself is slick and swanky (in keeping with its nightclub's exclusive vibe), serving pricey food and drink. You can also rent a very expensive sun bed, but it's much more affordable to bring your own towel and find a comfy patch of sand. Pay showers are nearby.

My favorite hidden beach—**St. Jakob**—takes a lot longer to reach, but if you're up for the hike, it's worth it to escape the

crowds. Figure about a 25-minute walk (each way) from the Old Town. Go through the Ploče Gate at the east end of the Old Town, and walk along the street called Frana Supila as it climbs uphill above the waterfront. At Hotel Argentina, take the right (downhill) fork and keep going on Vlaha Bukovca. Eventually you'll reach the small church of St. Jakob. You'll see the beach—in a cozy protected cove—far below. Curl around behind the church and keep an eye out for stairs going down on the right. Unfortunately, these stairs are effectively unmarked, so it might take some trial and error to find the right ones. (If you reach the rusted-white gateway of the old communist-era open-air theater, you've gone too far.) Hike down the very steep stairs to the gentle cove, which has rentable chairs and a small restaurant for drinks (and a WC). Enjoy the pebbly beach and faraway views of Dubrovnik's Old Town. In peak season, water taxis may be ferrying beachgoers between this beach and the Old Port, offering an easier trip (around 30 kn one-way).

Other, even more distant beaches are worth considering. If you're staying at—or visiting—the resorty zone of **Lapad Bay,** you'll find a fine beach there (near Hotel Kompas).

Locals prefer to swim on **Lokrum Island,** because there are (relatively) fewer tourists there. While there are no sandy or even pebbly beaches, there are several rocky ones, with ladders to lower yourself gingerly into the water. As the rocks here can be particularly jagged, you'll want to wear good water shoes, and beware of uneven footing (both underwater, and on your way to the ladders). For details on taking a boat to Lokrum, see page 345.

Finally, for the best sandy beach in this part of Croatia, you'll have to take a boat to the island of Lopud, then hike (or ride a golf cart) across the spine of the island to the gorgeous **Šunj Beach.** Making an all-day trek out here (by public ferry) is worth doing only if you're desperate for a long, lingering day at the beach. If you're cruising the Elaphite Islands, you'll likely stop on Lopud for two or three hours—enough time for a quick dip at Šunj. For more on Lopud and Šunj Beach, see page 347.

Sea Kayaking

Paddling a sleek kayak around the outside of Dubrovnik's imposing walls is a memorable experience. Several outfits in town offer half-day tours (most options 250-350 kn); popular itineraries include loops along the City Walls, to secluded beaches, and around Lokrum Island; many include a break for snorkeling, and some are timed to catch the sunset while bobbing in the Adriatic. Well-established companies include **Adriatic Kayak Tours** (www. adriatickayaktours.com), **Outdoor Croatia** (www.outdoorcroatia. com), and **Adria Adventure** (www.kayakingcroatia.com)—but new companies pop up all the time...check online or look for fliers locally.

Shopping in Dubrovnik

Most souvenirs sold in Dubrovnik—from lavender sachets to plaster models of the Old Town—are pretty tacky. Whatever you buy,

prices are much higher along the Stradun than on the side streets.

A classy alternative to the knickknacks is a type of local jewelry called *Konavoske puce* ("Konavle buttons"). Sold as earrings, pendants, and rings, these distinctive and fashionable filigree-style pieces consist of a sphere with several small posts. Though they're sold around town, it's least expensive to buy them on Od Puča street, which runs parallel to the Stradun two blocks toward the sea (near the Serbian Orthodox Church). The high concentration of jewelers along this lane keeps prices reasonable. You'll find the "buttons" in various sizes, in both silver (affordable) and gold (pricey).

You'll also see lots of jewelry made from red coral, which can only be legally gathered in small amounts from two small islands in northern Dalmatia. If you see a particularly large chunk of coral, it's likely imported. To know what you're getting, shop at an actual jeweler instead of a souvenir shop.

Gift-Shop Chains: Several gift shops in Dubrovnik (with additional branches throughout Dalmatia) hawk fun, if sometimes made-in-China, items. Look for these chains, which are a bit classier than the many no-name shops around town: **Aqua** sells pleasant nautical-themed gifts, blue-and-white-striped sailor shirts, and other gear. **Bonbonnière Kraš** is Croatia's leading chocolatier, selling a wide array of tasty candies. **Uje** has artisan olive oils and other boutiquey edibles.

Entertainment in Dubrovnik

MUSICAL EVENTS

Dubrovnik annually hosts a full schedule of events for its Summer Festival (July 10-Aug 25, www.dubrovnik-festival.hr), which is quickly followed by its Late Summer Festival. But the town also works hard to offer traditional music outside of festival time. The Cultural Information Desk, inside the Sloboda theater lobby at the bottom of the Bell Tower on Luža Square, is a good source of information on events (open long hours daily). For the latest on any of these festivals and concerts, check the events listings in *The Best in Dubrovnik* guide, or ask the TI.

Here are a few good choices:

Spirited **Linđo folk-music** concerts are performed for tourists twice weekly in Sloboda theater below the Bell Tower (100 kn, usually Tue and Fri at 21:30, www.lindjo.hr).

The **Dubrovnik Symphony Orchestra** performs crowd-pleasing classics three times weekly in summer (and once weekly through winter)—usually at the Rector's Palace in good weather, or the Dominican Monastery in bad weather (100-400 kn, typically at 21:00, www.dso.hr).

Various historic **churches** around town host touristy but enjoyable concerts (generally 100 kn, each venue hosts about 3/week at 21:00, mobile 098-244-264). Venues include St. Savior, just inside the Pile Gate; the simpler Domina Church, just up Od Domina street from the Stradun; and the little chapel near the Dominican Church at the Ploče Gate.

Also consider the folk dancing and market each Sunday morning at Čilipi, a small town near the airport (see page 352). Dubrovnik-based companies offer excursions that include transportation there and back.

NIGHTLIFE

Dubrovnik's Old Town is one big, romantic parade of relaxed and happy people out strolling. The main drag is brightly lit and packed

with shops, cafés, and bars, all open late. This is a fun scene. And if you walk away from the crowds or out on the port, you'll be alone with the magic of the Pearl of the Adriatic. Everything feels—and is—very safe after dark.

If you're looking for a memorable bar after dark, consider these:

▲▲▲Drinks with a View

Cold Drinks "Buža" offers, without a doubt, the most scenic spot for a drink. Perched on a cliff above the sea, clinging like a barnacle to the outside of the City Walls, this is a peaceful, shaded getaway from the bustle of the Old Town...the perfect place to watch cruise ships disappear into the horizon. *Buža* means "hole in the wall"—and that's exactly what you'll have to go through to get to these places. There are two different Bužas. **Buža II** is the older of the pair. Filled with mellow tourists and bartenders pouring wine from tiny screw-top bottles into plastic cups, Buža II comes with castaway views

and Frank Sinatra ambience. This is supposedly where Bill Gates hangs out when he visits Dubrovnik. When the seats fill up—as often happens around sunset—you can order a drink at the bar and walk down the stairs to enjoy it "on the rocks"...literally (30-70-kn drinks, summer daily 9:00-into the wee hours, closed mid-Nov-Jan). **Buža I,** with a different owner, is mellower, plays hip rather than romantic music, and has concrete stairs leading down to a beach on the rocks below. While lacking Buža II's shade, Buža I is bigger, less claustrophobic, and often a bit less crowded, making it a viable alternative (20-50-kn drinks).

Getting There: Both Bužas are well away from the bustle of the main drag, along the seaward wall. To reach them from the cathedral area, hike up the grand staircase to St. Ignatius' Church, then go left to find the lane that runs along the inside of the wall. To find the classic Buža II, head right along the lane and look for the *Cold Drinks* sign pointing to a literal hole in the wall. For the hipper Buža I, go left along the same lane, and locate the hole in the wall with the *No Toples No Nudist* graffiti.

Cocktails and People-Watching

The no-name square tucked behind the cathedral is jammed with tables from a half-dozen different cafés, which fill with tourists and locals each evening. Live jazz is provided nightly by **Jazz Caffè Troubadour,** but as their drink prices are outlandish (80-100-kn cocktails), most people prefer to sit at a nearby place where you can hear the music nearly as well.

Nonenina, a few steps from the cathedral on Pred Dvorom, is an outdoor lounge with big, overstuffed chairs at a fine vantage point for people-watching. They brag that they serve 180 different types of cocktails (60-80 kn, also 35-45-kn beers, daily 9:00-late, across from Rector's Palace).

The Gaffe Irish Pub, with a chummy, pubby interior and a small courtyard, is a rollicking spot to drain a pint and watch some rugby (Miha Pracata 4, mobile 098-196-2149, see full listing on page 337).

Restaurant Klarisa, tucked in a tight back corner of the Old Town (behind St. Claire's Convent, just up Gariste ulica from On- ofrio's Fountain), has live jazz each night outside. You can pay for an overpriced meal or drink, or just loiter and enjoy (Poljana Paska Miličevića 4, tel. 020/413-100).

D'Vino Wine Bar is an ideal place to nurse a drink while learning about Croatian wine, nibbling local tapas, and socializing; for details, see page 335.

Nightclubs

Several places are near or just beyond the Ploče Gate at the east end of town. Head under the Bell Tower, then up the street past the Dominican Monastery. You'll pass the hole-in-the- wall entrance (right) for the snobby, upscale **360°** cocktail bar (www.360dubrovnik.com). Then, after crossing the bridge, look (on the left) for the entrance to **Revelin**—a dance club that fills one of the city wall's fortress towers (www.revelinclub-dubrovnik. com). Then head out and up the street until you reach Banje Beach, half of which is occupied by the **EastWest** dance club (www.ew- dubrovnik.com). Note that some of these bars and clubs are more exclusive and may charge admission on weekends.

MOVIES

The Old Town has a variety of movie theaters showing Ameri- can blockbusters (usually in English with Croatian subtitles, un- less the film's animated or for kids; for the schedule, see www. kinematografi.org). Two modern cinemas in town have comfortable seating and show current movies year-round: the **Sloboda,** right under the Bell Tower on Luža Square; and **Visia,** just inside the Pile Gate.

In good summer weather, head for the fun outdoor **Jadran** cinema, where you can lick ice cream (B.Y.O.) while you watch a movie with a Dubrovnik-mountaintop backdrop. This is a cheap, casual, and very Croatian scene, where people smoke and chat, and the neighbors sit in their windowsills to watch the movie (most nights late June-early Sept, shows begin shortly after sundown; in the Old Town near the Pile Gate). Another outdoor movie venue, **Slavica,** is farther out of town, on the road leading away from the Pile Gate.

Sleeping in Dubrovnik

You basically have two options in Dubrovnik: a centrally located room in a private home *(soba);* or a resort hotel on a distant beach, a bus ride away from the Old Town. Dubrovnik hotels are generally a rotten value; consider your *sobe* options instead. For locations, see the map on page 328.

No matter where you stay, prices are much higher mid-June through mid-September, and highest in July and August. Reserve ahead for these peak times. Most accommodations prefer to list their rates in euros (and I've followed suit), but you'll pay in kunas.

SOBE (PRIVATE ROOMS): A DUBROVNIK SPECIALTY

In Dubrovnik, you'll almost always do better with a *soba* than with a hotel. Before you choose, carefully read the information on page 764. All of my favorite *sobe* are run by friendly English-speaking Croatians and are inside or within easy walking distance of the Old Town. Most of my listings come with private facilities, air-conditioning, kitchenettes, and satellite TV; while some are in family homes, you can be as anonymous as you like. Most *sobe* don't include breakfast, so I've listed some suggestions later, under "Eating in Dubrovnik."

To search from home, you can use the regular booking sites (such as TripAdvisor.com or Booking.com)—but if you want to book one of the places I've listed here, **please book direct** (by sending them an email), which saves both you and your host money. Another good place to search is www.dubrovnikapartmentsource. com, run by an American couple and offering a range of carefully selected, well-described accommodations.

In the Old Town, Above the Stradun Promenade

These are some of my favorite accommodations in Dubrovnik. All are located at the top of town, high above the Stradun, and all are good values. The first four are within a few steps of each other, along a little block dubbed by some "Rickova ulica." If you don't mind the very steep hike up, you'll find this to be a handy home base. When one of these places is full, they work together to find space for you. The last two listings are a few blocks over, and nearly as nice (and equally steep). Because all of these hosts live off-site, be sure to let them know when you'll arrive so they can let you in.

$$ Villa Ragusa offers good-value rooms in the Old Town. Pero and Valerija Carević have renovated a 600-year-old house at the top of town. The five comfortable, modern rooms come with wooden beams and antique furniture. There are three doubles with bathrooms (including a top-floor room with rooftop views over the Old Town for no extra charge—request when you reserve) and two singles that share a bathroom (S-€45/€40/€25, Db-€90/€80/€50, €8 breakfast can be eaten here or more scenically at nearby Stradun café, cash only, air-con, lots of stairs with no elevator, Žudioska ulica 15, mobile 098-765-634, www.villaragusadubrovnik.com, villa.ragusa@du.t-com.hr).

$$$ Apartments Paviša, next door to Villa Ragusa and run by Pero and Davorka Paviša, has three good, older-feeling rooms (Db-€100/€70-80/€50, book direct by email for these prices, no breakfast, cash only, air-con, lots of stairs, Žudioska ulica 19, mobile 098-427-399 or 098-175-2342, www.apartmentspavisa.com, pero.pavisa@gmail.com). They have two more rooms in the **Viktorija** neighborhood, about a 20-minute mostly uphill walk east of the Old Town. While it's a long-but-scenic walk into town, the views from these apartments are spectacular (same prices as in-town rooms, Frana Supila 59, bus stop nearby). Pero and Davorka also manage **Apartments Martecchini,** three units a bit closer to the main drag in the Old Town (small apartment-€100/€70-80/€50, bigger apartment-€120/€80-90/€60, biggest apartment-€130/€90-100/€60, prices depend on size and views, book direct by email for these prices, no breakfast, cash only, air-con, www.apartmentsmartecchini.com).

$$ Ivana and Anita Raič are sisters renting three apartments with kitchenettes and modern, stylish, pastel flourishes (Db-€90/€70-80/€50, no breakfast, cash only, air-con, Žudioska ulica 16, Ivana's mobile 098-996-0858, Anita's mobile 099-592-1568, www.apartments-raic.com, ivanaraic@gmail.com).

$$$ Apartments Kovač, a lesser value but decent, has two simple, older apartments just inside the upper wall (Db-€100/€90/€70,

Sleep Code

Abbreviations **(7 kn=about $1, €1=about $1.10, country code: 385)**
S=Single, **D**=Double/Twin, **T**=Triple, **Q**=Quad, **b**=bathroom
Price Rankings
$$$ **Higher Priced**—Most rooms €95 or more
$$ **Moderately Priced**—Most rooms €55-95
$ **Lower Priced**—Most rooms €55 or less

If I've listed two sets of rates, I've noted when the second rate applies (generally off-season, Oct-May); if I've listed three sets of rates, the first is for peak season (July-Aug), the second is for shoulder season (May-June and Sept-Oct), and the third is for off-season (Nov-April). The dates for seasonal rates vary by hotel.

These rates do not include the modest tourist tax (about 7 kn/person per night). Hotels generally accept credit cards and include breakfast in their rates; most *sobe* accept only cash and don't offer breakfast. While rates are listed in euros, you'll pay in kunas. Wi-Fi generally is free, and English is spoken at each place listed here. Prices change; verify current rates online or by email. For the best prices, always book directly with the hotel.

extra person–€10, no breakfast, cash only, air-con, Peline 1, mobile 098-975-4284, www.apartmentskovac-dubrovnik.com, info@apartmentskovac-dubrovnik.com, Ana and Zvonko).

$$ Plaza Apartments, run by Lidija and Maro Matić, rents three clean, well-appointed, modern apartments on a plant-filled lane—the steepest and most appealing stretch of stairs leading up from the Stradun. Lidija's sweet personality is reflected in the cheerful rooms, which are a fine value if you don't mind the hike (Db-€90/€80/€70, big two-story seaview apartment–€110/€85/€75, cheaper Nov-April, these prices for Rick Steves readers who book direct, no breakfast, cash only, air-con, all apartments have kitchenettes and laundry machines, climb the stairs past Dolce Vita gelato shop to Nalješkovićeva 22, tel. 020/321-493, mobile 091-517-7048, www.apartmaniplaza.com, lidydu@yahoo.com).

$$ Minerva Apartments has three cozy units near the top of a similar lane, in the home of Dubravka Vidosavljević-Vučić (Db-€90/€80/€70, cheaper Nov-April, cash only, no breakfast, air-con, laundry machine, Antuninska 14, mobile 091-252-9677, duvivu@gmail.com).

In the Old Town, near the Cathedral and St. John's Fort

The following places are south of the Stradun, mostly clustering around the cathedral and St. John's Fort, at the end of the Old Port.

DUBROVNIK

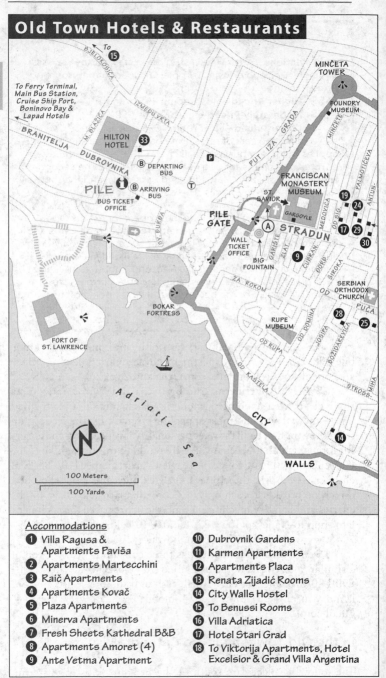

Old Town Hotels & Restaurants

MINČETA TOWER

To BJELOKOSICA
To 15

To Ferry Terminal,
Main Bus Station,
Cruise Ship Port,
Boninovo Bay &
Lapad Hotels

IZMEĐU VRTA

BRANITELJA

DUBROVNIKA

M. BLAŽIĆA

HILTON HOTEL

33

P

B DEPARTING BUS

T

PILE

i

B ARRIVING BUS

BUS TICKET OFFICE

GV. ĐURĐA

PILE GATE

WALL TICKET OFFICE

BIG FOUNTAIN

GARIŠTE

ZLAT

ZA ROKOM

OD DOMINA

OD RUPA

BOKAR FORTRESS

RUPE MUSEUM

OD KAŠTELA

FORT OF ST. LAWRENCE

FOUNDRY MUSEUM

PUT IZA GRADA

MINČETE

PALMOTIĆEVA

ANTUN.

FRANCISCAN MONASTERY MUSEUM

ST. SAVIOR

GARGOYLE

A STRADUN

OD SIG.

MEDOVIĆA

CUBRAN.

POBR.

ŠIROKA

19

24

17

29

30

9

SERBIAN ORTHODOX CHURCH

PUČA

OD

JOSIPA

BOŽIDAREVIĆA

28

25

STROSS. MIHA

CITY

14

WALLS

OD

Adriatic Sea

N

100 Meters
100 Yards

DUBROVNIK

To find the Karmen and Zijadić apartments from the cathedral, walk toward the big fort tower along the inside of the wall (follow signs for *akvarji*); for Dubrovnik Gardens, climb up the grand staircase to the Jesuit St. Ignatius Church.

$$$ Fresh Sheets Kathedral B&B, well-run by Canadian-Croatian couple Jon and Sanja, rents six bright, stylish, modern rooms in an ideally located building—next door to the cathedral and squeezed between two of Dubrovnik's most happening squares. Three of the rooms have shared bathrooms, and all have views over interesting squares and landmarks in the heart of the Old Town. While pricey, the hospitality, well-appointed rooms, and great location can make it worthwhile (D-€188, Db-€198, studio-€248, family suite-€348, less Oct-May, for best prices book direct by email, air-con, Bunićeva Poljana 6, mobile 091-896-7509, www.freshsheetskathedral.com, stay@freshsheetskathedral.com).

$$$ Apartments Amoret, run by all-business Branka Dabrović, rents pricey but quite comfortable apartments in four different buildings. All four classes of apartments are comparably good, with traditional wood furnishings, and all are central ("regular" apartments-€110/€100/€90; "standard" apartments-€130/€120/€100; "superb" apartments-€160/€150/€120; "royal" apartments for up to 4-€220/€200/€170, extra person-€20; cheaper Nov-April, 30 percent more for 1-night stays, 20 percent more for 2-night stays, 10 percent more for 3-night stays, no breakfast, cash only, air-con, mobile 091-530-4910, tel. 020/324-005, www.dubrovnik-amoret.com, amoret-dubrovnik@hotmail.com).

$$$ Ante Vetma and his mother Marija rent a modern one-bedroom apartment in a newer building tucked down a side street, just a few level steps from the Stradun (Db-€110/€100/€95, cash only, air-con, laundry machine, mobile 098-705-605, ante.vatma@gmail.com).

$$ Dubrovnik Gardens, conscientiously run by Roberto and his mother Marija (also recommended tour guides—see page 288), is unique and a top value. Hiding off of the big square in front of the Jesuit St. Ignatius Church is a rare private garden—a peaceful oasis smack-dab in the heart of the bustling city. Two units have their own exclusive slice of the garden: a cozy freestanding cottage (Db-€90/€80, can work for a family of up to 4); and an elegant, bright, spacious, artistically appointed studio apartment (Db-€100/€90). Unwind in your garden, and even order food from the neighboring restaurant (the recommended Kopun)...very cool, particularly in a city with virtually no green space. They also have a bigger, antique-furnished, two-room apartment (Db-€120, Qb-€140, garden views but no access, up several flights of stairs, sleeps up to 4; for all units: €10 more per extra person, €20 more for

1-night stay, cash only, air-con, kitchenette, mobile 091-541-6637, www.dubrovnikgardens.com, dubrovnikgardens@gmail.com).

$$$ Karmen Apartments are well-run by a Brit named Marc and his Croatian wife Silva, who offer four welcoming apartments just inside the big fort. While a bit pricey, the apartments are roomy, well-equipped, and homey-feeling, each with a bathroom and kitchen. The decor is eclectic but tasteful, drawing from Marc and Silva's extensive art collection; the stairwell has a virtual minimuseum of historic Dubrovnik maps and documents (smaller apartment-€95/€75/€55, mid-sized apartment-€145/€110/€85, bigger apartment-€175/€120/€100, ask about Rick Steves discount when you book direct, no breakfast, cash only, air-con, near the aquarium at Bandureva 1, tel. 020/323-433, mobile 098-619-282, www.karmendu.com, marc.van-bloemen@du.t-com.hr).

$$$ Apartments Placa (PLAH-tsah; not to be confused with Plaza Apartments, described earlier) is run by Tonči (TOHN-chee). He rents three apartments with some antique furnishings and some modern, overlooking the market square in the heart of the Old Town. You might get some early-morning noise from the market set-up, but the double-paned windows help, and the location is wonderfully central. Since Tonči lives elsewhere, clearly communicate your arrival time (Db-€100/€90/€80, cheaper Nov-April, no breakfast, cash only, no extra charge for 1- or 2-night stays, several flights of stairs, air-con, Gundulićeva poljana 5, mobile 091-721-9202, www.dubrovnik-online.com/apartments_placa, tonci.korculanin@du.t-com.hr).

$$ Renata Zijadić offers three older but well-located rooms with slanting floors. One modern, sleek apartment enjoys grand views over the Old Port (€130/€120); a smaller, older, simpler double features an ornate old cabinet and no views (Db-€75/€65); and a top-floor apartment, with low ceilings and fine vistas, is a lesser value (€130/€120; cheaper Oct-May, no extra charge for 1- or 2-night stays, no breakfast, cash only, air-con; follow signs for wall access and walk up the steps marked *ulica Stajeva* going over the street to find Stajeva 1; tel. 020/323-623, www.dubrovnik-online.net/house_renata, renatadubrovnik@yahoo.com).

$ City Walls Hostel, bright, stylish, and appealingly funky, is your best inexpensive option in the Old Town. The 18 bunks (two 6-bed dorms, one 4-bed dorm, and a double room) sit above a tight common area. Located at the very top of Dubrovnik just inside the City Walls, it's a steep hike up from the main drag, but worth it if you enjoy youthful backpacker bonding (bunk in dorm room-€22-36, bed in private room-€28-38, likely closed Nov-March, includes breakfast, lockers, kitchenette, Svetog Šimuna 15, mobile 091-799-2086, www.citywallshostel.com, citywallshostel@gmail.com, Marijana).

Outside Pile Gate, Just West of the Old Town

While the area in front of the Pile Gate is a congested tourist hub, one of my favorite Dubrovnik lodgings sits high on the hill above the chaos, offering a warm welcome to travelers hardy enough to make the hike.

$$$ Jadranka and Milan Benussi rent two apartments in a quiet, traffic-free neighborhood. Their delightful stony-chic home, complete with a leafy terrace, is a steep 10-minute hike above the Old Town—close enough to be convenient, but far enough to take you away from the bustle and into a calm residential zone. Jadranka speaks good English, enjoys visiting with her guests, and gives her place a modern Croatian class unusual for a *soba*. This is one of your most comfortable home bases in Dubrovnik, if you don't mind the walk (small apartment-€130/€120/€100, apartment with balcony-€140/€130/€110, these are Db prices—12 percent less for Sb, cheaper Nov-April, 30 percent extra for 1-night stays, no breakfast, cash only, air-con, kitchenettes, Miha Klaića 10, tel. 020/429-339, mobile 098-928-1300, www.dubrovnik-benussi.com, jadranka@dubrovnik-benussi.com). To find the Benussis, first go to the big Hilton Hotel just outside the Pile Gate. Walk up the little stepped lane called Marijana Blažića at the upper-left corner of the Hilton cul-de-sac. When that lane dead-ends, go left up ulica Don Iva Bjelokosića (more steps) until you see a little church on the left. The Benussis' house is just before this church.

Beyond the Ploče Gate, East of the Old Town

To reach these options, you'll go through the Ploče Gate and walk along the road stretching east from the Old Town (with fine views back on the Old Port). This area is shared by giant waterfront luxury hotels and residential areas, so it has a bit less character than the Old Town listings (which I prefer).

$$$ Apartments Paviša, described on page 326, has two fine apartments in the Viktorija neighborhood about a 20-minute walk or short bus ride from town.

$$$ Villa Adriatica is a bit pricey, but has one of the finest views in Dubrovnik. Its four old-fashioned rooms sit above a travel agency and a family home just outside the busy Ploče Gate, a few steps from the Old Town. The rooms are Old World-furnished, but have modern bathrooms, TVs, and air-conditioning. While less personal and a lesser value than my other listings, it could be worth it just for the huge, shared terrace with priceless Old Port views, plus a common living room and big kitchen furnished with museum-piece antiques. Teo manages the rooms; ask for him at the Perla Adriatic travel agency, just outside the Ploče Gate (Db-€110-120/€100-110/€80-90, cheaper Nov-April, price depends on size and view, no breakfast, cash only, air-con, Wi-Fi in some areas, Frana Supila 4, mobile 098-334-500, tel. 020/411-962, www.villa-adriatica.net, booking@villa-adriatica.net, Tomšić family).

HOTELS

If you must stay in a hotel, you have only a few good options. There are just two hotels inside the City Walls—and one of them charges $500 a night (Pucić Palace, www.thepucicpalace.com). Any big, resort-style hotel within walking distance of the Old Town will run you at least €200. These inflated prices drive most visitors to Boninovo Bay or the Lapad Peninsula, a bus ride west of the Old Town. In the mass-tourism tradition, many European visitors choose to take the half-board option at their hotel (i.e., dinner in the hotel restaurant). This can be convenient and a good value, but the Old Town is a much more atmospheric place to dine.

$$$ Hotel Stari Grad knows it's the only real hotel option inside the Old Town—and charges accordingly. It has eight extremely stylish rooms a half-block off the Old Town's main drag. The rooftop terrace enjoys an amazing view over orange tiles (Db-€299/€269/€220, includes breakfast, air-con, lots of stairs with no elevator, Od Sigurate 4, tel. 020/322-244, www.hotelstarigrad.com, info@hotelstarigrad.com).

$$$ Adriatic Luxury Hotels is a chain with several plush hotels near Dubrovnik. Location-wise, the most enticing are **Hotel Excelsior** (Frana Supila 12) and **Grand Villa Argentina** (Frana Supila 14)—which are a scenic 10-minute walk outside the Ploče Gate, east of the Old Town—as well as the **Hotel Bellevue** (on Boninovo Bay, a short bus ride or long walk west of the Old Town; see "Greater Dubrovnik" map on page 279). For top-of-the-top luxury lodgings without regard for the price tag, browse their options at www.adriaticluxuryhotels.com (top-season prices are around Db-€500-600—but you'll rarely pay that much).

Eating in Dubrovnik

While there are a few gems, Dubrovnik often disappoints diners with high prices, surly service, and mediocre quality. This is

a place to be choosy and do your homework; if you do, you'll enjoy a memorable meal for half the price of an overpriced tourist trap. Be sure to get the latest information—this city has a troubling trend of hot new eateries going swiftly downhill. The places I've recommended are well-established and provide a decent value. All of my recommendations are in or very near the atmospheric Old Town. Anywhere you dine, breezy outdoor seating is a no-brainer, and scrawny, adorable kittens beg for table scraps. In general, seafood restaurants are good only at seafood; if you want pasta, go to a pasta place.

Nishta ("Nothing"), featuring a short menu of delicious vegetarian-fusion cuisine with Asian flair, offers a welcome change of pace from the Dalmatian seafood-pasta-pizza rut. Busy Swiss owner/chef Gildas cooks, while his wife Ruža and their staff cheerfully serve a steady stream of return diners. This tiny place—which has been a reliable and affordable crowd-pleaser for years—has just a few cramped indoor and outdoor tables. Even if you're not a vegetarian, it's worth a visit; reserve the day ahead in peak season (40-kn starters, 70-90-kn main courses, Mon-Sat 11:30-22:00, closed Sun and Jan-Feb, on the restaurant-clogged Prijeko street—near the Pile Gate end of the street, tel. 020/322-088).

Dalmatino offers some of the best traditional Dalmatian cooking in the city, combined with some modern twists. This is quality food and attentive service at prices that, while not cheap, won't blow your budget. While there are only a few outdoor tables tucked along the alley, there's a spacious, classy-but-not-stuffy dining room (65-90-kn pastas, 110-180-kn main courses, daily 11:00-23:00, Miha Pracata 6, tel. 020/323-070, http://dalmatino-dubrovnik.com, Robert). Don't confuse Dalmatino's tables with its neighbors'.

Kopun just feels special, with an off-the-beaten-path setting on a gravelly square facing the Jesuit St. Ignatius Church. They serve up regional specialties (mostly seafood) with a touch of class. Several dishes make use of the restaurant's namesake, *kopun*—a rooster that's castrated young and plumps up (70-130-kn pastas and starters, 85-160-kn main courses, daily 11:00-23:00, Poljana Ruđera Boškovića 7, tel. 020/323-969, www.restaurantkopun.com).

Azur, tucked near the Buža bars just inside the City Walls, offers a break from the standard regional fare. The menu presents Mediterranean cuisine with an Asian twist (for example, swordfish in a black curry sauce). Owner Vedran has created a hit with discerning locals and travelers alike with careful preparation and service. Book a little ahead for an outside table (50-90-kn starters and snacks, 90-150-kn main courses, daily 11:00-24:00, Pobijana 10, tel. 020/324-806).

Lady Pi-Pi, named for a comical, anatomically correct, and slightly off-putting statue out front, sits high above town, barely inside the wall. Most diners come for the casual, young vibe and to enjoy a good meal on their vine-covered terrace. Many of the tasty dishes are prepared over an open grill. Several tables overlook the rooftops of Dubrovnik, but these fill up fast, and no reservations are possible—come early or be prepared to line up (80-130-kn main courses, daily May-Sept 9:00-24:00, closed Oct-April and in bad weather, Peline b.b., tel. 020/321-288).

Wine Bar with Finger Food: **D'Vino Wine Bar,** just a few steps off the main drag, has a relaxed atmosphere and a smart, easygoing approach to Croatian wines. Run by gregarious Aussie-Croat Sasha and his capable staff (including Anita), this cozy bar sells more than 60 wines by the glass (25-80-kn glasses; most around 40 kn). Their user-friendly menu highlights small producers with helpful descriptions of each wine, and the staff is happy to guide you through your options. The various three-taste wine flights (50 kn) make a good introduction to Croatian wines. Their tasty appetizers paired with your wine can make an appealing dinner; the smoked duck or swordfish plates go well with the reds. Sit in the get-to-know-your-neighbor interior or linger at the sidewalk tables. Reservations are smart if you'll be here during dining hours—after about 18:00 (100-kn 2-person cheese-and-meat plate, 100-kn *antipasti* plate; daily 10:30-late, Palmotićeva 4a, tel. 020/321-130, www.dvino.net). Sasha takes wine lovers on all-day wine tours to the Pelješac Peninsula (see page 356); also ask about the organized tastings and other events in his adjacent tasting room.

Bosnian Cuisine: For a break from Croatian fare, try the grilled meats and other tasty Bosnian dishes at the misnamed **Taj Mahal.** The menu offers an enticing taste of the Turkish-flavored land to the east. Choose between the tight interior, which feels like a Bosnian tea house, or tables out on the alley (60-75-kn salads, 90-135-kn main courses, daily 10:00-24:00, Nikole Gučetića 2, tel. 020/323-221). For a primer on Bosnian food, see the "Balkan Flavors" sidebar on page 421.

Pizza: Dubrovnik seems to have a pizzeria on every corner. Little separates the various options—just look for a menu and outdoor seating option that appeals to you. **Oliva Pizzeria,** just behind St. Blaise's Church, puts out consistently good food (45-90-kn pizzas, Lučarica 5, daily 10:00-24:00, tel. 020/324-594); around the side is a handy takeout window (20-kn slices). Close to the Old Town, but just far away to be frequented mostly by locals, **Tabasco Pizzeria** is tucked at the corner of the parking lot beneath the cable-car station. Unpretentious and affordable, this is the place to come if the pizza is more important than the setting—though the outdoor terrace does have views of the City Walls...over a sea of parked cars (40-50-kn pizzas, 70-85-kn "jumbo" pizzas, daily 9:00-23:00, Hvarska 48A, tel. 020/429-595).

Pasta: **Spaghetteria Toni** is nothing fancy, but it offers good pastas at reasonable prices. Choose between the cozy 10-table interior or the long alley filled with outdoor tables (60-kn salads, 60-

90-kn pastas, daily in summer 11:00-23:00, closed Sun in winter, closed Jan, Nikole Božidarevića 14, tel. 020/323-134).

Sandwiches: Buffet Škola is a rare bit of preglitz Dubrovnik just a few steps off the Stradun, serving takeaway or sit-down sandwiches on homemade bread. Squeeze into the hole-in-the-wall interior, or sit at one of the outdoor tables (30-kn sandwiches, skip the overpriced ham-and-cheese boards, daily 8:00-22:00, Antuninska 1, tel. 020/321-096).

Ice Cream: Dubrovnik has lots of great *sladoled*, but locals swear by the stuff at **Dolce Vita.** In addition to good ice cream, they have tasty crêpes (daily 9:00-24:00, a half-block off the Stradun at Nalješkovićeva 1A, tel. 020/321-666).

The Old Town's "Restaurant Row," Prijeko Street: The street called Prijeko, a block toward the mainland from the Stradun promenade, is lined with outdoor, tourist-oriented eateries—each one with a huckster out front trying to lure in diners. (Many of them aggressively try to snare passersby down on the Stradun, as well.) Don't be sucked into this vortex of bad food at worse prices. The only place worth seeking out here is Nishta (described earlier). Still, it can be fun to take a stroll along here—the atmosphere is lively, and the sales pitches are entertainingly desperate.

Forgettable Food with Stunning Old Town Views: **Komarda,** located just outside of the Ploče Gate, serves up mediocre food on a memorable terrace, with views of Dubrovnik's walls and Old Port. Tables are scattered around a tranquil garden just above the sea and a concrete beach. Drop by early to reserve the table of your choice for dinner—but skip it if you don't land a view table (75-90-kn pastas, 90-170-kn main courses, daily 7:00-24:00, reservations essential in summer, look for stairs on the right just after the travel agencies, mobile 098-428-239, http://komarda.hr).

Picnic Tips: Dubrovnik's lack of great restaurant options makes it a perfect place to picnic. You can shop for fresh fruits and veggies at the open-air produce market (each morning near the cathedral, on the square called Gundulićeva Poljana). Supplement your picnic with basic supplies from **Konzum grocery store** (one location on the market square near the produce vendors, another near the bus stop just outside Pile Gate, both open Mon-Sat 7:00-21:00, Sun 8:00-20:00). Good picnic spots include the shaded benches overlooking the Old Port; the Porporela breakwater (beyond the Old Port and fort—comes with a swimming area, sunny no-shade benches, and views of Lokrum Island); and the green, welcoming park in what was the moat just under the Pile Gate entry to the Old Town.

Breakfast: If you're sleeping in a *soba*, you'll likely be on your own for breakfast. Fortunately, you have plenty of cafés and pastry shops to choose from, and your host probably has a favorite he or she can recommend. In the Old Town, **Dubrava Bistro**—which locals call "Snack Bar"—has great views and fine outdoor seating at the most colorful end of the Stradun. While the food is nothing special, you can't beat the real estate. Locals who hang out here—catching up with their friends as they stroll by—call this their low-tech version of Facebook (basic 45-55-kn egg dishes, 24-kn caffè lattes, daily 8:00-24:00, Placa 6, tel. 020/321-229). Nearby, another scenic spot is **Gradska Kavana**—tucked between the Bell Tower and Rector's Palace (55-60-kn breakfasts, daily 8:00-24:00, Pred Dvorom 1). For better food in a less atmospheric setting, **The Gaffe Irish Pub** has a good menu of breakfast options (45-50 kn, served daily 9:00-11:00, also affordable weekday lunch specials for 35-40 kn, Miha Pracata 4, tel. 020/640-152, see map on page 329).

Dubrovnik Connections

While ferries and catamarans have traditionally used Dubrovnik's Port Gruž (a bus ride away from the Old Town), a planned redevelopment could relocate some or all boats to the far end of the port, under the big bridge. Ask locally for the latest.

By Catamaran: Two speedy catamarans connect Dubrovnik to points north. Schedules and ticket-buying procedures have been notoriously changeable in recent years—confirm all details online, or ask at the TI. Of the two options, the *Krilo* catamaran—which typically leaves Dubrovnik in the late afternoon—offers more departures (daily June-Sept, 3-4/week May and Oct, none Nov-April) and more destinations: It stops at Mljet National Park (1.5 hours), Korčula (2 hours), Hvar (3 hours), and Split (4 hours). You can buy *Krilo* tickets at www.krilo.hr; it's best to book several days ahead (in peak season, they can sell out up to 4 days before). A different catamaran, called *Nona Ana,* has a shorter season (June-Sept) and doesn't reach as far north. Every day, *Nona Ana* stops at two ports on Mljet Island: Sobra (1 hour) and Polače (closer to the national park, 1.5 hours). In July and August, it sometimes continues to Korčula (4/week, 2.5 hours). In winter (Oct-May), the boat goes only to Šipan (one of the Elaphite Islands near Dubrovnik) and Sobra (on Mljet). Tickets for the *Nona Ana*—which can sell out, especially in peak season—are sold at the kiosk next to the boat at Port Gruž. Try to be at the ticket window when it opens, one hour before departure, or even earlier in peak season. Confirm schedules at www.gv-line.hr.

By Bus to: Split (at least hourly, typically at the top of the hour, less off-season, 4.5 hours), **Korčula** (summer: 1/day at 15:00; Sun 2/day at 15:00 and 18:00, 3.5 hours; also consider the shuttle-bus service described next), **Rijeka** (4/day, 13 hours), **Zagreb** (10/day, overnight options, 10 hours), **Kotor** in Montenegro (2-3/day,

2.5 hours), **Mostar** (3/day, 5 hours), **Sarajevo** (2/day, 6 hours; includes a night bus in summer only at 22:30), **Pula** and **Rovinj** (1/day overnight departing at 15:30, 15 hours to Pula, 16 hours to Rovinj). As usual, schedules are subject to change—confirm locally before making the trip to the bus station. For bus information, check www.libertasdubrovnik.com or call 060-305-070 (a pricey toll line, but worth it).

By Shuttle Bus to Korčula: Korčula-based Korkyra Info Travel Agency runs a handy door-to-door shuttle service from your Dubrovnik accommodations to Korčula; reserve ahead (typically departs at 14:00 and at 17:00, daily May-Sept, by request only off-season, may stop briefly in Ston if you want, 2 hours, 150 kn one-way, mobile 091-571-4355, www.korkyra.info, info@korkyra.info). Korkyra Info can also arrange for a private transfer, including stops (such as wine-tastings and a quick visit to Ston; €150 for up to 8 people).

By Plane: To quickly connect remote Dubrovnik with the rest of your trip, consider a cheap flight. For information on Dubrovnik's airport, see page 281.

By Seaplane: For a scenic, swift, and memorable way to connect Dubrovnik to the rest of Croatia, consider European Coastal Airlines. They fly 19-seat propeller seaplanes to a variety of Croatian destinations. For details, see page 214 or visit www.ec-air.eu.

By Car: For tips on driving along the Dalmatian Coast between Dubrovnik and Split, see page 215 in the Split chapter.

Can I Get to Greece from Dubrovnik? Your best bet is to fly. There are direct flights to Athens on Aegean and Croatia Airlines. Even though Croatia and Greece are nearly neighbors, no direct boats connect them, and the overland connection is extremely long and rugged.

What About Italy? Flying is the easiest option, though there are only a few direct flights (on Croatia Airlines to Rome or Venice; or on easyJet to Rome or Milan). You can take a direct night boat from Dubrovnik to Bari, or head to Split for more boat connections (for more on all of these boats, see page 212). The overland connection is too long (figure 5 hours to Split, then 5 hours to Zagreb, then 7 hours to Venice).

NEAR DUBROVNIK

Excursions from Dubrovnik's Old Port • Cavtat • Trsteno Arboretum • Pelješac Peninsula • Mljet National Park

The longer you linger, the clearer it becomes: Dubrovnik isn't just a town, it's an entire region. Stretching up and down the glimmering Dalmatian Coast from Dubrovnik are a variety of worthwhile getaways. Just offshore from the city's Old Town—and accessible via scenic boat trip from its historic port—are enticing islands and villages, where time stands still for lazy vacationers: the playground islet of Lokrum and the archipelago of the Elaphite Islands. The serene resort town of Cavtat, just south of Dubrovnik, has some of the best art treasures of this part of Dalmatia (including a stunning mausoleum designed by Ivan Meštrović). To the north is a lush arboretum called Trsteno, with a playful fountain, a 600-year-old aqueduct, a villa, a chapel...and, of course, plants galore. Poking into the Adriatic is the vineyard-covered Pelješac Peninsula, where friendly vintners are eager to impress you with their wines, and where the mighty little town of Ston lures you to climb its sprawling fortifications. And out at sea is the sparsely populated island called Mljet, a third of which is carefully protected as one of Croatia's most appealing national parks, where you can hike, bike, boat, and swim to your heart's content. Best of all, there's no better place to "come home to" than Dubrovnik—after a busy day exploring the coastline, strolling the Stradun to unwind is particularly sweet.

PLANNING YOUR TIME

Give yourself at least a full day and two nights to experience Dubrovnik itself. But if you can spare the time, set up in Dubrovnik for several nights and use your extra days for some of these excursions. (This also gives you the luxury of keeping an eye on the

Dubrovnik Day Trips at a Glance

The international excursions to Bosnia-Herzegovina and Montenegro—which are worth considering for overnight stops—are covered in their own chapters.

In Bosnia-Herzegovina

▲▲▲**Mostar** The side-trip with the highest degree of cultural hairiness—but, for many, also the greatest reward—lies to the east, in Bosnia-Herzegovina. With its iconic Old Bridge, intriguing glimpse of European Muslim lifestyles, and still-vivid examples of war damage, Mostar is unforgettable. Allow a full day or more (best reached by bus or car).

Međugorje Devout Catholics may want to consider a trip to this pilgrimage site in Bosnia-Herzegovina, with a holy hill that some believe is visited regularly by an apparition of the Virgin Mary. Allow a full day or more (best reached by car or bus).

In Montenegro

▲▲**The Bay of Kotor** For rugged coastal scenery that arguably rivals anything in Croatia, head south of the border to Montenegro. The Bay of Kotor is a dramatic, fjord-like inlet crowned by the historic town of Kotor, with twisty Old World lanes, one of Europe's best town walls, and oodles of atmosphere. Allow a full day or more (best reached by car or bus).

The Montenegrin Interior A visit to Montenegro's scruffy but historic former capital, Cetinje, comes with a twisty drive up a mountain road and across a desolate, forgotten-feeling plateau. Allow a full day or more (best reached by car).

Budva Riviera Montenegro's best stretch of sandy beaches isn't worth a special trip, but it's a fun excuse for a drive if you've got extra time to kill. The highlight is the famous resort peninsula of Sveti Stefan. Allow a full day or more (best reached by car).

On the Mainland near Dubrovnik

▲Cavtat A charming resort/beach town, unassuming Cavtat holds a pair of wonderful and very local art experiences: an elaborate mausoleum designed by the sculptor Ivan Meštrović, and the house and museum of Cavtat-born modern painter Vlaho Bukovac. Allow a few hours (best reached by boat or bus).

▲Pelješac Peninsula This long, narrow, scenic spit of land—between the main coastal road and Korčula Island—is a favorite of wine lovers, who can joyride through its vineyards and sample its product (or just enjoy the beautiful scenery). Allow a half-day to a full day (best reached by car).

▲Trsteno Arboretum Plant lovers will enjoy this surprisingly engaging botanical garden just outside Dubrovnik, punctuated by a classical-style fountain and aqueduct. Allow a half-day (best reached by bus or car).

Ston A small town with giant fortifications, Ston (on the Pelješac Peninsula) is worth a short stop to scramble up its extensive walls. Allow an hour (best reached by car or bus).

Off the Coast of Dubrovnik

▲Mljet National Park While this largely undeveloped island is time-consuming to reach from Dubrovnik, Mljet offers an opportunity to romp on an island without all those tacky tourist towns. This is for serious nature lovers eager to get away from civilization. Allow a full day (best reached by boat).

Lokrum Island The most convenient excursion from Dubrovnik, this little island—just a short hop offshore from the Old Port—is a good chance to get away from (some of) the tourists. Allow a few hours (best reached by boat).

Elaphite Islands This inviting archipelago offers a variety of island experiences without straying too far from Dubrovnik. With more time, Korčula (for a small town) or Mljet (for a back-to-nature experience) are better, but the "Elafiti" are more convenient. Allow a half-day to a full day (best reached by boat).

NEAR DUBROVNIK

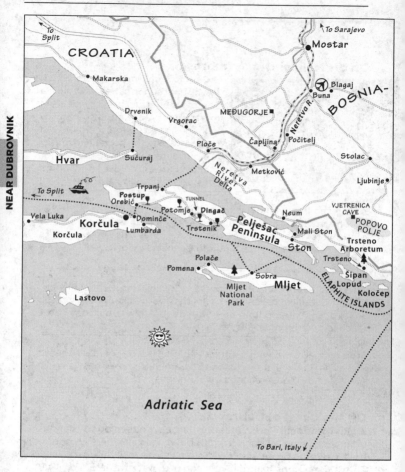

weather reports and saving the most weather-dependent activities for the sunniest days.) For suggestions on how much time to allow per destination, see the sidebar on page 340. Use a map to strategically line up these attractions—for example, you can easily do Trsteno, Ston, and the Pelješac Peninsula on a drive between Dubrovnik and Korčula, while Cavtat pairs nicely with a trip to the airport or Montenegro.

I've listed day trips in this chapter in order of ease from Dubrovnik—the farther down the list, the more difficult to reach (Montenegro and Mostar, the most time-consuming, are covered in their own chapters). Choose the trips that sound best to you, and ask locals and other travelers for their impressions...or for new leads.

Near Dubrovnik

GETTING THERE

Cavtat and the Elaphite Islands are easy to reach by private **excursion boat** from Dubrovnik's Old Port; Cavtat also works by bus. A **city-run boat** links the Old Port to nearby Lokrum. **Public ferries** connect Dubrovnik's Port Gruž to the Elaphite Islands (the most ap-

pealing is Lopud). The other destinations are farther afield, best reached by **boat** (Mljet) or by **car** or **bus** (Montenegro, Mostar, Trsteno, Pelješac Peninsula).

I've listed public transportation options for each, but consider **renting a car** for the day. Or you can splurge for your own **private**

driver (see page 288); to make it more affordable, rally other travelers to accompany you and split the cost.

Alternatively, a variety of travel agencies in Dubrovnik offer **guided excursions** (by bus and/or boat) to nearby destinations. Popular itineraries include everything mentioned in this chapter, plus Korčula and others. While these excursions can be a convenient way to see otherwise difficult-to-reach destinations, the quality can be hit-or-miss. The biggest companies are efficient mass-tourism machines—you'll be jammed into buses and boats until every seat is filled, and the guides typically do their spiel (mostly a memorized script) in several languages. Smaller outfits offer a more casual experience with more personal attention, but lack the polish of the big players. Since this scene is constantly evolving, check online reviews, look around for fliers, and ask locals for tips. (Be aware that many small travel agencies simply sell seats on the big companies' trips.)

Excursions from Dubrovnik's Old Port

At Dubrovnik's salty Old Port, captains set up tiny booths to hawk touristy boat trips. It's fun to chat with them, page through their sun-faded photo albums, and see if they can sell you on a short cruise. In addition to the islands noted below, you can also take a boat from the Old Port to **Cavtat** (described later).

PANORAMA CRUISE

The basic option is a 45-minute "panorama cruise" out on the water and back again (75 kn, departures about every hour). You'll loop around the City Walls—which offer a unique view on Dubrovnik's stout defenses—and do a circuit around Lokrum Island as well. Understandably, these cruises are most popular at or shortly before sunset.

You could just hop on whichever boat is departing next, but I enjoy the **Sv. Ivan,** a cargo boat dating from 1878. Prowling its decks and leaning back against rope railings just feels right in this seafaring town. They also offer a 20 percent discount to readers of this book (that is, you'd pay 60 kn for a 50-minute panorama cruise; look for their desk among the many sales kiosks at the Old Port, mobile 099-441-2054, www.dubrovnik-panoramacruise.com).

If you're a *Game of Thrones* fan, consider the *GoT*-themed cruise. You'll head to Port Gruž to meet the historic *Karka* boat, departing at 18:30 (or earlier in shoulder season, depending on sunset time). The one-hour cruise to the Old Town comes with a box of *GoT* costumes. You'll disembark at the Old Port and set off on a 1.25-hour walking tour of *GoT* sites in the Old Town (325 kn covers cruise and walk, does not include bus trip to Port Gruž, www. karaka.info).

I'd skip the pointless **glass-bottom boat** or "**minisubmarine**" versions of this cruise, which cost more and don't add much.

LOKRUM ISLAND

This island, just offshore from the Old Town, provides a handy escape from the city. When the Old Town just gets too jam-packed with tourists, locals hop a boat out here for some peace and quiet. They call it the "Island of Love," because it offers many secluded spots popular with courting couples. The main attractions here are hiking (on shaded paths that curl up, over, and around the thickly wooded island) and bathing (on jagged, rocky beaches—many of which are designated nude beaches).

Getting There: Lokrum is reachable only by an official city-run boat, which departs twice hourly from the end of the pier in Dubrovnik's Old Port (80 kn round-trip, 15-minute crossing, runs daily mid-June-Aug 9:00-20:00, shorter hours in shoulder season, stops running Nov-March).

Visiting the Island: From the Lokrum boat dock, walk up to the pink building—the visitors center—to buy a map of the island. Continuing up, you'll reach a fork: To head across the narrow middle of the island, continue straight ahead, where you'll find a monastery-turned-Habsburg-palace (today housing a humble *Game of Thrones* exhibit—see sidebar on page 287) and a small botanical garden. Just beyond this area, uneven rocks lead to ladders where you can ease yourself into the sea. There's also a small lake (fed by an underwater canal from the sea) called the "Dead Sea" (Mrtvo More) that's suitable for swimming.

Another option from the boat dock is to hook left and curl around the cove to the island's most popular beach, on the Bay of Portoč, that's famous for its nude sunbathing. If you'd like to (carefully) subject skin that's never seen the sun to those burning rays, follow the *FKK* signs from the boat dock for about five minutes to the slabs of waterfront rock, where naturists feel right at home. Continuing past this beach, you can work your way up and over to the other side of the island (on very rocky trails).

For an even more serious hike, head right from the boat dock for the two-hour hike that goes all the way around the island, and consider a detour to its highest point (at 315 feet above sea level), capped by Fort Royal, an old Austro-Hungarian military fortification.

You'll find a few cafés scattered around the island, mostly along the main path from the boat dock to the monastery complex.

ELAPHITE ISLANDS (ELAFITI)

This 13-island archipelago, just north of Dubrovnik, is popular among day-trippers because it allows you to hit three different islands in a single day: Koločep, Lopud, and Šipan. These "Deer Islands" (supposedly named for their shape—though I don't see it) are a bit overhyped and can't hold a candle to some of the more distant Dalmatian islands, such as Korčula and Hvar. But they're a decent choice if you need a break from Dubrovnik's crowds and want a lazy day cruising Dalmatia. Along the way, you'll discover fishing ports, shady forests, inviting beaches, and forgotten escape mansions of old Dubrovnik aristocracy. The two smaller islands (Koločep and Lopud) are traffic-free, making them a restful backwater getaway. While there's little to actually see on each island, each church, beach, and walking path is well-signed, making it easy to just wander. Bring decent footwear for hiking uneven trails, and pack along swimwear. Each island has some sort of beach relatively near the boat dock; on a hot day, you could just wear your swimsuit on the boat and make a point to take a dip at each stop.

Getting There: The easiest way to cruise the Elafiti is to buy an excursion at Dubrovnik's Old Port, which usually includes a "fish picnic" cooked up by the captain as you cruise (about 250 kn with lunch, several boats depart daily around 10:30-11:00, return around 15:45-19:30; so they can be sure to buy enough food, companies prefer you to reserve and pay a 50-kn deposit the day before). For a bigger and more memorable ship—and a more

corporate experience—you can pay a bit more to go on the *Karaka* or the *Sirena*, modern replicas of the traditional cargo ships once built here in Dubrovnik (advertised along with the others at the Old Port).

Regardless of which company you go with, you generally spend about two to three hours on Lopud and about an hour each on Koločep and Šipan, with about 2.5 hours on the boat. To get to the Elaphite Islands without a tour (on a cheap ferry), you'll sail from Dubrovnik's less convenient Port Gruž.

Koločep

The nearest island to Dubrovnik, and the sleepiest, Koločep's harbor arcs away from its boat dock. Walking around it, you'll quickly reach a small main square with al fresco cafés spilling out onto the seawall; beyond that is a sandy beach in front of a hotel, with rentable chairs. Near the boat dock, well-signed steps lead up into the hills, passing several small churches and Koločep's little museum of ecclesiastical art (the only museum I saw on the Elafiti).

On a short visit, you'll barely have time to stroll the harbor; if your excursion leaves you here a bit longer, consider a low-impact **hike** over the spine of the island to the village of Gornje Čelo, on the opposite side (about 1.5 miles away). You'll climb up stairs past an old guard tower, pass a pink stucco church near a cemetery, then follow the narrow path between high stone walls and past olive groves. You'll wind down to a little port town with an inviting beach; looping around to Placet takes you to a wall of dramatic cliffs. *Donje Čelo* signs lead you back to your boat.

▲Lopud

The main attraction of the Elaphite Islands, Lopud feels like a humbler Cavtat without all the great art. But Lopud's trump card is its fine beaches, including one of the nicest beaches in the area (a long hike or short golf-cart ride from the main boat dock). Lopud feels bigger, more vital, and more inviting than the other two islands. Most excursions give it far more time than Koločep or Šipan; it's also accessible by public ferry, and may be worth considering for an all-day beach getaway.

Your boat docks near the stout Franciscan monastery, which pokes out into the sea, dominating the townscape. From there, a picturesque promenade winds past several beaches (sand, then pebbles, then sand) and the entrance to a lush garden, before stretching all the way to a luxury hotel. Near the boat dock, you'll find a **TI** (Obala Iva Kuljevana 12, tel. 020/759-086).

For beach bums, the main attraction on Lopud is at the other end of the island: **Šunj Beach.** This gorgeous, shallow, sandy

beach—hemmed in on both sides by forested cliffs—splays serenely between beach bars and ritzy yachts that drop anchor to take a dip. The almost entirely sandy floor and gentle incline makes this beach ideal for waders and families. The catch is that it takes a bit of effort to reach: It's a moderately strenuous 1.5-mile walk over the scraggly spine of the island. Otherwise, golf carts zip arriving tourists over to the beach (usually around 20 kn/person each way). While you might see the carts waiting near the promenade, more likely you'll have to walk partway to reach them: Follow the promenade as far as the abandoned Grand Hotel, then head inland (on a drab, poorly maintained concrete trail), following signs for *Šunj Beach*. Soon you'll see the golf carts. From here, if you prefer, you can continue to hike the rest of the way. Given its distance from the main boat dock, it's not worth attempting to visit Šunj if you're on Lopud for less than two hours.

Šipan

By far the biggest island (at just over six square miles), and the northernmost, Šipan has two different port towns. Your ship will  most likely use the one facing Lopud, called Suđurađ (named for the local patron saint, George). Suđurađ's harbor is watched over by the fortified, castle-like 16th-century villa of a local aristocrat. A beach beckons just across the bay from the boat dock. Next to the harbor, the small Church of St. George—with a large covered porch—has a vivid fresco over the altar of George slaying the dragon while being watched over by two other locally revered saints, Blaise (Dubrovnik's protector) and Nicholas (the patron saint of sailors).

If you need an excuse for a short hike, head from the harbor straight up the street away from the water, following signs for the Church of Sv. Duh (Holy Spirit). After passing through a humble residential zone, you'll arrive at a stout, fortress-like church, with raw-stone walls. If it's open, poke inside to see the rough-and-tumble interior. The stairs to the right of the altar lead up to the rooftop, where you can see the large, fertile valley that sits in the middle of this island. If you're tempted to ring the bell, resist—locals ring it only when a member of the local community dies.

Cavtat

This sleepy resort town—just 12 miles to the south, near the Montenegrin border, and rated ▲—offers a milder alternative to bustling Dubrovnik. With its strategic location sheltered inside a nearly 360-degree bay, this settlement was thriving long before there was a Dubrovnik. The Greeks called it Epidaurus, while the Romans called it Epidaurum—but these days, it's Cavtat (TSAV-taht). The town is best known as a handy spot to find a room when Dubrovnik's booked up. But even those suffering from beach-resort fatigue will enjoy a side-trip to Cavtat, which is home to two gems of Croatian art: a breathtaking hilltop mausoleum by the great Croatian sculptor Ivan Meštrović, and the former home-turned-museum of the Cavtat-born, early 20th-century painter Vlaho Bukovac.

GETTING TO CAVTAT

Boats to Cavtat leave about hourly from Dubrovnik's Old Port (80 kn round-trip, 50 kn one-way, about 45 minutes each way, hourly return boats from Cavtat). The boat deposits you right along Cavtat's main seafront promenade. Note that a round-trip ticket is cheaper, but you'll have to return with the same company (rather than on whichever boat is leaving next).

You can also reach Cavtat by public **bus** #10, which leaves from Dubrovnik's main bus station and also stops at the "cable car" bus stop above the Old Town (1-2/hour, 30-40 minutes, 25 kn). The bus brings you to Cavtat's parking lot (described next). Returning by bus from Cavtat, hop off at the Dubrovnik bus stop that's along the main road high above the Old Town—about a 5- to 10-minute walk down into town.

For variety, consider going to Cavtat by boat (buy a one-way ticket), then returning by bus.

Drivers find Cavtat an easy detour when heading to points south, including Montenegro or the airport; the town is well-signed off the main road. The big parking lot is at the back of Cavtat's peninsula, just around the corner from the main part of town and seafront promenade: Just walk past the TI, hook right at the busy street, and head for the waterfront.

Orientation to Cavtat

Cavtat is set within an idyllic, horseshoe-shaped harbor hemmed in by a pair of peninsulas. Tucked around the back side of the peninsula is the parking lot, left-luggage office *(garderoba),* and **TI** (Zidine 6, tel. 020/479-025, www.tzcavtat-konavle.hr). Cavtat is basically a one-street town, but that street is a fine pedestrian promenade running along the harbor, with a few narrow lanes winding steeply up into the hill. Capping the hill above town is a cemetery with the Meštrović mausoleum.

Sights in Cavtat

Waterfront Wander

Strolling along Cavtat's waterfront, you'll be immersed in a wrap-around bay and surrounded by Europeans vacationing well. At

the near end of the promenade, notice the big water polo court roped off in the bay; Cavtat and Dubrovnik are the birthing ground for many of the core players of the Croatian national water-polo team. Across the street is **St. Nicholas Church,** with a humble, dull interior (though hanging high in the altar area are Vlaho Bukovac's paintings of the four evangelists). About halfway along the drag, one of the narrow lanes leading up the hill (appropriately named Bukovčeva) takes you to the fine **Vlaho Bukovac House** (described below). At the end of the main waterfront area is the **Church of Our Lady of the Snows,** commemorating a freak—and seemingly miraculous—midsummer snowstorm in ancient Roman times, believed to have been a sign sent by the Virgin Mary. Inside, above the altar, is a Vlaho Bukovac painting (from 1909) of Mary and the Baby Jesus watching over Cavtat.

Climbing the steep steps up to the right of the church leads you up to Ivan Meštrović's **Račić Mausoleum** (described later). With more time, consider continuing around the peninsula to its pointy tip for distant views of Dubrovnik's Old Town. This is one of the favorite spots in this area for watching the sunset. (If you continue all the way around the point, in about 20 minutes you'll wind up back at the parking lot at the start of town.)

▲Vlaho Bukovac House (Kuća Bukovac)

One of the joys of travel is learning about locally beloved artists who are little known outside their homelands. Cavtat proudly introduces you to native son Vlaho Bukovac (1855-1922), who grew up in this very house and went on to become the most important Croatian painter of the modern period. Bukovac moved to New York City with his uncle at age 11, beginning a life of great adventure. After a brief career as a sailor (traveling to Peru and San Francisco), he trained as an artist in Paris, then in Zagreb.

For his last 20 years, Bukovac spent his summers in Prague and his winters here in Cavtat.

Cost and Hours: 40 kn; May-Oct Tue-Sun 9:00-13:00 & 16:00-20:00; Nov-April Tue-Sat 9:00-13:00 & 14:00-17:00, Sun 14:00-17:00; closed Mon year-round; Bukovčeva 5, tel. 020/478-646, www.kuca-bukovac.hr.

Visiting the Museum: Touring the collection (with good English explanations), you'll get to know Bukovac's life and his works. Bukovac's paintings are mostly realistic (in accordance with his formal Salon training in Paris), but shimmer with a hint of Post-Impressionism; his later works echo the slinky Art Nouveau Slavic pride of the Czech painter Alfons Mucha, who was Bukovac's contemporary.

The ground floor displays photos of his early life; upstairs you'll find old furniture, early sketches, and portraits of Bukovac and his

family (the painting of his children's disembodied heads hanging on the wall is macabre but strangely tender). The top floor houses one big atelier room filled with canvases from various periods, allowing you to survey his impressive artistic development with a sweep of the head. Throughout the house are murals painted by Bukovac in his early days, offering a glimpse of a burgeoning artist who would go on to make Cavtat very proud.

▲▲Račić Family Mausoleum (Mauzolej Obitelji Račić)

This harmonious masterwork of Croatia's greatest artist is the gem of Cavtat, and worth ▲▲▲ to fans of Ivan Meštrović's powerful

sculptures. To learn more about Meštrović before you visit, read the sidebar on page 194.

Cost and Hours: 10 kn, Mon-Sat 10:00-17:00, closed Sun and mid-Oct-mid-April. If she's not too busy, helpful Nena will show you around.

Getting There: Capping the hill above town, it's a steep 10-minute walk from the Cavtat waterfront. From the Church of Our Lady of Snows at the far end of the waterfront, climb up the stairs (following *mauzolej* signs).

Visiting the Mausoleum: Over the course of one tragic year, all four members of the wealthy Račić family—father, mother, son, daughter—died in the 1918-19 Flu Pandemic. From 1920 to 1922, in accordance with their will, Ivan Meštrović was commissioned to craft their final resting place. He used the opportunity to create a cohesive meditation on Christian faith and death, made entirely of brilliant white stone from the island of Brač.

As you enter, take a moment to appreciate how the interior ponders birth, life, and death. The four inner walls of the octagonal hall hold the tombs of the departed; above each tomb, an angel lovingly carries their souls up to heaven—spiriting them into a cupola studded with angel heads. The floor has symbols for the four evangelists: Matthew (angel), Mark (lion), Luke (bull), and John (eagle). The chapel to the left holds a crucifix; to the right, an altar to St. Rok (the patron saint of illness, to whom the chapel is dedicated—the dog licking the wound in his leg is his symbol). Straight ahead is an altar with Mary holding the Baby Jesus above a relief of the Lamb of God, and below that, Jesus' body being taken down from the cross. Flanking this altar, notice the bases of the twisting candelabras: alternating angels look down to honor the dead.

The chapel rewards those who linger over the details, such as the bronze doors, with four saints, Glagolitic inscriptions, and the 12 Apostles. The saints chosen for this door preach both ecumenism and Yugoslav unity: Cyril and Methodius (the Byzantine missionaries who first brought Christianity to this region), along with a Catholic bishop (Bishop Gregory of Nin) and an Orthodox saint (St. Sava). Taken together, the mausoleum is an astonishing display of talent, especially considering it was Meštrović's first architectural work.

Nearby: The mausoleum sits in the middle of a tranquil cemetery that's still used for the funerals of Cavtat residents. As you exit the mausoleum, head straight out and a bit to the right to find two communal graves for the poor—with smaller markers lined up along a large plinth. Also in this cemetery is the grave of the artist Vlaho Bukovac.

NEAR CAVTAT
Čilipi
This nearby village hosts a Sunday-morning folk festival through the summer (Easter-Oct, starting at 9:00). There's a special Mass at the church, an open-air market, and—starting at 11:15—a costumed folk-dancing show (tel. 020/771-007, www.cilipifolklor.hr).

Trsteno Arboretum

Take a stroll through the shaded, relaxing botanical garden in Trsteno (worth ▲), just up the coast from Dubrovnik. Nongarden-

ers may find it a bit dull, but Trsteno is a horticulturalist's heaven. Spread over 63 acres on a bluff overlooking the sea, this arboretum features hundreds of different Mediterranean, Asian, and American plants (each one labeled in six languages, including English). The whole complex is laced with easy footpaths and sprinkled with fun attractions—a column-studded Renaissance Garden, a desolate villa, a little chapel, an old mill and olive-oil press, and a seaview pavilion. *Game of Thrones* fans will recognize it as the backdrop of many park-set scenes at King's Landing.

As you wander, the world melts away and you're alone with the sounds of nature: wind, water, birds, and frogs. The garden's centerpiece is the whimsical 18th-century Neptune Fountain, featuring the god of the sea flanked by water-spouting nymphs and fishes as he holds court over a goldfish-stocked, lily-padded pond. Circling around behind the fountain, you'll discover that it's fed by an impressive 230-foot-long aqueduct that was built in the 15th century.

Cost and Hours: 40 kn, daily May-Oct 7:00-19:00, Nov-April 8:00-16:00, tel. 020/751-019.

Nearby: On the waterfront below the arboretum, next to the little village harbor, you'll see the shell of a once-grand 18th-

century **palace,** which was damaged during the siege of Dubrovnik and is now abandoned. It's still owned by the government, but investors are lining up for a chance to buy this prime real estate—possibly the most desirable ruin in Croatia.

Getting There: Trsteno is best reached by car, particularly if you're taking your time driving to Dubrovnik from the north (the main coastal road goes through the town of Trsteno, right past the well-marked arboretum). You also have two bus options from Dubrovnik (20-30 minutes). Any long-distance northbound bus can drop you in Trsteno—ask about the next bus at the main station. Alternatively, the slower local buses #12 and #15 also reach Trsteno. Coming back from Trsteno to Dubrovnik is trickier: Wait at the bus stop with the glass canopy by the park entrance and wave down any Dubrovnik-bound bus that passes (at least hourly).

Pelješac Peninsula

North of Trsteno, the skinny, 55-mile-long Pelješac (PEHL-yeh-shahts) Peninsula—practically an honorary island and rated ▲—splits off from the Croatian coastline as if about to drift away to Italy. (The far tip of Pelješac comes within a stone's throw of Korčula island.) This sparsely populated peninsula, famous for its rugged terrain—and the grapes that thrive here—is worth a detour for wine lovers. But its heavily fortified town of Ston, just a short side-trip from the main coastal road, merits a stretch-your-legs visit for anyone. Notice that if you're connecting from Korčula to anywhere else in Croatia by car, you'll probably be taking the ferry to the Pelješac Peninsula anyway; consider slowing down to sample a few wines, to scramble up the walls at Ston, or to have a meal at Mali Ston.

Getting There: Buses between Dubrovnik and Korčula traverse the Pelješac Peninsula, but drivers have the option of stopping where they like (such as at Ston or a winery). Some public buses also stop at Ston.

STON

The town of Ston, at the base of the peninsula, is the gateway to Pelješac. This "Great Wall of Croatia" town is famous for the im-

pressive wall that climbs up the mountain behind it (about a half-mile encloses the town itself, while another three miles clamber up the hillsides). The unassuming town was heavily fortified (starting in 1333) for two reasons: to defend its strategic location, where mountains and bays create a bottleneck along the road from Dubrovnik to Pelješac, near the Republic of Dubrovnik's northern boundary; and to protect its impressive salt pans, which still produce the mineral. Filling a low-lying plain that sprawls in front of Ston's doorstep, these pans provided Dubrovnik with much of its wealth, back in the days when salt was worth more

A Bridge Too Far?

As you drive along the coast between Split and Dubrovnik, you may be surprised to reach a border checkpoint for Bosnia-Herzegovina at the resort town of Neum. How is it that Bosnia wound up with its very own five-and-a-half-mile stretch of the Dalmatian Coast?

During the heyday of the Republic of Dubrovnik, the city's leaders granted this land to the Ottoman Empire to provide a buffer between Dubrovnik's holdings and the Republic of Venice, to the north. (They knew the Venetians would never dare to enter the territory of the Ottomans, their feared enemy.) Later, as the borders of Europe were being redrawn in modern times, Bosnia retained possession of this strip of land.

For years, coastal Bosnians and their Croatian neighbors have coexisted, albeit with a bit of friction. Prices for hotel rooms, groceries, and other staples are slightly cheaper in Neum, whose rest stops lure tourist buses with low prices and generous bus-driver kickbacks. Visitors are inconvenienced by having to go through a passport checkpoint as they enter Bosnia and again, just a few minutes later, as they exit Bosnia. On busy days, lines can back up at this border—have your passport and rental car's "green card" (proof of insurance) ready. Beyond the red tape, Croatians are irritated by Neum merchants underselling Croatian alternatives nearby.

As Croatia extends its expressway southward, the most logical approach would be a route through Bosnia to Dubrovnik. But some Croatian politicians have been looking for a way to avoid Neum altogether. One solution is to build a 1.5-mile-long bridge from just north of Neum to the Peljes̆ac Peninsula, then rejoin the coastal road back in Croatia, just south of Neum—effectively bypassing Bosnian territory. It's a very expensive way to avoid a tiny strip of land, and environmentalists worry about the impact the bridge will have on the ecosystem around Mali Ston. Because of the proposed bridge's popularity with a certain segment of the voting population, talk about the bridge always escalates just before election season...then tapers off afterwards with nothing officially decided. Will the Bosnian bypass ever be built? Stay tuned.

than its weight in gold. The pans would be flooded with saltwater, then sealed and left to evaporate—leaving the salt easy to harvest.

Today, the sleepy town—with more than its share of outdoor cafés and restaurants—is notable only for the chance to scramble up its massive **fortifications** (park your car in the big lot, then cross the street into town and look right; the entrance to the walls is in the big tower). These walls are undergoing an extensive restoration, and the long, skinny strip running over the ridge to the town of Mali Ston (described next) is already complete. For a short wall experience, you can just do a circle around the stout lower walls (about 30 minutes); for a more serious hike, you can climb all the way up and over to Mali Ston (figure an hour or more). Be warned that the walls can be blazing hot—with all that glistening limestone reflecting heat—and there's virtually no shade (40 kn to enter walls regardless of how far you walk, daily April-Oct 8:00-19:30, Nov-March generally 9:00-15:00).

Other than the walls, there's not much to do in Ston. The town's deserted feel is a result of a devastating 1996 earthquake, from which Ston is still rebuilding. But there are several inviting cafés for a lazy drink and various places to grab a sandwich or pizza slice. If you want a serious sit-down meal, skip Ston's mediocre offerings and head over to Mali Ston instead.

Eating near Ston, in Mali Ston: From Ston, the walls scamper over a ridge to its little sister, the bayside village of Mali Ston ("Small Ston"). Surrounded by a similar, but smaller, fortified wall, Mali Ston is known for its many mussel and oyster farms, and for its good restaurants. A local favorite is **Kapetanova Kuća,** a memorable place with a fine location on Mali Ston's waterfront. Celebrity chef Lidija Kralj prides herself on her unpretentious but delicious food, made with fresh produce from the restaurant's own garden. For dessert, her bizarre *makaruli*—macaroni cake—is tastier than it sounds (10-kn cover charge, 100-130-kn seafood and meat dishes, daily 9:00-23:00, tel. 020/754-264).

Near the entrance to Kapetanova Kuća's parking lot, look for the simple **oyster shack/souvenir kiosk**, where local women sell fresh oysters and mussels from the adjacent bay and Pelješac wine decanted into plastic water bottles—all for cheap.

PELJEŠAC WINE COUNTRY

Farther along, the sparsely developed Pelješac Peninsula is blanketed with vineyards. Wine is the draw here, and a variety of vintners open their doors for passing visitors to sample their products. While it's a bit distant from Dubrovnik (about a two-hour drive to the heart of the wine-producing area), it's a worthwhile pilgrimage for wine lovers—or even just wine likers—and an easy stop-off for those driving from Korčula. Pelješac is an overlooked gem, and feels like a throwback to an age when wine tastings were relaxed, chatty, and fun, rather than corporate and rushed.

Tours of Pelješac: To really do the peninsula justice, consider hiring a guide to take you for a spin around Pelješac. **Sasha Lušić,** who runs the D'Vino Wine Bar in Dubrovnik, is a gregarious Aussie-Croat. He prides himself on taking you to a wide variety of vintners, who represent the best of what's happening here. Sasha's tours, which flex from day to day based on his customers' interests and stamina, can go late into the evening (other options include cheaper half-day tours to areas closer to Dubrovnik—prices depend on what's included—and traditional *peka* lunch or sunset seaside dinner, www.dvino.net, sasha@dvino.net). Other Dubrovnik-based drivers also do good wine tours (which also include several other worthwhile, scenic stops), including **Petar Vlašić** (see page 288).

⊖ Self-Guided Driving Tour

I've arranged this tour in the order you'll come from the tip of Pelješac (Orebić, just across the channel from Korčula). If you're doing it from Dubrovnik, begin by driving all the way to the village of Potomje (you can skip the section between there and Orebić) and visit the wineries on your way back (since it's a long, skinny peninsula, you'll have to backtrack anyway). I've included a detour to some of Croatia's finest (and largely undiscovered) vineyards. For a primer before you start, see "Croatian Wine" on page 32.

If you're crossing from Korčula Island, you'll begin the tour in **Orebić.** It's basically one main road from here back to Ston (where you'll meet up with the main coastal road to Dubrovnik or Split), so you can't really get lost—though we will make an off-the-beaten-path vineyard detour.

Follow the main road (toward Dubrovnik and Split) up, up, up for about 15 minutes to a dramatic **viewpoint** (there's a pullout on the right with benches—watch for the giant wine bottle) looking back toward Korčula. The jagged cliffs to your left are the Pelješac Peninsula (where we're about to drive), and the island poking out to the left is Mljet National Park. Straight ahead is Korčula, and behind that, the island of Lastovo. On a clear day, you can almost see to Italy. Below you and to the right, you can see some vineyards in the **Postup** wine-growing region; to the left (not quite visible from here) are the vineyards of **Dingač.** These are the two best wine-growing regions of Pelješac: Both areas are steeply angled, so they catch a maximum amount of sun, which creates very sweet grapes that produce high-alcohol, very dark (actually called "black" in Croatian) wine with strong legs (or, as Croatians call them, "tears"). The rugged, rocky limestone provides natural irrigation (since water can flow freely through it), and the high winds here keep off bugs and other pests. It all adds up to extremely healthy vines; because disease is rare, pesticides are not needed.

Continuing along the road, you'll crest the hill and pass the turnoff for Trpanj (where ferries connect to the mainland); soon after, watch on the left for the **Peninsula Wine Bar.** Owned by local vintners Boris and Baldo, and run by Rastafarian Pero, this

Sampling Pelješac Wines

Most Pelješac wines are made with *plavac mali* ("little blue") grapes, a distant relative of California zinfandel (they're called "son of zinfandel") and Italian *primitivo*. These wines are usually quite "big," with lots of tannins and high alcohol content (thank the warm climate for that).

Reds from the *plavac mali* grape are the real draw here, even though they account for just a third of the production (most are whites, with a few rosés). Winery staff enjoy explaining that this small area has three entirely different terroirs. The flat, easy-to-harvest Potomje valley produces cheaper, lower-quality wines; bottles are generally labeled simply with the type of grape (for example, *plavac mali*). Just over the mountains are the steep, sea-facing, sun-drenched Dingač and Postup areas (Dingač wines, a notch up in quality, tend to have more finesse than the coarser Postup wines). Bottles from these areas are usually labeled with the region rather than the grape.

Some vintners are starting to blend the *plavac mali* grape with other red grapes, like cabernet franc, merlot, and marselan, which creates a softer, less robust wine.

place feels like a glorified truck stop. But it's ideal for one-stop shoppers who want to learn about and try wine from a variety of producers. They usually have about 30 wines available. You can sample wine by the taste (figure 5-25 kn for premium wine, look for tasting flights listed on the chalkboard), by the glass (15-60 kn each—most about 25 kn), or by the bottle (40-250 kn, most about 50 kn). Tastings are free if you buy a few bottles. They also offer tastings of local olive oil and grappa (April-Oct daily 9:00-23:00, closed Nov-March, tel. 020/742-503, www.peninsula.hr).

After the wine bar, you'll drop down into a **plateau** surrounded by cliffs. The vines you'll see in this so-called "continental" area are the same *plavac mali* grapes as in Postup and Dingač, but they receive less sun and are less sweet. Notice that many of the vines appear to be almost wild; these are older vineyards, which aren't irrigated, so they must let the vines grow this way to help them survive the hot summer months. This method maximizes yield but reduces quality. Newer vineyards are irrigated and use guide wires, and generally look more manicured.

Soon you'll arrive in the village of **Potomje,** which is at the center of this important wine-growing area and makes a perfect stop for wine tasting. Four wineries here welcome visitors and offer a helpful introduction to Pelješac wines; taken together, they deliver a good range in experience, from mom-and-pop to state-of-the-art: Matković, Madirazza, Matuško, and Violić. Violić is an appealingly Back Door experience, and worth saving for last. All are staffed by friendly English speakers who are eager to introduce you to their wines; while the tastings are free, it's good form to buy a bottle or two. (If you want a more elaborate tasting with food pairings or for a small group, call ahead.) Unless otherwise noted, these places open around 8:00-20:00, but close earlier in shoulder season and are generally closed in winter (Nov-March—but call ahead and they may be able to open for you, cash only). Most wineries also have various brandies to try (including *travarica*, an herb-infused brandy).

Start your tasting at the beginning of town on the right, where you can pull into the small tasting room of **Vina Matković.** The gentle owner, Željka, can pour you a sample of their well-balanced and reasonably priced wines (reds only, don't miss her blend with marselan grapes, June-Nov daily 9:00-20:00, call ahead at other times, mobile 091-211-1230, www.vinamatkovic.com).

Next, near the far end of town, look for the big, pink building of the **Madirazza** winery. Notice the roses that line the vineyards—like a canary in a coal mine, these are more quickly affected by disease than the vines, offering an early-warning system in the event of an unwanted infestation. Madirazza's oaky, fairly acidic wines cost 45-100 kn per bottle (reserve bottles for 140-250 kn, mobile 098-212-163, www.dingac.hr, Mina).

Across the main road from Madirazza's parking lot is a smaller road (marked with *Matuško* and *Tunel Dingač* signs) leading to the **Matuško** winery. This handsome winery sports a library-like tasting room and makes finer, less coarse wines than Madirazza's. The range of wines available to taste is exceptional (including a chardonnay and tasty rosé—although red is what they do best and most). If you ask nicely, you can visit the sprawling network of atmospheric cellars where tour groups sip wines between aging barrels (25-130-kn bottles, reserve bottles for 200-900 kn, good place for a WC stop, tel. 020/742-393, mobile 098-428-676 www.matusko-vina.hr).

Backtrack to the road that leads to the tunnel. As you face the entrance to the tunnel, turn left, following *Boris Violić* signs to the unassuming **Violić** family home and winery. Offering a good contrast to the polished and more mainstream-feeling wineries described above, chatty Boris Violić-Matuško and his charming wife Marine invite passing visitors to slow down and enjoy some home-style hospitality. In addition to sampling their wines (four reds and two whites made the "old-fashioned" way, 30-150-kn bottles), consider buying some brandy, olive oil, or their delicious grandma-made treats (Potomje 6, tel. 020/753-031, mobile 091-525-3731, www.vinavukas.com).

When you're ready to move on, look for the **tunnel** through the mountain marked *Tunel Dingač,* with the picture of a donkey. Before this tunnel was dug, beasts of burden trod surefootedly up and over this mountain to carry the grapes from Dingač, on the far side, to this village. The donkey remains a symbol of this wine-growing region. In the 1970s, this tunnel was built to make everyone's lives easier. Take advantage of it by driving through the mountain and into another world.

Popping out at the sea, you're in the heart of the **Dingač** vineyards. Turn left (toward *Borak*) and drive on the one-lane road above all those vines, with a green and jagged waterline that looks almost Celtic. (Drive carefully: While it's a paved road, it's narrow, with a very steep shoulder.) Croatia's best reds are lovingly raised right here, soaking up ample sunshine as they struggle against a very rocky soil (ideal for wine grapes). Locals explain  that these grapes are bathed in sunlight from every angle—not just the sun above, but the reflection of those rays from both the sea and the white soil. Dingač never freezes (unlike the valley), and rainfall runs off immediately through its porous limestone soil, making these plants very disease-resistant. By the time they are harvested, Dingač grapes are withered by the sun—halfway to raisins, packed with sugar, and ideal for producing top-quality and highly alcoholic wines. At the fork, continue down to the right, toward *Dingač/ Borak;* at the next fork, when the Borak road turns sharply down and to the right, keep going straight onto the smaller road.

As you drive, keep enjoying dramatic views of Mljet Island. When you enter an area of trees, look across the harbor to see a  building perched on a cliff over the water—that's our next stop. Soon you'll come to the village of Trstenik; at the T-intersection, make a sharp right turn, then turn left to pass along its little waterfront. At the far end of town, on the way up the hill, turn into the parking lot for the **Grgić** winery. Perhaps the best-known and best-regarded Croatian vintner, Mike Grgić's facility is less appealing than the others we've visited, and you have to pay for the tasting (30 kn)... but the fame of the wine may be worth it for some. (See page 32 for the story of how Grgić revolutionized both American and Croatian winemaking.) This place is surprisingly humble. Keeping things simple, Grgić does a white wine (*pošip*, with grapes grown on Korčula but produced here, 135 kn per bottle) and a red wine (210 kn per bottle); breaking with convention, he names his red simply *plavac mali* partly to help promote this largely unknown and underappreciated grape. He also sells wines from his California winery, Grgich Hills, at or below their California prices (200-440 kn; daily 9:00-17:00, tel. 020/748-090).

Exiting the winery, turn right (uphill) and twist up to the main road, where you'll turn right, toward Ston. Cresting the hill, you'll see the other side of the peninsula and the channel separating it from the mainland—as if to emphasize the narrowness of this spit of land. From here, you'll continue straight along all the way to Ston. You may be tempted by the *vino* signs in **Janjina,** but these are aimed mainly at Croatians buying table wine in bulk—100 liters at a time.

Leaving Janjina, keep following signs for *Ston* and *Dubrovnik*. You'll twist down and follow the **Bay of Ston,** which is famous for its shellfish production. Here where the Neretva River (which runs under Mostar's Old Bridge) empties into the sea, conditions are perfect for cultivating mussels, oysters, and clams. (You'll spot many such farms out in the bay—look for the areas roped off with buoys.) The road climbs up once more, passing the aptly named Bella Vista viewpoint café (which overlooks the dock for the ferry to the national park on Mljet Island), before continuing into the walled town of **Ston.** For more on that town—and a good restaurant in nearby **Mali Ston**—see page 354.

Leaving Ston, turn right (toward Dubrovnik) once you hit the main road; from here, it's about an hour back into town. En route, watch out for the speed traps at the towns of Doli and Orešac.

Mljet National Park

Carefully protected against modern development, the island hideaway of Mljet National Park (rated ▲) offers a unique back-to-nature escape. With ample opportunities for hiking, swimming, biking, and boating—and without a nightclub, tacky T-shirt, or concrete "beach" pad in sight—Mljet (muhl-YAYT) is appreciated by active, outdoorsy travelers.

Though Mljet Island is one of Dalmatia's largest, it has fewer than 1,500 residents. Nearly three-quarters of the island is covered

NEAR DUBROVNIK

Mljet National Park

To Korčula
via Excursion Boat

To Dubrovnik
via Krilo Catamaran
& Excursion Boat

To Dubrovnik
via Nona Ana
Catamaran

800 Meters
800 Yards

To Sobra
(Car Ferries)

Polače

SMALL
BRIDGE

Pomena

Govedari

Babine
Kuće

Pristanište

Montokuc

Soline

G r e a t
L a k e

*Small
Lake*

VELIKI
MOST

ST. MARY'S
CHURCH

A d r i a t i c   S e a

——— Paved Road
- - -   Path
·······   Boat

in forest, leaving it remarkably untamed. Aside from its beautiful national park, Mljet has inspired some of the most memorable tales of the Croatian coast—the poet Homer, his protagonist Ulysses, and the Apostle Paul all spent time here...or so the locals love to boast.

PLANNING YOUR TIME

While you could spend the night, it's more efficient to visit Mljet as a side-trip. In summer, this can be done by public catamaran: either the *Nona Ana* from Dubrovnik or the *Krilo* from Korčula. At other times—or from other home bases—you may find it easier to sign up for a package excursion.

No matter how you arrive, one day is plenty for Mljet. Here's a good plan: Start at Pristanište and catch the boat to the island in the Great Lake. Take the boat back to Mali Most (Small Bridge), where you can rent a bike for a pedal along the shore of the Great Lake. If you're heating up, take a dip in the Small Lake at the beach near the Small Bridge. When you're ready for a bit of civilization, walk into Pomena and relax by the seaside, then take the hotel's shuttle bus or a minibus-taxi back to your starting point to catch the catamaran back home. With more energy, skip Pomena and hike to the island's high point at Montokuc (you can hike down to Polače on the other side).

Be warned that everything here is very seasonal and weather-dependent, so visiting outside of peak season (June-Sept) may come with some frustration.

Orientation to Mljet

The island of Mljet is long (23 miles) and skinny (less than two miles wide). The national park occupies the western third of the island. You're likely to reach Mljet via one of three port towns. **Polače** (POH-lah-cheh) and **Pomena** (POH-meh-nah) are handy entry points into the national park, while **Sobra** (SOH-brah) is much less convenient (a 1.25-hour bus trip across the island from the park). The *Nona Ana* catamaran from Dubrovnik puts in at both Polače and Sobra; the *Krilo* catamaran and most excursions use Pomena; and car ferries to the mainland use Sobra.

Polače and Pomena flank the heart of the national park, a pair of saltwater "lakes" called simply **Great Lake** (Veliko Jezero) and **Small Lake** (Malo Jezero). The two bodies of water meet at a cute little bridge, appropriately named **Small Bridge** (Mali Most), where you can rent kayaks and bikes and catch a boat out to the little **island** in the Great Lake. A 15-minute walk around the Great Lake from the Small Bridge brings you to **Pristanište** (meaning, roughly, "transit hub"), where you can also catch a boat to the island or a shuttle bus to Polače. The nearby cliff-climbing town of **Goveđari** is home to many of the people who work at the park, but is not interesting to tourists.

Everything's well-signed, but it's worth investing in a detailed park map (available at the entry kiosk).

TOURIST INFORMATION

The **TI** is in Polače, just across from where the *Nona Ana* catamaran from Dubrovnik docks (tel. 020/744-186). The island's lone hotel, the **Hotel Odisej** in Pomena, acts as a second tourist information point. The hotel is a hub of services for visitors (whether you stay there or not): bike, scooter, car, and boat rentals, scuba diving lessons, walking tours around the island, cruises to some of the island's caves, and even help finding private accommodations. For more on the hotel, see "Sleeping and Eating on Mljet," later.

The general-information website for the island (which covers the towns, Hotel Odisej, *sobe* and apartments, and more) is www.mljet.hr; for information on the national park, visit www.np-mljet.hr (or call 020/744-041).

ARRIVAL IN MLJET

At Polače: From the boat dock, you'll pass the TI, then walk a few minutes up the coast (near the Roman ruins) to a kiosk where you can buy your park entry ticket and catch a minibus to the Pristanište transit hub at the Great Lake (coordinated with boat arrival). Once at Pristanište, you can take a boat out to the island in the Great Lake (about hourly), or walk around the lake toward the Small Bridge, Small Lake, and on to Pomena.

At Pomena: If you arrive at Pomena, exit the boat to the left (passing Hotel Odisej) and buy your park entry ticket at the kiosk. A few steps up the road beyond the kiosk, you'll see a shortcut to the right that takes you up and down some steps on your way to the Small Lake; once at the lake, bear left and continue to the Small Bridge, where you can catch the boat to the island in the Great Lake or rent a bike or kayak.

Note that there's no official bus between Polače and Pomena, but Hotel Odisej operates a shuttle to coincide with the Dubrovnik catamaran. The island also has some informal minibus-taxis.

At Sobra: If you come on a car ferry into Sobra, it's about a 1.25-hour bus trip on twisty roads to reach the Polače/Pomena tourist hub. Avoid arriving via Sobra unless you're desperate.

Sights at Mljet National Park

The 70-kn **entry fee** (80 kn in July-Aug) includes access to the following sights, plus the shuttle bus from Polače to the Great Lake. The park is open daily May-mid-Oct 7:00-19:00 (shorter hours in shoulder season, closed Nov-Feb).

The Lakes

The "Great Lake" and "Small Lake" are technically saltwater bays—fed by the sea and affected by ocean currents (as you'll clearly see if you're at the little channel by the Small Bridge at the right time of day). Scientists love these lakes, which contain various shellfish species unique to Mljet.

The Island

The main activity in the park is taking a boat out to the Great Lake's little island-in-an-island (20 kn round-trip, boats depart about hourly from the Small Bridge and from Pristanište). The tiny island's main landmark is St. Mary's Church (Sv. Marija) and the attached monastery, left behind by Benedictine monks who lived on Mljet starting in the 12th century. Though the monastery complex has been modified over the ages, fragments of the original Romanesque structure still survive. You can hike the easy trail up to the top of the island, passing remains of fortifications and old chapels, and look for the island's only permanent residents: a hand-

The Tales of Mljet

For a mostly undeveloped island, Mljet has had a surprisingly busy history. Home to Illyrians, Greeks, Romans, Slavs, Venetians, Habsburgs, Yugoslavs, and now Croatians, the island has hosted some interesting visitors (or supposed visitors) that it loves to brag about.

Around the eighth century B.C., the Greek epic poet Homer possibly spent time here. He was so inspired by Mljet that he used it as the setting for one of the adventures of his hero Ulysses (a.k.a. Odysseus). This is the island where Ulysses fell in love with a beautiful nymph named Calypso and shacked up with her in a cave for seven years. Today there's a much-vaunted "Ulysses' Cave" (Odisejeva Spilja), a 40-minute hike below the island's main town, Babino Polje (at the far end of the island—skip it unless you're a Ulysses groupie).

Flash forward nearly a millennium, when a real-life traveler found his way to Mljet. According to the Bible (Acts 28), the Apostle Paul was shipwrecked on an island called "Melita"—likely this one—for three months. While on the island, Paul was bitten by a deadly snake, which he threw into a fire. The natives were amazed that he wasn't affected by the poison, and he proceeded to cure their ailments. This event was long believed to have happened on the similarly named isle of Malta, in the Mediterranean Sea. But more recently, many historians began to believe that Paul was on Mljet. The most convincing argument: Malta never had poisonous snakes. Incidentally, Mljet no longer does, either—the Habsburgs imported an army of Indian mongooses to rid the island of problematic serpents. Because of this historical footnote, people from Mljet are nicknamed "mongooses" by other Croatians.

The heroics continue with today's "mongooses." There have been more than 100 fires on the island in the last 20 years (most caused by lightning, some by careless visitors), but only three have spread and caused significant destruction. That's because the people of Mljet—well aware of the fragility of the island that provides their income—are also a crack volunteer firefighting force, ready to spring into action and save their home at the first wisp of smoke.

ful of goats, donkeys, and chickens. You'll have about an hour to explore, but it only takes half that to see everything—then relax with an overpriced drink at the restaurant by the boat dock.

Biking

The Great Lake is surrounded by a paved, mostly level road that's good for an hour or two of pedaling. (The path is broken by the channel connecting the lakes to the sea, but you can likely flag down a taxi boat to ferry you across for a small fee.) The unpaved path around the Small Lake is rough and rocky, making biking there more difficult. The handiest place to rent a bike for a quick ride around the Great Lake is right at the lake itself, by the Small Bridge. Other bike rental points are scattered around the island, including in both Polače and Pomena. But those towns are separated from the lakes—and from each other—by steep hills, making cycling from either town to the lakes a headache for casual bikers.

Swimming

Options are everywhere, most temptingly at the Great Lake and Small Lake. Even though it's fed by seawater, the Small Lake is always slightly warmer than the sea. The beach by the Small Bridge is particularly handy (but there are no showers or WCs).

Boating

You can rent kayaks at the Small Bridge. Motorized boats—except for the occasional local resident's dinghy—aren't allowed on the island's lakes.

Hiking to Montokuc

The most rewarding hike takes you up to the national park's highest point, Montokuc. At 830 feet above sea level, this is a serious hike up a steep hill—skip it unless you're in good shape, and be sure to bring water. The trail runs between Polače, at the north end of the island, and the village of Soline, beyond the far end of the Great Lake (past the old, broken bridge called Veliki Most). If you're doing this or any other hike, the park map is essential (sold at park entry kiosks and other merchants).

Sleeping and Eating on Mljet

($$ = €95 or more; $ = €95 or less)

$$ Hotel Odisej, the only hotel on the island, has more charm than most renovated communist hotels. Sitting right on the waterfront, with 157 rooms, it's a predictably comfortable home base (rates flex with demand, closed mid-Oct-mid-April, tel. 020/362-111, www.hotelodisej.hr).

$ Sobe *and Apartments:* Mljet has a wide range of private accommodations, with a few in each town or village. If you arrive without a room, the TI in Polače or Hotel Odisej in Pomena can help you find something. If you're looking in advance, check out the island website, www.mljet.hr. I'd choose a place in the population centers of Polače or Pomena (for their easy access to the park) or in the cute Great Lake-front village of Babine Kuće (near the Small Bridge).

For **eating,** many good restaurants are scattered around the island. There isn't one that's particularly worth seeking out—just eat when it fits your itinerary (or bring a picnic).

Mljet Connections

By Catamaran: Two catamarans connect Mljet to other major destinations (schedules vary from year to year, so be sure to confirm details carefully on each company's website). The *Krilo* cata-maran, which uses the dock at Pomena, offers more departures (daily June-Sept, 3-4/week May and Oct) and more destinations: From Mljet, it heads south to Dubrovnik (1.5 hours); and north to Korčula (1 hour), Hvar (2 hours), and Split (3 hours). For details on the *Krilo*—and to book tickets in advance—see www.krilo. hr. A different option, the *Nona Ana* catamaran, heads to Dubrovnik each afternoon in summer from both Sobra (1 hour) and Polače (the best choice for day-trippers, 1.5 hours). On some days in the peak months of July and August, the *Nona Ana* also heads north in the morning to Korčula (4/week, 1 hour). In winter (Oct-May), the boat runs only from Sobra to Dubrovnik. For more on the *Nona Ana*—which can sell out, especially in peak season—see www.gv-line.hr.

By Car Ferry: For drivers, a car ferry connects the town of Prapratno (near the base of the Pelješac Peninsula, not far from Ston) to Sobra on Mljet (for schedules, see www.jadrolinija.hr). Once at Sobra, it's at least a 30-minute drive to the park.

By Excursion: Many destinations are more conveniently connected to Mljet by excursion than by public transit. While you don't need a guide to enjoy the island, the simple convenience of round-trip transportation makes this worth considering.

MONTENEGRO
Crna Gora

MONTENEGRO

The Bay of Kotor • Kotor • The Montenegrin Interior
• The Budva Riviera

If Dubrovnik is the grand finale of a Croatian vacation, then Montenegro is the encore. One of Europe's youngest nations awaits you just south of the border, with dramatic scenery, friendly locals proud of their unique land, and a rough-around-the-edges appeal.

Crossing the border (with passport ready—Montenegro is not yet part of the EU), you know you've left sleek and tidy Croatia for a place that's gritty, raw, and a bit exotic. While Croatia's showpiece Dalmatian Coast avoided the drab, boxy dullness of the Yugoslav era, less affluent Montenegro wasn't so lucky. Between the dramatic cliffs and time-passed villages, you'll drive past grimy, broken-down apartment blocks and some truly unfortunate concrete architecture. Montenegro is also a noticeably poorer country than its northern neighbor.

Historically, Montenegro has been even more of a crossroads of cultures than Croatia. In some ways, there are two Montenegros: the remote, rugged, rustic mountaintop kingdom that feels culturally close to Serbia; and this chapter's focus, the sun-drenched coastline of staggeringly strategic importance that has attracted a steady stream of rulers over the millennia. At one point or another, just about every group you can imagine has planted its flag here—from the usual suspects (Venetians, Austrians, Russian czars) to oddball one-offs (Bulgarian kingdoms, Napoleon's Ljubljana-based Illyrian Provinces). In spite of their schizophrenic lineage, or maybe because of it, Montenegrins have forged a unique cultural identity that defies many of the preconceived notions of the Balkans. Are they like Serbs or Croats? Do they use the Cyrillic or the Roman alphabet? Do they worship the Roman Catholic God or the Eastern Orthodox one? Yes, all of the above.

Since Montenegro gained independence in 2006, its coast has become a powerful magnet for a very specific breed of traveler: multimillionaires from Russia and the Middle East, who have chosen to turn this impressionable, fledgling country—with its gorgeous coastline—into their very own Riviera. The Tivat airport is jammed with charter flights from Moscow, signs along the coast advertise Russian-language radio stations, and an extravagant luxury yacht marina recently opened near Tivat (Porto Montenegro, www.portomontenegro.com). And so Montenegro finds itself in an awkward position: trying to cultivate an image as a high-roller luxury paradise, while struggling to upgrade what is—in places—a nearly Third World infrastructure. Glittering new €500-a-night boutique hotels are built, then suffer power and water outages. Lower your expectations, and don't expect a fancy facade and high prices to come with predictable quality.

Still, nothing can mar the natural beauty of Montenegro's mountains, bays, and forests. For a look at the untamed Adriatic,

a spin on the winding road around Montenegro's steep and secluded Bay of Kotor is a must. The area's main town, also called Kotor, has been protected from centuries of would-be invaders by its position at the deepest point of the fjord—and by its imposing town wall, which scrambles in a zigzag line up the mountain behind it. Wander the enjoyably seedy streets of Kotor, drop into some Orthodox churches, and sip a coffee at an al fresco café.

With more time, romantics can corkscrew up into the mountains to sample the Balkans' best smoked ham at Njeguši and visit the remote, original capital of the country at Cetinje, beach bums can head for the Budva Riviera, and celebrity-seekers can daydream about past glories at the striking hotel-peninsula of Sveti Stefan.

GETTING TO MONTENEGRO

This chapter is designed for day-tripping to Montenegro from Dubrovnik; all of the sights are within about a three-hour drive of Dubrovnik, and within about an hour of each other. If you're arriving in Montenegro by cruise (as many visitors do these days), read the sidebar on page 376.

By Car: Driving is the best option, giving you maximum flexibility for sightseeing—but be aware of possible border delays (see "Helpful Hints," later). I've narrated a self-guided driving tour of the Bay of Kotor, and another for the most accessible slice of the

MONTENEGRO

Montenegro Almanac

Official Name: After being part of "Yugoslavia," then "Serbia and Montenegro," it's now the Republic of Montenegro (Republika Crna Gora)—which means "Black Mountain." It might have gotten its name from sailors who saw darkly forested cliffs as they approached, or it may have been named for a mythical mountain in the country's interior.

Snapshot History: Long overshadowed by its Croatian and Serbian neighbors, Montenegro finally achieved independence on June 3, 2006, in a landmark vote to secede from Serbia—its influential and sometimes overbearing "big brother."

Population: Montenegro is home to about 650,000 people. Of these, the vast majority are Eastern Orthodox Christians (45 percent Montenegrins, 29 percent Serbs), with minority groups of Muslims (including Bosniaks and Albanians, about 11 percent total) and Catholics (1 percent).

Area: 5,415 square miles (slightly smaller than Connecticut).

Red Tape: Americans and Canadians need only a passport (no visa required) to enter Montenegro.

Geography: Montenegro is characterized by a rugged, rocky terrain that rises straight up from the Adriatic and almost immediately becomes a steep mountain range. The country has 182 miles of coastline, about a third of which constitutes the Bay of Kotor. The only real city is the dreary capital in the interior, Podgorica (190,000 people). Each of Yugoslavia's six republics had a town called Titograd, and Podgorica was Montenegro's.

Economy: Upon declaring independence in 2006, Montenegro's economy was weak. But the privatization of its economy (includ-

---

Montenegrin interior. Even if you don't have a rental car during your Dubrovnik visit, consider renting one just for the day to visit Montenegro. Perhaps most satisfying—but more pricey—is to hire your own Dubrovnik-based driver to bring you here (my favorites are recommended on page 288). While this is expensive (€250 for the day), you can try to team up with other travelers to share the cost.

By Bus: Bus service between Dubrovnik and Montenegro is workable but infrequent (2-3/day each way between Dubrovnik and Kotor town, 2.5 hours). It's possible to day-trip from Dubrovnik to Kotor, but it's a long day on the bus: The first morning bus departs Dubrovnik at 7:00, arriving in Kotor around 9:30 (later if there are delays); the return bus departs Kotor at 14:45 (reaching Dubrovnik around 17:00). Keep in mind that if you ride the bus, you can't stop to explore the sights along the way. As the schedule is always in

ing its dominant industry, aluminum) and the aggressive development of its tourist trade (such as soliciting foreign investment—mostly Russian—to build new luxury hotels) have turned things around. In fact, in recent years, Montenegro has had one of the highest foreign investment rates in Europe. Still, it remains a poor place: Montenegro's unemployment rate hovers around 19 percent, and its per capita GDP is just $15,000.

Currency: Though it's not a member of the European Union, Montenegro uses the euro as its currency: €1 = about $1.10.

Language and Alphabet: The official language is Montenegrin, which is nearly identical to Serbian but predominantly uses "our" Roman alphabet (rather than Cyrillic). Still, you'll see plenty of Cyrillic here—targeting the country's large Serb minority as well as Russian tourists and investors.

Telephones: Montenegro's country code is 382. When calling from another country, first dial the international access code (00 from Europe, 011 from the US), then 382, then the area code (minus the initial zero), then the number. Note that Montenegro recently changed its area codes. If you see the former code for the Bay of Kotor area, 082, you'll have to replace it with the new one: 032.

Flag: It's a red field surrounded by a gold fringe. In the middle is the national seal: a golden, two-headed Byzantine eagle topped with a single crown, holding a scepter in one hand and a ball in the other (symbolizing the balance between church and state). The eagle's body is covered by a shield depicting a lion with one paw raised (representing the resurrected Christ).

flux, it's important to confirm times carefully at the Dubrovnik TI or bus station.

It's also possible to take a bus from Montenegro to **Mostar** in Bosnia-Herzegovina; it's a long journey (8-9 hours), but you can choose between two scenic routes: via Trebinje (the mountainous interior) or via Dubrovnik (coastal scenery). For details, see "Kotor Connections" on page 400.

By Excursion: As a last resort, consider taking a package excursion that follows basically the same route covered in this chapter (sold by various travel agencies in Dubrovnik; see page 344).

PLANNING YOUR TIME

Assuming you have your own car, for a straightforward one-day plan, drive to Kotor and back (figure about eight hours, including driving time and sightseeing stops). To extend your time, you can add as much Montenegro as you like. Get an early start (to avoid lines at the border, I'd leave Dubrovnik as early as 7:30). It takes about two hours to drive from Dubrovnik to Kotor (add about 1.5 hours if you stop in Perast for the boat trip out to the island). Kotor is worth two or three hours. From Kotor, you can return directly to Dubrovnik (about 1.5 hours if you use the ferry shortcut—see page 387); or drive another hour up to Njeguši and Cetinje in the Montenegrin interior, or a half-hour to the Budva Riviera (from either place, figure about 2.5-3 hours back to Dubrovnik). To cram everything into one extremely long day, you can do Dubrovnik-Kotor-Cetinje-Budva Riviera-Dubrovnik.

HELPFUL HINTS

Border Delays: The main Croatian-Montenegrin border is at Debeli Brijeg. When it's not busy, this border is relatively straightforward—just stop and show your passport and your car's "green card" (proof of insurance). However, there can be delays here on very busy days—especially on Saturdays in August, and to a lesser degree in July and early September. To avoid long backups, you have two options: Get an early start (locals suggest reaching the border by 8:00—leaving Dubrovnik around 7:30 or 7:45 to beat the tour buses); or use the secondary crossing, called Konfin, which rarely has much of a line (big buses are not allowed). While the Konfin border can save you time on a busy day, it's a bit less straightforward (with a few turn-offs rather than a straight shot on the main road), and takes a few more miles. I've narrated a scenic route ("Konfin Border Detour") in my self-guided driving tour, later.

Afternoon Delays: The Debeli Brijeg border crossing can also be severely delayed coming back to Dubrovnik in the afternoon. (Lines are worst in summer around 16:00 or 17:00—when a long chain of excursion buses all head back at the same time.) If this happens, use the secondary (and much less crowded) Konfin border crossing. For tips, see page 377.

Local Guide: While many Dubrovnik-based drivers/guides can bring you to Montenegro, if you really want the Montenegrin perspective, consider hiring a local guide here. I spent a great day learning about this area from **Stefan Đukanović,** a young, energetic, knowledgeable guide who speaks good English and has an infectious enthusiasm for his homeland. Hiring Stefan is a great value. The catch is that he can't come and get you in Dubrovnik, so it works best if you drive yourself to Montenegro and pick him up when you get there. Stefan is also an excellent choice if you're arriving in Kotor by cruise ship (guiding only: €60/half-day, €80/day, extra for driver if going outside of Kotor; several shore excursions possible—contact for details and rates, mobile 069-297-221 or 069-369-994, www.miroandsons.com, djukan@t-com.me).

The Bay of Kotor

With dramatic cliffs rising out of the glimmering Adriatic, ancient towns packed with history and thrilling vistas, an undeveloped ruggedness unlike anything in Croatia, and a twisty road to tie it all together, the Bay of Kotor represents the best of Montenegro. To top it off, it's easy to reach by car from Dubrovnik. (Don't forget your passport.)

Bay of Kotor Driving Tour

The Bay of Kotor (Boka Kotorska—literally the "Mouth of Kotor"; sometimes called "Boka Bay") is Montenegro's most enjoyable and convenient attraction for those based in Dubrovnik. This self-guided day trip—worth ▲▲—narrates the drive from the Croatian border to the town of Kotor, in the Bay of Kotor's deepest corner.

The Montenegrin border is about 40 minutes south of Dubrovnik. Simply follow the main coastal road south (signs to *Ćilipi*), past Cavtat and the airport.

From Dubrovnik to the Border

As you leave Dubrovnik, the jagged cliffs on your left eventually give way to a pastoral countryside called **Konavle** (literally "canal," recalling how the Romans built aqueducts through this area to supply their settlement at today's Cavtat). This farming region—effectively Dubrovnik's hinterland—was badly damaged during the Yugoslav Wars, when the Yugoslav People's Army invaded from the south, forcing villagers to flee to safety in Dubrovnik. But today it's bouncing back, and is home to many appealing *konobas* (taverns) serving traditional local food.

Soon after the turn-off for the Bosnian border, on the right, you'll pass **Kupari**, with one of the few buildings in the area that still has war damage. Originally Tito's villa, the building later became a vacation home for Yugoslav military officers. Now it's a ruin, awaiting investors.

From Kupari, you'll curl around the picturesque **Bay of Cavtat**, where some of the world's richest people tie up their yachts. Partway along the bay, after the village of Plat, you'll pass (on the left) an electrical plant, which harnesses the power of an underground river to generate more than enough clean energy for the entire city.

After the pleasant resort town of **Cavtat** (described on page

MONTENEGRO

MONTENEGRO

Cruising into Kotor

With cruise-ship crowds reaching capacity in nearby Dubrovnik, the Montenegrin town of Kotor has emerged as a hugely popular port of call on Mediterranean cruises. If you're one of them, here are some pointers.

Arrival in Kotor by Cruise Ship: It's easy. Ships either dock at or tender to the long pier that juts out directly in front of the Old Town. All passengers are funneled out of the same port gate, with the Old Town straight ahead. As you leave the port gate, look left to find an **ATM** in a freestanding orange kiosk (the main square of the Old Town, less than a five-minute walk away, also has ATMs); and look right to see an official **taxi** stand. (Unscrupulous taxis have been known to camp out near here to commandeer cruise passengers; be sure to use one at an official stand, and with a taxi logo and phone number on the side of the car.)

Exiting the port gate, continue straight ahead with the water on your right. Watch for the crosswalk (on your left, marked with brown *Kotor* sign) over the busy harborfront road, which you can use to get to the square in front of the Old Town, the TI, and the start of my self-guided walk.

Amenities: Free **Wi-Fi** is available near the TI kiosk. The two **pharmacies** in the Old Town are open long hours daily (for locations, see the map on page 389).

Sightseeing Options: The **Old Town of Kotor** itself is the obvious place to spend your day—though seeing everything, including my self-guided orientation walk and all of the museums—won't take you more than a couple of hours. Add a couple more hours if you're up for the stiff hike to the fortress above town (and maybe another hour or so just to recover). With more time, you may want to venture farther afield. The easiest choice is **Perast,** where you can explore a seaside village and ride a small boat out to one of the islands in the middle of the fjord (for details, see page 383); allow about four hours total for the round-trip to Perast and the island. Public buses connect Kotor town to Perast, or you can spring for a taxi (legitimate cabbies charge €20-25 one-way or €40-50 round-trip, including waiting time; negotiate a fixed price up front). For either of these trips—or to reach other, more distant Montenegrin destinations explained in this chapter—consider hiring a **local guide;** I recommend Stefan Đukanović, listed on page 374.

Sail-in and Sail-away: Cruisers visiting Kotor are treated to a spectacular sail-in and sail-away, through the fjordlike bay and the narrow Verige Strait. If the weather's good and you enjoy dramatic scenery, this is not a day to sleep in or nap during the sail-away.

348), then the airport, you have the option of turning off (on the right, toward *Molunat*) to take advantage of the less crowded border crossing at Konfin (described next). Otherwise, just cruise along the main road until you reach the primary Debeli Brijeg border crossing. (If there's a line-up when you arrive, it's easy to backtrack to the alternate crossing: Just after the town of Gruda, follow signs for *Pločice,* then *Vitaljina,* then *Herceg Novi,* joining up with the route described next.)

Optional Konfin Border Detour

If you suspect that there will be long lines at the primary border crossing (in the peak of summer)—or if you simply prefer a longer and more scenic route—consider this uncongested detour via the secondary border, at Konfin. Soon after passing the airport, take the turn-off on the right for *Molunat.* You'll pass through a tranquil, nearly Tuscan landscape of pointy cypresses, vineyards, olive groves, and fig trees. Just before the village of Radovčići, on the right, watch for **Kojan Koral,** a horse farm that has hosted movie-star equines for the HBO show *Game of Thrones.* They offer horseback rides and ATV safaris (www.kojankoral.hr).

Farther along, you'll enjoy fine views (on the right) down on the dramatic, elongated peninsula of **Molunat.** Notice that the H-shaped peninsula forms two protected bays. The larger one, facing north (toward Dubrovnik), is used to harbor ships in winter, while the smaller, south-facing one is better in summer.

When the road reaches a T-intersection, turn left for *Dubrovnik* and *Park Prevlaka,* then follow signs right for *Đurinići,* then right again for *Vitaljina.* As you continue on this road—through the villages of Đurinići, Višnjići, and Vitaljina—high on the mountains to your left is the point locals call **Tromeđe** ("Three Borders"), where Croatia, Bosnia-Herzegovina, and Montenegro converge.

Continue straight along this road all the way to the border, following signs for *Herceg Novi* and *GP Konfin.* You'll pass a turn-off on the right for **Park Prevlaka,** an old Austro-Hungarian and Yugoslav army fortress that has recently been converted into a park; you can see it at the tip of the peninsula poking out on your right—the southernmost point in Croatia.

Before long, you'll arrive at the Croatian border post, and then the Montenegrin one. After entering Montenegro, you'll curve along the small bay into Igalo, where you can pick up the self-guided driving tour.

• *From either border, you can make it to Kotor in about an hour without stopping, but with all the diversions en route you should plan for much more time. Navigating on this tour is really simple: It's basically*

MONTENEGRO

MONTENEGRO

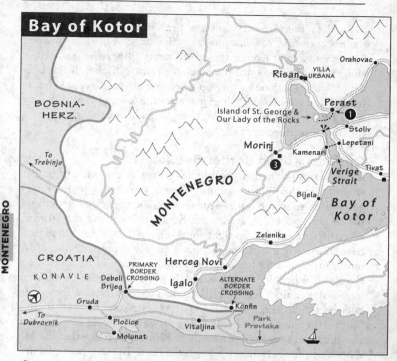

Bay of Kotor

Orahovac

VILLA URBANA

Risan

Island of St. George &
Our Lady of the Rocks

Perast ❶

Stoliv

Lepetani

Morinj

Kamenari

❸

Tivat

To Trebinje

MONTENEGRO

Verige Strait

Bijela

Bay of Kotor

BOSNIA-HERZ.

Zelenika

CROATIA

KONAVLE

PRIMARY BORDER CROSSING

Herceg Novi

Debeli Brijeg

Igalo

ALTERNATE BORDER CROSSING

Gruda

Konfin

To Dubrovnik

Pločice

Vitaljina

Park Prevlaka

Molunat

the same road, with no turn-offs, from Dubrovnik to Kotor. First, you'll approach the coast at the town called...

Igalo

Driving through Igalo, keep an eye out (on the right) for a big concrete hotel called **Institut Dr. Simo Milošević** (no relation to war-criminal Slobodan). This internationally regarded spa is one of the world's premier treatment facilities for arthritis and nerve disorders. Especially popular among Scandinavians, it's capable of hosting more than 1,000 patients at once. Yugoslav President-for-Life Tito had a villa nearby and took treatments here.

• *A couple of miles beyond Igalo, you enter the biggest city you'll see today...*

Herceg Novi

The drab economic and industrial capital of the Bay of Kotor, Herceg Novi (with 25,000 people) is hardly the prettiest introduction to this otherwise striking landscape. Herceg Novi flourished during the Habsburg boom of the late 19th century, when a railroad line connected it to Dubrovnik, Sarajevo, and Vienna. Back then, Austrians vacationed here—but more recent development has been decidedly less elegant than the Habsburgs'. While there is a walled Old Town core to Herceg Novi, it's not worth stopping to see; skip

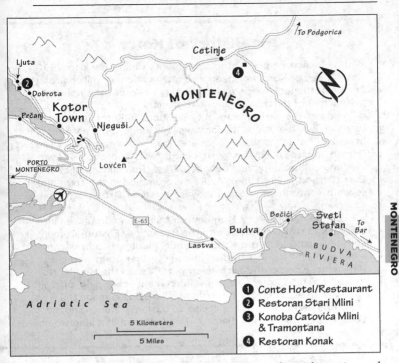

Map labels: To Podgorica · Cetinje · Ljuta · Dobrota · Kotor Town · Prčanj · Njeguši · MONTENEGRO · PORTO MONTENEGRO · Lovćen · E-65 · Lastva · Bečići · Budva · Sveti Stefan · To Bar · BUDVA RIVIERA · Adriatic Sea · 5 Kilometers · 5 Miles

1. Conte Hotel/Restaurant
2. Restoran Stari Mlini
3. Konoba Ćatovića Mlini & Tramontana
4. Restoran Konak

the turnoff for the town center, carrying on along the main road toward Budva.

Passing above Herceg Novi's Old Town, keep an eye out on the right for the town's stout 15th-century **fortress,** which was built by the Ottomans—who controlled this area, but never made it deeper into the bay.

Also in Herceg Novi, watch for tropical trees. Locals pride themselves on their particularly mild climate, sheltered by the fjord. Supposedly, "it never drops below 50 degrees Fahrenheit." Town symbols include banana trees and the mimosa flower, which blooms all winter long. Each February, as much of Europe (and most of Montenegro) is under a blanket of snow, Herceg Novi proudly hosts a Mimosa Festival.

Despite its tropical cachet, however, Herceg Novi is basically a mess. (Don't worry—the drive gets much prettier later on.) Why so much ugliness compared to Croatia? For one thing, Tito viewed Croatia's Dalmatian Coast as a gold mine of hard Western currency—so he was inclined to keep it Old World-charming. But in Montenegro, a heritage of corruption and bribery spurred some unfortunate construction. ("Would a few thousand dinar convince you to ignore my new hotel's code violations?") From an architectural point of view, it's a sad irony that gorgeous Dubrovnik was devastated by bombs while the gritty cities of Montenegro survived

The History of Kotor

With evidence of prehistoric settlements dating back to 2500 B.C., the Bay of Kotor has been a prized location for millennia. Its unique bottleneck shape makes the Bay of Kotor the single best natural harbor between Greece and Venice.

One of the earliest known civilizations in Kotor (third century B.C.) was that of the Illyrians, whose Queen Teuta held court here until her lands were conquered by the Romans. After the Roman Empire split in the fourth century A.D., Montenegro straddled the cultural fault line between West (Roman Catholic) and East (Orthodox Christian). As Rome crumbled in the sixth and seventh centuries, the Slavs moved in (some Orthodox, some Catholic).

By the 10th century, Montenegro's Slavs had organized into a sovereign state, affiliated with the Byzantine (Eastern Roman) Empire. Thanks to its protected location, medieval Kotor became a major city of the salt trade. The area further flourished in the 14th century, under the Serbian emperor Dušan the Mighty. Notorious for his aggressive law enforcement—chopping off the hand of a thief, slicing off the nose of a liar—Dušan made the Bay of Kotor a particularly safe place to do business. If a visiting merchant was robbed, the nobleman who controlled that land would

the war essentially unscathed. Today, Montenegro is encouraging the construction of top-end resort hotels to lure high rollers from around the world (such as James Bond, who came to "Montenegro" to join a poker tournament at the Casino Royale—actually filmed in the Czech Republic). But this new development is poorly regulated, threatening to turn Montenegro into a charmless, concrete Costa del Sol-style vacation zone. Enjoy the Bay of Kotor's pristine areas (which we'll enter soon) while you still can.

• As you go through Herceg Novi, at the roundabout, follow signs for Budva, Kotor, and Trajekt/Ferry.

After the tunnel, you'll pass through **Zelenika**, once the end of the line for the Habsburg rail line from Vienna, which first brought tourism to this area.

You'll carry on through a few more dreary towns. Entertain yourself by gazing across the strait on your right to look for caves burrowed into the cliff face at sea level. These once provided shelter for Yugoslav warships. Also along this cliff, you'll see naval barracks. In **Bijela**, you'll pass a big industrial shipyard on your right; in addition to the rusty, hardworking ships you'll likely see here, this slip also services luxury yachts—another example of Montenegro's odd juxtaposition of gritty industry and nouveau wealth.

Eventually, you'll emerge into a more rustic setting: This fjordside road is lined with fishing villages, some now developed as resorts (includ-

be ruthlessly punished. Soon 2,000-horse caravans could pass without a worry along this fjord.

But the Serbian Empire went into steep decline after Dušan. As the Ottomans threatened to invade in the 15th century, Kotor's traders turned to Venice for help. The Venetian Republic would control this bay for the next 450 years, and it was never taken by the Ottomans.

In the late 19th century, when Venice fell to Napoleon, the Bay of Kotor came briefly under the control of France, then Russia, then Austria. With the decline of feudal traditions and trading wealth, the Bay of Kotor entered a period of architectural stagnation—preserving many time-warp towns that travelers appreciate today.

When Montenegro became part of Yugoslavia following World War I, the Serbs (who felt a cultural affinity with the Montenegrins that wasn't always reciprocated) laid claim to the Montenegrin coast as their own little patch of seafront. This Serb connection helped Montenegro avoid the initial violence of the breakup of Yugoslavia. But a few years later, the Montenegrins decided it was time to part ways. For the rest of the story, see the "Montenegro: Birth of a Nation" sidebar, later.

MONTENEGRO

*ing a few with severe communist-era touches). Each waterfront house seems to have its own little boat dock sticking out into the glassy water. You'll pass through the town of **Kamenari**, which has a handy ferry that you could use to shave time off your return trip to Dubrovnik (described at the end of this drive). Two minutes after leaving Kamenari (just after the Kostanjica sign), watch for a convenient gravel pull-out on the right (likely packed with tour buses, by the small white lighthouse). Pull over to check out the narrowest point of the fjord, the...*

Verige Strait

Any would-be invaders had to pass through this strategic bottleneck to reach the port towns inside the bay. It's narrow enough to carefully monitor (not even a quarter-mile wide), but deep enough to allow even today's large megaships through (more than 130 feet deep). Because this extremely narrow strait is easy to defend, whoever controlled the inside of the fjord was allowed to thrive virtually unchecked.

Centuries before Christ, the Bay of Kotor was home to the Illyrians—the mysterious ancestors of today's Albanians. In the third century B.C., Illyrian Queen Teuta spanned this strait with an ingenious shipwrecking mechanism to more effectively collect taxes. To this day, many sunken ships litter the bottom of the bay. (Teuta was a little too clever for her own good: Her shrewdness and success attracted the attention of the on-the-rise Romans, who seized most of her holdings.)

In later times, chains were stretched across the bay here to control the entrance (the name "Verige" comes from a Slavic word for "chain"). Later still, the Venetians placed cannons on either side of the strait, with a clear shot at any entering ships. Looking across the wide part of the bay, notice the town of Perast (by the two islands). Perast—where we'll be stopping soon—was also equipped with cannons that could easily reach across the bay. This extensive defense network succeeded in keeping the Ottomans—and any other would-be invaders—out of the bay.

• *Continue driving around the fjord. You'll pass through the village of...*

Morinj

This town is known for two starkly different reasons: First, it's the home of a recommended restaurant with fine food in a gorgeous setting (Konoba Ćatovića Mlini); another, more casual eatery sits nearby (both described on page 400). And second, it was the site of a concentration camp for Croat prisoners captured during the 1991-1992 siege of Dubrovnik. Some 300 civilians from in and near Dubrovnik were forcibly brought here, where they lived in horrifying conditions. After the war, six of the guards from this camp were convicted of war crimes.

• *After going through Morinj and some other small villages, you'll pass through the larger resort town of...*

Risan

Back in Greek times, when the Bay of Kotor was known as *"Sinus Rhizonicus,"* Risan was the leading town of the bay. Later, during the Illyrian Queen Teuta's brief three-year reign, Risan was her capital. Today the town is still home to the scant remains of Teuta's castle (on the hilltop just before town), but it's mostly notable for its giant communist eyesore hotel—named, appropriately enough, Hotel Teuta.

In the town center, historians may want to turn off to the left (at the brown *Roman Mosaics* sign) for a quick look at a few partly intact mosaic floors of the second-century A.D. Roman **Villa Urbana** (€2, daily 8:00-20:00). You'll enter through a small modern building to access the large, covered footprint of the villa. Between the knee-high stone walls are mosaics of checkerboards, stylized marine life (including calamari), and—most significant—a small mosaic of reclining Hypnos, the god of dreams.

• *Continue on to Perast. As you approach the town, take the right fork (marked with brown sign) directly down into Perast; or you can first take the left fork to pass above town for sweeping views over the bay, then backtrack down into the town center.*

Perast

Called the "Pearl of Venetian Baroque," little Perast is a handy and scenic spot to stretch your legs and consider a boat trip. In high season (June-mid-Sept), you're required to pay to park near the entrance of town, and then walk 10 level minutes or ride the free shuttle bus into the town center; at other times, you may be allowed to drive along the waterfront road and park for free in front of the church.

Remember that Perast, with its cannons aimed at the Verige Strait across the bay, was an essential link in the Bay of Kotor's fortifications. In exchange for this important duty, Venice rewarded Perast with privileged tax-free status, and the town became extremely wealthy. Ornate mansions proliferated here during its 17th- and 18th-century heyday. But after Venice fell to Napoleon, and the Bay of Kotor's economy changed, Perast's singular defensive role disappeared. With no industry, no hinterland, and no natural resources, Perast stagnated—leaving it a virtual open-air museum of Venetian architecture.

Go to the tallest steeple in town, overlooking a long and narrow harborfront square. Perast is centered on its too-big (and incomplete) **Church of St. Nicholas**—dedicated to the patron saint of fishermen. It was originally designed to extend out into the sea (the old church, still standing, was to be torn down). But Napoleon's troops came marching in before the builders got that far, so the plans were scuttled—and this massive partial-church was instead simply grafted on to the existing, modest church.

Go inside (free, treasury-€1, sporadic hours, generally daily June-Sept 9:00-19:00, until 14:00 off-season and closed Dec-March except by request—ask locals around the church if someone can let you in, closed during Mass). Beyond the small sanctuary, you'll find a treasury with relics and icons. Look for the priceless crucifix from the school of the 18th-century Venetian artist Giovanni Battista Tiepolo

(#1, in the center display case), with Jesus on one side, and Mary and the saints on the other. Beyond the treasury is what was to be the main apse (altar area) of the unfinished massive church (notice

MONTENEGRO

it's at a right angle to the altar of the existing smaller church). The rough, unadorned brick walls make it clear that they didn't get very far. Check out the model of the ambitious but never-built church. The Baroque main altar is by Bernini's student Francesco Cabianca, who lived in this area and was always trying to earn money to pay off his gambling debts. The small room at the end displays old vestments.

You can pay €1 to climb the **church tower** for the view. I'd skip the Town Museum, farther down the waterfront (fills a grand old hall with paintings, furniture, model ships, and other historical bric-a-brac).

Eating in Perast: For a seafront meal, window-shop the restaurants with seating out on the water. **Conte,** filling a pier in the middle of town, is a classic choice (€10-14 pastas, €15-20 main dishes, tel. 032/373-687).

• *Before leaving Perast, take a close look at the two islands just offshore (and consider paying a visit).*

St. George (Sv. Đorđe) and Our Lady of the Rocks (Gospa od Škrpjela)

These twin islands—one natural, the other man-made—come with a fascinating story.

The **Island of St. George** (the smaller, rocky island with trees and a monastery—closed to tourists) was once part of the fortification of the Bay of Kotor. Nearby was an underwater reef with a small section poking  above the surface. According to legend, two fishermen noticed a strange light emanating from the reef in the early-morning fog. Rowing out to the island, they discovered an icon of Our Lady. They attempted to bring it ashore, but it kept washing back out again to the same spot. Taking this celestial hint, local seamen returning home from a journey began dropping rocks into the bay in this same place. The tradition caught on, more and more villagers dropped in rocks of their own, and eventually more than a hundred old ships and other vessels were loaded with stones and intentionally sunk in this spot. And so, over two centuries, an entire island was formed in the middle of the bay.

Flash forward to today's **Our Lady of the Rocks** (the flat island with the dome-topped Catholic church). In the 17th century, locals built this Baroque church on this holy site and filled it with symbols of thanks for answered prayers. Step inside (free entry) to explore the collection: silver votive plaques—many of them with images of ships in storms or battles—given by appreciative sail-

Montenegro: Birth of a Nation

Montenegro, like Croatia and Slovenia, was one of the six republics that constituted the former Yugoslavia. When these republics began splitting away in the early 1990s, Montenegro—always allied closely with Serbia, and small enough to slip under the radar—decided to remain in the union. When the dust had settled, four of the six republics had seceded, leaving only two united as "Yugoslavia": Serbia and Montenegro.

At first, Montenegrin Prime Minister Milo Đukanović was on friendly terms with Serbia's Slobodan Milošević. But in the late 1990s, as Milošević's political stock plummeted, Montenegro began to inch away from Serbia. Eager to keep its access to the coast (and the many Serbs who lived there), Serbia made concessions that allowed Montenegro to gradually assert its independence. In 1996, Montenegro boldly adopted the German mark as its official currency to bail out of the inflating Yugoslav dinar.

By 2003, the country of Yugoslavia was no more, and the loose union was renamed "Serbia and Montenegro." Thus began a three-year transition period that allowed Montenegro to test the waters of real independence. During this time, Serbia and Montenegro were united only in defense—legislation, taxation, currency, and most governmental functions were separate. And after three years, Montenegro would be allowed to hold a referendum for full independence.

That fateful vote took place on May 21, 2006. In general, ethnic Montenegrins tended to favor independence, while ethnic Serbs wanted to stay united with Serbia. To secede, Montenegro needed 55 percent of the vote. By the slimmest of margins—half a percent, or just 2,300 votes—the pro-independence faction won. On June 3, 2006, Montenegro officially declared independence. (To save face, two days later, Serbia also "declared independence" from Montenegro.)

Today, Montenegrins are excited to have their own little country and enthusiastic about eventually joining the European Union. But many view independence as an epilogue rather than a climax. Shortly after the referendum, I asked a Montenegrin when the countries would officially separate. He chuckled and said, "Three years ago."

MONTENEGRO

ors who survived; 1,700 silver and gold votive plaques from other grateful worshippers; 68 canvases by local Baroque painter Tripo Kokolja; and a huge collection of dried wedding bouquets given by those who had nothing else to offer (the church is a popular place for weddings). Take a close look at the main altar. That legendary icon, which refused to budge from this spot, still caps the altar today. The faithful squeeze into the very tight space behind the altar, where a hole in the back of the structure lets them reach

MONTENEGRO

through and touch the original reef where the icon was found. Give it a try—if you dare.

The adjacent **museum** is an entertaining mishmash of items. The entry price includes a fun little tour by Davorka, Nataša, or Sandra (€1, May-Oct daily 9:00-18:00, off-season opens sporadically with boat arrival—or call ahead to Davorka's mobile 069-621-322). Just inside, study the models of both islands. The artificial one—the one you're on—is shaped vaguely like a boat. The collection includes a wide range of ancient artifacts, including a glass case displaying fragments dating—staggeringly—from 3500 B.C. (found in the hills just above Perast). There's also a small modern-art gallery with various depictions of the two islands created by artists who came here and were inspired by this place; paintings of ships commissioned by local sailors (notice that most have a saintly image of Mary and the Baby Jesus hovering nearby); and other gifts given through the ages. Upstairs, near the gift shop counter, look for the amazing embroidery made by a local woman who toiled over it for more than 25 years. She used her own hair for the hair of the angels—which you can see fade from brown to gray as she aged (beginning at around 3 o'clock and going clockwise, you'll see the subtle change in color).

Getting There: Boats to Our Lady of the Rocks leave from in front of St. Nicholas' Church in Perast—look for the guys milling around the harborfront with boats ready to go. The going rate is €5/person round-trip, but Zoran (who has the boat with the red awning marked *Taxi Boat Perast*) says he'll charge only €4/person if you show this book. If it's quiet, they'll drop you on the island for about 30 minutes before returning to get you.

• *When you're ready to move on, continue driving around the fjord. After the large town of Orahovac, you'll see part of the bay roped off for a mussel farm; these farms do best when located where mountain rivers spill into the bay. And a hundred or so yards later, you cross a bridge spanning the don't-blink-or-you'll-miss-it...*

Ljuta River

According to locals, this is the "shortest river in the world"—the source is under the cliff just to the left of the bridge, and it meets the sea just to the right. Short as it is, it's hardly a trickle—in fact, its name means "Angry River" for its fierce flow during heavy rains. The river actually courses underground for several miles before emerging here. Like the Karst area south of Ljubljana, this is a karstic landscape—limestone that's honeycombed with under-ground rivers, caves, and canyons.

• *Immediately after the bridge, look for the turnoff (on the right) to the recommended Restoran Stari Mlini—a tranquil spot for a meal or drink. Fittingly, this "Old Mill" sits right where the river comes tum-bling out—the perfect spot to harness that hydropower.*

Continuing along the fjord, as you pass through the town of Do-brota, look across the bay to the village of...

Prčanj

This town is famous as the former home of many centuries' worth of wealthy sea captains. When the Bay of Kotor was part of the Austrian Empire, Emperor Franz Josef came to Prčanj. Upon being greeted by some 50 uniformed ship captains, he marveled that such a collection of seafarers had been imported for his visit...not real-izing that every one of them lived nearby.

• *Keep on driving. When you see the giant moat with the town wall, and the smaller wall twisting up the hill above, you'll know you've arrived in Kotor (see next page).*

Before leaving Kotor, make a decision about where you want to go next. You have three basic options: Budva Riviera; the mountainous Montenegrin interior; or back to Croatia (see instructions for the third option in the next section).

Continuing past Kotor's Old Town, you'll follow the edge of the fjord. At the far end of town (and the fjord), you'll come to a roundabout. Bearing left at the roundabout takes you toward the handy tunnel to the Budva Riviera—or, along this same road, if you turn right after the cemetery and just before the tunnel, you'll take the extremely twisty road up, up, up into the Montenegrin interior (Njeguši and Cetinje).

Once you're finished in Montenegro, it'll be time to head...

Back to Croatia: Lepetani-Kamenari Ferry Shortcut

When you're ready to return to Dubrovnik, you can go back the way you came. Or, for a quicker route, consider the ferry that cuts across the narrow part of the fjord (between the towns of Lepetani and Kamenari). On the Kotor side of the bay, the boat departs from the town of Lepetani.

From Kotor, you have two options to reach the ferry: The easi-est option is to leave Kotor, bear left at the roundabout at the far end of town, and take the tunnel toward Budva. Once through the tunnel, follow signs into Tivat, and continue straight through Tivat on the main road to reach Lepetani, which is a few miles be-yond the end of town. Or, for a more challenging but more scenic route, simply turn right at the roundabout and continue driving on the waterfront road clockwise around the bay (through Prčanj

MONTENEGRO

and Stoliv) until you land in Lepetani. But be warned that this road is extremely narrow (one lane, with an Adriatic shoulder) and can be exhausting. However, it also offers grand views back across the fjord at Kotor, Perast, and other picturesque towns you came through earlier.

No matter how you approach, remember that "ferry" is *trajekt* (it's also signed for *Herceg Novi*—the big city across the bay). The boat goes continuously (in slow times, you may have to wait briefly for enough cars to show up), and the crossing takes just four minutes (it takes longer to load and unload all the cars than it does to cross). A small car and its passengers pay €4.50 each way.

On your way back to Dubrovnik after the ferry, if there are long lines at the primary border crossing—or you want a quieter, more scenic return—use the Konfin alternate crossing described earlier: After exiting Igalo, just before the border, take the first left after the Hipermarket and Petrol gas station (following small yellow sign to *Višnjići*)—watch for the turn-off on the left that's marked *granični prijelaz Konfin*. From the Konfin border, follow signs to *Dubrovnik* (on back roads at first, later merging with the main road).

Kotor

Butted up against a steep cliff, cradled by a calm sea, naturally sheltered by its deep-in-the-fjord position, and watched over by an imposing network of fortifications, the town of Kotor is as impressive as it is well-protected. Though it's enjoyed a long and illustrious history, today's Kotor is a time-capsule retreat for travelers seeking an unspoiled Adriatic town.

The ancient town of Catarum—named for the Roman word for "contracted" or "strangled," as the sea is at this point in the gnarled fjord—was first mentioned in the first century A.D. Like the rest of the region, Kotor's next two millennia were layered with history as it came under the control of foreign powers: Illyrians, Romans, Serbs, Venetians, Russians, Napoleonic soldiers, Austrians, Tito's Yugoslavia...and now, finally, Montenegrins. Each group left its mark, and Kotor has its share of both Catholic and Orthodox churches.

Through all those centuries, Kotor avoided destruction by warfare. But it was damaged by earthquakes—including the same 1667 quake that leveled Dubrovnik (known here as the "Great Shaking"), as well as a devastating 1979 earthquake from which the city is still cleaning up.

With an extremely inviting Old Town that seems custom-built

Kotor

"PARKING BENOVO"

NORTHERN GATE

Škurda River

TOWN WALLS

ST. NICHOLAS' CHURCH

ST. MARY'S

WALK ENDS

❸ Hotel Marija

WC

ST. LUKE'S

Access to Upper Town Walls

❾ ❹

St. Luke's Square

❼

KARAMPANA WELL

MARITIME MUSEUM OF MONTENEGRO

To "Parking Benovo" "Parking Urc" & Perast

Square of Arms

WC

Trg od Kina

❷

❶

WALK BEGINS

MAIN TOWN GATE

ⓘ

POST

❻

CRUISE SHIP PORT

"PARKING RIVA"

Trg od Brašna

Pjaca Sv. Tripuna

CATHEDRAL OF ST. TRYPHON

CHURCH OF OUR LADY OF HEALTH

JADRANSKI PUT

❽

❿

Pjaca od Salate

Access to Upper Town Walls

N

B a y   o f   K o t o r

❺

100 Meters

100 Yards

To Bus Station, Budva & Cetinje

SOUTHERN GATE

MONTENEGRO

❶ Hotel Villa Duomo
❷ Hotel Vardar
❸ Hotel Marija
❹ D&Sons Apartments
❺ Old Town Hostel
❻ City Restaurant
❼ Cesarica
❽ Produce Market
❾ The Old Winery
❿ Pharmacies (2)

for aimless strolling, Kotor is an idyllic place to while away a few hours. Though it's sometimes called a "little Dubrovnik," Kotor is more low-key, less ambitious, less historic, flatter, and much smaller than its more famous neighbor. And yet, with its own special spice that's exciting to sample, Kotor is a hard place to tear yourself away from.

Orientation to Kotor

Kotor (or Cattaro in Italian) has a compact Old Town shaped like a triangle. The two sides facing the bay are heavily fortified by a thick wall, and the third side huddles under the cliff face. A meandering defensive wall climbs the mountainside directly behind and above town. While only 3,000 people live within the Old Town walls, greater Kotor has a population of about 12,000.

The Old Town's mazelike street plan is confusing, but it's so small and atmospheric that getting lost is more fun than frustrating. The natives virtually ignore addresses, including the names of streets and squares. Most Old Town addresses are represented simply as "Stari Grad" (Old Town) and a number, useless if you're trying to navigate by streets. To make matters worse, a single square can have several names—so one map labels it Trg od Katedrale (Cathedral Square), while another calls it Pjaca Sv. Tripuna (Piazza of St. Tryphon). My advice: Don't fret about street or square names. Simply navigate with a map and by asking locals for directions. Thanks to the very manageable size of the Old Town, this is easier than it sounds.

TOURIST INFORMATION

The TI is in a kiosk just outside the Old Town's main entrance gate (daily May-Oct 8:00-20:00, Nov-April 8:00-17:00, tel. 032/325-950, www.kotor.montenegro.travel/en). Pick up the free map and browse the collection of other brochures. There's a free Wi-Fi hotspot around this kiosk; look for the "TOKOTOR" network.

ARRIVAL IN KOTOR

By Car: Approaching town, you'll first see Kotor's substantial wall, which overlooks a canal. You can park in one of three pay lots: "Parking Riva," along the bay immediately across from the main gate, is the closest to the Old Town but also the most expensive (€1/hour, to the right just after crossing the bridge by the wall); "Parking Benovo," in the lot across the canal (€0.80/hour, on the left just before the bridge by the wall—you'll be sent back here if the first lot is full); or "Parking Urc" (€0.60/hour, a bit farther out and along the water). All three are easily walkable from the Old Town entrance. Be sure you've parked legally, in one of these designated lots; while locals brazenly leave their cars anywhere they like, tourists get towed without remorse.

By Bus: The bus station is about a half-mile (10-minute walk) south of the Old Town. Arriving here, simply exit to the right and walk straight up the road—you'll run into the embankment and town wall.

Sights in Kotor

Because of its tangled alleys and irregular street plan, Kotor feels bigger than it is. But after a few minutes of strolling, you'll discover you're going in circles and realize it's actually very compact.

(In fact, aimless wandering is Kotor's single best activity.) As you ramble, keep an eye out for these key attractions. I've listed them roughly in the order of a counterclockwise route through town, beginning outside the main entrance gate.

▲Main Town Gate (Glavna Gradska Vrata)

The wide-open **square** fronting the bay and waterfront marina now welcomes visitors. But for centuries, its purpose was exactly the opposite. As the primary point of entry into this heavily fortified town, it was the last line of defense. Before the embankment was built, the water came directly to this door, and there was only room for one ship to tie up at a time. If a ship got this far (through the gauntlet we saw back at the Verige Strait), it was carefully examined here again to levy taxes before its passengers could disembark. This double-checkpoint was designed to foil pirates who might fly the flag of a friend to get through the strait, only to launch a surprise attack once here. (The pirates' primary booty wasn't silver or gold, but men—kidnapped for ransom, or, if ransom wasn't paid, as slaves to row on ships.)

Check out the pinkish **gate** itself. The oldest parts of this gate date from 1555. It once featured a Venetian lion, then the double-

headed eagle of the Habsburg Empire. But today, most of the symbolism touts Tito's communism (notice the stars and the old Yugoslav national seal at the top). The big date (November 21, 1944) commemorates this area's liberation from the Nazis by Tito's homegrown Partisan Army. The Tito quote *(tuđe nećemo svoje nedamo)* means, roughly, "Don't take what's ours, and we won't take what's yours"—a typically provocative statement in these troubled Balkans.

• *Notice the* **TI** *in the kiosk just to the left of the gate. Then go through the gate into town. You'll emerge into the...*

Square of Arms (Trg od Oržja)

Do a quick spin-tour of the square, which is ringed with artifacts of the city's complex history. Looking to the left, you'll see a long building lined with cafés. This was once the palace of the rector, who ruled Kotor on behalf of Venice. Princes could watch the action from their long

balcony overlooking the square, which served as the town's living room. Later, the palace became the Kotor Town Hall. Beyond the long building, two other buildings poke out into the square (on either side of the lane leading out of the square). The one on the right is the Venetian arsenal, the square's namesake. The one on the left is the "French Theater," named for its purpose during the time this area was under Napoleon's control. Directly across from the gate you just came through, you'll see the town's Bell Tower, one of Kotor's symbols. The odd triangular structure at its base was once the town pillory, where wrongdoers would be chained and subjected to public ridicule of the rudest kind imaginable. In the little recessed square just right of that, you'll spot the recommended, copper-roofed Hotel Vardar. Handy ATMs around this square dispense euros.

• *Walk down the long part of the square directly ahead of where you entered (toward Hotel Vardar). Take the broad lane angling off to the right (paved with red-and-white-striped tiles), which leads past mansions of Kotor's medieval big shots. Cross a square (Trg od Brašna) and turn left down the little lane at its end. After one short block, you'll hit Pjaca Sv. Tripuna (a.k.a. Trg od Katedrale), home to the...*

▲Cathedral of St. Tryphon (Katedrala Sv. Tripuna)

Even though most of today's Kotorians are Orthodox, Kotor's most significant church is Catholic. According to legend, in 809, Venetian merchants were sailing up the coast from Nicea (in today's Turkey) with the relics of St. Tryphon—a third-century martyr and today's patron saint of gardeners. A storm hit as they approached the Bay of Kotor, so they took shelter here. Every time they tried to leave, the weather worsened...so they finally got the message that St. Tryphon's remains should remain in Kotor.

Cost and Hours: €2.50, daily June-Sept 9:00-19:00, April-May and Oct 9:00-18:00, Nov-March 9:00-15:00, Mass on Sun at 10:00.

Visiting the Cathedral: Take in the cathedral's **exterior.** The church has been rebuilt after four different earthquakes—most extensively after the 1667 quake, when it achieved its current Renaissance-Baroque blend. That earthquake, which also contributed to Dubrovnik's current appearance, destroyed three-quarters of Kotor's buildings. A fire swept the city, and all of the dead bodies attracted rats (and with them, the plague)—a particularly dark chapter in Kotor's history.

Why are the two **towers** different? There are plenty of legends, but the most likely answer is that restorers working after 1667 simply ran out of money before they finished the second one. Notice the Church of Our Lady of Health way up on the hill above this church—built in thanks to God by survivors of the plague (it also serves as part of the town fortifications—described later).

Within the cathedral, the **nave** of the church is marginally interesting, with stout columns; surviving Byzantine-style frescoes under the arches—all that's left of paintings that once covered the church; and a fine 15th-century silver-and-gold altar covered by a delicate canopy.

But the best part is the **reliquary** upstairs. Find the stairs at the rear and walk up to the chapel. Behind the Baroque altar (by Bernini's student Francesco Cabianca, whose work we saw in Perast) and the screen are 48 different relics. In the center is St. Tryphon—his bones are in a silver casket, and his head is in the golden chalice next to it. In the small room up the stairs, examine the fascinating icon of the Madonna and Child from the 15th century (it's in a freestanding wooden frame with a crucified Jesus on the other side; to find it, you may have to look around back or rotate the frame). The painting exemplifies this town's position as a bridge between Western and Eastern Christianity: The faces, more lifelike, are Western-style (Catholic) Gothic; the stiff, elongated bodies are more Eastern (Orthodox) and Byzantine-style. From here, take a slow walk around the upper gallery of the church to see its displays of relics (such as arms and feet covered in silver), paintings, vestments, and other ecclesiastical items.

• *Exit the church, veer right, and exit the square on the street near the recommended City Restaurant, marked by trees. In a block, you'll wind up on a little square that's home to the...*

Maritime Museum of Montenegro (Pomorski Muzej Crne Gore)

Like so many Adriatic towns, Kotor's livelihood is tied to the sea. This humble museum covers three floors and explores that important heritage. As you climb the stairway, notice the evocative maps and etchings of old Kotor. Portraits of salty swashbucklers, traditional costumes, and 98 coats of arms representing aristocratic families who have lived here (ringing the main room upstairs) are all reminders of the richness of Kotor's history. You'll see a display of rifles and swords (some with fun ornamental decorations illustrating the art of killing) and lots of model ships. The museum is housed in the Gregorina Palace, one of dozens of aristocratic mansions that dot the Old Town—yet another reminder of the historically high concentration of wealth and power in this little settlement.

Cost and Hours: €4, includes English audioguide; July-

Aug Mon-Sat 9:00-20:00, closes earlier off-season, Sun 9:00-13:00 year-round; on Trg Grgurina, tel. 032/304-720, www.museummaritimum.com.

• *Turn right out of the museum, and make a right again on the first lane. After 10 yards, you'll pass a well on your left called the...*

Karampana

This well served as Kotor's only public faucet until the early 20th century. As such, it was also the top place in town for gossip, like the office water cooler. It's said that if your name was mentioned here, you knew you had arrived. Today, though the chatter is no longer raging on this square, the town's gossip magazine is called *Karampana*. While the pump still works (swing the pendulum once and keep it there), it's sometimes disconnected to prevent tourists from swinging it back and forth too aggressively.

• *Continue straight past the well into the next square...*

▲St. Luke's Square (Trg Svetog Luke)

There are two Serbian Orthodox churches on this pretty square, each with the typical Orthodox church features: a squat design, narrow windows, and portly domes. Little **St. Luke's Church** (Crkva Sv. Luka), in the middle of the square, dates from the 12th century. Locals debate long and hard as to whether St. Luke's was originally built as a Catholic church or an Orthodox one. (Although it "looks" Orthodox, it was constructed at a time when even Catholic churches were built in the Orthodox style.) Regardless of its origin, during the Venetian era the church did double duty as a house of worship for both. These days, it's decidedly Orthodox. Step into the humble interior (free, daily May-Oct 10:00-20:00, Nov-April 8:00-13:00 & 17:00-19:00).

The bigger and much newer **St. Nicholas' Church** (Crkva Sv. Nikola), was built in 1909—because of its Neo-Byzantine design, it has similarly spherical domes and slitlike windows (free, same hours as St. Luke's).

Before entering, notice how the Orthodox crosses on the steeples of St. Nicholas' Church differ from the cross seen in Roman Catholic churches (known as a Latin cross). In addition to the standard crossbar, Orthodox crosses often also have a second, smaller crossbar near the top (representing the *I.N.R.I.* plaque that was displayed above Jesus' head). Sometimes Orthodox crosses also feature a third, angled crossbar at the bottom. Many believe that rather than being nailed directly to the cross, Jesus' feet were nailed to a crossbar like this one to prolong his suffering. The slanted angle represents Jesus' forgiveness of the thief crucified to his right (the side that's pointing up)...and suggests where the unrepentant thief on his left ended up.

Stepping into these (or any other Orthodox) churches, you'll immediately notice some key differences from Catholic churches: no pews (worshippers stand through the service as a sign of respect), tall and skinny candles (representing prayers), and a screen of icons, called an iconostasis, in the middle of the sanctuary to separate the material world from the holy world (where the Bible is kept). For more about Orthodox worship, see the sidebar on page 316.

Before continuing on, enjoy this square's lazy ambience. The big building fronting the square is a music school, and the students practicing here fill this already pleasant public space with an appealing soundtrack.

• *If you go down the street to your left as you face St. Nicholas, you'll wind up back at the Square of Arms. But first try getting lost, then found again, in Kotor's delightful maze of streets.*

The town's final attraction is above your head. To go there directly, face St. Nicholas' Church, turn right, and walk straight for two blocks until you reach St. Mary's Church (named for one of four Catholic saints who came from the Bay of Kotor—which some faithful locals call the "Bay of Saints"). If you skirt the church along its right side—down the narrow lane with two arches—you'll find the entrance to the town walls.

▲▲Town Walls (Gradske Zidine)

Kotor's fortifications begin as stout ramparts along the waterfront, then climb up the sheer cliff face behind town in a dizzying zigzag line. If there's a more elaborate city wall in Europe, I haven't seen it. A proud Kotorian bragged to me, "These fortifications cost more to build than any palace in Europe."

Imagine what it took to create this "Great Wall of Kotor." The wall is nearly three miles long and sits on some extremely inaccessible terrain. It was built in fits and starts over a millennium (9th-19th centuries, though most of it was completed during the Venetian occupation in the 17th and 18th centuries). Its thickness varies from 6 to 50

feet, and the tallest parts are 65 feet high. Sections higher on the hill—with thinner walls, built before the age of gunpowder—are the oldest, while the thick walls along the water are most recent. It was all worth it: The fortified town survived many attacks, including a two-month Ottoman siege in 1657.

If you're in great shape, consider scrambling along the walls and turrets above the Old Town.

Cost and Hours: Entry to the walls is €3 May-Oct daily 8:00-20:00; otherwise they're free.

Hiking the Walls: If you go all the way up to the top fortress and back again, it'll take around an hour and a half round-trip (depending on how fast you go). This involves climbing 1,355 steps (an elevation gain of more than 700 feet)—don't overestimate your endurance or underestimate the heat. ("Am-I-*that*-out-of-shape?" tourists routinely find themselves winded and stranded high above town.) Bring plenty of water, along

with a hat and sunscreen, and wear sturdy shoes. Most of the way, there's both a ramp and uneven stairs, but the route is in poor repair, with a lot of rough, rocky patches.

It's best to tackle the walls clockwise. (Even if you're not doing the hike, you can visually trace this route.) Find the entrance at the back-left corner of town (near St. Mary's Church, through the alley with the two arches over it). Pay the entry fee and begin hiking up. On the way up, notice the sign explaining that the fortress reconstruction was funded by the United States (Nov 2004)—if you're a US taxpayer, consider this hike your tax dollars at work.

First climb as high as the **Church of Our Lady of Health** (Crkva Gospe od Zdravlj). This is the halfway mark—about 20 minutes from the base at a good pace. While some believe this church has miraculous healing powers, most everyone agrees it offers some of the best views down over Kotor.

From this church, you can either cut back down toward the Old Town, or—if you're not exhausted yet—keep hiking up to the tippy-top **Fortress of St. John** (figure another 30 minutes from the church, if you're in decent shape). Built on the remains of fortifications from the Illyrians (you can scan the third-century B.C. remains just beyond the fort), this was the headquarters for the entire wall network below it. There's not much to see here, but it is fun to play "king of the castle" exploring the ruined shell—and the views, with 360 degrees of Montenegrin cliffs, are spectacular.

Then head back down, enjoying your reward: a downhill walk

Sleep Code

Abbreviations   (€1=about $1.10, country code: 382)
S=Single, **D**=Double/Twin, **T**=Triple, **Q**=Quad, **b**=bathroom.
Price Rankings
$$$ **Higher Priced**—Most rooms €100 or more.
 $$ **Moderately Priced**—Most rooms between €70-100.
  $ **Lower Priced**—Most rooms €70 or less.

If I've listed two rates, the first is for peak season (June-Sept) and the second for shoulder/off-season (Oct-May). Unless otherwise noted, credit cards are accepted, English is spoken, air-conditioning is available, breakfast is included, and free Wi-Fi and/or a guest computer is generally available. Prices change; verify current rates online or by email. For the best prices, always book directly with the hotel.

with head-on views of the Bay of Kotor. On the way down, watch your step on the slippery-even-when-dry marble stairs, highly pol-

ished by the feet of centuries of visitors. At the round terrace below the church, you can head to the right (back the way you came); or, for a different path, head left following *powder magazine* signs, then down (right) at the fork. The ticket-seller warned me that he's often seen people wipe out on the very last step on their way down—so exhausted after the demanding hike that they let their guard down.

Sleeping in Kotor

Kotor is an enjoyable place to spend the night. (Given its popularity as a cruise port, and among side-trippers from Dubrovnik, only a tiny fraction of visitors bother to sleep here.) However, the town has two big disadvantages: inexplicably high prices (you'll sleep more affordably in Dubrovnik) and lots of nighttime noise from boisterous bars. Assume it'll be loud anywhere, and pack earplugs.

$$$ Hotel Villa Duomo is a stylish refuge just down the street from the cathedral. The 13 stony-chic rooms share an interior terrace where breakfast is served in good weather (Db-€135/€120, Tb-€185/€170, more for bigger units, Stari Grad 358, tel. 032/323-111, www.villaduomo.com, villaduomo@yahoo.com).

$$$ Hotel Vardar has 24 rooms with mod bathrooms smack-dab in the middle of the Old Town. This classic old copper-roofed hotel has been renovated from top to bottom, leaving it tastefully chic. While convenient, the dead-central location can come with some noise, especially on weekends—request a quieter room (Sb-€115/€105, standard Db-€135/€125, larger Db with views on the square-€160/€150; 15 percent less Fri-Sat nights for two people, elevator, Stari Grad 476, tel. 032/325-084, www.hotelvardar.com, info@hotelvardar.com).

$$ Hotel Marija, an Old World throwback on an Old Town square, offers 17 rooms and wood-paneled halls. Request a quieter room in the back (Sb-€65/€50, Db-€90/€70, Tb-€103/€90, Qb-€130/€110, on Trg od Kina, Stari Grad 449, tel. 032/325-062, hotel.marija.kotor@t-com.me).

$ D&Sons Apartments has six good, modern apartments along an atmospheric, café-lined lane at the back edge of the Old Town (Db-€60/€50, bigger apartment-€100/€80, no breakfast but kitchenettes, Stari Grad 490, mobile 069-050-094, www.dandsons.com, dandsons@t-com.me, Dražan).

$ Old Town Hostel is a budget option in the Old Town, filling a stony, labyrinthine 13th-century building with 10 rooms, ranging from 10-bed dorms to overpriced private rooms. Youthful conviviality fills the inviting lounge (bunk in dorm room-€14-19/€9-12, D-€60/€40, Db-€80/€60; no breakfast but kitchen in each room, Stari Grad 284, tel. 032/325-317, mobile 067-737-825, www.hostel-kotor.me, info@hostel-kotor.me).

Eating in Kotor

In coastal, Italian-influenced Kotor, the cuisine is very similar to Croatia's: seafood, pasta, and pizza. There are a few local specialties to look for, and at the top of the list is *Njeguški pršut*, the delicious smoked ham from the village of Njeguši high in the mountains above town (described later, under "The Montenegrin Interior"). While *pršut* (prosciutto) is beloved throughout the Balkans, *Njeguški pršut*'s rich, salty, smoky flavor is perhaps the best. It goes well with the local cow's cheese—smoked, of course.

Montenegro produces some surprisingly good (and expensive) wines. The biggest producer in the country—and one of the biggest in the Balkans—is Plantaže Podgorica, which corks up some 20 million bottles each year. While that kind of volume often doesn't come with quality, Plantaže's vintages are quite good and worth trying (if not impossible to avoid). The most popular red-wine grape is the dry, medium-bodied *vranac* (VRAH-nahts), which is distantly related to Italian *primitivo*, Californian zinfandel, and Croatian *plavac mali*. For white, you'll see the dry, fruity *krstač* (kur-STACH), similar to riesling.

As far as choosing restaurants in Kotor, there's not much to recommend. Truly great cuisine is rare here—I'd just settle for something scenic and functional. For a better quality, memorable meal in a romantic setting, drivers can consider heading to Konoba Ćatovića Mlini or Restoran Stari Mlini (described later).

Simple and Tasty near the Cathedral: City Restaurant, with breezy outdoor tables next to the Cathedral of St. Tryphon, offers a fine, shady perch. Its well-varnished picnic tables are set within the little forest in the Old Town, and more tables fill a small square out front (€7-11 pizzas, pastas, and salads; €10-20 main courses; daily 8:00-1:00 in the morning; mobile 069-049-653).

Local Fish: Cesarica offers unpretentious seafood in a casual, stony interior buried deep in the Old Town. They enjoy bragging that the owner, Petar, was a fisherman, so he has a line on the freshest ingredients (€7-12 salads, €9-15 main dishes, daily 9:00-23:00, Stari Grad 375, mobile 069-049-733).

Market: Just outside the Old Town wall, facing the harbor, is a lively open market that hops each morning (typically 9:00-14:00, busiest on Sat). This is a great place to gather ingredients for a picnic, including the delicious local smoked ham, *Njeguški pršut*.

Wine Bar: The Old Winery (Stara Vinarija) fills an inviting stony-chic space on a tight Old Town lane with convivial indoor and outdoor seating. It's a chance to enjoy a limited but appealing range of dishes that work well with wines from throughout the former Yugoslavia—with an emphasis on Montenegrin vintages (€9-16 pastas, €15 seafood salads, €12-20 main courses). Hang out in the wine bar itself (about 20 wines available by the glass, €5-12/glass, most about €6; frequent live music—piano in the morning, blues after 21:00). Or stop in their wine shop—called Mon Ami—next door. Both are open long hours daily (Stari Grad 483, mobile 068-517-417, Goran). You can sample three wines in the shop for cheap, or spring for a more elaborate five-wine tasting in the bar (call or drop by in advance to reserve).

NEAR KOTOR

These very scenic options are situated on or near the bayside road. The first two restaurants sit in oasis-like settings near running water, which helps keep them cool during the hot summer months.

In Ljuta

Restoran Stari Mlini has a cozy interior and wonderful outdoor seating scattered around a spring-fed stream near an old, namesake water mill. Surrounded by trickling water, you'll dine on local cuisine, with an emphasis on seafood. If you prefer freshwater fish, you can choose your own trout from the pond (€14-19 pastas, €15-24 main courses, daily 12:00-24:00, tel. 032/333-555).

MONTENEGRO

MONTENEGRO

Near the Verige Strait, in Morinj

Konoba Ćatovića Mlini is a memorable restaurant worth going out of your way to reach. Hiding in a sparse forest off the main fjordside road, this oasis is situated amidst a series of ponds, streams, waterfalls, and bubbling springs. The traditionally clad waiters are stiffly formal, mindful of this place's good reputation. Choose between several different stony seating options, indoors and out. Family-run for 200 years, this place is a local institution, yet it

feels like a well-kept secret. Reservations are essential in summer (€10-18 pastas, €12-24 fish dishes, extensive wine list, daily 11:00-23:00, tel. 032/373-030, www.catovicamlini.me). The best plan might be to dine here on your way back to Dubrovnik from Kotor: At the town of Morinj, watch for burgundy *Konoba Ćatovića Mlini* signs leading away from the water.

Tramontana is a more affordable, still very scenic option overlooking a beach with grand fjord views, right along the main waterfront road on the way out of Morinj (€6 sandwiches, €8 salads, €9 pizzas and pastas, daily 8:00-24:00, mobile 068-737-737).

Kotor Connections

From Kotor by Bus to: Perast (hourly, usually at :15 past the hour, every 2 hours on Sun, departs from small bus stop near Old Town rather than bus station), **Herceg Novi** (2/hour, 1 hour), **Budva** (1-4/hour, 40 minutes), **Cetinje** (2/hour, 1 hour), **Dubrovnik** (daily at 8:30 and 14:45, one additional run in summer, 2.5 hours), **Mostar** (2/day via Trebinje—likely at 11:00 and 22:00, 9 hours; also 1/day via Dubrovnik—likely at 14:15, 8 hours; all operated by Globtour), **Zagreb** (daily at 14:45). Bus info: tel. 032/325-809, www.autobuskastanicakotor.me.

The Montenegrin Interior

Although Montenegro is trying to cultivate a glitzy beach-break cachet, for most of its history it has been thought of as a rugged mountain kingdom. While the coast—the focus of most of this chapter—was traditionally Venetian or Austrian, the true heart of Montenegro beat behind the sheer wall of mountains rising up from that seafront. And romantics, caught up in misty Balkan fantasies, still think of this inland area as the "real" Montenegro.

While the Bay of Kotor is the most accessible and appealing part of the country, if you have more time, consider a joyride up into the mountains. For a quick look at this area, the easiest loop takes you to the historic capital of Cetinje—a dull little town in its own right, but a fine excuse for a mountain drive. You could do this whole loop in about two and a half hours without stopping (about an hour from Kotor to Cetinje, then another hour to Budva, then a half-hour back to Kotor)—but if you want to stretch your legs in Njeguši or Cetinje, allow more time.

Self-Guided Driving Tour

THE ROAD INTO THE MOUNTAINS

The road to Cetinje twists you up the mountain face that stretches high above Kotor—it's an incredibly scenic, white-knuckle drive. (Particularly since it can be clogged with cruise excursion buses, timid drivers may want to skip it.)

From Kotor, leave town toward Budva (bearing left at the roundabout). At the edge of Kotor, after the cemetery but before the big tunnel, take a right (marked for *Cetinje*) and begin your ascent. Cresting the first hill, go left to get to Cetinje (also marked for *Njeguši*). You'll wind up and up (past a small Roma encampment) on 25 numbered switchbacks. The road is a souvenir from the Habsburg era (1884). While Venetian rule brought sea trade, Austrian rule brought fortresses and infrastructure. After switchback #13, you'll pass an old customs house marking the former border between the Austro-Hungarian Empire and the Kingdom of Montenegro—a reminder that the coastline was not historically an integral part of Montenegrin cultural identity. As you near the top, look across the canyon to the left to spot the impossibly rough little donkey path that once was Cetinje's connection with the coast... like a tenuous umbilical cord tethering the mountainous interior to the outside world.

As you crest the hill, the vegetation changes—you're high above the Adriatic, with commanding views of Kotor and its bay (and great photo-op pull-outs; the best is just after switchback #25). Continuing inland, you find yourself in another world: poor, insular, and more Eastern (you'll see more Cyrillic lettering). Country farmhouses sell smoked ham, mountain cheese, and *medovina* (honey brandy). Before long, you reach a broad plain and the hamlet of...

MONTENEGRO

MONTENEGRO

NJEGUŠI

The humble-seeming village of Njeguši (NYEH-goo-shee) is actually well-known among Montenegrins, with two very important claims to fame. This was the hometown of the House of Petrović-Njegoš, the dynasty that ruled Montenegro for much of its history (1696-1918). The family's favorite son was Petar II Petrović-Njegoš (1813-1851). Aside from ruling the country, Petar II is remembered most fondly as a great poet and playwright—sort of the Montenegrin Shakespeare.

Njeguši is also famous for producing its own special type of air-dried ham, called *Njeguški pršut*. Locals explain that, because this meadow overlooks the sea on one side, and the mountains on the other, the wind changes direction 10 times each day, alternating between dry mountain breeze and salty sea air—perfect for seasoning and drying ham hocks. For good measure, the *pršut* is also smoked with beech wood. The blocky, white buildings lining the road that look like giant Monopoly houses are actually smokehouses, jammed with five layers of hanging ham hocks—thousands of euros' worth—silently aging. (More industry than you realize hides out in sleepy villages.) A couple of traditional restaurants at the heart of the village are happy to serve passing tourists a lunch of this local specialty. For more on *pršut*, see the sidebar on page 530.

FROM NJEGUŠI TO CETINJE

Continuing through Njeguši toward Cetinje, you'll twist up into more mountains—soon arriving in an even more rugged and inhospitable landscape than you passed on the road that brought you here from the coast. Eyeing this desolate scenery, you can understand why the visiting Lord Byron said of this place, "Am I in paradise or on the moon?" Along the mountain road that drops you down into Cetinje, each rock has the phone number of a vulture-esque road repair service *(auto slep)* spray-painted onto it. Low-profile plaques mark the site of Tito-era ambush assassinations.

Keep an eye out (on the horizon to the right) for the pointy peak of the mountain called **Lovćen,** which is capped by an elaborate mausoleum, designed by the great Croatian sculptor Ivan Meštrović, and devoted to King Petar II Petrović-Njegoš. With more time, you could actually drive up to the top of this mountain for sweeping views across Montenegro.

Soon you reach the outskirts of...

CETINJE

Cetinje (TSEH-teen-yeh)—the historic capital of Montenegro—is a fine but fallen-on-hard-times little burg that sits cradled in a desolate valley surrounded by mighty peaks. (Run-down as Cetinje is, it's still more pleasant than the current, drab capital, Podgorica.)

Observing Cetinje from afar, it seems made to order as the historic capital of a remote and rustic people. It was the home of the Montenegrin king since the 15th century, but has always been pretty humble. In fact, it's said that when the Ottomans conquered it and moved in ready to rampage, they realized there wasn't much to pillage and plunder—so they just destroyed the town and moved on. The town was destroyed several other times, as well—and each time, the local people rebuilt it.

This "Old Royal Capital," once the leading city in the realm, is today recovering from its status as a victim of Tito's quirky economic program for Yugoslavia. It used to provide shoes and refrigerators for the country, but when Yugoslavia disintegrated, so did the viability of Cetinje's economy. As you explore the two-story town today, it seems there's little more than a scruffy dollop of tourism to keep its 17,000 people housed and fed. Many of its younger generation have left for employment along the coast in the tourism industry.

Park in the town center and stroll the main street (Njegoševa) past kids on bikes, old-timers with hard memories, and young adults with metabolisms as low as the town's. At the end of this drag is the main square (Balšića Pazar), surrounded by low-key sights with sporadic opening hours: the **Ethnographic Museum** (traditional costumes and folk life), **Historical Museum** (tracing the story of Montenegro), **Njegoš Museum** (dedicated to the beloved poet-king Petar II Petrović-Njegoš), and **National Museum,** which honors King Nikola I, who ruled from 1860 until 1918. While his residence is as poor and humble a royal palace as you'll see in Europe, Nikola I thought big. He married off five of his daughters into the various royal families of Europe.

A short walk from the palace is the birthplace of the town, **Cetinje Monastery.** It's dedicated to St. Peter of Cetinje, a legendary local priest who carried a cross in one hand and a sword in the other, established the first set of laws among Montenegrins, and inspired his people to defend Christian Montenegro against the Muslim Ottomans. The monastery also holds the supposed right hand of St. John the Baptist. You are free to wander respectfully through the courtyard and church of this spiritual capital of Serbian Orthodox Montenegro.

FROM CETINJE BACK TO THE COAST

To avoid backtracking down the same twisty road you came up, consider heading more directly back toward the coast from Cetinje. Just follow signs for *Budva*. A few miles outside of Cetinje along this road, look for the good **Restoran Konak,** which serves up tasty traditional dishes with indoor and outdoor seating (open long hours daily, tel. 041/761-011).

Continuing along this road, you'll pop out high above the **Budva Riviera.** Looking out to sea, you'll spot the distinctive peninsula of Sveti Stefan off to the left, and the town of Budva to the right. If you have even more time, linger along the coast to visit these sights (described next). Otherwise, head right to return to Kotor or Dubrovnik.

The Budva Riviera

Montenegrins boast, "Croatia's got islands, but we've got beaches!" Long swaths of coarse-sand and fine-pebble beaches surround the resort town of Budva, just south of Kotor. This 15-mile stretch of coast, called the "Budva Riviera," is unappealingly built up with a mix of cheap and luxury resort hotels—making it pale in comparison to the jagged saltiness of the Bay of Kotor or the romantic tidiness of Dalmatia. This region has recently become a mecca for super-wealthy Russians, staking their claim to this patch of Adriatic seafront. But the area isn't without its charms. Aside from the pleasant Old Town of the region's unofficial capital, Budva, you'll discover a near-mythical haunt of the rich and famous: the highly exclusive resort peninsula of Sveti Stefan (not possible to visit, but alluring from afar). For me, more time in Kotor or an earlier return to Dubrovnik would be more satisfying than the trek to the Budva Riviera. But beach lovers who have plenty of time and a spirit of adventure will find this area merits a look.

GETTING TO THE BUDVA RIVIERA

Budva is about a 30-minute drive south of **Kotor.** The easiest approach is to continue past Kotor along the fjord, left at the roundabout, then through the tunnel (following *Budva* signs; exiting the tunnel, notice the sign in Cyrillic letters for Russki Radio 107.3—catering to the Russian jet-setters). For a more scenic route, take a right before the tunnel for the upper road to Budva, which twists over the mountain (described earlier, under "The Montenegrin Interior"). After winding up several switchbacks (with giddy views back over the Bay of Kotor) and cresting the hill, go right (again following *Budva* signs). You'll coast down into a valley, through the town of Lastva, then back over another mild hill that deposits you above the beaches of Budva.

First you'll reach the town of **Budva** (turn right at traffic light, following brown *Stari Grad* signs to the Old Town; parking is well-marked in modern complex next to Old Town). Continuing around the bay, you'll pass the busy, modern resort cluster of Bečići before reaching **Sveti Stefan.**

Sights on the Budva Riviera

Between the strings of resort hotels are two towns that deserve a quick visit.

BUDVA

The Budva Riviera's best Old Town has charming Old World lanes crammed with souvenir shops and holiday-making Serbs and Rus-

sians. While less appealing than Kotor, Budva at least offers a taste of romance between the resort sprawl.

Budva began as an "emporium" (market and trading center) for Greek seamen, and extremely valuable jewelry uncovered here indicates that some pretty important people spent time here. Today, Budva's layout is simple and intuitive—a peninsula (flanked by beaches) with a big Venetian-style bell tower.

From the parking lot, head inside the Old Town walls and wander up the main drag, Njegoševa. Out at the tip of town, you'll pop out into a small café-lined square with a **Catholic church** (on the left, with an unusually modern 1970s mosaic behind the altar depicting St. John preaching on the Montenegrin coast) facing the Orthodox **Holy Trinity Church,** with gorgeous and colorful Orthodox decorations inside. Beyond that is a huge **citadel** that's imposing on the outside but dull on the inside; it's not worth paying to tour its museum of model ships, antiquarium (old library), restaurant, and less-than-thrilling sea views.

SVETI STEFAN

Like a mirage hovering just offshore, the famously exclusive luxury hotel that makes up the resort peninsula of Sveti Stefan beckons curious travelers to come, see, snap a photo...and then wish they'd spent more time elsewhere. While scenic, there's not much to actually experience at Sveti Stefan (unless you've got more than a thousand bucks to rent a room); while it's a great photo op, it disappoints many who make the trip. But for those caught up in

Robin Leach-ian memories of this hotel's glory days, it's worth a pilgrimage.

Once an actual, living town (connected to the mainland only by a narrow, natural causeway), Sveti Stefan was virtually abandoned after World War II. The Yugoslav government developed it into a giant resort hotel in the 1950s. As old homes were converted to hotel rooms, the novelty of the place—and its sterling location, surrounded by pebbly beaches and lush scenery—began to attract some seriously wealthy guests.

During this resort's heyday in the 1960s and 1970s, it ranked alongside Cannes and St-Tropez as *the* place to see and be seen on Europe's beaches. You could rent a room, a house, an entire block of houses, or even the entire peninsula. Anonymity was vigilantly protected, as the nicest "rooms" had their own private pools (away from public scrutiny), lockable gates, and security guards. Lured by Sveti Stefan's promise of privacy, celebrities, rock stars, royalty, and dignitaries famously engaged in bidding wars to decide who'd be granted access to the best suites: Whoever put the most money in a sealed envelope and slipped it to the manager, won. (According to local legend, Sly Stallone's money talked.) Guests were pampered—indulged no matter how outrageous their requests. Sophia Loren, Kirk Douglas, Doris Day, and Claudia Schiffer are just a few of the big names who basked on Sveti Stefan's beaches.

By the late 2000s, Sveti Stefan had experienced a dramatic decline. The Yugoslav Wars scared visitors away, its cachet faded, and the resort grew a bit rough around the edges. Then the Indian company Aman Resorts swept in with ambitious plans to restore the island to its former status as one of the world's most exclusive, crème-de-la-crème resorts (cheapest Db-€1,100 in high season, http://www.aman.com). These days, no-neck thugs guard the causeway, letting only guests (no exceptions) cross over into the fantasy world of Sveti Stefan. If you're desperate to check it out, you can reserve a table at the expensive restaurant. If you want to relax on the beaches flanking the causeway, most areas charge €30-50 per person for the day, but there are a few free areas—ask the guard for pointers.

Even if you can't enter the peninsula, let your imagination run as you gaze upon it. Strolling through the dead town, peeking through gates, visitors hope to spot a withered old celebrity who forgot to go home. "Rooms" come with varying degrees of privacy (each more expensive than the last): no fence, small fence, big fence. At the far end is the biggest and most famous "suite," where guests have an entire corner of the peninsula to themselves. At the top of the peninsula is a big Russian Orthodox church and a smaller Serbian Orthodox church—though both are little more than hotel decorations today.

Across the water from Sveti Stefan, on its own little cove, is one of Tito's former vacation villas (Villa Miločer, also part of the Aman resort). From here, you can enjoy the promenade that runs from the beach in front of the villa and to the next cove; eventually, this path will let you stroll along the water all the way to Budva.

Getting to Sveti Stefan: Sveti Stefan is just three miles beyond Budva. Coming around the bay from Budva (following signs toward *Bar*), you'll pass above the peninsula on the main road, watching for the well-marked pull-out on the right that offers classic views. After snapping your photos, if you want to get closer, continue down and turn off to the right, following signs to *Hotel Sveti Stefan*; you can park in the pay lot and walk along the beach as far as the causeway.

From Sveti Stefan to Dubrovnik: Figure 1.5 hours to the Croatian border (if you go via Tivat—rather than Kotor—and use the shortcut ferry across the Bay of Kotor, described on page 387), then another 45 minutes to Dubrovnik.

MONTENEGRO

BOSNIA-HERZEGOVINA

Bosna i Hercegovina

BOSNIA-HERZEGOVINA

 The 1990s weren't kind to Bosnia-Herzegovina: War. Destruction. Genocide. But apart from the tragic way it separated from Yugoslavia, the country has long been—and remains—a remarkable place, with ruggedly beautiful terrain, a unique mix of cultures and faiths, kind and welcoming people who pride themselves on their hospitality, and some of the most captivating sightseeing in southeastern Europe.

Little Bosnia-Herzegovina is a country with three faiths, three languages, and two alphabets. While the rest of Yugoslavia has splintered into countries dominated by one ethnicity, Bosnia remains an uneasy mix of scattered communities, with large contingents of all three major Yugoslav groups: Muslim Bosniaks, Eastern Orthodox Serbs, and Catholic Croats. These same three factions fought each other in that brutal war two decades ago, and today they're struggling to reconcile, work together, and put the country back on track.

A visit here offers a fascinating opportunity to sample the cultures of these three major faiths within a relatively small area. In the same day, you can inhale incense in a mystical-feeling Serbian Orthodox church, hear the subtle clicking of rosary beads in a Roman Catholic church, and listen to the Muslim call to prayer echo across a skyline of prickly minarets. Few places in Europe—or the world—cram so much diversity into such a small space.

About half of the people in Bosnia are "Bosniaks"—that is, Muslims. Travel in Bosnia offers an illuminating and unique glimpse into a culture that's both devoutly Muslim and fully European. Here, just a short drive from the touristy Dalmatian Coast, you can step into a mosque and learn about Islam directly from a Muslim. The country also holds one of the most important pilgrimage sites of the Roman Catholic world: Međugorje, where six residents have reported seeing visions of the Virgin Mary.

Bosnian coffee *(bosanska kafa)* is not just a drink, but a complex ritual that captures this culture's deliberate, stop-and-smell-the-tulips approach to life. Similar to what you might call "Turkish coffee," this unfiltered brew is prepared—and enjoyed—according

to a very specific routine: The fine grounds are stirred with water in a small copper-plated kettle with a long, straight handle (called a *džezva*). When it's ready to drink, it's done slo-o-o-owly: Carefully decant the coffee—easy now, don't pour off too many grounds—into a small ceramic cup. If you take sugar, put the sugar cube in the cup first, then pour the coffee over it. Sip your coffee gradually, and swirl the cup periodically to agitate and recaffeinate your brew. (If it's prepared—and drunk—properly, you won't even wind up with mud at the bottom of the cup.) Nibble on the Turkish delight candy *(rahatlokum)* that usually accompanies Bosnian coffee, and take time to chat with your travel partner or a new Bosnian friend. The point is not to slam down caffeine, but to have an excuse to slow your pulse and focus on where you are and who you're with. (In Mostar, Café de Alma is an ideal place to sample and learn more about Bosnian coffee—see page 432.)

Bosnian coffee is just one of the many facets of local culture that were adopted from the Ottomans (from today's Turkey) who ruled here for centuries. Thanks largely to this influence, Bosnian culture is permeated with a deep and abiding soulfulness that's rare in Europe. The Bosnian language features an entire lexicon of words that have no clear translation in other tongues or cultures.

Sarajevans embrace the concept of *raja*, meaning an unpretentious humility that stems from being one with a community or a circle of friends. *Merak* is enjoyment, particularly a relaxed atmosphere that arises when you're among friends—perhaps while listening to *sevdah* music (explained below) and sipping Bosnian coffee. Enjoying the company of friends while going out for snacks is called *mezetluk* (related to the Greek *mezedes*, or tapas-like small plates). And the insult *papak* (literally "hoof") means primitive, naive, tacky, or generally "outsider"—such as wearing white socks with dark shoes (a stereotypical Bosnian faux pas).

My favorite Bosnian word is *ćejf*, which means a sense of well-being while engaged in an enjoyable—and often highly idiosyncratic—routine. These rituals—from the way someone spins their worry beads, to their own unique procedure for preparing and drinking coffee or smoking a water pipe, to a dervish whirling in a worshipful trance—might be considered "OCD" (or simply "annoying") by many Americans...but Bosnians understand that it's simply *ćejf*. As long as your *ćejf* is not hurting anyone, it's tolerated—because everyone has one.

Sevdah—sometimes called "the Bosnian blues"—is a traditional folk music that mingles powerful emotions: sad and happy, convivial and nostalgic. Bosnians explain how the passionate, mournful strains of *sevdah* (which sounds distinctly eastern) pair perfectly with falling in love, drinking with friends, or contemplating loss. *Sevdah* is also the word for a poignant, melancholic mood—sort of the counterpoint to *merak*. Balancing these moods, Bosniaks explain, is key to emotional satisfaction.

To strike up a conversation, ask your new Bosnian friend to tell you more about what any of these terms means. All of them are examples of how Bosnians celebrate the "little things" that make life worth living...things that mainstream American and European cultures, all too often, see as barriers to progress.

In keeping with their generally relaxed culture, Bosnians are known for their gregarious sense of hospitality and their sharp sense of humor. Even during the darkest days of the war, they found ways to joke about the horrors unfolding around them. And today, they're quick to chuckle at their complicated political system and shambolic economy. Pointing to an ATM, your new Bosnian friend may say, "That's what we call our 'wailing wall.'" And they like to quip about their unfortunate circumstances in life: "Just our luck. Bosnia has so many Muslims—but no oil."

This unique Muslim culture seems fitting in this porous and mountainous land, where streams and rivers trickle endlessly. After all, the very name "Bosnia" comes from a term that means "running water" or "saturated"—and Muslim culture prizes constantly flowing water. While Christians bless still water and call it holy, for Muslims, the power of nature is in its movement; they prefer water to be continually flowing, cleansing, replenishing, circulating. Just as a dervish whirls to connect with the spirituality of the earth and the heavens, so, too, should water be in motion. When the Ottomans arrived here from their Turkish homeland, they must have felt right at home.

Bosnia rearranges your mental furniture more than any other country in this book. It offers an enticing glimpse at a completely different, very eastern worldview. And it comes with some in-your-face lessons about recent history.

While repairs are ongoing, you'll still be confronted by vivid and thought-provoking scars of the Yugoslav Wars, especially outside of the tourist zones. Poignant roadside memorials to fallen soldiers, burned-out husks of buildings, unmistakable starburst patterns in the pavement, and bullet holes in walls are a constant reminder that the country is still recovering—physically and psychologically. Driving through the countryside, you'll pass between Muslim, Croat, and Serb towns—each one decorated with its own provocative sectarian symbols. Bosnia teaches an essential lesson about how real—and destructive—war and interethnic strife truly are.

In this book I focus on a few key Bosnian destinations including several fascinating, user-friendly places within easy reach of the Dalmatian Coast: the Turkish-flavored city of Mostar (with its restored Old Bridge—one of Europe's most inspiring sights), some nearby attractions offering a more complete view of Herzegovina (Blagaj, Počitelj, and Stolac), and the Catholic shrine at Međugorje. A longer trip from Dalmatia—and well worth the trek—is the Bosnian capital of Sarajevo, with a spectacular mountain-valley setting, a multilayered history, powerful wartime stories, and a resilient populace of proud Sarajevans eager to show you their city.

Bosnia is highly recommended as a detour—both geographical and cultural—from the Croatian and Slovenian mainstream. Inquisitive visitors come away from a visit to Bosnia with a more

Bosnia-Herzegovina Almanac

Official Name: Bosna i Hercegovina (abbreviated "BiH"); the *i* means "and"—Bosnia and Herzegovina (the country's two regions). For simplicity, I generally call the whole country "Bosnia" in this book. "Bosna" (literally "running water") is the name of a major river here, while the tongue-twisting name "Herzegovina" (hert-seh-GOH-vee-nah) comes from the German word for "dukedom" (Herzog means "duke").

Snapshot History: Bosnia-Herzegovina's early history is similar to the rest of the region: Illyrians, Romans, and Slavs (oh, my!). In the late 15th century, Turkish rulers from the Ottoman Empire began a 400-year domination of the country. Many of the Ottomans' subjects converted to Islam, and their descendants remain Muslims today. Bosnia-Herzegovina became part of the Austro-Hungarian Empire in 1878, then Yugoslavia after World War I, until it declared independence in the spring of 1992. The bloody war that ensued came to an end in 1995. (For details, see the Understanding Yugoslavia chapter.)

Population: About 3.9 million. (There were about 100,000 identified casualties of the Yugoslav Wars in the 1990s, but many estimates of total casualties are double that number.) Someone who lives in Bosnia-Herzegovina, regardless of ethnicity, is called a "Bosnian." A southern Slav who practices Islam is called a "Bosniak." Today, about half of all Bosnians are Bosniaks (Muslims), about a third are Orthodox Serbs, and nearly 15 percent are Catholic Croats.

Area: 19,741 square miles (about the size of West Virginia). In both size and population, Bosnia is comparable to Croatia.

Geography: Bosnia and Herzegovina are two distinct regions that share the same mountainous country. Bosnia constitutes the majority of the country (in the north, with a continental climate), while Herzegovina is the southern tip (about a fifth of the total area, with a hotter Mediterranean climate). The nation's capital,

---

nuanced understanding of the former Yugoslavia. And Bosnia offers lower prices and a warmer welcome than you'll find on the Croatian coast. Overcome your jitters and dive in.

BOSNIAN HISTORY

With its mountainous landscape, remote from the more mainline areas of the western Balkans, Bosnia's evolution has followed a unique course. Even now, the people of Bosnia struggle with being outsiders—afloat on an oddball cultural island flanked by the Roman Catholic West (Croatia) and the Orthodox East (Serbia), borrowing elements from both but not fully belonging to either.

After periods of rule by the Illyrians and the Romans, Bos-

Sarajevo, has an estimated 310,000 people; Mostar is Herzegovina's biggest city (with approximately 130,000 people) and unofficial capital.

Red Tape: To enter Bosnia-Herzegovina, Americans and Canadians need only a passport (no visa required).

Economy: The country's economy has struggled since the war—the per capita GDP is just $9,800, and the official unemployment rate is around 44 percent.

Currency: The official currency is the Convertible Mark (Konvertibilna Marka, abbreviated KM locally, BAM internationally). The official exchange rate is $1 = about 1.80 KM. But merchants are usually willing to take euros, and (in Mostar) they'll often accept Croatian kunas, roughly converting prices with a simple formula:

2 KM = €1 = 7 kn (= about $1.10)

Telephones: Bosnia-Herzegovina's country code is 387. If calling from another country, first dial the international access code (00 in Europe, 011 in the US), then 387, then the area code (minus the initial zero), then the number.

Flag: The flag of Bosnia-Herzegovina is a blue field with a yellow triangle along the top edge. The three points of the triangle represent Bosnia-Herzegovina's three peoples (Bosniaks, Croats, Serbs), and the triangle itself resembles the physical shape of the country. A row of white stars underscores the longest side of the triangle. These stars—and the yellow-and-blue color scheme—echo the flag of the European Union (a nod to the EU's efforts to bring peace to the region). While this compromise flag sounds like a nice idea, almost no Bosnian embraces it; each group has its own unofficial but highly prized symbols and flags (such as the fleur-de-lis for the Bosniaks, the red-and-white checkerboard shield for the Croats, and the cross with the four C's for the Serbs)—many of which offend the other groups.

nia fostered its own thriving Slavic civilization during the Middle Ages. The local Bogomils were a homegrown branch of Christianity that was neither Catholic nor Orthodox—and was viewed with suspicion by both faiths. Literally "dear to God," the Bogomil faith was simple, ascetic, and somewhat mystic, combining elements of Slavic, Illyrian, and Celtic traditions. The Bogomils—who comprised a majority of the population of medieval Bosnia—had a thriving civilization. Vivid artifacts of the Bogomil kingdom still survive, such as their engraved burial grave markers, called *stećaks* (some of the best-preserved are in Stolac, near Mostar).

When the Ottomans (from today's Turkey) took over this land in the 15th century, they tolerated different faiths...but offered generous economic and political incentives to those who converted to Islam. In negotiating their religious freedoms with the sultans, Bosnia's Roman Catholics (who identified as Croats) and Eastern Orthodox (who identified as Serbs) both had the support of larger church hierarchies outside of Bosnia. But the Bogomils had no bargaining power, and were more likely to swap one monotheistic faith for another—creating the Muslim South Slav ethnicity that would come to be known as "Bosniak."

Under the Ottomans, Bosnia flourished. The Ottoman sultans invested in infrastructure (primarily bridges—including Mostar's Old Bridge—and fountains) and architecture, including many mosques, hammams (baths), caravanserais (inns), madrassas (theological schools), and so on. Bosnian Muslims rose through the ranks of the empire, becoming military generals, religious leaders, beloved poets, and even grand viziers (advisers to the sultans).

After four centuries of rule, the Ottoman Empire entered a steep decline. The Bosniak military hero Husein Gradaščević—nicknamed "The Dragon of Bosnia" (Zmaj od Bosne)—led an armed uprising in the 1830s. Though he died in battle, his movement eventually brought about the end of the archaic Ottoman system of rule in Bosnia, leading to a greater degree of autonomy.

But Bosnia was bound for even bigger changes. Unable to manage its vast holdings, in 1878 the Ottomans passed control of Bosnia-Herzegovina to their Habsburg rival, the Austro-Hungarian Empire (which already controlled neighboring Croatia and Slovenia). The Habsburgs quickly moved to modernize Bosnia, erecting buildings and investing in infrastructure. Sarajevo, Mostar, and many other Bosnian cities still show the impressive results of these efforts, which pulled Bosnia from their antiquated Ottoman ways into the modern world. Habsburg rule piped in mainstream European culture for the first time. Now Bosnian urbanites and aristocrats exchanged their ornate Turkish gowns for snazzy Austrian business suits...which they wore with their old fezzes and turbans.

Of course, not everybody bought what the Habsburgs were selling. Fierce underground resistance movements—such as the Black Hand—were determined to bring about self-rule for the South Slavs. Just 40 years after the Habsburgs took over, their empire began to topple—losing a Great War that began when the Habsburg heir, Archduke Franz Ferdinand, was assassinated in Sarajevo (see sidebar on page 495).

Following World War I, Bosnia was swept up in the movement to create a union of the South Slavs. The original incarnation of Yugoslavia, called "the Kingdom of the Serbs, Croats, and Slovenes," ignored the Bosniaks both in name and in political influence—they were merely along for the ride.

During World War II, Bosnia was part of the so-called "Independent State of Croatia" (run by the Nazis' puppet Ustaše government). Hitler's right-hand man, Heinrich Himmler, came to Bosnia to assess where the Bosniaks might fit into the Führer's ethnic vision. He determined that they were "Croats with Muslim culture"—that is, good ol' Aryans, who would be conscripted to fight. Himmler and the Ustaše leader, Ante Pavelić (a Bosnian-born Croat), squabbled over whether the Bosniaks would fight for the SS or the Ustaše. Ultimately they created an SS Hanjar/Handschar unit (named for a Turkish knife), issuing the conscripts a Germanic-style uniform with a ceremonial fez. The unit fought fiercely against Tito's Partisan Army, and participated in the Ustaše's genocidal efforts against Serbs, Jews, and other "undesirables." But as the war wore on, more and more of these troops became disillusioned with the Nazi cause, and deserted in large numbers.

Some of the most dramatic WWII battles between the Yugoslav Partisans and the Nazis took place here in Bosnia. One of the most famous was the Battle of the Neretva, in which Tito ingeniously saved more than 4,000 of his wounded troops—effectively turning the tide of the war (for more on this battle, see page 515).

The postwar communist country of Yugoslavia was born in the Bosnian town of Jajce on November 29, 1943, when Partisan generals met to outline the future of a hoped-for post-Nazi state. But in the new incarnation of Yugoslavia, many Bosniaks still felt like second-class citizens. Local Muslims recall that Yugoslav government-issued textbooks reinforced negative stereotypes. For example, they might say "Sasha [a typically Serb name] is working," but "Mujo [a typically Muslim name] is a bad boy."

Even after the outbreak of violence between breakaway republics Slovenia and Croatia and Serb-dominated Yugoslavia in 1991, things stayed strangely calm in Bosnia. But when the Bosnian conflict finally erupted in 1992, it was war of the most brutal kind. A three-way war exploded between Bosnian Croats (supported by Croatia proper), Bosnian Serbs (supported by Serbia proper), and Bosniaks (who, caught in the crossfire, realized they had no real European allies). The early to mid-1990s saw the worst human, architectural, and cultural devastation in Bosnian history. Sarajevo, Srebrenica, and Mostar became synonymous with sectarian strife, horrific sieges, and shocking genocide. (For more details on the war, see page 740 of the Understanding Yugoslavia chapter.)

The Dayton Peace Accords that ended the conflict here in 1995 gerrymandered the nation into three separate regions: the Federation of Bosnia and Herzegovina (FBiH, shared by Bosniaks and Croats, roughly in the western and central parts of the country), the Republika Srpska (RS, dominated by Serbs, generally to the north and east), and the Brčko District (BD, a tiny corner of the country, with a mix of the ethnicities). For the most part, each of the three native ethnic groups stay in "their" part of this divided country, but tourists can move freely among them.

On your visit, tune into the many ways that the Bosniaks, Croats, and Serbs of Bosnia are working to coexist. To satisfy the country's various factions, the currency uses both the Roman and the Cyrillic alphabets, and bills have different figureheads and symbols (some bills feature Bosniaks, others Serbs). Until very recently, the alphabet used on road signs changed with the territory: Roman alphabet in Muslim and Croat areas, Cyrillic alphabet in Serb lands. But now all road signs throughout Bosnia-Herzegovina are required to appear in both alphabets—though that doesn't prevent vandals from spray-painting over the alphabet they don't like. License plates also used different alphabets, but this led to vandalism. Today's license plates use only letters that are common to both alphabets.

Towns with mixed populations are either effectively divided in half, or have buildings clearly marked with symbols indicating the ethnicity of the occupant. Small-town schoolhouses often operate "two schools under one roof," with separate entrances and staggered shifts for the Bosniak and Croat kids...who, virtually from birth, are constantly reminded they are very different from each other. In some towns, a beautifully restored Orthodox church may sit across from the battered footprint of a long-gone mosque, or vice versa.

Bosnia has a central government, but each population group also has its own autonomous government and sub-agencies, resulting in four essentially redundant bureaucracies. The country is also divided into 10 state-like cantons, each of which also has some governmental authority. Imagine the inefficiency. On top of all this, Bosnia is still navigating the complex transition from communism to capitalism, and rebuilding from a devastating war. It's a miracle that things here work at all.

More than 20 years later, the delicate compromises that were necessary to end a horrifying war have become almost too complicated to maintain. For Bosnia-Herzegovina to fully recover, all three groups must learn to truly set aside their differences and work

Fundamentalist Islam in Bosnia?

Islam is a hot topic in today's Europe, where some citizens scapegoat Muslim immigrants. And even though Bosnia's Muslims are indigenous, they're not immune to criticism—especially from their Serb and Croat rivals. While Bosniaks have a long history as a peace-loving people, critics allege that elements of the population are experimenting with some alarming fundamentalist Islamic ideologies.

These allegations do have some basis in fact. During the war and genocide of the 1990s, many Bosniaks felt abandoned by Europe and the US, who were too timid to step in and "take sides" to end the violence. In his people's darkest hour, desperate Bosnian President Alija Izetbegović recruited assistance from the only group willing to offer help: Muslim fundamentalists from the Middle East and North Africa. Several hundred mujahideen (Islamic jihadists) came to Bosnia to train Bosniak soldiers—and participated in bloody massacres of Serbs and Croats. They brought with them the dangerous ideas of Wahhabism, an ultraconservative movement bent on "purifying" Islam, often through violent means. According to reports, Izetbegović was even in contact with Osama bin Laden. In some cases, the mujahideen offered donations to widows of šehids (Bosniak martyrs).

Today, while waning, these groups' influence persists. Muslim countries have helped to fund the postwar reconstruction of Bosnia, especially the rebuilding of mosques and madrassas. Just as the end of atheistic, communist Yugoslav rule kick-started a passion for Catholicism in Croatia and the Orthodox faith in Serbia, many Muslims in Bosnia are today actively pursuing their faith. You may even see women wearing traditional Muslim headscarves—a rare sight before the war, when most Bosniaks dressed just like their Serb and Croat neighbors. (But note that many veiled women are likely Muslim tourists from elsewhere.)

And what about those mujahideen fighters? Most left the country after the war, as dictated by the Dayton Peace Accords. But small pockets of Wahhabists still live in remote areas high in the mountains. The vast majority of practicing Muslims in Bosnia explicitly denounce the Wahhabists—just as any peaceful, moderate country looks with concern upon its lunatic fringe.

together. Pessimists (who are abundant in this region) don't like Bosnia's chances, and Bosnian Serbs still talk loudly about secession (Republika Srpska's president, Milorad Dodik, is an outspoken separatist). But others see signs of hope, such as the young people from the three faiths now beginning to cautiously intermingle, as their ancestors did for centuries. Will Bosniak, Serb, and Croat youth manage to transcend the fear and anger that tainted their parents' and grandparents' country in the 20th century? That history is yet to be written.

BOSNIAN FOOD

Bosnia-Herzegovina dines on grilled meat, stewed vegetables, soft cheeses, and other foods you may think of as "Turkish" or "Greek." On menus, look for the word *domaća*—"homemade." Another key term is *pod sača,* which means "under the bell" (similar to *peka* in Croatia); this means that it has been slow cooked under a copper lid covered with hot coals. For a rundown of the most common items you'll eat in Bosnia—and throughout the Balkans—see the "Balkan Flavors" sidebar.

Dolma is a bell pepper stuffed with minced meat, vegetables, and rice. A *sarma* or *sarmica* is similar, but stuffed in cabbage leaves rather than in a pepper, while *japrak* is stuffed grape leaves. *Begova čorba* ("nobleman's stew") is a meaty vegetable soup. *Grah* is bean soup. And one Bosnian institution—which you'll see at roadside truck stops across the country—is the whole lamb grilled on a spit.

While Balkan cuisine favors meat, a nice veggie complement is *đuveđ* (JOO-vedge)—a spicy mix of stewed vegetables, flavored with tomatoes and peppers. And the best salad option is *šopska salata*—a Greek-style salad of tomatoes, cucumbers, onions, and peppers, smothered in grated feta-like *sirene* cheese. *Srpska salata* ("Serb salad") is often the same thing, but may have extra cheese.

Bosnian desserts—typically sweetened with honey rather than sugar—are another local treat. Drop by a sweets shop and peruse your options. *Baklava,* a phyllo dough pastry with nuts and honey, is a familiar choice. *Kadaif* is similar, but made with shredded sheets of dough. *Tulumba* is a pastry cylinder drenched in honey, and *tufahija* is an apple stuffed with walnuts, soaked in honey, and topped with whipped cream. *Smokvača* is a dense, very sweet fig pie. You'll also see blocks of nougat-like *halva,* made from sesame paste. And every cup of Bosnian coffee comes with a Turkish delight candy.

Bosnia produces some wine, but it's mostly consumed domestically. Sarajevso Pivo, brewed in the capital, is the favored brand of beer. In Bosnia, "coffee" is *kafa* (not *kava,* as in Croatia and Slovenia). While you can easily get espresso-style coffee, *bosanska kafa* (unfiltered "Bosnian coffee") is more local—and more fun to drink. (For tips on this ritual, see earlier.)

BOSNIAN LANGUAGE

Technically, Bosnia-Herzegovina has three languages—Bosnian, Serbian, and Croatian. But all three are mutually intelligible variants of what was until recently considered a single language: Serbo-Croatian. The Croatian survival phrases on page 37 will work

Balkan Flavors

All of the countries of the Balkan Peninsula—from Slovenia to Greece—have several foods in common: The Ottomans who

controlled much of this territory for centuries imported some goodies that remained standard fare here long after they left town. Whether you're in Bosnia-Herzegovina, Slovenia, Croatia, Montenegro, or Serbia, it's worth seeking out some of these local tastes.

A popular, cheap fast food you'll see everywhere is **burek** (BOO-rehk)—phyllo dough filled with meat, cheese, spinach, or apples. *Burek* rivals pizza-by-the-slice as the most popular take-away snack food in southeastern Europe. The best *burek* is *pod sača*—cooked under a baking lid.

Grilled meats are a staple of Balkan cuisine. You'll most often see **ćevapčići** (cheh-VAHP-chee-chee), or simply **ćevapi** (cheh-VAH-pee)—minced meat (typically a mix of lamb and beef) formed into a sausage-link shape, then grilled. There are variations: Sarajevo-style *(sarajevski ćevapi)* is typically eaten with grilled onions and stuffed into a pita-like flatbread called **somun**; Banja Luka-style *(banjalučki ćevapi)* is one long, continuous *ćevap* with hot peppers on the side.

Ražnjići (RAZH-nyee-chee) are small pieces of steak on a skewer, like a shish kebab. **Pljeskavica** (plehs-kah-VEET-suh) is similar to *ćevapčići*, except the meat is in the form of a hamburger-like patty. **Pileći** is chicken, and **piščančje** is grilled chicken breast. **Sudžukice** are sausages, and **ćufte** are meatballs.

You just can't eat any of this stuff without the ever-present condiment **ajvar** (EYE-var). Made from red bell pepper and eggplant, *ajvar* is like ketchup with a kick. Many Americans pack a jar of this distinctive sauce to remember the flavors of the Balkans when they get back home. (You may even be able to find it at specialty grocery stores in the US—look for "eggplant/red pepper spread.")

Particularly in Bosnia, another side-dish you'll see is the soft, spreadable—and tasty—cheese called **kajmak**. **Lepinje** is a pita-like grilled bread, which is often wrapped around *ćevapčići* or *pljeskavica* to make a sandwich. **Uštipci** is a fry bread that's especially popular throughout Bosnia-Herzegovina.

Ajvar, *kajmak*, *lepinje*, and diced raw onions are the perfect complement to a **"mixed grill"** of various meats on a big platter—the quintessence of Balkan cuisine on one plate.

just fine throughout Bosnia-Herzegovina. Bosniaks and Croats use basically the same Roman alphabet we do, while Serbs use the Cyrillic alphabet. You'll see both alphabets on currency, official documents, and road signs, but the Roman alphabet predominates in virtually every destination covered in this book. Most people also speak English.

BOSNIA-HERZEGOVINA

MOSTAR AND NEARBY

Mostar • Blagaj • Počitelj • Stolac • Međugorje

Mostar (MOH-star) encapsulates the best and the worst of the former Yugoslavia. During the Tito years, its residents—Catholic Croats, Orthodox Serbs, and Muslim Bosniaks—enjoyed an idyllic mingling of cultures, all living together in harmony. Their differences were spanned by an Old Bridge that epitomized an optimistic vision of a Yugoslavia in which ethnicity didn't matter. But then, as the country unraveled in the early 1990s, Mostar was gripped by a gory three-way war among those same peoples...and that famous bridge crumbled into the Neretva River.

Mostar is still rebuilding, and the bullet holes and destroyed buildings are ugly reminders that the last time you saw this place, it was probably on the nightly news. Western visitors may also be struck by the immediacy of the Muslim culture that permeates Mostar, where minarets share the horizon with church steeples. During the Ottomans' 400-year control of this region, many Slavic subjects converted to Islam (see sidebar on page

419). And, although they retreated in the late 19th century, the Ottomans left behind a rich architectural, cultural, and religious legacy that has forever shaped Mostar. Five times each day, loudspeakers on minarets crackle to life, and the call to prayer warbles through the streets. In many parts of the city, you'd swear you were in Turkey.

Despite the scars of war, Mostar's setting is stunning: strad-

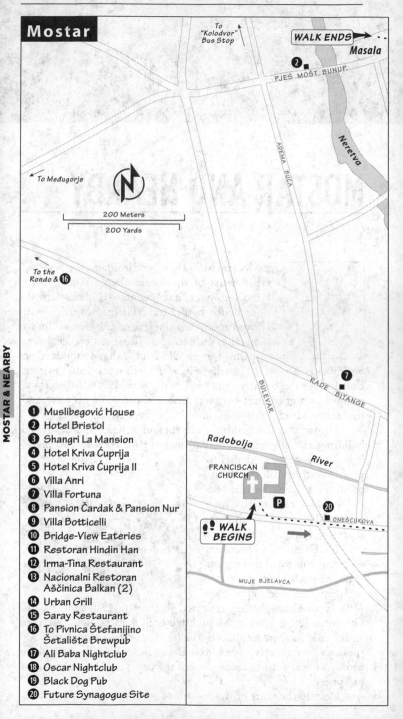

MOSTAR & NEARBY

Mostar

To "Kolodvor" Bus Stop

WALK ENDS →

Masala

❷

PJEŠ MOST BUNUP

ADEMA BUĆA

Neretva

To Međugorje

200 Meters

200 Yards

To the Rondo & ⓰

RADE BITANGE

❼

BULEVAR

Radobolja   River

FRANCISCAN CHURCH

P

❷⓪   ONEŠĆUKOVA

WALK BEGINS →

MUJE BJELAVCA

❶ Muslibegović House
❷ Hotel Bristol
❸ Shangri La Mansion
❹ Hotel Kriva Ćuprija
❺ Hotel Kriva Ćuprija II
❻ Villa Anri
❼ Villa Fortuna
❽ Pansion Čardak & Pansion Nur
❾ Villa Botticelli
⓾ Bridge-View Eateries
⓫ Restoran Hindin Han
⓬ Irma-Tina Restaurant
⓭ Nacionalni Restoran Aščinica Balkan (2)
⓮ Urban Grill
⓯ Saray Restaurant
⓰ To Pivnica Štefanijino Šetalište Brewpub
⓱ Ali Baba Nightclub
⓲ Oscar Nightclub
⓳ Black Dog Pub
⓴ Future Synagogue Site

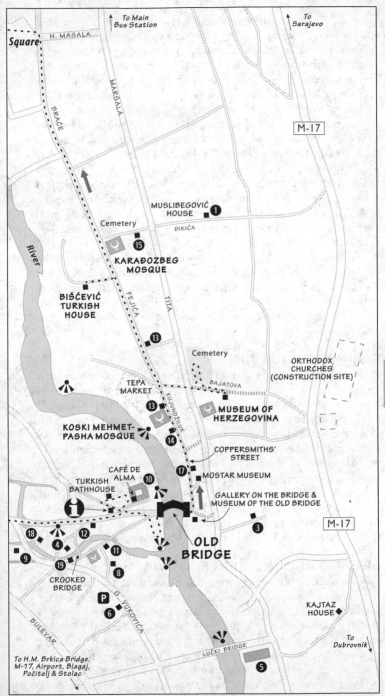

Square

To Main
Bus Station

To
Sarajevo

H. MASALA

BRAĆE

MARŠALA

M-17

MUSLIBEGOVIĆ
HOUSE ●1

Cemetery

ĐIKIĆA

●15

KARAĐOZBEG
MOSQUE

River

BIŠĆEVIĆ
TURKISH
HOUSE

FEJIĆA

TITA

●13

Cemetery

ORTHODOX
CHURCHES
(CONSTRUCTION SITE)

TEPA
MARKET

BAJATOVA

●13

KUJUNDŽILUK

MUSEUM OF
HERZEGOVINA

KOSKI MEHMET-
PASHA MOSQUE

●14

COPPERSMITHS'
STREET

CAFÉ DE
ALMA

●10

●17

MOSTAR MUSEUM

TURKISH
BATHHOUSE

GALLERY ON THE BRIDGE &
MUSEUM OF THE OLD BRIDGE

ℹ

●3

M-17

●18

●12

●4

OLD
BRIDGE

●9

●19

●11

CROOKED
BRIDGE

●8

P

G. VUKOVIĆA

●6

KAJTAZ
HOUSE ◆

BULEVAR

To H.M. Brkica Bridge,
M-17, Airport, Blagaj,
Počitelj & Stolac

LUČKI BRIDGE

●5

To
Dubrovnik

MOSTAR & NEARBY

dling the banks of the gorgeous Neretva River, with tributaries and waterfalls carving their way through the rocky landscape. The sightseeing—mosques, old Turkish-style houses, and that spine-tingling Old Bridge—is more engaging than much of what you'll find in Croatia or Slovenia. And it's cheap: Hotels, food, and museums cost less than half of what you'll pay in Dubrovnik or Ljubljana.

In this chapter, I've also included some worthwhile attractions near Mostar: the river spring and whirling dervish house at Blagaj, the striking fortified hill town of Počitelj, and workaday Stolac, which sits upon some very impressive history. The top Croat sight in Bosnia-Herzegovina is Međugorje, where Catholic pilgrims flock from around the world to hear tales of a Virgin Mary apparition. All of these places are within a half-hour's drive of Mostar; take your pick to fit into the drive between Mostar and coastal destinations.

While a visit to Mostar was depressing not that long ago, the city gets more uplifting all the time: Mostarians are rebuilding at an impressive pace, tentatively reintegrating, and working hard to make Mostar tourist-friendly. Mostar is well on its way to reclaiming its status as one of the premier destinations in the former Yugoslavia.

PLANNING YOUR TIME

Bosnia-Herzegovina is a major cultural detour on your Dalmatian vacation—but it's easy to reach, just a three-hour drive or four-hour bus ride from Dubrovnik or Split. To fit a Mostar overnight into your itinerary, consider a round-trip plan that takes you south along the coast, then back north via Bosnia-Herzegovina (for example, Split-Hvar-Korčula-Dubrovnik-Mostar-back to Split).

Mostar's Old Town is packed with day-trippers at midday, but empty in the morning and evening. You can get a good feel for Mostar in just a few hours, but a full day—and, ideally, an overnight—gives you time to linger and ponder. My self-guided walk provides a framework for a visit of any duration. With extra time, venture to the western (Croat) part of the city, which most tourists miss.

GETTING AROUND HERZEGOVINA

By Car: Coming with your own car gives you maximum flexibility, and a number of interesting routes connect Mostar to the coast (for detailed route information, see "Route Tips for Drivers" on page 453). If you do plan to drive here, let your car-rental company know in advance, to ensure you have the appropriate paperwork for crossing the border. If you're not up for driving yourself, consider splurging on a **driver** to bring you here (for drivers based in Dubrovnik, see page 288; for a Mostar-based driver, see page 429).

Drivers may suggest several detours en route. Do your homework to know which ones interest you (for example, Međugorje isn't worth the extra time for most visitors), and don't hesitate to say that you want to just max out on time in Mostar itself.

By Bus: Public buses work well to connect Mostar with destinations on the Dalmatian Coast (particularly Split and Dubrovnik). For details, see "Mostar Connections," page 451.

By Package Tour: Taking a package excursion from a Dalmatian resort town sounds like an efficient way to visit Mostar or Međugorje. But it has its cons: Count on lots of hours on a crowded bus, listening to a lackluster, multilingual tour guide reading from a script, and precious little time in the destinations themselves. I'd pick an itinerary focusing on Mostar itself, and avoid tours that include a pointless boat trip on the Neretva River or time in Međugorje. Those that add a quick visit to the worthwhile town of Počitelj are a better deal. Ask for details at any travel agency in Dalmatia.

Orientation to Mostar

Mostar (pop. 130,000) fills a basin surrounded by arid mountains and split down the middle by the emerald-green Neretva River. Bosniaks live mostly on the east side of the river (plus a strip on the west bank) and Croats in the modern sprawl to the west. The populations are beginning to mix again...tentatively. Virtually all of the sights are in the Bosniak zone, but visitors move freely throughout the city, and don't even notice the division. The cobbled, Turkish-feeling Old Town (called the "Stari Grad" or "Stara Čaršija") surrounds the town's centerpiece, the Old Bridge.

The skyline is pierced by the minarets of various mosques, but none is as big as the two major Catholic (Croat) symbols in town, both erected after the Yugoslav Wars: the giant white cross on the hilltop (marking the place from where Croat forces shelled the Bosniak side of the river, including the Old Bridge); and the enormous (almost 100-foot-tall) bell tower of the Franciscan Church of Sts. Peter and Paul. A monumental Orthodox cathedral on the hillside across the river, destroyed during the war, is now being rebuilt.

A note about safety: You'll see bombed-out buildings everywhere, even in the core of the city. A few are marked with *Warning! Dangerous Ruin* signs; for safety's sake, never wander into any building that appears damaged or deserted. Also, pickpockets operate in the tourist zone; watch your valuables, especially on the Old Bridge.

TOURIST INFORMATION

The virtually worthless TI shares a building with a tour office, but it does give out a free town map and a few other brochures on Mostar and Herzegovina (sporadic hours, a block from the Old Bridge at Rade Bitange 5, tel. 036/580-275, www.turizam.mostar.ba).

ARRIVAL IN MOSTAR

By Bus or Train: The **main bus station** sits next to the giant but mostly deserted **train station,** north of the Old Town on the east side of the river. At the bus station, you'll find ticket windows and a left-luggage counter in the Autoprevoz lobby facing the bus stalls. You can check schedules and buy tickets in this office for most buses *except* the many connections operated by Globtour, whose office is nearby (exit Autoprevoz, turn left, and walk to the end of the bus-station area). Because these two companies don't cooperate well, you may have to check with both to get the complete schedule. To find your way to the town center, walk through the bus stalls and parking lot and turn left at the big road, which leads you to the Old Town area in about 15 minutes. A taxi into town costs about 5-10 KM.

It's possible (though unlikely) that you'll arrive at Mostar's secondary bus station, called **"Kolodvor,"** on the west/Croat side of town. From here, it's a dreary 20-minute walk into town: Turn right out of the bus station area, turn left down the busy Dubrovačka street, and head straight to the river (which you can follow south into the Old Town). Globtour buses that stop at Kolodvor will likely continue to the main bus station; those run by other companies probably won't (in either case, ask).

For details on both stations, see "Mostar Connections," later.

By Car: For tips on driving to Mostar from the Dalmatian Coast, see page 453.

HELPFUL HINTS

Local Cash: Need Convertible Marks? The most convenient ATM in town is to the left of Fortuna Tours' door, right at the top of Coppersmiths' Street (but on a short visit, you can generally skip a trip to the ATM, as many vendors here also accept Croatian kunas and euros).

Travel Agency: The handy **Fortuna Tours** travel agency, right in the heart of the Old Town (at the top of Coppersmiths' Street), sells all the tourist stuff, can book a local guide or arrange a transfer, and answers basic questions (long hours daily, Kujundžiluk 2, tel. 036/551-887, main office tel. 036/552-197, www.fortuna.ba, headoffice@fortuna.ba).

Local Guides: Hiring a guide is an excellent investment to help you understand Mostar. I've enjoyed working with **Alma**

Elezović, a warm-hearted Bosniak who loves sharing her city and her wartime stories with visitors (€20/person, up to €70/group for 2-3-hour tour, mobile 061-467-699, http://almasguidedtours.blogspot.com, aelezovic@gmail.com). If Alma is busy, she may send you with her son **Jaz** (pronounced "yahz"), who speaks perfect English and offers a younger generation's perspective. Other companies around town can arrange for a local guide at extremely reasonable prices (2-hour tour—€30/2 people, €40/4 people, includes entry to mosque and/or Turkish house); try **Fortuna Tours,** listed previously.

Local Driver: Ermin Elezović, husband of local guide Alma (see above), is a gregarious, English-speaking driver who enjoys taking visitors on day trips from Mostar. You can also hire him for a transfer between Mostar and destinations anywhere in Croatia (prices for a van for up to 6 people: €120 for one-way transfer to Sarajevo, Split, or Dubrovnik with a few brief sightseeing stops on the way; €140 one-way to Split airport or the Korčula ferry; €240 for an all-day round-trip from Mostar to Sarajevo, Split, or Dubrovnik; also available for longer trips— contact Ermin and Alma for help planning out a multiday itinerary; mobile 061-908-597, elezovicermin@gmail.com).

Updates to This Book: For updates to this book, check www.ricksteves.com/update.

Sights in Mostar

CENTRAL MOSTAR

Mostar's major sights line up along a handy L-shaped axis. I've laced them together as an enjoyable orientation walk: From the Franciscan Church, you'll walk straight until you cross the Old Bridge. Then you'll turn left and walk basically straight (with a couple of detours) to the big square at the far end of town. This walk is designed to help you see both the main tourist zones, and the parts of workaday Mostar that many visitors miss.

• *Begin at the...*

▲Franciscan Church of Sts. Peter and Paul

In a town of competing religious architectural exclamation points, this spire is the tallest. The church, which adjoins a working Franciscan monastery, was built in 1997, after the fighting subsided (the same year as the big cross on the hill). The tower, which looks like a minaret on steroids, is modeled after typical Croatian/Venetian campanile bell towers. Step inside to see the cavernous interior, still not fully decorated. (Sunday Mass here is an inspiration.)

• *The church fronts the busy boulevard called...*

▲Bulevar

"The Boulevard" was once the modern main drag of Mostar. In the early 1990s, this city of Bosniaks, Croats, and Serbs began to fracture under the pressure of politicians' propaganda. In October of 1991, Bosnia-Herzegovina—following Croatia's and Slovenia's example, but without the blessing of its large Serb minority—began a process of splitting from Yugoslavia. Soon after, the Serb-dominated Yugoslav People's Army invaded. Mostar's Bosniaks and Croats joined forces to battle the Serbs and succeeded in claiming the city as their own, forcing out the Serb residents.

But even as they fended off the final, distant bombardments of Serb forces, Mostar's Bosniaks (Muslims) and Croats (Catholics) turned their guns against each other. This street became the front line—and virtually all of its buildings were destroyed. The area to the east of here (toward the river) was held by Bosniaks, while the western part of town was Croat territory.

While many of the buildings along here have been rebuilt, some damage is still evident. Stroll a bit, imagining the hell of a split community at war. Neighbors, friends, and even families fought among themselves. Mortar craters in the asphalt leave poignant scars. During those dark war years, the Croats on the hill above laid siege to the Bosniaks on the other side, cutting off electricity, blocking roads, and blaring Croatian rabble-rousing pop music and propaganda speeches from loudspeakers. Through '93 and '94, when the Bosniaks dared to go out, they sprinted past exposed places, for fear of being picked off by a sniper. Local Bosniaks explain, "Night was time to live"—cloaking themselves in black clothes, under cover of darkness. When people were killed along this street, their corpses were sometimes left here for months, because it wasn't safe to retrieve the bodies. Tens of thousands fled, many taking refuge elsewhere in Europe, in the US, and in Canada.

The stories are shocking, and it's difficult to see the war impartially. But looking back on this complicated war, I try not to broadly cast one side as the "aggressors" and another as the "victims." Bosniaks were victimized in Mostar, just as Croats were victimized during the siege of Dubrovnik (explained on page 296). And, as the remains of a destroyed Orthodox cathedral on the hillside above Mostar attest, Serbs also took their turn as victims. Every conflict has many sides, and it's the civilians who often pay the highest toll—no matter their affiliation.

Head down Onešćukova street, across the Bulevar from the church. A few steps down on the left, the vacant lot with the menorah-ornamented metal fence will someday be the **Mostar Synagogue.** While the town's Jewish population has dwindled to a handful of families since World War II, many Jews courageously served as aid workers and intermediaries when Croats and Bosniaks were killing each other. In recognition of their loving help, the community of Mostar gave them this land for a new synagogue.
• *Continue past the synagogue site, entering the Old Town and following the canyon of the...*

Radobolja River Valley

Cross the small river called Radobolja, which winds over waterfalls

and several mills on its way to join the Neretva, and enter the city's cobbled historic core (keeping the river on your right). As you step upon the smooth, ankle-twisting river stones, you suddenly become immersed in the Turkish heritage of Mostar. Around you are several fine examples of Mostar's traditional heavy limestone-shingled roofs. From the arrival of the Ottomans all the way through the end of World War II, Mostar had fewer than 15,000 residents—this compact central zone was pretty much all there was to the city. It wasn't until the Tito years that it became industrialized and grew like crazy. As you explore, survey the atmospheric eateries clinging to the walls of the canyon—and choose one for a meal or drink later in the day (I've noted a couple under "Eating in Mostar," later).

Walk straight ahead until you reach a break in the buildings on your right. Belly up to the wall (you may have to squeeze between souvenir stands). The mosque you see across the river is one of 10 in town. Before the Yugoslav Wars there were 36, and before World War II there were even more (many of those damaged or destroyed in World War II were never repaired or replaced, since Tito's communist Yugoslavia discouraged religion). But the recent war inspired Muslims to finally rebuild. Each of the town's reconstructed mosques was financed by a Muslim nation or organization (this one was a gift from an international association for the protection of Islamic heritage). Some critics (read: Croats) allege that these foreign Muslim influences—which generally interpret their faith more strictly than the typically progressive and laid-back Bosniaks—are threatening to flood the country with a rising tide of Islamic fundamentalism. For more on this debate, see page 419.

• *Look upriver. Spanning the river below the mosque (partly obscured by trees) is the...*

▲Crooked Bridge (Kriva Ćuprija)

This miniature Old Bridge was built nearly a decade before its more famous sibling, supposedly to practice for the real deal. Damaged—but not destroyed—during the war, the original bridge was swept away several years later by floods. The bridge you see today is a reconstruction.

• *Continue on the same street deeper into the city center. After a few steps, take a detour to the left, to the area I like to call...*

"Hammam Square"

Heading up this quiet eddy off the rushing river of the main tourist strip, you'll emerge into a small square. The glimmering domes mark the **hammam,** or Turkish bathhouse. Destroyed in World War II, this was only rebuilt a few years ago. A Turkish organization—as if restaking their original Ottoman claim here—has recently opened a Turkish bath museum in this space.

As you face the hammam, notice the long building to your right. If you go in the door near the left end of this building, then cross straight through the courtyard, you'll pop out at a **terrace** where various restaurants offer mediocre food with stunning views of the Old Bridge—a great spot for a floodlit dinner.

Near the right end of that same long building is one of Mostar's best-kept secrets. At **Café de Alma,** soulful Jaz ("yahz") loves to explain the rich heritage and traditions around Bosnian coffee (which you may think of as "Turkish coffee"). For 2 KM, he'll show you his coffee roaster (the only one in Mostar), then grind and pour you a cup of Bosnian coffee. The coffee is good, but learning about this important facet of Bosnian culture is even better. He also has teas and handmade syrups for refreshing drinks, and sells bags of his coffee (either beans or ground) and Bosnian coffee gear (daily 9:00-18:00 but may be closed sporadically).

• *Head back to the main drag and continue toward the bridge, passing several more market stalls. Because the bridge itself can be crowded with tourists (and pickpockets), I'd hike down to the **riverbank** below to read the following description while enjoying a dramatic view of the stunning structure. To get there, hook right at the Šadrvan restaurant, then watch for the steps down to the river on your left.*

▲▲▲Old Bridge (Stari Most)

One of the most evocative sights in the former Yugoslavia, this iconic bridge confidently spanned the Neretva River for more than four centuries. Mostarians of all faiths love the bridge and speak of "him" as an old friend. Traditionally considered the point where East meets West, the Old Bridge is as symbolic as it is beautiful. Dramatically arched and flanked by two boxy towers, the bridge is stirring—even if you don't know its history.

Before the Old Bridge, the Neretva was spanned only by a rickety suspension bridge, guarded by *mostari* ("watchers of the bridge"), who gave the city its name. Commissioned in 1557 by the Ottoman Sultan Süleyman the Magnificent, and completed just nine years later, the Old Bridge was a technological marvel for its time..."the longest single-span stone arch on the planet." (In other words, it's the granddaddy of the Rialto Bridge in Venice.) Because of its graceful keystone design—and the fact that there are empty spaces inside the structure—it's much lighter than it appears. And yet, nearly 400 years after it was built, the bridge was still sturdy enough to support the weight of the Nazi tanks that rolled in to occupy Mostar. Over the centuries, it became the symbol of the town and region—a metaphor in stone for the way the diverse faiths and cultures here were able to bridge the gaps that divided them.

All of that drastically changed in the early 1990s. Beginning in May of 1993, as the city became engulfed in war, the Old Bridge frequently got caught in the crossfire. Old tires were slung over its sides to absorb some of the impact from nearby artillery and shrapnel. In November of 1993, Croats began shelling the bridge from the top of the mountain (where the cross is now—you can just see its tip peeking over the hill from the top of the bridge). The bridge took several direct hits on November 8; on November 9, another shell caused the venerable Old Bridge to lurch, then tumble in pieces into the river. The mortar inside, which contained pink bauxite, turned the water red as it fell in. Locals said that their old friend was bleeding.

The decision to destroy the bridge was partly strategic—to cut off a Bosniak-controlled strip on the west bank from Bosniak forces on the east. (News footage from the time shows Bosniak soldiers scurrying back and forth over the bridge.) But there can be no doubt that, like the Yugoslav Army's siege of Dubrovnik, the attack was also partly symbolic: the destruction of a bridge representing the city's Muslim legacy.

MOSTAR & NEARBY

After the war, city leaders decided to rebuild the Old Bridge. Chunks of the original bridge were dredged up from the river. But the limestone had been compromised by soaking in the water for so long, so it couldn't be used (you can still see these pieces of the old Old Bridge on the riverbank below). Having pledged to rebuild  the bridge authentically, restorers cut new stone from the original quarry, and each block was hand-carved. Then they assembled the stones with the same technology used by the Ottomans 450 years ago: Workers erected wooden scaffolding and fastened the blocks together with iron hooks cast in lead. The project was overseen by UNESCO and cost over $13 million, funded largely by international donors.

It took longer to rebuild the bridge in the 21st century than it did to build it in the 16th century. But on July 23, 2004, the new Old Bridge was inaugurated with much fanfare and was immediately embraced by both the city and the world as a sign of reconciliation.

Since its restoration, another piece of bridge history has fully returned, as young men once again jump from the bridge 75 feet down into the Neretva (which remains icy cold even in summer). Done both for the sake of tradition and to impress girls, this custom carried on even during the time when the destroyed bridge was temporarily replaced by a wooden one. Now the tower on the west side of the bridge houses the office of the local "Divers Club," a loosely run organization that continues this long-standing ritual. On hot summer days, you'll see divers making a ruckus and collecting donations at the top of the bridge. They tease and tease, standing up on the railing and pretending they're about to jump...then getting down and asking for more money. (If he's wearing trunks rather than Speedos, he's not a diver—just a teaser.) Once they collect about €30, one of them will take the plunge.

• *Now hike across the Old Bridge. Watch your footing—the big, chunky steps, spaced at awkward intervals, seem designed to trip up distracted tourists.*

Inside the Halebija Tower at the near end of the bridge, up the stairs (above the Divers Club), the **War Photo Exhibition** displays 50 somber, poignant wartime images taken by photojournalist Wade Goddard. While small, the collection of black-and-white images puts a human face on the suffering by focusing not on the conflict itself, but on the everyday people whose lives were ripped apart by the war (6 KM, daily mid-July-mid-Oct 9:00-21:00; April-mid-July and mid-Oct-Nov 11:00-18:00, closed Dec-March).

From the top of the bridge, see how many of the town's 10 mosques you can spot (I counted seven minarets).

• *Once across the bridge, three exhibits are on your right; unless you have a special interest, I'd skip these and save your time for the more worth-while sights described later.*

Exhibits near the Old Bridge

The **Gallery on the Bridge** is a bookstore operated by the local Islamic cultural center, filling a former mosque for soldiers who guarded the bridge. Explore the good, free photo exhibition of powerful images of war-torn Mostar. The shop sells an impressively wide range of books about the former Yugoslavia and its troubled breakup. You can pay 2 KM to watch a seven-minute montage of videos and photos of the bridge, before, during, and after the war (entry free, daily 8:00-23:00).

Just beyond the bookstore, tucked into the corner on the right, look for the stairs leading up to the **Museum of the Old Bridge** (Muzej Stari Most). Located within one of the Old Bridge's tow-ers, this museum features a film and photos about the reconstruc-tion of the bridge, archaeological findings, and a few other paltry exhibits about the history of the town and bridge, all in English. The museum offers more detail than most casual visitors need (5 KM, daily April-Aug 8:00-18:00, Feb-March and Sept-Nov 8:00-16:00, closed Dec-Jan, lots of stairs, Bajatova 4, tel. 036/551-6021).

Finally, as you round the bend and proceed along Copper-smiths' Street (described next), you could head up the wide stair-case on your right, then hook to the left on the main road, to find the **Mostar Museum** (Muzej Mostar, or MuM for short). This offers a look at everyday lifestyles in Mostar and Herzegovina (5 KM, Tue-Sun 10:00-16:00 or earlier if the guy feels like it, closed Mon, www.muzejhercegovine.com).

• *After the Old Bridge, the street swings left and leads you along...*

▲▲Coppersmiths' Street (Kujundžiluk)

This lively strip, with the flavor of a Turk-ish bazaar, offers some of the most color-ful shopping this side of Istanbul. You'll see Mostar's characteristic bridge de-picted in every possible way, along with blue-and-white "evil eyes" (believed in the Turkish culture to keep bad spirits at bay), old Yugoslav Army kitsch (including spent bullet and shell casings engraved with images of Mostar), and hammered-copper decorations—continuing the long tradition that gave the street its name. Partway up, the homes with the color-

fully painted facades double as galleries for local artists. The artists live and work upstairs, then sell their work right on this street. Pop into the *atelier d'art* "Đul Emina" on the right (under wooden beams) to meet Sead Vladović and enjoy his impressive iconographic work. This is the most touristy street in all of Bosnia-Herzegovina, so don't expect any bargains. Still, it's fun. As you stroll, check out the fine views of the Old Bridge.

• *Continue uphill. After the street levels out, about halfway along the street on the left-hand side, look for the entrance to the...*

▲Koski Mehmet-Pasha Mosque (Koski Mehmet-Paša Džamija)

Step into this courtyard for a look at one of Mostar's many mosques. Dating from the early 17th century, this mosque is notable for its cliff-hanging riverside location, and because it's particularly accessible for tourists.

Cost and Hours: 5 KM to enter mosque, 5 KM more to climb minaret, daily April-Oct 9:00-18:00, until 19:00 at busy times, Nov-March 9:00-17:00. If it seems crowded with tour groups, you can enter a very similar mosque later on this walk instead (which has most of the same features).

Visiting the Mosque: The **fountain** *(šadrvan)* in the courtyard allows worshippers to wash before entering the mosque, as directed by Islamic law. This practice, called ablution, is both a literal and a spiritual cleansing in preparation for being in the presence of Allah. It's also refreshing in this hot climate, and the sound of running water helps worshippers concentrate.

The **minaret**—the slender needle jutting up next to the dome—is the Islamic equivalent of the Christian bell tower, used to call people to prayer. In the old days, the *muezzin* (prayer leader) would climb the tower five times a day and chant, "There is only one God, and Muhammad is his prophet." In modern times, loud-speakers are used instead. Climbing the minaret's 89 claustrophobic, spiral stairs is a memorable experience, rewarding you at the top with the best views over Mostar—and the Old Bridge—that you can get without wings (entrance to the right of mosque entry).

Because this mosque is accustomed to tourists, you don't need to take off your shoes to enter (but stay on the green carpet), women don't need to cover their heads, and it's fine to take photos inside. Near the front of the mosque, you may see some of the small, overlapping rugs that are below this covering (reserved for shoes-off worshippers).

Once **inside,** notice the traditional elements of the mosque. The niche (mihrab) across from the entry is oriented toward Mecca (the holy city in today's Saudi Arabia)—the direction all Muslims face to pray. The small stairway *(mimber)* that seems to go nowhere

The Muslims of Bosnia

Muslims have been an integral part of Bosnia's cultural tapestry for centuries. During the more than 400 years under Ottoman rule, the Muslim Turks did not forcibly convert their subjects (unlike some Catholic despots at the time). But many local Slavs were persuaded to become Muslims, for lower taxes and better business opportunities. Within 150 years of the start of Ottoman rule, half of the population of Bosnia-Herzegovina was Muslim. These people constitute an ethnic group called "Bosniaks," and many of them are still practicing Sunni Muslims today. Most Bosniaks are Slavs—of the same ethnic stock as Croats and Serbs—but some have ancestors who married into Turkish families.

The actions of a small but attention-grabbing faction of Muslim extremists have burdened Islam with a bad reputation in the Western world. But judging Islam based on ISIS and al-Qaeda is a bit like judging Christianity based on the Oslo gunman and the Ku Klux Klan. Visiting Mostar is a unique opportunity to get a taste of a fully Muslim society, made a bit less intimidating because it wears a more-familiar European face.

Here's an admittedly simplistic outline designed to help travelers from the Christian West understand a very rich but often misunderstood religion that's worthy of respect:

Muslims, like Christians and Jews, are monotheistic. They call God "Allah." The most important person in the Islamic faith is Muhammad, Allah's most important prophet, who lived in the sixth and seventh centuries A.D. Jesus is also one of the most revered prophets in Islamic tradition.

The "five pillars" of Islam are the same among Muslims in Bosnia-Herzegovina, Turkey, Iraq, the US, and everywhere else. Followers of Islam should:

1. Say and believe, "There is only one God, and Muhammad is his prophet."

2. Pray five times a day, while facing Mecca. Modern Muslims explain that it's important for this ritual to include several elements: washing, exercising, stretching, and thinking of God.

3. Give to the poor (one-fortieth of your wealth, if you are not in debt).

4. Fast during daylight hours through the month of Ramadan. Fasting is a great social equalizer and helps everyone to feel the hunger of the poor.

5. Visit Mecca. This is interpreted by some Muslims as a command to travel. Muhammad said, "Don't tell me how educated you are, tell me how much you've traveled."

Good advice for anyone, no matter what—or if—you call a higher power.

is symbolic of the growth of Islam—Muhammad had to stand higher and higher to talk to his growing following. This serves as a kind of pulpit, where the cleric gives a speech, similar to a sermon or homily in Christian church services. No priest ever stands on the top stair, which is symbolically reserved for Muhammad.

The balcony just inside the door is traditionally where women worship. For the same reason I find it hard to concentrate on God at yoga classes, Muslim men decided prayer would go better without the enjoyable but problematic distraction of bent-over women between them and Mecca. These days, women can also pray on the main floor with the men, but they must avoid physical contact.

Muslims believe that capturing a living creature in a painting or a sculpture is inappropriate. (In fact, depictions of Allah and the prophet Muhammad are strictly forbidden.) Instead, mosques are filled with ornate patterns and Arabic calligraphy (of the name "Muhammad" and important prayers and sayings from the Quran). You'll also see some floral and plant designs, which you'd never see in a more conservative, Middle Eastern mosque.

Before leaving, ponder how progressive the majority of Mostar's Muslims are. Most of them drink alcohol, wear modern European clothing (you'll see very few women wearing head scarves or men with beards—and those you do see are likely tourists from the Middle East), and almost never visit a mosque to pray. In so many ways, these people don't fit our preconceived notions of Islam...and yet, they consider themselves Muslims all the same.

The mosque's **courtyard** is shared by several merchants. When you're done haggling, head to the terrace behind the mosque for the best view in town of the Old Bridge.

• *Just beyond this mosque, the traffic-free cobbles of the Old Town end. Take a right and leave the cutesy tourists' world. Walk up one block to the big...*

▲▲New Muslim Cemetery

In this cemetery, which was a park before the Yugoslav Wars, every tomb is dated 1993, 1994, or 1995. As the war raged, more exposed cemeteries were unusable. But this tree-covered piece of land was relatively safe from Croat snipers. As the casualties

mounted, locals buried their loved ones here under cover of darkness. Many of these people were soldiers, but some were civilians. Strict Muslim graves don't display images of people, but here you'll see photos of war dead who were young, less-traditional members of the Muslim community. The fleur-de-lis shape of many of the tombstones is a patriotic symbol for the nation of Bosnia. The Arabic squiggles are the equivalent of an American having Latin on his or her tombstone—old-fashioned and formal.

• *Go up the wide stairs to the right of the cemetery (near the mosque). At #4 (on the right, just before and across from the bombed-out tower), you'll find the…*

Museum of Herzegovina (Muzej Hercegovine)

This humble little museum is made worthwhile by a deeply moving **film** that traces the history of the town through its Old Bridge: fun circa-1957 footage of the diving contests; harrowing scenes of the bridge being pummeled, and finally toppled, by artillery; and a stirring sequence showing the bridge's reconstruction and grand reopening on that day in 2004—with high-fives, Beethoven's *Ode to Joy*, fireworks, and more divers. (This includes much of the same footage as the similar film at the Gallery on the Bridge, described earlier, but doesn't focus solely on the wartime damage.)

The museum itself displays fragments of this region's rich history, including historical photos and several items from its Ottoman period. There are sparse English descriptions, but without a tour guide the exhibits are a bit difficult to appreciate. Topics include the Turkish period, Herzegovina under the Austro-Hungarian Empire, village life, and (in the basement) local archaeology. One small room commemorates the house's former owner, Dzemal Bijedić, who was Tito's second-in-command during the Yugoslav period until he was killed in a mysterious plane crash in 1977. (If Bijedić had lived, many wonder whether he might have succeeded Tito…and succeeded in keeping Yugoslavia together.)

Cost and Hours: 5-KM museum entry includes 12-minute film, no narration—works in any language, ask about "film?" as you enter; Mon-Fri 9:00-16:00, Sat 10:00-15:00, closed Sun; often closed in winter—call first; Bajatova 4—walking up these stairs, it's the second door that's marked for the museum, under the overhanging balcony, tel. 036/551-602, www.muzejhercegovine.com.

• *Backtrack to where you left the Old Town. Notice the **Tepa Market**, with locals buying clothing and produce, in the area just beyond the pedestrian zone. Now walk (with the market on your left) along the lively street called **Brače Fejića**. (There's no sign, but the street is level and busy with cafés.) You're in the "new town," where locals sit out in front of boisterous cafés sipping coffee while listening to the thumping beat of distinctly Eastern-sounding music.*

Stroll down this street for a few blocks. At the palm trees (about 50 yards before the minaret—look for sign to Ottoman House), you can side-trip a block to the left to reach...

▲Bišćević Turkish House (Bišćevića Ćošak)

Mostar has three traditional Turkish-style homes that are open for tourists to visit. The Bišćević House is the oldest, most interesting, and most convenient for a quick visit, but two others are described at the end of this listing. Dating from 1635, the Bišćević House is typical of old houses in Mostar, which mix Oriental style with Mediterranean features.

Cost and Hours: 4 KM, March-Nov Mon-Fri 8:00-19:00, Sat-Sun 9:00-18:00, generally closed Dec-Feb—but you can arrange a visit by calling ahead to Fortuna Tours, tel. 036/552-197, Bišćevića 13.

Visiting the House: First you'll step through the outer (or animals') garden, then into the inner (or family's) garden. This inner zone is surrounded by a high wall—protection from the sun's rays, from thieves...and from prying eyes, allowing women to take off the veil they were required to wear in public. Enjoy the geometrical patters of the smooth river stones in the floor (for example, the five-sided star), and keep an eye out for the house's pet turtles. It's no coincidence that the traditional fountain *(šadrvan)* resembles those at the entrance to a mosque—a reminder of the importance of running water in Muslim culture. The little white building is a kitchen—cleverly located apart from the house so that the heat and smells of cooking didn't permeate the upstairs living area.

Buy your ticket and take off your shoes before you climb up the wooden staircase. Imagine how a stairway like this one could be pulled up for extra protection in case of danger (notice that this one has a "trap door" to cover it). The cool, shady, and airy living room is open to the east—from where the wind rarely blows. The overhanging roof also prevented the hot sun from reaching this area. The loom in the corner was the women's workplace—the carpets you're standing on would have been woven there. The big chests against the wall were used to bring the dowry when the homeowner took a new wife. Study the fine wood carving that decorates the space.

Continue back into the main gathering room *(divanhan)*. This space—whose name comes from the word "talk"—is designed in a circle so people could face each other, cross-legged, for a good conversation while they enjoyed a dramatic view overlooking the Neretva. The room comes with a box of traditional costumes—

great for photo fun. Put on a pair of baggy pants and a fez and really lounge.

Other Turkish Houses: If you're intrigued by this house, consider dropping by Mostar's two other Turkish houses. The **Muslibegović House** (Muslibegovića Kuća) feels newer because it dates from 1871, just a few years before the Ottomans left town. This homey house—which also rents out rooms to visitors (see "Sleeping in Mostar," later)—has many of the same features as the Bišćević House. If they're not too busy, Sanela or Gabriela can give you an English tour (4 KM, mid-April-mid-Oct daily 10:00-18:00, closed to visitors off-season, just two blocks uphill from the Karađozbeg Mosque at Osman Đikića 41, tel. 036/551-379, www.muslibegovichouse.com). To find it, go up the street between the Karađozbeg Mosque and the cemetery, cross the busy street, and continue a long block uphill on the alley. The wall with the slate roof on the left marks the house.

The **Kajtaz House** (Kajtazova Kuća), hiding up a very residential-feeling alley a few blocks from the Old Bridge, feels lived-in because it still is (in the opposite direction from most of the other sights, at Gaše Ilića 21).

• *Go back to the main café street and continue to the...*

▲Karađozbeg Mosque (Karađozbegova Džamija)

The city's main mosque was completed in 1557, the same year work began on the Old Bridge. This mosque, which welcomes visitors,

feels less touristy than the one back in the Old Town. Before entering the gate into the complex, look for the picture showing the recent war damage sustained here. You'll see that this mosque has most of the same elements as the Koski Mehmet-Pasha Mosque (described earlier), but some of these decorations are original. Across the street is another cemetery with tombstones from that terrible year, 1993.

Cost and Hours: 5 KM to enter mosque, 5 KM more to climb minaret, daily May-Sept 9:00-18:00, Oct-April 10:00-16:00. You'll need to remove your shoes, but women don't have to cover their heads, and photos are allowed inside.

• *Now leave the tourists' Mostar and continue into modern, urban Mostar along the street in front of the Karađozbeg Mosque. This grimy, mostly traffic-free street is called...*

▲Braće Fejića

Walking along the modern town's main café strip, enjoy the opportunity to observe this workaday Bosniak town. Notice many cafés that serve drinks but no food. People generally eat at home before going out to nurse an affordable drink. (Café ABC has good cakes and ice cream; the upstairs is a popular pizza hangout for students and families.)

At the small mosque on the left, obituary announcements are tacked to the stone wall, listing the bios and funeral times for locals who have recently died. A fig tree grows out of the mosque's minaret, just an accident of nature illustrating how that plant can thrive with almost no soil (somehow, the Bosniaks can relate). Walking farther, look back and up to see a few ruins—still ugly more than two decades after the war. There's a messy confusion about who owns what in Mostar. Surviving companies have no money. Yugo Bank, which held the mortgages, is defunct. No one will invest until clear ownership is established. Until then, the people of Mostar sip their coffee in the shadow of these jagged reminders of the warfare that wracked this town a couple of decades ago.

Near the end of the pedestrian zone, through the parking lot on the right, look for the building with communist-era reliefs of 12th-century Bogomil tomb decor—remembering the indigenous culture that existed here even before the arrival of the Ottomans.

When you finally hit the big street (with car traffic), head left one block to the big **Masala Square** (literally, "Place for Prayer"). Historically, this was where pilgrims gathered before setting off for Mecca on their hajj. This is a great scene on balmy evenings, when it's a rendezvous point for the community. The two busts near the fountain provide perfect goal posts for budding soccer stars.

• *For a finale, you can continue one block more out onto the bridge to survey the town you just explored. From here, you can backtrack to linger in the places you found most inviting. Or you can venture into...*

WESTERN (CROAT) MOSTAR

Most tourists stay on the Bosniak side of town. But for a complete look at this divided city, it's well worth strolling to the west side. While there's not much in the way of sightseeing here, and much of this urban zone isn't particularly pretty, it does provide an interesting contrast to the Muslim side of town. As this is the location of some of Mostar's new shopping malls, this area feels more vital each year, and a few of the tree-lined streets seem downright elegant.

Crossing the river and the Bulevar, the scarred husks of destroyed buildings begin to fade away, and within a block you're immersed in concrete apartment buildings. When the city became divided, the Muslims holed up in the original Ottoman Old Town, while the Croats claimed this modern Tito-era sprawl. The relative lack of war damage here makes it clear which side of town had it worse. Also notice that there are more pizza and pasta restaurants

The Dawn of War in Mostar

Mostar was always one of the most stubbornly independent parts of the former Yugoslavia. It had one of the highest rates of mixed-ethnicity marriages in all of Bosnia-Herzegovina. In the early 1990s, Mostar's demographics were proportioned more or less evenly—about 35 percent of its residents were Bosniaks, 34 percent Croats, and 19 percent Serbs. But this delicate balance was shattered in a few brutal months of warfare.

On April 1, 1992, Bosnia-Herzegovina—led by Muslim president Alija Izetbegović—declared independence from Yugoslavia. Very quickly, the Serb-dominated Yugoslav People's Army moved to stake their claim on territory throughout the country, including the important city of Mostar. On April 3, Serb forces occupied the east end of town (including the Ottoman Old Town), forcing many residents—predominantly Croats and Bosniaks—to hole up in the western part of the city. Meanwhile, Serbian and Croatian leaders were secretly meeting to divvy up Bosnian territory, and by early May, they'd agreed that Croatia would claim Mostar.

Several weeks later, when the joint Croat-Bosniak forces crossed back over the river, the Serb forces mysteriously withdrew from the city (having been directed to capitulate), and retreated to the mountaintops above town. The Croats and Bosniaks, believing they'd achieved peace, began putting their city back together. During this time, some factions also rounded up, tortured, and killed Serbs still living in Mostar. Many Bosniaks moved back to their homes on the east side of town, but, rather oddly, many of the Croats who had previously resided there instead stayed in the west—in many cases, moving into apartments vacated by Serbs who had fled.

On May 9, 1993—the Yugoslav holiday of "Victory over Fascism Day"—Mostarians were rocked awake by the terrifying sounds of artillery shells. Croat military forces swept through the city, forcibly moving remaining Bosniaks from the west part of town into the east. Throughout that summer, Bosniak men were captured and sent to concentration camps, while the Croats virtually sealed off the east side of town—creating a giant ghetto with no way in or out. The long and ugly siege of Mostar had begun.

than *ćevapčići* joints—even the food over here is more Croat than Bosniak.

Looking at a map, you'll notice that many streets on this side of town are named for Croatian cities (Dubrovačka, Splitska, Vukovarska) or historical figures (Kneza Branimira, Kralja Tomislava, and Kralja Petra Krešimira—for the dukes who first united the Croats in the ninth and tenth centuries). This side of town also has several remnants of Mostar's brief period of Habsburg rule (1878–

1918). During this time, the empire quickly expanded what had been a sleepy Ottoman backwater, laying out grand boulevards and erecting genteel buildings that look like they'd be at home in Vienna.

All streets converge at the big roundabout (about a 15-minute walk from the Old Town) called the **Rondo,** which is a good place to get oriented to this neighborhood. Overlooking this lively intersection is the stately Hrvatski Dom ("Croatia House") cultural center. Notice how even the street signs are politically charged: *Centar* signs pointedly direct traffic *away* from the (Bosniak) Old Town, and many road signs point toward Široki Brijeg—a Croat stronghold in western Herzegovina.

The adjacent **Park Zrinjevac** is a pleasant place to stroll, and was the site of an infamously ill-fated attempt at reconciliation. In the early 2000s, idealistic young Mostarians formed the Urban Movement of Mostar, which searched for a way to connect the still-feuding Catholic and Muslim communities. As a symbol of their goals, they chose Bruce Lee, the deceased kung-fu movie star, beloved by both Croats and Bosniaks for his characters' honorable struggle against injustice. A life-size bronze statue of Lee was unveiled with fanfare in this park in November of 2005—but was almost immediately vandalized. The statue was repaired, and may or may not have been returned to its pedestal (which you'll still find in the park).

Several interesting sights lie close to this roundabout. A block toward the Old Town from the Rondo (on Kralja Višeslava Humskog), look for the big **Muslim cemetery** with tombstones from the early 1990s. These are the graves of those killed during the first round of fighting, when the Croats and Bosniaks teamed up to fight the Serbs.

If you head from the Rondo down Kneza Branimira (across from the park), you'll enjoy an inviting boulevard shaded by plane trees. When first built, this street was called **Štefanijino Šetalište**—"Stéphanie's Promenade," after the Belgian princess who married Austria's Archduke Rudolf (the heir apparent of the Habsburg Empire until he died in a mysterious murder-suicide pact with his mistress). Partway down the street on the left is the recommended Pivnica Štefanijino Šetalište, a good place for a microbrew or a meal.

If you head up Kralja Petra Krešimira IV from the Rondo, after two long blocks on the left you'll see an abandoned, derelict park leading to a gigantic **Partisan Cemetery and Monument.**

This socialist-style monument spreads all the way up the hill. It oozes with symbolism trumpeting the pivotal WWII Battle of the Neretva, when Tito and his Partisan Army turned the tables on Nazi forces (just 30 miles north of here—see page 515). It was designed by Bogdan Bogdanović, who created many such monuments and memorials throughout Yugoslavia, and dedicated by Tito himself in 1965. From the terrace at the top, which is scattered with symbolic gravestones for those who gave their lives to free Yugoslavia from the Nazis, small streams once trickled down to the large enclosure at the bottom, ultimately flowing beneath a stylized broken bridge representing the Bridge at the Neretva. Today the monument is overgrown and ignored—a tragic symbol of post-Tito ethnic discord. Local Croats—who have little nostalgia for the Yugoslav period, which they now view as a time of oppression—seem to intentionally neglect the place. This formerly hallowed ground is a mess of broken concrete and a popular place for drunken benders, garbage dumping, and drug deals (be careful if you decide to explore, and avoid it after dark). A pensive stroll here comes with a poignant reflection on how one generation's honored war dead can become the next generation's unwanted burden.

Nightlife in Mostar

Though Mostar is touristy, it's also a real urban center with a young population riding a wave of raging hormones. The meat market

in the courtyard next to the old Turkish bathhouse (on "Hammam Square") is fun to observe. The Old Bridge is a popular meeting place for locals as well as tourists. A stroll from the Old Bridge down the café-lined Braće Fejića boulevard to the modern Masala Square at the far end of town (described earlier) gives a great peek at Mostarians socializing away from the tourists. Wherever you wind up, order a cocktail or try a Turkish-style hubbly-bubbly (*šiša*, SHEE-shah). Ask to have one of these big water pipes fired up for you and choose your flavored tobacco: apple, cappuccino, banana, or lemon.

Ali Baba is an actual cave featuring a fun, atmospheric, and mellow hangout scene (look for low-profile entrance along Coppersmiths' Street, just

MOSTAR & NEARBY

down from the Old Bridge—watch for signs tucked down a rocky alley).

Oscar Nightclub is a caravanserai for lounge lizards—an exotic world mixing babbling streams, terraces, lounge chairs, and big sofas where young and old enjoy cocktails and *šiša* (open "nonstop" as long as the weather is good—usually June-mid-Sept, closed off-season, up from the Old Bridge on Onešćukova street, near the Crooked Bridge at the end of the pedestrian zone).

Black Dog Pub, the brainchild of Seattleite Stefan (who moved to Mostar as part of a humanitarian NGO during the war), fosters a lively, youthful scene that feels more international than "traditional Bosnian." They serve local microbrews (including several from the Oldbridz Brewery) and have live music most nights from around 20:00. Stefan makes a point of hiring locals from every different ethnic background, and his bar has become a hangout for Mostarians from both sides of town as well as tourists. Sit in the convivial interior, or head out to the riverside terrace (no food—just drinks, open long hours daily, just across the Crooked Bridge from Onešćukova street).

Sleeping in Mostar

Most of my listings are small, friendly, accessible, affordable guesthouses in or very near the Old Town. Many hotels and pensions in town promise "parking," but it's often street parking out front—private lots are rare. Mostar's Old Town can be very noisy on weekends, with nightclubs and outdoor restaurants rollicking into the wee hours. If you're a light sleeper, consider Villa Fortuna, the Muslibegović House, or Shangri La, which are quieter than the norm.

$$$ The **Muslibegović House,** a Bosnian national monument that also invites tourists in to visit during the day, is in an actual Turkish home dating from 1871. The complex houses 10 homey rooms and two suites, all of which combine classic Turkish style (elegant and comfortable old beds, creaky wooden floors with colorful carpets, lounging sofas; guests remove shoes at the outer door) with modern comforts (air-con, flatscreen TVs). Situated on a quiet residential lane just above the bustle of Mostar's main pedestrian drag and Old Town zone, this is a memorable experience (Sb-€60, Db-€90/€75, "pasha suite"-€105, includes a tour of the house, closed Nov-Feb, 2 blocks uphill from the Karađozbeg Mosque at

MOSTAR & NEARBY

Osman Đikića 41, tel. 036/551-379, www.muslibegovichouse.com, muslibegovichouse@gmail.com; Taž, Sanela, and Gabriela).

$$$ Hotel Bristol is the only business-class place near central Mostar. Its 48 rooms don't live up to their four stars, but the location is handy, overlooking the river, a 10-minute walk from the heart of the Old Town (Sb-€48, Db-€72, apartment-€91, extra bed-€16, air-con, elevator, some street noise, stuffy/smoky lobby, limited parking, Mostarskog Bataljona, tel. 036/500-100, www.bristol.ba, info@bristol.ba).

$$ Shangri La Mansion fills a gorgeously restored Austro-Hungarian building on a hill above the Old Town, squeezed between war ruins. The eight rooms come in all different sizes, but all of them are modern and nicely appointed. Thoughtfully run with modern flair by Nermin, it has a beautiful rooftop garden that's ideal for relaxing (Db-€49-63/€45-59/€36-49, price depends on size and amenities, breakfast-€6, air-con, free parking, Kalhanska 10, mobile 061-169-362, www.shangrila.com.ba, info@shangrila.com.ba).

$$ Hotel Kriva Ćuprija ("Crooked Bridge"), by the bridge of the same name, is tucked between waterfalls in a picturesque valley a few steps from the Old Bridge. It's an appealing oasis with 26 stylish rooms and a restaurant with atmospheric outdoor seating (Sb-€45, Db-€69, bigger "superior" Db-€75, apartment-€89, extra bed-€19, 10 percent discount on rooms and food with this book, can be noisy from surrounding nightlife, air-con, free parking, call to reconfirm if arriving after 19:00, enter at Onešćukova 23 or Kriva Ćuprija 2, tel. 036/360-360, mobile 061-915-915, www.motel-mostar.ba, krivacuprijamostar@gmail.com, Sami). Their second location—**Hotel Kriva Ćuprija II**—offers 10 modern rooms in a restored Habsburg-style building on a dreary urban street, about 200 yards to the south. As it's a less convenient location and lacks soul, I prefer the original (same prices, discount, amenities, and contact information as main hotel; some traffic noise, Maršala Tita 186, next to the Lučki Bridge, reception tel. 036/554-125).

$$ Villa Anri, a bit more hotelesque than other pensions in Mostar, sits a block farther from the bustle near the Bulevar. The stony facade hides eight rooms (six with balconies) combining old Herzegovinian style and bright colors. The big draw is the rooftop terrace, shared by two rooms, which enjoys grand views over the Old Bridge area (standard rooms: Db-€60/€50, Tb-€95/€80, €5 more for small balcony; huge top-floor terrace rooms: Db-€95/€80, Tb-€110/€85, cash only, air-con, free parking, Braće Đukića 4, tel. 036/578-477, www.motel-mostar.com, villa.anri@gmail.com).

$ Villa Fortuna is an exceptional value, located in a nondescript urban neighborhood a few minutes' walk farther away from the Old Bridge. Owners Nela and Mili Bijavica rent eight tasteful, modern rooms above the main office of Fortuna Tours. The courtyard in front offers free, secure parking, and in back there's a pleasant garden with a traditional Herzegovinian garden cottage (Sb-€30, Db-€40, apartment-€80, these prices if you book direct by email, breakfast-€5, non-smoking, air-con, Rade Bitange 34, tel. 036/580-625, mobile 063-315-017 or 063-299-189, www.villafortuna.ba, villa_fortuna@bih.net.ba). Fortuna Tours can also put you in touch with locals renting rooms and apartments.

$ Pansion Čardak, run by Suzana and Nedžad Kasumović, has five pleasant rooms sharing a kitchen and Internet nook in a stone house set just back from the bustling Crooked Bridge area (Db-€50-70/€45, price depends on size and terrace, Tb-€70/€60, Qb-€80/€70, cash only, breakfast at nearby restaurant-€3-4, air-con, free parking, Jusovina 3, tel. 036/578-249, mobile 061-385-988, www.pansion-cardak.com, info@pansion-cardak.com).

$ Pansion Nur, run by Feđa, a relative of Suzana and Nedžad (above), has four simpler but cheaper rooms and a shared kitchen (small Db-€40/€35, Db-€50/€40, Tb-€60/€50, suite-€70/€60, cash only, no breakfast, air-con, free parking, Jusovina 8b, tel. 036/580-296, mobile 062-160-872, www.pansion-nur.com, info@pansion-nur.com).

$ Villa Botticelli, overlooking a charming waterfall garden just up the valley from the Crooked Bridge, has five colorful rooms at affordable prices (Sb-€30, Db-€40, breakfast-€3, air-con, Muje Bjelavca 6, enter along the street facing the Crooked Bridge, mobile 063-319-057, www.villabotticelli.com, info@villabotticelli.com, Snježana and Zoran).

Eating in Mostar

Most of Mostar's tourist-friendly restaurants are conveniently concentrated in the Old Town. If you walk anywhere that's cobbled, you'll stumble onto dozens of tempting restaurants charging the same reasonable prices and serving rustic, traditional Bosnian food. In my experience, the menus at most places are virtually identical—though quality and ambience can vary greatly. As eateries tend to come and go quickly here, and little distinguishes these places anyway, don't be too focused on a particular spot. Grilled meats are especially popular—read the "Balkan Flavors" sidebar, on page 421, before you dine. Most local wines are made with one of two indigenous grapes: *blatina* (literally "muddy"; a thick, heavy, earthy red) and *žilavka* (literally "root"; a bright, fairly acidic white).

ON THE EMBANKMENT, WITH OLD BRIDGE VIEWS

For the best atmosphere, find your way into the several levels of restaurants that clamber up the riverbank and offer perfect views

of the Old Bridge. In terms of the setting, this is the most memorable place to dine in Mostar—but be warned that the quality of the food along here is uniformly low, and prices are relatively high (figure 8-18 KM for a meal). If you want a good perch, it's fun and smart to drop by earlier in the day and personally reserve the table of your choice.

To reach two of the most scenic eateries, go over the Old Bridge to the west side of the river, and bear right on the cobbles until you get to the old Turkish bathhouse (with the copper domes on the roof, at "Hammam Square"). To the right of the bathhouse is the entrance to a lively courtyard surrounded by cafés. Crossing straight through the courtyard, you'll find stairs leading down to several riverfront terraces belonging to two different restaurants: **Babilon** (my choice for better food) and **Teatar.** Poke around to find your favorite bridge panorama before settling in for a drink or a meal.

Two other places (including a pizzeria) are a bit closer to the bridge—to reach these, look for the alley on the left just before the bridge tower.

MOSTAR & NEARBY

NEAR THE OLD BRIDGE

While they lack the Old Bridge views, these places are just as central as those listed earlier, and serve food that's generally a step up. The first four places are in the atmospheric Old Town, while the last one is in the modern part of town.

Restoran Hindin Han is pleasantly situated on a woody terrace over a rushing stream. It's respected locally for its good cooking—with a wide variety, from grilled meats to seafood—and fair prices (big 12-20-KM salads, 10-18-KM main courses, Sarajevsko beer on tap, daily 11:00-24:00, Jusovina 10, tel. 036/581-054). To find it, walk west from the Old Bridge, bear left at the Šadrvan restaurant, cross the bridge, and you'll see it on the left.

Irma-Tima, run by the frenetic one-woman show Irma, grills up the best *ćevapčići* and other meats that I've had in Mostar. Its touristy, very scenic location—along the main shopping drag, a couple of blocks from the Old Bridge—belies the quality of the food (8-12-KM plates, long hours daily, Onešćukova b.b., mobile 062-958-539).

Nacionalni Restoran Aščinica Balkan ("Balkan National Restaurant/Cafeteria") is a convenient cafeteria-style eatery with two handy locations. They serve up tasty, home-cooked Bosnian specialties; you can order from the menu, but it's more fun to order a "mix" *(mješanac)* plate from the display case—the small 10-KM plate is plenty for a light meal (16-KM "medium" and 20-KM "large" plates also available, 3-KM salads, Bosnian coffee, tempting dessert display case, daily 10:00-23:00, one location right at the end of the Old Town cobbles before the market, the other a couple of blocks away on the new town's main drag at Braće Fejića 57, tel. 036/551-868).

Urban Grill's food is nothing special—it has basically the same menu as other places in town—but its terrace enjoys one of Mostar's best unobstructed views of the Old Bridge (8-16-KM grilled meat and other meals, 10-12-KM pastas and salads, Bosnian coffee, daily 8:00-22:00, enter along the main cobbled Old Town drag at Mala Tepa 26, tel. 036/552-235).

Saray is an untouristy, nondescript little eatery just uphill from the Karađozbeg Mosque in the modern part of town. They have a basic menu of cheap and very tasty grilled meats—specializing in the classic *ćevapčići*—and outdoor seating overlooking a playground that offers good people- and kid-watching while you eat (4-10-KM grilled meats, big 7-KM salads, daily 7:00-23:00, Karađozbegova 3, mobile 062-062-301).

IN THE WEST (CROAT) SIDE OF TOWN

While less charming and romantic, a stroll to the west side of town (still inhabited primarily by Croats) offers an interesting contrast to the cutesy Old Town—and a completely different array of restaurants. Here you'll find more pizza and pasta places than grilled meats, as well as shiny new shopping centers with modern food courts, and the following brewpub. For more on this neighborhood, see page 442.

Pivnica Štefanijino Šetalište ("Stéphanie's Promenade Brewpub"), named for the onetime Austro-Hungarian crown princess, mingles modern Croat class with Habsburg grandeur. It fills a stylish cellar and an inviting outdoor terrace with happy diners, sipping beers and digging into international fare. It sits along its gorgeous, tree-lined namesake boulevard (9-15-KM main dishes, daily 8:00-24:00, Kneza Branimira 11, tel. 036/319-319, www.stefanija.info).

Mostar Connections

BY BUS

Not surprisingly for a divided city, Mostar has two different, autonomous bus terminals, each served by different companies. Mostar's **main bus station** (called "Autobusna Stanica") is on the east/Bosniak side of the river, about a 15-minute walk north of the Old Town (for details, see "Arrival in Mostar," earlier). Most buses you're likely to take use this station; for information on the other station (on the west/Croat side of town), see the end of this section.

Schedules and Tickets: At the main station, two primary companies (one Bosniak, one Croat) operate independent offices, providing schedule information and tickets only for their own buses. Because the companies are reluctant to cooperate, there's no single information or ticket office for all Mostar buses—if you're unclear on your options, visit both companies to get details before buying tickets. As you face the bus station, near the left end is the Bosniak company **Autoprevoz** (tel. 036/551-900, www.autoprevoz-bus.ba); they also sell tickets for a few other companies (including Eurolines and Bogdan Bus). Near the right end is the Croat-owned **Globtour** (look for *Mediteran Tours* sign, tel. 036/550-065, www.globtour.com), which sells tickets only for its own buses. Local and regional connections (not listed below) are operated by Mostar Bus, whose buses depart from across the street from the main bus station (www.mostarbus.ba).

Tracking down reliable **schedule** information in Mostar is tricky, but you can start by checking the websites listed above, then calling or visiting both companies at the station to confirm your options and buy tickets. Note that buses to seasonal destinations (such as along the Dalmatian Coast) run more frequently in peak season, roughly June through mid-September.

From Mostar's Main Bus Station: Both Autoprevoz and Globtour operate buses to **Sarajevo** (6/day on Autoprevoz, 3/day on

Globtour, 2.5 hours), **Zagreb** (4/day on Globtour, 1/day on Auto-prevoz, 9 hours, includes a night bus), and **Split** (3/day on Autoprevoz, 2/day on Globtour, 4-4.5 hours; additional departures by Eurolines in summer). Globtour exclusively handles buses to **Međugorje** (5/day, 40 minutes), and **Dubrovnik** (3/day, 4-5 hours).

That important **Dubrovnik** connection is tricky: Most days, all Dubrovnik buses depart early in the day, making an afternoon return from Mostar to Dubrovnik impossible. However, in summer (June-Aug), Eurolines adds two more departures each day—including a handy 17:30 departure, which makes day-tripping from Dubrovnik workable (tickets sold at Autoprevoz office).

Globtour also runs a handy bus to Montenegro's **Bay of Kotor.** Two buses leave around the same time, at 7:00; one originates in Mostar and takes the inland route, via Herzegovina and Trebinje, passing only one border (but with much less coastal scenery) and is more likely to be on time, arriving in Kotor around 16:00. The other option takes the coastal route via Dubrovnik, with four borders and more scenery, but often arriving late. I'd request the Trebinje route. Another connection to Kotor leaves at 16:00, arriving around 1:00 in the morning.

From Mostar's West/Croat Bus Station: A few additional buses, mostly to Croatian destinations and to Croat areas of Bosnia-Herzegovina, depart from the west side of town. These use a makeshift "station" (actually a gravel lot behind a gas station) on Vukovarska street, called "Kolodvor." It's about a 15-minute walk due west of the main bus station. Most buses using the Kolodvor station are operated by the Euroherc company. In addition to one daily bus apiece to **Zagreb, Split,** and **Sarajevo,** this station has several departures to **Metković** (at the Croatian border, with additional connections to Croatian destinations) and to **Međugorje** (7/day Mon-Fri, 3/day Sat, none Sun). Additionally, some Croat buses leave from a bus stop near the Franciscan Church. But since the connections are sparse, the location is inconvenient, and the "station" is dreary, I'd stick with the main bus station and ignore this option unless you're desperate.

BY TRAIN

Mostar is on the train line that runs from Ploče (on the Croatian coast between Split and Dubrovnik) to Zagreb, via Mostar and Sarajevo. But the train tends to be cramped and slow; buses are typically much more efficient and comfortable. The train schedule changes frequently, but it's usually possible to go by train to **Ploče** (with good bus connections to elsewhere in Dalmatia; 2 hours) and **Sarajevo** (2.5 hours). Some trains continue from Sarajevo all the way to **Zagreb** (11.5 hours from Mostar; bus is faster). Train info: Tel. 036/550-608.

ROUTE TIPS FOR DRIVERS: FROM DUBROVNIK TO MOSTAR

You have two options for the drive between Dubrovnik and Mostar: easy and straightforward along the coast, or adventurous and off-the-beaten-path through the Herzegovinian mountains. I've narrated each route coming from Dubrovnik to Mostar, but you can do either one in reverse. (For driving directions from Mostar to Sarajevo, see the end of the Sarajevo chapter.)

The Main Coastal Road

The vast majority of traffic from Dubrovnik to Mostar follows the coastal road north, then cuts east into Bosnia. Because this is one of the most direct routes, it can be crowded (allow about 2.5 hours). It's also a bit inconvenient, as you have to cross the border three times (into and out of Bosnia at Neum, and into Bosnia again at Metković). Note that in the peak of summer (July-Aug), traffic can back up at Neum (worst at 9:00-11:00, when day-trippers from Dubrovnik are clogging the roads). If you expect busy borders, try leaving Dubrovnik early (before 8:00) or later (around 10:00, or leave earlier but make some stops—such as Trsteno or Ston—en route; your goal is to reach the border after 11:00).

Begin by driving north of Dubrovnik, passing some of the places mentioned in the Near Dubrovnik chapter: **Trsteno** (with its arboretum), and **Ston** and **Mali Ston** (with a mighty wall and waterfront restaurants, respectively). After passing the Ston turnoff, you'll see the long, mountainous, vineyard-draped **Pelješac Peninsula** across the bay on your left.

Soon you'll come to a surprise border crossing, at **Neum.** Here you'll cross into Bosnia-Herzegovina—then, six miles later, cross back out again (for details on this odd little stretch of Bosnian coast, see page 355).

You won't be back in Croatia for long. Just north of Neum, the main coastal road jogs away from the coast and around the striking **Neretva River Delta**—the extremely fertile "garden patch of Croatia," which produces a significant portion of Croatia's fruits and vegetables. The Neretva is the same river that flows under Mostar's Old Bridge upstream—but in Metković, it spreads out into 12 branches as it enters the Adriatic, flooding a vast plain and creating a bursting cornucopia in the middle of an otherwise rocky and arid region. Enjoying some of the most plentiful sunshine on the Croatian coast, as well as a steady supply of water for irrigation, the Neretva Delta is as productive as it is beautiful.

At the Neretva Delta, turn off for the town of **Metković;** at the far end of that town, you'll cross the border into **Bosnia-Herzegovina,** then continue straight on the main road (M-17) directly into Mostar. As you drive, you'll see destroyed buildings and occasional roadside memorials bearing the likenesses of fresh-faced soldiers who died in the recent war.

Along the way are a few interesting detours: In Čapljina, you can turn off to the left to reach **Međugorje** (see page 460). If you stay on the main road, keep your eyes peeled soon after the Čapljina turnoff for a mountaintop castle tower (on the right side of the road), which marks the medieval town of **Počitelj** (see page 458). With extra time, just before Mostar (in Buna), you can detour a few miles along the Buna River into **Blagaj** (see page 457).

Approaching **Mostar** on M-17, you'll pass the airport, then carry on straight toward *Sarajevo* (ignoring the first turn-off to the left for *Centar*). As you skirt the city, take the left turn for *Centar* and *Posušje*. When you come to the traffic light, you can turn right to reach the east side of the river (for the Muslibegović House or Hotel Kriva Ćuprija II); or continue straight to reach the west side of the river (for my other accommodations). If you continue straight, you'll bear right onto Bulevar street, and continue on that main artery for several blocks (passing several destroyed buildings). At the street called Rade Bitange, turn left and park in the pay lot next to the bulky Franciscan church (with the giant bell tower). From here, the start of my self-guided walk—which leads you straight through the middle of town—is just across the street. Signage can be confusing; if you get lost, try asking for directions to "Stari Most" (STAH-ree most)—the Old Bridge.

Rugged-but-Scenic Backcountry Journey Through Serb Herzegovina

While the coastal route outlined above is the most common way to connect Dubrovnik to Mostar, I enjoy getting out of the tourist rut by twisting up the mountains behind Dubrovnik and cutting across the scenic middle of Herzegovina. This route feels much more remote, but the roads are good and the occasional gas station and restaurant break up the journey. I find this route particularly interesting because it offers an easily digestible taste of the **Republika Srpska** part of Herzegovina—controlled by the country's Serb minority, rather than its Bosniak and Croat majorities. You'll see Orthodox churches and monasteries, the Cyrillic alphabet, and various symbols of the defiantly proud Serb culture (such as the red, white, and blue flag with the four golden C's). You can't get a complete picture of the former Yugoslavia without sampling at least a sliver of Serb culture. (Because this road goes through the Serbian part of Herzegovina, it's not popular among Bosniaks or Croats—in fact, locals might tell you this road "does not exist." It does.) If you want a little taste of Republika Srpska, consider just day-tripping into Trebinje—especially on Saturday, when the produce market is at its liveliest.

The first step is to climb up into the mountains and the charming market town of Trebinje. From there, two different roads lead to Mostar: via Stolac or via Nevesinje. If you take the Stolac route, the whole journey from Dubrovnik to Mostar takes about as long as the coastal road (and potentially even faster, thanks to the light traffic and lack of an extra border). The Nevesinje route takes a good hour longer than the Stolac route, and immerses you in an even more remote landscape.

Dubrovnik to Trebinje: From Dubrovnik, head south toward Cavtat, the airport, and Montenegro. Shortly after leaving Dubrovnik, watch for—and follow—signs on the left directing you to *Brgat Gornji*. (Signage completely ignores the large Serb town of Trebinje, just past this obscure border village.) As you drive through the border into Bosnia-Herzegovina, notice the faint remains of a long-abandoned old rail line cutting sharp switchbacks up the hill. This once connected Dubrovnik to Mostar and Sarajevo. The charred trees you may see are not from the war, but from more recent forest fires.

Carry on across the plateau, where you may begin to notice Cyrillic lettering on signs: You've crossed into the Republika Srpska. About 20 minutes after the border, you'll come upon **Trebinje** (Требиње)—a pleasant and relatively affluent town that's a good place to stretch your legs, get some Convertible Marks (ATMs are scattered around the town center), and maybe nurse a coffee while people-watching on the big, leafy, inviting main square. Out on the square, a smattering of humble open-air market stalls sell local produce (Saturday is the biggest market day, but there's always some action). There's a welcoming TI on the square, but in this small-time town, they don't have much to do (closed Sun, Jovana Dučića b.b., tel. 059/273-410, www.trebinjeturizam.com). From the bottom of the square, you can stroll through the fortified gate into the sleepy, almost completely untouristy Old Town (called Kaštel), with more cafés and the town mosque (vengefully demolished during the war, but later rebuilt). The Trebišnjica River is spanned by the graceful, Ottoman-built Arslanagica Bridge. Overlooking the town from its hilltop perch is the striking Orthodox Church of Nova Gračanica, built to resemble the historically important Gračanica Monastery in Kosovo. If you have time, drive up to the church's viewpoint terrace for great views over Trebinje and the valley, and step inside the church to immerse yourself in a gorgeously vibrant world of Orthodox icons.

MOSTAR & NEARBY

From Trebinje, you have two options for getting to Mostar: The faster route via Stolac, or the very rugged slower route via Nevesinje.

Stolac Route: As you enter Trebinje, after crossing the river, follow signs for *Mostar* and *Ljubinje*. Follow the Trebišnjica River into a high-altitude karstic basin, where evocative old water-wheels power a primitive irrigation system. From here, the river flows down to the coast—providing hydroelectric power for Dubrovnik—before detouring south and emptying into the sea near Herceg Novi, Montenegro...one river, three countries, in just a few miles. This area is blanketed with vineyards and dotted with old monasteries. Passing the village of Mesari ("Butchers"), you'll also see flocks of sheep. In this part of the Balkans, Croats were traditionally the city-dwellers, while Serbs were the farmers. There used to be sheep like these in the pastures near Dubrovnik, but when the Serbs left during the war, so did the sheep.

Pull over at one of the humble, slate-roofed Orthodox chapels by the road. (There's one in Staro Slano.) In the cemeteries, many of the gravestones are from 1991—when soldiers from this area joined the war effort against Dubrovnik.

The large, flat, sunken field you're driving along is called **Popovo Polje** ("Priests' Field"). Because it floods easily, the canal was built to remove floodwater. Watch for the turnoff to **Vjetrenica** (near Zavala), a karstic cave that was a big draw in Yugoslav times. Closed down during the war, it recently reopened. It's less spectacular than the famous caves in Slovenia, but has interesting water features that may be worth touring for spelunkers with time to kill (www.vjetrenica.ba).

At the fork, carry on straight to Ljubinje. Climbing up into the mountains, you'll see garbage along the side of the road—an improvised dump in this very poor land, where a fractured government struggles to provide even basic services. Twisting up through even higher mountains, you'll wind up in the town of **Ljubinje** (Љубиње). In this humble burg, roadside stands with *med* signs advertise homegrown honey. Also keep an eye out for drying tobacco. The partially built houses are not signs of war damage (the war didn't reach here); they're a form of "savings" in the Balkans, where people don't trust banks: Rather than deposit money in an account, they spend many years using any extra funds to gradually add on to a new house.

Continuing toward Mostar, you'll pass through more desolate countryside, then your ears will pop (and you'll pass a red, white, and blue sign marking the "border" of Republika Srpska) as you drop down into the town of **Stolac** (Столац); the town's defiant mosque minaret tells you that you've crossed from Serb territory into Bosnia's Muslim-Croat Federation. Stolac is home to some fascinating history, and worth a stroll if you have the time (see page 459). Leaving Stolac, keep an eye out (on the left, just before the *Poprati* sign) for its interesting **necropolis**—a cluster of centuries-old traditional Bosnian tombstones (worth a quick photo-op stop, and described on page 459).

Past Stolac, you'll climb up the hill, going through the village of Poprati. Soon you'll have the option of either turning off to the right to head directly to **Mostar,** or continuing along the main road to reach Čapljina, where you'll turn right to go past **Počitelj** (see page 458) on your way into Mostar. Either way, **Blagaj** (see below) is worth considering as a detour before ending in Mostar. (If you want to go to **Međugorje**—see page 460—go through Čapljina and follow signs.) For arrival tips in Mostar, see the end of the driving directions earlier.

Nevesinje Route: This longer, more remote, middle-of-nowhere routing takes about an hour longer than the Stolac route. But if you're adventurous, it's a fun ride. From Trebinje, drive north toward **Bilećko Lake**—a vast, aquamarine lake you'll see on your right (the Vikiovac Restaurant offers a great viewpoint). Then you'll go through the town of **Bileća** (Билећа), turning west at the gloomy industrial town of **Gacko** (Гацко, with a giant coal mine), and onward to the humble but proud little town of **Nevesinje** (Невесиње). From Nevesinje, it's a quick drive up over the mountains, then down into Mostar—passing spectacular views of Herzog Stjepan's imposing castle over the town of Buna. Follow signs on into Mostar.

Near Mostar

While Mostar has its share of attractions, there's also plenty to see within a short drive. Ideally try to splice one or two of these stops into your trip between Mostar and the coast (see my "Route Tips for Drivers," earlier, for tips on linking them up).

Blagaj

Blagaj (BLAH-gai, rhymes with "pie") was the historical capital of this region until the arrival of the Ottomans. This is the site of a mountain called Hum, which is topped by the ruins of a hilltop castle that once belonged to Herzog ("Duke") Stjepan, who gave Herzegovina its name.

Deep in Blagaj is an impressive cliff face with a scenic house marking the source of the Buna River. The building, called the **Tekija,** is a former monastery for Turkish dervishes (an order that

emphasizes poverty and humility, famous for the way they whirl in a worshipful trance). Built in the 15th century and recently restored, the house is surrounded by a modern visitors-center complex with a café, gift shop, and pay WCs. It's free to enter and look around the Tekija, which feels similar to the tourable Turkish houses in Mostar (for a description, see page 440). You'll take your shoes off and tiptoe across a patchwork of small rugs from room to room. Gazing out the windows at the towering cliff stretching to heaven, and hearing the constant, steady flow of water, it's easy to imagine how this could be considered a very spiritual place.

After seeing the house, stroll a bit along the river, which is crossed by several footbridges offering a grand view back on the Tekija and cliff. A handful of sprawling, touristy restaurants—with open-air terraces right along the refreshing river—serve up traditional Bosnian food, including trout pulled from their own river-fed ponds.

Getting There: Blagaj is easiest to see on the way to or from Mostar—just turn off from the main road and follow the Buna River, following *tekija* signs to the big parking lot.

Počitelj

Počitelj (POTCH-ee-tell) is an artists' colony filled with a compelling mix of Christian and Muslim architecture. Ideally situated right along the main Mostar-to-Croatia road, it's one of the most popular rest stops for passing tour buses, so it's hardly undiscovered. But it's still worth a stop for its dramatically vertical townscape and beautifully restored Ottoman architecture.

Park your car and hike across the riverstone cobbles to the open square at the base of town, with a handy restaurant, lots of gift shops, and aggressive vendors. The multi-domed building is an old hammam (bathhouse). Then hike up the steep stairs (dodging costumed vendors, and enjoying fine aerial views on those hammam domes) to reach the **mosque.** You can pay 3 KM to enter (women must cover their heads). The interior is bigger, though not necessarily better decorated, than the mosques in downtown Mostar (for a description of a typical Bosnian mosque interior, see page 436). A photo on the porch shows the building circa 1993, destroyed to its foundation.

Continue up the stairs behind the mosque, which lead steeply all the way up to the fortress, which was originally built in the 15th century by Hungar-  ian King Mátyás Corvinus (who pushed the Ottomans back, briefly reclaiming some territory— including this region—for the forces of Christian Europe). There's virtually nothing to see inside (the stairs inside the tower are extremely steep and narrow—tread carefully), but the views are sensational. The best views are from the flat terrace out front. It's clear just how strategic this location is, between steep cliffs and with perfect views up and down the Neretva Valley.

Stolac

One of the most historic spots in Herzegovina, Stolac (STOH-lats) was a cradle of early Balkan civilization. Unless you're fascinated by archaeology, Stolac isn't worth a long detour—but since it's on the way between Mostar and Dubrovnik (on the back-roads route), consider stopping off if you have a little time to spare.

About 15,000 to 16,000 years ago—long before the Greeks or Romans arrived in this region—the Illyrians (ancestors of to-  day's Albanians) lived in this area's caves, where they left behind some drawings. On a hill above the modern town are the overgrown remains of the once-fearsome drystone Illyrian fortress that watched over this strategic road in the third and fourth centuries B.C. The Romans were later supplanted by the local Bogomil civilization, an indigenous Christian society. Stolac's most impressive attraction dates from this era: On the outskirts of town (on the road toward Mostar), you'll find a **necropolis** with a bonanza of giant tombstones called *stećak*s (from the 13th-15th centuries), engraved with evocative reliefs. Soon after these were erected, the Ottomans arrived, and conversions to Islam followed.

Archaeological treasures aside, today's Stolac is a workaday village with little tourism—it trudges along, largely oblivious to the ancient treasures embedded all around. The town was particularly hard-hit during the Yugoslav Wars, when it was taken over by Croat forces and its majority Muslim residents forced to flee to Mostar. Today the war crimes tribunal in The Hague has an entire division devoted to "Stolac Crimes"—at least 80 civilians were killed here. The mosque and surrounding area were completely leveled; it's now rebuilt, and the town's population is divided evenly between Croats and Bosniaks. Tension still hangs heavy in the air. Local Croats have erected crosses in front of several buildings in town, and the main square features a giant monument engraved with the names of Croats killed in the fighting here. The new, super-modern Catholic church spire rockets up over town, evoking the one-upsmanship of the similar steeple in Mostar. In a recent soccer match between the Croatian and Turkish national teams, local Bosniaks backed the Turks...and things got very tense.

If you're interested in learning more, it's well worth hiring local guide **Sanel Marić** to show you around. Sanel is an industrious young man who works for a local organization that strives to help the people of Stolac transcend the scars of the recent war. He can both show you some of the ancient sights around town, and fill you in on recent events (€30 for a tour around town, mobile 061-071-830, sanell_m@yahoo.com).

Međugorje

Međugorje is an unassuming little village "between the hills" (as its name implies) that ranks with Lourdes, Fátima, and Santiago de Compostela as one of the most important pilgrimage sites in all of Christendom. To the cynical non-Catholic, it's just a strip of crassly commercial hotels, restaurants, and rosary shops leading up to a dull church, all tied together by a silly legend about a hilltop apparition. But if you look into the tear-filled eyes of the pilgrims who've journeyed here, it's clear that to some, the power of this place is real. Strolling through the grounds, you can hear the hushed sounds of prayer whispering through the bushes.

For true believers, Međugorje represents a once-in-a-lifetime opportunity to tread on sacred soil: a place where, for decades, the Virgin Mary has appeared to six local peo-

Međugorje Mary

What compels millions to flock to this little village in the middle of nowhere? The official story goes like this: On the evening of June 24, 1981, two young women were gathering their sheep on the hillside above Mostar. They came across a woman

carrying a baby who told them to come near. Terrified, they fled, only to realize later that this might have been a vision of the Virgin Mary. They returned the next night with some friends and saw the apparition again.

In the three-plus decades since, six different locals (including the two original seers) claim to have seen the vision, and some of them even say they see it regularly to this day. They also say that Mary has given them 10 secrets—predictions of future events that will portend Judgment Day. Written on a piece of parchment, these are kept safely at the home of one of the seers. They have said they will reveal each of these secrets, 10 days before the event occurs, to the local parish priest, who will then alert the world.

Doubting Thomases aren't convinced. One cause for suspicion is that the six seers, before witnessing the visions, were sometimes known to be troublemakers. (In fact, they later admitted that they went up the hill that fateful night not to chase wayward sheep, but to sneak a smoke.) One investigator suggested that they invented the story as a prank, only to watch it snowball out of control once they told it to the local priest.

For decades, the Vatican declined to confirm the sightings as miraculous in nature. (Priests were allowed to accompany pilgrimages to Međugorje, but not to *lead* them.) A three-year Vatican investigation wrapped up in 2015, but the results had not yet been announced as this edition went to press.

ple. Even though the Vatican has declined to recognize the apparitions, that doesn't stop hundreds of thousands of Catholics from coming here each year. More than 30 million pilgrims have visited Međugorje since the sightings began—summer and winter, war (which didn't touch Međugorje) and peace, rain and shine. People make the trek here from Ireland, Italy, Germany, Spain, the US, and just about anywhere else that has Catholics.

PLANNING YOUR TIME

Unless you're a pilgrim (or think you might be a pilgrim), skip Međugorje—it's an experience wasted on nonbelievers. The only "attractions" are an unexceptional modern church, a couple of hill-top hikes, and pilgrim-spotting.

If you do go, the easiest way is to take a day-trip excursion from the Dalmatian Coast (sold from Split, Dubrovnik, and Korčula). By public bus, you can day-trip into Međugorje from Split, but not from Dubrovnik. Consider spending the night here, or sleep in Mostar two nights and day-trip into Međugorje.

Orientation to Međugorje

Međugorje (MEDGE-oo-gor-yeh, sometimes spelled "Medju-gorje" in English) is basically a one-street town—most everything happens in the half-mile between the post office (where the bus stop is) and the main church, St. James (Crkva Sv. Jakova). On the hills behind the church are two trails leading to pilgrimage sites. Many travel agencies line the main strip; at any of these, you can find a room, rent a car, hire a local guide, buy ferry tickets for Croatia, and use the Internet.

Sights in Međugorje

The center of pilgrim activity is **St. James' Church** (Crkva Sv. Jakova), which was built before the apparitions. The interior, like the outside, is modern and monochromatic—with a soothing yellow color and stained-glass windows lining the nave. Out front are posted maps that are useful for getting oriented, and a white statue of the Virgin Mary that attracts a lot of attention from pilgrims. Notice the long row of multilingual confessional booths.

As you face the church, you'll see two trails leading up into the hills. Behind and to the left of the church is **Apparition Hill** (at Podbrdo), where the sightings occurred (a one-mile hike, topped by a statue of Mary). Directly behind the church is the **Great Hill** (Križevac, or "Cross Mountain"), where a giant hilltop cross, which predates the visions, has become a secondary site of pilgrimage (1.5-mile hike). If you wonder why they don't make these rocky paths easier to climb, remember that an act of pilgrimage is supposed to be challenging. In fact, pilgrims often do one or both of these hikes barefoot, as an act of penitence.

Around back of the church is a makeshift amphitheater with benches, used for outdoor services. Beyond that is a path, lined with scenes from the life of Jesus. Farther along, on the right, is an elongated, expressionistic statue of the **Resurrected Savior** (Uskrsli Spasitelj), also known as the "Weeping Knee."

Miraculously (or not), the statue's right knee is always wet—go ahead and touch the spot that's been highly polished by worshippers and skeptics alike.

Believers and nonbelievers both appreciate the parade of kitsch that lines the **main street** leading up to the church. While rosaries are clearly the big item, you can get basically anything you want stamped with Catholic imagery (Mary is particularly popular, for obvious reasons).

Eating in Međugorje

The main street is lined with straightforward, crank-'em-out eateries catering to tour groups. For something a little more atmospheric and fun, head for **Gardens Restaurant** (near the post-office end of the main drag). The ground-floor bar, which feels a bit like a transplanted British pub, serves only drinks; you can order tasty international cuisine in the classy dining room upstairs, and the namesake garden terrace out back. Somewhat youthful but still respectable, it's a nice place to unwind at the end of a long pilgrimage (10-14-KM pastas and pizzas, 14-24-KM main courses, daily 10:00-23:00, Antunovića 66, tel. 036/650-499, www.clubgardens.com).

Sleeping and Eating near Međugorje

$$$ Herceg Etno Selo (Herceg Ethno Village) is a completely artificial but undeniably appealing faux-village of new but old-looking Bosnian dry-stone buildings wedged between industrial areas and office parks. With slate roofs, inviting ponds, playgrounds, a vineyard, a small farm, and a big amphitheater, this sprawling complex includes 50 buildings, housing a restaurant, a big hotel, gift shops, and more. Designed as a retreat center for church groups on pilgrimage, it's a restful place. If Epcot had a low-rent "Croat Herzegovina" pavilion, it would look a lot like this—completely artificial but utterly charming. The industrial-size restaurant has a menu of very well-executed Bosnian and Croatian food (6-15-KM starters, 15-30-KM main courses), while the hotel has 71 rooms (Db-€72, Tromeđa b.b., tel. 036/653-400, www.etno-herceg.com, info@etno-herceg.com). Leaving town, follow signs for *Split/Ljubuški*, and look for it on the left between warehouses.

SARAJEVO

Spectacularly set in a mountain valley blanketed with cute Monopoly houses, Sarajevo (sah-rah-YEH-voh) is a sight to behold. It's a cruel irony that for a few short years, Sarajevo became synonymous with sectarian strife. For virtually its entire history, this beautiful city was a model of the opposite: Muslims, Catholics, Orthodox Christians, and Jews living together in cooperation and harmony. (One of its many nicknames is "Little Jerusalem.") Squeezed into its narrow valley, Sarajevo never even had the option of splitting itself up into ethnic ghettos, so people lived side-by-side. To this day, there are several places in the city where you can see a mosque, synagogue, Catholic church, and Orthodox church with a turn of the head.

Sarajevo is the delightful product of a rich, if occasionally tumultuous, history. The Ottoman-style Old Town, the Baščaršija, feels transplanted here from Istanbul. Then you'll turn a corner and suddenly feel lost in an almost Viennese cityscape. Strolling its streets is the next best thing to a time machine.

Though torn by war two decades ago, Sarajevo is a comfortable and safe place to visit. Listen to the Muslim call to prayer and watch Catholic and Orthodox church bells playfully jostle above the skyline. Step into historic houses of worship from each of this region's four major faiths, noticing the similarities. Visit the street corner where World War I began, climb up into the hills to the Olympic stadium that commanded the world's attention in 1984, or ascend even higher for sweeping views over one of Europe's most stunningly set capitals. Make friends with a gregarious Sarajevan—it's easy to do—and ask him the best way to prepare and drink Bosnian coffee. Ponder the scars of war, hunch over to squeeze through the tunnel that was the besieged Sarajevans' one lifeline to the world, and listen to a local relate personal stories from the harrowing time of the siege. Play a game of giant chess with the jeering old-timers in an urban park. Shop your way through the copper-laden canyons of the Turkish-style bazaar, bartering down the price of a hand-hammered Bosnian coffee set. Relax in a hidden caravanserai, take a slow drag on a *šiša* (water pipe spewing sweet plumes of fruity smoke), and sample some honey-dripping pastry treats. For dinner—or just a snack—nibble on some of the best *bureks* (savory, flaky pies) and *ćevapi* (grilled sausages) this side of the Bosphorus. Go ahead—it's OK to enjoy Sarajevo.

PLANNING YOUR TIME

Sarajevo demands a minimum of a day. Side-tripping here from Mostar lets you scratch the surface, but you won't regret having one, two, or even three nights here. With whatever time you have, begin in the characteristic Turkish quarter, the Baščaršija.

I've described two self-guided walks. If you only have time for one, take the first one, which provides a good orientation to Sarajevo and takes you all the way through town, with opportunities to stop at virtually all of the important sights (except the Sarajevo War Tunnel Museum, which requires a long but worthwhile detour). The second walk focuses on the urban, "downtown" zone called "Sniper Alley," with some harrowing tales of the Siege of Sarajevo.

Note that Sarajevo is a 2.5-hour trip beyond Mostar, making it a logistical dead-end that's not really "on the way" to other destinations in this book. To maximize efficient use of your time, consider flying in or out of here (for example, Croatia Airlines has reasonably priced flights to Zagreb). But be aware that in winter, heavy morning fog often grounds flights.

Orientation to Sarajevo

With approximately 310,000 people (660,000 in the greater Sarajevo area)—filling a city that held up to 525,000 at its prewar peak—Sarajevo is barely contained by its valley. It's surrounded by steep mountains on all sides, with houses scampering up the valley walls (more recently joined by wartime cemeteries occupying what once were forested parks). It's a long, skinny city, lining up along its humble Miljacka River and main thoroughfare. You can trace the city's historical and architectural development from

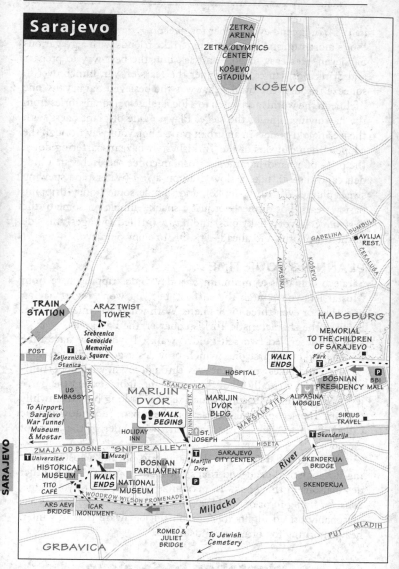

Sarajevo

ZETRA ARENA

ZETRA OLYMPICS CENTER

KOŠEVO STADIUM

KOŠEVO

GABELINA

SUMBULA

AVLIJA REST.

TEKALUŠA

ALIPAŠINA

KOŠEVO

HABSBURG

TRAIN STATION

ARAZ TWIST TOWER

Srebrenica Genocide Memorial Square

MEMORIAL TO THE CHILDREN OF SARAJEVO

POST

Željeznička Stanica

FRANCA LEHARA

KRANJCEVIĆA

HOSPITAL

WALK ENDS

Park

BOSNIAN PRESIDENCY

BBI MALL

US EMBASSY

MARIJIN DVOR

KUNINO STR.

MARIJIN DVOR BLDG.

MARŠALA TITA

ALIPAŠINA MOSQUE

WALK BEGINS

To Airport, Sarajevo War Tunnel Museum & Mostar

HOLIDAY INN

ST. JOSEPH

SIRIUS TRAVEL

Skenderija

HISETA

ZMAJA OD BOSNE

"SNIPER ALLEY"

Muzeji

SARAJEVO CITY CENTER

River

Univerziter

HISTORICAL MUSEUM

TITO CAFÉ

BOSNIAN PARLIAMENT

Marijin Dvor

SKENDERIJA BRIDGE

SKENDERIJA

WALK ENDS

NATIONAL MUSEUM

WOODROW WILSON PROMENADE

Miljacka

ARS AEVI BRIDGE

ICAR MONUMENT

ROMEO & JULIET BRIDGE

To Jewish Cemetery

PUT MLADIH

GRBAVICA

SARAJEVO

east to west, starting with the historic Old Town core, called the Baščaršija. West of that is the Austrian-feeling part of town (along Ferhadija street), and beyond that, the modern, concrete skyscraper zone called Marijin Dvor. From here, the city's busy main drag rumbles west (it's called Zmaja od Bosne close to downtown, and Bulevar Meše Selimovića farther out; in wartime it was known as "Sniper Alley").

Terminology: The terminology for the various parties involved in the Yugoslav Wars is particularly sensitive—and can vary

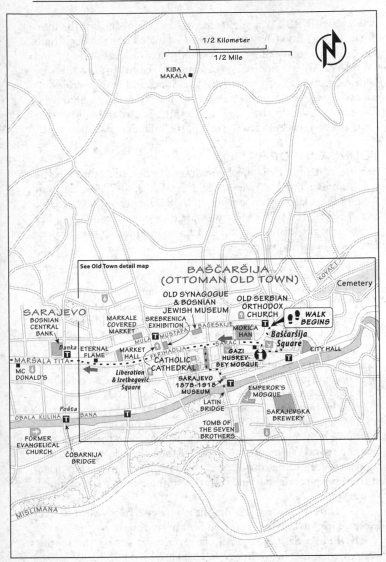

depending on whom you're talking to. During the siege, the citizens of Sarajevo were majority Muslim/Bosniak, but also included Croats, Serbs, Jews, and others; many think of themselves not as a specific ethnicity, but as "Sarajevans" or "Bosnians." Meanwhile, the army surrounding the city was made up almost entirely of Serbs, but not all Serbs supported them—so to call them simply "Serbs" is incomplete. Sarajevans (conscientious not to disrespect the many Serbs who were among those besieged) prefer to call the aggressors "the Bosnian Serb Army," "Army of Republika Srpska" (abbreviated VRS), "Karadžić's forces," or "Četniks." But the term "Četnik" is a loaded one: It was first used to describe the fierce Serb fighting force that ethnically cleansed parts of Yugoslavia during World War II. The troops who surrounded the city evoked this earlier image and called themselves "Četniks," and many Sarajevans have followed suit. However, in other contexts, calling a Serb (who was not involved in the siege) a "Četnik" is a serious insult that could put you on the receiving end of the infamous Balkan temper.

TOURIST INFORMATION

Sarajevo's helpful TI is on the main pedestrian drag through the old Ottoman quarter (May-Sept Mon-Fri 9:00-22:00, Sat-Sun 9:00-18:00; Oct-April Mon-Fri 9:00-18:00, Sat-Sun 9:00-16:00; Sarači 58, tel. 033/580-999, www.sarajevo-tourism.com). Another branch is at the airport. At either TI, you can pick up the *Sarajevo Navigator* monthly planner.

ARRIVAL IN SARAJEVO

By Bus or Train: Sarajevo's bus and train stations sit next to each other on one very long, urban block up from the Marijin Dvor area (former "Sniper Alley," US Embassy, Holiday Inn, and museums). They're about 2.5 miles west of the Baščaršija (Old Town, with my recommended hotels).

The **train station** looks out over a desolate-feeling plaza; simply walk out front, buy a tram ticket from the kiosk, and ride tram #1 to the Baščaršija. Alternatively, you can pay 6-10 KM for a taxi.

The **bus station** (Autobusna Stanica Sarajevo) has a small ticket lobby, a left-luggage desk *(garderoba)*, and a smattering of kiosks and cafés. Exit the building straight ahead, keeping the busy street on your right. Walk about 100 yards, then hook left around the big post office (near a row of cafés). You'll wind up at the big plaza in front of the train station, with the stop for tram #1 (explained above).

By Car: If you're driving into Sarajevo from Mostar, see "Route Tips for Drivers" at the end of this chapter.

By Plane: Sarajevo's small, sleepy airport sits on the southwestern edge of town (airport code: SJJ, tel. 033/289-100, www.sarajevo-airport.ba). It has ATMs and a TI kiosk. There's no handy public-transportation connection into town, so the easiest option is a taxi; the fair metered rate to downtown is around 15-20 KM, but most taxi drivers demand 30 KM. If you'd like to take public transit, walk straight out the front door of the airport and continue on foot about 10 minutes directly ahead to the Dobrinja neighborhood, where you can catch trolley bus #103 to the Latin Bridge in the Old Town, or bus #31E to near the old City Hall, also in the Old Town (both run about 3-4/hour, buy ticket from kiosk or driver, see tram description below). If you'll be at the airport, it's convenient to visit the nearby War Tunnel Museum (pay no more than 10 KM for the taxi ride from the airport).

GETTING AROUND SARAJEVO

Almost everything that's worth seeing in town (with the notable exception of the War Tunnel Museum) is within long walking distance of each other. But you may need to make use of the city's **public transportation** network, which includes trams, buses, and trolley buses. A single ticket costs 1.80 KM (buy at kiosk or on board, good for one ride only—if you transfer, you must buy a new ticket; when boarding, validate your ticket by stamping it in the green box). A day ticket for 5 KM is good for one calendar day (sold only at the kiosk behind the Catholic cathedral). The handy tram #3 does a big loop from one end of town to the other, starting in the Old Town (several stops, including at the Latin Bridge/Latinska Ćuprija, at the City Hall/Vijećnica, at the Baščaršija stop near the main square on Kovači street, and behind the cathedral), then along the main drag (former "Sniper Alley") to the west end of town (Ilidža stop, a short taxi ride to the Sarajevo War Tunnel Museum), and back again (7.5 miles and 40 minutes one-way). Tram #1 is also useful, connecting the train and bus stations with "Sniper Alley" and the Old Town.

Sarajevo is an excellent **taxi** town, with cheap fares and generally honest cabbies. Figure 1.50 KM for the drop, then 1 KM per kilometer. Short rides within town are typically a steal at 5-10 KM. To ensure you're getting an official, regulated taxi, confirm that the license plate starts with the letters "TA," and be sure the driver turns on the meter.

HELPFUL HINTS

Travel Agency: Sirius Travel, run by can-do Bakir and Sakiba Zagorica (who used to live in Florida), can arrange accommodations and transfers (€10 to the airport), tours around town (€50/2-hour walking tour, €80/4-hour walking tour plus drive to panoramic viewpoints), or anything else you might need in Sarajevo (along the river at Obala Kulina Bana 5, tel. 033/550-940, www.sirius-travel.ba, siriustravel@bih.net.ba).

Local Guidebook: Look for the informative, pocket-sized book called *The Siege of Sarajevo 1992-1996*. Designed to help visitors better understand this city's complex and tragic wartime story, it's concisely written, filled with powerful black-and-white photographs, and sold at bookstores around town.

War and Peace in Sarajevo

When the Ottomans arrived in this valley in the 15th century, what had been a humble settlement of Bogomil kings and Franciscans from Dubrovnik was swiftly converted into a major trading center—thanks to its strategic location between the Croatian coast and the Ottoman-held lands farther east. Sarajevo's location was near silver and coal mines, and came with an ample supply of fresh spring water and runoff from the mountains all around—providing constantly running water, which is so prized in Muslim culture. The Ottomans harnessed that water to build baths and fountains for Sarajevo's mosques. The town became a thriving population center and, eventually, the capital of the area.

As the Ottoman Empire declined in the late 19th century, the Habsburgs took over—dispatching urban planners and architects to spiff up the burg to Viennese standards. During its brief 40 years under the Austro-Hungarian Empire, Sarajevo was modernized and grew quickly. But the Habsburgs, too, fell from power—thanks to a war that started with the assassination of their heir in this very city (see page 495).

During the Yugoslav era, Sarajevo enjoyed a privileged status as a town that exemplified Tito's idealistic vision of the various Yugoslav ethnicities living and working together. It was chosen to represent Yugoslavia as the host of the 1984 Winter Olympics.

Tours in Sarajevo

▲▲▲Local Guides

With such a powerful and challenging-to-grasp recent history, and with the ready availability of extremely good and affordable local guides, it's virtually obligatory to hire a guide for your Sarajevo time. For the price of joining an organized walking tour in many European cities, you can hire your very own Sarajevan for the day, who will likely be willing to speak frankly about their experiences during the siege. If at all possible, arrange to hire **Amir Telibečirović,** a journalist, war veteran, and historian who explains Sarajevo's sights and history—from ancient to recent—with brilliant clarity. Amir can add immeasurably to your Sarajevo experience (30 KM or €15/person for a tour of any length, or 50 KM/€25 for just one person, mobile 061-304-966, teleamir@gmail.com). If Amir is busy, **Jadranka Šuster** is worth considering for her professional, by-the-book approach (€40/2 hours, €15/extra hour, €120/all day, more for 4 or more people; also offers special activities such as cooking classes, gastronomic tours, coppersmithing, and wood-burning crafts; mobile 061-828-400, www.sarajevo-tour.com, sarajevotour@gmail.com). Other guides

But then, less than a decade after its moment in the limelight, its fate took an appalling turn, as Sarajevo again seized the world's attention—for the worst possible reasons. As Yugoslavia broke apart, multiethnic Bosnia became ground zero for hashing out old ethnic grudges. Sarajevans woke up one morning in the spring of 1992 completely surrounded by the heavy artillery of Radovan Karadžić's Bosnian Serb army and paramilitary groups. Overnight, their besieged city became a shooting gallery, with Sarajevan civilians as the targets. During the longest siege in modern European history (three years and eight months), people here were bombarded to the edge of madness and picked off in the streets by distant snipers. The Sarajevans—Bosniaks, Croats, and Serbs alike—were forced to improvise to create shelter, heat, food, and entertainment. They dug a half-mile-long tunnel to get basic supplies and did whatever they could to keep going. For more on this dark time, see "The Siege of Sarajevo" on page 484.

Since 1996, peace has returned to Sarajevo. While you'll see some completely restored historical buildings and glass skyscrapers, there are also skeletons of bombed-out buildings, and lots of bullet holes and shrapnel scars. Sarajevo is a city in transition—and much remains to be done.

are also available for similar rates; to arrange, contact Sirius Travel (see "Helpful Hints," earlier).

Insider Tours

This company runs various itineraries around the city, departing from their office near the Latin Bridge (at Zelenih Beretki 30, open Mon-Fri 8:00-18:00—or 9:00-17:00 in winter, Sat-Sun 9:00-14:00). Options include their **introductory free tour** (tips expected, 1.5 hours, daily at 16:30); **Eat, Pray, Love,** an experiential tour that includes some food tasting and visits to Sarajevo's main houses of worship (€30, 4 hours, daily at 10:00); **Times of Misfortune,** detailing the siege (€27, includes entrance to War Tunnel Museum, 3 hours, daily at 11:00); a more specific tour of the **War Tunnel Museum** (€15, includes museum admission, 2 hours, daily at 14:00); **Sarajevo Assassination,** focusing on Franz Ferdinand and Princip sites (€19, 3 hours, daily at 10:30); **Islam You Did Not Know,** designed to demystify Bosnian Muslim culture (€10, 1 hour, daily at 10:00); and other tours available on request (such as their Jewish tour, €25, 4 hours). They also offer excursions to other parts of Bosnia, including the Srebrenica massacre site, a river-rafting trip, Olympics sights, Mostar and nearby towns, and a combo-tour of the towns of Jajce and Travnik. Call ahead to

SARAJEVO

confirm the schedule and to reserve—book at least an hour ahead for the in-town walks, or a day ahead for the out-of-town trips (mobile 061-190-591, tel. 033/534-353, www.sarajevoinsider.com). Their office also has a modest museum about the Siege of Sarajevo, with a few basic informational posters and a powerful, grisly eight-minute film (3 KM).

Adventure Excursions

Sarajevo's spectacular setting lends itself to adventure travel—hiking, mountain biking, river rafting, skiing, and so on. **Green Visions** offers eco-friendly excursions into the Bosnian countryside (tel. 033/717-291, www.greenvisions.ba).

Walks in Sarajevo

Below I've outlined two different self-guided walks that, when taken together, provide a useful spine for visiting virtually all of the sights mentioned under "Sights in Sarajevo," later (except the War Tunnel Museum, which is farther out). The first walk covers the historic core of town, including most of the museums. The second (which begins an easy five-minute walk from where the first leaves off) focuses on the Siege of Sarajevo.

▲▲▲WELCOME TO SARAJEVO

This walk begins where most tourist visits do, in the Ottoman-influenced Old Town—the Baščaršija—then strolls through history as it traverses the Habsburg quarter.

I've split the walk into three parts. If you're in a hurry and want to focus on the Old Town, just do Parts 1 (Ottoman zone) and 2 (Habsburg quarter); Part 3 takes you deeper into the workaday urban core, including some sights relating to the siege, and is designed to help you connect to the "Sniper Alley" area. Doing the entire walk without entering any of the sights could take as little as two hours—but with sightseeing stops, it can fill an entire day or more.

• *Begin at the main square of the Old Town (Baščaršija), with the wooden fountain at the top.*

Part 1: Ottoman Old Town (Baščaršija)

"Pigeon Square": Though it's nicknamed for its many winged residents, this square is officially called Baščaršija. Literally translated as "Main Marketplace," this unmistakably Ottoman-flavored square has given its name to the entire Old Town. The fountain (notice the small faucet at the base), called **Sebilj,** is an icon of Sarajevo. According to local legend, visitors who drink water from this fountain will return to Sarajevo someday. The original was built in 1753, but this restored version dates from the 19th century. Although it's the centerpiece of the "Turkish" Old Town, the fountain is more Persian in style. The Ottoman Empire (of which Sarajevo was a part) enjoyed influences from throughout both the Islamic and the European cultures: art, literature, and poetry from Persia (today's Iran); religious influence (i.e., Sunni Islam) from the Arabic world; diplomacy from the Germanic world; and herbal pharmacology and music from the Jewish world.

Turn with your back to the fountain and walk down the cobbled square. Look for the tight little lane on the left, just before the

mosque. This is the wonderfully authentic **Coppersmiths' Street** (Kazandžiluk), where craftsmen still carry out their work, hammering beautiful works of art out of copper—you can hear their little hammers tapping from their workshops. It's just the place to buy a copper Bosnian coffee set that you'll never use. This might be the most touristy street in Sarajevo, so the prices aren't a bargain, but it's a fun stroll.

Walk all the way down Coppersmiths' Street—jogging right at the end—until you pop out around the corner, on **Locksmiths' Street** (Bravadžiluk). Locals call this lane "Ćevapi Street" for its many ćevabdžinica (shops selling the tasty minced-meat, grilled sausages called ćevapčići). You'll also see several buregdžinica (shops selling the savory phyllo-dough pastry called burek; my favorite, the recommended Buregdžinica Sač, is just down a side lane off of this street).

Look left, to the yellow-and-brown-striped building at the end of the block. This is one of the city's main landmarks, the **City Hall** (Vijećnica)—the best example of Austrian Historicist-style architecture from the 40 years of Habsburg rule. While it looks Islamic, it was designed by a Czech architect who went to Morocco to find inspiration—so it has no connection at all to local culture. Later it became the City Library, and was also the local Nazi headquarters during World War II. But this landmark building—and its books—were destroyed by shells in 1992; in 2014, it reopened after a years-long restoration and now invites visitors to take in its gorgeous interior (described later). This building is also the place where, on June 28, 1914, the Habsburg heir, Archduke Franz Ferdinand, began a fateful drive through town. (We'll see where that trip ended later on this walk.)

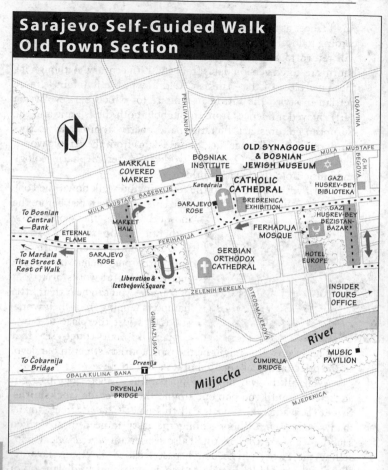

Sarajevo Self-Guided Walk
Old Town Section

Now turn right and walk a half-block down Locksmiths' Street, popping out at the bottom of the square where we started this walk. On your right is the **Baščaršija Mosque,** the first of many we'll see throughout town (though this one is closed to the public). Kitty-corner from the mosque, notice the copper domes on the roof of the covered market hall (Brusa Bezistan). Dating from 1551, this market hall now holds the **City History Museum,** with a great model of late 19th-century Sarajevo and other good exhibits (worth visiting for an introduction to the city, and described later under "Sights in Sarajevo").

• *Across from the mosque's gate, walk down the main street through town.*

Sarači Street: Lined with shops, more *ćevapi* joints, tempting desserts (for some Bosnian treats, see page 420), and the TI, this busy pedestrian street is a handy artery for sightseeing. Like so many streets in the Baščaršija, this is named for a type of

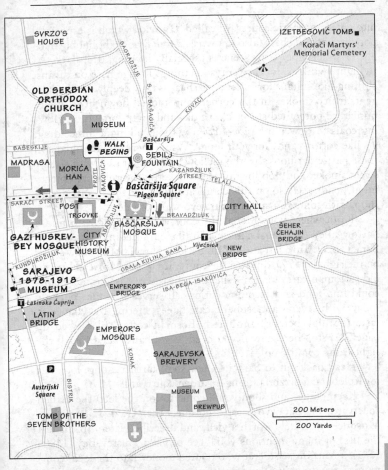

craftsman who worked here—in this case, "Leathermakers." After a short block, on the left, is the **TI.** Across the street is the lane

called **Prote Bakovića,** crammed with characteristic (if touristy) eateries. Bakovića also leads to the **Old Serbian Orthodox Church,** well worth a visit (described later). None of the four Serbian Orthodox Churches in Sarajevo was vandalized during the siege, though they were all damaged by shrapnel launched at nearby targets by the Bosnian Serb Army.

It's easy to miss the many **courtyards** *(han)* that burrow between blocks in the Old Town. Directly across Sarači street from Prote Bakovića, go down the little alley next to the TI. You'll pop into an atmospheric courtyard called **Trgovke**, which is especially popular with *šiša* bars (also known as *nargila*, hookah, hubbly bubbly, or water pipe). This scene is especially inviting after dark. As twilight twinkles, local twentysomethings lounge here on divans, chilling like sultans (or, at least, pashas) as they deeply inhale pungent, fruity smoke. In the corners and tucked down little alleys, miniature potbellied stoves churn day and night, providing glowing coals to power the pipes. Even without taking a direct drag, it's like cotton candy for your lungs. While there's no marijuana in these particular hookahs, the mellow hubbub, air rich with sickly-sweet smoke, and floodlit minarets rocketing overhead are plenty mind-bending. Also on this courtyard, look for the Egoist design shop, with some fun and hip Sarajevo stuff for sale.

From where you entered the courtyard, turn right to find a narrow alley (next to Damask Nargila Bar) leading back out to Sarači street. Turn left and continue along Sarači. After a few steps, on the right (at #77), dip into the courtyard of the **Morića Han,** an old Ottoman caravanserai—like an inn, where passing merchants could find food and accommodations. It serves a similar purpose today, with several atmospheric café tables offering the chance to taste the high-octane, unfiltered "Bosnian coffee" (described on page 511; stop here now if you need to get caffeinated for all the sightseeing coming up).

Head back out to Sarači. A few steps farther along, look left for Kolobara, a pizzeria filling a garden courtyard.

Keep going, and soon you'll come to (on the left) the walled courtyard of Sarajevo's top mosque, the **Gazi Husrev-Bey Mosque**—definitely worth a visit, and described later. This is just the first of many mentions you'll see of Gazi Husrev-Bey (1480-1541), a Muslim aristocrat who poured money into the local community. Many of the landmarks of the Old Town were built as part of Husrev-Bey's *vakuf,* or religious endowment; you'll notice plaques to this effect all over town. Thanks to his patronage, Sarajevo became the biggest city in the European part of the Ottoman Empire. If you'd like to pay your respects to this John-D-and-Catherine-T-MacArthur-style benefactor, his tomb is just to the left of the mosque (also described later).

Across the street from the mosque's middle gate (at #33, labeled *Muzej Gazi Husrev-Bey*) is the **Kuršumlija Madrasa,** originally built as an Islamic theological school by Husrev-Bey in the 1530s. Step into the outer courtyard for a better look at the building, which has multiple chimneys poking up above the roofline. Students lived in simple "dorms," each one individually heated by its own stove. You can peek into the inner courtyard, or pay 3 KM to go in and peruse its interesting but dry exhibit about Husrev-Bey (including a good film about his life and legacy) and the history of the building. The main classroom, straight ahead from the entrance, has a Star of David chandelier, suggesting the deep interfaith respect through much of Sarajevo's history (everything described in English, daily 9:00-13:00 & 13:30-20:00). The modern school next door (the yellow building, to the right) still teaches the Islamic faith.

Still in the courtyard, as you face the madrasa, look left to see the sparkling-new library, **Gazi Husrev-Bey Biblioteka.** While local Muslim bigwigs (the modern-day versions of Husrev-Bey) don't have the money to invest as they'd like in their home country, other Middle Eastern countries (in this case, Qatar) are keeping this tradition of endowment alive. Throughout Bosnia, many destroyed-then-rebuilt mosques and Muslim cultural institutions come with a plaque noting which Islamic country paid to resurrect it. In addition to being a fully operational archive and library, this gorgeous new complex includes a large auditorium and a museum that displays its treasures—including precious books that were hidden away in a bank vault to survive the siege (3 KM, daily 9:00-18:00, www.ghb.ba).

Head back out to Sarači street and continue to the corner. On the left is another covered bazaar, this one still functioning as a market: **Gazi Husrev-Bey Bezistan-Bazar.** Cut through the market hall—maybe browsing for a scarf, purse, necklace, watch, or sunglasses—and pop out the far end, turning right to find a field (squeezed between the market and Hotel Europe) littered with ruins from a 16th-century Ottoman caravanserai, called **Tašlihan.** Funded by (surprise, surprise) Gazi Husrev-Bey, this caravanserai hosted passing travelers, traders, and merchants—logically, since it was located next to the bazaar—until it was badly damaged by an 1879 fire.

• *Now walk back past the end of the covered market, take the first right, and walk a short block down to the...*

Miljacka River: The last building on your left before the riverfront houses the **Sarajevo 1878-1918 Museum** (described later). The museum outlines the brief but prolific four decades of Austrian Habsburg rule here—and, more importantly, the story of how Gavrilo Princip's assassination of the Habsburg heir, Archduke Franz Ferdinand, took place right on this corner. The shooting set off a chain reaction of allegiances and grudges that swiftly pulled all of Europe—and, eventually, much of the world—into a Great War that would end the age of empires and inaugurate a new era of modern nations. (For the full story, see "The Shot Heard 'Round the World" on page 495.)

Go across the street to the Turkish-style **Latin Bridge** (Latinska Ćuprija)—so named because during Ottoman times, this was an area populated by many Catholics (who said Mass in Latin).

After World War I, the bridge was renamed "Principov Most" for the assassin who had asserted Bosnian Serb nationalism against the Habsburgs. But after the 1992-1996 siege, Sarajevans couldn't stand calling the bridge after a Bosnian Serb, and went back to the old name.

Looking down, you'll see that the Miljacka is hardly a rushing river (like the Neretva in Mostar)—up here in the Bosnian highlands, this is still just a trickle. While not navigable for trade, the river's current was harnessed to spur the development of the old Ottoman town. From here, you're near three sights that may be worth a detour later. Looking across the bridge to the left, you'll see the minaret of the copper-domed **Emperor's Mosque** (Careva Džamija)—the city's most elegant and oldest, built in 1457 to honor the Ottoman Sultan Mehmet the Conqueror (though it's been rebuilt and expanded many times since then). Just behind the mosque, a short walk from here, is the **Sarajevsko Pivo** brewery, a huge facility that churns out every Bosniak's favorite brew. Because it's fed by a natural spring, this was one of the few factories that was able to keep working through the siege. It also has a fine little museum about the beer's history and an atmospheric old beer hall serving pub grub (see "Eating in Sarajevo," later). Those intrigued by Sarajevo's spiritual history might consider a five-minute detour from here to the **Tomb of the Seven Brothers** (described later; go straight across the river and up the hill, past the park with the charming little music pavilion/tea house, to the top of the parking lot).

• *Part 1 of our walk is finished. To continue with Part 2—and see a very different side of Sarajevo—backtrack all the way through the covered market to the main drag where we started, and turn left.*

This street has now changed its name from Sarači to Ferhadija. Without the slightest transition, you step from the extremely Ottoman-feeling "little Istanbul" of the Baščaršija into the Viennese-feeling Habsburg Quarter. Notice the Sarajevo: Meeting of Cultures *sign underfoot. You're encouraged to stand here and snap a selfie in one direction, with an Ottoman backdrop—then turn 180 degrees and snap a selfie in the other, with an Austrian backdrop.*

Part 2: Habsburg Sarajevo (Ferhadija Street)

With the precipitous decline of the Ottoman Empire in the late 1800s, the Habsburgs—who ruled the vast Austro-Hungarian Empire from Vienna—saw an opportunity to fill the vacuum left in this part of Europe. With the swirl of a pen in 1878, Bosnia went from Ottoman to Austrian rule. As they had throughout their realm, the Habsburgs stepped in and immediately began to modernize Sarajevo, rolling out new infrastructure and buildings like crazy. While they ruled Sarajevo for only 40 years, the Habsburgs left it a far more modern city than they'd found it.

After a few steps on Ferhadija, an alley on the right leads up to the **Old Synagogue and Bosnian Jewish Museum** (described later)—offering a fascinating look at another of this city's many faiths.

Just a bit farther, set back from the street on the left, is the small but pretty **Ferhadija Mosque.** If you go around behind the mosque and duck into the **Hotel Europe,** you'll find a genteel, chandeliered, Viennese-style coffeehouse interior. The architect who gave Sarajevo its Austrian look—including this hotel—was actually a Czech, Karel Pařík. He lived here for nearly 60 years and designed some 70 buildings in town, including the City Hall, the big Evangelical Church across the river, and the National Museum where this walk ends.

Continuing two more blocks along Ferhadija street, on the right, you can't miss the **Catholic Cathedral** (described later). Notice that this is the fourth different house of worship we've seen (Muslim, Orthodox Christian, Jewish, Catholic) in just the short distance since we began our walk. The silver statue out front celebrates Sveti Ivan Pavao II. "Papa"—that's St. John Paul II—came here on April 12, 1997, Bosnia's first-ever papal visit.

Around the right side of the cathedral is the very sobering **Srebrenica Exhibition,** documenting the heinous genocidal activities at that eastern Bosnian town. This sight is a must for visitors who want to better understand the atrocities that went on in this country so recently (exhibition described later).

Directly in front of the cathedral's main steps, look for the big **Sarajevo rose** in the pavement—a distinctive starburst indentation that's colored in red, and carefully preserved as a memorial, even after the surrounding pavement was replaced. Immediately following the war, about 1,000 of the impact craters in the streets of Sarajevo were filled with a red resin, instantly creating a poignant memorial. As the city has rebuilt, most of these Sarajevo roses have been replaced with new asphalt. Only a few remain, and those are tended to by a local preservation group. Another one is around the left side of the cathedral, just before the side door. I'll point out two more Sarajevo roses through the rest of this walk.

Behind the cathedral is an old Ottoman bathhouse *(hamam)*, with telltale copper domes. Today it's part of a private cultural center called the **Bosniak Institute.** It sometimes houses special exhibits; if one is going on, you can look around inside.

A block farther along Ferhadija, on the left, is a parklike square once called Liberation Square—since renamed **Liberation and Izetbegović Square** to honor the

wartime Bosnian president. The square is ringed with busts of important Bosnian writers, and the *Multicultural Man Builds the World* statue in the middle—of a naked man doing jumping jacks, with a highly polished member—was donated by an Italian artist to beautify the war-torn city. You'll see many such examples of donated public art through Sarajevo—quite a few of them are "white elephants" not entirely embraced by the cynical, siege-hardened Sarajevans. At the far end of the square, old-timers gather to play giant-size chess—carefully strategizing while a rogues' gallery of onlookers cheers and jeers for each move. It's an enjoyable scene that testifies to the resilience of the Bosnian spirit—and the ability of unemployed locals to find ways to entertain themselves in a miserable economy.

At the end of the square is yet another house of worship: The bold facade and towers of the **Serbian Orthodox Cathedral.** This was built from 1863 to 1869, during Otto-

man rule. In this ecumenical city, the funds came from all quarters: donations from the Romanovs, Russia's ruling family; from the Ottoman sultan; and from a Serbian prince. Like many houses of worship in this town, the church's architecture demonstrates the mingling of faiths: It looks like an Orthodox church with a Catholic bell tower. (Bell towers are atypical enough for Orthodox churches, but this one even uses Catholic-style Roman numerals.) While the postwar renovation may not quite be complete, the interior is cavernous and lavishly decorated, with beautifully painted domes and a stirring iconostasis—it's well worth a look (free, daily 8:00-17:30; for more on the Serbian Orthodox Church, see page 316).

Continuing along Ferhadija, just after the park on your right is an elegant yellow **market hall.** Go through (or alongside) this hall and emerge on the other side, then walk to the right one block along the busy street. On the left side of this street, look for Sa-

rajevo's **Markale covered market.** Browse your way through humble tables, heavy with produce, to the back corner, where a stone plaque and names engraved on a glass wall recall a pivotal moment in the Siege of Sarajevo. This busy, completely untouristy market gained infamy as the site of two cruel bombings that targeted civilians and claimed more than a hundred innocent lives—Sa-

rajevans who were simply shopping for paltry foodstuffs to keep their families fed and alive through impossibly tough conditions. Sixty-seven Sarajevans died during an attack on February 5, 1994 (plus another 144 wounded), and 43 more died (and 90 wounded) on August 28, 1995. (The blast pattern from one of the bombings, in the floor, is protected by a glass case.) These ruthless bombardments were a turning point in the siege—when the international community began to sit up and pay attention, and realize that this was not simply a standard-issue war between equal parties, but a barbaric siege that was destroying the lives of countless peace-loving civilians who wanted no part of the violence. It was the 1995 attack, in part, that prompted NATO air strikes against Karadžić's forces two days later. "Operation Deliberate Force" ultimately led to the Dayton Peace Accords, which finally ended the violence— although Sarajevans wish NATO hadn't been quite so "deliberate" as to wait three and a half years before taking action.

Head back to the main walking street, Ferhadija, and contin-

ue on your way. As you walk, in the pavement in front of the Tally Weijl shop (at #12, on the left), look for **another Sarajevo rose** (the red resin is worn off, but the impact crater survives). The plaque next to the door of the shop explains that on May 27, 1992, 26 *Građana Sarajeva* ("citizens of Sarajevo") were killed by an artil-

lery shell while waiting in line to buy bread at a bakery here.

The street angles and takes you up to an intersection with the busy Maršala Tita street, named for the WWII Partisan military hero and president-for-life of communist Yugoslavia—Marshal Tito. On the right at the corner is an **eternal flame** honoring

SARAJEVO

Partisan fighters. If you're here in cold weather, you may notice that the practical Sarajevans—who learned during the lean years of the siege never to waste resources—use it to warm up as they pass by.

• *Part 2 of our walk is finished. If you're pooped, or just want more time to check out the sights in this part of town, now's the time to bail out. But if you want to continue, Part 3 will send you in the direction of "Sniper Alley" (covered in my other self-guided walk).*

Part 3: Maršala Tita Street

Crowded with cars, trucks, trams, and buses, this artery feels more urban and less atmospheric than the Ottoman and Austrian zones we just left. During the siege, this was one of the safest major boulevards in town, since it's relatively narrow and well-protected from snipers by tall buildings. The exposed side-streets were blocked off to create what was called a "Road of Life," where people could walk without fear of being picked off by distant gunmen. We'll follow this street several blocks to ground zero of the former war zone.

After a block, on the right, his-and-hers Atlases flank the doors of the **Bosnian Central Bank** building—where the fledgling Convertible Mark currency is administered. The all-purpose lights spanning the street here are lit up to celebrate local festivals and (in this multifaith city) a wide range of religious holidays: Ramadan, Christmas, and New Year's.

Farther along, on the left, is **McDonald's,** which caused an uproar when it finally opened here in July of 2011. The opening was delayed for four years, as local *ćevapi* vendors—scandalized by the notion of a multinational conglomerate challenging the loyalty of Bosnian palates—did whatever they could to block it. For weeks after it opened, there were long lines down the street of Sarajevans curious to try the American burgers. But within a few weeks, the furor died down, the crowds dispersed, and the *ćevapi* sellers were satisfied that Bosnians wouldn't abandon the grilled meats they've enjoyed for centuries.

One block later, the street opens up. On the left is the slick, new BBI Centar shopping mall. On the right is a fine park with perhaps the most emotionally devastating memorial in this trag-

edy-laden city: the **Memorial
to the Children of Sarajevo.**
Look closely at the symbolism-
packed fountain. The glass
sculpture in the middle represents a sandcastle, but one that
is not—and never will be—finished...the innocent play of a

child cut short by an untimely death. The footprints embedded in
the concrete basin belong to the young siblings of children who
were killed in the war. The silver pillars to the left can be spun to
see names of young victims of the fighting. Nearly 1,600 children
were among those killed during the siege.

Scattered in the hillsides of the **park** beyond the fountain,
notice a few Ottoman-style gravestones, shaped like turbans—the
earliest dating from the early 17th century. In the pavement at the
far end of this park—about 30 yards before the crosswalk—look for
a Sarajevo rose.

Leaving the park, continue down the busy street. The brown-
and-orange building on the left is the **Bosnian Presidency** (the
local "White House"). During the early days of the war, this building was the focus of street-by-street fighting; if the Bosnian Serb
forces had claimed it, they could have declared victory. At one
point, they were within 50 yards of this building, but the defense
held. As part of the compromise to end the war, today Bosnia's
"Presidency" is made up of a committee of three members: one
Bosniak, one Croat, and one Serb, with a rotating chairmanship.
Difficult as it is to get things done with one president, imagine how
impossible the situation is when you need agreement among three
people who are predisposed to mistrust each other. While critical
for ending the war, this compromise has made it even more difficult
to move forward with postwar recovery.

In the park beyond the Presidency is the 16th-century Alipašina
Mosque. A long walk directly up the hill from here (with your back

to the mosque, about a mile up
Alipašina street) would take
you to the **Zetra Olympics
Center** (not worth a detour
now, but worth considering if
you're curious and have time
later). This complex includes
Koševo Stadium, which held
the opening ceremony for the
1984 Olympics (and, in 1997,

hosted visits by both Pope John Paul II and the band U2—both of
whom had spoken out in support of the besieged Sarajevans); and

The Siege of Sarajevo

Most travelers know that Bosnia-Herzegovina was torn apart by a war when Yugoslavia broke up in the early to mid-1990s (see the Understanding Yugoslavia chapter). But few realize that in that country's capital, Sarajevo, the "war" was not conventional fighting between armies, but a medieval-style siege designed to cut off the city from food, water, electricity, telephone, medicine, and other critical supplies. The Siege of Sarajevo lasted for more than 1,300 days, making it the longest siege in modern European history (longer than the infamous WWII-era Siege of Leningrad, a.k.a. St. Petersburg). How could a modern city of some 300,000 people be cut off in this way?

In early 1992, the people of Bosnia-Herzegovina voted in favor of independence from Yugoslavia; although many Serbs boycotted the ballot box, 64 percent of Bosnians turned out, and 98 percent of them voted yes. Over the next month, Bosnian Serb leader Radovan Karadžić and Bosnian President Alija Izetbegović traded heated rhetoric about what the new nation of Bosnia-Herzegovina would look like. Meanwhile, each one built a make-shift army: Izetbegović's Bosnian Army asserted control over Sarajevo's city center, while Karadžić's well-supplied Bosnian Serb troops from the Yugoslav People's Army fortified their positions on the hills ringing the capital.

On April 1, a Serb militia group invaded the town of Bijeljina in eastern Bosnia, massacring many innocent civilians. On April 5, some 100,000 Sarajevans—of all ethnic stripes—came to the busy intersection in front of the Bosnian Parliament to stage a peace rally. Karadžić watched nervously from his office in the Holiday Inn across the street. When the protesters turned their attention to his building, he commanded his snipers to open fire on the unarmed crowd, killing six. Karadžić fled to the hills above town, while Izetbegović's police moved in and arrested the snipers. After Izetbegović refused Karadžić's ultimatum to release the snipers, Karadžić began shelling the city.

For the next month, the situation degraded in other parts of the country, as Bosnian Serb paramilitary groups carried out ethnic cleansing. On May 2, 1992, the Bosnian Serb Army began their advance on the capital in earnest, bombarding Sarajevo's city center, blowing up its central post office to disable telephone communication, and erecting barricades, completely cutting off the Sarajevans from the outside world. The city was defended by a motley collection of policemen, professional soldiers who had defected from the Yugoslav army, and even criminal street gangs. About 12 percent of the army was made up of Serbs. It wasn't necessarily a "pro-Bosnia" army—just Sarajevans desperate to preserve their way of life. This wasn't patriotism: It was survival.

Both sides dug in for a long struggle. Yugoslavia's leader, Slobodan Milošević, sent a ruthless general, Ratko Mladić, to take command of the Bosnian Serb forces. His orders: "Target the Muslim neighborhoods...Shell them until they're at the edge of madness." Snipers monitored exposed streets, immediately firing upon any Sarajevan who dared to walk past.

Horrifying as the tales of besieged Sarajevo are, it's equally uplifting to hear about the irrepressible human spirit shown during these times. The people of Sarajevo survived thanks to the tireless efforts of those who dug and used a tunnel to break the siege (see page 505); and to international relief organizations, including the Red Cross as well as Islamic, Orthodox, Catholic, Jewish, and secular humanitarian groups.

Food was a major concern. The UN took responsibility for humanitarian aid through the siege, and about 90 percent of food was provided by UN airlifts. Sarajevans remember European Community-donated mystery meat in *ICAR* cans, which they ate happily while trying not to think of where it came from (now immortalized by a monument behind the Historical Museum).

Amazingly, people did not simply give up. Even if they lacked basic resources, they continued dressing well and keeping up appearances—if only to preserve their own sanity. Barbers, for example, had a very valuable skill that they could barter for other goods and services.

Throughout even the darkest days of the siege, Sarajevans had art galleries, cafés for socializing, and even a film festival (the famous Sarajevo Film Festival, still going strong, began in 1993). One well-known figure—Vedran Smailović, the "Cellist of Sarajevo"—played his instrument in the bombed-out ruins around town. In 1993, a "Miss Sarajevo" beauty pageant was held in a basement; at the end, all of the contestants held up a banner pleading, "Don't let them kill us." (The pageant was immortalized in U2's "Miss Sarajevo" music video.)

Sarajevans managed to keep their sense of humor even through the difficult times. When tensions were running high before the war broke out, one night a pro-Serb vandal spray-painted on a Sarajevo post office, "This is Serbia!" The next day, it was rebutted with a new message: "No, this is a post office, you idiot!" On another occasion, someone graffitied on a building: "Tito, come back!" The next day's response: "No thanks, I'm not crazy!" And on the day that Sarajevo beat Leningrad's record for the longest siege of modern times, a local radio station proudly played Queen's "We Are the Champions."

In mid-1995, thanks to NATO bombing raids and joint action by the Croatian and Bosnian armies, the siege started to weaken. On Feb. 29, 1996—the four-year anniversary of the independence referendum that had sparked the war—the government officially declared that the siege was over. It's impossible to know exact figures, but most estimates suggest that about 300,000 to 350,000 lived through the siege, including around 50,000 to 70,000 Serbs who decided to stay in their home city. During the siege, about 10,000 Sarajevans died—including nearly 1,600 children—and 56,000 to 70,000 were wounded.

Zetra Arena, which was used for Olympic skating events (this is where ice dancers Jayne Torvill and Christopher Dean thrilled the world with their "Bolero" routine) and for the closing ceremony. Today the complex houses a museum about those games. Poignantly, the stadium that once commanded the world's attention is now surrounded by a vast field of headstones—mostly of Sarajevans killed during the war. The ice arena's basement was used as a makeshift morgue, and its wooden seats were used to build coffins for the deceased.

• *Our walk is finished. From here, you can circle back to any of the sights you haven't yet seen. If you have stamina and interest left, you can continue directly on to the next walk, which covers the main sights of the Siege of Sarajevo. The starting point is just a five-minute walk away: Simply continue following Maršala Tita street, jogging left with the road and passing another park (with a conspicuously modern sculpture that was another artist's "white elephant" gift to Sarajevo). Soon after, you'll reach the major intersection with the huge, glassy Sarajevo City Center shopping mall on your left. Here Maršala Tita becomes the city's main thoroughfare (Zmaja od Bosne)—where the next walk begins.*

▲▲"SNIPER ALLEY": THE SIEGE OF SARAJEVO

This walk, which leads you through the broad boulevards and skyscraper jungle of modern Sarajevo, is designed to help you appreciate some of the key sites of the Siege of Sarajevo, and to provide an interesting way to get to the worthwhile Historical Museum (which further illustrates the way people lived during the siege) and the National Museum (which may be closed due to funding cuts). The walk begins in the shadow of the Bosnian Parliament building, which you can reach by walking five minutes from the end of the self-guided walk (above) or by riding a tram to the Marijin Dvor tram stop. This neighborhood is officially called Marijin Dvor (roughly "Maria's Castle," after a nearby palace that was built for an aristocrat's wife)—a strangely romantic name for a modern "downtown" turned war zone. These days it's better known as "Sniper Alley," the nickname given by foreign journalists who covered the besieged city.

• *Begin your visit to this part of Sarajevo with a...*

"Sniper Alley" Spin-Tour: Stand near the engraved medieval tomb at the corner of the big intersection in front of the Bosnian Parliament (the tall, glassy building). Look up to the hillside across the river. High on that hill, the patch of land with the grave markers is the city's main **Jewish cemetery;** during the siege, Karadžić's snipers found this an ideal position from which to rain bullets down on the innocent civilians below. People would cross this street only at night, by cover of darkness, or occasionally by running behind a moving UN armored vehicle that provided cover. Just over two decades ago, if you stood here long enough to read this paragraph, you'd be dead.

Spin to the right to see the blocky glass skyscraper—the **Bosnian Parliament.** While freshly rebuilt today, this was utterly destroyed during the war.

Looking farther to the right, up the big boulevard, you'll see the prominent, bright-yellow facade of the **Holiday Inn.** When it was built for the 1984 Olympics, this was the premier hotel in Sarajevo, fit for visiting dignitaries. But less than a decade later,

the first shots of the Bosnian War were fired right here. As tensions were rising throughout Bosnia-Herzegovina, tens of thousands of peace protesters filled this street on April 5, 1992. Karadžić instructed snipers positioned in the hotel to open fire on the unarmed crowd, killing six and wounding many others. Later, the hotel housed foreign journalists and dignitaries, and was therefore virtually the only safe space in the entire city center—though even this enclave suffered its share of incidental damage. Since the war, the hotel has been fully renovated.

Turning to the right, you see the Catholic **Church of St. Joseph** (built by the Czech architect Karel Pařík). The street to the left of the church, with a clear view from the sniper's nest in the Jewish cemetery, is called Tršćanska ("Trieste Street")—but locals began calling it Trćanska, "Running Street," where it was deadly to walk at a normal pace. Behind the church stands a **hospital.** While the side of the hospital facing away from the hillside sniper's nest was a safe place for injured and ill Sarajevans to recover, the side facing the hill was exposed to sniper fire...a lesson learned in the worst possible way when snipers shot through the windows to kill patients lying in their beds.

Finally, looking to the right you'll see the gigantic **Sarajevo City Center** shopping mall—super-modern and exclusive-feeling, this seems to trumpet to the world that Sarajevo's recovery is well underway. It's built (like so much in modern-day Sarajevo) by investors from the Middle East, who view Sarajevo as a comfortably Muslim enclave in the heart of Europe.

• *From here, if you want to go straight to the Historical Museum, continue up the main street past the Bosnian Parliament, then carry on two long blocks to reach the museum (on your left). But for a more interesting approach—dotted with significant siege locations—take the scenic back way along the river. With your back to the church, walk three minutes down the street to the river and the...*

"Romeo and Juliet Bridge": This bridge was originally named

"Vrbanja Bridge," but now it's officially called "Suada Dilberović and Olga Sučić Bridge" for the two young women who were the first documented victims of the Siege of Sarajevo. Dilberović was

a Dubrovnik-born Bosniak pursing her medical degree at the University of Sarajevo, and Sučić was a Croat resident of Sarajevo; both were killed by sniper bullets while standing on this bridge during the Holiday Inn peace rally massacre. But this bridge is internationally better known as "Romeo and Juliet Bridge," for two other victims of the war. Two young Sarajevans—Admira Ismić (a Bosniak) and Boško Brkić (a Serb)—were lovers who wanted to escape to a better life together. Brkić used his connections with Serb officials to obtain promise of safe passage out of the city. On May 19, 1993, the couple made it as far as this bridge before snipers opened fire; both were hit and fell to the ground. Boško died instantly; Admira crawled to her beloved, and died clutching his body in her arms. The bodies could not be retrieved and buried for fear of further sniper attacks, so they lay on the bridge for another week, locked in a heart-wrenching embrace. After four days, American war correspondent Kurt Schork issued a dispatch describing the corpses, grabbing the attention of people around the world with this example of the horrifying conditions in the Bosnian capital. The ill-fated "Romeo and Juliet of Sarajevo" have been immortalized in film, song, and news accounts. Sarajevans embrace the couple for the way they embody a united Sarajevo—with people of various ethnicities living together under siege. As Ismić's father said in Schork's dispatch, "Love took them to their deaths. That's proof this is not a war between Serbs and Muslims. It's a war between crazy people, between monsters."

Directly across this bridge is the **Grbavica** neighborhood, the closest Bosnian Serb forces got to the city center during the siege—which is why the area we just passed through was so deadly. The snipers were just a couple of blocks away. Notice the bullet holes that still pockmark the buildings facing Grbavica.

• *Turn right and stroll along the river for a couple of blocks, along the...*

Woodrow Wilson Promenade (Vilsonovo Šetalište): Though this was a deadly no-man's-land just two decades ago, today it's a pleasant, tree-lined riverside park. But here in Sarajevo, even a pretty park has a sinister edge: The trees here survived only because they were too close to enemy lines to safely cut down for fuel.

Enough siege talk. Stow your guidebook and just enjoy this romantic walk for a while. I'll meet you at the next bridge.

The **Ars Aevi Bridge** was designed by Paris' Pompidou Centre architect Renzo Piano, who has also drawn up plans for the nearby future home of Sarajevo's contemporary art museum.

At this bridge, turn right and head away from the river. You'll pass through a field that's the future site for the Ars Aevi con-

temporary art museum (www.arsaevi.ba). Just beyond that, tucked into the back wall of the Historical Museum, are the outdoor tables of the **Tito Café.** This kitschy hangout celebrates the dictator of communist Yugoslavia with preachy red flags, lots of old photos, camouflage stools, and a bust of the beloved leader, as well as an old jeep and other Yugoslav military vehicles scattered out front. (The tank you'll see out front is a WWII-era relic, which was actually put into use again during the siege.) The clientele seems split between those who really do miss Tito, and those who are here ironically...but either way, they're having fun.

(While nursing a drink here, read the "Tito" sidebar on page 734.)

In the park between the café and the river, look for the **monument** shaped like a giant tin can with an *ICAR* label. This is a (somewhat ironic) thank-you for international relief supplies sent to Sarajevo during the siege, including the canned meat that sometimes appeared in care packages from the European Community. Understandably, Sarajevans have a love-hate nostalgia for this "siege Spam."

From the big can, take the sidewalk through the park back toward the main drag. On the left, look for another ironic monument, a big **stone slab,** on the left (next to the stairs to the Historical Museum). This reads, "Under this stone there is a monument to the victims of the war and cold war."

The stairs next to this slab lead up to the gloomy concrete home of the **Historical Museum,** with a quirky but fascinating collection of everyday items used by Sarajevans to survive the siege (described later).

Exiting the Historical Museum, you're facing the side of the genteel mansion housing the **National Museum**—which has re-opened but can be sporadically closed due to lack of funds. Try going in the main door (middle of building, facing busy road) to check its status.

Across the street from the Historical Museum, you can see the sleek, low-slung **US Embassy** building, which fills a huge walled complex in the heart of downtown—keeping a cautious eye on a city that has seen more than its share of turmoil over the past generation or two. Hovering just beyond the embassy is the 580-foot-tall **Avaz Twist Tower,** which has a fine view from its 36th floor (see page 507).

• *Our walk is finished. From here, you can visit the Historical Museum; walk or ride a tram (#2, #3, or #5) back to your starting point in the Old Town; or, for one more poignant siege sight, take a taxi or tram #3 (plus a short taxi ride) out to the War Tunnel Museum (described later).*

Sights in Sarajevo

I've organized Sarajevo's main sights as you'll reach them while you follow my self-guided walks, above.

IN THE OTTOMAN OLD TOWN (BAŠČARŠIJA)
City Hall (Vijećnica)

This Karel Pařík-designed masterpiece of Neo-Moorish style was one of the main landmarks of Habsburg-era Sarajevo. Destroyed during the siege, it was meticulously rebuilt thanks partly to donations from Spain, Austria, and Hungary (the three big Habsburg countries). Reopened in 2014, today it once again houses the city hall and a library, and invites visitors to step inside and ogle its stunning interior atrium, with hand-painted details under colorful stained glass. In the basement, you'll find an exhibit on the history of the building and of Sarajevo, as well as temporary exhibits. While Sarajevo has better history museums, this is worth a visit if you're an aficionado of opulent Habsburg architecture.

Cost and Hours: 5 KM, June-Sept Tue-Sun 10:00-20:00, Oct-May until 17:00, closed Mon year-round, www.sarajevo.ba.

▲City History Museum
(in Brusa Bezistan Covered Market)

Filling a big indoor silk bazaar right on old Sarajevo's main square, this good museum features a giant model of the city in 1878, at the apex of the Ottoman period and just before the new Austrian rulers renovated and expanded Sarajevo. The rest of the collection offers a fine historical overview of the city in English, with actual artifacts, traditional costumes, and a good video tracing Sarajevo's story (with English subtitles).

Cost and Hours: 3 KM, mid-April-mid-Oct Mon-Fri 10:00-18:00—off-season until 16:00, Sat 10:00-15:00, closed

SARAJEVO

Sun, 5-KM guidebooklet, Abadžiluk 10, tel. 033/239-590, www. muzejsarajeva.ba.

Visiting the Museum: As you enter, you'll first circle clockwise around the ground floor for a quick look at prehistoric, Roman, and medieval Sarajevo. Near the end of this section (back near the entrance), notice the two big **Bogomil tombstones** (from the medieval Bosnian Christian civilization)—an older, horizontal one and a later, vertical one. The vertical tomb is a transitional piece that demonstrates how Bogomil culture began to take on Turkish customs after the arrival of the Ottomans. The tomb has been rotated upright (in keeping with the Muslim tradition) and displays a Muslim-style crescent moon. A man with a bow and arrow is a common motif on Bogomil tombstones. Here, we see the bow and arrow, but not the man (in keeping with the Muslim ban on depicting living things in art). But, in a sort of compromise, it does feature an animal. Nearby is an unusual wooden sarcophagus, which may have held the remains of an important person.

Upstairs, do another clockwise loop, beginning with the origins of the city of Sarajevo. One display case demonstrates the religious diversity of this city—from an Orthodox Easter egg, to a Torah and menorah, to a copy of the Old Testament. The traditional clothing exhibit shows how local styles were influenced by Venetian, Slavic, and Turkish trends, while the one on crafts and trade features items you may have found for sale in the bazaars. Under Ottoman rule, the city saw a flourishing of the arts (see the calligraphy) and education, but as that empire began to decline, illiteracy skyrocketed and Bosnia's neighbors sensed weakness (exemplified by the case full of weapons). Ultimately Bosnia became part of the Austro-Hungarian Empire (see the new flag of Sarajevo up above), which changed local lifestyles and fashions. Notice the paintings of Bosnian Muslims of this era, who wore Austrian-style suits, but with fezzes and turbans. The remaining exhibits show architecture from the Habsburg period, when the very Turkish-style Old Town was surrounded by a Viennese urban zone.

▲Old Serbian Orthodox Church

While fully Orthodox inside and out, this 16th-century church has features that resemble a synagogue or a mosque— hinting at the mingling of faiths that has characterized Sarajevo for most of its history. Stepping inside, notice that the church (which was built on the site of an even earlier one) is set about three feet below street level. Because the Ottomans wouldn't allow churches to be taller than mosques, the builders went down instead of up. Also notice how—with its split-level design and upstairs gallery—it feels like a synagogue with an iconostasis. Upstairs in the gallery (another feature more commonly seen in synagogues and mosques than in churches), you may see worshippers making a fuss over a small coffin, which contains the body of a child; this is believed to have healing power, especially for infertile women. Across the small courtyard is a museum with old icons, incense burners, vestments, and manuscripts in Cyrillic. Look for the document in squiggly Arabic script—a written confirmation from the Ottoman sultan permitting worshippers to practice the Orthodox Christian faith here. The wine shop keeps up the Bosnian tradition of Orthodox monks doubling as vintners.

Cost and Hours: 2 KM, includes church and museum, Mon-Sat 8:00-18:00, Sun 8:00-16:00, Mula Mustafe Bašeskije 59.

▲▲Gazi Husrev-Bey Mosque (Gazi Husrev-Begov Džamija)

Called "Begova Mosque" for short, this is Sarajevo's most important and most historic mosque. For more on Bosnia's Muslim faith, see page 437.

Cost and Hours: Outer courtyard-free; mosque-3 KM (or 6-KM combo-ticket with Kuršumilja Madrasa/Gazi Husrev-Bey Biblioteka)—buy ticket at little house to the right as you enter courtyard; opening times vary depending on prayer schedule and are posted at ticket office—generally May-Sept daily 9:00-12:00 & 14:00-15:30 & 16:45-18:45, Oct-April daily 9:00-11:00, shorter hours during Ramadan; Sarači, tel. 033/573-151, www.tourism-gazi.ba.

Visiting the Mosque: Start in the outer courtyard. The **fountain** in the middle (with water piped in from the mountains three miles away) is for washing before prayer. Around the left side, look for the two freestanding **mausoleums** (you can't enter them, but you can peek through the windows around the side). The larger one holds the remains of the mosque's founder and namesake, Gazi Husrev-Bey (1480-1541; *bey* is an Ottoman aristocratic title, like "Lord" or "Sir")—a governor of Bosnia who donated vast sums to improving Sarajevo. The smaller mausoleum holds his assistant and secretary, a highly educated Croat named Tardić who had been captured in a battle. He accepted Gazi Husrev-Bey's offer of a job, a precondition of which was that he convert to Islam, and went on to become the governor's most trusted advisor. The **cemetery** behind the mausoleums has graves both old and new; one of the most recent holds the remains of the imam from the destroyed mosque in Banja Luka, a Serb stronghold in northern Bosnia.

Now, let's go inside. Buy a ticket at the office, noticing the modern facility nearby for ablution (washing before prayer). Then step into the mosque's **interior** (women must cover their heads, but visitors can keep their shoes on). You'll see many of the same elements

found in other Bosnian mosques (see description on page 436). Appreciate the remarkably spacious-feeling architecture. Many of the carpets are gifts from Muslim nations and date from the Tito era. As an anchor of the nonaligned world, which included many Muslim countries (in North Africa and the Middle East),

Tito had particularly good relations with Islamic leaders. The electric lighting—the world's first in a mosque—was installed by the Habsburg rulers in 1898 (the same year they lit up Vienna's Schönbrunn Palace), suggesting how deeply the Habsburgs respected the local Islamic faith. The besieging Bosnian Serb forces in the 1990s didn't share this respect, and used the mosque's minaret for target practice. Looking through the windows, you can see the walls are six feet thick—which helped save it from utter destruction. The mosque was badly damaged, and renovated in 1996 using funds largely from Saudi Arabia; the interior—while covered in fine calligraphy—is still less ornately decorated than it once was.

Nearby: The **clock tower** across the narrow street is also part of the mosque complex; notice that its "noon" lines up with sunset—critical in establishing the five times each day that Muslims pray. Under the clock tower you'll find a free public WC and a little hole-in-the-wall bakery that's open late.

▲▲Sarajevo 1878-1918 Museum and Archduke Franz Ferdinand Assassination Site

Worth ▲▲▲ and ample goose bumps to historians with vivid imaginations, and interesting to anyone, this is the nondescript street corner where the heir to the vast but declining Austro-Hungarian

Empire met a bloody fate at the hands of a Bosnian Serb separatist, plunging Europe into the War to End All Wars (until the next war). The shots were fired as Franz Ferdinand and his wife Sophie sat, JFK-and-Jackie style, in an open-top car during a visit to the Bosnian capital (for the full story, see the sidebar). The street corner where it happened, across from the Latin Bridge (Latinska Ćuprija), is now home to a plaque and a humble one-room museum, which shows a good

video montage in its window that helps illustrate the story. The **Sarajevo 1878-1918 Museum** traces the four decades when this city was part of the Vienna-ruled Austro-Hungarian Empire, with a special emphasis on the assassination. Just inside the entrance, look for the symbolic footprints of the assassin, Gavrilo Princip. Beyond that, the museum holds one well-presented room featuring the trappings of the age, a map showing the sites relating to the assassination, life-size mannequins of Franz Ferdinand and Sophie, and clips from a 1970s-vintage Yugoslav film about the assassination, all with English labels.

Cost and Hours: 4 KM, Mon-Fri 10:00-18:00, Sat 10:00-15:00, closed Sun, Zelenih Beretki 1, tel. 033/533-288, www.muzejsarajeva.ba.

Near the Old Town (Baščaršija)
Tomb of the Seven Brothers

This nondescript mosque, at the top of the parking lot across the Latin Bridge from the Old Town, is a favorite spot for Sarajevo superstition. Along the right, outer wall of the mosque are a door

and seven windows marking tombs of (according to legend) innocent people who were unjustly sentenced to death; a strange light was reported to be emanating from their graves at night. It's believed that if you put a coin of the same value in each of these eight slots, you can make a wish or a request. Then you are supposed to walk around the top of the mosque, turn left, and walk down the little lane. Listen carefully—the first words you hear as you walk along this street will help you divine the answer you seek. Interestingly—but not surprisingly for this ecumenical town—even non-Muslim Sarajevans come here when they are searching for enlightenment.

Cemeteries and Viewpoint just Above the Baščaršija

If you walk about 10 minutes up Kovači street from the Sebilj fountain, you'll come to a fine viewpoint over the Old Town, as well as some large, thought-provoking cemeteries from the siege years. Looking even higher in the hills, you'll see more sprawling cemeteries blanketing the hillsides. People were buried in these

The Shot Heard 'Round the World

On June 28, 1914, Archduke Franz Ferdinand—heir to the throne of the massive Habsburg Empire—and his wife, Sophie, visited Sarajevo. While they were in town, a local pan-Slavic movement to liberate Bosnia from the Austro-Hungarian Empire (affiliated with a movement called the Black Hand) plotted an assassination. Early in the day, the attempt failed when a bomb intended for the archduke's car instead wounded other members of his party. Believing the plot to be foiled, the archduke continued on his way, visiting the City Hall a few blocks up the river.

A 19-year-old Bosnian Serb named Gavrilo Princip, who was in on the plot, was waiting for Ferdinand's car along the river by the Latin Bridge (across the street from today's museum, by the tram stop). But when that area became too crowded, he crossed to the corner now marked by a plaque, and stepped into a nearby delicatessen. Meanwhile, after leaving the City Hall, Franz Ferdinand decided at the last moment to change his schedule and visit the people who had been wounded by the bomb. Confused by the last-minute change, the driver took a wrong turn up this street and paused in a moment of indecision, causing the car to stall...directly in front of Princip. The assassin raised his gun and fired, killing both Franz Ferdinand and Sophie.

Princip and the other plotters were arrested. The Habsburgs wanted to send investigators into Serbia to root out the co-conspirators; Serbia's refusal to grant them access kicked off a chain reaction that brought all of Europe to war. While historians stress that Ferdinand's assassination was merely the event that ignited the tinderbox of World War I—not the "cause" of the war—its significance is undeniable.

The epilogue: Because Princip was too young to be executed, he was given a 20-year sentence at Theresienstadt prison outside of Prague (which the Nazis later converted into Terezín concentration camp). The terrible conditions at the camp led to Princip's early death at age 24. Much of the world considered him a monster, but by the end of World War I, the nascent nation of Yugoslavia—which emerged from the ashes of that war exactly as Princip and his accomplices had dreamed—celebrated him as a hero. They even gave his name to the bridge near the place where he happened to be standing when he stumbled into his opportunity to change history.

places either at night or in heavy fog, when gravediggers could be safe from snipers.

At the top of Kovači street, the **Kovači Martyrs' Memorial Cemetery** is worth a pensive wander. The billboard near the entrance labels each grave. High on the hill is the ceremonial metallic-domed grave of wartime president Alija Izetbegović, surrounded by a crescent-shaped fountain that feeds a stream that trickles downhill between the other headstones. (Just uphill, inside an old tower from the city wall, is a small museum dedicated to Izetbegović.)

Just above this area is a neighborhood called **Vratnik** (roughly "Gateway"), the oldest part of town.

Svrzo's House (Svrzina Kuća)

If you'd like to tour a traditional home from the Ottoman period, hike five minutes uphill from the Old Town to see this well-preserved, sprawling estate, built in the 17th century by a wealthy local Bosniak family. It's similar to the "Turkish houses" you'll see in Mostar—except that it's made of wood, as is typical of Bosnia, while Herzegovinian homes (like those in Mostar) are made of stone. First, you'll head upstairs to see the men's sitting room *(halvat)*, the women's room (where the ladies of the house did their embroidery), and the dining room (where guests sat on the floor around the low table, or up on the long divans all around the room). The *kamarija* (balcony) overlooks the inner courtyard, with its garden and well. Then head downstairs to see the big kitchen and large *halvat*—for big family gatherings.

Cost and Hours: 3 KM, Mon-Fri 10:00-18:00—off-season until 16:00, Sat 10:00-15:00, closed Sun, 5-KM guidebook, Glođina 8, tel. 033/535-264, www.muzejsarajeva.ba.

IN THE HABSBURG QUARTER

Immediately west of the Ottoman quarter is the more modern part of town, built at the end of the 19th century after Bosnia became part of the Austro-Hungarian Empire. While several of the sights scattered through this area are much older, most of the buildings here are evocative of those in the capital at the time, Vienna.

▲▲Old Synagogue (Stari Hram) and Bosnian Jewish Museum (Muzej Jevreja BiH)

Combining a classic old 16th-century synagogue with an excellent and insightful museum chronicling the Jewish faith in this country, this building was modeled after a synagogue in Toledo, Spain. Soon after the Jews were expelled from that kingdom in the late 15th century, Sephardic Jews made their way to Bosnia, which they found to be an unusually tolerant place (typical of its entire history). Unlike many Central and Eastern European cities, Sarajevo did not relegate its Jews to a ghetto; they lived amid their non-Jewish neighbors. Local Sephardi used "Ladino," a unique language mixing Spanish and Hebrew (even today, rabbis greet each other not with *Shalom,* but with *Buenos días*).

Cost and Hours: 3 KM, mid-April-mid-Oct Mon-Fri 10:00-18:00—off-season until 16:00, Sun 10:00-13:00, closed

Sat, 5-KM guidebook, Josipa Štadlera 32, tel. 033/475-740, www. muzejsarajeva.ba.

Visiting the Synagogue and Museum: Buy your ticket and step into the central hall, with the *bima* (altar-like raised area) in the center and the wooden doors that hold the Torah. Women, who in accordance with Jewish tradition worship separately from men, stand up in the arcades ringing the hall. Climb up the stairs to see the exhibits filling those arcades. On the first floor up, you'll see a replica of the important Sarajevo Haggadah book (see sidebar); a tombstone from a Jewish cemetery on the hill across the river, which is the second biggest in Europe (after Prague's) and was tragically used as a sniper's nest during the siege; and a model of the original appear-
ance of this synagogue. The next floor shows more Jewish religious items and illustrates how local Jews adopted local culture (for example, you'll see Jews wearing Muslim-style fezzes). The replica of an Ottoman-era "pharmacy" with herbal cures is a reminder that such businesses were typically run by Jewish Sarajevans.

The top floor focuses on the dark 20th century, including the Holocaust. The exhibit profiles Bosnians who were designated as "Righteous Among the Nations"—an honorific for non-Jews who risk their own lives to save their Jewish neighbors. Among these is Derviš Korkut, the Muslim museum curator who saved the Sarajevo Haggadah from Nazi investigators. Some Jewish women were smuggled out of Nazi-occupied areas by disguising themselves in Muslim veils. You'll also see Nazi-mandated armbands identifying Jews, photos of resistance fighters, and an exhibit on the reprehensible Jasenovac concentration camp on today's Bosnian-Croatian border—where Jews, Serbs, Roma (Gypsies), antifascist Muslims and Croats, communists, and other enemies of the Ustaše-controlled state were savagely executed. Jasenovac lacked the "high-tech" gas chambers of other Nazi camps, so they resorted to more medieval methods, murdering their victims by knife, sword, or even a hammer to the skull. And yet, even through that dark history, Sarajevo has remained a place where cultures coexist side-by-side: Position yourself so that you can look through the Star of David window to see a minaret.

Catholic Cathedral

Dating from 1884-1889, this Historicist structure mingles different "Neo-" architectural styles (typical of Viennese buildings of that age): a Neo-Gothic exterior and a Neo-Byzantine/Neo-

SARAJEVO

The Sarajevo Haggadah

An ancient Jewish text telling the story of the Exodus—used as a sort of "order of service" for the Passover Seder—the Haggadah is considered the third most important book of the Jewish faith (after the Torah and Talmud). The Sarajevo Haggadah is filled with colorful illustrations as well as wine stains—indicating that it has been used at many Passover dinner tables. While the book's exact origins are unclear, it likely dates from around 1350 and was brought here from Spain by Sephardic transplants in the 16th century.

Appropriately for a book about the Exodus, it has had quite an unlikely journey through a landscape of hardship. Bosnians—who, regardless of their ethnicity, consider the Sarajevo Haggadah a part of their national cultural heritage—proudly explain that the book has been protected time after time by people of a wide variety of faiths (not just Jews). During the WWII occupation, when an SS officer came here to claim the Haggadah, the Muslim curator of the museum lied about its whereabouts, and carried it on horseback into the mountains to hide it away under the doorstop of a village mosque. Soon after the siege began in 1992, the room in the National Museum that held the Haggadah was almost entirely destroyed by mortar shells—but the book itself survived, secured in a steel box. The building was exposed to sniper fire, so under cover of darkness, Bosnian Army troops snuck to the museum, rescued the book, and stored it in the vault of the Bosnian Central Bank.

Today, the National Museum still owns the book. But, in yet another chapter of its outlandish history, funding cuts have frequently closed the museum to the public in recent years. If you'd like to see the Haggadah (through a glass door), confirm with the TI that the National Museum is open.

Baroque interior. Notice the big gap across the street, offering a fine view of the adjacent hillside. During the siege, the church's front door was dangerously exposed—not only to snipers, but to antiaircraft machine guns, which were used to periodically spray bullets randomly over the town. Inside, the red-and-white-striped ribs—a Neo-Moorish style element—are rare in a Catholic church, but seem to fit here in ecumenical Sarajevo. Inside and on the left, look for the grave of the church's Croatian founder, Joseph Stadler, and a plaque commemorating St. John Paul II's 1997 visit here.

Cost and Hours: Free, daily 9:00-16:00, 2-KM guidebooklet, no shorts, Trg Fra Grge Martića 2.

▲▲Srebrenica Exhibition (Memorijalna Galerija 11/07/95)

Worth ▲▲▲ for anyone who wants to better understand the atrocities in Bosnia's recent history, this important, emotionally exhausting exhibition uses photographs and video clips to tell the story of the remote Bosnian village that experienced the worst massacre on European soil since World War II. You'll be shown around by a guide (departing about hourly—they'll tell you when the next tour begins, and you can pass any waiting time watching the powerful videos).

Cost and Hours: 12 KM, daily June-Sept 9:00-22:00, May 10:00-20:00, Oct-April 10:00-18:00, Trg Fra Grge Matića 2/III, tel. 033/953-170, www.galerija110795.ba.

Visiting the Exhibition: Because of the horrifying massacre that took place there (described in the sidebar on page 502), the name "Srebrenica" has become synonymous with some of the worst crimes against humanity in recent memory. The date you'll see everywhere—11/07/95—commemorates July 11, 1995, when Bosnian Serb forces invaded Srebrenica, beginning their genocidal attack. This exhibit, consisting mostly of haunting photographs by Tarik Samarah, documents the process of piecing together exactly what happened there. Photos show the faces of just 640 of the more than 8,000 victims; conditions in the refugee camps where survivors lived after the massacre; the process of exhuming, documenting, and investigating the many mass graves that have been discovered (mass funerals are held on July 11 each year to honor victims who were identified during that year); and some graphic and unsettling graffiti by UN troops from the Netherlands, which suggests that they felt more contempt than sympathy for the people they were assigned to protect.

Perhaps the most powerful parts of the exhibit are the wrenching movies that are shown at the far end of the exhibition hall (two screens, with movies alternating on a loop). Most powerful is *Srebrenica Massacre*, a 27-minute video that outlines (with English subtitles) the harrowing chain of events that led to the fall of Srebrenica and the ruthless murders of so many of its residents. Other films include *Miss Sarajevo* (30 minutes, about life in Sarajevo during the siege); a more academic film called *Mapping Genocide and Post-Genocide Society*; and slideshow videos of powerful Srebrenica photography.

Maps on the wall identify the locations of mass graves that have been found so far. Out in the hallway, a 50-foot-long wall lists the name and date of birth of each of the 8,372 victims who have been identified so far; the alphabetical list makes it clear that en-

SARAJEVO

tire extended families were wiped out. Nearby, touchscreens with headphones let you view individual testimonials from survivors and victims' relatives (subtitled in English). For even more information, sit at one of the terminals in the first room, where you can click through more than four hours of video documentation. The quote on the wall reminds visitors of a lesson that, it seems, needs to be repeated again and again: "All that is necessary for the triumph of evil is that good men do nothing."

NEAR "SNIPER ALLEY"

For the most interesting approach to this area from the Old Town (Baščaršija), see my self-guided walk, earlier.

▲Historical Museum of Bosnia-Herzegovina (Historijski Muzej BiH)

Filling a still-bombed-out-feeling, Tito-era building next to the National Museum, this museum features a small and ramshackle but fascinating exhibit explaining the Siege of Sarajevo—if you take the time to examine and appreciate the items and photos. While there are some English labels, they're sparse, and it helps to have a Sarajevan explain the items firsthand; this is a good place to come with a local guide.

Cost and Hours: 5 KM, Mon-Fri 9:00-19:00, Sat-Sun 9:00-14:00, 5-KM book, Zmaja od Bosne 5, tel. 033/226-098, www.muzej.ba.

Visiting the Museum: Formerly the "Museum of the Revolution," the building's stairwell still features Socialist Realist mosaics from the communist period, and a statue of Tito stands in the inner courtyard. Head upstairs to see the exhibit. Note that the collection is in flux, and they're hoping to secure funding that would help them install a more modern exhibit.

In the middle of the main hall, you'll likely find an exhibit about the war crimes tribunal in The Hague, with good English explanations and an engaging film that illuminates the process. All around is the **"Sarajevo Surrounded"** exhibit, with lots of artifacts from siege-time Sarajevo. Follow the chronological exhibit, which tells the story through photographs, news clippings, shells and weapons used in combat, and many actual items that show how Sarajevans improvised ways to carry on. Viewing these items, you'll be inspired by the desperate ingenuity of the besieged Sarajevans.

First you'll view a dry overview of the events leading up to the siege. Then, the display of **cigarettes** explains how smokes were used as a sort of currency; even through the siege, the local cigarette factory kept working, though the product sometimes had to be packaged in makeshift wrappers.

The elaborate **satellite telephone** was, for a time, the only way that Bosnian President Alija Izetbegović could communicate with the outside world. In the glass case nearby, you'll see the various ways that people created light, including a candle made of pork fat with a wick made from carpet fibers. Along the wall behind the satellite phone, notice the Monopoly-like money that was the city's ersatz legal tender during the siege. Nearby, look for photos of the "Sarafix" technique—invented here, out of necessity—which allowed doctors to set a broken bone with a metal frame with pins instead of a traditional cast.

Along the wall behind the rickety market stall, a case displays the paltry **foodstuffs** that Sarajevans considered themselves

lucky to find during wartime. Imagine picking over these meager offerings—rusty canned goods, military rations, plastic bags stuffed with grains—and trying to figure out how to use them to feed your family. Sarajevans learned how to stretch a "one-day ration" for up to two weeks. (Many nations sent old military rations—Sarajevans might find themselves eating leftover US rations from the Vietnam War.) Lawns were converted into makeshift produce gardens. Everyone came up with "siege recipes," replacing unavailable ingredients with whatever they could. For example, during a time when rice was relatively plentiful, they'd mix it with flour to make bread, or use it as filling for *bureks* (savory pastries). Instead of spinach filling for a *burek*, they might use greens from buttercup flowers. And when they had a taste for coffee, they'd burn rice, grind it, and mix it with hot water; they swear the taste was similar...even if it was missing the caffeine kick.

In the corner, the mockup of a typical siege-time **apartment** shows how people were forced to make do. The windows and roof

are covered with a plastic tarp donated by the international community. The TV, telephone, refrigerator, and other appliances were useless without electricity. (The power might come on sporadically, but never for very long.) Look around at the so-called "Sarajevo inventions," created by desperate and clever people to keep going. Notice the makeshift stove (a collection of several other, smaller stoves is nearby). During the frigid Sarajevo winters, trees were cut down to fuel fires. When the trees were gone, firewood was in short supply (a bundle might cost the equivalent of $50), so besieged residents

Srebrenica

Despite their hardships during the siege, many Sarajevans consider themselves fortunate not to have met the same fate as many of the Bosniaks living in eastern Bosnia during the war. These areas, bordering Serbia proper and intertwined with Serb-dominated parts of Bosnia, were aggressively targeted by the vicious military and paramilitary forces of Bosnian Serb President Radoran Karadžić. While many towns along the Foča River Valley were brutally besieged and overrun, the most notorious site of ethnic cleansing was in the town of Srebrenica.

Before the war, Srebrenica (SREB-reh-neet-seh, meaning "silver mine") was a mining center and spa town of about 36,000 people, which sat near the geographical center of Yugoslavia. While three-quarters of the population was Bosniak, it also had a large Serb community. There was nothing unique about Srebrenica that made it prime to become the poster child for ethnic cleansing—it simply got in the way of Karadžić's battle plans.

In 1993, as reports surfaced of Karadžić's forces using ethnic cleansing in multiple Bosniak villages in eastern Bosnia, the United Nations designated "safe areas" where civilian refugees could take shelter. Srebrenica was the first one. The UN dispatched a "protection force" (UNPROFOR) to these areas. But those UNPROFOR troops—including 400 Dutch soldiers sent to watch over Srebrenica—soon feared for their own lives as much as for those they were intended to guard. The UN demanded that their troops remain completely "neutral," even when directly attacked—dooming them to an ultimately pointless mission.

Conditions in the "safe areas" swiftly deteriorated, and by 1995, Srebrenica had become a highly vulnerable refugee-crammed island in a tight bottleneck valley, entirely surrounded by Bosnian Serb forces. In July, the noose began to close around Srebrenica, as General Ratko Mladić invaded. In the afternoon of July 11, 1995, Mladić marched triumphantly through the town, claiming Srebrenica for the Serb people. Most of the estimated 50,000 to 60,000 people living in the town fled.

Approximately 25,000 refugees—mostly women, children, ill or injured people, and the elderly—showed up in desperation at the UN peacekeeping base at the nearby village of Potočari. The terrified Dutch troops there, unable to provide for either the safety or the basic nutritional needs of so many, took in only about 5,000 of the refugees (predominantly mothers with babies) and turned the rest away—leaving the rest to fend for themselves.

Both at Potočari and in Srebrenica, Bosnian Serb forces culled out any men between the ages of 12 and 77. In that moment, families were ripped apart forever, as husbands, fathers, and sons were taken away to be summarily executed. Many survivors still don't know exactly what happened to their relatives; they simply never came back. In some cases, troops walked through the throngs of refugees, murdering Bosniak men right out in the open, then tossing their bodies into a pile. Bosniak women were forcibly raped in front of dozens of witnesses. Crying children who couldn't be silenced were slaughtered. Two days later, the Dutch forces evicted the rest of the refugees from inside their camp, including more than 200 men, dooming them to certain death. (The Dutch role in Srebrenica remains a matter of deep guilt in the Netherlands.)

Late in the evening of July 11, approximately 12,000 Bosniak men—about half of them military, and half civilian—headed into the hills surrounding town, with the intention of hiking through the mountains to the free city of Tuzla, 35 miles away. A human chain eight miles long trudged slowly across the difficult terrain. Mladić shelled the hillsides, killing many. Others died of malnutrition or exhaustion from hiking through sweltering summer heat. Some committed suicide. The next day, the column was split in half, and one large group was surrounded by Bosnian Serb forces, bombarded with artillery (and, some allege, chemical weapons), and told to surrender. Thousands did...and were executed. After five days, survivors finally stumbled into safety in the town of Tuzla. Others wandered in the mountains for months.

While captured Bosniak men were sometimes killed on the spot, more typically they were taken to holding areas (typically schools, warehouses, or soccer fields) until they could be moved to remote areas for a systematic, mass execution—often by lining them up, blindfolding them, shooting them or slitting their throats, and then bulldozing them into mass graves.

All told, at least 8,000 people, mostly men, were murdered by the forces of Karadžić and Mladić over the course of just a few days. Mass graves are continually being discovered. The remains of people who once called Srebrenica home are dutifully pulled out of the ground, identified through DNA testing, and given a proper burial in a collective funeral each year on July 11.

There's no silver lining, no happy ending to the tale of Srebrenica. The best that victims' families can hope for is that their loved ones' remains will someday be identified so they can bury them properly. The World War II concentration camp memorials, museums, and documentation centers around Europe all share the same message: Never again. Srebrenica tells us that, despite the best efforts of civilized people, that message still falls on deaf ears. Appallingly, many people in the former Yugoslavia still try to deny or justify the events at Srebrenica. Visiting the Srebrenica Exhibition in Sarajevo helps deflect that bogus propaganda with facts. And various companies in Sarajevo (including Sarajevo Insider) run educational tours to Srebrenica.

burned their furniture, shoes, old toys—anything flammable. And they bundled up in as many clothes as possible. After 1994, natural gas was available in some areas; notice the recycled IV tube (still bloody inside) used to power the gas lamp.

In other parts of the exhibition hall, you'll generally find temporary exhibits.

National Museum (Zemaljski Muzej)

This humble museum struggles to do justice to the illustrious history of this fascinating nation. As it's often closed due to funding cuts, check first (on their website or at the TI) to ensure it's open before making the trip. While the dusty collections of archaeology, natural science, and ethnology are less than thrilling, the main reason to visit is to peek at one of the world's most precious books, the Sarajevo Haggadah (see sidebar on page 498).

Cost and Hours: 6 KM, likely open Tue-Fri 10:00-19:00, Sat-Sun 10:00-14:00, closed Mon, Zmaja od Bosne 7, tel. 033/262-710, www.zemaljskimuzej.ba.

Visiting the Museum: The large museum—filling four buildings surrounding a central garden—can be seen quickly. From the entrance, turn right into the **Archaeology** section. On the ground floor, look for third-century mosaics from Stolac. Then head upstairs, go through the left door, and look left (through the glass door with blue light) to see the **Sarajevo Haggadah** in a display case. The rest of the upstairs has items from the Dark Ages and Middle Ages.

Head out into the central botanical garden and turn left to find the **Ethnology** section, which is like an open-air Bosnian folk museum moved inside—with six authentic, mostly wooden interiors from buildings around the country. The rooms are arranged to emphasize how the various cultures that lived here influenced each other. You'll learn about traditional Bosnian lifestyles: how people would sit on the floor around a table to eat, sharing one very long napkin, and how backyards were often connected so that Muslim women could pass between houses without covering up. On the steps out front are *stećak*s, large engraved tombstones from the Bogomil times of the 12th to the 14th centuries (the best collection of these is on the outskirts of Stolac, described on page 459).

The **Natural History** section (in the building directly across the garden from the main building) displays vast collections of butterflies and bugs, plant life, birds, and rocks.

OUTER SARAJEVO
▲▲Sarajevo War Tunnel Museum
(Sarajevski Ratni Tunel)

In the countryside on the southwestern outskirts of Sarajevo, near the airport, is a small but fascinating museum celebrating the ingenuity and determination of the besieged Sarajevans to continue

supplying their city. Here you can walk through a small stretch of the actual half-mile supply tunnel they dug to stay alive during the siege. The still battle-scarred house that marks its entrance holds a small museum, displaying actual items used in the tunnel.

Cost and Hours: 10 KM, daily April-Oct 9:00-17:00, Nov-March 9:00-16:00, Tuneli 1, mobile 061-213-760, tel. 033/778-670, info line tel. 033/778-672, www.tunelspasa.ba, info@tunelspasa. ba. Your ticket includes a free tour (usually lasting about 30 minutes), but only if you call a few days ahead to arrange a time.

Getting There: The tunnel is a long detour from anyplace else in town. Therefore, the most convenient option is to take a guided tour that includes transportation from downtown and a clear explanation of what happened here. Various companies offer these tours, including Insider Tours (see "Tours in Sarajevo," earlier). By taxi, the fair metered rate from downtown is 15-20 KM one-way—just tell them "*tunel*." Alternatively, you can take tram #3 or bus #32 from the Old Town to the end of the line (Ilidža stop, about 40 minutes one-way), then walk 2.5 miles or pay 5-10 KM one-way for a taxi from there. If you're flying into or out of the city, this combines well with your trip to the airport.

Background: With the city almost entirely surrounded by the Bosnian Serb Army, the Sarajevans' lone connection to the outside world was a mountain pass. But between them and that pass was the city's airport—which couldn't be crossed by either side because it was controlled by the impartial UN. So, rather than go through the airport, they went beneath it—digging a half-mile-long tunnel under the runway. Coal-mine engineers spent four months and four days in 1993 digging a passageway that was about five feet tall and three feet wide. Once completed, Sarajevans could enter the basement of an apartment building, hunch over and hike through

SARAJEVO

thickly humid air for 20 minutes, and emerge at a house on the other end. (After a heavy rain, the tunnel would fill with water, making the hike even more unpleasant.) From the house, they could hike over the mountains to get supplies. While money was scarce, cigarettes produced at Sarajevo's factory could be traded for what was needed, which was carried back over the mountains and through the tunnel. Eventually the tunnel was wired to also supply electricity and natural gas into the city, and was equipped with rails to more efficiently transport goods on wheeled carts. The tunnel was open to any Sarajevan—and people used it to shuttle back and forth, day and night—but it was carefully monitored for smugglers who might use it to profit from the tragedy inside the city. While the besieging enemy knew about the tunnel, its nonlinear course underground made it impossible for them to know exactly where it was—and even if they had known, to destroy it they'd have had to go through the UN-controlled airport. The best they could do was to relentlessly bombard the tunnel's entrances.

Visiting the Museum and Tunnel: After buying your ticket, you'll walk through the small three-room museum, then see the tunnel itself, and have the chance to watch a movie about this site's history.

The museum's first room displays military equipment, including shell casings (this area was bombarded with more than 300 grenades daily, with 3,777 being launched here in one day alone), and photos and orders relating to the tunnel's construction.

The second room displays the chair on wheels used to push the ailing President Izetbegović through the tunnel—hardly presidential transport, but the only way he could safely get in and out of the city for diplomatic meetings.

The third room displays various items representing the challenge of simply staying alive in Sarajevo while it was under siege. Notice the small display of paltry foodstuffs. The canisters—including a tin box with a spigot—demonstrate the struggle to find drinking water. In the frame you'll see the contents of an aid package that was expected to last one person for 10 to 15 days. Lighting was often as simple as oil and water in a glass jar with a wick. The broken glass window over the stove illustrates the absurdity of trying to keep warm through a frigid winter when basic insulation was an impossibility. Between the doors, notice the two uniforms that show how the initially improvised Bosnian defense forces evolved as the war went on: At first, they wore jeans and tennis shoes, while later they had real uniforms and boots. Also look for the photos of the many celebrities who have visited this place.

Along the back wall, you can see the various types of carts used to transport food, weapons, and sick people through the tunnel. It was used both by the military (the cart with artillery boxes), and by civilians (the dolly with backpacks and boxes). The makeshift canvas boots—roughly stitched together using material donated by the international community—were pulled on over regular shoes to trudge through the water that collected on the tunnel floor. Notice the cables and pipes along the back wall—a reminder that the tunnel was used not only for people and supplies, but also for electricity and gas.

Then follow the marked route to the tunnel itself (passing an artillery shell still embedded in the cement floor), where you can climb down the tight stairs and squeeze through an actual 80-foot-long stretch. Imagine yourself walking, crouched over, 30 times this far from one end to the other. If you'd like, you can hike through the tunnel wearing a backpack loaded with 65 pounds—roughly the amount that women typically carried through the tunnel (men would carry more than double that much).

Near the tunnel entrance (and in the open-air sheds out back), you can watch a good 20-minute film that illustrates the construction and use of the tunnel.

Out back are several places to sit and look at a map of the besieged city—superimposed, not without irony, over a map from the 1984 Olympic Games. The actual airport sits on the horizon. (Locals say that when they saw a UN plane taking off—likely carrying international officials to safety—they knew trouble was brewing.) In 1993, for the first time, Bosnia-Herzegovina selected a band to represent the newly independent country at the Eurovision **Avaz Twist Tower** Contest (a Europe-wide TV extravaganza somewhat like the finale to *American Idol*). The band, Fazla, was trapped in Sarajevo by the siege. Determined to make it to the show in Ireland, they ran across the UN-controlled airport runway with their instruments, which they then carried over the mountains to freedom. By the time the band returned, the siege tunnel under the airport was finished, and they were able to easily sneak back into the city. Even many people who managed to leave the city chose to return and remain under siege with their families and neighbors, rather than abandon their unique city and way of life.

▲▲City Views

This vertical city's gorgeous setting is best seen from high up. Unfortunately, most viewpoints are not easily reachable by public transportation. One option is to walk from the Old Town up Kovači street—lined with characteristic bars and a mix of local and touristy artisans—for a decent (if not sky-high) view over town (see page 494).

Or you can take a taxi up to the popular

SARAJEVO

viewpoint called **White Bastion** (Bijela Tabija), at an old fortress (a taxi from the Old Town should cost about 10 KM round-trip). Bus tours around Sarajevo include at least one panoramic viewpoint that offers grand vistas over one of Europe's most spectacularly set cities.

Closer to the modern "downtown," the **Avaz Twist Tower** (next to the train station) has a sky-high café with sweeping views over the city—just head inside and ride the elevator to floor 35 (3-KM coffee and soft drinks, 4-5-KM beers, 5-10-KM cocktails, daily 8:00-22:30). You can walk up one more flight of stairs to an outdoor view terrace (1-KM turnstile).

Two recommended restaurants—**Kibe Mahala** and **Park Prinčeva**—also offer great views over the Old Town area (see "Eating in Sarajevo," later).

Sleeping in Sarajevo

The city enjoys a wide variety of good accommodations, ranging from budget hostels to cozy and warmly run little pensions to plush hotels. All of my listings are in or very near the Old Town (Baščaršija) and the start of my self-guided walk. Places that are actually in the Baščaršija come with some nighttime noise.

$$$ Hotel Central is a plush splurge right in the heart of the Old Town. The public areas and 15 rooms are done in a very trendy, modern style. Given the central location, request a quiet room (Sb-€102, Db-€123, junior suite-€153, look online for cheaper deals, air-con, pool/sauna, Ćumurija 8, tel. 033/561-800, www.hotelcentral.ba, info@hotelcentral.ba).

$$ Ada Hotel is a soothing oasis with a charming facade and breakfast room. Its wooden staircase leads to· eight spartan but comfortable rooms. Warm Sofija and her crew pride themselves on offering exceptional hospitality (and here in friendly Bosnia, that's really saying something). As it's mostly used to house guests of various embassies, it tends to book up quickly—reserve ahead. It's a five-minute uphill walk above the Old Town, near a large wartime cemetery (Sb-€51, Db-€77, Tb-€87, apartment-€102, 10 percent cheaper if you pay cash, air-con, free parking, Abdesthana 8, tel. 033/475-870, www.adahotel.ba, adahotel@adahotel.ba).

$$ Hotel Old Town, tidy and businesslike yet still affordable, has 15 new-feeling rooms right in the heart of the Old Town (Sb-€60, Db-€89, Tb-€117; prices soft in slow times—more like Db-€72; air-con, free parking, Mali Čurćiluk 11A, tel. 033/574-200, www.hoteloldtown.ba, info@hoteloldtown.ba).

$$ Hotel Latinski Most ("Latin Bridge"), in an 1880s villa overlooking the embankment where Archduke Franz Ferdinand was assassinated in 1914, retains a Habsburg theme in its 10 classy

---

Sleep Code

Abbreviations **($1=about 1.80 KM, €1=about $1.10, country code: 387)**
S=Single, **D**=Double/Twin, **T**=Triple, **Q**=Quad, **b**=bathroom
Price Rankings
$$$ Higher Priced—Most rooms €100 or more
$$ Moderately Priced—Most rooms €70-100
$ Lower Priced—Most rooms €70 or less
Unless otherwise noted, credit cards are accepted, prices include breakfast, free Wi-Fi and/or a guest computer is generally available, and English is spoken. Sarajevo's hotels quote prices in euros. Prices change; verify the hotel's current rates online or by email. For the best prices, always book directly with the hotel.

---

rooms. It's just across the river from the Old Town in a pleasantly uncrowded neighborhood (Db-€80, pricier suites, air-con, free parking, Obala Isa Bega Isakovica 1, tel. 033/572-660, mobile 061-134-287, www.hotel-latinskimost.com, info@hotel-latinskimost.com).

$$ Hotel Michele is a friendly, quirky guesthouse facing a school in a quiet though slightly dingy neighborhood; it's a 10-minute uphill walk from Maršala Tita street. The 12 huge rooms and eight gargantuan apartments are gaudy, decorated with antique furniture. This place has hosted several celebrities in town for the Sarajevo Film Festival...it doesn't take much prompting to get the receptionist to do some name-dropping. On my last visit, I slept in the Richard Gere room (Sb-€75, Db-€85, much bigger "luxury" room for €20 more, apartments-€120-150, air-con, free parking garage, Ivana Cankara 27, tel. 033/560-310, mobile 061-338-177, www.hotelmichele.ba, contact@hotelmichele.ba).

$ Halvat Guest House is very tight but homey, offering five stylish-for-the-price rooms and one apartment squeezed into a modern shell. It's on a nondescript urban street that's a quick walk from the heart of the Old Town. The staff, led by Valida and Mumo, are friendly and welcoming (Sb-€46, Db-€68, Tb-€86; apartment-€46/person for up to three; skip breakfast to save €4/person, cash only, air-con, free parking, Kasima Efendije Dobrače 13, tel. 033/237-714, www.halvat.com.ba, halvat@bih.net.ba).

$ Kandilj Pension ("Candle") has 10 simple, small yet comfortable rooms in a traditional Ottoman-style house with a snug breakfast cellar. With a cozy and pleasant old-fashioned feel, it's up a gentle hill and next to the Tomb of the Seven Brothers, across the river from the Old Town (Sb-€40, Db-€62, Tb-€73, air-con, Bistrik/potok 12A, tel. 033/572-510, mobile 061-938-940, www.kandilj.com, info@kandilj.com, Adi). They also rent three modern, nicely equipped, well-priced apartments a steep five-minute walk above the pension (and 10 minutes above the river); if you don't mind the hike, these are a fine value (Db-€60-70, Tb-€70-80, price depends on size, check-in and breakfast at pension).

$ Hotel Safir, while more impersonal than the norm, is nicely located on a tiny lane near (but not *too* near) the Old Town action. The eight rooms are modern, with blue tile accents and small kitchenettes, but a bit sterile (Db-€65, breakfast-€2.50, air-con, Jagodića 3, tel. 033/475-040, www.hotelsafir.ba, info@hotelsafir.ba).

$ Vagabond Hostel, enthusiastically run by sisters Alvina and Aida, is fantastically located right along the main Ferhadija pedestrian street (so expect some noise). Unpretentious and youthful, it has 32 beds in six rooms (bunk in dorm room-€15, D-€45, Q-€80, cheaper off-season, cash only, no breakfast, air-con in most rooms, shared kitchen, Ferhadija 21, tel. 033/238-811, www.vagabond.ba, hostel@vagabond.ba).

Eating in Sarajevo

Cosmopolitan Sarajevo boasts a wide array of good eateries, serving not only traditional Bosnian food (which is delicious), but a wide range of international flavors as well. I've focused my recommendations on the area in and near the Old Town (Baščaršija).

TRADITIONAL BOSNIAN FOOD

The Baščaršija is crowded with tourist-oriented eateries slinging good Bosnian fare. For a primer, see the "Balkan Flavors" sidebar on page 421.

Several obvious choices line the street called **Prote Bakovića,** which juts up from the main drag just a block over from "Pigeon Square" (across from the TI). Along here are a variety of crowd-pleasing cafés and restaurants, including **Dveri, Pod Lipom,** and **Dženita.** Comparison-shop menus and take your pick. But first read up on the cheaper options below.

Burek: These delicious "Bosnian pies," made with flaky phyllo dough and savory fillings, are available throughout the Balkans. While there are several choices in the Baščaršija, my favorite is **Buregdžinica Sač,** a hole-in-the-wall where they're made with fresh ingredients and baked the traditional way, under a metal lid that's covered with hot coals *(ispod sača).* Order at the counter, then take away or grab a table outside—this is Sarajevo's best quick meal. Choose between spinach, meat, tangy cheese, or potato—or ask for a mix of all four (5 KM/portion, Mon-Sat 8:30-20:00, closed Sun, in the alley off of Bravadžiluk street called Bravadžiluk Mali).

Ćevapčići: Around every corner in the Baščaršija, you'll run into a *ćevabdžinica*—a cheap eatery selling the tasty little sausage-shaped minced-meat patties. Bosnians agree that this is the best place in the country to get the local answer to hot dogs and hamburgers. While you can barely go wrong here, keep an eye out for these options: The highest concentration is along Bravadžiluk street, including **Mrkva** ("Carrot"), a slick and more modern-feeling option that's part of a local chain (Bravadžiluk 15); and the more traditional **Petica** ("Five"), run by the Ferhatović family (just off Bravadžiluk at Oprkanj 2). Other good Old Town choices are **Galatasaray** (Gazi Husrev-Begova 44), a few steps off of Sarači street near the mosque; and **Željo**, named for a local soccer team, which hides in a less touristy zone near the river (Kundurdžiluk 12).

Aščinica: An *aščinica* is a Turkish-style cafeteria, where you survey your options at the display case and point to what you want. It's an efficient, affordable, and relatively untouristy way to get a taste of Bosnian cooking. The *aščinica* called **ASDž** is a good choice on a nondescript Old Town street (6-12-KM meals, daily 8:00-19:00, Mali Čurčiluk 3, tel. 033/238-500). For a completely untouristy experience, head for **Aščinica "H.E.M"**, a country-cutesy lunch counter near the workaday Markale Market (limited English—point to what looks good, 3-5-KM meals, Mon-Sat 8:00-16:00, closed Sun, Bašeskije 21).

Bosnian Coffee *(Bosanska Kafa):* Known elsewhere as "Turkish coffee," this thick, unfiltered, highly caffeinated sludge (which leaves a layer of "mud" at the bottom of your cup) is a Sarajevo staple. For tips on the proper ritual for drinking your Bosnian coffee—which is an integral part of Bosnian culture—see page 410. Choose any Baščaršija table with a view that you enjoy, or poke into the atmospheric **Morića Han** courtyard, a former caravanserai (which also has a restaurant).

OTHER OPTIONS

Apetit is a six-table dining room wrapped around a busy chef, who prepares Asian-European fusion cuisine with whatever he's found at today's market. There's no menu—you'll simply discuss what you want with the server. As this is a popular place, reservations are recommended (25-KM meals, Mon-Sat 12:00-22:00, closed Sun, Josipa Štadlera 6, mobile 062-868-131, www.apetit.ba).

To Be ~~Or Not~~ To Be, in the Old Town, is a popular, intimate little place (with six tables on two floors, plus some outdoor seating) where Amer serves up delicious home-cooked comfort food from an eclectic international menu. She'll take your order, then head over to her kitchen in the corner—which isn't much bigger than yours back home—and cook up your meal fresh. On the sign notice

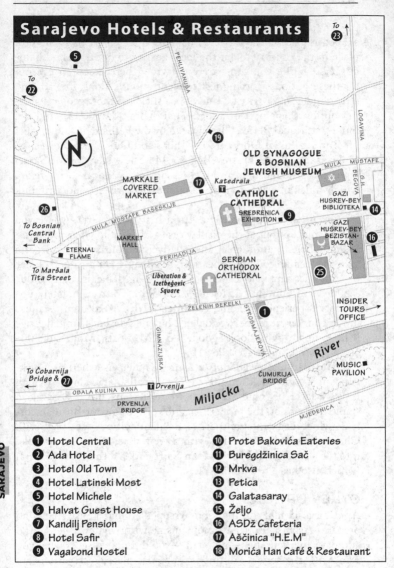

Sarajevo Hotels & Restaurants

OLD SYNAGOGUE & BOSNIAN JEWISH MUSEUM

MULA MUSTAFE

MARKALE COVERED MARKET

Katedrala

CATHOLIC CATHEDRAL

Srebrenica EXHIBITION

GAZI HUSREV-BEY BIBLIOTEKA

To Bosnian Central Bank

MULA MUSTAFE BAŠESKIJE

MARKET HALL

ETERNAL FLAME

FERHADIJA

SERBIAN ORTHODOX CATHEDRAL

GAZI HUSREV-BEY BEZISTAN-BAZAR

To Maršala Tita Street

Liberation & Izetbegović Square

ŽELENIH BERELKI

ŠTROĐMAJEROVA

INSIDER TOURS OFFICE

GIMNAZIJSKA

To Čobarnija Bridge &

OBALA KULINA BANA

Drvenija

ČUMURIJA BRIDGE

River

MUSIC PAVILION

Miljacka

DRVENIJA BRIDGE

MJEDENICA

PEHLIVANUŠA

LOGAVINA

G.H.

BEGOVA

To 23

To 22

To

❶ Hotel Central	❿ Prote Bakovića Eateries
❷ Ada Hotel	⓫ Buregdžinica Sač
❸ Hotel Old Town	⓬ Mrkva
❹ Hotel Latinski Most	⓭ Petica
❺ Hotel Michele	⓮ Galatasaray
❻ Halvat Guest House	⓯ Željo
❼ Kandilj Pension	⓰ ASDž Cafeteria
❽ Hotel Safir	⓱ Aščinica "H.E.M"
❾ Vagabond Hostel	⓲ Morića Han Café & Restaurant

SARAJEVO

that "or not" is crossed out—during the siege, everyone here decided they definitely wanted to be (10-15-KM omelets and pastas, 14-25-KM meat and fish dishes, daily 11:00-23:00, Čizmedžiluk 5, tel. 033/233-265, mobile 061-508-008).

Sarajevska Brewery's **Pivnica HS** brewpub is a big, rollicking beer hall that also manages to feel cozy. Tucked in the back of the sprawling, spring-fed Sarajevska complex, this place has two levels of diners, a double-decker bar, and a long menu of pub grub. Although their regular Sarajevska lager is available any-

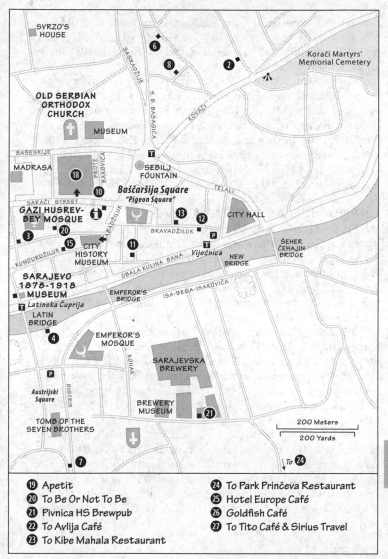

19 Apetit
20 To Be Or Not To Be
21 Pivnica HS Brewpub
22 To Avlija Café
23 To Kibe Mahala Restaurant

24 To Park Prinčeva Restaurant
25 Hotel Europe Café
26 Goldfish Café
27 To Tito Café & Sirius Travel

SARAJEVO

where, beer pilgrims come to the brewery to tap into the unfiltered wheat beer (sold only here) and the rare dark beer (8-10-KM pastas and starters, 12-24-KM main dishes, daily 10:00-24:00, can be closed for special events—consider calling ahead, Franjevačka 15, tel. 033/239-740). Next door is the

brewery's little **museum**—one well-presented room with old barrels, bottles, steins, photographs, and vintage ads (3 KM, 5 KM includes a drink in the bar, 25 KM includes lunch, daily 10:00-18:00, www.pivnicahs.com).

Avlija ("Courtyard") sits in an unassuming, untouristy neighborhood a short walk above Maršala Tita street (and about 10-15 minutes from the Old Town). This very local-feeling hangout fills its namesake courtyard with bright, funky colors, rustic wooden tables, and happy drinkers and diners. The cuisine is a mix of Bosnian and international—affordable and very good (6-12-KM pastas and salads, 10-22-KM meat dishes, Mon-Sat 8:00-23:00, closed Sun, Sumbula Avde 2, tel. 033/444-483).

DINING HIGH ABOVE SARAJEVO, WITH PANORAMIC VIEWS

Two good options sit in the residential hills above the Old Town, overlooking a stunning sunset and the twinkling hillsides at twilight. In each case, it's a long and steep hike up from town—or a quick and cheap taxi ride (figure around 5-7 KM each way). One feels fancy, the other is more casual, but at either one you'll want to reserve before making the trip.

Kibe Mahala is elegant, with sleek decor, a Sinatra soundtrack, and a romantic, glassed-in terrace. While service can be uneven, it's very affordable even though it feels like a splurge. Their specialty is lamb roasted on a spit; if you'd like to try this Balkan classic, order it when you reserve your table (12-20-KM main courses, Mon-Sat 11:00-23:00, closed Sun, Vrbanjuša 164, tel. 033/441-936, www.kibemahala.ba).

Park Prinčeva feels like a big beer garden, with long picnic tables overlooking the city, roving musicians, traditionally dressed servers, and a menu of hearty Bosnian food. With point-blank views of City Hall and the Sarajevo hillsides, it's a memorable setting. It may not be high cuisine, but it's high-up cuisine (14-25-KM meals, long hours daily, Iza Hrida 7, tel. 033/532-403, www.parkprinceva.ba).

CAFÉS

Being at the intersection of two cultures famous for enjoying a cup of coffee (Viennese and Ottoman), Sarajevo has more than its share of cozy cafés. Explore the streets—both in the Old Town and in the modern areas—to find just the right spot. For Ottoman atmosphere in the Baščaršija, peruse your options along both Sarači (Leathermakers' Street) and Bravadžiluk (Locksmiths' Street)—or just cut to the chase and head for the **Morića Han** courtyard (see page 512). For Viennese-style splendor, you'll stumble on many fine options, but likely none as impressive as the chandeliered café inside the **Hotel Europe.** Many modern cafés line lively Ferhadija street, which is great for people-watching. For a claustrophobic, cluttered old room that feels like the hipster version of *Antiques Roadshow*, head for the quirky, wildly decorated **Goldfish** (Kaptol 5). And if you're nostalgic for the Red old days, it's obligatory to visit **Tito Café** behind the Historical Museum (see page 500).

Sarajevo Connections

From Sarajevo by Bus to: Mostar (9/day, 2.5 hours), **Split** (2/day, 8 hours), **Dubrovnik** (2/day, 6 hours; includes a night bus in summer only), **Zagreb** (4/day, 8 hours, includes night bus), **Ljubljana** (1/day but not every day, sometimes overnight, 11 hours). Most (but not all) buses are operated by Centrotrans/Eurolines (www.centrotrans.com); the general number for bus information at the main station is tel. 033/213-100. A few additional buses depart from the predominantly Serb area of East Sarajevo (info tel. 057/317-377).

By Train: Sarajevo sits in the middle of a train line that goes south to **Mostar** and **Ploče** (on the Croatian coast between Split and Dubrovnik), and north to **Zagreb** (2.5 hours to Mostar, 4.5 hours to Ploče, 9 hours to Zagreb). As the specific schedule is constantly in flux, check your options at www.bahn.com. Most travelers find the bus more comfortable and faster than the train.

ROUTE TIPS FOR DRIVERS

From Mostar to Sarajevo: Whether you're driving or taking the bus, you're in for a scenic journey that also takes you past some interesting sights of historical note. The road is in excellent repair, and the glorious mountain views and intriguing villages will make you want to come back and stay longer in Bosnia. Even if you're not stopping along the way, keep track of these landmarks as you roll.

You'll begin by heading up the dramatically scenic **Neretva River Canyon,** which surrounds a thrusting river that powers four hydroelectric dams. The scenery crescendos as you twist your way through the canyon.

The first major town you pass is **Jablanica,** famous among Bosnians as the best place to enjoy spit-grilled lamb (look for restaurants along the road)—and as the site of the WWII Battle of Neretva, which demonstrated Tito's brilliance as a military tactician. Tito arrived here with his Partisan army, including some 4,000 injured troops and a squadron of desperate villagers and civilian refugees who had joined their ranks. Surrounded by his dual foes—Nazis and Četniks—Tito got clever: First, his troops destroyed five bridges across this river, leaving the clear impression that the Partisans planned to push away from the river. Then, as

SARAJEVO

the Nazis redeployed their troops, Tito's men quickly repaired one of the bridges overnight. This allowed the Partisans—including all of their wounded and hangers-on—to cross the river, destroy the bridge again, and swing around to catch the Nazis off-guard. Tito's victory at the Battle of the Neretva—and especially his pledge, "Wounded people we shall not leave"—still echoes in the collective memory of those living in what was once Yugoslavia. In 1969, the victory was immortalized in the Oscar-nominated *Battle of Neretva*, which featured Yul Brynner, Orson Welles, and other big names lured by the Yugoslav government's extremely generous funding.

To learn more about the battle, turn off at the brown *museum* sign in Jablanica to reach the **Museum of the Battle for the Wounded at Neretva** (Muzej Bitka za Ranjenike na Neretvi). This huge, abandoned-seeming building was erected overlooking the gorge and the site of the famous bridge in 1978...and, it seems, hasn't been renovated since. Inside you'll see dusty old exhibits including original helmets and rifles; life-size dioramas of the wounded being evacuated; a model showing how they used the wreckage of the original bridge to support their new, makeshift one; a small photo exhibit of the Yugoslav Wars in Mostar and Bosnia, honoring those lost in the fighting; and life-size models of Bosnian village life. Huge windows look over the river gorge, where you can see a replica of the bridge that was built for the movie and kept here as a memorial (4 KM, April-Oct Mon-Fri 8:00-16:00, Sat-Sun 9:00-16:00; Nov-March Mon-Fri 7:00-15:00, closed Sat-Sun; tel. 036/752-705, www.muzej-jablanica.com).

Continuing along the main road, the next major town is **Konjic,** known for its traditional woodworking. The mountains above Konjic are a popular place for whitewater rafting. Also in those mountains, Tito had a failsafe bunker—one of many such complexes throughout Yugoslavia where he could retreat in case of invasion or worse. This one has been opened as a museum, but it requires a reservation (call the Konjic TI at 036/728-123). Konjic's old bridge (which you'll see on the right as you drive over the modern bridge) dates from the same era as Mostar's Old Bridge. Both Jablanica and Konjic were held by Muslim forces during the Yugoslav Wars, which made them relatively safe havens, especially compared to Mostar or Sarajevo.

From Konjic, the road climbs up to **Ivan Planina** mountain, the geographical boundary between Herzegovina and Bosnia. Along this rugged road, you'll pass the deserted village of **Bradina;** soon after, just before the tunnel, is a huddle of abandoned homes. This is the birthplace of Ante Pavelić—the Bosnian Croat who led the ruthless Nazi-puppet Ustaše forces during World War II.

Passing through the **Ivan Tunnel** (nearly a half-mile long), you enter Kanton Sarajevo (*kanton*, based on the Swiss canton model, roughly means "county"). In addition to separating Herzegovina from Bosnia, this tunnel marks a dramatic weather divide—from the balmy, Mediterranean climate around Mostar to the chilly, continental climate of Sarajevo.

Winding down into the plain around **Sarajevo,** you'll enter the city limits. Just before the Hotel Radon Plaza (on the right) is a pink, destroyed, student building—marking what was the front line of the besieged area of wartime Sarajevo. Everything you'll pass from here on out was under constant sniper fire for three and a half years (you're driving straight up what was called "Sniper Alley"). As you continue into town along the main drag, watch for these landmarks: on the right, the wartime UN offices (in the former university student center); on the left, the national TV headquarters (with a huge antenna array on the roof); on the right, a huge new mosque built with donations from Malaysia (one of 10 in town financed by wealthy investors from the Muslim world); on the left, the distinctive, blue, and aptly named Avaz Twist Tower, hosting the offices of Bosnia's main newspaper (*Dnevni Avaz,* "Daily Voice"—you can ride the elevator up for a grand view, described on page 507); also on the left, the US Embassy, followed by the famous Holiday Inn (built for the 1984 Olympics, and later a safe refuge for wartime journalists); across the street from the Holiday Inn, the restored Bosnian Parliament building; and then the swanky Sarajevo City Center shopping mall. From here, keep following the river into the city center—going through the Austro-Hungarian part of town, passing the place where Archduke Franz Ferdinand was assassinated, and winding up at Sarajevo's Old Town, the Baščaršija.

It's important to find secure parking in Sarajevo. Most hotels have parking, and small public lots are scattered around the Old Town area; for a bigger, more secure garage, head for the BBI Centar shopping mall (on Maršala Tita street—see map on page 512).

SARAJEVO

SLOVENIA
Slovenija

SLOVENIA

Tiny, overlooked Slovenia is one of Europe's most unexpectedly charming destinations. At the intersection of the Slavic, German, and Italian worlds, Slovenia is an exciting mix of the best of each culture. Though it's just a quick trip away from the tourist throngs in Venice, Munich, Salzburg, and Vienna, Slovenia has stayed off the tourist track—making it a handy detour for in-the-know Back Door travelers. Be warned: Everyone I've met who has visited Slovenia wishes they'd allotted more time for this delightful, underrated land.

Today, it seems strange to think that Slovenia was ever part of Yugoslavia. Both in the personality of its people and in its landscape, Slovenia feels more like Austria. Slovenes are more industrious, organized, and punctual than their fellow former Yugoslavs...yet still friendly, relaxed, and Mediterranean. Locals like the balance. Visitors expecting minefields and rusting Yugo factories are pleasantly surprised to find Slovenia's rolling countryside dot-

ted instead with quaint alpine villages and the spires of miniature Baroque churches, with snowcapped peaks in the distance.

Only half as big as Switzerland, Slovenia is remarkably diverse for its size. Travelers can hike on alpine trails in the morning and explore some of the world's best caves in the afternoon, before relaxing with a glass of local wine and a seafood dinner while watching the sun set on the Adriatic.

Though not unaffected by the recent economic crisis, Slovenia enjoys a prosperity unusual for a formerly communist country. The Austro-Hungarian Empire left it with a strong work ethic and an impressive industrial infrastructure, which the Yugoslav government expanded. By 1980, 60 percent of all Yugoslav industry was in little Slovenia (which had only 8 percent of Yugoslavia's population and 8 percent of its territory). Of the 13 new nations that have

Slovenia

joined the European Union since 2004, Slovenia was the only one rich enough to be a net donor (with a higher per-capita income than the average), and the first one to join the euro currency zone (it adopted the euro in January 2007). Thanks to its longstanding ties to the West and can-do spirit, Slovenia already feels more "Western" than any other destination in this book.

The country has a funny way of making people fall in love with it. Slovenes are laid-back, easygoing, stylish, and fun. They won't win any world wars (they're too well-adjusted to even try)... but they're exactly the type of people you'd love to chat with over a cup of coffee.

The Slovenian language is as mellow as the people. While Slovenes use Serb, German, and English curses in abundance, the worst they can say in their native tongue is, "May you be kicked by a horse." For "Darn it!" they say, "Three hundred hairy bears!" In bad traffic, they might mutter, "The street is white!"

Coming from such a small country, locals are proud of the few things that are distinctly Slovenian, such as the roofed hayrack. Because of the frequent rainfall in the mountainous northwest, the hayracks are covered by a roof that allows the hay to dry thoroughly. The most traditional kind is the *toplar*, consisting of two hayracks

Slovenia Almanac

Official Name: Republika Slovenija, or simply Slovenija.

Snapshot History: After being dominated by Germans for centuries, Slovenian culture proudly emerged in the 19th century. In the aftermath of World War I, Slovenia merged with its neighbors to become Yugoslavia, then broke away and achieved independence for the first time in 1991.

Population: Slovenia's two million people (a count similar to Nevada's) are 83 percent ethnic Slovenes who speak Slovene, plus a smattering of Serbs, Croats, and Muslim Bosniaks. Almost 60 percent of the country is Catholic.

Latitude and Longitude: 46° N and 14° E (latitude similar to Lyon, France; Montreal, Canada; or Bismarck, North Dakota).

Area: At 7,800 square miles, it's about the size of New Jersey, but with one-fourth the population.

Geography: Tiny Slovenia has four extremely different terrains and climates: the warm Mediterranean coastline (just 29 miles long—about one inch per inhabitant); the snowcapped, forested alpine mountains in the northwest (including 9,400-foot Mount Triglav); the moderate-climate, central limestone plateau that includes Ljubljana and the cave-filled Karst region; and to the east, a corner of the Great Hungarian Plain (the Prekmurje region, near Maribor and Ptuj). If you look at a map of Slovenia and squint your eyes a bit, it looks like a chicken running toward the east.

Biggest Cities: Nearly one in five Slovenes lives in the two biggest cities: Ljubljana (the capital, pop. 270,000) and Maribor (in the east, pop. 158,000). Half of the population lives in rural villages.

Economy: Slovenia has a Gross Domestic Product of $60 billion and a GDP per capita of around $30,000. Slovenia's economy is based largely on manufactured metal products (trucks and machinery), which are traded with a diverse group of partners.

Currency: Slovenia uses the euro: €1 = about $1.10.

Government: The country is led by the prime minister (currently Miro Cerar), who heads the leading vote-getting party in legislative elections. He governs along with the figurehead president (currently Borut Pahor). Slovenia's relatively peaceful secession is credited largely to former president Milan Kučan, who remains a popular figure. The National Assembly consists of about 90 elected legislators; there's also a second house of parliament, which has much less power. Despite the country's small size, it is divided into some 200 municipalities—creating a lot of bureaucracy that locals enjoy complaining about.

Flag: Three horizontal bands of white (top), blue, and red. A shield in the upper left shows Mount Triglav, with a wavy-line sea below and three stars above.

The Average Slovene: The average Slovene skis in this largely alpine country, and is an avid fan of team handball (yes, handball). He or she lives in a 250-square-foot apartment, earns $1,400 a month, watches 16 hours of TV a week (much of it in English with Slovene subtitles), and enjoys a drink-and-a-half of alcohol every day.

Notable Slovenes: A pair of prominent Ohio politicians from the Cleveland area—perennial presidential candidate **Dennis Kucinich** and former senator **George Voinovich**—are each half-Slovene. (In 1910, Cleveland had the biggest Slovenian population of any city in the world—just ahead of Trieste and Ljubljana.) Classical musicians might know composers **Giuseppe Tartini** and **Hugo Wolf.** Even if you haven't heard of architect **Jože Plečnik** yet, you'll hear his name a hundred times while you're in Slovenia—especially in Ljubljana (see page 570). Perhaps most famous of all is the illustrious **Melania Knauss**—a *GQ* cover girl who's also the current Mrs. Donald Trump.

Sporty Slovenes: If you follow alpine sports or team handball, you'll surely know some world-class athletes from Slovenia. NBA fans might recognize basketball players **Primož Brezec** and **Bostjan Nachbar,** as well as some other less famous players. Slovenian hockey player **Anže Kopitar** plays in the NHL. The athletic Slovenes—perhaps trying to compensate for the minuscule size of their country—have accomplished astonishing feats: **Davo Karničar** has skied down from the "seven summits" (the highest points in each of the seven continents—that means the peaks of Everest, Kilimanjaro, McKinley, and so on). **Benka Pulko** became the first person ever to drive a motorcycle around the world—that is, all seven continents, including Antarctica, which is also the longest solo motorcycle journey by a woman (total trip: 111,856 miles in 2,000 days; for more, see www.benkapulko.com). **Dušan Mravlje** ran across all the continents. And ultramarathon swimmer **Martin Strel** has swum the entire length of several major rivers, including the Danube (1,775 miles), the Mississippi (2,415 miles), the Yangtze (3,915 miles), and the Amazon (3,393 miles; for more, see www.martinstrel.com).

SLOVENIA

connected by one big roof. It looks like a skinny barn with open, fenced sides. Hay hangs on the sides to dry; firewood, carts, tractors, and other farm implements sit on the ground inside; and dried hay is stored in the loft above. But these wooden *toplarji* are firetraps, and a stray bolt of lightning can burn one down in a flash. So in recent years, more farmers are moving to single hayracks *(enojni)*; these are still roofed, but have posts made of concrete rather than wood. You'll find postcards and miniature wooden models of both kinds of hayracks (a fun souvenir).

Another uniquely Slovenian memento is a creatively decorated front panel from a beehive *(panjske končnice)*. Slovenia has a

strong beekeeping tradition, and beekeepers believe that painting the fronts of the hives makes it easier for bees to find their way home. Replicas of these panels are available at gift shops all over the country. (For more on the panels and Slovenia's beekeeping heritage, see page 624.)

Slovenia is also the land of polka. Slovenes claim that polka music was invented here, and singer/accordionist Slavko Avsenik—from the village of Begunje near Bled—cranked out popular oompah songs that made him bigger than the Beatles (and therefore, presumably, Jesus) in Germany. You'll see the Avsenik ensemble and other oompah bands on Slovenian TV, where hokey Lawrence Welk-style shows are an institution.

To really stretch your euros, try one of Slovenia's more than 400 farmhouse B&Bs, called "tourist farms" *(turistične kmetije)*—similar to *agriturismi* in Italy. These are actual working farms (often organic) that sell meals and/or rent rooms to tourists to help make ends meet. You can use a tourist farm as a home base to explore the entire country—remember, the farthest reaches of Slovenia are only a day trip away. A comfortable, hotelesque double with a private bathroom—plus a traditional Slovenian dinner and a hearty breakfast—costs as little as €50.

Most visitors to Slovenia are, in my experience, completely charmed by the place. With all it has going for it, it's hard to believe that Slovenia is not already overrun with tourists. Somehow, this little country continues to glide beneath the radar. Exploring its mountain trails, savoring its colorful capital, and meeting its friendly locals, you'll feel like you're in on a secret.

HELPFUL HINTS

Sunday Closures: Slovenia can be extremely sleepy on Sundays, even in the larger towns and cities, where virtually all shops are closed. Plan ahead. Fortunately, many restaurants remain open, plus a select few grocery stores.

Smoking Ban: Smoking is prohibited in public places, unless it's a specially designated (and well-ventilated) smoking room. Larger hotels still have some smoking rooms, but smoking isn't allowed in public areas. Outdoors, all bets are off.

Telephones: Slovenian phone numbers beginning with 080 are toll-free; 090 and 089 denote expensive toll lines. Most mobile phone numbers begin with 03, 04, 05, or 07. For more details on how to dial to, from, and within Slovenia, see page 776.

Toll Sticker: To drive on Slovenia's expressways *(avtocesta)*, you'll need to display a toll sticker *(vinjeta,* veen-YEH-tah; €15/week, €30/month). If renting your car in Slovenia, it probably comes with a sticker (but make sure); if you're driving in from elsewhere, such as Croatia, you can buy one at a gas station, post office, or some newsstands (watch for *vinjeta* signs at gas stations as you approach the border). *Be warned:* This rule is taken very seriously. If you're found driving on expressways without the sticker, you'll immediately be fined €150.

Cruise Port: The Slovenian town of **Koper** (see page 724) is becoming a popular port of call for Mediterranean cruises. Given the country's size, it's possible to see just about any of the Slovenia destinations covered in this book in a day in port (provided you use your time efficiently and have a private driver—I recommend Tina Hiti and Sašo Golub, listed on page 598).

SLOVENIAN HISTORY

Slovenia has a long and unexciting history as part of various larger empires. After Illyrian, Celtic, and Roman settlements came and went, this region became populated by Slavs—the ancestors of today's Slovenes—in the late sixth century. But Charlemagne's Franks conquered the tiny land in the eighth century, and, ever since, Slovenia has been a backwater of the Germanic world—first as a holding of the Holy Roman Empire and later, the Habsburg Empire. But even as the capital, Ljubljana, was populated by Austrians (who called the city Laibach), the Slovenian language and cultural traditions survived in the countryside.

Through the Middle Ages, much of Slovenia was ruled by the Counts of Celje (highly placed vassals of the Habsburgs). In this era before modern nations—when shifting allegiances and strategic marriages dictated the dynamics of power—the Counts of Celje rose to a position of significant influence in Central and Eastern Europe. Celje daughters intermarried with some of the most powerful dynasties in the region: the Polish Piasts, the Hungarian Anjous, and the Czech Přemysls. Before long, the Counts of Celje had emerged as the Habsburgs' main rivals. In the 15th century, Count Ulrich II of Celje married into Serbia's ruling family and managed to wrest control of Hungary's massive holdings. Had he not been assassinated in 1456, this obscure Slovenian line—rather than an obscure Austrian one—may have emerged as the dominant power in the eastern half of Europe. (Instead, the Habsburgs consolidated their vanquished foe's fiefdoms into their ever-growing empire.) In homage, the three yellow stars of the Counts of Celje's seal still adorn Slovenia's coat of arms.

Soon after, with Slovenia firmly entrenched in the Counter-Reformation holdings of the Habsburg Empire, the local Reformer Primož Trubar (1508-1586) strove both to put the Word of God into the people's hands, and to legitimize Slovene as a written language. This Slovenian answer to Martin Luther secretly translated the Bible into Slovene in Reformation-friendly Germany, then smuggled copies back into his homeland.

Over the next several centuries, much of Slovenia was wracked by Habsburg-Ottoman wars, as the Ottomans attempted to push north through this territory to reach Vienna. Slovenia also found itself caught in the crossfire between Austria and Venice. Seemingly exhausted by all of this warfare—and by their own sporadic, halfhearted, and unsuccessful uprisings against Habsburg rule— Slovenia languished as a sleepy backwater.

When the port city of Trieste (in Slovenian territory) was granted free status in 1718, it boosted the economy of Slovenian lands. The Enlightenment spurred a renewed interest in the Slovenian culture and language, which further flourished when Napoleon named Ljubljana the capital of his "Illyrian Provinces"— Slovenia's own mini-empire, stretching from Austria's Tirol to Croatia's Dalmatian Coast. During this brief period (1809-1813), the long-suppressed Slovene language was used for the first time in schools and the government. This kicked off a full-throated national revival movement—asserting the worthiness of the Slovenian language and culture compared to the dominant Germanic worldview of the time. Inspired by the patriotic poetry of France Prešeren (1800-1849), Slovenian pride surged.

The last century saw the most interesting chapter of Slovenian history. Some of World War I's fiercest fighting occurred at the Soča (Isonzo) Front in northwest Slovenia—witnessed by young Ernest Hemingway, who drove an ambulance (see sidebars on pages 642 and 656). During World War II, Slovenia was divided among Nazi allies Austria, Italy, and Hungary—and an estimated 20,000 to 25,000 Slovenes perished in Nazi- and Italian-operated concentration camps.

Slo-what?-ia

The only thing I know about Slovakia is what I learned firsthand from your foreign minister, who came to Texas.

—George W. Bush, to a Slovak journalist (Bush had actually met with Dr. Janez Drnovšek, who was then Slovenia's prime minister)

Maybe it's understandable that many Americans confuse Slovenia with Slovakia. Both are small, mountainous countries that not too long ago were parts of bigger, now defunct nations. But anyone who has visited Slovenia and Slovakia will set you straight—they feel worlds apart.

Slovenia, wedged between the Alps and the Adriatic, is a tidy, prosperous country. Until 1991, Slovenia was one of the six republics that made up Yugoslavia. Historically, Slovenia has had very strong ties with Germanic culture—so it feels like its neighbor to the north, Austria.

Slovakia—two countries away, to the northeast—is slightly bigger. Much of its territory is covered by the Carpathian Mountains, most notably the dramatic, jagged peaks of the High Tatras. In 1993, the Czechs and Slovaks peacefully chose to go their separate ways, so the nation of Czechoslovakia dissolved into the Czech Republic and the Slovak Republic (a.k.a. Slovakia).

To make things even more confusing, there's **Slavonia**. This is the thick, inland panhandle that makes up the northeast half of Croatia, along Slovenia's southeast border. Much of the warfare in Croatia's 1991-1995 war took place in Slavonia (including Vukovar; see the Understanding Yugoslavia chapter).

Mixing them up is understandable, but doing just a little homework will make you feel smarter than a former president.

As Yugoslavia entered its Golden Age under war hero Marshal Tito, Slovenia's prime location where Yugoslavia meets Western Europe (a short drive from Austria or Italy)—and the diligent national character of the Slovenian people—made it a prime candidate for industrialization.

After Tito's death in 1980, the various Yugoslav republics struggled to redefine their role in the union. While many factions reverted to age-old, pre-Tito nationalistic fervor, the Slovenes grew increasingly focused on their own future...and began to press for real reforms of the communist system. Slovenia had always been Yugoslavia's smallest, northernmost, most prosperous republic. Slovenes realized that Yugoslavia needed Slovenia much more than Slovenia needed Yugoslavia.

In 1988, the iconoclastic Slovenian magazine *Mladina* pushed the boundaries of Yugoslavia's nominally "free" press, publishing articles critical of the Yugoslav People's Army. Four young reporters (including Janez Janša, who would later become Slovenia's prime minister) were tried, convicted, and imprisoned, spurring outrage among Slovenes. A few months later, the Slovenian delegation defiantly walked out of the Yugoslav League of Communists Congress.

The first-ever free elections in Slovenia on April 8, 1990, ended communist rule and swept reformer Milan Kučan into the presidency. Kučan attempted to pursue a Swiss-style confederated relationship with his fellow Yugoslav republics, but met with resistance from his counterparts who were more focused on their own ethnic self-interests. Later that year, in a nationwide referendum, 88 percent of Slovenes voted for independence from Yugoslavia.

And so, concerned about the nationalistic politics of Serbian strongman Slobodan Milošević and seeking the opportunity for true democracy and capitalism, Slovenia seceded. Because more than 90 percent of the people here were ethnic Slovenes—and because Slovenia was careful to respect the rights of its minority populations—the break with Yugoslavia was simple and virtually uncontested. Its war for independence lasted just 10 days and claimed only a few dozen lives. (For more details, see page 737 in the Understanding Yugoslavia chapter.)

In May of 2004 Slovenia became the first of the former Yugoslav republics to join the European Union. The Slovenes have been practical about this move, realizing it's essential for their survival as a tiny nation in a modern world. But there are trade-offs, and "Euroskeptics" are down on EU bureaucracy. As borders disappear, Slovenes are experiencing more crime. Traditional farms are grappling with strict EU standards. Slovenian businesses are having difficulty competing with big German and other Western European firms. Before EU membership, only Slovenes could own Slovenian land, but now wealthy foreigners are buying property, driving up the cost of real estate. Still, overall, most Slovenes feel that EU membership was the right choice.

After independence, Slovenia impressed its European neighbors with its powerhouse economy and steady growth. However, the global financial crisis revealed that some of the affluence was deceptive: Many of Slovenia's biggest companies had been running up huge debts. As all of Europe's bubble burst in 2008, those corporate debts were assumed by Slovenia's big banks—devastating the economy and sparking financial worries.

In recent years, Slovenes have grown weary of a string of corrupt and incompetent politicians. Janez Janša, who became prime minister for the second time in 2011, was swept out of office amid a wave of protests and eventually sentenced to a prison term for corruption. His successor, Alenka Bratušek, resigned after just a year in office. One popular figure—at least in Ljubljana—is the visionary mayor Zoran Janković, who has reshaped the capital during his tenure (see page 555).

In the fall of 2015, Slovenia became the focal point of a Europe-wide debate when a flood of refugees from Syria and other nations showed up at its border. Like its neighbors Croatia and Hungary, Slovenia grappled with the challenge of caring for the new arrivals even as it facilitated their passage to wealthy northern European countries. News reports suggested that Slovenia responded to this humanitarian crisis with pragmatic compassion.

While many of the refugees expressed relief at what a friendly and competent place Slovenia was, those of us who already love the country were hardly shocked. The Slovenes are adjusting to the 21st century with their characteristic sense of humor and easygoing attitude, just as they've done throughout their history.

SLOVENIAN FOOD

Slovenian cuisine offers more variety and better quality than Croatian fare. Slovenes brag that their cuisine melds the best of Italian

and German cooking—but they also embrace other international influences, especially French. Like Croatian food, Slovenian cuisine also features some pan-Balkan elements: The savory phyllo-dough pastry *burek* is the favorite fast food here, and when Slovenes host a backyard barbecue, they grill up *čevapčiči* and *ražnjiči,* topped off with the eggplant-and-red-bell-pepper condiment *ajvar* (see the "Balkan Flavors" sidebar on page 421). Slovenia enjoys Italian-style dishes, with a pizza or pasta restaurant on seemingly every corner. Hungarian food simmers in the northeast corner of the country (where many Magyars reside). And in most of the country, traditional Slovenian food has a distinctly Germanic vibe—including the "four S's": sausages, schnitzels, strudels, and sauerkraut.

Traditional Slovenian meals come with a hearty helping of groats—a grainy mush made with buckwheat, barley, or corn. Buckwheat, which thrives in this climate, often appears on Slovenian menus. You'll also see plenty of *štruklji,* a dumpling-like savory layer cake that can be stuffed with cheese, meat, or vegetables. *Repa* is turnip prepared like sauerkraut. Among the hearty soups in Slovenia is *jota*—a staple for Karst peasants, made from *repa,* beans, vegetables, and often sausage.

The cuisine of Slovenia's Karst region (the arid limestone plain south of Ljubljana) is notable. The small farms and wineries of this region have been inspired by Italy's Slow Food movement—

Pršut

In Slovenia, Croatia, and Montenegro, *pršut* (purr-SHOOT) is one of the essential food groups. This air-cured ham (like Italian prosciutto) is soaked in salt and sometimes also smoked. Then it hangs in open-ended barns for up to a year and a half, to be dried and seasoned by the howling Bora wind. Each region produces a slightly different *pršut*. In Dalmatia, a layer of fat keeps the ham moist; in Istria, the fat is trimmed, and the *pršut* is dryer.

Since Slovenia and Croatia joined the European Union, strict new standards have swept the land. Separate rooms must be used for the slaughter, preparation, and curing of the ham. While this seems fair enough for large producers, small family farms that want to produce just enough *pršut* for their own use—and maybe sell one or two ham hocks to neighbors—find they have to invest thousands of euros to be compliant.

their owners believe that cuisine is meant to be gradually appreciated, not rushed. The Karst's tasty air-dried ham *(pršut)*, available throughout the country, is worth seeking out (see sidebar). Istria (the peninsula just to the south of the Karst, in southern Slovenia and Croatia) produces truffles that, locals boast, are as good as those from Italy's Piedmont region (see page 150).

Voda is water, and *kava* is coffee. Radenska, in the bottle with the three little hearts, is Slovenia's best-known brand of mineral water—good enough that the word *Radenska* is synonymous with bottled water all over Slovenia and throughout the former Yugoslavia. It's not common to ask for (or receive) tap water, but you can try requesting *voda iz pipe*.

Adventurous teetotalers should forgo the Coke and sample Cockta, a Slovenian cola with an unusual flavor (which supposedly comes from berry, lemon, orange, and 11 herbs). Originally called "Cockta-Cockta," the drink was introduced during the communist period, as an alternative to the difficult-to-get Coca-Cola. This local variation developed a loyal following...until the Iron Curtain fell, and the real Coke became readily available. Cockta sales plummeted. But in recent years—prodded by the slogan "The Taste of Your Youth"—nostalgic Slovenes are drinking Cockta once more.

The premier Slovenian brand of *pivo* (beer) is Union (OO-nee-ohn), but you'll also see a lot of Laško

(LASH-koh), whose mascot is the Zlatorog (or "Golden Horn," a mythical chamois-like animal). For the full story on Slovenian wines, see the sidebar.

Regardless of what you're drinking, to toast, say, *"Na ZD-ROW-yeh!"*—if you can't remember it, think of "Nice driving!"

Slovenia's national dessert is *potica*, a rolled pastry with walnuts and sometimes also raisins. While traditionally eaten at Christmas, it's available year-round. Slovenes eat it from the hard outer crust in, saving the nutty center for last. For more tasty treats, see the "Bled Desserts" sidebar on page 615. Locals claim that Ljubljana has the finest gelato outside of Italy—which, after all, is just an hour down the road.

SLOVENIAN LANGUAGE

Slovene is surprisingly different from the languages spoken in the other former Yugoslav republics. While Serbian and Croatian are mutually intelligible, Slovene is gibberish to Serbs and Croats. Most Slovenes, on the other hand, know Serbo-Croatian because, a generation ago, everybody in Yugoslavia had to learn it.

Linguists have identified some 46 official dialects of Slovene, and there are probably another 100 or so unofficial ones. Locals can instantly tell which city—or sometimes even which remote mountain valley—someone comes from by their accent.

The tiny country of Slovenia borders Italy and Austria, with important historical and linguistic ties to both. For self-preservation, Slovenes have always been forced to function in many different languages. All of these factors make them excellent linguists. Most young Slovenes speak flawless English effortlessly—then admit that they've never set foot in the United States or Britain, but love watching American movies and TV shows (which are always subtitled, never dubbed).

Slovene pronunciation is very similar to Croatian (see page 773). Remember, *c* is pronounced "ts" (as in "cats"). The letter *j* is pronounced as "y"—making "Ljubljana" easier to say than it looks (lyoob-lyee-AH-nah). Slovene only has one diacritical mark: the *strešica*, or "little roof." This makes *č* sound like "ch," *š* sound like "sh," and *ž* sound like "zh" (as in "measure"). The letter *v* is pronounced like "u"—so the Slovenian word *avto* sounds like "auto," and the mountain Triglav is pronounced "TREE-glau" (rhymes with "cow").

The only trick: As in English, which syllable gets the emphasis is unpredictable. Slovenes use many of the same words as Croatians, but put the stress in much different places.

Learn some key Slovenian phrases (see the Slovenian survival phrases on the next page). You'll make more friends and your trip will go more smoothly.

Slovenian Wines

It should come as no surprise that Slovenia produces excellent *vino* (wine). After all, this little country abuts well-respected wine-growing neighbors Italy and Hungary. In fact, Slovenia's winemaking tradition originated with its pre-Roman Illyrian and Celtic inhabitants, meaning that wine has been grown much longer here than in most other European countries. As in Croatia, wine standards plummeted with Yugoslav-era collectivization, but in recent years ambitious vintner families have been determined to bring quality back to Slovenian wines—with impressive results.

Slovenia's three main wine-growing regions are Primorska, Posavje, and Podravje.

The best-known is the **Primorska** region, in the southwest. With a Mediterranean climate (hence its name: "by the sea"), Primorska is best known for its reds. Primorska's Goriška Brda ("Hillsides of Gorica") shares the terroir of Italy's Friuli/Venezia Giulia region (and its much-vaunted, DOC-classified Collio Goriziano wines). This area produces some of Slovenia's most respected wines, made mostly with internationally known grapes such as merlot and cabernet sauvignon. Goriška Brda also produces a good white using the *rebula* grape (also known by its Italian name, *ribolla gialla*). A bit farther south (and still within Primorska), the Karst grows lots of *refošk (refosco)* grapes, which thrive in iron-rich red soil *(terra rossa)*. The top product is the extremely full-bodied, "big" *teran*—infused with a high lactic acid content that supposedly gives the wine healing properties. Nearby coastal areas (around Koper) also grow *refošk*, along with the white *malvazija* grape that's also widely used in Croatian Istria.

To the northeast, near Hungary, is the **Podravje** region (the Drava River Valley), dominated by white grapes—especially *laški riesling* (known internationally as Welsh riesling) and *renski riesling* (what we'd call simply riesling). If you're visiting Ptuj or Maribor, you'll see local menus listing wines produced on the steeper right bank of the Drava River (Haloze) and the left bank (Slovenske Gorice, "Slovenian Hills").

And finally, a bit to the south of Podravje is the **Posavje** region (the Lower Sava River Valley, bordering Croatia). This area—which is still focused on quantity over quality—produces both white and red wines; it's known mostly for the light, russet-colored *cviček* wine (a blend of red and white grapes).

With any type of Slovenian wine, *vrhunsko* (premium) is a mark of quality, while *kakovostno* is a notch down, and *namizno* is a table wine. Other key terms are similar to Croatian: *suho* (dry), *sladko* (sweet), and *pol-* (half).

Slovenian Survival Phrases

In the phonetics, ī sounds like the long i in "light," and bolded syllables are stressed. The vowel "eh" sometimes sounds closer to "ay" (depending on the speaker).

English	Slovenian	Pronunciation
Hello. (formal)	Dober dan.	**doh**-behr dahn
Hi. / Bye. (informal)	Živjo.	**zheev**-yoh
Do you speak English?	Ali govorite angleško?	**ah**-lee goh-voh-**ree**-teh ahn-**glehsh**-koh
Yes. / No.	Ja. / Ne.	yah / neh
I (don't) understand.	(Ne) razumem.	(neh) rah-**zoo**-mehm
Please. / You're welcome.	Prosim.	**proh**-seem
Thank you (very much).	Hvala (lepa).	**hvah**-lah (**leh**-pah)
Excuse me. / I'm sorry.	Oprostite.	oh-proh-**stee**-teh
problem	problem	proh-**blehm**
No problem.	Ni problema.	nee proh-**bleh**-mah
Good.	Dobro.	**doh**-broh
Goodbye.	Na svidenje.	nah **svee**-dehn-yeh
one / two	ena / dve	**eh**-nah / dveh
three / four	tri / štiri	tree / **shtee**-ree
five / six	pet / šest	peht / shehst
seven / eight	sedem / osem	**seh**-dehm / **oh**-sehm
nine / ten	devet / deset	deh-**veht** / deh-**seht**
hundred / thousand	sto / tisoč	stoh / **tee**-sohch
How much?	Koliko?	**koh**-lee-koh
local currency	euro	**ee**-oo-roh
Write it?	Napišite?	nah-**peesh**-ee-teh
Is it free?	Ali je brezplačno?	**ah**-lee yeh brehz-**plahch**-noh
Is it included?	Ali je vključeno?	**ah**-lee yeh vuk-**lyoo**-cheh-noh
Where can I find / buy...?	Kje lahko najdem / kupim...?	kyeh **lah**-koh **nī**-dehm / **koo**-peem
I'd / We'd like...	Želel / Želeli bi...	zheh-**lehl** / zheh-**leh**-lee bee
...a room.	...sobo.	**soh**-boh
...a ticket to ___.	...vozovnico do ___.	voh-**zohv**-neet-soh doh ___
Is it possible?	Ali je možno?	**ah**-lee yeh **mohzh**-noh
Where is...?	Kje je...?	kyeh yeh
...the train station	...železniška postaja	zheh-**lehz**-neesh-kah pohs-**tī**-ah
...the bus station	...avtobusna postaja	**ow**-toh-boos-nah pohs-**tī**-yah
...the tourist information office	...turistično informacijski center	too-**rees**-teech-noh een-for-maht-**see**-skee **tsehn**-tehr
...the toilet	...vece (WC)	**veht**-seh
men / women	moški / ženski	**mohsh**-kee / **zhehn**-skee
left / right / straight	levo / desno / naravnost	**leh**-voh / **dehs**-noh / nah-**rahv**-nohst
At what time...?	Ob kateri uri...?	ohb kah-**teh**-ree **oo**-ree
...does this open / close	...se odpre / zapre	seh ohd-**preh** / zah-**preh**
(Just) a moment.	(Samo) trenutek.	(sah-**moh**) treh-**noo**-tehk
now / soon / later	zdaj / kmalu / pozneje	zuh-**dī** / kuh-**mah**-loo / pohz-**neh**-yeh
today / tomorrow	danes / jutri	**dah**-nehs / **yoo**-tree

In a Slovenian Restaurant

English	Slovenian	Pronunciation
I'd like to reserve...	*Rezerviral bi...*	reh-zehr-**vee**-rahl bee
We'd like to reserve...	*Rezervirali bi...*	reh-zehr-**vee**-rah-lee bee
...a table for one / two.	*...mizo za enega / dva.*	**mee**-zoh zah **eh**-neh-gah / dvah
Is this table free?	*Ali je ta miza prosta?*	**ah**-lee yeh tah **mee**-zah proh-stah
Can I help you?	*Izvolite?*	eez-**voh**-lee-teh
The menu (in English), please.	*Jedilni list (v angleščini), prosim.*	yeh-**deel**-nee leest (vuh ahn-**glehsh**-chee-nee) **proh**-seem
service (not) included	*postrežba (ni) vključena*	post-**rehzh**-bah (nee) vuk-**lyoo**-cheh-nah
cover charge	*pogrinjek*	poh-**green**-yehk
"to go"	*za s sabo*	zah **sah**-boh
with / without	*z / brez*	zuh / brehz
and / or	*in / ali*	een / **ah**-lee
fixed-price meal (of the day)	*(dnevni) meni*	(duh-**new**-nee) meh-**nee**
specialty of the house	*specialiteta hiše*	speht-see-ah-lee-**teh**-tah **hee**-sheh
half portion	*polovična porcija*	poh-loh-**veech**-nah **port**-see-yah
daily special	*dnevna ponudba*	duh-**new**-nah poh-**nood**-bah
fixed-price meal for tourists	*turistični meni*	too-**rees**-teech-nee meh-**nee**
appetizers	*predjedi*	prehd-yeh-**dee**
bread	*kruh*	krooh
cheese	*sir*	seer
sandwich	*sendvič*	**send**-veech
soup	*juha*	**yoo**-hah
salad	*solata*	soh-**lah**-tah
meat / poultry	*meso / perutnina*	meh-**soh** / peh-root-**nee**-nah
fish / seafood	*riba / morska hrana*	**ree**-bah / **mor**-skah **hrah**-nah
fruit	*sadje*	**sahd**-yeh
vegetables	*zelenjava*	zeh-lehn-**yah**-vah
dessert	*sladica*	slah-**deet**-sah
(tap) water	*voda (iz pipe)*	**voh**-dah (eez **pee**-peh)
mineral water	*mineralna voda*	mee-neh-**rahl**-nah **voh**-dah
milk	*mleko*	**mleh**-koh
(orange) juice	*(pomaranč ni) sok*	(poh-mah-**rahnch**-nee) sohk
coffee	*kava*	**kah**-vah
tea	*čaj*	chī
wine	*vino*	**vee**-noh
red / white	*rdeče / belo*	ahr-**deh**-cheh / **beh**-loh
sweet / dry / semi-dry	*sladko / suho / polsuho*	**slahd**-koh / **soo**-hoh / **pohl**-soo-hoh
glass / bottle	*kozarec / steklenica*	koh-**zah**-rehts / stehk-leh-**neet**-sah
beer	*pivo*	**pee**-voh
Cheers!	*Na zdravje!*	nah **zdrow**-yeh
More. / Another.	*Še. / Še eno.*	sheh / sheh **eh**-noh
The same.	*Isto.*	**ees**-toh
Bill, please.	*Račun, prosim.*	rah-**choon** proh-seem
tip	*napitnina*	nah-peet-**nee**-nah
Delicious!	*Odlično!*	ohd-**leech**-noh

LJUBLJANA

Ljubljana (lyoob-lyee-AH-nah) is irresistible. With a lazy Old Town clustered around a castle-topped hill, Slovenia's capital is often likened to Salzburg. It's an apt comparison—but only if you inject a healthy dose of breezy Adriatic culture, add a Slavic accent, and replace favorite son Mozart with local architect Jože Plečnik.

Ljubljana feels smaller than its population of 270,000. With a castle perched on a hill overlooking downtown and several clusters of good museums that try hard but have only so much to say, it does its best to please sightseers. But ultimately, this town is all about ambience. The cobbled core of Ljubljana is an idyllic place that sometimes feels too good to be true. The cityscape is slathered with one-of-a-kind architecture, festivals fill the summer, and people enjoy a Sunday stroll any day of the week. Fashion boutiques and al fresco cafés jockey for control of the Old Town, while the leafy riverside promenade crawls with stylishly dressed students sipping *kava* and polishing their near-perfect English. Laid-back Ljubljana is the kind of place where graffiti and crumbling buildings seem elegantly atmospheric instead of shoddy. But more and more of those buildings have been getting a facelift recently, as a spunky mayor has been spiffing up the place and creating gleaming traffic-free zones left and right—making what was already an exceptionally livable city into a true pedestrians' paradise.

Batted around by history, Ljubljana has seen cultural influences from all sides—most notably Prague, Vienna, and Venice. This has left the city a happy hodgepodge of cultures. Being the midpoint between the Slavic, Germanic, and Italian worlds gives Ljubljana a special spice.

The Story of Ljubljana

In ancient times, Ljubljana was on the trade route connecting the Mediterranean (just 60 miles away) to the Black Sea. (Toss a bottle off the bridge here, and it can float to the Danube and, eventually, all the way to Russia.) Legend has it that Jason and his Argonauts founded Ljubljana when they stopped here for the winter on their way home with the Golden Fleece. Some stories say Jason slayed a dragon here, while according to others, it was St. George; either way, the dragon remains the city mascot to this day.

Some of the area's earliest known inhabitants during the Neolithic and Bronze ages lived in rustic houses on tall wooden piles in the marshy lands surrounding today's city center. They poled around the shallow lagoons in dugout canoes. Sometimes called "crannog dwellers" (after similar homes in the Scottish Highlands), these earliest Ljubljanans left behind precious few artifacts, save for half of a wooden wheel and axle that's 5,200 years old.

The area was later populated by the Illyrians and Celts, and was eventually Romanized (and called Emona) before being over-run by Huns, only to be resettled by Slavs—the ancestors of to-day's Slovenes.

In 1335, Ljubljana fell under the Habsburg emperors, who called it Laibach and steered its development for the next six centuries. Slovenian language and culture were considered back-wards, as most of Laibach's inhabitants spoke German and lived essentially Austrian lifestyles. This Austrian vibe persists today, thanks to abundant Austrian Baroque and Viennese Art Nouveau architecture.

Napoleon put Ljubljana on the map when he named it the capital of his Illyrian Provinces, a realm that stretched from the Danube to Dubrovnik, and from Austria to Albania (for just four short years, 1809-1813). For the first time, the Slovene language was taught in schools, awakening a newfound pride in Slovenian

PLANNING YOUR TIME

Ljubljana deserves at least a full day. Rather than checking off a list of museums, spend most of your time strolling the pleasant town center, exploring the many interesting squares and architectural gems, browsing the produce market, shopping at the boutiques, and sipping coffee at sidewalk cafés along the river.

Here's the best plan for a low-impact sightseeing day: Begin on Prešeren Square, the heart of the city. Cross the Triple Bridge and wander through the riverside produce market before joining the town walking tour at 10:00 (at 11:00 in Oct-March). Then wander south along the Ljubljanica River and through the Kra-kovo gardens to tour the Jože Plečnik House (closed Mon). In

cultural heritage. People still look back fondly on this very brief era, which was the first (and probably only) time when Ljubljana rose to prominence on the world stage. (Despite spending more than 600 years as part of the Habsburg Empire, Ljubljana has no "Habsburg Square"...but it does have a "French Revolution Square.")

In the mid-19th century, the railway connecting Vienna to the Adriatic (Trieste) was built through town—and Ljubljana boomed. An earthquake hit the city in 1895, damaging many buildings. Locals cleverly exaggerated the impact (propping up buildings that were structurally sound, and even tearing down unwanted old houses that had been unharmed) in preparation for the visit of Emperor Franz Josef—who took pity on the city and invested generously in its reconstruction. Ljubljana was made over in the Art Nouveau style. A generation later, architect Jože Plečnik bathed the city in his distinctive, artsy-but-sensible, classical-meets-modern style.

In World War II, Slovenia was occupied first by the Italians, then by the Nazis. Ljubljana had a thriving resistance movement that the Nazis couldn't suppress—so they simply fenced off the entire city and made it a giant prison for three years, allowing in only basic food shipments. But the Slovenes—who knew their land far better than their oppressors did—continued to slip in and out of town undetected, allowing them to agitate through the end of the war.

In 1991, Ljubljana became the capital of one of Europe's youngest nations. Today the city is filled with university students, making it feel very youthful. Ljubljana is on the cutting edge when it comes to architecture, public art, fashion, and trendy pubs—a tendency embodied by its larger-than-life mayor, Zoran Janković (see page 555). And yet, Ljubljana's scintillating avant-garde culture has soft edges—hip, but also nonthreatening and user-friendly.

the afternoon, commit some quality time to people-watching at a riverside café, window-shop at some colorful boutiques (perhaps following my self-guided shopping walk in the Old Town), or do more sightseeing (good options include the City History Museum, near several Jože Plečnik landmarks downtown; the Serbian Orthodox Church and Tivoli Park, with the Contemporary History Museum, west of downtown; or the Slovenian Ethnographic Museum and other sights in Metelkova, north of downtown).

Plenty of good day trips are a short distance from Ljubljana. With a second day, visit Lake Bled (see next chapter), or head for one of the two impressive caves (Škocjan or Postojna) and nearby sights in the Karst region south of the city (see the Karst chapter).

Ljubljana is sleepy on Sundays (virtually all shops are closed and the produce market is quiet, but museums are generally open, a modest flea market stretches along the riverfront, and the TI's walking tour still runs). The city is also relatively quiet in August, when the students are on break and many locals head to beach resorts. They say that in August, even homeless people go to the coast.

Orientation to Ljubljana

Ljubljana's central zone is compact, and with a little wandering, you'll quickly get the hang of it. The Ljubljanica River—lined with cafés, restaurants, and a buzzing outdoor market—bisects the city, making a 90-degree turn around the base of a castle-topped hill. Most sights are either along or just a short walk from the river. Visitors enjoy the distinctive bridges that span the Ljubljanica, including the landmark Triple Bridge (Tromostovje) and pillared Cobblers' Bridge (Čevljarski Most)—both designed by Jože Plečnik. Between these two is a plain bridge (with great views) called Brv (roughly, "simple footbridge"). The center of Ljubljana is Prešeren Square, watched over by a big statue of Slovenia's national poet, France Prešeren.

I've organized the sights in this chapter based on which side of the river they're on: the east (castle) side of the river, which is where Ljubljana began and has more medieval charm; and the west (Prešeren Square) side of the river, which has a more Baroque/Art Nouveau feel and most of the urban sprawl. At the northern edge of the tourist's Ljubljana is the train station and Metelkova museum and nightlife zone; at the southern edge are the garden district of Krakovo and the Jože Plečnik House; and at the western edge is Tivoli Park.

Ljubljana's Two Big Ps: You'll hear the following two easy-to-confuse names constantly during your visit. Mind your Ps, and your visit to Ljubljana becomes more meaningful: **Jože Plečnik** (YOH-zheh PLAYCH-neek, 1872-1957) is the architect who shaped Ljubljana, designing virtually all of the city's most important landmarks. For more information, see page 570. **France Prešeren** (FRAHN-tseh preh-SHAY-rehn, 1800-1849) is Slovenia's greatest poet and the namesake of Ljubljana's main square.

TOURIST INFORMATION

Ljubljana's helpful, businesslike TI has a useful website (www.visitljubljana.com) and two branches: at the **Triple Bridge,** across from Prešeren Square (daily June-Sept 8:00-21:00, Oct-May 8:00-19:00, Stritarjeva 1, tel. 01/306-1215); and at the upper corner of the **market** (with bikes to rent and information about the rest of Slovenia; June-Sept daily 8:00-21:00; Oct-May Mon-Fri 8:00-19:00, Sat-Sun 9:00-17:00; Krekov trg 10, tel. 01/306-4575). At either TI, pick up a pile of free resources, including the big city map, the *Tourist Guide,* and the monthly events guide.

The **Ljubljana Tourist Card,** which includes access to public transportation and covers entry to many city museums as well as the TIs' walking tours and boat trips, could save busy sightseers some money (€23/24 hours, €30/48 hours, €35/72 hours).

ARRIVAL IN LJUBLJANA

By Train: Ljubljana's modern, user-friendly train station (Železniška Postaja) is at the northern edge of the city center. Emerging from the passage up to track 1a, turn right and walk under the long canopy to find the yellow arrivals hall. Everything is well-signed in English, including the handy train-information office (with useful handouts outlining journeys to several domestic and international destinations), lockers, and—near the front of the station—a big **ticket office** with clearly marked ticket windows and an **ATM.** Arrivals are *prihodi,* departures are *odhodi,* and track is *tir.*

You can **walk** to any of my recommended hotels within about 20 minutes (often less). To reach Prešeren Square at the city's center, leave the arrivals hall to the right and walk a long block along the busy Trg Osvobodilne Fronte (or "Trg O.F." for short, with the bus station in the middle). After passing the bus stalls, turn left across Trg O.F. and go down Miklošičeva, at the building with the round, red-brick columns. This takes you past some of Ljubljana's most appealing architecture to Prešeren Square.

Unscrupulous **taxis** crouch in front of the station, waiting to spring on unsuspecting tourists. The fair metered rate to any of my recommended hotels is around €3 (maybe up to €4-5 in heavy traffic or after hours). But, because the city refuses to regulate taxi tariffs, train-station taxis uniformly charge exorbitant rates—generally around €3-5 per kilometer (plus an extra fee of around €2-3 for bags). Simply put, it's impossible to hail a taxi on the street in front of the station and get anything resembling a fair fare. To avoid giving these crooks the satisfaction, call for a taxi that charges fair rates (tel. 080-1190, 01/511-2314, or 01/520-9704). Taking just a few more minutes to wait for your cab could easily save you €10 or more. For more on taxis—and how to avoid rip-offs—see "Getting Around Ljubljana—By Taxi," later.

By Bus: Ljubljana's bus station (Autobusna Postaja) is a low-profile building (with ticket windows, a bakery, and newsstands) in

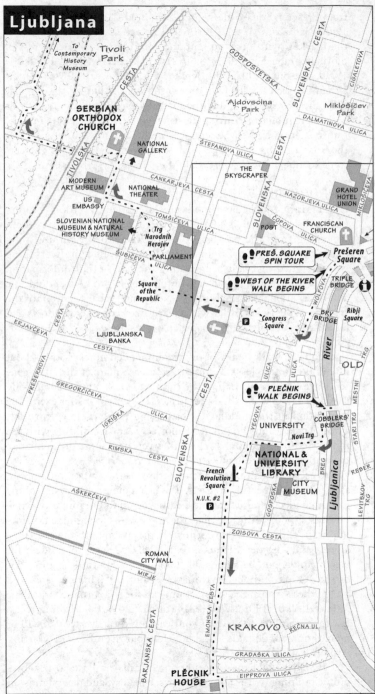

Ljubljana

To Contemporary History Museum

Tivoli Park

GOSPOSVETSKA

SLOVENSKA   CESTA

CIGALETOVA

SERBIAN ORTHODOX CHURCH

Ajdovscina Park

Miklošičev Park

NATIONAL GALLERY

ŠTEFANOVA   ULICA

DALMATINOVA   ULICA

CESTA

TIVOLSKA

MODERN ART MUSEUM

US EMBASSY

NATIONAL THEATER

CANKARJEVA   CESTA

THE SKYSCRAPER

SLOVENSKA

NAZORJEVA   ULICA

GRAND HOTEL UNION

MIKLOŠIČEVA

SLOVENIAN NATIONAL MUSEUM & NATURAL HISTORY MUSEUM

TOMŠIČEVA   ULICA

Trg Narodnih Herojev

POST

ČOPOVA   ULICA

FRANCISCAN CHURCH

ŠUBIČEVA   ULICA

PARLIAMENT

PREŠ. SQUARE SPIN TOUR

Prešeren Square

WEST OF THE RIVER WALK BEGINS

WOLFOVA

TRIPLE BRIDGE

Square of the Republic

Congress Square

BRV BRIDGE

Ribji Square

ERJAVČEVA   CESTA

CESTA

LJUBLJANSKA BANKA

River

OLD

MESTNI TRG

PREŠERNOVA

GREGORČIČEVA   ULICA

PLEČNIK WALK BEGINS

IGRIŠKA   ULICA

VEGOVA

University

COBBLERS BRIDGE

STARI TRG

RIMSKA   CESTA

Novi Trg

NATIONAL & UNIVERSITY LIBRARY

BREG

REBER

AŠKERČEVA

SLOVENSKA   CESTA

French Revolution Square

N.U.K. #2

CITY MUSEUM

GOSPOSKA

Ljubljanica

LEVITKOV TRG

ZOISOVA   CESTA

ROMAN CITY WALL

MIRJE

EMONSKA   CESTA

KRAKOVO

REČNA UL.

BARJANSKA   CESTA

GRADAŠKA   ULICA

PLEČNIK HOUSE

EIPRROVA   ULICA

LJUBLJANA

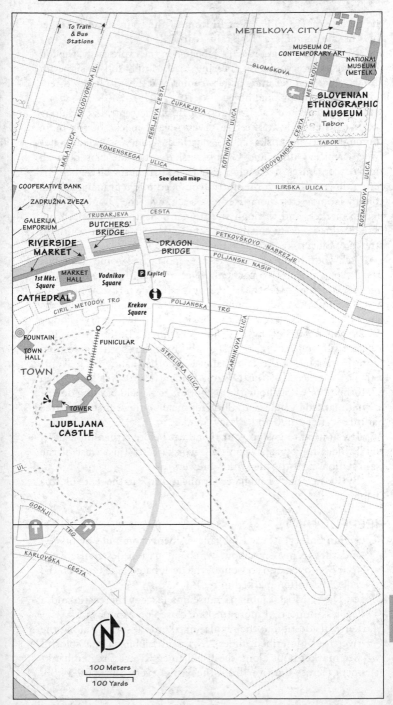

the middle of Trg O.F., right in front of the train station. To get into the city center, see "By Train," earlier.

By Car: As you approach Ljubljana on the expressway, the toll road ends. Once you're on the ring road, simply follow signs for *Center*. Once you get into the city center, you'll begin to see directional signs to individual hotels.

Ljubljana is not car-friendly; much of the central zone along the river is entirely traffic-free. Even several blocks of the main thoroughfare, Slovenska cesta—north of Congress Square, between Šubičeva ulica and Gosposvetska cesta—are closed to all traffic except buses. To reach the southern part of the city when entering downtown from the north, you need to circumnavigate the core by looping east along Resljeva cesta, over the Dragon Bridge by the market, and through the tunnel beneath the castle; from here, Karlovška cesta cuts back west over the river to the southern stretch of Slovenska cesta.

Ask your hotel about parking—most have some available, usually for a price. Two particularly central (and expensive) parking lots are the one beneath **Congress Square** (€1.20/hour for first 3 hours, then €2.40/hour, or €1.80/hour overnight) and the one called **N.U.K. #2,** near the National and University Library (€1.20/hour 7:00-19:00, €1.80/hour overnight). Both of these lots are accessible on Slovenska cesta only from the south—if coming from the north, see directions above. Another handy lot is **Kapitelj,** just southeast of the Dragon Bridge (€1.90/first hour, then €2.40/hour, or €1.50/hour 18:00-6:00). Legal, paid parking downtown is marked by blue lines (look for meters); these spaces are free Saturdays after 13:00 and all day Sunday.

If you need to gas up your rental car before returning it here, you'll find a huge gas station on Tivolska cesta (just west of the train station, near the big Union brewery).

By Plane: See "Ljubljana Connections," at the end of this chapter.

HELPFUL HINTS

Pedestrian Safety: Many Ljubljana residents commute by bike—and they're not shy about whizzing past pedestrians. Keep your eyes open and stay out of the designated bike lanes on the sidewalks (often marked in red).

Closed Days: Most Ljubljana museums (except the castle and a few less-important museums) are closed on Mondays.

Markets: In addition to the regular **market** that sprawls along the riverfront (described under "Sights in Ljubljana"), a colorful **flea market** hops along the Ljubljanica River's Breg embankment (across the river from the castle) every Sun 8:00-14:00.

On summer Saturdays, there's also a lively and colorful **arts and handicrafts market** in the same place (Sat 8:00-14:00).

Internet Access: The city's **WiFree** program—with Wi-Fi hotspots near Prešeren Square and along the river—lets you get online free for up to an hour. Pick up the brochure at the TI (you'll be texted a code to enter).

Post Office: The main post office *(pošta)* is in a beautiful yellow Art Nouveau building a block up Čopova from Prešeren Square, at the intersection with Slovenska cesta (Mon-Fri 8:00-19:00, Sat 8:00-12:00, closed Sun).

Laundry: The handiest option is **Emonec Launderette,** with self-service machines across the courtyard from the couldn't-be-more-central Hotel Emonec (described on page 581); this is a convenient spot to tumble-dry your undies while exploring (€5/load wash and dry, daily 16:00-20:00, Wolfova 12, tel. 01/200-1520). **Hostel Celica** also has self-service laundry—but it has only one machine, and hostel guests have priority (€8/load, not very central at Metelkova 8). For pricey full service, try **Tekstilexpress,** between the city center and Tivoli Park (€4.80/kilo, figure about €20-25 for a full load, takes 24 hours, Mon-Fri 7:00-19:00, Sat 9:00-13:00, closed Sun, Cankarjeva 10B, tel. 01/252-7354).

Car Rental: Handy options include **Hertz** (Trdinova 9, tel. 01/434-0147, www.hertz.si), **Europcar** (in City Hotel at Dalmatinova 15, mobile 031-382-052, www.europcar.si), **Avis** and **Budget** (both in Grand Hotel Union at Miklošičeva 3; Avis—tel. 01/241-7340, www.avis.si; Budget—tel. 01/421-7340, www.budget.si), and **Sixt** (at the train station, tel. 01/234-4650).

Best Views: The Skyscraper's observation deck offers the best views in town (see page 565). Views from the castle are nearly as good. At street level, my favorite views are from the bridge called Brv (between the Triple and Cobblers' bridges), especially at night. On sunny days, the colorful architecture on and near Prešeren Square pops, and you'll take photos like crazy along the river promenade.

GETTING AROUND LJUBLJANA

By Bus: Virtually all of Ljubljana's sights are easily accessible by foot. And using the buses is a bit of a headache: First, you have to buy a plastic "Urbana" card for €2, which you then load with credit to pay for rides (you can't pay the driver). A ride costs €1.20 (valid for up to 90 minutes, card shareable by up to three people). Buy the card at the TI, where you can return it to reclaim your €2 at the end of your trip. Transit info: www.lpp.si.

By Taxi: Always call for a cab, or you'll get ripped off. Because cabbies can legally charge whatever they want, even if they use the meter you'll still pay way too much. Legitimate taxis usually start at about €1.50, and then charge €1 per kilometer. But because city leaders refuse to regulate taxi tariffs, many unscrupulous cabbies (including all of those who wait at the train station) legally charge far more, and tack on bogus additional "surcharges." Crooked cabbies are a big problem in Ljubljana, but you can avoid this headache entirely by always calling a reputable taxi company instead of hailing one on the street. If you do this, Ljubljana is a fantastic taxi town with very affordable rates—a ride within the city center (such as from the station to a hotel) should run only a few euros, generally less than €5. Good companies include **Metro Taxi** (tel. 080-1190 or 041-240-200), **Laguna** (tel. 01/511-2314), or **Intertours** (tel. 01/520-9704). Don't be intimidated—dispatchers speak English, and your hotel, restaurant, or the TI can call a cab for you.

By Bike: Ljubljana is a cyclist's delight, with lots of well-marked bike lanes. It's easiest to rent bikes at the market square TI (€2/2 hours, €8/day; see "Tourist Information," earlier). Like many European cities, Ljubljana has a subsidized borrow-a-bike program (called BicikeLJ) with 30 locations around the city center. Once you register online with a credit card (€1 fee for a weekly subscription), rides are free or very cheap (free for the first hour, €1 for the second, €2 for the third, and so on). If you're planning on doing lots of biking, it's worth the hassle to sign up (http://en.bicikelj.si).

By Shuttle Bus: After Ljubljana pedestrianized much of its downtown core a few years back, the natives began to squawk about the hassle of getting around without a car. To mollify critics, the city subsidizes a network of green electric carts, called **Kavalir,** which anyone (even tourists) can flag down or call to take them anywhere within the pedestrian zone...for free. Just wave one down and tell them where you want to go (or phone them—April-Oct call 031-666-331 or 031-666-332; Nov-March call 031-666-299).

Tours in Ljubljana

To help you appreciate Ljubljana, taking a walking tour—either through the TI or by hiring your own local guide—is worth ▲▲.

Walking Tour

The TI organizes excellent two-hour guided town walks of Ljubljana in English, led by knowledgeable guides. In summer, the walk also includes either a trip up to the castle (by funicular or tourist train) or a 30-minute boat ride on the river. From April through September, there are three tours daily at 10:00, 14:00, and 17:00. From October through March, the walking tour goes daily at 11:00 (€10, or €9 if you pay at TI, meet at Town Hall around corner from Triple Bridge TI). They also offer a variety of other tours, including a food tour, a torchlight tour of Roman ruins, a Town Hall tour, and so on—get details at the TI.

Local Guides

Having an expert show you around his or her hometown for two hours for €70 has to be the best value in town. **Marijan Krišković,** who leads tours for me throughout Europe, is an outstanding guide (mobile 040-222-739, kriskovic@yahoo.com). **Barbara Jakopič,** thoughtful and extremely knowledgeable, also leads my tours (mobile 040-530-870, b_lucky2@yahoo.com). **Minka Kahrič,** who's traveled to the North Pole, also leads tours closer to home—including walks around Ljubljana and excursions into the countryside (€70/2-hour walking tour; driving: €100/up to 4 hours, €140/up to 8 hours; mobile 041-805-962, polarnimedo@yahoo.com). You can also book a guide through the TI (arrange at least 24 hours in advance).

Boat Cruise

Because Ljubljana is a small town that's easily seen on foot, a boat trip on the Ljubljanica River is more romantic than informative. You have two options for your one-hour cruise (weather permitting): with English commentary from a live guide (€10, 2/day in summer, departs from near the Triple Bridge—about one block along the embankment away from the market, get details from TI), or unguided (€8, may have audioguides, 2-3/hour in summer 10:00-20:00, operated by various companies and from various docks—they'll approach you as you walk past).

Excursions from Ljubljana

Many worthwhile sights near Ljubljana are tricky to reach by public transportation. To hit several efficiently in one day, join an excursion. Three relatively well-established outfits are **Roundabout** (their one-day "Karst and Coast Mystery" tour takes you to Predjama Castle, Škocjan Caves, Lipica, and Piran for €49 plus admission to the caves and an optional wine tasting; www.roundabout.si; their "off the beaten track" tours delve deeper into local culture), **Slovenia Explorer** (their ambitious "Slovenia in 1 Day" trip visits Lake Bled, Postojna Caves, and Predjama Castle for €119; www.slovenia-explorer.com), and **Nature Adventures** (focused on active trips including rafting, paragliding, skydiving, and horseback riding; www.adventures-nature.com). For multiday trips around the country, check out the **Loopyslovenia** hop-on, hop-off bus service (www.loopyslovenia.com).

Prešeren Square Spin Tour

The heart of Ljubljana is the people-friendly, traffic-free Prešeren Square (Prešernov trg, rated ▲▲), which is described in this self-guided spin tour.

The city's meeting point is the large **statue of France Prešeren,** Slovenia's greatest poet, whose works include the lyrics to the Slovenian national anthem (and whose silhouette adorns Slovenia's €2 coin). The statue shows Prešeren, an important catalyst of 19th-century Slovenian nationalism, being inspired from above by a Muse. This statue provoked a scandal and outraged the bishop when it went up a century ago—a naked woman sharing the square with a church! To ensure that nobody could be confused about the woman's intentions, she's conspicuously depicted with typical Muse accessories: a laurel branch and a cloak. Even so, for the first few years citizens covered  the scandalous statue with a tarp each night. And the model who posed for the Muse was so disgraced that no one in Slovenia would hire her—so she emigrated to South America and never returned.

Stand at the base of the statue to get oriented. The bridge crossing the Ljubljanica River is one of Ljubljana's top landmarks, Jože

Plečnik's **Triple Bridge** (Tromostovje). The middle (widest) part of this bridge already existed, but Plečnik added the two side spans to more efficiently funnel the six streets of traffic on this side of the bridge to the one street on the other side. The bridge's Venetian vibe is intentional: Plečnik recognized that Ljubljana, located midway between Venice and then-capital Vienna, is itself a bridge between the Italian and Germanic worlds. Across the bridge are the TI, WCs, ATMs, market and cathedral (to the left), and the Town Hall (straight ahead).

Now turn 90 degrees to the right, and look down the first street after the riverbank. Find the rose-colored woman in the picture frame on the second floor of the first yellow house. This is **Julija,** the unrequited love of Prešeren's life. Tour guides spin romantic tales about how the couple met. But the truth is far less exciting: He was a teacher in her father's house when he was in his 30s and she was 4. Later in life, she inspired him from afar—as she does now, from across the square—but they never got together. She may have been his muse, but when it came to marriage, she opted for wealth and status.

When Ljubljana was hit by an earthquake in 1895, locals took the opportunity (using an ample rebuilding fund from the Aus-tro-Hungarian Empire) to remake

their city in style. Today Ljublja-na—especially the streets around this square—is an architecture-lover's paradise. The **Hauptmann House,** to the right of Julija, was the only building on the square to survive the quake. A few years later, the owner redecorated it in the then-trendy Viennese Art Nouveau style you see today, using bright colors (since his family sold dyes). All that remains of the original structure is the little Baroque balcony above the entrance.

Just to the right of the Hauptmann House is a car-sized **model** of the city center—helpful for orientation. The street next to it (with the McDonald's) is **Čopova,** once the route of Ljubljana's Sunday promenade. A century ago, locals would put on their Sun-day best and stroll from here to Tivoli Park, listening to musicians and dropping into cafés along the way. Plečnik called it the "lifeline of the city," connecting the green lungs of the park to this urban center. Through the 20th century, this route became less pedestri-an-friendly, as Slovenska cesta and railroad tracks were both laid across it. Things are getting better with the closure of Slovenska to all traffic except buses, but Ljubljana's best evening *paseo* thrives along the river from the Triple Bridge all the way up the river.

Continue looking to the right, past the big, pink landmark Franciscan Church of St. Mary. Next door, the characteristic glass

awning marks **Galerija Empo-rium**—the first big post-quake department store, today govern-ment-protected. At the top of the building is Mercury, god of com-merce, watching over the square that has been Ljubljana's commer-cial heart since the city began. (If you look carefully, you can see the mustachioed face of the building's owner hiding in the folds of cloth by Mercury's left foot.) Since this area was across the river from medieval Ljubljana (beyond the town's limits...and the long arm of its tax collector), it was the best place to buy and sell goods. Today this sumptuously restored building houses a top-end fashion mall, making it the heart of Lju-

Ljubljana at a Glance

▲▲▲**People-Watching** Ljubljana's single best activity is sitting at an outdoor café along the river and watching the vivacious, stylish, fun-loving Slovenes strut their stuff. **Hours:** 24/7.

▲▲**Riverside Market** Lively market area in the Old Town with produce, clothing, and souvenirs. **Hours:** Best in the morning, especially Sat; market hall open Mon-Fri 7:00-16:00, Sat 7:00-14:00, closed Sun. See page 550.

▲▲**Serbian Orthodox Church of Sts. Cyril and Methodius** Beautifully decorated house of worship giving insight into the Orthodox faith. **Hours:** Daily 8:00-19:00. See page 563.

▲▲**National and University Library** Jože Plečnik's pièce de résistance, with an intriguing facade, piles of books, and a bright reading room. **Hours:** Main staircase open Mon-Fri 8:00-20:00, Sat 9:00-14:00, closed Sun; student reading room open to the public only mid-July-mid-Aug Mon-Sat 14:00-18:00. See page 567.

▲▲**Jože Plečnik House** Final digs of the famed hometown architect who shaped so much of Ljubljana, explained by an enthusiastic guide. **Hours:** Tue-Sun 10:00-18:00, English tours begin at

bljana's boutique culture. Step inside for a glimpse at the grand staircase.

The street between Galerija Emporium and the pink church is **Miklošičeva cesta,** which connects Prešeren Square to the train station. When Ljubljana was rebuilding after the 1895 earthquake, town architects and designers envisioned this street as a showcase of its new, Vienna-inspired Art Nouveau image.

Up Miklošičeva cesta and on the left is the prominent **Grand Hotel Union,** with a stately domed spire on the corner. When these buildings were designed, Prague was the cultural capital of the Slavic world. The new look of Ljubljana paid homage to "the golden city of a hundred spires" (and copied Prague's romantic image). The city actually had a law for several years that new corner buildings had to have these spires. Even the trees you'll see around town were part of the vision. When the architect Plečnik designed the Ljubljanica River embankments a generation later, he planted tall, pointy poplar trees and squat, rounded willows—imitating the spires and domes of Prague.

Detour a block up Miklošičeva cesta to see two more architec-

the top of each hour, last tour departs at 17:00, closed Mon. See page 569.

▲▲Slovenian Ethnographic Museum Engaging, well-presented collection celebrating Slovenian culture. **Hours:** Tue-Sun 10:00-18:00, closed Mon. See page 571.

▲Cathedral Italian Baroque interior and bronze doors with intricate, highly symbolic designs. **Hours:** Open long hours daily but closed 12:00-15:00. See page 554.

▲Ljubljana Castle Tower with good views and so-so 3-D film. **Hours:** Grounds open daily April-Sept 9:00-23:00, Oct-March 10:00-21:00; castle open daily June-Sept 9:00-21:00, April-May and Oct 9:00-20:00, Nov 10:00-19:00, Dec-March 10:00-18:00. See page 557.

▲Contemporary History Museum Baroque mansion in Tivoli Park, with exhibit highlighting Slovenia's last 100 years. **Hours:** Tue-Sun 10:00-18:00, closed Mon. See page 564.

▲City Museum of Ljubljana Modern, high-tech exhibit covering the city's history. **Hours:** Tue-Sun 10:00-18:00, Thu until 21:00, closed Mon. See page 566.

---

tural gems of that era (across from the Grand Hotel Union): First is a Secessionist building—marked **Zadružna Zveza**—with classic red, blue, and white colors (for the Slovenian flag). Next is the

noisy, pink, zigzagged **Cooperative Bank.** The bank was designed by Ivan Vurnik, an ambitious Slovenian architect who wanted to invent a distinctive national style after World War I, when the Habsburg Empire broke up and Eastern Europe's nations were proudly emerging for the first time.

Prešeren Square is the perfect springboard to explore the rest of Ljubljana. Now that you're oriented, visit some of the areas listed next.

Sights in Ljubljana

Ljubljana is bursting with well-presented, we-try-harder museums celebrating Slovenian history and culture. These include the Slovenian History Exhibition at the castle, the City Museum of Ljubljana, and the Contemporary History Museum in Tivoli Park. As these are similar and largely overlapping, if you get museumed out easily, just pick the one that's handiest to your sightseeing plan.

THE MARKET AND OLD TOWN

The castle (east) side of the river is the city's most colorful and historic quarter, packed with Old World ambience.

▲▲Riverside Market (Tržnice)

In Ljubljana's thriving Old Town market, big-city Slovenes enjoy buying directly from the producer. Prices go down as the day gets late and as the week goes on. The market, worth an amble anytime, is best on Saturday mornings, when the townspeople take their time wandering the stalls. In this tiny capital of a tiny country, you may even see the president searching for the perfect melon.

➲ **Self-Guided Walk:** Begin your walk through the market at the Triple Bridge (and TI). The riverside **colonnade,** which echoes

the long-gone medieval city wall, was designed by (who else?) Jože Plečnik. This first stretch—nearest the Triple Bridge—is good for souvenirs: woodcarvings, replica painted frontboards from beehives, honey products (including honey brandy), and lots of colorful candles (bubbly Marta will gladly paint a special message on your candle for no extra charge). For lots more shopping tips—here and nearby—see "Shopping in Ljubljana," later.

Farther in, the market is almost all local, and the colonnade is populated by butchers, bakers, fishermen, and lazy cafés. Peek down at the actual river and see how the architect wanted the town and river to connect. The lower arcade (which you can access directly from the Triple Bridge or by going down the spiral staircase by the beehive panels) is a people zone, with public WCs, inviting cafés, and a stinky fish market *(ribarnica)* offering a wide variety. The recommended restaurant just below, **Ribca,** serves fun fishy plates, beer, and coffee with great riverside seating.

Across from the stairs that lead down into the fish market, about where the souvenir stands end, you reach the first small market square. On your right, notice the 10-foot-tall concrete **cone.** Plečnik wanted to make Ljubljana the "Athens of the North" and imagined a huge cone-shaped national acropolis—a complex for government, museums, and culture. This ambitious plan didn't make it off the drawing board, but part of Plečnik's Greek idea came true: this marketplace, based on an ancient Greek *agora*. Plečnik's cone still captures the Slovenes' imaginations...and adorns Slovenia's €0.10 coin.

At the top of this square, you'll find the 18th-century **cathedral** standing on the site of a 13th-century Romanesque church (check out its finely decorated doors—and, if they're open, go inside; for a complete description, see later).

The building at the end of the first market square is the seminary palace. In the basement is a **market hall** *(pokrita tržnica),* with vendors selling cheeses, meats, baked goods, dried fruits, nuts, and other goodies (Mon-Fri 7:00-16:00, Sat 7:00-14:00, closed Sun). This place is worth a graze—walk all the way through. Most merchants are happy to give you a free sample (point to what you want, and say *probat, prosim*—"a taste, please").

Leaving the market hall at the opposite end, turn left to reach the modern **Butchers' Bridge.** Jože Plečnik designed a huge roofed bridge to be built here, but—like so many of his designs—the plans were scuttled. Decades later, aware of Plečnik's newfound touristic currency, some town politicians dusted off the old plans and proposed building the bridge. The project stalled for years until the arrival of Mayor Zoran Janković, who swiftly constructed this modern version of the bridge. While it looks nothing like Plečnik's original plans, the bridge kept the old name and has been embraced by the community (there's a handy public WC down below on the lower level). The sculptures on the bridge, by local artist Jakov Brdar, were originally intended to be temporary—but people loved them, so they stayed. (The wild-eyed, wild-bearded Brdar often hangs out near the bridge, asking passersby how they like his creations.) Notice the mournful pose of the Adam and Eve statues (being evicted from the Garden of Eden) at the market end of the bridge. And don't miss the bizarre smaller sculptures along the railing—such as the ones that look like mischievous lizards breaking out of their eggs. Almost as soon as it was built, the bridge's railings were covered with padlocks—part of the recent Europe-wide craze for young couples to commemorate their love by locking a padlock to a bridge railing. But all those locks put too much strain on the railing—they are regularly cut off, soon to be replaced by new ones.

Sprawling up from the bridge is the **main market square,** packed with produce and clothing stands. (The colorful flower market hides behind the market hall.) The vendors in the row near-

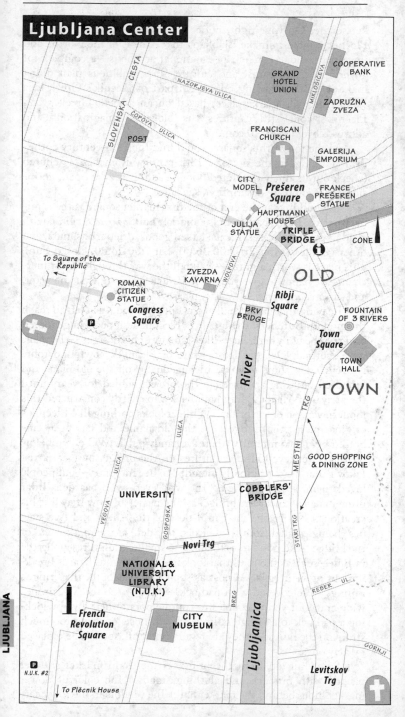

Ljubljana Center

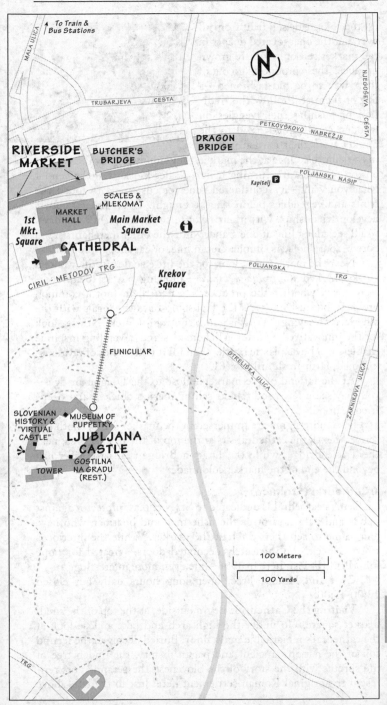

To Train & Bus Stations

MALA ULICA

TRUBARJEVA CESTA

NJEGOŠEVA CESTA

PETKOVŠKOVO NABREŽJE

DRAGON BRIDGE

RIVERSIDE MARKET

BUTCHER'S BRIDGE

POLJANSKI NASIP

Kapitelj P

SCALES & MLEKOMAT

1st Mkt. Square

MARKET HALL

Main Market Square

CATHEDRAL

CIRIL - METODOV TRG

POLJANSKA TRG

Krekov Square

FUNICULAR

STRELIŠKA ULICA

ŽARNIKOVA ULICA

SLOVENIAN HISTORY & "VIRTUAL CASTLE"

MUSEUM OF PUPPETRY

LJUBLJANA CASTLE

TOWER

GOSTILNA NA GRADU (REST.)

100 Meters

100 Yards

TRG

est the colonnade sell fruit from all over, but the ones located deeper in the market sell only locally grown produce. These producers go out of their way to be old-fashioned—a few of them still follow the tradition of pushing their veggies on wooden carts (called *cizas*) to the market from their garden patches  in the suburbs. Once at the market, they simply display their goods on top of their cart, turning it into a sales kiosk. Tell the vendor what you want—it's considered rude for customers to touch the fruits and vegetables before they're bought. Over time, shoppers develop friendships with their favorite producers. On busy days, you'll see a long line at one stand, while the other merchants stand bored. Your choice is simple: Get in line, or eat subpar produce.

Near the market hall, look for the little **scales** in the wooden kiosks marked *Kontrolna Tehtnica*—allowing buyers to immediately check whether the producer cheated them (not a common problem, but just in case). The Habsburg days left locals with the old German saying, "Trust is good; control is better." Nearby, look for the innovative "Nonstop Mlekomat" stand, a vending machine that lets you buy a plastic bottle, then fill it with a liter of raw, unskimmed, farm-fresh milk for €1.

At the far end of the market—close to the Dragon Bridge—you may see a few **food trucks** selling roasted chicken and deep-fried seafood.

Two more sights are immersed in the market action (both described next); the cathedral sits at the top of the market area, near the Triple Bridge, while the Dragon Bridge spans the river just beyond the end of the market colonnade.

▲Cathedral (Stolnica)

Ljubljana's cathedral is dedicated to St. Nicholas, protector against floods and patron saint of the fishermen and boatmen who have long come to sell their catch at the market. While the interior is worth a peek, the intricately decorated doors—created for Pope John Paul II's visit here in 1996—are even more interesting.

Cost and Hours: Free, open long hours daily but closed 12:00-15:00.

Visiting the Cathedral: Begin outside, at the top of the small market square. Go under the high arch and take a close look at the cathedral's remarkable **main door**. Buried deeply in the fecund soil of the nation's ancient and pagan history, the linden tree of life sprouts with the story of the Slovenes. The ceramic pots represent the original Roman settlement here. Just to the left, above

Zoran Janković

The latest chapter in Ljubljana's story has been written by its mayor, Zoran Janković. Sort of the Michael Bloomberg of Slovenia, this successful businessman transformed himself into a broadly supported mayor who is unafraid to pursue an ambitious civic agenda.

As chairman of the huge Mercator supermarket chain, Janković was famous for prowling around the front lines of his stores, micromanaging all the day-to-day business. After corporate political shuffling forced him out, Janković turned his attention to the municipal realm—and, in 2006, was elected mayor of Ljubljana in a landslide.

The people of this city had grown accustomed to well-intentioned but ineffectual leaders who would propose and then cancel ambitious projects. But Janković's no-nonsense follow-through finally made things happen. Project after project materialized, on time and under budget: the funicular to the castle, several new bridges (including the Butchers' Bridge at the market), the creation of quaintly cobbled traffic-free zones throughout almost the entire town center, the rejuvenation of miles of riverfront embankment for pedestrians, and closing a several-block stretch of one of Ljubljana's most heavily used downtown streets (Slovenska cesta) to all car traffic. The sweeping changes have had their critics, among them elderly people who can no longer easily drive to their homes in the now-traffic-free center. Janković has attempted to assuage them with free shuttle buses. Ultimately, most Ljubljanans are thrilled with the transformation of their city—he was reelected in another landslide in 2012. Janković embodies the ideal of how a progressive electorate can trust a capable leader to wisely invest public funds in urban-beautification projects that benefit the common good.

the tree, are the Byzantine missionaries Cyril and Methodius, who came here to convert the Slavs to Christianity in the ninth century. Just above, Crusaders and Ottomans do battle. Near the top, see the Slovenes going into the cave—entering the dark 20th century (World War I, World War II, and communism). At the top is Pope John Paul II (the first Slavic pontiff, who also oversaw the fall of communism). Below him are two men who are on track to becoming Slovenia's first saints; the one on the right is Frederic Baraga, a 19th-century bishop who became a missionary in Michigan and codified Chippewa grammar (notice the Native American relief on the book he's holding). In the upper right-hand corner is a sun, which has been shining since Slovenia gained its independence in 1991. Around back of the cathedral is a similar door, carved with images of the six 20th-century bishops of Ljubljana.

The cathedral's **interior** is stunning Italian Baroque. The transept is surrounded by sculptures of four bishops of Roman Ljubljana (when it was called Emona, or Aemon). Left of the main altar, notice the distinctive chair. This was designed by the very religious Jože Plečnik, whose brother was a priest here. Look up over the nave to enjoy the recently restored, gorgeous ceiling fresco.

▲Dragon Bridge (Zmajski Most)

The dragon has been the symbol of Ljubljana for centuries, ever since Jason (of Argonauts and Golden Fleece fame) supposedly

slew one in a nearby swamp. This is one of the few notable bits of Ljubljana architecture *not* by Plečnik (but by Jurij Zaninović, a fellow student of Vienna architect Otto Wagner). While the dragon is the star of this very photogenic Art Nouveau bridge, the bridge itself was officially dedicated to the 40th anniversary of Habsburg Emperor Franz Josef's reign (see the dates on the side: 1848-1888). Tapping into the emp's vanity got new projects funded—vital as the city rebuilt after the 1895 earthquake. But the Franz Josef name never stuck; those dragons are just too darn memorable.

From the Dragon Bridge, it's an easy funicular ride or steep hike up to Ljubljana Castle (described later). Or you can head back through the market to reach the Town Square and Old Town (see next), where I've narrated a self-guided shopping tour.

▲Town Square (Mestni Trg) and the Old Town

Ljubljana's Town Square, just across the Triple Bridge and up the street from Prešeren Square, is home to the **Town Hall** (Rotovž), highlighted by its clock tower and pillared loggia. Step inside the Renaissance courtyard to see paintings, artifacts, and a map of late 17th-century Ljubljana. Studying this map, notice how the river, hill, and wall worked together to fortify the town. Courtyards like this (but humbler) are hidden throughout the city. As rent in these old places is cheap, many such courtyards host funky and characteristic little businesses. Be sure to get off the main drag and poke into Ljubljana's nooks and crannies.

In the square between the Town Hall and the cathedral is a recent replica of the **Fountain of Three Carniolan Rivers,** inspired

in style and theme by Rome's many fountains. The figures with vases represent this region's three main rivers: Ljubljanica, Sava, and Krka. This is one of many works in town by Francesco Robba, an Italian who came to Ljubljana for a job, fell in love with a Slovene, and stayed here the rest of his life—decorating the city's churches with beautiful Baroque altars. At the nearby corner, check out the wild interior of the Nova KBM Bank, which looks more like a cutting-edge nightclub.

Now turn with your back to the fountain. You're staring down the single street that constitutes Ljubljana's Old Town. In the early 19th century, Ljubljana consisted mainly of this solitary main drag, running along the base of Castle Hill (plus a small "New Town" across the river). Stretching south from here are two other "squares"—Stari trg (Old Square) and Gornji trg (Upper Square)—which have long since grown together into one big, atmospheric promenade lined with quaint boutiques, great restaurants, and cafés. Virtually every house along this drag has a story to tell of a famous resident or infamous incident. As you walk, keep your eyes open for Ljubljana's mascot dragon—it's everywhere.

For a self-guided shopping stroll that runs the length of this delightful street—and highlights several fine shops en route—see "Shopping in Ljubljana," later.

▲Ljubljana Castle (Ljubljanski Grad)

The castle above town offers enjoyable views of Ljubljana and the surrounding countryside. There has probably been a settlement on

this site since prehistoric times, though the first true fortress here was Roman. The 12th-century version was gradually added on to over the centuries, until it fell into disrepair in the 17th century. Today's castle—rebuilt in the 1940s and renovated in the 1970s—is a hollow-feeling replica, lacking any sense of real history. However, in recent years they've filled this shell with four worthwhile attractions and some respectable restaurants. It also offers a fine view, looking out over Ljubljana's rooftops and to the Alps on the horizon. The castle is home to

LJUBLJANA

the Ljubljana Festival, with concerts throughout the summer (tel. 01/306-4293, www.ljubljanafestival.si).

Cost and Hours: The grounds are free to visit and open daily April-Sept 9:00-23:00, Oct-March 10:00-21:00. Tickets and hours for the history exhibition, film, castle tower, and puppetry museum change from year to year. Most likely, you can pay €7.50 (or €10 with the round-trip funicular) for admission to all four. To add an audioguide or a guided tour (described next), you'll pay a total of €10 (or €12 with the funicular). The attractions are open daily June-Sept 9:00-21:00, April-May and Oct 9:00-20:00, Nov 10:00-19:00, Dec-March 10:00-18:00, tel. 01/232-9994, www. ljubljanskigrad.si.

"Time Machine" Tours: Guides dressed as historical figures lead one-hour tours of the castle (€10 combo-ticket with castle sights, or €12 to add funicular; July-Sept 4/day, May-June 2/day, Oct-April 2/day Sat-Sun only, confirm schedule at information office or funicular ticket desk, tours depart from castle information center).

Getting to the Castle: A slick **funicular** whisks visitors to the top in a jiff (€2.20 one-way, €4 round-trip, also included in combo-tickets described above, runs every 10 minutes, 1-minute ride, daily April-Sept 9:00-23:00, Oct-March 10:00-21:00, catch it at Krekov trg—across the street from the market square TI). From the top, you'll find free WCs and a few easy flights of stairs up into the heart of the castle complex (or take the elevator). Another sweat-free route to the top is via the **tourist train** that leaves at the top of each hour (or more frequently with demand) from the street in front of the Town Hall (€4 round-trip, daily in summer 9:00-21:00, shorter hours off-season, doesn't run in snow or other bad weather). There are also two handy **trails** to the castle. The steeper-but-faster route begins near the Dragon Bridge: Find Študentovska lane, just past the statue of Vodnik in the market. This lane dead-ends at a gravel path, which you'll follow up to a fork. Turn left to zigzag up the steepest and fastest route, which deposits you just below the castle wall; from here, turn left again and curl around the wall to reach the main drawbridge. Slower but a bit less steep is Reber, just off Stari trg, a few blocks south of the Town Hall: Walk up to the top of Reber, and, at the dead end, turn right and start climbing up the stairs. From here on out, keep bearing left, then go right when you're just under the castle (follow *Grad* signs).

Visiting the Castle: The castle's information office is on the courtyard above the top of the funicular. Across the way are the well-stocked Rustika gift shop and three eateries (the fancy Strelec; Gradska Kavana, the "castle café"; and the recommended Gostilna na Gradu, with traditional Slovenian cuisine). The upper floors house two wedding halls—Ljubljana's most popular places to get married (free for locals).

Most of the sights worth seeing at the castle are in the opposite wing, clustered around the base of the tallest tower. As you face the tower, the entrance to the history exhibit is to the left, while the "Virtual Castle" film and tower climb itself are to the right. The Museum of Puppetry is near the information office.

The **Slovenian History Exhibition** offers a concise but engaging overview of this little country's story. As you enter, ask to borrow the free audioguide, then head downstairs and work your way up. Dark display cases light up when you approach, revealing actual artifacts, video clips, and touchscreens with more information. A unique feature of the museum is that you're invited to touch replicas of important historic items (in many cases, the originals are in other Ljubljana museums). Don't miss the top floor of the exhibit (go up the glassed-in staircase), which is the most interesting—covering the tumultuous 20th century. You'll learn about topics ranging from the battlefields of World War I, to the creation of the first Yugoslavia, to the fascist occupation and harrowing Italian-run concentration camps of World War II, to the cult of personality around Partisan war hero-turned-Yugoslav president Tito, to Slovenia's bid for independence.

Entering the door to the right of the tower, you'll first find the small **penitentiary** exhibit, recalling the post-Napoleonic era, when the castle was converted to a prison. It saw the most action during World War I, when it housed political prisoners (including the beloved Slovenian writer Ivan Cankar) and POWs. Modest exhibits inside actual former cells describe the history and list the names of past inmates.

If you head downstairs from the entrance, you'll find a Gothic **chapel** with Baroque paintings of St. George (Ljubljana's patron saint, the dragon-slayer) and coats of arms of the various aristocratic families that have called this castle home.

Heading up the stairs, you'll find the informative, entertaining, and nicely animated **"Virtual Castle" film,** in which Ljubljana's mascot dragon describes this hill's layers of history (12 minutes, plays all day on the half-hour; often in English, but otherwise borrow English headset).

Finally, climb the 92 spiral steps up to the **castle tower,** with one of the best views in town.

Don't miss the oddly fascinating **Museum of Puppetry** (ride up the elevator inside the gift shop near the castle information office). This traces the history of puppetry as an art form, which flourished in the Modernist milieu of early-20th-century Ljubljana. You'll step into a surreal world of marionettes, shadow puppets, and other creations. This is not a goofy attraction for kids; in fact, some of the puppets are quite grotesque and disturbing. You'll see marionettes of Adolf Hitler and Partisan troops, watch grainy footage of famous puppet masters (including Milan Klemenčič, who pioneered the form here in 1910), then climb up to the mezzanine and put on a show of your own.

Eating: Combine your visit to the castle with a meal at the recommended **Gostilna na Gradu,** with the best traditional Slovenian food in town (in the castle courtyard; described later, under "Eating in Ljubljana"). I'd skip the pricey and pretentious **Strelec** restaurant that offers little more than an overly complicated theme and menu.

THE MUSEUM ZONE AND TIVOLI PARK

The Prešeren Square (west) side of the river is the heart of modern Ljubljana, and home to several prominent squares and fine museums. These sights are listed roughly in order from Prešeren Square and can be linked to make an interesting walk.

• *Leave Prešeren Square in the direction the poet is looking, bear to your left (up Wolfova, by the picture of Julija), and walk a block to...*

Congress Square (Kongresni Trg)

This grassy, tree-lined square hosts big events. It's ringed by some of Ljubljana's most important buildings: the University headquarters, the Baroque Ursuline Church of the Holy Trinity, a classical mansion called the Kazina, and the Philharmonic Hall. The green belt at the heart of the square, called Park Zvezda ("Star Park") for its radiating paths, is fronted by several inviting cafés and restaurants; the recommended **Zvezda Kavarna** is a top spot for its local cakes and ice cream.

At the top end of the square, by the entry to a pedestrian underpass, a Roman sarcophagus sits under a gilded statue of a **Roman citizen**—a replica of a Roman tomb sculpture from 1,700 years ago, when this town was called Emona. The busy street above you has been the site of the main trading route through town since ancient Roman times. Information boards tell you more.

Take a few steps into the underpass, and look left to find the easy-to-miss **Chopin Passage** (Chopinov Prehod), which displays exposed parts of the original Roman-era road and a model of Emona in ancient times.

• *Continue the rest of the way through the underpass beneath Slovenska cesta, then walk straight through the gap in the Maxi shopping mall into the...*

▲Square of the Republic (Trg Republike)

This unusual plaza is ringed by an odd collection of buildings. While hardly quaint, the Square of the Republic gives you a good taste of a modern corner of Ljubljana. And it's historic—this is

where Slovenia declared its independence in 1991.

The **twin office towers** (with the world's biggest digital watch, flashing the date, time, and temperature) were designed by Plečnik's protégé, Edvard Ravnikar. As harrowing as these structures seem, imagine if the builders had followed the original plans—the towers would be twice as tall as they are now and connected by a bridge, representing the gateway to Ljubljana. These buildings were originally designed as the Slovenian parliament, but they were scaled back when Tito didn't approve (since it would have made Slovenia's parliament bigger than the Yugoslav parliament in Belgrade). Instead, the **Slovenian Parliament** is across the square, in the low-profile office building with the sculpted entryway. The carvings are in the Socialist Realist style, celebrating the noble Slovenian people conforming to communist ideals for the good of the entire society. Completing the square are a huge conference center (Cankarjev Dom, the white building behind the skyscrapers), a shopping mall, and some public art.

• *Just a block north, across the street and through the grassy park (Trg Narodni Herojev), you'll find the...*

Slovenian National Museum (Narodni Muzej Slovenije) and Slovenian Museum of Natural History (Prirodoslovni Muzej Slovenije)

These two museums share a single historic building facing a park behind the Parliament. They're both average but worth considering if you have a special interest or if it's a rainy day.

The **National Museum** occupies the ground floor, featuring a lapidarium with carved-stone Roman monuments and exhibits on Egyptian mummies. (Temporary exhibits are also on this level.) Upstairs and to the right are more exhibits of the National Museum, with archaeological findings ranging from old armor and pottery to the museum's two prized possessions: a fragment of a 45,000-year-old Neanderthal flute fashioned from a cave bear's femur—supposedly the world's oldest musical instrument; and the "figural situla," a beautifully decorated hammered-bronze bucket from the fifth century B.C. Embossed with scenes of everyday Iron Age life, this object has been a gold mine of information for archaeologists.

Upstairs and to the left is the **Natural History** exhibit, featuring the flora and fauna of Slovenia. You'll see partial skeletons of a mammoth and a cave bear, plenty of stuffed reptiles, fish, and birds, and an exhibit on "human fish" (*Proteus anguinus*—long, skinny, pale-pink, sightless salamanders unique to caves in this part of Europe).

Cost and Hours: €6 for National Museum, €4 for Natural History Museum, or €8.50 for both, some English descriptions, both open daily 10:00-18:00, Thu until 20:00, Prešernova 20, tel. 01/241-4400, www.nms.si and www.pms-lj.si.

• *At the far end of the building is a glassed-in annex displaying Roman stone monuments (free). Turning left around the museum building and walking one block, you'll see the...*

US Embassy

This pretty yellow chalet (with brown trim and a red roof, at Prešernova cesta 31) wins my vote for quaintest embassy building in the world. Resist the urge to snap a photo...those guards are all business.

• *Just up Prešernova cesta from the embassy are two decent but skippable art museums.*

National Gallery (Narodna Galerija)

This museum has three parts: European artists (in the new building), Slovenian artists (in the old building), and temporary exhibits. Find the work of Ivana Kobilca, a late 19th-century Slovenian Impressionist. Art lovers enjoy her self-portrait in *Summer*. If you're going to Bled, you can get a sneak preview with Marko Pernhart's huge panorama of the Julian Alps.

Cost and Hours: €5, special exhibits typically cost extra, permanent collection free first Sun of the month, open Tue-Sun 10:00-18:00, closed Mon; if main entrance at Cankarjeva 20 is closed for renovation, use the other entrance at the big glass box between two older buildings at Prešernova 24; tel. 01/241-5418, www.ng-slo.si.

Museum of Modern Art (Moderna Galerija Ljubljana)

Newly renovated, this museum has a permanent collection of modern and contemporary Slovenian artists, as well as temporary exhibits by both homegrown and international artists. To explore the "Continuities and Ruptures" permanent collection (aptly named for a place with such a fractured, up-and-down recent history), borrow the English floor plan and take a chronological spin through the 20th century. Unusual for a "modern" art museum is the room with Partisan art, with stiff, improvised, communist-style posters from the days when Tito and his crew were just a ragtag militia movement.

Cost and Hours: €5, ask about combo-ticket with contemporary branch at Metelkova—see page 573, Tue-Sun 10:00-18:00, Thu until 20:00 in July-Aug, closed Mon, Tomšičeva 14, tel. 01/241-6800, www.mg-lj.si.

• *By the busy road near the art museums, look for the distinctive Neo-Byzantine design (tall domes with narrow slits) of the...*

▲▲Serbian Orthodox Church of Sts. Cyril and Methodius

Ljubljana's most striking church interior isn't Catholic, but Orthodox. This church was built in 1936, soon after the Slovenes joined a political union with the Serbs.
Wealthy Slovenia attracted its poorer neighbors from the south—so it built this church for that community. Since 1991, the Serb population continues to grow, as people from the struggling corners of the former Yugoslavia flock to prosperous Slovenia. Its gorgeous interior—which feels closer to Moscow than to Rome—offers visitors a taste of this important faith.

Cost and Hours: Free, daily 8:00-19:00; divine liturgy Sun at 11:00, other days services at 8:30 and 18:00; Prešernova cesta 35, www.spc-ljubljana.si.

Visiting the Church: Step inside for the best glimpse of the Orthodox faith this side of Dubrovnik. The church is colorfully decorated without a hint of the 21st century, mirroring a very conservative religion. Many of the church's colorful frescoes are copies of famous frescoes that decorate medieval Serbian Orthodox monasteries throughout the Balkans. On the balcony (at the back of the nave), you'll see Cyrillic script that explains the history of the church. Notice that there are no pews, because worshippers stand throughout the service. On the left, find the little room with tubs of water, where the faithful light tall, skinny beeswax candles (purchased at the little window in the back corner). The painted screen, or iconostasis, is believed to separate our material world from the spiritual realm behind it. Ponder the fact that several centuries ago, before the Catholic Church began to adapt to a changing world, all Christians worshipped this way. For more on the Orthodox faith, see the sidebar on page 316.

• *On the other side of the busy street is...*

Tivoli Park (Park Tivoli)

This huge park, just west of the center, is where Slovenes relax on summer weekends. The easiest access is through the graffiti-covered underpass from Cankarjeva cesta (between the Serbian Orthodox Church and the Museum of Modern Art). As you emerge, the Neoclassical pillars leading down the promenade clue you in that this part of the park was designed by Jože Plečnik. Along this "main boulevard" of the park, various changing photographic exhibitions are displayed.

• *Aside from taking a leisurely stroll, the best thing to do in the park is visit the...*

▲Contemporary History Museum (Muzej Novejše Zgodovine)

In a Baroque mansion (Cekinov Grad) in Tivoli Park, a well-done exhibit called "Slovenians in the 20th Century" traces the last hundred years of Slovenia—essentially from the end of World War I to independence in 1991. Out front is a T-55 Yugoslav tank that was commandeered by the Slovenes during their war for independence. Inside, the ground floor displays temporary exhibits, and upstairs you'll find several rooms using models, dioramas, light-and-sound effects, and English explanations to creatively tell the story of one of Europe's youngest nations. While it's a little difficult to fully appreciate, the creativity and the spunky spirit of the place are truly enjoyable.

Cost and Hours: €3.50, permanent exhibit free first Sun of the month, guidebook-€5, open Tue-Sun 10:00-18:00, closed Mon, in Tivoli Park at Celovška cesta 23, tel. 01/300-9610, www. muzej-nz.si.

Getting There: The museum is a 20-minute walk from the center, best combined with a wander through Tivoli Park. The fastest approach: As you emerge from the Cankarjeva cesta underpass into the park, climb up the stairs, then turn right and go straight ahead for five minutes. You'll continue straight up the ramp, then turn left after the tennis courts and look for the big pink-and-white mansion on the hill.

Visiting the Museum: The exhibit begins at the dawn of the 20th century, during Slovenia's waning days as part of the Austro-Hungarian Empire. You'll walk through a simulated trench from the Soča Front, then learn about the creation of the post-World War I Kingdom of Serbs, Croats, and Slovenes (or, as this exhibit pointedly puts it, "Kingdom of Slovenes, Croats, and Serbs").

Your footfalls echo loudly as you enter the room describing Slovenia's WWII experience (ask them to start the 12-minute "multivision" wrap-around slideshow, with music and sound effects). You'll learn how during that war, Slovenia was divided between neighboring fascist powers Germany, Italy, and Hungary. Each one tried (but failed) to exert linguistic and cultural control over the people, hoping to eradicate the Slovenian national identity. Video screens show subtitled interviews with people who lived through those war years.

Passing through the ballroom, you reach the "Slovenia 1945-1960" exhibit, outlining both the good (modernization) and the bad (prison camps and secret police) of the early Tito years. Despite his ruthless early rule, Tito remains popular here; under his stern bust, page through the photo album of Tito's visits to Slovenia. Find the display of the country's former currencies. Examining the Yugoslav dinar, notice that the figureheads on that communist currency were generic, idealized workers, farmers, and other members of the proletariat...except for a few notable individuals (including Tito). Meanwhile, Slovenia's short-lived post-Yugoslav currency, the *tolar* (1991-2006, R.I.P.), featured artists and scientists rather than heads of state and generals.

The most evocative room has artifacts from the Slovenes' brave declaration of independence from a hostile Yugoslavia in 1991. The well-organized Slovenes had only to weather a 10-day skirmish to gain their freedom. It's chilling to think that at one point bombers were en route to level this gorgeous city. The planes were called back at the last minute, by a Yugoslav People's Army officer with allegiances to Slovenia.

• *Hungry? Straight ahead and down the stairs from the museum, look for the "Hot Horse" food kiosk, selling €4 horseburgers (no joke). A local institution, this is a popular place to get together with friends and neighbors. The giant, modern, blocky, light-blue building across the busy road is the Pivovarna Union—the brewery for Ljubljana's favorite beer.*

On your way back to the center, you could stop by...

▲The Skyscraper (Nebotičnik)

This 1933 building was the first skyscraper in Slovenia, for a time the tallest building in Central Europe, and one of the earliest European buildings that was clearly influenced by American architecture. Art Deco inside and out, it's a thrill for architecture fans and anyone who enjoys a great view—the top floor, which hosts a pricey restaurant, café, and observation deck, offers the best panorama of Ljubljana's skyline. Zip up in the elevator just to take a peek, or stay for a drink or meal.

There are three levels: The best is floor #12, where you can sit outside (or, in bad weather, head up the spiral stairs to the glassed-in terrace) and enjoy a drink with unobstructed views over the city and castle (€3 beer/wine/coffee, €5-8 cocktails, €5-7 light food). One floor below (#11) is the indoor club/lounge, with a similar menu. And on the next floor down (#10) is the restaurant, with pricey food (€10-19 main courses) and less-impressive views. The good-value €8 lunch deals are available in either place. I'd skip the restaurant and the club, and just grab a drink or snack up on the terrace.

Cost and Hours: Free to ride the elevator up for a peek, but you should buy at least a drink if you want to stick around; terrace and club open daily 9:00-very late; restaurant open Mon-Sat 12:00-21:00, closed Sun; 2 blocks from Prešeren Square at Štefanova 1, tel. 040-601-787, www.neboticnik.si.

• *A few blocks south, near several Jože Plečnik sights (see next section) at the river end of French Revolution Square, you'll find the...*

▲City Museum of Ljubljana (Mestni Muzej Ljubljana)

This thoughtfully presented museum, located in the recently restored Auersperg Palace, offers a high-tech, in-depth look at the story of this city. Though everything is well-described in English (and touchscreens provide even more information), a student on the museum's staff might be able to show you around if it's not too busy—ask.

Cost and Hours: €6, Tue-Sun 10:00-18:00, Thu until 21:00, closed Mon, kid-friendly, Gosposka 15, tel. 01/241-2510, www.mgml.si.

Visiting the Museum: You'll begin your visit in the cellar, with Roman ruins (including remains of the original Roman road and sewer system, found right here) and layers of medieval artifacts. A model of the modern city—sitting upon footprints of the Roman (red) and medieval (blue) settlements—illustrates Ljubljana's many layers of history. If it's not traveling to other museums (as it usually is), you may see the world's oldest wooden wheel on an axle, dating from around 3200 B.C. and discovered in the Ljubljana marshlands. Upstairs are the mayor's room (with a few exhibits) and the ever-evolving permanent collection, called Faces of Ljubljana. Exhibits on economy and trade include communist-era advertisements, while another section explains how Ljubljana has belonged to 10 different states over the last 200 years, ranging from the genteel Habsburg Empire to the oppressive Nazi regime to membership in the benevolent EU. You'll also see an actual Fiat Zastava 750 car, the classic "Fičko" car that everyone owned—or wanted to own—in communist Yugoslavia (sort of a proto-Yugo). Rounding out the collection is a range of temporary exhibits.

Nearby: Your ticket includes admission to two archaeological sites nearby (summer only)—pick up a map at the front desk.

• *If visiting the museum, don't miss the nearby National and University Library and French Revolution Square—both described in the next section.*

JOŽE PLEČNIK'S ARCHITECTURE

Jože Plečnik is to Ljubljana what Antoni Gaudí is to Barcelona: a homegrown, amazingly prolific genius who shaped his town with a unique and beautiful vision. And Plečnik's mark on Ljubljana, much like Gaudí's on Barcelona, has a way of turning people who couldn't care less about architecture into fans. There's plenty to see. In addition to the Triple Bridge, the riverside market, and the sights listed here, Plečnik designed the embankments along the Ljubljanica and Gradaščica rivers in the Trnovo neighborhood; the rebuilt Roman wall along Mirje street, south of the center; the Church of St. Francis, with its classicist bell tower; St. Michael's Church on the Marsh; Orel Stadium; Žale Cemetery; and many more buildings throughout Slovenia.

Some of the best Plečnik sights are near the river, just south of Congress and Prešeren squares. I've linked them into a short self-guided walk.

• *From Prešeren Square, stroll south along the river. After the plain bridge called Brv, you'll come to the...*

▲Cobblers' Bridge (Čevljarski Most)

Named for the actual cobblers (shoemakers) who set up shop along the river in olden times, the bridge encapsulates Plečnik's style per-

haps better than any other structure: simple, clean lines adorned with classical columns. Ideal for people-watching (with the castle hovering scenically overhead), this is one of Ljubljana's most appealing spots.

• *Continue past Cobblers' Bridge on the right side of the river, past the fountain. After about a block, turn right up the parked-up street called Novi trg. At the top of this street, on the left, is a red-brick building embedded with gray granite blocks in an irregular checkerboard pattern. This is the...*

▲▲National and University Library
(Narodna in Univerzitetna Knjižnica, or NUK)

Widely regarded as Plečnik's masterpiece, this building is a bit underwhelming...until an understanding of its symbolism brings it to life.

Cost and Hours: Free, staircase open Mon-Fri 8:00-20:00, Sat 9:00-14:00, closed Sun. The quiet main reading room is officially open for visitors only mid-July–mid-Aug Mon-Sat 14:00-18:00.

Visiting the Library:
Begin by standing outside and surveying the **exterior.** On the surface, the red-and-gray color scheme evokes the red soil and chunks of granite of the Karst region, south of Ljubljana. But on a deeper

level, the library's design conveys the theme of overcoming obstacles to attain knowledge. In the facade, the blocks of irregular size and shape represent a complex numerological pattern that suggests barriers on the path to enlightenment. The sculpture on the river side is Moses—known for leading his people through 40 years of hardship to the Promised Land. On the right side of the building, find the horse-head doorknobs—representing the winged horse Pegasus (grab hold, and he'll whisk you away to new levels of enlightenment).

Step **inside**. The main staircase is dark and gloomy—modeled after an Egyptian tomb. But at the top, through the door marked

Velika Čitalnica, is the bright, airy main reading room: the ultimate goal, a place of learning. The top-floor windows are shaped roughly like open books. Sadly, except for one month a year when the students are on summer break, you can't actually enter the reading room; you'll just have to look at postcards in the shop, and imagine young Ljubljanans hunched studiously over their books, surrounded by Plečnik's bookshelves, railings, and high windows.

Aside from being a great work of architecture, the building also houses the most important library in Slovenia, with more than two million books (about one per Slovene). The library is supposed to receive a copy of each new book printed in the country. In a freaky bit of bad luck, this was the only building in town damaged in World War II, when a plane crashed into it. But the people didn't want to see their books go up in flames—so hundreds of locals formed a human chain, risking life and limb to save the books from the burning building.

• *Directly behind the library is a mellow square with an obelisk in the middle. This is...*

French Revolution Square (Trg Francoske Revolucije)

Plečnik designed the **obelisk** in the middle of the square to commemorate Napoleon's short-lived decision to make Ljubljana the capital of his Illyrian Provinces. It's rare to find anything honoring Napoleon outside of Paris, but he was good to Ljubljana. Under his rule, Slovenian culture flourished, the Slovene language became widely recognized and respected for the first time, schools were established, and roads and infrastructure were improved. The monument contains ashes of the unknown French soldiers who died in 1813, when the region went from French to Austrian control.

The Teutonic Knights of the Cross established the nearby **monastery** (Križanke, ivy-capped wall and gate, free entry) in 1230. The adaptation of these monastery buildings into the Ljubljana Summer Theatre was Plečnik's last major work (1950-1956).

• *From here, it's a scenic 10-minute walk to the next sight. From the obelisk, walk down Emonska toward the twin-spired church. You'll pass (on the left) the delightful Krakovo district—a patch of green countryside in downtown Ljubljana. Many of the veggies you see in the riverside market come from these carefully tended gardens. When you reach the Gradaščica stream, head over the bridge (also designed by Plečnik) and go around the left side of the church to find the house.*

▲▲Jože Plečnik House (Plečnikova Zbirka)

One of Ljubljana's most interesting sights is the house of the architect who redesigned much of the city. Today the house is

decorated exactly as it was the day Plečnik died, containing much of his equipment, models, and plans. The house can be toured only with a guide, whose enthusiasm brings the place to life. There are very few barriers, so you are in direct contact with the world of the architect. Still furnished with unique, Plečnik-designed furniture, one-of-a-kind inventions, and favorite souvenirs from his travels, the house paints an unusually intimate portrait of an artist. While the house initially underwhelms some visitors, it's a ▲▲▲ pilgrimage for those who get caught up in Ljubljana's idiosyncratic sense of style.

Cost and Hours: €6, Tue-Sun 10:00-18:00—last tour departs at 17:00, closed Mon, 45-minute English tours begin at the top of each hour, Karunova 4, tel. 01/280-1600, www.mgml.si.

Getting There: It's directly behind the twin steeples of the Trnovo Church. The 15-minute stroll from the center—the same one Plečnik took to work each day—is nearly as enjoyable as the house itself. You can either walk south along the river, then turn right onto Gradaška and stroll along the stream to the church; or, from French Revolution Square, head south on Emonska. Either way, you'll pass through the garden-patch district of Krakovo, where pea patches and characteristic Old World buildings gracefully cohabitate. On the way to or from the museum, it's enjoyable to get a meal in Krakovo (two great restaurants—Pri Škofu and Manna—are described later, under "Eating in Ljubljana").

Background: Ljubljana's favorite son lived here from 1921 until his death in 1957. He added on to an existing house, building a circular bedroom for himself and filling the place with bric-a-brac

Jože Plečnik (1872-1957)

There is probably no other single architect who has shaped one city as Jože Plečnik (YOH-zheh PLAYCH-neek) shaped Ljubljana. From libraries, office buildings, cemeteries, and stadiums to landscaping, riverside embankments, and market halls, Plečnik left his mark everywhere.

Plečnik was born in Ljubljana to a cabinet maker. He worked as a furniture designer and dabbled as a self-trained architect, catching the eye of the great Secessionist architect Otto Wagner—who invited him to study in Vienna. Plečnik's first commissions, done around the turn of the 20th century in Vienna, were pretty standard Art Nouveau stuff. Then Tomáš Masaryk, president of the new nation of Czechoslovakia, decided that Prague Castle could use a new look. But he didn't want an Austrian architect; it had to be a Slav. In 1921, Masaryk chose Jože Plečnik, who sprinkled the castle grounds with his distinctive touches. By now, Plečnik had perfected his simple, eye-pleasing style, which mixes modern and classical influences, with lots of columns and pyramids—at once austere and playful.

By the time Plečnik finished in Prague, he had made a name for himself. His prime years were spent creating for the Kingdom of Yugoslavia (before the ideology-driven era of Tito). Plečnik re-

he designed, as well as artifacts, photos, and gifts from around the world that inspired him as he shaped Ljubljana. Living a simple, almost monastic lifestyle, Plečnik knew what he liked, and these tastes are mirrored in his house.

Visiting the House: While waiting for your tour to begin, explore the modest but engaging **museum,** offering biographical details about Plečnik. In one room, a model of Ljubljana locates the many structures he designed all around the city. You'll also see descriptions and photos of his greatest works, and large wooden models of two of his biggest "unrealized projects" that never made it off the drawing board: the cone-shaped national acropolis and the roofed Butchers' Bridge at the market.

The **tour** takes you through the actual rooms where Plečnik lived: kitchen, circular bedroom, sitting room, studio, and greenhouse. As you tour the place, be patient. Listen to its stories. Appreciate the subtle details. Notice how reverently your guide (and other Slovenes) speaks of this man. Contrast the humbleness of Plečnik's home with the dynamic impact he had on the cityscape of Ljubljana and the cultural heritage of Slovenia. Wandering

turned home to Ljubljana and set to work redesigning the city, both as an architect and as an urban planner. He lived in a humble house (now a recommended museum) behind the Trnovo Church. On his walk to work every day, he pondered ways to make the city

even more livable. As you wander through town, notice how thoughtfully he incorporated people, nature, the Slovenian heritage, town vistas, and symbolism into his works—it's feng shui on a grand urban scale.

For all of Plečnik's ideas that became reality, even more did not. After World War II, the very religious Plečnik fell out of favor with the new communist government. (It's fun to imagine how this city might look if Plečnik had always gotten his way.) After his death in 1957, Plečnik was virtually forgotten by Slovenes and scholars alike.

But in 1986, an exposition about Plečnik at Paris' Pompidou Center jump-started interest in the architect. Within a few years, Plečnik was back in vogue. Today, scholars laud him as a genius who was ahead of his time...while locals and tourists enjoy the elegant simplicity of his works.

Plečnik's hallways, it's hard not to be tickled by this man's sheer creativity and by the unique world he forged for himself to live in. As a visitor to his home, you're in good company. He invited only his closest friends here—except during World War II, when Ljubljana was occupied by Nazis and the university was closed, and Plečnik allowed his students to work with him here.

IN METELKOVA

Three museums face each other on a slick modern plaza next to the park called Tabor, about a 15-minute walk northeast of Prešeren Square in the dull but up-and-coming district of Metelkova. Nearby, you can explore the funky squatters' colony of Metelkova City (with Ljubljana's famous prison-turned-youth hostel).

▲▲Slovenian Ethnographic Museum (Slovenski Etnografski Muzej)

Housed in a state-of-the-art facility, this delightful museum is Ljubljana's most underrated attraction. With both permanent and temporary exhibits, the museum strives to explain what it is to be Slovene, with well-presented and well-described cultural artifacts from around the country. If you've caught the Slovenian folk culture itch, this is the place to scratch it.

Cost and Hours: €4.50, free first Sun of month, Tue-Sun 10:00-18:00, closed Mon, great café, Metelkova 2, tel. 01/300-8745, www.etno-muzej.si.

Visiting the Museum: The ground and first floors have good temporary exhibits, while upstairs you'll find two permanent exhibits.

The best exhibit, filling the third floor, is called **"Between Nature and Culture."** As you exit the elevator, turn left and find the shrunken head, which comes with a surprisingly frank exhibit that acknowledges the shortsighted tendency for museum curators—including at this museum—to emphasize things that are foreign or different. Continue through collections of "Reflections of Distant Worlds" (non-European cultures) to reach the core of the collection, which focuses on Slovenia. A good but slow-moving film visits the country's four major regions. Another exhibit ponders how people half a world away—in Slovenia and in North America—simultaneously invented a similar solution (snowshoes) for a common problem. One display deconstructs Slovenian clichés (including this country's odd fascination with its traditional hayracks). The arrangement of the collection emphasizes the evolution of an increasingly complicated civilization, from basic farming tools to ceramics to modern technology. You'll see exhibits on traditional Slovenian beekeeping, blacksmithing, weaving, shoemaking, costumes and customs, pottery, furniture, and religious objects. The children's "Ethnoalphabet" area features an A-to-Ž array of engaging, hands-on activities.

The other permanent exhibit, on the second floor (from the elevator, turn left to find the entrance), is called **"I, We, and Others."** A bit too conceptual for its own good, this heady exhibit ponders the notion of belonging. Designed for Slovenes more than foreigners (with very limited posted English information—borrow the free English audioguide from the ticket desk before heading up), it explores various aspects of how people define who they are, from individual and family to community and nation. Videos and sounds enhance the exhibits, and the curators neatly juxtapose well-known icons from different cultures (such as various national parliament buildings) in thought-provoking ways. While it's easy to get lost amid the navel-gazing, there is something particularly poignant about this topic here in the identity-obsessed Balkans.

Slovenian National Museum-Metelkova (Narodni Muzej Slovenije)

Next door to the Ethnographic Museum is this facility, where items from the Slovenian National Museum that were formerly tucked away in storage are now displayed on two floors. The very pretty historical bric-a-brac is neatly presented without much context—it's just an excuse to get a bunch of interesting stuff out into public view. Each room has a different collection: furniture, pottery and ceramics, church vestments, weapons and armor, and more. The painting gallery is nicely organized by century and style. The museum also features temporary exhibits. Everything's labeled in English, and a guide can show you around, if they're not too busy.

Cost and Hours: €6, Tue-Sun 10:00-18:00, closed Mon, Maistrova 1, tel. 01/230-7032.

Museum of Contemporary Art-Metelkova (Muzej Sodobne Umetnosti Metelkova, MSUM)

This cutting-edge branch of the Museum of Modern Art opened in 2012 to showcase changing exhibitions of present-day, mostly Slovenian and Eastern European artists. In addition to temporary installations, it populates its permanent "The Present and Presence" exhibit with a variety of pieces from its collection. The modern space is at once sleek and playful, making this museum worth a visit for art lovers who appreciate works from the 1960s to the present.

Cost and Hours: €5, ask about combo-ticket with Museum of Modern Art, Tue-Sun 10:00-18:00, closed Mon, Maistrova 3, tel. 01/241-6825, www.mg-lj.si.

Metelkova City (Metelkova Mesto)

The heart of Slovenia's counterculture, this former military installation is now a funky, graffiti-and-wild-art-slathered squatter's colony, billed as an "autonomous cultural center." Built by the Habsburgs in the 1880s, the complex—with barracks, warehouses, and a prison—was used by a laundry list of later occupiers, from Italian fascists to Nazis to the Yugoslav People's Army. After Yugoslavia pulled its troops out of Slovenia (following the Ten-Day War), the cluster of buildings sat derelict and abandoned. In 1993, transient artists moved into the sprawling complex and set up galleries, theaters, bars, and nightclubs. While controversial at first, Meltelkova City has gradually become accepted by most Ljubljanans, and the city (which owns the property) not only tolerates but, in subtle ways, encourages this hotbed of youthful artistic expression. While edgy, this place is fascinating to explore—it's sleepy by day and lively by night (www.metelkovamesto.org).

Anchoring the area is **Hostel Celica,** one of Europe's most unusual youth hostels, which fills a former prison building. Twenty artists were invited to decorate cells that have been turned into accommodations, and the ground floor features vibrant public spaces, a good and affordable restaurant (a nice place for a lunch or a light dinner), and a shoes-off "Oriental café." The message: Thoughtful art and architecture can transcend an ugly history. You can drop by to see the building anytime, and ask to borrow a flashlight to explore the dank and gloomy basement solitary confinement cells, with a small but interesting exhibition on the history of the building (and the various prisoners who have called it home—including Janez Janša, who did time here during communism and later became Slovenia's prime minister). But if you're interested in this place, make a point to visit at 14:00 for a free guided tour of the entire complex (tours run daily; you can also try calling to arrange a tour at other times, tel. 01/230-9700, www.hostelcelica.com).

Shopping in Ljubljana

Ljubljana, with its easygoing ambience and countless boutiques, is made to order for whiling away an afternoon shopping. It's also a fun place to stock up on souvenirs. Popular items include wood carvings and models (especially of the characteristic hayracks that dot the countryside), different flavors of schnapps (the kind with a whole pear inside—cultivated to actually grow right into the bottle—is a particularly classy gift), honey mead brandy (*medica*—sweet and smooth), bars of soap wrapped in wool (good for exfoliating), and those adorable painted panels from beehives (described on page 624). Rounding out the list of traditional Slovenian items are wrought-iron products from Kropa, crystal from Rogaska, lace from Idrija, salt from Piran, and Peko shoes (similar to high-fashion Italian models, but cheaper; the name is an abbreviation of its founder's name: Peter Kozina).

There are two convenient areas in the city center that offer abundant shopping opportunities: at **Ciril-Metodov trg and near the market;** and, beginning a few steps away, the **Old Town** pedestrian lane that cuts through the downtown core. I've described options in both places below. (A third street worth exploring—with a bit more funky student style—is the graffiti-slathered **Trubarjeva cesta,** a block up from the river and easy to find from Prešeren Square.)

AT CIRIL-METODOV TRG AND NEAR THE MARKET

The most atmospheric trinket-shopping is in the first stretch of the **market colonnade,** along the riverfront next to the Triple Bridge (described earlier, under "Sights in Ljubljana").

If you're looking for serious handicrafts rather than trinkets, drop by the **Rustika** gallery, just over the Triple Bridge (on the castle side). In addition to beehive panels, they also have lace, painted chests and boxes, and other tasteful local-style mementos (daily 9:00-21:00, Stritarjeva 9, mobile 031-459-509). There's another

Rustika location up at the castle courtyard. A somewhat more downscale souvenir shop with a wide variety is **Dom Trgovina,** across from the TI on the main market square (Mon-Sat 9:00-21:00, Sun 10:00-21:00, Ciril-Metodov trg 5).

Kraševka sells high-quality artisanal products (mostly foods) from the Karst region, and also acts as a sort of information office for that area (Mon-Fri 9:00-19:00, Sat 9:00-15:00, closed Sun, Ciril-Metodov trg 10, tel. 01/232-1445).

Trgovina Ika, a small artisan boutique with its own hip and idiosyncratic sense of style, is a delightful place to browse for truly authentic Slovenian stuff that goes beyond souvenirs. Its unique items by local designers—jewelry, hats, scarves, shoes, and so on—are modern and fashionable (Mon-Fri 10:00-19:30, Sat 9:00-18:00, Sun 10:00-14:00, Ciril-Metodov trg 13, tel. 01/123-21743).

IN THE OLD TOWN

Ljubljana's main Old Town street—which changes names from Mestni trg to Stari trg, then Gornji trg—is also lined with several characteristic shops, selling a few of the unique gift items produced in this proud little country. Here's a lightly narrated tour of this inviting street, from start to finish. Unless otherwise noted, all of these shops are open long hours on weekdays (often until 20:00); most close a bit earlier on Saturdays (around 17:00), and close in the early afternoon on Sundays (usually by 13:00 or 14:00).

◆ Self-Guided Shopping Stroll: Begin in front of the Town Hall. Before you start the walk, take the opportunity to browse the shops along Ciril-Metodov Trg, noted above (all of which are within a five-minute walk of here). When you're ready, head down the street.

First, on the left at Mestni trg 6, look for two fun shops: **Dvorec Trebnik** sells cosmetics and bath products handmade by people with disabilities; **Smile** is a colorful design/concept store. A few steps farther along at #7, **Honey House** sells products harvested by beekeeper Luka (closed Sun). For tips on browsing your honey options, see page 624.

Just beyond at #8, **Piranske Soline** sells products from the giant salt pans that sit just south of Piran on Slovenia's tiny coastline (see page 721). You can pick up some locally harvested sea salt, or peruse their salt-based beauty products (bath salts, body milk, and other exfoliants, www.soline.si).

Across the street at #19, **Güjžina** highlights food, wines, and other products from the Hungarian-influenced region of Slovenia called Prekmurje (also called Pannonia). While the restaurant (on the left, €11-16 meals) is hit-or-miss, their wine bar (on the right) is a good place to learn more about the products of one of Slovenia's top wine-growing regions. If you want a dessert, this is a fine place to try the cake called *gibanica*—originating in Prekmurje, and beloved throughout Slovenia.

Back on the left, at #8, **La Chocolate** is the first of two artisanal *čokoladnice* (chocolate shops) along this strip (www.lachocolate.si).

Farther along, on the right (at #17), **Galerija Idrijske Čipke** shows off handmade lace from the town of Idrija (www.idrija-lace.com).

Continuing past various clothes boutiques, look for (on the left, at #11) another chocolate shop, **Čokoladnica Cukrček.** A bit pricier than La Chocolate, this shop is best known for its foil-wrapped "Prešeren Balls" chocolates—a clever and civic-minded takeoff on Salzburg's "Mozart Balls," replacing the composer with Slovenia's greatest poet (www.cukrcek.si).

Continue along the street (which here changes names from Mestni trg to Stari trg), passing more clothes shops. On the left, at Stari trg 3, look for **Cha** tea shop, which sells over 100 varieties of tea, plus porcelain teapots and cups from all over. It's attached to the recommended Čajna Hiša teahouse.

A few steps down on the left (at #5), **Cafetino** is the best place in town for coffee. They have more than 20 types available—espresso or Turkish-style, plus beans to take home.

Next door, follow the passage to reach **Za Popen't Pivoteka,** a "bottle shop" selling 200 kinds of beer in individual bottles. While they stock a few Slovenian beers, they focus on international microbrews—including several American brands. Even if it's not authentically Slovenian, this shop is a fun browse for beer lovers. The name is a play on words, loosely meaning "foamy goodness" (www.zapopent.si). In the same courtyard is the stylish **Formadoma** design shop, specializing in housewares (closed Sun, www.formadoma.eu).

Now you'll wade through a stretch of enticing restaurants with wonderful outdoor tables (for my recommendations here, see page 582). Notice Julija and Romeo, facing each other wistfully across the street.

After the little "restaurant row," the lineup of shops resumes. On the left at Stari trg 11A, look for **Patrizia** jewelry; a few doors down, **Wool Art Knitwear** has unique (and very well-insulated) Serbian-style clothing. Across the street at #18, **Babushka Boutique** sells creative prints and Pinteresty gifts (www.babushkaboutique.com).

From here, you'll pass a few more funky shops, as well as some rare books and antiques shops. On the right at #26, don't miss **Woodway**, with locally made wooden jewelry, sunglasses, and phone cases, and cork handbags and wallets from Portugal (www.woodway.si).

The cobbled charm culminates at the square called **Gornji trg.**

Sleep Code

Abbreviations   (€1=about $1.10, country code: 386)
S=Single, **D**=Double/Twin, **T**=Triple, **Q**=Quad, **b**=bathroom
Price Rankings
  $$$ **Higher Priced**—Most rooms €110 or more
   $$ **Moderately Priced**—Most rooms €70-110
    $ **Lower Priced**—Most rooms €70 or less
Unless otherwise noted, Wi-Fi is generally free, credit cards
are accepted, and breakfast is included, but the modest tour-
ist tax (about €1/person, per night) is not. Everyone listed here
speaks English.

   Prices change; verify current rates online or by email. For
the best prices, always book directly with the hotel.

Look uphill and notice the village charms of some of the oldest
buildings in town: four medieval houses with rooflines slanted at
the ends, different from the others on this street.

Sleeping in Ljubljana

Ljubljana has a good range of accommodations in all price ranges.
I've focused my listings in or within easy walking distance of the
city center. To get the best value, book ahead. The most expensive
hotels raise their prices even more during conventions (Sept-Oct,
and sometimes also June).

   $$$ *Boutique Hotels in the Old Town:* Three similar (but un-
related) boutique hotels cluster idyllically on a cobbled square in
Ljubljana's Old Town. While quite overpriced (catering to deep-
pocketed business travelers), they offer Old World charm with
upscale touches. All of these are in old buildings with period
touches; expect lots of stairs and no elevators (the rates listed are
for May-mid-June and Sept-Oct, followed by mid-June-Aug, then
Nov-April). **Hotel Angel,** part of the Lesar group, is the plush-
est of the bunch. Its 12-plus rooms have crisp white decor (Db-
€180/€150/€130, €10 more for a bigger superior room on the top
floor, pricier suites, air-con, parking-€15, Gornji trg 7, tel. 01/425-
5089, www.angelhotel.si, info@angelhotel.si, warm Jovan). **Alle-
gro Hotel** has a musical theme and 17 rooms with hardwood floors
around a checkerboard-tiled garden courtyard (Sb-€100/€80/€65,
"economy" D with private bathroom across the hall-€115/€85/€70,
classic Db-€140/€130/€100, superior Db-€170/€150/€120, air-
con, prebook for €15 parking, Gornji trg 6, mobile 059-119-620,
www.allegrohotel.si, info@allegrohotel.si). The family-run **Antiq
Hotel** is a bit older, with less polish and 16 idiosyncratically deco-
rated rooms sprawling through two buildings with lots of stairs

Ljubljana Hotels & Restaurants

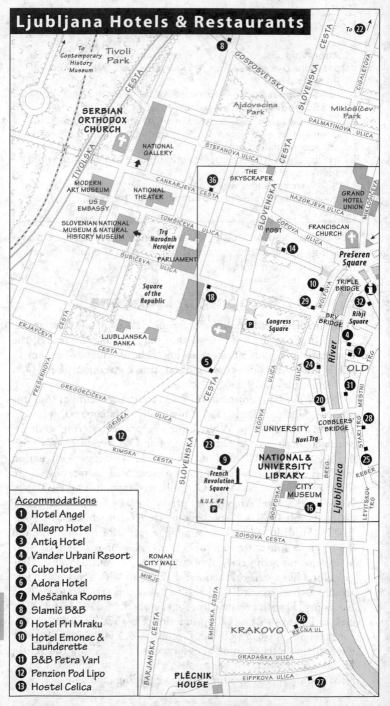

To ② →

To
Contemporary
History
Museum

Tivoli
Park

GOSPOSVETSKA

CESTA

SLOVENSKA

CESTA

CIGALETOVA

Ajdovscina
Park

Miklošičev
Park

DALMATINOVA ULICA

SERBIAN
ORTHODOX
CHURCH

TIVOLSKA

NATIONAL
GALLERY

ŠTEFANOVA ULICA

CANKARJEVA CESTA

THE
SKYSCRAPER

MODERN
ART MUSEUM

NATIONAL
THEATER

TOMŠIČEVA

US
EMBASSY

SLOVENIAN NATIONAL
MUSEUM & NATURAL
HISTORY MUSEUM

Trg
Narodnih
Herojev

PARLIAMENT

SLOVENSKA

CESTA

ULICA

NAZORJEVA ULICA

ČOPOVA

POST

FRANCISCAN
CHURCH

GRAND
HOTEL
UNION

MIKLOŠIČEVA

Prešeren
Square

⑭

⑩

TRIPLE
BRIDGE

WOLFOVA

①

SUBIČEVA

Square
of the
Republic

⑱

㉙

㉜

Ribji
Square

BR
BRIDGE

④

⑦

ERJAVČEVA CESTA

LJUBLJANSKA
BANKA

P

Congress
Square

River

OLD

㉔

㉛

PREŠERNOVA

GREGORČIČEVA

ULICA

⑤

CESTA

⑳

COBBLERS'
BRIDGE

㉘

IGRIŠKA

⑫

RIMSKA CESTA

SLOVENSKA CESTA

VEGOVA ULICA

UNIVERSITY

Novi Trg

STARI TRG

MESTNI

REBER

㉕

㉓

⑨

French
Revolution
Square

NATIONAL &
UNIVERSITY
LIBRARY

GOSPOSKA

BREG

Ljubljanica

LEVSTIKOV TRG

N.U.K. #2

P

CITY
MUSEUM

⑯

ROMAN
CITY WALL

MIRJE

ZOISOVA CESTA

Accommodations

1. Hotel Angel
2. Allegro Hotel
3. Antiq Hotel
4. Vander Urbani Resort
5. Cubo Hotel
6. Adora Hotel
7. Meščanka Rooms
8. Slamič B&B
9. Hotel Pri Mraku
10. Hotel Emonec & Launderette
11. B&B Petra Varl
12. Penzion Pod Lipo
13. Hostel Celica

BARJANSKA CESTA

EMONSKA CESTA

KRAKOVO

REČNA UL.

㉖

GRADAŠKA ULICA

PLEČNIK
HOUSE

EIPPROVA ULICA

㉗

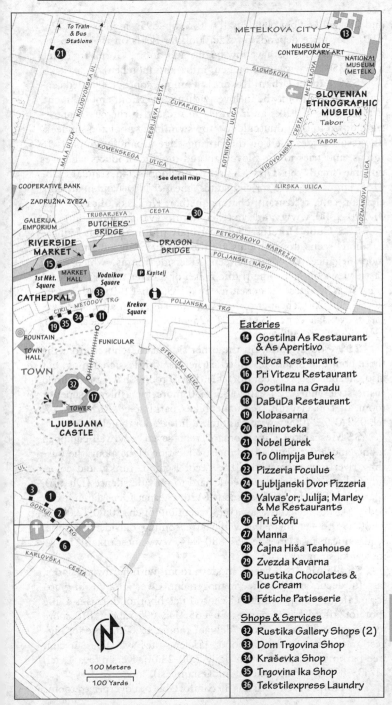

METELKOVA CITY

MUSEUM OF
CONTEMPORARY ART

NATIONAL
MUSEUM
(METELK.)

SLOMŠKOVA

SLOVENIAN
ETHNOGRAPHIC
MUSEUM
Tabor

TABOR

To Train
& Bus
Stations

KOLODVORSKA UL.

REGLJEVA CESTA

ČUFARJEVA

KOTNIKOVA

ULICA

VIDOVDANSKA CESTA

ROZMANOVA

ULICA

MALA ULICA

KOMENSKEGA ULICA

ILIRSKA ULICA

COOPERATIVE BANK
ZADRUŽNA ZVEZA
GALERIJA
EMPORIUM

See detail map

TRUBARJEVA CESTA

BUTCHERS'
BRIDGE

PETKOVŠKOVO NABREŽJE

POLJANSKI NASIP

RIVERSIDE
MARKET

DRAGON
BRIDGE

1st Mkt.
Square

MARKET
HALL

Vodnikov
Square

Kapitelj

CATHEDRAL

CIRIL - METODOV TRG

Krekov
Square

POLJANSKA TRG

FOUNTAIN

TOWN HALL

TOWN

FUNICULAR

STRELIŠKA ULICA

GORNJI

TRG

TOWER

LJUBLJANA
CASTLE

KARLOVŠKA CESTA

UL.

N

100 Meters
100 Yards

Eateries
14 Gostilna As Restaurant & As Aperitivo
15 Ribca Restaurant
16 Pri Vitezu Restaurant
17 Gostilna na Gradu
18 DaBuDa Restaurant
19 Klobasarna
20 Paninoteka
21 Nobel Burek
22 To Olimpija Burek
23 Pizzeria Foculus
24 Ljubljanski Dvor Pizzeria
25 Valvas'or; Julija; Marley & Me Restaurants
26 Pri Škofu
27 Manna
28 Čajna Hiša Teahouse
29 Zvezda Kavarna
30 Rustika Chocolates & Ice Cream
31 Fétiche Patisserie

Shops & Services
32 Rustika Gallery Shops (2)
33 Dom Trgovina Shop
34 Kraševka Shop
35 Trgovina Ika Shop
36 Tekstilexpress Laundry

LJUBLJANA

and a mazelike floor plan (small S-€75, Sb-€95, small D-€90, Db-€110-165, price depends on size, look for deals on their website, air-con, some rooms have low beams and doors, Gornji trg 3, tel. 01/421-3560, www.antiqhotel.eu, info@antiqhotel.eu).

$$$ Vander Urbani Resort is a unique concept: Nestled central as can be just off the in-love-with-life riverfront embankment, it really does feel like an intensely hip resort in the city center—right down to the minuscule rooftop swimming pool and sundeck. The resort prides itself on the cutting-edge urban design of its 16 rooms, and tries to use Slovenian and organic products wherever possible (small "zen" Db with hardwood floors-€145, standard Db-€155, larger Db-€175, pricier suites, cheaper Nov-March, air-con, elevator, café, restaurant, champagne bar, Krojaška ulica 6-8, tel. 01/200-9000, www.vanderhotel.com, info@vanderhotel.com).

$$$ Cubo Hotel is a jolt of trendy minimalism on Ljubljana's hotel scene. Its 26 rooms are the best place in town for sleek, mod elegance. Choose between streetside rooms, which enjoy castle views but get some traffic noise, or quieter courtyard rooms (very flexible rates but generally Sb-€135, Db-€140-180, palatial suite-€200-250, cheaper off-season, non-smoking, air-con, elevator, Slovenska cesta 15, tel. 01/425-6000, www.hotelcubo.com, reception@hotelcubo.com).

$$$ Adora Hotel, on the other side of the church from the three boutique hotels described earlier, is a bit less charming, but also cheaper and very comfortable. Its 10 rooms have a restrained rustic style (Db-€124/€109/€85, €30 more for a bigger superior room, air-con, elevator, free loaner bikes, parking-€9, Rožna ulica 7, tel. 082-057-240, www.adorahotel.si, info@adorahotel.si).

$$ Meščanka ("City Woman") rents seven cozy, well-equipped rooms and apartments in a fantastic location right along the bustling riverfront promenade. The decor is mod, funky, and colorful, and the good windows work hard to provide silence (Db-€70, apartment-€90, bigger apartment-€120, cheaper Oct-March, extra bed-€20, no breakfast, air-con, reception open 10:00-12:00 & 14:00-19:00—let them know if you're coming outside that time, Ključavničarska 4, mobile 051-880-044, www.mescanka.si, info@mescanka.si, Saša).

$$ Slamič B&B has 17 modern rooms with hardwood floors, tasteful decor, and absentee management. Over an appealing upscale café in a nondescript but central neighborhood, this is a fine spot for affordable elegance (Sb-€65, Db-€95, about €10 more for bigger and slightly nicer "deluxe" rooms, or €20 more for biggest and newest "deluxe" rooms, pricier suites available, air-con, free parking, reception open daily 7:00-23:00, Kersnikova 1, tel. 01/433-8233, www.slamic.si, info@slamic.si).

$$ Hotel Pri Mraku has 35 comfortable but overpriced rooms in a pleasant neighborhood near French Revolution Square. While it's a bit rough around the edges and not without its quirks, this trusty old place is my sentimental favorite in Ljubljana (Sb-€77, Db-€98, ground-floor and top-floor rooms have air-con and cost €4-5 extra, 8 percent discount for Rick Steves readers if you reserve ahead, extra bed-€23, cheaper mid-Oct-April, non-smoking floor, elevator, restaurant with terrace under an old vine, Rimska 4, tel. 01/421-9650, www.daj-dam.si, hotelmrak@daj-dam.si).

$$ Hotel Emonec (eh-MOH-nets), with some of the most centrally located cheap beds in Ljubljana, hides just off Wolfova lane between Prešeren and Congress squares. Its 54 rooms—in two buildings across a courtyard from each other—feel like a cookie-cutter chain hotel, with tight bathrooms and a shoestring staff. But the price and ideal location make it worth considering (Sb-€64, small Db-€67, bigger "standard" Db-€77, Tb-€90-96, Qb-€105-111, price depends on demand, cheaper Nov-April, parking garage-€7, they also run a handy self-service launderette—see page 543, Wolfova 12, tel. 01/200-1520, www.hotel-emonec.com, hotelemonec@siol.net).

$ B&B Petra Varl offers comfortable, affordable, nicely appointed rooms on a courtyard across from the bustling riverside market. Petra, an artist who speaks good English, will help you feel at home. As this place is Ljubljana's top budget option, book early (Db-€67, extra bed-€10, includes kitchenette with basic do-it-yourself breakfast, cash only, air-con, go into courtyard at Vodnikov trg 5 and look for *B&B* sign at 5A, mobile 031-851-842, bb@varl.si).

$ Penzion Pod Lipo has 10 rooms above a restaurant in a mostly residential area about a 12-minute walk from Prešeren Square. While the rooms are old and simple, it's thoughtfully run by Marjan (Db-€63, Tb-€77, Qb-€98, breakfast in restaurant-€4.50, cash only, sometimes unstaffed—let them know when you'll arrive, non-smoking, guest kitchen, putting green on terrace, tel. 01/251-1683, mobile 031-809-893, www.penzion-podlipo.com, info@penzion-podlipo.com).

$ Hostel Celica, a proud, innovative, and lively place, is owned by the city and run by a nonprofit student organization.

This former military prison's 20 cells *(celica)* have been converted into hostel rooms—each one unique and decorated by a different designer (free tours of the hostel daily at 14:00). The top floor features more typical hostel rooms (each with its own bathroom, for 4-12 people). The building also houses an art gallery, tourist information, self-service laundry (€8/load), and a variety of eateries. For more on the history of this site, see page 573 (bunk bed in dorm–€24-29; per-person price in private "cell" rooms: S-€63, D-€33, T-€31; includes breakfast, sheets, towels, and tax; no curfew, non-smoking, bike and car rental, active excursions around Slovenia, Metelkova 8, a dull 15-minute walk to Prešeren Square, 8 minutes to the train station, tel. 01/230-9700, www.hostelcelica.com, info@hostelcelica.com). The hostel hosts live music events one night a week until around 24:00, but otherwise maintains "quiet time" after 23:00. However, the surrounding neighborhood—a bit run-down and remote, but safe—is a happening nightlife zone, which can make for noisy weekends.

Eating in Ljubljana

At this crossroads of cultures (and cuisines), Italian and French flavors are just as "local" as meat-and-starch Slovenian food. This cosmopolitan city also dabbles in other cuisines; you'll find Thai, Indian, Chinese, Mexican, and more. Most places seem to offer a similar menu of Slovenian/Mediterranean fare with international flourishes. To locate these restaurants, see the map on page 578.

Lunch Deals: Ljubljana has many of the best restaurants in this book. However, they tend to be quite expensive. To stretch your budget, make a point to have your main meal at lunch, when most of Ljubljana's top eateries serve a high-quality three-course meal (starter, main, dessert) at a very affordable price—usually €9-10, typically not including drinks. You won't have much choice (they may only have one or two options each day; some places don't offer this deal on weekends, so check before you sit down), but the quality is high and the value is outstanding. After a big lunch, you can have a light dinner—picnic, *burek*, pizza, sandwich...or just gelato. Places I recommend that offer these lunch deals include Pri Vitezu, DaBuDa, Valvas'or, Julija, Marley & Me, Pri Škofu, Manna, and the restaurant at the top of The Skyscraper (I've noted "lunch special" where applicable below).

IN THE CITY CENTER

Gostilna As ("Ace"), tucked into a courtyard just off Prešeren Square, offers fish lovers the best blowout in town. It's dressy, pricey, and pretentious (the service is deliberate, and waiters ignore the menu and recommend what's fresh). Everything is specially prepared each day and beautifully presented. It's loosely based on the

Slow Food model: Servings are small, and you're expected to take your time and order two or three courses. The dining room is old-fashioned and a bit stuffy, but in good weather, their rooftop terrace is gorgeous (mostly fish and Italian dishes, €10-21 starters, €15-28 main courses, daily 12:00-24:00, reservations smart, Čopova 5A, or enter courtyard with *As* sign near image of Julija on Wolfova, tel. 01/425-8822, www.gostilnaas.si). For cheaper food and drinks from the same kitchen, eat at the attached **As Aperitivo,** a much livelier, more casual spot. You'll sit in the leafy courtyard or the winter garden, with big windows that stay open in the summer (€10-15 salads and sandwiches, €8-12 pastas, €11-23 main courses, food served daily 12:00-24:00, longer hours for drinks, good gelato counter inside). The courtyard also has a couple of other fun eateries—and, in the summer only, live music.

Ribca ("Fish") hides under the first stretch of market colonnade near the Triple Bridge. This is your best bet for a relatively quick and cheap riverside lunch. Choose between the two straightforward menus: grilled fillets or fried small fish. With the fragrant fish market right next door, you know it's fresh. If you just want to enjoy sitting along the river below the bustling market, this is also a fine spot for a coffee or beer (€6-7 salads, €4-6 seafood appetizers, €7-10 main courses, €8 lunches, Mon 8:00-16:00, Tue-Sat 8:00-21:00, Sun 11:00-18:00, tel. 01/425-1544).

Pri Vitezu is well-respected for its seasonal menu of classic Mediterranean dishes. It sits along the newly spiffed-up Breg embankment, just beyond Cobblers' Bridge; sit out on the pedestrian mall or in the Old World-elegant interior. Although a bit pretentious and quite expensive at dinner, this place is especially worthwhile for its good-value lunch special (€9-16 starters, €16-26 main dishes, Mon-Sat 11:00-23:00, closed Sun; shorter hours in winter and closed Sat-Sun; Breg 18-20, tel. 01/426-6058, www.privitezu.si).

Traditional Slovenian Food: Because Slovenes head into the countryside when they want traditional fare, Ljubljana isn't the best place to find authentic Slovenian grub. But if you'd like to try some, your best budget bet may be **Klobasarna**, listed later. For a more formal sit-down meal, head for **Gostilna na Gradu,** in the castle courtyard high above town—if you don't mind going up to the castle to get it (the handy funicular costs €4 round-trip). Run by a well-respected chef, it serves up a seasonal menu of traditional flavors with modern flair. The portions are small, but the prices are surprisingly affordable. Choose between the dull vaulted interior, the glassed-in arcade, or the outdoor tables. Reservations are recommended before you make the trip up here (€10-13 starters, €9-17 main dishes, €30 four-course meal lets you sample several flavors, Mon-Sat 10:00-24:00—food served until 22:00, Sun 9:00-

18:00—food served until 17:00, Grajska Planota 1, mobile 031-301-777, www.nagradu.si).

Asian Fusion: **DaBuDa** is the best spot in Ljubljana for Asian cuisine, featuring a well-described menu of good Thai dishes (salads, curries, wok meals, and noodles) in a very mod, dark-wood, split-level setting frequented by hip young professionals (lunch special, €9-12 main courses, daily 12:00-23:00, also a few outdoor tables, between Congress Square and Square of the Republic at Šubičeva 1A, tel. 01/425-3060).

Fast and Cheap: **Klobasarna** is a budget foodie option specializing in *kranjska klobasa*—traditional Carniolan sausage, from the Slovenian uplands. The menu is simple—one wiener for €3.50, two for €5.90, extra for *jota* (hearty turnip stew)—and delicious. They also serve the Slovenian dumplings called *štruklji* (Mon-Sat 10:00-23:00, Sun 10:00-15:00, Ciril-Metodov trg 15, mobile 051-605-017). **Paninoteka,** with wonderful outdoor seating overlooking Cobblers' Bridge and fine interior seating, has affordable and tasty €3-4 sandwiches; their full menu is good, but much more expensive (daily 9:00-22:00, Jurčičev trg 3, mobile 040-349-329). *Burek,* the typical Balkan phyllo-dough snack (see the "Balkan Flavors" sidebar on page 421), can be picked up at street stands around town. Most are open 24 hours and charge about €2-3 for a hearty portion. An easy choice is **Nobel Burek,** next to Miklošičeva cesta 30; but many locals prefer **Olimpija Burek,** around the corner at Pražakova 14 (across from the post office).

Pizzerias: Ljubljana has lots of great sit-down pizza places. Expect to pay €5-10 for an average-sized pie (wide variety of toppings). **Pizzeria Foculus,** tucked in a boring alleyway a few blocks up from the river, has a loyal local following, a happening atmosphere, an innovative leafy interior, a few outdoor tables, and Ljubljana's best pizza (over 50 types, daily 11:00-24:00, just off French Revolution Square across the street from Plečnik's National and University Library at Gregorčičeva 3, tel. 01/251-5643). **Ljubljanski Dvor** enjoys the most convenient and scenic location of any pizzeria in town. On a sunny summer day, the outdoor riverside terrace is unbeatable; I'd skip the dull interior and the pricier pasta restaurant higher up (Mon-Sat 10:00-24:00, Sun 12:00-24:00, 50 yards from Cobblers' Bridge at Dvorni trg 1, tel. 01/251-6555). Ljubljanski Dvor also has a handy, cheap pizza **takeout window** (go around back to the walk-up window on Congress Square). Enjoy a €2 slice at one of their outdoor tables facing Congress Square, or get it to go and munch it along the river.

IN THE OLD TOWN

The main drag through the Old Town (which starts at the Town Hall and changes names as it goes: Mestni trg, then Stari trg, then

Gornji trg) is lined with inviting eateries. Tables spill into the cobbled pedestrian street, filled with happy diners. If you're at a loss for where to eat in town, stroll here to survey your options, then pick your favorite menu and ambience. As many restaurants along here are uniformly good, no one place really has the edge.

Several popular options cluster in one particularly atmospheric stretch; all except Romeo offer a similar menu of Mediterranean-Slovenian cuisine and wonderful outdoor seating: **Valvas'or,** the upscale option, has a dressy dining room and a posh gold color scheme (€10 weekday lunch deal, €10-15 starters, €14-22 main courses, €40 degustation menu, Mon-Sat 12:00-22:00, closed Sun, Stari trg 7, tel. 01/425-0455). **Julija** features homey country-Slovenian decor inside (€9 lunch deals, €9-12 starters, €12-19 main courses, daily 12:00-22:00, Stari trg 9, tel. 01/425-6463). **Romeo,** across the street, is a lowbrow bar serving unexceptional Mexican food...but the name sure is clever (get it? "Romeo and Julija"). And **Marley & Me** comes with a warm welcome from Matej (€7-9 weekday lunch specials, €9-14 pastas, €12-22 main courses, daily 11:00-23:00, Stari Trg 9, tel. 08/380-6610). I've also enjoyed a great salad lunch at the nearby **Čajna Hiša** teahouse (described later, under "Coffee, Tea, and Treats.")

IN KRAKOVO

The Krakovo district—just south of the city center, where garden patches nearly outnumber simple homes—is a pleasant area to wander. It's also home to two tasty restaurants. If the nearby Jože Plečnik House is open during your visit, you could combine your visit there with a meal at one of these options.

Pri Škofu ("By the Bishop") is a laid-back, leafy place with appealing outdoor seating, a nondescript modern interior, and a focus on freshness, serving international cuisine with a Slovenian flair. This hidden gem is deliciously memorable; reserve ahead (creative €3 soups, €8 lunches, €9-11 pastas, €15-22 main courses at dinner, €4 homemade desserts, Mon-Fri 10:00-24:00—but may be closed on Mon, Sat-Sun 12:00-24:00, Rečna 8, tel. 01/426-4508).

Manna, with artfully presented, seasonal Slovenian-Mediterranean fusion cuisine, sits along the pleasant Gradaščica canal. The interior is pure Secession—the Gustav Klimt-era, early 20th-century, gold-accented Viennese style that was so influential in Ljubljana. I prefer the more artistic, café-like downstairs to the stuffy upstairs dining room, but the seating out front is hard to beat on a nice day (lunch special, €18-24 main courses, Mon-Sat 11:00-24:00, Sun 11:00-21:00, Eipprova 1A, tel. 05/992-2308).

COFFEE, TEA, AND TREATS

Riverfront Cafés: Enjoying a coffee, beer, or ice-cream cone along the Ljubljanica River embankment (between the Triple and Cobblers' bridges) is Ljubljana's single best experience—worth ▲▲▲. Tables spill into the street, and some of the best-dressed, best-looking students on the planet happily fill them day and night. (A common question from first-time visitors to Ljubljana: "Doesn't anybody here have a job?") This is some of the top people-watching in Europe. Just explore and find the spot with the breezy ambience you like best. When ordering, the easiest choice is a *bela kava* (white coffee)—a caffè latte.

Teahouse: If coffee's not your cup of tea, go a block inland to the teahouse **Čajna Hiša.** They serve about 50 different types of tea, light food (including great salads), and desserts (€2-4 cakes and sandwiches, €7-9 salads, Mon-Fri 8:00-22:00, Sat 8:00-15:00, Sun 10:00-14:00, on the atmospheric main drag in the Old Town a few steps from Cobblers' Bridge at Stari trg 3, tel. 01/421-2444). They also have an attached tea shop, **Cha** (described on page 576).

Cakes: **Zvezda Kavarna,** a trendy, central place at the bottom of Congress Square, is a local favorite for cakes, pastries, and ice cream. A nostalgic favorite here—once popular in communist times, and recently reintroduced to great acclaim—is the *emona kocka* (Emona cube), a layer cake with nuts, cake, and chocolate (€3-5 cakes, Mon-Sat 7:00-23:00, Sun 10:00-20:00, a block up from Prešeren Square at Wolfova 14, tel. 01/421-9090). Their **Deli,** one door toward Prešeren Square, has takeaway coffee and smoothies, a wide variety of cakes to go, and some of the most decadent ice cream in town (same hours). And their **Bistro,** around the corner facing Congress Square, has a full menu.

Chocolates and Ice Cream: **Rustika** is a local chain that sells tasty homemade chocolates, cookies (including one kind with four different types of chocolate), and a wide variety of unusual and delicious artisanal ice cream flavors. The menu changes from day to day, but highlights can include balsamic vinegar with vanilla or strawberry, very dark chocolate, Kanada (with maple syrup and walnuts), and Greek yogurt with honey and nuts. The handiest location is about an eight-minute walk from Prešeren Square, and comes with a delightful stroll along colorful Trubarjeva cesta (ice cream available summer only, Mon-Fri 8:00-19:00, Sat 9:00-13:00, closed Sun, Trubarjeva cesta 44, mobile 059-935-730). Don't confuse this sweet shop with the Rustika gift shop.

More Ice Cream: Ljubljana is known for its Italian gelato-style ice cream. You'll see fine options all along the Ljubljanica River embankment, but many places serve ice cream only in summer. **Romantica**, just up the steps from the river, is the foodies' choice, with creative and delicious artisanal flavors (just uphill from Ljubljanksi Dvor pizzeria at Dvorni trg 1). **Fétiche Patisserie,** along the riverfront café embankment, is another good choice, with some unusual, pungent, Asian-themed flavors. Other favorites include **Rustika** and **Zvezda Kavarna** (both described earlier).

Ljubljana Connections

As Slovenia's transportation hub, Ljubljana is well-connected to both domestic and international destinations. When checking schedules, be aware of city name variations: In Slovene, Vienna is "Dunaj," Budapest is "Budimpešt," and Venice is "Benétke."

GETTING TO CROATIA'S ISTRIAN PENINSULA
To reach **Istria** (just south of Slovenia) by public transportation, you have two relatively straightforward options: In summer, direct buses depart Ljubljana for Rovinj each day (3-4/day late June-Aug, 1/day Sept, none Oct-late June). From late June through late September, there's also a train connection to Pula (1/day, transfer in Hrpelje-Kozina); once in Pula, you can connect by bus to other Istrian destinations. On off-season weekends, you might have to get creative (try connecting through Rijeka).

BY TRAIN
From Ljubljana by Train to: Lesce-Bled (roughly hourly, 40-60 minutes—but bus is better because it goes right to Bled town center), **Postojna** (nearly hourly, 1 hour), **Divača** (close to Škocjan Caves and Lipica, nearly hourly, 1.75 hours), **Sežana** (close to Lipica, nearly hourly, 2 hours), **Piran** (direct bus is better—see next; otherwise allow 4 hours, train to Koper, 4/day, 2.5 hours; then bus to Piran, 7/day, 30 minutes), **Maribor** (hourly, 2-3 hours, most with a transfer in Zidani Most), **Ptuj** (1/day direct, 2.5 hours, more with transfer in Pragersko and sometimes additional change in Zidani Most), **Zagreb** (4/day direct, 2.5 hours), **Rijeka** (2/day direct, 3 hours), **Pula** (1/day late June-late Sept, 5 hours, transfer in Hrpelje-Kozina), **Split** (1/day, 9 hours, transfer in Zagreb), **Vienna** (that's **Dunaj** in Slovene, 1/day direct, 6 hours; otherwise 3/day with transfer in Villach or Maribor, 6-6.5 hours), **Budapest** (that's **Budimpešta** in Slovene; 1/day direct, 9 hours, other connections possible with 1-2 changes but complicated, no convenient night train), **Venice** (called **Benétke** in Slovene; fastest by bus—see next; otherwise 2/day with a transfer in Villach, 6 hours), **Salzburg** (2/day direct, 4-5 hours, an additional 2/day possible with transfer in Villach), **Munich** (2/day direct,

6 hours, including 1 night train; otherwise transfer in Salzburg). Train info: Toll tel. 01/291-3332, www.slo-zeleznice.si.

BY BUS

The bus station is a low-profile building in front of the train station. Buses depart from the numbered stalls in the middle of the street. For any bus, you have to buy tickets at the bus station ticket windows or at the automated e-kart kiosk (pay with credit card or cash), not from the driver. For bus information, pick up one of the blue phones inside the station to be connected to a helpful English-speaking operator. Bus info: www.ap-ljubljana.si, toll tel. 1991 (€1.50/call), from the US call +386-1-234-4600.

By Bus to: **Bled** (Mon-Sat hourly—usually at the top of each hour, fewer on Sun, 1.25 hours), **Postojna** (at least hourly, 1 hour), **Divača** (close to Škocjan Caves and Lipica, about every 2-3 hours, 1.5 hours), **Piran** (5/day Mon-Fri, 2/day Sat, 4/day Sun, 2.5 hours), over the **Vršič Pass** to **Bovec** (2/day July-Aug at 6:30 and 15:00, June and Sept Sat-Sun only at 6:30, 4.25 hours to Bovec, none Oct-May), **Kobarid** (1/day in July-Aug over Vršič Pass, 5 hours; otherwise faster but less scenic via Idrija, 3.5 hours), **Rijeka** (1/day in summer, none off-season, 2.5 hours), **Zagreb** (10/day, less on weekends, 2.5 hours). To reach Croatia's Istria—specifically **Rovinj**—the bus is your best option (3-4/day late June-Aug, 1/day Sept, none Oct-late June, 4-5.5 hours, buses also stop in **Piran** and **Poreč**; off-season: 2/week to **Poreč** or **Pula** and change there to Rovinj, generally Mon and Fri, departs at 16:00). DRD runs a handy direct bus from Ljubljana to the **Venice-Mestre** train station (on the mainland, with easy and frequent train connections to the island; 1/day each way, departs at 8:15, 3.75 hours).

BY SHARED SHUTTLE SERVICE

If bus and train schedules don't quite get you where you need to go, **GoOpti**—a company with an innovative business model for shared minibus transfers—can be a convenient and inexpensive option for somewhat flexible travelers. First, go to www.goopti.com and select your destination, date, and preferred time of arrival or departure. Then, 24 hours before departure, you'll get an update of the specific pickup time, based on the needs of other passengers. Prices can flex dramatically, but it's quite affordable (for example, an advance nonrefundable purchase from Ljubljana could be €17 to Piran, €20 to Venice, or €22 to Zagreb; for the best price, book two months ahead). For a few euros extra, they can pick you up at your hotel rather than the train or bus station. To lock in a specific time, you can pay extra for a "VIP" transfer ("VIP flex" is similar, but refundable).

GoOpti reaches destinations throughout Slovenia (including

Ljubljana, the airport, Lake Bled, Lake Bohinj, Bovec in the Julian Alps, towns in the Karst such as Postojna and Sežana, and Piran and other Slovenian coastal destinations), but it's also handy for farther-flung international destinations—such as Venice or its airport, Trieste, various Austrian cities (Vienna, Salzburg, Klagenfurt, etc.), and Croatian cities such as Zagreb and Pula.

BY PLANE

Slovenia's only **airport** (airport code: LJU) is 14 miles north of Ljubljana, about halfway to Bled. Confusingly, the airport goes by three names: Ljubljana Airport (the international version); Brnik (for the town that it's near); and Jože Pučnik Airport (a politician for whom it was controversially renamed in 2007). Most flights are operated by Slovenia's national airline, Adria Airways (www.adria-airways.com), but additional flights are run by easyJet (www.easyjet.com), Wizz Air (www.wizzair.com), and various national carriers (Air France, Turkish Airlines, Finnair, and so on). The airport is small and manageable. Morning flights tend to cluster around the same time frame (between 6:45 and 7:30); as the airport doesn't open until 5:00, there's no need to show up before then. If you need to kill time here, follow signs (around to the left as you exit the terminal) to *Razgledna Terasa* and *Terasa Avionček* and ride the elevator up to the rooftop terrace with a café (daily 9:00-19:00). Here you can sip a coffee while you watch planes land and take off. Airport info: tel. 04/206-1000, www.lju-airport.si.

Getting Between Downtown Ljubljana and the Airport: Two kinds of buses connect the airport with Ljubljana's bus station: **public bus** #28 (to the right as you exit the airport; Mon-Fri hourly until 20:00, only 7/day Sat-Sun, 45 minutes, €4.10), and a **minibus** (to the left as you exit the airport, scheduled to depart after various arriving flights—look for schedule posted near bus stop). Two different companies run the minibus transfers, which take about 30 minutes and cost €9 to downtown: Markun (mobile 041-792-865, www.prevozi-markun.com) and Marko Nowotny (mobile 040-771-771, www.mnj.si). I'd take whichever one is departing first. For a transfer *to* the airport, your hotel or any TI can make arrangements with one of these companies a day or so in advance (same price)—or you can try GoOpti, described earlier. Unfortunately, certain evening arrivals don't coordinate well with either the bus or the minibus, so you might have to wait a while or take a pricey **taxi** (figure €25-35 to the airport if you call a reputable company, but more like €42 *from* the airport—since you have to use the pricey taxi stand out front).

To Lake Bled: For tips on going from the airport directly to Lake Bled, see page 616.

The Austrian Alternative: Since Ljubljana's airport is the only one in the country (and thus charges extremely high taxes and airport fees), many Slovenes prefer to fly out of Austria. The airport in **Klagenfurt** (airport code: KLU, also known as "Alpe-Adria Airport"), just over the Austrian border to the north, is subsidized by the local government to keep prices low and compete with Ljubljana's airport. Especially if you're connecting to Bled, it's somewhat handy to reach (from Ljubljana or Bled, take the train to Villach, then to Klagenfurt's Annabichl station, which is a 5-minute walk from the airport; total trip 3 hours from Ljubljana, or 2 hours from Bled; www.klagenfurt-airport.com). A taxi transfer to Bled runs a hefty €120 and takes about an hour (see "By Taxi" on page 598). Austrian Airlines (www.austrian.com) flies from Klagenfurt, as does low-cost carrier Germanwings (www.germanwings.com).

LAKE BLED

Lake Bled—Slovenia's leading mountain resort—comes complete with a sweeping alpine panorama, a fairy-tale island, a cliff-hanging medieval castle, a lazy lakeside promenade, and the country's most sought-after desserts. And the charms of its glorious mountain vistas and traditional folk life only crescendo as you explore the surrounding areas. Taken together, there are few more enjoyable places to simply be on vacation.

Since the Habsburg days, Lake Bled (locals pronounce it "blayd") has been *the* place where Slovenes wow visiting diplomats. In the late 19th century, local aristocrats—who knew how to find a fine mountain resort—surrounded the humble lakefront village with classy villas. Tito also had one of his vacation homes here (today's Hotel Vila Bled), where he entertained illustrious guests. But above all, Lake Bled feels like a place that Slovenes enjoy alongside their visitors.

Lake Bled has plenty of ways to idle away an afternoon. While the lake's main town, also called Bled, is more functional than quaint, it offers postcard views of the lake and handy access to the region. Hike up to Bled Castle for intoxicating vistas. Make a wish and ring the bell at the island church. Wander or bike the dreamy path around the lake. Sit on a dock, dip your feet in the water, and feed some of the lake's resident swans. Then dive into some of Bled's famous cakes while you take in the view of Triglav, Slovenia's favorite mountain (see the "Mount Triglav" sidebar on page 640). Bled quiets down at night—there's no nightlife beyond a handful of pubs—giving hikers and other holiday makers a chance to recharge.

Bled is also a great jumping-off point for a car trip through the Julian Alps (see next chapter), and a wide variety of other worthwhile side-trips are right at its doorstep. These include the less developed lake named Bohinj, even deeper in the mountains; a spectacular (yet easy) hike in the nearby mountain gorge of Vintgar; the pleasant Old Town of Radovljica, with its fascinating little beekeeping museum; and the ironworking town of Kropa, boasting a museum that attracts the kind of people who wonder how things work.

PLANNING YOUR TIME

Bled and its neighboring mountains deserve at least two days. With one day, spend it in and around Bled (or, spend a quick morning in Bled and an afternoon day-tripping). With a second day and a car, drive through the Julian Alps using the self-guided tour in the next chapter. The circular route takes you up and over the stunning Vršič Pass, then down the scenic and historic Soča River Valley. Without a car, skip the second day, or spend it doing nearby day trips: Bus or bike to Radovljica and its bee museum, hike to Vintgar Gorge, or visit Lake Bohinj (all described under "Near Lake Bled," at the end of this chapter).

Orientation to Lake Bled

The town of Bled is on the east end of 1.5-mile-long Lake Bled. The lakefront is lined with soothing parks and chunky resort hotels. A 3.5-mile path meanders around the lake. As no motorized boats are allowed, Lake Bled is particularly peaceful.

The tourists' center of Bled has two parts, which melt into each other: a ragtag village and a cluster of giant hotels. The main thoroughfare, called **Ljubljanska cesta,** leads out of Bled town toward Ljubljana and most other destinations. Just up from the lakefront is the modern **commercial center** (Trgovski Center Bled), with a supermarket, ATM, shops, and a smattering of lively cafés. Nicknamed "Gaddafi," the commercial center was designed for a city in Libya, but the deal fell through—so the frugal Slovenes built it here instead.

Bled's less-touristy Old Town, under the castle, has a web of tight streets and big but humble old houses surrounding the pointy spire of St. Martin's Church. Here you'll find the bus station, some good restaurants, a few hostels, and more locals than tourists.

The mountains poking above the ridge at the far end of the lake are the Julian Alps, crowned by the three peaks of Mount Tri-

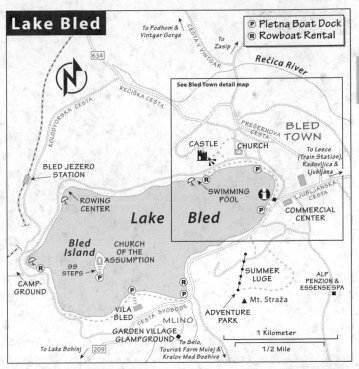

glav. The big mountain behind the town of Bled is Stol ("Chair"), part of the Karavanke range that defines the Austrian border.

TOURIST INFORMATION

Bled's most central TI is in the long, lakefront casino building across the street from the big, white Hotel Park (as you face the lake, the TI is hiding around the front at the far left end, overlooking the lake). Pick up the map with the lake on one side and the whole region on the other and the free Bled information booklet, with up-to-date details on local attractions and transportation options. Get advice on hikes and day trips, confirm transit schedules, and if you're doing any serious hiking, spring for a good regional map. They also have free Wi-Fi and rent cars (July-Aug Mon-Sat 8:00-21:00, Sun 9:00-17:00; May-June and Sept-Oct Mon-Sat 8:00-19:00, Sun 11:00-17:00; Nov-April Mon-Sat 8:00-18:00, Sun 8:00-13:00; Cesta Svobode 10, tel. 04/574-1122, www.bled.si).

The TI's other branch is harder to reach for nondrivers—on the main road out of town—but it conveniently shares an office with the **Triglav National Park Information Center,** which offers lots of helpful advice for those heading into the mountains (free information, maps and guidebooks for sale; daily mid-April-mid-

LAKE BLED

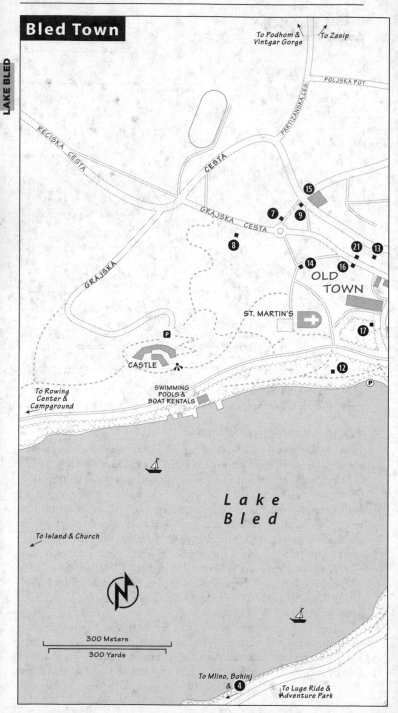

Bled Town

To Podhom & Vintgar Gorge

To Zasip

POLJSKA POT

RECIŠKA CESTA

CESTA

GRAJSKA CESTA

PARTIZANSKA CES.

GRAJSKA

15

7

9

8

21

13

14

16

OLD TOWN

17

ST. MARTIN'S

CASTLE

P

To Rowing Center & Campground

SWIMMING POOLS & BOAT RENTALS

12

P

Lake Bled

To Island & Church

N

300 Meters

300 Yards

To Mlino, Bohinj & 4

To Luge Ride & Adventure Park

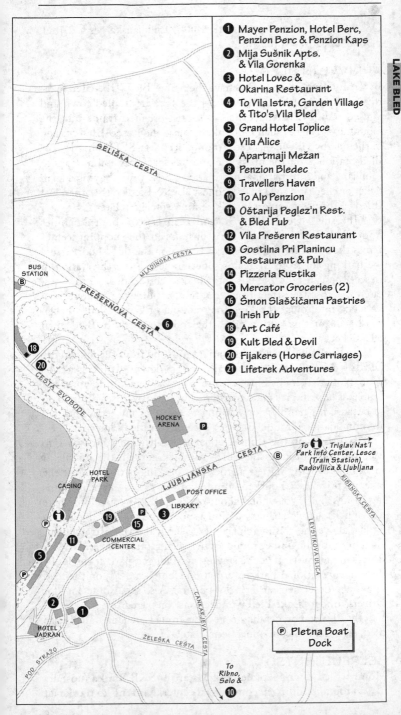

1. Mayer Penzion, Hotel Berc, Penzion Berc & Penzion Kaps
2. Mija Sušnik Apts. & Vila Gorenka
3. Hotel Lovec & Okarina Restaurant
4. To Vila Istra, Garden Village & Tito's Vila Bled
5. Grand Hotel Toplice
6. Vila Alice
7. Apartmaji Mežan
8. Penzion Bledec
9. Travellers Haven
10. To Alp Penzion
11. Oštarija Peglez'n Rest. & Bled Pub
12. Vila Prešeren Restaurant
13. Gostilna Pri Planincu Restaurant & Pub
14. Pizzeria Rustika
15. Mercator Groceries (2)
16. Šmon Slaščičarna Pastries
17. Irish Pub
18. Art Café
19. Kult Bled & Devil
20. Fijakers (Horse Carriages)
21. Lifetrek Adventures

BUS STATION

SELIŠKA CESTA

MLADINSKA CESTA

PREŠERNOVA CESTA

CESTA SVOBODE

HOCKEY ARENA

To 🛈, Triglav Nat'l Park Info Center, Lesce (Train Station), Radovljica & Ljubljana

LJUBLJANSKA CESTA

ŠIBENIŠKA CESTA

LEVŠTIKOVA ULICA

HOTEL PARK

CASINO

POST OFFICE

LIBRARY

COMMERCIAL CENTER

HOTEL JADRAN

CANKARJEVA CESTA

ŽELEŠKA CESTA

POD STRAŽO

To Ribno, Selo &

Ⓟ **Pletna Boat Dock**

Oct 8:00-18:00; off-season until 16:00; Ljubljanska cesta 27, tel. 04/578-0205, www.tnp.si).

ARRIVAL IN BLED

By Train: Two train stations have the name "Bled." The **Bled Jezero** ("Bled Lake") Station is across the lake from Bled town and is used only by infrequent, slow, tourist-oriented trains into the mountains. You're much more likely to use the **Lesce-Bled** Station in the nearby village of Lesce (pronounced lest-SEH). The Lesce-Bled Station is on the main line and has far better connections to Ljubljana and international destinations. So if you're buying a train ticket or checking schedules, request "Lesce-Bled" rather than just "Bled." (This is so important, I'll remind you again later.)

The small **Lesce-Bled Station** is in Lesce, about 2.5 miles from Bled. The nearest ATM is upstairs in the shopping center across the street (at the Gorenjska Banka on the third floor, across the parking lot from Mercator supermarket). From the station in Lesce, you can take the bus into Bled town (2/hour, 10 minutes, catch it across the street from the train station); or pay about €14 for a taxi into town. If taking the train out of Lesce-Bled, you can buy tickets at this station or on the train—nobody in Bled town sells tickets.

By Bus: Bled's main bus station is just up from the lake in the Old Town. To reach the lake, walk straight downhill on Cesta Svobode. Note that many buses also stop on the way into town, along Ljubljanska cesta; it's good to ask if your bus driver is willing to do so because it's handier for walking to many of my recommended accommodations (for details, see "Sleeping in Bled," later).

By Car: Coming from Ljubljana, you'll wind your way into Bled on Ljubljanska cesta, which rumbles through the middle of town before swinging left at the lake. Parking is tricky; near the lake, it's pricey (€2/hour) and limited to short stays. If you're sleeping in town, ask your hotel about parking. But if you're only here for a quick visit, you can try to find a spot in the short-term parking lot just above the commercial center (2-hour limit); to stretch your visit, head for the underground lot between Hotel Krim and the ice rink (4-hour limit). If you're staying even longer, park at the lot by the Triglav National Park Information Center and TI, on the road into town (described earlier; €5/24 hours). Also see "Route Tips for Drivers" under "Lake Bled Connections" on page 616.

By Plane: For details on getting from Ljubljana's airport to Bled, see "Lake Bled Connections," later.

HELPFUL HINTS

Money: Bled town's handiest ATMs are at **SKB Banka** (upstairs in round building at commercial center), **Gorenjska Banka** (at far end of Hotel Park), and **NLB** (on the main road into town, at Pension Union).

Post Office: It's just above the commercial center on Ljubljanska cesta (Mon-Fri 8:00-19:00, Sat 8:00-12:00, closed Sun, July-Aug slightly longer, tel. 04/575-0200).

Laundry: Most hotels can do laundry for you, but it's expensive (priced by the piece). You'll get a better deal from a can-do local, **Anže Štalc.** Call Anže to arrange drop-off, and pick it up cleaned and folded 24 hours later (€15/load, €5 more for same-day express service, mobile 041-575-522).

Car Rental: The Julian Alps are ideal by car. Several companies have branches in Bled, including **Europcar** (mobile 031-382-055), **Budget** (mobile 041-578-0320), **Sixt** (mobile 030-645-350), **Hertz** (tel. 04/201-6999), and the local **Avantcar** (mobile 041-400-980); as the offices tend to move around, inquire in Bled about the current locations.

Massage: If you're here to relax, consider a massage at the **Essense** wellness center at the recommended Alp Penzion. This modern, classy facility—hiding in the countryside about a 15-minute walk or 5-minute taxi ride above the lake—offers a wide range of spa treatments, including pedicures and Thai massage. A standard 50-minute massage will run you about €45 (call first to arrange, Cankarjeva cesta 20A, tel. 04/576-7450, www.essense.si, info@essense.si). You'll also find wellness centers with massage, saunas, and whirlpools at a few of the newer big hotels, including the recommended **Hotel Lovec,** as well as **Hotel Astoria** and **Golf Hotel** (open to nonguests for an additional charge).

GETTING AROUND LAKE BLED (LITERALLY)

By Bike: You can rent a mountain bike at the TI (€3.50/hour, €6/3 hours, €8/half-day, €11/day). The TI also has electric bikes, which give you a much-appreciated boost once you get them moving (€5/1 hour, €10/4 hours, €15/8 hours). While walking around the lake is slo-mo bliss, biking it lets you fast-forward between the views of your choice. Biking is also a great way to reach Vintgar Gorge—about three mostly level miles one-way, perfect for combining a countryside pedal with a walk immersed in nature. For a longer pedal, ask for the TI's excellent biking map, with various great bike trips clearly marked and described. The separated bike path to the nearby town of Radovljica (and its bee museum) is about four level miles one-way (get details at the TI).

By Horse and Buggy: Buggies called *fijakers* are the romantic, expensive, and easy way to get around the lake. Hire one along the lakefront between Hotel Park and the castle (see map on page 594 for location; around the lake-€40, one-way up to castle-€40, round-trip to castle with 30-minute wait time-€50, mobile 041-710-970).

By Tourist Train: A little train makes a circuit around the lake every 40 minutes in summer (€4, daily 9:00-21:00 in peak season, shorter hours off-season, weather-dependent, mobile 051-337-478).

By Tourist Bus: A handy but pricey shuttle bus passes through Bled daily in the summer. It starts from the main bus station, stops at a few hotels (including Grand Hotel Toplice), then goes up to the castle and on to the Vintgar Gorge entrance (€2.30 one-way to Vintgar, €1.80 just to the castle, departs at 10:00 June-Sept and also at 9:00 July-Aug, confirm schedule at TI or bus station or check www.alpetour.si).

A different summertime bus is designed to reach villages to the east that are otherwise poorly served by public transportation, including Kropa (ironwork museum) and the musical village of Begunje, along with some larger towns such as Radovljica. The bus runs only a few days a week, with a different route each day (€4/day, July-mid-Aug only, ask for schedule at TI in Bled or Radovljica).

By Taxi: Your hotel can call a taxi for you. Or contact **Bled Tours,** run by friendly, English-speaking driver Sandi Demšar and his girlfriend Cvetka (€10 to the castle or to Lesce-Bled train station, €14 to Radovljica, €50 to Ljubljana airport, €120 to Klagenfurt airport in Austria, office in Hotel Krim, Ljubljanska cesta 7, mobile 031-205-611, www.bledtours.si, info@bledtours.si).

By Boat: For information on renting your own boat, see "Boating" on page 606. For details on riding the characteristic *pletna* boats, see listing for "The Island" (page 601).

By Private Plane: If you have perfect weather and deep pockets, there's no more thrilling way to experience Slovenia's high-mountain scenery than from a small propeller plane soaring over the peaks. Flights depart from a grass airstrip near the village of Lesce, a 10-minute drive or taxi ride from Bled. Expensive...but unforgettable (€90 for 15-minute hop over Lake Bled only, €150 for 30-minute flight that also buzzes Lake Bohinj, €210 for deluxe 45-minute version around the summit of Triglav, arrange at least a day in advance, tel. 04/532-0100, www.alc-lesce.si, info@alc-lesce.si).

Tours at Lake Bled

Local Guides

Tina Hiti and **Sašo Golub,** an energetic young couple, are both excellent guides who enjoy sharing the town and region they love with American visitors. Hiring one of them can add immeasurably to your enjoyment and understanding of Bled and the surrounding area (€45 for 2-hour tour of Bled, arrange several days in advance, info@pg-slovenia.com, Tina's mobile 040-166-554, Sašo's mobile 040-524-774, www.pg-slovenia.com). Tina and Sašo are especially handy for side-tripping into the countryside if you don't want to drive yourself. I've spent great days with both of them and was thankful they were behind the wheel. Their most popular trip is a day in the Julian Alps (€190 round-trip from Bled, €230 to pick up or drop off in Ljubljana, extra charge for 8 or more people, ask about adding a picnic lunch for a small extra charge). They also offer many other options, including all-day shore excursions from the cruise port in Koper (€300 for a day visiting Ljubljana and Bled, up to 3 people) and trips in the Slovenian countryside to research your roots (price depends on distance). As Tina and Sašo both lead tours for me in Europe—and have two young kids—they may send you off with a well-trained substitute. Tina's father **Gorazd,** a former Yugoslav Olympian in ice hockey, brings the older generation's perspective to the trip; **Ervin** provides a younger view; and **Petra** is well-versed in mountain herbs.

Excursions

To hit several far-flung day-trip destinations in one go, consider a package tour from Bled. Destinations range from Ljubljana and the Karst region to the Austrian Lakes to Venice. For example, an all-day Julian Alps trip to the Vršič Pass and Soča Valley runs about €40 per person (sold by various agencies around town—ask the TI). This tour is handy, but two people can rent a car for the day for about the same price and do it at their own pace using the self-guided driving tour in the next chapter.

Adventure Trips

Various Bled-based companies specialize in taking tourists on active, outdoorsy excursions into the surrounding countryside and mountains. One popular, all-day trip is white-water rafting on the Soča River (around €90/person). Other options include canyoning, river tubing, mountain biking, paragliding, rock climbing, and more. Outfits include **Lifetrek Adventures** (near the bus station at Grajska 4, mobile 040-508-853, www.lifetrek-slovenia.com) and **TinaRaft** (based in Radovljica, mobile 041-646-255, www.tinaraft.si). Note that these companies tend to attract a young, sometimes rowdy crowd that enjoys lubricating their adventures with alcohol.

Sights at Lake Bled

Bled doesn't have many sights, but there are plenty of rewarding and pleasant activities.

▲▲▲Walk Around the Lake

Strolling the 3.5 miles around the lake is enjoyable, peaceful, and scenic. At a leisurely pace, it takes about an hour and a half...not

counting stops to snap photos of the ever-changing view. On the way, you'll pass some great villas, mostly from the beginning of the 19th century. The most significant one was a former residence of Marshal Tito—today the Hotel Vila Bled, a fine place to stop for a coffee and pretend Tito invited you over for a visit (described next). For the more adventurous, hiking paths lead up into the hills surrounding the lake (ask TI for details and maps; or hike to—and through—Vintgar Gorge, described on page 618).

▲Tito's Vila Bled

Before World War II, this villa on Lake Bled was the summer residence for the Yugoslav royal family. When Tito ran Yugoslavia, the part-Slovene communist leader took over the place and had it renovated using plans from the architect Jože Plečnik. During his heyday, Tito entertained international guests here (big shots from the communist and nonaligned world, from Indira Gandhi to Nikita Khrushchev to Kim Il Sung to Raúl Castro). Since 1984, it's been a classy hotel and restaurant, offering guests grand Lake Bled views and James Bond ambience. The garden surrounding the villa is filled with exotic trees, brought here by Tito's guests from distant lands.

The terrace has a restaurant that welcomes visitors to drop in for a meal, a piece of cake, or just a cup of coffee (reservations smart if you're dining; likely closed Nov-March). Tito fans might want to splurge for an overnight (standard Db-€195, tel. 04/575-3710, www.vila-bled.si). But even if you're not a guest here, the hotel's

staff is generally tolerant of curious tourists poking around the public areas inside.

From the marbled lobby, head upstairs. This is where Tito sympathizers have a nostalgic opportunity to send an email from his desk, sip tea in his lounge, and gawk at his **Social-**

ist **Realist wall murals.** Those murals, decorating the upper walls of a vast ballroom on the second floor, are a fascinating peek at the propaganda of the time. Follow the rousing story of the origins of postwar Yugoslavia, starting on the upper left as you enter: First you see the Nazi destruction of Belgrade in 1941, a dark moment that inspired the South Slavs to band together to fight these foreign occupiers. See Tito raising his ragtag army, then leading them into pivotal battles in Bosnia-Herzegovina (notice the minaret and the destroyed bridge over the Neretva River), followed by a winter spent enduring hardship. At the end of this long wall, Tito's victorious Partisans crush the final vestiges of the Nazis; in the upper-right corner, the spring blossoms represent a promising future for the people of Yugoslavia. The large panel at the end of the room trumpets the idealized postwar world that Tito envisioned: proud workers from all walks of life coming together for the betterment of Yugoslavia. In the shadow of a mighty factory—a symbol of heavy industry, which communists embraced as the way of the future—notice that the ironworker and the farmer are holding hands in unity. The room's focal point is the mother hoisting a young child with one arm, and the flag of the nascent Socialist Federal Republic of Yugoslavia with the other.

Getting There: The villa is a 20-minute lakeside walk from the town of Bled at Cesta Svobode 26 (it's the big, white villa with the long staircase at the southern end of the lake, just beyond the village of Mlino). You can also ask your *pletna* gondolier to drop you off here after visiting the island. Those hiking around the lake will pass the gate leading up through Tito's garden to the restaurant and lobby.

▲▲The Island (Blejski Otok)

Bled's little island—capped by a super-cute church—nudges the lake's quaintness level over the top. Locals call it simply "The Island" *(Otok)*. While it's pretty to look at from afar, it's also fun to visit.

The island has long been a sacred site with a romantic twist. On summer Saturdays, a steady procession of brides and grooms, cheered on by their entourages, heads for the island. Ninety-nine steps lead from the island's dock up to the Church of the Assumption on top. It's tradition for the groom to carry—or try to carry—his bride up these steps. About four out of five are successful (proving themselves "fit for marriage"). During the communist era, the church was closed and weddings were outlawed here. But the tradition reemerged—illegally—even before the regime ended, with a clandestine ceremony in 1989.

Cost and Hours: Free to visit island, church-€6, ticket includes tower climb, daily May-Sept 9:00-19:00, April and Oct until 18:00, Nov-March until 16:00.

Getting There: The most romantic route to the island is to cruise on one of the distinctive *pletna* boats (€12/person round-trip, includes 30-minute stay on the island; catch one at several spots around the lake—most convenient from in front of Grand Hotel Toplice or just below Hotel Park, might have to wait for more passengers to fill the boat; boats generally run from dawn, last boat leaves one hour before church closes; replaced by enclosed electric boats in winter—unless the lake freezes, in which case you can rent ice skates; mobile 031-316-575). Other places to catch a *pletna* include the village of Mlino, partway around the lake; the bottom of the grand staircase leading up to Vila Bled (it's a shorter trip from here, but the same cost); and at the campground. For more on these characteristic little vessels, see the "*Pletna* Boats" sidebar. Note that *pletna* boatmen stick close to the 30-minute waiting time on the island—which can go very fast. For more time, you can **rent your own boat** and row to the island (see Boating listing, later). It's even possible to **swim,** especially from the end of the lake nearest the island (see "Swimming" listing, later), but you're not allowed into the church in your swimsuit. Guess you'll just have to go in naked.

Visiting the Island: At the top of the stairs, the **Potičnica café** sells *potica*, the Slovenian nut-roll cake that's traditional at Christmastime but delicious any day of the year. The attached **souvenir shop** is the best in Bled, well-stocked with a variety of high-quality Slovenian gifts, trinkets, and keepsakes.

Upstairs in the same building is the worthwhile but easy-to-miss **art gallery,** which displays changing exhibits as well as a wonderful permanent exhibit commemorating Slovenia's membership in the EU. Local sculptor Ladina Kurbor has created finely

detailed clay figurines clad in the traditional national costume from each of the European Union member nations. The attached room houses figurines wearing traditional dress from various parts of Slovenia (identified on the map and explained by the posted descriptions).

The island's main attraction is the **church.** An eighth-century Slavic pagan temple dedicated to the goddess of love and fertility once stood here; the current Baroque version (with Venetian flair—the bell tower is separate from the main church) is the fifth to occupy this spot. Go inside and find the rope for the church bell, hanging in the middle of the aisle just before the altar. A local superstition claims that if you can get this bell to ring three times with one big pull of the rope, your dreams will come true. Worth a try—but be careful if you're slight of build, as the rope can take you for a ride.

If you're waiting for a herd of tourists to ring out their wishes, pass the time looking around the area in front of the altar. When the church was being renovated in the 1970s, workers dug up several medieval graves (you can see one through the glass under the bell rope). They also discovered Gothic frescoes on either side of the altar, including, above the door on the right, an unusual ecclesiastical theme: the *bris* (Jewish circumcision ritual) of Christ.

Your ticket also includes the **bell tower.** At 91 steps, it's a shorter climb than the one up from the boat dock. Up top, you'll find a restored pendulum mechanism from 1890 and fine lake views that are marred by a mesh covering that makes it impossible to snap a clear picture.

To descend by a different route, walk down the trail behind the church (around the right side), then follow the path around the island's perimeter back to where your *pletna* boat awaits.

▲Bled Castle (Blejski Grad)

Bled's cliff-hanging castle, dating in one form or another from 1,000 years ago, was the seat of the Austrian bishops of Brixen, who

controlled Bled in the Middle Ages. Today it's merely a fine tourist attraction with a little history and lots of big views. The various sights at the castle—a decent history museum, a frescoed chapel, an old-fashioned printing press, and a wine cellar—are more cute than interesting, but the real reason to come up here is to bask in the sweeping panoramas over Lake Bled and the surrounding mountainscapes.

Cost and Hours: €9, daily May-Oct 8:00-20:00, Nov-April 9:00-18:00, printing press and wine cellar close one hour earlier; tel. 04/572-9782, www.blejski-grad.si.

Getting There: To really earn those views, you can **hike** up the steep hill (20-30 minutes). The handiest trails are behind big St. Martin's Church: Walk past the front door of the church with the lake at your back, and look left after the first set of houses for the *Grad* signs marking the steepest route (follow the wooden stakes all the way up the steep switchback steps); or, for a longer but less steep route, continue past the church on the same street about five minutes, bearing uphill (left) at the fork, and

Pletna Boats

The *pletna* is an important symbol of Lake Bled. In addition to providing a pleasant way to reach the island, these boats also carry on a tradition dating back for generations. In the 17th century, Habsburg Empress Maria Theresa granted the villagers from Mlino—the little town along the lakefront just beyond Bled—special permission to ferry visitors to the island. (This provided a much-needed source of income for Mlino residents, who had very limited access

to farmland.) They built their *pletnas* by hand, using a special design passed down from father to son for centuries—like the equally iconic gondolas of Venice. Eventually, this imperial decree and family tradition evolved into a modern union of *pletna* oarsmen, which continues to this day.

Today *pletna* boats are still hand-built according to that same centuries-old design. There's no keel, so the skilled oarsmen work hard to steer the flat-bottomed boat with each stroke—boats piloted by an inexperienced oarsman can slide around on very windy days. There are 21 official *pletnas* on Lake Bled, all belonging to the same union. The gondoliers dump all of their earnings into one fund, give a cut to the tourist board, and divide the rest evenly amongst themselves. Occasionally a new family tries to break into the cartel, underselling his competitors with a "black market" boat that looks the same as the official ones. While some see this as a violation of a centuries-old tradition, others view it as good old capitalism. Either way, competition is fierce.

find the *Grad 1* sign just after the Penzion Bledec hostel on the left. Once you're on this second trail, don't take the sharp-left uphill turn at the fork (instead, continue straight up, around the back of the hill). If you'd rather skip the hike, you can take the morning **tourist bus** (see "Getting Around Lake Bled," earlier), your **rental car**, a **taxi** (around €12), or—if you're wealthy and romantic—a **horse and buggy** (€40, €10 extra for driver to wait 30 minutes and bring you back down). However, all of these options take you only to the parking lot, from which it's still a steep and slippery-when-wet five-minute hike up to the castle itself.

Eating: The **restaurant** at the castle is pricey, but worth the splurge for the views and excellent menu featuring regional cuisine. Come for dinner while it's still light out and savor the setting. There's good seating inside, but it's even better on the outside terrace. Call ahead to book a view table (€12 splittable appetizers, €12-16 pastas, €20-25 main courses, €20 fixed-price meal, daily in summer 10:00-22:00, less off-season, tel. 04/579-4424). Paupers can bring their own **picnic** to munch along the wall with million-dollar views over Lake Bled (buy sandwiches at the Mercator grocery store in the commercial center before you ascend—see page 614).

Visiting the Castle: After buying your ticket, go through the gate and huff the rest of the way up to the outer courtyard. We'll tour the castle clockwise, starting from here. As the castle is continually being spruced up, some details may be different than described.

Turning left at the entrance, you'll pass WCs, then the door to Mojster Janez's working replica of a **printing press** *(grajska tiskarna/manufaktura)* from Gutenberg's time. You can buy your own custom-made souvenir certificate using this very old technology. While this may seem like a tourist gimmick, there's actually some interesting history here. As in many lands, the printing press was a critical tool in the evolution of Slovenia's culture. Look above the press for a life-size mannequin of Primož Trubar (1508-1586), a Slovenian cross between Martin Luther and Johannes Gutenberg. In Trubar's time, Slovene was considered a crude peasants' language—not just unworthy of print, but actually illegal to print. So this Reformer went to Germany and, in 1550—using presses like this one—wrote and printed the first two books in the Slovene language: *Abecedarium* (an alphabet primer to teach illiterate Slovenes how to read) and *Catechismus* (a simplified version of the New Testament). Trubar smuggled his printed books back to Slovenia (hidden in barrels of playing cards) and, en route to Ljubljana, was briefly given refuge in this castle. (Trubar is still much-revered today, appearing on the Slovenian €1 coin.) Up the stairs is an exhibition in English about early printing methods and the importance of moveable type for advancing the Protestant Reformation, whose goal was to get the Word of God more easily into the hands of everyday people. You'll also see one of those first Trubar books—notice it was printed in Tübingen, Germany, an early enclave of the Reformation.

Just past the printing press is the castle's oldest tower—from the 11th century—and a **café terrace** offering pricey drinks with grand views.

Continue past the café and begin climbing the stairs up to grander and grander **views** over the lake. Reaching the terrace at the very top, you'll find the best vistas; the restaurant; a tiny chapel with 3-D frescoes that make it seem much bigger than it is (next to the museum entrance); a small shop selling iron items that are still forged the traditional way; and the well-presented castle **museum,** which strains to make the story of Bled, the castle, and the surrounding region of Carniola interesting. The ground floor has exhibits about geology, prehistoric artifacts, ironworking, and the seasonal life cycle of the region, while the upstairs has a cool 3-D model of the surrounding mountains, smaller models illustrating the growth of the building, more prehistory, and exhibits on the development of tourism at Lake Bled (including its many fine vacation villas). While video screens and some English information are helpful, there's only so much to say.

When you're done up here, head down the stairs between the museum and restaurant (passing WCs). Coming back down into the lower courtyard, turn left down the ramp to find the **wine cellar,** where you can pay a hefty €14-17 to bottle and cork your own souvenir bottle of wine (you're paying for the experience more than the wine). Slovenian wines are well-explained by one of two guys (both, coincidentally, named Andrej) who dress as monks, since winemaking was a monastic responsibility in the Middle Ages.

Before leaving the castle, climb the stairs up to the wooden **defensive gallery** for the best views in town of the mountains east of Bled. The biggest one is called Stol ("Chair"). In the foreground, you can see the steeple marking the town of Podhom; just to the left, the folds in the hills hide the dramatic Vintgar Gorge (see page 618).

Boating

Bled is the rowing center of Slovenia. Town officials even lengthened the lake a bit so it would perfectly fit the standard two-kilometer laps, with 100 meters more for the turn (on maps, you can see the little divot taken out of the far end). Bled hosted its fourth world championship in August 2011. The town has produced many Olympic medalists, who've won gold in Sydney, silver in Athens, and bronze in London. Notice that local crew team members, whom you'll likely see running or rowing, are characters—with a tradition of wild and colorful haircuts. This dedication to rowing adds to Bled's tranquility, since no motorized boats are allowed on the lake.

If you want to get into the action, you'll find **rental rowboats** at various points around the lake (€10-20/hour). Look for them at Pension Pletna in the lakeside village of Mlino (a scenic 15-minute walk around the lake from Bled); at the swimming pool under the castle (the closest but priciest option); and in the modern building just before the campground on the far end of the lake.

Swimming

Lake Bled has several suitable spots for a swim. The swimming pools under the castle are filled with lake water and routinely earn  the "blue flag," meaning the water is top-quality (swim all day-€7, less for afternoon only, mid-June-Sept daily 8:00-19:00, closed Oct-mid-June and in bad weather, tel. 04/578-0528). Lake Bled's main beach is at the campground at the far end of the lake, though you can also swim near the village of Mlino. If you swim to the island, remember that you can't enter the church in your swimsuit.

Luge Ride (Poletno Sankanje)

Bled's "summer toboggan" luge ride, atop Mount Straža overlooking the lake, allows you to scream down a steep, curvy metal rail track on a little plastic sled. This is a really scary one—speedy, with lots of tight turns, and with great views over the lake—but it's quite pricey. A chairlift takes you to the top of the track, where you'll sit on your sled, take a deep breath, and remind yourself: Pull back on the stick to slow down, push forward on the stick to go faster. You'll drop 480 feet in altitude on the 570-yard-long track, speeding up to about 25 miles per hour as you race toward the lake.

Cost and Hours: €9/ride, cheaper for multiple rides, chairlift only-€4, weather-dependent—if it rains, you can't go. In summer, it's open daily (late June-Aug 10:00-20:00, early Sept 11:00-18:00). In shoulder season, it's Sat-Sun only (mid-April-late June generally 11:00-18:00, late Sept-mid-Oct 11:00-17:00). It's closed off-season (mid-Oct-early April).

Getting There: The base of the chairlift is on the hillside just south of town, beyond Grand Hotel Toplice and just behind the Hostel Vila Viktorija.

Adventure Park (Pustolovski Park)

Next to the luge at the top of Mount Straža, this park has a series of five high-ropes courses designed for everyone from five-year-olds to adults. You'll get rigged up in a safety harness and go through a training course, then be set loose on your choice of courses (with help from spotters on the ground); plan on spending about two hours to do all of them. It's a steep hike up the hill, or you can pay €4 to ride the chairlift for the luge ride (or pay €8 to ride the chairlift up and luge back down).

Cost and Hours: €20 for adults, €16 for kids 7-14, €10 for kids under 7, late June-Aug daily 10:00-20:00, first half of Sept daily 11:00-18:00, shorter hours and Sat-Sun only rest of season, closed late Oct-early April, last entry two hours before closing, mobile 031-761-661, www.pustolovski-park-bled.si.

▲Kralov Med Beehive Demonstration

Tucked in Selo village, a long walk or short drive from Bled, this fascinating countryside sight is worth ▲▲▲ (or zzz) for fans of the apicultural arts. (First, read up on beekeeping on page 624.) Local beekeeper Blaž Ambrožič has built an apiary (freestanding house of beehives) and teaches visitors all about this very Slovenian form of agriculture. First you'll see the painted panels, with bees buzzing in and out. Blaž's prize possession is a gigantic Winnie-the-Pooh-style hive that he transplanted from a tree trunk. He'll demonstrate how you can hold your hand within inches of the buzzing hive without getting stung, thanks to the peaceful nature of the indigenous Carniolan bee. Inside, you can watch through a big (and safe) window as Blaž pulls out the honeycomb frames from the hive and works with his bees. You can sample (and buy) different types of honey, along with other bee-related gifts. Outside is a perennial garden that demonstrates when various plants blossom, providing much-needed pollen for the bees.

Cost and Hours: €4/person, call or email a day ahead to arrange a time, demonstrations usually last an hour or more and may even run for just two people, Selo pri Bledu 26, tel. 041-657-120, www.kralov-med.si, blazambrozic@gmail.com.

Getting There: Blaž's beehives are in the village of Selo, a five-minute drive or taxi ride or 40-minute walk from Bled town. Head out of town along the lake (past Grand Hotel Toplice), then turn left (inland) at the village of Mlino. In the next village, Selo, look for the two colorful beehive apiaries along the main road, just above the recommended Tourist Farm Mulej.

Nightlife in Bled

BLED PUB CRAWL

Bled is quiet after hours. However, the town does have a few fun bars that are lively with a young crowd (all open nightly until late). Since many young people in Bled are students at the local tourism school, they're likely to speak English...and eager to practice with a native speaker. Try a Smile, a Corona-type Slovenian lager. *Šnops* (schnapps) is a local specialty—popular flavors are plum *(slivovka)*, honey *(medica)*, blueberry *(borovničevec)*, and pear *(hruškovec)*.

Kick things off with the fun-loving local gang at **Gostilna Pri Planincu** near the bus station (described later, under "Eating in Bled"). Then head down Cesta Svobode toward the lake; just below Hotel Jelovica, you'll find the rollicking **Irish Pub** (a.k.a. "The Pub"), with Guinness and indoor or outdoor seating. For the hippest scene in town, duck across the street and wander a few more steps down toward the lake to find the **Art Café,** with a mellow ambience reminiscent of a Van Gogh painting. Around the lake near the commercial center, **Bled Pub** (a.k.a. "The Cocktail Bar" or "Troha"—for the family that owns it) is a trendy late-night spot where bartenders sling a dizzying array of mixed drinks to an appreciative, youthful crowd (between the commercial center and the lake, above the recommended Oštarija Peglez'n restaurant). If you're still standing, several other bars and cafés percolate in the commercial center, including **Kult Bled,** facing the main road. Slathered with iconic film images and neon colors, it attracts a thirtysomething crowd and occasionally hosts live music. **Devil** is open even later (also in the commercial center, near the ATM).

Sleeping in Bled

Bled has more hotel beds, per capita, than anywhere in Slovenia—and most of them are in huge, renovated convention hotels (originally dating from the communist period). I prefer staying in smaller, more characteristic, pension-type accommodations on the town's fringe—most of them an easy walk from the lake. These quaint little family-run places book up early with Germans and Brits; reserve well ahead. I've listed the high-season prices (May-Oct) unless noted. Off-season, prices are typically 10-20 percent lower. For even cheaper beds, consider one of the many *sobe* (rooms in private homes) scattered around the lake; look for signs in the neighborhood just above Prešernova cesta.

ABOVE THE LAKE

These friendly, cozy, characteristic accommodations are Bled's best values. The only catch is that they're perched on a hilltop a 5- to 10-minute climb up from the lake (easier than it sounds). There are two ways to find these from the town center: Walk around the lake to Grand Hotel Toplice, then go up the stairs around the right side of the Hotel Jadran (on the hill across the street from Grand Hotel Toplice). Or, from the main road into town (Ljubljanska cesta), take the small service road just above the commercial center (in front of Hotel Lovec), and loop up around the big Kompas and Golf hotels. If arriving by bus, ask nicely if your driver will let you disembark along Ljubljanska cesta (just above the traffic light) to avoid the long walk from the bus station. From this bus stop, you can walk down Ljubljanska cesta and take the road just above the post office, which leads up to this area. If you're sleeping up here, Penzion Berc and Mayer Penzion both have great restaurants (described later, under "Eating in Bled").

$$ Mayer Penzion, thoughtfully run by the Trseglav family, comes with 13 great-value rooms, a helpful staff, a tasty restaurant, an atmospheric wine-tasting cellar, and beautifully handcrafted Slovenian woodwork. They book up fast in summer with return clients, so reserve early (Sb-€58, Db-€85, extra bed-€20, family deals, elevator, Želeška

cesta 7, tel. 04/576-5740, www.mayer-sp.si, penzion@mayer-sp.si). They also rent a cute, newly restored two-story Slovenian farm cottage next door (Db-€120, Tb/Qb-€150).

$$ Hotel Berc and **Penzion Berc** (pronounced "berts"), run by the Berc brothers, are next door to Mayer Penzion and flank a romantic outdoor restaurant. Both have cozy public spaces, balconies off every room, and free loaner bikes, and are worth reserving ahead (both cash only). The hotel building has 15 rooms with pleasantly woody decor (Sb-€45-55, Db-€75-85—price depends on size, season, and length of stay; Pod Stražo 13, tel. 04/576-5658, www. berc-sp.si, hotel@berc-sp.si, run by Luka). The adjacent *penzion* offers 10 very sharp rooms (Db-€85-120, closed Nov-Christmas and sporadically off-season, Želeška cesta 15, tel. 04/574-1838, www. berc-sp.si, penzion@berc-sp.si; run by Miha, who also offers local excursions).

$$ Penzion Kaps, owned by Peter (whose father, Anton, is a great craftsman), has 13 comfortable rooms with balconies, modern bathrooms, and classic old wood carvings in a Shangri-La kind of place. The inviting breakfast room clusters around a giant ceramic stove (Sb-€50-60, Db-€75-83, Tb-€90-97 cash only, free loaner bikes, Želeška cesta 22, mobile 059-117-746, www.penzion-kaps. si, info@penzion-kaps.si).

$ Friendly **Mija Sušnik** rents out two comfortable apartments. Modern, tidy, and equipped with kitchens, these are a good budget choice for families (Db-€57, Tb-€68, Qb-€79, 20 percent extra for fewer than 3 nights, includes tax, breakfast not included but available at Hotel Berc next door, cash only, laundry service, free parking, Želeška cesta 3, tel. 04/574-1731, susnik@bled-holiday. com). It's just toward the lake from the bigger pensions, with a big crucifix out front. Her sister Ivanka also rents apartments, but they're farther from the lake.

$ Vila Gorenka is your nonhostel, low-budget, no-frills option. The Žerovec family's old-fashioned house has eight faded and musty rooms; three of them have their own bathrooms, while the rest share two other bathrooms. Room #10 has a grand-view balcony (S-€17-25, Sb-€30, D-€34-40, Db-€50, cash only, price depends on season, no extra charge for 1-night stays, self-service continental breakfast-€6, closed Nov-Easter, just below the bigger

> # Sleep Code
>
> **Abbreviations**   **(€1=about $1.10, country code: 386)**
> **S**=Single, **D**=Double/Twin, **T**=Triple, **Q**=Quad, **b**=bathroom
> **Price Rankings**
> **$$$** **Higher Priced**—Most rooms €100 or more
>   **$$** **Moderately Priced**—Most rooms €60-100
>   **$** **Lower Priced**—Most rooms €60 or less
> Unless otherwise noted, Wi-Fi is available and free, credit cards are accepted, and breakfast is included, but the modest tourist tax (about €1/person, per night) typically is not. Everyone listed here speaks English. Prices change; verify the hotel's current rates online or by email. For the best prices, always book directly with the hotel.

pensions at Želeška cesta 9, mobile 040-958-624, http://freeweb.siol.net/mz2, vilagorenka@gmail.com, Janez).

ON OR NEAR THE LAKE

You'll pay a premium to be closer to the lake—but it's hard to argue with the convenience.

$$$ Hotel Lovec (LOH-vets), a Best Western Premier, sits in a convenient (but non-lakefront) location just above the commercial center. Gorgeously renovated inside and out, and run by a helpful staff, it's professional yet welcoming and cheery. Its 60 plush rooms come with all the comforts and a respected restaurant (Sb-€128, Db-€160, €20 more for a lakeview balcony, very soft rates fluctuate with demand—email to ask for best price, cheaper Nov-Feb, family and "executive" suites available, delicious breakfast, elevator, indoor pool, free parking, Ljubljanska cesta 6, tel. 04/620-4100, www.lovechotel.com, reservations@kompas-lovec.com).

$$$ Vila Istra is your elegant lakeside splurge, housed inside a prominent and gorgeously restored Art Nouveau villa from 1887. The remarkably spacious rooms include one double and five sprawling suites. Room furnishings gild the lily a bit, but respect the history of the building. It's a scenic 15-minute walk outside of the town center, almost to the village of Mlino (Db-€110-130, suite-€190-250, price based on demand, air-con, Cesta Svobode 35, mobile 059-080-808, www.vila-istra.info, booking@bled.net).

$$$ Grand Hotel Toplice (TOHP-leet-seh) is the grande dame of Bled, with 87 high-ceilinged rooms, parquet floors, a genteel lakeview café/lounge, posh decor, all the amenities, and a long list of high-profile guests—from Madeleine Albright to Jordan's King Hussein to Slovene-by-marriage Donald Trump (ask to see their "wall of fame"). Once elegant, this place is a bit faded these days, but it's still a classic. Rooms in the back are cheaper, but have no lake views and overlook a noisy street—try to get one as high up as possible (nonview Db-€210, lakeview Db-€280, suites with lake views-€310, very flexible rates—check online, air-con, elevator, free one-hour boat rental for guests, free parking, Cesta Svobode 12, tel. 04/579-1000, www.hotel-toplice.com, ghtoplice@ hotelibled.com). The hotel's name—*toplice*—means "spa"; guests are free to use the hotel's swanky, natural-spring-fed indoor swimming pool (a chilly 72 degrees Fahrenheit).

NEAR THE OLD TOWN

$$$ Vila Alice, a beautifully appointed option on a busy road in the sleepy upper part of town, offers seven rooms in a classy villa with elegant public spaces, a private garden, and a sauna (standard Db-€120, superior Db-€155, deluxe Db-€178, pricier suite, air-con in some rooms, free parking, reception open daily 7:00-22:00, convenient for drivers at Prešernova cesta 26, mobile 040-231-303, www.vila-alice.com, info@vila-alice.com).

$ Apartmaji Mežan, run by welcoming Janez and Saša, has four family-friendly apartments in a modern home buried in the middle of town, just uphill from the church. As it's next to an old barn, it's technically a tourist farm (Db-€50, cash only, no breakfast, Riklijeva 6, mobile 041-210-290 or 041-516-688, www. apartmaji-mezan.si, sasa.mezan@gmail.com).

$ Penzion Bledec (BLED-ets), a family-run, official IYHF hostel, is just below the castle at the top of the Old Town. Each of the 12 rooms has its own bathroom. They have dorms (bunk in dorm room-€22-24) as well as rooms that can be rented as doubles (though "doubles" are actually underutilized triples and quads, with separate beds pushed together—so they might not be reservable July-Aug or at other busy times, Db-€54, Tb-€72; cheaper Nov-April, members pay 10 percent less, includes sheets, breakfast-€5, great family rooms, full-service laundry for guests-€9/load, restaurant, Grajska 17, tel. 04/574-5250, www.bledec.si, info@bledec.si).

$ Travellers Haven is a low-key hostel run with a smile by Mirjam. The 31 beds fill eight rooms in a nicely renovated hundred-year-old villa in the Old Town. The lodgings are well-maintained and the hangout areas are inviting, though the tight bathrooms offer little privacy (bunk in dorm room-€22, D-€48, cheaper off-season, no breakfast but guest kitchen, reception open 8:00-13:00 & 16:00-23:00, laundry machines, rental bikes, Riklijeva cesta 1, mobile 041-396-545, www.travellers-haven.si, travellers-haven@t-2.net).

OUTSIDE TOWN

The following listings are a bit farther out: Alp Penzion is a 20-minute walk from the lakefront, but still doable for nondrivers, while the tourist farm and "glampground" are best for drivers.

$$$ Garden Village is very expensive...but very cool. Alternately billed as a "glampground" and a "green resort," this splurge combines the closeness to nature of camping with the amenities of a hip resort. From the main lodge, restaurant, and rustic pond/pool, the complex tumbles down a ravine toward a gushing river, connected by slippery plank walks. You can choose between the tree house (with a loft and netted hammock area up top for kids, €290/€230); the glamping tents, with canvas walls and nestled in an abundant produce garden (€340/€250); or the simpler pier tents, actually on stilts over the river (€110/€90). All of these include breakfast, Wi-Fi, and other amenities, but additional charges for cleaning and shorter stays can really add up (on the road toward Lake Bohinj, turn off on the left just before Vila Bled, Cesta Gorenjskega odreda 16, tel. 08/389-9220, www.gardenvillagebled.com, reservations@gardenvillagebled.com).

$$ Alp Penzion makes the most of a peaceful countryside setting amid hayfields, within a 20-minute, partly uphill walk of the lake (better for drivers or for those who don't mind the walk). With 12 rooms (some with balconies), this kid-friendly place is enthusiastically run by the Sršen family, who offer lots of fun extras, including a summer barbecue grill/outdoor pub (June-Sept: Sb-€60, Db-€75-85—higher price is for rooms with balcony; Oct-May: Sb-€45, Db-€70; extra bed-€15, 3 percent cheaper if you pay cash, prices can be flexible—based on demand, family rooms, dinner possible in summer—ask when you book, air-con, free loaner bikes, Cankarjeva cesta 20A, for location, see the map on page 595, tel. 04/574-1614, www.alp-penzion.com, bled@alp-penzion.com). Just next door is the relaxing Essense spa (described earlier, under "Helpful Hints").

$ Tourist Farm Mulej, possible for hardy walkers but much better for drivers, is a new but traditional farmhouse in a tranquil valley about a half-mile from the lake (1.5 miles from Bled town). Damjana and Jože, who run this working farm (with 70 milk cows...and their smells), also rent out eight modern rooms and four apartments—all with balconies—and serve breakfasts and dinners made with food they produce. Be sure to see the udderly fascinating, fully automated cow-milking machine called Lely, who's practically a member of the family (Db-€60, or €80 with dinner; 20 percent extra for 1- or 2-night stays in June-Aug, cash only, family rooms, air-con, free loaner bikes, horseback riding free for experienced guests, Selo pri Bledu 42a, tel. 04/574-4617 or 04/022-4888, www.mulej-bled.com, info.mulej@gmail.com). It's in the farm village of Selo—drive along the lakeside road south from Bled, then turn off in Mlino toward Selo, and look for the signs (to the right) once in the village. For the location, see the map on page 619.

Eating in Bled

Bled has several good restaurants, but most everything is quite similar. For variety, wait for Ljubljana.

Okarina, run by charming, well-traveled Leo Ličof (who may be retiring soon), serves a diverse array of cuisines, all of them well-executed: international fare, traditional Slovenian specialties (with an emphasis on game), and Indian (Himalayan) dishes. Leo has a respect for salads and vegetables and a passion for fish. Creative cooking, fine presentation, friendly service, and an atmosphere as tastefully eclectic as the food make this place a great splurge (€9-14 pastas, €11-24 main courses, plus a few pricier indulgences, Mon-Fri 12:00-15:00 & 18:00-23:00, Sat-Sun 12:00-23:00, next to recommended Hotel Lovec at Ljubljanska cesta 8, tel. 04/574-1458). Daily 18:00-23:00 and maybe also for lunch, June-Sept only, closed off-season and in bad weather.

Oštarija Peglez'n ("The Old Iron"), conveniently located on the main road between the commercial center and the lake, cooks up tasty Slovenian and Mediterranean meals, with an emphasis on fish and fun, family-style shareable plates. Choose between the delightful Slovenian cottage interior or the shady streetside terrace. Reservations are smart in summer (€8-12 salads and pastas, €11-23 main courses, daily 12:00-23:00, Cesta Svobode 19A, tel. 04/574-4218).

Vila Prešeren is the best lakeside choice, featuring mod decor, good international cuisine (as well as some traditional Slovenian dishes), and tables on a giant terrace reaching down to the lakefront. This is a great spot to linger over a meal, a drink, or a classic Lake Bled dessert (€10-13 salads, €14 pastas and starters, €14-24 main courses, daily 7:00-23:00, Veslaška promenada 14, tel. 04/575-2510). They also rent eight overpriced but well-located rooms upstairs (Db-€150, www.vilapreseren.si).

In the B&B Zone Above Town: Just up the hill from the lakefront, two recommended B&Bs run restaurants ideal for dinner in a lovely setting. At either place, it's smart to reserve ahead—especially in summer. **Penzion Berc** operates a dreamy splurge restaurant. You'll dine at white-tablecloth tables positioned just so on the lush lawn or in the cutesy interior—both come with live piano music (€10-14 pastas, €16-28 main courses, May-Sept daily 17:00-23:00, Želeška cesta 15, tel. 04/574-1838). Next door, **Mayer Penzion** runs a classy restaurant with fine traditional cooking and good seating inside and out. This is where a Babel of international tour-

Bled Desserts

While you're in Bled, be sure to enjoy the town's specialty, a cream cake called **kremna rezina** (KRAYM-nah ray-ZEE-nah; often referred to by its German-derived name, **kremšnita**, KRAYM-shnee-tah). It's a layer of cream and a thick layer of vanilla custard artfully sandwiched between sheets of delicate, crispy crust. Heavenly. Slovenes travel from all over the country to sample this famous dessert. You may also see some new-fangled strawberry and chocolate kremšnita variations, but purists swear by the original.

Slightly less renowned—but just as tasty—is **grmada** (gur-MAH-dah, "bonfire"). This dessert was developed by Hotel Jelovica as a way to get rid of their day-old leftovers. They take yesterday's cake, add rum, milk, custard, and raisins, and top it off with whipped cream and chocolate syrup.

There's also prekmurska gibanica—or just **gibanica** (gee-bah-NEET-seh) for short. Originating in the Hungarian corner of the country, gibanica is an earthy pastry filled with poppy seeds, walnuts, apples, and cheese, and drizzled with rum.

Yet another dessert is the very traditional **potica** (poh-TEET-seh), a walnut roll that's usually eaten at Christmastime. While it's rare to find this in bakeries, the café on the island in the lake sells several varieties.

Desserts are typically enjoyed with a lake-and-mountains view—the best spots are the terrace at Vila Prešeren, the Panorama restaurant by Grand Hotel Toplice, and the terrace across from Hotel Park (figure around €5 for cake and coffee at any of these places). For a more local but non-lakeview setting, consider the recommended Šmon Slaščičarna (only slightly cheaper).

ists comes to swap hiking tips and day-trip tales (limited menu, €10-22 main courses; €38 fixed-price meal with salad bar, main course, and dessert; Tue-Sun 18:00-24:00, closed Mon, Želeška cesta 7, tel. 04/576-5740).

Gostilna Pri Planincu ("By the Mountaineers") is a homey, informal bar coated with license plates and packed with fun-loving and sometimes rowdy natives. A larger dining area sprawls behind the small, local-feeling pub, and there's outdoor seating out front and on the side patio. The menu features huge portions of stick-to-your-ribs Slovenian pub grub, plus Balkan grilled-meat specialties (€10-20 main courses). Look for their €6-9 daily specials—huge, home-style traditional dishes. Upstairs is a timbered pizzeria selling €6-10 wood-fired pies (daily 9:00-23:00, pizzeria open from

11:00, Grajska cesta 8, tel. 04/574-1613). The playful cartoon mural along the outside of the restaurant shows different types of mountaineers (from left to right): thief, normal, mooch ("gopher"), climber, and naked (...well, almost).

Pizzeria Rustika, in the Old Town, offers wood-fired pizzas and salads. Its upstairs terrace is relaxing on a balmy evening (€6-10 pizzas, daily 12:00-23:00, service can be slow when it's busy, Riklijeva cesta 13, tel. 04/576-8900).

Supermarket: The **Mercator** grocery store, in the commercial center, has the makings for a bang-up picnic. They sell sandwiches to go for about €3, or will make you one to order (point to what you want). This is a great option for hikers and budget travelers (Mon-Fri 7:30-20:30, Sat 7:00-15:00, Sun 8:00-12:00). There's another location closer to the Old Town and castle (Mon-Sat 7:00-20:00, Sun 8:00-16:00).

Dessert: While tourists generally gulp down their cream cakes on a hotel restaurant's lakefront terrace, local residents favor the desserts at **Šmon Slaščičarna** (a.k.a. the "Brown Bear," for the bear on the sign). It's nicely untouristy, but lacks the atmosphere of the lakeside spots (€2-3 cakes, daily 7:30-21:00, near bus station at Grajska cesta 3, tel. 04/574-1616).

Splurge Restaurant Near Bled

Vila Podvin, in the village of Mošnje (about a 15-minute drive from Lake Bled, just past Radovljica), has gained a big culinary reputation in recent years. The talented celebrity chef, UrošŠ (who has hosted some popular Slovenian cooking shows), prides himself on melding traditional Slovenian recipes with modern techniques and flavors. The dressy but inviting interior and fine garden are equally enjoyable places to dine. Their €15 three-course lunch special—available until 15:00—is a nice way to affordably sample their menu. Reservations are smart (fixed-price meals-€40/4 courses, €60/6 courses; otherwise €15 starters, €25-30 main courses; €2 cover, Tue-Sat 12:00-22:00, Sun 12:00-17:00, closed Mon, Mošnje 1, tel. 08/384-3470, www.vilapodvin.si). They also rent very sharp rooms and offer cooking classes (explained on their website).

Lake Bled Connections

The most convenient train connections to Bled leave from the Lesce-Bled Station, about 2.5 miles away (see details under "Arrival in Bled," earlier). Remember, when buying a train ticket to Lake Bled, make it clear that you want to go to the **Lesce-Bled Station** (not the Bled Jezero Station, which is poorly connected to the main line). No one in the town of Bled sells train tickets; buy them at the station just before your train departs (open Mon-Fri

5:30-21:00, Sat 7:00-15:00, Sun 14:30-19:30). If the ticket window there is closed, buy your ticket on board from the conductor (who will likely waive the surcharge).

Note that if you're going to **Ljubljana,** the bus (which leaves from Bled town itself) is better than the train (which leaves from the Lesce-Bled train station).

From Lesce-Bled by Train to: Ljubljana (roughly hourly, 40-60 minutes), **Salzburg** (3/day, 4 hours, some change in Villach, Austria), **Munich** (3/day, 5.5 hours, some change in Villach), **Vienna** (that's **Dunaj** in Slovene, 3/day, 5.25-6 hours, transfer in Villach), **Venice** (2/day with transfers in Villach—one partway by bus, 6-6.5 hours; instead consider a GoOpti minibus—described on page 588), **Zagreb** (4/day direct, 3-3.5 hours).

By Bus to: Ljubljana (Mon-Sat hourly—usually at :30 past the hour, fewer on Sun, 1.25 hours), **Radovljica** (Mon-Fri at least 2/hour, Sat hourly, Sun almost hourly, 15 minutes), **Lesce-Bled train station** (2/hour, 10 minutes), **Lake Bohinj** (hourly, 40 minutes to Bohinj Jezero stop, 50 minutes to Bohinj Vogel or Bohinj Zlatorog stop, 3/day in summer continue all the way to Savica Waterfall trailhead), **Podhom** (15-minute hike away from Vintgar Gorge, Mon-Fri 5/day in the morning, 1/day Sat, none Sun, 15 minutes), **Spodnje Gorje** (also 15-minute hike from Vintgar Gorge, take bus in direction of Krnica, hourly, 15 minutes). Confirm times at the TI or by using the schedules posted at the unstaffed Bled bus station. Buy tickets on the bus.

By Plane: Ljubljana Airport (airport code: LJU) is between Lake Bled and Ljubljana, about a 45-minute drive from Bled. Connecting by taxi costs around €60 (set price up front—since it's outside of town, they don't use the meter; be sure to use a Bled-based taxi because a Ljubljana-based taxi will likely be more expensive). The Zup Prevozi shuttle bus is a more affordable option at €13, but it runs only a few times each day (generally coordinated to meet easyJet flights—see schedule at www.zup-prevozi.eu). Another option is to prearrange a shared shuttle service with either GoOpti (see description on page 588) or Zup Prevozi. The public bus connection from Bled to the airport is cheap (total cost: about €6) but complicated and time-consuming: First, go to Kranj (Mon-Fri 12/day, Sat-Sun 8/day, 35 minutes), then transfer to a Brnik-bound bus (at least hourly, 20 minutes). Many Bled residents prefer to fly from Klagenfurt, Austria. For details on both the Ljubljana and Klagenfurt airports, see page 589.

Route Tips for Drivers: Bled is less than an hour north of Ljubljana on the slick A-2 expressway. The exit is marked for *Lesce,* but you'll also see signs for *Bled,* which will lead you directly to the lake (where the road becomes Ljubljanska cesta).

To reach **Radovljica** (bee museum) or **Lesce** (train station), drive out of Bled on Ljubljanska cesta toward the expressway. Watch for the turnoff to *Lesce* on the right. They're on the same road: Lesce first (to reach train station, divert right when entering town), then Radovljica. (Signs to *Radovljica* will divert you out to the main road that parallels the expressway, then back down into Radovljica; instead, you could follow signs to Lesce, and drive through that town for the more direct route.) Also along this road, between Lesce and Radovljica, is the well-marked turnoff to the road to **Kropa** (with its Iron Forging Museum).

Near Lake Bled

The countryside around Bled offers several day trips that can be done easily without a car (bus connection information is described in each section). The four trips listed here are the best (two small-town/museum experiences, two hiking/back-to-nature options). They're more convenient than can't-miss, but each is worthwhile on a longer visit, and all give a good taste of the Julian Alps. For a self-guided driving tour through farther-flung (and even more striking) parts of the Julian Alps, see the next chapter.

Vintgar Gorge

For those seeking an easy yet spectacular walk, Vintgar (VEENT-gar), worth ▲▲, is one of my favorite low-impact hikes in Slovenia or Croatia. Just north of Bled, the river Radovna has carved this mile-long, picturesque gorge into the mountainside. Boardwalks and bridges put you right in the middle of the magic in this "poor man's Plitvice." Shaded and relatively cool, this is a refreshing place for a walk on a hot day.

The gorge—easily reachable from Bled by bus or foot—works well for those who are itching for a hike but don't have a car. From the entrance, allow about 1.5 hours for a round-trip hike, including time for photos (and there will be photos). On sunny days, the gorge can be crowded (and less idyllic) after about 11:00—if you anticipate crowds, get an early start.

Cost and Hours: €4 to enter gorge, open daily April-Oct 8:00-19:00 or until dusk, June-Aug maybe until 20:00, closed Nov-March, tel. 04/572-5266.

Getting to Vintgar Gorge: The gorge is 2.5 miles north of

Bled. To reach the gorge entrance, you can walk (takes at least one hour one-way), pedal a rental bike (about 30 minutes, easiest with an electric bike), take a bus (15-minute ride plus 15-minute walk, or 30-minute ride on summer tourist bus), or drive (less than 10 minutes).

Walkers and **cyclists** leave Bled on the road between the castle and St. Martin's Church and take the uphill (left) road at the fork. Just after the little yellow chapel, turn right on the road with the big tree, then immediately left at the Mercator grocery store. When the road swings left, continue straight onto Partizanska (marked for *Podhom* and a walking sign for *Vintgar;* ignore the bus sign for *Vintgar* pointing left). At the fork just after the little bridge, go left for Podhom, then simply follow signs for *Vintgar*.

In summer, the easy **tourist bus** takes you right to the gorge entrance (only runs in the morning; see "Getting Around Lake Bled," page 597). Otherwise, you can take a **local bus** to one of two stops: Podhom (Mon-Fri 5/day in the morning, 1/day Sat, none Sun, 15 minutes) or Spodnje Gorje (take bus in direction of Krnica, hourly, 15 minutes). From either the Podhom or the Spodnje Gorje bus stop, it's a 15-minute walk to the gorge (follow signs for *Vintgar*).

Drivers follow signs to *Podhom*, then *Vintgar* (see walking/cycling instructions), and park for free right at the gorge entrance.

Gorge Hike: After buying your ticket, you'll hit the board-walk trail (sometimes a bit slippery) and crisscross over the most dramatic and narrow stretch, tiptoeing over several waterfalls and marveling at the clarity of the water. Then the gorge—and the trail—flattens out and passes under a high stone footbridge and over a scenic dam. Finally, at the end of the gorge, you'll reach a footbridge over a plunging waterfall (next to a snack stand and WCs). For more views, continue on five minutes downhill (following the *Pod Slap* signs), then circle over the river again to reach a knoll where you can peer up at the waterfall and bridge you just crossed.

When finished, you can simply go back the way you came, or take a prettier return to Bled (described next).

Scenic Hike Back to Bled: If you still have energy once you reach the end of the gorge, consider this longer hike back with pan-oramic views. Behind the snack stand deep in the gorge, find the trail marked *Pod Katarina*. You'll go uphill for 25 strenuous min-utes (following the red-and-white circles and arrows) before crest-ing the hill and enjoying beautiful views over Bled town and the region. Continue straight down the road 15 minutes to the typical, narrow old village of Zasip, then walk (about 30 minutes) or take the bus back to Bled.

Radovljica

The town of Radovljica (rah-DOH-vleet-suh, "Radol'ca" for short), perched on a plateau above the Sava River, has the charming Old Town that Bled lacks (refreshingly, it also lacks much of Bled's sum-mer crowds). The traffic-free core of the town, once hemmed in by a stout wall (still faintly visible in some areas), is jammed with his-toric buildings that surround the long, skinny main square called Linhartov trg. While Radovljica's

Old Town is a pleasant place to stroll or nurse a coffee, you can see it all in a few minutes. The main reason to visit here is to tour its small but strangely fascinating beekeeping museum—despite hav-ing only a few rooms, it still ranks as one of Europe's biggest on the apiarian arts. Skip the town on Mondays, when the museum is closed (and be aware that the museum has shorter hours off-season).

Tourist Information: The enthusiastic TI loves to help visitors appreciate the town of "Radol'ca" (May-Sept daily 9:00-19:00; Oct-

April Mon-Fri 9:00-16:00, Sat-Sun 9:00-18:00; Linhartov trg 1, tel. 04/531-5112, www.radolca.si).

GETTING TO RADOVLJICA

Buses to Radovljica generally leave Bled every half-hour (fewer on weekends, buy ticket from driver, trip takes about 15 minutes). To reach the town center and the bee museum from the bus station, leave the station going straight ahead, cross the bus parking lot and the next street, then turn left down the far street (following brown sign for *Staro Mesto*). In five minutes, you'll reach the start of the pedestrianized Linhartov trg (with the TI—on the right—and the start of my "Old Town Stroll").

Drivers leave Bled on Ljubljanska cesta and follow the directions under "Route Tips for Drivers" on page 617. The road dead-ends at Radovljica's pedestrian zone, where you'll find a parking lot (by the rustic garage), the TI, and the start of my "Old Town Stroll."

A handy **bike** path scenically and peacefully connects Bled with Radovljica (about 4 miles, get details at TI).

Sights in Radovljica

Old Town Stroll

Whether arriving by bus or by car, you'll enter the Old Town next to the TI. If you curl around below the main road, you'll find the scant remains of the city's original **moat**—the only surviving one in Slovenia.

On the left, just as you enter the Old Town, **Vinoteka Sodček** offers a handy opportunity to sample Slovenian wines. Their €12 tasting includes five wines, plus cheese and *pršut* (air-dried ham)—it's best to call ahead to arrange this. You can also buy bottles of wine here for €10-15. Owner Aleš knows his stuff (Mon-Sat 9:00-21:00, closed Sun, Linhartov trg 8, tel. 04/531-5071).

Continuing into the Old Town, after a half-block you'll pass a fun little **secondhand shop** on the right—crammed with everything from beat-up modern appliances to genuine Slovenian antiques.

Beyond that, the street opens up into **Linhartov trg**, a charming square fronted by historic buildings. On the left is the **Magušarjeva Hiša,** a fine old Gothic house where potter Urban Magušar lives, has a studio and exhibition space, and teaches pottery classes—if you're curious, step into the courtyard and ask him if you can see the house (Trubarjeva 1, mobile 041-734-808).

The **Vidičeva Hiša** café serves great ice cream and cakes. Farther along is the traditional, recommended **Lectar** restaurant, with a "living museum" in the basement where you can watch bakers making traditional gingerbread ornaments (€1.50 entry).

Across the street is a monument with a student holding a big medallion image of **Josipina Hočevar,** a Radovljica native who later helped fund the town's water system (see the old well nearby) and a school and many important buildings in Krško, near Zagreb. Next to that is the **Šivičeva Hiša,** an atmospheric late-Gothic house that's open to the public. If you go a block down any street to the right, you'll come to a fine valley **viewpoint** emphasizing Radovljica's dramatic position on a long promontory.

Dominating the main part of the square is the big, yellow **town "castle"** (actually a mansion); upstairs you'll find the **Apicultural Museum** (described next), the Linhart Museum, and the Baroque Hall—once divided into 10 small offices, but recently restored to its previous grandeur.

Beyond the mansion (and connected to it by a gallery) is **St. Peter's Church;** to its right is its rectory, where you can dip into the pretty courtyard.

Circle all the way around the church, then go through the gate to the edge of the ravine. Burrowed into the hillside is a **WWII-era bunker** left behind by the Nazis. Peeking into the window of the bunker, you'll see it's been turned into a chapel dedicated to Edith Stein, a 20th-century Polish Jew who became a Carmelite nun but was arrested by the Nazis and executed at Auschwitz. She was later made a saint by Pope John Paul II (notice the menorah and Star of David inside the chapel, on the right). While she has no official ties to Radovljica, locals are inspired by Edith's example.

▲▲Apicultural Museum (Čebelarski Muzej)

This museum celebrates Slovenia's long and very proud beekeeping heritage. While the exhibits about the history of beekeeping are oddly fascinating, the highlight is the extensive collection of colorfully painted frontboard panels (used on the front of hives)—one of Slovenia's most cherished folk arts. Replicas of these panels are sold in souvenir shops nationwide, but these are the real deal.

Cost and Hours: €3, good English descriptions, €1.60 English guidebook is a nice souvenir; May-Oct Tue-Sun 10:00-18:00, closed Mon, shorter hours off-season, Jan-Feb closed Sat-Mon; clean and easy WCs, upstairs at Linhartov trg 1, tel. 04/532-0520, www.muzeji-radovljica.si.

Visiting the Museum: Everything is well-described in English, but this commentary will help you locate the highlights.

The **first room** of the museum traces the history of beekeeping, from the time when bees were kept in hollowed-out trees to the present day. The bust celebrates beekeeper extraordinaire Anton Janša. On the nearby wall, you'll see excerpts from his first-ever textbook on beekeeping, as well as documents from other VIBs (very important beekeepers).

In the **second room** are old-fashioned tools. When a new queen bee is born, the old queen takes half the hive's bees to a new location. Experienced beekeepers used the long, skinny instrument (a beehive stethoscope) to figure out when the swarm was working up a steady buzz, indicating they were ready to fly the coop. Then, once the bees had moved to a nearby tree, the beekeeper used the big spoons to retrieve the queen—surrounded by an angry ball of her subjects—from her new home before she could get settled in. The beekeeper transferred the furious gang into a manmade hive designed for easier, more sanitary collection of honey. You can also see the tools beekeepers used to create smoke, which makes bees less aggressive. Even today, some of Slovenia's old-fashioned beekeepers simply light up a cigarette and blow smoke on any bees that get ornery. The life-size model of a man carrying a box on his back illustrates how dedicated beekeepers would trudge uphill with their hives to help them reach higher and higher blossoms as the summer wore on. You'll also see a variety of old beehives (and a press used to squeeze every last drop of honey out of that comb), as well as photos of apiaries—large, freestanding buildings that house multiple hives. The map on the wall shows how the Carniolan bee—favored by beekeepers for its relatively mellow personality and fast growth in springtime—has been exported far and wide throughout the world, thanks to its adaptability to new climates.

The **third room** features the museum's highlight: whimsically painted beehive frontboards (called *panjske končnice*). Beekeepers,

 believing these paintings would help the bees find their way home, developed a tradition of decorating their hives with religious, historical, and satirical folk themes. The oldest panel dates from 1758, but the practice really took off in the 19th century. Take your time perusing these delightful illustrations. The depiction of a hunter's funeral shows all the animals happy...except his dog. In another panel, animals shave the hunter—evoking an old Slovenian saying about "shaving the fool." Panels also reveal professional stereotypes of the time: One popular panel shows two farmers fighting over a cow, while a lawyer milks it. Another features a giant snail running over very slow-moving tailors (who were considered extremely lethargic in

Slovenian Beekeeping

Since the days before Europeans had sugar, Slovenia has been a big honey producer. Slovenian farmer Anton Janša (1734-1773) is considered the father of modern beekeeping. Habsburg Empress Maria Theresa brought him to Vienna to become Europe's first official teacher of this art. And even today, beekeeping is considered a crucial part of Slovenian culture. The area around Lake Bled (Carniola) has about 6,000 inhabitants, including 65 beekeepers who manage 5,000 hives—the most bees per capita of any place in Europe.

Most Slovenian beekeepers maintain large buildings called apiaries, which hold banks of smaller hives (as opposed to beekeepers in North America, who tend to have a few separate large hives). This innovation—one of many by Janša—allows beekeepers to maximize efficiency. The front panel of each individual hive is painted in bright colors, often depicting creative folk scenes. This is designed to help both the bees and the beekeepers (who were, traditionally, often illiterate) distinguish the hives from each other. (While bees may not be able to tell a painting of a bear from one of a flower, they can distinguish enough patterns and colors to keep themselves from accidentally going to the wrong hive—in which case they'd be attacked as an outsider.)

Replicas of those characteristic **beehive panels** are available at shops in Bled and Ljubljana and make for appealing souvenirs. Basic reproductions of the beehive panels cost around €12-15, while better-quality, hand-painted ones run €20-30 or more. When perusing your options, it helps to know the stories behind each one (see page 622 for a run-down on some of the designs).

The other apian souvenir is **honey**. In 2013, Slovenian honey

sewing new clothes). Historical panels include a bloody beheading during a local battle and several scenes of troublesome Turks. There's everything from portraits of Habsburg emperors, to a "true crime" sequence of a man murdering his family as they sleep, to proto-"Lockhorns" cartoons of marital strife, to awkward depictions of foreign lands (based on likely incomplete or faulty descriptions of the day), to 18th-century erotica (one with a woman showing some leg and another with a flip-up, peek-a-boo panel). A few panels blur the line between humorous and misogynistic: Look for the devil sharpening a woman's tongue on a wheel; the mill where old women are put in and young women are pulled out; or the man

was designated as a unique product by the European Union—a certification that means only honey produced in a certain place and manner can carry that name. Taste can differ tremendously from hive to hive, and is determined by the specific flowers and blossoms a hive's bees gather pollen from. Ideally find a shop that will let you sample several. In general, honeys made from mixed flowers and linden blossoms (which tend to be cloudy from a natural crystallization process) have the sweetest, mildest flavor; those made from chestnut or pine trees can have a bitter after-taste. The honeys that appear creamy are infused with flavors and are most often eaten on bread or pancakes; plain honey is more versatile.

Besides honey, beekeepers also make money by raising new queen bees. Each hive has one, and they can't be bred—one of the larvae is simply fed special "royal jelly" that encourages her to become a leader. In the springtime, when bees are born, the beekeeper keeps a close eye on the hive to figure out whether there are any potential queens about to emerge. If he finds one, he'll move the old queen—who brings half the hive with her—to a new home (before she can find one on her own).

Slovenes still reserve an importance and affection for bees that's rare in modern times. For example, the Slovene language has two different words for "to give birth" and "to die": One they use exclusively for humans and bees, and a different one for all other animals. If a beekeeper dies, it's believed (with some pretty incontrovertible evidence) that the new beekeeper must formally "introduce" himself to the hive by going there and explaining to the bees what has happened; otherwise, they become confused and agitated, and often die themselves.

To learn more about Slovenian beekeeping, visit the insightful Apicultural Museum in Radovljica. For an even more vivid, practical experience, call Blaž at Kralov Med near Bled for a demonstration (see page 608). At either place, you'll get a sense for just how proud Slovenes are of their bees.

carrying a cross—and his wife—on his back. (Equal-opportunity offenders, beekeepers also painted scenes of drunk men being yanked out of bars and away from card games by their wives.) The life-size wooden statues were used to "guard" the beehives—and designed to look like fearsome Ottoman and Napoleonic soldiers.

The **fourth room** examines the biology of bees. In the summer only, look for the actual, functioning beehive. Try to find the queen—she's usually marked with a dot on her back. The surround-sound hive nearby lets you step inside to hear the noise of a buzzing queen. You'll also see bee-related products, including wax items, ornaments, and pastries. Another exhibit shows how bees—so respected here in Slovenia, and around the world—are a popular decorative motif, adorning everything from coins to buildings (in many cultures, diligent bees, who store their honey, are symbolic of banks).

The **final room** features a modern beekeeper's house, special exhibits, and a good but dry, detailed 14-minute film about the Carniolan bee.

Back at the entrance, the ticket desk sells a few choice souvenirs, including hand-painted replicas of frontboards, honey brandy, candles, ornaments, and other bee products.

Nearby: Sharing a ticket desk with the bee museum, the skippable **Linhart Museum** celebrates one of Slovenia's leading Enlightenment thinkers: Radovljica-born Anton Linhart, the 18th-century politician and historian who wrote some of the first plays in the Slovenian language, setting the stage for France Prešeren (€5 combo-ticket with Apicultural Museum, same hours).

Eating in Radovljica

Several Radovljica restaurants near the bee museum have view terraces overlooking the surrounding mountains and valleys.

Lectar offers pricey, hearty Slovenian fare in a rural-feeling setting with a user-friendly, super-traditional menu. Its several heavily decorated rooms are often filled with tour groups, but in good weather, don't miss the terrace out back. Come here if you want to linger over rustic Slovenian specialties—not if you're in a hurry. The restaurant is known for its heart-shaped gingerbread cookies (called *lect*), inscribed with messages of love. In the cellar is a €1.50 "living museum" where you can watch costumed bakers make and decorate these hearts according to the traditional recipe (€6-11 starters, €9-13 main courses, Wed-Mon 12:00-22:00, closed Tue, family-friendly, Linhartov trg 2, tel. 04/537-4800).

Gostilna Avguštin, across the street, is the simpler local alternative for unpretentious, stick-to-your-ribs Slovenian fare. Their terrace in back enjoys an even better view than Lectar's (€6-9 starters, €11-20 main dishes, daily 11:00-24:00, Linhartov trg 15, tel. 04/531-4163).

Kropa

Tucked in a narrow gully below the Jelovica Plateau, the modest metalworking village of Kropa has a big history as one of the earliest and most prolific industrial centers of Europe. Kropa thrills engineers—for whom it merits ▲▲—but may leave others cold.

GETTING TO KROPA

Kropa is poorly connected by bus, other than the summer-only, infrequent tourist bus from Bled (see page 596) and sporadic weekday connections to Radovljica; skip Kropa unless you have a car. Drivers can find the well-marked road to Kropa off the road that runs between Lesce and Radovljica.

BACKGROUND

Beginning in the 15th century, the people of Kropa harnessed their substantial natural resources: iron ore from nearby mines; plenty of wood to keep the furnaces burning; and water from their rushing river, which they diverted into channels to power waterwheels. By the 16th century, Kropa was already known as one of the most important blacksmithing towns in Europe, and was granted a prized semi-autonomous status by the Habsburg Empire. Blacksmiths here specialized in spikes and nails, producing 127 different types—from small tacks for shoes, to bigger nails for horseshoes, to huge spikes used for major construction projects all over Europe. The romantic wooden pilings in the Venice lagoon are held together with Kropa spikes.

By the 18th century—still well before the dawn of the Industrial Age—Kropa was one of the most industrially developed

places in Europe. Its 70 houses were packed with 1,400 men, women, and children, who all worked in the foundries. But by the late 18th century, local iron ore deposits were depleted, the industry collapsed, and some 800 local residents died of disease and other poverty-related causes. The 19th century saw another boost, as Kropa spikes were in demand to build the Vienna-Trieste railway. By modern times, the nail and spike industry had been replaced by decorative blacksmithing (especially at the big Uko factory across from the museum), which included items such as fancy gates and mailboxes. Today, Kropa's 90 houses hold a more reasonable population of 200.

Sights in Kropa

▲Iron Forging Museum (Kovaški Muzej)

This modest but engaging exhibit traces the history of this metalworking burg. Filling two floors of a typical old Kropa house, the displays have little English explanation but capture the blacksmithing spirit of Kropa.

Cost and Hours: €3, May-Oct Tue-Sun 10:00-18:00, closed Mon, shorter hours off-season, Kropa 10, tel. 04/533-7200, www.muzeji-radovljica.si.

Visiting the Museum: When you buy your ticket, ask the attendant if she's willing to show you around the museum—this really helps bring the (otherwise poorly explained) exhibits to life. If she's busy, the following describes some things to look for on your own.

Go up to the first floor and enter the room with the big town model of Kropa as it was in the 19th century. Notice just how ingeniously the town channeled its water supply to use its raw power for its foundries. The next room shows big chunks of iron ore, and the buckets used to gather and carry it. (Many workers here farmed during the summer and were miners in the winter.) Although the big model of a blast furnace seems fairly sophisticated and "modern," it was used in Kropa all the way back in the mid-15th century. A waterwheel pumped bel-

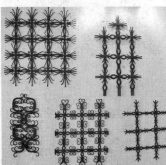

lows onto a wood fire, superheating it to melt down the raw iron ore to create impure "pig iron." The second, smaller chimney was a furnace that further refined the iron. Look at the blacksmiths' tools and pass through the room with several huge bellows, then enter the room with decorative iron gratings and other decorations. These date from Kropa's later era of blacksmithing, between the two World Wars. Near the base of the stairs is a big music box with a piano, drums, and cymbals (ask the ticket seller to start it for you).

Climb the stairs to the top floor, where you'll see a model of a typical family home, as well as mannequins of the family in period dress. The next room displays the vast range of nails and spikes that were produced here. A worker was expected to produce 2,000 of these spikes in one day.

Strolling the Town

Walk from the museum up through this hardworking yet charming village. Notice the **canals** that have been split off from the main river to channel water to turn waterwheels (you'll see a replica waterwheel by the Uko factory).

The main **bridge** through town offers a good view up and down the thundering river—making it clear why this was an attractive place for early industry. The blocky, boldly communist-era **monument** next to the bridge honors the Partisans who died during World War II while evicting the Nazis from Yugoslavia. Although its aesthetic is off-putting Socialist Realism, its content—with locally made iron decorations—is unique to Kropa. Notice the Kropa resident handing over his hammer in exchange for a rifle. Locals have long enjoyed military exemption because their metalworking prowess was so valuable to the war effort. The communist Yugoslav government—always eager to celebrate industry's role in advancing the cause of the proletariat—made Kropa Slovenia's first town to be protected as a cultural monument, in 1953.

Crossing the bridge and continuing up the road, near the top of town on the left you'll pass a traditional **spike forge** with firewood stacked out front. This working facility—which still merges the power of wood, water, and a blacksmith's arm to create spikes—is part of the Iron Forging Museum, but unfortunately, it's rarely open to individual visitors (ask at the museum). For most of its history, Kropa had 15 such forges.

Lake Bohinj

The pristine alpine Lake Bohinj (BOH-heen), 16 miles southwest of Bled, enjoys a quieter scene and (in clear weather) even better vistas of Triglav and the surrounding mountains. This is a real back-to-nature experience, with just a smattering of hotels and campgrounds, rather than the well-oiled resort machine of Bled. Some people adore Bohinj; others are bored by it. While spectacular in clear, sunny weather, it's disappointing in the clouds (and, because of its position deep in the mountains, it can be socked-in here even when it's clear in Bled). But if the weather is great and you're finding Bled too touristy to allow you to really enjoy nature, go to Bohinj.

GETTING TO LAKE BOHINJ

From Bled, hourly **buses** head for Bohinj, stopping at three different destinations: Bohinj Jezero (the village of Ribčev Laz, 40 minutes), then Bohinj Vogel (a

10-minute walk from the base of the Vogel Mountain cable car, 50 minutes), and finally a few hundred yards more to Bohinj Zlatorog (Hotel Zlatorog and the one-hour hike to the Savica Waterfall trailhead, 50 minutes). In summer, a few buses continue all the way to the Savica Waterfall trailhead (see

details under "Savica Waterfall," later). Off-season, there are fewer buses—confirm times before you depart.

Drivers leave Bled going south along the lakefront road, Cesta Svobode; in the village of Mlino, you'll peel off from the lake and follow signs to *Boh Bistrica* (a midsize town near Lake Bohinj). Once in the town of Bohinjska Bistrica, turn right, following *Boh Jezero* signs. The road takes you to the village of Ribčev Laz and along the lakefront road with all the attractions—the drive from Bled to the lake takes about 30 minutes. You can follow this road all the way to the Vogel cable-car parking lot; at the Vogel turnoff, you can continue straight ahead to reach the Savica Waterfall trail-head, or turn right and cross the bridge to curl around the far end of the lake and see the pristine river that feeds the lake (which flows out of the pool at the base of the Savica Waterfall).

Sights at Lake Bohinj

A visit to Bohinj has three parts: a village (offering boat trips on the lake), a cable car (and nearby cemetery), and a waterfall hike. I've listed them as you'll reach them along the main road from Bled, which runs along the south side of the lake. If you plan to do every-thing (boat trip, cable car, waterfall hike), ask at the TI in Ribčev Laz about a combo-ticket to save some money.

Ribčev Laz Village

Coming from Bled, your first views of Bohinj will be from the little village called Ribčev Laz (loosely translated as "Good Fishin' Hole") at the southeast corner of the lake. Here you'll find a TI, a handful of hotels and ice-cream stands, and the Bohinj Jezero bus stop.

On the way into town, on a small hill to the right, is a **monument** to the four Bohinj-area mountaineers who first summited Mount Triglav on August 26, 1778.

The town's main landmark is its picturesque lakefront church, **St. John the Baptist** (to your right as you face the lake, past the stone bridge; not open to visitors).

A five-minute stroll down the main lakefront road is a dock where you can catch an electric **tourist boat** to make a silent circuit around the lake (€10.50 round-trip, €7.50 one-way, daily 10:00-18:00, runs hourly, less off-season). The boat stops at the far end of the lake, at Camp Zlatorog—a 10-minute walk from the Vogel cable car (see below).

Across from the Ribčev Laz dock is a fun concrete 3-D model of Triglav. Finally, a few more steps down the road, just beyond a boat rental dock, is a statue of **Zlatorog**, the "Golden Horn"—a mythical chamois-like creature native to the Julian Alps.

▲Vogel Mountain Cable Car

For a mountain perch without the sweat, take the cable car up to the top of Vogel Mountain, offering impressive panoramic views of Mount Triglav and the Julian Alps. On a

clear day, this is the best mountain pan-orama you can get without wings (the light is best in the morning).

Cost and Hours: €13.50 round-trip, Dec-Oct daily 8:00-18:00, runs every 30 minutes in summer and continuously in winter, closed Nov, www.vogel.si.

Getting There: To reach the cable-car station, drivers follow signs to *Vogel* (to the left off the main lakefront road, marked *1915* and *1917*); by bus, get off at the Bohinj Vogel stop (request this stop from driver) and hike about 10 minutes up the steep road on the left (away from the lake).

Visiting the Summit: After you arrive at the top, savor the views from the metal platform where you exit the cable car...just don't look down. Walking up through the cable-car station (past the Viharnik snack bar, with basic food and far-from-basic views), you'll pop out at the summit, a ski-in-winter, hike-in-summer area with a pasture filled with grazing cows and smaller chairlifts to various recreation areas.

The first chairlift is designed for skiers and doesn't run in sum-mer, but if you hike down into the little valley, you can take the second chairlift up the adjacent summit (Orlove Glave) for views into another valley on the other side. Then, from Orlove Glave, you can hike or ride the chairlift back to where you started. With plenty of time and very strong knees, you could even hike from Orlove Glave all the way back down to Lake Bohinj.

If you need a break near the cable-car station, the alpine hut Merjasec ("Wild Boar") offers tasty strudel and a wide variety of local brandies (including the notorious "Boar's Blood"—a concoc-tion of several different flavors guaranteed to get you snorting).

World War I Cemetery

Back down below the cable car, on the main road just beyond the Bohinj Vogel bus stop, look for the metal gate on the left marking the final resting place for some WWI Soča Front soldiers (see sidebar on page 656). While no fighting occurred here (it was mostly on the other side of these mountains), injured soldiers were brought to a nearby hospital, and those who didn't recover ended up here. Notice that many of the names are not Slovenian, but Hungarian, Polish, Czech, and so on—a reminder that the entire multiethnic Austro-Hungarian Empire was involved in the fighting. If you're walking down from the cable-car station, the cemetery makes for a poignant detour on your way to the main road (look for it through the trees).

Savica Waterfall (Slap Savica)

Up the valley beyond the end of the lake is Bohinj's final treat, a waterfall called Slap Savica (sah-VEET-seh). Hardy hikers enjoy

following the moderate-to-strenuous uphill trail (including 553 stairs) to see the cascade, which dumps into a remarkably pure pool of aquamarine snowmelt.

Cost and Hours: €2.50, daily in summer from 8:00 until dusk, allow up to 1.5 hours for the round-trip hike.

Getting There: Drivers follow the lakefront road to where it ends, right at the trailhead. Without a car, getting to the trailhead is a hassle. Boats on the lake, as well as most public buses from Bled, take you only as far as the Bohinj Zlatorog stop—the end of the line, and still a one-hour hike from the trailhead (from the bus stop, follow signs to *Slap Savica*). However, three buses a day (Mon-Sat July-Sept only, none Sun or off-season) run from Bled all the way to the Savica trailhead (likely departing Bled at 10:00, 14:20, and 16:20, about an hour to the trailhead, returning at 15:30 and 18:30—but confirm times locally before making the trip). Frankly, if the connections don't fit your itinerary, it's not worth worrying about.

Sleeping at Lake Bohinj

If you'd like to get away from it all and settle in at Bohinj, consider **$$ Stare Pension** (STAH-reh). Well-run by mild-mannered Jože, it has 10 older, rustic-but-well-maintained rooms (five of them with balconies) in a pristine setting at the far end of the lake (Db-€80 July-Aug, €70 May-June and Sept, €60 Oct-April, €5 less without balcony, half-board-€10 per person, Ukanc 128, mobile 040-558-669, www.impel-bohinj.si, info@impel-bohinj.si). They also rent an eight-person villa for longer stays (info@rent-villa-slovenia.com).

To get higher into the forested hills, you can head for **$$ Penzion Resje,** which sits above Bohinjska Bistrica. Simple but cozy, it has 14 affordable rooms, a great restaurant, and an away-from-it-all local feel, nestled in a tiny village called Nemški rovt—"German road" (Db-€70 in July-Aug, €50 off-season, Nemški rovt 21A, tel. 04/572-1079, www.penzion-resje.si, resje21a@gmail.com, Jože).

THE JULIAN ALPS

Vršič Pass • Soča River Valley • Bovec • Kobarid

The countryside around Lake Bled is plenty spectacular. But to top off your Slovenian mountain experience, head for the hills. The northwestern corner of Slovenia—within yodeling distance of Austria and Italy—is crowned by the Julian Alps (named for Julius Caesar). Here, mountain culture has a Slavic accent.

The Slovenian mountainsides are laced with hiking paths, blanketed in deep forests, and speckled with ski resorts and vacation chalets. Beyond every ridge is a peaceful alpine village nestled around a quaint Baroque steeple. And in the center of it all is Mount Triglav—ol' "Three Heads"—Slovenia's national symbol and, at 9,396 feet, its tallest mountain.

The single best day in the Julian Alps is spent driving up and over the 50 hairpin turns of breathtaking Vršič Pass (vur-SHEECH, open May-Oct) and back down via the Soča (SOH-chah) River Valley, lined with offbeat nooks and Hemingway-haunted crannies. As you curl on twisty roads between the cut-glass peaks, you'll enjoy stunning high-mountain scenery, whitewater rivers with superb fishing, rustic rest stops, thought-provoking WWI sights, and charming hamlets.

A pair of Soča Valley towns watch over the region. Centrally situated Bovec is all about good times (it's the whitewater adventure-sports hub), while Kobarid has Old World charm and better restaurants, and attends to more serious matters (WWI history). Though neither is a destination in itself, both Bovec and Kobarid are pleasant, functional, and convenient home bases for lingering in this gloriously beautiful region.

PLANNING YOUR TIME

Most visitors do this area as a surgical strike on a full-day side-trip from Lake Bled or Ljubljana—and even that quick glimpse is very satisfying. But there's plenty here to make it worth slowing down and spending a night (or possibly more). If you'd like to take advantage of the Soča Valley's hiking trails and many adventure sports (especially whitewater rafting on the Soča River), give yourself more time.

GETTING AROUND THE JULIAN ALPS

The Julian Alps are best by **car.** Even if you're doing the rest of your trip by train, consider renting a car here for maximum mountain day-trip flexibility. I've included a self-guided driving tour that incorporates the best of the Julian Alps (Vršič Pass and the Soča Valley).

If you're without your own wheels, hiring a **local guide with a car** can be a great value, maximizing not only what you see, but what you learn. Or you can choose a cheaper but less personalized day-trip **excursion** from Bled. (Both options are explained under "Tours at Lake Bled," page 598.)

In the summer, a public **bus** follows more or less the driving-tour route over the Vršič Pass described below (departs Ljubljana daily July-Aug at 6:30 and 15:00, June and Sept Sat-Sun only at 6:30, 4.25 hours to Bovec, afternoon bus also continues to Kobarid in 5 hours total, road closed Oct-May). Additional Vršič Pass buses leave from Kranjska Gora at the foot of the mountains, which is also connected by bus to Ljubljana and Bled. (Yet another option is to take a direct bus from Ljubljana to Bovec that uses the somewhat less scenic southerly route via Idrija—but then you'd miss going over the Vršič Pass.) To check or confirm schedules, see www.ap-ljubljana.si.

If you lack the time or transport to reach the Vršič Pass and Soča Valley, you could stay closer to Bled, and get a taste of the Julian Alps with a more convenient day trip to the Vintgar Gorge or Lake Bohinj (reachable with easy and frequent bus connections; see "Near Lake Bled" in the previous chapter).

Julian Alps Driving Tour

This all-day, self-guided driving tour—rated ▲▲▲—takes you over the highest mountain pass in Slovenia, with stunning scenery and a few quirky sights along the way. From waterfalls to hiking trails, WWI history to queasy suspension bridges, this trip has something for everyone.

ORIENTATION TO THE JULIAN ALPS

Most of the Julian Alps are encompassed by Triglav National Park (Triglavski Narodni Park). This drive is divided into two parts: the Vršič Pass and the Soča River Valley. While not for stick-shift novices, all but the most timid drivers will agree that the scenery is worth the many hairpin turns. Frequent pull-outs offer plenty of opportunities to relax, stretch your legs, and enjoy the vistas.

Planning Your Time: This drive can be done in a day, but consider spending the night along the way for a more leisurely pace. You can start and end in Bled or Ljubljana. You can return to your starting point, or do this trip one-way as a very scenic detour between these two destinations.

Length of This Tour: These rough estimates do not include stops: Bled to the top of Vršič Pass—1 hour; Vršič Pass to Trenta (start of Soča Valley)—30 minutes; Trenta to Bovec—30 minutes; Bovec to Kobarid—30 minutes; Kobarid to Ljubljana or Bled—2 hours (remember, it's an hour between Ljubljana and Bled). In other words, if you started and ended in Bled and drove the entire route without stopping, you'd make it home in less than five hours...but you'd miss so much. It takes at least a full day to really do the region justice.

Tourist Information: The best sources of information are the Bled TI (see page 593), the Triglav National Park Information Centers in Trenta (page 642), and the TIs in Bovec and Kobarid (both listed in this chapter).

Maps: Pick up a good map before you begin (available at local TIs, travel agencies, and gas stations). The all-Slovenia *Autokarta Slovenija* or the TI's *Next Exit: Goldenhorn Route* map both include all the essential roads, but several more detailed options are also available. The 1:50,000 Kod & Kam *Posoče* map covers the entire Vršič Pass and Soča Valley (but doesn't include the parts of the drive near Bled and Ljubljana).

OK...let's ride.

PART 1: VRŠIČ PASS

From Bled or Ljubljana, take the A-2 expressway north, enjoying views of Mount Triglav on the left as you drive. About 10 minutes past Bled, you'll approach the industrial city of **Jesenice**, whose iron- and steelworks once filled this valley with multicolored smoke. The city, which was known as the "Detroit of Yugoslavia," plans to convert these old factories (most of which closed in the 1980s) into a sort of theme park.

Just after the giant smokestack with the billboards, the little gaggle of colorful houses on the right (just next to the freeway) is **Kurja Vas** ("Chicken Village"). This unassuming place is locally famous for producing hockey players: 18 of the 20 players on the 1971 Yugoslav hockey team—which went to the World Championships—were from this tiny hamlet.

As you zip past Jesenice, keep your eye out for the exit marked *Jesenice-zahod, Trbiž/Tarvisio, Kr. Gora,* and *Hrušica* (it's after the gas station, just before the tunnel to Austria). When you exit, turn left toward *Trbiž/Tarvisio* and *Kranjska Gora* (yellow sign).

Just after the exit, the big blue building surrounded by tall lights was the former border station (the overpass you'll go under leads into Austria). Locals have fond memories of visiting Austria during the Yugoslav days, when they smuggled back forbidden Western goods. Some items weren't available at home (VCRs, Coca-Cola, designer clothes), while other goods were simply better in Austria (chocolate, coffee, dishwasher soap).

Slovenes brag that their country—"with 56 percent of the land covered in forest"—is Europe's second-greenest. As you drive toward Kranjska Gora, take in all this greenery...and the characteristic Slovenian hayracks (recognized as part of the national heritage and now preserved; see page 572). The Vrata Valley (on the left) is a popular starting point for climbing Mount Triglav. Paralleling the road on the left is a "rails-to-trails" bike path—converted from an old railway bed—that loops from here through Italy and Austria, allowing bikers to connect three countries in one day. On the right, watch for the statue of Jakob Aljaž, who actually bought Triglav— back when such a thing was possible (he's pointing at his purchase). Ten minutes later, in Gozd Martuljek, you'll cross a bridge and enjoy a great head-on view of Špik Mountain.

Kranjska Gora was once Yugoslavia's leading winter resort, and remains popular with Croatian skiers. As every Slovene and Croatian wants a ski bungalow here, it has some of the highest property values in the country. Entering Kranjska Gora, you'll see a turnoff to the left marked for *Bovec* and *Vršič*. This leads up to the pass, but winter sports fanatics may first want to take a 15-minute detour to see the biggest ski jump in the world, a few miles ahead (stay straight through Kranjska Gora, then turn left at signs for **Planica**, the last stop before the Italian border; you'll likely pay a small parking fee to drive in and see it, or you can park before the payment booth and walk in). Every few years, tens of thousands of sports fans flock here to watch the ski-flying world championships. This is where a local boy was the first human to fly more than 100

JULIAN ALPS

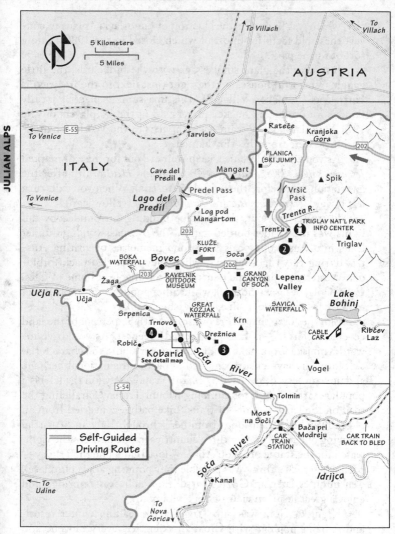

meters on skis. Today's competitors routinely set new world records (currently 784 feet—that's 17 seconds in the air). Nearby is a newly built Nordic center, used as a home base for a wide range of winter sports. From the ski jump, you're a few minutes' walk from Italy or Austria. This region—spanning three nations—lobbied unsuccessfully under the name Senza Confini (Italian for "without borders") to host the 2006 Winter Olympics. This philosophy is in tune with the European Union's vision for a Europe of regions, rather than nations.

Back in Kranjska Gora, follow the signs for *Vršič*. Before long, you'll officially enter **Triglav National Park** and come to the first

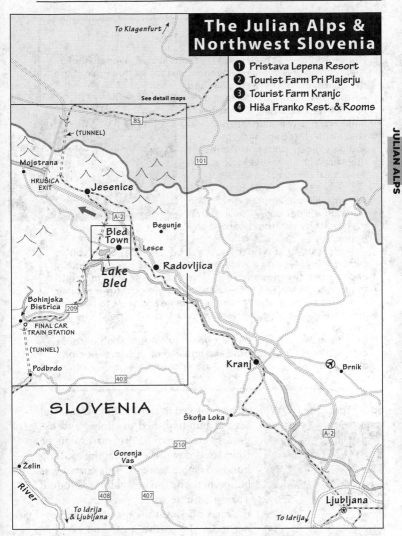

JULIAN ALPS

The Julian Alps & Northwest Slovenia

1 Pristava Lepena Resort
2 Tourist Farm Pri Plajerju
3 Tourist Farm Kranjc
4 Hiša Franko Rest. & Rooms

of this road's 50 hairpin turns (24 up, then 26 down)—each one numbered and labeled with the altitude in meters. Notice that the turns are cobbled to provide better traction. If the drive seems daunting, remember that 50-seat tour buses routinely conquer this pass...if they can do it, so can you. Better yet, imagine—and watch for—the bicyclists who regularly pedal to the top. The best can do it in less than 30 minutes—faster than driving.

After switchback #8, with the cute waterfall, park your car on the right and hike up the stairs on the left to the little **Russian chapel.** This road was built during World War I by at least 10,000 Russian POWs of the Austro-Hungarian Empire to supply the

Mount Triglav

Mount Triglav ("Three Heads") stands watch over the Julian Alps, and all of Slovenia. Slovenes say that its three peaks are the guardians of the water, air, and earth. This mountain defines Slovenes, even adorning the nation's flag: You'll often see the national seal, with three peaks (the two squiggly lines under it represent the Adriatic). Or take a look at Slovenia's €0.50 coin.

From the town of Bled, you'll see Triglav peeking up over the ridge on a clear day. (You'll get an even better view from nearby Lake Bohinj.)

It's said that you're not a true Slovene until you've climbed Triglav. One native took these words very seriously and climbed the mountain 853 times...in one year. Climbing to the summit—at 9,396 feet—is an attainable goal for any hiker in decent shape. If you're here for a while and want to become an honorary Slovene, befriend a local and ask if he or she will take you to the top.

If mountain climbing isn't your style, relax at an outdoor café with a piece of cream cake and a view of Triglav. It won't make you a Slovene...but it's close enough on a quick visit.

Soča Front. The POWs lived and worked in terrible conditions, and several hundred died of illness and exposure. On March 8, 1916, an avalanche thundered down the mountains, killing hundreds more workers. This chapel was built where the final casualty was found. Take a minute to pay your respects to the men who built the road you're enjoying today. It's a Russian Orthodox chapel—notice that the crosses topping the steeples have three crossbars. (For more on the Orthodox faith, see page 316.)

Back on the road, after #17, look up as high as you can on the cliff face to see sunlight streaming through a **"window"** in the rock. This natural formation, a popular destination for intrepid hikers, is big enough for the Statue of Liberty to crawl through.

After #22, at the pullout for Erjavčeva Koča restaurant, you may see tour-bus groups making a fuss about the mountain vista. They're looking for a ghostly face in the cliff wall, supposedly belonging to the mythical figure **Ajda.** This village girl was cursed by the townspeople after correctly predicting the death of the Zlato-rog (Golden Horn), a magical, beloved, chamois-like animal. Her tiny image (with a Picasso nose) is just above the tree line, a little to the right—try to get someone to point her out to you (you can see her best if you stand at the signpost near the road).

After #24, you reach the **summit** (5,285 feet). Consider getting out of the car to enjoy the views (in peak season, you'll pay an

attendant a €3 "ecological tax" to park here). Hike up to the hut for a snack or drink on the grand view terrace. On the right, a long gravel chute gives hikers a thrilling glissade. (From the pullout just beyond #26, it's easy to view hikers "skiing" down.) If you have time and energy to burn, from the summit consider hiking about 20 minutes uphill

to the Poštarski Dom ("Fifth Hut," with good food). Along the way, you'll see the ruins of a telpher cable-car line, which was used to run supplies between here and the valley floor during World War I. You'll also enjoy some of the best possible views of the Ajda face.

As you begin the descent, keep an eye out for old WWI debris. A lonely guard tunnel stands after #28, followed by a tunnel marked *1916* (on the left) that was part of the road's original path. Just after, watch for the turnoff at the right, at a little gravel parking lot with a picnic table. From the platform viewpoint, you can see mountain valleys formed in two different ways: To the left, the jagged V-shaped Soča Valley, carved by a raging river; and on the right, the gentle U-shaped Trenta Valley, gouged by a glacier.

Continuing down, you'll see abandoned checkpoints from when this was the border between Italy and the Austro-Hungarian Empire. At #48 is a statue of **Julius Kugy,** an Italian botanist who wrote books about alpine flora.

At #49, the road to the right (marked *Izvir Soče*) leads to the **source of the Soča River.** If you feel like stretching your legs after all that shifting, drive about five minutes down this road to a restaurant parking lot. From here, you can take a challenging 20-minute uphill hike (which includes some stretches where you'll cling to guide wires) to the Soča source. This is also the starting point for the well-explained, 12-mile Soča Trail (Soška Pot), which leads all the way to the town of Bovec.

Nearing the end of the switchbacks, follow signs for *Bovec.* Crossing the Soča River, you begin the second half of this trip.

Hemingway in the Julian Alps

It was against the scenic backdrop of the Slovenian Alps that a young man from Oak Park, Illinois, first came to Europe—the continent with which he would forever be identified. After graduating from high school in 1917 and working briefly as a newspaper reporter, young Ernest Hemingway wanted to join the war effort in Europe. Bad vision kept him out of the army, but he craved combat experience—so he joined the Red Cross Ambulance Corps instead.

After a short detour through Paris, Hemingway was sent to the Italian Front. On his first day, he was given the job of retrieving human remains—gruesomely disfigured body parts—after the explosion of a munitions factory. Later he came to the Lower Piave Valley, not far from the Soča Front. In July 1918, his ambulance was hit by a mortar shell. Despite his injuries, he saved an Italian soldier who was also wounded. According to legend, Hemingway packed his own wound with cigarette butts to stop the flow of blood.

Sent to Milan to recuperate, Hemingway fell in love with a nurse, but she later left him for an Italian military officer. A decade later, Hemingway wrote about Kobarid (using its Italian name, Caporetto), the war, and his case of youthful heartbreak in the novel *A Farewell to Arms*.

PART 2: SOČA RIVER VALLEY

During World War I, the terrain between here and the Adriatic made up the Soča (Isonzo) Front. As you follow the Soča River south, down what's nicknamed the "Valley of the Cemeteries," the scenic mountainsides around you tell the tale of this terrible warfare. Imagine a young Ernest Hemingway driving his ambulance through these same hills (see sidebar).

But it's not all so gloomy. There are plenty of other diversions—interesting villages and churches, waterfalls and suspension bridges, and more. Perhaps most impressive is the remarkable clarity and milky-blue color of the Soča itself, which Slovenes proudly call their "emerald river."

After switchback #49, you'll cross a bridge, then pass a church and a botanical garden of alpine plants (Alpinum Juliana, summer only). Across the street from the garden (on the right) is the parking lot for the Mlinarica Gorge. While the gorge is interesting, the bridge leading to it was damaged in a severe storm and hasn't yet been rebuilt—so it's best left to hardy hikers.

The last Vršič switchback (#50) sends you into the village of **Trenta.** As you get to the cluster of buildings in Trenta's "downtown," look on the left for the **Triglav National Park Information Center,** which also serves as a regional TI (daily July-Aug 9:00-

19:00, May-June and Sept-Oct 10:00-18:00, Dec-April 10:00-14:00, closed Nov, tel. 05/388-9330, www.tnp.si). The €5 museum here provides a look (with English explanations) at the park's flora, fauna, traditional culture, and mountaineering history. An AV show celebrates the region's forests, and a poetic 15-minute slide-show explains the wonders and fragility of the park (included in museum entry, ask for English version as you enter).

After Trenta, you'll pass through a tunnel; then, on the left, look for a classic **suspension bridge.** Pull over to walk out for a bounce, enjoying the river's crystal-clear water and the spectacular mountain pan-orama.

About five miles beyond Trenta, in the town of Soča, is the **Church of St. Joseph** (with reddish-brown steeple, tucked behind the big tree on the right). Step inside to see some fascinating art. During World War II, an artist hiding out in the mountains filled this church with patriotic symbolism. The interior is bathed in Yugoslav red, white, and blue—a brave statement made when such nationalistic sentiments were dangerous. On the ceiling is St. Michael (clad in Yugoslav colors) with Yugoslavia's three WWII enemies at his feet: the eagle (Germany), the wolf (Italy), and the serpent (Japan). The tops of the walls along the nave are

lined with saints, but these are Slavic, not Catholic. Finally, look carefully at the Stations of the Cross and find the faces of hated Yugoslav enemies: a lederhosen-clad Hitler (pulling a rope to up-right the cross; fourth from altar on left) and Mussolini (seated, as Herod; first from altar on right). Behind the church, the stylized cross on the hill marks a **WWI cemetery**—the final resting place of some 600 Austro-Hungarian soldiers who were killed in action.

For another good example of how the Soča River cuts like God's band saw into the land, stop about two minutes past the church at the small gravel lot (on the left) marked *Velika Korita Soče* (**"Grand Canyon of Soča"**). While the entire Soča Valley is dra-matic, this half-mile, 30- to 50-foot deep stretch is considered the most impressive. Venture out onto the suspension bridge over the gorge...and bounce if you dare. If the water's high, notice the many side streams pouring into the churning river in a series of mini-wa-terfalls. For more views, cross over the bridge and hike down along the treacherously uneven and narrow, rocky path downstream to another bridge.

Just beyond the suspension bridge is the turnoff (on the left) to the Lepena Valley, home of the recommended Pristava Lepena ranch, with accommodations and Lipizzaner horses (described later, under "Sleeping in Bovec"). If you head up this valley, you'll find a big gravel pullout on the right (marked *Velika Korita*) that lets you cross another springy bridge over a particularly wide stretch of the river. This is a popular place for those who enjoy hiking up alongside the "Grand Canyon" we passed earlier (about 5 miles round-trip, uneven terrain).

Soon after the Lepena Valley turnoff, watch on the left for the large **barn** (marked *Žičnica Golobar*). Pull over here if you'd like a close look at one of the stations for a primitive, industrial telpher cable-car line, which was used mostly for logging.

Roughly five miles after the town of Soča, you exit the national park, pass a WWI graveyard (on the left), and come to a fork in the road. The main route leads

to the left, through Bovec. But first, take a two-mile detour to the right (marked *Trbiž/Tarvisio* and *Predel/Kluže*), where the WWI **Kluže Fort** keeps a close watch over the narrowest part of a valley leading to Italy (€3; July-Aug daily 9:00-20:00; June and Sept Sun-Fri 9:00-17:00, Sat 9:00-18:00; May and Oct Sat-Sun 10:00-17:00, closed Mon-Fri; closed Nov-April; www.kluze.net). In the 15th century, the Italians had a fort here to defend against the Ottomans. Half a millennium later, during World War I, it was used by Austrians to keep Italians out of their territory. Notice the ladder rungs fixed to the cliff face across the road from the fort—allowing soldiers to quickly get up to the mountaintop.

Back on the main road, immediately after the Kluže turnoff, watch for the gravel pullout on the left with the little wooden hut (look for the green sign with old photos). To see some original **WWI-era fortifications,** pull over here and hike on the gravel path 10 minutes through the woods to reach the Ravelnik Outdoor Museum. Here you can see trenches dug into the dirt and rocks, abandoned pillboxes, rusty sheds, and other features of an evocative wartime landscape. While not entirely typical of Soča Front embattlements (remember, those were mostly high on the mountaintops and remain challenging to reach), Ravelnik offers a taste of those times.

Continue following the main road to **Bovec.** This town, which saw some of the most vicious fighting of the Soča Front, was hit hard by earthquakes in 1994 and 1998 (and by another tremor in 2004). Today, it's been rebuilt and remains the adventure-sports capital of the Soča River Valley—also known as the "Adrenaline Valley," famous for its whitewater activities. (Since the water comes from high-mountain runoff, the temperature of the Soča never goes above 68 degrees Fahrenheit.) For a good lunch stop in Bovec, turn right at the roundabout as you first reach the town; you'll pass Martinov Hram's inviting restaurant terrace on the right, and soon after, the Letni Vrt pizzeria (for details on both, see "Eating in Bovec," later). But if you're not eating or spending the night in Bovec, you could skip the town entirely and not miss much (continue along the main road to bypass the town center).

About three miles past Bovec, as you cross the bridge (with the yellow *Boka* sign), look carefully high up on the rock wall in the gorge to your right to spot the **Boka waterfall,** which carves a deep gouge into the cliff as it tumbles into the valley. (Hardy hikers can climb up for a better view of this fall—the trailhead is just after the bridge on the right—but it's an extremely strenuous hike.)

Head south along the river, with water somehow both perfectly clear and spectacularly turquoise. When you pass the intersection at the humble village of **Žaga,** you're just four miles from Italy. Continuing south, you'll pass a pullout (just before Srpenica) that is a popular put-in point for kayaking trips along the river. Keep an eye out for happy kayakers. Soon after, on the left, you'll pass the giant TKK caulk factory.

Soon you'll see signs for **Kobarid,** home to a sleepy main square and some fascinating WWI sights. Don't blink or you'll miss the Kobarid turnoff on the right—it lets you skirt into town past the highly recommended Kobarid Museum, which tells the tale of the WWI-era Soča Front. Farther along, you'll reach the tidy main square. Driving up to the Italian mausoleum hovering over the town is a must. (These sights are described later, under "Sights in Kobarid.")

Leaving Kobarid, continue south along the Soča to **Tolmin.** Before you reach Tolmin, decide on your preferred route back to civilization...

FINISHING THE DRIVE

While you could go back over the pass the way you came, there are various ways to make your trip a loop by circling through some more varied scenery. Which way you go depends on your final destination: Ljubljana or Bled.

To Ljubljana (or Southern Slovenia/Croatia)

From Tolmin, you have two possible driving routes to the capital.

Either option brings you back to the A-1 expressway south of Ljubljana, and will get you to the city in about two hours (though the second route has fewer miles).

Nova Gorica Route: The option you'll encounter first (turnoff to the right before Tolmin) is the smoother, longer route southwest to Nova Gorica. Along this road, you'll pass a hydroelectric dam and go under a 1906 rail viaduct that once connected this area to the port of Trieste (now in Italy). In the charming town of Kanal, you'll cross over the Soča on a picturesque bridge that's faintly reminiscent of Mostar's (as in that city, young people stage a competition that involves jumping off this bridge into the raging river below). Farther along, the striking Solkan Bridge (another link in the Trieste rail line) is the longest single-span stone arch bridge in the world. Soon after, you arrive in Nova Gorica. This fairly dull city is divided in half by the Italian border (the Italian side is called "Gorizia"). Because Italians aren't allowed to gamble in their hometowns, Nova Gorica is packed with casinos catering to Italian gamblers. In fact, it's home to Europe's biggest casino. Rocks spell out the name "TITO" on a hillside above town—a strange relic of an earlier age. From Nova Gorica, you can hop on the H-4 expressway, which links easily to the main A-1 expressway. Also notice that the road from Nova Gorica to Ljubljana takes you through the heart of the Karst region—if you have time and daylight to spare, you could tour a cave, castle, or Lipizzaner stud farm on your way back up to Ljubljana (see the Karst chapter).

Idrija Route: For a more off-the-beaten-path, ruggedly scenic approach, take this rural option: Continue through Tolmin, then head southeast through the hills back toward Ljubljana. Along the way, you could stop for a bite and some sightseeing at the town of Idrija (EE-dree-yah), known to all Slovenes for three things: its tourable mercury mine, fine delicate lace, and tasty *žlikrofi* (like ravioli). Back at the expressway (at Logatec), head north to Ljubljana.

To Bled

To reach Bled, you could follow either of the Ljubljana-bound routes outlined above, then carry on northward for another hour to Bled (allow about 3 hours total). But the following options are more direct.

Car Train: The fastest option is to load your car onto a "Car Train" (Autovlak) that cuts directly through the mountains. The train departs at 18:31 from Most na Soči (just south of Tolmin, along the Idrija route described above) and arrives at Bohinjska Bistrica, near Lake Bohinj, at 19:09 (€14 for the car; afternoon departure late April-late Sept only, also departs year-round at 7:34 and 10:35, confirm schedule at the Bled TI before making the trip).

No reservations are necessary, but arrive at the train station about 30 minutes before the scheduled departure to allow time to load the car. Note: This is a very old train that can be quite jerky and bumpy. You'll stay inside your car the entire time. If you're claustrophobic, prone to motion sickness, or both, consider giving this train a miss.

To get to the car train, drive through Tolmin, then Most na Soči (turning left for *Ljubljana*). About a mile out of Most na Soči, watch on the right for the big bridge over the river, marked for *Čepovan* and *železniška postaja* (train station). Crossing the bridge, turn right to find the train station; once there, go around the far-left side of the long station building and drive up the ramp to wait your turn to load. You'll buy your ticket, load on your car, pull your hand brake, and put the car in gear. Then you'll stay in the car and enjoy the scenery. Taking off, you'll cross a scenic viaduct, then twist through the mountains, going through multiple tunnels including a final 10-minute passage from Podbrdo beneath the mountains to Bohinjska Bistrica, where you'll unload your car. From Bohinjska Bistrica, it's less than a half-hour drive back to Bled, or a 10-minute drive (in the opposite direction) to Lake Bohinj.

Through Italy via Predel Pass: Although this route requires some backtracking, it also includes a detour through Italy. From Kobarid, drive back the way you came (through Bovec), then turn off for the Kluže Fort (described on page 644), marked for *Predel* and Italy. In a few miles, after passing the fort, the road curves up through two small villages (first Log pod Mangartom, then Strmec na Predelu directly above it). Continue past the ruined fortress and cross the Italian border (there's no need to stop). Then curl down a few hairpin turns past the end of tranquil, scenic Lake Predel, and continue straight through the ghost city of Cave del Predil (a heavily industrialized former lead-mining town; overhead are the five rounded peaks of the Cinque Punte formation) and along the valley road, following signs for Slovenia. Approaching Tarvisio, turn right (continuing to follow signs for *Kranjska Gora* and Slovenia); from here, it's about a half-hour (10 miles) back across the Slovenian border to Kranjska Gora. This is where you first began your ascent of the Vršič Pass—just retrace your steps back to Bled.

Other Driving Routes: The fastest route (about 2 hours) essentially follows the car train route, but goes over rather than through the mountains. This route is partially on a twisty, rough, very poor-quality road (go through Tolmin, turn off at Bača pri Modreju to Podbrdo, then from Petrovo Brdo take a very curvy road through the mountains into Bohinjska Bistrica and on to Bled). For timid drivers, it's more sane and not too much longer to start out on the Idrija route toward Ljubljana (described above), but turn off in Želin (before Idrija) toward Skofja Loka and Kranj, then continue on to Bled.

Bovec

The biggest town in the area, Bovec (BOH-vets) has a happening main square and all the tourist amenities. It's best known as a hub for whitewater adventure sports. While not exactly quaint, Bovec is pleasant enough to qualify as a good lunch stop or overnight home base. If nothing else, it's a nice jolt of civilization wedged between the alpine cliffs.

Orientation to Bovec

TOURIST INFORMATION
The helpful TI is on the main square (June-Sept daily 8:30-20:30, Oct-May daily 9:00-16:00 except closed Sat-Sun in Nov-April, Trg Golobarskih Žrtev 8, tel. 05/384-1919, www.bovec.si).

ARRIVAL IN BOVEC
The main road skirts Bovec, but you can turn off (watch for signs on the right) to take the road that goes through the heart of town, then rejoins the main road farther along. As you approach the city center, you can't miss the main square, Trg Golobarskih Žrtev, with the TI and a recommended restaurant. You'll find a big free parking lot behind the Mercator supermarket (on the left on the way into town, just before the main square), and a few pay parking spaces on or near the square itself.

Activities in Bovec

As the de facto capital of Slovenia's "Adrenaline Valley," Bovec offers many opportunities to enjoy the nature all around it.

Adventure Sports
The main activity in the Soča Valley is getting out on the rushing, crystal-clear waters of the river. The main options are rafting, kayaking, and hydrospeeding (a masochistic variation on boogie boarding—lying face-down on a short surfboard and shooting headfirst toward the rapids). The official season is March 15 until October 31, but outside of summer, the frigid water is less appealing and fewer companies operate. From an adrenaline perspective, these activities are best in spring—when the water is highest—and tamer in summer. By fall, water levels are even lower.

When conditions are ideal, most **rafting** companies put in near the Boka waterfall (just downriver from Bovec), and pick up at the village of Trnovo ob Soči. (When water levels are low, companies put in near Sprenica instead.) Most rafting trips last about 2.5-3 hours, with about 1.5 hours actually on the river and extra time to swim.

Kayaking is available at various points along the river, which vary dramatically in level of difficulty; the TI's free *Water-Adventure-Sport* map outlines your options and notes areas that are unsafe. To get a glimpse of kayakers, hang out at Napoleon Bridge, just outside of Kobarid.

The most popular place for **canyoning**—a risky activity that involves wading and rappelling in rushing rivers—is in Canyon Sušec, about halfway between Bovec and Kobarid.

Other popular options include skydiving and paragliding; biking (Bovec Šport Centar rents electric mountain bikes); ziplines (there's a course above Bovec and another high in the Učja Valley); and even—gasp!—golf (Bovec has a 9-hole course, www. golfbovec.si). Of course, all of these activities come with some degree of risk (except, perhaps, golf); use common sense and investigate the safety record of any company that offers trips. The Bovec TI is a good source of information about any of these, and an ever-changing roster of local adventure travel companies run a variety of tours. Well-established outfits include Bovec Šport Centar (www. bovec-sc.si) and Soča Rafting (www.socarafting.si).

Sightseeing Flights

Aero Taxi runs scenic sightseeing flights from Bovec's little airport (€79/20-minute "introductory" flight, €140/30-minute mountain-scenery flight, longer itineraries available, prices are for up to 3 people, mobile 041-262-726, www.janezlet.si).

Fly Fishing

The Soča River is a popular spot for fishing, predominantly for the endemic marble trout. Only fly fishing is allowed; some areas are catch-and-release, and all areas require a permit. **Soča Fly** offers information, fly-fishing gear, and tours (mobile 031-705-552).

Sleeping in Bovec

Dobra Vila and Hotel Sanje ob Soči are situated near the turnoff from the main road into central Bovec (about a 10-minute walk into town). Martinov Hram and Stari Kovač are closer to the main square, in the town center.

$$$ Dobra Vila, run with class by brothers Juri and Matjaš, has 11 plush, boldly stylish yet classic rooms, and a generous rear terrace. You'll stay in a gorgeously restored former telephone office that feels like an enticing whisper of ages past (Db-€120-145 de-

JULIAN ALPS

Sleep Code

Abbreviations   (€1=about $1.10, country code: 386)
S=Single, **D**=Double/Twin, **T**=Triple, **Q**=Quad, **b**=bathroom
Price Rankings
  $$$ **Higher Priced**—Most rooms €100 or more
  $$ **Moderately Priced**—Most rooms €60-100
  $ **Lower Priced**—Most rooms €60 or less
Unless otherwise noted, Wi-Fi is available and free, credit cards are accepted, and breakfast is included, but the modest tourist tax (about €1/person, per night) is not. Everyone listed here speaks English. Prices change; verify the hotel's current rates online or by email. For the best prices, always book directly with the hotel.

pending on size and amenities, cheaper off-season, air-con, Mala vas 112, tel. 05/389-6400, www.dobra-vila-bovec.si, welcome@dobra-vila-bovec.si). They also have the most elegant restaurant in town (€36 dinner; see "Eating in Bovec," later).

$$$ Hotel Sanje ob Soči means "Dreams by the Soča"—which describes both what you'll do here and the vision that entrepreneurial owners Boštjan and Valentina have for their sleek, modern, spa-like lodgings. The 10 rooms (Db-€98-124, includes breakfast) and nine apartments (€110-180, includes kitchenette, optional breakfast-€8) fill a pine-clad, Scandinavian-feeling shell on the edge of Bovec. The rooms—all with terraces, and each one named for the mountain that dominates its view—are fairly simple and Ikea-furnished (price depends on size, 20 percent cheaper in spring and fall, air-con, children's play area, Mala vas 105a, tel. 05/389-6000, mobile 031-331-690, www.sanjeobsoci.com, info@sanjeobsoci.com).

$$ Martinov Hram has 12 nice, modern rooms over a popular restaurant a few steps from Bovec's main square. While the rooms are an afterthought to the busy restaurant (reception at the bar), they're comfortable (very flexible rates, in peak season figure Sb-€46, Db-€74, a few euros less off-season, no extra charge for 1-night stays, rooms on sunny side have air-con, Trg Golobarskih Žrtev 27, tel. 05/388-6214, www.martinov-hram.si, sara.berginc@gmail.com).

$ Stari Kovač B&B is your basic budget option, with eight rooms in an old-feeling guesthouse a steep block downhill from the main square (Db-€58, cheaper off-season and for 3 nights or more, kitchens in each room or pay €8/person for breakfast, cash only, Rupa 3, tel. 05/388-6699, mobile 041-646-427, www.starikovac.com, info@starikovac.com).

NEAR BOVEC

$$$ Pristava Lepena is a relaxing oasis hiding out in the Lepena Valley just north of Bovec. Well-run by Milan and Silvia Dolenc, this place is its own little village, with a series of rustic-looking cabins, a restaurant, a small exercise room, a kids' play area, a tennis court, an outdoor swimming pool, and a sauna/whirlpool. Milan and Silvia organize regular events for their guests (such as musical performances, a barbecue night, and activities for kids). Hiding behind the humble split-wood shingle exteriors is surprising comfort: 13 cozy rooms (with wood-burning stoves, TV, telephone, and all the amenities) that make you feel like relaxing. This place whispers "second honeymoon" (Db-€144 in July-Aug or €126 in shoulder season, more for larger apartments, closed in winter, multinight stays preferred, single-night stays may be possible for 20 percent extra, dinner-€23, lunch and dinner-€38, nonrefundable 30 percent advance payment when you reserve; just south of the village of Soča, exit the main road at the sign for *Lepena,* and follow the white horses to Lepena 2; tel. 05/388-9900, mobile 041-671-981, www.pristava-lepena.com, pristava.lepena@siol.net). Milan and Silvia also have three Welsh ponies and four purebred Lipizzaner horses that guests can ride (experienced riders-€25/hour, riding lesson-€30; nonguests may be able to ride—call ahead and ask). Kids love their mascot mountain goats.

$ Tourist Farm Pri Plajerju is on a picturesque plateau at the edge of Trenta (the first town at the bottom of the Vršič Pass road). Run by the Pretner family (gregarious Marko is a park ranger, shy Stanka is "the boss"), this organic farm raises sheep and rents five apartments in three buildings separate from the main house. As the Soča Valley doesn't have many tourist farms, this is one of your best options if you want to stay at one. However, its location deeper in the mountains makes it a bit less convenient for side-tripping—it's 30 minutes to Bovec and an hour to Kobarid (July-Aug: Db-€50-70, Tb-€60-80, Qb-€70-85; Sept-June: Db-€45-60, Tb-€55-70, Qb-€65-75; price depends on size, breakfast-€7, dinner-€11—available some but not all nights; watch for signs to the left after coming over the pass and going through the village of Trenta, Trenta 16a; tel. 05/388-9209, mobile 041-600-590, www. eko-plajer.com, info@eko-plajer.com).

Eating in Bovec

Inexplicably, little Bovec's restaurants tend to charge a cover of €1-1.50—a greedy practice otherwise rare in Slovenia, but perhaps influenced by the town's proximity to Italy.

Martinov Hram, run by the Berginc family (sisters Sara and Suzi), has an inviting outdoor terrace under a grape trellis. Inside, the nicely traditional decor goes well with regional specialties with a focus on lamb, delicious pancakes, and homemade bread (€8-13 pastas, €9 pancakes, €10-20 main courses, daily 10:00-23:00 except closed Mon in Oct-May; on the main road through Bovec, just before the main square on the right at Trg Golobarskih Žrtev 27; tel. 05/388-6214).

Letni Vrt is big, with an outdoor terrace facing Bovec's main intersection, and sprawling indoor dining rooms—including a nice winter garden that's inviting on cold days. The menu is almost comically lengthy—I'd stick with the good and affordable pizzas (€7-11 pizzas and pastas, €9-20 main courses, daily 11:00-23:00, Fri-Sun only in winter, Trg Golobarskih Žrtev 1, tel. 05/389-6383).

Dobra Vila, also a recommended hotel, is the only place in town for an elegant, upscale meal of thoughtfully presented international cuisine with local flair. It's smart to call ahead (€36 fixed-price dinner, daily 19:00-22:00, see contact information earlier).

Bovec Connections

From Bovec by Bus to: Kobarid (4-6/day, 30 minutes), **Ljubljana** (direct over scenic Vršič Pass: 2/day July-Aug, 1/day Sat-Sun only June and Sept, none off-season, 4.25 hours; some additional buses may go over Vršič Pass to Kranjska Gora, where you can change to other destinations; otherwise less scenic via Idrija).

Kobarid

Kobarid (KOH-bah-reed) feels older, and therefore a bit more appealing, than its big brother Bovec. This humble settlement was immortalized by a literary giant, Ernest Hemingway, who drove an ambulance in these mountains during World War I. He described Kobarid as "a little white town with a campanile in a valley. It was a clean little town and there was a fine fountain in the square." Sounds about right. Even though Kobarid loves to tout its Hemingway connection, historians believe that Papa did not actually visit Kobarid until he came back after the war to research his book.

Aside from its brush with literary greatness, Kobarid is known as a hub of information about the Soča Front (with an excellent WWI museum, a hilltop Italian mausoleum, and walks that connect to surrounding sites). You won't find the fountain Hemingway

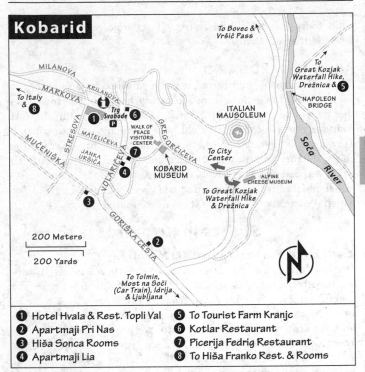

Kobarid

To Bovec & Vršič Pass

To Great Kozjak Waterfall Hike, Drežnica & ⑤

NAPOLEON BRIDGE

MILANOVA

MARKOVA

KRILANOVA

To Italy & ⑧

ITALIAN MAUSOLEUM

Trg Svobode ⑥

WALK OF PEACE VISITORS CENTER

STRESOJA

MATELIČEVA

MUČENIŠKA

JANKA URŠIČA

VOLARIČEVA

GREGORČIČEVA

⑦

KOBARID MUSEUM

To City Center

ALPINE CHEESE MUSEUM

To Great Kozjak Waterfall Hike & Drežnica

Soča River

③

200 Meters

200 Yards

GORIŠKA CESTA

②

N

To Tolmin, Most na Soči (Car Train), Idrija & Ljubljana

① Hotel Hvala & Rest. Topli Val
② Apartmaji Pri Nas
③ Hiša Sonca Rooms
④ Apartmaji Lia
⑤ To Tourist Farm Kranjc
⑥ Kotlar Restaurant
⑦ Picerija Fedrig Restaurant
⑧ To Hiša Franko Rest. & Rooms

JULIAN ALPS

wrote about—it's since been covered up by houses (though the town government hopes to excavate it as a tourist attraction). You will find a modern statue of Simon Gregorčič (overlooking the main intersection), the beloved Slovenian priest-slash-poet who came from and wrote about the Soča Valley.

Orientation to Kobarid

The main road, Gregorčičeva, cuts right through the heart of little Kobarid, bisecting its main square (Trg Svobode). The Kobarid Museum is along this road, on the left before the square. To reach the museum from the main square, simply walk five minutes back toward Bovec.

TOURIST INFORMATION

The TI has good information on the area, and free Internet access and Wi-Fi (July-Aug daily 9:00-20:00; May-June and Sept Mon-Fri 9:00-13:00 & 14:00-19:00, Sat-Sun 9:00-13:00 & 16:00-19:00; Oct-April Mon-Fri 9:00-13:00 & 14:00-16:00, Sat 10:00-14:00, closed Sun; on the main square at Trg Svobode 16—follow the white footprints behind the statue of Gregorčič, tel. 05/380-0490, www.dolina-soce.com).

ARRIVAL IN KOBARID

Driving into town from Bovec, watch carefully on the right for the poorly marked first turnoff into Kobarid (they want you to stay on the main road bypass around town; if you miss the turnoff, just continue on this, then turn right later to reach the main square). Turning into town, you could make a sharp left turn to reach the cheese factory (marked by the big modern tower), or continue straight ahead to pass the Kobarid Museum, then the main square. You'll find parking on the main square (free for up to 2 hours), from which it's an easy five-minute stroll to the museum.

Sights in Kobarid

▲▲Kobarid Museum (Kobariški Muzej)

This modest but world-class museum—worth ▲▲▲ for history buffs—offers a haunting look at the tragedy of the Soča Front. The tasteful exhibits, with fine English descriptions and a pacifist tone, take an even-handed approach to the fighting—without getting hung up on identifying the "good guys" and the "bad guys." The museum's focus is not on the guns and heroes, but on the big picture of the front and on the stories of the common people who fought and died here.

Cost and Hours: €6, good selection of books, daily April-Sept 9:00-18:00, Oct-March 10:00-17:00, Gregorčičeva 10, tel. 05/389-0000, www.kobariski-muzej.si.

Tours: History buffs can call ahead to arrange a private guide to lead them through the collection (€20/hour), or tour the sights outside (€25/hour). You can also arrange a guide through the Walk of Peace Visitors Center, listed later.

Visiting the Museum: The entry is lined with hastily made cement and barbed-wire gravestones, flags representing all the nationalities involved in the fighting, and pictures of soldiers and nurses from diverse backgrounds who were brought together here (for example, the men wearing fezzes were from Bosnia-Herzegovina, which was annexed by the Austro-Hungarian Empire shortly before the war). The rooms in this front part of the museum show off typically good temporary exhibits about the war.

Buy your ticket and ask to watch the English version of the 19-minute film on the history of the Soča Front (informative but dry, plays on top floor).

The first floor up is divided into several rooms, which you'll tour counterclockwise. The White Room—filled with rusty crampons, wire-cutters, pickaxes, and shovels—explains wintertime conditions at the front. What looks like a bear trap was actually used to trap enemy soldiers. The Room of the Rear shows the day-to-day activities away from the front line, from supplying troops to more mundane activities (milking cows, washing clothes, getting a shave, lifting weights, playing with a dog). The Black Room is the museum's most somber, commemorating the more than one million casualties of the Soča Front. These heartbreaking exhibits honor the common people whose bodies fertilized the battlefields of Europe. Horrific images of war injuries are juxtaposed with a display of medals earned—prompting the question, was it worth it? The little altar was purchased by schoolchildren, who sent it to the front to offer the troops some solace.

Through the door marked *The Krn Range Room* (also on the first floor up), pass the small model of the mountaintop war zone and find your way to the Kobarid Rooms, which trace the history of this region from antiquity to today. High on the wall, look for the timelines explaining the area's turbulent past. The one in the second room shows wave after wave of invaders (including Ottomans, Habsburgs, and Napoleon). In the next room, above a display case with military uniforms, another timeline shows the many flags that flew over Kobarid's main square during the 20th century alone.

On the top floor, across from the room where the film plays (described above), you'll see a giant model of the surrounding mountains, painstakingly tracing the successful Austrian-German *Blitzkrieg* attack during the Battle of Kobarid. Crawl into the small cave and press the button to hear a patriotic song about a soldier, who reads a letter he's written to his family about the conditions here.

▲▲Italian Mausoleum (Kostnica)

The 55 miles between here and the Adriatic are dotted with more than 75 cemeteries, reminders of the countless casualties of the

Soča Front. One of the most dramatic is this mausoleum, overlooking Kobarid. The access road, across Kobarid's main square from the side of the church, is marked by stone gate towers with the word *Kostnica*—one tower is topped with a cross and the other with a star for the Italian army.

Take the road up Gradič Hill—passing Stations of the Cross—to the mausoleum. Built in

The Soča (Isonzo) Front

The valley in Slovenia's northwest corner—called Soča in Slovene and Isonzo in Italian—saw some of World War I's fiercest fighting. While the Western Front gets more press, this eastern border between the Central Powers and the Allies was just as significant. In a series of 12 battles involving 22 different nationalities along a 60-mile-long front, 300,000 soldiers died, 700,000 were wounded, and 100,000 were declared MIA. In addition, tens of thousands of civilians died. A young Ernest Hemingway, who drove an ambulance for the Italian army in nearby fighting, would later write the novel *A Farewell to Arms* about the battles here (see "Hemingway in the Julian Alps" sidebar on page 642).

On April 26, 1915, Italy joined the Allies. A month later, it declared war on the Austro-Hungarian Empire (which included Slovenia). Italy unexpectedly invaded the Soča Valley, quickly taking the tiny town of Kobarid, which it planned to use as a home base for attacks deeper into Austro-Hungarian territory. For the next 29 months, Italy launched 10 more offensives against the Austro-Hungarian army, which was encamped on higher ground on the mountaintops. All of these Italian offensives were unsuccessful, even though the Italians outnumbered their opponents three to one. This was unimaginably difficult warfare—Italy had to attack uphill, waging war high in the mountains, in the harshest of conditions. Trenches had to be carved into rock instead of mud. The fighting coincided with one of the most brutal winters in centuries; many unprepared conscripts—brought here from faraway lands and unaccustomed to the harsh winter conditions atop the Alps—froze to death. Some 60,000 soldiers were killed by avalanches.

Visitors take a look at this tight valley, hemmed in by seemingly impassible mountains, and wonder: Why would people fight so fiercely over such inhospitable terrain? At the time, Slovenia was the natural route from Italy to the Austro-Hungarian capitals

1938 (when this was still part of Italy) around the existing Church of St. Anthony, this octagonal pyramid holds the remains of 7,014 Italian soldiers. The stark, cold Neoclassical architecture is pure Mussolini. Names are listed alphabetically, along with mass graves for more than 1,700 unknown soldiers *(militi ignoti)*.

Walk behind the church and enjoy the **view.** Scan the WWI battlements high on the mountain's rock face. Incredibly, the fighting was done on these treacherous ridges; civilians in the valleys

at Vienna and Budapest. The Italians believed that if they could hold this valley and push over the mountains, Vienna—and victory—would be theirs. Once committed, they couldn't turn back, and the war devolved into one of attrition—who would fall first?

In the fall of 1917, Austro-Hungarian Emperor Karl appealed to his ally Germany, and the Germans agreed to assemble an army for a new attack to retake Kobarid and the Soča Valley. In an incredible logistical accomplishment, they spent just six weeks building and supplying this new army by transporting troops and equipment high across the mountaintops under cover of darkness...above the heads of their oblivious Italian foes dozing in the valley below.

On October 24, Austria-Hungary and Germany launched an attack that sent 600,000 soldiers down into the town of Kobarid. This crucial 12th battle of the Soča Front, better known as the Battle of Kobarid, was the turning point—and saw the introduction of battlefield innovations that are commonplace in the military today. German field commanders were empowered to act independently on the battlefield, reacting immediately to developments rather than waiting for approval. Also, for the first time ever, the Austrian-German army used elements of a new surprise-attack technique called *Blitzkrieg*. (One German officer, Erwin Rommel, made great strides in the fighting here, and later climbed the ranks to become famous as Hitler's "Desert Fox" in North Africa.)

The attack caught the Italian forces off-guard, quickly breaking through three lines of defense. Within three days, the Italians were forced to retreat. (Because the Italian military worked from the top down, the soldiers were sitting ducks once they were cut off from their commanders.) The Austrians called their victory the "Miracle at Kobarid." But Italy felt differently. The Italians see the battle of Caporetto (the Italian name for Kobarid) as their Alamo. To this day, when an Italian finds himself in a mess, he might say, "At least it's not a Caporetto."

A year later, Italy came back—this time with the aid of British, French, and US forces—and easily retook this area. On November 4, 1918, Austria-Hungary conceded defeat. After more than a million casualties, the fighting at Soča was finally over.

only heard the distant battles. Looking up and down the valley, notice the "signal churches" evenly spaced on hilltops, each barely within view of the next—an ancient method for quickly spreading messages or warnings across long distances.

If the **church** is open, go inside and look above the door to see a brave soldier standing over the body of a fallen comrade, fending off enemies with nothing but rocks.

When Mussolini came to dedicate the mausoleum, local

revolutionaries plotted an assassination attempt that they believed couldn't fail. A young man planned to suicide-bomb Mussolini as the leader came back into town from this hilltop. But as Mussolini's car drove past, the would-be assassin looked at his fellow townspeople around him, realized the innocent blood he would also spill, and had a last-minute change of heart. Mussolini's trip was uneventful, and fascism continued to thrive in Italy.

▲Walk of Peace (Pot Miru)

This walking route—which extends more than 140 miles from these mountains all the way to the Adriatic—is designed to link museums, cemeteries, churches, and other sites related to the warfare of the Soča Front. But it also has a secondary purpose of celebrating and introducing visitors to all aspects of regional culture and natural sites. In addition to the excellent museum here in Kobarid, several other "outdoor museums" in the area let you get close to the places where the fighting actually occurred. Some are reachable by car, while others require a challenging mountain hike.

To learn more about all of these options, visit the **Walk of Peace Foundation Visitors Center,** across the street from the Kobarid Museum. They hand out good, free maps and booklets about these sites, and sell a fine guidebook to WWI sights in the area. Tour their engaging, state-of-the-art exhibition (free, July-Aug Mon-Fri 9:00-13:00 & 14:00-19:00, Sat-Sun 10:00-13:00 & 14:00-19:00, April-June and Sept-Oct slightly shorter hours, closed Nov-March—but you can try knocking on weekdays, Gregorčičeva 8, tel. 05/389-0167, www.potmiru.si).

They also arrange **guides** to join you for part of the walk (€25/hour). Contact them at least one day ahead to check their schedule and/or arrange a tour.

Kobarid Historical Walk

This shorter walk to WWI sights around Kobarid is well-explained by the free brochure available at the TI, museum, and information center (3 miles, mostly uphill, allow 3-5 hours; or you can just do a shorter, easier stretch along the river, 1-2 hours).

Alpine Cheese Museum

This humble exhibit, at the big Planika ("Edelweiss") dairy at the edge of town, examines the history of cheesemaking in this area since ancient times.

Cost and Hours: €2.50; May-Sept Mon-Sat 10:00-12:00 & 17:00-19:00, closed Sun except July-Aug 10:00-12:00; Oct shorter hours and closed Sun; closed Nov-April; Gregorčičeva 32, tel. 05/384-1013, www.mlekarna-planika.si/muzej. To get here, turn right into Kobarid, then take the sharp left turn that leads you down beneath the underpass to the cheese factory (marked by the tall modern tower).

Great Kozjak Waterfall (Veliki Kozjak) Hike

If you have time to kill in Kobarid and want to go for a sturdy hike, consider trekking to the Great Kozjak Waterfall—a dramatic cascade that flows through an extremely narrow gorge and plunges 50 feet into a beautiful pool. While local signs clock the hike at 30 minutes from the town center, plan on closer to 45 minutes each way. The trailhead is at the Bovec end of Kobarid: As you approach the town from Bovec, turn right into the town, then take an immediate and sharp left to go back under the main road, passing the cheese factory and following signs for *Kamp Koren*. Wind down to cross the Napoleon Bridge over the Soča (watch for kayakers), then turn left and head up the hill (you'll pass Kamp Koren). You can park in the big gravel lot across the street from the camp, or, to get closer to the trailhead, turn left just after Kamp Koren at the *Slap Kozjak* sign and follow the gravel road (park your car at the pullout after the multicolored beehives). Continue walking along the gravel path down into the ravine, passing views of a smaller waterfall. Go right at the fork, continue into the gorge, and take the high, narrow bridge over the stream (which has no railing—a little nerve-wracking for those afraid of heights). Finally, follow the boardwalk as it curls around a cliff for great views of the falls. A different, longer trail follows the Soča River Valley, eventually looping up and around to Kozjak.

Sleeping in Kobarid

My first listing is right on the main square. The other two hide on side streets about a block off the main road through town, between the museum and the main square (about a three-minute walk to either).

$$$ Hotel Hvala is the only real hotel in town. Run by the Hvala family, its 32 contemporary rooms are comfortable, and the location can't be beat. The mural on the wall in the elevator shaft tells the story of the Soča Valley as you go up toward the top floor (Sb-€76, Db-€112, €4 less/person off-season; cheaper third-floor "mansard" Sb-€45, Db-€70; pricier superior Db with air-con and sleek new decor-€135/€160/€200 depending on size; hotel closed parts of Feb and Nov, elevator, Trg Svobode 1, tel. 05/389-9300, www.hotelhvala.net, topli.val@siol.net).

$$ Apartmaji Pri Nas ("Our Place") has six very stylish apartments in a pleasant suburban home along the main road that skirts the town center of Kobarid (Db-€70/€50-60, 2-night minimum, no breakfast but kitchens in each unit, air-con, Goriška cesta 5, mobile 031-377-585, www.pri-nas.si, prinas.kobarid@gmail.com).

$ Hiša Sonca ("House of the Sun"), in a cheery, yellow family home along the main road, has two comfortable rooms (Db-€50) and one big apartment that sleeps up to eight (€140-200 depending on number of people; breakfast-€7, cash only, 2 blocks from main square at Mučeniška 1, mobile 031-664-253, www.apartma-hisasonca.com, hisasonca@gmail.com, Natalija).

$ Apartmaji Lia, run by sweet Alenka Likar, has three tidy apartments in two buildings in the town center (Db-€40, 1-night stay-€10 extra, extra adult-€20, kids under 15-€10, cash only, no breakfast, air-con, main house at Volaričeva 9, mobile 041-953-366, www.apartmaji-lia.si, apartmajilia@gmail.com).

IN THE MOUNTAINS HIGH ABOVE KOBARID

One of my favorite Soča Valley accommodations hides in a tiny village a twisty 10-minute drive up from Kobarid's main square. **$ Tourist Farm Kranjc** is a remote but scenic, well-run working sheep farm with eight comfortable rooms, organic meals prepared with their own produce, and a huge shared-view terrace. While this farm—which feels traditional, but has modern style—is a bit less convenient to the sights, it's ideal if you want to really feel like you're huddled high in the mountains (Db-€56, bigger "superior" Db-€76, includes breakfast, dinner-€12/person, air-con in attic rooms only; also ask about their "glamping" cots with private bathroom; Koseč 7, tel. 05/384-8562, mobile 041-946-088, www.turizem-kranjc.si, info@turizem-kranjc.si, Urška and the Kranjc family). It's in the village of Koseč, above Kobarid. From Kobarid, leave town by crossing the Napoleon Bridge (toward Kamp Koren and Great Kozjak Waterfall—see directions under "Great Kozjak Waterfall Hike"). Just after that bridge, turn left and twist up to Drežnica, where you'll turn right to reach Koseč; once in the village, look for signs directing you up the steep road to the left.

Eating in Kobarid

Kobarid prides itself on its restaurants, hosting a few of the best-regarded eateries in the region. (And arguably the best of them all is Hiša Franko, just outside of town and described in the next section.) Kotlar and Topli Val serve up elegant, borderline-pretentious, overpriced but generally good meals that are worth the splurge. Picerija Fedrig is your budget alternative.

Kotlar Restaurant, on the main square, has a classy interior that sprawls around the prow of a faux sailboat. The emphasis is on seafood and locally sourced meats (€10-13 pastas, €12-25 main courses, Mon 18:00-23:00, Thu-Sun 12:00-15:00 & 18:00-22:00, closed Tue-Wed, Trg Svobode 11, tel. 05/389-1110, www.kotlar. si). Kotlar also rents rooms if you're in a pinch (Db-€70).

Topli Val ("Heat Wave"), Hotel Hvala's restaurant, is pricey but good, with a menu that emphasizes fish (€8-13 pastas, €9-22 main courses, lengthy list of Slovenian wines, Tue-Sun 12:00-15:00 & 18:00-23:00, closed Mon, Trg Svobode 1, tel. 05/389-9300).

Picerija Fedrig serves up good €5-7 pizzas (Mon-Tue 17:00-22:00, Wed-Sun 12:00-22:00; off-season Thu-Fri 17:00-22:00, Sat-Sun 12:00-21:30, closed Mon-Wed; a block south of the main square at Volaričeva 11, tel. 05/389-0115).

Sleeping and Eating near Kobarid

$$$ Hiša Franko is a gourmet restaurant that also rents 13 rooms less than a five-minute drive outside of Kobarid. The modern-style rooms in the main building are upscale and comfortable (Db-€135-148 depending on size and amenities), while the three rooms in the adjacent yellow house are much simpler, dated, and affordable (Db-€90; all rooms include breakfast, bike rental-€7, Staro Selo 1, tel. 05/389-4120, www.hisafranko.com, info@hisafranko.com).

What brings most people here is the upscale **restaurant**, which combines Slovenian cuisine and ingredients with modern international influences to create a memorable, if pricey, meal (five courses-€60, nine courses-€80, no à la carte). The dining room is spiffy but casual and unpretentious, and the service is attentive and welcoming. Reserve ahead, especially in summer (Tue-Fri 19:00-23:00, Sat-Sun 12:00-15:00 & 19:00-23:00, closed Mon, also closed Tue off season, closed entirely Jan-March).

Getting There: To reach Hiša Franko, leave Kobarid following signs for *Italija* and *Robič* on the pleasant tree-lined road, and look for the restaurant's sign on the right.

Kobarid Connections

From Kobarid by Bus to: Bovec (4-6/day, 30 minutes), **Ljubljana** (1/day in July-Aug over Vršič Pass, 5 hours; otherwise faster but less scenic via Idrija, 3.5 hours).

LOGARSKA DOLINA AND THE NORTHERN VALLEYS

The Julian Alps around Lake Bled are Slovenia's most accessible and most famous pincushion of peaks. But the high-mountain thrills don't end there. Stretching to the east, along the border with Austria, is the Kamniško-Savinjske range—home to several very remote valleys. One particularly inviting nook between the cut-glass peaks is the time-passed valley called Logarska Dolina. To get way, way, way off the beaten track—with gravel roads, unpasteurized milk, and the few Slovenes who still don't speak English—head to Logarska Dolina, its surrounding valleys, and the breathtaking Panoramic Road above them all.

Logarska Dolina—very loosely translated as "Woodsman's Valley"—thrills adventurous drivers, true back-to-nature nuts, and those intrigued by old-fashioned farming lifestyles...or, better yet, travelers who are all of the above. Most of all, Logarska Dolina is the ideal excuse for a long drive on high-mountain roads to one of Slovenia's most traditional corners.

Traveling here, you come to appreciate the vibrant culture and history that pervades even this remote and rugged corner of a tiny country. Some 25,000 years ago, hardy Ice Age people already lived in Logarska Dolina. Archaeologists have uncovered some remarkable remains from these prehistoric times—mostly tools made from bone, among them a flute and the oldest needle ever discovered. Today's residents focus on sheep, and locally made products—from cheese to thick felt hats, vests, and slippers—are a proud Logarska Dolina symbol. Other treasured aspects of the local culture include woodcarving, marble carving, rollicking zither sing-alongs, and huge ceramic stoves that work hard to keep mountain folk warm through the frigid winter.

With some effort and a bit of extra time, you can enjoy two other interesting sights in this part of Slovenia. On the way between Ljubljana and Logarska Dolina, it's a fairly short detour to the rugged, extremely above-it-all herders' settlement of Velika Planina—which feels even more remote and rugged than Logarska Dolina. And to the east, Velenje Castle has a fine little museum.

If you want to dig deep into the Slovenian mountains—like the glaciers that carved Logarska Dolina during the last Ice Age— these northern mountains are the place. Slovenes like to keep this getaway a secret; it's one of their favorite escapes from the daily grind (and, along with Lake Bled, one of the country's most popular places to get married). Travelers who find Lake Bled too touristy prefer Lake Bohinj (see page 629). But travelers who think Bohinj is too touristy...*love* Logarska Dolina.

PLANNING YOUR TIME

A trip to Logarska Dolina can be done as a long, full-day circular drive from either Bled or Ljubljana. But to really escape to the mountains, spend the night. If you're heading between Ljubljana/ Bled and Ptuj/Maribor on the A-1 expressway, Logarska Dolina is roughly on the way (though it's still an hour off the expressway). Velika Planina combines conveniently with Logarska Dolina, but makes for a very long day.

GETTING TO LOGARSKA DOLINA

I'd skip this region without a car. Public transportation to the northern valleys is extremely time-consuming. In summer only, one **bus** each weekday goes from the city of Celje to Solčava, then on to Logarska Dolina. But once you're there, many of the region's best attractions (such as the Panoramic Road) are unreachable by public bus. In the summer, the Center Rinka in Solčava may be able to help arrange a shared shuttle bus (€75/person from Ljubljana; see contact info later, under "Tourist Information").

On the other hand, Logarska Dolina is made to order by **car.** The valley is nearly due north from Ljubljana. But because of the mountains that lie between them, you'll need to boomerang substantially to the east to get there. From Ljubljana, take the A-1 expressway east (toward Celje) to the Šentrupert exit. From here, most of the route is well-marked with brown *Log Dolina* signs. Head north on road 225 along the Savinja River, past Mozirje and Nazarje, then continue northwest on road 428 through Ljubno, Luče, and Solčava. (For details on getting around the valleys once you're in Solčava, see "Route Tips for Drivers," later.) Figure about an hour from Ljubljana to the Šentrupert exit, then another hour to Solčava.

A good, detailed map is essential. The *Avtokarta Slovenija* map

LOGARSKA DOLINA

Logarska Dolina

—— Road
----- Path

Not to scale:
Solčava to Entry Kiosk
is a 7-Minute Drive.

*Cable Car to
Velika Planina*

To Ljubljana

Luče

Raduha
6,765'

Kamniško

Ojstrica
7,710'

Robanov Kot

SAVINJA

Solčava

RIVER

CENTER
RINKA

PANORAMIC
ROAD

1 Hotel/Restaurant Plesnik
2 Vila Palenk
3 Lenar Tourist Farm
4 Ojstrica Country House & Rest.
5 Na Razpotju Guesthouse &
   Fairytale Forest
6 Tourist Farm Govc-Vršnik
7 Firšt Gostišče Rooms,
   Rest. & Museum
8 Tourist Farm Žibovt
9 Tourist Farm Perk
10 Tourist Farm Klemenšek
11 Orlovo Gnezdo Mountain Hut

will do, but consider getting one with even more detail for this
region (such as the 1:50,000 *Zgornja Savinjska Dolina* map, available locally).

The route I've described earlier is the most straightforward.
Detailed maps will show some seeming "shortcuts" that appear to
take you more directly between Ljubljana and Logarska Dolina.
These are scenic but slow. Two variations are the road through
Kamnik, then over the mountains via Gornji Grad to pick up the
main road into Solčava (near Ljubno); and the even more dramatic version of this route, cutting the corner from Krivčevo north
through Podvolovljek to Luče, which lets you tie in a detour to
Velika Planina. Another seeming shortcut via Kranj—dipping into
Austria on the impossibly twisty Jezersko-Pavličevo Sedlo road,
through Villach—is also possible, and also time-consuming.

Orientation to Logarska Dolina

This area—also called Solčavsko—is tucked in the northern corner
of Slovenia, just a few miles from Austria. Although vast (about
40 square miles), the area has only 580 inhabitants. This chapter's
core sights branch off from an east-west axis formed by the valley
of the Savinja River. The main attraction here is the valley called

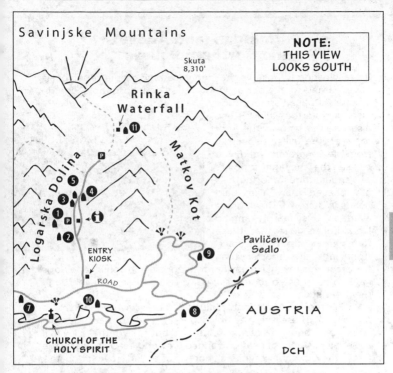

Logarska Dolina, which cuts through the mountainscape south from the Savinja River Valley. Roughly parallel to Logarska Dolina are two smaller valleys: gentle **Robanov Kot** to the east and rugged **Matkov Kot** to the west. (*Dolina* means "valley;" *kot*—literally, "corner"—is a short valley.) Running along the top of the Podolševa ridge above the Savinja River is the rough, gravelly **Panoramic Road** (Panoramska Cesta)—with spectacular views over the entire region.

TOURIST INFORMATION

The region's best source of information is in **Solčava,** at the **Center Rinka,** which hands out maps and brochures, has a good exhibit about the region, can help you find a room or plan a hike, and can arrange activities such as guided hikes, bike rental, horseback riding, rock climbing, archery, and paragliding (daily June-Aug 8:00-20:00, April-May and Sept 8:00-18:00, Oct-March 8:00-15:00, Solčava 29, tel. 03/839-0710, www.solcavsko.info, info@solcavsko.info). For more on the Center Rinka, see "Sights in Logarska Dolina," later.

Within **Logarska Dolina,** there's a modest **TI kiosk** across the parking lot from Hotel Plesnik (very flexible hours but generally May-Oct daily 9:00-15:00, closed Nov-April and in bad weather,

Farming in (and Above) the Northern Valleys

It's fascinating to observe the ingenious ways that intrepid locals have learned to eke out a living in such an inhospitable land. In Logarska Dolina, farmers don't just cultivate the valleys—they also use the land at the very tops of the hills. Especially from the Panoramic Road, you can see that the highest points of various ridges and foothills are shaved bare—like bald heads in a crowd. Cows graze even on this sharply angled land. Locals joke that these farms are so steep that cows' front legs are shorter than  their rear legs to make it easier for them to climb uphill—and dogs have to hang on to the grass with their teeth and bark through their rear ends.

This region's abundant traditional houses have wooden roofs and siding. These shingles are generally made of hard, durable larch wood, and the boards are not cut, but split. In the fall, you'll see endless stacks of neatly arranged firewood, ready to warm the family through the winter. Each house has a tiled stove for heat.

take left fork to hotel after you enter Logarska Dolina to Logarska Dolina 9, tel. 03/838-9004, www.logarska-dolina.si). If it's closed, the nearby Hotel Plesnik also provides basic tourist information. There's also a **TI** along the main road in **Luče** (tel. 03/839-3555).

Sights in Logarska Dolina

The road running along the Savinja River and the Panoramic Road running above it are connected at both ends—forming a handy loop that allows drivers to see everything efficiently. I suggest driving the Panoramic Road first, to get a good overview of the region, then winding down along the Savinja River to dig into the valleys. (If you have bad morning weather that may clear up in the afternoon, do the opposite.)

Route Tips for Drivers: The town of Solčava is the gateway to the region and has the handy and interesting Center Rinka. From Solčava, you can twist up to the Panoramic Road (follow signs to *Podolševa*). At the far (west) end of this sky-high road, you'll come to a fork: Going left drops you directly down into Logarska Dolina, while going right takes you toward the Austrian border at Pavličevo

It's a rough lifestyle. A farming family's primary source of income is mostly cows used for milk and meat, but also pigs and goats. Some of the farms in the Savinja River Valley raise yaks imported from Scotland, which are bred for their meat. A second source of income is forestry: The trees on a farm's property can be harvested and sold. Finally, farmers make a living from you and me, in the form of overnights or meals eaten at their farms.

The many tourist farms *(turistična kmetija)* in this region are a recent phenomenon. During the Yugoslav era, people who lived here stopped farming and moved or commuted into nearby towns in the valley to work in factories. But Slovenia's industry was designed to work as a cog in the Yugoslav machine—other regions provided raw materials, and a large, ready-made market to buy the finished product. After the Slovenes declared independence from Yugoslavia, many of the factories closed, and the farmers-turned-workers returned to their ancestral farming ways. To supplement their income, many families have converted their working farms into tourist farms, inviting guests to visit, stay, and dine with them, and appreciate their unique lifestyles. (I've listed several of these farms in this chapter.) Even though many of the farms in Logarska Dolina seem as though they could be generations old, some date from only the mid-1990s.

Sedlo, and a very rugged, gravelly loop around the top, then bottom, of Matkov Kot (easy to miss—follow signs for tourist farms).

After visiting Logarska Dolina, take the Savinja River road back to Solčava. If you have time, you can detour into the valley of Robanov Kot when you head south from Solčava.

▲▲▲Panoramic Road (Panoramska Cesta)

The Logarska Dolina valley itself (described later) is beautiful. But the region's spectacular highlight is the Panoramic Road, twisting along the top of the cliff above it. At an altitude of around 4,000 feet (compared to about 2,500 feet in Logarska Dolina), this road offers one thrilling drive. For a sneak preview, see www.solcavska-panoramska-cesta.si.

As you rattle along the rough road, all around you are vast swaths of mountain forests, broken only by hilltops covered with patches of green grass. Each of these hills is its own farm that raises grass to feed livestock (see sidebar). You're just an avalanche's tumble from the Austrian border. Several stretches of the Panoramic Road are what Slovenes poetically call "white roads"—that is, unpaved gravel.

About halfway along the Panoramic Road, the late 19th-century **Church of the Holy Spirit** (Sveti Duh) hovers on a hilltop above the hamlet of Podolševa. Climb up to the church for sweeping views over Logarska Do-

lina. If the church is open, duck inside and find a very unusual relief of three men representing the Holy Trinity. God is in the center, Jesus is on the left, and on the right, it's the Holy Spirit, depicted not as a dove but as a balding man.

Watch for pullouts offering stunning views all along the Panoramic Road; the best stretch is between the Klemenšek and Žibovt tourist farms. Pack along a picnic, or consider stopping off at a tourist farm for a meal (Tourist Farm Klemenšek owns some of the best views in the region—listed under "Eating in Logarska Dolina," later). Some farms serve *kislo mleko,* or "soured milk"...which is exactly what it sounds like. Fresh, unpasteurized milk is set out in the open air, usually in a darkened room. The fat rises to the top and forms a skin on top. The bottom of the milk is like yogurt, white and relatively flavorless. Meanwhile, the yellowish top layer comes with a kick: a pungent barnyard aftertaste. I tried it—once—and enjoyed it...the experience, if not the flavor.

▲▲Logarska Dolina

This valley, 4.5 miles long and about a quarter-mile wide, is the region's main draw. A flat, broad meadow surrounded on all sides by sheer alpine cliffs, it's an idyllic place for a drive, hike, or bike

ride. Various sights—caves, waterfalls, old log cabins, and so on—surround the valley, but it's most appealing simply as a place to commune with gorgeous Slovenian nature.

Though you can enter the valley year-round, you'll pay a €7 entry fee per car from April through October (at other times, or if there's bad weather and the entry kiosk is closed, it's free). After the valley entrance, the road forks. Take the left fork to reach the TI kiosk (see "Tourist Information," earlier) and hotels; or take the right fork to bypass them (the two forks eventually rejoin).

At the far end of the valley, you'll find a parking lot with some snack stands. From here, you can follow the *Slap Rinka—10 min* signs up the moderately strenuous path to the **Rinka Waterfall.** This is where mountain runoff tumbles into the valley, feeding the Savinja River, which courses through the valley and region. Relax at the little mountain hut called Orlovo Gnezdo ("Eagle's Nest") and enjoy a drink with a view of the falls, which plunge 300 feet down from the adjacent cliffs.

With more time, Logarska Dolina offers an inviting, mostly level place to go for a longer **hike,** surrounded by cow-filled meadows and towering peaks. The "Nature-Ethnographic Trail" is a two-hour, four-mile (one-way) hike that starts near the entrance of the valley and leads to the end of the valley. A brochure that describes the route is available at the Logarska Dolina TI kiosk and at the Center Rinka, along with information about more adventurous hikes up into the region's mountains.

▲Center Rinka

This sleek building sits along the main road in the village of Solčava, just 50 yards from the twisty route up to the Panoramic Road. Named for the big waterfall that feeds the Savinja River (which carved out this region's beauty), it's a state-of-the-art visitors center that celebrates the local landscape and culture. A small but endearing—and free—exhibition on the natural area includes displays about area caves and the prehistoric findings unearthed in them, local handicrafts (felt and woodworking), trees, wildflowers, and animals. It provides a good foundation for exploring the region, and the 15-minute film makes you wish you had more time here. The center also offers a free Internet terminal and Wi-Fi, a café/bar selling some locally made products (meats, cheeses, and cookies), a shop with an enjoyable variety of local handicrafts, and a children's play area. A visit here is smart both in good weather (to plan your high-mountain fun) and in bad weather (to learn about the region without getting wet).

Cost and Hours: Free, daily June-Aug 8:00-20:00, April-May and Sept 8:00-18:00, Oct-March 8:00-15:00, Solčava 29, tel. 03/839-0710, www.solcavsko.info.

Nearby: The village of **Solčava** itself is a pleasant place, hemmed in tightly by alpine cliffs and capped by the picturesque Church of Christ the King.

Robanov Kot and Matkov Kot

These smaller, sleepier valleys, dotted with traditional farm build-ings, flank Logarska Dolina. They offer the same surrounded-by-mountains feeling, but they're less cultivated and less crowded than Logarska during the peak season. With extra time, poke into one or both of these minivalleys simply to enjoy the peaceful views.

Robanov Kot, near Solčava, is more gentle and accessible, with better and more level roads. This valley is well-marked with a brown sign just south of Solčava; it's home to the recommended Tourist Farm Govc-Vršnik.

The **Matkov Kot** road is more rugged, with cliff-hanging gravel portions that can feel like little more than tractor ruts. But the valley scenery is breathtaking (sometimes literally)—and argu-ably rivals the Panoramic Road. Adventurous drivers who enjoy mountain vistas will find it worth the grinding gears. It's easy to miss this poorly marked valley—look for signs to the tourist farms (the recommended Tourist Farm Perk is on this road) and for *Mat-kov Škaf.*

Other Sights

If you have ample time here, you can consider some other offbeat attractions that are more charming than thrilling.

The **Firšt Gostišče**—which has a restaurant and rents rooms on the road between Solčava and Logarska Dolina—has a cave on their property called Fidova Zijalka, the residence of a 19th-cen-tury hermit and medicine man named Fida. Much higher on the hill is another cave called Potočka Zijalka, where prehistoric find-ings have helped advance our modern understanding of life during the last Ice Age. Honoring this heritage, the Firšt family operates their own modest, dry, two-room museum of prehistoric cave find-ings and folk medicine (€2, same hours as restaurant—see page 673). They also have an "ethnographic park": Pay €4 and pick up the essential English guidebooklet at the main building, then hike steeply up into the hills behind for a one-hour loop that takes you to the cave, with commentary en route about local flora, fauna, and farming lifestyles.

If you're traveling with kids, consider paying a visit to the **Fai-rytale Forest,** next to and run by the recommended Na Razpotju Guesthouse in the middle of Logarska Dolina. Speckled through a gentle wood are 35 wood carvings illustrating local fairy tales, all explained in English (€2.50/child, €3.50/adult, April-Nov daily 10:00-18:00; listed under "Sleeping in Logarska Dolina," next).

Sleep Code

Abbreviations (€1=about $1.10, country code: 386)
S=Single, **D**=Double/Twin, **T**=Triple, **Q**=Quad, **b**=bathroom
Price Rankings
  $$$ Higher Priced—Most rooms €100 or more
   $$ Moderately Priced—Most rooms €55-100
    $ Lower Priced—Most rooms less than €55
Hotels accept credit cards, but tourist farms are cash only and charge extra for stays of fewer than three nights. Wi-Fi generally is available and free and breakfast is included, but the modest tourist tax (about €1/person, per night) is not. Everyone listed here speaks English. Prices change; verify the hotel's current rates online or by email. For the best prices, always book directly with the hotel.

Sleeping in Logarska Dolina

All of my listings are in Logarska Dolina or within about a 15-minute drive. Many accommodations in this region have their own restaurants, and it's common (and typically a good value) to take "half-board" at your accommodation—dinner (or sometimes lunch) for a fixed additional price. There are no restaurants in this area that are worth going out of your way for, so eating where you sleep makes sense.

IN LOGARSKA DOLINA

These options sit in the valley of Logarska Dolina itself. They're listed in the order you'll reach them as you drive down the valley.

$$$ Hotel Plesnik and **Vila Palenk,** both part of the only big hotel outfit in the area, sit proudly in the middle of Logarska Dolina. The hotel, with lively public spaces and 30 modern rooms with traditional farmhouse furnishings, is a big, classy, overpriced splurge (Sb-€89, Db-€144, elevator). The nearby, smaller Vila Palenk has 11 rustic rooms with more character (Sb-€50, Db-€90, family room-€150, no elevator, breakfast at the main hotel). Reservations for both are handled through the same office (€12/person for dinner at hotel restaurant, check online for discounts, indoor swimming pool, Logarska Dolina 10, tel. 03/839-2300, www. plesnik.si, info@plesnik.si). After entering Logarska Dolina, you'll come to a fork; bear left to reach the hotel.

$$ Lenar Tourist Farm rents six rooms and three apartments with cozy farmhouse decor in two adjacent homes with nice views over a small orchard and the grand valley of Logarska Dolina (Db-€60, apartment for up to 6 people-€100, breakfast-€5, cash only,

Logarska Dolina 11, mobile 041-851-829, www.lenar.si, tk.lenar@
siol.net).

$$ Ojstrica Country House has nine simple rooms and a res-
taurant halfway along Logarska Dolina (Db-€64, €82 with dinner,
cheaper for multinight stays with dinner packages, Logarska Do-
lina 13a, tel. 03/838-9051, mobile 041-664-455, www.logarska-
ojstrica.si, info@logarska-ojstrica.si).

$$ Na Razpotju Guesthouse ("At the Crossroads") is especially good for families, with 10 colorful rooms named for moun-
tain herbs and a small theme park of carved fairy tales (Sb-€50,
Db-€80, dinner-€12/person, a quarter-mile from Hotel Plesnik
toward the far end of the valley, Logarska Dolina 14, mobile 031-
249-441, www.logarska-narazpotju.si, razpotje@siol.net).

NEAR LOGARSKA DOLINA

In Robanov Kot: **$$ Tourist Farm Govc-Vršnik** (pronounced
"goats vurshnick")—in this smaller, relaxing valley (a scenic
15-minute drive from Logarska Dolina)—is my favorite option
in the region, and the most modern and accessible of my tourist
farm listings. English-speaking Marjana and the Vršnik family run
this farm with a soft-spoken, warmhearted hospitality. They have
cows, a traditional beehive, and 10 cozy rooms with bright, woody
decor (Db-€60, €80 with dinner, 20 percent more for 1- or 2-night
stays, cheaper mid-Oct-late April, cash only, Robanov Kot 34, tel.
03/839-5016, www.govc-vrsnik.com, govc.vrsnik@siol.net). As
you enter the valley of Robanov Kot (just south of Solčava), watch
for signs (it's the second tourist farm on the left).

Between Solčava and Logarska Dolina: **$ Firšt Gostišče**, sit-
uated along the picturesque riverside road just outside Logarska
Dolina, feels like a rural rest stop, with a popular restaurant, six
straightforward rooms, and a small museum about local prehistoric
finds (Db-€50, 1-night stay-€12 extra, 2-night stay-€6 extra, din-
ner-€9/person, cheaper Oct-May, Logarska Dolina 1a, tel. 03/839-
4678, www.first-logarska.si).

On the Panoramic Road: **$ Tourist Farm Žibovt** is dramati-
cally situated at the far end of the Panoramic Road, a few minutes'
walk from the Austrian border. It perches on a ledge with fine views
of a tranquil meadow that ends at a sheer cliff plunging to the bot-
tom of Logarska Dolina. In addition to renting six cheery rooms,
the Poličnik family serves meals and turns out a wide range of dairy
products—including the unforgettable *kislo mleko* ("soured milk").
They also make traditional wooden games and have beehives that
produce homemade honey; a small marble quarry is nearby (Db-
€52, extra for 1-night stays, cash only, closed mid-Oct-mid-April,
Logarska Dolina 24, tel. 03/584-7118, www.nad1000m.si/zibovt,
kmetija.zibovt@gmail.com, Žarko and Martina Poličnik). The

farm is well-marked at the far end of the Panoramic Road (near the Austrian border crossing at Pavličevo Sedlo).

Overlooking Matkov Kot: **$ Tourist Farm Perk** is the most rustic of my listings, with seven simple, older-feeling, but budget-priced rooms (some of which have a private bathroom on the hall). It's scenically perched on the particularly remote-feeling gravel road high above Matkov Kot (D/Db-€52, €60 with dinner, cash only, Logarska Dolina 23, tel. 03/584-7120, mobile 041-282-485, www.perk.si, info@perk.si, Krivec family speaks limited English).

Eating in Logarska Dolina

Many of the region's tourist farms serve full meals to passersby in summer and light meals and snacks at other times. The food here is traditional and heavy, and no place is worth a long drive for a meal. Base your decision on convenience.

Picnics: The best option is to bring a picnic with you and eat whenever you find the scenic perch you like best. If you wait to buy your picnic until you reach the valley, you're too late. Instead, shop at one of the small grocery stores along the main road in Luče or Solčava. Also in Solčava, the Center Rinka's café/bar sells locally produced meats and cheeses to supplement your picnic. Spectacularly located picnic benches punctuate the Panoramic Road, including ones a few hundred yards on either side of the recommended Tourist Farm Klemenšek.

In Logarska Dolina: Several of my recommended accommodations also have food, including **Hotel Plesnik** (big restaurant with pricey food—€7-10 pastas, €13-24 main courses, daily 12:00-15:00 & 18:00-20:00) and **Ojstrica Country House** (woody, convivial space with a bar frequented by locals, affordable €8-10 meals, daily 12:30-15:00 & 18:00-20:00). On the road between Logarska Dolina and Solčava, **Firšt Gostišče** serves up €6-8 small meals and €9-18 main courses (Tue-Sun 12:00-21:00, closed Mon).

On the Panoramic Road: **Tourist Farm Klemenšek,** set on a grassy ridge with spectacular views, has the classic Logarska Dolina setting, home cooking, and indoor or outdoor tables (July-Aug daily 11:00-21:00; May-June and Sept-mid-Oct Sat-Sun only 11:00-21:00, closed Mon-Fri; closed mid-Oct-April; halfway between Sveti Duh and the end of the Panoramic Road, tel. 03/838-9024, www.na-klemencem.si).

Velika Planina

This extremely remote and rustic herdsmen's settlement sits on a mile-high island, surrounded by 360 degrees of cut glass. Accessible only by a cable-car ride, chairlift, and short hike—or by driving a very rough road and taking a longer hike—Velika Planina is an alpine wonderland, offering a scenic and insightful look at farming lifestyles. While it takes some effort to reach, it's worth the trip for those lingering in the mountains. Velika Planina is also very loosely on the way between Ljubljana (or Lake Bled) and Logarska Dolina (the cable car is a five-mile detour from the Kamnik-Luče road, described earlier, under "Getting to Logarska Dolina").

Orientation: A large meadow with houses (the literal meaning of its name), Velika Planina feels like you're at the end of the world—and yet, on a clear day you can see Ljubljana on the horizon. The focal point for tourists is Pastirsko Naselje (Pastors' Settlement); also known as Veliki Stan (Big Town) and Tiha Dolina (Silent Valley). This is where about 35 farmers—who live most of the year in a dozen different villages scattered throughout the valley below—bring their 400 cows for high-altitude grazing each summer (early June-mid-Sept). At other times, it's scenic but very desolate—I'd skip it if the cows aren't up. For more information, and to confirm cable-car timetables, see www.velikaplanina.si.

Getting There: North of Ljubljana is the city of Kamnik, and north of that is the village of Kaminška Bistrica. From here, you can ride a **cable car** up into the mountains (€11 round-trip for cable car, €15 for cable car and chairlift, cable car runs at the top of each hour mid-June-mid-Sept 8:00-20:00, shorter hours off-season, chairlift coordinated with cable car arrival, tel. 031/680-862). From the top of the cable car (4,655 feet), you have various ways to get to the Pastirsko Naselje village. One option is a long 40-minute hike. But most visitors prefer to continue on to a chairlift: From the chairlift's first station (Zeleni rob), it's a level 20-minute hike to the village, and from the second/top station (Gradišče, 5,472 feet), it's a downhill 20-minute hike.

It's also possible to **drive** most of the way to Velika Planina, but it requires negotiating a confusing maze of steep and unpaved roads; because locals don't want cars anywhere near the village (which would ruin the rustic ambience), you'll have to park a long hike away. If you'd like to try, from the Kamnik-Luče road, near Podvoljovek, watch for the turnoff to *Tiha Dolina*. Once on this maze of roads, carefully track signs to *Veliki Stan* until you see the "do not enter" sign—from here, you'll have to hike in.

Visiting Velika Planina: Here in the "big village," farmers reside in unique traditional houses: tiny residential quarters in the center, surrounded by stables for the animals (which helps heat the living area), all covered by a unique oval roof. The homes are made of larch wood, which helps provide natural weatherproofing. One of the huts, the **Preskar Hut**, hosts a small museum of 19th-century farming lifestyles; others, including the **Pri Gradišekovih** (near the top of town), may be open to sell cheese and other food.

Perched on a ridge just above the settlement, just enjoying the view, is the rustic, wooden **Chapel of St. Mary of Snows** (which was destroyed during WWII and rebuilt in 1988). A priest still comes up each Sunday throughout the summer to say Mass for this tiny community.

Velika Planina has its own very distinctive and proud culture. The farmers' traditional costume is a cloak made of overlapping corn stalks (which almost looks like a giant hula skirt) and a floppy hat—both of which provide protection from the elements. While here, they produce a unique, pear-shaped cheese called *trnič*, which tastes like a very young Swiss cheese—mild and semicrumbly. It's often served with a buckwheat mush called *žganci*, and eaten with a wooden spoon that's another one of this area's local traditions. The soured milk *(kislo mleko)* from Logarska Dolina is also produced here.

Herdsmen gather and socialize in a common hut called "The Parliament." They are keeping up with modern times: They only wear the traditional costume as a photo op for tourists, and many of the huts have been modernized (solar panels are the only source of electricity). But old-timers are concerned that the next generation isn't eager about carrying on the tradition. High-maintenance cows require 24/7 attention, and most young people have other jobs now. Visit now, while this last vestige of traditional herding still survives.

Velenje Castle

This scenic, 700-year-old, hill-capping castle seems out of place over the modern industrial town of Velenje (which was once named "Titovo Velenje" for the Yugoslav dictator, Tito). Even more unusual is the eclectic, extensive, and endearing museum it houses. While it's not worth going far out of your way to see, a trip to the castle makes a good rainy-day activity or a fine diversion if you've got extra time at the end of your Logarska Dolina day.

Cost and Hours: €2.50, Tue-Sun 10:00-18:00, closed Mon, Ljubljanska cesta 54, tel. 03/898-2630, www.muzej-velenje.si.

Getting There: Velenje Castle is easy to visit en route to or from Logarska Dolina, especially if you're headed east on the expressway. From the road connecting Logarska Dolina to the expressway, you can detour east just south of Mozirje (via Gorenje) into Velenje, where you'll look for easy-to-miss brown signs to turn off for the castle. From Velenje, you can head south straight to the expressway.

Visiting the Castle: If the guides aren't busy, one of them can show you around (included in ticket price). Otherwise, borrow the English descriptions.

You'll find a surprising diversity of exhibits surrounding the

LOGARSKA DOLINA

tranquil castle courtyard: replicas of a circa-1930s general store and pub; a Czech professor's three-room collection of African art and everyday items; a survey of regional history through the Middle Ages, including a replica of a countryside home; a city history overview (the town was founded only after World War II, so much of its story dates from Tito's Yugoslav era); an exhibit on the WWII experience in the local area; various Slovenian paintings and sculptures; and temporary exhibits. Separate buildings house a collection of Baroque church art and an exhibit on mastodons (the remains of two of these extinct tusked mammals were found near here in 1964).

PTUJ AND MARIBOR

The vast majority of Slovenia's attractions are concentrated in the western third of the country: the mountains, the sea, the capital city, and the Karst. East of Ljubljana, the mountains gradually fade into cornfields, the towns and cities become less colorful, and "oh, wow!" turns into "so what?" But there's hope, in the form of Slovenia's oldest town (and winner of the "funniest name" award): Ptuj (puh-TOOey—the "P" is almost silent; and yes, it really does sound like someone spitting). This small, sleepy, pleasant town boasts a creaky Old Town and a hilltop castle packed with museum exhibits. For a big-city complement to Ptuj, drop into Maribor—the country's second city, and the de facto capital of eastern Slovenia. Expect some contrasts from the more popular parts of Slovenia. Even in this tiny country, rivalry rages between cities—and people here in the "02 Zone" (the area-code-derived nickname that Slovenes use for this region) have their own personality, dialect, and political priorities.

PLANNING YOUR TIME

With a week or more in Slovenia and a desire to delve into the less-touristed areas of the country, Ptuj deserves a short visit. A few hours are enough to feel you've mastered the town; if you're a restless sightseer, it's tough to fill an entire day here. Begin by touring the castle, then enjoy a wander through the Old Town and consider Ptuj's other museums, or relax at the thermal baths across the river. If you can't sit still that long, consider spending a few more hours on a side-trip into Maribor.

Ptuj and Maribor are conveniently located on the train network, and are easy to reach from Ljubljana, as well as from international destinations like Zagreb, Vienna, and Budapest.

Ptuj

With a storied past, a much-vaunted castle, and easygoing locals who act like they've never met a tourist, Ptuj is charming. Populated since the early Stone Age, Ptuj has a long and colorful history that reads like a Who's Who of Central Europe: Celts and Romans, Dominican friars and Habsburg counts, Nazis and Yugoslavs...not to mention a fuzzy monster named Kurent. The people of Ptuj are particularly proud of their Roman era, when "Poetovio" was a bustling metropolis of 40,000 people (nearly quadruple today's size). But even as it clings to its noble past, today's Ptuj is refreshingly real, with a sleepy small-town ambience and an interesting castle/museum.

While it hosts plenty of visitors (mostly Germans and Austrians, who call it "Pettau"), Ptuj is hardly a tourist town. Real people, not nightclubs or souvenir shops, populate the Old Town. If this makes Ptuj feel a bit less polished than the big-name sights in western Slovenia, so much the better—think of it as a diamond in the rough.

Orientation to Ptuj

Ptuj is squeezed between its historic castle and the wide Drava River. With just 11,000 people (23,000 in greater Ptuj), it still ranks as Slovenia's eighth-largest town. The Old Town is shaped roughly like a triangle, with the castle and two monasteries as its three points. You can walk from one end of the Old Town to the other in about 10 minutes, but since the town slopes uphill from the river to the castle, there's a bit of up and down.

TOURIST INFORMATION

Ptuj's TI shares the square called Slovenski trg with its landmark City Tower. They hand out a good town map and *A Short Guide Through Ptuj*, with historical and sightseeing information (daily May-Sept 9:00-20:00, Oct-April 9:00-18:00, Slovenski trg 5, tel. 02/779-6011, www.ptuj.info).

ARRIVAL IN PTUJ

The humble **train station** is about a 10-minute walk from the center. Exit the station to the left, then cross the busy road to the **bus station.** From the bus station, the Old Town is just on the other

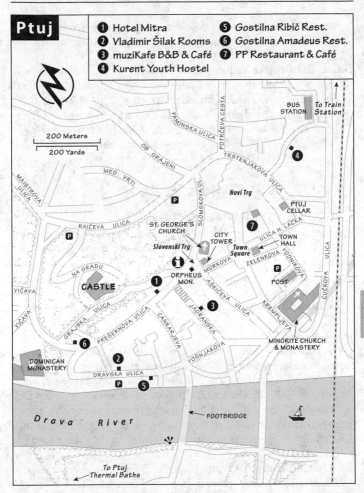

Ptuj

1. Hotel Mitra
2. Vladimir Šilak Rooms
3. muziKafe B&B & Café
4. Kurent Youth Hostel
5. Gostilna Ribič Rest.
6. Gostilna Amadeus Rest.
7. PP Restaurant & Café

side of the big commercial center. If you're **driving** in from the expressway, cross the big bridge into town and then watch for *P* signs to the left. Street parking in town is abundant and affordable—look for blue lines—but it's limited to two hours. If you want to visit the castle, follow brown *Grad* signs to twist up the road and park just below it.

HELPFUL HINTS

Internet Access: The town has a few Internet cafés, but the easiest access is at the free terminal inside the TI (see earlier).

Local Guide: Anja Cuznar, a likeable, knowledgeable, can-do native, offers walking tours of the town (€60/2 hours) and can also help arrange any other tours or excursions in this often-overlooked corner of Slovenia—including wine-tastings, food tours, and so on (mobile 031-776-440, anja.cuznar@ capriturizem.si).

Tours: The **Ptujske Vedute agency** handles most guided-tour options in Ptuj. They try to offer regularly scheduled two-hour walking tours, which include a tasting of three wines (€11, more if few people show up, ask TI for latest schedule). They can also book you a private guide (€40 for up to a one-hour tour of the Old Town, also possible for half-day or full-day tours; tel. 02/778-8780, www.vedute.si, ptuj@vedute.si).

Sights in Ptuj

▲▲PTUJ CASTLE (PTUJSKI GRAD)

The modest castle is Ptuj's top sight, and it proudly claims to be Slovenia's most-visited museum. Overlooking the town from its perch over the Drava River, it's less than thrilling from afar. But the horseshoe-shaped castle complex hosts a series of surprisingly rich and engaging exhibits.

Cost and Hours: €5, daily 9:00-17:00, May-mid-Oct until 18:00, July-Aug Sat-Sun until 20:00, tel. 02/748-0360, www. pmpo.si.

Information and Tours: Good English descriptions are posted in most rooms. English tours are rare, but you can call to ask if one is scheduled that you can join (included in entry fee). Or you can call ahead to arrange your own private tour for €15 extra (depends on guide availability, email at least one day ahead to ptujski.grad@pmpo.si). But my self-guided tour, below, covers the highlights. For more in-depth information, buy the thorough guidebook.

Getting There: You can't miss the castle, sitting over the city. It's about a 10-minute cobbled hike above the Old Town. Several trails lead up from the Old Town, all well-marked with *Grad* signs (easiest to find is the lane called Grajska ulica, near the TI).

❂ Self-Guided Tour: The core of the Ptuj Castle collection shows off the lifestyles of the castle's historic residents, while other exhibits display weapons, musical instruments, and traditional costumes used for the annual Kurentovanje festival. You'll follow a one-way route. The entrances to each exhibit are not all well-marked, but attendants are always around to direct you to what you want to see. Touring the whole shebang takes about two hours.
• *Buy your ticket in the long building just below the main part of the castle. This same building also has the castle's highlight, the...*

Collection of Traditional Carnival Masks: Ptuj's Mardi Gras celebration, called Kurentovanje, is well-known for its processions of fanciful masked characters (see sidebar on page 682).

This exhibit—as colorful as an episode of *Sesame Street*—offers an entertaining look at the complete Kurentovanje experience. The various costumes are all lined up in one long hall, as if reenacting the processional that stomps through Ptuj's streets each spring. First come the spearmen, dressed more or less like normal folks. Soon after, the plow is used to symbolically "wake up the soil" and set the stage for a season of bountiful crops. Then you'll see a group of striking Kurent costumes—from old homemade ones (turn an old coat inside-out to reveal the fur lining) to today's store-bought versions (they run about €500). After the giant hen comes the bear, a reminder of times when Roma (Gypsy) entertainers actually did bring trained bears to town. The horse (called Rusa) is taken by a farmer from house to house, trying to "sell" it to neighbors. But the horse is unruly and obnoxious—supposedly good luck for the health and fertility of livestock. The costume of the old woman carrying the old man on her back seems whimsical, but it represents a powerful theme: We carry the memory of the deceased with us always. Near the end are Jürek (swaddled in greenery, representing spring) and Rabolj (a Kurent-like monster, representing winter); these two do battle—and, of course, the spring always wins.

• *Now head up into the main part of the castle, climbing the cobbled road into the courtyard. Show your ticket to go through the gate, and then climb the main stairs (on the left side of the courtyard) one floor up.*

Courtyard: Look over the courtyard for this quick history lesson: In the 11th century, the archbishops of Salzburg built a

fortress here. In the 12th century, the Lords of Ptuj, who watched over the Salzburgers' land, moved in. The LoP's died out in the mid-15th century, and from then on, the castle changed hands frequently. Over the next several centuries, Ptuj Castle gradually acquired its current appearance: a Romanesque core (part of a 14th-century fortress, barely visible now) with a Renaissance arcaded courtyard (designed by Italian experts who came to fortify the castle against the Ottomans), accentuated by an austere Baroque addition (the outermost wing, with the decorated stone window frames). Most of what you'll see in today's exhibit dates from the time of the Counts of Herberstein (1873-1945).

Now look over the door at the end of the arcade to see the **castle seal,** a hodgepodge of symbols representing previous owners. What's an English phrase (in the banner at the top) doing on a seal for a castle in Slovenia? It's because of a Hungarian princess. In the Middle Ages, when a princess of Hungary moved to Scotland to be

Kurentovanje

Ptuj is famous for its distinctive Mardi Gras celebration, called Kurentovanje (koo-rent-oh-VAWN-yeh). Locals dress up in elaborate costumes and parade through the streets, celebrating the end of winter and heralding the arrival of spring. Nearby villages have similar, smaller, and more traditional processions.

It seems quaint today, but in the Middle Ages, Kurentovanje was deadly serious. The winter is particularly harsh here, so when spring began to approach, the peasants wanted to offer encouragement. They'd put on frightening masks and costumes and parade around making as much noise as possible to scare off the winter.

Kurentovanje's most notable character is Kurent, a fun-loving Slavic pagan god of hedonism—sort of the Slovenian Bacchus. A Kurent is covered with fur and has a long, red tongue, horns, a snout, whiskers, red-ringed eyes, a wooden club with a spiny hedgehog skin wrapped around one end, and red or green socks. It wears a chain of five bells around its waist, and jumps around and swings its hips to get them clanging as loudly as possible. Kurents travel together in packs, so the combined noise can be deafening.

Traditionally the role of Kurent was played by young men of the village, who used it as an opportunity to catch the eye of a potential wife. (Young women still toss handkerchiefs to the Kurents as they pass by.) Each young man makes his own costume in secret—making the big reveal all the more frightening. Traditionally, they'd use the stinkiest animal hides they could find, to make the beast smell as hideous as it looked and sounded.

These processions have evolved into modern extravaganzas. These days, men and women of any age buy their Kurent costumes in a store, and Kurentovanje's daytime parades are followed by evenings of music, celebration, and general debauchery. In recent years, in a sort of "creature exchange" program, characters from Mardi Gras celebrations in other countries have come to take part in Kurentovanje.

Imagine about 350 of these hairy beasts, each one with five huge bells clanging at top volume, stomping down Prešernova street. Or come the Sunday before Ash Wednesday, and see for yourself. For details on all the festivities, check out www.kurentovanje.net.

Kurentovanje ends at midnight on Shrove Tuesday (before Ash Wednesday), when people move into the more pensive season of Lent...confident that spring will soon return.

with her new husband, she took with her a particularly protective chamberlain. When the chamberlain buckled the princess to her horse for a treacherous river crossing, he'd fasten her on with three belts instead of just one, and shout "Grip fast!" when they came to any rough patches. That chamberlain's descendants took the name Leslie and eventually bought this castle in 1656. The family crest became those three buckles the chamberlain had used to protect his princess (in the left shield). You'll spot this insignia throughout the castle.

• *Going through the door, you enter the...*

Feudal Dwelling Culture Collection: This exhibit displays artifacts belonging to the castle's previous owners. The route takes you more or less clockwise in a roughly chronological order, from the 16th to the 19th century. In the first few rooms—where receptions were held and guests were (hopefully) impressed—you'll see several 17th-century tapestries from Brussels depicting the travels of Ulysses. Notice that nearly every big room has its own ceramic stove (fed from behind the wall by servants). Looking up, you'll see that while some of the rooms have exposed wooden-beam ceilings, others are adorned with cake-frosting stucco work—it's original, was created by highly skilled masters, and is still intact after nearly 300 years. At the end of the first hall is a gallery of portraits of the Herbersteins, who furnished this part of the castle and were eager to establish their legitimacy as a ruling family.

• *Looping back to where you began, head down the hallway into the residential part of the castle (in the hall, notice the yellowed, 700-year-old Herberstein family tree on your right). The first big room is the...*

Countess' Salon: Also called the "Chinese Salon," this room reveals the fascination many 17th- and 18th-century Europeans had for foreign cultures. But the European artists who created these works never actually visited China, instead basing their visions on stories they heard from travelers who may or may not have had firsthand experience there. The results—European depictions of imagined Chinese culture—are highly inaccurate at best, and flights of pure fantasy at worst (look around for animals and instruments that never existed). This European interest in Chinese culture is known as *chinoiserie*. We'll see a similar fixation on Turkish culture soon.

• *Head through the next few rooms (countess' bedroom, countess' dressing room, old chapel, chambermaid's room). Before entering the 14th-century core—and oldest part—of the castle, keep your head up to see a very unusual chandelier: an anatomically correct (or surgically enhanced, by the look of it) female dragon. Continue into the...*

Bedrooms: The first shows off what prim and proper 17th-century Europeans considered to be "erotic" art (with a mythical creature trying to woo a woman), while the second is decorated in

Napoleonic-era Empire-style furniture. In this room, pay special attention to the stove: Water (which could be scented) was poured into the top, and emerged at the bottom in the form of steam. Fancy. The third bedroom brings the survey of furniture up to date: 19th-century Biedermeier...simple, practical, comfortable, but still beautiful.

• *Going into the arcade, turn left to find the...*

Festival Hall: Then as now, this hall was a preferred place for banquets and concerts. Decorating the walls is Europe's biggest collection of *turqueries*. Like the faux-Chinese stuff we saw earlier, this is a (usually highly inaccurate) European vision of Turkish culture. After the Habsburg armies defeated the Ottomans and forced them out of Central Europe, the two powers began a diplomatic relationship. In the late 17th century, many Austrian officers went to Turkey and came back with souvenirs and tall tales, which were patched together to form the idiosyncratic vision of the Ottoman Empire you see here.

The left wall shows Ottoman politicians of the day—many with European features (presumably painted by artists who'd never laid eyes on an actual Turkish person). Along the back wall, we see portraits of four sultans' wives. Imagine how astonishing the notion of a harem must have been in the buttoned-down Habsburg days. But even though these paintings are unmistakably titillating, they're still appropriately repressed. The first woman (on left) wears two different layers of semitransparent clothing (what's the point?). And the fourth woman (on right) reaches for some fruit (symbolic of...well, you know) and teasingly pulls open her dress so we can see what's underneath, which is...more clothes.

Finally, look on the right wall, with 17th-century Eurofied visions of people from other cultures: Africans, Native Americans, and Asians, all with exaggerated features. This quirky collection is typical of Slovenian museums: Since they can't afford great works by famous artists, they collect items that may seem obscure, but actually have an interesting story to tell.

At the far end of the Festival Hall, you can poke into the castle's chapel.

• *Exiting the Festival Hall, go straight ahead along the arcade to its end, where you'll take the tight, medieval spiral staircase up one level. At the top, the row of sandstone dwarves leads to two skippable rooms of paintings. Instead, turn left into...*

Medieval Knights, Founders, and Patrons of the Arts: This exhibit tells you more than you ever wanted to know about the Lords of Ptuj. Touring its several rooms, you'll see family trees and crests, artifacts from lords gone by, models of local buildings, and a fine 1380 statue of St. George (Ptuj's patron saint) slaying the dragon. The darkened rooms highlight the Middle Ages, with some precious statues by the greatest local masters of the day.

• *Exit to the right, and walk to the end of the arcade.*

Castle Gallery: This painting gallery features works from the Baroque period, the 16th to the 18th century. As most of these are lesser painters' copies of famous works by great masters, you likely won't recognize many names in here. One name in particular you won't recognize is Johann Christian Schröder (1655-1702), a Prague court painter whose depictions of biblical scenes constitute the majority of the collection.

• *Head back down to the courtyard. Ask one of the attendants to direct you (across the courtyard from the main staircase) to the...*

Collection of Musical Instruments: This fun and well-presented exhibit groups instruments by type of music, which you'll hear as you enter each room. The first section celebrates Ptuj's civic marching band, a prized local tradition. The next section displays ancient Roman instruments. The tibia (in the display case), dating from the second century A.D., is the only one ever found; it had two pipes made of bone leading to a single mouthpiece (illustrated on the wall). The next section features woodwinds and strings, including a rare, preserved lute. And the last section shows off a Bösendorfer piano and other keyboard instruments.

• *As you exit, you can ask to be directed to the anticlimactic finale (to the right), the...*

Collection of Arms: Squeezed into one corner of a huge, vaulted room is an armory collection spanning several centuries, from the 1400s through World War I. They're displayed on racks, as they would have been in a real armory. Also in this hall, look for models of the castle as it appeared in 1657 and in 1812.

• *Your castle visit is over. Enjoy the views, then head back down into town.*

OLD TOWN

The sights in Ptuj's Old Town are simple and not very time-consuming. Wander around, take them in at your own pace, then reward yourself with a relaxing drink on a square.

▲Slovenski Trg

Once Ptuj's main square, and now its most atmospheric, Slovenski trg is fronted by the TI, Hotel Mitra, and the City Tower. Around this square are several reminders of Ptuj's Roman past.

The white marble slab in the middle of the square, known as the **Orpheus Monument,** was commissioned by a Roman mayor in the second century A.D. to honor an esteemed figure: himself. Notice the musician playing the lyre (near the top, center of slab, below the naked woman). Since the lyre is commonly associated with Orpheus, the monument's nickname stuck. When Rome fell, so did many of its structures, including this one. It became buried in history, only to reappear in the 16th century as the town pillory, where criminals were punished (secured by chains that were embedded in the holes you still see in the slab). In the Middle Ages, the town judge would come out onto the balcony over the door of his white house, at the top of the square (at #6), to witness justice being served.

The **City Tower** was built in the late 16th century to defend against Ottoman invaders (who were likely to pass by here on their way to lay siege to Vienna). The tower used to be a story taller, but the top burned in a fire (one of four that swept the city in the late 17th and early 18th centuries). The shortened tower was capped with this jaunty Baroque steeple.

Embedded in the staircase at the back of the tower are more fragments from Ptuj's Roman era. This so-called **"open-air museum"** is just a taste of the vast Roman material unearthed in Ptuj. In the middle of the staircase, make out the letters: POETOVIONA—a longer version of Ptuj's Roman name, Poetovio.

Just behind the City Tower is **St. George's Parish Church** (Cerkev Svetega Jurija, open daily 7:00-11:00 & 18:00-18:30), which dates back before any other building in Slovenia. The current Gothic version is packed with diverse ecclesiastical art. Inside, notice (on your left) the gorgeous circa-1380 statue of St. George, Ptuj's patron saint, slaying the dragon. Then go to the first big pillar on the right, where you'll see a glass-covered relief depicting throngs of admirers adoring the Baby Jes...wait—where's Jesus? (Not to mention Mary's hands?) Several years ago, Jesus was stolen from this pillar. To help prevent further vandalism, the priests reduced the opening times (notice the seven-hour midday break).

Prešernova Street (Prešernova Ulica)

Stretching away from the City Tower is Ptuj's main drag and oldest street. It's wider than most streets in town because it led to what was once the medieval market square (now Slovenski trg), and merchants would set up market stalls all along the street. Many of the houses here have long since been renovated

PTUJ & MARIBOR

in Renaissance or Baroque style, making it Ptuj's most picturesque thoroughfare.

Town Square (Mestni Trg)

Today Ptuj's main square, this lively people zone (just down Murkova street from Slovenski trg) is a hub of activity. Major events and festivals—including the Kurentovanje Mardi Gras festival—take place here.

The square is watched over by the distinctive **Town Hall,** built by a visionary mayor a century ago. The three flags represent (left to

right) the European Union, Slovenia, and the Municipality of Ptuj. Over the left door (on the corner) are two statues commemorating Ptuj's Roman history: on the right, Emperor Trajan, who granted Ptuj city-status in the early second century A.D.; and on the left, St. Viktorin, a Ptuj bishop who wrote scholarly works on ecclesiastical themes during the late third century A.D., until he was martyred by Emperor Diocletian.

Facing the Town Hall in the middle of the square is a statue of **St. Florian,** who traditionally protects towns against fire. Ptuj was devastated by four fires in the late 17th and early 18th centuries. This statue is a 1993 replica of one that was built here after the fourth fire, in 1744. Miraculously, the town never burned again...or maybe not so miraculously, since they rebuilt it with stone instead of wood. Largely as a result of Ptuj's frequent fires, its rival Maribor (to the north) gradually supplanted it as the region's main center of commerce and winemaking. Ptuj's fate was sealed a century later, when the rail line between Vienna and Trieste was routed through Maribor. Today Maribor has 10 times as many people as Ptuj—and 10 times the industry, congestion, and urban gloominess. Hmm... maybe Ptuj got the better end of the deal, after all.

Ptuj Cellar (Ptujska Klet)

Ptuj is highly regarded for its wines, and this is the main facility for the major Pullus brand. Simple wine was produced in this region as far back as the Celts. The Romans advanced the art, only to have it disappear in the Dark Ages, then be revived in the 13th century by Minorite monks. Today this enormous cellar, branching out under the Old Town, continues this proud tradition—and holds a staggering 1.3 million gallons of wine (about 85 percent of it white). The cellar is also home to a "wine archive" with bottles dating back to 1917. This precious archive survived World War II because it was sealed off from the Nazis behind a giant barrel.

The winemakers sell a wide variety of bottles (€3-15). They're proudest of their award-winning sauvignon blanc, but their best seller—at a million bottles a year—is a local wine called Haložan (a semidry blend of four whites).

Tours and Tastings: Cellar tours and wine-tastings are possible if you call ahead (€9, Mon-Sat 9:00-17:00, call Tanja at mobile 041-394-896). While these are often available in English, you may wind up joining a German- or Slovene-language tour. The cellar tour comes with some hokey lighting effects and is followed by an even hokier audio-visual presentation during the tasting.

Shop: If you just want to pick up a bottle, stop by their wine shop, around the corner from the cellar (Mon-Fri 9:00-17:00, Sat 9:00-12:00, closed Sun, Vinarski trg 1, tel. 02/787-9827, www.pullus.si).

Minorite Church and Monastery (Minoritski Samostan)

This church, dedicated to Saints Peter and Paul, was one of the only buildings in town destroyed in World War II. (The Allies believed that the occupying Nazis were storing munitions here.) Only the foundation at the back end of the church survived, and it was left in ruins for decades. In 1989, friars celebrated their 750th anniversary in Ptuj by rebuilding the back part of the church. About a decade later, the front half was also reconstructed, and the statues in the niches above the door were replaced only a few years ago. Step into the contemporary, minimalist interior, with its modern stained-glass windows and Stations of the Cross. At the altar are the original statues that once adorned the church facade. Go through the door on the right into the peaceful cloister. A handful of friars can still be seen roaming these tranquil halls, and you're welcome to stroll here, too.

Cost and Hours: Free, daily 7:30-18:30, Minoritski trg.

Ptuj Thermal Baths (Terme Ptuj)

This gigantic bath complex, a 15-minute walk across the river from Ptuj's Old Town, is a fun place to splash around. It's a hit with locals and tourists, kids and oldsters. The "Thermal Park" has multiple swimming pools, whirlpools, and slides, including the "longest slide in Slovenia." The complex also offers indoor pools, saunas, and various spa treatments. Naturally fed by thermal springs, the pools vary in temperature, from warm to hot. When you buy your ticket, you're given a plastic card that you use to enter and lock your locker. Then go and have fun. Additional indoor pools are available at the hotel across the street.

Cost and Hours: €15/all day, cheaper for shorter visits, towel rental, outdoor pools daily 9:00-20:00, indoor pools daily 8:00-22:00, Pot v Toplice 9, tel. 02/749-4100, www.terme-ptuj.si.

Sleep Code

Abbreviations   **(€1=about $1.10, country code: 386)**
S=Single, **D**=Double/Twin, **T**=Triple, **Q**=Quad, **b**=bathroom
Price Rankings
   $$$ **Higher Priced**—Most rooms €80 or more
    $$ **Moderately Priced**—Most rooms €30-80
     $ **Lower Priced**—Most rooms €30 or less
Unless otherwise noted, credit cards are accepted, breakfast is included, free Wi-Fi and/or a guest computer is generally available, and English is spoken. The tourist tax (about €1/person, per night) is not included in the rates I've quoted. Prices change; verify current rates online or by email. For the best prices, always book directly with the hotel.

Sleeping in Ptuj

Central Ptuj has only a few hotels, a hostel, and a handful of *sobe*/guesthouses. While the options seem limited, the rooms are generally a good value compared to the western part of the country.

$$$ Hotel Mitra offers Ptuj's nicest rooms and best location: right on its most appealing street, a few steps from the landmark City Tower. It's the closest thing in town to a business-class hotel. Each of the 29 rooms—well-appointed, with cushy decor—has its own historical theme (Sb-€65, bigger Sb-€73, Db-€112, Db suite-€150, €5 less per person mid-Oct-April, for best prices reserve direct by email, air-con, elevator, limited free parking, Prešernova 6, tel. 02/787-7455, www.hotel-mitra.si, info@hotel-mitra.si).

$$ Vladimir Šilak rents 16 comfortable rooms around a charming courtyard in his gorgeously renovated Old Town home. The building dates from sometime between the 12th and 15th centuries, and Vladimir has lovingly restored it using quality materials. If you want to sleep in a centuries-old house with huge medieval vaults and three-foot-thick walls, this is the place (small Sb-€35, standard Sb-€38-44, small Db-€50, standard Db-€58-63, Tb-€85, Qb-€98, cheaper mid-Oct-April, apartments with kitchenettes also available for not much more, breakfast included in rooms but €5/person extra in apartments, air-con, free parking, bike rental, Dravska 13, tel. 02/787-7447, mobile 031-597-361, www.rooms-silak.com, info@rooms-silak.com).

$$ muziKafe B&B rents seven fun, colorful, funky (in a good way) rooms above a lively café in the heart of the atmospheric Old Town. After traveling around the world for a year, the owners decided to open a place where fellow globetrotters feel at home (Sb-€40-62, Db-€52-85, Vrazov trg 1, tel. 02/787-8860, www.muzikafe.si, info@muzikafe.si).

$ **Kurent Youth Hostel** is institutional, comfortable, and clean with 53 bunks. Each dorm room has its own bathroom (bunk in dorm room-€16, €1.50 less with IYHF membership, breakfast extra, self-service laundry-€4.50/load; reception open Mon-Fri 8:00-16:00, Sat-Sun 8:00-14:00; Osojnikova 9, tel. 02/771-0814, www.youth-hostel.si, yhptuj@csod.si). It's hiding in the big, pinkish commercial center (with the Spar supermarket) near the bus station.

Eating in Ptuj

Little Ptuj isn't known for its high cuisine. You'll spot several breezy cafés and packed pizzerias, but high-quality eateries are in short supply.

Gostilna Ribič is every local's first recommendation for a splurge dinner. One of the most popular (and expensive) places in town, it has a short menu that's focused on fresh, local dishes, with an emphasis on fish. Sit in the classy interior or outside on the relaxing riverside terrace (€10-12 small meals, €10-22 main courses, Tue-Sun 12:00-23:00, closed Mon, Dravska ulica 9, tel. 02/749-0635). If you're ready for a break from Slovenian cuisine, the Chinese restaurant (Kitajski Vrt) across the street is surprisingly good.

Gostilna Amadeus serves up traditional Slovenian cuisine to tour groups, individual tourists, and a few locals. They're especially proud of their €5 *štruklji* (ravioli-like filled dumplings). The bar, with outdoor seating and drinks only, is downstairs; to eat a meal, head upstairs to their nicely appointed dining room (€7-8 pastas, €8-18 main courses, Mon-Sat 12:00-23:00—except closed Tue Oct-May, Sun 12:00-16:00, Prešernova 36, tel. 02/771-7051).

PP is frequented by locals who enjoy its inexpensive, unpretentious, stick-to-your-ribs fare—lots of meat and potatoes, plus fried...everything. With a gaudy pub ambience, this Slovenian answer to T.G.I. Friday's is on the town's main shopping square (Novi trg), surrounded by supermarkets and malls. The **Kavarna** (café) has light food and outdoor seating; to eat a full meal, head indoors (filling €4-7 main courses, Mon-Sat 9:00-20:00, closed Sun, café open until 22:00; off-season, restaurant closes at 16:00 and café closes at 18:00; Novi trg 2, tel. 02/749-0622). The name stands for Perutnina Ptuj, a chicken conglomerate that owns half the town (including this place, Gostilna Ribič, and the big wine cellar)—you'll see their logo everywhere.

muziKafe, which also rents rooms (see earlier), is a cool hangout with an artistic spirit right in the center of the creaky Old Town. They serve drinks, light food, snacks, and cakes in a colorful, convivial atmosphere. Their vaulted cellar also hosts musical performances a few nights each week (Mon-Sat 8:00-23:00, Sun 10:00-22:00, Vrazov trg 1, tel. 02/787-8860, www.muzikafe.si).

Ptuj Connections

From Ptuj by Train to: Maribor (8/day, 1 hour, additional connections—sometimes faster—possible with transfer in Pragersko), **Ljubljana** (1/day direct, 2.5 hours; more with transfer in Pragersko and sometimes additional change in Zidani Most, 2-3 hours), **Zagreb** (3/day, 3-4 hours, usually requires 2 transfers), **Budapest** (that's **Budimpešt** in Slovene, 1/day direct, 6 hours; other connections take longer and require more changes), **Vienna** (that's **Dunaj** in Slovene, 1/day with transfer in Pragersko, 4.5 hours; 1/day with transfer in Maribor, 6.5 hours; additional connections require more changes, 5-6 hours). For destinations in western Slovenia, first go to Ljubljana.

Maribor

The second-biggest city in Slovenia (with 158,000 people), Maribor lives forever in the shadow of its much glitzier big sister, Ljubljana. Maribor is too small to offer an exciting big-city experience and too big to be charming. But this home of industry, business, and one of Slovenia's three universities is worth a quick look if you want to round out your Slovenian experience.

The lazy provincial town of Maribor woke up fast in 1846, when the Habsburgs built the train line from Vienna to the coast through here. It quickly modernized, losing some of its quaintness but gaining an urban, industrial flavor. However, Maribor was devastated in World War II (unlike other Slovenian cities), when it served as a headquarters for occupying Nazi forces. Since the city's factories also produced plane engines and other supplies, it became a "secondary target," where Allied warplanes—mostly American—would drop their bombs if unable to hit their primary targets in Germany or Austria.

Today, rebuilt Maribor feels mellow for its size. Nestled up against a gentle vineyard-covered hill, it's almost cozy. From a tourist's perspective, the town is pleasant enough, but pretty dull—

there's little to do other than wander its pedestrians-only streets. The city doesn't merit a detour, but it's worth a couple of hours for a stroll if you're passing through or have run out of diversions in Ptuj.

The countryside surrounding Maribor—called Mariborsko Pohorje—is an inviting recreational area, with vine-strewn hills lively with hikers and bicyclists in summer and with skiers in winter. Maribor is also the center of a thriving wine-growing region—especially popular among Austrians, who flow over the border to sample wines here, then stumble home. If you have time to spare, ask the TI for details about either of these outlying activities.

Orientation to Maribor

Maribor lines up along the bank of the Drava River. At the center of its concrete sprawl is the mostly traffic-free Old Town, with a variety of fine squares.

TOURIST INFORMATION

The main TI, at the northeast corner of the Old Town can give you a list of hotels or help you arrange for a local guide (Mon-Fri 9:00-19:00, Sat-Sun 9:00-18:00, Partizanska 6a—on the far side of the Franciscan Church from Trg Svobode, tel. 02/234-6611, www. maribor-pohorje.si).

ARRIVAL IN MARIBOR

The train station (which has big lockers) is a 10-minute walk east of the Old Town. Exit the station to the left and head up busy Partizanska cesta. Follow Partizanska as it swings right at the bus station, then continue three more blocks toward the Franciscan Church, with its twin red-brick spires. The main TI is in front of the church, and the Old Town is immediately behind the church.

Maribor Walk

Maribor's Austrian-feeling Old Town lacks big-league sights, but its squares and lanes are worth a wander. This lightly narrated self-guided walk gives you the lay of the land. You could do it in less than a half-hour, not including stops.

Entering the Old Town from the train station (on Partizanska, passing the Franciscan Church with its two red-brick spires—see "Arrival in Maribor," earlier), you find yourself on **Trg Svobode.** The oddly bulbous monument honors local Partisans (Yugoslav freedom-fighters) who were executed by Nazis during World War II. Wine cellars honeycomb the earth under this square.

At the end of the square, with the tall tower, is the town's **castle** (Mestni Grad), which houses a good regional museum.

Adjoining Trg Svobode is a second square, **Grajski trg**—Maribor's liveliest, bustling with cafés and restaurants (including the recommended Štajerc brewpub, just down the street from the bottom of the square). At the top of the square is the venerable **Café Astoria,** a local landmark.

Recent-history buffs may want to take a detour from here to Maribor's most interesting museum: the **Maribor National Liberation Museum** (Muzej Narodone Osvoboditve Maribor), about a five-minute walk up the street that's at the top of Grajski trg (between Café Astoria and the castle). The ground floor features generally good temporary exhibits. Upstairs, the permanent collection holds a hodgepodge of items from the city's history, mostly focusing on Slovenia's turbulent 20th century (€2, Mon-Fri 8:00-17:00, Sat 9:00-12:00, closed Sun, Ulica Heroja Tomšiča 5, tel. 02/235-2600, www.muzejno-mb.si).

Back on Grajski trg, follow lively **Slovenska ulica,** lined with characteristic cafés, sweet shops, and happy al fresco diners. Take a left at Tyrševa/Gosposka, passing some fun student-oriented boutiques. Then turn right on 10 Oktobra to find the big parking-lot square called Slomškov trg, with the city **cathedral** (skip the tower climb—the view is nothing special).

From the cathedral, walk straight down toward the river, cutting through Rotovški trg. You'll wind up on the long, narrow **Glavni trg,** surrounded by historic buildings (including the City Hall) and presided over by an impressive 18th-century plague column.

If you continue down to the riverbank, you'll find yourself in the district called **Lent,** where vintners traditionally offer tastings of their wines. While it's usually pretty quiet, this area hops each summer when Maribor hosts its Lent Festival (late June-early July, www.festival-lent.si). Along this embankment, look for the locally revered "old vine" stretching along a railing—it's supposedly 400 years old and still produces wine-worthy grapes.

Eating in Maribor

Štajerc is a popular local watering hole that brews its own beer and serves up heavy, starchy, traditional food. They're particularly known for their distinctive emerald-green beer, Štajerc Zeleno (though they also have light and dark variations). Sit inside, or enjoy the outdoor seating on Maribor's most happening square, Grajski trg (€4-8 meals, open long hours daily, Vetrinjska 30, tel. 02/234-4234).

Maribor Connections

From Maribor by Train to: Ptuj (8/day, 1 hour, more with transfer in Pragersko), **Ljubljana** (hourly, 2-3 hours, most with transfer in Zidani Most), **Vienna** (that's **Dunaj** in Slovene, 2/day direct, 4 hours, additional connections require changes in Spielfeld-Strass and Graz).

THE KARST

Caves, Castles, and Horses

In Slovenia's Karst region, about an hour south of Ljubljana on the A-1 expressway, you'll find some of the most impressive cave systems on the planet, have a chance to get to know the famous Lipizzaner stallions up close and personal (and for a fraction of what you'd pay in Vienna), and see one of Europe's most dramatically situated castles—built into the face of a mountain.

The word "karst" is used worldwide to refer to an arid limestone plateau, but Slovenia's is the original. In fact, that term comes from the Slovenian word "Kras"—a specific region near the Italian border. Since this limestone terrain is easily dissolved by water, karstic regions are punctuated by remarkable networks of caves and underground rivers.

Your top Karst priority is a cave visit. Choose between Slovenia's two best caves, Škocjan or Postojna—each with a handy side-trip nearby (to help you pick, see the sidebar on page 705). In the neighborhood of Škocjan is Lipica, where the Lipizzaner stallions strut their stuff. Just up the road from Postojna is Predjama Castle, picturesquely nestled into the side of a cliff.

I've listed public-transit possibilities, but most recommended destinations are very challenging to reach without a car. To efficiently hit several in one day, consider taking a guided excursion from Ljubljana (see page 545).

Sleeping and Eating in the Karst

$$ Majerija is the region's most enticing splurge, filling an 18th-century farmhouse in the Vipava Valley, about a 30-minute drive from either cave. They have both a fine restaurant focusing on high-quality updated Slovenian fare (figure €80-100 for dinner for two with wine, open Thu-Sat 12:00-15:00 & 18:00-22:00, Sun 12:00-17:00, closed Mon-Wed, also closed Thu off-season) and 10 modern, stylish, comfortable rooms (Db-€96, breakfast-€10, Slap 18, in Vipava, tel. 05/368-5010, mobile 041-405-903, www.majerija.si, info@majerija.si).

$ Pr'Vncki, a welcoming pension run by young parents Tamara and Ervin is within walking distance of Škocjan Caves and an easy drive to the other Karst sights. This 270-year-old typical Karst home has four simple but comfortable rooms. They also offer their guests drinks and seasonal meals, served in good weather on the front terrace under a grape arbor (Db-€58, includes breakfast, cash only, relaxing garden, in village of Matavun—adjacent to the Škocjan Caves entrance—at #10, tel. 05/763-3073, mobile 040-697-827, pr.vncki.tamara@gmail.com).

$ Tourist Farm Hudičevec (hoo-DEE-cheh-vets), midway between Škocjan and Postojna (15 minutes from either) is a simpler option. This kid-friendly complex, with seven rooms and two apartments, is run by the farming Simčič family (Db without dinner-€52, Db with dinner-€70, ask about larger apartments, tel. 05/703-0300, www.hudicevec.si, info@hudicevec.si). Idyllic and remote as this place sounds, it's actually right next to the expressway (which makes it easy to reach, but also comes with some road noise, and large tour groups may show up for dinner). Take the Razdrto exit from the expressway, turn right toward Postojna, then start looking right away for the low-profile sign directing you back under the road.

Škocjan Caves and Lipica Stud Farm

Drivers can easily combine these two attractions, which are just a short drive from each other. By public transportation, it's more challenging. The main transit hubs for this area are the towns of Divača and Sežana, both served by train and bus from Ljubljana. A shuttle bus goes between the Divača train station and Škocjan Caves (4/day June-Sept, less off-season, 10 minutes, coordinated to meet some trains—check schedules at Ljubljana TI). To reach Lipica, you'll have to take a taxi from one of the train stations (try the Sežana-based Taxi Šeki, tel. 041/621-347).

▲▲▲ŠKOCJAN CAVES (ŠKOCJANSKE JAME)

Škocjan (SHKOHTS-yahn) offers fantastical formations and a spectacularly vast canyon with a raging underground river. The main attraction is a guided hike through the caves; this hike is about two miles long, goes up and down more than 400 steps, and is mostly underground. For a few euros more, you can extend your hike through two adjacent valleys and the less remarkable Mahorčič Cave, just above river level.

While anyone in good shape can enjoy Škocjan, those who have trouble walking or tire easily are better off touring the Postojna Caves instead (described later).

Cost and Hours: Take the €16 two-hour **tourist path 1**—billed as "Through the Underground Cavern"—with English commentary (June-Sept tours daily at the top of each hour 10:00-17:00, Oct-May tours daily at 10:00 and 13:00 and sometimes also at 15:00 or 15:30). Call or pick up the current brochure—which you'll find everywhere in Slovenia—to confirm schedule before making the trip; tel. 05/708-2104, www.park-skocjanske-jame.si.

To extend the hike, you can buy the €21 ticket for **tourist path 2**—called "Following the Reka River Underground"—which gives you access to more valleys and the Mahorčič Cave and takes 1-1.5 additional hours. This can be done on your own June-Sept (10:00-15:00), but for safety reasons, you must go with a guide in April-May and Oct (at 11:00 and 14:00), and it's closed Nov-March.

You'll need to decide whether you want to pay for the extension before buying your ticket. Consider this: Path 1 alone provides enough hiking (and plenty of caves) to exhaust most visitors. But those with abundant stamina and time, a love of caves, and a spirit of exploration will feel that the extension for €5 is money well-spent.

Getting to Škocjan: By car, take the A-1 expressway south from Ljubljana about an hour and get off at the Divača exit (also marked with brown signs for *Lipica* and *Škocjanske jame*) and follow signs for *Škocjanske jame*. (Before or after Škocjan, drivers can easily visit the Lipica Stud Farm, described next.) The caves have free and easy parking.

By public transportation, it's trickier. Take the train or bus to Divača (see "Ljubljana Connections," page 587), which is about three miles from the caves. To get from the Divača train station to the caves, you can either take the local shuttle bus (4/day June-Sept, 2/day off-season, typically coordinated to meet certain arriving trains); hike about 45 minutes; or take a taxi (around €10-15, try calling Taxi Šeki, tel. 041/621-347).

Services: You'll find WCs at the ticket office and at the starting point for tourist path 1, but none in the caves themselves. The ticket office has free lockers—ask for the key.

KARST

Eating: A snack bar at the cave ticket office sells basic, over-priced sandwiches and other snacks.

Expect Changes: Trails at Škocjan are being repaired and new ones are planned, so details may change. The staff are helpful about explaining your options.

Visiting the Caves: Upon arrival, get a ticket for the next tour (including tourist path 2 if you choose). You'll pass waiting time at a covered terrace with an info kiosk, gift shop, café, and interactive educational center with exhibits about the caves.

Tourist Path 1: At tour time, your guide (toting an industrial-strength flashlight) calls everyone together, and you march silently for 10 minutes to the cave entrance. There you split into language groups and enter the cave.

The first half of the experience is the **"Silent Caves"** (so called for the lack of running water), with a wide array of wondrous for-mations and what seem like large caverns. The experience builds and builds as you go into ever-more-impressive grottoes, and you think you've seen the best.

But then you get to the truly colossal final cavern—the **"Murmuring Water Cave"**—with a mighty river crashing through the bottom. You feel like a bit player in a sci-fi thriller. It's a world where a thousand evil *Wizard of Oz* monkeys could comfortably fly in formation. You hike high above the river for about a mile, crossing a breathtak-ing (but stable-feeling) footbridge 150 feet above the torrent. Far below, the scant remains of century-old trails from the early days of tourism are evocative. The cave finally widens, sunlight pours in, and you emerge—like lost creatures seeking daylight—into a lush canyon. This is the **Big Collapsed Valley,** which used to be part of the Škocjan network until its roof fell in.

After Your Tour: Exiting the cave, your options are a bit con-fusing, but guides are generally standing by. The basic choice is a speedy return, or a slow and scenic one (which may include tourist path 2). Regardless of your route, *P* and *i* signs direct you back to the ticket office.

To **return to the surface** as quickly as possible, turn right and follow signs steeply uphill to the small funicular, which lifts you back to the ticket office. (From the top of the funicular, you can also head straight and walk gently uphill 10 minutes to the muse-ums, which are included in your ticket and described later.)

For a **longer, more strenuous, and more scenic return,** turn left and loop around the perimeter of the Big Collapsed Valley. After passing a fountain (marking the entrance of the off-limits Tominc Cave), you'll come to a fork: The tunnel on the left is a round-trip detour (returning to this point) that takes you to the thundering waterfall at the bottom of the canyon, illustrating how the Reka River grinds like God's band-saw into the land. The stairs in the middle lead to the upper part of the canyon; from here, more stairs on the left lead up to the ticket booth. If you head straight past these stairs, you'll cross a modern bridge and reach the entrance to the tour extension, described next.

Tourist Path 2 (Mahorčič Cave and Small Collapsed Valley): Following the directions above, you'll wind up along the rim of the Big Collapsed Valley across from the Škocjan exit (at a modern bridge). Here, a ticket-taker will ask to see your ticket. You'll hike along a "natural bridge" (actually a short stretch of cave) from the Big Collapsed Valley to the Small Collapsed Valley; circling through here, you'll wind down to the entrance to Mahorčič Cave, where you'll walk just above the Reka River. Compared to the main cave on tourist path 1, Mahorčič is smaller, but very atmospheric, as it's short enough to let in evocative rays of natural light—and you're much closer to

the surface of the river. Exiting this cave, you'll hike uphill about a half-mile, across farm fields, to get back to the ticket office.

Museums: Two small, skippable museums sit high on the hill in the village of Škocjan, a 15-minute, mostly uphill walk from the Škocjan Caves ticket office or a 10-minute uphill walk on a gravel path straight ahead from the top of the funicular—just follow the church icon and *Muzej* signs. First, in the thatched stone house, is an **ethnological collection**—one small, rustic room with primitive local farming tools and a video re-creating hand-scythes (pick up the English flier). Second, in the white house across the way, is a museum of the **history of cave exploration.** You'll see a model of the valleys and villages of the region, along with a cutaway model of the caves, plus lots of old photographs (admission to both parts covered by cave ticket in summer, open June-Sept daily 11:30-19:30, Oct and April-May Sat-Sun 11:30-18:30; Nov-March open by request only, €4). A bit higher is the humble Škocjan village church, boldly perched on a bulb of land that overlooks cliffs in all directions.

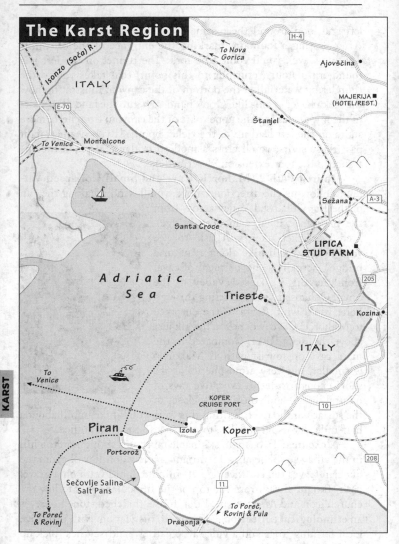

The Karst Region

To Nova
Gorica

H-4

Isonzo (Soča) R.

ITALY

Ajovščina

MAJERIJA ■
(HOTEL/REST.)

E-70

Štanjel

To Venice   Monfalcone

Sežana   A-3

Santa Croce

LIPICA
STUD FARM

*A d r i a t i c
S e a*

205

Trieste

Kozina

ITALY

To
Venice

KOPER
CRUISE PORT

10

Piran   Izola   Koper

Portorož

208

Sečovlje Salina
Salt Pans

11

To Poreč
& Rovinj

To Poreč,
Rovinj & Pula

Dragonja

▲▲LIPICA STUD FARM (KOBILARNA LIPICA)

The Lipica (LEE-peet-suh) Stud Farm, a
10-minute drive from the Škocjan Caves,
was founded in 1580 to provide horses for the
Habsburg court in Vienna. Today you can tour
the Lipizzaner stables to visit these magnificent animals, whose stalls are labeled with their
purebred bloodlines. While the stuffy Viennese cousins of Slovenia's Lipizzaners perform
under chandeliers, a visit to Lipica is a more

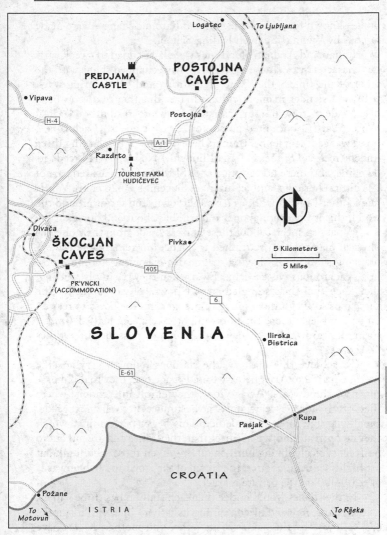

intimate experience: You can get nose to nose with the stallions, learn how they're raised and trained, and—on most days—watch them train or perform. The Lipizzaners' clever routine—stutter-stepping sideways to the classical beat—thrills visitors. Horse lovers will be in heaven here; even those who don't know a mare from a gelding will find it interesting.

Background: In 1580, horse-loving Habsburg Archduke Charles II wanted to create the perfect animal: He imported Andalusian horses from his homeland of Spain, then bred them with a local line of Karst horses to come up with an extremely intelligent and easily trainable breed. Charles' creation, the Lipizzaner stallions—known for their noble gait and Baroque shape—were made famous by Vienna's Spanish Riding School.

Italian and Arabian bloodlines were later added to tweak various characteristics. These regal horses have changed shape with the tenor of the times: They were bred strong and stout during wars, frilly and slender in more cultured eras. But they're always born black, fade to gray, and turn a distinctive white in adulthood. Until World War I, Lipica bred horses for Austria's needs. (Each time a horse was sent to Vienna, trainers here honored it by planting three linden trees; *lipica* means "small linden.") Now Austria breeds its own line, and these horses prance for Slovenia—a treasured part of its cultural heritage (and featured on Slovenia's €0.20 coin). While many other Lipizzaner lines have their own stud farms around the world, this is the original one, and still has about 360 horses.

What's so special about these horses? Aside from their obvious physical majesty, they're trained to "dance" in remarkable ways—prancing sideways, sashaying diagonally, or joining another horse in a synchronous pas de deux. Even when they're simply trotting, they keep their heads angled steeply down, oh so genteelly. The three most difficult moves involve first getting the horse to rear up on its hind legs; then, the horse might take a step (called *larada*), spring upward *(kapriola)*, or jump as high as possible three times *(kurbetta)*.

To achieve this mastery, the stallions follow a very specific lifetime regimen: After being weaned at age one, they roam in pastures for three years. At age four, they enroll in "school," where they "study" for five years; only the best move up to the next grade. Finally, at age nine, the valedictorians begin performing, which they do until around age 25; after that, they retire and are put out to pasture (typically living until about 30). Even those who flunk out are highly valuable as sires; the cream of the crop can fetch upwards of €200,000 on the private market.

In the stables, you'll notice that each stallion has three names: its own name (created by combining its father's line with its mother's) followed by the names of its father and mother. Males have only six bloodlines (and females 17), so many names are recycled—which is why many horses have numbers after their names.

Speaking of breeding, while the stallions are studying, the Lipizzaner mares freely roam the pastures; they're trained to return to their stables with a single whistle at the end of each day. But they have an important job as well. Mares are pregnant basically all of the time: After the 11 months and one week of gestation, they give birth, are given eight days off, and are impregnated again on the ninth day.

By the way, the hills less than a mile away are in Italy. Aside from the horses, Lipica's big draw is its casino. Italians across the border are legally forbidden from gambling in their own town's casinos—for fear of addiction—so they flock here to Slovenia to try their luck.

Getting to Lipica: The Lipica Stud Farm is in Slovenia's southwest corner (a stone's throw from Trieste, Italy). By car, exit the A-1 expressway at Divača and follow brown *Lipica* signs. As you drive into the farm, you'll go through pastures where the stallions often roam. Park in front of the hotel/casino, then walk through the trees, following signs to the ticket office.

It's a hassle by public transportation. You can take the train or bus from Ljubljana to Divača (about six miles from Lipica) or to Sežana (about four miles from Lipica). From those places, you can hire a taxi (€15 from Divača, €10 from Sežana).

Visiting the Stud Farm: There are three activities at Lipica—you can tour the farm for a look at the horses, watch a training session, and, on some days, see a more elaborate performance of the prancing stallions. No matter when you come, the tour is a must to really understand the horses. Whether you view a training session or a performance depends on the day of the week; plan your day carefully to ensure that you get to see one or the other. Note that in summer, Monday is the only day you can't see the horses training or performing (but the tour still runs).

Cost: Stud farm tour only-€12, tour plus training session-€14, tour plus performance-€19, tel. 05/739-1580, www.lipica.org.

Tours: The essential 50-minute guided tour gives you a firm background to help you understand just how special these beasts are. You'll learn about the breed's history, walk through some of the gelding and mare stables, enjoy a brief guided tour of the museum (described later), and then—as a grand finale—see the very best stallions, who live in luxurious, spacious stables. English tour schedule: April-Oct daily on the hour 10:00-17:00; Nov-March daily at 10:00, 11:00, 13:00, 14:00, and 15:00.

Training Sessions: On most days, these provide your best chance to see the horses in action (May-Sept Wed-Thu and Sat at 10:00-10:45 and 11:00-11:45; April and Oct Tue-Sat at 10:00-10:45 only; none Nov-March). Time your visit to do the training session and tour back-to-back. These are not performances—they are true training sessions, with young, gray-mottled stallions (and red-shirted jockeys) mixing in with more mature, pure-white stallions, whose jockeys wear black vests. While you likely won't see a complete routine, the sessions are narrated in English by an expert, so they're more educational than performances. For maximum information, get close to the expert and don't be afraid to ask questions.

Performances: The choreographed performances take place only three afternoons a week in high season (May-Sept Tue, Fri, and Sun at 15:00; April and Oct Sun only at 15:00; none Nov-March), but if you're nearby on one of those days, they're worth planning your day around. As with the training sessions, it's smart to precede a performance with the 14:00 tour, which gives you background information to better appreciate the horses' moves.

Lipikum Museum: Included in your tour ticket is this small, state-of-the-art museum. Succinct, insightful, and all in English, the museum uses informative panels, video screens, and interactive components to illustrate all aspects of the Lipizzaner. Notice that—like the horses themselves—the museum rooms begin black, then turn gray, and end white as you proceed through the exhibit. A Lipizzaner skeleton shows anatomy, and 18th-century paintings illustrate how the breed used to vary in color (until a mutation crept into the bloodline, turning all of them white). The guided tour dips into the museum briefly, but it's worth coming back afterward to linger over the exhibits.

Eating: There's a small self-service café just above the ticket booth, and a restaurant inside the hotel.

Postojna Caves and Predjama Castle

These two sights are easy for drivers to connect, since they're along the same road. If you're using public transportation, it's not too difficult to reach the caves, and in summer there is a shuttle between the caves and the castle included in the combo-ticket for both sights.

▲▲POSTOJNA CAVES (POSTOJNSKA JAMA)

Postojna (poh-STOY-nah) is the most accessible—and most touristy—cave experience in the region. It's the biggest cave system in Slovenia, with more than 12 miles of explored caves (three of which you'll see on the tour). It's also the easiest to visit, since much of the tour is on a fast-moving train, and the rest is well-paved, well-lit, and not too steep. All of this makes it Slovenia's single most popular tourist attraction.

Cost and Hours: €23, €32 combo-ticket covers caves, castle, and summer-only shuttle between them; tours leave daily at the top of each hour July-Aug 9:00-18:00; May-June and Sept 9:00-17:00; April and Oct at 10:00, 12:00, 14:00, and 16:00; Nov-March at 10:00, 12:00, and 15:00; tours last 1.5 hours, call to confirm schedule or pick up brochure at any TI, Jamska cesta 30, tel. 05/700-0100, www.postojna-cave.com. If you're visiting several sights here—including the Vivarium and Predjama Castle interior—do the math to see if the advertised combo-tickets save you money.

Crowd Control: From mid-May through mid-September, try

Postojna vs. Škocjan: Which Caves to Visit?

The recipe for creating a cave is simple: Begin with limestone. Then, just add water and wait for 2 million years. (Serves half a million tourists each year.)

The Karst has two big cave systems: Postojna and Škocjan. Each one is massive. Stalagmites and stalactites—in a slow-motion love story—silently work their way toward each other, a third of an inch per century, until that last drip never drops. Minerals picked up by the water as it seeps through various rocks create the different colors (iron makes red, limestone makes white, and so on). Both caves were excavated and explored in the mid-19th century.

However, what you'll see inside each cave system—and how you'll see it—is quite different. Slovenes debate long and hard about which cave system is better. The formations at Postojna are slightly more abundant, varied, and colorful, with stalagmites and stalactites as tall as 100 feet. Postojna is easier to reach by public transportation and far less strenuous to visit than Škocjan—of the three-mile route, you'll walk only about a mile (the rest of the time, you're on a speedy underground train). But Postojna is also more expensive and much more touristy (they get a half-million visitors each year, five times as many as Škocjan)—you'll wade through tour buses and tacky souvenir stands on your way to the entrance. Most importantly, Postojna lacks Škocjan's spectacular, massive-cavern finale. Škocjan also comes with a fairly strenuous hike, leaving you feeling like you really did something adventurous. Finally, the choice of a likely side-trip might help you decide: Near Postojna is the cliff-hanging Predjama Castle, while Škocjan is closer to the Lipica Stud Farm.

No matter which cave you visit, you'll find it chilly, but not really cold (a light sweater is fine). Both caves technically forbid photography (a laughable rule that nobody takes seriously).

These caves are also home to a unique little cave-dwelling creature—the so-called "human fish" (a.k.a. olm or *Proteus anguinus*), which is a long, skinny, pale-pink salamander-like creature with fingers and toes. The world's biggest cave-dwelling animal, these amphibians can grow up to a foot long, live for about a century, and survive up to a decade without eating (the live specimens on display in Postojna are never fed during the four months they're on view). As they're endemic to Slovenia, the "human fish" are celebrated as a sort of national mascot.

to show up 30 to 40 minutes early for the morning tours (popular with tour buses); at other times, aim for 15 minutes ahead.

Adventure Tours: If you'd like to do some more adrenaline-fueled spelunking in Postojna, check their website for details on booking one of the more adventurous routes through the caves.

Getting to Postojna: The caves are just outside the town of Postojna, about 45 minutes south of Ljubljana on the A-1 expressway. By **car,** take the expressway south from Ljubljana and get off at the Postojna exit. Leaving the expressway, turn right and follow the *jama/grotte/cave* signs through town until you see the tour buses. Drivers pay to park a third of a mile from the cave entry. By **train,** you'll arrive at the train station in the town of Postojna; from here, you can walk to the caves in about 20 minutes, or pay for a taxi. If coming on the bus from Ljubljana, you'll be dropped just a five-minute walk from the caves.

Visiting the Caves: A visit here is basically an easy, lightly guided stroll through an amazing underground cavern. The optional audioguide offers more information than the official tour-guide spiel. Whether you arrive by car, tour bus, or on foot, you'll walk past a paved outdoor souvenir mall to the gaping hole in the mountain. Buy your ticket, then climb up the stairs and wait with the mob to board the little open-air train, which slings you deep into the mountain, whizzing past wonderful formations. (The ride alone is exhilarating.) Then you get out, assemble into language groups, and follow a guide on a well-lit, circular, paved path through more formations.

First you'll hike uphill into the "Big Mountain"—the highest point inside the caves, and (surprisingly) actually higher than where you entered. You're surrounded

by a sea of fairy-chimney stalagmites and stalactites, some of them a hundred feet tall. Then you'll hike downhill and cross a bridge over a canyon into "Spaghetti Hall," named for the long, skinny stalactites that seem to be dripping from the ceiling. Also in this area are some amazing, translucent "curtains" of rock. Circling down beneath the bridge you just crossed, you'll come to some huge, white, melting-ice-cream formations (including one called "The Organ," for obvious reasons). You'll wind up in the impressively vast cavern called the "Concert Hall," peering into an aquarium with the strange "human fish." Then you'll load back onto the train and return to the bright daylight. Exiting the train, notice that the ceiling of this part of the cavern is charred black.

KARST

The only coloring in the cave caused by humans, this is residue from a huge WWII explosion; the Partisan Army blew up a fuel and ammo depot the Nazis kept here.

"Vivarium": This disappointing exhibit, which fills a smaller cave next to the ticket booth, gives you the chance to learn more about karstic caves and speleobiology (the study of cave-dwelling animal life). You'll be given a flashlight and sent to look for 17 different species of animals—but since the cave-dwellers (naturally) hide from view, you just wind up squinting into empty aquariums most of the time. One interesting feature is a wall with graffiti signatures from past visitors—some dating all the way back to the 13th century. Upstairs is a "butterfly collection"—two dozen frames filled with samples of butterflies around a big conference room. While troglodytes, science nuts, and those who just can't get enough of those human fish may get a charge out of this exhibit, it's basically just an attempt to wring a little more cash out of gullible tourists (€8, opens 30 minutes before first cave tour, closes 30 minutes after the last tour).

▲PREDJAMA CASTLE (PREDJAMSKI GRAD)

Burrowed into the side of a mountain close to Postojna is dramatic Predjama Castle (prehd-YAH-mah), one of Europe's most scenic castles (despite its dull interior). Predjama is a hit with tourists for its striking setting, exciting exterior, and romantic legend.

Notice as you approach that you don't even see Predjama—crouching magnificently in its cave—until the last moment. The

first castle here was actually a tiny ninth-century fortress embedded deep in the cave behind the present castle. Over the centuries, different castles were built here, and they gradually moved out to the mouth of the cave. While the original was called "the castle in the cave," the current one is *pred jama*—"in front of the cave."

While enjoying the view, ponder this legend: In the 15th century, a nobleman named Erasmus killed the emperor's cousin in a duel. He was imprisoned under Ljubljana Castle and spent years nursing a grudge. When he was finally released, he used his castle—buried deep inside the cave above this current version—as a home base for a series of Robin Hood-style raids on the local nobility and merchants. (Actually, Erasmus stole from the rich and kept for himself—but that was good enough to make him a hero to the peasants, who hated the nobles.)

Soldiers from Trieste were brought in to put an end to Erasmus' raids, laying siege to the castle for over a year. Back then, the only way into the castle was through the cave in the valley below—then up, through an extensive labyrinth of caves, to the top. While the soldiers down below froze and starved, Erasmus' men sneaked out through the caves to bring in supplies. (They liked to drop their leftovers on the soldiers below to taunt them, letting them know that the siege wasn't working.)

Eventually, the soldiers came up with a plan. They waited for Erasmus to visit the latrine—which, by design, had to be on the thin-walled outer edge of the castle—and then, on seeing a signal by a secret agent, blew Erasmus off his throne with a cannonball. Erasmus is supposedly buried under the huge linden tree in the parking lot.

As the legend of Erasmus faded, the function of the castle changed. By the 16th century, Predjama had become a castle for hunting more than for defense—explaining its current pictur-esque-but-impractical design.

After driving all the way here, it seems a shame not to visit the interior—but it's truly skippable. The management (which also runs the nearby Postojna Caves) is very strict about keeping the interior 16th-century in style, so there's virtually nothing inside except 20th-century fakes of 16th-century furniture, plus a few forgettable paintings and cheesy folk displays. English descriptions are sparse, and the free English history flier is not much help. But for most, the views of the place alone are worth the drive. Also skip the "cave under Predjama Castle"—it's redundant if you're going to Postojna or Škocjan.

Cost and Hours: €12 to go inside, daily July-Aug 9:00-19:00, May-June and Sept 9:00-18:00, April and Oct 10:00-17:00, Nov-March 10:00-16:00. Tel. 05/751-6015, www.postojnska-jama.eu.

Getting to Predjama: Predjama Castle is on a twisty rural road 5.5 miles beyond Postojna Caves. By car, just continue on the winding road past Postojna, following signs for *Predjama* and *Predjamski Grad* (coming back, follow signs to *Postojna*). If using public transportation, you can take the train to the town of Posto-jna; in the summer, you can buy a €32 combo-ticket that includes the caves, the castle, and a shuttle bus trip between them (departs about hourly). If you're in a pinch, consider hitching a ride between Predjama and Postojna with a friendly tour bus or tourist's car, as most visitors do both sights.

PIRAN

Croatia's 3,600-mile-long coast gets all the acclaim, but don't overlook Slovenia's own 29 miles of Adriatic coastline. The Slovenian coast has only a handful of towns: big, industrial Koper; lived-in and crumbling Izola; and the swanky but soulless resort of Portorož. But the Back Door gem of the Slovenian Adriatic is Piran (pee-RAHN). Most Adriatic towns are all tourists and concrete, but Piran has kept itself charming and in remarkably good repair while holding the tourist sprawl at bay. Its glassy square feels tugged at the top by a stout Venetian-style bell tower—as if without this anchor, the whole thing might just slide off into the tidy, picturesque harbor. Even though the town can be crowded with a United Nations of vacationers (especially Italians) in peak season, as you get to know it, Piran becomes one of the most pleasant and user-friendly seaside towns this side of Dubrovnik.

PLANNING YOUR TIME

You can see everything in Piran (including a pop into the Maritime Museum and a hike up the bell tower) in just a couple of hours. Then feel free to just bask in the town's ambience. Enjoy a gelato or a *kava* (coffee) on the sleek, marbled Tartini Square, surrounded by Neoclassical buildings and watched over by the bell tower. Go for a swim at one of its rocky beaches. Wander Piran's piers and catch its glow at sunset.

Piran also works as a base for visiting the caves, horses, and castles of the nearby Karst region (see previous chapter). Notice, too, that it's conveniently on the way between Ljubljana/the Karst and Croatia's Istria (see "Route Tips for Drivers" on page 721).

Orientation to Piran

Piran is small; everything is within a few minutes' walk. Crowded onto the tip of its peninsula, the town can't grow. Its population—7,500 a century ago—has dropped to about 4,200 today, as many young people find more opportunity in bigger cities.

Piran clusters around its boat-speckled harbor and main show-piece square, Tartini Square (Tartinijev trg). Up the hill behind Tartini Square is the landmark bell tower of the Cathedral of St. George. A few blocks toward the end of the peninsula from Tartini Square is the heart of the Old Town, May 1 Square (Trg 1 Maja).

From Tartini Square and the nearby marina, a concrete prom-enade—lined with rocks to break the storm waves, and with expen-sive tourist restaurants to break your budget—stretches along the town's waterfront, inviting you to stroll.

TOURIST INFORMATION

The TI—with brochures about Piran, the adjacent resort of Portorož, and the entire region—is inside the grand Venetian-style Town Hall on Tartini Square (daily July-Aug 9:00-22:00, Sept-June 9:00-17:00, at #2, tel. 05/673-4440, www.portoroz.si).

ARRIVAL IN PIRAN

By Car: Driving and parking in Piran is a headache; park your car as quickly as possible and forget about it. Fortunately, the city makes this relatively easy by offering a free shuttle bus connecting the parking options with downtown (4/hour).

If you're overnighting in town and don't want to haul your bags from the garage, take a ticket at the parking barrier, drive into the Old Town, drop off your bags, and pick up a voucher from your hotel; if you leave within 15 minutes, the voucher gets you out free. Then park at the big garage described next. If you're day-tripping to Piran, simply park at the garage when you arrive.

As you drive into town, you'll pass the big **parking garage** on the hill. Most visitors wind up parking here (€1.70/hour, €17/day, typically discounted with a voucher from your hotel). From the garage, ride the elevator down to floor 1, exit, and walk about 50 yards to the waterfront parking lot for locals (called Fornače), where you'll see a stop for the free shuttle bus into town; an elec-tronic board notes how many minutes until the next bus comes. The shuttle zips you right to Tartini Square. (If you've packed light, you can also walk to Tartini Square in about 15 minutes—just follow the water.)

If you're feeling lucky, you could continue driving down the hill past the garage, where you'll stop at a gate marking the entrance to the Old Town. It's possible to park within this area, but options are minimal and extremely expensive (€5/hour in summer, €3/hour in winter; be sure you're in a legitimate space).

By Bus: Piran has two bus stops. Shuttle buses from the parking garage and nearby towns (such as Portorož) stop right at Tartini Square; intercity buses (such as those to Ljubljana) use the low-profile main bus station along the water, near the entrance to town.

HELPFUL HINTS

Laundry: Piran has no launderette. If you're desperate, try asking very nicely to use the washer at the recommended **Val Youth Hostel** (unless it's being used by guests).

Bike Rental: The **TI** rents basic bikes for low prices; this works fine for a quick spin along the coast. For a more serious adventure on two wheels, rent a pricier trekking bike from **Luma Šport,** across the street from the intercity bus station (daily June-Aug 9:00-12:00 & 17:00-21:00, shoulder season 9:00-18:00 in good weather, less off-season, Dantejeva 3, mobile 041-781-414, Magda). The TI hands out a free map illustrating ambitious rides in the region.

Sights in Piran

▲▲Tartini Square (Tartinijev trg)

Tartini Square was once part of a protected harbor. In 1894, the harbor smelled so bad that they decided to fill it in. Today, rather

than fishing boats, it's filled with skateboarding kids. While traffic used to clog this square, it was recently pedestrianized. The "square"—a shiny marble oval surrounded by a tidy geographical grid pattern—is one of Slovenia's most appealing public spaces. Be sure to nurse a coffee while you're here. Survey the many café vantage points and take your pick.

The dynamic statue in the middle honors **Giuseppe Tartini** (1692-1770), a composer and violinist once known throughout Europe. Behind Tartini, the Neo-Renaissance **Town Hall** (housing the TI) dates from the 1870s.

The fine little red palace in the corner (at #4, where Tartini's left hand is gesturing) is the **"Venetian House"** (c. 1450), the oldest preserved house on the square. Classic Venetian Gothic, it comes with a legend: A wealthy Venetian merchant fell in love with a simple local girl when visiting on business, became her sugar daddy,

and eventually built her this flat. When the townsfolk began to gossip about the relationship, he answered them with the relief you see today (with the Venetian lion, between the two top windows): *Lassa pur dir* ("Let them talk").

Today the Venetian House's ground floor hosts a branch of the enticing **Piranske Soline shop,** selling a classy range of culinary and health aids produced using the salt that's gathered just around the bay from here. While those salt pans are worth a visit (Sečovlje Salina Nature Park, described later), this shop offers a chance to get a feel for that age-old local industry with minimal effort (open long hours daily, ulica IX Korpusa 2, tel. 05/673-3110, www.soline.si).

▲Cathedral and Bell Tower of St. George (Stolna Cerkev Sv. Jurija)

Piran is proud of its many churches, which number more than 20. While none is of any real historic or artistic importance, the Cathedral of St. George—dominating the town from the hilltop just above Tartini Square—is worth a look. This cathedral dates from the 14th century and was decorated in the Baroque style by Venetian artists in the 17th century. It dominates the Old Town with its bell tower *(cam-*

panile), a miniature version of the more famous one on St. Mark's Square in Venice. Why such a big church for such a little town? So that would-be invaders, surveying Piran from the sea, would spot a huge church and assume it marked a big city...not worth the risk to plunder.

Cost and Hours: Church and museum—€1, July-Aug Mon and Wed-Fri 10:00-16:00, Sat-Sun 10:00-18:00, May-June and Sept-Oct Wed-Mon 10:00-16:30, closed Tue year-round; closed Nov-April; bell tower—€1 to go up and "€0 to go down," July-Aug daily 10:00-20:00, closes earlier off-season.

Church and Museum: While you can peek into the church

Piran

SWIMMING
PUBLIC BEACH
LIGHTHOUSE
Tursicev Square
PREŠERNOVO NABREŽE
PUSTERLA
GRAJSKA
ST. GEORGE CATHEDRAL & BELL TOWER
TEGOYA BONAFACIJEVA
HARBOR PROMENADE
GREGORCICEVA
TRUBARJEVA
ADAMIČEVA
May 1 Square
VERDIJEVA
SWIMMING
OBZIDNA ULICA
Market Square
UL. IX KORPUSA
VENETIAN HOUSE
200 Meters
200 Yards
ZELENJAVNI TRG
TOMAŽIČEVA
Tartini Square
BOLNIŠKA
A d r i a t i c   S e a
STJENKOVA ULICA
SHUTTLE BUSES
MARITIME MUSEUM
ROZMANOVA ULICA
SWIMMING
POST
Marina
CANKARJEVO NABREŽJE
TOMŠIČEVA ULICA
MARXOVA
MATTEOTIJEVA ULICA
MOGORON
LONG-DISTANCE BUSES
SWIMMING
SHUTTLE BUSES
TOWN GATE
Fornače
To Parking Garage, Portorož, Salt Pans & Croatia

1. Hotel Tartini
2. Hotel Piran
3. PachaMama Pleasant Stay
4. Bevk Apartments (2)
5. Miracolo di Mare B&B
6. Val Youth Hostel & Internet Access
7. Restaurant Neptun
8. Pri Mari Restaurant
9. Pizzeria Petica
10. Sarajevo '84
11. Bakery & Supermarket
12. Café Teater
13. Bike Rental
14. Aquarium

PIRAN

through a grate at the far end, you'll need to enter through the door on the side (facing town) and buy a ticket for the church museum. The modest museum contains treasury items (including an elaborately decorated silver-and-gold statue of the church's namesake, St. George, slaying a dragon) and a little crypt displaying some early foundations of the church building along with archaeological finds. Head up the stairs into the church interior, which is serenely decorated in proper Venetian Renaissance and Baroque style. You'll see several dynamic interpretations of George and his dragon-slaying (including a giant statue left of the nave, and a painting on the ceiling). But the church's prized possession hides in the presbytery: Stand directly in front of the altar, close up, and look right. This *Piran Crucifixion*, dating from the 14th century, is powerful and emotive. Nailed to a Y-shaped cross, Christ is at once expressionistic (with gnarled toes, awkwardly disjointed shoulders, and an elongated frame that exaggerates his agony) and gruesomely medieval. When the crucifix was restored recently, historians found countless layers of additions and modifications (including 10 layers of paint), suggesting how its appearance has flexed with the tenor of the times. Now protected in its glass box from the fickle seaside air, the crucifix is explained in detail by a free brochure available in the museum.

Bell Tower: The tower (with bells dating from the 15th century) welcomes tourists willing to climb 146 rickety steps for the best view in town and a chance for some bell fun. Stand inside the biggest bell. Chant, find the resonant frequency, and ring the clapper ever so softly. Snap a portrait of you, your partner, and the rusty clapper. Brace yourself for *fortissimo* clangs on the quarter-hour.

View Terrace: Even if you don't ascend the tower, head to the grassy terrace behind the cathedral for sweeping views of the bays that flank Piran. First, looking over the rooftops of Piran, you'll see a long peninsula jutting out. This is the northern edge of Croatia's Istria.

Then, looking in the opposite direction, you'll see a huge port city in the distance: Trieste, Italy. Until 1920, this metropolis (the main port of the Austro-Hungarian Empire) had close ties to Slovenia—much of its population spoke Slovene. After it was annexed by Italy, many Slovenes moved closer to their compatriots in Yugoslavia, but a large Slovene-speaking minority still lives here (mostly in the rural areas on the city's outskirts).

Ponder how tiny Slovenia's coastline is—wedged between Italy and Croatia (two nations with some of the longest coastlines in all of Europe). For years, Croatia maintained that, in accordance with the letter of international maritime law, a country with such a short coastline should not be allowed to operate a port—and yet, Slovenia does (its busy port town, Koper, is tucked just behind the peninsula in front of Trieste). Croatia said "the law's the law!"—but Slovenes, along with many international observers, perceived it as bullying. After years of wrangling, in 2009, when Croatia needed Slovenia's support to join the EU, the Slovenes said, "Not so fast..." and vetoed Croatia's EU bid for 10 months. Eventually US Secretary of State Hillary Clinton intervened, and cooler heads prevailed—Croatia is in the EU, and Slovenia's port is still busy.

Looking back to the base of Piran's peninsula, you'll get a good view of the crenellated castle that protected this strategic location.

PIRAN

Piran History

Piran was named for the fires (*pyr* in Greek) that were lit at the tip of its peninsula to assist passing ships. Known as "Pirano" in *Italiano*, the town is home to a long-standing Italian community (about 1,500 today)—so it's legally bilingual, with signs in two languages. As with most towns on the eastern Adriatic, it has a Venetian flavor. Piran wisely signed on with Venice as part of its trading empire in 933, and because of its valuable salt industry and strong trade, managed to enjoy some autonomy in later centuries. After plagues killed most of Piran's population in the 15th century, local Italians let Slavs fleeing the Ottomans repopulate the town. Piran's impressive walls were built to counter the growing Ottoman threat. Too much rain ruined the town's valuable salt basins, but in the 19th century, the Austrian Habsburg rulers rebuilt the salt industry (these salt fields are still open for tourist visits—see page 722). With that change came a new economic boom, and Piran grew in importance once again. After World War I, this part of the Habsburg Empire was assigned to Italy, but fascism never sat well with the locals. After World War II, the region was made neutral, then became part of Yugoslavia in 1956. In 1991, with the creation of Slovenia, the Slovenes of Piran were finally independent.

Sergej Mašera Maritime Museum
(Pomorski Muzej Sergej Mašera)

This humble museum—worth considering only on a rainy day—faces the harbor and the square, filling three floors of an elegant old building with faintly endearing exhibits. The first floor contains a darkened room of "underwater finds," including a collection of amphorae from antiquity that are visible through a glass floor. The second floor is a series of dusty rooms on the history of seafaring, with a wide assortment of model ships, and a town model that illustrates how today's Tartini Square was once an enclosed and fortified harbor. And the top floor hosts a modern exhibit honoring illustrious Slovenian seamen, with historical documents and uniforms. The exhibits are described only in Slovene and Italian, but you can borrow English descriptions for each floor (or buy the cheap, illustrated English booklet).

Cost and Hours: €3.50; July-Aug Tue-Sun 9:00-12:00 & 17:00-21:00, Sept-June Tue-Sun 9:00-17:00, closed Mon year-round; Cankarjevo nabrežje 3, tel. 05/671-0040, www.pomorskimuzej.si.

Aquarium

Piran's small, modern aquarium is well-presented, convenient (right off Tartini Square), and another decent rainy-day activity.

PIRAN

You'll stroll through a few rooms with tanks clearly labeled in English and filled with Adriatic sea life.

Cost and Hours: €5, mid-June-Aug Tue-Sun 9:00-21:00, shorter hours off-season, closed Mon year-round, Kidričevo nabrežje 4, tel. 05/673-2572, www.aquariumpiran.si.

May 1 Square (Trg 1 Maja)

This square, deep in a warren of cobbled lanes in the middle of the Old Town's peninsula, marks the center of medieval Piran, where its main streets converged. Once the administrative center of town, today it's the domain of local kids and ringed by a few humble eateries. The stone rainwater cistern dominating the square's center was built in 1775 after a severe drought. Rainwater was captured here with the help of drains from roofs and channeled by hard-working statues into the system. The water was filtered through sand and stored in the well, clean and ready for townspeople to draw—or, later, pump—for drinking.

Harborfront Stroll

Wandering along the harborfront, with its chunky breakwater, is a delight: almost no pesky mopeds or cars, and virtually no American or Japanese tourists—just Slovenes and Italians. Children sell shells on cardboard boxes. Husky sunbathers lie like large limpets on the rocks. Walk around the lighthouse at the tip of the town and around the corner, checking out the cafés and fish restaurants along the way.

Swimming

Piran has clear, warm, enticing water. And, while the town is too small and skinny to have a conventional "beach," tourists find plenty of ways to go for a swim. Here are a few ideas, listed in geographical order from Tartini Square:

The big concrete pad in front of **Hotel Piran,** with a half-dozen ladders descending directly into the deep, may be the easiest choice. Coin-op showers, two nearby cafés (one in the hotel itself, and the adjacent Teater Café), and rentable beach chairs (€10 buys you two chairs and an umbrella) make this spot especially handy. It's a public beach, so you can spread out a towel on the concrete and lounge for free.

If you continue past Hotel Piran along the embankment **promenade** (lined with restaurants), you'll see plenty of swimmers and sunbathers trying to get comfortable on the big breakwater; try to find a flat rock to spread out on. (A few sunbathers scramble for space along the walkway, but this can get crowded.) Along here, several ladders provide easy access to the sea. While there's no shower on the promenade, it's a quick walk to the others noted here.

If you continue to the end of the promenade and hook around the lighthouse at the tip of town, you'll soon come to an even bigger **concrete pad.** A bit less inviting than the one in front of Hotel Piran, it's quite large, making this a good choice if the first two options are crowded. Cafés and free showers are nearby. Just past the end of the concrete is a small pebbly/rocky beach, but it's less clean and less inviting.

Other options are a bit farther afield. Right near the traffic gate and parking lot at the **entrance to town,** you'll find a small pebbly beach (with free showers); beyond that is a long stretch—basically the entire length of the Fornače parking lot—of concrete pad with ladders providing easy access into the sea. While not exactly serene, it's uncrowded. To get to this area quickly, just hop on the free shuttle bus from Tartini Square.

If you walk about 10 minutes past the Fornače parking lot and garage, you'll reach a public beach in front of the **Bernardin** hotel complex.

With a car, you can drive to the **town center of Portorož,** which has a pleasant boardwalk and a sandy beach that's arguably more appealing than anything in Piran itself.

Sleeping in Piran

Piran's accommodations options are limited, but I've listed the best in each price range.

$$$ Hotel Tartini faces Piran's gorgeous main square 50 yards from its tidy harbor. Its 46 simple rooms—jaunty, colorful, and a bit faded—feel like an Italian resort hotel. Though it's not elegant, the hotel works hard to please its guests. Don't miss the upstairs terrace, with great views over Tartini Square (Sb-€88/€82/€76, Db-€138/€118/€102; €10 more for seaside room with balcony, 10 percent discount for Rick Steves readers who book direct; air-con, elevator, discount for town parking garage, Tartinijev trg 15, tel. 05/671-1000, www.hotel-tartini-piran.com, info@hotel-tartini-piran.com, well-run by Andreja).

$$$ Hotel Piran, the waterfront grande dame of Piran, owns the best sea views in town. Its 89 rooms feel fresh and upscale, if a bit soulless. The non-view rooms face a gloomy street; all of the seaview rooms come with a little balcony—worth paying extra for (viewless Db-€160/€140/€125, seaview Db-€200/€170/€155, air-con, elevator, pay-for-use rooftop terrace, discount for town parking garage, Stijenkova 1, tel. 05/666-7100, www.hotel-piran.si, info@hotel-piran.si).

$$ PachaMama Pleasant Stay is a vibrant guesthouse run with a youth-hostel mentality by well-traveled Mitja (who named the place for "Mother Earth" in an Incan language). The 12 rooms, just a block off Tartini Square, are modern, woody, sleek, small, straightforward, and well-priced. They share a multilevel terrace out back, in the shadow of the town bell tower (Db-€60, likely €10 more in July-Aug, shared kitchen, ask about breakfast, air-con, lots of stairs, Trubarjeva 8, tel. 05/918-3495, mobile 041-776-576, www.pachamama.si, info@pachamama.si).

$$ Bogdan and Jana Bevk rent six good apartments in two different buildings with roof terraces; both are buried in a quiet part of the Old Town. As they live elsewhere, call when you arrive so Bogdan can meet you and take you to the apartment (Db-€60/€50/€40, €10 more for newer apartments with sauna, 50 percent more for 1-night stays, 5-night minimum in July-Aug, no breakfast, air-con, lots of stairs, discount for town parking lot, Marxova 13 and Prežihova 4, mobile 051-623-682, tel. 05/902-2111, www.bevk.si, info@bevk.si). They also have a much bigger, two-room apartment closer to Tartini Square (€120/€100/€80).

$$ Miracolo di Mare B&B, at the bus-station end of the Old Town, has 12 straightforward but comfortable rooms—each one a bit different—in a historic building. In good weather, breakfast is served in the inviting garden, under a 75-year-old kiwi tree (Db-€70/€60, reception open 8:00-12:00 & 15:00-20:00, air-con in some rooms, Wi-Fi in lobby, free loaner bikes, Tomšičeva 23, tel. 05/921-7660, mobile 051-445-511, www.miracolodimare.si, bbstudio@elcatel.si, Borut).

$ Val Youth Hostel is a friendly slumbermill a short block off the waterfront. The rooms are small, basic, and a bit dated, but perfectly sleepable and affordably priced (47 beds in 20 dorm rooms;

PIRAN

bunk in dorm room-€22-€25, lower price is for Sept-May, €5 more for 1-night stays in peak season, includes breakfast and sheets, prices are the same regardless of room size, free self-service laundry, kitchen, 20 yards in from waterfront near tip of peninsula at Gregorčičeva 38A, tel. 05/673-2555, www.hostel-val.com, yhostel.val@siol.net). Some services are available to nonguests: You can eat breakfast here (€5), use their guest computer or Wi-Fi (free, but buy a drink), and—if they're not busy and if you ask nicely—use their laundry facilities (likely for a small fee).

Eating in Piran

Pricey tourist bars and restaurants face the sea (figure about €20/main course), while the laid-back, funky, and colorful local joints seem to seek an escape from both the tourists and the sun in the back lanes. Get off the beaten track to find one of my recommended restaurants, and you'll enjoy a seafood-and-pasta feast for half what you'd pay in Venice (just across the sea).

Restaurant Neptun, with fresh seafood and pastas served in a fishnet-strewn dining room, is my favorite eatery in town. I find it far classier than the tacky tourist fish joints. The Grilj family works hard to please six tables of diners (plus two more outside in the nondescript alley in good weather). Everything's made to order with fish straight out of the Adriatic—nothing's frozen. I can't resist their gnocchi with scampi as a starter. Consider splurging on a whole fish, grilled to perfection (€7-10 pastas, €8-20 meat and fish dishes, daily 12:00-16:00 & 18:00-22:00, Župančičeva 7, tel. 05/673-4111). Don't confuse this with Neptun Café, at the waterfront bus station.

Pri Mari Restaurant is about a 10-minute walk from Tartini Square, near the entrance to town. Gregarious Mara and Tomaž will welcome you into their cheery dining room like an old friend, then treat you to tasty Venetian-style cooking (€8-12 pastas, €9-17 meat and fish dishes, Tue-Sat 12:00-16:00 & 18:00-22:00, Sun 12:00-18:00—or until 22:00 in July-Aug, closed Mon, Dantejeva 17, tel. 05/673-4735).

Pizzeria Petica, tucked down a back lane, is atmospheric and tasty. Dine in the cozy interior, or sit outside (€5-8 pizzas, daily 11:00-23:00, Župančičeva 6, mobile 080-3588).

Sarajevo '84, part of a small Slovenian chain, oozes Yugonostalgia for the year that the Bosnian capital hosted the Olympics. This is the spot for a break from fish and pasta—the menu features gigantic portions of inexpensive, stick-to-your-ribs Bosnian grilled meats (for help navigating the menu, read the "Balkan Flavors" sidebar on page 421). Sit in the Bosnian-themed interior, or out on the terrace, overlooking a busy street and the sailboat harbor (filling—and splittable—€5-7 meals, Mon-Sat 9:00-24:00, Sun 9:00-22:00, Tomšičeva 43, tel. 05/923-5044).

Quick Bites and Picnics: For food on the go, duck behind the Town Hall (which houses the TI). You'll find an outdoor market (Mon-Sat 7:00-13:00); a bakery selling pizza slices, sandwiches, and *burek* to go (Naša Pekarna, daily 7:00-18:00); a Mercator supermarket (Mon-Fri 7:00-20:00, Sat 7:00-13:00, Sun 8:00-12:00); and a pay WC.

Drinks: **Café Teater** is *the* place for drinks with Adriatic views and a characteristic old interior. Catching the sunset here is a fine way to kick off your Piran evening (pricey cocktails, open long hours daily, Stjenkova 1). If you prefer to sit out on Tartini Square, you can take your pick of cafés. **Hotel Tartini** has a hidden terrace, called Altana, high above the scene, with dynamite views over the square and church bell tower; while officially open only in peak season (July-Aug daily 18:00-22:00), at other times you can buy a drink down on the square, then take it up to the terrace to enjoy (elevator to floor 2, then go outside and head up the stairs).

Piran Connections

Piran has a small, unstaffed bus station, right along the water near the entrance to town.

The best way to connect Piran with **Ljubljana** is by **bus** (5/day Mon-Fri, 2/day Sat, 4/day Sun, 2.5 hours, www.ap-ljubljana.si). By **train,** the trip takes four hours (bus between Piran and Koper, then train between Koper and Ljubljana).

TO CROATIA'S ISTRIA

By Bus: Piran has decent connections to Croatian Istria, but the specific schedule tends to fluctuate from year to year; it's smart to confirm your plans at www.ap-ljubljana.si, or ask the Piran TI. In summer, daily buses connect Piran to **Rovinj** (3-4/day late June-Aug, 1/day Sept, none Oct-late June, 2-3 hours, buses also stop in **Poreč** en route). Year-round, there are also buses going from Piran to Poreč and Pula (2/day Mon-Fri, 1/day Sat-Sun); from those towns, you can transfer to reach Rovinj. Other options to Istria connect through Portorož (the large resort town next to Piran) or Umag (just over the border, in Croatia). Or consider the boat (see next).

BY BOAT

Trieste Lines runs boats from Trieste (Italy) to Piran, Poreč, and Rovinj—potentially handy for connecting Piran to those Istrian destinations (www.triestelines.it).

A boat called the *Prince of Venice*—designed for day-trippers, but also convenient for one-way transport—sails from the nearby town of Izola to Venice, but the schedule is sparse (1-2/week in summer, shuttle bus connects Piran to boat in Izola, book through Kompas Travel Agency, www.kompas-online.net).

Commodore Cruises also runs sporadic boats between Piran and Venice (www.commodore-cruises.hr).

ROUTE TIPS FOR DRIVERS

Piran is a natural stopover between Ljubljana and Croatia's Istria. You can do the Karst sights on the way down (lined up conveniently along the A-1 expressway), sleep in Piran, then continue to Istria; or simply make a beeline to Piran and see the town before moving on to sleep in Istria.

From Ljubljana to Piran: Piran is about 1.5 hours from Ljubljana. From Ljubljana, take the A-1 expressway south to Koper; when the expressway ends at the outskirts of Koper, follow *Portorož/Portorose* signs—enjoying grand views over the bay to Trieste on your right, and passing the charming old town of Izola—then *Piran/Pirano* signs. For arrival and parking instructions, see "Arrival in Piran," earlier.

From Piran to Croatia's Istria: Leaving Piran, go through Portorož, then Lucija, then follow signs to *Pula*. Just after you enter Seča, signs on the right point to the salt pans of Sečovlje Salina Nature Park (described next). The border is just a few minutes straight ahead. (If you want to see the salt museum, remember that it's between the Slovenian and Croatian border posts—just after leaving Slovenia, keep an eye on the right for the very easy-to-miss gravel road.) Once in Croatia, follow *Pula* signs to get on the *ipsilon* highway that zips you down through the middle of Istria.

PIRAN

Near Piran

While Piran is easily the most worthwhile destination on Slovenia's coast, the historic and well-presented salt pans at **Sečovlje Salina Nature Park**—a short drive or boat ride to the south—are interesting and convenient, especially if you're heading to Croatia. The big city of **Koper** is skippable, but unavoidable, if you're visiting this region by cruise ship. Fortunately, if you do come to Koper on a ship, it's easy to get to Piran, and possible to reach other attractions in Slovenia.

Sečovlje Salina Nature Park

A few miles south of Piran, a literal stone's throw from the Croatian border, the Sečovlje Salina Nature Park (Krajinski Park Sečoveljske Soline) features enormous salt pans, which have been used since the Middle Ages for harvesting this precious mineral. Back in the days before refrigeration, salt's preservative powers made it more valuable than gold. As you drive by on the way to Croatia, you'll wonder what this massive complex is...so why not stop for a visit?

The "nature park" has two parts: Lera, to the north, harvests salt using 700-year-old techniques, and has a fine visitors center and a saltwater spa; Fontanigge, to the south (closer to Croatia), has a good museum to explain traditional salt-harvesting methods to tourists. I never thought salt could be so interesting. The only catch is that, in order to preserve the unique landscape around the salt pans, visitors aren't allowed to drive all the way to the attractions; you'll have to walk (20-30 minutes to Lera, farther to Fontanigge) or hitch a ride on a golf cart (Lera only).

Cost and Hours: €7 (€6 Nov-March) covers entry to both Fontanigge and Lera salt fields, the visitors center, and the museum; salt fields and visitors center open daily 8:00-21:00 in summer, closes earlier off-season; museum open daily April-Oct 9:00-18:00, closed Nov-March; tel. 05/672-2341, www.kpss.si.

Getting There: The nature park is between Piran and the Croatian border. For **drivers** heading south toward Croatia (see "Route Tips for Drivers," earlier), you'll pass the entrance to the Lera salt field on your right, just after entering the town of Seča (watch for brown *Sečoveljske soline* signs). To visit Lera, go down a steep cobbled stretch, then cross a bridge over a channel to reach the ticket booth (from here, it's a 15-minute walk—described later). For Fontanigge—farther along the main road—it's more complicated: You'll actually have to cross the Slovenian border, then a few feet later, just before you reach the Croatian border post, you'll see a gravel road on the right, leading to the salt field. It's a five-minute drive to the gate, where you'll park and walk about 30 minutes to the museum.

Fit cyclists can **bike** from Piran to the salt fields in about an hour (for bike-rental information, see "Helpful Hints," earlier).

If you don't have your own wheels, the only possibility is to take the very sporadic *Solinarka* **boat** from Piran (goes right to the museum, typically runs in summer only, frequency depends on demand—ask for schedule at the Piran TI).

Visiting the Park: Remember, there are two parts to the nature park, which are a drive, bike ride, or long hike away from each other. If you're choosing just one, make it Lera, which is easier to reach (since it's a shorter walk and has a golf-cart option). Fortanigge—which requires a long hike—is for die-hards.

Lera: The Lera section has a multimedia visitors center, small café, and salt-products shop, and gives you a good look at the salt pans themselves.

Buy your ticket at the small wooden kiosk near the parking lot. From here, it's just over a mile (20-30-minute walk) to the attractions, passing a shop selling products made with the salt harvested here. If you'd rather skip the walk, you can pay €1 per person to ride a golf cart (scheduled to depart at the top of each hour, but they can typically request one for you at other times—ask).

It's enjoyable to walk at least one way through the neat patchwork of vast, wood-framed salt pans, connected by a series of canals with little doors. Keep an eye out for workers harvesting salt just as it was done from medieval times up until the Austrians arrived in 1904. Museum docents do it the way their ancestors did: First, they fill up the shallow pans with seawater, then they seal them off and allow the water to naturally evaporate, leaving behind those precious deposits. Once most of the water is gone, they use large rake-like tools to sweep the salt into big piles. You'll most likely see salt gatherers at work during the peak of summer (July-Aug), when the hot sun speeds evaporation. (Be aware that the walk can be blazing hot, with nearly no shade—perfect conditions for harvesting salt.)

The **multimedia center** shows a mesmerizing 30-minute film (with English subtitles) of modern-day locals harvesting salt the same way their ancestors did. "In 700 years," they note, "only the clothing has changed." Traditional tools decorate the walls. In the adjoining hall, you can see a model of the entire area of the salt pans; learn more about the history and ecology of salt-gathering; and watch short video clips about local birds (which thrive in this salty ecosystem). Everything is nicely presented and well-described in English.

Next to the multimedia center is a small **café** (selling affordable meals and drinks—not surprisingly, all those piles of salt just seem to make people thirsty). Climbing the spiral staircase on the adjacent building, you'll reach a **rooftop viewpoint** offering panoramic views over the entire area. Also nearby are WCs.

To get the most out of your visit, consider booking an affordable **guided tour** (€25/person, 1.5-hour guided walk through the salt fields, reserve 2 days ahead at www.kpss.si).

In a different part of Lera (about a mile from the ticket booth) is the **Thalasso Lepa Vida Spa,** where you can soak in salty water and order a range of other treatments, such as salt-pan mud wraps and other salty exfoliations (€18/up to 2 hours, includes €5 museum ticket and free golf-cart ride from ticket booth, other treatments cost extra, April-Oct daily 9:00-20:00, weather-dependent and closed Nov-March, tel. 05/672-1360, www.thalasso-lepavida.si).

Fontanigge: This part of the park—within a few feet of the Croatian border, which is just over the little river—is home to the Salt-Making Museum. From the parking lot, it's a long two-mile hike along a bumpy gravel road to the museum. Well-explained by posted English information and a knowledgeable docent, the exhibit demonstrates tools and methods, illustrating the lifestyles of the people who eked out a hard living on these salty marshes (for example, since they all shared a communal oven, each family had their own stamp for marking their loaves of bread).

Koper (Cruise Port)

The big city a half-hour to the north of Piran, Koper, is a gloomy industrial burg (pop. 25,000) that is emerging as a popular cruise port. I wouldn't bother coming here unless you're arriving by cruise ship—in which case, you can follow my instructions below.

Ships put in right in front of the Old Town. You'll exit the terminal building into a tidy collection of tourist stalls and a small TI kiosk (TI tel. 05/664-6403, www.koper.si). Across the street, you'll see fragments of Koper's stout town wall. The bus stop directly in front of the port gate serves a hop-on, hop-off tourist train that does a loop around the Old Town perimeter (€2/ride, four stops, but basically pointless). Free Wi-Fi is available in the port area.

While **Koper** itself is worth a quick stroll, most cruisers will want to move on to more enticing destinations farther afield. The easiest (and probably best) choice is **Piran,** well-connected by bus; also consider riding a bus to **Trieste,** or hiring a guide for a busy day driving all over Slovenia (**Ljubljana, Lake Bled,** the famous **caves,** and more). Each option is described below.

Koper: While this big city lacks charm, its main square is worth a quick peek, and it has a fine harborfront promenade. To explore, turn right as you exit the port, then turn left at the speed bump just past the big, blocky wall. Climbing up the stairs and turning left, you can walk to the view terrace overlooking the cruise port. From here, do a 180 and follow brown *Center/Centro* signs directly away from the port. After a long block, you'll pop out in Koper's main square, **Titov trg.** On this square, you'll find a climbable, 204-step bell tower; a TI (inside the crenellated castle, Praetorian Palace/Pretorska Palača); a loggia with café tables; and a Mercator supermarket with an ATM by the front door. After exploring here, head to the most scenic stretch of Koper's waterfront: Facing the palace with the TI, turn right down Kuričeva ulica. You'll head through the atmospheric Old Town (and pass another ATM on your right) until you reach a little square with a loggia. Just beyond this is the waterfront; if you follow it to the left, you'll find a broad and nicely manicured promenade.

To Piran: Slovenia's most charming coastal town is easily reached by bus (departs every 20-30 minutes Mon-Fri, hourly Sat-Sun, 45 minutes). The bus to Piran leaves from a stop that's about a 10-minute walk from your ship. Exiting the port area, turn left and walk alongside a long, multicolored building on your left. At the end of this building, watch for the covered bus stop across the street, on your right. This is where you can catch the bus to Piran. If, instead, you prefer to explore Koper's downtown core a bit, you can follow the instructions above, looping through the main square and following Kuričeva ulica down to the waterfront. When you reach the water, turn left and head along Pristaniska ulica, with the cement-colored market on your right-hand side. When you reach the roundabout, turn right and head for the bus stop on the right side of the street (next to the parking lot), where you can catch the Piran-bound bus.

To Trieste or Ljubljana: While the bus to Piran leaves from Koper's town center, other connections depart from Koper's adjacent train and bus stations, which sit beyond the far end of the Old Town. To avoid the long walk, you can hop on any public bus, all of which head for this station. From the main bus station, you can ride the bus into the nearby Italian port city of **Trieste** (6/day, none on Sun, 45-60 minutes)—the historic port of the Austro-Hungarian Empire, with a fine Old Town and a romantic harbor. To go farther afield, you can head north to **Ljubljana.** Reaching the capital takes about 2.5 hours by bus or by train, but connections are sparse (about 4/day on either, though the only times convenient for cruisers are the 10:03 train or the 10:50 bus—both Mon-Fri only).

To Elsewhere in Slovenia: As the drive to Ljubljana takes an hour less (about 1.5 hours each way), hiring your own **guide/driver** is a smart splurge to efficiently link together several worthwhile Slovenian stopovers. A popular round-trip from Koper is to visit both Ljubljana and Lake Bled before returning to your ship; if you skip Bled, you'll have time to tour one of the great caves (Škocjan or Postojna) or other sights (such as the Lipica Stud Farm) between the coast and Ljubljana. Bled-based guides Tina Hiti and Sašo Golub can take you on an all-day excursion to see Ljubljana and Bled for €300 (price for up to 3 people; for details, see page 598).

UNDERSTANDING YUGOSLAVIA

Americans struggle to understand the complicated breakup of Yugoslavia—especially when visiting countries that have risen from its ashes, such as Croatia, Slovenia, and Bosnia-Herzegovina. Talking to the locals can make it even more confusing: Everyone seems to have a slightly different version of events, and mildly plausible (but specious) conspiracy theories run rampant. A very wise Bosniak once told me, "Listen to all three sides—Muslim, Serb, and Croat. Then decide for yourself what you think." A Serb told me a similar local saying: "You have to look at the apple from all sides." That's the best advice I can offer. But since you may not have time for that on your brief visit, here's an admittedly oversimplified, as-impartial-as-possible history to get you started.

BALKAN PENINSULA 101

For starters, it helps to have a handle on the different groups who've lived in the Balkans—the southeastern European peninsula between the Adriatic and the Black Sea, stretching roughly from Hungary to Greece. Despite its current, somewhat sinister connotations, the word "Balkan" probably comes from a Turkish term meaning, simply, "wooded mountains." The Balkan Peninsula has always been a crossroads of cultures. The Illyrians, Greeks, Celts, and Romans had settlements here before the Slavs moved into the region from the north around the seventh century. During the next millennium and a half, the western part of the peninsula—which would become Yugoslavia—was divided by a series of cultural, ethnic, and religious fault lines.

The most important religious influences were **Western Christianity** (i.e., Roman Catholicism, first brought to the western part of the region by Charlemagne and later reinforced by the Austrian Habsburgs), **Eastern Orthodox Christianity** (brought to the east

Yugoslav Succession

Legend:
- Former Yugoslavia Border
- Current Borders
- Province within Serbia
- SLOVENE Language
- "Serbian Krajina" (Serb-Controlled Croatia 1991-1995)
- Republika Srpska (Serb territory in Bosnia-Herz.)

100 Kilometers
100 Miles

from the Byzantine Empire), and **Islam** (brought to the south by the Ottomans).

Two major historical factors made the Balkans what they are today: The first was the **split of the Roman Empire** in the fourth century A.D., dividing the Balkans down the middle into Roman Catholic (west) and Byzantine Orthodox (east)—roughly along today's Bosnian-Serbian border. The second was the **invasion of the Islamic Ottomans** in the 14th century. The Ottoman victory at the Battle of Kosovo Polje (1389) opened the door to the region and kicked off five centuries of Islamic influence in Bosnia-Herzegovina and Serbia, further dividing the Balkans into Christian (north) and Muslim (south).

Because of these and other events, several distinct ethnic identities emerged. The major ethnicities of Yugoslavia—Croat, Slovene, Serb, and Bosniak—are all considered South Slavs. The huge Slav ethnic and linguistic family—some 400 million strong—is divided into three groups: South (the peoples of Yugoslavia, explained next, plus Bulgarians), West (Poles, Czechs, and Slovaks), and East (Russians, Ukrainians, and Belarusians).

The South Slavs, who are all descended from the same ancestors and speak closely related languages, are distinguished by their religious practices. Roman Catholic **Croats** or **Slovenes** are found mostly west of the Dinaric Mountains (Croats along the Adriatic coast and Slovenes farther north, in the Alps); Orthodox Christian **Serbs** live mostly east of the Dinaric range; and Muslim **Bosniaks** (whose ancestors converted to Islam under the Ottomans) live mostly in the Dinaric Mountains. Two other, smaller Orthodox ethnicities have been influenced by other large groups: the **Montenegrins** (shaped by centuries of Croatian and Venetian Catholicism) and the **Macedonians** (with ties to Bulgarians and Greeks). To complicate matters, the region is also home to several non-Slavic minority groups, including **Hungarians** (in the northern province of Vojvodina) and **Albanians,** concentrated in Kosovo (descended from the Illyrians, who lived here long before the Greeks and Romans).

Of course, these geographic divisions are extremely general. The groups overlapped a lot—which is exactly why the breakup of Yugoslavia was so contentious. One of the biggest causes of this ethnic mixing came in the 16th century. The Ottomans were threatening to overrun Europe, and the Austrian Habsburgs wanted a buffer zone. The Habsburgs encouraged Serbs who were fleeing from Ottoman invasions to settle as a "human shield" along today's Croatian-Bosnian border (known as *Vojna Krajina*, or "Military Frontier").

Imagine being a simple Croat farmer in a remote village. One day your new neighbors move in: big, tough, highly trained Serb refugees with chips on their shoulders after having been kicked out of their ancestral homeland. And imagine being one of those Serbs: angry, frightened, and struggling to make a new life far from home. The cultural clash between these two groups reverberated for centuries.

Another legacy of the Ottomans—which directly resulted in the strife of the 1990s and continued tension today—was their occupation of Kosovo. This southern province is considered the ancestral homeland of the Serbs, whose civilization began here before they moved their capital north to Belgrade, fleeing the Ottomans after the Battle of Kosovo Polje. Under Ottoman rule, Kosovo was opened up to settlement by Muslim Albanians, who quickly came to represent a majority of the population. Centuries later, Kosovo—today 95 percent Albanian—looms large in the Serb consciousness, and their loss of this land still deeply offends them.

After the Ottoman threat subsided in the late 17th century, some of the Balkan states (basically today's Slovenia and Croatia)

Who's Who in Yugoslavia

Yugoslavia was made up of six republics, which were inhabited by eight different ethnicities (not counting small minorities such as Jews, Germans, and Roma). This chart shows each ethnicity and the republic(s) in which they were most concentrated. Not coincidentally, the more ethnically diverse a region was, the more conflict it experienced.

	Serbia*	Croatia	Bosnia-Herz.	Slovenia	Montenegro	Macedonia
Serbs (Orthodox)	X	X	X		X	
Croats (Catholic)		X	X			
Bosniaks (Muslims)			X			
Slovenes (Catholic)				X		
Macedonians (like Bulgarians)						X
Montenegrins (like Serbs)					X	
Albanians	X		X			X
Hungarians	X	X		X		

*Within Serbia were two "autonomous provinces," each of which was dominated by a non-Slavic ethnic group: Hungarians in Vojvodina and Albanians in Kosovo.

became part of the Austrian Habsburg Empire. The Ottomans stayed longer in the south and east (today's Bosnia-Herzegovina and Serbia)—making the cultures in these regions even more different. By the mid-19th century, the Ottoman Empire had become the dysfunctional "Sick Man of Europe," allowing Serbia to regain its independence through diplomatic means. Meanwhile, Bosnia-Herzegovina was taken into the Habsburg fold (frustrating the Serbs, who already had visions of uniting the South Slav peoples).

But before long, World War I erupted, after a disgruntled Bosnian Serb nationalist—with the aim of uniting the South Slavs—killed the Austrian archduke and heir to the Habsburg throne during a visit to Sarajevo (see page 495). This famously kicked off a chain of events that caused Europe, and the world, to descend into a Great War. During the war, the Serbs fought valiantly (alongside England, France, and the US) with the Allies, while their Slovene and Croat cousins—citizens of the multiethnic Austro-Hungarian Empire—were compelled to take up arms against them. Many Serbs, already eyeing a hypothetical future union of South Slavs, felt betrayed to see their would-be compatriots fighting against them.

SOUTH SLAVS UNITE

When the Austro-Hungarian Empire fell at the end of World War I, the map of Europe was redrawn for the 20th century. After centuries of being governed by foreign powers, the South Slavs began to see their shared history as more important than their differences. The Serbs pushed for the creation of an independent South Slav state, recognizing that a tiny country of a few million Croats or Slovenes couldn't survive on its own. And so, rather than be absorbed by a non-Slavic power, the South Slavs decided that there was safety in numbers, and banded together to form the Kingdom of the Serbs, Croats, and Slovenes (1918), later known as the Kingdom of Yugoslavia (Land of the South Slavs—*yugo* means "south"). "Yugoslav unity" was in the air. But this new union was fragile and ultimately bound to fail (not unlike the partnership between the Czechs and Slovaks, formed at the same time and for similar reasons).

From the very beginning, the various ethnicities struggled for power within the new Yugoslavia. The largest group was the Serbs (about 45 percent), followed by the Croats (about 25 percent). Croats often felt they were treated as lesser partners under the Serbs. For example, many Croats objected to naming the country's official language "Serbo-Croatian"—why not "Croato-Serbian"? Serbia already had a very strong king, Alexander Karađorđević, who assumed that his nation would have a leading role in the federation. A nationalistic Croat politician named Stjepan Radić, pushing for a more equitable division of powers, was shot by a Serb during a parliamentary session in 1928. Karađorđević abolished the parliament and became dictator. Six years later, infuriated Croat separatists killed him. By the time World War II came to Yugoslavia, the kingdom was already on the verge of collapse. The conflicts between the various Yugoslav groups had set the stage for a particularly complex and gruesome wartime experience.

WORLD WAR II

Observers struggle to comprehend how it was possible for interethnic conflict to escalate so quickly here in the early 1990s. Most of the answers can be found in the war that shook Europe 50 years earlier. In the minds of many combatants, the Yugoslav Wars of the 1990s were a continuation of unresolved conflicts from World War II.

YUGOSLAVIA

Capitalizing on a power struggle surrounding Yugoslavia's too-young-to-rule king, and angered by a popular uprising against the tenuous deals that Yugoslavia had struck with Nazi Germany, Hitler sent the Luftwaffe to air-bomb Belgrade on April 6, 1941. This classic blitzkrieg maneuver was followed by a ground invasion, and within 11 days, Yugoslavia had surrendered. The core of the nation (much of today's Croatia and Bosnia-Herzegovina) became the misnamed Independent State of Croatia, which was run by a Nazi puppet government called the Ustaše. Much of today's Serbia was occupied by Nazi Germany, Slovenia had a Quisling-like puppet dictator, and Montenegro was folded into Mussolini's Italy.

Many Croat nationalists supported the Ustaše in the hopes that it would be their ticket to long-term independence from Serbia. Emboldened by their genocide-minded Nazi overlords, Ustaše leaders used death camps to exterminate their enemies—specifically, the Serbs who, they felt, had wronged them in the days of the Kingdom of Yugoslavia. Not only were Jews, Roma, and other Nazi-decreed "undesirables" murdered in Ustaše concentration camps, but also hundreds of thousands of Serbs living in Croatia and Bosnia. (Estimates range from 800,000—the highball figure taught to Yugoslav schoolkids—to the offensively low 40,000 posited by nationalistic Croatian leaders in the 1990s.) Other Serbs were forced to flee the country or convert to Catholicism. Most historians consider the Ustaše camps to be the first instance of ethnic cleansing in the Balkans. (Half a century later, the Serbs justified their ruthless treatment of Croats and Bosniaks as retribution for these WWII atrocities.)

In the chaos of war, two distinct resistance movements arose, with the shared aim of reclaiming an independent Yugoslavia—but starkly different ideas of what that nation would look like.

First, in the eastern mountains of Yugoslavia rose the Četniks—a fearsome paramilitary band of mostly Serbian men fighting to reestablish a Serb-dominated monarchy. Wearing long beards and traditional mountain garb, and embracing a skull-and-crossbones logo adorned with the motto "Freedom or Death" in Cyrillic, the Četniks were every bit as brutal as their Ustaše enemies. In pursuit of their goal to create a purely Serb state, the Četniks expelled or massacred Croats and Muslims living in the territory they held. (To this day, if a Croat wants to deeply insult a Serb, he'll call him a "Četnik." And a Serb might use "Ustaše" to really hit a Croat where it hurts.)

The second resistance group—fighting against both the Četniks and the Ustaše—was the ragtag Partisan Army, led by Josip Broz, who was better known by his code name, Tito. The clever and determined Partisans had dual aims: to liberate Yugoslavia as a free nation on its own terms, and to make that new state a communist one. Even while the war was still underway, the Partisan leadership laid the foundations for what would become a postwar, communist Yugoslavia.

After years of largely guerrilla fighting among these three groups, the Partisans emerged victorious. And so, as the rest of Eastern Europe was being "liberated" by the Soviets, the Yugoslavs regained their independence on their own. Soviet troops passed through, in pursuit of the Nazis, but were not allowed to stay.

After the short but rocky Yugoslav union between the World Wars, it seemed that no one could hold the southern Slavs together in a single nation. But one man could, and did: Tito.

TITO'S YUGOSLAVIA

Communist Party president and war hero Tito emerged as a political leader after World War II. With a Slovene for a mother, a Croat for a father, a Serb for a wife, and a home in Belgrade, Tito was a true Yugoslav. Tito had a compelling vision that this fractured union of the South Slavs could function.

But Tito's new Yugoslavia could not be forged without force. In the first several years of his rule, Tito sometimes resorted to ruthless strong-arm tactics to forcibly persuade his subjects. Many soldiers who had fought against the Partisans were executed to create an intimidating example. To this day, Croatians—many of whose grandparents fought proudly with the Ustaše, furthering their ideal of an independent Croatian state—feel that they were disproportionately targeted by Tito, and in some cases, denied development funding in retaliation for their prior support of Partisan enemies. In particular, Croats resented Tito's treatment of Cardinal Alojzije Stepinac, the spiritual leader who (like many Croats) had supported the Ustaše. Stepinac was arrested, sham-tried, convicted, and died under house arrest. (Today, Croatia is the Yugoslav successor state where you'll find the least Tito nostalgia.) Similarly, the Četniks—who had also fought Tito's Partisans in the war—felt bruised as they gave up on their dreams of reinstalling the Serbian king.

Ultimately Tito prevailed, and while many Yugoslavs weren't entirely convinced of his vision, they went along with it...for the time being.

Tito's new incarnation of Yugoslavia aimed for a more equitable division of powers. It was made up of six republics, each with its own parliament and president: **Croatia** (mostly Catholic Croats), **Slovenia** (mostly Catholic Slovenes), **Serbia** (mostly Orthodox Serbs), **Bosnia-Herzegovina** (the most diverse—mostly Muslim Bosniaks, but with very large Croat and Serb populations), **Montenegro** (mostly Orthodox—sort of a Serb/Croat hybrid), and **Macedonia** (with about 25 percent Muslim Albanians and 75

Tito (1892-1980)

The Republic of Yugoslavia was the vision of a single man, who made it reality. Josip Broz—better known as Marshal Tito—presided over the most peaceful and prosperous era in this region's long and troubled history. Three decades after his death, Tito is beloved by many of his former subjects...and yet, he was a communist dictator who dealt brutally with his political enemies. This love-him-and-hate-him autocrat is one of the most complex figures in the history of this very complicated land.

Josip Broz was born in 1892 to a Slovenian mother and a Croatian father in the northern part of today's Croatia (then part of the Austro-Hungarian Empire). After growing up in the rural countryside, he was trained as a metalworker. He was drafted into the Austro-Hungarian army, went to fight on the Eastern Front during World War I, and was captured and sent to Russia as a prisoner of war. Freed by Bolsheviks, Broz fell in with the Communist Revolution... and never looked back.

At war's end, Broz returned home to the newly independent Yugoslavia, where he worked alongside the Soviets to build a national Communist Party. As a clandestine communist operative, he adopted the code name he kept for the rest of his life: Tito. Some believe this was a Spanish name he picked up while participating in that country's civil war, while others half-joke that the name came from Tito's authoritarian style: "*Ti, to!*" means "You, do this!" But one thing's clear: In this land where a person's name instantly identifies his ethnicity, "Tito" is ethnically neutral.

When the Nazis occupied Yugoslavia, Tito raised and commanded a homegrown, communist Partisan Army. Through guerilla tactics, Tito's clever maneuvering, and sheer determination, the Partisans liberated their country. And because they did so mostly without support from the USSR, Yugoslavia was able to set its own postwar course.

The war hero Tito quickly became the "president for life" of postwar Yugoslavia. But even as he introduced communism to his country, he retained some elements of a free-market economy—firmly declining to become a satellite of Moscow. He also pioneered the worldwide Non-Aligned Movement, joining with nations in Africa, the Middle East, Asia, and Latin America in refusing to ally with the US or USSR (see page 138). Stubborn but suitably cautious, Tito expertly walked a tightrope between East and West.

There was a dark side to Tito. In the early years of his regime, Tito resorted to brutal, Stalin-esque tactics to assert his control. Immediately following World War II, the Partisan Army massacred tens of thousands of soldiers who had supported the Nazis. Then Tito systematically arrested, tried, tortured, or executed those who did not accept his new regime. Survivors whose lives were ruined during this reign of terror will never forgive Tito for what he did.

But once he gained full control, Tito moved away from strong-arm tactics and into a warm-and-fuzzy era of Yugoslav brother-hood. Tito believed that the disparate peoples of Yugoslavia could live in harmony. For example, every Yugoslav male had to serve in the People's Army, and Tito made sure that each unit was a mi-crocosm of the complete Yugoslavia—with equal representation from each ethnic group. Yugoslavs from diverse backgrounds were forced to work together and socialize, and as a result, they became friends. He also worked toward economic diversification: Yugoslav tanks, some of the best in the world, were made of parts assem-bled in five different republics.

Tito's reign is a case study in the power of the cult of person-ality. Rocks on hillsides throughout Yugoslavia were rearranged to spell "TITO," and his portrait hung over every family's dinner table. Each of the six republics renamed one of its cities for their dictator. The main street and square in virtually every town were renamed for Tito. Each year, young people would embark on a months-long, Olympics-style relay, from each corner of Yugoslavia, to present a ceremonial baton to Tito on his official birthday (May 25). Tito also had vacation villas in all of Yugoslavia's most beautiful areas, including Lake Bled, the Brijuni Islands, and the Montenegrin coast. People sang patriotic anthems to their Druža (Comrade) Tito: "Comrade Tito, we pledge an oath to you."

Tito died in 1980 in a Slovenian hospital. His body went on a grand tour of the Yugoslav capitals: Ljubljana, Zagreb, Sarajevo, and Belgrade, where he was buried before hundreds of thousands of mourners, including more heads of state than at any other funer-al in history. At his request, his tomb was placed in the greenhouse where he enjoyed spending time.

The genuine outpouring of grief at Tito's death might seem unusual for a man who was, on paper, an authoritarian communist dictator. But even today, many former Yugoslavs—especially Slo-venes and Bosniaks—believe that his iron-fisted government was a necessary evil that kept the country strong and united. The even-tual balance Tito struck between communism and capitalism, and between the competing interests of his ethnically diverse nation, led to this region's most stable and prosperous era. In a recent poll in Slovenia, Tito had a higher approval rating than any present-day politician, and 80 percent of Slovenes said they had a positive im-pression of him.

And yet, the Yugoslavs' respect for their former leader was not enough to keep them together. Tito's death began a long, slow chain reaction that led to the end of Yugoslavia. As the decades pass, the old joke seems more and more appropriate: Yugoslavia had eight distinct peoples in six republics, with five languages, three religions (Orthodox Christian, Catholic, and Muslim), and two alphabets (Roman and Cyrillic), but only one Yugoslav—Tito.

YUGOSLAVIA

percent Orthodox Macedonians). Within Serbia, Tito set up two autonomous provinces, each dominated by an ethnicity that was a minority in greater Yugoslavia: Albanians in **Kosovo** (to the south) and Hungarians in **Vojvodina** (to the north). By allowing these two provinces some degree of independence—including voting rights—Tito hoped they would balance the political clout of Serbia, preventing a single republic from dominating the union.

Each republic managed its own affairs, but always under the watchful eye of president-for-life Tito, who said that the borders between the republics should be "like white lines in a marble column." "Brotherhood and unity" was Tito's motto, nationalism was strongly discouraged, and Tito's tight—often oppressive—control kept the country from unraveling. For more on Tito, see the sidebar on page 734.

Tito's Yugoslavia was communist, but it wasn't Soviet communism; you'll find no statues of Lenin or Stalin here. Despite strong pressure from Moscow, Tito broke away from Stalin in 1948 and refused to ally himself with the Soviets—and therefore received good will (and $2 billion) from the United States. He ingeniously played the East and the West against each other. He'd say to both Washington and Moscow, "If you don't pay me off, I'll let the other guy build a base here." Everyone paid up.

Economically, Tito's vision was for a "third way," in which Yugoslavia could work with both East and West without being dominated by either. Yugoslavia was the most free of the communist states. While large industry was nationalized, Tito's system allowed for small businesses. Though Yugoslavs could not become really rich, through hard work it was possible to attain modest wealth to buy a snazzy car, a vacation home, Western imports, and other niceties. By some GDP and other economic measures, Yugoslavia was at times more prosperous than poorer capitalist European countries like Italy or Greece. This experience with a market economy benefited Yugoslavs when Eastern Europe's communist regimes eventually fell.

Even during the communist era, Yugoslavia remained a popular tourist destination for visitors from both East and West, keeping its standards more in line with Western Europe than the Soviet states. Meanwhile, Yugoslavs, uniquely among communist citizens, were allowed to travel to the West. In fact, because Yugoslavs could travel relatively hassle-free in both East and West, their "red passports" were worth even more on the black market than American ones.

THINGS FALL APART

With Tito's death in 1980, Yugoslavia's six constituent republics gained more autonomy, with a rotating presidency. But before long, the fragile union Tito had held together started to unravel.

The breakup began in the late 1980s, with squabbles in the autonomous province of Kosovo between the Serb minority and the ethnic-Albanian majority. Remember that the Serbs consider Kosovo the cradle of their civilization—the medieval homeland of their most important monasteries and historic sites. Most significantly, it was the location of the Battle of Kosovo Polje ("Field of Blackbirds"), an epic 14th-century battle that formed the foundation of Serbian cultural identity...even though the Serbs lost to the Ottoman invaders (sort of the Serbian Alamo). One Serb told me, "Kosovo is the Mecca and Medina of the Serb people." But by the 1980s, 9 of every 10 Kosovans were Albanian, and the few Serbs still living there felt oppressed and abused by the Albanian leadership. To many Serbs, this was the most offensive of the many ways in which they felt they'd been victimized by their neighbors for centuries.

Serbian politician Slobodan Milošević saw how the conflict could be used to Serbia's (and his own) advantage. In April of 1987, Milošević delivered a rabble-rousing speech to aggrieved Serbs in Kosovo, pledging that Serbia would come to the aid of its brothers (famously asserting, "No one has the right to beat you"). He returned two years later for the 600th anniversary of the Battle of Kosovo Polje, arriving by helicopter to evoke old prophecies of a winged savior coming to unite the Serb people. Once there, he delivered another inflammatory speech ("Six centuries later, now, we are being again engaged in battles...they are not armed battles, although such things cannot be excluded yet"). With these visits, Milošević upset the delicate balance that Tito had so carefully sought, while setting the stage for his own rise to the Serbian presidency.

When Milošević-led Serbia annexed Kosovo soon after, other republics (especially Slovenia and Croatia) were concerned. The Croats and Slovenes had always had reservations about Yugoslav unity, and with the sea change signaled by Milošević's rhetoric, they decided it was time to secede. Some of the leaders—most notably Milan Kučan of Slovenia—tried to avoid warfare by suggesting a plan for a loosely united Yugoslavia, based on the Swiss model of independent yet confederated cantons. But other parties, who wanted complete autonomy, refused. Over the next decade, Yugoslavia broke apart, with much bloodshed.

The Slovene Secession

Slovenia was the first Yugoslav republic to hold free elections, in the spring of 1990. Voters wanted the communists out, and they wanted their own independent nation. The most ethnically homogeneous of the Yugoslav nations, Slovenia was also the most Western-oriented, prosperous, and geographically isolated—so secession just made sense. But that didn't mean it would be achieved without violence.

After months of stockpiling weapons, Slovenia closed its borders and declared independence from Yugoslavia on June 25, 1991. Belgrade sent in the Yugoslav People's Army to take control of Slovenia's borders with Italy and Austria, figuring that whoever controlled the borders had a legitimate claim on sovereignty. Fighting broke out around these borders. Because the Yugoslav People's Army was made up of soldiers from all republics, many Slovenian troops found themselves fighting their own countrymen. (The army had cut off communication between these conscripts and the home front, so they didn't know what was going on—and often didn't realize they were fighting their friends and neighbors until they were close enough to see them.)

Slovenian civilians bravely entered the fray, blockading the Yugoslav barracks with their own cars and trucks. Most of the Yugoslav soldiers—now trapped—were young and inexperienced, and were terrified of the improvised (but relentless) Slovenian militia, even though their own resources were far superior.

After 10 days of fighting and fewer than a hundred deaths, Belgrade relented. The Slovenes stepped aside and allowed the Yugoslav People's Army to leave with their weapons and to destroy all remaining military installations as they went. When the Yugoslav People's Army cleared out, they left the Slovenes with their freedom.

The Croatian Conflict

In April of 1990, a retired general and historian named Franjo Tuđman—and his highly nationalistic, right-wing party, the HDZ (Croatian Democratic Union)—won Croatia's first free elections (for more on Tuđman, see page 28). Like the Slovenian reformers, Tuđman and the HDZ wanted more autonomy from Yugoslavia. But Tuđman's methods were more extreme than those of the gently progressive Slovenes. Tuđman invoked the spirit of the Ustaše, who had ruthlessly run Croatia's puppet government under the Nazis. He removed mention of the Serbs as equal citizens of the new nation. He reintroduced symbols that had been embraced by the Ustaše, including the red-and-white checkerboard flag and the kuna currency. (While many of these symbols predated the Ustaše by centuries, they had become irrevocably tainted by their association with the Ustaše.) The 600,000 Serbs living in Croatia, mindful that their grandparents had been massacred by the Ustaše, saw the writing on the wall and began to rise up.

The first conflicts were in the Serb-dominated Croatian city of Knin. Tuđman had decreed that Croatia's policemen must wear a new uniform, which was strikingly similar to Nazi-era Ustaše garb. Infuriated by this slap in the face, and prodded by Slobodan Milošević's rhetoric, Serb police officers in Knin refused. Over the next few months, tense negotiations ensued. Serbs from Knin and elsewhere began the so-called "tree trunk revolution"—blocking important Croatian tourist roads to the coast with logs and other barriers. Meanwhile, the Croatian government—after being denied support from the United States—illegally purchased truckloads of guns from Hungary. (A UN weapons embargo, which was designed to prevent the outbreak of violence, had little effect on the Serb-dominated Yugoslav People's Army, which already had its own arsenal. But it was devastating to separatist Croatian and—later—Bosnian forces, which were just beginning to build their armies.) Croatian policemen and Serb irregulars from Knin fired the first shots of the conflict on Easter Sunday 1991 at Plitvice Lakes National Park.

By the time Croatia declared its independence (on June 25, 1991—the same day as Slovenia), it was already embroiled in the beginnings of a bloody war. The Yugoslav People's Army (now dominated by Serbs, as many Croats and Slovenes had defected) swept in, ostensibly to put down the Croat rebellion and keep the nation together. The ill-prepared Croatian resistance, made up mostly of policemen and a few soldiers who defected from the People's Army, were quickly overwhelmed. The Serbs gained control over the parts of inland Croatia where they were in the majority: a large swath around the Bosnian border (including Plitvice) and part of Croatia's inland panhandle (the region of Slavonia). They declared their own independence from Croatia, and called this territory—about a quarter of Croatia—the **Republic of Serbian Krajina** (*krajina* means "border"). This new "country" (hardly recognized by any other nations) minted its own money and raised its own army, much to the consternation of Croatia—which was now worried about the safety of Croats living in Krajina.

As the Serbs advanced, more than 200,000 Croats fled to the coast and lived as refugees in resort hotels. The Serbs began a campaign of ethnic cleansing, systematically removing Croats from contested territory—often by murdering them. (Many thousands of Croat civilians were killed.) The bloodiest siege was at the town of **Vukovar,** which the Yugoslav People's Army surrounded and shelled relentlessly for three months. By the end of the siege, thousands of Croat soldiers and civilians had disappeared. Many were later discovered in mass graves; hundreds remain missing, and bodies are still being found.

In a surprise move, Yugoslav forces also laid siege to the tourist resort of **Dubrovnik**—which resisted and eventually repelled the invaders (see page 296). By early 1992, both Croatia and the Republic of Serbian Krajina had established their borders, and a tense ceasefire fell over the region.

The standoff lasted until 1995, when the now well-equipped Croatian army retook the Serb-occupied areas in a series of two offensives—**"Lightning"** *(Blijesak),* in the northern part of the country, and **"Storm"** *(Oluja),* farther south. Some Croats retaliated for earlier ethnic cleansing by doing much of the same to Serbs—torturing and murdering them, and dynamiting their homes. Croatia quickly established the borders that exist today, and the Erdut Agreement brought peace to the region. But the country's demographics are forever changed: Of the 600,000 Serbs who had once lived in Croatia, approximately half were forced out, and more than 6,000 died in the war. Today, fewer than 200,000 Serbs—one-third of the original number—live in Croatia.

The War in Bosnia-Herzegovina

As violence erupted in Croatia and Slovenia, Bosnia-Herzegovina was suspiciously quiet. Even optimists knew it couldn't last. At the crossroads of Balkan culture, Bosnia-Herzegovina was even more diverse than Croatia; it was populated predominantly by Muslim Bosniaks (43 percent of the population), but also by large numbers of Serbs (31 percent) and Croats (17 percent). Bosniaks tended to live in the cities, while Serbs and Croats were more often farmers.

In the fall of 1991, Bosnia-Herzegovina's president, Alija Izetbegović, began to pursue independence. While most Bosnian Croats and virtually all Bosniaks supported this move, Bosnia's substantial Serb minority resisted it. Bosnian Serbs preferred to remain part of an increasingly dominant ethnic group in a big country (Yugoslavia) rather than become second fiddle in a new, small country (Bosnia-Herzegovina). And so the Serbs within Bosnia-Herzegovina created their own "state," called the **Republic of the Serb People of Bosnia-Herzegovina.** Its president, Radovan Karadžić, enjoyed the semisecret military support of Slobodan Milošević and the Yugoslav People's Army. The stage was set for a bloody secession.

In the spring of 1992, as a referendum on Bosnian independence loomed, the Serbs made their move. To legitimize their territorial claims, the Serbs began a campaign of ethnic cleansing against Bosniaks and Croats residing in Bosnia. Initially Karadžić's forces moved to take control of a strip of Muslim-majority towns (including Foča, Goražde, Višegrad, and Zvornik) along the Drina River, between Serbia proper and Serb-controlled areas closer to Sarajevo. They reasoned that their claim on this territory was legitimate, because the Ustaše had decimated the Serb population there during World War II. The well-orchestrated Karadžić forces secretly notified Serb residents to evacuate before they invaded each mixed-ethnicity town. Then troops would encircle the remaining Bosniaks and Croats with heavy artillery and sniper fire in an almost medieval-style siege. Many people were executed on the spot, while others were arrested and taken to concentration camps. Survivors were forced to leave the towns their families had lived in for centuries.

It was during this initial wave of Bosnian Serb ethnic cleansing—orchestrated by Radovan Karadžić and his generals—that the world began to hear tales as horrifying as anything you can imagine. Militia units would enter a town and indiscriminately kill anyone they saw—civilian men, women, and children. Pregnant women mortally wounded by gunfire were left to die in the street. Fleeing residents crawled on their stomachs for hours to reach cover, even as their family and friends were shot and blown up right next to them. Soldiers rounded up families, then forced parents to watch as they slit the throats of their children—and then the parents were killed, too. Dozens of people would be lined up along a bridge to have their throats slit, one at a time, so that their lifeless bodies would plunge into the river below. (Villagers downstream would see corpses float past, and know their time was coming.) While in past conflicts houses of worship had been considered off-limits, now Karadžić's forces actively targeted mosques and Catholic churches. Perhaps most despicable was the establishment of so-called "rape camps"—concentration camps where mostly Bosniak women were imprisoned and systematically raped by Serb soldiers. Many were intentionally impregnated and held captive until they had come to term, when they were released to bear and raise a child forced upon them by their hated enemy. These are the stories that turned "Balkans" into a dirty word.

The Bosnian Serb aggressors were intentionally gruesome and violent. First, leaders roused their foot soldiers with hate-filled propaganda (claiming, for example, that the Bosniaks were intent on creating a fundamentalist Islamic state that would do even worse to its Serb residents). Then, once the troops were furious and motivated, they were ordered to carry out unthinkable atrocities. For some people who carried out these attacks, the war represented a cathartic opportunity to exact vengeance for decades-old perceived injustices. Everyday Serbs—who, for centuries, have been steeped in messages about how they have been the victims of their neighbors—saw this as an opportunity to finally make a stand. But their superiors had even more dastardly motives. They sought not only to remove people from "their" land, but to do so in such a heinous way as to ensure that the various groups could never again tolerate living together.

Bosnia-Herzegovina was torn apart. Even the many mixed families were forced to choose sides. If you had a Serb mother and a Croat father, you were expected to pick one ethnicity or the other—and your brother might choose the opposite. The majority of people, who did not want this war and couldn't comprehend why it was happening, now faced the excruciating realization that their neighbors and friends were responsible for looting and burning their houses, and shooting at their loved ones. As families and former neighbors trained their guns on each other, proud and beautiful cities such as Mostar were turned to rubble.

Even as the Serbs and Croats fought brutally in the streets, their leaders—Slobodan Milošević and Franjo Tuđman, respectively—were secretly meeting to carve up Bosnia into Serb and Croat sectors, at the Bosniaks' expense (the so-called Karađorđevo Agreement). Bosniak President Alija Izetbegović—who was completely left out of the conversation—desperately pleaded with the international community to support the peaceful secession of a free Bosnian state. Motivated more by fear than by nationalism, Izetbegović insisted that the creation of an independent Bosnia-Herzegovina was the only way to protect the lives of the Bosniak people.

At first, the Bosniaks and Croats teamed up to fend off the Serbs. But even before the first wave of fighting had subsided, Croats and Bosniaks turned their guns on each other. The Croats split off their own mini-state, the **Croatian Republic of Herzeg-Bosnia**. A bloody war raged for years among the three groups: the Serbs (with support from Serbia proper), the Croats (with support from Croatia proper), and—squeezed between them—the internationally recognized Bosniak government, with little support from anybody.

The United Nations Protection Force (UNPROFOR)—dubbed "Smurfs" both for their light-blue helmets and for their ineffectiveness—exercised their very limited authority to provide humanitarian aid. Their charge allowed them only to feed civilians caught in the crossfire—an absurd notion in places like Sarajevo, where civilians were forced to live like soldiers. (A political cartoon from the time shows a Bosnian Serb preparing to murder a Bosniak with a knife. A UN solider appears and says, "Not so fast!" He proceeds to feed the Bosniak...then walks away, mission accomplished, while the Serb butchers his victim.) Later, the UN tried to designate "safe areas" where civilians were protected, but because the UNPROFOR troops were forbidden to use force—even in self-defense—they became helpless witnesses to atrocities. This ugly situation was brilliantly parodied in the film *No Man's Land* (which won the Oscar for Best Foreign Film in 2002), a very dark comedy about the absurdity of the Bosnian war.

For three and a half years, the capital of Sarajevo—still inhabited by a united community of Sarajevans (which included Bosniaks, Croats, and Serbs)—was surrounded by Karadžić's Bosnian Serb army (for more on the "Siege of Sarajevo," see page 484). Other Bosniak cities were also besieged, most notoriously Srebrenica in July of 1995. While a Dutch unit of UNPROFOR troops sat impotently by, General Ratko Mladić invaded Srebrenica and oversaw the murder of at least 8,000 of its residents, mostly men. Additionally, 35,000 to 40,000 Bosniak women and children were forcibly removed from the city; many of them (including babies) died en route. For more on this particularly dark chapter, see the "Srebrenica" sidebar on page 502.

After four long years, the mounting mass of atrocities—including the siege of Srebrenica and the bombing of innocent civilians at a market in Sarajevo—finally persuaded the international community to act. In the late summer of 1995, NATO began bombing Bosnian Serb positions, forcing them to relax their siege and come to the negotiating table. The Dayton Peace Accords—brokered by US diplomats at Wright-Patterson Air Force Base near Dayton, Ohio—finally brought an end to the wars of Yugoslav succession.

The Dayton Peace Accords carefully divided Bosnia-Herzegovina into three different units: the Federation of Bosnia and Herzegovina (Bosniaks and Croats), the Serb-dominated Republika Srpska, and the mixed-ethnicity Brčko District. While this compromise helped bring the war to an end, it also created a nation with four independent and redundant governments—further crippling this war-torn and impoverished region.

The Fall of Milošević

After years of bloody conflicts, Serbian public opinion had decisively swung against their president. The transition began gradually in early 2000, spearheaded by Otpor, a nonviolent, grassroots, student-based opposition movement, and aided by similar groups. Using clever PR strategies, these organizations convinced Serbians that real change was possible. As anti-Milošević sentiments gained momentum, opposing political parties banded together behind one candidate, Vojislav Koštunica. Public support for Koštunica mounted, and when the arrogant Milošević called an early election in September 2000, he was soundly defeated. Though Milošević tried to claim that the election results were invalid, determined Serbs streamed into their capital, marched on their parliament, and—like the Czechs and Slovaks a decade before—peacefully took back their nation.

In 2001, Milošević was arrested and sent to The Hague, in the Netherlands, to stand trial before the International Criminal Tribunal for the Former Yugoslavia (ICTY). Milošević served as his own attorney as his trial wore on for five years, frequently delayed due to his health problems. Then, on March 11, 2006—as his trial was coming to a close—Milošević was found dead in his cell. Ruled a heart attack, Milošević's death, like his life, was controversial. His supporters alleged that Milošević had been denied suitable medical care, some speculated that he'd been poisoned, and others suspected that he'd intentionally worsened his heart condition to avoid the completion of his trial. Whatever the cause, in the end Milošević escaped justice—he was never found guilty of a single war crime.

More War Leaders on Trial

On July 18, 2008, Serbian police announced that they had captured Radovan Karadžić, the former leader of the Bosnian Serb state who is considered one of the worst culprits in the brutal ethnic cleansing.

Karadžić, who went into hiding shortly after the war (in 1996), had been living for part of that time in a residential neighborhood of Belgrade, posing as an alternative-medicine healer named Dr. Dragan David Dabić. (Karadžić had previously received training as a psychiatrist.) This expert on what he called "Human Quantum Energy" had his own website and even presented at conferences.

How did one of the world's most wanted men effectively disappear in plain sight for 12 years? He had grown a very full beard and wore thick glasses as a disguise, and frequented a neighborhood bar where a photo of him, in his earlier life, hung proudly on the wall...and yet, he was undetected even by those who saw him every day. It's alleged that at least some Serb authorities knew of his whereabouts, but, considering him a hero, refused to identify or arrest him.

In May of 2011, the last "most wanted" criminal of the conflict—Karadžić's military leader, General Ratko Mladić—was found and arrested. As of this writing, Karadžić and Mladić are standing trial in The Hague.

Montenegro and Kosovo: Europe's Newest Nations

After the departures of Croatia, Slovenia, Bosnia-Herzegovina, and Macedonia (which peacefully seceded in 1991), by the late 1990s only two of the original six republics of Yugoslavia remained united: Serbia (which still included the provinces of Kosovo and Vojvodina) and Montenegro. But in 2003, Montenegro began a gradual secession process that ended when it peacefully tiptoed its way to independence in 2006. (For all the details, see "Montenegro: Birth of a Nation" on page 385.)

The Yugoslav crisis concluded in the place where it began: the Serbian province of Kosovo. Kosovo's majority Albanians rebelled against Serbian rule in 1998, only to become victims of Milošević's ethnic cleansing (until US General Wesley Clark's NATO warplanes forced the Serbian army out). For nearly a decade, Kosovo remained a UN protectorate within Serbia—still nominally part of Serbia, but for all practical purposes separate and self-governing (under the watchful eye of the UN). Reading between the lines, Serbs point out that independent Kosovo quickly became a very close ally of the US, allowing one of Europe's biggest military bases—Camp Bondsteel—to be built in their territory.

On Sunday, February 17, 2008, Kosovo's provisional government unilaterally declared its independence as the "Republic of Kosovo." The US, UK, France, Germany, and several other countries quickly recognized the new republic, but the UN didn't officially endorse it. Serbia opposed the move, and was backed by several countries involved in their own internal disputes with would-be breakaway regions: Russia (areas of Georgia), China (Taiwan), and Spain (Catalunya, the Basque Country, and others).

The new Kosovo government carefully stated that it would protect the rights of its minorities, including Serbs. But the Serbs deeply believed that losing Kosovo would also mean losing their grip on their own history and culture. They also feared for the safety of the Serb minority there (and potential retribution from Albanians who had for so long been oppressed themselves). For a few tense months, international observers watched nervously, worrying that war might erupt in the region once more. There have been a few scuffles, especially in some of the larger Serb settlements. But Kosovo's independence appears to be holding—representing, perhaps, the final chapter of a long and ugly Yugoslav succession. Kosovo is the seventh country to emerge from the breakup of Yugoslavia.

YUGOSLAVIA

FINDING THEIR WAY:
THE FORMER YUGOSLAV REPUBLICS

Today, Slovenia and Croatia are as stable as many Western European nations, Bosnia-Herzegovina has made great strides in putting itself back together, Macedonia feels closer to Bulgaria than to Belgrade, and the sixth and seventh countries to emerge from "Yugoslavia"—Montenegro and Kosovo—are fledgling democracies.

And yet, nagging questions remain. Making the wars even more difficult to grasp is the uncomfortable reality that there were no clear-cut "good guys" and "bad guys"—just a lot of ugliness on all sides. In the war between the Croats and the Serbs, it's tempting for Americans to take Croatia's "side" because we saw them in the role of victims first; because they're Catholic, so they seem more "like us" than the Orthodox Serbs; and because we admire their striving for independence. But in the streets and the trenches, it was never that straightforward. The Serbs believe that *they* were the victims first—back in World War II, when their grandparents were executed in Croat-run Ustaše concentration camps. And when Croats retook the Serb-occupied areas in 1995, they were every bit as brutal as the Serbs had been a few years before. Both sides resorted to genocide, both sides had victims, and both sides had victimizers.

Even so, many can't help but look for victims and villains. During the conflict in Bosnia-Herzegovina, several prominent and respected reporters began to show things from one "side" more than the others—specifically, depicting the Bosniaks (Muslims) as victims. This reawakened an old debate in the journalism community: Should reporters above all remain impartial, even if "showing all sides" might make them feel complicit in ongoing atrocities?

As for villains, it's easy to point fingers at Slobodan Milošević, Radovan Karadžić, Ratko Mladić, and other political or military leaders who have been arrested and tried at The Hague. Others condemn the late Croatian President Franjo Tuđman, who, it's now known, secretly conspired with Milošević to redraw the maps of their respective territories. And of course, the foot soldiers of those monstrous men—who followed their immoral orders—cannot be excused.

And yet, you can't paint an entire group with one brush. While some Bosnian Serbs did horrifying things, only a small fraction of all Bosnian Serbs participated in the atrocities. Travelers to this region quickly realize that the vast majority of people they meet here never wanted these wars. And so finally comes the inevitable question: Why did any of it happen in the first place?

Explanations tend to gravitate to two extremes. Some observers consider this part of the world to be inherently warlike—a place where deep-seated hatreds and age-old ethnic passions unavoidably flare up. This point of view sees an air of inevitability about the recent wars...and the potential for future conflict. And it's hard to deny that the residents of the region tend to obsess about exacting vengeance for wrongdoings (real or imagined) that happened many decades or even centuries in the past.

For others, however, this theory is an insulting oversimplification. Sure, animosity has long simmered in the Balkans, but for centuries before World War II, the various groups had lived more or less in harmony. The critical component of these wars—what made them escalate so quickly and so appallingly—was the single-minded, self-serving actions of a few selfish leaders who shamelessly and aggressively exploited existing resentments to advance their own interests. It wasn't until Milošević, Karadžić, Tuđman, and others expertly manipulated the people's grudges that the region fell into war. By vigorously fanning the embers of ethnic discord, polluting the airwaves with hate-filled propaganda, and carefully controlling media coverage of the escalating violence, these leaders turned what could have been a healthy political debate into a holocaust.

Tension still exists throughout the former Yugoslavia—especially in the areas that were most war-torn. Croatians and Slovenes continue to split hairs over silly border disputes, Bosnia-Herzegovina groans under the crippling inefficiency of four autonomous governments, and Serbs ominously warn that they'll take up arms to reclaim Kosovo. Observers can't deny the painful possibility that, just as grudges held over from World War II were quickly ignited in the 1990s, holdover tensions from the recent wars could someday ignite a new wave of conflict. When the people of this region encounter other Yugoslavs in their travels, they instantly evaluate each other's accent to determine: Are they one of us, or one of them?

For the visitor, it's tricky to get an impartial take on the current situation, or even on historical "facts." As the people you meet will tell you their stories, sometimes it's just as important to listen to the tone and subtext of their tale as it is to try to judge its veracity. Are they preaching a message of reconciliation or one of provocation?

With time, hard feelings are fading. The appealing prospect of European Union membership is a powerful motivator for groups to set aside their differences and cooperate. The younger generations don't look back—teenaged Slovenes no longer learn Serbo-Croatian, have only known life in an independent little country, and get bored (and a little irritated) when their old-fashioned parents wax nostalgic about the days of a united Yugoslavia. A middle-aged Slovene friend of mine thinks fondly of his months of compulsory service in the Yugoslav People's Army, when his unit was made up of Slovenes, Croats, Serbs, Bosniaks, Albanians, Macedonians, and Montenegrins—all of them compatriots, and all good friends. To the young Yugoslavs, ethnic differences didn't matter. My friend still often visits with an army buddy from Dubrovnik—600 miles away, not long ago part of the same nation—and wishes there had been a way to keep the country all together. But he says, optimistically, "I look forward to the day when the other former Yugoslav republics also join the European Union. Then, in a way, we will all be united once again."

PRACTICALITIES

This chapter covers the practical skills of European travel: how to get tourist information, pay for things, sightsee efficiently, find good-value accommodations, eat affordably but well, use technology wisely, and get between destinations smoothly. To study ahead and round out your knowledge, check out "Resources."

Tourist Information

BEFORE YOUR TRIP

National tourist offices are a wealth of information. Before your trip, visit each country's website for events, activities, and attractions by region. Explore information on Croatia's islands and active tourism (tel. 212/279-8672, http://us.croatia.hr), Slovenia's outdoor activities and tourist farms (www.slovenia.info), and Bosnia-Herzegovina's hiking opportunities and well-preserved historical sites (www.bhtourism.ba).

IN CROATIA, SLOVENIA, AND BOSNIA-HERZEGOVINA

A good first stop in every town is generally the tourist information office—abbreviated **TI** in this book (though locally, you may see them marked *TZ*, for *turistička zajednica*). Throughout Croatia and Slovenia, you'll find TIs are usually well-organized and always have an English-speaking staff; in Bosnia and Montenegro, TIs can be more hit-or-miss.

TIs are good places to confirm opening times, pick up a city map, and get information on public transit (including bus and train schedules), walking tours, special events, and nightlife. Prepare a list of questions and a proposed plan to double-check. Many TIs have information on the entire country or at least the region, so try to pick up maps for destinations you'll be visiting later in your trip.

Local TIs are not allowed to make money by running a room-booking service. But they can almost always give you a list of local hotels and private rooms, and if they're not too busy, they can call around for you to check on availability. If you're in a pinch and need a room, online booking sites are helpful, and every major town has at least one travel agency with a room-booking service.

Travel Tips

Emergency and Medical Help: For medical or other emergencies, dial 112 in Croatia, Slovenia, Montenegro, and Bosnia-Herzegovina. If you get sick, do as the locals do and go to a pharmacist for advice. Or ask at your hotel for help—they'll know of the nearest medical and emergency services.

Theft or Loss: To replace a passport, you'll need to go in person to the appropriate embassy or consulate (see page 797). If your credit and debit cards disappear, cancel and replace them (see "Damage Control for Lost Cards" on page 756). File a police report, either on the spot or within a day or two; you'll need it to submit an insurance claim for lost or stolen rail passes or travel gear, and it can help with replacing your passport or credit and debit cards. For more information, see www.ricksteves.com/help. To minimize the effects of loss, back up your digital photos and other files frequently.

Borders: Even though Croatia and Slovenia are both in the EU, you'll still have to stop and show your passport when you cross the border between them (or when crossing into Bosnia-Herzegovina or Montenegro). But whether by car, train, or bus, you'll find that border crossings are generally a nonevent: Flash your passport, maybe wait a few minutes, and move on. Drivers may be asked to show proof of car insurance ("green card"), so be sure you have it when you pick up your rental car. Because Slovenia belongs to the Schengen open-borders agreement, you don't have to stop or show a passport when crossing between Slovenia and Austria, Italy, or Hungary. (Croatia may join Schengen as early as 2017.) Crossing from Croatia into Bosnia-Herzegovina or Montenegro is fairly straightforward, if occasionally a bit slow. When you change countries, you change phone cards, postage stamps, and, in most cases, money.

Time Zones: Croatia, Slovenia, Bosnia-Herzegovina, and Montenegro, like most of continental Europe, are generally six/nine hours ahead of the East/West Coasts of the US. The exceptions are the beginning and end of Daylight Saving Time: Europe "springs forward" the last Sunday in March (two weeks after most of North America) and "falls back" the last Sunday in October (one week before North America). For a handy online time converter, try www.timeanddate.com/worldclock.

Business Hours: Particularly in seasonal resort areas along the coast, business hours can be very unpredictable—dictated entirely by demand. A shop may be open daily from 9:00 to 24:00 in August, with its hours becoming progressively shorter in the shoulder season until it closes entirely in mid-October. In larger, less touristy cities and towns—and in most of Slovenia—hours are a bit more predictable (typically Mon-Fri from around 8:00 or 9:00 until 17:00, Sat mornings from 8:00 or 9:00 until 12:00 or 13:00, and closed Sun). In both Croatia and Slovenia, you will find a few businesses open on Sundays, but generally only in touristy areas or in large cities (especially near bus or train stations). Friday and Saturday evenings are rowdy; Sunday evenings are quiet.

Watt's Up? Europe's electrical system is 220 volts, instead of North America's 110 volts. Most newer electronics (such as laptops, battery chargers, and hair dryers) convert automatically, so you won't need a converter, but you will need an adapter plug with two round prongs, sold inexpensively at travel stores in the US. Avoid bringing older appliances that don't automatically convert voltage; instead, buy a cheap replacement in Europe.

Discounts: While discounts are not listed in this book, youths (under 18) and students (with International Student Identity Cards, www.isic.org) often get discounts—but only by asking.

Online Translation Tips: You can use Google's Chrome browser (available free at www.google.com/chrome) to instantly translate websites. With one click, the page appears in (very rough) English translation. You can also paste the URL of the site into the translation window at www.google.com/translate. The Google Translate app converts spoken English into most European languages (and vice versa) and can also translate text it "reads" with your mobile device's camera.

Smoking Bans: Both Croatia and Slovenia have enacted

smoking bans in most public places, though patrons at outdoor tables can still smoke. Bosnia-Herzegovina and Montenegro have no such bans, so be ready for lots of smoke, indoors and out, in those countries.

Money

This section offers advice on how to pay for purchases on your trip (including getting cash from ATMs and paying with plastic), dealing with lost or stolen cards, VAT (sales tax) refunds, and tipping.

WHAT TO BRING

Bring both a credit card and a debit card. You'll use the debit card at cash machines (ATMs) to withdraw local cash for most purchases, and the credit card to pay for larger items. Some travelers carry a third card, in case one gets demagnetized or eaten by a temperamental machine.

For an emergency stash, bring several hundred dollars in hard cash in $20 bills. If you have to exchange the bills, go to a bank; avoid using currency exchange booths because of their lousy rates and/or outrageous (and often hard-to-spot) fees.

CASH

Cash is just as desirable in Europe as it is at home. Small businesses (hotels, restaurants, mom-and-pop cafés, shops, etc.) prefer that you pay your bills with cash. Some vendors will charge you extra for using a credit card, some won't accept foreign credit cards, and some won't take any credit cards at all. Cash is the best—and sometimes only—way to pay for bus fare, taxis, and local guides.

Throughout Europe, ATMs are the standard way for travelers to get cash. They work just like they do at home. To withdraw money from an ATM (known as a *Bankomat* in Croatia and Slovenia), you'll need a debit card (ideally with a Visa or MasterCard logo for maximum usability), plus a PIN code (numeric and four digits). For increased security, shield the keypad when entering your PIN code, and don't use an ATM if anything on the front of the machine looks loose or damaged (a sign that someone may have attached a "skimming" device to capture account information). Try to withdraw large sums of money to reduce the number of per-transaction bank fees you'll pay.

When possible, use ATMs located outside banks—a thief is less likely to target a cash machine near surveillance cameras, and

Exchange Rates

Slovenia and Montenegro both use the euro, while Croatia and Bosnia-Herzegovina have different currencies. (Check www. oanda.com for the latest exchange rates.)

Croatia

Croatia's currency is called the kuna (abbreviated kn locally, HRK internationally):

7 Croatian kunas (kn) = about $1

To roughly convert Croatian kunas into dollars, divide by seven (e.g., 7 kn = about $1; 70 kn = about $10; 200 kn = about $29).

A kuna is broken into 100 smaller units, called lipas. There are coins of 1, 2, 5, 10, 20, and 50 lipas; and 1, 2, and 5 kunas.

Croatia doesn't officially use the euro, and many vendors there (frustrated by thousands of cruise passengers who don't want to visit an ATM) flat-out refuse to take euros. If you try to spend euros in Croatia, don't be surprised if you're turned away. Confusingly, most hotels quote prices in euros for the convenience of their international guests. But they'll convert the bill to kunas to determine your final payment.

Slovenia and Montenegro

Slovenia and Montenegro use the euro currency:

1 euro (€) = about $1.10

To convert prices in euros to dollars, add 10 percent: €20 is about $22, €50 is about $55. Just like the dollar, one euro (€) is broken down into 100 cents. Coins range from €0.01 to €2, and bills from €5 to €500.

Bosnia-Herzegovina

In this country, you'll use the Bosnian convertible mark (abbreviated KM locally, BAM internationally):

1.80 Bosnian convertible mark (KM) = about $1

To very roughly determine prices in US dollars, subtract about half (for example, 10 KM is about $5, and 50 KM is about $25). A convertible mark is broken down into 100 feninga. There are bills of 1, 5, 10, 20, 50, 100, and 200 marks, and coins of 1, 2, and 5 marks and 5, 10, 20, and 50 feninga. Most Bosnian merchants are willing to take euros, and some (especially in Mostar) will also accept Croatian kunas.

So, that 50-kn bottle of Croatian wine is about $7, the €25 Slovenian feast is about $27, the 60-KM Bosnian coffee set is around $30, and the 300-kn taxi ride through Zagreb is...uh-oh.

if your card is munched by a machine, you can go inside for help. Stay away from "independent" ATMs such as Travelex, Euronet, YourCash, Cardpoint, and Cashzone, which charge huge commissions, have terrible exchange rates, and may try to trick users with "dynamic currency conversion" (described at the end of "Credit and Debit Cards," next). Although you can use a credit card to withdraw cash at an ATM, this comes with high bank fees and only makes sense in an emergency.

Because the countries in this region have different currencies, you may wind up with leftover cash. Coins can't be exchanged once you leave the country, so spend them before you cross the border. Bills are easy to convert to the "new" country's currency, but remember that regular banks have the best rates for the conversion. Post offices and train stations usually change money if you can't get to a bank.

While traveling, if you want to monitor your accounts online to detect any unauthorized transactions, be sure to use a secure connection (see page 775).

Pickpockets target tourists. To safeguard your cash, wear a money belt—a pouch with a strap that you buckle around your waist like a belt and tuck under your clothes. Keep your cash, credit cards, and passport secure in your money belt, and carry only a day's spending money in your front pocket.

CREDIT AND DEBIT CARDS

For purchases, Visa and MasterCard are more commonly accepted than American Express. Just like at home, credit or debit cards work easily at larger hotels, restaurants, and shops. I typically use my debit card to withdraw cash to pay for most purchases. I use my credit card sparingly: to book hotel reservations, to buy advance tickets for events or sights, to cover major expenses (such as car rentals or plane tickets), and to pay for things online or near the end of my trip (to avoid another visit to the ATM). While you could instead use a debit card for these purchases, a credit card offers a greater degree of fraud protection.

Ask Your Credit- or Debit-Card Company: Before your trip, contact the company that issued your debit or credit cards.

• Confirm your **card will work overseas,** and alert them that you'll be using it in Europe; otherwise, they may deny transactions if they perceive unusual spending patterns.

• Ask for the specifics on transaction **fees.** When you use your credit or debit card—either for purchases or ATM withdrawals—you'll typically be charged additional "international transaction" fees of up to 3 percent (1 percent is normal) plus $5 per transaction. If your card's fees seem high, consider getting a different card just for your trip: Capital One (www.capitalone.com) and most credit unions have low-to-no international fees.

• Verify your daily ATM **withdrawal limit,** and if necessary, ask your bank to adjust it. I prefer a high limit that allows me to take out more cash at each ATM stop and save on bank fees; some travelers prefer to set a lower limit in case their card is stolen. Note that foreign banks also set maximum withdrawal amounts for their ATMs.

• Get your bank's emergency **phone number** in the US (but not its 800 number, which isn't accessible from overseas) to call collect if you have a problem.

• Ask for your credit card's **PIN** in case you need to make an emergency cash withdrawal or encounter Europe's chip-and-PIN system; the bank will not reveal your PIN over the phone, so allow time for it to be mailed to you.

Chip and PIN: While much of Europe is shifting to a chip-and-PIN security system for credit and debit cards, the countries in this region still use the old magnetic-stripe technology. (European chip-and-PIN cards are embedded with an electronic security chip, and require a four-digit PIN to make a purchase.) If you happen to encounter chip and PIN, it will probably be at automated payment machines, such as those at toll roads or unattended gas pumps. On the outside chance that a machine won't take your card, find a cashier who can make your card work (they can print a receipt for you to sign), or find a machine that takes cash. Most travelers who use only magnetic-stripe cards don't run into problems. Still, it pays to carry local cash; remember, you can always use an ATM to withdraw cash with your magnetic-stripe card.

US banks are now issuing credit cards with chips. Many of these are not true chip-and-PIN cards, but instead are chip-and-signature cards, for which your signature verifies your identity. These cards also have a magnetic stripe and should work in Europe for live transactions and at most payment machines, but won't work for offline transactions such as at unattended gas pumps. If you're concerned, ask if your bank offers a true chip-and-PIN card. Andrews Federal Credit Union (www.andrewsfcu.org) and the State Department Federal Credit Union (www.sdfcu.org) offer these cards and are open to all US residents.

Dynamic Currency Conversion: If merchants or hoteliers offer to convert your purchase price into dollars (called dynamic currency conversion, or DCC), refuse this "service." You'll pay even more in fees for the expensive convenience of seeing your charge in dollars. If your receipt shows the total in dollars only, ask for the transaction to be processed in the local currency. If the clerk refuses, pay in cash—or mark the receipt "local currency not offered" and dispute the DCC charges with your bank.

Some ATMs and retailers try to confuse customers by presenting DCC in misleading terms. If an ATM offers to "lock in" or "guarantee" your conversion rate, choose "proceed without conversion." Other prompts might state, "You can be charged in dollars: Press YES for dollars, NO for euros" (or "kunas" or "Bosnian convertible marks"). Always choose the local currency in these situations.

DAMAGE CONTROL FOR LOST CARDS

If you lose your credit, debit, or ATM card, you can stop people from using your card by reporting the loss immediately to the respective global customer-assistance centers. Call these 24-hour US numbers collect: Visa (tel. 303/967-1096), MasterCard (tel. 636/722-7111), or American Express (tel. 336/393-1111). In Croatia, to make a collect call to the US, dial 0800-220-111. In Bosnia, dial 00-800-0010. In Slovenia, dial 1180—but this number only works from Slovenian phone numbers. It's not possible to make collect calls from Montenegro—dial the above numbers direct. Press zero or stay on the line for an English-speaking operator. European toll-free numbers (listed by country) can be found at the websites for Visa and MasterCard.

Try to have this information ready: full card number, whether you are the primary or secondary cardholder, the cardholder's name exactly as printed on the card, billing address, home phone number, circumstances of the loss or theft, and identification verification (your birth date, your mother's maiden name, or your Social Security number—memorize this, don't carry a copy). If you are the secondary cardholder, you'll also need to provide the primary cardholder's identification-verification details. You can generally receive a temporary card within two or three business days in Europe (see www.ricksteves.com/help for more).

If you report your loss within two days, you typically won't be responsible for any unauthorized transactions on your account, although many banks charge a liability fee of $50.

TIPPING

A decade ago, tipping was unheard of in Croatia and Slovenia. But then came the tourists. Today, some waiters and taxi drivers have learned to expect Yankee-sized tips when they spot an American. Tipping the appropriate amount—not feeling stingy, but also not contributing to the overtipping epidemic—can be nerve-wracking to conscientious visitors. Relax! Many locals still don't tip at all, so any tip is appreciated. As in the US, the proper amount depends on your resources, tipping philosophy, and the circumstances, but some general guidelines apply.

Restaurants: You don't need to tip if you order your food at a counter. At restaurants that have a waitstaff, round up the bill 5-10 percent after a good meal. For details on tipping in restaurants, see page 772.

Taxis: For a typical ride, round up your fare about 5 percent (for instance, if the fare is 71 kn, pay 75 kn). If the cabbie hauls your bags and zips you to the airport to help you catch your flight, you might want to toss in a little more. But if you feel like you're being driven in circles or otherwise ripped off, skip the tip.

Services: In general, if someone in the service industry does a super job for you, a small tip of a euro (or the local equivalent) is appropriate...but not required. If you're not sure whether (or how much) to tip for a service, ask a local for advice.

GETTING A VAT REFUND

Wrapped into the purchase price of your souvenirs is a Value-Added Tax (VAT) of 25 percent in Croatia, 22 percent in Slovenia, 17 percent in Bosnia, and 19 percent in Montenegro ("VAT" is called "PDV" in this part of the world). You're entitled to get most of that tax back if you purchase more than a certain amount (for example, 740 kn in Croatia, €175.01 in Slovenia) of goods at a store that participates in the VAT refund scheme. Typically, you must ring up the minimum at a single retailer—you can't add up your purchases from various shops to reach the required amount.

Getting your refund is usually straightforward and, if you buy a substantial amount of souvenirs, well worth the hassle. (Note that if the store ships the goods to your US home, VAT is not assessed on your purchase.) You'll need to:

Get the paperwork. Have the merchant completely fill out the necessary refund document. You'll have to present your passport. Get the paperwork done before you leave the store to ensure you'll have everything you need (including your original sales receipt).

Get your stamp at the border or airport. Process your VAT document with the customs agent at your last stop in the country in which you made your purchase (or, if you bought it in the European Union, at your last stop in the European Union), such as at the airport. Arrive an additional hour before you need to check in for your flight to allow time to find the local customs office—and to stand in line. It's best to keep your purchases in your carry-on. If they're too large or dangerous to carry on (such as knives), pack them in your checked bags and alert the check-in agent. You'll be sent (with your tagged bag) to a customs desk outside security; someone will examine your bag, stamp your paperwork, and put your bag on the belt. You're not supposed to use your purchased goods before you leave. If you show up at customs wearing your brand-new Slovenian shoes, officials might look the other way—or deny you a refund.

Collect your refund. You'll need to return your stamped document to the retailer or its representative. Many merchants work with a service, such as Global Blue or Premier Tax Free, that have offices at major airports, ports, or border crossings (either before or after security, probably strategically located near a duty-free shop). These services, which extract a 4 percent fee, can refund your money immediately in cash or credit your card (within two billing cycles). If the retailer handles VAT refunds directly, it's up to you to contact the merchant for your refund. You can mail the documents from home, or more quickly, from your point of departure (using an envelope you've prepared in advance or one that's been provided by the merchant). You'll then have to wait—it could take months.

CUSTOMS FOR AMERICAN SHOPPERS

You are allowed to take home $800 worth of items per person duty-free, once every 31 days. You can take home many processed and packaged foods: vacuum-packed cheeses, dried herbs, jams, baked goods, candy, chocolate, oil, vinegar, mustard, and honey. Fresh fruits and vegetables and most meats are not allowed, with exceptions for some canned items. As for alcohol, you can bring in one liter duty-free (it can be packed securely in your checked luggage, along with any other liquid-containing items).

To bring alcohol (or liquid-packed foods) in your carry-on bag on your flight home, buy it at a duty-free shop at the airport. You'll increase your odds of getting it onto a connecting flight if it's packaged in a "STEB"—a secure, tamper-evident bag. But stay away from liquids in opaque, ceramic, or metallic containers, which usually cannot be successfully screened (STEB or no STEB).

For details on allowable goods, customs rules, and duty rates, visit http://help.cbp.gov.

Sightseeing

Sightseeing can be hard work. Use these tips to make your visits to Croatia's and Slovenia's finest sights meaningful, fun, efficient, and painless.

PLAN AHEAD

Set up an itinerary that allows you to fit in all your must-see sights. For a one-stop look at opening hours, see the "At a Glance" sidebars for Istria, Dubrovnik, and Ljubljana. The hours at sights tend to fluctuate with demand from season to season (especially in coastal towns), but you can easily confirm the latest by checking with the TI or museum websites.

Don't put off visiting a must-see sight—you never know when a place will close unexpectedly for a holiday, strike, or restoration. Many museums are closed or have reduced hours at least a few days a year, especially on holidays such as Christmas, New Year's, and Labor Day (May 1). A list of holidays is on page 798; check online for possible museum closures during your trip. In summer, some sights may stay open late. Off-season, most museums have shorter hours.

Going at the right time helps avoid crowds. This book offers tips on the best times to see specific sights. Try visiting popular sights very early or very late. Evening visits are usually peaceful, with fewer crowds.

Study up. To avoid redundancy, many cultural or historical details are explained for one sight in this book and not repeated for another; to get the full picture, read the entire chapter for each destination before you visit.

AT SIGHTS

Here's what you can typically expect:

Entering: Be warned that you may not be allowed to enter if you arrive 30 to 60 minutes before closing time. And guards start ushering people out well before the actual closing time, so don't save the best for last.

Photography: If the museum's photo policy isn't clearly posted, ask a guard. Generally, taking photos without a flash or tripod is allowed. Some sights ban photos altogether.

Temporary Exhibits: Museums may show special exhibits in addition to their permanent collection. Some exhibits are included in the entry price, while others come at an extra cost (which you may have to pay even if you don't want to see the exhibit).

Expect Changes: Artwork can be on tour, on loan, out sick, or shifted at the whim of the curator. Pick up any available free floor plans as you enter, and ask museum staff if you can't find a particular item.

Audioguides and Apps: Many sights rent audioguides, which generally offer recorded descriptions in English (sometimes included in the price, otherwise about $6-8). If you bring your own earbuds, you can enjoy better sound and avoid holding the device to your ear. To save money, bring a Y-jack and share one audioguide with your travel partner. Increasingly, museums and sights offer apps—often free—that you can download to your mobile device (check their websites).

Services: Important sights may have an on-site café or cafeteria (usually a good place to rejuvenate during a long visit). The WCs at sights are free and generally clean.

Before Leaving: At the gift shop, scan the postcard rack or thumb through a guidebook to be sure you haven't overlooked something that you'd like to see.

Every sight or museum offers more than what is covered in

this book. Use the information in this book as an introduction—not the final word.

Sleeping

The accommodations scene in Croatia and Slovenia is quirky and complicated. In most Croatian destinations, you have two basic choices: either a big hotel or what locals call "private accommodations"—a rented apartment (*apartman*, plural *apartmani*) or a room in a private home (*soba*, pronounced SOH-bah; plural *sobe*, SOH-bay). I've explained the ins and outs of each in this section.

I favor accommodations and restaurants that are convenient to your sightseeing activities. I look for places that are friendly, comfortable, clean, professional-feeling, English-speaking, relatively quiet at night, and family-run. A major feature of this book is its extensive and opinionated listing of good-value rooms. My favorites are small, family-run hotels (which are rare) and friendly local people who rent "hotelesque" private rooms without a reception desk (which are, thankfully, abundant). I'm more impressed by local character, a handy location, and a fun-loving philosophy than flat-screen TVs and a pricey laundry service. Obviously, a place meeting every criterion is unusual, and all of my recommendations fall short of perfection. But I've listed the best values I could find for each price range.

Book your accommodations well in advance if you'll be traveling during busy times. See page 798 for a list of major holidays and festivals; for tips on making reservations, see page 766.

RATES AND DEALS

In Croatia, most hotels are outrageously expensive, but private accommodations are an excellent value. My recommendations range from $15 bunks to $500-plus splurges, but most cluster somewhere in between: For a well-located standard double room in peak season on the Croatian coast, plan on spending $150-250 in a big resort hotel; $80-130 in a small hotel or a hotelesque private room or apartment (with your own bathroom, TV, and other amenities); or $50-80 for a more basic private room with a shared bathroom. While most Croatian accommodations quote their rates in euros, when you check out, payment is expected in kunas (or, occasionally, by credit card).

Slovenia has a wider range of affordable small hotels (about

$90-130 in Ljubljana, and $70-90 in small towns and the countryside), which make private accommodations a lesser value there.

I've described my recommended accommodations using a Sleep Code (see sidebar). Rates vary wildly by season, with August being the most expensive. Short stays (of less than three nights) are discouraged, especially in peak season. Expect to pay 20-50 percent extra if you're staying just one or two nights, and don't be surprised if some places have a multinight minimum in summer. But if you can fill a gap in their reservations schedule, they might waive this surcharge.

Three or four people can save money by requesting one big room. Traveling alone can be expensive: A single room is often only 20 percent cheaper than a double.

For most of my recommended accommodations, I provide a website (which may have a built-in booking form) and an email address; you can expect a response in English within a day (and often sooner). Always book directly with your host—it saves you and them money (see the sidebar on page 765).

As explained in the Sleep Code, for most accommodations I've listed three prices: high, middle, and low season. If you're on a budget, it's smart to email several hotels to ask for their best price. Comparison-shop and make your choice. Many larger hotel chains use "dynamic pricing," a computer-generated system that predicts the demand for particular days and sets prices accordingly: High-demand days can be more than double the price of low-demand days. This makes it impossible for a guidebook to list anything more accurate than a wide range of prices. I regret this trend. In general, for these hotels I've listed only the top-season price (for the sake of comparison); for the specific rate, go on their website and punch in your dates. While you can assume that hotels listed in this book are good, it's difficult to say which are the better values unless you email to confirm the price.

In general, prices can soften if you do any of the following: offer to pay cash, stay at least three nights, or mention this book. You can also try asking for a cheaper room or a discount, or offer to skip breakfast.

HELPFUL HINTS

Get help finding your accommodations. On the Croatian coast, most of my recommendations are small family homes with just a few rooms, often tucked up narrow lanes from the main square or main drag. As these can be tricky to find, use the maps in this book, get careful directions from your host, and ask anyone you pass as you're looking. If they offer to come meet you at the ferry... accept! Even if the *soba* owner is not there to meet you, someone at the bar next door can track him or her down for you.

Sleep Code

To help you sort easily through my listings, I've divided the accommodations into three categories based on the price for a double room with bath during high season:

$$$	**Higher Priced**
$$	**Moderately Priced**
$	**Lower Priced**

I always rate hostels as $, whether or not they have double rooms, because they have the cheapest beds in town.

Prices can change without notice; verify the hotel's current rates online or by email.

Accommodations throughout this region—especially in Croatia—tend to fluctuate wildly by season. For most, I have listed multiple price ranges, separated by a slash—signifying top season (often July-Aug), middle season (typically May-June and Sept-mid-Oct), and low season (mid-Oct-April). However, keep in mind that the specific dates when rates change can vary from hotel to hotel, so these ranges are intended to help you roughly compare your options; for specific rates, check the accommodations' websites or email them a request. For the best prices, always book directly with the hotel.

When a price range is given for a type of room (such as double rooms listing for €80-100), it generally means the price fluctuates with the size of room. A modest tourist tax (roughly €1/person, per night) is added to room rates.

B.Y.O.B. (bring—or buy—your own breakfast). Many of my accommodations don't provide breakfast. In each town, I've recommended some places to buy your own. But if you'd like a simple "picnic breakfast" in your room, bring along or buy some individual instant coffee pouches (like Nescafé or Starbucks Via) for a few kunas.

Bring earplugs. Discos and nightclubs fill the old town centers of many cities in this book—including Dubrovnik, Split, and Ljubljana. I've noted the specific hotels that suffer the worst noise. If you're a light sleeper, make a point of requesting a quiet room.

Expect odors. Croatia and Slovenia both have a smoking ban for most accommodations (though larger hotels may have some designated smoking rooms). However, guests can still smoke on balconies and other outdoor areas, so it may not be possible to completely escape a somewhat smoky room.

Throughout this region, many accommodations have Yugoslav-era septic-tank systems that aren't properly vented. On rainy

Abbreviations

To pack maximum information into minimum space, I use the following code to describe accommodations in this book. Prices listed are per room, not per person.

- **S** = Single room (or price for one person in a double).
- **D** = Double or Twin room. Double beds can be two twins sheeted together and are usually big enough for nonromantic couples.
- **T** = Triple (generally a double bed with a single).
- **Q** = Quad (usually two double beds; adding an extra child's bed to a T is usually cheaper).
- **b** = Private bathroom with toilet and shower or tub.

According to this code, a couple staying at a "Db-€90/€70/€60" place in Dubrovnik would pay a total of €90 (about $99) in July and August, €70 (about $77) in spring and fall, or €60 (about $66) in winter for a double room with a private bathroom. At hotels, unless otherwise noted, breakfast is included, staff speak basic English, and credit cards are accepted. Most private accommodations come with several flights of stairs; unless I note "elevator," assume you'll have to climb stairs to your room. Note that private accommodations rarely accept credit cards or include breakfast; virtually all the ones I list are run by English-speakers, but a few proprietors may rely on relatives or neighbors to help translate.

Almost every accommodation I list has free Wi-Fi for guests (if they don't, I've noted it in the listing).

days, an unpleasant sewage smell may drift into rooms. This isn't harmful, but it's impossible to predict and can be unpleasant. Nothing can be done about it, so don't bother complaining (unless you want to try to switch to a less-smelly room).

Perhaps because of poor ventilation—or because they tend to be located in musty old stone buildings—many hotels and *sobe* in Croatia use heavily perfumed air fresheners in their rooms. It's usually easy to locate and unplug these, but if you are very sensitive to fragrances, try asking your *soba* host to remove them before you arrive.

Bring bug spray. Window screens are rare in this area, so in warm weather be prepared to share your room with mosquitoes and other bugs.

Shower smartly. If there seems to be no hot water, try flipping the switch with a picture of a water tank, usually next to the light switch. (Ideally, discover this switch long before you need to shower, and keep it on—otherwise you'll have to wait 20-30 minutes for the water to heat up.) In many *sobe*, the hot-water tank is tiny—barely big enough for one American-length shower. So two people traveling together may want to practice the "navy shower" method (douse yourself, turn off water, soap up, then turn water back on for a quick rinse)...or the second person may be in for a chilly surprise. The incredibly high water pressure in most Croatian showers just makes the hot water go that much faster (turn the faucet on only partway to help stretch the precious hot water).

In private accommodations and some hotels, towels aren't replaced, so hang them up to reuse. The cord that dangles over the tub or shower in big resort hotels is not a clothesline—you pull it if you've fallen and can't get up.

General Tips—From Arrival to Checkout: If you're arriving in the morning, your room probably won't be ready. Drop your bag safely at the hotel and dive right into sightseeing.

Hoteliers and *soba* hosts can be a great help and source of advice. Most know their city well, and can assist you with everything from public transit and airport connections to finding a good restaurant, the nearest launderette, or a Wi-Fi hotspot.

Even at the best places, mechanical breakdowns occur: Air-conditioning malfunctions, sinks leak, hot water turns cold, and toilets won't flush. Report your concerns clearly and calmly. For more complicated problems, don't expect instant results.

To guard against theft in your room, keep valuables out of sight. A few rooms come with a safe, and other hotels have safes at the front desk. I've never bothered using one.

Checkout can pose problems if surprise charges pop up on your bill. If you settle your bill the afternoon before you leave, you'll have time to discuss and address any points of contention.

Above all, keep a positive attitude. Remember, you're on vacation. If your accommodations are a disappointment, spend more time out enjoying the places you came to see.

TYPES OF ACCOMMODATIONS
Private Accommodations (*Sobe* and Apartments)

Private accommodations offer travelers a characteristic and money-saving alternative for a fraction of the price of a hotel. You have two options: *sobe* (rooms) or *apartmani* (apartments). Often, a house renting both types is called a *vila* or *villa*—like a small guesthouse or pension.

Often run by empty-nesters, private accommodations are similar to British bed-and-breakfasts...minus the breakfast (ask your host about the best nearby breakfast spot). Generally the more you pay, the more privacy and amenities you get: private bathroom, TV, air-conditioning, kitchenette, and so on. The simplest *sobe* allow you to experience Croatia on the cheap, at nearly youth-hostel

Always Book Direct

For the best price, send your email straight to the *soba* host or hotelier who rents the rooms. The rates I list in this book assume you're booking directly.

You may be tempted to book through a third-party website (such as the popular Booking.com), but—because these take a hefty commission—your host will often charge you higher rates to make up the difference.

The importance of booking direct can't be overstated. Several *soba* hosts I list in this book told me that some of my readers have emailed them to check availability, and then proceeded to book through a third party. This makes zero sense and costs everybody more money—except the middleman. Making your reservation directly with the host also gives you the opportunity to ask any questions you have about the accommodations, and to start to get to know the person you're staying with. Perhaps most important, many *soba* hosts offer lower prices if you book direct. Any special prices or discounts I've negotiated for this book are invalidated if you use a middleman.

As you look over the listings, you'll notice that some accommodations promise special prices to Rick Steves readers who book directly with the soba host or hotelier. To get these rates, you must email or call your host directly, mention this book when you reserve, and then show the book upon arrival. Rick Steves discounts apply to readers with ebooks as well as printed books. Because we trust hosts and hotels to honor this, please let me know if you don't receive a listed discount. Note, though, that discounts understandably may not be applied to promotional rates.

prices, while giving you a great opportunity to connect with a local family. The fanciest *sobe* are downright swanky and offer near-hotel anonymity. Apartments are bigger and cost slightly more than *sobe*, but they're still far cheaper than hotels. At most places, the only real difference between a *soba* and an apartment is that the apartment comes with a kitchenette.

Registered *sobe* are rated by the government using a system that assigns stars based on amenities. Three or more stars means that you'll have your own bathroom, while two stars puts the bathroom down the hall. (Apartments always have private bathrooms.) Many *sobe* and apartments also have TV and air-conditioning (but usually no telephone). The prices for private accommodations generally fluctuate with the seasons, and remember that stays of fewer than three nights often come with a 20-50 percent surcharge (though this can be waived outside peak season).

Since the best-value *sobe* deservedly book up early, reservations are highly recommended. It's important to **book directly** with your

Making Reservations

It's possible to travel most of the year without reservations, especially if you arrive early in the day (although popular tourist towns can be completely full in late July and August). But given the good value of the accommodations I've found for this book, I'd recommend that you reserve your rooms several weeks in advance—or as soon as you've pinned down your travel dates. Note that some national holidays merit your making reservations far in advance (see "Holidays and Festivals" on page 798).

Because my favorite accommodations tend to be small-time entrepreneurs renting only a few rooms, they book up fast with my readers. I've tried to list several good options, so if your first choice is full, you can simply try others on the list. Sometimes one of my listings might offer to find you somewhere else to stay. This can be convenient, but don't feel obligated—you'll have more control over your options if you book direct, using my recommendations.

Requesting a Reservation: To make a reservation, contact hotels and *sobe* directly by email or phone. It's easiest to book your room through the hotel's website. (For the best rates, always use the hotel's official site and not a booking agency's site.) If there's no reservation form, or for complicated requests, send an email (see opposite page for a sample request). Most recommended hotels take reservations in English.

The hotelier or *soba* host wants to know:

- the number and type of rooms you need
- the number of nights you'll stay
- your date of arrival (use the European style for writing dates: day/month/year)
- your date of departure
- any special needs (such as bathroom in the room or down the hall, cheapest room, twin beds vs. double bed)

host (see the sidebar). After you've reserved, keep in mind that your host loses money if you don't show up. For this reason, some hosts may request your credit-card number to secure the reservation. (They'll generally ask for payment in cash when you're there; your credit card won't be charged.) A few hosts might ask you to wire or mail money as a deposit.

From:	rick@ricksteves.com
Sent:	Today
To:	info@hotelcentral.com
Subject:	Reservation request for 19-22 July

Dear Hotel Central,

I would like to reserve a room for 2 people for 3 nights, arriving 19 July and departing 22 July. If possible, I would like a quiet room with a double bed and a bathroom inside the room.

Please let me know if you have a room available and the price.

Thank you!
Rick Steves

Mention any discounts—for Rick Steves readers or otherwise—when you make the reservation.

Confirming a Reservation: Most places will request a credit-card number to hold your room. If they don't have a secure online reservation form—look for the *https*—you can email it (I do), but it's safer to share that confidential info via a phone call or two emails (splitting your number between them).

Canceling a Reservation: If you must cancel, it's courteous—and smart—to do so with as much notice as possible, especially for smaller family-run places and *sobe*. Be warned that cancellation policies can be strict; read the fine print or ask about these before you book. Internet deals may require prepayment, with no refunds for cancellations.

Reconfirming a Reservation: Always call or email to reconfirm your room reservation a few days in advance. For smaller hotels and *sobe,* I call again on my day of arrival to tell my host what time I expect to get there (especially important if arriving late—after 17:00).

Phoning: For tips on calling hotels overseas, see page 776.

Because wiring money can come with substantial fees—which you (rather than the *soba* host) will incur—it usually works better to mail them a check or travelers check. Ask your *soba* host which options they accept.

Soba hucksters who accost you on the street can be very aggressive about luring travelers away from their reserved rooms. But if you've already booked a room at a particular place, you owe it to them to show up.

If you like to travel spontaneously, during most of the year

Keep Cool

If you're traveling in the summer, the extra expense of an air-conditioned room can be money well spent, particularly in the south. Most hotel rooms with air-conditioners come with a control stick (like a TV remote) that generally has similar symbols and features: fan icon (click to toggle through wind power, from light to gale); louver icon (choose steady airflow or waves); snowflake and sunshine icons (cold air or heat, depending on season); clock ("O" setting: run X hours before turning off; "I" setting: wait X hours to start); and the temperature control (21 or 22 degrees Celsius is comfortable; also see the thermometer diagram on page 803). When you leave your room for the day, turning off the air-conditioning is good form.

you'll have no problem finding *sobe* as you go (late July and August are the exceptions). Locals hawking rooms meet each arriving boat, bus, and train. The quality can be hit or miss, but many of these are good options. In fact, I've found some of my favorite *sobe* in this book this way. The person generally shows photos of her place, you haggle for a price, then she escorts you to your new home. Be sure you understand exactly where it's located (i.e., within easy walking distance of the attractions) before you accept. Because Europeans tend to dramatically lowball walking estimates, ask to see the location on a map.

You can also keep an eye out for rooms as you walk or drive through town—you'll see blue *sobe* and *apartmani* signs everywhere. While it takes nerve to just show up without a room, this is standard operating procedure for many backpackers.

Third-party sites such as Booking.com and TripAdvisor are another popular way to find a bed. However, because of the quirky nature of Croatian accommodations, similar places may be shuffled, somewhat arbitrarily, between multiple classifications ("Hotels," "B&Bs and Inns," "Specialty Lodging," and "Vacation Rentals")—making it difficult to compare apples to apples. While these sites are useful as a second opinion, I've found many of their top-ranked places to be mysteriously lackluster in person. (See "The Good and Bad of Online Reviews" sidebar, later.) And remember: Even if you find your accommodations on one of these sites, you'll always get a better deal if you book directly.

As a last resort, you can enlist the help of a travel agency on the ground to find you a room—but you'll pay 10-30 percent extra.

Note that *sobe* aren't as common or as much of a good value in Slovenia as they are in Croatia, but the Slovenes have their own cheap option: tourist farms *(turistične kmetije)*. At these working farms, you can get a hotelesque room, plus breakfast and dinner, for a surprisingly low cost. For more on tourist farms, see page 666.

Hotels

For most travelers, Croatian hotels are a bad value—they tend to be big, impersonal, and overpriced. While most hotels have been renovated, they still carry on the old Yugoslav aesthetic of mass tourism. That means crowded "beach" access (often on a concrete pad), less-than-enthusiastic staff, a travel-agency desk selling excursions in the lobby, corny live music in the lounge a few nights each week, and a seaview apéritif bar. More money buys you a friendlier, more polished staff and newer decor.

The hotel situation is more straightforward in Slovenia and Bosnia, which have a wider range of small, reasonably priced hotels. While you will find a few communist-era holdover hotels in resorty parts of these countries, they don't dominate the scene as they do in Croatia.

Hostels

A hostel provides cheap dorm beds where you sleep alongside strangers for about $25-35 per night. Travelers of any age are welcome if they don't mind dorm-style accommodations and meeting other travelers. Most hostels offer kitchen facilities, guest computers, Wi-Fi, and a self-service laundry. Nowadays, concerned about bedbugs, hostels are likely to provide all bedding, including sheets. Family and private rooms may be available on request.

Hostels are a relatively new concept in Croatia. Official Hostelling International (IYHF) hostels are usually poorly located, in bad repair, and institutional, while independent hostels are loosely run, tend to attract a youthful party crowd, and are grungier than the European norm. If you need a cheap bed and aren't into the party scene, you'll probably do better for only a little more money by sleeping in basic private accommodations (rooms in private homes with shared bathrooms, described earlier).

Slovenia has a more appealing range of hostels. For example, one of Europe's most innovative hostels is Ljubljana's Celica, a renovated former prison (see page 573).

In each town, I've tried to list the best-established, most reputable hostel options, both independent and official. But this scene is evolving so fast that avid hostelers will do better getting tips

The Good and Bad of Online Reviews

User-generated travel review websites—such as TripAdvisor, Booking.com, and Yelp—have quickly become a huge player in the travel industry. These sites give you access to actual reports—good and bad—from travelers who have experienced the hotel, restaurant, tour, or attraction.

My hotelier friends in Europe are in awe of these sites' influence. Small hoteliers who want to stay in business have no choice but to work with review sites—which often charge fees for good placement or photos, and tack on commissions if users book through the site instead of directly with the hotel.

While these sites work hard to weed out bogus users, my hunch is that a significant percentage of reviews are posted by friends or enemies of the business being reviewed. I've even seen hotels "bribe" guests (for example, offer a free breakfast) in exchange for a positive review. Also, review sites are uncurated and can become an echo chamber, with one or two flashy businesses camped out atop the ratings, while better, more affordable, and more authentic alternatives sit ignored farther down the list. (For example, I find review sites' restaurant recommendations skew to very touristy, obvious options.) And you can't always give credence to the negative reviews: Different people have different expectations.

Remember that a user-generated review is based on the experience of one person. That person likely stayed at one hotel and ate at a few restaurants, and doesn't have much of a basis for comparison. A guidebook is the work of a trained researcher who has exhaustively visited many alternatives to assess their relative value. I recently checked out some top-rated TripAdvisor listings in various towns; when stacked up against their competitors, some are gems, while just as many are duds.

Both types of information have their place, and in many ways, they're complementary. If a hotel or restaurant is well-reviewed in a guidebook or two, and also gets good ratings on one of these sites, it's likely a winner.

from fellow travelers and searching sites such as www.hostels.com, www.hostelworld.com, and www.hostelz.com.

At any hostel, cheap meals are sometimes available, and kitchen facilities are usually provided for do-it-yourselfers. Expect crowds in the summer, snoring, and lots of noisy backpacker bonding in the common room while you're trying to sleep. Hosteling is ideal for those traveling solo: Prices are per bed, not per room, and you'll have an instant circle of friends. At most hostels, you can reserve online or by phoning ahead (usually with a credit card).

OTHER ACCOMMODATION OPTIONS

Renting an apartment, house, or villa can be a fun and cost-effective way to go local. Websites such as Booking.com, Airbnb, VRBO, and FlipKey let you browse properties and correspond directly with European property owners or managers.

Airbnb.com and Roomorama also list rooms in private homes. Beds range from air-mattress-in-living-room basic to plush-B&B-suite posh. If you want a place to sleep that's free, Couchsurfing. com is a vagabond's alternative to Airbnb. It lists millions of outgoing members who host fellow "surfers" in their homes.

Eating

Croatia and Slovenia offer good food for reasonable prices—especially if you venture off the main tourist trail. When restaurant-hunting, choose a spot filled with locals, not the place with the big neon signs boasting, "We Speak English and Accept Credit Cards." Venturing even a block or two off the main drag leads to higher-quality food for a better price. This is affordable sightseeing for your palate.

While not quite high cuisine, the food of this region is surprisingly diverse. Choosing between strudel and baklava on the same menu, you're constantly reminded that this is a land where East meets West. I've listed the specific specialties in the introduction to each country in this book, but throughout Croatia and Slovenia you'll sink your teeth into lots of tasty Italian-style food (pizzas and pastas),

as well as seafood and fine local wines. You'll also find some pan-Balkan elements, such as grilled meats and phyllo dough, that distinguish the cuisine throughout the former Yugoslavia (see the "Balkan Flavors" sidebar on page 421).

At fish restaurants, seafood is often priced by weight—either by kilogram (just over two pounds) or by hectogram (about 3.5 ounces). A one-kilogram portion feeds two hungry people or three light eaters. When I list price ranges for main dishes at restaurants, I don't include the super-top-end splurges (such as lobster or truffles). For tips on ordering seafood, see "Croatian Food" on page 30.

While bread, cover, and service charges haven't traditionally been applied in these countries, a few tourist-oriented restaurants have started to pad their bills with these extra fees. If you're concerned about this, ask up front.

When you're in the mood for something halfway between a restaurant and a picnic meal, look for bakeries selling *burek* (the savory phyllo-dough pastry) and other goodies, or shops advertising "pizza cut" (pizza by the slice). Many grocery stores sell premade sandwiches, and others might be willing to make one for you from what's in the deli case.

Tipping: You only need to tip at restaurants that have table service. If you order your food at a counter, don't tip. At restaurants that have a waitstaff, it's common to tip after a good meal by rounding up the bill 5-10 percent. My rule of thumb is to estimate about 10 percent, then round down slightly to reach a convenient total. For a 165-kn meal, I pay 180 kn—a tip of 15 kn, or about 9 percent. That's plenty. A 15 percent tip is overly generous, verging on extravagant. At some tourist-oriented restaurants, a 10 or 15 percent "service charge" may be added to your bill, in which case an additional tip is not necessary. If you're not sure whether your bill includes the tip, just ask.

Staying Connected

Staying connected in Europe gets easier and cheaper every year. The simplest solution is to bring your own device—mobile phone, tablet, or laptop—and use it just as you would at home (following the tips below, such as connecting to free Wi-Fi whenever possible). Another option is to buy a European SIM card for your mobile phone—either your US phone or one you buy in Europe. Or you can travel without a mobile device and use European landlines and computers to connect. Each of these options is described below, and you'll find even more details at www.ricksteves.com/phoning.

USING YOUR OWN MOBILE DEVICE IN EUROPE

Without an international plan, typical rates from major service providers (AT&T, Verizon, etc.) for using your device abroad are about $1.50/minute for voice calls, 50 cents to send text messages, 5 cents to receive them, and $20 to download one megabyte of data. But at these rates, costs can add up quickly. Here are some budget tips and options.

Use free Wi-Fi whenever possible. Unless you have an unlimited-data plan, you're best off saving most of your online tasks for Wi-Fi. You can access the Internet, send texts, and even make voice calls over Wi-Fi.

Many cafés (including Starbucks and McDonald's) have hotspots for customers; look for signs offering it and ask for the Wi-Fi password when you buy something. You'll also often find

Hurdling the Language Barrier

Croatia and Slovenia have one of the smallest language barriers in Europe. You'll find that most people in the tourist industry—and virtually all young people—speak excellent English. When only a few million people on the planet speak your language, it's unrealistic to expect others to learn it—so instead, you learn English early and well. (In Croatia, all schoolchildren start learning English in the third grade.) And since TV is subtitled rather than dubbed, people get plenty of practice hearing everyday American English. Some Croatians and Slovenes are more proficient in slang than many Americans. Of course, not *everyone* speaks English. Be reasonable in your expectations, especially when trying to communicate with clerks or service workers. (Throughout the region, German and Italian often work where English fails.)

Even when dealing with an English-speaker, it's polite to know a few words of the local language. "Hello" is *dobar dan* in Croatian, and *dober dan* in Slovene. *Hvala* means "thank you" in both languages. I've listed the essential phrases in each country introduction (Croatian on page 35, and Slovene on page 531).

Croatians and Slovenes pronounce a few letters differently than in English, and they add a few diacritics (little pronunciation markings). Here are a few rules of thumb:

J / j sounds like "y" as in "yellow"

C / c sounds like "ts" as in "bats"

Č / č and **Ć / ć** sound like "ch" as in "chicken"

Š / š sounds like "sh" as in "shrimp"

Ž / ž sounds like "zh" as in "leisure"

Đ / đ (only in Croatian) is like the "dj" sound in "jeans"

Croatian and Slovene are notorious for their seemingly unpronounceable consonant combinations. Most difficult are hv (as in *hvala,* "thank you") and nj (as in Bohinj, a lake in Slovenia). Don't over-pronounce these. In **hv,** the h is nearly silent; to approximate it, simply turn the hv into an f (for *hvala,* just say "FAH-lah"). When you see **nj,** the j has a very slight "y" sound that can be omitted: for Bohinj, just say BOH-heen. Listen to locals and imitate.

A few key words are helpful for navigation: *trg* (pronounced "turg," square), *ulica* (OO-leet-sah, road), *cesta* (TSEH-stah, avenue), *autocesta* (OW-toh-tseh-stah, expressway), *most* (mohst, bridge), *otok* (OH-tohk, island), *trajekt* (TRAH-yehkt, ferry), and *Jadran* (YAH-drahs, Adriatic).

Note that Bosnia and Montenegro each have their own languages, but both are very closely related to Croatian—using virtually all of the same letters and words listed above. English is common in those countries, as well.

Don't be afraid to interact with locals—give it your best shot, and they'll appreciate your efforts.

Wi-Fi at TIs, city squares, major museums, public-transit hubs, airports, and aboard trains and buses.

Sign up for an international plan. Most providers offer a global calling plan that cuts the per-minute cost of phone calls and texts, and a flat-fee data plan that includes a certain amount of megabytes. Your normal plan may already include international coverage (T-Mobile's does).

Before your trip, call your provider or check online to confirm that your phone will work in Europe, and research your provider's international rates. A day or two before you leave, activate the plan by calling your provider or logging on to your mobile phone account. Remember to cancel your plan (if necessary) when your trip's over.

Minimize the use of your cellular network. When you can't find Wi-Fi, you can use your cellular network—convenient but slower and potentially expensive—to connect to the Internet, text, or make voice calls. When you're done, avoid further charges by manually switching off "data roaming" or "cellular data" (in your device's Settings menu; if you don't know how to switch it off, ask your service provider or Google it). Another way to make sure you're not accidentally using data roaming is to put your device in "airplane" or "flight" mode (which also disables phone calls and texts, as well as data), and then turn on Wi-Fi as needed.

Don't use your cellular network for bandwidth-gobbling tasks, such as Skyping, downloading apps, and watching YouTube—save these for when you're on Wi-Fi. Using a navigation app such as Google Maps can take lots of data, so use this sparingly.

Limit automatic updates. By default, your device is constantly checking for a data connection and updating apps. It's smart to disable these features so they'll only update when you're on Wi-Fi, and to change your device's email settings from "auto-retrieve" to "manual" (or from "push" to "fetch").

It's also a good idea to keep track of your data usage. On your device's menu, look for "cellular data usage" or "mobile data" and reset the counter at the start of your trip.

Use Skype or other calling/messaging apps for cheaper calls and texts. Certain apps let you make voice or video calls or send texts over the Internet for free or cheap. If you're bringing a tablet or laptop, you can also use them for voice calls and texts. All you have to do is log on to a Wi-Fi network, then contact any of your friends or family members who are also online and signed into the same service. You can make voice and video calls using Skype, Viber, FaceTime, and Google+ Hangouts. If the connection is bad, try making an audio-only call.

You can also make voice calls from your device to telephones

Tips on Internet Security

Using the Internet while traveling brings added security risks, whether you're getting online with your own device or at a public terminal using a shared network.

First, make sure that your device is running the latest version of its operating system and security software. Next, ensure that your device is password- or passcode-protected so thieves can't access your information if your device is stolen. For extra security, set passwords on apps that access key info (such as email or Facebook).

On the road, use only legitimate Wi-Fi hotspots. Ask the hotel or café staff for the specific name of their Wi-Fi network, and make sure you log on to that exact one. Hackers sometimes create a bogus hotspot with a similar or vague name (such as "Hotel Europa Free Wi-Fi"). The best Wi-Fi networks require entering a password.

Be especially cautious when checking your online banking, credit-card statements, or other personal-finance accounts. Internet security experts advise against accessing these sites while traveling. Even if you're using your own mobile device at a password-protected hotspot, any hacker who's logged on to the same network may be able see what you're doing. If you do need to log on to a banking website, use a hard-wired connection (such as an Ethernet cable in your hotel room) or a cellular network, which is safer than Wi-Fi.

Never share your credit-card number (or any other sensitive information) online unless you know that the site is secure. A secure site displays a little padlock icon, and the URL begins with *https* (instead of the usual *http*).

worldwide for just a few cents per minute using Skype, Viber, or Hangouts if you prebuy credit.

To text for free over Wi-Fi, try apps like Google+ Hangouts, WhatsApp, Viber, and Facebook Messenger. Apple's iMessage connects with other Apple users, but make sure you're on Wi-Fi to avoid data charges.

USING A EUROPEAN SIM CARD IN A MOBILE PHONE

This option works well for those who want to make a lot of voice calls at cheap local rates. Either buy a phone in Europe (as little as $40 from mobile-phone shops anywhere), or bring an "unlocked" US phone (check with your carrier about unlocking it). With an unlocked phone, you can replace the original SIM card (the microchip that stores info about the phone) with one that will work with a European provider.

In Europe, buy a European SIM card. Inserted into your

How to Dial

Many Americans are intimidated by dialing European phone numbers. You needn't be. It's simple, once you break the code.

Dialing Rules

Here are the rules for dialing, along with examples of how to call one of my recommended B&Bs in Dubrovnik (tel. 020/321-493). The 020 is Dubrovnik's area code.

Dialing Internationally to Croatia, Slovenia, Bosnia, or Montenegro

Whether you're phoning from a US landline, your own mobile phone, a Skype account, or a number in another European country, you're making an international call. Here's how to do it:

1. Dial the international access code (011 if calling from a US or Canadian phone; 00 if calling from Europe). If dialing from a mobile phone, you can enter a + in place of the international access code (press and hold the 0 key).
2. Dial the country code (385 for Croatia, 386 for Slovenia, 387 for Bosnia-Herzegovina, or 382 for Montenegro).
3. Dial the phone number (drop the initial 0).
   Examples:
   • To call my recommended hotel from a US or Canadian phone, dial 011, then 385, then 20/321-493.
   • To call from any European phone, dial 00, then 385, then 20/321-493.
   • To call from any mobile phone, dial +, then 385, then 20/321-493.

Dialing Within Croatia, Slovenia, Bosnia, or Montenegro

To make a domestic call (either from a local mobile phone or land-

phone, this card gives you a European phone number—and European rates. SIM cards are sold at mobile-phone shops, department-store electronics counters, some newsstands, and even at vending machines. Costing about $5-10, they usually include about that much prepaid calling credit, with no contract and no commitment. You can still use your phone's Wi-Fi function to get online. To get a SIM card that also includes data costs (including roaming), figure on paying $15-30 for one month of data within the country you bought it. This can be cheaper than data roaming through your home provider. To get the best rates, buy a new SIM card whenever you arrive in a new country.

I like to buy SIM cards at a mobile-phone shop where there's a clerk to help explain the options and brands. Certain brands—including Lebara and Lycamobile, both of which operate in multiple

line), you'll generally dial both the area code (including the initial 0) and the local number. If you're calling within the same area code, you could drop the area code and just dial the local number. But, I keep things simple by always dialing the full phone number, including the area code or prefix.

Example: To call my recommended Dubrovnik hotel from any Croatian landline or mobile phone, dial 020/321-493. If dialing from within the same 020 area code, you can just enter 321-493.

Calling from any European Country to the US

To call the US or Canada from Europe (either from a mobile phone or landline), dial 00 (Europe's international access code), 1 (US/Canada country code), and the phone number, including area code. If calling from a mobile phone, you can enter a + instead of 00.

Example: To call my office in Edmonds, Washington, from anywhere in Europe, I dial 00-1-425-771-8303; or, from a mobile phone, +-1-425-771-8303.

More Dialing Tips

In Croatia, mobile phone numbers begin with 09, and numbers beginning with 060 are pricey toll lines. Slovenian phone numbers beginning with 080 are toll-free; 090 and 089 denote expensive toll lines. Mobile phone numbers in Slovenia usually begin with 03, 04, 05, or 07. Note that Montenegro recently changed its area codes. If you see the former code for the Bay of Kotor area, 082, you'll have to replace it with the new one: 032.

The "Phoning Cheat Sheet" on the next page shows how to dial per country, or you can check www.countrycallingcodes.com or www.howtocallabroad.com.

European countries—are reliable and economical. Ask the clerk to help you insert your SIM card, set it up, and show you how to use it. In some countries you'll be required to register the SIM card with your passport as an antiterrorism measure (which may mean you can't use the phone for the first hour or two).

When you run out of credit, you can top it up at newsstands, tobacco shops, mobile-phone stores, or many other businesses (look for your SIM card's logo in the window), or online.

USING LANDLINES AND COMPUTERS IN EUROPE

It's easy to travel in Europe without a mobile device. You can check email or browse websites using public computers and Internet cafés, and make calls from your hotel room and/or public phones.

Phones in your **hotel room** can be inexpensive for local calls

Phoning Cheat Sheet

Just smile and dial, using these rules.

Calling a European number

- **From a mobile phone** (whether you're in the US or in Europe): Dial + (press and hold 0), then country code and number*
- **From a US/Canadian number:** Dial 011, then country code and number*
- **From a different European country** (e.g., German number to French number): Dial 00, then country code and number*
- **Within the same European country** (e.g., German number to another German number): Dial the number as printed, including initial 0 if there is one

* Drop initial 0 (if present) from phone number in all countries except Italy

Calling the US or Canada from Europe

Dial 00, then 1 (country code for US/Canada), then area code and number; on mobile phones, enter + in place of 00

Country	Country Code	Country	Country Code
Austria	43	Italy	39 [2]
Belgium	32	Latvia	371
Bosnia-Herzegovina	387	Montenegro	382
Croatia	385	Morocco	212
Czech Republic	420	Netherlands	31
Denmark	45	Norway	47
Estonia	372	Poland	48
Finland	358	Portugal	351
France	33	Russia	7 [3]
Germany	49	Slovakia	421
Gibraltar	350	Slovenia	386
Great Britain & N. Ireland	44	Spain	34
Greece	30	Sweden	46
Hungary	36 [1]	Switzerland	41
Ireland	353	Turkey	90

[1] For long-distance calls within Hungary, dial 06, then the area code and number.
[2] When making international calls to Italy, do not drop the initial 0 from the phone number.
[3] For long-distance calls within Russia, dial 8, then the area code and number. To call the US or Canada from Russia, dial 8, then 10, then 1, then the area code and number.

and calls made with cheap international phone cards (relatively rare in Croatia and Slovenia; sold at post offices, newsstands, street kiosks, tobacco shops, and train stations). You'll either get a prepaid card with a toll-free number and a scratch-to-reveal PIN code, or a code printed on a receipt; to make a call, dial the toll-free number, follow the prompts, enter the code, then dial your number.

Most hotels charge a fee for placing local and "toll-free" calls, as well as long-distance or international calls—ask for the rates before you dial. Since you're never charged for receiving calls, it's better to have someone from the US call you in your room.

If you're sleeping in my recommended *sobe* (rooms in private homes) or apartments, be aware that you're unlikely to have a telephone in your room.

You'll see **public pay phones** in post offices and train stations, but be aware that with the prevalence of mobile phones, public phones are getting harder to find. The phones generally come with multilingual instructions, and most work with insertable phone cards (sold at post offices, newsstands, etc.). To use the card, take the phone off the hook, insert the card, wait for a dial tone, and dial away. With the exception of Great Britain, each European country has its own insertable phone card—so your Croatian card won't work in a Slovenian phone.

It's always possible to find **public computers**: at your hotel (many have one in their lobby for guests to use), or at an Internet café or library (ask your hotelier or the TI for the nearest location). If typing on a European keyboard, use the "Alt Gr" key to the right of the space bar to insert the extra symbol that appears on some keys. If you can't locate a special character (such as @), simply copy it from a Web page and paste it into your email message.

Mail

You can mail one package per day to yourself worth up to $200 duty-free from Europe to the US (mark it "personal purchases"). If you're sending a gift to someone, mark it "unsolicited gift." For details, visit www.cbp.gov and search for "Know Before You Go."

The Croatian and Slovenian postal services work fine, but for quick transatlantic delivery (in either direction), consider services such as DHL (www.dhl.com).

Transportation

BY CAR OR PUBLIC TRANSPORTATION?

If you're debating between using public transportation, renting a car, or flying between destinations in Europe, consider these factors: Cars are best for three or more traveling together (especially families with small kids), those packing heavy, and those delving

PRACTICALITIES

Public Transportation in Croatia & Slovenia

To Salzburg — To Graz & Vienna — To Budapest — To Budapest

AUSTRIA   HUNGARY

Tarvisio, Villach, Jesenice, Spielfeld, Maribor, Ptuj, Hodoš, Murska Sobota, Pécs
Udine, Bled, Koba-rid, Lecce, Logarska Dolina, Pragersko, Gyékényes
Gorizia, Nova Gorica, Sež., Ljubljana, Zidani M., Zagreb, Koprivnica
Trieste, Piran, Div., Postojna, Pivka, CROATIA, Osijek, SERBIA
Koper, Poreč, Opatija, Rijeka, Ogulin, Slavonski Brod, Vinkovci, To Belgrade
Rovinj, Pazin, Rab, Novi Grad, Doboj, Šid
Brijuni Islands, Pula, Stinica, Plitvice Lakes National Park, Banja Luka
BOSNIA-HERZEGOVINA
Adriatic Sea, Zadar, Knin, Sarajevo
Split, MEĐUGORJE
Trogir, Mostar
Ancona, Hvar, Ploče, MONTE-NEGRO
ITALY, Korčula, Mljet, Kotor
Dubrovnik, Bay of Kotor, Sveti Stefan
To Bari, Italy

Legend:
- — Rail
- - - Bus
- ···· Boats
- ✈ Airport

100 Kilometers
100 Miles

into the countryside. Trains, buses, and boats are best for solo travelers, blitz tourists, city-to-city travelers, and those who don't want to drive in Europe. While a car gives you more freedom, trains, buses, and boats zip you effortlessly and scenically from town to town, usually dropping you in the center, often near a TI. Don't overlook intra-European flights, which can be an affordable way to cover long distances (especially to skip the long overland journeys between places like Dubrovnik, Sarajevo, and Zagreb).

Cars are a worthless headache in places like Ljubljana and Dubrovnik. But in some parts of Croatia and Slovenia, a car is helpful, if not essential: Istria (especially the hill towns), the Julian Alps, Logarska Dolina, the Karst, and Montenegro's Bay of Kotor. A trip into Mostar (and on to Sarajevo) is best by car—allowing you to stop off at interesting places en route—but doable by public transportation. In other areas, a car is unnecessary: Ljubljana, Zagreb, and most of the Dalmatian Coast (Dubrovnik, Split, Hvar, and Korčula). For most trips, the best plan is a combination: Use public transportation in some areas, then strategically rent a car for a day or two in a region that merits it. (I've noted which areas are best by car, and offered route tips and arrival instructions throughout this book.)

PUBLIC TRANSPORTATION

Throughout this book, I've suggested whether trains, buses, or boats are better for a particular destination (in the "Connections" section at the end of each chapter). When checking timetables *(vozni red)*, arrivals are *prihodi* and departures are *odhodi; svaki dan* means "daily," but some transit doesn't run on Sundays *(nedjeljom)* or holidays *(praznikom)*. You'll notice that many posted schedules list departure times, but not the duration of the trip; try asking for this information at the ticket window.

Trains

Trains are ideal for certain routes in Croatia and Slovenia (such as between Ljubljana and Zagreb) and for connecting to some other countries. But their usefulness is limited, and you'll find buses, boats, and flights better for most journeys.

Schedules and Tickets: Pick up train schedules from stations as you go. To study ahead on the Web, check www.bahn.com (Germany's excellent Europe-wide timetable). You can also check www.slo-zeleznice.si for Slovenia, and www.hzpp.hr for Croatia. Buy tickets at the train station (or on board, if the station is unattended)—you rarely need a reservation.

Rail Passes: While rail passes can be a good deal in some parts of Europe, they usually aren't as useful in Croatia or Slovenia. Point-to-point tickets are affordable and often the better option. If your travels are taking you beyond Croatia and Slovenia, consider the flexible Eurail Select Pass, which covers unlimited travel for up to 10 travel days (within a two-month period) in two to four adjacent countries (Croatia and Slovenia are considered a single "country"). Again, none of these passes is likely to save you much money, but if a pass matches your itinerary, give it a look and crunch the numbers. For options and prices on pertinent Eurail passes, see www.ricksteves.com/rail.

Buses

Buses often take you where trains don't. For example, train tracks run only as far south as Split; for destinations on the

Dalmatian Coast farther south, you'll rely on buses (or boats). Even on some routes that are served by trains, buses can be a better option. For instance, Ljubljana and Lake Bled are connected by both train and bus—but the bus station is right in the town center of Bled, while the train station is a few miles away. Buses can even be convenient for connecting to islands (via ferry, of course). For example, if heading from the island of Korčula to Dubrovnik, the bus connection runs more frequently than the comparable boat connection, and takes about the same amount of time.

Confusingly, a single bus route can be operated by a variety of different companies, making it difficult to find comprehensive schedules. These online-timetable sites are helpful: www.autobusni-kolodvor.com for Croatia and www.ap-ljubljana.si for Slovenia. For smaller towns, the TI can also help you sort through your options. Get creative with checking schedules: If you're going from a small town to Split, and that town doesn't have its own online timetable, try checking the "arrivals" schedules on the Split website (www.ak-split.hr) instead. If your trip involves a connection at an intermediate station, don't be surprised if it's difficult to get the schedule details for your onward journey. Be patient, and try calling that town's TI (or the TI or bus station at your final destination) for details.

Prices vary among companies, even for identical journeys. For popular routes during peak season, drop by the station to buy your ticket a few hours in advance—or even the day before—to ensure getting a seat (ask the bus station ticket office or the local TI how far ahead you should arrive). Buses have some overhead bag storage on board, but you'll likely check your big bag under the bus (for the extra cost of about $2 per bag).

If you're headed south along the coast, sitting on the right side comes with substantially better scenery (sit on the left for northbound buses). When choosing a seat, also take the direction of the sun into consideration.

Boats

All along the Croatian coast, slow car ferries and speedy catamarans inexpensively shuttle tourists between major coastal cities and quiet island towns. Boats run often in summer (June-Sept), but frequency drops sharply off-season.

A **ferry** *(trajekt)* takes both passengers and cars; while pokey, it can run in almost any weather. The number of cars is limited, but there's virtually unlimited deck space for walk-on passengers. Watching the ferry crew scurrying around to load and unload cars and trucks onto their boat—especially if it's a small one—is a ▲▲▲ Croatian experience.

Increasingly, popular tourist destinations in Croatia are connected by much faster, passenger-only **catamarans.** These are efficient, but they have to slow down (or sometimes can't run at all) in bad weather. Catamarans are smaller, with limited seats, so they tend to sell out quickly. Because of the high speeds, you'll generally have to stay inside the boat while en route, rather than being outside on the deck.

If you're island-hopping in Dalmatia, you'll choose between boats operated by three companies. Most of Croatia's boats—big

and small—are operated by the state-run company called **Jadrolinija** (yah-droh-LEE-nee-yah, www.jadrolinija.hr, tel. 051/666-111). Jadrolinija has a virtual monopoly on the big car-ferry routes, and also runs some handy high-speed catamarans. Two other privately run catamarans—which often have more tourist-friendly schedules than Jadrolinija—are *Krilo* (www.krilo.hr) and *Nona Ana* (www.gv-line.hr). Because schedules can change dramatically from season to season, and no single website can show you all of your options, carefully review each of these three sites when making your island-hopping plans. Local TIs are the best source of information for how their town is connected to the rest of the coast.

You'll be competing with lots of other travelers for a few precious seats on the most convenient catamarans. Book your ticket as far ahead as possible; on the popular routes, tickets will sell out—sometimes very quickly. You can book advance tickets for most of these boats on their websites. If you have to buy tickets in person (a common policy for *Nona Ana*), find out when they go on sale, and get there as early as possible. The closer to peak season (July-Aug) you're traveling, the more important this becomes. I've tried to list the correct place and time to buy tickets for each boat, but as this changes from year to year, you may have to ask around.

Because all boats have open seating, it's smart to show up 30-60 minutes before departure time to get a good seat. Advance reservations are not necessary for walk-on passengers on car ferries; you can almost always find a seat on the deck or in the onboard café.

Boat rides are cheap for deck passengers. A short hop, such as from Split to the island of Hvar or Korčula, costs around $5-10 on a catamaran or a ferry. For a longer trip, such as from Split to Dubrovnik, figure $20.

Drivers cannot reserve a car space in advance on most routes. This means that drivers will want to arrive at the dock up to a few  hours early, especially in peak season. Because volumes flex with the season, the local TI is your best resource for advice on how early to get in line. Notice that on some islands, the car ferry port is a long drive from the main tourist town (for example, Vela Luka on Korčula Island is a 1-hour drive from Korčula town; Stari Grad on Hvar Island is a 20-minute drive from Hvar town).

You can buy overpriced, low-quality food and drinks on board most boats. Bring your own snacks or a picnic instead.

RENTING A CAR

If you're renting a car, bring your driver's license. In Slovenia, Croatia, and Bosnia, you're also technically required to have an International Driving Permit—an official translation of your driver's license (sold at your local AAA office for $15 plus the cost of two passport-type photos; www.aaa.com). While that's the letter of the law, I generally rent cars without having this permit. How this is enforced varies from country to country: Get advice from your car rental company.

Rental companies require you to be at least 21 years old and to have held your license for at least one year. Drivers under the age of 25 may incur a young-driver surcharge, and some rental companies do not rent to anyone 75 or older.

Research car rentals before you go. It's cheaper to arrange most car rentals from the US. Consider several companies to compare rates.

Most of the major US rental agencies (including Avis, Budget, Enterprise, Hertz, and Thrifty) have offices throughout Europe. Also consider the two major Europe-based agencies, Europcar and Sixt. It can be cheaper to use a consolidator, such as Auto Europe/Kemwel (www.autoeurope.com) or Europe by Car (www. europebycar.com), which compares rates at several companies to get you the best deal—but because you're working with a middleman, it's especially important to ask in advance about add-on fees and restrictions.

Always read the fine print carefully for add-on charges—such as one-way drop-off fees, airport surcharges, or mandatory insurance policies—that aren't included in the "total price." You may need to query rental agents pointedly to find out your actual cost.

For the best deal, rent by the week with unlimited mileage. To save money on fuel, you can request a diesel car. I normally rent the smallest, least-expensive model with a stick shift (generally cheaper than an automatic). Almost all rentals are manual by default, so if you need an automatic, request one in advance; be aware that these cars are usually larger models (not as maneuverable on narrow, winding roads).

Figure on paying roughly $230 for a one-week rental. Allow extra for supplemental insurance, fuel, tolls, and parking. Note that short rentals cost significantly more per day, while longer rentals can be cheaper per day. For trips of three weeks or more, leasing can save you money on insurance and taxes (see "Leasing," later).

Be warned that international trips—say, picking up in Ljubljana and dropping in Dubrovnik—while efficient, can be expensive (see the "Rental-Car Conundrum" sidebar for ways around this). I prefer to connect long distances by train or bus, then rent cars for a day or two where they're most useful. But be aware that some companies have a minimum rental period (generally three days); you can keep the car for a shorter time, but you'll pay for the minimum period anyway. If you want the car for just a day or two, try to find a company that allows short rentals.

Always tell your car-rental company up front exactly which countries you'll be entering. Some companies levy extra insurance fees for trips taken in certain countries with certain types of cars (such as BMWs, Mercedes, and convertibles). Or the company may prohibit driving the car in off-the-beaten-track destinations, such as Bosnia-Herzegovina. As you cross borders, you may need to show the proper paperwork, such as proof of insurance (called a "green card"). Double-check with your rental agent that you have all the documentation you need before you drive off.

Picking Up Your Car: Big companies have offices in most cities, but small local rental companies can be cheaper.

Compare pickup costs (downtown can be less expensive than the airport) and explore drop-off options. Always check the hours of the location you choose: Many rental offices close from midday Saturday until Monday morning and, in smaller towns, at lunchtime.

When selecting a location, don't trust the agency's description of "downtown" or "city center." In some cases, a "downtown" branch can be on the outskirts of the city—a long, costly taxi ride from the center. Before choosing, plug the addresses into a mapping website. You may find that the "train station" location is handier. But returning a car at a big-city train station or downtown agency

The Rental-Car Conundrum

Virtually everyone planning a trip by car to this region runs into the same problem: International drop-off fees for rental cars are astronomical (usually several hundred dollars). Generally there's no extra charge for picking up and dropping off a car in different towns within the same country (for example, the long 9-hour drive between Zagreb and Dubrovnik), but you'll pay through the nose to drop off across the border (including the quick 2-hour drive from Zagreb to Ljubljana). This is especially frustrating when connecting some car-friendly parts of southern Slovenia (such as the Karst) with similar areas in nearby northern Croatia (such as Istria or Plitvice Lakes National Park).

First, compare rates at various rental companies to see if one happens to offer a lower drop-off charge (it happens, but it's rare). If there's no way around the high fee, think creatively to avoid this huge and unnecessary expense.

Let's say you want to pick up a car in Ljubljana, drive through Slovenia's Karst to Istria, then continue to Split and drop your car...but the drop-off fee is $400. Here are two possible alternatives: First, you could do a circuit around the sights of southern Slovenia, then head back up to Ljubljana (fast and easy, thanks to the short distances and speedy expressways), drop your Slovenian car there, and take public transit to northern Croatia (such as the bus to Rovinj, or the train to Zagreb, Rijeka, or Pula). After sightseeing there, you could pick up a second car for your Croatian driving (for example, take the bus from Rovinj—which doesn't generally have handy car-rental offices—to a nearby city that does, such as Pula or Poreč). Another option is to begin your trip in Croatia, pick up your rental car there, then loop back up into Slovenia with the Croatian car before continuing to Croatia.

There's no doubt that these solutions add some hassle to your itinerary, but they could save you hundreds of dollars.

can be tricky; get precise details on the car drop-off location and hours, and allow ample time to find it.

When you pick up the rental car, check it thoroughly and make sure any damage is noted on your rental agreement. Find out how your car's lights, turn signals, wipers, and fuel cap function, and know what kind of fuel the car takes (diesel vs. unleaded). When you return the car, make sure the agent verifies its condition with you. Some drivers take pictures of the returned vehicle as proof of its condition.

Navigation Options

When renting a car in Europe, for a digital navigator you can use the mapping app that's already on your cellular-connected device, or download a mapping app that's designed to be used offline. As an alternative, you could rent a GPS device (or bring your own GPS device from home).

To use your mobile device for pulling up maps or routes on the fly, for turn-by-turn directions, or for traffic updates, you'll need to go online—so it's smart to get an international data plan (see page 772). But just using GPS to locate your position on a map doesn't require an Internet connection (and therefore doesn't require Wi-Fi or cellular data). This means that once you have the map in your phone, you can navigate with it all day long without incurring data-roaming charges.

Using Your Device's Mapping App: The mapping app you use at home (such as Google Maps or Apple Maps) will work just as well for navigating Europe.

The most economical approach is to download information while you're on Wi-Fi (at your hotel, before setting out for the day). Google Maps' "save map to use offline" feature is useful for this, allowing you to view a map when you're offline (though you can't search for an address or get directions). Apple Maps doesn't offer a save-for-offline feature, though it does automatically cache (save) certain data. So if you bring up the maps you need or plan your route while on Wi-Fi in the morning, the Apple Maps app may end up caching those maps and not using data roaming much during the day.

No matter which app you use, view the maps in standard view (not satellite view) to limit data use. And consider bringing a car charger: Even offline, mapping services gobble up battery life.

Using a Third-Party Offline Mapping App: A number of well-designed apps allow you much of the convenience of online maps without any costly data demands. City Maps 2Go is popular; OffMaps and Navfree also offer good, zoomable offline maps—similar to Google Maps—for much of Europe. You need to be online to download the app, but once that's done, the maps are accessible anywhere (note that you won't get turn-by-turn directions, which require a data connection).

Using GPS: Some drivers prefer using a dedicated GPS unit—not only to avoid using cellular data, but because a stand-alone GPS can be easier to operate (important if you're driving solo). The downside: It's expensive—around $10-30 per day. Your car's GPS unit may only come loaded with maps for its home country—if you need additional maps, ask. And make sure your device's language is set to English. If you have a portable GPS device at home, you can take that instead, but you'll need to buy and download European maps before your trip. This option is far less expensive than renting.

Driving in Croatia and Slovenia

To Salzburg — 145m • 2.5h

To Vienna — 250m • 4h

AUSTRIA

To Vienna — 260m • 4.5h

Ptuj

300m • 6h

To Vienna

Logarska Dolina — 35m 1h — Velenje — 20m 5h

Bled — 45m • 1.25h — 55m • 1h

Kobarid — 60m 2.5h

Ljubljana — 30m • 1h — 40m • .75h — Šentrupert exit

ITALY

70m • 2h

70m • 1.75h

90m • 2h

SLOVENIA

Zagreb

220m • 5h

155m • 3h

To Venice — 125m • 3h

Škocjan Caves — 35m • 1h

50m • 1h

75m 2h

100m • 2h

140m • 4h

85m • 2h (via expressway)

165m • 3h (via expressway)

Piran

25m 1h

45m • 1.25h — Rijeka/Opatija

110m • 2.5h (via expressway)

45m 1.5h

65m • 2.5h — Plitvice Lakes Nat'l Park

85m • 1.75h

45m 1.5h — Motovun — 40m 1.25h

30m 1h

Rovinj

55m • 1.5h

30m .75h — Pula

Rab (town)

Senj

110m • 3h

Adriatic Sea

Zadar

100m • 2h (via expressway)

CROATIA

ITALY

m = miles
h = hours
····· = car ferry

Note: Your times may vary based on traffic, construction, and road conditions.

Car Insurance Options

When you rent a car, you are liable for a very high deductible, sometimes equal to the entire value of the car. Limit your financial risk with one of these three options: Buy Collision Damage Waiver (CDW) coverage with a low or zero deductible from the car-rental company, get coverage through your credit card (free, if your card automatically includes zero-deductible coverage), or get collision insurance as part of a larger travel-insurance policy.

Basic **CDW** includes a very high deductible (typically $1,000-1,500). Though each rental company has its own variation, basic CDW costs $10-30 a day (figure roughly 30 percent extra) and reduces your liability, but does not eliminate it. When you reserve or pick up the car, you'll be offered the chance to "buy down" the basic deductible to zero (for an additional $10-30/day; this is sometimes called "super CDW" or "zero-deductible coverage").

If you opt for **credit-card coverage,** there's a catch. You'll technically have to decline all coverage offered by the car-rental company, which means they can place a hold on your card (which can be up to the full value of the car). In case of damage, it can be time-consuming to resolve the charges with your credit-card company. Before you decide on this option, quiz your credit-card company about how it works.

If you're already purchasing a **travel-insurance policy** for your trip, adding collision coverage is an option. For example, Travel Guard (www.travelguard.com) sells affordable renter's collision insurance as an add-on to its other policies; it's valid everywhere in Europe except the Republic of Ireland, and some Italian car-rental companies refuse to honor it, as it doesn't cover you in case of theft.

For more on car-rental insurance, see www.ricksteves.com/cdw.

Leasing

For trips of three weeks or more, consider leasing (which automatically includes zero-deductible collision and theft insurance). By technically buying and then selling back the car, you save lots of money on tax and insurance. But leases aren't available in Croatia or Slovenia—you'll have to pick up and drop off the car elsewhere in Europe (such as in Germany or Italy). Leasing provides you a brand-new car with unlimited mileage and a 24-hour emergency assistance program. You can lease for as little as 21 days to as long as five and a half months. Car leases must be arranged from the US. One of many companies offering affordable lease packages is Europe by Car (www.europebycarblog.com/lease).

DRIVING

Drivers should be prepared for twisty seaside and mountain roads, wonderful views, and plenty of tempting stopovers.

Road Rules: Seat belts are required, and two beers under those belts are enough to land you in jail. Be aware of typical European road rules; for example, many countries—including all those in this book—require headlights to be turned on at all times (even in broad daylight), and it's generally illegal to drive while using your mobile phone without a hands-free device. In Eu-

rope, you're not allowed to turn right on a red light, unless there is a sign or signal specifically authorizing it, and on expressways it's illegal to pass drivers on the right. Ask your car-rental company about these rules or check the US State Department website (www.travel.state.gov, search for your country in the "Learn about your destination" box, then click on "Travel and Transportation").

Fuel: Gas is expensive—often about $6 per gallon. Diesel cars are more common in Europe than back home, so be sure you know what type of fuel your car takes before you fill up (diesel is *dizel* in both languages). Fuel pumps are color-coded for unleaded gasoline or diesel.

Tolls: Croatia and Slovenia are crisscrossed by an impressive network of expressways (*autocesta* in Croatian, *avtocesta* in Slovene). I don't call them "freeways" because they're not—you'll pay to use them.

In Croatia, you'll pay about 0.50 kunas per kilometer—so a 100-kilometer trip (60 miles), which lasts about an hour, costs 50 kunas ($7). You'll take a toll-ticket when you enter the expressway, then submit it when you get off (but don't lose your ticket, or you'll pay the maximum).

Slovenia has done away with its tollbooth system. Instead, drivers who use Slovenia's expressways are required to buy a toll

sticker, called a vignette (Slovene: *vinjeta*, veen-YEH-tah; €15/week, €30/month). Vignettes are sold at gas stations, post offices, and some newsstands. Your rental car might already come with one—ask. A few of my readers have reported waiting too long to buy one, and getting slapped with a €150 fine, plus €15 for the sticker. If you're coming into Slovenia on an expressway, watch for *vinjeta* signs at gas stations as you approach the border, and purchase the sticker before you cross.

Bosnia-Herzegovina and Montenegro don't levy tolls—in fact, they don't even have expressways.

Road Conditions: Croatian, Slovenian, and even Bosnian roads are extremely well-engineered and typically in excellent repair. (The less said about Montenegrin roads, the better.) Croatia is still working on finishing its speedy A-1 expressway from Zagreb all the way south to Dubrovnik; currently it ends about 80 miles south of Split, where you'll have to transfer to the winding coastal road. For the latest on new expressways in Croatia, see www.hac.hr and www.hak.hr; for Slovenia, see www.dars.si. Secondary roads can be very twisty—especially along the coast or through the mountains. If you get way off the beaten track, you might find gravel. Locals poetically describe these as "white roads." (Get it? No asphalt.) Keep a close eye out for bikers. You'll see scads of them on mountain roads, struggling to earn a thrilling downhill run.

Maps and Signage: A good map is essential (see page 796). While most roads are numbered, the numbers rarely appear on signs. Instead, do as the Croatians and Slovenes do, and navigate by town name—at every major intersection, directional signs point to nearby towns and cities. The color of the sign tells you what type of road you're approaching: yellow is a normal road, while blue (in Croatia) or green (in Slovenia) indicates that the route is via expressway. Brown indicates a cultural or natural attraction (such as a castle or a cave). On expressways, each tunnel and bridge is identified and labeled with its length in meters. Learn the universal road signs. As you approach any town, follow the *Centar* signs (usually also signed with a bull's-eye symbol).

STOP AND LEARN THESE ROAD SIGNS

Speed Limit (km/hr) — Yield — No Passing — End of No Passing Zone

One Way — Intersection — Main Road — Expressway

Danger — No Entry — Cars Prohibited — All Vehicles Prohibited

No Through Road — Restrictions No Longer Apply — Yield to Oncoming Traffic — No Stopping

Parking — No Parking — Customs or Toll Road — Peace

Bosnian Detour: If you'll be driving along the Dalmatian Coast, notice that between Split and Dubrovnik, you'll actually pass through Bosnia-Herzegovina for a few miles (through the town of Neum). Don't stress about this international detour—it lasts about 20 minutes, and the borders are a breezy formality (you may need to show your passport, but generally you'll just be waved through; for details, see page 355).

Parking: Get parking advice from your hotel, or look for the blue-and-white *P* signs. Street parking marked with blue lines must be paid for (look for pay-and-display parking meters, or ask at a nearby newsstand if you can pay for parking there). Parking is a costly headache in big cities. You'll pay about $15-25 a day to park safely. Rental-car theft can be a problem in cities, so ask at your hotel for advice. Many coastal towns—such as Rovinj and Piran—are off-limits to cars...unless you're sleeping in the city center, in which case you may be granted permission to drive in just long enough to drop off your bags, then return to the parking lot outside of town. Ask your hotelier about this in advance.

FLIGHTS

Croatia is a little country with long distances (for example, it's at

least a seven-hour drive from Zagreb to Dubrovnik), so flying can save you a lot of time. Flying also makes sense if you're going to Sarajevo, which is relatively far from other destinations in this book, but easily connected to Zagreb by two daily flights on Croatia Airlines.

Each country has its own national air carrier: Croatia's is **Croatia Airlines** (www.croatiaairlines.com), while Slovenia has **Adria Airways** (www.adria-airways.com). Both offer flights within Croatia and Slovenia, and to most major European capitals. And both carriers sell a handful of seats on certain flights at deeply discounted promotional rates. For example, a Croatia Airlines "FlyPromo" ticket from Zagreb to Split or Dubrovnik can cost as little as $60—cheaper and much faster than taking the bus. These cheap seats sell out fast, so book several weeks ahead.

The best comparison search engine for both international and intra-European flights is www.kayak.com. For inexpensive flights within Europe, try www.skyscanner.com or www.hipmunk.com; for inexpensive international flights, try www.vayama.com.

Flying to Europe: Start looking for international flights four to five months before your trip, especially for peak-season travel. Off-season tickets can be purchased a month or so in advance. Depending on your itinerary, it can be efficient to fly into one city and out of another. If your flight requires a connection in Europe, see our hints on navigating Europe's top hub airports at www.ricksteves.com/hub-airports.

Flying Within Europe: Other than Croatia Airlines and Adria Airways, well-known cheapo carriers that fly to this region include **easyJet** (www.easyjet.com), **Ryanair** (www.ryanair.com), **Wizz Air** (www.wizzair.com), and **Norwegian Air** (www.norwegian.no). If you're not sure who flies to your destination, check its airport's website for a list of carriers. But be aware of the potential drawbacks of flying with a discount airline: nonrefundable and nonchangeable tickets, minimal or nonexistent customer service, pricey and time-consuming treks to secondary airports, and stingy baggage allowances with steep overage fees. If you're traveling with lots of luggage, a cheap flight can quickly become a bad deal. To avoid unpleasant surprises, read the small print before you book.

Flying to the US and Canada: Because security is extra tight for flights to the US, be sure to give yourself plenty of time at the airport. It's also important to charge your electronic devices before you board because security checks may require you to turn them on (see www.tsa.gov for the latest rules).

Resources

RESOURCES FROM RICK STEVES

Rick Steves Croatia & Slovenia is one of many books in my series on European travel, which includes country guidebooks, city guidebooks (Rome, Florence, Paris, London, etc.), Snapshot guides (excerpted chapters from my country guides), Pocket Guides (full-color little books on big cities), and my budget-travel skills handbook, *Rick Steves Europe Through the Back Door*. Most of my titles are available as ebooks. My phrase books—for German, French, Italian, Spanish, and Portuguese—are practical and budget-oriented. My other books include *Europe 101* (a crash course on art and history designed for travelers); *Mediterranean Cruise Ports* and *Northern European Cruise Ports* (how to make the most of your time in port); and *Travel as a Political Act* (a travelogue sprinkled with tips for bringing home a global perspective). A more complete list of my titles appears near the end of this book.

Video: My public television series, *Rick Steves' Europe*, covers

Begin Your Trip at RickSteves.com

My mobile-friendly **website** is *the* place to explore Europe. You'll find thousands of fun articles, videos, photos, and radio interviews organized by country; a wealth of money-saving tips for planning your dream trip; monthly travel news dispatches; my travel talks and travel blog; my latest guidebook updates (www.ricksteves.com/update); and my free Rick Steves Audio Europe app. You can also follow me on Facebook and Twitter.

Our **Travel Forum** is an immense, yet well-groomed collection of message boards, where our travel-savvy community answers questions and shares their personal travel experiences—and our well-traveled staff chimes in when they can be helpful (www.ricksteves.com/forums).

Our **online Travel Store** offers travel bags and accessories that I've designed specifically to help you travel smarter and lighter. These include my popular bags (rolling carry-on and backpack versions, which I helped design...and live out of four months a year), money belts, totes, toiletries kits, adapters, other accessories, and a wide selection of guidebooks and planning maps.

Choosing the right **rail pass** for your trip—amid hundreds of options—can drive you nutty. Our website will help you find the perfect fit for your itinerary and your budget: We offer easy, one-stop shopping for rail passes, seat reservations, and point-to-point tickets.

Want to travel with greater efficiency and less stress? We organize **tours** with more than three dozen itineraries and up to 900 departures reaching the best destinations in this book...and beyond. We offer a 14-day Adriatic tour that visits Slovenia, Croatia, and a bit of Bosnia-Herzegovina, as well as a 16-day Eastern Europe tour. You'll enjoy great guides, a fun bunch of travel partners (with small groups of 24 to 28 travelers), and plenty of room to spread out in a big, comfy bus when touring between towns. You'll find European adventures to fit every vacation length. For all the details, and to get our Tour Catalog and a free Rick Steves Tour Experience DVD (filmed on location during an actual tour), visit www.ricksteves.com or call us at 425/608-4217.

Europe from top to bottom with over 100 half-hour episodes. To watch full episodes online for free, see www.ricksteves.com/tv. Or to raise your travel I.Q. with video versions of our popular classes (including my talks on travel skills, packing smart, European art for travelers, travel as a political act, and individual talks covering most European countries), see www.ricksteves.com/travel-talks.

Audio: My weekly public **radio show**, *Travel with Rick Steves*, features interviews with travel experts from around the world. A complete archive of 10 years of programs (over 400 in all) is available in the radio section of www.ricksteves.com/radio. Most of this audio content is available for free through my **Rick Steves Audio Europe** app (see page 12).

Maps: The black-and-white maps in this book are concise and simple, designed to help you locate recommended places and get to local TIs, where you can pick up more in-depth maps of towns and regions (usually free). Better maps are sold at newsstands and bookstores. Before you buy a map, look at it to be sure it has the level of detail you want. Map apps for your smartphone or tablet are also handy (see "Navigation Options," earlier).

If you prefer paper maps and are driving, you'll want to pick up a good, detailed map in Europe. A 1:500,000-scale Croatia map covers everything in this book (including Slovenia, Bosnia-Herzegovina, and most of Montenegro) with all the detail you'll need. If you'll be hiking, especially in the Slovenian Alps, you'll find no shortage of excellent, very detailed maps locally.

APPENDIX

Useful Contacts

Emergency Needs

For medical or other emergencies, dial 112 in Croatia, Slovenia, Montenegro, and Bosnia-Herzegovina.

US Embassies

In Croatia: Ulica Thomasa Jeffersona 2, Zagreb, tel. 01/661-2400, consular services tel. 01/661-2300, http://zagreb.usembassy.gov

In Slovenia: Prešernova 31, Ljubljana, passport services available Mon-Fri 9:00-11:30 & 13:00-15:00, tel. 01/200-5500, http://slovenia.usembassy.gov

In Montenegro: Džona Džeksona 2, Podgorica, must call for appointment, tel. 020/410-500, http://podgorica.usembassy.gov

In Bosnia-Herzegovina: Ulica Robert C. Frasure 1, Sarajevo, passport services available Mon-Fri 14:00-15:30 plus Fri 8:00-11:30, tel. 033/704-000, http://sarajevo.usembassy.gov. There's also a branch office in Mostar (Husnije Repca 3, tel. 036/580-580).

Canadian Embassies and Consulates

In Croatia: Prilaz Đure Deželića 4, Zagreb, Mon-Thu 10:00-12:00 & 13:00-15:00, Fri 10:00-13:00, tel. 01/488-1200, after-hours emergencies call collect Canadian tel. 613/996-8885, www. canadainternational.gc.ca/croatia-croatie

In Slovenia: Linhartova cesta 49a, Ljubljana, Mon, Wed, Fri 8:00-12:00, tel. 01/252-4444, after-hours emergencies call collect Canadian tel. 613/996-8885, some services provided through Canadian Embassy in Budapest, Hungary, www.canadainternational. gc.ca/hungary-hongrie

In Montenegro: Contact the Canadian Embassy in Belgrade, Serbia; from Montenegro dial 00-381-11-306-3000, after-hours emergencies call collect Canadian tel. 613/996-8885, www. canadainternational.gc.ca/serbia-serbie

In Bosnia-Herzegovina: Contact the Canadian Embassy in Budapest, Hungary; from Bosnia-Herzegovina dial 00-36-1-392-3360, for after-hours emergencies call collect Canadian tel. 613/996-8885, www.canadainternational.gc.ca/hungary-hongrie

Directory Assistance

Dial 988 in Croatia or Slovenia.

Holidays and Festivals

This list includes selected festivals in this region, plus national holidays. Many sights and banks close down on national holidays. As both Croatia and Slovenia are predominantly Catholic, religious holidays—Easter, Ascension Day, Whitsunday, and Whitmonday—are a big deal, and frequent. In the Muslim areas of Bosnia (including Mostar and Sarajevo), locals observe the month of Ramadan. Before planning a trip around a festival, verify its dates by checking the festival's website or contacting the national tourist office in Croatia (http://us.croatia.hr) or Slovenia (www.slovenia. info). Unless stated otherwise, all holidays listed here apply to both Croatia and Slovenia.

Jan 1	New Year's Day
Jan 6	Epiphany
Feb	Kurentovanje Carnival, Ptuj, Slovenia (11 days leading up to Ash Wednesday, www. kurentovanje.net)
Feb 8	National Day of Culture, Slovenia (celebrates Slovenian culture and national poet France Prešeren)
Late March	Ski Flying World Championships, Planica, Slovenia (3 days, www.planica.si)
March/April	Easter and Easter Monday: March 27-28, 2016; April 16-17, 2017

April 27	National Resistance Day, Slovenia
May 1	Labor Day, Croatia and Slovenia
May	Ascension: May 5, 2016; May 25, 2017
May/June	Pentecost and Whitmonday: May 15-16, 2016; June 4-5, 2017
May/June	Corpus Christi: May 26, 2016; June 15, 2017
May/June/July	Ramadan (Muslim holy month): June 6-July 4, 2016; May 27-June 24, 2017; Bosnia-Herzegovina
Mid-June	Dance Week Festival, Zagreb, Croatia (www.danceweekfestival.com)
June 22	Antifascist Struggle Day, Croatia
June 25	National Day, Slovenia; Statehood Day, Croatia
July-Aug	Dubrovnik Summer Festival, Croatia (www.dubrovnik-festival.hr)
Early July-Sept	Ljubljana Festival, Slovenia (www.ljubljanafestival.si)
Late July	International Folklore Festival, Zagreb, Croatia (5 days, costumes, songs, dances from all over Croatia; www.msf.hr)
Late July or early Aug	Motovun Film Festival, Istria, Croatia (www.motovunfilmfestival.com)
Aug 5	National Thanksgiving Day, Croatia
Aug 15	Assumption of Mary
Late Aug	Diocletian Days, Split, Croatia (toga-clad celebrations)
Mid-Sept-early Nov	White Truffle Days, Livade, Croatia (Istrian truffle festival, weekends only)
Oct 8	Independence Day, Croatia
Oct 31	Reformation Day, Slovenia
Nov 1	All Saint's Day/Remembrance Day (religious festival, some closures)
Nov 11	St. Martin's Day (official first day of wine season)
Dec 24-25	Christmas Eve and Christmas Day
Dec 26	Boxing Day/St. Stephen's Day; Independence and Unity Day, Slovenia

Recommended Books and Films

To learn about Croatia and Slovenia past and present, check out a few of these books and films.

Books: Lonnie Johnson's *Central Europe: Enemies, Neighbors, Friends* is the best historical overview of Croatia, Slovenia, and their neighboring countries. The most readable history of Croatia itself is Benjamin Curtis' *A Traveller's History of Croatia*. Rebecca West's classic, bricklike *Black Lamb and Grey Falcon* is the definitive travelogue of the Yugoslav lands (written during a journey between the two World Wars). For a more recent take, Croatian journalist Slavenka Drakulić has written a quartet of insightful essay collections from a woman's perspective: *Café Europa: Life After Communism; The Balkan Express; How We Survived Communism and Even Laughed;* and *A Guided Tour Through the Museum of Communism*. Drakulić's *They Would Never Hurt a Fly* profiles Yugoslav war criminals. For a thorough explanation of how and why Yugoslavia broke apart, read *Yugoslavia: Death of a Nation* (by Laura Silber and Allan Little). Joe Sacco's powerful graphic novel, *Safe Area Goražde,* describes the author's actual experience living in a mostly Muslim town in Bosnia-Herzegovina while it was surrounded by Serb forces during the wars of the 1990s. Sacco's follow-up, *The Fixer and Other Stories,* focuses on real-life characters he met in siege-time Sarajevo.

Films: To grasp the Yugoslav Wars that shook this region in the early 1990s, there's no better film than the Slovene-produced *No Man's Land,* which won the 2002 Oscar for Best Foreign Film. The BBC produced a remarkable five-hour documentary series called *The Death of Yugoslavia,* featuring actual interviews with all of the key players (it's difficult to find on home video, but try searching for "Death of Yugoslavia" on YouTube; the book *Yugoslavia: Death of a Nation,* noted above, was a companion piece to this film). BBC also produced a harrowing documentary about the infamous Bosnian massacre, *Srebrenica: A Cry From the Grave* (also available on YouTube). *In the Land of Blood and Honey*—Angelina Jolie's intense, difficult-to-watch directorial debut—tells the story of the Bosnian conflict through the eyes of a civilian woman held in a "rape camp." And *The Diplomat* is a documentary about Richard Holbrooke, the American who negotiated the peace to end the Yugoslav Wars.

On a lighter note, a classic from Tito-era Yugoslavia, *The Battle of Neretva* (1969), imported Hollywood talent in the form of Yul Brynner and Orson Welles to tell the story of a pivotal and inspiring battle in the fight against the Nazis. More recent Croatian films worth watching include *Border Post* (*Karaula*, 2006), about various Yugoslav soldiers working together just before the war broke out, and *When Father Was Away on Business* (1985), about a prisoner on the Tito-era gulag island of Goli Otok, near Rab. Other local movies include *Armin* (2007), *How the War Started on My Island* (1996), *Underground* (1995), and *Tito and Me* (1992).

Fans of HBO's *Game of Thrones* may recognize locations in Dubrovnik and other Croatian coastal towns, where much of the series is filmed (for details, see page 287).

Conversions and Climate

NUMBERS AND STUMBLERS
- Europeans write a few of their numbers differently than we do. 1 = 1, 4 = 4, 7 = 7.
- In Europe, dates appear as day/month/year, so Christmas 2017 is 25/12/2017.
- Commas are decimal points and decimals are commas. A dollar and a half is 1,50, one thousand is 1.000, and there are 5.280 feet in a mile.
- When counting with fingers, start with your thumb. If you hold up your first finger to request one item, you'll probably get two.
- What Americans call the second floor of a building is the first floor in Europe.
- On escalators and moving sidewalks, Europeans keep the left "lane" open for passing. Keep to the right.

METRIC CONVERSIONS
A kilogram is 2.2 pounds, and l liter is about a quart, or almost four to a gallon. A kilometer is six-tenths of a mile. I figure kilometers to miles by cutting them in half and adding back 10 percent of the original (120 km: 60 + 12=72 miles, 300 km: 150 + 30=180 miles).

1 foot = 0.3 meter	1 square yard = 0.8 square meter
1 yard = 0.9 meter	1 square mile = 2.6 square kilometers
1 mile = 1.6 kilometers	1 ounce = 28 grams
1 centimeter = 0.4 inch	1 quart = 0.95 liter
1 meter = 39.4 inches	1 kilogram = 2.2 pounds
1 kilometer = 0.62 mile	32°F = 0°C

CLOTHING SIZES
When shopping for clothing, use these US-to-European comparisons as general guidelines (but note that no conversion is perfect).
- Women's dresses and blouses: Add 30
  (US size 10 = European size 40)
- Men's suits and jackets: Add 10
  (US size 40 regular = European size 50)

- Men's shirts: Multiply by 2 and add about 8
  (US size 15 collar = European size 38)
- Women's shoes: Add about 30
  (US size 8 = European size 38-39)
- Men's shoes: Add 32-34
  (US size 9 = European size 41; US size 11 = European size 45)

CLIMATE

First line is the average daily high; second line, average daily low; third line, average days without rain. For more detailed weather statistics for destinations in this book (as well as the rest of the world), check www.wunderground.com.

J	F	M	A	M	J	J	A	S	O	N	D

CROATIA • Dubrovnik

J	F	M	A	M	J	J	A	S	O	N	D
53°	55°	58°	63°	70°	78°	83°	82°	77°	69°	62°	56°
42°	43°	57°	52°	58°	65°	69°	69°	64°	57°	51°	46°
18	15	20	20	21	24	27	28	23	20	14	16

SLOVENIA • Ljubljana

J	F	M	A	M	J	J	A	S	O	N	D
36°	41°	50°	60°	68°	75°	80°	78°	71°	59°	47°	39°
25°	25°	32°	40°	48°	54°	57°	57°	51°	43°	36°	30°
18	17	20	17	15	14	19	19	20	17	15	16

BOSNIA-HERZEGOVINA • Sarajevo

J	F	M	A	M	J	J	A	S	O	N	D
36°	42°	52°	59°	68°	75°	79°	80°	73°	62°	48°	39°
23°	25°	32°	38°	45°	51°	53°	53°	48°	41°	33°	27°
15	14	18	17	15	16	19	23	21	19	15	16

Fahrenheit and Celsius Conversion

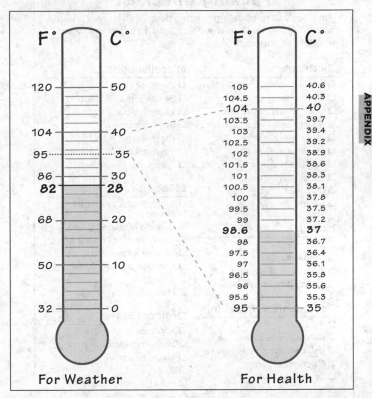

For Weather

For Health

Europe takes its temperature using the Celsius scale, while we opt for Fahrenheit. For a rough conversion from Celsius to Fahrenheit, double the number and add 30. For weather, remember that 28°C is 82°F—perfect. For health, 37°C is just right. At a launderette, 30°C is cold, 40°C is warm (usually the default setting), 60°C is hot, and 95°C is boiling.

Packing Checklist

Whether you're traveling for five days or five weeks, you won't need more than this. Pack light to enjoy the sweet freedom of true mobility.

Clothing

- ❑ 5 shirts: long- & short-sleeve
- ❑ 2 pairs pants or skirt
- ❑ 1 pair shorts or capris
- ❑ 5 pairs underwear & socks
- ❑ 1 pair walking shoes
- ❑ Sweater or fleece top
- ❑ Rainproof jacket with hood
- ❑ Tie or scarf
- ❑ Swimsuit
- ❑ Sleepwear

Money

- ❑ Debit card
- ❑ Credit card(s)
- ❑ Hard cash ($20 bills)
- ❑ Money belt or neck wallet

Documents & Travel Info

- ❑ Passport
- ❑ Airline reservations
- ❑ Rail pass/train reservations
- ❑ Car-rental voucher
- ❑ Driver's license
- ❑ Student ID, hostel card, etc.
- ❑ Photocopies of all the above
- ❑ Hotel confirmations
- ❑ Insurance details
- ❑ Guidebooks & maps
- ❑ Notepad & pen
- ❑ Journal

Toiletries Kit

- ❑ Toiletries
- ❑ Medicines & vitamins
- ❑ First-aid kit
- ❑ Glasses/contacts/sunglasses (with prescriptions)
- ❑ Earplugs
- ❑ Packet of tissues (for WC)

Miscellaneous

- ❑ Daypack
- ❑ Sealable plastic baggies
- ❑ Laundry soap
- ❑ Spot remover
- ❑ Clothesline
- ❑ Sewing kit
- ❑ Travel alarm/watch

Electronics

- ❑ Smartphone or mobile phone
- ❑ Camera & related gear
- ❑ Tablet/ereader/media player
- ❑ Laptop & flash drive
- ❑ Earbuds or headphones
- ❑ Chargers
- ❑ Plug adapters

Optional Extras

- ❑ Flipflops or slippers
- ❑ Mini-umbrella or poncho
- ❑ Travel hairdryer
- ❑ Belt
- ❑ Hat (for sun or cold)
- ❑ Picnic supplies
- ❑ Water bottle
- ❑ Fold-up tote bag
- ❑ Small flashlight
- ❑ Small binoculars
- ❑ Insect repellent
- ❑ Small towel or washcloth
- ❑ Inflatable pillow
- ❑ Some duct tape (for repairs)
- ❑ Tiny lock
- ❑ Address list (to mail postcards)
- ❑ Postcards/photos from home
- ❑ Extra passport photos
- ❑ Good book

Pronouncing Place Names

Remember that *j* is pronounced as "y," and *c* is pronounced "ts." For the special characters, *č* is "ch," *š* is "sh," *ž* is "zh," and *đ* is similar to "j."

Name	Pronounced
Bohinj	BOH-heen
Bovec	BOH-vets
Brijuni (Islands)	bree-YOO-nee
Brtonigla	bur-toh-NEEG-lah
Cavtat	TSAV-taht
Cetinje	TSEH-teen-yeh
Dubrovnik	doo-BROHV-nik
Grožnjan	grohzh-NYAHN
Herzegovina	hert-seh-GOH-vee-nah
Hum	hoom
Hvar	hvahr
Istria	EE-stree-ah
Jadrolinija (Ferry Company)	yah-droh-LEE-nee-yah
Kobarid	KOH-bah-reed
Korčula	KOHR-choo-lah
Krka	KUR-kuh
Lipica (Lipizzaner Stud Farm)	LEE-peet-suh
Ljubljana	lyoob-lyee-AH-nah
Međugorje	medge-oo-gor-yeh
Mljet (National Park)	muhl-YET
Motovun	moh-toh-VOON
Mostar	MOH-star
Njeguši	NYEH-goo-shee
Opatija	oh-PAH-tee-yah
Otočac	OH-toh-chawts
Pelješac	PEHL-yeh-shahts
Piran	pee-RAHN
Plitvice (National Park)	PLEET-veet-seh
Polače	POH-lah-cheh
Pomena	POH-meh-nah

(continued on next page)

APPENDIX

(continued from previous page)

Name	Pronounced
Poreč	poh-RETCH
Postojna (Caves)	poh-STOY-nah
Predjama (Castle)	prehd-YAH-mah
Ptuj	puh-TOO-ey
Pula	POO-lah
Rab	Rob
Radovljica	rah-DOH-vleet-suh
Rijeka	ree-YAY-kah
Rovinj	roh-VEEN
Sarajevo	sah-rah-YEH-voh
Senj	sehn
Škocjan (Caves)	SHKOHTS-yahn
Soča (River Valley)	SOH-chah
Vršič (Pass)	vur-SHEECH
Zagreb	ZAH-grehb
Poreč	poh-RETCH

INDEX

INDEX

INDEX

MAP INDEX

Explore Europe

At ricksteves.com you can browse through thousands of articles, videos, photos and radio interviews, plus find a wealth of money-saving travel tips for planning your dream trip. And with our mobile-friendly website, you can easily access all this great travel information anywhere you go.

TV Shows

Preview the places you'll visit by watching entire half-hour episodes of Rick Steves' Europe (choose from all 100 shows) on-demand, for free.

ricksteves.com

your travel dreams into affordable reality

Radio Interviews

Enjoy ready access to Rick's vast library of radio interviews covering travel

tips and cultural insights that relate specifically to your Europe travel plans.

Travel Forums

Learn, ask, share! Our online community of savvy travelers is a great resource for first-time travelers to Europe, as well as seasoned pros. You'll find forums on each country, plus travel tips and restaurant/hotel reviews. You can even ask one of our well-traveled staff to chime in with an opinion.

Travel News

Subscribe to our free Travel News e-newsletter, and get monthly updates from Rick on what's happening in Europe.

Audio Europe™

Pack Light and Right

Gear up for your next adventure at ricksteves.com

Light Luggage

Pack light and right with Rick Steves' affordable, custom-designed rolling carry-on bags, backpacks, day packs and shoulder bags.

Accessories

From packing cubes to moneybelts and beyond, Rick has personally selected the travel goodies that will help your trip go smoother.

Shop at ricksteves.com

Experience maximum Europe

Save time and energy

This guidebook is your independent-travel toolkit. But for all it delivers, it's still up to you to devote the time and energy it takes to manage the preparation and logistics that are essential for a happy trip. If that's a hassle, there's a solution.

Rick Steves Tours

A Rick Steves tour takes you to Europe's most interesting places with great

great tours, too!

with minimum stress

guides and small groups of 28 or less. We follow Rick's favorite itineraries, ride in comfy buses, stay in family-run hotels, and bring you intimately close to the Europe you've traveled so far to see. Most importantly, we take away the logistical headaches so you can focus on the fun.

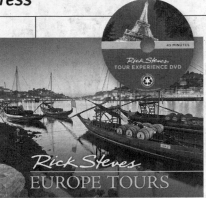

customers—along with us on 40 different itineraries, from Ireland to Italy to Istanbul. Is a Rick Steves tour the right fit for your travel dreams? Find out at ricksteves.com, where you can also get Rick's latest tour catalog and free Tour Experience DVD.

Join the fun

This year we'll take 18,000 free-spirited travelers— nearly half of them repeat

Europe is best experienced with happy travel partners. We hope you can join us.

See our itineraries at ricksteves.com

BEST OF GUIDES

Best of France
Best of Germany
Best of Ireland
Best of Italy
Best of Spain

EUROPE GUIDES

Best of Europe
Eastern Europe
Europe Through the Back Door
Mediterranean Cruise Ports
Northern European Cruise Ports

COUNTRY GUIDES

Croatia & Slovenia
England
France
Germany
Great Britain
Ireland
Italy
Portugal
Scandinavia
Scotland
Spain
Switzerland

CITY & REGIONAL GUIDES

Amsterdam & the Netherlands
Belgium: Bruges, Brussels, Antwerp & Ghent
Barcelona
Budapest
Florence & Tuscany
Greece: Athens & the Peloponnese
Istanbul
London
Paris
Prague & the Czech Republic
Provence & the French Riviera
Rome
Venice
Vienna, Salzburg & Tirol

SNAPSHOT GUIDES

Basque Country: Spain & France
Berlin
Copenhagen & the Best of Denmark
Dublin
Dubrovnik
Edinburgh
Hill Towns of Central Italy
Italy's Cinque Terre
Krakow, Warsaw & Gdansk
Lisbon

Nearly all Rick Steves guides are available as ebooks. Check with your favorite bookseller.
Rick Steves guidebooks are published by Avalon Travel, a member of the Perseus Books Group.

Maximize your travel skills with a good guidebook.

Credits

RESEARCHER
Steve Smith

Steve manages tour guides for the Rick Steves' Europe tour program and has been researching guidebooks with Rick for over two decades. Fluent in French, he's lived in France on several occasions, and is the co-author of four of Rick's books covering France. Steve owns a restored farmhouse in rural Burgundy that serves as his home base for guidebook research in Europe.

CONTRIBUTOR
Gene Openshaw

Gene is the co-author of a dozen Rick Steves books. For this book, he wrote material on Europe's art, history, and contemporary culture. When not traveling, Gene enjoys composing music, recovering from his 1973 trip to Europe with Rick, and living everyday life with his daughter.

SPECIAL THANKS
The authors would like to thank our Slovenian, Croatian, and Bosnian friends for their invaluable insights. *Hvala lepa* to Marijan Krišković, Tina Hiti, Sašo Golub, Amir Telibečirović, Bojan Kočar, Barbara Jakopić, and Gorazd Hiti.

Avalon Travel
An imprint of Perseus Books
A division of Hachette Book Group
1700 Fourth Street
Berkeley, CA 94710

Text © 2016 by Rick Steves
Cover © 2016 by Avalon Travel. All rights reserved.
Maps © 2016 by Rick Steves' Europe
Printed in Canada by Friesens. First printing June 2016.

For the latest on Rick's lectures, guidebooks, tours, public radio show, and public television series, contact Rick Steves' Europe, 130 Fourth Avenue North, Edmonds, WA, 98020, 425/771-8303, www.ricksteves.com, rick@ricksteves.com.

ISBN 978-1-63121-301-4

Rick Steves' Europe

Special Publications Manager: Risa Laib
Managing Editor: Jennifer Madison Davis
Editors: Glenn Eriksen, Tom Griffin, Katherine Gustafson, Mary Keils, Suzanne Kotz, Cathy Lu, John Pierce, Carrie Shepherd
Editorial & Production Assistant: Jessica Shaw
Editorial Intern: Grace Swanson
Researcher: Steve Smith
Graphic Content Director: Sandra Hundacker
Maps & Graphics: David C. Hoerlein, Lauren Mills, Mary Rostad

Avalon Travel

Senior Editor & Series Manager: Madhu Prasher
Editor: Jamie Andrade
Associate Editor: Sierra Machado
Copy Editor: Patrick Collins
Proofreader: Patty Mon
Indexer: Stephen Callahan
Production & Typesetting: Rue Flaherty
Cover Design: Kimberly Glyder Design
Maps & Graphics: Kat Bennett, Mike Morgenfeld

Photo Credits

Front Cover: Placa stradun in Dubrovnik © Jean-Pierre Lescourret
Title Page: © Cameron Hewitt
Full-page photos: p. 17, Rovinj; p. 369, Perast; p. 409, Coppersmiths' Street, Mostar; p. 519, Julian Alps
Additional Photography: Cameron Hewitt, Rick Steves, Sandra Hundacker, Rhonda Pelikan, Pat O'Connor, Wikimedia Commons (PD-Art/PD-US). Photos are used by permission and are the property of the original copyright owners.